The Indispensable PC Hardware Book

Your Hardware Questions Answered

The Indispensable PC Hardware Book
Your Hardware Questions Answered

Hans-Peter Messmer

ADDISON-WESLEY
PUBLISHING
COMPANY

Wokingham, England • Reading, Massachusetts • Menlo Park, California • New York
Don Mills, Ontario • Amsterdam • Bonn • Sydney • Singapore
Tokyo • Madrid • San Juan • Milan • Paris • Mexico City • Seoul • Taipei

Cover designed by Chris Eley
and printed by The Riverside Printing Co. (Reading) Ltd.
Typeset by someTimes GmbH, Munich.
Printed in The United States of America.

First printed 1993.

ISBN 0-201-62424-9

British Library Cataloguing in Publication Data
A catalogue record for this book is available from the British Library.

Library of Congress Cataloging in Publication Data
Messmer, Hans-Peter
    [PC-Hardwarebuch. English]
    The indispensable PC hardware book : your hardware questions
answered / Hans-Peter Messmer.
        p.   cm.
    Translation of: PC-Hardwarebuch.
    Includes index.
    ISBN 0-201-62424-9
    1. Computer input-output equipment. 2. Microcomputers.
I. Title.
TK7887.5.M4613 1993   93-45763
004.165--dc20   CIP

Contents

Introduction

Dear Reader,

Thank you for consulting this introduction. As a long preface is a waste of time, I just want to give you a short glance at the contents of this – what I hope to be – Indispensable PC Hardware Book.

Who should read this book

This book aims to address a wide range of people who are interested in knowing more about the inner workings of a personal computer. Even beginners should not shy away from the extensive number of pages – they will be introduced gradually to the subject from a basic level of knowledge in Part 1. This book is for:

–   Everybody who wants to or who has to understand the structure and functioning of a personal computer, either as a professional or as a private user;

–   programmers who want to access hardware components at a very low level;

–   users who want to upgrade their PCs and who would like to understand what they are about to do;

–   dealers who wish to advise their customers well;

and last but not least,

–   curious people who want to look somewhat beyond the horizon and hear about the ideas behind such magic words as, for example, «protected and virtual 8086 mode» or the methods of packing hundreds of Mbytes into a pocket-sized box called HDD.

The indispensable contents of this book

The book is divided into four major parts which are self-contained and can be used independently.

Part 1, Basics, introduces the subject of personal computer hardware and takes a short tour through all the major components, so that beginners are prepared for the following more demanding parts.

Part 2, which includes Chapters 2 to 7, presents the motherboard components, that is, the Intel microprocessors from the ancestor 8086 up to the i486DX2 as well as memory and support chips. They form the heart and brain of a PC. Part 2 focuses on the technology and the ideas behind these chips as well as the programming practice of the support elements. Also the various architectures from the legendary PC/XT up to EISA, microchannel and local buses are explained.

Part 3, including Chapters 8 and 9, is dedicated to mass storage. Floppy drives as well as hard disk and optical drives are discussed. Modern recording and reliable encoding techniques are presented and widely used drive interfaces are included, for example SCSI and IDE.

Part 4, comprising Chapters 10 to 12, presents interfaces, keyboards and mice as well as modern graphics adapters. The structure, functioning and programming – indispensable in the case of interfaces – of these components are discussed.

The extensive appendices provide a lot of practical information, especially for programmers. They can use Appendices E to L as a programming manual for DOS, BIOS and register-programmed functions.

Finally, the Glossary is a small but nevertheless comprehensive computer encyclopedia which explains most terms and concepts related to personal computer hardware.

Acknowledgements

This book is the result of a lot of work – not only by the author but also by many other people whom I would like to thank very warmly. They are, particularly, Nicky Jaeger who looked after me and the manuscript at all times and Karl-Heinz Höfner, who encouraged me to publish this book, both from Addison-Wesley. I also have to thank Jeremy Thompson and Annette Abel for carefully copy-editing and proofreading the manuscript. Mereover, I would like to thank all the companies and people who assisted me in writing the book by providing written or verbal information.

Hans-Peter Messmer
Lindenberg, December 1993

Part 1
Basics

This chapter outlines the basic components of a Personal Computer and various related peripherals as an introduction to the PC world. Though intended for beginners, advanced users would also be better prepared for the later and more technically demanding parts of the book.

1 Main Components

1.1 The Computer and Peripherals

Personal Computer (PC), by definition, means that users actually work with their own «personal» computer. This usually means IBM-compatible computers using the DOS or OS/2 operating system. Mainframe users may wonder what the difference is between a PC and a *terminal*: after all, a terminal also has a monitor, a keyboard and a small case like the PC, and looks much the same as (Figure 1.1). Where there is a difference is that the PC contains a small but complete computer, with a processor (hidden behind the names 8086/8088, 80286 or i486, for example) and a floppy disk drive. This computer carries out data processing on its own, that is, it can process files, do mathematical calculations, and much more besides. On the other hand, a terminal only establishes a connection to the actual computer (the mainframe). The terminal can't carry out data processing on its own, being more a monitor with poor input and output capabilities that can be located up to a few kilometres away from the actual computer. That a small PC is less powerful than a mainframe occupying a whole building seems obvious, but that is only true today. One of the first computers (called *ENIAC*, developed between 1943 and 1946, which worked with tubes instead of transistors) occupied a large building, and consumed so much electricity that the whole data processing institute could be heated by the dissipated power! Nevertheless, ENIAC was far less powerful than today's PCs.

Because PCs have to serve only one user, while mainframes are usually connected to more than 100 users (who are *logged in* to the mainframe), the lack of data processing performance in the PC is thus reduced, especially when using powerful Intel processors. Another feature of PCs (or microcomputers in general) is their excellent graphics capabilities, which are a necessary prerequisite for user-friendly and graphics-oriented programs like Microsoft's Windows. In this respect, the PC is superior to its «big brother».

Figure 1.1 shows a basic PC workstation. The hub, of course, is the PC, where you find not only the above-mentioned processor but one or more floppy disk drives, hard drives, interfaces and other devices. These are dealt with in some detail in Section 1.2. Because you can't enter commands into the actual PC, or receive data from it, a *keyboard* (for entering commands and data) and a *monitor* (for data output) are also present. High quality computer monitors are far more powerful (and therefore much more expensive) than a TV.

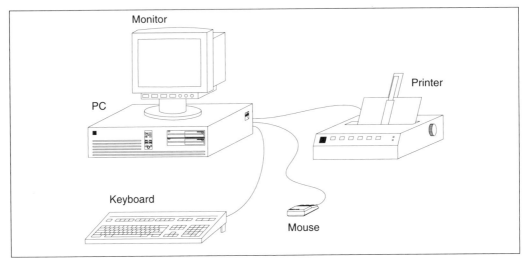

Figure 1.1: Basic PC Equipment.

With this equipment you can start work: for example, entering text files, doing mathematical calculations, or playing computer games. To use the PC's graphics capabilities (with Windows, for example) a *mouse* is usually needed. In this book, «PC» always means the sum total of these components, because without a keyboard and a monitor you can't control the machine.

For printing text files, of course, you need a printer. By using various *interfaces* you can connect additional *peripherals* like a *plotter* (for drawing plans with coloured pencils) or a *modem* (for worldwide data communication). «Peripherals» means all those units located outside the PC's case.

1.2 Inside the Personal Computer

This chapter deals with the various components of a PC, starting with basic definitions of concepts like the motherboard, the controller etc; their functions are outlined. Also, an overall picture of the interworkings between individual components is given.

1.2.1 How to Open the Case

In order to work with a PC or to understand how it works, you don't, of course, need to open the case. But I think there are a lot of curious users who will soon want to look inside. The following gives some tips on doing this, while trying to avoid burnt-out electric components and rather unpleasant electric shocks. To open the case you'll need a screwdriver and some common sense. It is best to use a magnetic screwdriver because, in my own experience, one or more screws will inevitably fall into the case. With a magnetic screwdriver you can get them out quite easily.

You may have heard that magnetic objects should never be placed near a PC. I would like to comment on this:

- the Earth has a magnetic field;
- if you scratch your disk with a sharp object you do so at your own risk; it doesn't matter whether it is a knitting needle, a hammer or a magnetic screwdriver;
- opening a hard disk drive means losing the data simply because of the dust that is always present in the air; whether the hard disk is disturbed magnetically afterwards is completely insignificant;
- the distance between the read/write heads and the disk surface is less than about 1 μm.

In principle, the Earth's magnetic field is shielded by the PC's metal case, but as soon as you remove the cover the magnetic field penetrates all the components. As all electronic and magnetic components are exposed to the Earth's magnetic field when the computer is assembled, this obviously can't have an adverse influence. Floppy and hard disks are coated with a thin magnetizing layer: if someone deliberately scratches off this coating, he really doesn't know what he is doing. The data medium of the hard disk drives is enclosed in a case so that dust particles in the air don't act as a sort of scouring powder. Therefore, the hard disk is destroyed not by magnetic but by mechanical action. Whether you are additionally damaging the still present magnetic pattern with a magnetic object after the mechanical destruction of the data medium would seem to be unimportant.

Finally, the distance between the read/write heads and the data medium is less than about 1 μm. Because of the protective envelope the closest you can bring the screwdriver to the data medium of a floppy disk is one millimeter away at most. That is one thousandth of the head-data medium distance. According to magnetostatic laws, the strength of the magnetic field decreases in proportion to the square of the distance. This means that the screwdriver must have a local field strength which is one millionth of the field of the read/write head. Perhaps someone could show me this monster of a screwdriver with its superconducting magnet! In the case of hard disk drives, this ratio is much greater because of the additional separation provided by the drive's case.

The dangers of mechanical destruction are clearly far more likely. I always use a magnetic screwdriver because I always lose a screw in the case, and because of the danger of a short circuit caused either by the screw or by a rash action after having tried to get the screw out.

Advice: **If your case is sealed and there is a notice advising that breaking the seal will invalidate the warranty, you should open the case only after having contacted your dealer.**

Figure 1.2 shows three examples of PC cases (two desktops and one tower), which are the most common types.

If you are one of those lucky PC buyers who got a technical reference book or at least a user handbook when you bought your PC, you should have a look at this handbook first to find out how to open the case. If you've found this information, then follow the manual and ignore the next paragraph.

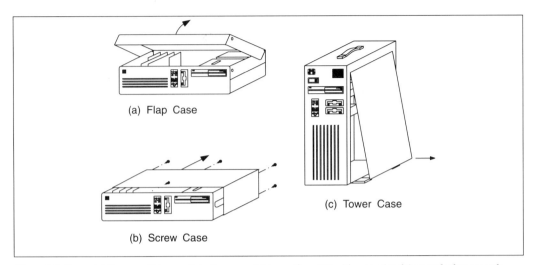

Figure 1.2: Cases: (a) flap case, (b) normal desktop case, (c) tower for a PC with extensive drives and adapter cards.

Advice: **Unplug all cables going into the PC before opening the case. If you damage a cable with your screwdriver an unpleasant electric shock may be the result. However, even if you have unplugged your PC, you should still be careful not to damage any cables or circuit boards.**

Figure 1.2a shows a case with a flap cover. To open the case you must press the buttons on each side and flip the cover off. If the case is screwed on, you'll have to remove the screws located at the sides and then flip away the cover. On the desktop case (Figure 1.2b), several screws are located on the back. Only remove those screws arranged at regular intervals from the edge of the case. Sometimes, the power supply and other peripherals are fixed onto the back with screws, so don't unscrew these by mistake.

Tower cases (shown in Figure 1.2c) usually have a side that can simply be removed, as it is held only by sheet springs. If you can't see any screws, try removing the side with some force (don't be too violent!).

Take Care Against Electric Shocks

Remember that inside the PC most parts are sensitive. You may have had a slight electric shock after getting out of your car or walking over a carpet. This is because you have been charged with *frictional electricity*. Most electronic circuits in a PC would not survive a discharge of such *static electricity*. Therefore, don't touch any internal components if you are not discharged completely.

But now you have a dilemma: either unplug the computer and risk «flash-overs» caused by static electricity, destroying the computer's circuits, or keep the PC plugged in and risk an electric shock. The best solution is to buy an earthing bracelet (see Figure 1.3). You are thus always earthed and no static electricity can accumulate. Otherwise, plug your computer into an electric socket protected by a circuit-breaker and avoid using both hands simultaneously so that no current path between hand-heart-hand can occur. Before picking up circuit boards you should always touch the case of your power supply to discharge yourself. If you want to examine boards with electronic circuitry more closely and you take the boards out, only handle them by their edges.

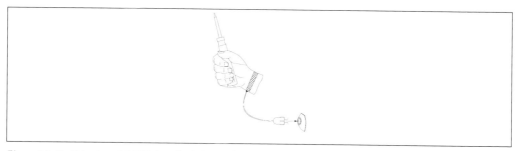

Figure 1.3: Earthing bracelet: This bracelet is inserted into a electric socket that is earthed so that charges can flow away from the user.

Inside the PC there are various circuit boards (see Figure 1.4). With some imagination you can also locate the components in an exotic-looking PC. To find out whether a certain board is a controller, a parallel or serial interface or a graphics adapter, it is best to investigate which devices the board is connected to. The individual components are presented below in greater detail.

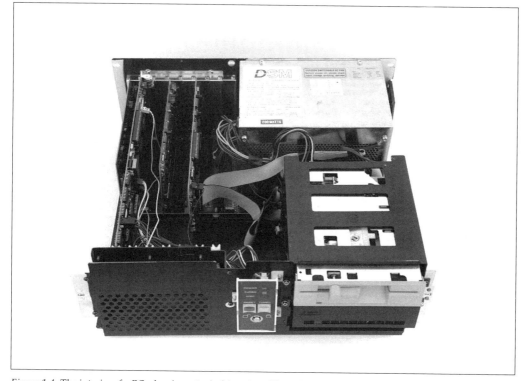

Figure 1.4: The interior of a PC, showing a typical interior with various adapter cards and drives.

1.2.2 Data Flow inside the PC

Personal Computers, like other computers, are used for *electronic data processing* (*EDP*). For this, data must be input into the PC, and the PC has to supply (the resulting) data. Between input and output, a varying amount of data processing take place using a *program*. Figure 1.5 shows a typical PC with the most important functional units necessary for data processing.

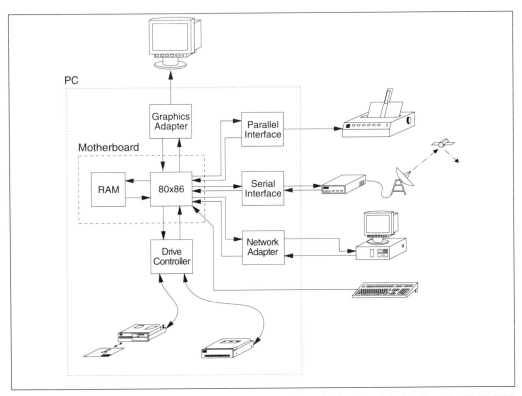

Figure 1.5: Block diagram of a PC with peripherals. The arrows indicate the direction of the data flow. The 80x86 CPU and the RAM are located on the motherboard. All parts surrounded by the broken line are normally inside the PC case.

The main part is the processor, also called the 80x86 Central Processing Unit (*CPU*) (x is a dummy variable from «#» to «4» to denote the 8086/8088, 80186, 80286, 80386, 80486 family of Intel processors used in IBM-compatible PCs). Because of the large number of incoming and outgoing arrows, it can be seen that this processor represents (so to speak) the heart of the computer, in which all data processing events take place. Immediately next to the CPU is the *main memory*, or Random Access Memory (RAM) that the CPU uses to store or read inter-mediate results of the data processing or programs to/from. The CPU and RAM are the main components of the *motherboard*. The processor is connected to the keyboard, with which you enter data (text, for example) or commands (DIR, for example). To display such inputs visually, the CPU is further connected to a *graphics adapter*, which accepts the data to display, and proces-ses it so it can be displayed on the monitor. At this point I want to mention that a computer doesn't necessarily need a monitor to output data; the monitor mainly supports the user. There are a lot of computers (the engine control Motronic, for example) that are very powerful, but which have neither a keyboard nor a monitor. In this case, the computer is usually called a *process computer*. To read more extensive datasets, or to store them for a longer time, *floppy* and *hard disk drives* are included. The processor may read data from them or write data to them with a *controller*. This is necessary because (apart from CMOS-RAM and the main memory of some laptops) all RAMs lose their contents when the PC is powered down. All data stored in that memory is thus irrevocably lost.

Nearly all PCs have at least one *parallel interface* (called PRN, LPT1, LPT2 or LPT3 under DOS) to which a printer may be connected, and at least one *serial interface* (called COM1–COM4 under DOS). The serial interface is also often called the *communication interface* because a modem can be connected to it, and with an appropriate program you can exchange data with other computers via public telephone or data networks. For example, it is possible to access a database in another country via satellite. In this way, your tiny (and seemingly unimportant) PC becomes a member of an international data network. (You can see what unexpected possibilities a PC offers beyond computer games!) Many PCs also have a *network adapter*, with which you embed your computer into a *local area network (LAN)*, that is, you may exchange data with another or several computers that are also equipped with a network adapter. Nevertheless, the other computer does not also have to be a PC. With your network adapter and appropriate software you may easily access a supercomputer and start to work on it.

1.2.3 The Motherboard

Figure 1.6: The Motherboard comprises all the central parts of a Personal Computer like, for example, the CPU, main memory and extension slots for additional adapter cards.

As the name implies the motherboard is the heart of your PC, on which all components that are absolutely necessary are located. Figure 1.6 shows a typical motherboard, though the layout of motherboards may vary considerably.

You can see the motherboard and several *slots* into which the circuit boards of the graphics adapter and the interfaces are located (the slots are often called *bus slots*). If your motherboard has such bus slots but no further electronic components, you have a PC with a so-called *modular board*. The motherboard in a modular PC is divided into a *bus board* (which has the slots) and a separate *processor board*. The latter is inserted into a slot in the same way as all the other boards, but its internal structure is the same as the motherboard described below. Figure 1.7 shows the motherboard in diagrammatic form. As mentioned earlier, the 80x86 processor is the central unit of the board. It executes all the data processing, that is, numbers are added, subtracted, multiplied or divided, logic operations with two items are executed (logical AND, for example) and therefore their relations (equal, above, below, etc.) are determined, or data is input and output. For extensive mathematical operations such as, for example, the calculation of the tangent of two real numbers with very high accuracy, a mathematical *coprocessor* or *processor extension* is available. Intel calls the coprocessors belonging to the 80x86-family 80x87, for example, the 80287 is the coprocessor for the 80286 chip. Other companies also supply mathematical coprocessors (Weitek, Cyrix).

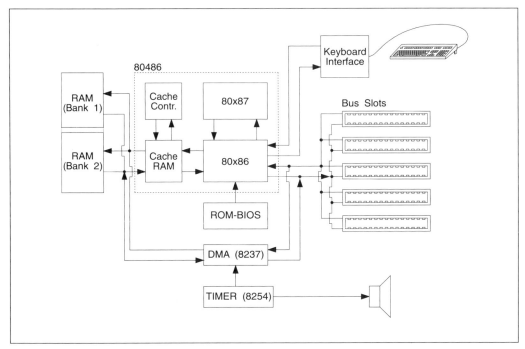

Figure 1.7: Diagram of a motherboard. The diagram shows the typical structure of a motherboard. The central part is the CPU 80x86. The CPU can be associated with an 80x87 coprocessor for mathematical applications and a cache controller and cache RAM to enhance performance. The newest 80x86 processor – the i486 – integrates all these parts on a single chip. Additionally, on the motherboard there are the memory (RAM), the ROM BIOS, the 8237 and 8254 support chips, a keyboard interface, and the bus slots.

Usually, PCs are not equipped with a coprocessor when shipped, only with a socket for it. You can buy the corresponding chip afterwards and put it into this socket. The 80x86 automatically recognizes whether a coprocessor is present, and transfers the corresponding commands to it; the 80x87 then calculates the requested mathematical value. Coprocessors may calculate the tangent of an arc up to 100 times more quickly than «normal» processors. So if you are doing extensive mathematical applications (like, for example, three-dimensional computer graphics or CAD) this gives an enormous advantage.

Another important motherboard component is the main memory or RAM. Usually, the RAM is divided into several *banks*, though recently it has been made up of memory modules (SIMM or SIP). Each bank has to be fully equipped with memory chips, meaning that the main memory may only be extended bank-by-bank – the memory of a partially equipped bank will not be recognized by the PC. The lowest value for the main memory size of an AT today is 1 Mbyte; fully equipped 386 and 486 PCs have at least 8 Mbytes of RAM. The CPU stores data and intermediate results, as well as programs, in its memory and reads them later. For this, the processor has to tell the memory which data it wants to read (for example). This is done by an *address*, which is something like the house number of the data unit requested. Transferring this address to the memory is carried out by an *address bus*, and the transfer of the data by a *data bus*. Generally, in computer terms a *bus* means a number of lines through which data and signals are transferred. Therefore, the address bus consists of several lines, in the PC generally 20 (PC/XT), 24 (AT) or 32 (i386, i486) lines.

In the context of main memory you will often hear the expression *access time*. This is the time period between the CPU's command to the memory that data should be read and these data being transferred to the processor. Modern memory chips have an access time of about 60–100 ns, which for humans is a minute time period (batting the eyelid takes at least one 100th of a second, that is, 100 000 * 100 ns), but not so for modern computers with a high clock frequency. Actually, the access time is one of the most important restrictions on the operational speed of a PC.

Therefore, powerful and fast-clocked computers (25 MHz and above) have a so-called *cache* or *cache memory*. Usually, this cache is significantly smaller than the main memory, but much faster (with an access time of 15–25 ns). The cache holds data that is frequently accessed by the CPU so it is available to the processor more quickly. The CPU, therefore, doesn't have to wait for its relatively slow main memory. If the CPU reads data out of main memory, the cache controller first checks to see whether this data is held in the cache memory. If it is, the data is immediately transferred to the CPU; otherwise, the cache controller reads the data from the main memory and transfers it to the processor simultaneously. If the CPU wants to write data it is written into the cache memory at a high speed. Later, the cache controller writes it into the main memory. You sometimes demonstrate similar behaviour yourself; for example, if you are programming some routines you take off the shelf those documents that you are likely to need. In this case, your desk is the cache memory and you are the cache controller. When a problem arises you take additional documents off the shelf and put them on your desk. If the desk is full (the cache memory is exhausted) you put those documents you are unlikely to need back onto the shelf. Other documents that you need may then be placed on your desk. In these circumstances it is important that the cache memory is *transparent* to the processor, that is, the CPU doesn't recognize that a fast cache memory is installed between itself and the main memory. In other words, the processor operates as if no cache memory were present. On the new and powerful 80x86 family processors, the processor, coprocessor, an 8 kbyte cache memory and a cache controller are integrated on a single chip to form the 80486 CPU, or i486.

The motherboard also includes a *Read Only Memory* (ROM). Located on this chip are the programs and data that the PC needs at power-up (because it loses the contents of its main memory when it is powered down). The processor reads these programs and executes them at power-up. In the ROM there are also various support routines for accessing the keyboard, graphics adapter, etc. – known collectively as the *ROM-BIOS*.

If you enter data via the keyboard, the keyboard interface communicates directly with the processor (for advanced readers, it issues a hardware interrupt; see Section 7.1), and informs it that a character has been input. The CPU can then read and process that character.

As mentioned above, data is exchanged via the address and data buses. To control the data transfer processes, additional control signals are required; for example, the CPU must tell the memory whether data should be read or written. This is carried out by a so-called *write-enable* signal, for which one bus line is reserved. Because of the various signals, the slot has, for example, 62 contacts for the XT bus (the XT's system bus) and 98 contacts for the AT bus. (Note that the bus slots therefore have different lengths.) The lines for the control signals are guided in parallel to the address and data buses and lead to the bus slots. The data bus, address bus and all the control lines are known as the *system bus*, which ensures that all inserted adapter cards are informed about all the operations taking place in the PC.

For example, a memory expansion card may be inserted in one bus slot. The CPU accesses the memory on this adapter card in the same way as it accesses the memory on the motherboard. Therefore, the bus slots must have all the signals necessary to control the PC components (and this expansion card, for example, is one of them). Theoretically, it does not matter into which free slot an adapter card is inserted, as long as all the contacts fit into the bus slot. In practice (especially if you are using a low quality motherboard or adapter card), an adapter card may only run correctly in a certain bus slot, as it is only in this bus slot that all the bus signals arrive at the appropriate time.

Frequently, extensive amounts of data must be transferred from a hard or floppy disk into the main memory, as is the case when a text is loaded into a word processor, for example. For such minor tasks an 80x86 processor is too valuable a chip, because it can carry out far more complex operations than this. For this reason, the motherboard has one (PC/XT) or two (AT) chips optimized for data transfer within the computer – the *Direct Memory Access* (DMA) *chips*. They are connected to the main memory and the data bus, and to certain control lines that are part of the bus slots. Using these control lines, the DMA chips can be activated to carry out data transfer from a hard disk into main memory, for example, at a very high speed. In this process the CPU is bypassed and is not allocated the data transfer operation.

You have probably realized that your PC can also be used as a clock, telling the date and time (DOS commands DATE and TIME). To implement this function a *timer chip* is present, which periodically tells the processor that the DOS-internal clock has to be updated. (This chip also controls memory refresh and the speaker.) In a dynamic RAM *(DRAM)*, the information stored vanishes as time passes (typically within a period of 10 ms to 1 s). To avoid this, the DRAM has to be periodically refreshed to regenerate the memory contents. DRAMs are used in the PC as main memory. Bus slots are vitally important in making PCs flexible. Besides the standard plug-in graphics adapters, controllers, etc., you can also insert other adapters, such as a voice synthe-sizer to program spoken output on your PC. This might be a first step towards a *multimedia PC*.

1.2.4 Graphics Adapters and Monitors

For a user, an essential part of a PC is the monitor, as well as the accompanying graphics or dis-play adapter card. Strictly speaking, a graphics adapter is electronic circuitry for displaying graphics. A display adapter is the generic term, and it also includes electronic devices that can only display text (that is, no free lines, circles etc.), though because text adapters are no longer used in PCs, this strict distinction has vanished. The graphics adapter is usually constructed as a plug-in card for a bus slot. Figure 1.8 shows a VGA adapter card.

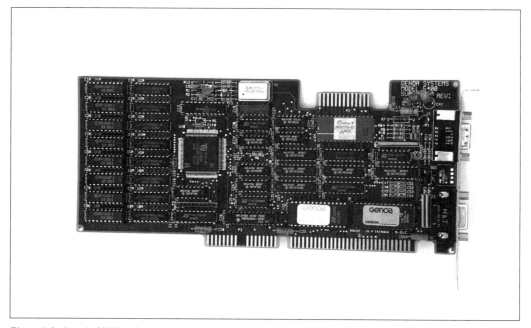

Figure 1.8: A typical VGA adapter card for displaying text and graphics on-screen.

Although it is possible to run a PC without a monitor and to output directly to a printer, this is a painstaking process. If graphics are to be printed, a dot matrix printer is usually occupied for several minutes, and a laser printer will be tied up for many seconds. Moreover, in the age of the «paperless office» it is inappropriate to output all draft documents to paper immediately. Therefore the monitor, with its short response time and the vibrancy of its displayed data, is far better as an output medium. If, for example, a line has to be inserted into a drawing, only this new line has to be formed, not the whole displayed image. Under DOS, the monitor and the keyboard are regarded as a single entity because of their special usage as standard input/output devices, and are thus called the console (DOS-unit CON).

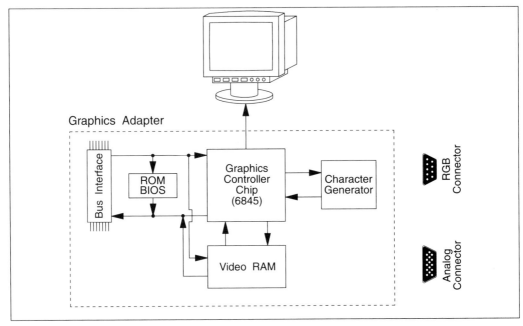

Figure 1.9: Graphics adapter. The central part is a graphics control chip, which controls the character generator and the video RAM. The CPU can access the control chip and the video RAM via the bus interface.

The hub of a graphics adapter is the *graphics control chip*, usually a Motorola 6845 (Figure 1.9). You'll find this or a compatible chip on nearly all adapters. It is responsible for driving the monitor, that is, supplying pulses for horizontal and vertical retraces, displaying the cursor, controlling the number of text lines and columns, as well as the display of text and graphics. The picture on the monitor is written by an electron beam similar to that in a TV, which scans the screen line by line. If the beam reaches the lower right corner, it returns to the upper left corner, that is, a new page.

The graphics adapter has two operation modes: text and graphics. Characters are displayed as a fixed pattern of points, graphics as a free pattern. If a certain character is to be displayed in *text mode*, the CPU need pass only the number or *code* of this character to the graphics control chip. The *video RAM* holds data (codes) that determine the character to be displayed on-screen. The job of the *character generator* is to convert this code into a corresponding pattern of pixels so that the character can be displayed on-screen by the graphics control chip. On the other hand, in *graphics mode* the video RAM is read out directly and the character generator is not enabled. Therefore, far more complex «patterns» (i.e. graphics) may be displayed.

The data for the screen contents is written into the video RAM by the CPU. The CPU may also read data out of the video RAM, for example to determine the character at a certain location on-screen. For this the graphics adapter has a bus interface, which detects whether data for the graphics adapter is present on the system bus. Via the bus interface, the CPU can write data into the video RAM which, for example, is displayed as text on-screen. On the other hand, the CPU may read data about to be overwritten by a new window under MS-Windows and store it in main memory. It is thus possible to restore the original state by retransferring, after closing the window, the data stored in main memory back into the video-RAM. Moreover, the graphics control chip can be reprogrammed via the bus interface so that, for example, instead of the usual 25 lines and 80 columns each, a new mode with 60 lines and 132 columns each is displayed.

Because reprogramming the graphics control chip from a standard mode to the mode mentioned above is dependent upon the particular hardware on the graphics adapter, high-resolution EGA and VGA adapter cards have their own BIOS. This is located in a ROM, and supports the ROM-BIOS on the motherboard. It includes routines to switch between different display modes (modern graphics adapters may have up to 80 different such modes), to set points with a certain colour at a certain location on the screen, or to use various pages in video memory. For this, the CPU on the motherboard calls the corresponding program in the ROM-BIOS of the graphics adapter via the bus interface.

On the back of the graphics adapter there are usually one or more jacks. Connectors for monochrome and RGB monitors (*red-green-blue*) have two rows of holes; connectors for analog monitors have three rows. Monochrome and RGB monitors are driven by digital signals so that a maximum of 16 different colours may be displayed simultaneously: two each for red, green and blue, and an additional intensity signal (high, low). Therefore, $2^4 = 16$ different signal combinations are possible. With an EGA adapter card, these 16 colours may be chosen from a *palette* containing 64 colours. This means that only 16 of these 64 colours can be displayed simultaneously. The VGA card and other new adapters drive an analog monitor with an analog signal. In principle, any number of colours may now be displayed simultaneously, but for technical reasons the VGA standard limits them to 256 simultaneously displayable colours. The 256 colours may be selected from a palette of 262 144 (64 red * 64 green * 64 blue) different colours. Extremely high-resolution graphics adapters with a resolution of 1280 * 1024 points drive the correspondingly more powerful monitors by an analog signal, which is transmitted via a BNC cable. The cable is shielded against external influences so that the driving signals are not disturbed and the cable doesn't act as an antenna and influence other equipment. Some graphics adapters have all three jacks. On the Hercules and other compatible graphics cards, a parallel interface is integrated onto the adapter card. You will see this if a jack for connecting a printer with a parallel interface is present. Figure 1.15 shows the layout of the parallel interface jack.

1.2.5 Drive Controllers, Floppy and Hard Disk Drives

As already mentioned, the main disadvantage of main memory is the volatility of the stored data. When the PC is switched off, or if the power supply is interrupted, all the data is lost. Therefore, RAM is unsuitable for long-term data storage. For this reason, magnetic memories were developed very early on. Before the invention and the triumphant progress of semiconductor memories and integrated memory chips, even main memory consisted of magnetic drums. Later, these drums were replaced by magnetic core memories, tiny magnetic rings through which run read and write wires. In the PC field, floppy disks and hard disk drives are now generally established (see Figure 1.10).

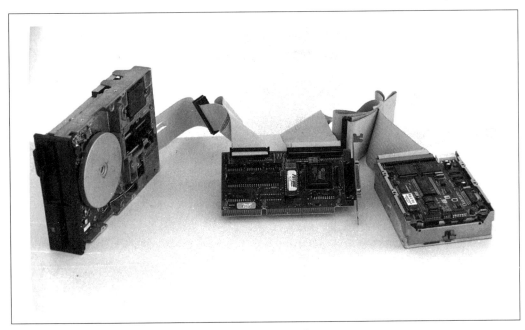

Figure 1.10: A typical floppy drive, hard disk drive and combicontroller.

Floppy disk drives belong to the group of drives with so-called *removable data volume*, because different floppies (data volumes) can be inserted into a single drive and removed later. The actual floppy disk is a circular and flexible disk, coated with a magnetic material and housed in a protective envelope (see Figure 1.11).

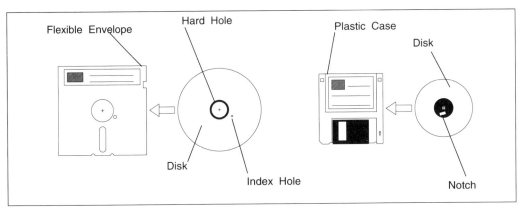

Figure 1.11: Floppy disks. Presently for the PC, 5 1/4" floppy disks in a flexible envelope with capacities of 360 Kbytes and 1.2 Mbytes as well as 3 1/2" floppy disks in hard plastic cases with capacities of 720 Kbytes and 1.44 Mbytes are available.

For IBM-compatible PCs, floppy disks 5 1/4" and 3 1/2" in diameter are available. The smaller 3 1/2" floppies are enclosed in a hard plastic case, and are inserted together with the case into the drive, which writes data to it or reads data from it. On 5 1/4" floppy drives, the drive flap must be locked down as otherwise no data can be read or written; 3 1/2" drives automatically lock the floppy disk in place.

On the other hand, on *hard disk drives* or *hard disks* the data volume cannot be removed; it is fixed in the drive. Furthermore, the data volumes are no longer flexible, but stiff («hard») disks. Typically, a hard disk holds 100 times more data than a floppy disk.

Floppy and hard disk drives are also used in other computers, such as the Apple Macintosh, Commodore Amiga, or mainframes. Therefore, the technique of floppy and hard disk drives is completely independent of the technology of a PC. To read and write data with the CPU on the motherboard, it is necessary to control the drives. For this, a *controller* is inserted into one bus slot to control the floppy and hard disk drives, and to transfer data between the drive and main memory. Figure 1.12 shows a block diagram of a controller.

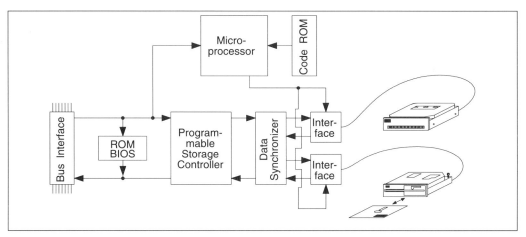

Figure 1.12: A controller and drives. The microprocessor controller controls the components according to the microprogram in the ROM code. Data is transferred beween the drive and controller via an interface.

The controller is the link between the CPU and the drives. For this reason it has two interfaces: the bus interface (which we met in the section on graphics adapters) for data exchange with the CPU; and one interface for every floppy or hard disk drive. Today's PCs usually have a *combicontroller*, with which two or more floppy drives and two hard disk drives can be connected. The combicontroller has its own microprocessor, with programs stored in ROM to control the electronic components on the controller card. To avoid any confusion, I must emphasize that this microprocessor is not identical to the 80x86 CPU on the motherboard, but is sited independently on the controller. Therefore, the controller is actually a small and independent computer (a further example of a computer without a monitor), to which the CPU on the motherboard supplies «commands» via the bus interface. Similarly, you enter commands for the CPU via the keyboard (interface). We shall meet this idea of independent, small computers that support the central processor on the motherboard again, hence the name *Central* Processor Unit.

The microprocessor now controls data flow between the bus and drive interfaces by driving the programmable storage controller and the data synchronizer appropriately. On floppy and hard disks, the data is held in a form that is especially suited for data recording on these magnetic data carriers. For processing in a PC this form is, however, completely unsuitable. Therefore, the data synchronizer carries out a conversion between these two incompatible formats. The programmable storage controller controls the read and write operations, and checks the read data for correctness.

In order to use and control the drives effectively, many controllers have their own ROM-BIOS. As for ROM-BIOS on a graphics adapter, this ROM-BIOS holds several routines for accessing the hard disk controller. The control routines for the floppy drives are already located in the ROM-BIOS on the motherboard – do not confuse this ROM-BIOS with the ROM code. The routines in the ROM code control the microprocessor on the controller and cannot be accessed by the CPU on the motherboard, whereas the routines in the ROM-BIOS on the controller *support* the CPU on the motherboard.

With intelligent drives like the AT bus, SCSI or ESDI, the controller is fixed to the drive so that drive and controller together form an entity. Therefore, instead of a controller being inserted into a bus slot, there is a *host adapter* in the slot; this host adapter establishes a connection between the system bus and the controller. Usually, the host adapter has its own BIOS. In the mainframe field, the actual computer is called «the host», and the user is connected to the host via a terminal.

Because a standard controller can be connected to many different drives, the controller has to be constructed in a very general and simple way. A controller that is fixed to a certain drive, however, may be adapted specially to that drive. Because of the low prices of today's electronic components, using a fixed controller (which requires one controller per drive) influences the overall price only a little.

Some host adapters or controller cards have a jack on the reverse to connect an external drive. SCSI adapters often have an additional jack on the back which directly connects to the internal SCSI bus; thus external SCSI units may also be connected, for example, an external streamer drive can be used.

1.2.6 Streamers and Other Drives

Data backup is enormously important for users. Using floppy disks means spending a lot of time on data backups because floppy drives are slow compared to hard disk drives; also, the capacity of a floppy disk is roughly 100 times smaller than that of hard disks – to back up a hard disk of about 100 Mbytes capacity you would need 100 floppy disks. It is particularly frustrating because almost every minute the filled floppy disk has to be removed and a new one inserted!

To overcome this restriction, and so that a qualified programmer is not occupied as a sort of «disk jockey», streamer drives (*streamers*) were developed (see Figure 1.13). As the name indicates, a regular streaming of data from the hard or floppy drives to a magnetic tape enclosed in a streamer cartridge takes place. Magnetic tapes have been unbeatable up to now in view of their simple handling, insensitivity, storage capacity and price, so they are well-suited for data backup. The tapes used have an enormous storage capacity (up to 250 Mbytes) and are enclosed in a highly accurate case. This virtually guarantees that the read/write head will be able to locate the data tracks again later. Simple streamer drives may be connected to a floppy disk controller. Very powerful streamers with a higher data transfer rate, on the other hand, have their own controller, which is inserted into a bus slot and controlled by the accompanying software. With such a system, a medium-sized hard disk can be backed up in less than 15 minutes.

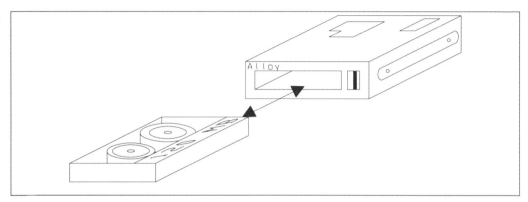

Figure 1.13: Streamer drive and cartridge. In the PC domain, tape drives are used in the form of cartridge drives. Such streamer cartridges have a capacity of up to 250 Mbytes.

In recent years, many other drive types and corresponding data carriers have come onto the market, largely optical data volumes. They allow an even greater enhancement of storage capacity compared to high density hard disks. For distributing huge and unchangeable data sets (like databases, program libraries, etc.), *CD-ROM* is especially well-suited. The name is derived from the well-known CD player (Compact Disc), but instead of music signals, data is transferred to the PC. In principle this is the same, as music can also be regarded as a data set. With only one of these shiny CD-ROM disks, data that would normally occupy a large pack of floppy disks can be shipped. The CD-ROM drive scans the surface of the disk with a laser beam and converts the back-scattered laser light into a data stream. Depending on the technical design, CD-ROM drives can be connected to existing floppy disk controllers or have a separate controller that has to inserted into a bus slot.

One big disadvantage with CD-ROMs is that data can be read but not modified. Progress towards «real» optical data recording is offered by WORMs (Write Once, Read Many). In such drives, data may be written onto an optical disk once and read an infinite number of times afterwards. If a data record is to be modified it must be written in the modified form at another, free location. The original data remains on the disk but will be ignored. You can imagine that the disk will fill within a short time, and will have to be replaced quite soon. If we consider the development of hard drives (the first 10 Mbyte hard disk for the XT was extraordinarily expensive), we can expect cheap optical data carriers that will be freely erasable and writable to arrive within the next few years.

One relic of the PC's ancient past should be mentioned: the cassette recorder. The first PC was delivered by IBM in 1980 without a floppy drive but with a cassette recorder! This, of course, had a specially adapted interface so that the CPU could read and write data. When loading a program from the cassette recorder, which today's hard drives carry out within a second, the user could go out for a cup of coffee. Not least because of this, office work today has become much more hectic....

Obviously the bus slots allow an enormous flexibility of expansion for your PC. In principle, such seemingly exotic components as magnetic bubble or holographic memories can also be embedded into your PC – but by doing this you would already be crossing into the next century.

1.2.7 Parallel Interfaces and Printers

A PC is equipped with at least one parallel interface, which may be located on the monochrome or Hercules graphics card (see Section 1.2.4) or on a separate interface adapter card (see Figure 1.14). On a separate interface adapter card, in most cases, you'll find an additional serial interface.

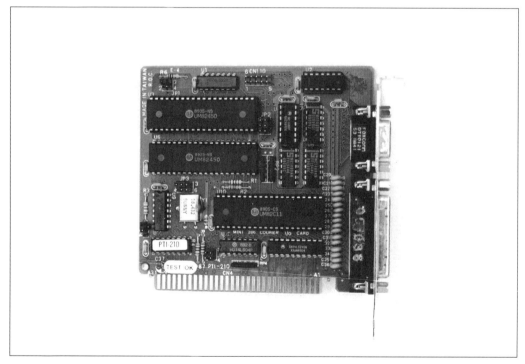

Figure 1.14: Typical interface adapter card on which a parallel interface and a serial interface are integrated.

Via the system bus, data is transmitted in units of one (PC/XT), two (AT bus) or four bytes (EISA bus, 32-bit microchannel). The bus interface (see Figure 1.15) of a parallel interface is therefore always one byte (or eight bits) wide. This means that one byte (or eight bits) are transferred to the interface at a time (also true for graphics adapters, hard disk controllers, serial interfaces, etc.) They are supplied with data in units of one byte. In the case of a graphics adapter for the 32-bit EISA bus, for example, four such units may be transferred simultaneously. On the other hand, a graphics adapter for the 8-bit XT bus must be supplied with four such units in succession.

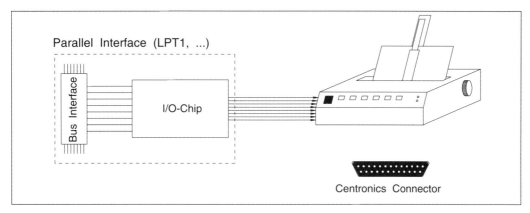

Figure 1.15: A parallel interface card has an I/O chip or an equivalent circuit that transmits or receives data at the contacts of the Centronics connector to or from a printer.

The I/O-chip on the interface card accepts these eight bits together and transfers them together, (that is, in parallel) to the connected device (usually a printer) so that eight data lines are present. Besides this data byte, control signals are also transmitted to indicate whether the data has arrived. Up to 100 kbytes of data can thus be transferred every second if the parallel interface and connected peripheral hardware is correctly adapted. On the interface is a jack with 25 holes, which supply signals according to the *Centronics standard*. The standard actually claims 36 contacts, but the PC occupies only 25: the remaining 11 were not used by IBM, and are therefore omitted. Because all manufacturers orient to «Big Blue», in time this has led to a «reduced» standard with only 25 contacts.

You should be able to recognize a parallel interface by this jack, if in doubt. The disadvantage of the Centronics standard is that cables with individual shielded wires are not used. The maximum distance between the PC and printer is therefore limited to about 2 m. Of particular importance is that the data is exchanged via *handshaking*, that is, the receiver confirms the reception of every data byte, and a clock signal (*strobe*) is transmitted together with the data signals.

The printer accepts the transmitted data and prints the corresponding text or graphics. In doing this, it generally responds to certain data patterns in the received data stream. In particular, it checks whether so-called «printer control characters» or «escape sequences» are included, which indicate a control command for the printer. The printer then reacts accordingly. For example, the character sequence 0dh 0ah means a carriage return and line feed (*CR = Carriage Return, LF = Line Feed*).

Other peripherals may also be connected to a parallel interface, assuming that the receiving interface satisfies the Centronics standard. Usually, the parallel interface only supplies data, but doesn't receive any. Actually, the older I/O-chips of parallel interfaces are unable to receive data, but more recently, versions of these chips can receive data, and it is thus possible to exchange data between computers via the parallel interface (and suitable software). IBM uses this method in its PS/2 series to transfer data between computer systems with 5 1/4" and 3 1/2" floppy disk drives, because their floppy formats are wholly incompatible.

1.2.8 Serial Interfaces and Modems

As well as a parallel interface, a PC usually has one or more serial interfaces. These are integrated on an interface adapter card together with a parallel interface (see Figure 1.14). Figure 1.16 shows a diagram of a serial interface.

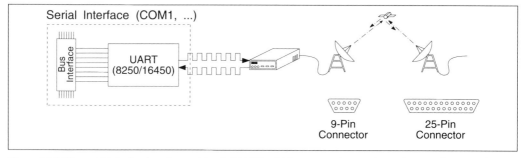

Figure 1.16: The serial interface largely consists of a UART, which executes the transformation to or from serial data. With a serial interface a modem for data communications can be connected, for example. The PC has a serial port with nine or 25 contacts.

The central component is a so-called UART. Older PC/XTs have an 8250 chip; the AT has the more advanced 16450. Via the bus interface, the CPU on the motherboard may access the UART and read or transmit data. In the case of a serial interface, like the parallel interface, data is transferred to the bus interface, and from there to the UART, in units of one byte. Unlike the parallel interface, however, the UART doesn't transfer the data to the peripheral in a parallel way, but converts each byte into a serial stream of individual bits. This stream is transmitted via a single data line, not eight as is the case for the parallel interface. Moreover, the UART adds additional bits, if necessary: start, stop and parity bits. A data packet consisting of eight data bits and the additional UART control bits is thus formed. The number of signal changes per second is called the *baud rate*. The parity bit serves as a simple validity check for the transmitted data. In this way, much longer distances compared to the parallel interface are possible (up to 100 m without signal amplification). Moreover, the cable between the serial interface and any peripheral is more convenient, as only one data line is present. However, the transfer rate is therefore lower (in a PC up to 115 200 baud). Unlike connection via the parallel interface, no synchronization signal is transmitted.

Serial interfaces in PCs conform to the *RS232C standard*, which defines the layout and meaning of the connections, and which requires 25 contacts. However, serial interfaces in PCs only occupy 14 at most, even if the corresponding plug has 25 pins. Additionally, a reduced version with only nine pins exists, but this is sufficient only for use in PCs defined by IBM. Note that the contacts on the reverse of the interface adapter card are, unlike the parallel interface, formed into a plug (that is, there are pins, not holes). You can thus easily tell serial and parallel interfaces apart.

One feature of UART, and therefore of the serial interface, is that the transmission and reception of data may take place asynchronously. If data is arriving, the UART is activated without intervention from the CPU, and it accepts the data. Afterwards, it tells the processor that data has been received and is to be transferred to the CPU. If you connect a modem to your serial interface (also called the communications interface, COM), you can exchange data with other computers of any size via the public telephone or data networks (your friend's PC, or the computing centre of a database service provider, for example). Your PC then behaves like a terminal that may be up to 20 000 km (or taking into account satellite transmissions, up to 100 000 km) away from the actual computer. In this case, data is sent to the UART by the CPU in your PC. The UART converts it into a serial bit stream and transfers the stream to the modem. In the modem a carrier signal is modulated and transmitted via the telephone network and satellite to another modem, which is connected to the destination computer. That modem demodulates the signal (hence the name modem, MOdulator/DEModulator), extracts the data, and transfers it as a serial bit stream to the UART of the destination computer. The UART accepts this bit stream, converts it into one byte, and transfers that byte to the destination computer's CPU. If that computer is to supply data to your PC, the process works in the opposite direction. This only works, of course, if the transmission parameters (baud rate, number and values of start, stop and parity bits) of your serial interface and the destination computer coincide.

Because data reception may take place asynchronously (that is, the UART need not know that data is arriving at 15:01 GMT), a communications program may run in the background. Therefore, you may, for example, input text while your PC is transmitting a message or receiving an image. Using the serial interface, a simple local area network can be made to exchange small amounts of data among several PCs. This method is popular for transferring data between laptops and «normal» PCs (Laplink, for example, does this).

I should mention that a serial interface often connects a mouse, trackball or a joystick to the PC. If the user changes the position of these devices they output a serial data stream to the UART, like a modem. The UART accepts it and supplies the data byte to the CPU. Because of the rather long distances (compared to the parallel interface) that can be spanned with a serial interface, devices in another room or even another building may be driven. Nevertheless, the data transmission is very reliable, especially at low baud rates.

1.2.9 Network Adapters and LANs

The basic concept of the PC was to put an individual computer at every user's disposal. At that time (planning started in the mid 1970s), the PC was (according to today's standard) very expensive, and a method of mass storage of extensive databases beyond most users' means. This led to typically only one computer being present in an office, and much work was done manually or with a typewriter. Problems of data exchange could not arise because all data were managed on this single computer. As the price of PC hardware rapidly decreased and very powerful programs for word processing, databases, etc., appeared, the PC replaced manual work and typewriters more and more, leading to the introduction of innovative methods (like, for example, CAD in the field of architecture or engineering). According to Figure 1.1, every user would get their own printer and modem. That is, of course, a pure waste of resources, as a laser printer, for example, is more expensive today than the PC (and out of order for more than 90% of the time!) Moreover, the data cannot be managed centrally, resulting in data chaos. As a pure typewriter, a PC is far too good. Instead, its use for data processing and data exchange with other PCs is unavoidable.

For this reason, local area networks (LANs) are being used more and more. As the name implies, computers are networked locally (within a room, building or area) so that data (text files, database records, sales numbers, etc.) may be interchanged among individual PCs. The central part of a LAN is the *server* (see Figure 1.17).

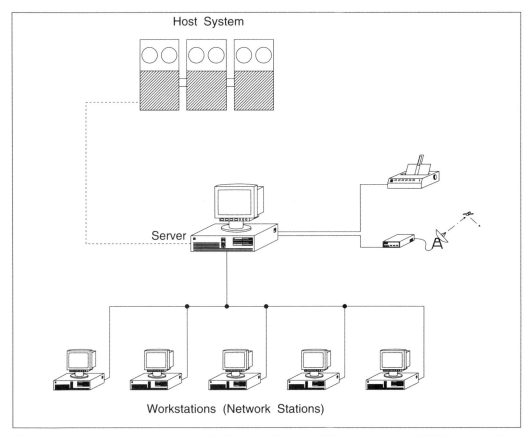

Figure 1.17: Structure of a local area network. LANs are locally bounded. The central part of a LAN is a server, which manages all the common data of all the network nodes, and establishes connections to peripherals or other computers.

The counterpart of a LAN is – what else – a *wide area network* (WAN). Computers are thus networked over long distances, for instance, the new passenger booking system AMADEUS with which you can reserve airline tickets all over the world. The AMADEUS computer centre is located in Erding, near Munich, with network nodes on all five continents.

On the server, all data which is accessible by more than one user is managed centrally. For this, the server has a high-capacity hard disk drive on which to hold all the data. Via cables and network adapters, data may be transferred from the server to the *netnodes*, that is, the PCs connected to the server, and vice versa. Moreover, a data exchange among the individual netnodes is also possible. Therefore, it is no longer necessary to copy the data onto a floppy disk, carry the floppy disk to the destination PC, and restore the data there. With a network, data can be transmitted from your workstation to one or more destinations, as over a pneumatic dispatch system. You can also fetch data from another netnode via the server. Unlike working on a PC, which doesn't usually have any password protection against illegal access, in a network you need an access entitlement to be able read or write certain data.

One particular advantage of the network as compared to a terminal is when the central computer (here the server) fails: with a terminal you are brought to a complete standstill, but as a user in a LAN you can go on working with your own, local PC. A further advantage is that on the server, all common data is managed centrally (and is backed up in one go there). Your personal data stock is at your disposal on your own PC. Therefore, a maximum of data security (by central management and backup) and, on the other hand, a maximum of flexibility, is possible. Usually, all netmembers share one or more printers so that considerable savings are possible, and the printer works to capacity. You may also exchange data via the server, so only one telephone line is required.

Like a controller (see Figure 1.12), a network adapter also has two interfaces: one bus interface for connection to the PC's CPU, and a network interface for accessing the network (see Figure 1.18). Like any other extension adapter card (graphics adapter, controller), the network adapter may be inserted into any free bus slot.

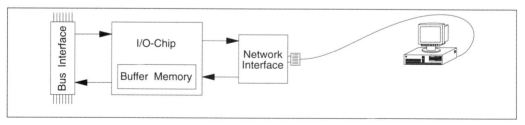

Figure 1.18: A network adapter card has a (more or less) complicated I/O chip, which normally has a buffer in which to temporarily store incoming or outgoing data. The network interface depends on the network used, e.g. Ethernet or Token Ring.

The CPU on the motherboard transfers data and commands to the I/O-chip or buffer memory on the network adapter card via the bus interface. This I/O-chip converts the data into a form that is adapted for transmission via the network, and it supplies the data to the network interface. The network now transfers the data to the intended computer (server or netnode). If, on the other hand, a command for transmitting data to the server or a netnode arrives at the I/O chip, the command is placed into the buffer memory and the CPU is informed about it at a suitable time.

The CPU interrupts the ongoing process (the calculation of a mathematical expression, for example), carries out the requested enquiry, and then restarts the interrupted process. If the bus interface for a PC on the network adapter card is replaced by an interface for another kind of computer (a UNIX machine, for example) and you insert this newly set-up adapter card in the other computer, very different computers may be networked. Any computer can thus be accessed via a network adapter, as is the case with a serial interface and a modem. Because network adapters are much more powerful (the data throughput is up to 100 times higher), the data is much faster.

1.2.10 CMOS RAM and Real-Time Clock

From the previous sections you can see that a PC may be equipped with an endless variety of extension adapters such as graphics adapters, hard disk controllers, interfaces, etc. If the computer is switched off, the PC loses its memory, and therefore doesn't know what components are installed. At power-up, all drives and components must be initialized, that is, set to a defined start-up state. You can imagine that there is a significant difference as to whether a 10 Mbytes or 300 Mbytes hard disk drive, or a main memory with 256 kbytes or 8 Mbytes, is present at initialization.

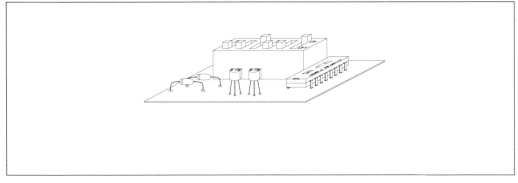

Figure 1.19: DIP switches. On adapter cards or the motherboard you often find small DIP switches. These are used to configure the adapter card or the motherboard.

In the first PCs and XTs the configuration could be set by different positions of so-called *DIP switches* (see Figure 1.19). At power-up, the processor reads the switch positions and determines which drives are installed and how much main memory is available. Because these switches are located on the motherboard, they are often hidden by extension adapter cards, so it is difficult to make new settings.

Beginning with the AT, this information was then held by a chip on the motherboard, the *CMOS RAM* (see Figure 1.6). The feature of this chip is that it needs relatively little power compared with other memory chips. In ATs and all newer IBM-compatibles, a battery or accumulator is present to supply power to this CMOS RAM (see Figure 1.20).

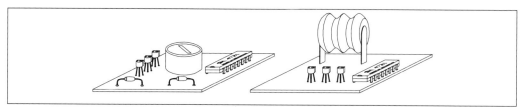

Figure 1.20: Battery and accumulator. Today's PCs generally have a battery or an accumulator to backup the configuration data of the CMOS RAM when the PC is switched off, and to periodically update the internal real-time clock.

But the CMOS chip has another function: it includes a *real-time clock* (see Figure 1.21). When the PC is switched off (or even unplugged) this clock is powered by the battery or accumulator, and is therefore able to update time and date independently. Today you don't have to provide the time or date at power-up, as the computer reads the CMOS RAM (where, in addition to the configuration data, the time and date are stored), and sets the DOS-internal system clock automatically. A correct system time is necessary because DOS appends a time mark to all files, indicating the time and date of the last file change. Backup programs like Backup may use this mark to determine which data to back up.

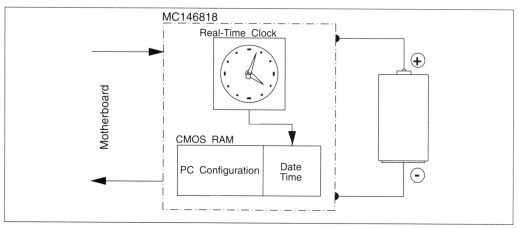

Figure 1.21: CMOS RAM and real-time clock. The PC has an MC146818 chip that has a real-time clock and a battery buffered CMOS RAM in which to store the configuration data.

The CMOS RAM and real-time clock are integrated on a single chip, Motorola's MC146818 or compatible. The CMOS RAM usually has 64 bytes, and works for two or three years with one battery.

1.2.11 Keyboard

The keyboard has remained the most important input device despite advances in graphics-oriented user shells (such as Windows or SAA standards). Figure 1.22 shows an opened MF II keyboard.

Figure 1.22: An opened MF II keyboard. You can see the keyboard chip, the scan matrix and the small switches at the crossings of the matrix.

Like the controller, the keyboard is also a small «computer» specialized for the conversion of key hits into a bit stream (Figure 1.23).

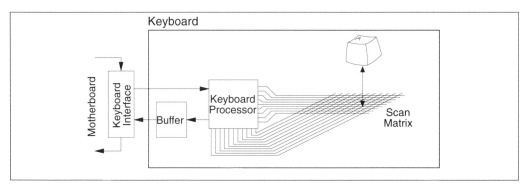

Figure 1.23: The keyboard has a keyboard processor to supervise the scan matrix, and a buffer in which to store the characters. The characters are transferred to the keyboard interface on the motherboard. Programmable keyboards can also receive data from the motherboard.

The main part of the keyboard is a microprocessor (8042 for PC/XT and 8048 for AT and MF II keyboards). This supervises the so-called *scan matrix* of the keyboard, which is made up of crossing lines each connected to the keyboard processor. At the crossing points, small switches are located, and on every switch a key is fixed. If you press a key the switch closes a contact between the crossing lines of the scan matrix. Now the microprocessor can determine the coordinates of the pressed switch, and therefore the activated key. This is done in the form of a *scan code*, which is transmitted via a buffer to the keyboard interface on the motherboard; thus the

CPU knows which key has been pressed. Conversion of the scan code into the corresponding character (letter A in Figure 1.23) is carried out by a program called the *keyboard driver* (in the case of DOS, keyb.com). Using this method, a lot of different keyboard layouts may be realized: without needing to change the keyboard hardware, and especially the scan matrix, keyboards for various languages can be realized simply by adjusting the keyboard driver for the language concerned. With DOS you may choose American (US), British (UK), German (GR), etc. keyboards.

1.2.12 Mice and other Rodents

With the advance of graphic-oriented user shells, so-called *pointing devices* have become more important. For the operation of many programs (Windows) they are very useful or even necessary (for example, AutoCAD). The oldest pointing device is the *mouse*, so called because of its plump body and long tail. Usually, a mouse is connected to the serial interface of the PC, but there are versions with their own adapter card for a bus slot, so-called *bus mice*. Originally, Microsoft planned three buttons for the mouse, but only two were used. Therefore, many mice have only two buttons. Well-known compatible mice are manufactured by Genius, Logitech and other companies.

The mouse is of no use on its own: to move the *mouse pointer* (usually an arrow or rectangle on-screen), every mouse needs (like the trackball or tablet) a program called a *mouse driver*. This converts the signals from the mouse into commands for the CPU on the motherboard. The CPU then drives the graphics adapter so that the pointer is actually moved.

As you may already have seen from looking at the outside, the mouse includes a gummed ball. Figure 1.24 shows the inside of a mouse.

The ball is in contact with two small rollers. When you move the mouse the ball is rotated, and the movement transmitted to the rollers. At the other end of the roller axis a disk with small holes located at regular distances is fixed. On both sides of the disk there is a transmitter and a receiver photosensor assembly. When the rollers are rotated by the ball, the disk interrupts the photosensor assembly and opens it, depending on whether a hole in the disk is located between the transmitter and receiver of the photosensor assembly. The number of such interruptions is proportional to the number of ball rotations, and therefore to the distance the mouse is moved. Because the two rollers are located perpendicular to each other (thus constituting a Cartesian coordinate system), any oblique movement of the mouse is converted into two numbers by the mouse's electronic controls. These describe the number of interruptions and openings of the photosensor assembly for both disks, thus the mouse knows exactly how far it has been moved. Now the values are transmitted via the cable to the serial interface, which then transfers the values received to the CPU.

In addition to this kind of mouse there are «tailless» mice that transmit the signal via an infra-red signal (similar to the remote control of a TV) to a receiver. The receiver is connected to the serial interface or an adapter card. Moreover, *optical mice* have recently come onto the market. These don't have a ball, but determine the direction and amount of movement using the pattern on a special *mouse pad* on which they are moved. In contrast to the rollers of a conventional mouse, the sensors necessary for this don't wear out, and because of the loss of the iron ball they are lighter. The optical pattern is converted into a number by the mouse's electronics, which represent the direction and the amount of movement. This conversion is rather complicated, and requires more expensive electronic equipment, therefore optical mice are, unfortunately, far more expensive than mechanical ones.

Figure 1.24: An opened mouse, with the ball and photosensor assembly for sensing movement.

If you put a mouse onto its «back» you virtually get a *trackball*. Actually, the interior of a trackball is very similar to that of a mouse, but in general the ball is considerably larger. You can rotate this ball in different directions with your fingers, and thus move the mouse pointer on the screen. In some keyboards or notebooks the trackball has already been integrated.

For professional CAD and graphics applications a *tablet* is recommended. Here, conversion of the sledge movement into pointer movement on-screen is executed purely by electronics. Below the surface of the tablet there is a matrix made of wires through which run current pulses. These pulses are detected by the magnifying glass and delivered to the PC. The advantage of this matrix is the very high resolution. A high-quality mouse reaches up to 400 dots per inch (dpi); a tablet, on the other hand, reaches 1000 dpi. Because the CPU knows exactly where each pulse is at what time, the CPU can determine the exact position of the magnifying glass on the tablet using the time at which the magnifying glass supplies a pulse. Unlike the mouse, which may be placed anywhere on the desk and only returns the direction and the amount of its movement, the tablet returns the absolute position (or coordinates). Usually, a tablet is divided into a central part, which serves as a drawing area and a peripheral part, where symbol fields are located. The symbol fields depend on the application (AutoCAD, for example). If you click on a point in the drawing area, AutoCAD draws a point. If, on the other hand, you click a symbol field in the peripheral area, AutoCAD executes a certain command (which is symbolized by the field).

There are further pointing devices such as the *joystick*, with which you may move a pointer on-screen similar to the mouse. Another, older pointing device is the so-called *light pen*. This takes the form of a pencil with which you can «press» certain optical keys or draw lines on the screen. The light pen works in a similar way to a tablet, but here no electrical pulses run through a wire matrix. Instead, the light pen detects the light-up of the screen at that position where the electron beam of the monitor hits the screen surface. Therefore, the light pen (or better, the graphics adapter) can determine its location (line, column) on the screen. As a user, you do not recognize the light-up as the eye is too slow.

1.2.13 The Power Supply

Of course, the components described above have to be supplied with energy in some way. Therefore, the power supply is explained here in brief. Figure 1.25 shows a standard power supply. (Depending on the computer manufacturer, there are many different shapes, of course.)

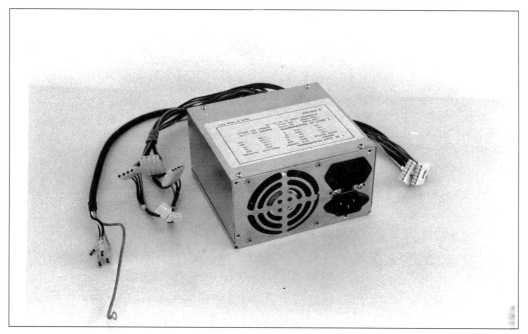

Figure 1.25: The power supply.

Usually, the power supply has one or two plugs for the motherboard, through which the motherboard is supplied with the necessary power. Adapter cards connected and inserted into the bus slots are usually supplied via the bus slots. Because the floppy and hard disk drives require far more current (power dissipation of 10–30 W each), the power supply additionally has up to four equal wire groups with appropriate plugs for the drives. Power supplies also include a thin wire with a further plug for the motherboard, through which the so-called *power-good signal* is transmitted to an electronic switch on the motherboard. The signal indicates that all necessary voltages are stable after power-up. A low voltage may lead to undefined states in initialization of the memory chips or the CPU, and therefore to disastrous failures. Thus, the electronic switch releases the 80x86 processor only if the power supply signals a stable voltage with the power-good signal. Not until then does the CPU call the BIOS to initialize all chips and boot the PC. The usual supply voltages in a PC are ±5 V and ±12 V. Some power supplies also include a socket for inserting the monitor power cable, but bigger monitors with a correspondingly higher power dissipation are usually plugged into their own socket.

1.3 Documentation

A very poor aspect of Personal Computers, especially of compatible products bought from the smaller shops, is the usually low-quality documentation. As a respectable PC user you have, of course, got a licensed operating system (MS-DOS, PC-DOS or DR-DOS, in most cases). Along with this licence you normally get a detailed description of the system commands and, in most cases, a BASIC interpreter (like GWBASIC or BASICA). Any hints about which of all the plugs and sockets is the serial interface, or where the main switch of your computer is located (don't laugh, the main switch can be hidden very efficiently) are missing in most manuals.

Therefore, you should make sure that you invest in an additional *user manual*, besides all the DOS manuals, which covers the following information:

- care and transportation of your PC;
- diagnostics software and instructions;
- memory extension and installation capabilities;
- type and resolution of the graphics adapter;
- type of connectable monitors;
- number and type of hard disk drive(s), and installation;
- number and type of floppy drives;
- opening the case and exchanging adapter cards;
- number and location of interfaces;
- type and layout of the keyboard;
- setting the clock frequency;
- calling the SETUP program and adjusting the system configuration.

IBM and some other manufacturers usually deliver such a manual along with their products, but with most of the cheaper products you rarely get any technical information about what you are buying. Also, some howlers seem to be unavoidable when translating manuals from Chinese into English. Also, dig a little deeper when you are buying expansion devices (another hard disk, more powerful graphics adapter, etc.), and ask for documentation. If, when you've installed the new device, the PC stops working, this information may be invaluable. For example, interface adapter cards installed later have to be configured according to the number and type of the previously installed adapters. Without documentation you will not be able to locate the jumpers for the configuration setting.

Further, the manual should include information on diagnostics software. This may detect the reason for failure in the case of technical failures and, for example, checks whether the hard disk controller is working correctly. Because this diagnostics software is dependent on the hardware, only the hardware manufacturer's software is useful.

A *technical reference* is beyond the scope of a user manual. In a technical reference, details are listed (in varying degrees of quality) that are of interest to programmers, for example. Only renowned PC manufacturers deliver such a technical reference, though, unfortunately, you may often only understand its contents when you know the facts.

Essential documentation which must accompany your PC includes:

– operating system manual;
– interpreter manual;
– user manual with diagnostics software;
– technical reference manual.

1.4 Taking Care of Data and Users

Personal Computers are sensitive devices. It is obvious that you shouldn't leave your PC or printer in the rain, expose it to enormous heat, or play football with it. Yet water and other liquids, such as coffee or orange juice, may lead to a short-circuit. A glass of orange juice tipped over the keyboard makes all the keys sticky. If such a mishap has happened, switch off the PC immediately and remove the liquid straight away with absorbent fabric. Rinse with distilled water if necessary.

Put on an earthing bracelet when opening the case (see Section 1.2.1) or discharge yourself by touching the power supply. This, of course, also holds if you want to insert memory chips, for example. Avoid touching the connections and pins as far as possible.

Shocks of all kinds are dangerous for the read/write heads, and the data media of floppy and hard disk drives. If you want to ship your PC, use the head parking of your hard disk drive. Today, nearly all hard disk drives have an *autopark* function, where the heads are automatically moved to a safe parking location upon power-down. But be careful; older hard disks don't have this function. Whether your hard disk drive implements such a function and which precautions have to be taken should be listed in the user manual. Utilities are available for hard disk drives without autopark functions that «park» the read/write heads manually at a certain track. These programs are usually called something like *park.exe* or *diskpark.exe*. Call the appropriate program in advance of each move. You can protect 5 1/4" disk drives by inserting a specially-shaped piece of cardboard (usually delivered with the drive), and locking it in. If necessary, you can use an unused floppy disk instead of cardboard. No special transport protection is required for 3 1/2" drives.

Handle all floppies with care. Labels must be written before they are stuck onto the envelope. If the label is already stuck on the floppy disk, only use a felt pen, never a ballpoint pen as the hard steel ball damages the surface of the disk. There is a slit in 5 1/4" floppy disks through which the disk surface is exposed. Never touch this magnetic surface as dust and fat particles may be deposited and damage the surface, thus destroying the data. Because of their plastic case, the newer 3 1/2" floppy disks are more stable and have a metal lock. If you move it aside, the floppy disk is exposed. In this case, never touch the surface.

Many users don't pay attention to an important point – data backup. This may have disastrous consequences. Like all other preventive actions, data backup is tiresome and the catastrophe may possibly never happen. As a private computer user usually it is only private data, computer games or some smaller programs that are lost, but bigger engineers' offices and legal chambers, for example, are controlled more and more by computers and the information they store. A complete loss may lead directly to ruin, or at least several months of data recovery. For small amounts of information, floppy disks are adequate, but large amounts of data should be managed centrally and periodically backed up by a powerful backup system, such as a streamer with appropriate software. Attention should also be given to some rare dangers such as fire. All the backup copies in the office are of no value if they burn along with the original data, or if they are destroyed by water damage. Therefore, important information should not only be backed up regularly, but also stored in another safe place. These hints, incidentally, evolve from practice.

Besides physical data damage (by fire, wear or negligence), logical damage may also arise. This is the product of incorrectly working hardware, user faults or malicious damage. If your PC is telling you that it is full of water but you didn't actually spill your coffee, it is probably infected by a computer virus. Some viruses are very dangerous and may destroy all your data within a few seconds. If you are only using licensed software from respectable suppliers, the probability of infecting your computer with a virus is very low. However, if you are using the one-hundredth unlicensed copy from a copying freak, such damage can't be excluded. Even so, in this case backups and some expert knowledge are usually enough to restore the data.

1.5 Operating System, BIOS and Memory Organization

The previous sections demonstrate that a PC may include a multitude of hardware components. In most cases, a user is not interested in all the details of their hard disk drive and how it is controlled by the hard disk controller. Instead, he or she uses an application program (such as CorelDRAW!) and wants to save data (drawings, in this case) as well as reread, alter or print them, if necessary. Figure 1.26 shows the different levels for accessing your PC's hardware.

Application programs are usually programmed with the help of high-level languages (C, BASIC, Pascal and COBOL, for example). Characteristic of high-level languages are commands adapted to human thinking, which may be used for searching and opening files and transferring parts (records) of them into memory. Skilful programming of the application hides this process behind a menu entry like *open file*. To do this, most high-level languages incorporate commands (or library routines) such as OPEN file FOR INPUT AS #1 in BASIC. One main feature of high-level languages is that they are portable, meaning that Pascal on a PC scarcely differs from Pascal on a supercomputer (the hardware is very different, of course). This is possible because an *operating system* (here DOS) supplies certain functions that make up the interface to the drives and the data on the volume. Thus, the program (or the user) doesn't need to locate the individual data on the volume, or read one or more records into memory. Instead, the operating system returns the requested data to the application (and therefore to the user) after a system call (here a command to DOS). Moreover, the operating system allows input and output of data through the parallel and serial interfaces, and displays text and graphics on the screen. It manages main memory and allocates part of it to application programs. Therefore, the system controls and supervises the operation of the whole computer. For these tasks, the «tiny» operating system DOS for your PC doesn't differ significantly from a big operating system (VMS, for example) for a mainframe. In a mainframe, the operating system also controls the computer, allocates memory, processor and other system elements to application programs, etc.

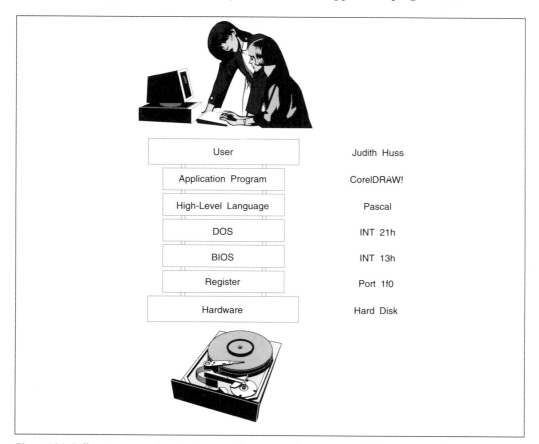

Figure 1.26: Different access levels. On the left are shown the different access levels between user and hardware. On the right is an example for each level. The top level is the application, which is the interface to the user. The bottom level is the registers that directly control the hardware.

All of these tasks are carried out by DOS in the background. If your *autoexec.bat* contains a line that automatically calls an application program you will never be confronted with the *prompt* C:>. Instead, the input mask or shell of the application program is loaded immediately. Many users confuse the C:> command and commands like DIR, CHDIR and DEL with the operating system or DOS. The prompt, as well as the internal DOS commands are, in fact, part of the *command interpreter* or *user shell*. Figure 1.27 shows a diagram of DOS components.

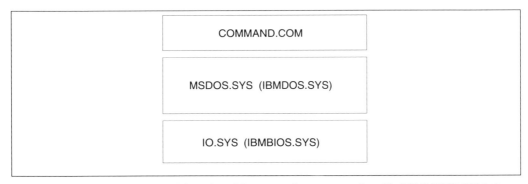

Figure 1.27: The DOS components. DOS consists of three parts: the most user-oriented is COMMAND.COM; the most hardware-oriented IO.SYS.

The «real» DOS with its interfaces to hardware and the management of memory, interfaces, etc. is located in the bottom two parts. Microsoft calls them IO.SYS and MSDOS.SYS (IBM IBMBIOS.SYS and IBMDOS.SYS). The lowest, and therefore the most hardware-oriented, level is IO.SYS. Here the routines for accessing the BIOS and registers are located. The interfaces that are important for programmers and application programs, such as file opening, byte output via the parallel interface, etc., are integrated in MSDOS.SYS. These instructions are converted into a command sequence for IO.SYS, therefore it is possible to adapt DOS to various hardware environments simply by changing the hardware-oriented IO.SYS part. Thus, the manufacturers of PCs have the opportunity to choose different technical solutions. By adapting IO.SYS accordingly, DOS (MSDOS.SYS) is then able to access this different hardware in exactly the same way as an original IBM PC because IO.SYS converts all instructions into correct commands for the different hardware. However, the passion of the Taiwanese for copying has made the adaptation of IO.SYS unnecessary, as at least 99.9999% of the hardware functions have been copied. Therefore, no different registers or additional instructions are needed.

For a user, the command interpreter is of great importance. In DOS its name is *COMMAND.COM*. This program displays the prompt (typically C:>), accepts your commands (DIR, COPY, etc.), or loads and calls programs. Within the command interpreter the so-called *internal DOS commands* are incorporated. If you issue such a command (for example, DIR), COMMAND.COM executes an internal routine (which, for example, executes a system call to read the directory of the floppy or hard disk). On the other hand, the *external DOS commands* are present as autonomous and complete programs that are loaded and executed, as are all other application programs (Word, for example), by COMMAND.COM. Unlike IO.SYS and MSDOS.SYS, COMMAND.COM may be replaced by another command interpreter (by means of the CONFIG.SYS command SHELL=...). This again emphasizes that DOS is made up of the files IO.SYS and MSDOS.SYS, or IBMBIOS.SYS and IBMDOS.SYS. They are located in the root directory as hidden files. With a suitable utility (such as Norton Utilities or PCTools) which locates hidden files, you should be able to track them down.

DOS, in turn, uses the BIOS to access certain hardware components. Usually, the BIOS supplies programs for accessing drives, the graphics adapter and parallel/serial interfaces on a physical (that is, hardware) level. Now you can see a distinct hierarchy: the menu item *open file* with CorelDRAW! is converted by the high-level language (at compile time) into system calls to DOS (at runtime), where DOS in turn internally converts these calls and uses BIOS programs to execute the menu item. In turn, the BIOS accesses the hardware by so-called *registers*. Registers are certain interfaces that are directly assigned to hardware. Commands that directly control the hardware operation are placed in registers. For example, the DMA chip, timer chip, graphics controller chip and drive controllers are accessed via registers. By using appropriate values, data exchange, the sound of a certain frequency, or various line frequencies on the monitor may be set. The address, size and meaning of the registers are, of course, largely dependent on the hardware. The job of the BIOS is to convert a defined function call into a corresponding command sequence for the registers concerned. Thus, the hierarchical concept of Figure 1.19 can be understood: if you program an application by directly accessing registers, the resulting pro-gram code can be executed only on a certain PC, and is therefore completely incompatible with other machines because the manufacturer is, in principle, free to choose any address and meaning for the registers. However, the access hierarchy, with its exactly defined interfaces between the different levels, allows (from the viewpoint of the application) a floppy drive with a 360 kbytes capacity to be accessed in the same way as a modern hard disk with a capacity of several gigabytes. BIOS and IO.SYS execute the necessary adapations to the physical drive. That the internal conversion of the menu item *open file* is very different for these two cases seems to be natural.

It should be noted that with the aid of hardware-oriented high-level languages like C, for example (and nowadays even with Pascal or BASIC), you have the opportunity to access the BIOS and registers of a PC directly. Direct access to the BIOS in particular became established with graphics applications or tools such as Norton Utilities or PCTools. Programmers want to speed up the performance of their programs and use the graphics capabilities of a PC (DOS doesn't incorporate any system call to output a graphics point on-screen, for example). As can be seen from Figure 1.26, you move around the operating system. In a PC with DOS this is not critical, because you are always working alone and only one application is running at a time. DOS is a *singletasking operating system*. More powerful computer systems (i386/i486 PCs with OS/2 or UNIX also belong to this group), on the other hand, run with a *multitasking operating system*. Popular resident programs such as the external DOS command PRINT or Borland's Sidekick occupy a position somewhere in the middle. PRINT prints files independent of the actual application running but, in contrast to a background program in a multitasking envi-ronment, the activation of PRINT is not carried out by the operating system (DOS) but by the periodic timer interrupt. PRINT catches this interrupt to activate *itself* for a certain self-defined time period. In contrast, with a multitasking operating system, all the applications residing in memory are activated by the *operating system* for a time period defined by the system. Thus, with OS/2 you can print a text while your CAD application is calculating the reinforcement of a house in the background and you are editing a letter in the foreground. Therefore, it is obvious that a multitasking system cannot allow any bypassing. In this case, there may be events run-ning in the computer that are not controlled by (and therefore hidden from) the operating system. Actually, memory resident programs like PRINT and Sidekick for DOS give the user some feeling of a multitasking environment.

A serious disadvantage of DOS is the so-called 640 kbytes border. This means that for all programs (including the operating system) only 640 kbytes are available at most. The reason is not some problem with space for memory chips or that memory is very expensive above 640 kbytes, but the *memory organization* defined by the designers of DOS (see Figure 1.28 for a description of this organization).

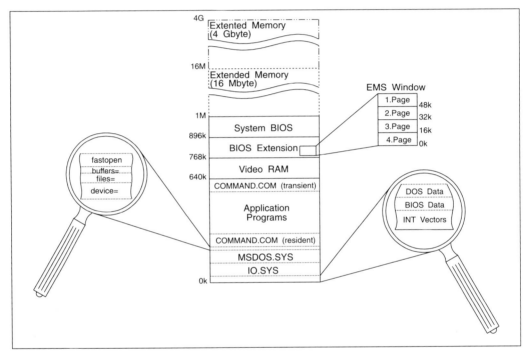

Figure 1.28: DOS memory organization. With DOS the first 640 kbytes are reserved for the operating system and application programs. Above the first 640 kbytes there is the video RAM, and starting with 768 kbytes there follow various (and optional) BIOS extensions. Above 1 Mbytes extended memory starts, which can be up to 4 Gbyte on an i386 or an i486.

You can see that the first 640 kbytes (addresses 0000h to 9999h) are reserved for programs. In the lowest parts reside interrupt vectors, BIOS and DOS data areas, IO.SYS, MSDOS.SYS, drivers and the resident part of COMMAND.COM. The *application programs area* (reserved for programs like Word or CorelDRAW!) runs on from this. At the upper end the transient part of COMMAND.COM overlaps with the application program area. To use memory as efficiently as possible, COMMAND.COM is divided into two parts: the resident part holds the routines that are, for example, necessary to load the transient part after completion or abortion of an application; the transient part holds the internal commands like DIR and COPY that are not necessary during execution of the application program, and which thus may be overwritten. Resident means that the corresponding code remains in memory even when the application is loaded: the code will not be overwritten under any circumstances; transient means that the corresponding program code can be overwritten to enhance the memory space for the application's code and data. Starting with DOS 4.0, you may determine the occupation of the first 640 kbytes by system and application programs, drivers, buffers, etc. using the command MEM /PROGRAM or MEM /DEBUG.

Above the 640 kbyte border are the 128 kbytes of the video RAM (see also Figure 1.9). The next 128 kbytes are reserved for BIOS extensions on graphics adapters and controllers (see also Figures 1.9 and 1.12). Above this there are 128 kbytes for the system BIOS on the motherboard (see Figure 1.7). In the original IBM PC, the ROM BASIC is also integrated into this area. All memory areas in total give a memory of 1 Mbyte.

The first two processors (8088 and 8086) had 20 lines for the address bus, and they could address a maximum of $2^{20} = 1$ Mbyte. Therefore, an *address space* (the number of addressable bytes) of 1 Mbyte was assumed and divided in the way described above. This separation was completely arbitrary, but you should notice that the first PC was delivered with 64 kbytes (!) of main memory. The reservation of the lower 640 kbytes for application programs and DOS (with 16 kbytes at that time) seemed as if it would to be enough to last for decades. The designers of DOS were caught completely unawares by later developments in computing, and therefore we are now struggling with this 640 kbyte border in the era of cheap and high-capacity memory chips.

In particular, it is worth nothing that the individual areas of the memory organization need not be completely filled. For example, it is possible to limit the main memory (the reserved lower 640 kbytes) to 256 kbytes instead of using the full 640 kbytes. That doesn't change the address A000h of the video memory in any way. The 384 kbytes in between remain empty and virtually constitute a «hole» in the address space. In the same way, the amount of the reserved areas for video RAM and ROM BIOS actually used has no influence on their location in the address space.

Unfortunately, because of the concept of the PC (and DOS), it is impossible to fill these holes with additional RAM. The CPU may not be able to access the corresponding memory chips, therefore all DOS programs are limited to a size of 640 kbytes less the memory area occupied by the system. Meanwhile DOS, together with all its drivers (for printer, screen, mouse, etc.) occupies a large amount of memory, so that less and less memory remains for application programs. Version 5.0 together with at least an 80286 chip offers progress to some extent. Here a large part of DOS is moved to the HIMEM area or extended/expanded memory. Application programs then have the opportunity to use a «fabulous» 620 kbytes of memory.

In the application area, the called program is stored and may itself request memory for its own purposes, for example to load a text file into memory. As the extent of the text file can't be foreseen at programming time, memory is assigned dynamically. This means that the application has to inform DOS how much memory is needed for the text file, and DOS assigns it to the application. That is the reason why some programs display the message *Not enough memory!*, although enough memory was available for loading the program. A request to DOS to provide additional memory for the text file can't be fulfilled by the operating system if there is too little memory available.

An important advance with the AT – or better, the 80286 processor and higher – is that the 80286, with its 24 address lines, can now address 16 Mbytes of memory (and the i386/i486 with 32 address lines can address 4 Gbytes). But this only works in the so-called *protected mode*. Memory above 1 Mbyte is called extended memory, and may be accessed by an 80286/i386/ i486 processor in protected mode only. This advanced protected mode is wholly incompatible with DOS. To retain compatibility, even the i386 and i486 are operated in *real mode*. Here they can only address 1 Mbyte of memory, even though 32 address lines are present. Therefore, PCs with i386 or i486 processors are also subject to the 640 kbyte border for application programs. However, Windows and OS/2 successfully attempt to break through this barricade. Switching between real and protected mode is possible to allow access to extended memory for at least a certain time. This method is used by programs like RAMDRIVE.SYS or VDISK.SYS for virtual drives. Another possibility is that a 64 kbyte region of memory may be inserted into free memory above the 640 kbyte border (into a hole in the address space); this region constitutes a so-called *window* into a much larger memory (up to 8 Mbytes). This large memory is called expanded memory, or EMS memory. By means of appropriate commands to registers on an EMS memory expansion adapter, the window (which consists of four partial windows) may be moved within the EMS memory. Therefore, the 8 Mbytes are available in sections of 64 kbytes (or 4*16 kbytes) each. Details about real and protected mode, as well as extended and expanded memory, are given later.

Part 2
The Motherboard

The motherboard is basically all those components that make up the actual computer. Important units such as hard disk drives and interfaces are already known as peripherals. It is only because the integration of electronic elements is so advanced today that the motherboard doesn't seem to be as important as it should. Before the integration of a million elements on a finger-nail sized chip was possible, the «motherboard» occupied a whole room! Therefore, it isn't surprising that discussing the motherboard will take up a large part of this book.

2 The Processor

The processor – often also called the CPU – is the heart or brain of a PC. In the processor, data processing takes place, which requires at least a minimum of intelligence. All other, sometimes rather complicated, chips are simply slaves of the processor which, together with the memory chips, is one of the highest integrated elements in a PC. But let us first turn to the unavoidable basics for understanding these seemingly very intelligent chips.

2.1 The Field-Effect Transistor

For highly integrated circuits such as microprocessors or memory chips, the MOS Field-Effect Transistor (MOSFET) is particularly suitable. It is small and easy to manufacture, yet has a very low power consumption, which is the difference between supplied power (from a battery, for example) and the power output by the circuit (for operating a light bulb, for example). This difference is entirely converted into heat, and heats up the circuit. Note that it is not primarily a high current that destroys the circuit, but the heating caused by an excessively high current which burns the elements. Figure 2.1a shows an n-channel MOSFET.

This MOSFET consists of a p-doped silicon substrate in which two n^+-doped regions are formed, called *source* and *drain*. The distance between source and drain in an IC is usually about 0.5–5 μm. P-doping means that the substrate accommodates more positively charged ions than negatively charged electrons as charge carriers for the current flow inside the substrate. This is achieved by implanting *impurities*. These atoms have less (p-doping with boron, etc.) or more (n-doping with phosphorous, arsenic, etc.) electrons compared to a silicon atom. The «+» indicates that the corresponding regions are highly doped (have a high concentration of these impurities). Between the two regions the so-called *channel* is located. The conductivity of the channel (and therefore the resistance of the MOSFET) is controlled by a *gate* formed of metal or polycristalline silicon, which is separated (and thus isolated) from the substrate by an oxide layer. Reading from top to bottom, the layer sequence reads metal-oxide-semiconductor; that is where the name MOS transistor comes from. If a control voltage is applied to the gate, free charge carriers arise through something like a «sucking effect». The higher the voltage, the more charge carriers are available, that is, the lower is the resistance of the channel. Note that transistor is the abbreviation of *tran*sfer re*sistor*. If a voltage U_{GS} is applied between the source and drain, then the current I_D (and therefore also the voltage output by the MOSFET) is governed by the gate voltage. The current flow does not start until the threshold voltage V_{th} has been exceeded. If the saturation value V_{st} is reached, current through the MOSFET no longer rises, even if the voltage U_{GS} between the gate and source rises further. The MOSFET operates in the saturation region. The currently described MOSFET is, more exactly, called an n-channel enhancement-type field-effect transistor (see Figure 2.1a).

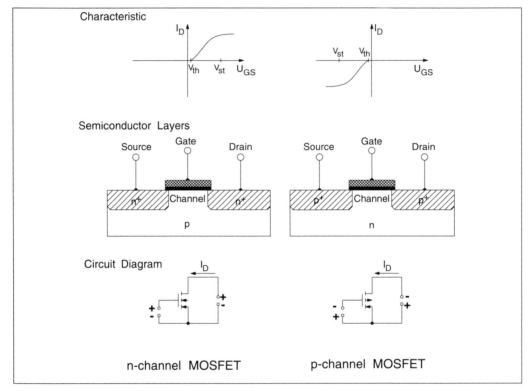

Figure 2.1a: n-channel field-effect transistor; Figure 2.1b: p-channel field-effect transistor. The characteristics of n-channel and p-channel transistors are complementary to each other. A field-effect transistor comprises two doped regions called source and drain in a lightly doped substrate. The conductivity of the channel between source and drain is altered by means of the gate voltage.

In the same way, a p-channel enhancement-type MOSFET may be constructed by exchanging the n- and p-layers (see Figure 2.1b). A significant difference between them is the opposite course of the conductivity with the voltage U_{GS} between the gate and source: a rising U_{GS} means a rise in conductivity for an n-channel MOSFET, but the decline of the conductivity for a p-channel MOSFET to zero. Pictorially, the gate voltage drives the charge carriers out of the channel and thus increases its resistance.

According to individual characteristics, it is apparent that from the threshold voltage V_{th} up to the saturation voltage V_{st}, a linear dependency between the applied voltage and the current through the MOSFET (and therefore the voltage output by the MOSFET) appears. The MOSFET is operated in this proportional region if it is installed in an *analog* circuit. This is, for example, the case for a radio or TV receiver. Here an indefinite number of intermediate levels between minimum and maximum values (minimum and maximum loudness of music, for example) is possible. But because the current through the MOSFET (and thus its resistance) can only be determined down to a certain finite precision, the intermediate levels are smudged. Therefore, no exact value of an intermediate level can be indicated, only its range.

In a *digital circuit*, however, the MOSFET is operated in a completely different way. Here the voltage U_{GS} between the gate and source is either below (or in the region of) the threshold voltage V_{th} or above (or in the region of) the saturation voltage V_{st}. Thus, two stable and unambiguous states of the transistor are defined: the off- and on-states, respectively. In the off-state, the MOSFET is completely turned off (has an indefinite resistance value), and a maximum voltage occurs between the source and the drain. In the on-state, the MOSFET leads the maximum current (has a resistance value of zero) and the voltage between the source and drain is minimal (equal to the threshold voltage V_{th}). Therefore, the transistor is used as a switch with two switching positions (on/off). For logic circuits, the existence of clearly defined and stable switching positions is essential because logic doesn't allow any woolly terms such as maybe, nearly, etc. With two clearly defined and distinguishable switching positions (and therefore output currents and voltages), we get digital circuits with dual or binary (that is, two-valued) logic.

To complete the picture, I want to mention that in very fast circuits (supercomputers, for example) a substrate made of gallium-arsenide (GaAs) instead of silicon is used. Further, in the context of so-called *fuzzy logic*, ambiguous terms like nearly, possible, etc. are also allowed. Up to now, this logic has mainly been of interest in research, but some minor applications, such as in the field of autofocus cameras, are already on the market. In the original field of data processing, this logic is not used in applications yet. The on/off logic states of a MOS transistor are converted using corresponding biasing voltages, resistance combinations, etc. to certain voltage values. In Table 2.1, the voltages for logical «1» and logical «0» for the NMOS and CMOS family, as well as for three additional bipolar families, are given.

Family	U0 [V]	U1 [V]
NMOS	−1...+1	5...10
CMOS	1...2	4...15
TTL	0...0.5	2.5...5
ECL	ca. 3	4...5
IIL	ca. 1	2...5

NMOS: logic with n-channel MOS transistors
CMOS: logic with complementary MOS transistors
TTL: (bipolar) transistor-transistor logic
ECL: (bipolar) emitter-coupled logic
IIL: (bipolar) integrated injection logic

Table 2.1: Logic levels of different logic families

2.2 Basics of Machine-Related Information Representation

An essential point in the last section was that a transistor in digital circuits (including the processors, memory, controllers etc. of your PC) is only operated in the on and off states. Thus, it seems natural to use a binary (two-valued) information representation in which each kind of information must be expressed by a series of on/off states, or 1/0.

At first glance this seems to be somewhat abstract. However, we are daily confronted with this process of information representation, but have adapted to it over the years so that it is no longer apparent to us. For example, in this book information about PC hardware is given in the form of a series of letters and punctuation marks. The only difference is that 26 different letters (a to z) and six punctuation marks (.,:;?!) are available. The electronic chips in your PC know only the on/off states, or 1/0; this means that letters and punctuation marks have to be converted to 1/0 states.

This conversion is done by means of a *code*. If you look at the following line

     5       $\circlearrowleft$

you assume that it means two completely different things: first the number five and then a donut-like symbol. Depending on your viewpoint, this may be false. The donut is the Arabic symbol for the digit 5. Therefore, the two symbols *mean* the same, but the item is *represented* differently. This also remains true with a secret code. The encoded text means the same as it did prior to encoding, but the representation has completely changed and the text is meaningless for most people. Of course, in the field of computers different codes also exist (and are used). The most common code (and in the case of a PC the only one used) is *ASCII*, which assigns certain characters a number (namely the code).

2.2.1 Decimal and Binary System

As well as characters, numbers must also be represented in some way. Don't confuse the terms digit and number: a digit is one of the symbols 0–9, but a number denotes a value. The *decimal numbers* familiar to us are represented by the digits 0 to 9 (ten, therefore decimal numbers). In other words, ten different states 0–9 can be distinguished, but in the case of a computer only two such states are available: 0 and 1. To understand the number representation in a computer we have to analyse the interpretation of a decimal number first. Our number system is also called a *positional system* because every position of a decimal number corresponds to a certain value. Generally the rightmost (first) position represents the value 1, the second position the value 10, the third position the value 100, etc. The number of such values per position is expressed by the corresponding digit.

Example: ```The interpretation of the number 318 is```
                        ```3 x 100 + 1 x 10 + 8 x 1```
                        ```or expressed by powers```
                        $3 \times 10^2 + 1 \times 10^1 + 8 \times 10^0$

This scheme may be extended to any number of an arbitrarily high value, of course. The «ten» represents the *base* of the number system and is equal to the number of distinguishable digits. In a computer, on the other hand, only two such digits are available for the base. Therefore the «ten» has to be replaced by «two». This directly leads to the *binary* or *dual system*. Numbers in the binary system are characterized by the suffix b:

Example: The number 100111110b means
                $1 \times 2^8 + 0 \times 2^7 + 0 \times 2^6 + 1 \times 2^5 + 1 \times 2^4 + 1 \times 2^3 + 1 \times 2^2 + 1 \times 2^1 + 1 \times 2^0$

                or in more detail
                $1 \times 256 + 0 \times 128 + 0 \times 64 + 1 \times 32 + 1 \times 16 + 1 \times 8 + 1 \times 4 + 1 \times 2 + 0 \times 1 = 318$

Thus we get two different representations of the decimal value 318: 318 in the decimal system and 100111110b in the binary or dual system. As for decimal numbers, the binary scheme can be extended to any number of an arbitrarily high value. However, you can immediately see a big disadvantage of the binary system as compared to the decimal system: the numbers become «longer», that is, you need more room to write them down.

In computing it became established to bundle eight such digits or *bits* (abbreviation for *binary digit*) into one *byte*. Half a byte, or four bits, is called a *nibble*; two bytes are called a *word*; and four bytes are called a *double-word*. With one byte a total of $2^8 = 256$ different numbers between 0 and 255 can be represented.

By grouping several bytes, numbers with higher values may also be represented. For example, the bundling of two bytes to one word leads to numbers in the range $0 - 65\,535$ ($2^{16}-1$). They are called *unsigned integers* (abbreviated to *unsigned*). A double-word with four bytes may express numbers from $0-4\,294\,967\,295$ ($2^{32} - 1$). This grouping leads to *unsigned long integers* (abbreviated to *unsigned long*).

2.2.2 ASCII Code

With the ASCII code, every one of these 256 different values of 1 byte is assigned a character; in other words, 256 chosen symbols are enumerated. Strictly speaking, the ASCII code only defines 128 characters; the first 32 are so-called *control characters* used to give messages concerning the transmitted data to the receiver. For example, the control character ^D (EOT=End Of Transmission) indicates the end of the current data transfer. But in the field of PCs, the *extended ASCII code* (introduced by IBM) has become firmly established. Here, even codes 128–255 are occupied by fixed characters. Furthermore, the first 32 codes (0–31) are assigned certain symbols. Appendix A gives a table with the symbols, characters and codes for the extended ASCII code according to IBM. It should be mentioned that the assignment of numbers and characters has been done completely arbitrarily. Beyond some practical considerations (you unavoidably need letters and digits), there is no particular reason why, for example, code 65 is assigned to uppercase A:

Example: ASCII code 65:   uppercase A
                (ext.) ASCII code 203:   graphics symbol ╦
                ASCII code 10 (LF):   control code for line feed

You can see that ASCII is very useful for representing text files (actually, text files are often called ASCII files). If you compose a chain of several continuous ASCII codes or, in other words, a chain of characters, you get a *string*. Because strings (which may correspond to a sentence, for example) may be of different lengths, usually the length of the string concerned must be specified. In BASIC this is done by a string descriptor which has, as one entry, the length of the string belonging to the descriptor. With DOS and some programming languages (C, for example), every string is terminated by ASCII code 0 (zero). Such a string is also called an *ASCIIZ string*. Besides the ASCII code there are, of course, other codes. Of importance for mainframes in particular is the so-called *EBCDIC code*, mainly used by IBM for its mainframes. Naturally, every user may construct his own code and may, for example, assign the letter A the code 1. By doing this, however, all compatibility is lost.

2.2.3 Negative Integers and Two's Complement

As well as the positive integers in arithmetic, negative integers are also of significance. One may think of introducing negative integers simply by a preceding bit that indicates whether the sign is positive (sign bit = 1) or negative (sign bit = 0). But in the field of computers, another representation has been established for practical reasons, the so-called two's complement representation (also written 2' complement representation). A negative integer is represented by replacing all 0s by 1s and all 1s by 0s in the corresponding positive number (forming the complement), and adding the value 1 to the complement's result:

```
Example:     positive integer 256:  0000 0001 0000 0000b

             negative integer −256:
             complement             1111 1110 1111 1111b
             add one           +                      1b
             result                 1111 1111 0000 0000b
```

Note that *signed integers* (abbreviated to *integer*) may have values in the range −32 768 (-2^{15}) to 32 767 ($2^{15}-1$). If the high-order (leftmost) bit is equal to 1, the signed integer represented is negative. The interpretation of signed integers is very different from the interpretation of unsigned integers:

```
Example:     binary number 1111 1111 1111 1111b
             interpretation as an unsigned integer:
```
$1\times2^{15}+1\times2^{14}+...+1\times2^1+1\times2^0 = 65,535$
```
             interpretation as a signed integer:
             high−order bit equals 1, therefore the number is negative;
             thus the procedure of the example mentioned above has to be inverted:

             binary           1111 1111 1111 1111b
             subtract one     1111 1111 1111 1110b
             complement       0000 0000 0000 0001b
             result                          −1
```

Actually, in the two's complement representation of signed integers, something like a sign is present (the most significant bit). But the rest of the number must not be interpreted as the absolute value of the number (in the example mentioned above this would lead to the value

−32,766). The two's complement representation is applied in exactly the same way to signed long integers. Thus they have a range of values between −2,147,483,648 (-2^{31}) and +2,147,483,647 ($2^{31}-1$). The reason for using the two's complement representation for negative numbers is that the subtraction of a number (the subtrahend) from another number (the minuend) can be accomplished by the addition of the two's complement of the subtrahend and the minuend. A possible carry is ignored. Strictly mathematical (in an axiomatic sense), this also holds in a similar form for normal addition: the subtraction of a number is put down to the addition of its inverse (represented as −number). Therefore the subtraction rule for binary numbers is:

```
minuend - subtrahend = minuend + two's complement(subtrahend)
```

```
Example:      calculate difference 15 - 1
                    15d = 0000 0000 0000 1111b
                     1d = 0000 0000 0000 0001b
    2'complement(1d)    = 1111 1111 1111 1111b
    therefore 15 - 1    = 0000 0000 0000 1111b
                         +1111 1111 1111 1111b
                        1 0000 0000 0000 1110b
    the leading 1 (carry) is ignored; thus the result is
0000 0000 0000 1110b or 14 decimal.
```

2.2.4 Hexadecimal Numbers

The representation of numbers by a series of 0s and 1s is rather tedious, and with a longer series you may soon lose track of your position. Therefore, it has become established practice to group four bits (one nibble), which means the introduction of a number system with the base 16, because four bits may represent 16 digits (0–15). Thus, the nibble constitutes the base of the *hexadecimal system*. All information units (byte, word, double-word) are multiples of one nibble. Because our familiar decimal system only knows digits 0–9, symbols for the new hexadecimal digits «10» to «15» must be added. Usually, the (uppercase or lowercase) letters a (10) to f (15) are used for this. To characterize a hexadecimal number an *h* or *H* (for hexadecimal) is added on (as in 2Fh, for example) or a *0x* is put in front (0x2F in C, for example). Conversion to the decimal system is carried out analogously to the conversion of binary numbers, only the base is now 16 instead of 2:

```
Example:      unsigned decimal integer    65,535
              binary number               1111 1111 1111 1111b
              hexadecimal numb            ffffh
```

```
Example:      hexadecimal number    9BE7h
              binary number         1001 1011 1110 0111b
              decimal number        9x16³+11x16²+14x16¹+7x16⁰
                                    = 39,911 (unsigned integer) or
                                    = −25,625 (signed integer)
```

You therefore get a more compact notation without losing the reference to computer hardware (which can only «think» in 0s and 1s) because each digit of a hexadecimal number may be represented by a nibble (four bits, half a byte). Thus, a hexadecimal number can be readily converted into a binary number (and therefore into the contents of a register, for example). Note that a hexadecimal number, like its binary counterpart, is unsigned. No minus sign exists, and only the interpretation of a binary or hexadecimal number can decide whether the number is positive or negative. Actually, the common decimal number system has something like an 11th digit in addition to 0–9, the sign «–», to distinguish positive and negative values.

2.2.5 BCD Numbers

Another important representation of numbers is given by the *binary coded decimals* (abbreviated to *BCD* or *BCD numbers*). With these numbers, the value of a byte represents the corresponding decimal digit:

```
Example:        decimal number 28
                BCD          0000 0010  0000 1000

                The first byte 0000 0010 indicates the digit 2 and
                the second byte 0000 1000 the digit 8.
```

One advantage of the binary coded decimals is that no conversion between decimal and binary numbers is necessary, as each digit is represented by its own byte. Note that the bytes indicate the *binary value* of the digits, and not their ASCII or EBCDIC codes. The main disadvantage is obvious: with one byte, 256 different numbers (or digits) can be represented, but BCDs only use ten of them. To reduce this wastefulness, *packed BCDs* are often used. Here, each nibble of a byte represents a digit.

```
Example:        decimal number 28 (compare to the example above)
                packed BCD    0010 1000

                The first nibble 0010 of the byte indicates the
                digit 2 and the second nibble 1000 the digit 8.
```

Note that in the case of packed BCDs, the nibbles also represent the binary value of the corresponding digit. With one byte, 100 numbers (0–99) can be represented here. The interpretation of a byte as a (packed) binary coded decimal leads, of course, to a completely different value compared to interpretation as an unsigned binary number (40 in the example).

Further different interpretations of bytes, words and other information units also exist. Of particular importance are the *instruction codes* for a processor, composed of one or more bytes which instruct the processor to execute a certain process (transfer data, compare, add, etc.). You can see that a few «bare» bytes may, depending on their interpretation, have very different meanings and consequences.

2.2.6 Little Endian Format and Intel Notation

Intel's processors use the *little endian format*, meaning that a word or double-word always starts with the low-order byte and ends with the high-order byte. In other words, the high-byte of a multiple-byte unit is stored at a higher address than the low-order byte. When writing a word or double-word we write the high-order byte at the leftmost position and the low-order byte at the rightmost. But storage addresses increase from left to right, therefore the 80x86 processors seemingly exchange the individual bytes compared to the «natural order» in words or double-words. Because the processor stores data in the same way as in main memory and on disk, they are also exchanged there (you may confirm this with the hex editor of Norton Utilities or PCTools). This only has consequences if the word or double-word represents a number and you want to split it up into the individual digits, because the order then becomes important (remember that all number systems used are positional systems):

Example: the hexadecimal word 1234h (decimal 4660) is stored in memory and on disk as
              3412h;
              the hexadecimal double—word 12345678h (decimal 405 419 896) is stored as
              78563412h.

In contrast, with *big endian format* a word or double-word always starts with the high-order and ends with the low-order byte. In other words, the high-byte of a multiple-byte unit is stored at a lower address than the low-order byte. Motorola's 68000 family uses the big endian format.

2.3 80x86 Microprocessors

Figure 2.2: The i486, currently one of the most powerful members of the 80x86 family, which combines CPU, coprocessor, cache controller and cache memory on a single chip.

The 80x86 as the CPU is the most essential part of a PC. In the 80x86, all logical and arithmetical operations are executed. In general, the processor reads data from memory, processes it in a way defined by an instruction, and writes the result into memory again. The following briefly describes the general structure of a microprocessor. The i486 is shown in Figure 2.2.

2.3.1 General Structure of a μP (Microprocessor)

To execute the above-mentioned logical and arithmetical operations (processes), a microprocessor has (see Figure 2.3) a Bus Unit (*BU*), an Instruction Unit (*IU*), an Execution Unit (*EU*) as well as an Addressing Unit (*AU*). Among other things, the bus unit includes a so-called *prefetch queue*. The execution unit is responsible for the data processing (add, compare, etc.), and for this purpose has a Control Unit (*CU*), an Arithmetical and Logical Unit (*ALU*), and various registers.

The bus unit establishes the connection to the outside world, that is, the data, address, and control bus. It fetches instructions from memory into the prefetch queue which, in turn, transfers them to the instruction unit. The IU then controls the execution unit so that the instructions fetched are actually executed by the ALU. Here, the control unit supervises the registers as well as the ALU to ensure trouble-free execution.

With the data bus, the microprocessor can read data out of or write data into memory. The memory location to read or write is accessed by an *address*. The processor calculates the address in the addressing unit, and supplies it via the address bus. Reading and writing is carried out via the bus unit. For this, the BU outputs the address and supplies the data to write, or fetches the data to read. The memory is addressed in the same way to fetch an instruction. In contrast, the data read (the instructions) are transferred into the prefetch queue, not into one or more of the registers in the execution unit, as is the case in normal data reading. The instruction unit reads the instruction from the prefetch queue, decodes it, and transfers the decoded instruction to the execution unit.

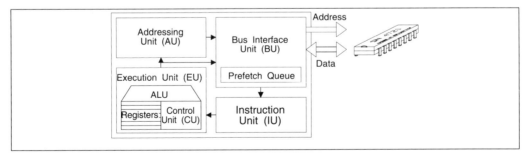

Figure 2.3: Structure of a microprocessor. A microprocessor comprises a bus interface with a prefetch queue for reading and writing data and instructions, an instruction unit for controlling the execution unit with its registers, and an addressing unit for generating memory and I/O addresses.

An essential point here is that instructions and data reside in the same memory. This means that there is no strict separation of instruction and data memory: each memory chip may serve as a data as well as an instruction memory. This is not obvious. The Z4 of Konrad Zuse (the first free-programmable electro-mechanical computer for numerical applications) had a program and a data memory that were strictly separate. In the instruction memory only instructions (and in the data memory only data) could be stored. Later, the mathematician John von Neumann developed the concept of mixed data and program memory.

2.3.2 Processors, Bus-Widths and other Characteristics from PC to EISA

Table 2.2 gives an overview of the use of 80x86 processors in various PCs. The table lists processor type, internal register width, width of address and data bus, maximum address space, and those PCs that use the processor concerned.

Processor	Register width	Address bus	DATA bus	Address space	Max. clock frequency	Used in
8088	16 bits	20 bits	8 bits	1Mbytes	10 MHz	PC
8086	16 bits	20 bits	16 bits	1Mbytes	10 MHz	XT, PS/2
80188	16 bits	20 bits	8 bits	1Mbytes	10 MHz	_1)
80186	16 bits	20 bits	16 bits	1Mbytes	10 MHz	_1)
80286	16 bits	24 bits	16 bits	16 Mbytes	16 MHz	AT, XT286, PS/2
80386SX	32 bits	24 bits	16 bits	16 Mbytes	20 MHz	AT, PS/2
386DX	32 bits	32 bits	32 bits	4 Gbytes	40 MHz	AT, PS/2, EISA
i486	32 bits	32 bits	32 bits	4 Gbytes	66 MHz	AT, PS/2, EISA
486SX	32 bits	32 bits	32 bits	4 Gbytes	25 MHz	AT, PS/2, EISA
Pentium	32 bits	32 bits	64 bits	4 Gbytes	66 Mhz	EISA, PS/2

1) Hardly used in PCs.

Table 2.2: Characteristics of the various processors

2.3.3 80x86 Registers

The 80x86 processor follows the general concept of a processor. Besides the control unit, the 80x86 has several registers, each with a width of 16 bits in an 8088/86/286, and some of 32 bits in an i386/i486. Figure 2.4 lists all the general-purpose, segment and flag registers. Starting with the 80286, many additional registers are also available for memory management, although they have a meaning only in protected mode. Here I first want to describe all 80x86 registers that can be used in real mode. Of course, the processor has a lot of further internal registers (for example, for storing temporary results) but these are not accessible by the programmer and are therefore not discussed here.

The 8088 to 80286 processors each have eight general-purpose registers AX to SP, four segment registers CS to ES, an instruction pointer, and a flag register. The 16-bit registers AX to DX are each divided into a pair of individually accessible 8-bit registers AH, AL to DH, DL, by which an individual data byte can be processed. Of some importance is the AX register (AH, AL), the so-called *accumulator*. For this register, the largest number of instructions and the most highly optimized instructions are available. The CX register serves as a *count register* for repeatedly executing instructions or loops. Every repetition or loop iteration decreases the value in CX by 1, until it reaches 0 and no further repetition is executed. Table 2.3 lists the usual names of the various registers, as well as their functions.

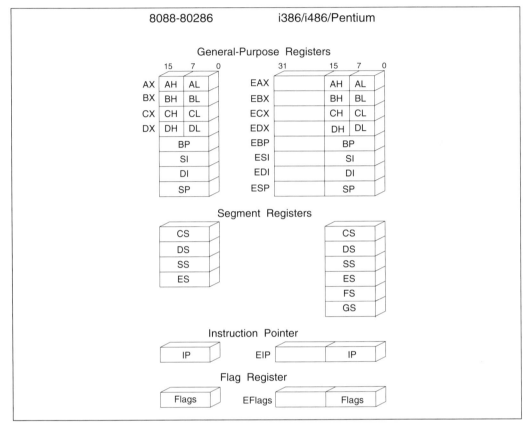

Figure 2.4: 80x86 processor registers. The general-purpose registers of 8088 to 80286 are 16 bits wide, those of the i386 and i486 processors 32 bits. Additionally, there are four to six segment registers and an instruction pointer, which addresses the instruction to be executed next, as well as a flag register storing the current processor status flags.

Register	Name	Function
AX (AH, AL)	accumulator	multiplication/division, I/O, fast shifts
BX (BH, BL)	base register	pointer to base address in data segment
CX (CH, CL)	count register	count values for repetitions, shifts, rotations
DX (DH, DL)	data register	multiplication, division, I/O
BP	base pointer	pointer to base address in stack segment
SI	source index	source string and index pointer
DI	destination index	destination string and index pointer
SP	stack pointer	stack pointer
CS	code segment	segment of instructions
DS	data segment	standard segment of data

Table 2.3: The 80x86 registers and their functions.

Register	Name	Function
SS	stack segment	segment of stack
ES	extra segment	free usable segment
FS	extra segment	free usable segment
GS	extra segment	free usable segment
IP	instruction pointer	offset of instructions
Flags	flags	flags for processor status and operation results

Table 2.3: cont.

As 32-bit processors, the i386/i386SX and i486 include general-purpose registers with a width of 32 bits, characterized by a preceding E (for *extended*). Note that registers EAX to EDX are also divided into AH, AL to DH, DL. Further, the i386/i386SX and the i486 may be operated in 16-bit mode, in which registers AX to SP are available as 16-bit registers without any change. The 16-bit mode is, of course, a pure waste, but indispensable for DOS compatibility. A special feature of all 80x86 processors is their *downward compatibility*. This means that anything that an older processor (with a lower number) can do may also be done by a newer processor (with a higher number). As there is a continuous progression in technology, the reverse does not hold, of course.

In the following sections the general-purpose and segment registers are discussed in more detail.

Accumulator AX

The accumulator is mainly used for temporary data storage. The special importance of the accumulator has historical reasons. In older and therefore simpler microprocessors, only one register (the accumulator) was available for adding (accumulating) data, for example. Today, the only remaining aspect of this limitation is that many instructions are only optimized for use by the accumulator, and are executed faster if the accumulator rather than another register is referenced. Also, some instructions with a register reference are only valid in connection with the accumulator (input/output from/to ports, for example).

In a multiplication, the accumulator contains one of the factors in advance of the execution, and part of or the complete result afterwards. In a division, the accumulator stores the whole or part of the divisor before the division, and the quotient afterwards. If data has to be input or output via an I/O port, the accumulator accepts the incoming data or holds the data which is to be output, respectively.

In the 8086 to 80286 16-bit processors the AX accumulator is divided into two 8-bit partial accumulators, AH (high-order byte of AX) and AL (low-order byte of AX). In the i386/i386SX/ i486/i486SX 32-bit processors, this division was retained. Additionally, the accumulator may be operated here with a width of 32 bits. In this case, the accumulator is called an EAX.

Example:

```
OUT 70h, al     ; the value in the accumulator;
                ; al is output via port 70h
```

Base Register BX

The base register can be used for temporary data storage, or as a pointer to the base of a data object (the beginning of an array, for example) in the indirect addressing mode.

Example:

```
MOV ax, [bx]    ; load accumulator with the value
                ; at the base address BX
```

Count Register CX

The count register usually holds the repetition count for loops (LOOP), string instructions (REP) or shifts and rotations (SHL, ROL, etc.). The value of CX is decremented by one with every iteration. Further temporary data may be stored in CX.

Example:

```
MOV cx, 10h    ; load CX with 10h (=16)
start:         ; label for return
OUT 70h, al    ; output value in al via port 70h
LOOP start     ; 16 repetitions (until CX equal 0)
```

Data Register DX

The data register is mainly used for temporary data storage. In a multiplication of two 16-bit numbers DX holds the high-order word of the result after execution. In dividing 32-bit numbers in the 8086 to 80286 16-bit processors, DX holds the high-order word before and the remainder after the division. If data is input or output via an I/O port, DX holds the I/O address (0 to 65 535) of the port to be accessed. Using the register DX is the only way to access ports with an I/O address above 255.

Example:

```
MUL BX ; multiplication of BX with AX (implicitly)
       ; after the multiplication DX:AX holds the product
       ; (high-order word in DX, low-order word in AX)
```

Base Pointer BP

Although the base pointer may used in the same way as the BX, CX or DX registers for temporary data storage, it shows its main power when used as a pointer. In this case, BP usually serves as a pointer to the base of a stack frame, and is employed to access the procedure arguments. For this purpose, the stack segment (SS) is assumed as the assigned segment register, that is, a memory access always uses the pair SS:BP. With a segment override, however, the SS can be replaced by any other segment.

Example: procedure call with argument passing and BP as a stack frame base (MASM 5.0)

```
        PUSH arg1    ; push first argument onto stack
        PUSH arg2    ; push second argument onto stack
```

```
        PUSH  arg3          ; push third argument onto stack          arrangement of arguments
        CALL  summe         ; calculate sum of all three arguments    and IP on the stack
        .
        .
Summe   PROC  NEAR          ; near call, therefore only two bytes     bp+8
                            ; for return address (old IP)
        PUSH  bp            ; save old base pointer                   bp+6
        MOV   bp, sp        ; load stack into base pointer, sp
                            ; points to old base pointer bp on stack  bp+4
        MOV   ax, [bp+4]    ; load arg1 into ax
        ADD   ax, [bp+6]    ; add arg2 and arg1 in ax                 bp+2
        ADD   ax, [bp+8]    ; add arg3 to arg1+arg2 in ax
        POP   bp            ; restore old base pointer                bp
        RET                 ; return
summe   ENDP
```

bp+8	arg1
bp+6	arg2
bp+4	arg3
bp+2	IP
bp	alt.bp

Source Index SI

As for BP, the source index SI may also be used for temporary data storage or as a pointer. In most cases, SI is used as the index of a data object within an array or similar structure, whose base is usually defined by the base register BX. In string instructions SI points to single bytes, words or double-words within the source string. Repeated execution (with REP) automatically decrements or increments SI, depending upon the direction flag. A MOVS instruction with a REP prefix is the fastest way of transferring data between two memory locations via the processor.

Example: output string "abcdefghij" on monochrome monitor in underlined form

```
string  DB    20 DUP ('a⊙b⊙c⊙d⊙e⊙f⊙g⊙h⊙i⊙j⊙') ; string to move (⊙ = ASCII code 1 is the
                                               ; attribute for underlined display)
        MOV   ax, @data           ; load string data segment into ax
        MOV   ds, ax              ; set ds to data segment
        MOV   ax, b800h           ; load segment of monochrome video RAM into ax
        MOV   es, ax              ; load video segment into extra segment es
        CLD                       ; proceed from a to j (ascending order)
        MOV   cx, 10              ; transfer 10 words each of 2 bytes (character + attribute)
        MOV   si, OFFSET string   ; load address of string into source index SI
        MOV   di, 00h             ; output string in upper left corner on screen
                                  ; (corresponding offset 0 in video RAM)
        REP   MOVSW               ; ten transfers of one word each
```

By means of the instruction REP MOVSW, DI and SI are increased by two after every transferred word, and therefore always point to the word to be transferred.

Destination Index DI

The destination index is the counterpart of the source index SI, and may therefore be used as a general temporary data storage as well as a pointer. In most cases, DI is employed as the index of a data object within an array or similar structure, whose base is usually defined by the base register BX. In string instructions SI points to single bytes, words or double-words within the destination string. Repeated execution (with REP) automatically decrements or increments DI, depending on the direction flag.

Example: see source index.

Besides the general-purpose registers, the 80x86 processors also incorporate *segment registers*. The 8088 to 80286 have four, the i386 and i486 processors six.

Code Segment CS

The code segment comprises the instructions and data that are addressed immediately. The instructions within the segment are addressed by the instruction pointer (IP), and the code segment is automatically changed during the course of a far call or an INT.

Data Segment DS

The data segment contains data assigned to the currently running program. Many instructions (MOV, for example) use the data segment implicitly to address data in memory. A segment override with another (extra) segment cancels this automatic segment assignment.

Stack Segment SS

The stack segment contains data accessed by stack instructions such as PUSH, POP, PUSHALL, etc. These instructions use the value in SS implicitly to write data into memory (onto the stack), or to read data from it. When data is stored on the stack, the accompanying stack pointer (SP) is *decreased* according to the size (in bytes) of the newly stored data. Thus, the stack grows from higher to lower memory addresses.

Extra Segments ES, FS, GS

These segment registers are available for string instructions. Furthermore, ES, FS and GS may be employed to override the standard data segment DS, so as to access the data of a memory cell that is not within DS without altering the value in DS. ES is often used by DOS and the BIOS to pass the segment of a string or a buffer to a function. For example, a buffer must be supplied before INT 13h; function 02h can be called to read one or more sectors from disk. The buffer's segment is passed in the ES register.

The segment registers are essential in accessing the memory. Let us turn now to the 8086 «ancestor».

2.4 Memory Addressing on the 8086

The following descriptions relate to the 8086, the simplest member of the 80x86 family. In later sections, all features and extensions of the newer family members (80286, i386 and i486) are explained in more detail.

2.4.1 Segments

The 8086 divides the available memory into *segments*. As the 8086 has 20 address lines in all it can address a maximum memory of 2^{20} bytes = 1Mbyte, therefore its *physical address space* has 1 Mbyte of memory. However, every general-purpose register is only 16 bits wide, and therefore can address only 2^{16} bytes = 64 kbytes at most. Thus, the 8086 divides the physical address space into segments with a size of 64 kbytes each. Within one segment the location of a byte is determined by an *offset*, which is held by the general-purpose registers.

Segments are accessed via segment registers CS to ES. For an access to memory, segment:offset pairs are formed. The segment of a certain byte is determined by the segment register, and the offset within the segment concerned is given by a general-purpose register.

As is the case with the 16-bit offset registers, the 16-bit segment registers can address 64k = 65 536 segments, the size of each segment being 64 kbytes. Consequently, one might expect an address space of 64 k*64 kbytes = 4 Gbytes. However, because of the 20-bit address bus, the physical address space of the 8086 is only 1 Mbyte. Therefore, the segments are interleaved every 16 bytes (see Figure 2.5).

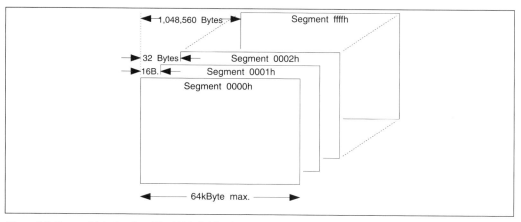

Figure 2.5: Segment interleaving. The 8086 divides the address space of 1 Mbyte into 64k segments of 64 kbytes each, thus subsequent segments are shifted 16 bits each and overlap; they are interleaved.

If the value in a segment register is increased by one, the segment is shifted by 16 bytes, whereas increasing the value in an offset register shifts the memory object by only one location. Thus, the segment register has a larger «transmission ratio». The determination of segment and offset is carried out in *real mode*.

The address of a byte (or general memory object) is calculated according to the formula

$$16 * segment + offset \qquad (2.1a)$$

or (equally)

$$10h * segment + offset \qquad (2.1b)$$

This is the same as shifting the segment register four bits to the left and adding the offset. The newly appearing bits are set to zero. This conversion is carried out in the addressing unit: the segment address is shifted by four bits to the left and an adder adds up the shifted segment address and the offset to form a *linear address* (see Figure 2.6).

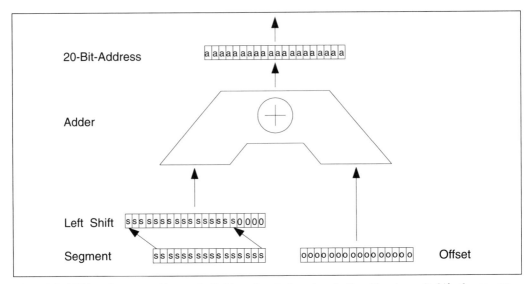

Figure 2.6: Addition of segment address and offset in real mode. In real mode, the addressing unit shifts the segment register value four bits to the left, thus multiplying the segment value by 16, and adds the offset. The result is a 20 bit address.

Segment and offset are generally expressed hexadecimally in the form *segment:offset*.

Example: 1F36:0A5D means segment 1F36, offset 0A5D
              according to the formula above the address is
              1F36h * 16 + 0A5Dh = 7990 * 16 + 2653 = 130,493

              If one uses the segment shifting of four bits
              then the following holds
                    1F360h
               +   0A5Dh
                    1FDBDh = 130,493

Note that two different segment:offset pairs may determine the same memory location.

Example: 1FB1:02AD means segment 1FB1, offset 02AD
              therefore the effective address is (as above)
              1FB1h * 16 + 02ADh = 8113 * 16 + 685 = 130,493

The main advance of the 80286 compared to the 8086/88/186/188 is the innovative *protected mode*. In this mode, segment and offset are completely decoupled: the segment registers have a different meaning, and no mapping acoording to formula (2.1) takes place. Thus, the 80286 actually has a *logical address space* of 1 Gbyte per task (program); this increases to 64 Tbytes for an i386/i486. A special address translation logic maps this logical address space onto a physical address space of 16 Mbytes at most with an 80286 or i386SX, because these processors have an address bus with 24 lines (2^{24} = 16 M). With an i386 or an i486, 4 Gbytes of physical memory is (theoretically) possible, as the address bus has 32 bits here. But, of course, you must take into account that the actual available memory may be significantly below these maximum values (especially with i386/i486).

With the i386/i386SX another new operating mode was developed, the so-called *virtual-8086-mode*. The i386 behaves in this mode almost as if it had several ordinary 8086 processors. Therefore, several real-mode applications may run at the same time without disturbing each other. In addition, protected and virtual modes are downward compatible. For example, the i486 may be operated in both virtual 8086 protected and real modes. For the technophiles among you, I shall discuss some details of these innovative modes (which are an essential basis for Windows, OS/2 or UNIX/XENIX) in Chapters 3 and 4.

2.4.2 Code Segment and Instruction Pointer

I have already mentioned that the processor reads (fetches) instructions from memory and executes them. The key to this fetching is formed by a code segment and instruction pointer. The code segment (of course) determines the segment from which the next instruction is to be read. The instruction pointer is the offset of the next instruction to be read. Thus, the segment:instruction pointer pair code makes up the address of the instruction in the memory to be executed next. The processor fetches this instruction and executes it, recognizing according to the instruction code how many bytes it has to read to fetch the complete instruction. The 80x86 instructions comprise 1–15 bytes.

Once the instruction has been executed, the instruction pointer is incremented by the number of bytes that the instruction just executed comprised. With a short 2-byte instruction the instruction pointer is thus incremented by 2. Now the segment:instruction pointer pair code points to the instruction to be executed next. This instruction is fetched and executed in the same way. Afterwards, the instruction pointer is again incremented. This fetching and incrementing is carried out independently by the microprocessor, without any intervention from another unit. Once started, the CPU continues to fetch and execute instructions. Here the prefetch queue and the bus unit play an important role. As mentioned above, instructions are read into the prefetch queue first, and the prefetch queue transfers them to the instruction unit later. If the number of bytes equal to the width of the processor's data bus is free in the prefetch queue, the bus unit reads a corresponding number of bytes from memory into the prefetch queue. For example, the 8086 has a data bus comprising two bytes (16 bits), thus it fetches two bytes if two bytes are free in the prefetch queue.

By doing this the processor uses the data bus to its optimum: if the processor is executing an instruction which doesn't require a memory access, such as, for example, the addition of two register values, then the bus unit may reload the prefetch queue without hindering the execution of the currently active instruction. Thus, immediately after completion of the instruction, the next instruction is available for execution, and does need not to be read from memory. Of course, a memory access by an active instruction (MOV register, memory, for example) takes precedence over reloading the prefetch queue. Simultaneously with executing the active instruction and reloading the prefetch queue, the instruction unit may decode the next instruction and prepare it for execution in the EU. The execution unit now executes the instruction within a certain number of clock cycles. Primitive instructions such as CLI require only two clock cycles; more elaborate ones like IDIV need up to 200 with the 8088 processor.

With the aid of the prefetch queue we get a regular *instruction stream* from memory to the processor. This stream can be interrupted and continued at another location by means of conditional and unconditional jumps. For this purpose, the value of the instruction pointer (and possibly that of the code segment) must be altered. With a NEAR call or jump the code segment remains unchanged; only the value of IP is reloaded. On the other hand, with a FAR call or jump the value of the code segment is also changed, and a so-called *intersegment call* or *jump* is executed. The processor continues at another program location in the memory. Note that such a jump also completely empties the prefetch queue because the bytes read in advance don't coincide with the jump's target instruction.

Example: The value of the code segment CS is 24D5 and the value of the instruction pointer 0108. Thus, the next instruction is located at address 24D5:0108. The code at this address is equal to 8CC0. The control unit CU decodes this and determines the instruction MOV AX, ES.

That is, the value of the extra segment ES has to be transferred into the accumulator register AX. After execution of the instruction, the value of the instruction pointer is incremented by two because MOV AX, ES was a 2-byte instruction. Thus, the value of IP is 010A and the value of the code segment CS remains unchanged.

Example: The value of the code segment CS is 80B8 and the value of the instruction pointer is 019D. Thus the next instruction is located at address 80B8:019D. The code at this address is equal to 7506. The control unit CU decodes this code and determines the instruction JNZ 01A5.

That is, the instruction is a conditional jump (jump if **n**ot **z**ero) to the instruction at address 01A5. The code segment is not changed in any case. For such conditional jumps the flag register is of great importance. Usually, a comparison of two values takes place in advance of a conditional jump. According to the comparison result, certain flags are set or cleared in the flag register. If the comparison leads to a «not zero» then the jump is executed: the instruction pointer IP is loaded with the value 01A5. Thus, the processor continues execution at 80B8:01A5. If the comparison leads to «equals zero» then no jump occurs and the instruction stream continues as normal. For this purpose, IP is incremented by two up to 019F because the conditional jump was a 2-byte instruction.

With the 16-byte instruction pointer IP, only programs comprising 64 kbytes of code would be possible. Changing the code segment by means of a special instruction (load CS with a certain value) allows more extensive programs. Note that the instruction pointer can only be set implicitly by a conditional or unconditional jump, not directly as is the case with the code segment. In addition, FAR calls or jumps automatically alter the value of the code segment register.

The instruction set for the 8086/88 has 123 instructions, the 80286 has 151, the i386/i386SX 206, and the i486 (including mathematical coprocessor instructions) has 255. Among these there are very powerful instructions for the transfer of a complete string by means of the source and destination index, the call of a procedure with CALL, or the explicit calling of a software interrupt with INT, for example. It is obvious that a detailed description of all the instructions would go far beyond the scope of this book. Therefore, Appendix B only lists the 80x86 instructions without giving any further detailed descriptions. Extensive descriptions should be given in good books dealing with assembler programming, or in the original Intel manuals.

2.4.3 Programming on a Processor Level: Mnemonics and the Assembler

In the preceding sections, instructions such as MOV or CALL have already been mentioned. If you investigate a program with the aid of a suitable editor or the internal DOS command TYPE, you will search in vain for such instructions. JNZ, MOV, etc. are called *mnemonic code* (or *mnemonics*), and are only used to assist a programmer in remembering the instructions, because mnemonics indicate the operation of the instruction concerned in a short form (compared to a home-made C routine with the name _lets_fetch_data_now).

An *assembler* understands these mnemonic codes and carries out a corresponding encoding into a *machine instruction*. Machine instructions are a series of 0s and 1s with a length of one or more bytes. If you want to display a program using TYPE, these codes are interpreted as ASCII characters and TYPE seems to supply nonsense. For example, instead of the instruction JNZ 01A5 mentioned above, the following is displayed: U♠. However, with an assembler a lot of other things can also be simplified. For example, many assemblers can process macros (hence the name *macroassembler*), carry out various addressing schemes, and access variables, jump targets (JNZ proceed_here) and procedures (CALL sub_routine) in a symbolic way. The assembler then converts these instructions into corresponding machine instructions. An assembler is the closest you can get to the hardware when writing programs; you can influence hardware directly at the register level. Programs written in assembler are usually very compact and extremely fast (important for real-time applications for machine control). Pure programming in machine language doesn't lead to any further control over the microprocessor, but only makes the matter more difficult and fault-prone. In all further descriptions of machine instructions, I use the mnemonic codes and elements of assembler programming (for example, symbolic jump targets or names of procedures). In Appendix B there is a list of the 80x86 instructions, which you are advised to study to get an appreciation of what your processor can do.

2.4.4 The Flags

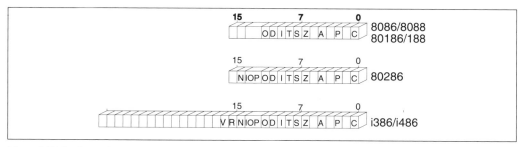

Figure 2.7: The flags. The 80x86 microprocessors have (depending on the actual processor type) several flags, which indicate the result of the previous operation or the present processor status. By introducing new operation modes, the number of flags has been increased from the 8086 to the i486.

Conditional jumps or branches are usually preceded by the logical comparison of two items (checking of a condition), as the word «conditional» implies. These instructions correspond, for example, to the commands GOTO... or IF...THEN GOTO... in BASIC. In this case the flag register is important because certain flags are set (flag = 1) or cleared (flag = 0) according to the comparison's result. Moreover, some instructions (ADC, addition with carry, for example) set or clear certain flags. Figure 2.7 shows all the flags of the 80x86 processors.

The following briefly describes the individual flags.

Carry
Carry is set if an operation generates a carry or a borrow for the destination operand. This is true if the sum in the 8-bit addition of two 8-bit operands leads to a result of more than 255, for example. Carry can be set by the instruction STC (set carry), cleared by CLC (clear carry), or complemented by CMC (complement carry).

Parity
Parity is set if the result of an operation has an even number of bits set. Parity is set by the processor.

Auxiliary Carry
This flag is used for BCD arithmetic and is set if an operation generates a carry or a borrow for the lower four bits of an operand. Remember that BCD numbers only use the lower four bits of a byte (see Section 2.2.5).

Zero
Zero is set by the processor if the result of an operation = 0. One example is the subtraction of two numbers of equal value, or the logical bit-by-bit AND of a value with zero.

Sign
Sign is equal to the most significant bit of an operation's result (0 = positive, 1 = negative result), and therefore only makes sense for signed numbers. If the difference between two numbers is negative, sign is set to one by the processor. Using this, two numbers may be compared, for example.

Trap
If trap is set the processor generates an interrupt 1 after every step (interrupts are explained later). Many DEBUG programs set trap and intercept the interrupt to execute a program step-by-step. Using this, the effects of the individual program steps can be investigated. Trap may not be set or cleared directly by an instruction. This can be circumvented with the aid of the instructions PUSHF (push flags onto stack) and POPF (write flags back from stack into flag register). The flags are pushed onto the stack by PUSHF, manipulated there, and the manipulated flags written back into the flag register with POPF.

Interrupt Enable
If interrupt enable is set, the processor accepts hardware IRQs and services them. This flag may be cleared using the instruction CLI or set by STI. Interrupts must be locked out during applications which don't allow any interruption during execution. If the lock-out is too long, problems may arise in real-time applications (for example, a byte arriving at the serial port may be lost).

Direction

The direction flag defines the direction of string operations (MOVS, for example). If direction is set, the strings are processed from higher to lower address, and vice versa. The direction flag may be set by STD and cleared by CLD.

Overflow

Overflow is set by the processor if the result of an operation is too big or too small for the destination operand. For example, the addition of two 16-bit numbers may lead to a value which no longer fits into a 16-bit register.

I/O Protection Level

This 2-bit flag defines the minimum required protection level for input and output operations in protected mode, and is managed by the operating system (OS/2, UNIX, etc.). This is discussed in some detail in Sections 3.3.9 and 4.2.6.

Nested Task

Nested task is used in protected mode to supervise the chaining of interrupted and reactivated tasks, and is managed by the operating system (OS/2, UNIX etc.). Some detailed information for technophiles will be given in Section 3.3.

Resume

If resume is set the i386 debug tasks are temporarily disabled. More about this is given in Section 4.2.5.

Virtual 8086 Mode

If the virtual 8086 mode flag is set, the i386 (or higher) is running in virtual mode and may execute several real-mode applications (such as DOS programs) concurrently. The processor behaves as if it incorporates several 8086 processors in parallel. Each of these «processors» works with its own copy of DOS so that the real-mode applications don't influence each other. If the flag is cleared, the i386 (or higher) runs in ordinary protected or real mode.

Nearly all instructions for conditional jumps test the value of the flag which reflects the result of the previous comparison.

Example:
```
If the value of register AX is equal to 5 then branching to TARAMTATAM occurs:
CMP ax, 5    ; compare register AX with value 5
JZ TARAMTATAM ; jump to TARAMTATAM
```

The processor executes the comparison CMP ax, 5 by subtracting the value 5 from AX and setting the flags accordingly. In the example, 5 is thus subtracted from the value of register AX. If AX is equal to 5 the zero flag is set. If AX is more than 5 (the subtraction's result is more than 0), then the 80x86 clears the sign and zero flags. If, on the other hand, AX is less than 5 (the subtraction's result is less than 0), zero is cleared and sign is set to 1.

Some instructions (such as JBE, jump if below or equal) test several flags (here: sign and zero) to determine whether the jump condition is fulfilled. Therefore, the flags supply extensive information concerning the current processor status or the result of an operation.

2.4.5 Stack Segment and Stack Pointer

Of some importance are the stack segment and accompanying stack pointer. Usually, every program has its own stack segment where the value of a register or a memory word can be stored with PUSH. The flags may be pushed onto the stack with PUSHF, and the general-purpose registers with PUSHA (80186 and higher). With POP, POPF and POPA (80186 and higher) the corresponding data can be retrieved from the stack.

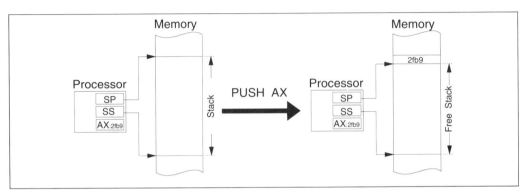

Figure 2.8: Stack and stack pointer. The 80x86 mainly uses the stack for storing return addresses and register values. An instruction PUSH AX pushes the value of the accumulator AX onto the stack and the stack pointer is decremented by two. Thus the stack is growing downwards, that is, to lower addresses.

Note that the stack is «growing» downwards, that is, to lower values of the stack pointer SP (see Figure 2.8). If data is pushed onto the stack the value of SP is decreased by two, because a whole word (two bytes) is always placed on the stack. If the i386/i486 32-bit processors are operated in 32-bit mode, of course, four bytes are always pushed onto the stack, and the value of SP is decreased by four with every PUSH. A completely empty stack therefore means the highest possible value of SP. After pushing a word, the stack pointer points to the last word pushed onto the stack.

Because of the downward growth of the stack, a stack overflow can easily be detected: if SP=0 the stack is full and application programs that regularly check the stack display the message *stack overflow!*. Usually, programmers reserve sufficient memory area for the stack (a sufficiently high value of SP to start with) so that such a stack overflow will only arise because of a pro-gramming error or faulty program use. In protected mode the processor's hardware (starting with the 80286) checks whether a stack overflow occurs, thus a very fast check is possible without any program overhead for software check routines.

The stack may be used as a temporary memory for data which is difficult to access without PUSH and POP (the trap flag, for example). On the whole, though, the stack is used to pass parameters to procedures and subroutines. For this purpose, the calling program pushes the parameters to be passed onto the stack using one or more PUSH instructions. The called proce-dure fetches these parameters with one or more POP instructions, or by addressing with the base pointer BP. Further, the called procedure stores its local variables on the stack. Depending on the programming language, the called procedure or the calling program cleans up the stack on its return from the subroutine, that is, it restores the stack state before the call. Thus, the parameters and local temporary variables stored on the stack are destroyed with the next procedure or subroutine call.

Most BIOS routines don't have their own stack, but use the stack of the calling program. On the other hand, DOS uses three internal stacks in total for its functions. The way in which 80x86 processors execute a PUSH SP instruction (that is, the stack pointer itself is pushed onto the stack) is quite different from the 8086/88 and all the other 80x86 processors:

−   The 8086/88 updates SP first (decreases SP by two) and copies the value of SP onto the stack afterwards.
−   Starting with the 80186/88 SP is copied onto the stack first and then the SP is updated (decreased by two or four).

2.4.6 Data Segment DS and Memory Addressing

Besides the code and stack segment registers, there is also the data segment register (DS). This register is important if an instruction reads data from or writes data into the memory. Usually, the offset of the data is held in one of the general-purpose registers, and the DS:offset pair points to the data to read or write. If data belonging to another segment has to be read or written, the segment register DS has to be loaded with the value of the new segment, or a so-called *segment prefix* must be used (more about this in the following sections). The data of the code segment will only be executable and (at most) readable. Overwriting code unavoidably means crashing the program. Execute-only data may be fetched into the prefetch queue, but not into general-purpose or segment registers, therefore a program cannot use them in the sense of data that is processed.

The use of different segments for code, stack and data allows the separation of the different sections of a program. The protected mode makes intensive use of this to avoid any erroneous overwriting of code by a program error (a main cause of crashed programs). Of course, all segment registers may hold the same value. In this case, no separation of code, stack and data occurs. The COM-programs of DOS are structured like this. COM-programs are relics from the days of CP/M, which was an operating system (control program) for simple 8-bit processors. COM-programs don't support a memory divided into segments, so segment registers in COM-programs have no meaning. The program deals only with offsets and all segment registers hold the same value, thus the address space for code and data is limited to 64 kbytes (one 8086 segment) in total.

2.4.7 Addressing Schemes

If a register (here AX, for example) is to be loaded with a value by means of MOV AX, three possibilities are available:

−   **Immediate:** MOV AX, 2h
The AX register is loaded with the value 2h. This value is fixed and stored in the code, that is, it appears as part of the instruction stream that is loaded into the prefetch queue by the bus unit.

– **Register Operand:** `MOV AX, BX`

The AX register is loaded with the value in the BX register.

– **Memory Operand: MOV AX, mem**

mem means the *effective address* (see below) of the operand that is to be loaded into the accumulator. If the effective address is fixed (that is, a quantity known at assembling time) it is precalculated by the assembler. In this case, mem is a *direct memory operand*. With a macroassembler, direct memory operands are usually assigned a fixed symbol (array, for example). If the effective address comprises a variable part, for example a register with a variable value, the CPU calculates the effective address at runtime. In this case, mem is an *indirect memory operand*.

The effective address is the offset of the operand within the selected segment (here DS). The effective address is made of up to four elements:

– **Displacement:** `MOV AX, array[0]`

The first element of the array is loaded into the accumulator. `array[0]` is a symbolic name that a macroassembler can process to assist the programmer in his work. In the assembled program you will find a number instead of `array[0]`, which indicates the address of the symbolic array[0]. If, for example, `array[0]` is at address 0f2h, the instruction reads as `MOV AX, 0f2h`.

– **Base Register:** `MOV AX, [BX]`

The operand at the address given by the value in register BX is loaded into the accumulator. If, for example, BX holds the value 0f2h, this instruction is equivalent to `MOV AX, array[0]`. The difference between `[BX]` and `array[0]` is that the value of BX may be altered dynamically by the program, but `array[0]` represents a fixed and constant value during program execution. For example, by changing BX and using a loop, the whole array can be processed. This is similar to the command `FOR I=0 TO 99 ... NEXT I` in BASIC. Base registers BX and BP (or EBX and EBP) are valid.

– **Index Register:** `MOV AX, [SI]`

In this basic form the use of the index register is equal to the use of the base register BX. Starting with the i386, a scaling factor (see below) may additionally be assigned. Index registers SI and DI (or ESI and EDI) are valid.

– **Scaling Factor (i386 and above):** `MOV AX, [SI*4]`

To calculate the effective address the value of the index register SI is multiplied by four, thus arrays whose elements consist of four bytes can be indexed. The scaling (multiplication) by a factor larger than 1 is carried out within the processor without any loss of time. Valid factors are 1, 2, 4 and 8.

Displacement, base register, index register and (starting with the i386) scaling factors can be used in any combination, therefore array elements may be addressed very efficiently.

Example: Assume an array with 100 elements that define 100 different bodies; each element has the structure height:width:depth:cross-section; height, etc. 1 byte each. The array starts at 0a24h. Using the following program fragment, the depth of an element can be transferred into the accumulator AX:

```
MOV BX, 0a24h        ; loads base address into BX
MOV SI, nr           ; load element number into SI
```

```
MOV AX, [BX+SI*4+2]   ; load depth (displacement 2 relative to the start of the element)
                      ; of element nr (element size = 4 bytes, therefore scaling 4)
                      ; of the array (starting at the base address in BX) into
                      ; accumulator AX
```

For the example indicated above, normally the segment register DS is used (or SS if the BP register is employed as the base register). Instead of these segment registers, ES and CS (and starting with the i386, additionally FS and GS) may also be used if, for example, the value of ES or CS is loaded into the DS register. But this method is only advantageous if there are many instructions which reference the segment stored in the ES register still to be executed. However, if the ES register is only used occasionally, a *segment override* may be employed. This override is performed in an assembler by specifying the data segment before the memory operand. Data segment and memory operand are separated by a colon. If applied to the example described above, the instruction MOV AX, ES:[BX+SI*4+2] would access an array in a segment defined by the segment register ES.

In the section on displacement it was mentioned that the assembler converts the instruction MOV AX, array[0] of the example described into MOV AX, 0f2h. But how can the assembler recognize that 02fh is a displacement (an address) and has no value (that is, the processor loads the value at address DS:02fh and not the value 02fh itself into the AX register)? The key to this is the encoding of instructions.

2.4.8 Encoding of Machine Instructions

The processor doesn't know any instructions like MOV AX, ES:[BX+SI*4+2], only bytes and series of bytes. Therefore, the assembler (or compiler in the case of high-level languages) must convert the instructions written in «unencoded text» into a quite lengthy series of bytes. For this purpose, every instruction is divided into four main parts:

prefix	opcode	operand(s)	displacement/data

The central part is the so-called *opcode* (operation code), which has one or two bytes and defines the instructions in an unambiguous manner. If the first byte is equal to 00001111b the opcode consists of two bytes. If the first byte starts with the bit combination 11011b (27 decimal corresponding to ESC), the instruction is for the mathematical coprocessor only. Simple instructions without operands such as CLC (clear carry) consist solely of the opcode and occupy only one byte. More extensive instructions with prefixes and several operands/displacement/data may, however, be up to 15 bytes on an i386/i486. Prefix, operand(s) and displacement/data are supplied if the opcode indicates that the processor needs such information. The two low-order bits of the opcode often define the direction of the data transfer (register to register/memory, or memory to register) as well as the use of 8-bit or 16-bit operands (AL or AX, for example).

The *operand(s)* field holds information concerning which registers use which direct or indirect memory operand. The *displacement/data* field defines a displacement that is fixed at assembling time or an immediate operand.

Example: The encoding into the opcode for the instruction MOV AX, 02fh mentioned above may be different, depending on whether 02fh is a displacement or an immediate operand:
    displacement: opcode 10100011 00101111
    immediate: opcode 10111000 00101111
That is, the byte 00101111 may be the displacement 02fh and also the immediate operand (value) 02fh.

The instruction unit (IU) can determine, according to the different opcodes, whether a MOV instruction with displacement or with an immediate operand is present. Thus the IU instructs the execution unit (EU) to handle the MOV instruction accordingly. If a displacement is present, then the EU drives the addressing unit to load the value at address DS:02fh from memory via the bus unit into the accumulator. If 02fh is an immediate operand, then 02fh is loaded into AX as part of the instruction stream from the prefetch queue.

If, in the case of a displacement, the operand at 02fh is to be loaded from segment ES instead of the standard segment DS, the same opcode is used but a *prefix* is put in front. This prefix issues a segment override. Valid segment override prefixes are listed in Table 2.4.

Segment	Prefix
CS	00101110 (2eh)
DS	00111110 (3eh)
SS	00110110 (36h)
ES	00100110 (26h)
FS	01100100 (64h)
GS	01100101 (65h)

Table 2.4: Segment override prefixes

In addition to the segment override prefixes, repetitions of string operations (using REP), the locking of the bus (using LOCK) and, with an i386/i486, the alteration of the operand (16 or 32 bits) and address size (16 or 32 bits) are also indicated by a prefix. The advantage of prefixes over an encoding in the opcode is obvious: prefixes are only used if an operation actually requires them. Encoding in the opcode would unavoidably lead to an opcode of at least two bytes to incorporate the additional encoding positions. Therefore, occasionally encoding with prefixes needs less storage capacity and the programs are more compact. Apart from the fact that a more extensive memory access is required by the segment override prefix, all instructions with reference to a segment other than the standard data segment are executed in the same time. Because the prefetch queue is continuously reloaded in the background, even the additional memory access slows down the execution speed only in very unfavourable circumstances (for example, if the prefetch queue has been cancelled after a jump or call).

Assemblers automatically recognize which operand size or which segment is applicable according to symbols like EAX or ES. They carry out a corresponding encoding of opcode, operand(s) and displacement/data, as well as the insertion of the required prefixes. Programming with a powerful assembler and the very extensive instruction set of the 80x86 processors sometimes gives the feeling of dealing with a high-level language.

2.5 The Physical Access to Memory and Peripherals

Until now we have only discussed the logical addressing of memory with offset and segment. The memory is, for example, accessed by means of the instructions MOV reg, mem or MOV mem, reg. Besides the memory space, the 80x86 also knows a so-called I/O space, which is accessed by means of the instructions IN, OUT, etc. via *ports*. The access may be byte-by-byte or word-by-word. In total, the 8086 can address 65 536 (= 64 k) 8-bit ports with addresses 0–65 535 or 32 768 (= 32 k) 16-bit ports with addresses 0, 2, 4, ..., 65 532, 65 534. In the PC, only the lower 1024 (1k) ports from 000h up to 3ffh are used. Also, a mixture of 8-bit and 16-bit ports is possible, but the corresponding 8-bit equivalent may not exceed 64 k. Thus, we get two completely separate address spaces: the memory and the I/O space, both addressed via the data and address bus. In contrast to the memory address space, which is addressable with any register, the I/O address space can only be addressed by the accumulator. Further, the segment registers have no meaning for the I/O address space. On the other hand, it is possible to regard the 64 k ports as a separate «segment» that is accessed with IN and OUT.

Ports and the I/O address space are largely used to access *registers* in peripherals. The IN and OUT instructions, together with their variations, establish a direct connection between the accumulator and the register of the peripheral, as well as transferring data among them. This data transfer, the differentiation between whether data has to be read or written, and similar processes, are told the processor's environment via connections. Figure 2.9 shows a pin arrangement diagram for the 8086 processor; their meanings are described in the next section.

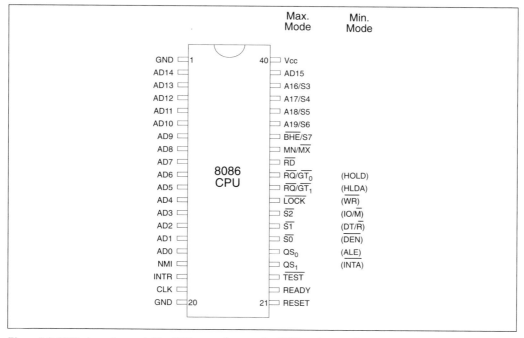

Figure 2.9: 8086 pin assignment. The 8086 comes in a standard DIP package with 40 pins. Some connections provide different signals in minimum and maximum mode.

One characteristic of the 8086 and 8088 compared to other 80x86 processors is that they can be operated in *maximum* or *minimum mode*. Selection is carried out by the MN/MX pin 33. If it is fixed at the supply voltage V_{cc} of +5 V, the 8086/88 operates in maximum mode. If it is grounded (0 V, GND), the 8086/88 runs in minimum mode. Because the structure of a computer is very different, depending upon the operation mode of the processor, this pin is usually soldered to one of these two potentials at the time of the computer's manufacture. In PCs with the 8088 processor (and the XT with the 8086 processor) the CPU always operates in maximum mode, but in other computers which use an 8086/88 the processor may be running in minimum mode.

The difference between minimum and maximum mode is how the bus is driven. In minimum mode, the 8086/88 generates the necessary control signal for the bus on its own. In maximum mode, it only outputs status signals to the accompanying *bus controller*. The bus controller interprets these status signals and generates the necessary signals for the bus. The predecessors of the 8086/88 were the simpler 8-bit processors (for example, the 8080), which generated the bus signals themselves. These chips were built into simple computers (compared to today's state-of-the-art) without much extension capability and poor memory size. Therefore, the chips didn't need to supply high currents for driving the individual components; that is why no additional bus controller was necessary. With an 8086/88 in minimum mode, a very compact computer is possible.

The flexible and more extensive design of the PC, however, requires an additional bus controller to supply all bus signals with the necessary power. Further, Intel (the processor family manufacturer) introduced a new bus design called MULTIBUS, which enables the cooperation of several processors – so-called *multi-processing*. This is, however, not used in the PC (with the exception of an additional coprocessor).

Besides the bus controller, many other chips are present that support the processor in its work. The most important are:

- the 8288/82288 bus controller
- the 8237 DMA controller
- the 8253 programmable interval timer
- the 8259 programmable interrupt controller
- the 8284 clock generator.

Every member of the processor family has its own set of support chips, but some support chips for older processors may also be used for new members of the family. For example, the 8237 DMA controller was used in the first PC and is still used in today's i486 computers.

For the overall performance of a computer, the processor is not the only decisive component – the support chip also plays an important role.

2.5.1 8086 Connections and Signals

The following explains the connections of the 8086 and the meanings of the corresponding signals. First, we cover the pins, which have the same meaning both in maximum and minimum mode. High indicates a logical high level, usually equal to V_{cc}, that is, +5 V. Low indicates a logical low level, normally equal to ground (GND) or 0 V. A signal without bar (such as *signal*) is active high, that is, has the indicated function at the high level. A signal with a bar (such as $\overline{\text{signal}}$) is active low. In the field of electronics, inverted signals are commonly characterized by a bar.

AD15–AD0 (pins 2–16, 39)

These 16 connections form the 16 data bits when the 8086 is reading or writing data as well as the lower 16 address bits when the 8086 is addressing memory or peripherals. The address signals are always supplied first and at a later time the data signals are output or read. Therefore these 16 pins form a *time-divisionally multiplexed* address and data bus, so the 40 pins of the 8086 package can be used very efficiently.

A19–A16/S6–S3 (pins 35–38)

These four pins form the four high-order bits of the address bus as well as four status signals which indicate the processor's current activity. Thus, these four lines form a time-divisionally multiplexed address and control bus. If the pins supply status information, S5 (pin 36) indicates the value of the interrupt flag in the processor's flag register, and S4/S3 indicates the segment register that is used for the access.

Valid status signals starting with the middle of T2 until the end of T4 (see Section 2.5.3) are shown in Table 2.5.

A17/S4	A16/S3	Register for data access
0 (low)	0	ES
0	1	SS
1 (high)	0	CS or none
1	1	DS

S5 = status of the IE flag (interrupt enable)
S6 = 0 (low) always

Table 2.5: Valid status signals

$\overline{\text{BHE}}$/S7 (pin 34)

This signal indicates whether a whole word (2 bytes) is present on the data lines AD15–AD0, one byte with an odd address on the data lines AD15–AD8 or one byte with an even address on the lines AD7–AD0. Because the 8086 has a 16-bit data bus but is also able to address 8-bit units (via AL, for example), it is necessary to tell the memory control in a write operation on which data lines the byte is transmitted. Equally, the processor needs to know, when reading a byte, on which data lines the byte is supplied. For the combination ($\overline{\text{BHE}}$/S7, A0) the following meanings hold (0 means low, 1 high):

```
(00) one complete word (2 bytes) is transferred via D15–D0
(01) one byte on D15–D8 is transferred from/to an odd byte address
(10) one byte on D7–D0 is transferred from/to an even byte address
(11) invalid
```

RD (pin 32)
This connection (READ) indicates whether the processor is reading data from memory or from an I/O register (RD high), or writing data (RD low).

READY (pin 22)
If the accessed memory or peripheral has completed the data transfer from or to the memory or peripheral, READY is set high to indicate that state to the processor. Therefore, slow memory chips or peripherals can cause the processor to insert wait states if they are unable to supply or accept the data in time. This ensures that the processor does not output data until it can be accepted, or that the processor delays its read until, for example, the memory has read data from one of its cells. Only when READY is high does the processor read data in or continue with data output, respectively. The asynchronous READY signal output by a memory chip or peripheral is supplied by the clock generator. The clock generator synchronizes the signal and supplies it as a synchronous READY signal to the processor.

INTR (pin 18)
This input signal is checked after completion of each instruction to determine whether an interrupt request from a hardware unit is pending. This check may be masked by a cleared interrupt flag. If a signal with high level is applied, a procedure is invoked to service the hardware interrupt request.

$\overline{\text{TEST}}$ (pin 23)
This input is continuously checked by the WAIT instruction. If the level of $\overline{\text{TEST}}$ is low, the processor continues to execute the program. Otherwise, it executes dummy cycles until $\overline{\text{TEST}}$ is low. Thus, the processor can be stopped, by means of the WAIT instruction, until the coprocessor has completed the corresponding calculation. Hardware interrupt requests are not locked out in this case, because the coprocessor requires up to 1000 clock cycles for calculating a logarithm and hardware interrupts might otherwise be lost.

NMI (pin 17)
A change of this signal from low to high causes an interrupt 2. This interrupt cannot be masked by the interrupt flag. The interrupt is executed immediately after completion of the current instruction. In the PC, for example, memory parity errors issue an NMI.

RESET (pin 21)
If this input is high for at least four clock cycles, the processor aborts its operation immediately and executes a processor reset as soon as the RESET signal becomes low. All internal registers are set to a defined value, and the processor starts execution at address 0f000:fff0.

CLK (pin 19)
CLK is the clock signal for the processor and the bus controller.

V_{CC} (pin 40)
This pin is supplied with the supply voltage of +5V.

GND (pins 1, 20)
These pins are earthed (usually 0V).

MN/$\overline{\text{MX}}$ (pin 33)

MN/$\overline{\text{MX}}$ indicates the operating mode. If MN/$\overline{\text{MX}}$ is earthed the 8086 is running in maximum mode. If the pin is fixed to V_{cc} the 8086 is operating in minimum mode.

The following signals and pin assignments are valid for maximum mode only.

$\overline{S}_2$, $\overline{S}_1$, $\overline{S}_0$ (pins 26–28)

The 8288 bus controller uses these three control signals to generate all necessary memory and I/O control signals that control a read or write access to memory or I/O space. For the combinations ($\overline{S}_2$, $\overline{S}_1$, $\overline{S}_0$) the following interpretations hold (0 means low, 1 high):

```
(000) a hardware interrupt request via INTR is accepted (interrupt acknowledge)
(001) an I/O port is read
(010) an I/O port is written
(011) the processor is stopped or disabled (HALT)
(100) an access to program code is taking place to reload the prefetch queue
(101) data is read from memory
(110) data is written into memory
(111) passive state
```

$\overline{\text{RQ}}/\overline{\text{GT}}_0$, $\overline{\text{RQ}}/\overline{\text{GT}}_1$ (Pins 30, 31)

These signals serve for switching the *local bus* between various *bus masters*. The local bus is the bus between different processors, but not the bus which establishes a connection to memory or peripherals. The bus master is a processor or control chip that may get control of the local bus to transfer data, and which supplies all necessary bus control signals (examples are the 8086 and the DMA controller).

The $\overline{\text{RQ}}/\overline{\text{GT}}_0$ connection has a higher priority than $\overline{\text{RQ}}/\overline{\text{GT}}_1$. If another processor wants to get control of the local bus, it outputs a request signal via $\overline{\text{RQ}}/\overline{\text{GT}}_x$ (x = 0,1) to the currently active processor (current bus master). If the addressed processor can release control (after completing its own instructions) it supplies an acknowledge signal via the same $\overline{\text{RQ}}/\overline{\text{GT}}_x$ pin.

Thus, the requesting processor takes control of the local bus. This procedure is necessary if several processors and I/O chips use a common storage and/or common I/O address space.

$\overline{\text{LOCK}}$ (pin 29)

If $\overline{\text{LOCK}}$ is active (that is, low) the processor may not release the local bus to another processor. $\overline{\text{RQ}}/\overline{\text{GT}}_x$ doesn't respond to the request with an acknowledge. Using the LOCK instruction, the $\overline{\text{LOCK}}$ signal may be activated explicitly. Some memory-critical instructions such as XCHG activate the $\overline{\text{LOCK}}$ signal on their own. If the 8086 releases control of the local bus during the course of an XCHG instruction, for example, the values to exchange may possibly be incorrectly defined. Depending on the exact timing involved when releasing the local bus the values may be exchanged, or not exchanged, or only partially exchanged as a result.

QS_1, QS_0 (pins 24, 25)

These signals indicate the status of the prefetch queue. Thus, the internal prefetch queue of the 8086 can be seen externally. For the possible combinations (QS_1, QS_0) the following interpretations hold (0=low, 1=high):

(00) no operation takes place; the prefetch queue is not active
(01) the first byte of the opcode in the prefetch queue is processed
(10) the prefetch queue is cancelled
(11) the next byte of the opcode in the prefetch queue is processed

The signals and pin assignments for 8086 operation in minimum mode are listed in Figure 2.9 on the right-hand side. Because the 8086 in the PC/XT is run in the maximum mode, these signals are not described here. You may deduce their meaning easily, as the 8288 bus controller generates the same signals (see the next section).

2.5.2 8288 Bus Controller

The 8288 bus controller is a support chip for 8086/8088 processors and is responsible for generating all necessary bus control signals. Figure 2.10 gives a pin assignment diagram for the 8288.

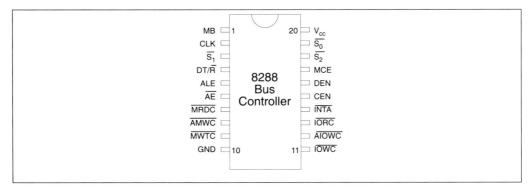

Figure 2.10. 8288 bus controller. The 8288 generates the necessary bus control signals for an 8086 CPU in maximum mode. The 8288 comes in a DIP package with 20 pins.

The following explains the most important pins and the meaning of the signals output or supplied in a PC.

MB (pin 1)
If this pin is fixed to V_{cc} then the 8288 supplies bus signals compatible with Intel's MULTIBUS specification. If MB is earthed then the 8288 optimizes the bus control signals with the aim of attaining the shortest possible bus cycles. In the PC, the 8288 supplies MULTIBUS-compatible control signals. Because the design of a computer is very dependant on the coordination of the bus signals, this pin is usually soldered to one of these two voltages.

CLK (pin 2)
This pin is supplied with the system clock signal from the 8284 clock generator.

$\overline{S}_2$, $\overline{S}_1$, $\overline{S}_0$ (pins 19, 18, 3)
These pins are supplied with the corresponding control signals from the processor. Depending on these signals, the 8288 bus controller outputs the control signals for the bus.

DT/$\overline{\text{R}}$ (pin 4)
(Data Transmit/Receive) If this pin is high then data is written; if it is low then data is read. Therefore, the signal at this pin indicates the direction of the data transfer on the bus.

ALE (pin 5)
(Address Latch Enable) ALE activates the address buffer. The buffer then accepts the address supplied by the processor and latches onto it. Thus, throughout the whole bus cycle the address is available and will not be altered until a new ALE signal is active.

$\overline{\text{MRDC}}$ (pin 7)
(Memory Read) If this pin (and therefore the control signal) is low, then data is transferred from memory to the processor.

$\overline{\text{MWTC}}$ (pin 9)
(Memory Write) If this pin is low, the bus transfers data from the processor to memory.

GND (pin 10)
This pin is supplied with the ground potential (usually 0 V).

$\overline{\text{IOWC}}$ (pin 11)
(I/O Write) If this pin is low, the bus transfers data from the processor to a register (port) in the I/O address space.

$\overline{\text{IORC}}$ (pin 13)
(I/O Read) If this pin is low, the bus transfers data from a register (port) in the I/O address space to the processor.

$\overline{\text{INTA}}$ (pin 14)
Confirms the acknowledges of a hardware interrupt request.

DEN (pin 16)
(Data Enable) If this pin is low, data is written into the data buffer and latched there.

MCE (pin 17)
This pin serves to correctly process a hardware interrupt if several cascaded interrupt controllers are present (see Chapter 7).

The internal logic of the bus controller interprets the status signals $\overline{\text{S}}_2$–$\overline{\text{S}}_0$ from the processor and activates the corresponding control signals for the bus. Furthermore, the 8288 coordinates those signals to enable the various buffers. Thus, an exactly defined data transfer between processor and memory or I/O address space is possible.

Example: If data is to be read from memory, the 8288 activates the signals MRDC (memory read), ALE (latch address into address buffer) and DEN (fetch read data into data buffer).

2.5.3 Accessing the Main Memory

To ensure a trouble-free data read process, the processor does not access the memory directly: for perfect coordination, buffer and control chips are necessary (see Figure 2.11). You have just learned about one of them: the 8288 bus controller. The memory chips must also be controlled in a specific manner. Details on reading and writing data into or from memory chips are given in Chapter 6.

If the 8086 accesses the main memory, the 8288 bus controller activates the output $\overline{\text{MRDC}}$ (read data) or **MWTC** (write data).

Besides the bus and memory controllers there is a *clock generator*, which generates the *system clock* for the processor, the buffer chips and all other components such as the interrupt controller. In the first PC the system clock was 4.77 MHz, but in newer XTs it can be up to 10 MHz. In Figure 2.12 the system clock is indicated by CLK.

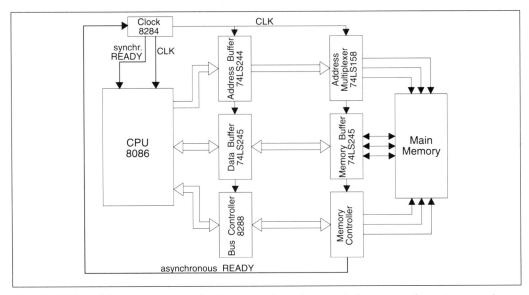

Figure 2.11: The path between processor and main memory. In maximum mode the processor does not access main memory directly. Instead, a bus controller generating the control signals for the bus and several buffers for temporary storage and for amplifying the data and address signals between 8086 and RAM are provided. The memory controller controls the main memory to read data from or write data to the intended address correctly.

If the 8086 CPU wants to read data from the memory, it outputs an address to an *address buffer* via its address bus. This buffer accepts the address and latches it to the bus controller activation signal ALE. Thus, the address buffer holds the address even if the time-divisionally multiplexed data/address bus of the 8086 is already transferring data. In the same way, data is transferred from the processor to the *data buffer* if the 8288 bus controller activates the signal DEN. To access the intended word in the main memory an *address multiplexer* is implemented, which selects the intended word in the main memory with the aid of the *memory controller*. The data read in this way is transferred from the main memory to the *memory buffer*. Afterwards, the memory buffer transmits the data read to the data buffer, from which, in turn, the CPU may fetch it.

The coordination of all these processes (that is, the driving of the buffer and control circuits) is carried out using the clock signal from the clock generator. Without this signal, complete chaos would arise, and correct data transfer would be impossible. However, the clock signals lead to correct execution, and give the individual circuits enough time to fulfill their tasks. If the clock frequency is increased, at some time a point is reached where one or more circuits is unable to keep up, and completely unpredictable values are read. The computer crashes.

Perhaps you have wondered why the upper 384 kbytes of main memory (with a total of 1 Mbyte) don't start immediately above the lower 640 kbytes but instead continue above 1 Mbyte? Of course, you have inserted memory chips without leaving any «hole» between 640 k and 1 M. The memory chips are correctly located side-by-side. Responsible for this «hole» in the address space is the address multiplexer. It passes all accesses to the lower 640 kbytes of main memory to the inserted chips, but an access to the section between 640 kbytes and 1Mbyte is handled according to the mapping shown in Figure 1.28. Thus, the address multiplexer (or an equivalent chip), for example, accesses the video RAM in the graphics adapter if a write to address B800:0210 occurs. Similarly, accesses to the ROM chips of the BIOS, to the extension adapters for networks, and to others are also diverted. For an address above 1 M, the address multiplexer again accesses the main memory chips on the motherboard. This assignment is wired and has nothing to do with the logical mapping of the address space, which we will meet later in chapters referring to the 80286 and i386.

As you can see from Figure 2.11, the data and control bus can transmit signals in both directions. Thus, they constitute a *bidirectional bus*. On the control bus it is mainly the READY signal which runs from the memory controller via the clock generator back to the processor that is transmitted. On the other hand, the processor supplies addresses but it never reads any, therefore this part of the bus is *unidirectional*. Figures 2.12 and 2.13 show the course of the main signals on the system bus for reading and writing data. With reference to Figure 2.13, the term «wait state» is now discussed.

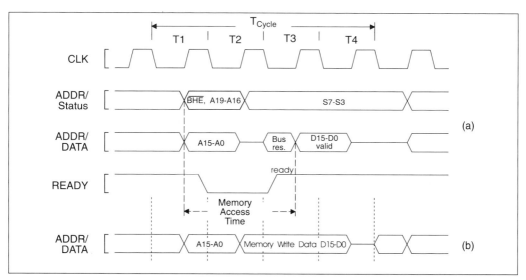

Figure 2.12: Signals on the system bus in a memory access cycle without wait states. (a) Memory read: the processor supplies the address and waits for the main memory data; the access time is the period between output of the address by the microprocessor and delivery of the data by the main memory.(b) Memory Write: The processor outputs the address, immediately by the data.
Both bus cycles are completed within four clock cycles, therefore no wait state T_{WAIT} is inserted.

2.5.4 Reading Data out of Memory

How does the reading of data without wait states work? Let's have a look at section (a) of Figure 2.12. For this process, four signals are essential:

- the clock signal CLK from the clock generator,
- address and status signals ADDR/Status from the processor,
- address and data signals ADDR/DATA from the processor and memory, and
- the READY signal to indicate the completion of data reading.

Every bus cycle consists of at least four clock cycles, thus with a 10 MHz XT 2.5 million bus cycles per second are possible at most. A bus cycle is divided into four parts comprising one clock cycle each: T1 to T4. In cycle T1 the 8086 outputs the address of the data to be read. These data are transferred to the processor during the course of cycles T3 and T4. In cycle T2 the transfer direction of the bus is inverted. In the following, these four cycles are explained in more detail.

T1

The processor outputs the control signals $\bar{S}_2$ to $\bar{S}_0$ to the bus controller, which in turn activates the address and data buffers. Afterwards, the address of the intended data is supplied by the pins A_0 to A_{19} and fetched into the address buffer. The $\overline{\text{BHE}}$ signal indicates whether a whole word or only one byte is read. Therefore, the read process has been started and the READY signal drops to low. The signal will rise to high only once the memory has supplied the intended data. The memory controller starts an internal read process of the main memory, and the address multiplexer addresses the corresponding data in the memory. Of course, this addressing and reading process needs some time.

T2

Now an inversion of the transmission direction on the bus takes place. Up to now the processor has supplied an address, but now it fetches data. For this purpose, the lines $\overline{\text{BHE}}$ and A_{19}–A_{16} are switched by the processor in such a way that they output the corresponding status information. The combined address/data bus of the pins A_{15}–A_0 is switched from address bus mode to data bus mode. This lasts some time.

T3

Now the data transfer cycle begins. First, the data bus (ADDR/DATA) is reserved for the data transfer from memory. The bus waits until the data is supplied. In this state D_{15}–D_0 are not yet valid, and the status signals S_7–S_3 are output. When the memory has completed its internal read process and has transferred the data to the memory buffer, the memory controller raises the READY signal to high. Usually, this rise occurs asynchronous to the clock signal CLK. Therefore, the READY signal must be synchronized first and, for this purpose, is supplied by the 8284 clock generator. Then the clock generator applies a synchronized READY signal to the processor. Thus, the data is transferred from the memory buffer to the data buffer. The data signals at the pins D_{15}–D_0 are thus valid, and the processor starts to fetch data.

T4

The processor finishes the read-in process after the half clock cycle. The buffers are disabled but the processor continues to output the status signals S_7–S_3. After the end of cycle T4, the system bus is again in the initial state. Now a further read or write process may be started. If no data has to be transferred the bus remains in a standby state until the processor again signals that data should be read or written.

Figure 2.12 shows the *access time* for the memory, that is, the time that the memory needs to answer a read request with the output of the intended data. The access time is the period between the supply of a valid address signal to, and the delivery of the data by, the main memory. The clock frequency and the response times of the circuits are fixed by the electronic design of the PC, therefore only memory chips whose access time is no longer than that defined by the design may be used. From Figure 2.12 it can be seen that the access time of the memory chips in a PC and XT without wait states may only be two clock cycles. This is the period between the address output and the validity of the data on the bus. Because the signal propagation times in the buffer circuits supervene, in practice only memory chips whose access time is about half of this memory access time may be used. In a 4.77 MHz PC, memory chips with an access time of 200 ns can be employed, but in a newer 10 MHz XT chips with a shorter 100 ns access time are necessary. If the chips operate more slowly then read and write errors occur.

2.5.5 Writing Data into Memory

If the CPU is writing data into memory without wait states, very similar processes are carried out. In Figure 2.12b only the behaviour of the ADDR/DATA signal is shown, because all other signals coincide with the signals in the case of data reading.

T1

All processes are identical to that indicated above, and only the bus controller is affected by the fact that data is to be written. Accordingly, it prepares the buffers and the memory controller for a data write.

T2

The direction of the combined address/data bus (ADDR/DATA) need not be switched because both the address and the data have to be output. Therefore, immediately after supplying the address the processor may output the write data to the data buffer at the clock signal CLK in T2. The data buffer transfers it to the memory buffer. Simultaneously, the memory controller drives the main memory to carry out an internal data write.

T3

If the main memory has completed its internal write process the memory controller raises the READY signal to indicate completion to the processor.

T4

The processor terminates the write process. The buffers are disabled but the processor continues to supply the status signals S_7–S_3. After the end of cycle T4, the system bus is again available for the next bus cycle.

The READY signal enables a flexible response to delays in the accessed memory by inserting so-called *wait states*. Main memory and slow peripherals such as the video RAM on the graphics adapter or the registers of the hard disk controller use this signal to indicate that they are ready to accept or output data. With a conventional main memory the number of wait states is usually fixed, or may be chosen with a jumper depending upon which memory chips are supplied in the PC. The memory controller handles wait states by releasing the READY signal later.

Modern and powerful concepts such as cache memories or page-interleaved memories, however, require flexible output of the READY signal, and therefore enable a flexible number of wait states depending upon the actual situation. For example, no wait state is necessary in a cache memory access, but an access to ordinary main memory requires two wait states.

2.5.6 Memory Access with Wait States

The following describes what happens when a READY signal is late, and how the processor inserts wait states. In Figure 2.13 the main signals that appear if the processor has to insert two wait states into a main memory access are shown.

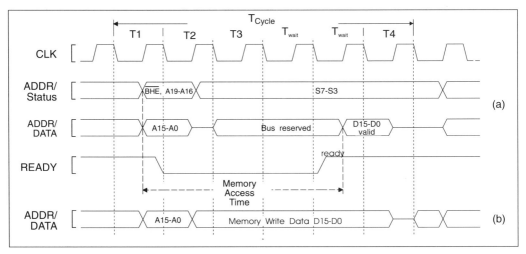

Figure 2.13: The signals on the system bus in a memory access cycle with two wait states. (a) Memory read: the processor supplies the address and waits for the data of the main memory; the main memory is not able to deliver the data in time, and therefore deactivates READY until the data is available on the data bus. (b) Memory Write: the processor outputs the address and immediately afterwards the write data; also in this case, the main memory is not working fast enough to take the data off the data bus; it therefore deactivates READY until the data is written into memory. Both bus cycles are completed within six clock cycles, therefore two wait states T_wait are inserted.

First, the signals when data is read with two wait states (Figure 2.13) is described. During the T1 and T2 clock cycles, processor and bus behave in the same way as in an access without wait states. The processor outputs control signals to the bus controller to enable the buffers and controllers; then it supplies the address of the data to be read. The memory controller issues an internal main memory read process.

But here the memory chips are too slow (or the clock frequency is too high), and the T3 cycle ends without any data being delivered by the main memory. Therefore, the memory controller doesn't raise the READY signal to a high level. The 8086 recognizes that no data is yet available and carries out a wait cycle T_{wait}. This cycle lasts exactly one clock cycle CLK. If the memory controller doesn't raise the READY signal within this wait state, the processor inserts another wait cycle T_{wait}. In principle, this may continue for any length of time.

However, as the main memory of the example illustrated completes the internal read process within the second wait cycle, the memory controller therefore raises the READY signal, and the last T4 cycle is now executed as described above. Thus the processor has inserted two wait cycles, and the computer is running with two wait states when accessing main memory.

The memory access time is accordingly longer. Here it comprises four clock cycles. In the example of Figure 2.12 it lasted for only two clock cycles. The number of wait states indicated in commercials usually gives the number of wait states for an access to main memory in the most advantageous case.

In data writing the same applies, of course. In Figure 2.13b the signals for a main memory access with two wait cycles for data writing are illustrated. In contrast to Figure 2.12b the READY signal is not raised until the second wait cycle T_{wait}, therefore the last T4 cycle is completed two clock cycles (CLK) later.

Of course, the number of wait states may be different for data reading and writing. Often, memory chips can read data faster than they are able to write it. Furthermore, the number of wait states may be dependent on the location of the memory: main memory on the motherboard usually runs with fewer wait states compared to the video RAM on the graphics adapter. Here up to 30(!) wait states are normal with a fast-clocked i386 PC. The reason in this case is the «bottleneck» of the slot connection to the adapter. This connection runs much more slowly than the connection between processor and main memory. Using the READY signal, components varying in their operating speed can be integrated into one PC. A special wait state logic that is dependent upon the individual hardware manufacturer performs the necessary speed adaptations.

To integrate slow components a decrease of the processor's clock frequency would also be possible, of course. The first PC was clocked with 4.77 MHz, but today's i486 computers reach 50 MHz, and in the future a further increase can be expected. Inserting wait cycles allows the processor to execute instructions internally with maximum speed, only being slowed down in an access to slower memory. But what's slow? During one movement of your eyelid (about 0.01 s) an average memory chip with an access time of 100 ns carries out 100,000 accesses. Also, take into account that one wait cycle in a 10 MHz computer leads to the same access rate as no wait state with a 4.77 MHz PC.

2.5.7 Word Boundary

Because the 8086 is a 16-bit processor with a 16-bit data bus, main memory is physically organized as a 16-bit memory. This means that the 8086 always accesses the memory physically at the byte addresses 0, 2, 4, ..., 1 048 574. Logically, data words (16 bits) may start at odd addresses, but physically the word at the odd address can't be accessed all at once. If a word is to be stored at an odd address, the bus unit of the 8086 divides this word access into two separate byte accesses. This process is completely transparent for software, that is, the hardware carries out the separation and the double memory access without any intervention from the software. Thus, the programmer may arrange data in any form without taking word boundaries into account.

During the two separate byte accesses memory is physically addressed in even-numbered portions, but only the required byte is fetched. The processor informs the memory controller of this using $\overline{\text{BHE}}$ and A_0 (the least significant address bit). Thus, an individual byte (low or high) at an even address 0, 2, ... ($\overline{\text{BHE}} = 1$, $A_0 = 0$) or an odd address 1, 3, ... ($\overline{\text{BHE}} = 0$, $A_0 = 1$) may be read or written. The same applies for $\overline{\text{BHE}}$ and A_0, of course, in cases where only a single byte is to be read (MOV al, [bx], for example) or written.

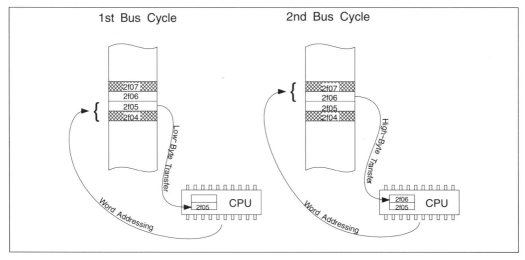

Figure 2.14: Word access with odd address. As the memory of the 16-bit 8086 processor is organized in 16-bit portions, the 8086 is unable to access odd word addresses, but has to divide such an access into two succeeding byte accesses. During each of these accesses a whole word is addressed but only one byte is actually transferred to the processor. The processor combines these two bytes into one 16-bit word internally. The 8086 bus unit performs this automatically.

In Figure 2.14 this process is shown for a read access. For access to the word with odd address 2f05h, the unit carries out a double byte access. First, the byte at 2f05h is read. For this the processor outputs the address 2f04h and sets $\overline{\text{BHE}} = 0$ and $A_0 = 1$ at the same time. Thus, the byte at address 2f05h is read. Because the least significant address bit $A_0 = 1$, the address bus actually outputs an odd address (address 2f05h, in this case). But the memory controller only uses the address bits A_{19}–A_1 (corresponding to address 2f04h), and combines A_0 and $\overline{\text{BHE}}$ to transfer one byte. Immediately afterwards, the CPU outputs the address 2f06h and at the same time sets $\overline{\text{BHE}}=1$ and $A_0=0$. Thus, the byte at address 2f06 is read. The bus unit combines the two bytes into one word at address 2f05h. Finally, one word at an odd address is read like this. To write one word at an odd address, the same procedure is executed in reverse.

You can see that reading or writing one word at an odd address requires two bus cycles. In contrast to this, reading or writing one word at an even address lasts for only one bus cycle. Therefore, it is advantageous (but not necessary, as mentioned above) to arrange data words at even storage addresses.

Incidentally, these explanations only apply to data words. The prefetch queue always fetches the code in portions of one word, which start at even storage addresses. Because of this, the prefetch queue is reloaded only if at least two bytes are free. To get even storage addresses the processor may eventually read one single byte, for example, because of a jump or call with an odd target address.

2.5.8 Accesses to the I/O Address Space

If the 8086 attempts to access a port, the 8288 bus controller activates the output $\overline{\text{IORC}}$ (read data) or $\overline{\text{IOWC}}$ (write data). Writing data to a port or reading data from a port are carried out in the same way as writing data into or reading data from memory. In Figure 2.15 the path for data transfer between processor and the ports is shown.

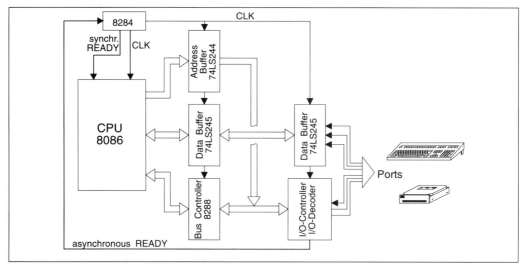

Figure 2.15: The path between processor and ports. The processor does not access the I/O address space directly, but indirectly via the 8288 bus controller, which generates the control signals for the bus and various buffers for temporary storage and for amplifying the data and address signals, as is also the case for the main memory.

As is the case in reading and writing data from and into memory, the CPU outputs an address to the address buffer and drives the bus controller by means of the status signals. If data has to be transmitted to a port (OUT), the processor additionally outputs data to the data buffer during the T2 cycle. With the control signals $\overline{\text{IORC}}$ and $\overline{\text{IOWC}}$, the logic on the motherboard recognizes that an access to the I/O address space and not the memory is required. Therefore, the I/O controller is activated instead of the memory controller. The I/O controller decodes the address signal from the address buffer and accesses the corresponding port. Usually, this port is assigned a register in a peripheral (keyboard or hard disk drive, for example), or in a hardware chip (mode control register in a DMA chip, for example). Thus, data may be exchanged between the processor and a register in the I/O address space of the PC. Because the 8086 can access 64 k ports at most, the four high-order address lines A_{19}–A_{16} are low during access to ports. Further, in the PC, the address lines A_{15}–$A_{10} = 0$ because only the first 1024 ports are used.

The bus cycle and the accompanying signals are the same as in Figures 2.12 and 2.13. Again, the READY signal is used to insert wait cycles as required. This is necessary, in particular, because access to registers in a chip in a peripheral (hard disk controller, for example) is usually much slower than the access to main memory. The term memory access time in Figures 2.12 and 2.13 should be replaced by I/O access time. Also, in most i386 and i486 computers with a 33 MHz clock frequency and above, the bus slots that establish the connection to the adapter cards run at only 8 MHz. An unsuitable coordination of bus slot and peripheral can lead to further delays so that a well-coordinated 80286 AT may carry out an access to a peripheral faster than an i386 AT. Chapter 3 gives further information on the overall performance of a computer.

2.6 Processor Reset

A processor reset is issued by setting the RESET pin high for at least four clock cycles. Once the signal has returned to low, the processor carries out an internal initialization. During the course of this initialization the registers are loaded wih the values indicated in Table 2.6.

flags	0002h
instruction pointer IP	fff0h
code segment CS	f000h
data segment DS	0000h
extra segment ES	0000h
stack segment SS	0000h

Table 2.6: Register values after a processor RESET

After the internal initialization, the CS:IP pair points to the memory address f000:fff0 or, combined, ffff0h. At this location the entry point to the start routine of the BIOS is usually present. Because only 16 bytes are available between ffff0h and the addressing limit fffffh (= 1 Mbyte), one of the first instructions is usually an unconditional jump (JMP) to the «real» target address. Now the BIOS boots the PC.

A processor reset (sometimes also called *cold-boot*) is issued by operating the main switch (power on of the PC) or the RESET key. Note that the three-finger-control Ctrl-Alt-Del only gives rise to a *warm-boot* by issuing an interrupt 19h. In this case, no processor reset occurs. The INT 19h only reloads the operating system but doesn't check the hardware components such as memory, interrupt controller, etc. You may recognize a cold-boot by the memory check: the memory addresses are counted up. For a warm-boot this time-consuming check is bypassed.

Because of the value 1234h at memory address 0040:0072h the start routine is able to determine whether a cold- or warm-boot is in progress. If the value 1234h is stored at this address then a warm-boot has to be executed. All other values indicate a cold-boot. The probability that at power-on (that is, completely random values in memory) the word 1234h is present at this location is 1 to 65536. Statistically speaking, you have to switch your PC on and off 65536 times before the BIOS interprets a cold-boot as a warm-boot. If you need one minute for one cold-boot then you will be occupied for 45 days and nights switching your PC on and off to provoke one such mistake. Thus, the security «built-in» is – statistically – more than enough. But what are statistics? If you are playing a lottery and you do one lottery every minute then it will take nearly 27 (!) years to get six correct numbers. Nevertheless, every week several people succeed in doing this, and among them are some who are not yet 27 years old!

2.7 Interrupt – The Break

A brief consideration of the cooperation between bus unit, prefetch queue, execution unit, etc. immediately shows that the processor executes never-ending instructions. If it has completed one instruction, the next is loaded and executed. Also, in situations where the PC seems to wait for an instruction (for example, DIR) or text from you, this doesn't mean that the processor has really stopped working with your input. Instead, a routine is executed in the background which continuously checks the keyboard to determine whether you have operated a key and input a character. Thus a program loop is carried out.

To interrupt the processor in its never-ending execution of these instructions, a so-called *interrupt* is issued. For example, a periodic interrupt (the timer interrupt) is used to activate the resident program PRINT regularly for a short time. For the 80x86 256 different interrupts (0–255) are available in total. Intel has reserved the first 32 interrupts for exclusive use by the processor but this unfortunately didn't stop IBM placing all hardware interrupts and the interrupts of the PC BIOS in exactly this region. I cannot see any real reason for this, and it may give rise to some strange consequences. If you are checking the index into an array against the array boundaries by means of the BOUND instruction on an AT and the index is outside, then the 80286 issues an exception which corresponds to interrupt 5. Therefore, your AT starts to print the screen. You may test this if you like with DEBUG by explicitly writing the opcode of BOUND into memory and loading the necessary registers with values that lead to an index outside the array boundaries. With G for Go you issue the index check, and as a consequence a usually unwanted screen print is produced. You'll be reassured that printing via the PrtScrn key is carried out according to a completely different principle. PrtScrn therefore also works on a PC/XT which only incorporates an 8086/88, and therefore doesn't yet know the instruction BOUND.

Depending on the source of an interrupt, one can distinguish three categories:

- software interrupts
- hardware interrupts
- exceptions.

2.7.1 Software Interrupts

A software interrupt is issued explicitly by an INT instruction. For example, using the instruction INT 10h the interrupt with hex number 10h is called. Figure 2.16 shows the procedure that is executed during an interrupt in real mode.

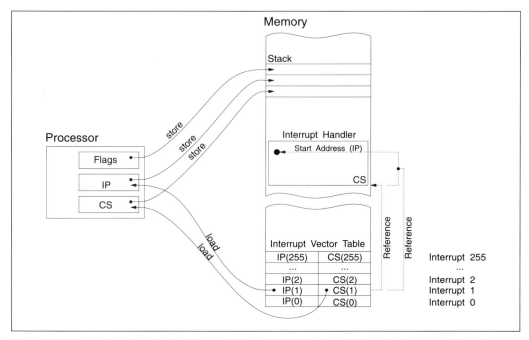

Figure 2.16: Interrupt in real mode. If an interrupt is issued the 8086 automatically pushes the current flags, the instruction pointer IP and the code segment onto the stack. The interrupt number is internally multiplied by four, and therefore indicates the offset in segment 00h where the interrupt vector for handling the interrupt is located. An interrupt vector is an address with the format segment:offset, which points to the start address of the corresponding handler. The 8086 loads IP and CS with the values specified in the table.

In the address space of the 80x86 the first 1024 (1 k) bytes are reserved for the interrupt vector table. This table holds a so-called *interrupt vector* for each of the 256 possible interrupts. Every interrupt vector occupies four bytes and indicates, in Intel format, the address segment:offset of the *interrupt handler*, which services the interrupt. Because an interrupt usually has a specific purpose, for example, calling an operating system function or dealing with the arrival of a character at the serial interface, the interrupt handler processes it accordingly. Thus the handler, for example, executes the operating system function or accepts the incoming character.

The assignment of interrupt and interrupt vector is one-to-one, that is, interrupt 0 is assigned the interrupt vector 0 (at address 0000:0000), the interrupt 1 is assigned the interrupt vector 1 (at address 0000:0004), etc. Thus, the interrupt number need only be multiplied by 4 to get the offset of the corresponding interrupt vector in segment 0000h. The processor carries out exactly this multiplication to determine the interrupt vector address from the interrupt number. As you can see, as well as the area f000:fff0 to f000:ffff for the processor reset we now have a second address section reserved for use by the 8086. These address areas are not available for application programs. Overwriting the interrupt vector table with invalid addresses has disastrous consequences. The next interrupt call crashes the computer.

During an interrupt call the following takes place (see Figure 2.16):

- the processor pushes flags, CS and IP (in this order) onto the stack,
- interrupt and trap flags are cleared,
- the processor addresses the interrupt vector in the interrupt vector table corresponding to the interrupt number and loads IP and CS according to the entry.

CS:IP of the interrupt vector specifies the target address of the interrupt handler. Thus, the processor continues program execution with the interrupt handler. The return to the calling program is carried out by an IRET.

Example: `INT 10h`

```
The processor pushes the current flags, CS and IP onto the stack, clears the interrupt and trap
flag, and reads the interrupt vector at address 0000:0040. The two bytes at 0000:0040 are
loaded into IP, and the two bytes at 0000:0042 are loaded into CS (taking into account the
Intel format low–high).
```

Also important is the encoding of the INT instruction, which is:

The bit sequences 11001100 and 11001101, respectively, are the opcodes and *vvvvvvvv* indicates the number of the interrupt. Thus, the instruction INT 3 comprises only one byte. Section 2.7.3 gives more information on this compactly encoded interrupt. All other INT instructions require an immediate address, that is, the interrupt number is part of the instruction stream. Therefore, the interrupt number cannot be held by a register or a memory operand.

Software interrupts occur synchronously to program execution, that is, every time the program reaches an INT instruction an interrupt is issued.

2.7.2 Hardware Interrupts

As the name implies, these interrupts are issued by a hardware chip (the timer interrupt by the timer chip, for example) or a peripheral such as the hard disk controller. Generally, two different types of hardware interrupt are distinguishable: the *non-maskable interrupt NMI* and the (maskable) *interrupt requests IRQ*. For *servicing* such an IRQ, the *PIC 8259 interrupt controller* plays an important role (see Section 7.1).

If the computer issues an NMI then the processor's NMI connection (pin 17) is supplied with a signal. The processor completes the current instruction and issues an interrupt 2 in the same way as described above. In the PC an NMI is issued if a parity error occurs during the course of a memory read.

Then the computer displays the following (or an equivalent) message:

```
Parity Error at xxxx:xxxx
```

xxxx:xxxx indicates the byte with the parity error. A characteristic of the NMI is that (as the name already implies) it cannot be masked. An NMI always takes priority. Because the NMI is usually only issued in connection with a serious hardware malfunction, this is understandable and correct. A PC with untrustworthy memory contents must be stopped from committing data suicide.

On the other hand, IRQ interrupt requests can be masked off by clearing the interrupt flag IE. Only when the opposite instruction STI has been issued are such interrupts enabled again. Note that the instruction INT xx for a software interrupt implicitly executes a CLI. Normally, interrupt requests are issued by a peripheral, for example if the serial interface wants to inform the processor that it has just received a character. The processing of such an interrupt request is described in detail in Section 7.1.3.

Hardware interrupt requests are managed by an interrupt controller. If this chip receives a signal indicating the issue of a hardware interrupt, then the interrupt controller applies a request signal (*interrupt request*) to the INTR input (pin 18) of the 8086. If the processor is able to service the interrupt (that is, the IE flag is set), then it supplies an acknowledge signal (*interrupt acknowledge*) either directly (minimum mode) or via the bus controller (maximum mode). The interrupt controller then returns the number of the interrupt to be executed. Now the processor continues in the same way as described above, and calls the interrupt handler.

Unlike software interrupts, the hardware interrupts (NMI and IRQ) are completely asynchronous to program execution. For example, a memory parity error doesn't always occur at the same program point. Further, the hard disk drive needs various time periods, depending on the current position of the read/write heads, before data can be transferred to the processor. The detection of program bugs which arise only in connection with hardware interrupts is thus made enormously complicated.

2.7.3 Exceptions

So far we have only got to know two interrupt sources. A third source is the processor itself. Interrupts that are generated by the processor are called *exceptions*. The consequences of an exception correspond to those of a software interrupt, that is, an interrupt is called whose number is supplied by the processor itself. Appendix D.3 gives a list of exceptions valid for the 80x86 family.

Many of the exceptions are reserved for processor operation in protected mode, starting with the 80286. In real mode, only the following exceptions are possible:

– Division by 0: if the divisor is equal to zero in a DIV or IDIV instruction, the operation's result is not defined. The ALU of the processor would need an infinite time to calculate such a quotient. If the division is not completed after a certain number of clock cycles, the control unit determines a division by zero and issues an interrupt 0.

– Single step: if the trap flag has been set then the processor issues an interrupt 1 after every executed instruction. Because the trap flag is automatically cleared with an interrupt call, the processor may execute the interrupt routine without a stop. Often, debuggers set the trap flag and intercept the interrupt to execute a program step-by-step.

−   Breakpoint (i386 and above): the i386 has internal debug registers to eventually generate an interrupt 3 (see Section 4.2.5). Of course, every processor may issue a software interrupt 3 by means of the instruction INT 3. As mentioned above, the INT 3 instruction comprises only one byte. Therefore, a debugger may set a breakpoint at the location of an instruction by overwriting the instruction (or its first byte) with the opcode 11001100, corresponding to INT 3. When the program execution reaches this point, an interrupt 3 is issued and the program execution is interrupted. To restart the program the debugger replaces the opcode 11001100 with the byte originally present at this location and executes an IRET.

−   Overflow detection with INTO: if the overflow flag is set and the INTO instruction is executed, then the processor issues an interrupt 4.

−   BOUND (80186 and higher): if the index checked by the BOUND instruction is outside the array boundaries, then the processor generates an interrupt 5.

−   Invalid opcode (80286 and higher): if the instruction unit detects an opcode that has no instruction assigned to it, then the processor issues an interrupt 6.

−   Coprocessor not present: if the instruction unit detects an opcode that specifies an instruction for the coprocessor and no coprocessor is installed, then the processor issues an interrupt 7.

2.8 The 8088

The 8088 is something like a «cut down» form of the 8086. Its internal structure with a bus unit, instruction unit, etc. is nearly identical to that of the 8086. Further, the 8088 has the same instruction set, knows the same addressing schemes, and handles segments and offsets in the same way as the 8086. Like its «big brother», the 8088 is also a 16-bit processor, that is, it processes data with a maximum width of 16 bits (one word).

The only difference from the 8086 is that the 8088 has only an 8-bit data bus (see Figure 2.17). Remember that the 8086 implements a 16-bit data bus. Because only one byte at a time can be transferred via an 8-bit data bus, the 8088 has to access memory or a port twice when it is reading or writing a 16-bit word.

Example: During the course of executing an instruction MOV ax, [bx] the 8088 accesses the memory twice to load the word at offset [bx] into the 16-bit accumulator ax.

This twice repeated access is completely transparent for software, that is, the bus unit automatically accesses the memory or port twice if a whole word has to be transferred. Therefore, all discussions concerning the word boundary in connection with the 8086 are irrelevant. Independent of whether the data word begins at an odd or an even address, two bus cycles are always required to transfer one 16-bit word. The bus cycles are executed in the same way as for the 8086 (see Figures 2.12 and 2.13).

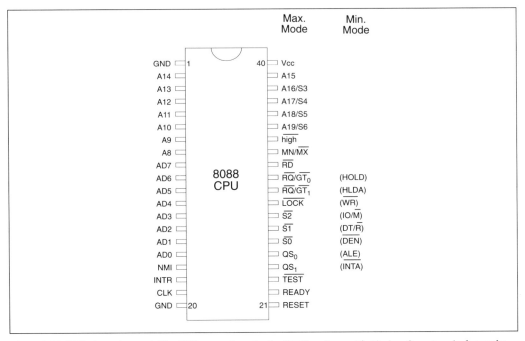

Figure 2.17: 8088 pin assignment. The 8088 comes in a standard DIP package with 40 pins. Some terminals supply different signals in maximum and minimum mode.

Compared to the 8086, all instructions that involve the transfer of a 16-bit word last at least four clock cycles longer (corresponding to a bus cycle without wait states). Thus, the 8088 processes data more slowly, on average.

Example: MOV ax, [bx] needs at least four additional clock cycles compared to the 8086; MOV al, [bx], on the other hand, needs an equal number of cycles because only one byte is transferred from memory into the 8–bit accumulator.

Another difference from the 8086 processor is that the prefetch queue of the 8088 has only four bytes (compared to six bytes in the 8086). Because of the 8-bit data bus, the prefetch queue is reloaded if only one byte is free (two bytes with the 8086). The smaller prefetch queue and the slower data transfer may therefore give rise to the processing speed of the processor being limited not by the internal program execution but by the speed with which the prefetch queue is reloaded. If several instructions that can be executed in a few clock cycles (for example, CLC, AND, CBW) occur in succession, then the processor has already completed the instruction after two clock cycles. But the bus unit needs at least four clock cycles to reload the prefetch queue. Therefore, the processor has to wait for the bus unit to fetch the next instruction.

The development of an 8086 with an 8-bit data bus (namely the 8088) has historical reasons. When the 8086 came onto the market in the mid-1970s to replace the 8-bit processors common at that time, hardly any support chips with a data width of 16 bits were available, or they were very expensive. Moreover, the construction of a board with a full 16-bit data bus is far more costly than a board with only an 8-bit data bus. For example, all data buffers must have a double capacity. To give an 8086 the chance to use the existing 8-bit technology further, the 16-bit data buffer was integrated onto the processor chip. Now the processor appeared to be an 8-bit processor – hence the 8088! Before you dismiss this solution as nonsense, be aware of the extremely fast development in computer technology during the last 15 years. The whole PC world was steamrollered by this development. The results are (among others) the 640 kbyte boundary of MS-DOS, the 8-bit DMA chips in an AT, and an i486 running in real mode.

2.9 Number Excursion – The Representation of Floating-Point Numbers

In Section 2.2 we have already come across the internal representation of positive and negative integers, as well as the binary coded decimals. But for extensive arithmetical calculations, broken numbers like 1/4 or −0.06215 or mixed numbers like −1 5/7 or 19456.208 are missing.

2.9.1 Scientific Notation and Biased Exponent

The basis for the representation of such numbers in a computer is so-called *scientific notation* or *floating-point representation*. In this (decimal) notation, every number is represented by a signed number between 1 and 10 (the *mantissa* ±M) and a power to the *base* B with a value of 10 with a signed *exponent* ±E:

```
number = ±M * B±E
```

At first glance this seems to be pure mathematics. To calm you down I therefore want to give a brief example with the numbers mentioned above.

```
Example: scientific notation with decimal base 10
1/4 = 0.25 = 2.5 * 0.1 = 2.5 * 10-1              mantissa 2.5, base 10, exponent -1
-0.06215 = -6.215 * 0.01 = -6.215 * 10-2         mantissa -6.215, base 10, exponent -2
-1 5/7 = -1.71428... = -1.71428 * 1 = -1.71428 * 100    mantissa -1.71428, base 10, exponent 0
19456.208 = 1.9456208 * 10.000 = 1.9456208 * 104  mantissa 1.9456208, base 10, exponent 4
```

Now the reason for the name floating-point representation also becomes apparent. The point is moved until the mantissa has one digit before and the rest of the digits after the decimal point. The number's value is maintained by increasing or decreasing the exponent accordingly. Unlike the so-called fixed-point numbers, the position of the decimal point is (as the name already implies) fixed. In today's computers, usually only floating-point numbers are used. But with the third number in the above example, you can see the disadvantage of scientific notation. A number that is not representable as a finite decimal fraction (and all broken numbers whose divisor is not a pure product of 2s and 5s belong to this group) is simply «cut off» after a certain number of digits. In the example, −1 5/7 is not simply equal to −1.71428 but must be infinitely continued with the periodical digit sequence 5714... On the other hand, 1/4 can be represented exactly because the divisor 4 is equal to 2*2 and therefore a pure product of only 2s. Of course, you have neither a pencil and paper nor the time to write down an infinite digit series, which, in most cases, would be pointless anyway. Instead, we are content with a finite number of mantissa digits. The number of these mantissa digits is called the *precision*. In the example, therefore, the numbers have a precision of two, four, six and eight decimal digits, respectively.

For a better understanding of broken numbers in a PC we should first analyse the interpretation of a number in floating-point notation, as we did previously for the integers. The integer decimal 2806 was interpreted as $2*10^3+8*10^2+0*10^1+6*10^0$. In the case of the floating-point number $6.215*10^{-2}$, we proceed in a similar way:

```
6.215*10⁻² = [6*10⁰+2*10⁻¹+1*10⁻²+5*10⁻³]*10⁻²
= [6*1+2*0.1+1*0.01+5*0.001]*0.01 = 0.06215
or
= 6*10⁻²+2*10⁻³+1*10⁻⁴+5*10⁻⁵
= 6*0.01+2*0.001+1*0.0001+5*0.00001 = 0.06215
```

You can see that the interpretations are similar. The value of each digit decreases from left to right with one power of ten. One starts with the value given by the exponent. The same applies for floating-point numbers with a value greater than 1.

```
1.9456208*10⁴ = [1*10⁰+9*10⁻¹+4*10⁻²+5*10⁻³+6*10⁻⁴+2*10⁻⁵+0*10⁻⁶+8*10⁻⁷]*104
= [1*1+9*0.1+4*0.01+5*0.001+6*0.0001+2*0.00001+0*0.000001+8*0.0000001]*10000
= 19456.208
or
= 1*10⁴+9*10³+4*10²+5*10¹+6*10⁰+2*10⁻¹+0*10⁻²+8*10⁻³
= 10,000+9,000+400+50+6+0.2+0.00+0.008 = 19456.208
```

Floating-point numbers are represented in a computer in a similar way, except the «2» corresponding to the binary system replaces the «10» of the decimal system.

```
Example:  1.1011001*2¹⁰⁰¹¹ in the binary system means
[1*2⁰+1*2⁻¹+0*2⁻²+1*2⁻³+1*2⁻⁴+0*2⁻⁵+0*2⁻⁶+1*2⁻⁷]*2¹⁹
=[1*1+1*0.5+0*0.25+1*0.125+1*0,0625+0*0.03125+0*0.015625+1*0.0078125]*524,288
= [1.6953125]*524,288 = 888,832
In "normal" binary representation this would be 888,832 = 1101 1001 0000 0000 0000b.
```

The example illustrates the principle of the representation of floating-point numbers in the binary system, but negative numbers and numbers with negative exponent (that is, numbers below 1) are not covered completely. Generally, the scientific notation is number $=\pm$ mantissa*base$^{\pm\text{exponent}}$. Therefore, two negative numbers are possible. For the representation of negative numbers we have (according to Section 2.2.3) two possibilities: sign bit and 2'complement representation.

Although the 2'complement representation turned out to be very advantageous, another method is used in the representation of floating point numbers. For the mantissa a sign bit is used, and for the exponent a so-called *biased exponent* is employed. Thus, a floating-point number in the binary system has the following form:

```
number = ±mantissa * 2exponent-bias
```

The sign $\pm$ of the mantissa is indicated by a sign bit and a fixed bias value is subtracted from the indicated exponent.

Example: floating–point representation with bias 127 of number 888,832:
$1.1011001*2^{10010010}$
value in "normal" representation therefore:
$1.1011001*2^{10010010-1111111}=1.1011001*2^{10011}$

As you can see, the result coincides with the example mentioned above.

The fact that the two binary floating-point numbers $1.1011001*2^{10010010}$ and $1.1011001*2^{10011}$ indicate the same value is a further example that not only the digit sequence is essential but particularly its interpretation. Of course, you can introduce a self-made «John-Smith-representation» of binary floating-point numbers by, for example, using 2'complement for the mantissa as well as for the exponent. Your imagination can run riot here, but whether the result is, first, sensible, second, useful and, third, generally acknowledged is another matter.

2.9.2 The Standard – IEEE Formats

As is the case for integers and long integers, for floating-point numbers you have to reserve a certain number of bits. In principle, you are free to choose an «odd» number of bits for a floating-point number, for example 43 bits. However, to enable an easy exchange for binary floating-point numbers as well, one generally uses the so-called *IEEE formats* today. Nearly all compilers and computers use this standard. Only Microsoft's BASIC interpreters traditionally use Microsoft's own format, the Microsoft binary format (MSBIN).

In the following sections these representation standards are discussed in detail. Figure 2.18 shows the IEEE formats for the number types short real, long real and temporary real. They occupy 32, 64 and 80 bits, respectively, and all use biased exponent.

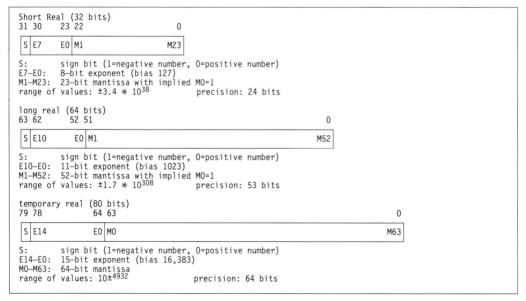

Figure 2.18: IEEE-formats for short real, long real and temporary real.

The values represented by the IEEE formats are, in general:

```
value = (-1)ˢ * (1 + M1*2⁻¹ + M2*2⁻² + ... + M23/M52/M63*2⁻²³/⁵²/⁶³) * 2^E7/E10/E14...E1E0-127
```

The short real format actually has a 24-bit mantissa but integrates only 23 bits of them into the four bytes of the defined format. Where is bit M0 of the mantissa? The answer is simple but inspired. It was mentioned above that in scientific notation a number between 1 and 10 is always in front of the decimal point. This representation is called *normalized* representation. If one does the same with binary floating-point numbers, the number 1 should be in front of the point because only 0 and 1 are available here. 0 does not apply, as by decreasing the exponent the point is moved through the number until a 1 is in front.

Example:
```
0.001011 * 2⁰¹¹⁰¹
Move point until 1 is in front
-> 0.1011 * 2⁰¹¹⁰⁰ -> 1.011 * 2⁰¹⁰¹¹
in normalized form therefore the number is 1.011 * 2⁰¹⁰¹¹
```

Therefore, in normalized representation *every* floating-point number starts with a 1. The IEEE format only uses normalized floating-point numbers so that the first digit M0 of the mantissa (that is, the digit before the point) is always equal to 1. It need not be integrated into the number explicitly but is implicitly known to be 1. Thus, the stored mantissa indicates only the digit after the point. Bits 23–30 hold the biased exponent: to get the «real» exponent you must subtract the value 127 from the stored exponent. Values smaller than 127 lead to negative exponents, and therefore represent numbers smaller than 1. The choice of 127 as the bias is arbitrary, but with 127 the exponent 0 for the number 1 is between the highest and the lowest possible exponents in the IEEE format. Finally, the S bit indicates the sign of the whole number.

Example: `70.457 = 7.0457 * 10¹` in short real format is:

```
428ce9fc = 0100 0010 1000 1100 1110 1001 1111 1100b
                 └──┘ └─┘
                          └─mantissa: 2⁻⁴+2⁻⁵+2⁻⁸+2⁻⁹+2⁻¹⁰+2⁻¹²+2⁻¹⁵
                                      +2⁻¹⁶+2⁻¹⁷+2⁻¹⁸+2⁻¹⁹+2⁻²⁰+2⁻²¹ = 0.1008906
                                      add the implicit 1: 1.1008906
                          ─exponent: 133-bias(127) = 6
                         ─sign: 0 = positive number
   Therefore the number is +1.1008906*2⁶ = +1.1008906*64 = 70.457
```

The same applies to the long real format. Bits 0–51 hold the mantissa digits after the decimal point. Here, too, the M0 bit is always equal to 1, and the format is therefore normalized. Together with the biased exponent, which is enhanced to 11 bits and has a bias value of 1023, the range of values is much larger than with the short real format. For most applications the long real format is enough. Even with the short real format, the ratio of the highest and the smallest possible values is much larger than the ratio between the size of the universe and that of an atom. And the precision of nearly 16 decimals in the long real format exceeds the experimental accuracy of all known constants of nature.

The values 255 and 2048 for the biased exponent in the short and long real formats are reserved by definition. A floating-point number with these exponents is called *NAN* (**not a n**umber) and is not regarded as a number. Coprocessors or software emulations of coprocessors report an error message if such a number occurs, or instead they process a predefined number.

Coprocessors such as Intel's 80x87 family (and software emulations of coprocessors) often use the temporary real format with a width of 80 bits. This format does not need to be normalized. The M0 bit of the mantissa is actually stored in the format, and is not presupposed implicitly as being 1. The range of values and precision of this format are enormous. With the 80 bits of the temporary real format, $2^{80} = 1.2 * 10^{24}$ different numbers can be represented. Even a very fast PC that can load one million different numbers in the temporary real format per second into the coprocessor would need more than 30 billion years to read every possible number – that is, twice the age of the universe. The 80 bits should also be enough for very ambitious program-mers.

But now something confusing seems to occur: a positive and a negative zero, (that is, two zeros). Mathematically speaking, this is nonsense; there is *exactly one* and only one zero (moreover, with no + or – sign). The reason for the sudden existence of two zeros is that the floating-point formats and coprocessors define numbers by way of their *representation*, but in mathematics numbers are defined abstractly by way of their *properties*. Both the long and the short real formats hold a sign bit. If all other 31 bits are equal to 0, then obviously the number 0 will be represented. However, because of the sign bit two representations seem to be possible: +0 with the sign bit cleared and –0 with sign bit set. The same also applies for the other floating point formats. It becomes even more complicated with floating-point numbers in normalized form. Here, the leading 1 of the mantissa is never stored. But how can one know whether the short real number 00000000h really has the value zero, or whether it is, by way of the implicit M0 = 1, the value $1*2^{-127}$?

The only way out of this is a strict definition: for a floating-point number in normalized form with the smallest possible exponent, the mantissa must be also equal to 0. Then the number represents the value 0. If, on the other hand, the exponent has the smallest possible value and the mantissa is not equal to 0, then it is presupposed that the mantissa is not in normalized but in «real» representation. This leads to a number that may be represented in the intended format only by gradual underflow. The number is too small for normalized representation, but can still be represented if the normalization is cancelled and leading zeros are allowed. However, in this way the precision is degraded.

```
Example: 00000001h
Sign 0b        -> positive number
Biased exponent 0000 0000b -> exponent -127, therefore no normalization of the mantissa
Mantissa 000 0000 0000 0000 0000 0001 = 2⁻²²
Value of the not-normalized number: mantissa * 2^Exponent = 2⁻²² * 2⁻¹²⁷ = 2⁻¹⁴⁹ = 1.4012985 * 10⁻⁴⁵
But in normalized representation the end is already reached with 00800000h=1*2⁻¹²⁶=1.1754944 *
10⁻³⁸.
```

2.9.3 BASIC Programmers Pay Attention – The MSBIN Format

Besides the IEEE format, the MSBIN format is also of some importance because the BASIC interpreters GWBASIC and BASICA of Microsoft and IBM, respectively, use this format for the internal representation of floating-point numbers. Figure 2.19 shows the MSBIN format of float-ing-point numbers.

```
short real (32 bits)
31      24 23 22                        · 0

 E7     E0 S M1                    M23

E7–E0:   8–bit exponent (bias 129)
S:       sign bit (1=negative number, 0=positive number)
M1–M23:  23–bit mantissa with implied M0=1
range of values: ±3.0 * 10⁻³⁹ ... ±1.7 * 10³⁸   precision: 24 Bit

long real (64 bits)
63 62       52 51                                        0

 E7     E0 S M1                                    M55

E7–E0:   8–bit exponent (bias 129)
S:       sign bit (1=negative number, 0=positive number)
M1–M55:  55–bit mantissa with implied M0=1
range of values: ±3.0 * 10⁻³⁹ ... ±1.7 * 10³⁸   precision: 56 Bit
```

Figure 2.19: MSBIN formats for short real and long real.

The bias value in the MSBIN format is 129 compared to 127 in the IEEE format. The values represented by the MSBIN formats are, in general:

$$\text{value} = (-1)^S * (1 + M1*2^{-1} + M2*2^{-2} + \ldots + M23/M55*2^{-23/55}) * 2^{E7\ldots E0-129}$$

The long real format has nearly twice the precision but no more extensive a range of values than the short real format. As some compensation, the precision is three bits higher than that of the IEEE long real format. Converting MSBIN's long real format to IEEE's long real format is always possible, but the reverse is only possible if the absolute value of the number in the IEEE format doesn't exceed $1.7 * 10^{38}$ and doesn't fall below $3.0 * 10^{-39}$.

All real formats require extensive calculation capabilities because real numbers must first be separated into their parts: sign, exponent and mantissa. Thereafter exponent and mantissa are calculated separately and the result is combined into a new real number again. Therefore, it is better to use long integers instead of real numbers even if a coprocessor is installed. That is especially advantageous for financial applications: it is faster to calculate the amount of money with long integers in units of cents or pennies (or even a hundredth of them) instead of employing real numbers. The result is converted into dollars or pounds sterling for display at the end by dividing by 100 or 10,000.

The length and structure of the real formats are dependent upon the computer employed. If you are writing assembler programs for real formats, or if you want to manipulate individual bits and bytes of a real number, then be aware that the Intel processors store the bytes in little endian format.

Example: `70.457=428ce9fch (IEEE short real format)` is stored in memory as `fce98c42h`.

2.10 The 8087 Mathematical Coprocessor

The 8087 supports the 8086 and 8088 processor for calculating mathematical expressions with floating-point numbers. The tasks of addition, subtraction, multiplication and division of floating-point numbers, the calculation of the square root and of logarithms, etc. belong to the coprocessor. Further, all 8086/88 addressing schemes for memory operands are also available for the 8087.

The four basic arithmetical operations with integers are already integrated on the 8086/88. Because the whole of mathematics from basic multiplication tables up to transcendent logarithmic functions is based on integers, all mathematical calculations may be carried out, in principle, with the 8086/88 alone. Programs that carry out the functions of the 8087 mathematical coprocessor in the same way, and supply the same results, are called *software emulations* of the 8087. But the 8087 carries out floating-point operations much faster than the 8086/88: for typical floating-point operations, Intel specifies the execution times indicated in Table 2.7.

Floating point operation	8087	Emulation with 8086/88
Addition/subtraction	10.6	1,000
Multiplication (single precision)	11.9	1,000
Division	24.4	2,000
Square root	22.5	12,250
Tangents	56.3	8,125
Exponentiation	62.5	10,687
Load (double precision)	6.3	1,062
Store (single precision)	13.1	750

Typical values are indicated for the emulation; more or less effective programming with 8086/88 instructions can increase or decrease these values.

Table 2.7: Floating point operations with 8087 and 8086/88 processors (execution time in μs at 8 MHz clock speed)

You can see the enormous speed-up by a factor of between 50 and 500 times. Application programs that intensively use mathematical calculations with floating-point numbers, such as CAD or the numerical control of machine tools and robots, are executed much more quickly with an 8087 processor. But the speed-up factors between 50 and 500 are related to the mathematical calculations only. An application, on the other hand, is also heavily occupied with the input and output of data, user guidance and other tasks. Therefore, don't expect all operations to be carried out 50 or 500 times faster. A realistic value, taking into account all of these tasks, is speed-up by a factor somewhere between two and ten. For example, for displaying a circle in a CAD program it is necessary to calculate all those points that make up the circle – here a coprocessor speeds up the calculation. On the other hand, the points must be displayed. The necessary accesses to the video memory are not supported by the coprocessor, so this access proceeds just as quickly without an 8087 processor.

I have called the 8087 a *mathematical* coprocessor several times. There are other coprocessors besides the 8087 (e.g. the 8089 or, in a newer version, the 82389) that are I/O coprocessors, and which support data exchange between the CPU (the 8086/88) and the system bus. In general, each processor that supports the CPU efficiently for a certain task is called a coprocessor. For example, coprocessors exist for mathematical, I/O, graphics and other applications.

2.10.1 Number Formats and Numerical Instruction Set

The 8086/88 is already able to handle numbers and, for this purpose, supports the following number formats:

- signed and unsigned integers (16 bits)
- long signed and unsigned integers (32 bits)
- packed and unpacked binary coded decimals (8 and 16 bits).

But arithmetic with floating-point numbers can only be emulated. The 8086/88 handles them as a string internally. Only the coprocessor emulation program separates the 32-, 64- or 80-bit floating point number into its constituents sign, mantissa and exponent, and processes them according to the four basic arithmetic operations for integers separately. Thereafter, the emulation program recombines the result into a string according the format of the floating-point number.

As a mathematical coprocessor, the 8087 can process floating-point numbers directly without dividing them into the sign, mantissa and exponent constituents. But the 8087 goes one step further and represents all numbers from the integer with 16 bits up to the temporary real number occupying 80 bits internally by the temporary real format according to the IEEE standard. Figure 2.20 shows the number formats that are supported by the 8087. The 8087 strictly implements the IEEE formats for floating-point numbers. Among the 8087 instructions (see Appendix C.1), two are of major importance for managing the number formats: *LOAD* and *STORE*. Using the LOAD instruction a number in one of the formats shown in Figure 2.20 is loaded into an 8087 register and simultaneously converted into the 80-bit temporary real format. Now the 8087 executes all calculations internally with this number format, from a simple comparison up to the very extensive calculation of a logarithm. The STORE instruction is the counterpart of LOAD. STORE (as the name implies) writes a number held in the 8087 in temporary real format into memory in one of the formats shown in Figure 2.20. For this purpose, the 8087 automatically carries out a format conversion. Therefore, the number formats of Figure 2.20 only apply to the format conversions supported by the 8087, and not to the internal representations. You can imagine that the conversion of the number formats is very calculation-intensive. For example, loading one short real number from memory into the 8087, and the accompanying format conversion, lasts up to 56 clock cycles. In the case of a BCD, the expenditure increases up to 310 clock cycles. Storing the number lasts even longer. For simple calculations like the addition, subtraction and multiplication of floating-point numbers the expenditure for format conversion is higher than the gain achieved through directly processing the floating-point numbers in the 8087. Because of this, some application programs execute simple floating-point operations by means of a software emulation on the 8086/88. Only operations that require more extensive calculations (for example, the logarithm) are executed on the 8087, and the 8087 carries out these tasks much faster than the 8086/88. Simple spreadsheet operations such as determining a sum and averaging the value of a column or line then go ahead with and without the coprocessor at the same speed. On the other hand, three-dimensional CAD applications often need trigonometric functions like sine and tangent to

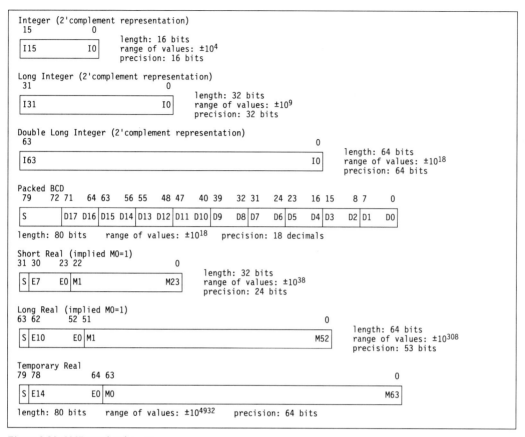

Figure 2.20: 8087 number formats.

calculate projections onto a certain plane. The sine of a (floating-point) quantity can be calculated using the following sum:

$$\sin x = x - x^3/3! + x^5/5! - x^7/7! + - \ldots \quad (3!=1*2*3=6,\ 5!=1*2*3*4*5=120\ \text{etc.})$$

Depending on the value of x, more or fewer terms $x^n/n!$ are necessary to determine the value of sin x with the required precision. The formula shows that a lot of very calculation-intensive floating-point multiplications for the powers x^n and floating-point divisions by the factorials n! are necessary. Software emulations with the 8086/88 need a lot of time for this. With such functions the 8087 can show its power impressively. Without a coprocessor the PC would be calculating a three-dimensional projection in a CAD or ray-tracing application for several days, but with an 8087 it would «only» take a few hours.

When reading the 8087 instruction set you may notice that the 8087 has no instruction to transfer data from one of its registers into a register of the 8086/88. For example, it is not possible to transfer a 16-bit integer from the 8087 into the AX accumulator of the 8086/88. This data exchange only works via the main memory, and is thus correspondingly slow. This is another reason why simple calculations with floating-point numbers are emulated on an 8086/88 in the same time as they are executed on an 8087.

2.10.2 8087 Connections and Signals

Like the 8086/88, the 8087 has 40 pins in all for inputting and outputting signals and supply voltages. Usually, the 8087 comes in a 40-pin DIP package. Figure 2.21 shows the pin assignment of the 8087.

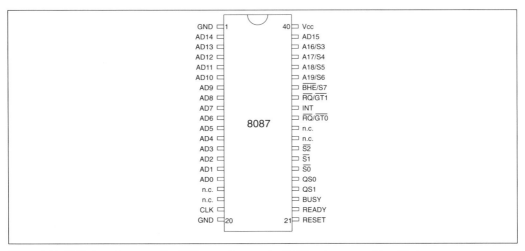

Figure 2.21: 8087 pin assignment. The 8087 comes in a standard DIP package comprising 40 pins.

AD15–AD0 (pins 39, 2–16)
These 16 connections form the 16 data bits when the 8087 is reading or writing data, as well as the lower 16 address bits for addressing memory. The address signals are always supplied first, and later the data signals are output or read. As is the case with the 8086, these 16 pins form a *time-divisionally multiplexed* address and data bus.

A19–A16/S6–S3 (pins 35–38)
These four pins form the four high-order bits of the address bus, as well as four status signals, and form a time-divisionally multiplexed address and control bus. During bus cycles controlled by the 8087, the S6, S4 and S3 signals are reserved and held on a high level. Additionally, S5 is then always low. If the 8086/88 is controlling the bus then the 8087 observes the CPU activity using the signals at pins S6 to S3.

$\overline{BHE}$/S7 (pin 34)
This signal indicates whether a whole word (2 bytes) is present on the data lines AD15–AD0, one byte with an odd address on the data lines AD15–AD8 or one byte with an even address on the lines AD7–AD0. When the 8086/88 is in control of the bus the 8087 observes the signal at pin S7 supplied by the CPU.

$\overline{S2}$, $\overline{S1}$, $\overline{S0}$ (pins 28–26)
The 8288 bus controller uses these three control signals to generate all necessary control signals for a read or write access of the 8087 to memory. For the combinations (S_2, S_1, S_0) the following interpretations hold for bus cycles controlled by the 8087:

```
(0xx) invalid
(100) invalid
(101) data is read from memory
(110) data is written into memory
(111) passive state
```

If the 8086/88 is controlling the bus, the 8087 observes the CPU activity using the signals at pins S2 to S0.

$\overline{RQ}/\overline{GT0}$ (pin 31)

The 8087 uses this pin to get control of the local bus from the 8086/88 so as to execute its own memory cycles. $\overline{RQ}/\overline{GT0}$ is connected to the CPU's $\overline{RQ}/\overline{GT1}$ pin. Normally, the 8086/88 is in control of the bus to read instructions and data. If the 8087 accesses the memory because of a LOAD or STORE instruction, it takes over control of the local bus. Therefore, both the 8086/88 and the 8087 can act as a local bus master.

$\overline{RQ}/\overline{GR1}$ (pin 33)

This pin may be used by another local bus master to get control of the local bus from the 8087.

QS1, QS0 (pins 24, 25)

The signals at these pins indicate the status of the prefetch queue in the 8086/88. Thus, the 8087 can observe the CPU's prefetch queue. For (QS1, QS0) the following interpretations hold:

```
(00) no operation takes place, the prefetch queue is not active
(01) the first byte of the opcode in the prefetch queue is processed
(10) the prefetch queue is cancelled
(11) a next byte of the opcode in the prefetch queue is processed.
```

INT (pin 32)

The signal output at this pin indicates that during the execution of a numerical instruction in the 8087, a non-maskable exception has occurred, for example an overflow. The output of the signal can be suppressed by interrupt masking in the 8087.

BUSY (pin 23)

If the signal at this pin is high then the 8087 is currently executing a numerical instruction. Usually, BUSY is connected to the $\overline{TEST}$ pin of the 8086/88. The CPU checks the $\overline{TEST}$ pin and therefore the BUSY signal to determine the completion of a numerical instruction.

READY (pin 22)

The addressed memory confirms the completion of a data transfer from or to memory with a high signal. The signal is guided through the 8284 clock generator for synchronization purposes, and is applied to this pin afterwards. Therefore, like the 8086/88, the 8087 can also insert wait cycles if the memory doesn't respond quickly enough after an access.

RESET (pin 21)

If this input is high for at least four clock cycles, the 8087 aborts its operation immediately and carries out a processor reset.

CLK (pin 19)

CLK is the clock signal for the coprocessor.

V$_{cc}$ (pin 40)
This pin is supplied with the supply voltage of +5V.

GND (pins 1, 20)
These pins are earthed (usually 0 V).

2.10.3 8087 Structure and Functions

The 8087 supports an 8086/88 CPU in maximum mode with 68 new mnemonics, therefore the coprocessor is also called a *processor extension*. The 8087 is thus regarded as an extension by the 8086/88, which makes additional registers, data types and instructions available to the CPU by a strictly defined cooperation between the 8086/88 and the 8087 on a pure hardware level. For a programmer (also for an assembler or machine language programmer) the 8086/88/87 combination appears to be only a single processor. This «new» processor, though, is much more powerful in mathematical calculations when compared to the 8086/88. This combination might also be regarded as one processor on *two* chips. Figure 2.22 shows the internal structure of the 8087.

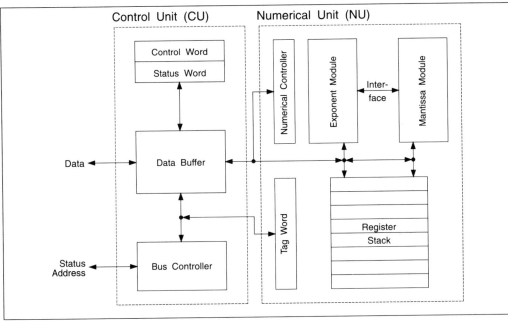

Figure 2.22: Internal structure of the 8087. The 8087 comprises a control unit for controlling the bus and the numerical unit. The numerical unit carries out calculations with floating-point numbers in an exponent and a mantissa module. Unlike the 8086/88, the 8087 has a register stack instead of discrete registers.

The 8087 is divided into two main functional groups: the *control unit (CU)* and the *numerical unit (NU)*. The numerical unit carries out the mathematical calculations. The control unit fetches and decodes the instructions, reads and writes memory operands, and excecutes the 8087 control instructions. Therefore, the CU can synchronize with the CPU while the heavy numerical work is done by the NU.

For mathematical reasons, the exponent and mantissa of a floating-point number are subject to different operations. For example, the multiplication of two floating-point numbers $\pm M1*B^{\pm E1}$ and $\pm M2*B^{\pm E2}$ can be put down to the addition of the exponents and the multiplication of the mantissas. The result is therefore

$$\pm M1*B^{\pm E1} \, * \, \pm M2*B^{\pm E2} \, = \, (\pm M1 \, * \, \pm M2) \, * \, B^{(\pm E1 \, + \, \pm E2)}$$

The ALU of the NU is therefore divided into an exponent module and a mantissa module. The interface between them serves, for example, to normalize the result by increasing or decreasing the exponent.

The control unit largely comprises a unit for bus control, data buffers, and a prefetch queue. The prefetch queue is identical to that in the 8086/88 in a double sense:

– It has the same length. Immediately after a processor reset the 8087 checks by means of the **BHE**/S7 signal whether it is connected to an 8086 or 8088. The 8087 adjusts the length of its prefetch queue according to the length in the 8086 (six bytes) or 8088 (four bytes), respectively.

– The prefetch queue contains the same instructions. By synchronous operation of the 8086/88 and 8087, the same bytes (and therefore also the same instructions) are present in the prefetch queues of both CPU and coprocessor.

Thus, the CU of the coprocessor attends the data bus synchronously to and concurrently with the CPU and fetches instructions to decode them. But the 8086/88 and the coprocessor 8087 differ significantly. The 8087 cannot execute any 8086/88 instructions, and vice versa. One could therefore expect that two different instruction streams are supplied for the CPU and the coprocessor; one stream with instructions for the CPU and one stream with (pure mathematical) instructions for the coprocessor. But that's not the case. Moreover, the instructions for the two different processors are mixed in only one instruction stream. The coprocessor instructions, though, differ in an essential respect from the 8086/88 instructions: They always start with the bit sequence 11011 (=27) and are therefore called *ESC instructions*. On the other hand, the instructions and prefixes for the 8086/88 may begin with any bit sequence except 11011.

In the 8086/88, there are several individual accessible general-purpose registers AX, BX etc., as well as segment registers CS, DS and SS, whereas the numerical and control unit of the 8087 implements a register stack with eight 80-bit registers R1 to R8, as well as various control and status registers (see Figure 2.23).

Each of the eight data registers is divided into three bit groups according to the temporary real format. The eight data registers are managed as a stack and not as individual registers. The 3-bit TOP field in the status word (see Figure 2.24) points to the register currently on top of the stack (**top of stack**). Therefore TOP has similar characteristics and tasks to the stack pointer SP in the 8086/88. You may decrease TOP by 1 and store one value in the corresponding register with 8087 instructions, for example, FLD (floating-point load and push), which is similar to the 8086/88 PUSH instruction. On the other hand, you can increase TOP by 1 and pop the value of the corresponding register from the stack with the FSTP instruction (floating-point store and pop), which is similar to the 8086/88 POP instruction. As is the case with the 8086/88, the stack «grows» downwardly to registers with smaller numbers. Most coprocessor instructions address the register on top of the stack implicitly, that is, the register with the number held in the TOP field of the status register.

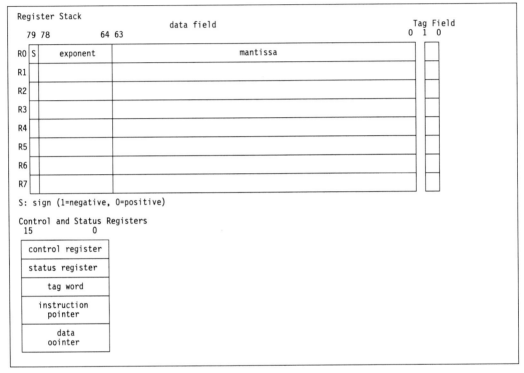

Figure 2.23: 8087 internal registers.

But with many 8087 instructions you are also free to specify a register explicitly. But be careful: the explicit specification is relative to TOP and not absolute.

Example: FLD st(3) addresses the third register, but which one of the registers R0 to R7 will really be accessed is dependent on the current TOP. If, for example, TOP is equal to 5 then register R2 is addressed. If TOP is equal to 1 then FLD st(3) means an invalid operation because register R–2 doesn't exist.

The data transfer between registers R0–R7 in the 8087 is carried out very quickly because the coprocessor has an 84-bit wide data path, and in the 8087 itself no format conversion is necessary.

In the status word the 8087 stores information concerning its current state. Using the FSTSW/FNSTSW instructions (store status word) the coprocessor may write the status word into memory. Then the CPU can investigate the status word to determine, for example, the source of an exception and the resulting NMI.

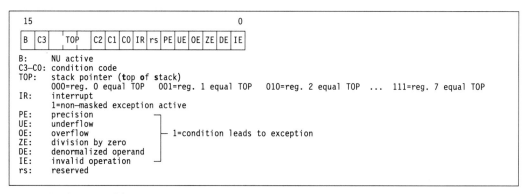

Figure 2.24: Status word format.

If bit *B* is set the numerical unit NU is occupied by a calculation or has issued an interrupt that hasn't yet been serviced completely. Bits *C3–C0* indicate the condition code of a comparison operation in the 8087, or an operation similar to this. They are thus equal to the 8086/88 flags. Note that two different zeros are possible. Table 2.7 shows the interpretations of the condition codes. The three *TOP* bits form the stack pointer mentioned above, which points to the «top» register of R7–R0. If the *IR* bit is set, a non-maskable exception has occurred and the 8087 has activated its INT output. In the PC/XT an NMI is issued. The *PE, UE, OE, ZE, DE* and *IE* bits specify the source of this exception.

instruction type	C3	C2	C1	C0	Meaning
Compare	0	0	x	0	TOP > operand (instruction FTST)
Test	0	0	x	1	TOP < operand (instruction FTST)
	1	0	x	0	TOP = operand (instruction FTST)
	1	1	x	1	TOP cannot be compared
Examine	0	0	0	0	valid, positive, denormalized
	0	0	0	1	invalid, positive, exponent=0 (+NAN)
	0	0	1	0	valid, negative, denormalized
	0	0	1	1	invalid, negative, exponent=0 (–NAN)
	0	1	0	0	valid, positive, normalized
	0	1	0	1	infinite, positive (+∞)
	0	1	1	0	valid, negative, normalized
	0	1	1	1	infinite, negative (–∞)
	1	0	0	0	zero, positive (+0)
	1	0	0	1	unused
	1	0	1	0	zero, negative (–0)
	1	0	1	1	unused
	1	1	0	0	invalid, positive, exponent=0 (+ denormalized)
	1	1	0	1	unused
	1	1	1	0	invalid, negative, exponent=0 (– denormalized)
	1	1	1	1	unused

Table 2.7: 8087 condition codes

The 8087 generates an exception under various circumstances, but some exceptions may be masked. Further, you are free to define various modes for rounding, precision and the representation of infinite values. For this purpose, the 8087 has a control word, shown in Figure 2.25.

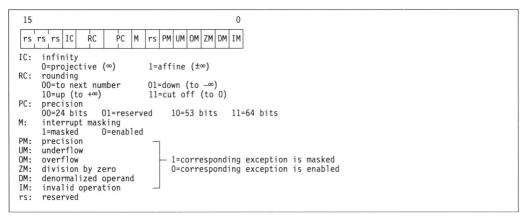

Figure 2.25: Control word format.

The *IC* bit controls the processing of infinite values. Projective infinity leads to only one value, namely ∞. If you set IC equal to 0, then the 8087 operates with affine infinity, and two infinite values +∞ and -∞ are possible. The term «infinite» must be used with care because in a strict mathematical sense no infinite qualities exist, only quantities which are *not limited* upwardly (+∞) or downwardly (-∞), or Riemann's far-point. The two *RC* bits control the rounding in the manner indicated. The precision of calculations in the 8087 can be set by means of the *PC* bits to retain compatibility with older mathematical coprocessors whose calculational capabilities are less than that of the 8087.

All other bits in the control word refer to exceptions and the consequent hardware interrupt. The 8087 detects and processes six different exceptions in all, which usually lead to a hardware interrupt (request). With the *M* bit, you can mask interrupts globally, in which case the 8087 ignores all exceptions and doesn't execute an on-chip exception handler. The *PM, UM, OM, ZM, DM* and *IM* bits mask exceptions individually. The coprocessor then carries out a standard routine for handling the corresponding error – a so-called *standard on-chip exception handler*. It is implemented on the chip. The following briefly lists the reasons for each exception and the action taken by the accompanying standard exception handler. If a non-masked exception occurs, the corresponding bits are set in the status word (see Figure 2.24):

– Precision (PE, PM): the result of an operation can't be represented exactly with the predefined format. If the PM bit is set, the coprocessor continues with no further action.
– Underflow (UE, UM): although the result is not zero it is too small to be represented with the predefined format. If UM is equal to 1, the 8087 cancels the result's normalization and shifts the leading 1 of the mantissa until the exponent corresponds to the selected format. Each shift to the right by one digit means a division of the mantissa by 2. Therefore, the value of the exponent must be increased accordingly. This process is called *gradual under-flow*.

- Overflow (OE, OM): the result is too big for the predefined format. If the exception is masked, the 8087 generates an encoding for ∞ internally, and continues processing with this number.
- Division by zero (ZE, ZM): the divisor was equal to zero but the dividend was not. For mathematical reasons, the result is not defined (not ∞). It is hard to work with undefined things, and with a masked exception the 8087 generates an encoding for ∞, as is the case for overflow. This solution seems to be better than none.
- Denormalized operand (DE, DM): at least one of the operands or the result of the operation could not be represented in normalized form (smallest possible exponent with a mantissa not equal to zero). If DM is set to 1, the 8087 continues without any further action and uses the denormalized quantity.
- Invalid operation (IE, IM): an overflow or underflow of the register stack has occurred (PUSH onto a full stack or POP with an empty stack), a mathematically undefined operation such as $0 \div 0$, $\infty \div \infty$ or $\infty - \infty$ is to be executed or the operand is a value characterized as NAN. With a masked exception the 8087 generates a certain NAN value or outputs a NAN value as the operation result.

```
 15                                                    0
┌──────────────────────────────────────────────────────┐
│ Tag7│ Tag6│ Tag5│ Tag4│ Tag3│ Tag2│ Tag1│ Tag0│
└──────────────────────────────────────────────────────┘
Tag7-Tag0:  tag values for register stack R7 ... R0
00=valid       01=zero
10=NAN, infinite, denormalized value or non-supported number format   11=empty
```

Figure 2.26: Tag word format.

A further status register is available in the coprocessor: the *tag word* (see Figure 2.26). In *Tag7–Tag0* the 8087 stores information concerning the contents of the eight data registers R7–R0. The coprocessor uses this information to execute certain operations faster. For example, the 8087 can distinguish empty and non-empty registers on the stack very quickly, or it can determine certain values such as NAN, infinite, etc. at high speed without the need to decode the value in the corresponding register. You can write the tag word into memory using the FSTENV /FNSTENV instruction (store environment state).

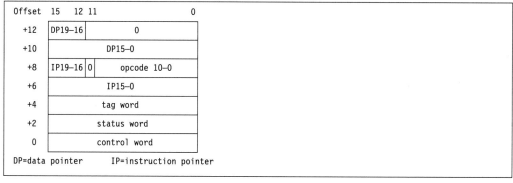

Figure 2.27: Memory image of instruction and data pointer.

Upon executing a numeric instruction, the coprocessor's control unit (CU) holds the addresses of the instruction and the operand, the opcode, and the control, status and tag words internally. If a coprocessor exception occurs and if the 8087 consequently issues an interrupt, the handler can write this environment state into memory using the FSTENV/FNSTENV instruction. The format is shown in Figure 2.27. Afterwards, the handler may determine the reason for the exception. The handling of a coprocessor error becomes far simpler using this strategy.

2.10.4 8087 Memory Cycles

Like 8086/88 instructions, 8087 instructions may also include a memory operand (for example, the instruction STORE array[bx]). The 8086/88 distinguishes such instructions from pure arithmetical instructions handed by the 8087. The CPU calculates the operand address according to the addressing scheme indicated, and then the 8086/88 executes a *dummy read cycle*. This cycle differs from a normal read cycle only in that the CPU ignores the data supplied by the memory. If the CPU recognizes a coprocessor instruction without a memory operand, it continues with the next instruction after the 8087 has signalled via its BUSY pin that it has completed the current instruction.

The 8087 also behaves differently for instructions with and without a memory operand. In the first case, it simply executes an instruction such as FSQRT (square root of a floating-point number). For an instruction with a memory operand it uses the 8086/88 dummy read cycle in the following way:

- Fetching an operand from memory: the 8087 reads the address supplied by the CPU in the dummy read cycle via the address bus and stores it in an internal temporary register. Then the 8087 reads the data word that is put onto the data bus by the memory. If the operand is longer than the data word transferred within this read cycle, the 8087 requests control of the local bus from the 8086/88. Now the 8087 carries out one or more succeeding read cycles on its own. The coprocessor uses the memory address fetched during the course of the dummy read cycle and increments it until the whole memory operand is read. For example, in the case of the 8088/87 combination, eight memory read cycles are necessary to read a floating-point number in long real format. Afterwards, the 8087 releases control of the local bus to the 8086/88 again.

- Writing an operand into memory: in this case the coprocessor also fetches the address output by the CPU in a dummy read cycle, but ignores the memory data appearing on the data bus. Afterwards, the 8087 takes over control of the local bus and writes the operand into memory, starting with the fetched address in one or more write cycles.

Because of the dummy read cycle the 8087 doesn't need its own addressing unit to determine the effective address of the operand with segment, offset and displacement. This is advantageous because the 8087, with its 75 000 transistors, integrates far more components on a single chip compared to the 28 000 transistors of the 8086/88, and space is at a premium.

The 8087 also uses the 8086/88 addressing unit if new instructions have to be fetched into the prefetch queue. The CPU addresses the memory to load one or two bytes into the prefetch queue. These instruction bytes appear on the data bus. The processor status signals keep the

8087 informed about the prefetch processes, and it monitors the bus. If the instruction bytes from memory appear on the data bus, the 8087 (and also the 8086/88, of course) loads them into the prefetch queue.

2.10.5 8086/8087 System Configuration

Figure 2.28 shows typical wiring of the 8087 coprocessor and CPU 8086/88. As they are bus masters, both chips access the same local bus that is connected to memory, the I/O address space and the bus slots via the 8288 bus controller. The 8086/88 and the 8087 read and decode the same instruction stream at the same speed, thus they operate *synchronously* and are supplied with the same clock signal (CLK) by the 8284 clock generator. All higher coprocessors, however, such as the 80287, i387, etc., run asynchronously to the CPU. For synchronous operation of the 8086/88 and 8087, the 8087 must always know the current state of the 8086/88.

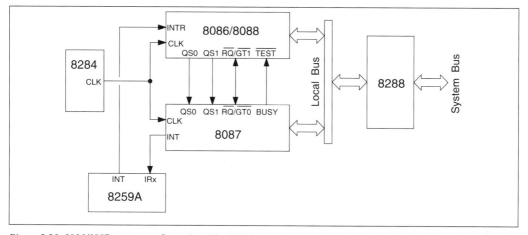

Figure 2.28: 8086/8087 system configuration. The 8087 harmonizes especially well with the 8086/88, and can therefore be connected to the 8086/88 without difficulties. The 8087 uses the same bus controller, the same clock generator, and the same interrupt controller as the CPU.

The 8087 can process its instructions independently of the CPU. Even concurrent (parallel) execution of instructions is possible, but here the problem of resynchronization arises after completion of the coprocessor instruction. After decoding the current ESC instruction, the 8086/88 would prefer to execute the next instruction at once, but cannot do so because the CPU has to wait for the coprocessor. Because of this, the BUSY pin of the 8087 is connected to the $\overline{\text{TEST}}$ pin of the 8086/88. When the coprocessor executes an instruction it activates the BUSY signal. When it has completed the instruction, it deactivates the signal. The WAIT instruction of the 8086/88 causes the CPU to check the $\overline{\text{TEST}}$ pin continuously to observe the BUSY state of the coprocessor. Only when the 8087 has deactivated BUSY to signal to the 8086/88 that the current instruction is completed and the 8087 is ready to accept further numeric instructions does the CPU continue with the next instruction. Via the QS0 and QS1 pins, the 8087 detects the status of the 8086/88's prefetch queue to observe the CPU's operation. Thus, the 8086/88 and 8087 always operate synchronously.

If an error or an exception occurs during a numerical calculation in the coprocessor, such as overflow or underflow, the 8087 activates its INT output to issue a hardware interrupt request to the CPU. Usually, the INT signal of the 8087 is managed by an interrupt controller (the 8259A, for example) and then applied to the 8086/88. But the PC/XT does it in another way: the 8087 hardware interrupt request is supplied to the NMI input of the 8086/88. The PC/XT has only one 8259A PIC and must therefore save IRQ channels. Note that besides the coprocessor interrupt, an error on an extension adapter or a memory parity error may also issue an NMI corresponding to interrupt 2. Thus, the interrupt handler must be able to locate the source of an NMI.

Figure 2.28 demonstrates that both the 8086/88 and the 8087 can access the local bus, to read data from memory, for example. 8086/88 instructions such as MOV reg, mem or the LOAD instruction of the 8087 carry out a memory access. Thus there are two bus masters, each using the local bus independently. A simultaneous access of the local bus by the CPU and coprocessor would give rise to a conflict between them, with disastrous consequences. Therefore, only one of these two processors may control the local bus, and the transfer of control between them must be carried out in a strictly defined way. Because of this, the $\overline{\text{RQ}}/\overline{\text{GT1}}$ pins of the 8086/88 and $\overline{\text{RQ}}/\overline{\text{GT0}}$ pins of the 8087 are connected. From Section 2.5 and the description above you can see that these pins serve to request and grant local bus control. The 8087 uses the $\overline{\text{RQ}}/\overline{\text{GT0}}$ pin to get control of the local bus for data transfers to and from memory. The $\overline{\text{RQ}}/\overline{\text{GT1}}$ pin is available for other bus masters, for example the I/O 8299 coprocessor. Therefore, CPU and coprocessor may alternate in controlling the local bus. The 8087 bus structure and its bus control signals are equivalent to that of the 8086/88.

2.11 PC/XT Architecture

After such an enormous amount of basic information on processors, bus controllers, etc. I now cover the actual use of the chips in a PC/XT. You can, of course, combine the chips described earlier and construct a robot or a laser printer controller, for example: one advantage of microprocessors is their flexibility. You may also meet the chips described in this book in other products, for example in your washing machine or in an aeroplane. But let us now turn to the actual architecture of the PC/XT.

2.11.1 The Components and their Cooperation

Figure 2.29 shows a block diagram of a PC/XT. If you have looked in vain for the chip names indicated in the figure on your motherboard, this doesn't mean that you didn't buy a PC! Instead, the chips will have been provided by a third-party manufacturer, or the functions of several chips integrated into a single chip. But the functional construction, and therefore the architecture, remains the same. Therefore, I only want to describe the basic configuration.

The central part is of course the processor. In a PC you will find an 8088 and in an XT the 8086. For a short time, an XT/286 was also on the market with the newer and more powerful 80286, but it did not have any other modification. This XT/286 was soon replaced by the more power-ful and modern AT.

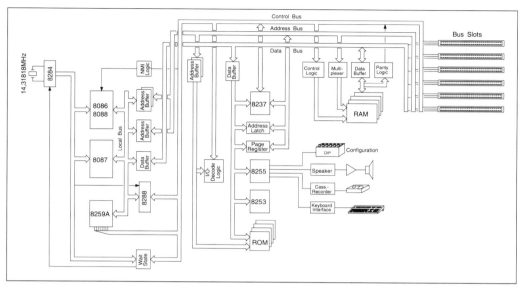

Figure 2.29: The PC/XT architecture.

In addition to the 8086/88, a mathematical 8087 coprocessor can be installed, or at least a socket for it may be present on the motherboard. An 8284 clock generator generates the system clock, and in the first PC was supplied with a crystal signal of 14 318 180 Hz. The 8284 divides this frequency by three to generate the effective system clock of 4.77 MHz. In more modern turbo-PC/XTs an oscillator with a higher frequency is present, which enables a system clock of 8 MHz or even 10 MHz. Further, an NEC CPU called V30 or V20 may be present instead of the 8086/88. The V30 and V20 are faster and have a slightly extended instruction set compared to the 8086/88, but are entirely downwards compatible with the Intel CPUs. The enhanced instruction set is of no use in a PC, as it can't be used for compatibility reasons.

A further essential component of the computer is the main memory. The processor is connected to it via the data, address and control buses. The CPU addresses the memory by means of the address bus, controls the data transfer with the control bus, and transfers the data via the data bus. The necessary control signals are generated by the 8288 bus controller according to instructions from the 8086/88. In order to carry out data exchange in as error-free and orderly a way as possible, the signals are buffered and amplified in various address and data buffer circuits.

In the PC/XT four different address buses can be distinguished:

- local address bus: comprises the 20 address signals from the 8086/88. External address buffers and address latches separate the local bus from the system address bus.

- system address bus: this is the main PC/XT address bus and represents the latched version of the local address bus. The signal for latching the address signals on the local address bus into the latches for the system address bus is ALE. In the PC/XT the system address bus leads to the bus slots.

– memory address bus: this is only implemented on the motherboard, and represents the multiplexed version of the system address bus. Via the memory address bus, the row and column addresses are successively applied to the DRAM chips (see Chapter 6).

– X-address bus: this is separated from the system bus by buffers and drivers, and serves to address the I/O units and the ROM BIOS on the motherboard. These may, for example, be the registers of the interrupt controller, the timer or an on-board floppy controller. I/O ports and BIOS extensions on expansion adapters are accessed by the system address bus.

Besides the four address buses there are four different data buses:

– local data bus: comprises the 16 data signals from the 8086/88. Additionally, a bus logic is necessary to distinguish byte and word accesses. External data buffers and data latches separate the local data bus from the system data bus. In the PC the local data bus is eight bits wide, and in the XT it is 16 bits wide.

– system data bus: is the latched version of the local data bus in the PC/XT, and has eight bits in the PC and 16 bits in the XT. One byte of the system data bus leads to the bus slots.

– memory data bus: this is only present on the motherboard, and establishes the connection between main memory and the system data bus. In the PC the memory data bus is eight bits wide, and in the XT it is 16 bits wide.

– X-data bus: this is separated from the system bus by buffers and drivers and accesses I/O units and the ROM BIOS on the motherboard. I/O ports and BIOS extensions on expansion adapters are accessed by the system data bus.

As already mentioned, the difference between the 8086 and the 8088 is the different width of their data buses. The 8086 has a 16-bit data bus, but the 8088 only has an 8-bit one. Therefore, in the PC the data bus on the motherboard for an access to main memory is only eight bits wide, but in a XT it is 16 bits wide. Besides the main memory on the motherboard, the CPU can also access chips on the adapter cards in the bus slots. A more detailed explanation of the structure and functioning of the bus slots is given below. Here, I only want to mention that all essential signals of the system bus lead to the bus slots, for example address, data and certain control signals necessary to integrate the adapter cards into the PC system.

In this respect, it is also important that in an XT the data bus is guided into the bus slots with only eight bits. In a 16-bit access via the complete 16-bit data bus of the 8086, an 8/16-converter must carry out the separation of one 16-bit quantity into two 8-bit quantities, or has to combine two 8-bit quantities into one 16-bit quantity. On the XT motherboard this is not necessary. The memory access is always carried out with the full width of 16 bits. On an XT this has, of course, enormous consequences for accesses to on-board memory on the one hand and to memory on an adapter card which is located in one of the bus slots on the other. Because of the limited 8-bit width for accesses to memory on the adapter card, less data is transferred each time. Thus, the data transfer rate is smaller. If 16-bit values are to be transferred then these values must be separated into two 8-bit values, or they must be combined from them. This takes some time, and the access time for accessing the memory expansion adapter card increases further compared to the on-board memory. This is especially noticeable on a turbo XT. The ancestor PC only ran at 4.77 MHz; with this clock rate the bus slots and inserted adapter cards don't have any problem in following the clock, but with the 10 MHz turbo clock this is not the case. In most cases, the slow bus slots are run at only half the turbo clock speed, that is, 5 MHz. An access to expansion memory on the adapter card is therefore slower in two ways: the 8/16-bit conversion lasts one bus cycle, and halving the bus frequency decreases the transfer rate further. Therefore, you should always choose to expand the on-board memory as long as the motherboard can accommodate additional memory chips. That is especially true for fast-clocked i386 and i486 computers. Even in these PCs, the bus slots run at 8 MHz at most. What a shock for the proud owners of a 50 MHz computer! Some PC have a dedicated memory slot besides the normal bus slots. Special memory adapter cards may be inserted into these memory slots to run at a higher frequency than the bus slots.

To decode the processor's addresses in a memory access, the PC/XT includes an address multiplexer. Together with the memory buffer, it drives the memory chips on the motherboard. The check logic for memory parity issues an NMI if the data doesn't conform to the additionally held parity bit at the time of data reading. The parity check is carried out on a byte basis, that is, each individually addressable byte in main memory is assigned a parity bit. When you extend your storage, therefore, you not only have to insert the «actual» memory chips, but also an additional chip for every eight memory chips. This 9th chip holds the corresponding parity bits. Generally, the memory is divided into *banks* which must always be completely filled. How many chips correspond to a bank depends on the number of data pins that one chip has for outputting or inputting data.

The older 64 kbit or 256 kbit chips usually have only one data pin. If memory is organized in eight bits, as is the case for a PC (that is, if it has an 8-bit data bus), then one bank is usually made up of eight memory chips plus one chip for parity. The reason is that in a read or write access, one byte is always transferred at a time, and therefore eight data connections are necessary. With a 16-bit organization, 18 chips (16 data chips plus two parity chips) are required. If you don't fill a bank completely then the address multiplexer accesses «nothing» for one or more bits, and the PC unavoidably crashes.

The PC/XT also has a ROM, where code and data for the boot-up process and the PC's BIOS routines are stored. The 8086/88 accesses the BIOS in ROM in the same way as it does with main memory. Wait cycles during an access to main memory, ROM or the I/O address space are generated by the wait state logic.

For supporting CPU and peripherals an 8259A Programmable Interrupt-Controller (PIC) is present in the PC/XT. It manages external hardware interrupts from peripherals such as the hard disk controller or timer chip. The 8259A has eight input channels connected to a chip, each of which may issue an interrupt request. In the PC these channels are called IRQ0–IRQ7. Table 2.9 shows the assignment of interrupt channel IRQx and the corresponding peripheral or support chip. How the 8259A works and how you may program it is explained in Chapter 7.

Channel	Interrupt	Used by
NMI	02h	parity, 8087 fault
IRQ0	08h	channel 0 of timer 8253
IRQ1	09h	keyboard
IRQ2	0ah	reserved
IRQ3	0bh	COM2
IRQ4	0ch	COM1
IRQ5	0dh	hard disk controller
IRQ6	0eh	floppy disk controller
IRQ7	0fh	LPT1

Table 2.9: Hardware interrupt channels

Another support chip is also present, the 8253 programmable interval timer (PIT) (or timer chip). It has three individually programmable counters in all (see Table 2.10). Counter 0 is used in the PC/XT to update the internal system clock periodically. For this purpose, this counter is connected to IRQ0 of the PIC. The hardware interrupt issued in this way updates the internal clock. This clock may be read or written using the DOS commands TIME and DATE. Counter 1 together with the DMA chip carries out the memory refresh, and counter 2 generates a tone frequency for the speaker. In Sections 7.2 and 7.4, details on the operation modes and programming of the PIT 8253 and speaker are given.

Channel	Used by
0	internal system clock (IRQ0)
1	memory refresh
2	speaker frequency

Table 2.10: PC/XT timer channel

Besides the processor, there is another chip able to carry out memory and I/O accesses: the 8237A DMA chip. It enables fast data transfer between main memory and I/O units such as the floppy controller. Unlike the 8086/88, the 8237A cannot process data but only transfer it (at high speed). The 8237A has four separately programmable transfer channels, used as indicated in Table 2.11.

Channel	Usage
0	memory refresh
1	SDLC adapter
2	floppy disk controller
3	hard disk controller

Table 2.11: PC/XT DMA channels

Channel 0 is reserved for memory refresh, and is activated periodically by the 8253A PIT to carry out a dummy access to memory. The memory chips are thus refreshed. The remaining three channels are available for data transfer. If, for example, the hard disk controller has read one sector then it activates channel 3 of the 8237A and hands the data transfer over to it without any intervention from the CPU. Besides the 8086/88 CPU, the 8237A is another, independent chip for carrying out bus cycles; thus it is a *bus master* – but with a limited function. The function, programming, and transfer protocol of the DMA chip are described in Chapter 7. The CPU and DMA chip are located on the motherboard. The PC/XT bus doesn't support external bus masters that may be located on an adapter card in a bus slot. It would be useful, for example, if the processor of a network adapter could access the main memory independently and without intervention from the motherboard's CPU in order to deliver data to the network, or to transfer data from the network into main memory. But in a PC/XT (and also in an AT), the adapter must issue a hardware interrupt to indicate the required data transfer to the CPU. Then the CPU carries out this transfer. With the advent of EISA and the microchannel, though, bus masters may be located on an external adapter card. They are then able to control the EISA bus or the microchannel on their own.

The keyboard is connected to the PC/XT's system bus by an 8255 programmable peripheral interface (PPI) (see Section 7.5). With the same chip, the BIOS can check the system configuration, which is set by DIP switches. But newer turbo XTs, like the AT, have a real-time clock and a CMOS RAM, which holds all necessary configuration data. Thus, DIP switches are no longer necessary. However, the PC/XT accesses the keyboard through the 8255. Also connected to the PPI are the speaker and the cassette logic for driving the cassette drive. Using the 8255, the speaker is either enabled or disconnected (the cassette drive is only of historical importance today).

The whole PC is powered by a power supply that outputs voltages of –12 V, –5 V, 0 V, +5 V and +12 V. The adapter cards in the bus slots are usually powered by corresponding contacts in the bus slots. Only «current eaters», for example FileCards with integrated hard disk drives, must be directly connected to the power supply.

As hardware components, the support chips mentioned above are accessed via ports in the I/O address space. Thus, the PC/XT uses *I/O mapped input/output (I/O)*. Table 2.12 shows the port addresses of the most important hardware components in the PC/XT.

Port address	Used by
000h–00fh	DMA chip 8237A
020h–021h	PIC 8259A
040h–043h	PIT 8253
060h–063h	PPI 8255
080h–083h	DMA page register
0a0h–0afh	NMI mask register
0c0h–0cfh	reserved
0e0h–0efh	reserved
100h–1ffh	unused
200h–20fh	game adapter
210h–217h	extension unit
220h–24fh	reserved
278h–27fh	parallel printer

Table 2.12: PC/XT port addresses

Port address	Used by
2f0h–2f7h	reserved
2f8h–2ffh	COM2
300h–31fh	prototype adapter
320h–32fh	hard disk controller
378h–37fh	parallel interface
380h–38fh	SDLC adapter
3a0h–3afh	reserved
3b0h–3bfh	monochrome adapter/parallel interface
3c0h–3cfh	EGA
3d0h–3dfh	CGA
3e0h–3e7h	reserved
3f0h–3f7h	floppy disk controller
3f8h–3ffh	COM1

Table 2.12: cont.

The registers of hardware components on adapter cards that are inserted into the bus slots (for example, the UART on the serial interface adapter or the 6845 on the graphics adapter) are also accessed via port addresses. The PC/XT hands over all accesses to the I/O address space to the bus slots in the same way as for accesses to memory on adapter cards. Note that any address, no matter whether in the memory or I/O address space, may only be assigned a single component. If you assign the same I/O address to, for example, the UART registers of COM1 and COM2, the chips disturb each other because they respond to the CPU's instructions (nearly) at the same time. Thus the interfaces don't work at all, or at least not correctly.

2.11.2 I/O Channel and Bus Slots

Most of the PC/XT system bus leads into the bus slots, all of which have the same structure. Theoretically, it doesn't matter into which slot you insert your brand-new adapter card, but in practice some adjoining adapter cards may disturb each other, so you could have to insert one adapter into another slot. During bus cycles that only refer to components on the motherboard, the slots are usually cut off from the system bus to minimize the load for the driver circuits, and to avoid any noise induced by the slots. Using the bus slot contacts, a PC/XT may be configured very flexibly. The inserted adapter cards behave like components that have been integrated onto the motherboard. Figure 2.30 shows the structure and contact assignment of a bus slot.

The following sections discuss the contacts and the meaning of the supplied or accepted signals.

OSC
This contact supplies the oscillator's clock signal of 14 318 180 Hz.

CLK
CLK is the system clock of the PC/XT. In the first PC, OSC was divided by three to generate the system clock with a frequency of 4.77 MHz.

RESET DRV

This contact supplies a reset signal to reset the whole system at power-up or during a hardware reset.

A19–A0

These contacts form the 20-bit address bus of the PC/XT, and either indicate the state of the 8086/88 address signals directly, or are generated by DMA address logic.

D7–D0

These signals form an 8-bit data bus for data transfer from or to adapter cards.

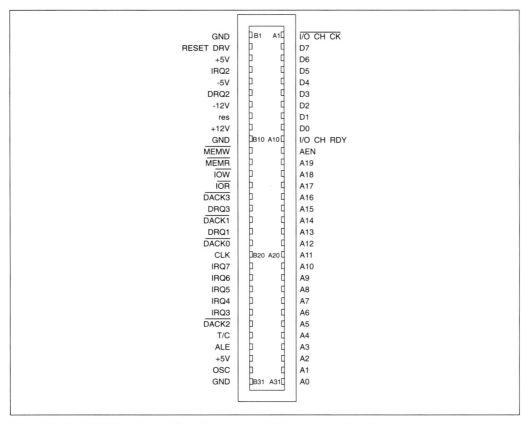

Figure 2.30: The PC/XT bus slot is laid out for an external 8-bit data bus, and has 62 contacts.

ALE

(Address Latch Enable) The ALE signal is generated by the 8288 bus controller, and indicates that valid address signals are present on the bus. Adapter cards may now decode these signals.

I/O CH CK

(I/O Channel Check) With this contact the adapter cards flag errors to the motherboard to indicate, for example, a parity error on a memory expansion board, or a general error on an adapter card. An active $\overline{\text{I/O CH CK}}$ signal (that is, a low level signal) issues an NMI corresponding to interrupt 2 in the PC/XT.

I/O CH RDY

(I/O Channel Ready) The contact receives the ready signal from addressed units on an adapter card. If I/O CH RDY is low, the processor or DMA chip extends the bus cycle by inserting one or more wait states.

IRQ2–IRQ7

These contacts transmit the hardware interrupt requests corresponding to channels IRQ2–IRQ7 to the PIC on the motherboard. For example, the hard disk controller activates IRQ5 after reading data from the disk into an internal buffer. The IRQ0 and IRQ1 lines are assigned channel 0 of the timer chip and the keyboard, respectively. Therefore, they do not need to be integrated into the bus slots.

$\overline{\text{IOR}}$

(I/O Read) The signal at this contact indicates that the processor or the DMA controller wants to read data, and the addressed peripheral should supply data onto the data bus. An active $\overline{\text{IOR}}$ corresponds to an active $\overline{\text{IORC}}$ of the 8288 bus controller, which indicates a read access to the I/O address space.

$\overline{\text{IOW}}$

(I/O Write) The signal at this contact indicates that the processor or the DMA controller wants to write data, and that the addressed peripheral should take the data off the data bus. An active $\overline{\text{IOW}}$ corresponds to the active $\overline{\text{IOWC}}$ of the 8288 bus controller, which indicates a write access to the I/O address space.

$\overline{\text{MEMR}}$

(Memory Read) By an active $\overline{\text{MEMR}}$ (that is, a low level signal), the motherboard tells the adapter cards that the processor or DMA controller wants to read data from main memory. An active $\overline{\text{MEMR}}$ corresponds to the active $\overline{\text{MRDC}}$ of the 8288 bus controller, which indicates a read access to memory address space.

$\overline{\text{MEMW}}$

(Memory Write) By an active $\overline{\text{MEMW}}$ (that is, a low level signal), the motherboard tells the adapter cards that the processor or DMA controller wants to write data into main meory. An active $\overline{\text{MEMW}}$ corresponds to the active $\overline{\text{MWTC}}$ of the 8288 bus controller, which indicates a write access to memory address space.

DRQ3–DRQ1

(DMA Request) With these contacts a peripheral on an adapter card indicates to the motherboard system that it wants to transfer data via one of the three DMA channels. Channel 0 of the DMA chip is connected on the motherboard with channel 1 of the timer chip to periodically carry out memory refresh. Therefore, DRQ0 doesn't lead to the bus slots. Lines DRQ3 to DRQ1 must be held active until the corresponding DACK signal also becomes active; otherwise the DMA request is ignored.

DACK3–DACK0
(DMA Acknowledge) These four contacts are used for acknowledging DMA requests DRQ3 to DRQ1, and for the memory refresh (DACK0). Once a DRQx request has been acknowledged by the corresponding DACKx, the data transfer via the corresponding DMA channel may take place.

AEN
(Address Enable) If the signal at this contact is active the DMA controller is controlling the bus for a data transfer. The processor and other peripherals are cut off from the bus.

T/C
(Terminal Count) If the counter of a DMA channel has reached its final value, the DMA transfer is complete and the T/C terminal supplies a pulse to indicate the end of the DMA cycle.

2.12 The 80186/88

To complete the picture, I want to briefly mention the successor of the 8086/88, the 80186/88. The relationship between the 80186 and 80188 is the same as for the 8086 and 8088, the only difference being that the 80186 has a 16-bit and the 80188 only has an 8-bit data bus. However, the 80186/88 is not just a microprocessor. Intel additionally integrated an interrupt controller, a DMA controller and a timer onto this single chip. Therefore, the 80186/88 is more of an integrated microcontroller. The instruction set has been expanded compared to the 8086/88 and some instructions are optimized so that an 80186/88 is about 25% faster than an equivalent 8086/88. The new 80186/88 instructions are listed in Appendix B.2. As is the case for the 8086/88, the 80186/88 also operates in real mode only, and has an address space of 1 Mbyte. It was not until the 80286 that protected mode was introduced and the address space extended to 16 Mbytes.

The main disadvantage of using the 80186/88 in a PC is that the register addresses of interrupt, DMA and timer chip are entirely incompatible with the corresponding register addresses in the PC. Therefore, integration of the 80186/88 would only be possible with additional and extensive decode logic. Because of this, the 80186/88 is hardly ever used in PC/XTs or compatibles. Instead, most manufacturers use the much more powerful 80286. As a stand-alone microprocessor on adapter cards for PCs (for example, facsimile adapters), the 80186/88 is, nevertheless, popular. Incompatibilities between the 8086/88 and the other support chips do not play a role here.

Integrated microcontrollers or chip sets such as the 80186/88 are becoming more and more popular, especially for very compact notebooks. It was only with these integrated solutions that the development of laptops and notebook computers became possible. Leading this field at the moment is Intel's 386SL together with the accompanying I/O subsystem, the 82360SL.

3 The 80286

The structure of the 80286 is basically the same as the 8086: it has a bus unit (BU), an instruction unit (IU), an execution unit (EU) and an addressing unit (AU). The main innovation is a new operating mode; so-called protected virtual address mode (or *protected mode* for short). In protected mode the processor hardware checks a program's access to data and code and allows such accesses on a total of four *privilege levels*. Data and code are therefore protected, and a PC crash is normally impossible. Moreover, the 80286 has a more extensive instruction set than the 8086. To this enhanced set belong instructions that have a meaning only in protected mode, or at least give different results here. All other instructions are identical in both the real and protected modes. Therefore, the same addressing schemes are available for the application programmer without the need to take into account the features of protected mode. All memory management tasks and memory accesses are carried out by the operating system with the aid of the 80286 hardware.

The access checks in protected mode indicated above provide hardware support for *multitasking operating systems*, such as OS/2. In a multitasking operating system environment, several programs (tasks) run concurrently (in parallel). Strictly speaking, the individual tasks are activated periodically by the operating system, are executed for a short time period, and are interrupted again by the operating system. Then the system activates another task. Unlike the TSR (Terminate and Stay Resident) programs of MS-DOS (PRINT, for example), the programs are activated by the operating system. TSR programs, on the other hand, activate themselves, usually by intercepting the periodic timer interrupt. Thus, a multitasking operating system often switches between the individual tasks within a short time (that is, a *task switch* is carried out), and users have the impression that the programs are running in parallel. With the 80286 hardware support in protected mode, these task switches may be carried out both quickly and efficiently.

Like the 8086 and 8088, the 80286 is a 16-bit processor (that is, its registers are 16 bits wide), and data processing is carried out with a width of 16 bits at most. Unlike the 8086, the 80286 has a 24-bit address bus, thus 16 Mbytes of memory can be addressed. However, this is only possible in protected mode; in real mode the 80286 only works at the speed of an 8086. The higher execution speed is the result of the higher processor clock frequency (newer types reach up to 25 MHz) and the optimized electronic circuitry in the instruction, execution and addressing units, as well as a modified bus cycle. This bus cycle enables a faster read and write through pipelined addressing. The 80286 can address 64 k 8-bit ports at addresses 0–65 535 or 32 k 16-bit ports with addresses 0, 2, 4, ..., 65 532, 65 534, or an equivalent mixture of 8-bit and 16-bit ports until 64 k is reached. As is the case for a PC/XT, in an AT only the lower 1024 (1 k) ports are used, that is, the AT's I/O decoder can only decode the port addresses 0–1023 (3ffh).

In real mode the physical address is generated in the same way as in the 8086, by shifting the segment value to the left by four bits (corresponding to a multiplication by a factor of 16), and adding the offset afterwards. It should be noted that the 80286 may already break through the 1 Mbyte boundary in real mode (for a few bytes). Unlike the 8086, the 80286 always runs in maximum mode, that is, it always needs a bus controller – in this case, therefore, the 82288. Further, the 80286 has no combined address and data bus; all address and data signals are input and output via a dedicated pin, thus switching between address and data bus mode has been dropped, and the BU runs more quickly.

3.1 80286 Connections and Signals

The 80286 comes in two different packages: a *plastic leaded chip carrier* (PLCC) or a *pin grid array* (PGA). The PLC carrier has contacts on all four edges of the package (Figure 3.1), whereas the pin grid array has 68 pins on the bottom of the package (Figure 3.1). The internal structure of the processor is identical in both cases; only the sockets into which it is inserted differ in shape and contact assignment. Because of the higher pin density, the pin grid package is smaller.

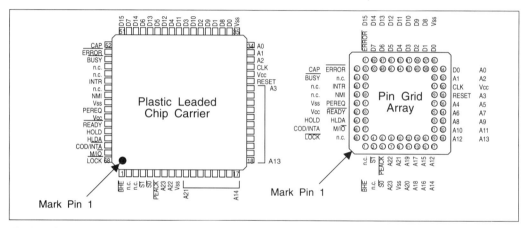

Fig. 3.1: The 80286 terminals. The 80286 comes in a PLCC or a PGA package with 68 contacts.

The following discusses the 80286 terminals. To avoid repetition only new or altered signals are mentioned.

$\overline{S1}$, $\overline{S0}$ (pins 4, 5)
These signals, together with M/$\overline{IO}$ and COD/$\overline{INTA}$, define the current state of the executed bus cycle. Depending on these signals, the 82288 bus controller generates the necessary control signals for the bus. The combinations (COD/$\overline{INTA}$, M/$\overline{IO}$, $\overline{S1}$, $\overline{S0}$) have the following meanings (0 = low, 1 = high):

```
(0000) a hardware interrupt request IRQ is acknowledged;
(0100) if A1 (address bit 1) is equal to 1 (high), then the processor is in the halt state,
       else it is in the shutdown state;
(0101) data is read from memory;
(0110) data is written into memory;
(1001) an I/O port is read;
(1010) an I/O port is written;
(1101) an instruction or an instruction fragment (one word of an instruction) is fetched from memory.
```

All other combinations do not appear or are invalid.

M/$\overline{\text{IO}}$ (pin 67)

This signal distinguishes an access to memory (M/$\overline{\text{IO}}$ high) from an access to the I/O address space (M/$\overline{\text{IO}}$ low).

COD/$\overline{\text{INTA}}$ (pin 66)

This signal distinguishes between bus cycles that *fetch* an instruction and similar bus cycles that *read data* from memory. Further, it distinguishes between an interrupt bus cycle and an access to I/O address space.

HOLD (pin 64), HLDA (pin 65)

These signals serve as the 8086 signals $\overline{\text{RQ}}/\overline{\text{GT}}_0$ and $\overline{\text{RQ}}/\overline{\text{GT}}_1$, for switching the local bus among various bus masters. If another processor or, for example, a DMA chip wants to take control of the local bus, it issues a request signal via the HOLD pin to the 80286. If the 80286 can release control, after completing several instructions it eventually outputs an acknowledge signal via the HLDA pin. Thus the requesting processor takes control of the local bus until it deactivates the signal to the HOLD input of the 80286 again. Now the 80286 deactivates HLDA and takes control of the local bus once more. While the other processor is controlling the local bus, data may neither be read nor written, of course. This is also true for fetching instructions into the prefetch queue. However, the 80286 can execute instructions internally that don't need any memory or I/O access, for example CLD or MOV bx, ax.

PEREQ (pin 61), $\overline{\text{PEACK}}$ (pin 6)

(Processor Extension Request, Processor Extension Acknowledge) If the coprocessor (80287) of the 80286 attempts to read data from or write it into memory, it activates the PEREQ signal. As soon as the 80286 has transferred the data from or to memory, it applies the $\overline{\text{PEACK}}$ signal to the coprocessor. This is necessary because the coprocessor has no dedicated units for protected mode and the corresponding memory access checks, thus the 80286 carries out the data transfer, including all necessary access right checks. (These points are discussed further in Section 3.3.)

$\overline{\text{BUSY}}$ (pin 54), $\overline{\text{ERROR}}$ (pin 53)

These signals inform the 80286 about the status of the current coprocessor. If $\overline{\text{BUSY}}$ is active the coprocessor is executing an instruction. The 80286 operation is stopped for some ESC instructions, as is the case for an active WAIT instruction. If the $\overline{\text{ERROR}}$ signal is active the 80286 issues a coprocessor interrupt when it executes certain ESC or a WAIT instruction. Because in protected mode the interrupts are subject to the same check conditions as all other program sections, these signals serve to integrate the 80287 into the check processes for access rights to data and program code (see Section 3.5.4).

CAP (pin 52)

Between this connection and ground (0 V) a capacitor with a capacity of 0.047 μF must be connected to correctly operate the internal bias generator of the 80286. This is carried out, of course, by the computer manufacturer. The CMOS version of the 80286 (the 80C286) doesn't need a capacitor, and the pin may be floating.

3.2 High Memory Area and HIMEM.SYS

Starting with DOS 4.00 an additional device driver was delivered to access the first 64 kbytes (approximately) above the 1 Mbyte limit. Therefore this memory area is already located in *extended memory*. The device driver is called HIMEM.SYS.

Because both the segment and the offset registers have a width of 16 bits, their maximum value is ffffh each. If we add the segment value ffffh and the offset ffffh in real mode to form a physical address, we get the following value:

| Segment ($* 2^4$) | ffff0h |
+ Offset	ffffh
Physical address	10ffefh

Because the 8086/88 only has a 20-bit address bus, and therefore in the addressing unit (AU) only a 20-bit adder is present, the leading 1 is ignored as a carry and ffefh remains as the physical address. This address falls into the first 64 kbyte segment of the address space, so a *wraparound* occurs.

But the 80286 now has a 24-bit address bus, and therefore a 24-bit address adder. Thus the leading 1 is not ignored as a carry but 21 address lines are activated instead. The 80286 operates in real mode with a «limited» 21-bit address bus, and the bytes with addresses between 10000h and 10ffefh may be accessed in extended memory. The 1 Mbyte limit in real mode is broken through by fff0h (65 520) bytes, or nearly 64 kbytes (see Figure 3.2). Of course, this is not equivalent to a «real» 21-bit address bus because with 21 address bits all bytes from 00000h up to 1fffffh can be addressed, not only those up to 10ffefh.

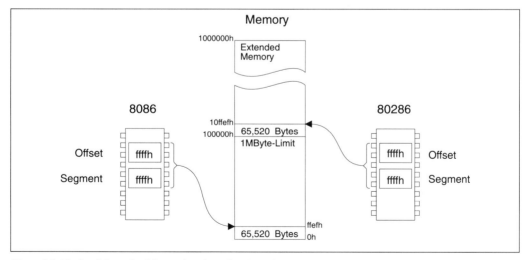

Figure 3.2: The breakthrough of the 1 Mbyte boundary in real mode. In real mode when the value of a segment register is multiplied by 16 and the offset is added, the result may be above 1 M. Because of the 24 address lines of the 80286 (unlike the 8086 20-bit address bus), this address above 1 M is actually output.

Because of the downward compatibility of all newer 80x86 processors, these processors can also access the first 65 520 bytes of extended memory in real mode.

The HIMEM.SYS device driver supplies a well-defined interface to access these 64 kbytes in real mode. Because other device drivers like SMARTDRV.SYS or RAMDRIVE.SYS also use this memory area, an access without HIMEM.SYS may give rise to a data collision. Another problem arises with certain MS-DOS versions. Some DOS-internal and undocumented functions rely on the wrap-around of the 8086/8088, but in an 80286 this never occurs. It is possible to outwit the 80286 by pulling address line A20 with the 21st address bit to a low level (0) by an external logic gate. Memory is then addressed as if a wrap-around at an address above 1 M has occurred. Control of the logic gate for activating and disabling the A20 address line is carried out in the AT by the keyboard controller (see Chapter 11). Among other things, HIMEM.SYS is responsible for ensuring that only in an intended access to the first 64 kbytes of extended memory is the A20 address line activated. In all other cases, A20 is disabled by HIMEM.SYS to emulate a wrap-around in the processor.

SMARTDRV.SYS and RAMDRIVE.SYS use the protected mode to access extended memory. In protected mode, all 24 address lines are available with no restrictions. Further, certain HIMEM.SYS functions may be used to access extended memory in protected mode. In the following chapter, this innovative 80286 operating mode is discussed in more detail.

3.3 80286 Protected Mode

For protected mode, the 80286 was given a few additional registers (see Figure 3.3): the task register (TR), and registers for the machine status word (MSW), the local descriptor table (LDT), the interrupt descriptor table (IDT) and the global descriptor table (GDT).

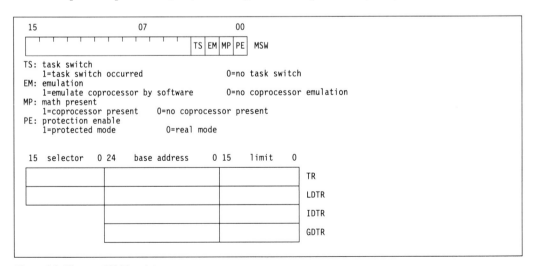

Figure 3.3: The new 80286 registers.

Therefore, the 80286 has two status registers, the flags and MSW. The MSW plays a role only in protected mode, but the flags always indicate the current processor state. In the following, the four MSW bits are briefly described. After a processor reset the MSW contains the value fff0h, that is, all non-reserved bits are cleared.

PE (protection enable)
If this bit is set the 80286 switches to protected mode.

MP (monitor coprocessor)
If the MP bit is set a WAIT instruction may issue the exception «no coprocessor present» corresponding to interrupt 7.

EM (coprocessor emulation)
If the EM bit is set all coprocessor functions are emulated by software. This means that, for example, the logarithm is not calculated by the 80287 floating-point functions but by a mathematical function library that only uses 80286 integer arithmetic.

TS (task switch)
If this bit is set a task switch has occurred, therefore it can be determined whether the coprocessor is still executing an instruction for the former task, or if it is ready for the new task. Because some 80287 instructions need up to 1000 clock cycles, it is possible that the 80286 switches to another task, services this task, and returns to the old task before the coprocessor has executed this instruction.

3.3.1 Processor Reset and Switching to Protected Mode

After a reset the 80286 always starts in real mode. All registers are set to the values indicated in Table 2.6. Furthermore, the machine status word is loaded with the value fff0h. GDTR, LDTR, IDTR and the task register have no meaning, therefore the 80286 starts as an 8086 for the moment. Moreover, after a reset the four most significant address lines A23–A20 are activated (that is, set to 1), thus the 80286 starts program execution at the physical 24-bit address fffff0h (16 bytes below 16 Mbytes). The four address lines A23–A20 are not disabled until the code segment (CS) is changed, for example by a FAR-jump. Thus, the entry point of the startup BIOS is located at the upper end of the 80286 physical address space. After the code segment's first change, this point is no longer accessible, unless a processor reset is carried out again.

If a switch to protected mode is to be carried out, it is the job of the ROM BIOS to set up the necessary tables in the memory and load at least the GDTR and IDTR registers with appropriate values. The meaning of the register and table entries is described in the following sections. If these settings are completed, the PE bit in the machine status word is set with the instruction LMSW (load MSW). Now the 80286 switches to protected mode. You are free to carry out this mode switch by function 89h of interrupt INT 15h (listed in appendix L.)

However, be aware that the inverse is **not** possible. Once in protected mode the PE bit cannot be cleared to reset the 80286 into real mode. Only the i386 (and i486) has a new function to reset the processor into real mode directly. On the 80286 a processor reset is the only possibility. The initialization routine is called and the processor again runs in real mode. You can imagine that this procedure is rather time-consuming because the processor has to carry out a lot of initializations. But the ROM BIOS recognizes (according to the entry shutdown state in the AT's CMOS RAM) whether the PC must be booted or the real mode set again. Intel's engineers implemented the real mode in the 80286 mainly for the ROM BIOS startup routine to prepare the system tables, etc. for protected mode. They did not expect that in the PC the next processor generation but one (the i486) would still be operating in real mode more than ten years later! Further, the return from protected to real mode is a violation of protection principles, because a virus or other aggressor may prepare itself in real mode for unrestricted access to all system elements that are also in protected mode. The operating system in real mode has no chance of recognizing and avoiding this attack.

Starting with the AT, the BIOS has an interrupt function (INT 15h, function 87h) for moving data between the first 1 Mbyte of memory and extended memory by means of the protected mode (the function is described in Appendix L). For this purpose, the BIOS builds the necessary tables, switches the processor to protected mode, transfers the data, executes a processor reset, intercepts the initialization, and returns to the calling program. RAMDRIVE.SYS, for example, works in a similar way. The time-consuming mode switches mean that storing small amounts of data on a virtual disk may often be slower than storing it on a hard disk with a short access time.

The main job of a program in real mode, either the ROM BIOS or a device driver, etc., is to set up at least the global and the interrupt descriptor tables before the 80286 can be switched to protected mode. It does not matter where these tables are located in the memory because the processor can access their addresses from the entries in GDTR and IDTR. Afterwards, the operating system loader, for example, may initialize all other tables, reserve memory for the system and application programs, etc. Thus the computer is booted completely.

3.3.2 Segment Descriptors, Global and Local Descriptor Table

In real mode the value of a segment register was simply multiplied by 16 to get the base address of the corresponding segment. The address within such a 64 kbyte segment was indicated by the offset, but in protected mode the values in the segment registers have a completely different meaning: they are so-called *selectors* and no longer «real» addresses. Figure 3.4 shows the structure of such a segment selector.

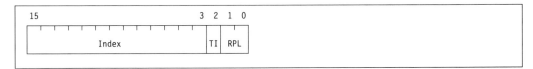

Figure 3.4: The structure of a segment selector.

As in real mode, the selector is 16 bits wide. The two least significant bits 0 and 1 indicate the *selector privilege level* or *requested privilege level (RPL)*. Only programs with a higher privilege are allowed to access the corresponding segment. Here we are confronted with access checks in protected mode for the first time. The value of the RPL field in the segment selector of the code segment (CS) is called the *current privilege level (CPL)*, because the currently active program is assigned this privilege level. Therefore, the active program may access data segments whose privilege level value is equal to or more than CPL. The value of RPL may be higher than that of CPL, that is, the segment defined with the selector is accessed by a lower privilege level. The higher of the CPL and RPL values defines the *effective privilege level (EPL)* of the task. The 80286 and all succeeding processors like the i386 know four privilege levels (PL), 0–3, in total; 0 characterizes the most privileged and 3 the least privileged level, so a higher value means a lower privilege, and vice versa. An RPL with a value 0, therefore, doesn't restrict the privilege level of a task, but a selector with an RPL of 3, independently of CPL, may only access segments with a privilege level 3.

Programs with a lower privilege level (higher CPL) are allowed to access segments of a higher level (lower CPL) only in a few exceptional cases. For this purpose, *gates* are defined. Thus the protection within one task is carried out by means of different privilege levels. Figure 3.5 outlines the concept of the various privilege levels graphically.

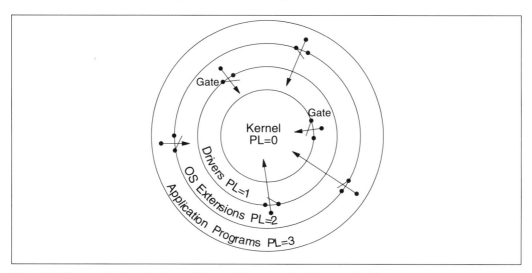

Figure 3.5: The concept of privilege levels. To protect the various tasks in a multitasking environment against malfunctions of another task, each task is assigned one of four privilege levels. The operating system kernel has the highest privilege PL=0; application programs, on the other hand, have the lowest privilege PL=3. A jump to a task with a higher privilege level is only possible via a gate.

Usually, the critical part or the *kernel* of the operating system has the highest privilege level 0. The kernel comprises at least the routines for memory management, executing task switches, handling critical errors, etc. Many instructions that directly influence the status of the processor or computer (for example, LGDT (load global descriptor table) or LMSW (load MSW)) may be executed in protected mode only by a program with a privilege level 0. This avoids application programs destroying the operating system because of a program bug, or a hacker getting uncontrollable access to data.

Operating systems not only manage the computer but also supply certain functions for data management, character output, etc. In the PC this is done by the interrupt 21h, for example, the so-called *DOS function interrupt*. Such *operating system functions* usually run at PL = 1. Also, unit and device drivers (for example, for accessing interfaces and drives) often run at this level. Less critical operating system functions such as the support of a graphics-oriented user shell may be assigned level 2.

The lowest privilege level is assigned to *application programs* because they only use the computer, and don't control it. Because of the low level (high PL), the data and codes of the operating system and other programs are well protected against program errors. For example, with MS-DOS a program error that erroneously overwrites the interrupt vector table leads to a complete system crash. In protected mode the operating system reacts by displaying an error message and aborting only the erroneous program. All other tasks stay running with no further destruction or influence. Therefore, bugs (that is, program errors) may be detected more easily. However, this is only true if the operating system (OS/2, for example) is error-free. Unfortunately, this is by no means a matter of course, because multitasking operating systems are very complex.

A task is the corresponding program (Microsoft Word, for example), its data (the text) as well as the necessary system functions (for data management at the hard disk level, for example). With Windows you can start WinWord and load a text. To edit another text file you may load this text into Word (started before), and then switch between the Word windows. Now you have two texts loaded into one program, therefore Word and the two text files constitute **one** task. Another possibility for editing the second text file is to start Word again, and to assign it a second window. Now you are loading the second text file into the Word version that was started last. Also, in this case you are free to switch between the two windows. The main difference, though, is that now you have started two programs (namely Word twice), and you have loaded a text file into each program. Every program, together with the corresponding text file, constitutes one task. Although you have started the same program twice, now **two** tasks are running on your PC.

For every privilege level of a task the 80286 uses its own stack. In the example mentioned above, one stack is necessary for the application program Word (PL=3), the functions of the user shell (PL=2), the operating system functions for data management (PL=1), and the kernel (PL=0). For a controlled program access to data and code in segments with a higher privilege level, gates are available. The gates supply maximum protection against unauthorized accesses to another's data and programs. If, for example, an application program uses operating system functions to open or close files – thus the application accesses another's functions – the gates ensure that the access is carried out without any faults. If the application program were to attempt to call the functions with an incorrect entry address, unpredictable behaviour of the computer is likely to occur. Therefore, the gates define (what else) «gates» through which the application program has access to the operating system or other routines.

Bit 2 of the segment selector (Figure 3.4) is the table indicator (TI). TI defines whether the global (TI = 0) or local (TI = 1) descriptor table has to be used to locate the segment in memory. The *global descriptor table* is a table in memory that describes the size and address of segments in the form of *segment descriptors*. The structure of such a segment descriptor is shown in Figure 3.6. Each descriptor comprises eight bytes.

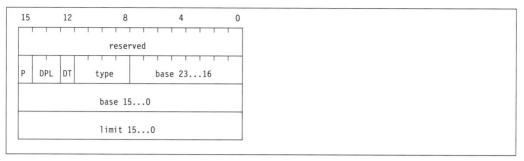

Figure 3.6: Structure of segment descriptors.

The 24 base bits of the segment descriptor indicate the starting address of the segment in memory (see Figure 3.7). These 24 base address bits correspond to the 24 address lines of the 80286. Therefore in protected mode, 2^{24} bytes, or 16 Mbytes, may be addressed. The base entry of a segment descriptor indicates the starting address of the segment concerned in this 16 Mbyte address space.

In real mode each segment has 64 kbytes even if only a little data is held in a segment. Because of the fixed interleaving of the segments, 15 bytes at most may be lost because the segments are successive every 16 bytes. Because of the decoupling of segments in protected mode, this no longer holds. Therefore, every segment descriptor has an entry *limit* in the low-order byte of the descriptor that indicates the segment size in bytes (see Figure 3.7). With the 16 bits of the limit entry in protected mode, segments with a maximum size of 64 kbytes are possible.

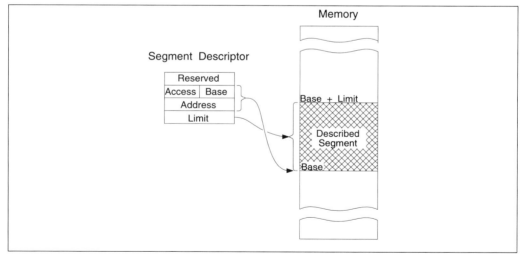

Figure 3.7: Base and limit of the segment descriptors. In protected mode the segment descriptor defines a segment. The base address indicates the physical beginning of the segment and the limit its size.

The *DT* bit in the segment descriptor indicates the descriptor type. If DT is equal to 0 then the descriptor describes a system segment or an application segment. The *type* field in the segment descriptor defines the segment type, and *DPL* the accompanying privilege level (from 0 to 3).

(DPL is also called the descriptor privilege level.) Finally, the P bit indicates whether or not the segment is actually in memory. The two most significant bytes are reserved. For compatibility with the i386 and later processors they should always be set equal 0. Because the i386 with its 32-bit offset registers may process much larger segments than the 80286, the i386 additionally uses these two bytes.

The index (that is, the 13 high-order bits of the segment selector) (see Figure 3.4) indicates the number of the segment descriptor in the descriptor table, which describes the corresponding segment. With 13 bits, 8192 different indices at most are possible, so the global descriptor table comprises 8192 entries with eight bytes each, or 64 kbytes at most. Therefore, up to 8192 segments may be defined. Because the structure and size of the segment descriptors in the local descriptor table (LDT) are identical to the structure and size in the global descriptor table (GDT), the explanations indicated above are also valid for the LDT. Whether the segment selector refers to the GDT or LDT is specified by the table indicator (TI) in the selector.

If the processor wants to access an entry in the GDT or LDT, it multiplies the index value by eight (the number of bytes per descriptor) and adds the result to the base address of the corresponding descriptor table. (The base address is held by the GDT or LDT register.) These registers are loaded by the operating system loader (in the case of the GDTR) or by the operating system itself (in the case of the LDTR). Unlike the LDT, in the setup of the GDT the 0th entry (beginning at the GDT base address) must not be used. Referencing the 0th entry leads to an exception «general protection error». Therefore, the erroneous use of an uninitialized GDTR will be avoided.

The main characteristic of the GDT is that the whole segment, and therefore memory management, is built up from the GDT. In the GDTR (Figure 3.3) are stored the base address as well as the limit (the GDT's size in bytes) of the global descriptor table. Thus the GDTR points to the GDT. On the other hand, the local descriptor table is managed dynamically, therefore several LDTs are possible, contrary to the GDT. For every local descriptor table an entry in the GDT exists, therefore the LDTs are managed similarly to segments (see Figure 3.8).

The GDTR may be loaded with the *segment descriptor* mem64 by means of the LGDT mem64 instruction. This step is necessary before the operating system loader switches the 80286 into protected mode. The LDTR is loaded with a *segment selector* by means of the instruction LLDT reg16 or LLDT mem16. This segment selector indicates the entry in the global descriptor table which holds the descriptor for the local descriptor table. But the consistent management of the descriptor tables is the job of the operating system only (OS/2, for example).

The application programmer has no influence upon these processes. For loading the descriptor table registers LDTR and GDTR, the privilege level 0 is necessary in protected mode – and this level is only assigned to the kernel. However, any attempt to alter these registers from an application program immediately gives rise to an exception «general protection error», and therefore to an interrupt 0dh.

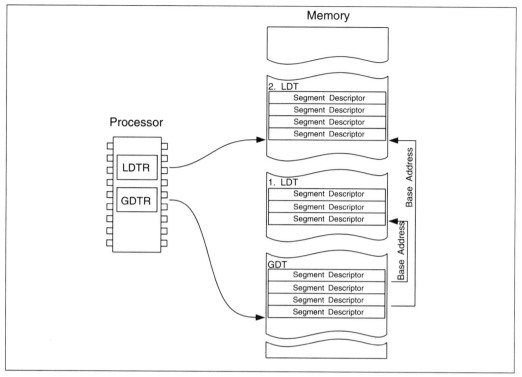

Figure 3.8: The local descriptor table (LDT). The 80286 GDTR points to the GDT in which segment descriptors for various LDTs may also be held. The LDTR indicates the number of the segment descriptor in the GDT, which in turn holds the LDT.

For every task both the global and local descriptor tables are supplied by the operating system. It is advantageous to describe segments commonly used by several tasks (segments with operating system functions, for example) in the GDT. All segments only used by their respective tasks should be defined with the LDT. The various tasks can therefore be isolated from each other, and two complete descriptor tables with 8192 entries each or 16 384 segments in total are available for one task. Because every segment may hold up to 64 kbytes, the maximum *logical address space* per task is 1 Gbyte. This value is, of course, much higher than the actual *physical address space* of the 80286 with 16 Mbytes. In such a case, not all the segments can be present in memory. If a segment is swapped to a hard disk drive by the operating system, the P bit in the segment descriptor of the corresponding LDT or GDT descriptor table is set to 0. If the processor attempts to access this segment, the hardware issues an exception «segment not present» corresponding to interrupt 0bh. The called interrupt handler may reload the intended segment into memory again. Eventually another segment is swapped. Therefore a much bigger *virtual address space* than that actually physically present can be generated.

If the 80286 loads a new segment selector into a segment register, the 80286 hardware automatically checks whether the program is allowed to access this segment. For this check it is necessary that the effective privilege level EPL is less than or equal to the descriptor privilege level DPL of the segment to be loaded. If this is true then the processor loads the base address and the limit of the segment described by the selector into the corresponding *segment descriptor cache register* (see Figure 3.9). Because of the extensive access right checks and the loading of the cache registers, all instructions that alter a segment register require far more clock cycles in protected mode than in real mode. For example, for the instruction LDS si, fpointer (load far-pointer fpointer into the register pair DS:SI), Intel specifies only 7 clock cycles in real mode but 21 clock cycles in protected mode.

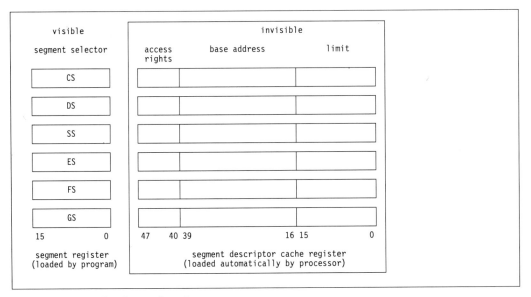

Figure 3.9: Segment descriptor cache register.

In protected mode every segment register is assigned a segment descriptor cache register. These cache registers are only used internally by the processor; the programmer has no access to them. The processor automatically (that is, without any software instructions) reads the limit, base address and the eight bits of the segment's access rights from the GDT or LDT. Throughout this memory access, the LOCK signal is automatically activated by the 80286. Because of the cache registers the processor no longer needs to access the entry in the descriptor table in memory when it is calculating an operand address or checking the access right. Instead, the 80286 can fetch the necessary data from an internal processor register at higher speed. In the description I have written «segment descriptor in the GDT or LDT», but you should always remember that the 80286 actually accesses the GDT or LDT only during the first access, and in all subsequent accesses the internal cache registers are referenced.

3.3.3 Memory Addressing in Protected Mode

In real mode the determination of a memory address is very easy: the value of the segment register concerned is multiplied by 16 and an adder adds the offset. In protected mode, the equivalent process is much more complicated. The following steps are carried out for this purpose (see Figure 3.10):

– With the aid of the segment selector in the corresponding segment register, it is determined whether the global or local descriptor table is to be used.

– With the memory management registers the base address of the descriptor table is determined.

– The index of the segment selector is multiplied by 8 and added to the base address of the descriptor table. Further, the 80286 checks whether this value exceeds the segment limit. If it exceeds the limit, the processor issues an interrupt 0dh (exception «general protection error»).

– With the segment descriptors (8 bytes) in the descriptor table, the base address and limit of the segment are determined.

– In the address adder of the addressing unit this base address and the offset are added. Further, it is checked whether this value exceeds the limit of the segment concerned. If this is the case the processor issues an interrupt 0dh (exception «general protection error»).

– The address thus determined is output as the physical address of the referenced memory object.

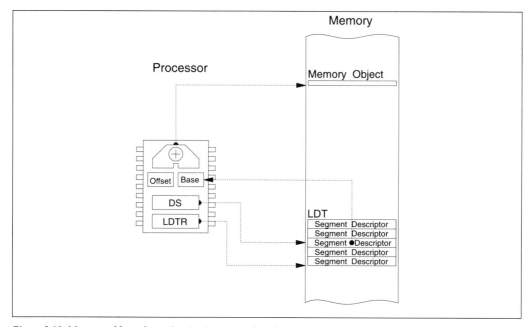

Figure 3.10: Memory address determination in protected mode.

Using the segment descriptor cache register the descriptors do not actually have to be read during the course of the above-mentioned steps. But the method described does indicate the logical strategy of the 80286 as it determines a physical address. Because all checks are executed in parallel to the address calculations, and as all important data is available in the cache registers, this extensive calculation and check procedure does not give rise to a delay when compared to the easy address determination in real mode. Except for instructions that load a new segment descriptor explicitly or implicitly, all memory accesses are carried out in protected mode at the same speed as in real mode.

3.3.4 Segment and Access Types

The DT bit as well as the four type bits of the segment descriptor (see Figure 3.6) indicate type and access to the segment described. If the DT (*descriptor type*) is equal to 1 the segment is also called an *application segment*, that is, the segment contains data and code for a program. The system routines that are part of the computer management down to the kernel level also belong to this kind of program. *System segments* and *gates* (DT = 0) describe data structures used for the control and supervision of several active tasks in the computer, or for calling procedures and jumping to segments with a different privilege level.

If the DT is equal to 1 (that is, the segment concerned is an application segment), the *type* field in the segment descriptor has the following structure:

```
 11  10   9   8
EXE E/C W/R  A
```

Table 3.1 shows various combinations of these bits and their meaning.

Number	EXE	Type	E	W	A	Description
0	0	data	0	0	0	read-only
1	0	data	0	0	1	read-only, accessed
2	0	data	0	1	0	read/write
3	0	data	0	1	1	read/write, accessed
4	0	data	1	0	0	read-only, expand-down
5	0	data	1	0	1	read-only, expand-down, accessed
6	0	data	1	1	0	read/write, expand-down
7	0	data	1	1	1	read/write, expand-down, accessed
8	1	code	0	0	0	execute-only
9	1	code	0	0	1	execute-only, accessed
10	1	code	0	1	0	execute/read
11	1	code	0	1	1	execute/read, accessed
12	1	code	1	0	0	execute-only, conforming
13	1	code	1	0	1	execute-only, conforming, accessed
14	1	code	1	1	0	execute/read, conforming
15	1	code	1	1	1	execute/read, conforming, accessed

Table 3.1: Application segment types (DT = 1)

If the term *data* is interpreted in a wide sense, then any set of information is meant that has a certain meaning. In this sense, programs are also data because they represent (of course) a set of information (a bit sequence) that has a meaning (namely, what the computer has to do). That this kind of information is not always obvious to us is immaterial in this respect.

But in a narrower sense, one distinguishes data and programs: data is information that has to be processed; programs, on the other hand, are the tools which process the data. The main difference between these two categories is that the data set «program» is usually not changed during the course of program execution, but data should be processed and altered. This differentiation of «data» is also reflected in the segment descriptors: there are executable (that is, program) as well as non-executable (that is, data) segments. This difference is marked by the bit *EXE*: if EXE is equal to 1 then it is a program segment.

Implicitly, data segments are always characterized as readable, but they may only be written if the bit *W* (*write*) is set. A write attempt to a segment with a write bit cleared (W = 0) issues an exception «general protection error», and therefore an interrupt 0dh. Stack segments must thus always be marked as writeable (W = 1) because the stack is periodically written by PUSH and read by POP. Data segments may differ in the direction in which they «grow». If the *E* (*expand-down*) bit is set, the segment grows downwards, otherwise it grows upwards. The interpretation of the limit differs in these two cases. With a segment growing upwards (E = 0) the offset must always be smaller than or equal to the limit. On the other hand, with a segment growing downwards (E = 1), the offset must always exhibit a value above the limit. If these conditions are not fulfilled the 80286 issues an exception «general protection error», and therefore an interrupt 0dh. One example of a segment growing downwards is the stack segment, because the stack grows downwards during an expansion (a PUSH instruction) by the decremented stack pointer (SP). Most other segments, however, grow upwards.

If the processor accesses data in a segment it automatically sets bit *A* (*accessed*). The 80286 is thus able to determine what data has been used and what has not. This is important if a segment has to be swapped to external storage (hard disk) to free memory for another segment. The *swap routine* uses these bits to determine segments which are not accessed and whose accessed bit is therefore cleared. If segments that are rarely accessed are swapped, the read/write overhead for the hard disk is reduced and the computer's performance is enhanced.

Unlike data segments, program segments are always characterized implicitly as non-writeable, or read-only. Therefore, the processor can never carry out a write access to such a code segment. This serves as protection against program errors. With MS-DOS, bugs often give rise to a program code overwrite, and the PC therefore crashes. However, it is possible to overlap a data and a code segment, for example by characterizing a segment as a code segment and defining another segment with the same base and the same limit as a data segment. In this case, the processor may overwrite code because the data segment is acting as an *alias* and may, of course, be written. That this procedure may lead to enormous problems if programming is not perfect seems to be obvious. If the *R* (*read*) bit in the segment descriptor of a code segment is set (R = 1), the segment may not only be executed (that is, fetched into the prefetch queue by the bus unit), but can also be transferred directly into a general-purpose register by means of a MOV instruction. This is, for example, necessary if the program code contains data. The ROM BIOS often holds some tables for hard disk types, base address of the video memory, etc., which must be read at power-up by the BIOS startup program. To realize the most effective swapping of code segments onto external mass storage, the segment descriptor for a code segment also contains an accessed bit. Instead of the expand-down bit (bit E) of the data segment descriptors, a code segment descriptor holds the C (*conforming*) bit. Program segments that are characterized as conforming may be directly accessed by less privileged code segments without the intervention of a gate. Typically, system functions that do not use any protected part of the system (for example, libraries and encoding functions) are located in conforming segments. Thus, application programs may access less critical functions without the time-consuming detour via a call gate.

3.3.5 System Segments

The 80286 implements three system segment types in all (see Table 3.2). The *task state segments* (*TSS*) define the status of active (busy) and interrupted (available) tasks, therefore they are of importance for the 80286's multitasking functions. TSS and LDT descriptors as well as system segments are only allowed in the GDT. For example, a local descriptor table is described by a system segment descriptor that has an entry 2 in the type field.

Type	Description
1	available 80286 TSS
2	LDT
3	busy 80286 TSS

Table 3.2: System segment types (DT = 0)

The entry base address in a system segment descriptor for an LDT defines the beginning of the table in memory. Because the LDT consists of entries with eight bytes each, the limit value in the system segment descriptor is the corresponding multiple of eight.

3.3.6 Control Transfer and Call Gates

During the course of a near call or a near jump, control is transferred to a procedure or an entry point located in the same segment as the corresponding CALL or JMP instruction. Therefore, only the value of the instruction pointer (IP) is altered and the 80286 checks whether this new value exceeds the limit of the segment. If the offset is valid the call or jump is carried out, otherwise the 80286 issues an exception «general protection error».

However, tasks rarely consist of only one code segment; usually, several code segments are present. If the program has more than 64 kbytes (one segment) then several segments can't be avoided. An access to another code segment within the task takes place, for example, in a far call, a far jump, or an interrupt. In all these cases the code segment is loaded with a new segment selector. In real mode the IP and the code segment (CS) are just loaded with new values during the course of such an *intersegment call*, which indicates the entry point of the routine. In protected mode the procedure is somewhat more complicated.

For a far call or a far jump three possibilities are available:

- If the target segment has the same privilege level (PL) as the source segment, the far call can be executed directly by loading the target segment descriptor into the code segment (CS). In this case, the 80286 only checks whether the new value of the IP exceeds the target segment limit, and whether the target segment type (EXE = 0 or 1) is consistent with the call.

- If the target segment is characterized as conforming, and if its privilege level is higher (the value of PL is lower) than that of the source segment, the far call is carried out in the same way as indicated above. But the code of the conforming segment is executed with a privilege level CPL corresponding to the less privileged level of the calling program and not to the more privileged level of the conforming segment. This prevents less privileged programs from getting a higher privilege level through the loophole of a conforming segment and becoming able to access more sensitive data.

- If the target segment has a different privilege level from that of the source segment, and if it is not characterized as conforming, only a call via a call gate is possible.

In the first two cases the 80286 just loads the segment selector into the CS register and continues program execution. In the last case the new segment selector does not directly point to the target segment but to a so-called *call gate*.

The handling of interrupts is a general task of the operating system kernel so that a call is usually connected with a change of the privilege level. The interrupt must use an *interrupt* or *trap gate* to activate the interrupt handler (see below). The task gate is described in Section 3.3.8, which is about multitasking.

These gates form a «gate» for entry into a routine of another segment with a different privilege level. Gates are defined by a DT = 0 bit in the segment descriptor and a value in the type field between 4 and 7. Table 3.3 lists the 80286 gate descriptors.

Type	Description
0	reserved
4	80286 call gate
5	task gate
6	80286 interrupt gate
7	80286 trap gate
8–15	reserved

Table 3.3: Gate descriptors (DT = 0)

The structure of the 80286 *gate descriptors* is shown in Figure 3.11. Call gates are not only used for procedure calls, but also for all conditional and unconditional jump instructions. They may reside in the local or global descriptor table, but not in the interrupt descriptor table; only interrupt, trap and task gates are allowed there.

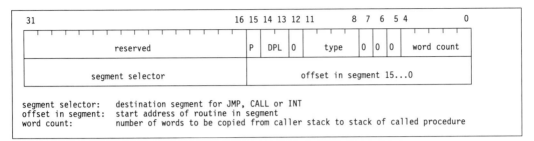

Figure 3.11: 80286 gate descriptor.

Thus the structure of a gate descriptor is very different from that of a «normal» segment descriptor: the segment's base address is missing. Instead, a 5-bit *word count* field is present, and bits 5 to 7 in the third descriptor word are set to 0. Further, the second word is reserved for a segment selector. This segment selector, together with the offset in the least-significant word, defines the entry point into the target routine. Thus two segment descriptor references are carried out during the course of a far call via a call gate (see Figure 3.12).

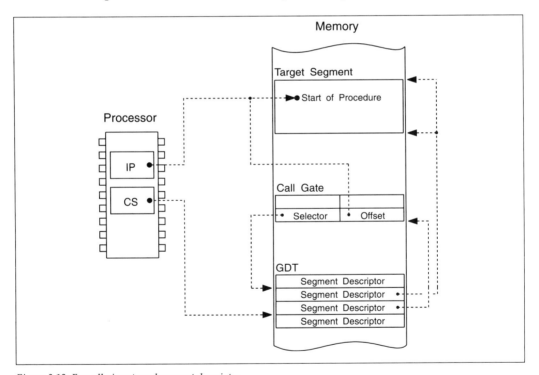

Figure 3.12: Far call via gate and segment descriptor.

The first reference loads the gate descriptor and the second determines the base address of the segment concerned. The base address of the target segment defined by the segment selector in the gate descriptor and the offset indicated in the gate descriptor are combined into the entry address by the processor's addressing unit. If the processor loads the target segment descriptor for a far call or a far jump into the CS register, it determines (by means of the entry in the type field) whether a gate descriptor or a code segment directly is described. In the first case, it automatically loads the segment descriptor indicated in the call gate (but only, of course, if the call can be carried out).

The reason for and purpose of this strategy are obvious. A strictly defined entry point is specified so that the calling program may not erroneously indicate an invalid entry point. This is especially important if operating system functions are called. An incorrect entry point into these routines usually leads to a system crash.

I have already mentioned that every task generates its own stack for each of the four different privilege levels. Data must frequently be transferred between these stacks so that a routine of a different privilege level has access to the data of the calling program. To enable this, the number of words to copy (two bytes each) is written into the *word count* field. During a call gate call, the 80286 automatically transfers these words from the calling stack to the stack of the called procedure. With five bits, 31 words (that is, 62 bytes) can be transferred at most. It is the fault of the programmer if he needs more bytes for parameter passing. However, passing a far pointer to a data structure containing the intended parameters may help. Of course, the 80286 also carries out an access check in a call via gates. The following privilege levels participate in this check:

– CPL,
– RPL of the segment selector for the call gate,
– DPL of the gate descriptor,
– DPL of the segment descriptor for the call's target segment.

The DPL entry of the gate descriptor defines from which privilege levels the gate may be used.

Gates may by used to pass control to more privileged levels (the operating system, for example), or to code of the same privilege level. In the latter case they are not absolutely necessary (see above), but this strategy is still possible. It is important, however, that only CALL instructions can use gates to activate routines with a lower privilege level (higher PL value). Jump instructions may use call gates only to pass control to a code segment at the same privilege level or to a conforming segment with an equal or higher level.

For a jump instruction to a segment that is not characterized as conforming, the following conditions must hold:

– the effective privilege level EPL (the greater of CPL and RPL) must be less than or equal to the DPL of the gate descriptor;
– the DPL of the target segment descriptor must be equal to the CPL of the calling program.

For a CALL or a jump instruction to a conforming segment, on the other hand, the following two conditions must be fulfilled:

– the effective privilege level EPL (the greater of CPL and RPL) must be less than or equal to the DPL of the gate descriptor;
– the DPL of the target segment descriptor must be less than or equal to the CPL of the calling program.

While calling a procedure with a higher privilege level via a call gate, the 80286 additionally carries out the following procedures:

− CPL is altered to reflect the new privilege level;
− control is passed to the called procedure;
− the stack is switched to the stack of the new privilege level.

The stacks of all privilege levels are defined by the task state segment of the task concerned (see below).

As can be seen, many more functions have been added to the 80286, as one would expect, simply because of the enhanced instruction set (16 new instructions). For example, the 80286 carries out the word transfer between the stacks *automatically and on its own*. No corresponding software commands are required in the instruction stream.

3.3.7 The Interrupt Descriptor Table

Besides registers for the global and local descriptor tables and the task register, the 80286 has a new register for the *interrupt descriptor table* (*IDT*, see Figure 3.3). In real mode the 1024 (1 k) low-order bytes of the address space are reserved for the 256 entries (interrupts) of the interrupt vector table. Every entry contains the entry address (target) of the corresponding interrupt handler in the segment:offset format.

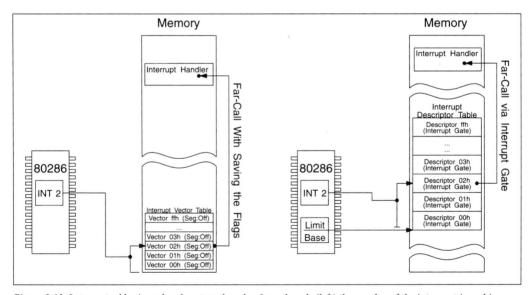

Figure 3.13: Interrupt tables in real and protected modes. In real mode (left) the number of the interrupt issued is simply multiplied by four to determine the offset in segment 00h where the corresponding interrupt vector is located. In protected mode, on the other hand, the IDTR points to a descriptor table, which stores gates to the corresponding interrupt handlers.

In protected mode also, 256 interrupts from 0–255 are available. The interrupt handlers are no longer accessed by a double word in the segment:offset format but via gates. Only task, interrupt and trap gates are valid entries in the IDT. Therefore each entry now requires eight bytes, compared to four bytes in real mode. Using the entry limit in the IDTR (Figure 3.3), the size of the interrupt descriptor table can be adjusted according to actual needs. If, for example, a system needs only interrupts 0–63, an IDT with 64 entries of eight bytes each (that is, 512 bytes) is sufficient. If an interrupt is issued for which no entry exists in the IDT (in the above indicated case, for example, INT 64) then the 80286 enters shutdown mode, signalling this by means of corresponding levels for the COD/$\overline{\text{INTA}}$, M/$\overline{\text{IO}}$, $\overline{\text{S1}}$, $\overline{\text{S0}}$ and A1 signals. Because the base address of the IDT is stored in the IDTR this table may reside anywhere in memory (see Figure 3.13).

Before the 80286 is switched to protected mode, the initialization program running in real mode has to build up the IDT as well as the GDT, and must load its base address and limit into the IDTR. If this is not carried out the processor is likely to crash before the IDT can be built up in protected mode, because every exception or interrupt points to an uninitialized location or issues another error exception that cannot be handled. During the course of a processor reset, the IDTR is loaded with the value 000000h for the base address and 03ffh for the limit. These values are consistent with the reserved area for the interrupt vector table in real mode.

The interrupt, trap and task gates have the same structure as the call gates (see Figure 3.11), but the word count entry has no meaning. The interrupt and trap gates define the entry point in the same way as the call gate, by means of the offset and the segment selector. The segment selector points to the segment descriptor in the LDT or GDT, which contains the base address of the segment concerned (as is the case with the call gate). Thus, the entry point of the interrupt handler is also exactly defined. The difference between interrupt and trap gates is that an interrupt call via an interrupt gate clears the IE and T flags, but the trap gate does not.

The following describes the special processes carried out when the processor meets a task gate during the course of an interrupt, or a call or jump instruction.

3.3.8 Multitasking, TSS and Task Gate

All the protection functions of the 80286 are mainly implemented for one aim: multitasking. This means that several tasks are run in parallel (concurrently) or, as already described above, the individual tasks are interrupted periodically and restarted at the same location after a short time. To facilitate this the state of a task at the time of interruption must be stored in its entirety because otherwise the task cannot be restarted at the same location later.

A similar process also takes place with MS-DOS: if a hardware interrupt (for example, the timer interrupt) occurs, then all registers are pushed onto the stack, the interrupt is serviced, and all registers are restored with the old values from the stack. It is important that the CS:IP register pair is stored because it defines the point in the program at which it has been interrupted.

You may have guessed that because of the extensive 80286 protection functions, it is not enough to simply store *some* registers. Instead, for this purpose the system segment (called the *task state segment, TSS,* which has not been explained in detail yet) is necessary. As the name implies, it retains the state of a task completely. Figure 3.14 shows the structure of a TSS.

15 0
task LDT selector
DS selector
SS selector
CS selector
ES selector
DI
SI
BP
SP
BX
DX
CX
AX
flag word
IP (start of task)
SS for CPL2
SP for CPL2
SS for CPL1
SP for CPL1
SS for CPL0
SP for CPL0
back-link to preceding TSS

Figure 3.14: 80286 Task state segment (TSS).

The TSS, for example, stores the SP pointers and SS segments for the stacks of the various privilege levels, the local descriptor table used for this task and an entry that points to the previously executed task. If the corresponding TSS descriptor in the LDT or GDT has a value of 1 in the type field, then the TSS described by the descriptor is available. This means that the task defined by the TSS may be started. If the type field holds an entry of 3, then the TSS is busy. Thus the task described by the TSS is active and need not be activated again, indeed it must not be activated again because the TSS still contains the old values. Therefore, unlike procedures, tasks are not reentrant in principle. Once the currently active task is interrupted, the 80286 *automatically and on its own* writes all current values of the active task into the corresponding TSS, and loads the values of the task to be started from its TSS into the registers. But now, how does the processor «know» if and eventually which task it has to activate?

The key is located in the task gates (Figure 3.15 shows their structure).

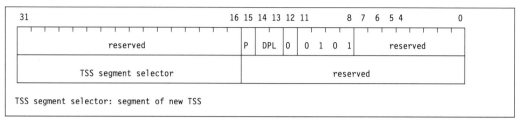

Figure 3.15: 80286 task gate descriptor.

The TSS segment selector in the task gate points to the segment descriptor, which defines the TSS of the task to activate. If the 80286 meets such a task gate during a CALL instruction, a jump instruction or an interrupt, it executes a *task switch* by storing the current state of the active task in the TSS defined by the task register TR (see Figure 3.3), and assigns the type field in the accompanying TSS descriptor the value 1. Thus, the TSS is characterized as an available TSS. The 80286 then loads the new TSS segment selector of the task gate descriptor into the TR, and reads the base address, limit and access rights of the task gate descriptor from the LDT or GDT (depending on which table the segment selector references in the task gate). To complete the task switch, the processor now characterizes the type field of the corresponding TSS descriptor as busy (type 3), and loads the values held by the new TSS into the corresponding registers. Afterwards, the 80286 continues with execution of the new task.

Example: The active task is the word processor Word which is currently laying out a document. Now a timer interrupt occurs. In the interrupt handler the 80286 meets a task gate that points to dBASE. Thus the processor suspends Word by writing all register values to the corresponding TSS. Then it loads all necessary data from the TSS for dBASE and restarts this task, which had been interrupted earlier. After a short time another timer interrupt occurs. But now dBASE is interrupted and the C compiler is activated. This interrupting and restarting of tasks takes place all the time.

It is the job of the operating system to assign a corresponding amount of processor time to the individual programs. Because the task switches are carried out frequently and very quickly, the user has the impression that all three programs are executed simultaneously. Control of these task switches, however, is the exclusive job of the operating system. If a new program is started the operating system supplies a new TSS for this task. You will appreciate that a multitasking operating system must carry out very complex processes at very high speed. Examples of such operating systems or operating system extensions are OS/2, UNIX and, in a limited sense, Windows. They are supported very efficiently by an 80286: to execute a task switch the operating system must «only» supply a task gate, a TSS descriptor, and a TSS. Storing the old register contents and loading the new values is carried out automatically by the processor. No software instructions from the operating system are necessary, although during a task switch 44 bytes of the old TSS must be stored, and 44 bytes of the new TSS have to be loaded.

Now an important warning: the well-known and popular DOS operating system doesn't use any of the functions indicated above. Also, the SMARTDRV.SYS and RAMDRIVE.SYS drivers only build up one GDT and one IDT to move byte groups between the lower 1 Mbyte of memory and extended memory. Task switches and the extensive and very useful access checks are not employed in any form.

Besides these checks and special properties when calling procedures, or during the course of switching between several tasks, a system programmer has to pay attention to many other restrictions and precautions. It is now possible to program a fully functional operating system that uses all the features of the 80286. This subject could fill two books with no problem: I want to be content with this basic course. In the next section, only the protection strategies for the second 80286 address space (namely the access checks for the I/O address space) are described.

3.3.9 Protection for the I/O Address Space

Registers of PC hardware components, such as the hard disk controller, are usually accessed via the I/O ports. Because control and supervision is one of the operating system's main jobs and, in most cases, drivers with privilege level PL = 1 are used for this purpose, the I/O address space is also subject to an access protection. Unlike «normal» memory, no segments are available here.

Rather, protection of the I/O address space is carried out using the IOPL flag in the flag register (see Figure 2.7). The value of this flag indicates the minimum privilege level that a code segment must have to be able to access the I/O address space. If the CPL of the current task is higher (lower privilege level), the I/O instructions IN, OUT, INS and OUTS lead to a «general protection error» exception. Application programs often carry out an access to ports using the operating system. Besides the four I/O instructions, CLI and STI are also dependent upon the IOPL flag. These six instructions are called *IOPL-sensitive* instructions, because the value of IOPL has an influence on their execution.

The reason and purpose of this restriction is obvious if we look at the case where a system function, for example, reads a record from the hard disk but is interrupted by a task switch, and the newly started task intervenes by a direct access to the control register of the controller. The state of the interrupted system routine is, after a further task switch, completely unpredictable. The PC crashes or even destroys data.

A task may only change the IOPL flag by means of the instructions POPF (POP flags) and PUSHF (PUSH flags), but these two instructions are *privileged* (that is, they can only be executed by a code segment with CPL = 0). This level is usually dedicated to the operating system kernel. The application programs are therefore unable to change the IOPL. Any attempt to do so results in an exception «general protection error» in the processor. However, as the flags are part of the TSS, and may therefore be different from task to task, it is possible that one task has access to the I/O address space and the other has not.

To complete the picture, I want to mention that the i386, besides global protection of the I/O address space by means of the IOPL flag, has another option to protect ports individually. Details are given in Chapter 4.

3.3.10 Summary of Protected Mode Protection Mechanisms

The 80286 protection mechanisms in protected mode largely affect instructions that control and determine the CPU state or that access code and data segments. These mechanisms prevent an erroneous or inadequate instruction from locking the CPU (for example, the HLT instruction), or data and code segments being used incorrectly. For this purpose, three groups of protection mechanisms are provided:

– Restricted use of segments: for example, in principle, code segments may not be overwritten and even data segments may only be overwritten if the write bit (bit W) is set. All accessible segments are described by the GDT or LDT; all other segments are inaccessible.
– Restricted access to segments: by using different privilege levels and CPL, DPL, EPL and RPL, the access by programs of a certain privilege level (CPL, RPL, EPL) to the data and code of other segments (DPL) is restricted. Exceptions are only possible through well-controlled call mechanisms (call gate, etc.).
– Privileged instructions: Instructions that directly influence the state of the CPU (for example, LGDT and LLDT) or the alteration of descriptor tables may only be carried out by programs whose CPL or IOPL indicate a high privilege level.

A violation of these protection mechanisms in protected mode immediately gives rise to an exception.

3.4 Pipelining and the 80286 Bus Cycle

Like the 8086, the 80286 also performs a bus cycle to access memory or the I/O space. A bus controller especially designed for the 80286 supports the processor: the 82288.

3.4.1 82288 Bus Controller

The 82288 bus controller is one of the support chips designed for the 80286 processor, and generates the control signals for the bus. Figure 3.16 shows the pin assignment of the 82288.

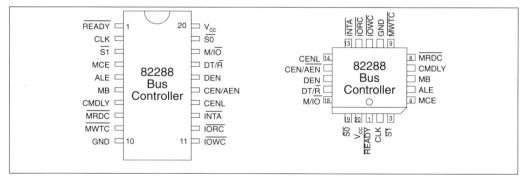

Figure 3.16: The 82288 bus controller. The 82288 is the counterpart of the 8288, and generates the bus control signals from the control signals supplied by the CPU.

In the following, only the new or altered pins as compared to the 8288 are explained, as well as the meaning of the signals supplied or accepted by them.

$\overline{\text{READY}}$ (pin 1)

$\overline{\text{READY}}$ indicates completion of the current bus cycle. If $\overline{\text{READY}}$ is on a high level (V_{cc}), the addressed memory chip or the peripheral is not yet ready to supply or accept data. Therefore, wait states or wait cycles must be inserted. This pin only accepts signals; it does not supply any.

CMDLY (pin 7)

If a high level signal is applied to this pin the 82288 delays the output of a command. Therefore, the following circuits and buffer (that is, those between the bus controller and the memory or I/O subsystem) have more time to prepare for the supply of the address, data and control signals (for example, $\overline{\text{ALE}}$).

CENL (pin 14)

An active signal at CENL is used to select the bus controller. This is necessary if several buses (and therefore also several bus controllers) are available for one processor. Generally, the PC implements only one bus, and thus only one 82288. The CENL pin is usually fixed to V_{cc} to select the bus controller all the time.

M/$\overline{\text{IO}}$ (pin 18)

(Memory/IO) This pin is used together with $\overline{S1}$, $\overline{S0}$ and COD/$\overline{\text{INTA}}$ to inform the bus controller about the type of bus cycle. The 82288 interprets the possible combinations of these four signals and generates the corresponding control signals for the bus. The M/$\overline{\text{IO}}$ signal distinguishes memory accesses from accesses to the I/O space. In the case of the 8086/8288, the $\overline{S2}$ signal was used instead.

As is the case for the 8288, the bus controller interprets the status signals $\overline{S1}$, $\overline{S0}$, COD/$\overline{\text{INTA}}$ and M/$\overline{\text{IO}}$ received from the processor in order to activate the corresponding control signals for the bus. It further coordinates the signals for activating the various buffers. Thus an error-free and strictly defined data transfer between processor and memory or I/O space is possible.

3.4.2 80286 Bus Cycle

The 80286 bus cycle differs considerably from the 8086 bus cycle. Additionally, the 80286 internally divides the clock signal from the 82284, the clock generator for the 80286, by two. This means that with a *system clock* CLK of the clock generator at 20 MHz the processor runs at 10 MHz only. These 10 MHz define the *processor clock* PCLK. It is usual to indicate the effective processor clock PCLK as the clock frequency of a Personal Computer and not the system clock CLK of the 82284 clock generator. By halving the PCLK compared to CLK the internal circuits such as the ALU and BU are not overstressed. On the other hand, the various internal and external signals may be better coordinated by the higher frequency of CLK. A similar effect is used, for example, with a digital watch. The clock is supplied with an external crystal frequency of typically 32 767 Hz, but the display is updated only every 0.01 s at most.

In Figure 3.17 a typical 80286 bus cycle for reading data from memory without wait states is shown. Like the 8086, the 80286 also needs at least four system clock cycles for one bus cycle, but this corresponds to only **two** processor bus cycles. Thus, a 10 MHz 80286 may carry out 5 million bus cycles per second, but a 10 MHz 8086 can execute only 2.5 million. Theoretically, the 80286 with its 16-bit data bus may transfer up to 10 Mbytes per second.

In Figure 3.17 the bus cycle #n and the successive bus cycle #(n+1) are shown. Every bus cycle is separated into two parts, T_S and T_C. T_S indicates the so-called *status cycle* and T_C the so-called *command cycle*. Both cycles last exactly one processor clock cycle, or two system clock cycles φ_1 and φ_2 each. During the status cycle T_S, the control and address signals are output; if data is written as well, data signals D15–D0 are supplied. During the course of the command cycle T_C, the memory or the peripheral carries out the read or write request and returns the read bytes to the data buffers in the case of data reading. If the memory or the peripheral is unable to complete the read or write request within the time available, it holds the READY signal on a high level (as was the case with the 8086). The 80286 is thus told that it should insert a wait cycle to give memory or the peripheral more time to complete the cycle. The processor then carries out further command cycles T_C.

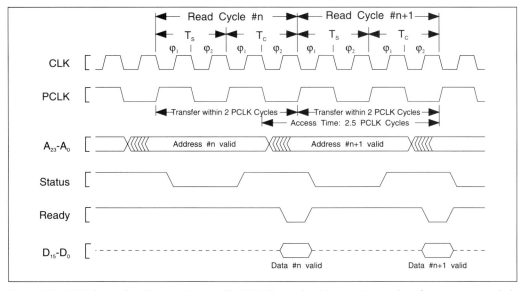

Figure 3.17: 80286 bus cycle without wait states. The 80286 bus cycle without wait states lasts for two processor clock cycles only. Furthermore, the cycles #n and #n+1 overlap so that pipelined addressing is carried out.

Figure 3.18 shows a write bus cycle with one wait state. The bus cycle #n in the Figure gives rise to a wait cycle; the bus cycle #(n+1), however, does not. The 80286 holds the write data active at least until the end of the first system clock cycle after the last T_C of the current bus cycle. If two bus cycles immediately succeed each other, this means that the write data is active at least until the end of the first system clock cycle of the *next* bus cycle.

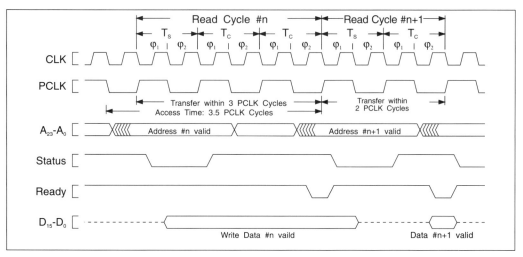

Figure 3.18: 80286 bus cycle with one wait state. Similar to the 8086/88, the 80286 can also insert wait states if the addressed unit is not fast enough, and deactivates READY.

As soon as the data becomes available during a read, READY falls to low (0 V). Thus, data signals D15–D0 on the data bus are valid and are amplified and latched onto the data buffer. Now the 80286 fetches this data from the data buffer and completes the bus cycle. As is the case for the 8086, the READY signal is synchronized by means of the 82284 clock generator.

If, on the other hand, the addressed unit needs more time to accept the address and data signals from the processor, the command cycle T_C can be delayed. For this purpose, the memory or peripheral (not the 80286 processor!) activates the CMDLY signal (*command delay*). With every fall of the system clock signal CLK the 82288 bus controller checks whether the CMDLY pin is on a high level. If this is the case the bus controller does not activate the signals of the command cycle. Not until the level of CMDLY is low does the 82288 continue with the T_C cycle. In this way, the command cycle may be delayed by a multiple of the system clock cycle CLK.

If data is to be written into memory or an I/O port, the 80286 outputs a data signal along with the address signals during the status cycle T_S. Because, unlike the 8086, no time-divisional multiplexed data/address bus is used (that is, the data and address pins are completely separate), the bus need not be switched. Thus the access to memory and ports may be carried out much faster compared to the 8086.

Besides the three «normal» bus cycles for reading and writing data and the passive bus cycle (if the prefetch queue does not need to be reloaded or the currently executed instruction does not need a memory or I/O access), there are shutdown and halt cycles. These are indicated by the combination (0100) of the signals COD/$\overline{\text{INTA}}$, M/$\overline{\text{IO}}$, $\overline{\text{S1}}$, $\overline{\text{S0}}$ and distinguished by the value A1. The shutdown cycle appears if several exceptions occur during execution of an instruction and the processor is unable to handle them any longer: it «strikes». The halt state may also be issued by the instruction HLT. In this case the processor is stopped and does not execute any more instructions. If the hardware IRQs are activated (that is, the IE flag is set), the processor can be forced out of the halt state by issuing a hardware interrupt request. For example, in the PC such an IRQ can be activated by the keyboard. The shutdown state is not affected by this, and the processor ignores the request.

To leave the shutdown state either an NMI or a processor reset must be issued. They also terminate the halt state. The difference is that with an NMI the processor mode is not altered. If the 80286 was running in protected mode before the shutdown, the operation is restarted in protected mode after an NMI and the interrupt handler 2 corresponding to the NMI is called. A processor reset always sets the 80286 to real mode, and the processor starts program execution at CS = f000h, IP = fff0h and additionally activates address lines A23–A20. A shutdown only occurs after a very, very serious problem, which is usually accompanied by a hardware malfunction. Such serious malfunctions may be caused, for example, by a power break, a flash of lightning, or a damaged chip. With the external issuance of an NMI or reset, the processor usually calls a *restart* or *recovery routine* to save what can be saved. However, application programmers are rarely confronted with such problems.

The physical path between processor and memory or I/O space is identical to that for the 8086 (see Figures 2.11 and 2.15). Also, for an 80286 a clock generator (the 82284 in this case), a bus controller (the 82288), data and address buffers, as well as memory and I/O controllers, must be present. The transfer of address, data and control signals between the various circuits is carried out in the same way as with the 8086. Because of the 24-bit address bus, the address buffers are also wider by four bits, of course.

3.4.3 Pipelined Addressing

To execute the access to memory and ports as quickly as possible, the 80286 bus unit supports pipelined addressing, also called *address pipelining*. Let's look at figures 3.17 and 3.18. In these figures you can see that the address signals for a bus cycle are already output before completing the preceding bus cycle. This is possible because the processor has to supply the address of the memory location or port to access only during the status cycle. The signals are fetched into the address buffers and decoded by the address decoder. In this connection, it is important that the decoder completes its operation, that is, has decoded the address, before the memory or port has accepted data (writing) or supplied data to the processor (reading). During reading or writing of the addressed memory location or port, the «address part» of the connection processor–memory or processor–port is more or less «out of work», and waits for the next address to decode. In the same way the «data transfer part» is not active when the address decoder decodes the next address.

Thus, the address decoder may accept the next address while the data transfer part is still occupied by reading or writing data. Therefore, the decoder logic and the address buffers can operate in advance. Successive accesses are interleaved in this way: the addressing part receives the new address one processor clock cycle before completion of the current bus cycle. Actually, the successive bus cycles last for three processor cycles but by means of interleaving the bus cycles the effective time is reduced to two cycles. This interleaved successive inputting and outputting of data and addresses is called *pipelined addressing*, because the signals «flow» in the same way as in a pipeline without stopping. Figure 3.19 shows this interleaving or overlapping of bus cycles.

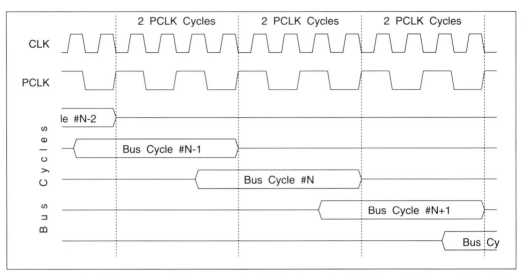

Figure 3.19: Pipelined addressing. With the 80286 pipelined addressing mode the CPU supplies the next address before the present bus cycle is completed. The addressed unit can therefore decode the address while the preceding data is still being transferred.

Pipelining is only possible because the 80286 has, unlike the 8086, no combined address/data bus. In the 8086 the pins are always occupied by the address or the data. Additionally, the pipelining is only effective if several memory or I/O accesses are carried out successively. During the first access the 80286 must start the pipelining by outputting the address of the first access. This is similar to the production line of General Motors: several hours have passed before the first completed car leaves the production line. But if the production line (or «car pipeline») is loaded once, a car leaves the production hall every five minutes. The extensive memory accesses during the course of a task switch or for loading the processor cache registers in protected mode are executable very quickly using this pipelined addressing.

3.4.4 Word Boundary

As is the case with the 8086, the 80286 also has a 16-bit data bus, but it can also address memory byte-by-byte. Thus we are confronted with the problem of word boundaries again. During an access to a word at an odd address, the 80286 has to execute two bus cycles. This is carried out in the same way as with the 8086, and is completely transparent to software. The bus unit executes the two bus cycles automatically and on its own, and combines the two bytes read into one word (reading) or divides the word to be written into two bytes (writing).

Bytes with an even address are transferred via lines D7–D0 of the data bus, and bytes with an odd address via lines D15–D8. If a word with an even address is to be transferred, the 80286 uses data pins D15–D0 and completes the transfer within one bus cycle. Oddly addressed words are transferred within two bus cycles, where the first access is carried out via D15–D8 (byte with an odd address) and the second access via D7–D0 (byte with an even address).

The same also applies for ports: 8-bit ports with an even I/O address are connected to the data lines D7–D0, and 8-bit ports with an odd address to the data lines D15–D8.

3.4.5 Reading Instructions and Prefetching

Because access to words with an odd address gives rise to two bus cycles, the bus unit usually reads a whole word at an even address. The only exception is when a CALL or jump instruction to an odd memory address is executed. In this case the BU fetches only one byte, namely the byte at this odd address. Afterwards, a whole 16-bit word with an even address is always read (if two bytes are free in the prefetch queue).

The 80286 aborts this *prefetching*, as does the 8086, if the processor's instruction unit (IU) detects a CALL or jump instruction. In this case, the 80286 cancels the prefetch queue and restarts the fetching of new instructions at the jump target address. In real mode the BU fetches instructions up to six bytes beyond the last CALL, jump or HLT instruction of a code segment. But in protected mode the BU terminates with the last word of the code segment to avoid an exception. Otherwise, the processor would attempt to access memory beyond the limit of the current code segment. If the last byte of the code segment has an even address, the BU carries out a word access and therefore also fetches the first byte *beyond* the limit of the code segment. But this byte is ignored because it does not belong to the current code segment.

3.5 The 80287 – Mathematical Assistance in Protected Mode

Real and protected mode are completely incompatible operating modes. So it is not surprising that the 8087 doesn't cooperate with the 80286. To operate its successor, the 80287, in a multitasking environment with the 80286 protected mode, Intel's engineers completely redesigned the interface between CPU and coprocessor. This mainly affects the control unit. The internal structure of the 80287 numeric unit, however, hardly differs from that of the 8087. Thus the 80287 doesn't calculate any faster than the 8087.

Meanwhile, a further coprocessor had been developed, the 80287XL. As well as a better numeric unit for faster execution of mathematical calculations, it also incorporates all the new functions of the i387 and strictly implements the new IEEE standard for handling rounding and infinite values. The interface to the 80286 remained the same. (If 80287 is indicated in the following, all the facts apply to the 80287 as well as the 80287XL. If 80287XL is written explicitly, only this enhanced coprocessor is concerned).

Unlike the 8087, the 80287 doesn't carry out any access to memory. The 8087 used the 8086/88 to evaluate the address of an operand or an instruction. With the 80286/287 combination the 80286 not only determines the memory address, but also executes all necessary accesses to memory on its own. Therefore, all data runs through the memory management unit in the 80286. That is necessary because memory addressing in protected mode may lead to far more problems and errors, such as an access denial for a task, than is the case in real mode. To access memory on its own the 80287 would not only need a rather simple addressing unit, like the 8087, but also extensive 80286 memory management functions in protected mode. Therefore, it is more economical to hand over all memory accesses to the 80286. The 80287 only accepts data from the CPU or delivers it to the 80286.

The 80287 supports the same number formats as the 8087 (see Figure 2.20), and represents all numbers internally in the temporary real format with 80 bits. As for the 8087, all numbers are converted according to whether they are read by a load or written by a store instruction.

As mentioned in Section 3.1, the 80286 divides the supplied clock signal CLK by two to generate the internal processor clock. The 80287 behaves in a similar way, but here the clock signal CLK is divided by three. Thus the 80287 runs at only two thirds of the CPU's speed. Therefore, the oft-complained-of clock reduction is not the result of a lower external clock frequency, but built into the 80287. Remember that the numeric unit does not differ from that in an 8087, and originally the 8087 cooperated with a 4.77 MHz 8086 CPU. The jump up to 12.5 MHz, at which a normal 80286 operates without any problems, is very large. Thus Intel's engineers were careful not to destroy their «old» 8087 in the new look of the 80287.

The division by three may be cancelled in principle by fixing the CKM pin (see the next section) on V_{cc} (high). Then the 80287 uses the external clock signal CLK directly without any division, but this option is for combination with another CPU and not with an 80286. In the PC the CKM pin is always low, and the external clock signal CLK is always divided by three if you insert an 80287 into the coprocessor socket on your motherboard. As is the case with the 80286, all specifications of the 80287 clock frequency apply to the effective frequency after the division by three. Thus, in a 10 MHz AT you need a coprocessor with an indicated clock frequency of 2/3*10 MHz = 6.67 MHz.

One possibility to increase the clock frequency of the coprocessor is the installation of a so-called piggyback board. Usually, this board is inserted into the 80287 socket on the motherboard, and has its own oscillator and an 82284 clock signal generator with a higher frequency as well as the 80287 coprocessor. If you install a piggyback board with a 10 Mhz 80287 and a clock signal generator with 30 MHz in a 10 MHz AT, then both the CPU and the coprocessor will run at an effective processor clock of 10 MHz.

The 80287XL, as a further development of the 80287, takes a more direct and better route. Unlike the normal 80287, in the 80287XL the external clock CLK is divided not by three but by two to generate the effective coprocessor clock, as is the case in the 80286. That is possible because the electronic components became far more powerful in the 80287XL. You can never install a 10 MHz 80287XL in an 80287 piggyback board with a 30 MHz oscillator. The effective clock frequency of 15 MHz greatly exceeds the specification of 10 MHz, and the 80287XL no longer operates correctly, or may be damaged.

3.5.1 80287 Connections and Signals

The 80287 comes in a 40-pin DIP or a 44-pin PLCC package. Figure 3.20 shows the pin assignment of the 80287.

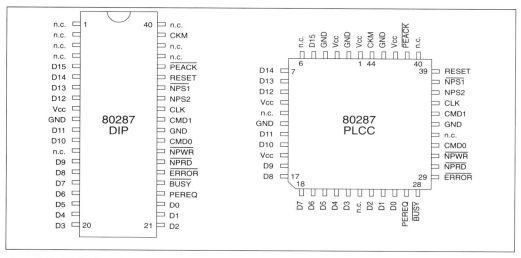

Figure 3.20: 80287 pin assignment.

In the following only the new 80287 connections and signals or the altered ones compared to the 8087 are discussed.

D15–D0 (pins 5–8, 11, 12, 14–23 or 5, 7–9, 13, 14, 16–22, 24–26)
These 16 connections form the bidirectional 16-bit data bus for data exchange between the 80286 CPU and 80287 coprocessor. Unlike the 8087, the 80287 does not supply any address bits.

PEREQ (pin 24 or 27)
(Processor Extension Request) If PEREQ is active (that is, the pin is on a high level potential), the 80287 informs the 80286 that it can accept data from or may supply data to the CPU. If all data has been transferred, the 80287 disables the PEREQ signal again.

$\overline{\text{PEACK}}$ (pin 36 or 41)
(Processor Extension Acknowledge) If the 80287 is executing a coprocessor instruction (that is, an ESC instruction), and if it activates the PEREQ signal to supply data to or to accept data from the CPU, then the 80286 responds with a $\overline{\text{PEACK}}$ signal to inform the coprocessor that the request has been acknowledged and the data transfer is in progress.

$\overline{\text{BUSY}}$ (pin 25 or 28)
If this signal is high the 80287 is currently executing an ESC instruction.

$\overline{\text{ERROR}}$ (pin 26 or 29)
If $\overline{\text{ERROR}}$ is active (that is, low), a non-masked exception has occurred. Thus, $\overline{\text{ERROR}}$ indicates the value of the ES bit in the status register (see below).

$\overline{\text{NPRD}}$ (pin 27 or 30)
(Numeric Processor Read) If the signal at this pin is low (active) then data may be transferred from coprocessor to CPU. For this purpose, the signals $\overline{\text{NPS1}}$ and NPS2 must additionally be active. Otherwise, $\overline{\text{NPRD}}$ will be ignored.

NPWR (pin 28 or 31)
(Numeric Processor Write) If the signal at this pin is low (active) then data may be transferred from the CPU to the coprocessor. For this purpose, the signals $\overline{\text{NPS1}}$ and NPS2 must additionally be active. Otherwise, $\overline{\text{NPRW}}$ will be ignored.

CMD0, CMD1 (pins 29, 31 or 32, 35)
(Command Select) Together with pins $\overline{\text{NPS1}}$, NPS2, $\overline{\text{NPRD}}$ and $\overline{\text{NPWR}}$, the CPU can control the coprocessor's operation. For the combinations (NPS1 NPS2 CMD0 CMD1 $\overline{\text{NPRD}}$ $\overline{\text{NPWR}}$) the following meanings apply:

```
(x0xxxx)  80287 not activated
(1xxxxx)  80287 not activated
(010010)  opcode is transferred to the 80287
(010001)  80287 transfers control or status word to the CPU
(011001)  80287 transfers data to the CPU
(011010)  CPU transfers data to the 80287
(010110)  exception pointer is written
(010101)  reserved
(011101)  reserved
(011110)  reserved
```

$\overline{\text{NPS2}}$, NPS1 (pins 33, 34 or 37, 38)
(Numeric Processor Select) If both pins are active (that is, $\overline{\text{NPS2}}$ is low and NPS1 is high), then the 80286 has detected an ESC instruction, and it activates the 80287 to execute the instruction.

CKM (pin 39 or 44)
(Clocking Mode) Usually this pin is fixed (by soldering) on Vcc (+5 V) or GND (0 V). In the first case, the 80287 uses the external clock signal CLK directly without any division. In the latter case the 80287 divides CLK by three, and the 80287XL by two, to generate the effective processor clock.

Unlike the 8087, the 80287 doesn't have, for example, an INT pin to issue a hardware interrupt. This job is taken over by the $\overline{\text{ERROR}}$ signal. If the 80287 signals the CPU by means of $\overline{\text{ERROR}}$ that an exception has occurred, the 80286 issues an interrupt at the next ESC or WAIT instruction on its own. Interrupts in protected mode are very delicate. They must be carried out within the frame of a completely different communication between CPU and coprocessor compared to the 8087 in real mode.

3.5.2 80287 Structure and Functioning

The internal 80287 structure is very similar to that of the 8087 (see Section 2.10.3); only the bus unit has changed according to the data exchange with the CPU. To be compatible with the 8087, the 80287 supports the same ESC instructions, and the 80287XL further supports the new i387 instructions. Also, the 80287 implements a register stack with eight 80-bit registers, which are accessed and managed in the same way as with an 8087. Additionally, a status, control and tag word are implemented. The status and control words differ only slightly from those of the 8087; the tag word remains the same. Figure 3.21 shows the format of the 80287 control word. Unlike the 8087, the 80287 may issue an interrupt only indirectly by means of the $\overline{\text{ERROR}}$ signal and the CPU. Therefore, the interrupt mask bit M is without any meaning, and is not used by the 80287. All other bits have the same meaning in an 80287 as in an 8087, but in the 80287XL the IC bit for infinity control is also different from that of the 8087.

```
 15                                                    0
┌──┬──┬──┬──┬─────┬──────┬──┬──┬──┬──┬──┬──┬──┬──┐
│rs│rs│rs│IC│  RC │  PC  │rs│rs│PM│UM│OM│ZM│DM│IM│
└──┴──┴──┴──┴─────┴──────┴──┴──┴──┴──┴──┴──┴──┴──┘
/80287 and 80287XL
RC:  rounding
     00=to next number          01=to lower (to -∞)
     10=to upper (to +∞)        11=cut off (to 0)
PC:  precision
     00=24 bits    01=reserved  10=53 bits   11=64 bits
PM:  precision     ┐
UM:  underflow     │
OM:  overflow      ├ 1=corresponding exception masked
ZM:  division by zero  0=corresponding exception enabled
DM:  denormalized operand
IM:  invalid operation ┘
rs:  reserved

/80287
IC:  infinity
     0=projective (∞)       1=affine (±∞)

/80287XL
IC:  no meaning
```

Figure 3.21: Control word format.

In the 80287, the IC bit for the handling of infinite quantities has the same meaning as in the 8087. As the 80287XL strictly implements the IEEE standard for floating-point numbers, the IC bit is without any meaning here. For compatibility reasons, you can program the bit in the same way as with an 8087 or 80287, but a changed value of IC has no consequence. The 80287XL always handles infinite quantities in the affine sense (±∞) even if IC is set to 0.

```
 15                                        0
┌─┬──┬────┬──┬──┬──┬──┬──┬──┬──┬──┬──┬──┬──┐
│B│C3│ TOP│C2│C1│C0│ES│SP│PE│UE│OE│ZE│DE│IE│
└─┴──┴────┴──┴──┴──┴──┴──┴──┴──┴──┴──┴──┴──┘
B:     busy bit
C3-C0: condition code
TOP:   stack pointer (top of stack)
       000=reg. 0 equal TOP   001=reg. 1 equal TOP   010=reg. 2 equal TOP  ...  111=reg. 7 equal TOP
ES:    error status
       1=non-masked exception active
SP:    stack flag
       1=invalid operation by register stack overflow or underflow
       0=invalid operation because of other reason
PE:    precision          ┐
UE:    underflow          │
OE:    overflow           ├ 1=condition generated exception
ZE:    division by zero   │
DE:    denormalized operand│
IE:    invalid operation  ┘
```

Figure 3.22: 80287 status word format.

As already mentioned, the 80287 handles exceptions in a different way compared to the 8087. It indicates an error to the CPU by means of the $\overline{\text{ERROR}}$ signal, which then indirectly issues an interrupt. On the other hand, with the 8087 the coprocessor can request a hardware interrupt on its own. Therefore, the interrupt bit IR in the 80287 status word is without any meaning; the 80287 status word differs only slightly in the ES and SP bits from the 8087 status word. Figure 3.22 shows the format of the 80287 status word. The *B* bit is implemented only for compatibility with the 8087, and is always equal to the ES bit. Therefore, B doesn't hold any information about the state of the numeric unit and thus of the $\overline{BUSY}$ pin. The new *ES* bit indicates the 80287's error status. If ES is set, a non-masked exception has occurred whose source is represented by the SP to IE bits. Bit *SP* is used to distinguish invalid operations (flag IE) by a register stack overflow or underflow, and invalid operations caused by other reasons. If SP is set, and therefore a register stack overflow or underflow has occurred, then you may distinguish an overflow (C1 = 1) and an underflow (C1 = 0) by means of the C1 bit. The interpretation of the condition code *C3–C0* is the same as that for the 8087 indicated in Table 2.8, but for an 80287XL additional codes are possible because of the enhanced instruction set. A description of all of these codes would go far beyond the scope of this book, therefore readers interested in this subject are referred to a good manual on 80287/80287XL programming.

The 80287 may be switched to protected mode by the FSETPM (floating set protected mode) instruction, and switched back to real mode with FRSTPM (floating return from protected mode). Note that the 80286 may be switched to protected mode immediately, but it can be switched back to real mode only by a processor reset. The 80287 executes the coprocessor instructions in real and protected mode in the same way because the 80286 memory management unit carries out all addressing work and access checks. The 80287 gets the instruction code and the operands after the CPU has addressed memory and read in the data.

The only difference between real and protected mode applies to the format in which the memory image of instruction and data pointer are stored. You can store the most important control and status registers using the instructions FLDENV (load environment), FSTENV (store environment), and with the 80287XL additionally with the instructions FSAVE and FRSTOR. Therefore, an exception handler is able to locate the error that led to the exception. Figure 3.23 shows the corresponding formats in real and protected mode.

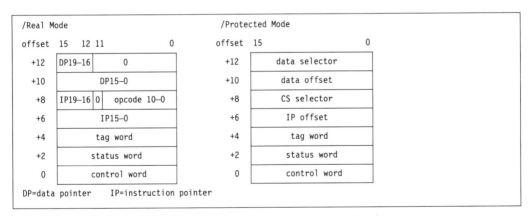

Figure 3.23: Memory image of instruction and data pointer in real and protected modes.

After an 80287 reset that is issued by a high-level signal at the RESET pin lasting for at least four 80287 CLK cycles, the coprocessor executes an internal reset. For the reset the 80287 needs 25

CLK cycles, during which it is not able to accept external instructions. Thus, the CPU has to wait for at least 25 coprocessor clock cycles after a coprocessor reset before it may hand over the first opcode. Also, the instruction FNINIT (initialize coprocessor) resets the 80287 internally into a strictly defined state. After the coprocessor reset, the 80287 should always be initialized with an FNINIT instruction. For the current 80287 types this is not absolutely necessary, but Intel recommends it to ensure compatibility with future versions. Table 3.4 lists the values of various 80287 registers after a reset or a FNINIT instruction.

Register	Value	Interpretation
Control word	37fh	all exceptions masked, precision 64 bit, rounding to next value
Status word	xy00h[1]	all exceptions cleared, TOP=000b[2], condition code undefined, B=0
Tag word	ffffh	all registers empty

[1] x = 0 or x = 4, 0 ≤ y ≤ 7
[2] after the first PUSH instruction TOP points to register 7 (111b), thus the stack is growing downwards

Table 3.4: Register values after RESET/FNINIT

3.5.3 80287 Exceptions

On an 8087 a non-masked exception immediately gives rise to an interrupt. For this purpose, the 8087 has an INT pin whose signal may issue a hardware interrupt. In protected mode interrupts are very delicate, and therefore in most cases part of the operating system or at least of near-system code elements. The 80287 has an $\overline{\text{ERROR}}$ pin that informs the CPU about an exception in the coprocessor, but which may not directly issue an interrupt. Instead, the CPU executes a predefined software interrupt when the 80287 indicates (by an active $\overline{\text{ERROR}}$ signal) that an error has occurred. Therefore, all interrupt protection mechanisms of the protected mode are available for the 80287 exceptions. For the 80287 exceptions four interrupts are reserved in total: 7, 9, 13 and 16. In the following the assigned exceptions are listed:

– Interrupt 7: in the CPU the EM (emulate coprocessor) bit or TS (task switch) was set when the CPU detected an ESC instruction in the instruction stream. If EM = 1 the coprocessor instruction must be emulated by software. Thus, the interrupt handler carries out a coprocessor emulation or calls such an emulation. If TS = 1 an ESC or WAIT instruction calls this interrupt to indicate that the current coprocessor context may possibly not correspond to the current task. The operating system must handle this state accordingly.
– Interrupt 9: in protected mode an operand spans an address area that is not completely covered by the operand's segment, or the operand is partially at the top/bottom of the segment and continues at the bottom/top (wrap around).
– Interrupt 13: in protected mode the first word of a numeric operand is partially outside the segment.
– Interrupt 16: the preceding numeric instruction led to a non-masked exception. The instruction's address and the address of the operand are stored in the instruction and data pointer register. Only ESC and WAIT instructions may issue this interrupt. Thus, with an 80287 only the *next* coprocessor or WAIT instruction gives rise to an interrupt. Depending upon the

application as well as the type and number of loaded tasks, a rather long time may pass before the coprocessor error leads to an interrupt. The 8087, on the other hand, issues an interrupt immediately after the occurrence of an exception.

If some exceptions are masked in the control register, the 80287 (like the 8087) executes a standard on-chip exception handler with the same results as is the case with the 8087. Note that the 80287XL only implements affine infinity ($\pm\infty$), no projective (∞) one. Therefore, infinite results because of a division by zero or overflow always have a sign. With an 8087 or 80287 (without XL) the result of the on-chip handler may also be a projective infinity without a sign, depending on the IC bit in the control register.

3.5.4 Communication Between CPU and 80287

As is the case with an 8087, the control unit (CU) carries out the communication with the 80286 CPU. But from the pin assignment (see Figure 3.20) you see that the 80287 is unable to address memory on its own. Also, the 8087 cannot access memory completely autonomously, but needs a dummy read cycle to determine the start address. Afterwards, the 8087 can execute all further memory addressing of a load or store cycle on its own. The 80287 is not even able to carry this out, but is completely dependent upon the CPU to carry out a memory access. Thus the 80287 doesn't communicate with memory in any way, only with the CPU.

The communication between CPU and coprocessor is carried out by means of I/O bus cycles. The control unit (or better, the bus interface of the control unit) behaves like a special I/O peripheral from the 80286's point of view. If the CPU detects an ESC instruction in the instruction stream that is fetched into the prefetch queue, the 80286 automatically carries out an I/O bus cycle to transfer the opcode to the coprocessor. For this purpose, the 80286 uses three reserved I/O addresses, listed in Table 3.5. Through these three coprocessor ports, the complete data transfer between memory and coprocessor also takes place. Addressing is carried out in the 80286 memory management unit, so that all protection mechanisms of the protected mode are also available for the 80287:

– Data reading: the 80286 addresses the memory and reads the addressed data by means of a normal memory read cycle. Afterwards, it transfers the data in an I/O bus cycle via the coprocessor ports to the 80287.
– Data writing: the CPU reads the data during the course of an I/O bus cycle via the coprocessor ports from the 80287. Then the 80286 addresses memory and writes the data into it by means of a normal memory write cycle.

```
                 Signals at 80287 pins
  I/O address
                 NPS2    /NPS1    CMD1    CMD0
  0f8h           1       0        0       0
  0fah           1       0        0       1
  0fch           1       0        1       0

  Be careful that you do not transfer data to these reserved port addresses. Otherwise, the 80287 can
  behave very strangely.
```

Table 3.5: 80287 reserved I/O addresses

The 80286 and the 80287 are in special tune with each other: to reach a very fast data exchange via the ports, this I/O bus cycle is carried out without wait cycles. For data transfer between memory and coprocessor, the I/O bus cyles between CPU and 80287 also have to be taken into account when compared to the 8087. Thus the load and store instructions need more time on an 80287 than on an 8087. With the 80287XL the necessary format conversions connected to the load and store instructions have been optimized so that the number of clock cycles here is fewer. Don't be surprised if a 10 MHz XT with an 8087 coprocessor runs nearly as fast as a 10 MHz AT with an 80287 coprocessor for pure mathematical applications. The 80287 (without XL) only runs with two thirds of the CPU clock (6.67 MHz). Further, it needs the additional I/O bus cycles between CPU and 80287 for a memory access. But the 80286/80287 combination compensates for this disadvantage by a more effective bus cycle, with two clock cycles per data transfer at 0 wait states compared to four clock cycles for the 8086/8087 combination. In the end, both PC types run at about the same speed.

3.5.5 80287 Memory Cycles

Strictly speaking, there are no 80287 memory cycles. All the data exchange with memory is routed through the CPU. The 80287 runs completely asynchronous to the CPU as far as the local bus is concerned, that is, the coprocessor must indicate explicitly by means of the PEREQ signal that it needs a memory access. With the 8086/8087 combination, on the other hand, the CPU was always informed about the processes in the coprocessor, and vice versa.

If the 80286 wants to carry out a data transfer such as the transfer of the opcode of an ESC instruction, the CPU starts an I/O bus cycle for communication with the 80287 by activating the two coprocessor signals $\overline{\text{NPS1}}$ and NPS2. Then the 80287 investigates the signals at the $\overline{\text{NPRD}}$ and $\overline{\text{NPWR}}$ pins to determine the direction of the data transfer (to the CPU and from the CPU, respectively), and to prepare the internal data buffers for output or input of data. According to the potentials at the CMD0 and CMD1 pins, the coprocessor further detects whether the opcode of an ESC instruction, an operand, or the memory image of the control and status registers is to be transferred.

If the coprocessor is ready for data transfer it activates the PEREQ signal. The CPU carries out, on the one hand, the transfer between coprocessor and 80286, and on the other the transfer between memory and CPU. If all data has been transferred the 80286 reacts with a PEACK, the 80287 deactivates the PEREQ signal and the data transfer between memory and coprocessor or between coprocessor and memory is completed.

3.5.6 80286/80287 System Configuration

Figure 3.24 shows the typical connection of the 80287 coprocessor and 80286 CPU. By means of data pins D15–D0 both access the same local bus but the addressing and therefore the output of the address signals A23–A0 is only carried out by the 80286 CPU. With the configuration indicated, both CPU and coprocessor receive the same clock signal from the same 82284 clock generator. Because 80287 and 80286 run asynchronously, the 80287 may also be clocked by a separate clock generator, which does not need to be an 82284.

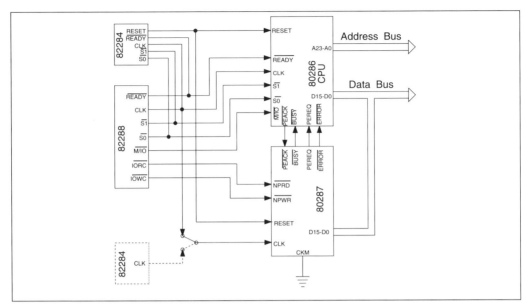

Figure 3.24: 80286/80287 system configuration. The 80287 harmonizes best with the 80286 and can therefore be connected to the 80286 without any problem. Unlike the 8086/8087 combination, the 80287 runs asynchronous to the CPU, and thus can be clocked by a separate clock generator.

An asynchronous operation of CPU and coprocessor is possible because, unlike the 8087, the 80287 is unable to control the local bus on its own. Instead, it receives all instruction code and data from the 80286. For this purpose the 80287 has a data bus that establishes the connection between CPU and coprocessor. The connections $\overline{\text{ERROR}}$, $\overline{\text{BUSY}}$, PEREQ, $\overline{\text{PEACK}}$, $\overline{\text{NPRD}}$, $\overline{\text{NPWR}}$, NPS2, $\overline{\text{NPS1}}$, CMD0 and CMD1 form a control bus for the 80287, which controls the data transfer from and to the CPU.

If an error or an exception occurs in the coprocessor during a numeric calculation (for example, an overflow or an underflow), then the 80287 activates its $\overline{\text{ERROR}}$ output to issue an interrupt in the 80286. On the other hand, the 8087 requests a hardware interrupt using a dedicated INT pin. You may see that the 80287, unlike the 8087, is no bus master. Therefore, no $\overline{\text{RG}}/\overline{\text{GT}}$ pins are present for getting control of the local bus. Thus, the 80287 is more directly conceived of as a «processor extension», as is the case with an 8087.

3.6 AT Architecture

There are no major differences between a PC and an AT, except that the PC with its 8088 processor only has an 8-bit data bus internally on the motherboard. On the other hand, the XT data bus internally comprises 16 bits. But in both PCs only 8 bits lead into the bus slots. Also, the internal structure is the same as far as the number and connections of the support chips 8237A, 8259A, 8253, etc. are concerned. Compared to the XT, the AT is a significant advance (AT actually means **a***dvanced* **t***echnology*), and its architecture is quite different from that of the PC/XT. The following sections briefly present these main differences.

3.6.1 Components and Their Cooperation

Figure 3.25 gives a block diagram of an AT. In most of today's ATs or AT-compatibles, several chips are integrated into one single chip, but the functional groups remain the same. Therefore, you may not find any of the chips shown in Figure 3.25. If you look at the data sheet of your motherboard, though, you will recognize that in chip X the functions of, for example, the two interrupt controllers, etc. have been integrated. It is the aim of Figure 3.25 to represent the functional structure of the AT as it was originally realized by individual chips, before the development of large-scale integration technology.

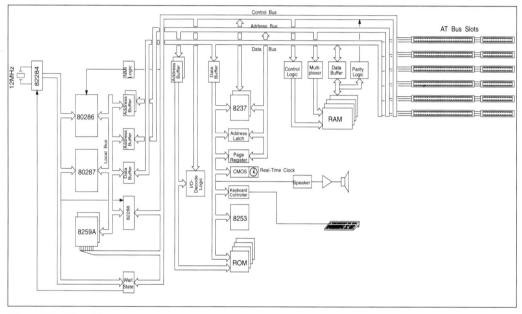

Figure 3.25: AT architecture.

Here, the central part is also the processor. In the AT you will find the 80286, with 24 address lines. Thus, the AT may have 16 Mbytes of memory at most. Further, with the 80286 the AT can operate in protected mode to run with advanced operating systems like OS/2 or UNIX. The A20 address line is controlled by the 8042 keyboard controller. It can be locked so that the 80286 in real mode strictly addresses only the lowest 1 Mbyte of memory, and carries out a wrap-around like the 8086/88. Unfortunately, some DOS-internal functions dating from the PC's Stone Age rely on this wrap-around, but compatibility with the Stone Age may be, in my opinion, a matter of taste.

In addition to the 80286, the 80287 mathematical coprocessor can be installed. Normally, there is at least one socket for it present on the motherboard. The system clock is supplied by the 82284 clock generator, which is the successor of the PC/XT's 8284. The first AT ran with an effective processor clock of 6 MHz, so that the clock generator had to supply twice this frequency (12 MHz). The processor clock frequency was increased up to a giant 8 MHz with the AT03 model. Meanwhile, there are 80286 CPUs on the market (Harris or AMD, for example) which run with an effective processor clock of up to 25 MHz. But the support chips and the AT bus are nowhere near this frequency, so wait states are often required.

A further component of the AT (as in every computer) is the main memory. The processor is connected to it by means of data, address and control buses, as is the case in the PC/XT. The CPU addresses the memory via a 24-bit address bus, controls the data transfer with the control bus, and transfers the data via a 16-bit data bus. The necessary control signals are generated by the 82288 bus controller, which is the successor of the PC/XT's 8288, and which is dedicated to the 80286. To carry out the data exchange in as error-free and orderly a manner as possible, the signals are buffered and amplified in various address and data buffers.

In the AT and its all successors up to the EISA PC, five different address buses can be distinguished:

– Local address bus: comprises the 24 address signals from the 80286. External address buffers and address latches separate the local bus from the system address bus.

– System address bus: as is the case for the PC/XT, this bus is the main address bus and represents the latched version of the bits A0 to A19 of the local address bus. Thus the system address bus in the AT is a 20-bit address bus. The signal for latching the address signals on the local address bus into the latches for the system address bus is ALE. In the AT, the system address bus is led to the bus slots as A0 to A19.

– Memory address bus: this address bus is only present on the motherboard, and represents the multiplexed version of the system address bus. Via the memory address bus, the row and column addresses are sucessively applied to the DRAM chips (see Chapter 6).

– X-address bus: this bus is separated from the system bus by buffers and drivers, and serves to address the I/O units and the ROM BIOS on the motherboard. These may, for example, be registers of the interrupt controllers, the timer or an on-board floppy controller. On the other hand, I/O ports and ROM BIOS on extension adapters are accessed by the system address bus.

– L address bus: this bus comprises the seven high-order (L = large) and non-latched address bits A17–A23 of the local address bus. It leads into the AT slots as LA17–LA23.

Besides these, there are four different data buses implemented in the AT:

– Local data bus: comprises the 16 data signals from the 80286. Additionally, a bus logic is necessary to distinguish byte and word accesses. External data buffers and data latches separate the local data bus from the system data bus.

- System data bus: this is the latched version of the local data bus in the AT, and it is 16 bits wide. The system data bus leads into the bus slots.

- Memory data bus: this data bus is only present on the motherboard, and establishes the connection between main memory and the system data bus.

- X-data bus: this bus is separated from the system bus by buffers and drivers, and accesses I/O units and the ROM BIOS on the motherboard. I/O ports and BIOS extensions on extension adapters are accessed by the system data bus.

Besides the main memory on the motherboard the CPU can also access chips on the adapter cards in the bus slots. A more detailed explanation of the construction and function of the AT slots is given below. Unlike the XT, the data bus leads into the bus slots with the full width of 16 bits. The additional control and data signals are located in a new slot section with 38 contacts. However, older XT adapters with an 8-bit data bus can also be inserted into the AT slots by means of the two new control signals *MEM CS16* and $\overline{I/O\ CS16}$. The bus logic automatically recognizes whether a 16-bit AT or an 8-bit PC/XT adapter is present in the bus slot. An 8/16-bit converter carries out the necessary division of 16-bit quantities into two 8-bit quantities, and vice versa.

Like the PC/XT bus, the AT or ISA bus also supports only the CPU and the DMA chips on the motherboard as bus masters which can arbitrate directly, without using a DMA channel. On external adapter cards in the bus slots, no bus master may operate and control the AT bus. The arbitration is carried out only indirectly, via a DMA channel, and not directly by a master request. It was not until EISA and the microchannel that such bus masters could also operate from peripheral adapter cards.

The first AT model ran at a processor clock of only 6 MHz. The bus slots and the inserted extension adapters have no problem in following the clock, but the situation is different with a turbo clock of, for example, 16 MHz. The inert bus slots then usually run with only half the turbo clock, that is, 8 MHz. Problems mainly arise with «half»-turbo clocks of 10 MHz or 12.5 MHz. In most cases, the bus slots also run at this frequency, but only very high quality adapters support 10 MHz or even 12.5 MHz.

The consequence is frequent system crashes, especially if the PC has been running for a long time and the warmer chips of the peripheral adapters can no longer follow the clock. Meanwhile, the ISA standard (which corresponds to the AT bus in most respects) requires a clock frequency for the bus slots of 8.33 MHz at most. Even adapter cards that could run more quickly are supplied in ATs which strictly implement this standard, with only 8.33 MHz.

Unlike the bus slots, the main memory on the motherboard runs with the full processor clock, even if this is 25 MHz. The main memory controller may advise the CPU at most to insert wait cycles if the RAM chips are too slow. But advanced memory concepts such as paging or interleaving (see Chapter 6) shorten the memory access times. Thus, an access to memory expansions on adapter cards is much slower than an access to the on-board memory (remember this if you want to extend your memory).

You should always prefer an extension of the on-board memory as long as the motherboard can integrate more chips. This applies particularly to very fast-clocked i386 and i486 models. Some PCs have a special memory slot besides the normal bus slots into which special memory adapter cards may be inserted, largely running with the full CPU clock so that no delays occur compared to the on-board memory.

To decode the processor's addresses in a memory access, the AT also has an address multiplexer. Together with the memory buffer, it drives the memory chips on the motherboard. The check logic for memory parity issues an NMI if the data does not conform with the additionally held parity bit at the time of data reading.

Also, additional memory on an adapter card may issue this memory parity error. Other sources for an NMI in an AT may be errors on an adapter card, indicated by $\overline{I/O}$ $\overline{CH}$ $\overline{CK}$. In the PC/XT the memory refresh was carried out only via channel 0 of the DMA chip. This channel is activated periodically by channel 1 of the timer chip. In the AT, the refresh interval is further defined by channel 1 of the timer chip, but the refresh itself is usually carried out by a dedicated refresh logic driven by the timer channel 1. Thus, channel 0 would normally be available, but certain manufacturers do use it further for refresh. For this purpose, the lines $\overline{DACK0}$ and $\overline{REF}$ lead into the AT slots (see below).

Like the PC/XT, the AT also has a ROM for holding boot code and data and the AT's BIOS routines. Unlike the 8086/88, in the PC/XT the AT's 80286 may also be operated in protected mode. These two operation modes are completely incompatible, which is, unfortunately, bad news for the BIOS: BIOS routines in real mode cannot be used by the 80286 in protected mode. Only the original AT, or other manufacturers' ATs, incorporate an *advanced BIOS*, which holds the corresponding routines for protected mode.

The advanced BIOS is located in the address space just below 16 Mbytes. If you buy a freely available version of OS/2 then usually the disks not only hold the operating system, but also the BIOS for protected mode. Thus, during the OS/2 boot process not only the operating system is loaded, but also the BIOS for protected mode. The BIOS routines present in ROM are only used for booting as long as the 80286 is not switched to protected mode. As you know, the BIOS implements the interface between operating system and hardware. Even tiny incompatibilities have disastrous consequences; the BIOS must be 100% compatible with the hardware. IBM's OS/2, which is available in the market, therefore only runs on a 100% compatible machine. With DOS, a 99% compatibility is usually enough.

For supporting the CPU and peripherals, the AT also has several support chips. Instead of one 8259A programmable interrupt controller (PIC), two are present in an AT: one *master PIC* and one *slave PIC*. The INTRPT output of the slave is connected to the master's IR2 input, thus the two PICs are cascaded. Therefore, 15 instead of eight IRQ levels are available in the AT. Table 3.6 shows the assignment of the interrupt channels IRQx to the various peripherals or support chips. Besides the IRQs, the NMI also is listed as a hardware interrupt, but the NMI directly influences the CPU, and no 8259A PIC is used for this purpose. Section 7.1 describes how the 8259A operates and how it may be programmed.

Channel	Interrupt	Used by
NMI	02h	parity, error on extension card, memory refresh
IRQ0	08h	channel 0 of timer 8253
IRQ1	09h	keyboard
IRQ2	0ah	cascade from slave PIC
IRQ3	0bh	COM2
IRQ4	0ch	COM1
IRQ5	0dh	LPT2
IRQ6	0eh	floppy disk controller
IRQ7	0fh	LPT1
IRQ8	0fh	real time clock
IRQ9	0fh	redirection to IRQ2
IRQ10	0fh	reserved
IRQ11	0fh	reserved
IRQ12	0fh	reserved
IRQ13	0fh	coprocessor 80287
IRQ14	0fh	hard disk controller
IRQ15	0fh	reserved

Table 3.6: AT hardware interrupt channels

Besides the PICs, a 8253/8254 programmable interval timer (PIT), or for short, timer chip, is present. The 8254 is the more developed successor to the 8253 but has the same function set. It includes three individually programmable counters (see Table 3.7). Counter 0 is used for periodically updating the internal system clock, as is the case in the PC/XT, and is connected to the IRQ0 of the master PIC. The hardware interrupt issued thus updates the internal clock, which can be checked by means of the DOS commands TIME and DATE. Timer 1 periodically activates the memory refresh, which is indicated by an active signal $\overline{\text{REF}}$ in the AT bus slot. Counter 2 generates the tone frequency for the speaker. In Sections 7.2 and 7.4 some details about the operation modes and the programming of the 8253 PIT and the speaker are given.

Channel	Used by
0	internal system clock (IRQ0)
1	memory refresh
2	speaker frequency

Table 3.7: AT timer channels

For memory and I/O accesses without any intervention of the CPU the AT has two 8237A DMA chips which are cascaded so that seven DMA channels are available. The use of the separately programmable transfer channels is shown in Table 3.8. The first four channels serve 8-bit peripherals and the other three channels 5–7 are implemented for 16-bit peripherals.

Channel 0 is reserved for memory refresh, although in most ATs its own refresh logic is present for the refresh process. The remaining three 8-bit channels are available for an 8-bit data transfer. Usually, the DMA chips run with a much lower clock frequency than the CPU. The frequency is typically about 5 MHz (even in cases where the CPU is clocked with 25 MHz). Some ATs enable a DMA frequency of up to 7 MHz, not very exciting compared to the CPU clock.

Thus it is not surprising that most AT hard disk controllers do not transfer data by DMA but by means of programmed I/O, because the 80286 runs much faster than an 8086/88 and the DMA chips. But the 16-bit hard disk controllers are sometimes served by one of the DMA channels 5–7. The function, programming and the transfer protocol of the DMA chips are explained in Section 7.3.

Channel	Used by	Width
0	reserved (memory refresh)	8 bits
1	SDLC adapter/tape drive	8 bits
2	floppy disk controller	8 bits
3	reserved	8 bits
4	cascade DMA1->DMA2	–
5	reserved	16 bits
6	reserved	16 bits
7	reserved	16 bits

Table 3.8: AT DMA channels

Unlike the PC/XT, the more modern and programmable keyboard of the AT is connected by a keyboard controller to the AT system bus. In the PC/XT, an 8255 programmable peripheral interface (PPI) was included for this purpose. The functions of the AT keyboard and its successor, the MF II keyboard, may be programmed (details are discussed in Chapter 11).

Instead of the DIP switches you will find a CMOS RAM in the AT. The CMOS RAM holds the system configuration and supplies it at power-up. EISA and microchannel further extend this concept: here you may even set up the DMA and IRQ channels used by EISA or microchannel adapters by means of an interactive program. These set-ups are stored in an extended CMOS RAM, and no jumpers need to be altered (after de-installing all adapters to expose the mother-board...). Together with the CMOS RAM, a real-time clock is integrated which periodically updates date and time, even if the PC is switched off. The two DOS commands DATE and TIME are no longer necessary at power-up for setting the current date and time. They are mainly used for checking these values.

The whole AT is powered in the same way as the PC/XT, by means of a power supply that supplies voltages of –12 V, –5 V, 0 V, +5 V and +12 V. In the AT, too, the adapter cards in the bus slots are usually powered by corresponding contacts in the bus slots. Only «current eaters» like FileCards with integrated hard disk drives must be directly connected to the power supply.

As hardware components, the support chips mentioned are accessed via ports in the I/O address space. Thus, the AT as well as the PC/XT uses *I/O mapped input/output (I/O)*. Table 3.9 shows the port addresses of the most important hardware components in the AT.

Besides the 80286, ATs often also include an i386 or i486 processor. With these processors some on-board data and address buses (the memory address bus, for example) may be 32 bits wide. But only 24 address lines and 16 data lines lead into the bus slots, as is the case for an original AT. The conversion to 32-bit quantities is carried out by special swappers and buffers. In principle, the architecture of these i386 or i486 ATs therefore doesn't differ from that of a conventional AT. Only the internal address and data buses may be adapted accordingly.

Port address	Used by
000h–00fh	1st DMA chip 8237A
020h–021h	1st PIC 8259A
040h–043h	PIT 8253
060h–063h	keyboard controller 8042
070h–071h	real-time clock
080h–083h	DMA page register
0a0h–0afh	2nd PIC 8259A
0c0h–0cfh	2nd DMA chip 8237A
0e0h–0efh	reserved
0f0h–0ffh	reserved for coprocessor 80287
100h–1ffh	available
200h–20fh	game adapter
210h–217h	reserved
220h–26fh	available
278h–27fh	2nd parallel interface
2b0h–2dfh	EGA
2f8h–2ffh	COM2
300h–31fh	prototype adapter
320h–32fh	available
378h–37fh	1st parallel interface
380h–38fh	SDLC adapter
3a0h–3afh	reserved
3b0h–3bfh	monochrome adapter/parallel interface
3c0h–3cfh	EGA
3d0h–3dfh	CGA
3e0h–3e7h	reserved
3f0h–3f7h	floppy disk controller
3f8h–3ffh	COM1

Table 3.9: AT port addresses.

3.6.2 I/O Channel and Bus Slots

Similar to the PC/XT, here also a main part of the system bus leads into the bus slots. The AT bus slots incorporate 36 new contacts, compared to the XT bus slot, to integrate the additional address, data, DMA and IRQ lines. Thus, 98 contacts are present in total. The additional AT contacts are included in a separate section, which is always arranged immediately behind the slot with the conventional XT contacts. Usually, each AT or AT-compatible has several pure XT and several pure AT slots with corresponding contacts. Also, it is completely insignificant (in theory) into which slot you insert an adapter card in the AT. You only have to ensure that you really do insert an AT adapter (discernible by the additional contacts on the bottom) into an AT slot and not into an XT slot. Figure 3.26 shows the structure and assignment of an AT bus slot.

In the following sections only the new contacts and the meaning of the supplied or accepted signals are presented. The assignment of the XT part of an AT slot (with the exception of the $\overline{\text{0WS}}$ and $\overline{\text{REF}}$ contacts) is given in Section 2.11.2. $\overline{\text{0WS}}$ has been added instead of the reserved XT bus contact B8 to service fast peripherals without wait cycles.

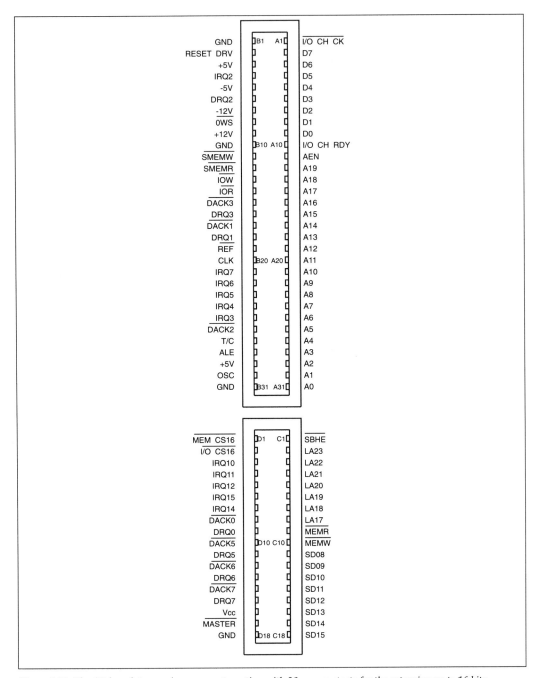

Figure 3.26: The AT bus slot comprises a separate section with 38 new contacts for the extension up to 16 bits.

$\overline{0WS}$

The signal from a peripheral indicates that the unit is running quickly enough to be serviced without wait cycles.

$\overline{REF}$

(Refresh) The signal at this contact indicates that the memory refresh on the motherboard is in progress. Thus, peripherals may also carry out a memory refresh simultaneously with the motherboard.

LA17–LA23

(Large Address) The contacts supply the seven high-order bits of the CPU address bus. Compared to the normal address contacts A0–A19 of the conventional XT bus, the signals at these contacts are valid much earlier, and may be decoded half a bus clock cycle in advance of the address bits A0–A19. Note that LA17–LA19 and A17–A19 overlap in their meaning. This is necessary because the signals on A17–A19 are latched and therefore delayed. But for a return of the signals $\overline{MEM\ CS16}$ and $\overline{I/O\ CS16}$ in time it is required that the address signals A17–A19 are also available very early.

SD8–SD15

(System Data) These eight contacts form the high-order byte of the 16-bit address bus in the AT.

$\overline{SBHE}$

(System Bus High Enable) If data is output onto or read from the high-byte SD8–SD15 of the data bus by the CPU or another chip, then $\overline{SBHE}$ is active and has a low level.

$\overline{MEM\ CS16}$

A peripheral adapter card must return a valid $\overline{MEM\ CS16}$ signal in time if it wants to be serviced with a data bus width of 16 bits. Using $\overline{MEM\ CS16}$, therefore, 8-bit and 16-bit adapters may be inserted into an AT slot without any problem. The AT bus logic recognizes whether the adapter must be accessed with 8 bits or 16 bits.

$\overline{I/O\ CS16}$

The signal at this contact has a similar meaning to MEM CS16. $\overline{I/O\ CS16}$ applies to I/O ports and not memory addresses.

$\overline{MEMR}$

(Memory Read) An active **MEMR**, (that is, low level) signal indicates that the processor or DMA controller wants to read data from memory with an address between 0 M and 16 M. On the other hand, the $\overline{SMEMR}$ signal in the XT slot only applies to the address space between 0 M and 1 M. With an address above 1 M $\overline{SMEMR}$ is inactive (that is, high).

$\overline{MEMW}$

(Memory Write) An active $\overline{MEMW}$ (that is, a low level signal) indicates that the processor or DMA controller wants to write data into memory with an address between 0 M and 16 M. On the other hand, the $\overline{SMEMW}$ signal in the XT slot only applies to the address space between 0 M and 1 M. With an address above 1 M $\overline{SMEMW}$ is inactive (that is, high).

IRQ10–IRQ12, IRQ14, IRQ15
These contacts transmit the hardware interrupt requests according to the channels IRQ10–IRQ12 and IRQ14, IRQ15 to the slave PIC on the motherboard. IRQ13 in the AT is reserved for the 80287 coprocessor, which is located on the motherboard. Therefore, this signal doesn't lead into the bus slots.

DRQ0, DRQ5–DRQ7
(DMA Request) With these contacts a peripheral on an adapter card may tell the system on the motherboard that it wants to transfer data via a DMA channel. Channel 0 of the first DMA chip is designed for an 8-bit transfer, the three additional channels 5–7, on the other hand, for 16-bit transfers. Channel 4 is used for cascading the two DMA chips.

$\overline{\text{DACK0}}$, $\overline{\text{DACK5}}$–$\overline{\text{DACK7}}$
(DMA Acknowledge) These four contacts are used for the acknowledgement of the DMA requests DRQ0 and DRQ5–DRQ7. Compared to the XT, $\overline{\text{DACK0}}$ has been replaced by $\overline{\text{REFR}}$ because the memory refresh is carried out via $\overline{\text{REFR}}$ in the AT.

$\overline{\text{MASTER}}$
The signal at this contact serves for bus arbitration. Thus, bus masters on adapter cards have the opportunity to control the system bus. For this purpose they must activate $\overline{\text{MASTER}}$, (that is, supply a low level signal). In the AT the integration of a bus master is carried out by an assigned DMA channel. Via this channel the bus master outputs a signal DRQx. The DMA chip cuts the CPU off the bus by means of HRQ and HLDA, and activates the $\overline{\text{DACKx}}$ assigned to the bus master. The bus master responds with an active $\overline{\text{MASTER}}$ signal and thus takes over control of the bus.

3.6.3 AT Bus Frequencies and ISA Bus

The concept and architecture of the AT have been very successful during the last few years. This makes it worse that no strictly defined standard for the bus system has actually existed. That became especially clear as the clock frequencies were increased more and more, and therefore problems with the signal timing became heavier. IBM never specified the AT bus in a clear and unambiguous way. All standards in this field are therefore rather woolly. For IBM that was not very serious, because Big Blue went over to the PS/2 series before its AT products exceeded the 8 MHz barrier. It was only after this barrier was broken that users of AT compatibles had to deal with bus problems. I have already mentioned that the bus slots run at 8.33 MHz at most, even in a 25 MHz AT. Before the AT manufacturers agreed to this strict definition, every manufacturer chose their own standard – not very pleasant for AT users. The consequence was that in many older turbo-ATs the bus as well as the CPU ran at 10 MHz or even 12.5 MHz. Such frequencies are only handled by a very few adapter cards. They cannot follow the clock, especially if the chips get warm after a certain time. A warmer chip usually has a lower operating speed, even if only a by few nanoseconds. This is enough, though, and the computer crashes. Things get even more confusing if we remember that the 8237A DMA chips and the 8259A PICs run at 5 MHz at most. Even the faster types only reach 8 MHz. Moreover, the timer chip is operated at 1.193180 MHz, namely 1/4 of the PC/XT base clock of 4.77 MHz, even in a 50 MHz i486 PC. That some misalignments and therefore unnecessary wait cycles occur with a

CPU clock of 25 MHz, a bus frequency of 10 MHz, a DMA frequency of 5 MHz and a timer frequency of 1.19 MHz seems to be obvious.

Seven years after presenting the AT the computer industry has become reconciled to a clearer, but unfortunately not very strict, standard for the AT bus. The result now is the *ISA bus* which is about 99% compatible with the AT bus in the original IBM AT. ISA is the abbreviation for *Industrial Standard Architecture*. Thus, ISA will really define an obligatory bus standard for all AT manufacturers.

This standard specifies that the bus slots should run at 8.33 MHz at most. If a 33 MHz i386 wants to access the video RAM, it must insert a lot of wait states. A reading bus cycle, for example, needs two bus cycles, but one bus clock cycle lasts four CPU clock cycles so that eight CPU clock cycles are necessary. If the memory on the graphics adapter has an (optimistic) access time of 80 ns, about five wait cycles are additionally necessary (the cycle time of a 80 ns DRAM lasts for about 150 ns, and the cycle time of the CPU clock is 30 ns; this leads to five wait cycles). If the two CPU cycles are subtracted, which a memory access always needs, then even with the optimum cooperation of a graphics adapter and a bus, eleven (!) wait states are necessary. Drivers, buffers etc. connected in between and misalignments may readily increase this value up to 20 wait cycles. The transfer rate with an ISA bus width of 16 bits is decreased to 3 Mbytes/s compared to a memory transfer rate of 66 Mbytes/s. A Windows window of 640*512 pixels with 256 colours is filled within 100 ms; a time period which is clearly recognized by the eye. No wonder that even 33 MHz i486 ATs do not always operate brilliantly with Windows. The enormous number of wait cycles during reads and writes from and to video RAM slows down the high-performance microprocessor. Whether the CPU needs some additional cycles for calculating a straight line is thus of secondary importance. Only special motherboards and graphics adapters where the video memory is (more or less) directly connected to the memory bus, and not accessed indirectly via the ISA bus, may solve this problem. But possibly Microsoft will «invent» a reasonable graphics interface for Windows that really exhausts the capabilities of the graphics processor on 8514/A and TIGA graphics adapters.

The bus frequency is generated by dividing the CPU clock, thus the ISA bus largely runs synchronous to the CPU. This is different, for example, from the microchannel, which uses its own clock generator for the bus so that the microchannel runs asynchronous to the CPU. The ISA bus also operates asynchronous cycles, for example if a DMA chip that runs at 5 MHz initiates a bus cycle. The big disadvantage of synchronous ISA cycles is that a whole clock cycle is lost as soon as an adapter becomes too slow even for only a few nanoseconds. Therefore, EISA enables the stretching of such cycles to avoid unnecessary wait states. Actually, a bus is much more than a slot on a motherboard.

Besides the layout of the bus slots and the signal levels, the ISA standard also defines the time period for the rise and fall of the address, data and control signals. But these properties are only important for developers of motherboards and adapter cards, therefore a vast number of signal diagrams and exact definitions are not given here. Signal freaks should consult the original ISA specification.

3.7 Interface to Hardware in Protected Mode – the ABIOS

All routines of the conventional Personal Computer BIOS are programmed in real mode, and therefore cannot be used by the 80286 in protected mode. Moreover, the BIOS was designed for a single tasking operating system so that every BIOS call must be completed before the BIOS routine returns control to the calling task. Thus the BIOS processes a call in one stage (also called *single-staged processing*). For fast executable functions such as reading the internal system clock, this is of no importance. But in a multitasking environment, processes that have to wait for the reaction of a rather slow hardware device (for example, the floppy drive) lock the PC. The time necessary to start the drive motors alone is nearly infinitely long for a fast-clocked 80286. The *ABIOS* (*advanced **BIOS***) has to solve these problems and to implement an interface to hardware for a multitasking operating system in protected mode. For calls that may last for a longer time, the ABIOS implements a so-called *multistaged processing*. Figure 3.27 shows a comparison of the various processing models for the conventional BIOS (also called *CBIOS*) and for the ABIOS.

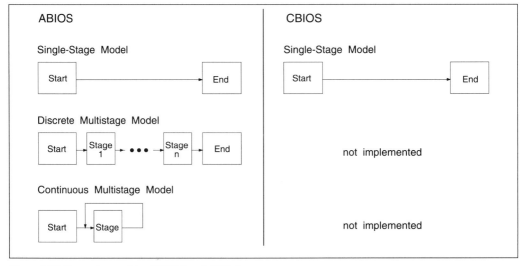

Figure 3.27: Processing models of CBIOS and ABIOS.

The CBIOS only implements the already mentioned single-staged model in the form of a *call-processing-return*. The call of a CBIOS function dedicates the CPU to the processing of this call. Only hardware interrupts are serviced. The ABIOS only uses the single-staged model for functions that can be completed at once, such as reading the internal system clock (here only an immediately executable memory access to the data structure of the system clock is necessary).

All other ABIOS calls proceed according to a discrete or continuous multistaged model, where each stage can be executed at once. All necessary wait processes are carried out between the individual stages, thus the CPU is not locked. For example, during an access to the hard disk, in one stage the seek instructions for the read/write heads are transferred to the controller. Then the ABIOS immediately returns control so that the CPU is available for another task. Once the drive has positioned the heads correctly, the controller issues an interrupt and the next stage of the ABIOS function is called. This example shows how the individual stages are called, that is, how the multistaged functions are driven. One possibility is a hardware interrupt that the accessed device issues if it is ready for the next function stage (floppy and hard disk drives, for example). Another possibility is the activation of individual stages after the elapse of a predefined time period (time period driven function). One example of this would be writing of the complete VGA colour register block, where only one register block is written during each stage.

Continuous multistaged functions are different from discrete ones in that after completing a stage, the same stage is called again in the next activation of the function. Thus, the continuous multistaged function is never terminated; it is always in a request state. Both multistaged models are only implemented by the ABIOS. The CBIOS only supports the single-staged model.

Every multistaged ABIOS function consists of three routines: start routine, interrupt routine, and time-out routine. The start routine is called if the corresponding function is started. The hardware interrupts assigned to the various stages, or the elapse of a predefined time period, activates the interrupt routine. A hardware time-out in interrupt-driven functions calls the time-out routine.

The ABIOS usually supports 16 devices and units that are defined by a corresponding ID number. Table 3.10 lists these devices and units. Additionally, the ABIOS uses the ID = 0 for internal function calls.

ID	Device/service	ID	Device/service
00h	internal ABIOS functions	0ah	NMI
01h	floppy drive	0bh	mouse
02h	hard disk drive	0ch–0dh	reserved
03h	graphics adapter	0eh	CMOS RAM
04h	keyboard	0fh	DMA
05h	parallel interface	10h	POS
06h	serial interface	11h	error tracking
07h	system clock	12h–15h	reserved
08h	real-time clock	16h	keyboard lock
09h	system functions	17h–ffffh	reserved

Table 3.10: Devices and units supported by the ABIOS

The call of ABIOS services is no longer carried out by registers, as was the case with the CBIOS. Instead, the ABIOS uses four data structures: function transfer table, device block, common data area, and request block. Every ABIOS service is assigned a *function transfer table*, which includes a table of pointers to the start, interrupt and time-out routines assigned to the ABIOS service. Additionally, it holds a table of pointers to the beginning of the individual functions of the ABIOS service. An ABIOS service is assigned a *unit block* corresponding to the serviced physical device that holds the interrupt and arbitration level of the hardware device, and other important information. In the *common data area* a table of pointers to the function transfer table and the device block of each ABIOS service is stored. Such a pointer pair in the table is identified by a unique ID. During ABIOS initialization the logical IDs are assigned. Calling programs use the logical IDs as an index to the common data area to call ABIOS services and functions. All function transfer tables, all device blocks and the common data area are generated and initialized during ABIOS initialization.

The *request block* constitutes the interface between the calling task and an ABIOS function. All input and output parameters are transferred via this data structure (for example, the logical ID, the function number, or the return code). Before a task can start an ABIOS function, it has to initialize the request block. The request block remains in memory until the call is completed, thus the request block takes over the job of the CPU registers for parameter passing (as is the case with the CBIOS). Table 3.11 lists the correspondences between ABIOS and CBIOS.

Process	ABIOS	CBIOS
parameter passing	request block	CPU registers
identification of the BIOS service by	logical ID	interrupt number
location of the BIOS service by	logical ID as an index into common data area	interrupt vector table
location of the BIOS function	vector in the function transfer table	internal jump table into CBIOS code

Table 3.11: Correspondences between ABIOS and CBIOS

Every ABIOS service has nine standard functions (see Table 3.12). The other numbers are available for device-dependent functions.

Number	Function
00h	standard interrupt handler
01h	return logical ID
02h	reserved
03h	read device parameters
04h	set device parameters
05h	reset/initialize
06h	activate
07h	deactivate
08h	read
09h	write

Table 3.12: ABIOS standard functions

After the calling task has initialized the request block, it can call the intended ABIOS function and pass control to the ABIOS. The actual call is then (for example, with OS/2) executed by the operating system function ABIOSCommonEntry or ABIOSCall. Readers interested in details on ABIOS should consult a programmer's reference for OS/2 (or another operating system) that uses the ABIOS.

4 The i386 – Entering the 32-Bit World

With the introduction of the i386, PC users could utilize power that not more than ten years before was available only on computers that filled a whole room! The significant performance jump from the 80286 to i386 is a result of doubling the register width to 32 bits. Data elements twice as large as on an 80286 can thus be processed at once; for example, you can multiply two 32-bit quantities with one MUL instruction – with an 80286 you need two MULs with a temporary storage of interim results. The prefetch queue has grown to 16 bytes, and can thus fetch more instructions for decoding in advance. This also increases the performance.

The memory management unit (MMU) already implemented in the 80286 has been expanded by a *paging unit* (*PU*). Together with an operating system that supports demand paging, undreamt-of possibilities are now available. But unfortunately, software development is nearly ten years behind the hardware. There are only a few operating systems such as UNIX or XENIX that use the 32-bit architecture and all the i386's advantages. The world's most popular operating system, DOS, uses virtually none of the advanced capabilities, being content with those functions already available on the 8086/88. All attempts to make more than 640 kbytes of application memory available for DOS with an i386 are pure nonsense, and nothing more! But unfortunately, we have to be compatible....

For the i386 an enhanced and more powerful mathematical coprocessor is available, the i387. It operates faster than its predecessor and strictly implements the IEEE 754-1985 standard for floating-point numbers. Besides Intel, Weitek, Cyrix and AMD have also developed floating-point accelerators for the i386. The i386 communicates with its environment via a 32-bit address and 32-bit data bus, thus it addresses a physical memory of 4 Gbytes and reads and writes data more quickly because of the wide data bus. On the other hand, the I/O address space is still limited to 64 k ports – the same number as for the 80286. Besides, the 8-bit and 16-bit ports, the i386 can also access 32-bit ports.

For compatibility reasons, the i386 can be operated in 8086 real mode. The processor then addresses 1 Mbyte of memory plus the lowest 64 kbyte in extended memory, behaving like a very fast 8086. The 32-bit architecture of the i386 can also be used in real mode; for example, you can access the EAX accumulator with its full width of 32 bits. The i386 protected mode is downwards compatible with the 80286 protected modes, but because of the larger physical address space of 4 Gbytes (compared to 16 Mbytes with the 80286), Intel defined additional and somewhat altered segment and gate descriptors. Further, the i386 can operate in a completely new mode, virtual 8086 mode. In this mode the processor calculates the address in the same way as in real mode, that is, it multiplies the segment value by 16 and adds the offset. However, because the virtual 8086 mode is embedded into protected mode, all protection mechanisms of the protected mode are available.

4.1 Terminals and Signals

Together with the control signals and supply voltages, the i386 needs 124 terminals. DIP and PLCC packages are no longer applicable, so the i386 comes in a *pin grid array package* with 132 pins. Pin grid arrays don't have pins or contacts on the side surfaces, but a corresponding number of pins on the bottom. Because of progess in the integration of electronic circuits, the connections of a chip, in most cases, occupy a larger area than the chip itself. Pin grid arrays occupy less area than all the other package types. Figure 4.1 shows the i386 pin assignment.

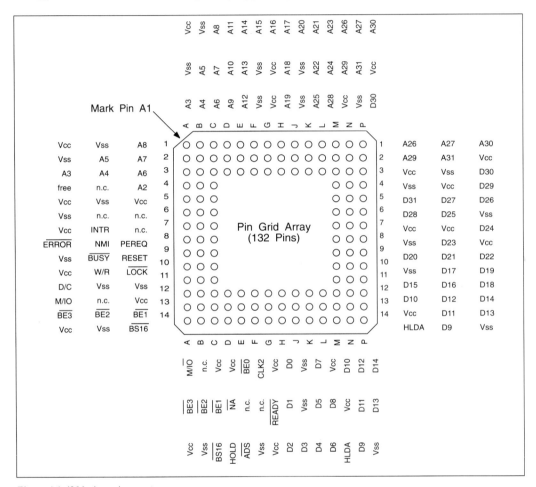

Figure 4.1: i386 pin assignment.

The terminals of the i386 are discussed below. To avoid any unnecessary repetition, only those new signals and pins or, compared to the 80286, altered ones are described.

CLK2
This pin is supplied with the clock signal. As for the 80286, the i386 also divides the clock signal internally by two to generate the effective processor clock.

D31–D0
These 32 pins form the bidirectional 32-bit data bus of the i386 for data input and output. By means of the $\overline{BS16}$ input the data bus may be configured as a 32- or 16-bit data bus. Note that

the i386 nevertheless drives all 32 signals during write operations, even if the bus size is set to only 16 bits.

A31–A2

These 30 pins form the 30 high-order bits of the 32-bit address bus. The two least-significant address bits A1 and A0 must be determined from the signals at the pins BE0–BE3.

BE0–BE3

(Byte Enable) The signals at these four pins indicate which bytes of the 32-bit data bus are active during the current bus cycle, that is, transfer valid data. $\overline{BE0}$ corresponds to the least significant data byte D0–D7, and $\overline{BE3}$ to the high-order data byte D24–D31. All combinations of the $\overline{BEx}$ (x = 0 to 3) are allowed as long as no inactive $\overline{BEx}$ is located between two active $\overline{BEx}$. If the i386, for example, outputs a word (2 bytes) via data pins D23–D8, then it sets $\overline{BE2}$ and $\overline{BE1}$ to a low level (active) and $\overline{BE3}$ and $\overline{BE0}$ to a high level (inactive). From $\overline{BE0}$–$\overline{BE3}$ you can determine the two least significant address bits A1 and A0 with no problem.

M/$\overline{IO}$, D/$\overline{C}$, W/$\overline{R}$

(Memory/IO, Data/Control, Write/Read) The signals at these pins indicate the type of the current bus cycle. The following combinations are valid:

```
(000) interrupt acknowledge sequence
(001) invalid
(010) read data from I/O port
(011) write data to I/O port
(100) fetch instruction from memory (prefetching)
(101) halt if /BE0=/BE1=/BE3=high, /BE2=low or shutdown if /BE0=low, /BE1=/BE2=/BE3=high
(110) read data from memory
(111) write data into memory
```

LOCK

If $\overline{LOCK}$ is active (low) the processor cannot release the local bus to another processor. The i386 doesn't respond with an acknowledge (HLDA) to a request.

ADS

(Address Status) The signal here indicates that the i386 outputs valid signals at the pins W/$\overline{R}$, D/$\overline{C}$ and M/$\overline{IO}$ that define the type of the current bus cycle and valid address signals at the pins $\overline{BE0}$–$\overline{BE3}$ and A31–A2. The computer system must ignore all bus definition and address signals if this signal is inactive, that is, at a high level.

NA

(Next Address) This signal is used for pipelined addressing. Low (active) indicates that the address decode system of the computer waits for new values for $\overline{BE0}$–$\overline{BE3}$, A2–A31, W/$\overline{R}$, D/$\overline{C}$ and M/$\overline{IO}$ and is ready to accept them for decoding even if the current bus cycle is not yet completed by a $\overline{READY}$. The i386 thus carries out pipelined addressing.

READY

The signal at this pin indicates whether the addressed peripheral system (for example, main memory or an I/O device) has completed the access ($\overline{READY}$=low) or needs some more time for this ($\overline{READY}$=high). With slow memories or peripherals the i386 can insert wait cycles flexibly.

This is carried out in the same way as on the 80286, that is, one wait state always lasts for one processor clock cycle or two CLK2 clock cycles.

$\overline{\text{BS16}}$

(Bus Size 16) If this pin is supplied with a signal with a low level then the i386 operates its data bus only with a width of 16 instead of 32 bits. The i386 can thus be connected directly to a system that has only a 16-bit data bus. No additional chips are necessary to divide a 32-bit quantity into two 16-bit quantities, or to combine two 16-bit quantities into one 32-bit quantity. With an 8086 and an 80286, for example, a 16/8-bit converter is necessary to enable an access to the XT slots with a data bus width of 8 bits by the processor with a 16-bit data bus.

HOLD, HLDA

(Bus Hold Request, Bus Hold Acknowledge) The signals at these pins serve for bus arbitration, that is, passing control of the local bus between various bus masters. If another bus master wants to take control it activates the i386 HOLD input. If the i386 can release control (that is, the release is not locked by an active $\overline{\text{LOCK}}$ signal) the processor responds with an HLDA signal to pass control of the local bus to the requesting bus master. The new bus master keeps the HOLD signal active as long as it needs control of the local bus. Afterwards, it deactivates HOLD and the i386 can take over the local bus again, for example to read data from memory.

$\overline{\text{BUSY}}$, $\overline{\text{ERROR}}$

These signals inform the i386 about the coprocessor's status. If $\overline{\text{BUSY}}$ is active then the coprocessor is currently executing an instruction and cannot accept another. If the $\overline{\text{ERROR}}$ signal is active, the i386 issues a coprocessor interrupt if it executes certain ESC or WAIT instructions.

PEREQ

(Processor Extension Request) The signal at this pin informs the i386 that data in the coprocessor is ready for transfer via the i386. The i386 carries out all data transfers including access checks and paging.

INTR

This input pin is checked after completing every instruction to determine whether a hardware unit interrupt request is pending. The check can be blocked (masked) by clearing the interrupt flag IE.

NMI

A transition of this signal from a low to a high level causes an interrupt 2. This interrupt cannot be masked by the interrupt flag IE. The i386 aborts program execution immediately after completing the current instruction.

RESET

If this input is on a high level for at least 15 clock cycles of CLK2, the processor immediately stops operation and carries out a processor reset.

V_{cc}

These pins are supplied with the supply voltage (usually +5 V).

GND

These pins are earthed (usually at 0 V).

4.2 New Internals

Besides expansion of the registers up to 32 bits and the implementation of a paging unit, the i386 implements additional features compared to the 80286, including the processor self-test at power-up and hardware support of debuggers, as well as somewhat altered protection mechanisms for the I/O address space. The following section gives more information on these subjects.

4.2.1 Processor RESET and Self-Test

If the processor is initialized or a processor reset is carried out, then the registers hold the values indicated in Table 4.1. The i386 starts program execution in real mode at the address fffffff0h. After the first JMP or CALL instruction beyond a segment border, the address lines A31–A20 drop to low. Then the i386 can only address objects below 1 M. After the reset and an eventual self-test, the DX register contains a 16-bit processor identification number with the value 03xxh. The high-order byte 03h indicates that the current processor is an i386. The eight bits xx indicate the i386 version. Usually, the value xx rises with newer i386 versions.

Register	Value			
EFLAG	uuuuuuuu uuuuuu00 00000000	00000010	=	uuuu0002h
CR0	0uuuuuuu uuuuuuuu uuuuuuuu	uuuu0000	=	uuuuuuu0h
IP	00000000 00000000 11111111	11110000	=	0000fff0h
CS	11110000 00000000	=	f000h*)	
DS	00000000 00000000	=	0000h	
SS	00000000 00000000	=	0000h	
ES	00000000 00000000	=	0000h	
FS	00000000 00000000	=	0000h	
GS	00000000 00000000	=	0000h	
DX	processor identification number			
all others	uuuuuuuu uuuuuuuu uuuuuuuu	uuuuuuuu	=	uuuuuuuuh
u: undefined				
*) base address = ffff0000h, limit = ffffh				

Table 4.1: Register values after a processor reset

Using a reset, the i386 can be directed to execute an internal self-test. This test is carried out by holding the $\overline{BUSY}$ pin on a low level for at least eight CLK2 clock cycles before and after the falling edge of the reset signal. The self-test checks the microcode ROM on the processor as well as a main part of the logic circuitry. To execute the self-test the i386 needs about 2^{19} clock cycles, which corresponds to about 20 ms with a 25 MHz i386. If the self-test has been completed without any error, the EAX register holds the value 0. Any other value indicates an internal processor error, that is, the chip is damaged.

4.2.2 General-Purpose Registers, Segment Registers and i386 Descriptors

Figure 4.2 shows all i386 registers accessible to the programmer. Besides these registers, the i386 has some further internal registers, for example the segment descriptor cache registers and others. You can see that among all those registers that are known from the 80286, only the general-purpose registers, flags and the instruction and stack pointers have grown to 32 bits. The segment registers still comprise 16 bits. Newly implemented in the i386 are the two segment registers FS and GS for addressing data, the control registers CR0–CR3, the debug registers DR0–DR7, and the test registers TR6 and TR7. The 80286 machine status word (MSW) is now embedded in the control register CR0.

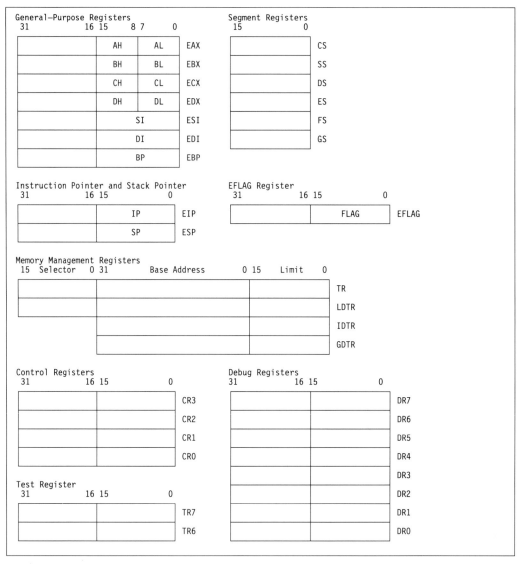

Figure 4.2: The i386 registers.

Among the 32-bit general-purpose registers EAX to EDX, the two low-order bytes may be accessed as 16-bit registers AX to DX. Further, the registers AX to DX are divided into a most significant register byte AH to DH and a least significant register byte AL to DL. From all other 32-bit registers, which represent an extension of the former 16-bit registers, the two low-order bytes can be accessed with the same name as for the 8086/80286. With the maximum size of the general-purpose registers of 32 bits, offsets with a length of 32 bits are now possible. These indicate values from 0 up to 4G–1. Thus, segments may be much larger with an i386 than with an 80286.

In protected mode the i386 uses the segment selectors in the segment registers (in the same way as the 80286) as an index to the descriptor table. While the structure of the segment selectors compared to the 80286 has not changed, some bits that were previously reserved are now used to reflect the 32-bit addresses of the i386. Figure 4.3 shows the format of an i386 segment descriptor.

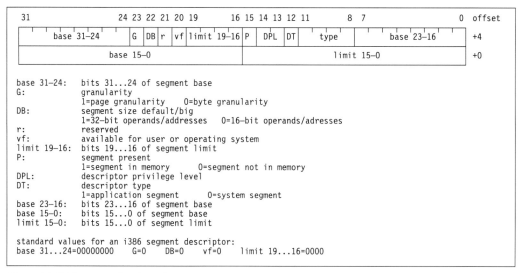

Figure 4.3: i386 segment descriptor format.

You can see that the most significant descriptor byte is no longer equal to 00000000, as was the case with the 80286, but indicates bits 31–24 of a 32-bit base. This extension was necessary because the i386 has a physical address space of 4 Gbytes compared to 16 Mbytes for the 80286. Because of the entry 00000000 in the field base 31–24, the i386 detects that an 80286 segment descriptor is present. Further, the entry limit has been extended by the four bits *limit 19–16*. For the interpretation of the limit, and therefore of the size of the segment defined by the descriptor, the granularity bit G is of major importance. With the G bit cleared the entry limit indicates the segment size in bytes. If G = 1 holds, then limit means the size in pages where one page occupies 4 kbytes (=4096 bytes).

Example: limit=1000, G=0:   segment limit 1000 bytes
                  limit=1000, G=1:   segment limit 1000*4kbyte=4,096,000 bytes

Thus with a cleared G bit, segments with a maximum size of $2^{20}*1$ byte (=1 Mbyte) are possible; but with a set G bit, segments that occupy up to $2^{20}*4$kbyte (=4 Gbytes) are available. Therefore, the complete address space of the 32-bit offset registers is only used with page granularity, but in this case the smallest allocation unit for a segment is already 4 kbytes, that is, memory is divided into segments in units of 4 kbytes. This is only favourable for larger systems. With a cleared G bit the maximum logical address space of a task on the i386 thus comprises 16 383 segments with 1 Mbyte each, that is, more than 16 Gbytes. With a set G bit the logical address space is 4096 times larger. It has nearly 64 Tbytes. To clarify this huge number: if every bit of these 64 Tbytes were to be represented by a grain of rice with a mass of 10 mg, then more than 5 trillion (5 000 000 000 000) tons of rice would be necessary. That's enough to feed mankind for 1000 years. Also closely related to the segment size is the *DB* bit, which indicates whether 16- or 32-bit operands are to be used as standard for a data segment defined by the descriptor, or whether 16- or 32-bit addresses are to be standard for a code segment defined by the descriptor. If DB = 0 the i386 uses 16-bit operands or 16-bit addresses. Note that in an 80286 segment descriptor, the DB bit is always equal to 0, thus 80286 code can be ported to the 32-bit architecture of the i386 with no problem. The i386 then uses all operands and addresses as 16-bit quantities. However, operands and addresses may also be enhanced by a so-called *operand size prefix 66h* or an *address size prefix 67h* for certain instructions if the DB bit is cleared.

The operand size prefix reverses the definition through the DB bit in the current *data* segment, and the address size prefix reverses the definition through the DB bit in the *code* segment. If DB is cleared (that is, the segment concerned operates with 16-bit quantities – operands or addresses), the prefixes force the i386 to use a 32-bit quantity instead of the usual 16-bit quantities. If, on the other hand, the DB bit is set, the segment operates with 32-bit quantities as standard, and the prefix advises the i386 to use a 16-bit quantity instead of the usual 32-bit quantities. Using the DB bit and the prefixes, the i386 doesn't need different opcodes for instructions, such as MOV, which sometimes process 16-bit and sometimes 32-bit quantities. The number of necessary opcodes is reduced, and therefore the instruction length is also reduced. For the same reason, the 80x86 in general uses segment override prefixes if another segment is to be used instead of the data segment DS for a data access.

Example: The opcode for the two instructions MOV eax, [01h] and MOV ax, [01h] is the
             same (10111000b). The i386 distinguishes them according to the DB bit and the
             operand size prefix. For the encoding example it is assumed that the DB bit
             in the code segment descriptor is cleared, that is, the i386 is operating
             with 16-bit displacements.

If the DB bit in the data segment descriptor is cleared, then in the first case the operand size prefix 66h must precede the opcode. Therefore the encodings are:

MOV eax, 01h: 66 b8 00 01
A 32-bit quantity at offset 01h is transferred into eax.

`MOV ax, 01h:`   `b8 00 01`

A 16-bit quantity at offset 01h is transferred into ax. If the DB bit in the data segment descriptor is set, then in the second case the operand size prefix 66h must precede the opcode because now the i386 uses 32-bit quantities as standard. Therefore, the encodings are:

`MOV eax, 01h:`   `b8 00 01`

A 32-bit quantity at offset 01h is transferred into eax.

`MOV ax, 01h:`   `66 b8 00 01`

A 16-bit quantity at offset 01h is transferred into ax.

In the *type* field of the segment descriptor (see Figure 4.3), more possibilities are available for a system segment (DT = 0) than for the 80286. Table 4.2 lists all system segment descriptors that are valid on the i386.

Type	Description
0	reserved
1	available 80286 TSS
2	LDT
3	active 80286 TSS
4	80286 call gate
5	task gate (286+386)
6	80286 interrupt gate
7	80286 trap gate
8	reserved
9	available 386 TSS
10	reserved
11	active 386 TSS
12	386 call gate
13	reserved
14	386 interrupt gate
15	386 trap gate

Table 4.2: i386 system segment types (DT=0)

It is clear that most gates and task state segments (TSS) differ between the 80286 and i386. The reason is the 32-bit architecture of the i386 which, for example, enables 32-bit offsets and 32-bit stack values. Details on the gates and TSS are indicated below.

The *vf* bit in the segment descriptor may be freely used by the user or the operating system. The i386 does not use this bit, and Intel did not reserve it for future use. All other entries have not changed in comparison to the 80286 segment descriptor.

Besides the segment descriptors, the gate descriptors also have changed when compared to the 80286, to support the 32-bit architecture of the i386. But for compatibility reasons, the i386 also supports all the 16-bit gate descriptors of the 80286. Figure 4.4 shows the format of the i386 gate descriptors. As you can see, the offset into the target segment has been extended to 32 bits.

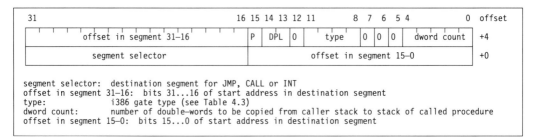

Figure 4.4: i386 gate descriptor format.

Furthermore, because of the 32-bit registers of the i386, not 16-bit words but 32-bit double-words are copied from the stack of the calling procedure to the stack of the called procedure. Thus, the field *dword count* indicates the number of double-words to copy. The calling mechanism via a gate and the meaning of the gates has remained the same. Table 4.3 lists all gate types valid for the i386.

Type	Description
4	80286 call gate
5	task gate (80286+i386)
6	80286 interrupt gate
7	80286 trap gate
12	i386 call gate
14	i386 interrupt gate
15	i386 task gate

Table 4.3: i386 gate types

The i386 task state segment has been altered in two ways: the i386 TSS has been adapted to the 32-bit architecture of the i386, and a second protection mechanism for the I/O address space has been introduced, which is implemented in the i386 TSS. Figure 4.5 shows the format of an i386 TSS.

For the two new segment registers FS and GS two new entries, FS selector and GS selector, are reserved. Moreover, the i386 TSS also stores the CR3 register, which indicates the base address of the page directory for the task described. The entry *I/O map base* indicates the address of an I/O map, which serves, besides the IOPL flag, for the protection of the I/O address space in protected mode.

Section 4.2.6 gives more information on this subject. By means of the 32-bit offset registers, all corresponding entries in the i386 TSS are expanded to 32 bits. The *back link* field (as in the 80286 TSS) contains a segment descriptor that points to the TSS of the previously interrupted task. This entry, however, is only valid if the NT (nested task) bit in the EFLAG register is set.

31	16	15	0	offset
I/O map base		0 0 0 0 0 0 0 0 0 0 0 0 0 0 0 T		+100 (64h)
0 0 0 0 0 0 0 0 0 0 0 0 0 0 0 0		LDT selector of task		+96 (60h)
0 0 0 0 0 0 0 0 0 0 0 0 0 0 0 0		GS selector		+92 (5ch)
0 0 0 0 0 0 0 0 0 0 0 0 0 0 0 0		FS selector		+88 (58h)
0 0 0 0 0 0 0 0 0 0 0 0 0 0 0 0		DS selector		+84 (54h)
0 0 0 0 0 0 0 0 0 0 0 0 0 0 0 0		SS selector		+80 (50h)
0 0 0 0 0 0 0 0 0 0 0 0 0 0 0 0		CS selector		+76 (4ch)
0 0 0 0 0 0 0 0 0 0 0 0 0 0 0 0		ES selector		+72 (48h)
EDI				+68 (44h)
ESI				+64 (40h)
EBP				+60 (3ch)
ESP				+56 (38h)
EBX				+52 (34h)
EDX				+48 (30h)
ECX				+44 (2ch)
EAX				+40 (28h)
EFLAGS				+36 (24h)
EIP				+32 (20h)
CR3 (PDBR)				+28 (1ch)
0 0 0 0 0 0 0 0 0 0 0 0 0 0 0 0		SS for CPL2		+24 (18h)
ESP for CPL2				+20 (14h)
0 0 0 0 0 0 0 0 0 0 0 0 0 0 0 0		SS for CPL1		+16 (10h)
ESP for CPL1				+12 (0ch)
0 0 0 0 0 0 0 0 0 0 0 0 0 0 0 0		SS for CPL0		+8 (08h)
ESP for CPL0				+4 (04h)
0 0 0 0 0 0 0 0 0 0 0 0 0 0 0 0		back link to preceeding TSS		+0 (00h)

Figure 4.5: i386 task state segment (TSS).

4.2.3 The EFLAGs

The flag register has also been enlarged to 32 bits to reflect the 32-bit architecture of the i386 and to provide enough space for the new flags necessary for virtual 8086 mode and debugger support. Figure 4.6 outlines the structure of the i386 EFLAG register.

Compared to the 80286, the *VM* and *RF* flags have been added, but the meaning of all the other flags has remained the same. To switch the i386 into virtual 8086 mode, the operating system must set the VM (**v**irtual **m**ode) flag to protected mode. This is only possible using a gate (Section 4.5 gives additional information on this). The RF (**r**esume **f**lag) controls restart after a breakpoint via the i386 debug registers. Readers interested in this subject will find more information in Section 4.2.5.

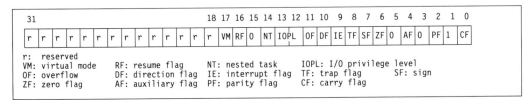

Figure 4.6: i386 EFLAGs.

4.2.4 Control and Memory Management Registers

The 80286 has only one control register: the machine status word (MSW), largely used to control the protected mode. Because of the newly added i386 paging unit, the i386 requires more control registers. In all, the i386 has four 32-bit control registers CR0–CR3. Figure 4.7 shows the structure of these registers.

The 80286 MSW is now included in the low-word of control register CR0, thus the meaning of bits TS, EM, MP and PE is the same as on the 80286. For compatibility reasons, the low-order word of the CR0 register can be further accessed by the instructions LMSW (load MSW) and SMSW (store MSW). Note that these instructions may not change or read the PG bit.

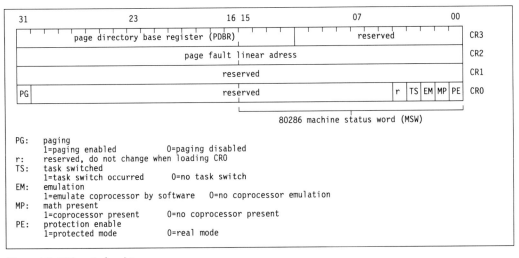

Figure 4.7: i386 control registers.

The *PG* bit activates (PG = 1) or disables (PG = 0) the paging unit (PU) of the memory management unit. With a deactivated PU no address transformation is carried out and the linear address after adding the offset and segment base is the physical address of the memory object. With an activated paging unit, though, the i386 carries out an additional address transformation besides memory segmentation to convert the linear address into a physical address. In Section 4.4 more information on this subject is given.

If you want to access the PG bit in the CR0 register or the new registers CR1–CR3, you must use a MOV instruction. Thus, the LMSW and SMSW instructions form (more or less) «sub-instructions» of MOV CR0, value and MOV value, CR0, respectively.

Example: Switch the i386 into protected mode by setting the PE bit in CR0.
1st possibility: MOV CR0, 0001h ; set PE bit by a MOV instruction with 32–bit operand
2nd possibility: LMSW 01h   ; set PE bit by an LMSW instruction with a 16–bit operand

If paging is active, the i386 stores the 20 high-order bits of the page directory address (the first order page table) in the control register CR3. If a page fault occurs during the course of executing an instruction, the i386 stores the linear address that caused the page fault in register CR2. Section 4.4 discusses the page directory, page table and page fault further.

Besides the control registers, the i386 (like the 80286) has four additional memory management registers (see Figure 4.8). Their structure and function is identical to that of the 80286. Important information on these registers is given in Section 3.3.

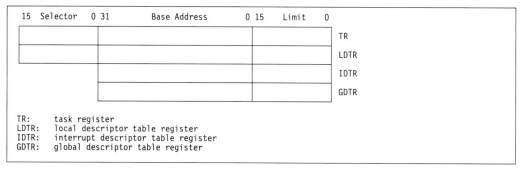

Figure 4.8: Memory management registers.

Here I also want to mention test registers TR6 and TR7. These are used for testing an internal buffer, the so-called *translation lookaside buffer (TLB)*. The TLB serves for caching page table entries when paging is active. Because these are far-reaching hardware concepts that are not guaranteed by Intel for future processors, readers interested in this subject should consult an original manual.

4.2.5 Debug Registers

Debugging in a multitasking environment is very delicate because a program has to be investigated while several other programs are running, and without those programs being affected by breakpoints, register alterations and other debugger influences. Real mode debuggers often overwrite the byte at an intended breakpoint with the code 11001100 of the instruction INT 3. If program execution reaches such a breakpoint, the processor issues an interrupt 3, which is caught by the debugger. To continue program execution the debugger overwrites the code 11001100 with the byte originally stored at this location. But in protected mode a major problem arises: all code segments are implicitly non-writeable, that is, the debugger may neither replace the original byte by the opcode 11001100 of INT 3, nor can it cancel this replacement to continue program execution without causing a protection error. A further disadvantage is that access to certain data areas cannot be detected by the strategy indicated above, although this would be very advantageous for detecting pointers in a program.

To alleviate the problems with debugging in protected mode mentioned above, Intel has equipped the i386 with eight debug registers DR0–DR7. These enable debugger support on a hardware level. Thus efficient debugging is possible in protected or virtual 8086 mode. Figure 4.9 shows the structure of the debug registers.

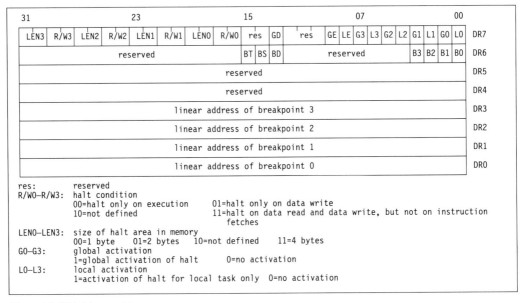

Figure 4.9: i386 debug registers.

The following briefly explains the meaning of the register entries. If you wish to look more closely at this interesting i386 hardware aspect, I recommend that you refer to a detailed i386 programmer's reference book (there is not enough room in this book to describe all the details).

Up to four breakpoints can be defined. The linear address of the four chosen breakpoints is stored in the *debug address registers* DR0–DR3. Debug registers DR4 and DR5 are reserved for future use. With *debug status registers* DR6 and DR7 you can control the i386's behaviour upon reaching a breakpoint for each breakpoint separately. For every breakpoint, entries R/W0–R/W3 separately define under which circumstances the i386 issues a debug exception according to Interrupt 1. You can choose from instruction execution, read data and write data. In a similar way, entries LEN0–LEN3 define the breakpoint «size» separately for every breakpoint. With bits G0–G3 you can globally activate the breakpoints. Then the i386 issues a debug exception if a task references the memory location indicated. This is advantageous if you wish to investigate the cooperation of several tasks. With bits L0–L3, on the other hand, you may activate the breakpoints locally. Then the i386 issues a debug exception only if a certain task references the memory location indicated. Entries GD, BT, BS and BD are used to control the restart of program execution after a debug exception, and to investigate its cause.

4.2.6   i386 Protection of the I/O Address Space with the IOPL Flag and I/O Permission Bit Map

In the i386 the I/O address space is globally protected in the same way as for the 80286, by means of the IOPL flag in the EFLAG register. A program accesses the I/O area with instructions IN, INS, OUT and OUTS, and executes the instructions STI and CLI only if its current privilege level (CPL) is at least the I/O privilege level (IOPL), that is, CPL ≤ IOPL must hold. Note, however, that each task has its own EFLAGs, and therefore each task may have another value for IOPL.

Moreover, the i386 employs a further protection mechanism for access to the I/O address space, the *I/O permission bit map*. It is stored in the TSS of the task concerned, thus different tasks can have different I/O permission bit maps. The entry *I/O map base* in the TSS descriptor indicates the offset within the TSS where the I/O permission bit map begins. The map occupies the area between the offset and the end of the TSS which is defined by the limit entry in the i386 TSS descriptor. The space between the entry I/O map base and the beginning of the I/O permission bit map may be used by the operating system to store its own information. Fig 4.10 shows the principle of the I/O permission bit map in the i386 TSS. Note that the most significant byte of the map (that is, the byte immediately below the end of the TSS) must be equal to 11111111b (=0ffh). For the I/O permission bit map only an i386 TSS can be used; an 80286 TSS is not allowed.

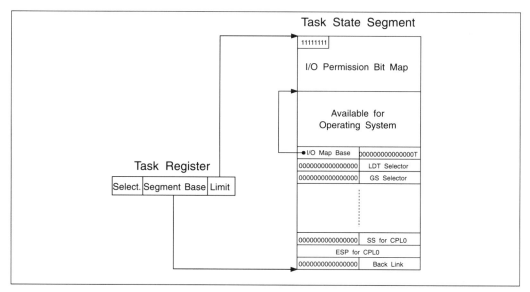

Figure 4.10: The I/O permission bit map in an i386 TSS. The i386 protects the I/O address space not only via the IOPL flag, but additionally by means of the I/O permission bit map. It is stored in the i386 TSS. A set bit protects the corresponding port and issues an exception if an illegal access attempt occurs.

A valid I/O permission bit map is always present if the I/O map base in the TSS indicates a location within the TSS. If the base value points beyond the TSS, the i386 ignores all checks concerning the I/O permission bit map, and the access protection for the I/O address space is carried out by the IOPL flag alone.

Thus the I/O permission bit map more or less represents a second level access protection: if the CPL and IOPL values allow an access to the I/O address space of the active task, the i386 additionally checks the I/O permission bit map to determine whether the intended port may really be accessed. This check is carried out based on a one-to-one assignment of the I/O address and the corresponding bit in the map. The port with address 0 is assigned the bit with offset 0 within the map, the port with address 1 is assigned the bit with offset 1, etc. If the bit corresponding to a certain port is set (equal to 1), the i386 issues a «general protection error» exception if this port is accessed. If the bit is cleared (equal to 0), the processor continues with the I/O operation.

The length of the map thus defines the number of ports additionally protected in this way, so it is not necessary for the I/O permission bit map to cover all I/O addresses. All I/O ports not covered by the map are automatically assigned a set bit, that is, an access to ports outside the map always leads to an exception. In the PC, for example, it is sufficient to cover the lower 3ffh ports by a map. An access to ports with higher addresses issues an exception. To cover the complete I/O address space, (64 k ports)/(8 bits per byte) + (8 bits 11111111), that is, 8193 bytes are necessary.

Note that 16-bit ports are assigned two successive bits and 32-bit ports are assigned four successive bits. Only if all two or four assigned bits are cleared simultaneously is the i386 able to continue I/O operations. But if only one of these bits is already equal to 1, the processor issues an exception.

```
Example: The bit map is   11111111 11001101 00110000 11010100
                          └───┬──┘ └──────────────┬──────────┘
                          end of map              map

1st case: 8-bit ports
protected ports:     2, 4, 6, 7, 12, 13, 16, 18, 19, 22, 23;
unprotected ports:   0, 1, 3, 5, 8, 9, 10, 11, 14, 15, 17, 20, 21
2nd case: 16-bit ports
protected ports:     2, 4, 6, 12, 16, 18, 22
unprotected ports:   0, 8, 10, 14, 20
3rd case: 32-bit ports
protected ports:     0, 4, 8, 12, 16, 20
unprotected port:    8
```

The 8-bit, 16-bit and 32-bit ports may be mixed, of course, depending on at which address an I/O device with the corresponding register width is located.

The virtual 8086 mode doesn't use the IOPL flag; protection of the I/O address space is solely carried out by the I/O permission bit map. The I/O behaviour of the 8086 can thus be emulated for an 8086 program running in the environment of a protected mode operating system.

4.3   The Flexible i386 Bus – 16-Bit Data Bus, Write Data Duplication and Pipelining

From Section 2.8 you already know that Intel developed an 8086 variant with an 8-bit data bus (the 8088) because of the lack of 16-bit support chips when introducing the 8086 into the market. Similarly, when introducing the i386 with a 32-bit data bus the 32-bit support chips were very expensive or even unavailable. Because of the very fast development of microelectronics, though, it could be estimated that only a short time after presenting the i386, 32-bit support chips would become available at a reasonable price. Thus (and for other reasons, too) Intel implemented a very flexible data bus for the i386 that can be operated either at 16 bits or at the full width of 32 bits. Further, the i386 can be connected to a 16-bit and a 32-bit data bus simultaneously because the switching need not be carried out by fixed wiring, but can be chosen individually for every bus cycle. Thus it is possible, for example, to operate the i386 for an access to main memory with a 32-bit data bus, and for an access to the I/O address space with a 16-bit data bus.

If a low level signal is applied to the $\overline{BS16}$ pin, the current bus cycle is limited to the 16 lower bits D15–D0 of the data bus. Addressing via $\overline{BE2}$ and $\overline{BE3}$ that applies to the 16 high-order bits D31–D16 of the data bus is correspondingly redirected to the low-order bits D15–D0. If values are to be transferred that have more than 16 bits, the i386 carries out several bus cycles in succession until the data transfer is complete.

$\overline{BE3}$	$\overline{BE2}$	$\overline{BE1}$	$\overline{BE0}$	D31–D24	D23–D16	D15–D8	D7–D0	duplication
low	low	low	low	b31–b24	b23–b16	b15–b8	b7–b0	no
low	low	low	high	b23–b16	b15–b8	b7–b0	undef.	no
low	low	high	high	b15–b8	b7–b0	b15–b8	b7–b0	yes
low	high	high	high	b7–b0	undef.	b7–b0	undef.	yes
high	high	high	low	undef.	undef.	undef.	b7–b0	no
high	high	low	low	undef.	undef.	b15–b8	b7–b0	no
high	low	low	low	undef.	b23–b16	b15–b8	b7–b0	no
high	high	low	high	undef.	undef.	b7–b0	undef.	no
high	low	low	high	undef.	b15–b8	b7–b0	undef.	no
high	low	high	high	undef.	b7–b0	undef.	b7–b0	yes

b31–b24: write data bits 31–24   b23–b16: write data bits 23–16
b15–b8: write data bits 15–8   b7–b0:   write data bits 7–0
undef.: value is undefined

Table. 4.4: i386 write data duplication

A further feature of the i386 for enhancing system throughput is the automatic duplication of write data. By means of the signals $\overline{BE0}$–$\overline{BE3}$, the processor determines which 8-bit groups of its 32-bit data bus transfer valid data. If the i386 starts a bus cycle for writing data where the write data arises on the high-order word (D31–D16) of the data bus only (that is, only $\overline{BE2}$ and $\overline{BE3}$ are active), the i386 automatically outputs the same data on the low-order half, D15–D0, of the data bus. In a system with a 16-bit data bus, the throughput can be enhanced independently of $\overline{BS16}$, because usually the 16/32-bit converter of the 16-bit bus system has first to transfer the data bytes from the high-order half of the data bus to the low-order half. With the automatic write data duplication, this transfer is unnecessary and the bus system thus runs more quickly. If the write data is output on the low-order half of the data bus (that is, D15–D0 only), no write data duplication onto the high-order half occurs. Table 4.4 lists the connection between the $\overline{BE0}$–$\overline{BE3}$ signals and the write data duplication.

With the 80286 we have already come across pipelined addressing. With the i386 the system designer can choose addressing either with or without pipelining. This choice may be made flexibly and separately for every bus cycle during processor operation using the $\overline{NA}$ signal. Thus the i386 may be switched between an access with and without pipelined addressing. Figure 4.11 shows three 0-wait-state read cycles without (Figure 4.11a) and with (Figure 4.11b) pipelined addressing.

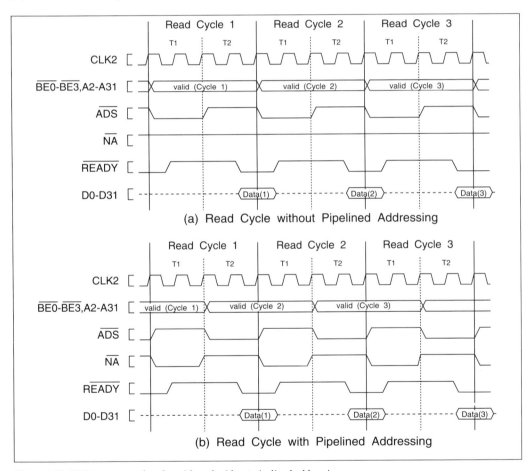

Figure 4.11: i386 memory read cycles with and without pipelined addressing.

You can see that without pipelined addressing the $\overline{NA}$ signal is always on a high level, that is, inactive. The address signals $\overline{BE0}$–$\overline{BE3}$ and A31–A2 are output at the begining of the read cycle and are valid until the end of this cycle. The time period between the output of the address signals and the transfer of the data (that is, the access time) is about three CLK2 cycles.

In a read cycle with pipelined addressing the i386 is instructed by the $\overline{NA}$ signal with a low (that is, active) level to output the address signals during the second half of the preceding bus cycle. Thus the read cycles are interleaved: by the earlier output of the address signals, the decode logic of the memory system may operate in advance while the addressed memory chip reads the data from an internal memory cell. The period between address output and data delivery is five CLK2 cycles, in this case, therefore two more CLK2 cycles (or one internal processor clock cycle) are available. Stated differently: the number of wait cycles for an access to memory can be reduced by one, or slower memory chips may be employed without increasing the number of wait states.

Pipelined addressing is thus very advantageous for access to slower memory chips. In general, the i386 runs with pipelined addressing in an access to slow DRAM chips. If a cache memory with very short access time is implemented, however, no pipelined addressing is necessary because the SRAM chips of the cache are fast enough to deliver the data without pipelined addressing at 0 wait states.

4.4 Paging

Besides the 32-bit architecture, a significant extension of the i386 from the 80286 is the implementation of a paging unit in the memory management unit. The features of paging and the new possibilities that arise are described in the following sections.

4.4.1 Logical, Linear, Physical Addresses and Paging

With the 32-bit offset registers and the 16-bit segment registers the i386 has a logical address space of 64 Tbytes per task. Because the base address in the segment descriptors is 32 bits wide, these 64 Tbytes are mapped to an address space with 4 Gbytes at the most. The combination of the segment's base address and the offset within the segment in the address adder leads to a so-called *linear address*. This means that the address indicates the address of a memory object in a linear fashion. Thus, with a larger address you find the memory object higher up in memory. The segment number, that is, the segment selector, doesn't indicate linearity. A selector larger in value may directly point to a segment at the lowest segment address. Mapping the 64 Tbytes onto the 4 Gbytes is possible because not all segments of the 64 Tbytes must be actually present (P bit of the segment descriptors). The rest may, for example, be swapped onto a (really very large) hard disk.

If all 32 i386 address lines are used, this linear 32-bit address can be converted to a *physical address*, which in turn has 32 bits. Then, each address in the logical address space of 4 Gbytes corresponds to a memory object in one of these countless memory chips – countless because to realize a physical memory of 4 Gbytes, without taking into acount the chips for the parity bits, 32,768 (!) 1 Mb memory chips are necessary. The chips alone weigh 164 kg (at 5g/chip) and cost (even with a bulk discount) about $150,000. No computer, except for massively parallel computers like the Connection Machine with its 65 536 processors, comes into such a category. For a PC, such storage is nonsense (even with Windows and OS/2).

Typical i386 PCs are presently equipped with 4 Mbytes. This is not very much for extensive database applications, DTP or powerful graphics programs. Such memories may generate data amounts internally that exceed the computer's available main memory.

We have already met one possibility to enlarge the virtual address space beyond the actual physical memory during the discussion on protected mode and the segment descriptors connected to it. In the segment descriptors a P (present) bit is available which indicates whether the segment is actually in memory. If the processor attempts to access a segment whose P bit is cleared (that is, the intended segment is not in memory), the «segment not present» exception is issued. Now the operating system can load the segment concerned into memory, and give the instruction the chance to access the segment again. It is therefore possible to generate more segments for a program than may simultaneously fit into the memory. The swapped segments are only loaded if needed. If not enough space is available in memory, one or more other segments must be swapped to make memory available for the newly read segment.

But now new problems arise. The data may only be swapped and loaded segment-by-segment. Further, the size of the segments coincides with the size of the data structures they hold. The data segment for an extensive drawing or the code segment of a powerful program module may be very large. On the other hand, the data segment that is the address text for a letter, or a code segment that holds a simple procedure, is usually very small. If a large segment is now to be loaded from the hard disk into memory, then possibly numerous small segments must be swapped. This is becoming very awkward, particularly if only one byte or word has to be accessed in the loaded segment but then immediately afterwards an access to the code or data in one of the segments just swapped takes place. The segment must be swapped again and the code or data segment reloaded. If the program needs data from the data segment that has just been swapped again, then everything has to be carried out again from the beginning, etc. You can see what this means in the case of a 1 Mbyte database segment: a long coffee break!

Another problem arises with low memory configuration: for the database segment there remains only that memory which has been left by the operating system, drivers, system tables and at least one code segment of the current program. If the swapped segment is larger than this remaining memory, it is impossible to read the whole segment into memory.

Thus the operating system has to do a lot of things: determine what segment it is best to swap, whether the now available memory is sufficient, eventually swap another segment, etc. The swapping process is very slow.

By now, though, you have surely guessed that a better method exists: *paging*. Because all segments must be present in the physical memory, which is usually much smaller than 4 Gbytes, the base addresses of all the segments are also within the address space of the physical memory. With a main memory of, for example, 4 Mbytes, all base addresses are lower than 4 M, that is, the complete linear address space between 4 Mbytes and 4 Gbytes is not used. In other words, about 99.9% of the linear address space remains unused. A lot of memory for many, many segments!

Paging maps a very large linear address space onto the much smaller physical address space of main memory, as well as the large address space of external mass storage (usually a hard disk). Hard disks, though, rarely have a capacity that corresponds to the i386 virtual address space. This mapping is carried out in «portions» of a fixed size called *pages*. In the case of the i386, a page size of 4 kbytes is defined (this size is fixed by processor hardware and cannot be altered). Thus the complete linear address space consists of one million pages. In most cases, only a few of them are occupied by data. The occupied pages are either in memory or swapped to the hard disk. Whether the i386 actually uses this paging mechanism is determined by the PG bit in the CR0 register. If the PG bit is set then paging is carried out; otherwise it is not. Because the operating system must manage and eventually swap or reload the pages, it is not sufficient to simply set the PG bit. The i386 hardware only supports paging analogous to the protection and task switch mechanisms. The operating system must intercept the paging exceptions and service them accordingly, look for the swapped pages, reload them, etc.

Thus a double address mapping is carried out in the i386. The segment and offset (virtual address) of a memory object are combined to form a linear address in the linear 4 Gbytes address space corresponding to one million pages. Then, these one million pages corresponding to the linear address are converted into a physical address or an exception «page not present» for reloading the page concerned.

4.4.2 Page Directory, Page Tables, Page Frames and CR3 Register

To determine a linear address from a segment and an offset one needs information as to where the segment concerned begins. This information is stored in the descriptor tables. Two levels of such tables exist: the global descriptor table (GDT) forms the «root directory», where the local descriptor tables (LDT) may arise as «subdirectories». The address of the descriptor tables is stored in the GDTR and LDTR, respectively. With the information held, segment and offset can be combined into a linear 32-bit address, which is used unaltered as the physical address.

Let us assume, for example, that we have a PC with an i386 processor and 4 Mbytes of main memory: the segment begins at 1b0000h and the offset is d23a0h, thus the linear address is 2823a0h. Therefore, the byte with number 2 630 560 or 0000 0000 0010 1000 0010 0011 1010 0000b is addressed. Because main memory is limited to 4 Mbytes, the ten most significant address bits are always equal to 0, that is, the address is always 0000 0000 00xx xxxx xxxx xxxx xxxx xxxx. Instead of x a hex-number between 0 and f is present.

The mapping between the linear and physical addresses is similarly implemented by a two-level directory and a register, which indicates the «root directory». One table defines the mapping of the linear to the physical address. For this, another interpretation of the linear address is required (see Figure 4.12).

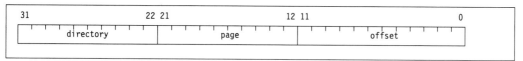

Figure 4.12: Linear address with paging.

If paging is active then the ten most significant bits of the linear address indicate the number of the page table concerned in the page directory, which corresponds to the current linear address. The following ten bits define the number of the page within the page table. Finally, the 12 low-order bits specify the offset within the thus defined page directly and unaltered. A linear address is thus mapped onto a physical address, where *directory* indicates a page table, *page* a page within this page table, and finally, *offset* an offset within this page (see Figure 4.13). This could also be expressed in the following manner: paging remaps the 20 high-order address bits onto new values, while the twelve low-order address bits are accepted in an unchanged manner.

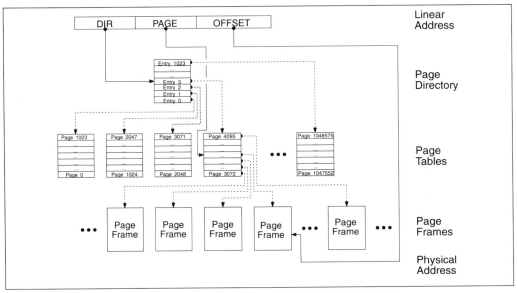

Figure 4.13: Mapping of linear address onto a physical address. After combining segment and offset, the resulting linear address is separated into a 10-bit page directory address, a 10-bit page address, and a 12-bit offset if paging is active. Each page holds 4 kbytes, so the whole address space is divided into one million 4 kbyte blocks.

The reason for two page table levels is immediately apparent. Every page table entry occupies four bytes (see Figure 4.14). If each page (with 4 kbytes each) of the 4 Gbyte linear address space corresponding to one million pages were to be mapped by means of a single page table in memory, then a memory of 4 Mbytes capacity would be necessary just for the page tables. Implementing two levels, on the other hand, enables the process to manage the second level page tables in the same way as pages, because they occupy 4 kbytes, as «normal» pages do. Thus, the second level page tables may be swapped like normal pages. Only the page directory with its 4 kbytes must be held in memory all the time. Its base address is stored in the CR3 register.

Like the page directory, the page table holds 1024 (1 k) entries with a length of four bytes each, in this case, page table entries. Figure 4.14 shows the structure of such a page table entry.

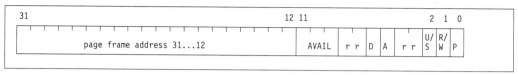

Figure 4.14: Page table entry.

The P (page present) bit indicates whether the page concerned is actually in memory (P = 1) or swapped (P = 0). In the latter case, the remaining 31 bits of the page table entry hold information on where the page is located on the hard disk or other mass storage device. The following entries have no meaning in this case.

If the page is in memory (P = 1), the 20 high-order bits define the address of the *page frame*. A page frame is a memory area with the size of a page (4 kbytes) that holds the data of a page. The addresses of such page frames are always multiples of 4096 (1000h): 0, 4096, 8192, ... or 0000h, 1000h, 2000h, ... You are free to imagine this pictorially as a «frame» (of a picture, for example). In the same way, a sheet («page») with information may be inserted into a frame; the paging mechanism inserts pages with various contents into the page frames. The frames remain the same (and are located on the same wall, to follow the metaphor through), but the information is changed.

The paging mechanism therefore replaces the 20 high-order address bits in the physical 32-bit address by these 20 bits of the page frame address. The twelve least significant bits of the physical address indicate the offest of the memory object within that page. The twelve low-order bits in the page table entry, on the other hand, serve to manage the page. If paging is active the i386 combines the 20 page frame address bits and the twelve offset bits of the linear address into a physical 32-bit address. If the page is swapped (P = 0) the i386 issues a «page fault» exception corresponding to interrupt 0eh. Now the paging routine of the operating system can load the required page into a free or freed page frame.

You may wonder how this works with memory objects such as double-words that don't fit into one page but overlap with another page.

Example: a double–word (4 bytes) at offset fffdh (decimal 4094). The two low–order bytes of the double–word are stored in the two high–order bytes of the page. But the two high–order bytes of the double–word are already held by another page which, moreover, may be swapped.

Recall that the i386 always accesses memory at addresses 0, 4, 8, ... If a double-word does not begin at such a double-word boundary, then the i386 carries out two memory accesses, which each start at a double-word boundary. In the above-mentioned example; the last four bytes of the page are thus accessed, in which the two high-order bytes of the double-word are stored. Then the processor accesses the first four bytes of the other page. If this page is not present in memory, it is reloaded. Thus the processor can also access the two least significant bytes of the double-word. The granularity of the pages with 4 kbytes therefore gives rise to no difficulties.

The advantages compared to swapping complete segments are obvious. The smaller sections with 4 kbytes each can be reloaded or stored very quickly. Further, programs usually access data that is quite close together. Even with the rather small page size of 4 kbytes compared with the linear address space of 4 Gbytes (a factor of one million), the probability is high that the intended data is already present in memory. For large segments, only those parts that are currently processed or executed must be loaded. A complete swapping and immediate reloading, as described above, does not occur with paging. The computer therefore runs much faster.

One could be of the opinion that the new address conversion that is necessary with paging, in addition to forming the linear address from the segment and offset, may lead to delays for address determination. This is not true in most cases, however. The i386 contains a cache memory where the last used page table entries are stored. This cache memory is called the *translation lookaside buffer* (*TLB*). Only if a page table entry is to be used that is not present in the TLB, and thus has to be reloaded from memory, is the address translation delayed by the memory access. But if the page table with the entry is swapped onto disk, the access takes much more time because the page table first has to be loaded into memory, and its entry must be read into the processor. Using intelligent algorithms in the operating system for managing page tables and their entries, this case rarely occurs and there are only a few delays. The gain of a very large linear address space compared to a small physical one by means of paging is really very significant.

For the management of pages and the second order page tables, several bits are reserved in the page table entries (see Figure 4.14). If the processor has accessed a page once (that is, if it reads or writes data), the A (accessed) bit in the corresponding page table entry is set. If the operating system regularly clears these A bits it may determine which pages are used often. Thus it only swaps the less used pages to cause as few read and write accesses of the hard disk drive as possible. Therefore, paging runs with hardly any delay.

The D (**d**irty) bit characterizes pages whose contents have been altered, that is, overwritten. If this bit is cleared the page need not be written onto disk when swapped, because there is still an unaltered former copy of that page on the disk. If the D bit is set, however, the operating system detects a change of data and writes (as well as information for relocating the page on disk) the data of the page itself onto the disk.

As is the case for segments, pages can also be protected against an access by programs. Unlike the segments (where four privilege levels 0–3 are available), the protection mechanism for pages only implements two levels: user and supervisor. Programs with privilege levels CPL = 0 to CPL = 2 (that is, operating system, device drivers and operating system extensions) use the supervisor level. Application programs, on the other hand, usually have the user privilege level. The privilege level of pages is indicated by the U/S (user/supervisor) bit, therefore U/S = 0 holds for operating system, system software, etc. (CPL = 0, 1, 2) and U/S = 1 holds for application code and data (CPL = 3).

With the R/W (read/write) bit, pages are marked as read-only (R/W = 0) or as readable and writeable (R/W = 1). A violation (for example, a write access to a read-only page (R/W = 0) leads to a «page fault» exception. The three AVAIL bits are available for the operating system to manage the pages; all other bits are reserved.

By means of segmentation and paging, a double address conversion is carried out in the i386. With segmentation the base address of the segment concerned is determined according to the descriptor tables and segment descriptors, and by adding the offset a linear address in a large linear address space is formed. Paging translates this linear address to a physical address for the much smaller physical address space, or to a «page fault» exception. This process is shown in Figure 4.15. Because of the segment descriptor cache register and the translation lookaside buffer, this translation is carried out in most cases without any delay.

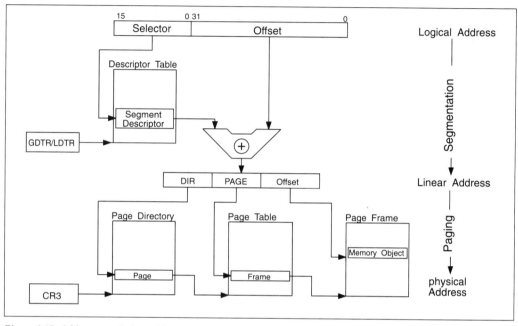

Figure 4.15: Address translation with segmentation and paging.

4.5 The i386 Virtual 8086 Mode – Myth and Reality

With the i386 a new operating mode was introduced which, as was the case for the 80286 protected mode, led to some confusion and a few myths. In the following sections I want to try to clarify the virtual mode. Together with the paging mechanisms, extensive capabilities for multitasking are available even for programs that are actually unable to use multitasking (what a contradiction!).

The incentive for the implementation of the virtual mode came from the enormous variety of program for PCs running under MS-DOS, which is a purely real mode operating system. Remember also that powerful i486 PCs with MS-DOS always operate in real mode, and therefore use only the first of all the 4,096 Mbytes of the 32-bit address space. Moreover, neither the extensive protection mechanisms of the protected mode nor the i386 paging mechanisms are used. Therefore, the virtual mode now enables the execution of unaltered real mode applications, as well as the use of protected mode protection mechanisms. The *virtual 8086 tasks* may run in parallel with other virtual 8086 tasks or i386 tasks, that is, *multitasking* with programs not designed for multitasking is taking place. 8086 programs running with MS-DOS are not designed for multitasking because DOS as the operating system is *not reentrant*. If a DOS function is interrupted by an interrupt, which in turn calls a DOS function, then the PC frequently crashes because after an IRET the original stack is destroyed. Because of this, the programming of resident (TSR) programs is very complicated. By means of the virtual mode and paging these problems can be avoided.

4.5.1 Virtual Machines and Virtual 8086 Monitor

In virtual mode the i386 hardware and the *virtual 8086 monitor* constitute a so-called *virtual machine*. The virtual machine gives the program or user the impression that a complete computer is dedicated to its use alone, even if it is only a member in a multiuser environment. The complete computer, for example, has its own hard disk, its own tape drive, or its own set of files and programs. Actually, the system may generate and manage many of these virtual machines. The system divides the physically present hard disk into sections each dedicated to one of the virtual machines. Thus, the user has the impression that he/she is in possession of a complete hard disk.

With a multiuser system such as UNIX/XENIX, many users can work on the computer. But every user has the impression that he is currently the only one. A mainframe succeeds with more than 1000 (!) such users. In a single-user system with multitasking such as OS/2, virtual machines are not generated for several *users*. Instead, the system generates its own virtual machine for each *task*. Because virtual machines are only serviced for a short time period, multitasking occurs. Thus, for example, a compiler, the printer spooler and an editor may run in parallel. Windows/386 or Windows 3.0 (and higher) on an i386, as well as the 32-bit version of OS/2, use such virtual machines on the basis of the virtual 8086 mode to execute real mode applications in parallel.

The virtual 8086 monitor is a system program that generates and manages the virtual 8086 tasks. For this purpose, the i386 hardware supplies a register set by means of a TSS, as well as a virtual memory area mapped to the first Mbyte of the task's linear address space. Additionally, the processor executes the instructions that apply to these registers and the address space of the task. It is the job of the virtual 8086 monitor to observe the interfaces of the virtual machine or the virtual 8086 task to the outside world. The interfaces are formed by interrupts, exceptions and I/O instructions. This monitor ensures that the virtual 8086 machine is embedded in the larger i386 system running in protected mode without disturbing other tasks or even the i386 operating system.

4.5.2 Entering and Leaving Virtual 8086 Mode

The i386 is switched to virtual mode when the *VM* (*virtual* **machine**) flag in the EFLAG register is set. This is only possible by code of privilege level 0, a task switch by means of an i386 TSS, or an IRET instruction that pops the EFLAGS with a set VM bit from the stack. (An 80286 TSS does not change the high-order word of the EFLAG register where the VM flag is located.) The i386 leaves virtual mode when the VM flag is cleared. This is carried out by an i386 TSS and an interrupt or exception which calls a trap or interrupt gate.

In virtual mode all 8086 registers, and additionally the new i386 registers like FS, GS, debug registers, etc., are available. Further, the new instructions implemented by the 80186/286/386 (for example, BOUND, LSS, etc.) can be used. A switch to virtual 8086 mode, however, is only possible if the i386 is already operating in protected mode. A direct entry from real mode to virtual 8086 mode is not possible. If the VM flag is cleared to leave virtual 8086 mode, the processor returns to protected mode to execute other (protected mode) tasks.

4.5.3 Addresses in Virtual 8086 Mode

The main incompatibility between real and protected mode is the different address determination methods. In real mode the value of the segment register is simply multiplied by 16. In protected mode, however, the segment register is used as an index to a table, where the «real» address of the segment is stored.

If the i386 now enables execution of 8086 applications in virtual 8086 mode, then it must determine the address in the same way as the 8086 running in real mode. In virtual 8086 mode the i386 generates the address by multiplying the segment register value by 16 and adding the offset. Note that the i386 recognizes 32-bit offset registers but the 8086 does not, therefore virtual 8086 tasks may generate linear 32-bit addresses by means of the address override prefix. If the value of an i386 offset register exceeds 65 535 (or ffffh) in virtual 8086 mode, the i386 issues a pseudo-protection exception 0ch or 0dh without supplying an error code. As is the case with the 80286, the combination of segment ffffh and offset ffffh leads to an address 10ffefh. In virtual 8086 mode the 1 Mbyte boundary is thus also broken through by about 64 kbytes.

4.5.4 Tasks in Virtual 8086 Mode

To form a virtual machine with the i386 that executes an 8086 application we need the following, as well as the i386 hardware:

– an 8086 program (real mode),
– a virtual 8086 monitor,
– operating system functions for the 8086 program.

Let us look at the example of an editor for MS-DOS; this is the 8086 program. The virtual 8086 monitor is part of the protected mode operating system for the i386. Further, the editor needs operating system functions to open and close files which, up to now, have been carried out by DOS.

These three parts together form a *virtual 8086 task*, which is represented by an i386 TSS. Thus, the virtual 8086 task can be called in the same way as a task designed especially for protected mode, that is, by a task switch via the i386 TSS. Multitasking with a previously single-tasking program (here the MS-DOS editor) takes place.

The virtual 8086 monitor runs in protected mode with a privilege level of 0, and it contains routines for loading the 8086 program and for handling interrupts and exceptions. On the other hand, the «actual» 8086 program runs with a privilege level of CPL = 3. As is the case with real mode, in virtual 8086 mode the first 10fff0h bytes of the i386 linear address space (of 4 Gbytes or 100 000 000h bytes) are also occupied by the 8086 program. Addresses outside this area cannot be generated by the 8086 program, so that the addresses beyond 10ffefh are available for the virtual 8086 monitor, the i386 operating system and other software.

For the virtual 8086 task, only the operating system functions of the 8086 operating system (MS-DOS, for example) are missing. There are two options for their implementation:

– The 8086 operating system runs as a part of the 8086 program, that is, the 8086 program and MS-DOS (for example) together form one virtual 8086 task. Thus, all operating system functions required are automatically available.

– The 8086 operating system is emulated by the i386 operating system, or is already implemented as a part of it.

The advantage of the first option is that the previous real mode operating system can be used in a nearly unaltered form. Every virtual 8086 task has its own MS-DOS copy (or the copy of another real mode operating system) exclusively dedicated to it. Several different operating systems may therefore run in an i386 machine: the overall i386 operating system for protected mode programs as well as the various 8086 operating systems for 8086 programs in virtual 8086 mode. But there remains a serious problem: the operating system functions of MS-DOS and other systems are called by means of interrupts; and interrupt handlers are very critical sections of the *i386* operating system, which runs in protected mode. The way in which the problem is solved is described below.

If several virtual 8086 tasks are to run in parallel, their coordination is easier if we use the second option above. In this case, the real mode operating system of the 8086 tasks is emulated by calls to the i386 operating system in most cases.

In protected mode, the I/O instructions are sensitive as to the value of the IOPL flag. A value of CPL above IOPL gives rise to an exception. In virtual 8086 mode, these I/O instructions are not sensitive to the IOPL flag, however. Protection of the I/O address space is carried only by means of the I/O permission bit map. Instead, the instructions PUSHF, POPF, INTn, IRET, CLI and STI now respond to the IOPL value, as the instructions PUSF, POPF, CLI and STI may alter flags. In the wider i386 environment, with possibly several virtual 8086 and protected mode tasks running, changing flags is the job of either the virtual 8086 monitor or the i386 operating system alone.

Because of the dependency of the INTn and IRET instructions on IOPL, the virtual 8086 monitor may intercept operating system calls from the 8086 program via interrupts. If the value of IOPL is lower than 3 (that is, lower than the CPL of the 8086 program), the monitor intercepts the interrupt. If the 8086 operating system is part of the 8086 program, the monitor hands the interrupt over to it. Call and result may eventually be adapted to the i386 environment. Alternatively, the monitor may emulate the function of the 8086 operating system concerned directly. Remember, however, that interrupts in real and protected mode appear very different.

Because the 8086 program has been written for an 8086 processor (or an 80286/i386 in real mode), the virtual 8086 task has an interrupt vector table in real mode format. It starts at linear address 00h and occupies 1 kbyte. The i386 doesn't use this table in virtual 8086 mode directly.

Instead, during an 8086 program INT instruction the i386 first calls the corresponding operating system handler by means of the IDT, and thus leaves virtual mode. As usual, the i386 pushes the EFLAGS onto the stack, thus the called handler can determine whether the VM flag has already been set (that is, whether the interrupt has interrupted a virtual 8086 task). If VM is set, the interrupt handler transfers control to the virtual 8086 monitor. Now this handler may service the interrupt on its own, or it may pass control to the interrupt handler of the 8086 program again. For this purpose it investigates the interrupt vector table of the interrupted 8086 task to locate the entry point of the real mode interrupt handler. Using IRET, the i386 switches back to virtual 8086 mode and calls this handler. The IRET instruction of the real mode handler leads to the virtual 8086 monitor again. After realigning the stacks for the return it executes an IRET. The i386 thus continues the interrupted program. Here the interrupt has been serviced by the real mode handler of the 8086 task by means of the IDT – monitor – handler detour.

Many MS-DOS programs set and clear the IE interrupt flag to control the servicing of hardware interrupts while executing critical code sections. An i386 operating system responsible for the whole machine may not tolerate such an intervention, of course. Therefore, the instructions PUSHF, POPF, CLI and STI are also dependent upon IOPL. The virtual 8086 monitor intercepts such instructions that affect the response of the whole system, and handles them in a way which doesn't influence the larger i386 system in a disadvantageous way. The intervention of the monitor concerning the IOPL-dependent instructions for the 8086 program is completely transparent, though: the 8086 program gets the impression that these instructions have been executed conventionally.

A further very critical section for multitasking systems is the I/O ports, because they access the registers of the hardware elements. This is another area where the i386 operating system may not allow any tricks from the 8086 program, but many real mode programs actually access I/O ports directly. In multitasking systems, however, most programs are only allowed to access I/O ports via the operating system that coordinates the accesses. In virtual mode this problem is solved by protecting the critical ports with the I/O permission bit map, but not with the IOPL flag. The virtual 8086 monitor may therefore allow the 8086 programs to access uncritical I/O ports directly. If, for example, an 8086 program configures an adapter for the control of a robot and the adapter's registers are not used by any other program, conflicts never occur. The detour via the operating system would only give rise to delays, but doesn't provide any advantages. On the other hand, critical ports like the registers of the video or hard disk controller are protected by the map. The virtual 8086 monitor intercepts such accesses, and handles them so that the other tasks in the system are not affected.

4.5.5 Paging and Virtual 8086 Mode

As long as only one task is running, no problems arise concerning the use of main memory. The first 10fff0h bytes of the linear address space are reserved for the virtual 8086 task. The operating system and all other tasks occupy the addresses above. But what happens with the video memory? Many 8086 programs directly write into the video RAM to speed up text and graphics output, and they prefer to do this from the upper left to the lower right corner for the whole screen. If several tasks running in parallel output data onto the screen, a hopeless confusion is the result. This is especially true if some of these tasks output data in text mode and others output it in graphics mode (and, very likely, using various graphics modes). These problems led to the development of the Presentation Manager for OS/2 or Windows, which supplies a unique interface to the screen for all programs. An older 8086 program, of course, doesn't know anything about this!

The solution for this problem is paging; the address space reserved for the video RAM (see Figure 1.29) can be mapped to a video buffer in main memory. This video buffer forms a «virtual» screen. Then the virtual 8086 monitor can decide which data in the video buffer is actually transferred to which location in the real video RAM. It is thus possible to assign an 8086 program a window on the screen for data output. For this purpose, the data need not even be available in the same form. The virtual 8086 monitor, for example, may convert the data delivered by the 8086 program in text mode into a graphics representation suitable for output in a Windows window or OS/2 Presentation Manager window.

In most cases, 8086 programs don't occupy all the memory that is available with MS-DOS. Thus, a further advantage of paging even with only one virtual 8086 task is that the unoccupied sections of the 10fff0h bytes can be used by other tasks. Without paging, the memory chips at the free locations are not filled with data, yet are unavailable for the storage of data and code for other tasks. As already mentioned, the 8086 program of a virtual 8086 task occupies the lower 10fff0h bytes of linear address space. If several virtual 8086 tasks run in parallel they must be swapped completely during a task switch to avoid the collision of the address and data of the various tasks. The only option to solve these problems is the i386 paging mechanism.

Each of the various virtual 8086 tasks must map the lower 10fff0h bytes of linear address space to different physical address spaces. This can be achieved by different page table entries for the first 10fff0h bytes corresponding to 272 pages with 4 kbytes each for the individual virtual 8086 tasks. Thus the individual virtual 8086 tasks, and therefore also the 8086 programs, are isolated. Additionally, the other advantages of paging, for example, a large virtual address space and protection of the pages, can be used. If the 8086 programs do not alter the 8086 operating system (that is, they don't overwrite its code), then several 8086 programs may share one copy of the 8086 operating system and the ROM code. The program code always remains the same, but the differences of the 8086 operating systems for the individual tasks are only the different values of registers CS, IP, SS, SP, DS, etc. These register values are stored in the TSS of the individual virtual 8086 tasks, and therefore define the state of the codes for the individual tasks without the need for several operating system codes. Therefore, a very economical use of the available memory is possible.

In the case of a bug in an 8086 program, it is possible that the 8086 operating system has been overwritten erroneously. Thus, an error in one program also affects the execution of another. This is a clear violation of the i386's protection philosophy! It can be avoided by marking the pages for the 8086 operating system in the page table as read-only (R/W = 0) so that any write attempt leads to an exception. If the attempt is a legal update of an 8086 operating system table, the monitor can carry out this job. If an illegal attempt to write occurs, the monitor aborts the 8086 program. Program errors can therefore be detected very quickly.

A destruction by overwriting the 8086 program or the 8086 operating system which is exclusively dedicated to the task concerned is not very serious. Only the erroneous program crashes. The virtual 8086 monitor, on the other hand, remains operable if one of the following precautions has been observed.

–   The first 10fff0h bytes of the linear address space are exclusively reserved for the 8086 program and the 8086 operating system. Addresses beyond this section cannot be generated without issuing an exception.

–   The pages of the virtual 8086 monitor are marked as a supervisor (U/S = 0) in the corresponding page table. Because the 8086 program of the virtual 8086 task always runs at CPL = 3, corresponding to the user level, the monitor cannot be overwritten. Any attempt to do this leads to an exception, which is intercepted by the monitor to abort the erroneous 8086 program.

In real mode with MS-DOS the programmer can easily bypass the operating system. For example, the programmer can directly manipulate the interrupt vector table to redirect an interrupt to a program's routine. Usually, function 25h of interrupt 21h is available for this. For a virtual 8086 task a very delicate situation thus arises. While the virtual 8086 monitor can intercept a change by means of the DOS interrupt, and therefore a change of the interrupt vector table, it does not recognize anything in the case of a direct overwrite (with MOV, for example). If the monitor emulates the 8086 operating system, the altered interrupt is possibly not serviced correctly because the monitor handles the interrupt in the original manner. 8086 programs do not always run correctly in the compatibility box of OS/2. This is especially the case for programs where the programmer has used his detailed knowledge about Personal Computers and DOS to construct a particularly fast and tricky program. That the i386 operating system or the virtual 8086 monitor is also tricked is obvious, but it was not intended by the programmer.

The virtual 8086 mode is a very powerful tool that leads to greater (and easier) compatibility with older real mode programs, thus enabling multitasking without the need to completely rewrite all programs. That not every nuance and each DOS trick is handled correctly should really be expected.

4.6 The Floating-Point Accelerator i387

Unlike the 80286, the i386 also recognizes 32-bit numbers but like its predecessor, it lacks the floating-point format. Therefore, for mathematical applications employing floating-point numbers a numerical coprocessor is necessary. For the i386 this is the i387 (what else?). The i387 is a major advance in comparison to the 80287. It performs mathematical calculations far more quickly and strictly implements the IEEE standard for floating-point numbers. The new 80287 version, the 80287XL, is internally nearly identical to the i387, but operates with only a 16-bit data bus and a much lower clock frequency. The i387 has a 32-bit data bus for data transfer between CPU and coprocessor, and is available for clock frequencies between 16 MHz and 40 MHz.

As is the case with the 80287, the i387 accesses memory only via the CPU. All numbers are represented internally by 80-bit floating-point numbers. During the execution of load and store instructions, the i387 automatically carries out the format conversions required.

To keep the power consumption of the i387 as low as possible it is implemented using CMOS technology, therefore it draws only 1.5 W. That is less than its ancestor the 8087, which has a power consumption of about 2.5 W. In conventional NMOS technique the power consumption would be at least ten times higher. The resulting 15 W would make the chip heat up, and the chip would burn.

4.6.1 i387 Connections and Signals

Figure 4.16 shows the pin assignment of this «accelerator» for floating-point applications.

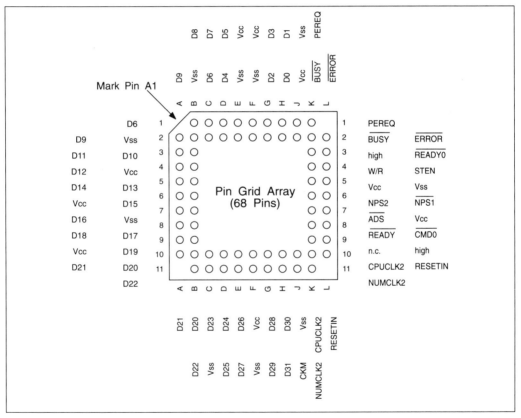

Figure 4.16: i387 connections.

The i387 terminals are discussed below. To avoid any unnecessary repetition, only new or altered (compared with the 80287) signals and pins are described. If you are unfamiliar with some points, study Section 3.1 first.

CPUCLK2

This pin is supplied with the external clock signal CLK2 of the CPU. The i387 uses CLK2 for the time-period coordination of its bus control logic. If CKM is set to a high level, the i387 runs synchronous to the CPU, and the other coprocessor components are also clocked with this signal.

NUMCLK2

If CKM is set low the i387 operates in an asynchronous mode, and uses the signal at this input for clocking all components except the bus control, which always runs synchronously. The ratio of NUMCLK2 and CPUCLK2 must be in the range between 0.625 and 1.400.

CKM

If this pin is on a high level (V_{cc}) the i387 runs in synchronous mode, that is, all components are clocked with CPUCLK2. If the mass potential is applied to this pin, only the bus unit uses the external processor clock CLK2; all other components are clocked by NUMCLK2. In this case, an additional clock generator is necessary.

D31–D0

These 32 pins form the bidirectional data bus for data exchange between the CPU and coprocessor.

$\overline{ADS}$

(Address Strobe) The signal at this pin, together with $\overline{READY}$, indicates when the i387 bus unit can check the W/$\overline{R}$ signal and the chip select signals of the CPU, that is, when the i386 supplies valid address signals. Generally, the $\overline{ADS}$ pin of the coprocessor is connected to the CPU's $\overline{ADS}$ pin.

STEN

(Status Enable) The signal at this pin selects the coprocessor chip. If STEN is active the i387 responds to the other addressing signals M/$\overline{IO}$, A31, A2, W/$\overline{R}$, $\overline{ADS}$ etc. from the CPU. For the possible combinations (STEN $\overline{NPS1}$ NPS2 $\overline{CMD0}$ W/$\overline{R}$) of the coprocessor control signals, the following meanings hold:

```
(0xxxx) i387 not selected
(11xxx) i387 not selected
(1x0xx) i387 not selected
(10100) i387 control or status word is read
(10101) opcode is written to the i387
(10110) data is read from the i387
(10111) data is written into the i387
```

STEN is mainly used for on-board checking of chips in systems incorporating an i387. If STEN is inactive the i387 can be completely deactivated for test purposes. It behaves as if it were physically not present.

PEREQ

(Processor Extension Request) An active signal (that is, a high level signal) at this pin indicates that the i387 expects data from the CPU, or that data is ready for output to the i386. As soon as all bytes have been transferred, the i387 disables the signal to inform the i386 about the completion.

READYO
(Ready Output) The i387 activates the signal at this pin so that write cycles are completed after two clock cycles and read cycles after three clock cycles. Thus, $\overline{\text{READYO}}$ indicates when an i387 bus cycle can be completed if no additional wait cycles are required. This is necessary because different ESC instructions last for different times before, during or after the operand transfer.

The meaning and function of all other pins are the same as for the 80287 coprocessor, so they are not repeated here.

4.6.2 Differences and Similarities between the i387 and 80287

When compared with the 80287, the i387 includes several new instructions. The i387 is able, for example, to evaluate sine and cosine, as is the new 80287XL. The differences mainly concern the formats and handling of infinite values by the i387. These points have been already mentioned in Chapter 3 in connection with the 80287XL.

The internal i387 registers are the same as those of the 80287 or 80287XL. The structure of the i387 control word coincides with that of the 80287XL, but the normal 80287 has an additional flag for handling the control of infinite values. In the i387 and 80287XL, such values are always handled in the affine sense, that is, as ±∞. The condition codes and the handling of exceptions has remained the same as in the 80287.

The memory image of the instruction and data pointers differs in two respects from those in the 80287. By means of the 32-bit registers in the i386, the format is also enlarged up to 32 bits. Additionally, the registers with the instruction and data pointers are no longer located inside the coprocessor (as is the case with the 80287), but inside the CPU. As a programmer you don't recognize this change because their storage and reading is carried out by the same ESC instructions. Therefore, you have the impression that the registers are located inside the coprocessor.

The only difference between real and protected mode in the i387 is that during the course of a pointer read or write, the real mode or protected mode format of memory addresses must be fetched or stored. Thus, not only the 80286 but also the 80287 had to be switched to protected mode to execute a program in protected mode that uses the coprocessor. With the i387 this is no longer required, as the i387 operates in real and protected mode in the same way.

Because the pointer registers are located inside the CPU, which is always aware of the current operating mode, the i386 carries out a pointer read or write without intervention from the coprocessor. The i387 only transfers data, not addresses, to the CPU, thus it need not be switched into protected mode to support the special address translation of the protected mode. For compatibility reasons, the i387 further «supports» the FSETPM instruction by ignoring it: no «invalid opcode» error message is issued.

Figure 4.17 shows the memory image format for 16- and 32-bit pointers in real and protected mode.

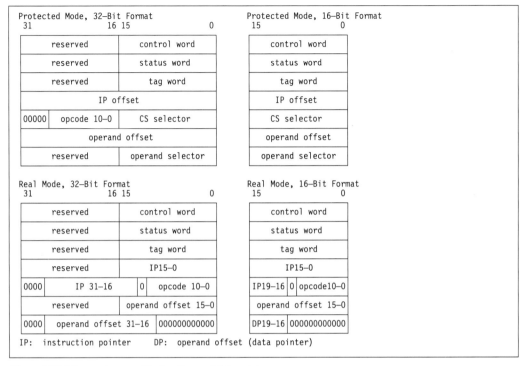

Figure 4.17: Memory images of instruction and data pointer.

4.6.3 Communication Between CPU and Coprocessor

The i387 is always supplied with the external CPU clock signal CLK2 to clock the bus unit, thus the bus unit runs synchronous to the CPU. For data exchange between processor and coprocessor, the i387 supports bus cycles with as well as without pipelined addressing. As is the case with the 80287, data exchange between i386 and i387 is carried out via reserved I/O ports, here outside the normal I/O address space. Table 4.5 gives the I/O addresses used by the i386, as well as the corresponding registers. The processor communicates with them by means of the assigned ports.

80386 I/O port	80387 register
800000f8h	opcode register
800000fch	operand register

Table 4.5: Coprocessor port addresses

Because of the leading «8» it can be seen that the i386 activates the address line A31 to access the coprocessor. But for an access to the normal I/O address space only the 16 low-order address bits are available (that is, A15–A2 as well as $\overline{BE3}$–$\overline{BE0}$). The two ports are 32-bit ports because the i387 is directly connected to the local 32-bit bus of the i386, and the data exchange among

CPU and coprocessor is carried out via the local data bus with a width of 32 bits. Figure 4.18 shows the i386/i387 system configuration.

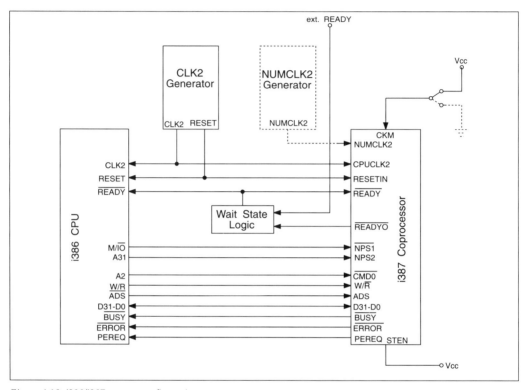

Figure 4.18: i386/i387 system configuration.

The processor addresses the i387 by means of the signals M/$\overline{\text{IO}}$, A2, W/$\overline{\text{R}}$, $\overline{\text{ADS}}$ and A31 (the most significant address bit). Data transfer is then carried out by the 32-bit data bus D31–D0. The STEN pin is always supplied with the supply voltage to activate the coprocessor. The wait state logic generates wait cycles for the CPU, and uses the coprocessor's $\overline{\text{READYO}}$ signal as well as other READY signals (from peripherals or slow memory components, for example) for this purpose.

4.7 Caching – Cooperation with High Speed Memories

Fast-clocked processors of course need fast memories. Where is the advantage of a 33 MHz CPU if it has to insert five wait cycles with every memory access? Today's DRAM chips have access times of 60–120 ns. That is too long for a 33 MHz clock frequency, especially if one considers the DRAM cycle time. One way out of this is SRAM chips with an access time of typically 20–25 ns. For supercomputers, high performance SRAMs are available that have an access time of only 12 ns, a time period in which an airplane traveling at 560 miles per hour moves no more than

0.003mm or one tenth of the diameter of a hair per second. SRAM chips, however, are much more expensive and far larger than DRAMs.

4.7.1 The Cache Principle

Caching now attempts to combine the advantages of fast SRAMs and cheap DRAMs to achieve a memory system that is as efficient as possible. Figure 4.19 shows the cache principle.

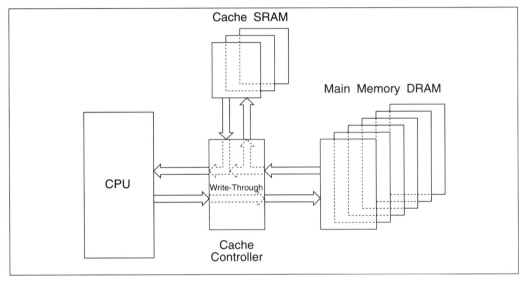

Figure 4.19: The cache principle. Between CPU and the main memory DRAM is interposed a fast cache SRAM which temporarily stores frequently used data and supplies it to the CPU in a short time.

Between the CPU and the main memory a cache unit is interposed, which comprises a cache controller and a cache SRAM. Typically, the cache memory is 10–100 times smaller than the main memory. Because most successive memory accesses refer only to a relatively small address area, the frequently accessed data is held in a small high-speed memory. Thus, one uses the advantage of a very short access time which, summed up over the many adjoined memory accesses, leads to a significant increase of the memory's access speed. Most of the data is rarely accessed successively, therefore it is possible to store the lion's share in the slow main memory without significantly decreasing the performance. The cache principle with a small high-speed memory and a large but slow main memory reconciles the advantages of both memories without exploding the costs.

If the CPU reads data it outputs the corresponding memory address to the cache controller. This controller determines whether the data is present in the cache SRAM. If this is the case, then a so-called *cache hit* has occurred. If, on the other hand, the data is only held in main memory, then this is a *cache miss*. In the former case, the cache controller reads the data required from the fast cache memory and transfers it to the CPU. Because of the high speed of the SRAM and cache controller, fast-clocked CPUs can also be supplied with data without any wait cycles. If a cache miss occurs, on the other hand, then the cache controller first has to read the data from the main memory. For this purpose, it indicates by an inactive READY signal that CPU wait cycles are necessary, and addresses the main memory. Because of the internal cache organization, generally several data bytes (a so-called *cache line*) is read from the main memory into the cache SRAM. The data byte addressed by the CPU is immediately handed over to the CPU. Thus, the cache controller is intelligent enough to issue bus cycles for reading data from memory on its own.

If the CPU writes data then the cache controller also determines whether this data is present in the SRAM. If it is the data is written into the cache SRAM. Unlike a read access, a cache miss is ignored here (that is, the cache controller does not carry out any bus cycles to transfer the data with the address indicated from the main memory into the SRAM). A CPU write process with a cache hit always also leads to a data transfer to main memory. This is called *write-through*. Depending on the system architecture, other cache strategies are possible, for example, data is only written into main memory if it is not present in cache memory, or in a write access the data from main memory is copied into the cache SRAM if a cache miss occurs. The above indicated write-through strategy is generally used for smaller computer systems today, and the PC caches exclusively use this method. The i486 on-chip cache can carry out various cache strategies that are mainly implemented with a multiprocessor environment in mind.

If other system elements also have an access to main memory (this is the case for DMA, for example) and can overwrite the main memory contents, the cache controller must invalidate any SRAM data whose counterpart in main memory has been overwritten. This is called *cache invalidation*. If the cache controller does not carry out the write-through strategy, but writes data from the CPU only into the cache SRAM, then in the case of a cache hit the cache's contents must be transferred to the main memory under certain circumstances. This is the case if, for example, a DMA chip is about to transfer data from the main memory to a peripheral and the current values of this data is present only in SRAM. This process is called a *cache flush*.

Software caches implemented on your PC will have similar properties. DOS, for example, uses internal buffers for floppy and hard disk accesses. You may define the number of such internal buffers by means of the CONFIG.SYS command BUFFERS. These buffers serve as a cache between CPU, main memory, and the floppy or hard disk controller. They don't use a write-through strategy so that in a system crash some data which has not yet been written to disk may be present in the buffer. Only once the file concerned is closed, or the buffer is required for another file or record, does DOS actually write the buffer contents onto disk. With the functions 0dh, 5d01h and 68h of INT 21h, you can force DOS to carry out a cache flush. Most software caches for hard disks (for example, former versions of SMARTDRV that emulate a cache for hard disk accesses) in main memory, on the other hand, use a write-through strategy. All write processes are thus handed over to disk but a read only accesses the copy in main memory. Newer versions of SMARTDRV.SYS use the write-back strategy. In this case, write accesses are effective for the disk at a later time as soon as the write-back can be carried out without affecting other programs.

Unlike the write-through strategy, writing one value with a cache system employing the *write-back strategy* doesn't immediately give rise to a main memory access if a cache hit occurs. Instead, the value is only written into the cache. Later, the cache controller also writes the new value into the slow main memory. This is carried out automatically upon replacing the cache line concerned with another line from main memory, or explicitly by means of a cache flush. Particularly in systems that have several bus masters sharing a common main memory, or using it at least partially for a data exchange, system designers have to ensure that the main memory contents are updated when a second bus master attempts to access it. If the cache controller with a write-back strategy misses updating the main memory entry in time, the active bus master accesses out-dated values.

4.7.2 Cache Organization and Associative Memory

This section covers some mysterious terms such as 4-way, tag and associative memory (CAM), and the strategy for supplying data temporarily stored in the SRAM. These can best be described using an example. For this, a cache for an i386 with a capacity of 16 kbytes and a cache line of 16 bytes is assumed.

The cache controller separates the 32-bit address from the i386 internally into a 20-bit tag address A31–A12, an 8-bit set address A11–A4 and a 2-bit double-word address. The 2-bit byte address A1–A0 addresses one of the four bytes within the double-word which is addressed by the DW address (and, of course, the other high-order address bits). Further, a cache entry has a 20-bit tag address, a write-protection bit, a valid bit, three LRU bits (shared, however by all four cache options) and four double-words with 32 bits each, which constitute the cache line concerned. Figure 4.20 shows this in a graphical form.

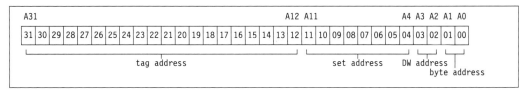

Figure 4.20: Cache entry and 4-way cache directory.

The most important terms are briefly discussed below.

Tag

The tag is a memory element in the cache directory. Using the tag the controller determines whether a cache hit or a cache miss has occurred. The tag holds the tag address, which indicates the address bits A31–A12 of the assigned cache line. Only with the tag valid bit set is the tag address actually valid; otherwise the tag address or the cache line holds invalid data. With a set write protection bit the assigned cache line may not be written. This is necessary, for example, so that cache line fills are not disturbed and the cache line fill cycle does not overwrite data that has been updated by the CPU before the cache line has been completely loaded into the SRAM.

Set

Each tag and the assigned cache line form an element of a set. The 8-bit set address A11–A4 determines the intended set from 256 possible sets.

Way

This term indicates the degree of the cache system's associativity. For a given set address, all the tag addresses are simultaneously compared with the tag part of the address supplied by the CPU to determine either a cache hit or a cache miss. In the example, a 4-way associative cache is assumed, that is, the cache has four ways. Each way holds 256 sets, with a cache line size of 16 bytes each. Together they lead to a 16 kbyte cache memory. One set entry for the four ways is assigned one LRU entry with three bits in common. The cache controller uses the LRU entry to determine the cache line that must be replaced in a cache miss. Details of this strategy are discussed in Section 4.7.3. The sets of all the ways, together with the LRU bits, form the cache directory for managing the cache lines in the SRAM cache. The cache directory may be held in the cache controller either internally or in an external SRAM.

Cache Line

The cache line forms the data unit, which is exchanged between the cache and the main memory as a whole. The CPU address is always directed to a cache line; within one cache line the double-word for the 32-bit data bus is further indicated by the address bits A3 and A2. A cache line is either valid as a whole or invalid as a whole. Even if the CPU only wants to read one byte, all 16 bytes of the cache line concerned must be present in the SRAM; otherwise a cache miss occurs. The cache lines make up the actual cache memory; the cache directory serves only to manage them.

Associative or Content Addressable Memory

We have already met the term associative or *content addressable memory* (*CAM*) in connection with caches. The expression already defines its operative principle. Usually, information in a memory is accessed explicitly by indicating the address. In an associative memory this is carried out by part of the information in the memory itself – hence the term CAM. To read information from the CAM an information section that coincides with the corresponding section of the addressed data is input into the memory. If data is held in the CAM that coincides at the concerned locations with the delivered addressing information, then the CAM supplies all the information assigned to this section. Because the addressing section contains only part of the information, it may be the case that different information «fits» and that they are also output. Thus, the result may be ambiguous (but this is not a surprising effect of association). For example, you can associate several things with the expression (information) «forest», such as tree, free time, trekking, etc. On the other hand, the CAM delivers no information if no coincidences occur. In real life you may also have some problems in associating something with «wafpwfwhen fc» (besides the standard exception «nonsense», perhaps).

In the cache the form of associative addressing is carried out on a set-base only. The association is carried out using the four ways, but addressing the set by explicitly indicating the set address A4–A11. The information section for associative addressing is specified by the tag addresses in the set. These tag addresses are compared to the tag address A12–A31 supplied by the CPU. If a coincidence occurs the cache controller «associates» the complete cache entry (that is, the cache line that belongs to the corresponding way of the set with the correct tag address). Figure 4.21

demonstrates the principle of determining a cache hit or a cache miss in a 4-way set associative cache.

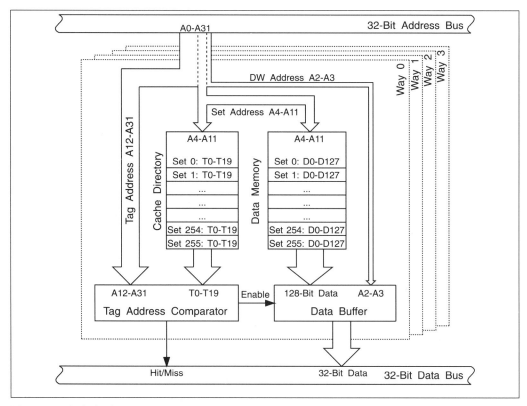

Figure 4.21: Cache hit determination.

The CPU puts the 32-bit address of the data to be read onto the address bus. The address is accepted and divided by the cache controller. The tag address A12–A31 is immediately transferred to the tag-address comparator. The controller uses the set address A4–A11 to select one set in the cache directory, and to output the tag address held by the set to the tag-address comparator. Additionally the cache controller uses the set address to transfer the cache line according to the set indicated from the SRAM data memory into a 128-bit data buffer. In the data buffer a double-word within the cache line is selected by means of the double-word address A2, A3. The tag-address comparator compares (that is, «associates») the tag address from the CPU with the cache directory's tag address. If they coincide then the comparator applies an enable signal to the data buffer so that the buffer transfers the double-word concerned to the 32-bit data bus. If the two tag addresses are different, the output is blocked and a cache miss is reported by means of the HIT/MISS signal. This selection and comparison operation is carried out in the same manner for all four ways. If the CPU's tag address coincides with the tag address in one of the four ways, a cache hit has occurred; otherwise a cache miss has occurred.

Because of its 20-bit width the tag address divides the i386 address space into 2^{20} cache pages with a 4 kbyte capacity each. Every page is further divided into 16-byte cache lines by means of the 256 sets. Each one of these four ways holds 256 of these cache lines.

Of course, other cache organizations are also possible besides the 4-way cache. With a 2-way cache, for example, only ways 0 and 1 exist. Further, other sets may be formed instead of 256. If only 64 sets are implemented then only six address bits are incorporated in the set address.

4.7.3 LRU Bits and Pseudo LRU Replacement Strategy

The cache controller uses the three LRU bits assigned to a set of cache lines for marking the last addressed (most recently accessed) way of the set. If the last access was to way 0 or way 1, the controller sets the LRU bit B0. For an access to way 0, bit B1 is set; for addressing way 1, B1 is cleared. If the last access was to way 2 or way 3, the controller clears bit B0. For an access to way 2 the LRU bit B2 is set; for addressing way 3, B2 is cleared. The LRU bits are updated upon every cache access and cleared upon each cache reset or cache flush.

If a cache miss now occurs during the course of a data read, the cache controller replaces a cache line by the cache line containing the data read. To find out which cache line should be replaced, the controller carries out the following pseudo-LRU strategy, which is shown in Figure 4.22 as a flow diagram.

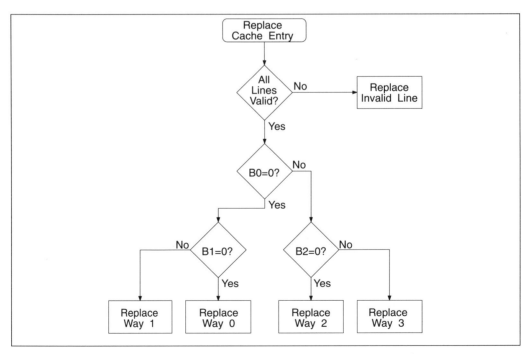

Figure 4.22: Pseudo LRU replacement strategy.

Using B0 the cache controller determines which pair of ways 0 and 1 or ways 2 and 3 have not been accessed for the longest time. Then, the controller (with the help of B1 or B2) determines which of the two assigned cache lines hasn't been accessed for the longest time, and marks the corresponding line as replaceable. The cache controller now reads one cache line from main memory and writes it into the SRAM, overwriting the cache line that has been marked as replaceable by the pseudo LRU algorithm.

4.8 The SX Variants of the Processors

Only a short time after presenting the i386 and i387 32-bit processors, Intel also developed two «cut down» variants of these chips: the i386SX and the accompanying i387SX coprocessor. Internally, they are identical to their big brothers, with the exception of an altered bus unit. Thus the i386SX can run in real, protected and virtual 8086 modes; it comprises the same control, debug and test registers, and carries out demand paging if the paging unit is active. Internally, it has the same 32-bit registers as the i386, and can thus manage a virtual address space of 64 Tbytes per task, and may also execute 32-bit instructions. Moreover, the prefetch queue with its 16 bytes is the same size as in the i386. The i387 recognizes the same instructions, has the same registers, and exchanges data with the CPU in the same way as the i387. Table 4.6 lists the main differences, which exclusively refer to the address space and the data bus.

	i386/i387	i386SX/i387SX
Address bus	32 bits	24 bits
Physical address space	4 Gbytes	16 Mbytes
I/O address space	64 kbytes	64 kbytes
Coprocessor port	800000fxh	8000fxh
Data bus	32 bits	16 bits
Data transfer rate[*)]	80 Mbytes/s	25 Mbytes/s
Max. clock speed	40 MHz	25 MHz

[*)] at max. clock speed with zero wait states.

Table. 4.6: SX processor model differences

You can see that the «normal» processor variants are far more powerful. The i386 is currently available with clock frequencies up to 40 MHz compared to 25 MHz for the i386SX. Together with the twice as wide data bus, the fastest i386 is therefore able to transfer nearly four times more data than the fastest i386SX. While the physical address space of 4 Gbytes seemed as if it would be enough for decades, there are already PCs on the market that have a main memory of 16 Mbytes, that is, the maximum for the i386SX. Because such a large storage capacity is only necessary for a very powerful system (EISA, OS/2), and a complete i386 is usually employed, this disadvantage is only of a theoretical nature. PCs, and especially notebooks with an i386SX base, have been successfully developed recently because all the innovative features of paging and the virtual 8086 mode are available to the user, but the system hardware, because of the smaller bus width, is easier and therefore cheaper. Only a 16-bit data bus and a 24-bit address bus are needed on the motherboard, as was already the case for a normal 80286 AT. Thus, the i386SX and its derivatives are very useful for compact notebooks. However, using paging and the virtual 8086 mode, more advantages (together with innovative programs such as Windows or OS/2) are available with the i386SX compared to the 80286. An i386SX-based PC is therefore a good compromise between power and money.

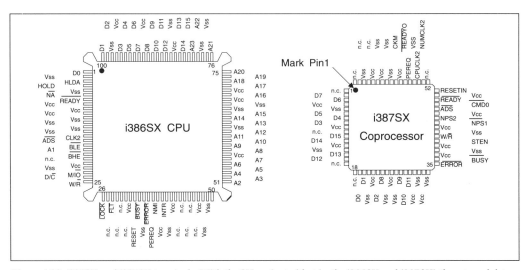

Figure 4.23: i386SX and i387SX terminals. With the SX variants (that is, the i386SX and i387SX) the external data bus is only 16 bits wide, although the data are processed internally with 32 bits, as is the case for the i386/i387. Because of the address bus reduction to 24 address lines, the i386SX/i387SX physical address space comprises only 16 Mbytes compared to 4 Gbytes.

The i386SX comes in a plastic quad flatpack package (PQFP) with 100 pins, and the i387SX in a PLCC package with 68 pins. Figure 4.23 shows the pin assignments of these two SX chips.

It is immediately noticeable that these processors have fewer connections when compared to their counterparts. In the following section the altered pins and signals that are not self-explanatory are briefly discussed.

$\overline{\text{BHE}}$, $\overline{\text{BLE}}$ (Pins 19, 17)

(Bus High Enable, Bus Low Enable) These signals indicate which part (low-order and/or high-order) of the data bus supplies or accepts valid data. On an i386 this job is carried out by the pins $\overline{\text{BE0}}$–$\overline{\text{BE3}}$.

$\overline{\text{FLT}}$ (28)

(Float) An active signal at this pin (that is, a low level signal) forces all i387SX pins that are able to output signals into an inactive state. This signal is largely applied for test purposes.

As for the i386, the i386SX can also carry out an internal self-test. It is issued in the same way, and lasts for about 2^{20} clock cycles, that is, about 30 ms with a 20 MHz i386SX. After the self-test the DX register contains a signature byte. The eight high-order bits have the value 23h. The «3» characterizes the i386 family and the «2» indicates that this is the second member of the family, that is, the i386SX. The low-order byte indicates the i386SX version number.

The i386SX and i387SX cooperate in the same way as the i386 and i387, thus the i386SX accesses the coprocessor with reserved I/O ports located outside the normal I/O address space. But because the i386SX has only 24 address lines instead of 32, the address line A23 instead of A31 is now activated. The I/O addresses for communication between CPU and coprocessor therefore comprise only three bytes (see Table 4.7). The transfer protocol is the same as for the i386/i387 combination, but the data transfer for 32-bit operands lasts longer as more bus cycles must be carried out because of the 16-bit data bus.

i386SX I/O port	i387SX register
8000f8h	opcode register
8000fch	operand register
8000feh[*]	operand register

[*] used during the second bus cycle in a 32-bit operand transfer.

Table 4.7: Coprocessor port addresses

4.9 BIOS Access to Extended Memory

The AT BIOS has two functions for interrupt INT 15h that may be used to move a data block between base memory below 1 Mbyte and extended memory. Further, the processor may be switched to protected mode. The functions are described in Appendix L. Readers interested in this subject should consult that appendix and Chapter 3 concerning protected mode, because you are at least partially responsible for the appropriate generation of the descriptor tables required.

4.10 386SL Chipset – A Two-Chip-AT

The steadily increasing integration density of transistors and other electronic elements not only refers to RAM chips or the CPU (the number of integrated transistors rose from the 30 000 on an 8086 up to more than three million (!) for the P5 or i586). Another trend is that more and more single elements (for example, DMA controller, interrupt controller, timer, etc.) are integrated on one or two chips. PCs are therefore not only getting more compact, but the power consumption has also decreased significantly; an obvious advantage for notebooks. The provisional summit of this development is Intel's 386SL chipset, which has the CPU chip 386SL and the I/O sub-system 82360SL, and integrates nearly all CPU, support and peripheral chips on these two chips.

4.10.1 386SL and 82360SL Internal Structure

Figure 4.24 schematically shows the internal structure of the 386SL and 82360SL.

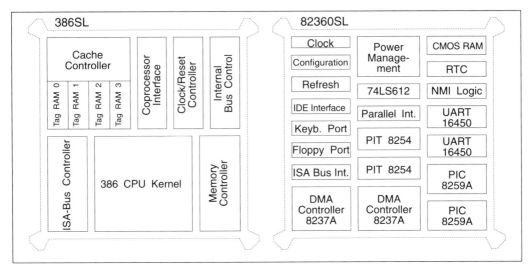

Figure 4.24: Internal structure of 386SL and 82360SL.

The 386SL integrates an improved i386 CPU core, a cache controller and tag RAM, an ISA bus controller, and a memory controller on a single chip. The CPU core is implemented in static design, and may be clocked down to 0 MHz to save power. Presently, the 386SL is available in two versions for clock frequencies of 20 MHz and 25 MHz. The cache interface may be directly connected to a 16, 32 or 64 kbyte cache. The cache organization is programmable as direct mapped, 2-way or 4-way set associative. The 20 MHz version may also be delivered without a cache controller and tag RAM.

The memory controller accesses the main memory via a 24-bit address bus and a 16-bit data bus. To its environment, the 386SL CPU therefore behaves like an i386SX. Main memory can be organized with one-way, two-way or four-way interleaving, and the number of wait states is programmable in the 386SL. Additionally, the memory controller incorporates an EMS logic, which implements LIM-EMS 4.0. The controller may also carry out ROM BIOS shadowing. An external shadow logic is not required – the ISA bus controller generates all necessary signals for the ISA bus. In the 386SL sufficiently powerful driver circuits are integrated for this purpose so that no external buffers and drivers are necessary. This significantly simplifies the design of a PC. Additionally, a *peripheral interface bus (PI bus)* is implemented. The 386SL may exchange data with fast peripherals (for example, the integrated 82370SL VGA controller) or flash memories by means of this bus. For controlling the PI bus the pins (and signals) PCMD, PM/$\overline{\text{IO}}$, $\overline{\text{PRDY}}$, $\overline{\text{PSTART}}$ and PW/$\overline{\text{R}}$ are implemented.

For a lower power consumption the 386SL can operate in a *power management mode* in which, for example, the 386SL clock frequency can be decreased, or even switched off. The power management is carried out by a non-maskable interrupt SMI of a higher priority. The handler of this interrupt is located in its own system power management RAM, which is completely separate from the ordinary main memory. The 386SL may access this memory only by means of the $\overline{\text{SMRAMCS}}$ signal. Thus, this concept is similar to that which AMD and Chips & Technologies follow with their low-power versions of the i386 (see Section 4.11).

On the 82360SL a real-time clock, a CMOS RAM, two 8254 timers with three channels each, two 8237A DMA controllers with improved page register 74LS612, a bidirectional parallel interface, two 8259A interrupt controllers, two serial interfaces (a UART 16450 and a support interface for a floppy controller), a keyboard controller and an IDE interface are integrated. Of significance is the additional power management control. This always activates only the currently driven unit, and thus reduces the power consumption significantly. Instead of the internal real-time clock, an external clock may also be used.

The 386SL chipset is already prepared for the integration of a VGA, and the 386SL outputs a special interface signal $\overline{\text{VGACS}}$ when it accesses the address space where the VGA is usually located. With the 386SL and 82360SL chips, some DRAMs and a high-integrated graphics controller (for example, the 82370SL VGA controller) you can build a complete AT. Thus the PW (Personal Workstation) on your wrist seems to be only a short time away.

4.10.2 Terminals and Signals

To avoid repetition and to save space, the connections and signals of the 386SL and 82360SL are discussed group-by-group.

386SL

Figure 4.25 shows the pin assignment of the 386SL in a PQFP with 196 pins. Additionally, the 386SL is also availabe in a pin grid array package with 227 connections.

CA15–CA1, CD15–CD0, $\overline{\text{CCSH}}$, $\overline{\text{CCSL}}$, $\overline{\text{COE}}$, $\overline{\text{CWE}}$
(Cache Address, Cache Data, Cache Chip Select High Byte, Cache Chip Select Low Byte, Cache Output Enable, Cache Write Enable). These 34 connections form the cache bus to the cache SRAM.

CMUX0–CMUX 14
(CPU Multiplexed Bus) These 15 connections form the memory control bus and supply the CAS, RAS, and parity signals if the main memory is implemented with DRAMs. If the main memory consists of SRAM chips only, CMUX0–CMUX14 provide the control signals for the SRAM chips.

$\overline{\text{BUSY}}$, $\overline{\text{NPXRDY}}$, $\overline{\text{NPXCLK}}$, $\overline{\text{NPXADS}}$, $\overline{\text{ERROR}}$, NPXRESET, NPXW/$\overline{\text{R}}$, PEREQ
(Busy, NPX Ready, NPX Clock, NPX Address Strobe, NPX Error, NPX Reset, NPX Write/Read, Processor Extension Request) These eight signals constitute the coprocessor interface to an i387SX.

BALE, HLDA, HRQ, IOCHRDY, $\overline{\text{IOCS16}}$, $\overline{\text{IOR}}$, $\overline{\text{IOW}}$, LA23–LA17, $\overline{\text{MASTER}}$, MEMCS16, MEMR, MEMW, SA19–SA0, SBHE, SD15–SD0, ZEROWS
(Bus Address Latch Enable, Hold Acknowledge, Hold Request, I/O Channel Ready, I/O Chip Select 16, I/O Read, I/O Write, Latchable Address, ISA Master, Memory Chip Select 16, Memory Read, Memory Write, System Address, System Byte High Enable, System Data, Zero Wait States) These 56 connections form the ISA bus interface of the 386SL.

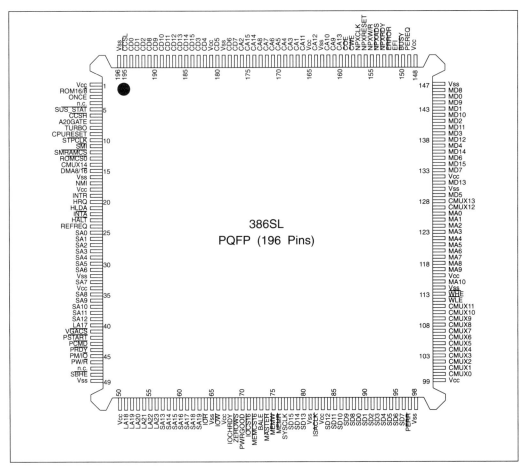

Figure 4.25: Pin assignment of the 386SL in PQFP.

MA10–MA0, MD15–MD0, $\overline{PERR}$, $\overline{WHE}$, $\overline{WLE}$

(Memory Address, Memory Data, Parity Error, Write High Enable, Write Low Enable) These 30 connections constitute the local memory bus between the CPU and main memory.

A20GATE, CPURESET, DMA8/16, $\overline{HALT}$, $\overline{INTA}$, INTR, NMI, $\overline{ONCE}$

(Address Line 20 Gate, CPU Reset, DMA Width 8/16, CPU HALT, Interrupt Acknowledge Sequence, Interrupt Request, Non-Maskable Interrupt, On-Board Circuit Emulation) These eight pins accept various control signals for the CPU.

EFI

(External Frequency Input) The clock frequency supplied is divided by two inside the 386SL, and then used as the internal processor clock.

PCMD, PM/$\overline{IO}$, $\overline{PRDY}$, $\overline{PSTART}$, PW/$\overline{R}$

(PI-Bus Command, PI-Bus Memory/IO, PI-Bus Ready, PI-Bus Start, PI-Bus Write/Read) These five connections form the control bus for PI cycles.

PWRGOOD

(Power Good) A high-level signal indicates a sufficient power supply.

REFREQ

(Refresh Request) A high-level signal indicates that the 386SL should issue a refresh cycle for main memory.

ROM16/8, ROMCS0

(ROM-Size 16/8, ROM Chip Select 0) These two connections provide the signals for accessing the ROM BIOS.

SMI, SMRAMCS, STPCLK, SUS_STAT

(System Power Management Interrupt, System Power Management RAM Chip Select, Stop Clock, Suspend Status) These signals implement the system's power management.

ISACLK2

(ISA Clock Two) This connection is supplied twice with the frequency of the ISA bus (usually 16 MHz).

SYSCLK

(System Clock) This pin provides the ISA system clock (usually 8 MHz), that is, half the frequency of the ISACLK2 signal.

TURBO

A high level signal forces the 386SL to run at maximum clock rate.

VGACS

(VGA Chip Select) The 386SL outputs a low-level signal if it accesses the VGA address space.

82360SL

Figure 4.26 shows the pin assignment of the 82360SL in a PQFP with 196 pins.

A20GATE, CPURESET, DMA8/16, HALT, INTA, INTR, NMI, ONCE

(Address Line 20 Gate, CPU Reset, DMA Width 8/16, CPU HALT, Interrupt Acknowledge Sequence, Interrupt Request, Non-Maskable Interrupt, On-Board Circuit Emulation) These eight connections provide or accept various control signals for or from the CPU.

BALE, AEN, DACK7–5, DACK3–0, DRQ7–5, DRQ3–0, HLDA, HRQ, IOCHCK, IOCHRDY, IOCS16, IOR, IOW, IRQ15, IRQ14, IRQ12–IRQ9, IRQ7–IRQ3, IRQ1, LA23–LA17, MASTER, MEMR, MEMW, OSC, REFRESH, RESETDRV, SA16–SA0, SBHE, SD7–SD0, SMEMR/LOMEM, SMEMW, TC, ZEROWS

(Bus Address Latch Enable, Address Enabled, DMA Acknowledge, DMA Request, Hold Acknowledge, Hold Request, I/O Channel Check, I/O Channel Ready, I/O Chip Select 16, I/O Read, I/O Write, Interrupt Request, Latchable Address, ISA Master, Memory Read, Memory Write, Oscillator, System Refresh, Reset Drive, System Address, System Byte High Enable, System Data, System Memory Read, System Memory Write, Terminal Count, Zero Wait States) These connections constitute the ISA bus interface of the 82360SL.

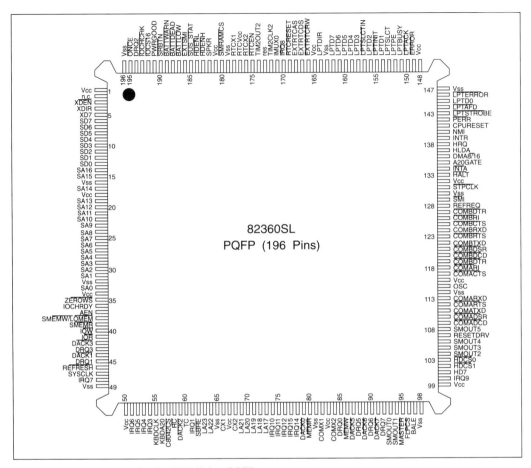

Figure 4.26: Pin assignment for the 82360SL in a PQFP.

BATTDEAD, BATTLOW, BATTWARN

(Battery Dead, Battery Low, Battery Warning) These three signals inform the 82360SL of the current power status of the battery or accumulator.

PERR, RC, REFREQ

(Parity Error, Reset CPU, Refresh Request) These connections directly accept signals from the CPU or provide them to the CPU.

PWRGOOD

(Power Good) A high-level signal indicates a sufficient power supply.

RTCEN

(RTC Enable) If this pin is provided with a low-level signal, the 82360SL enables the internal clock; otherwise it enables an external real-time clock.

RTCRESET, RTCVCC, RTCX1, RTCX2

(RTC Reset, RTC Vcc, RTC External Crystal Oscillator) These four connections drive the internal real-time clock.

SPKR

(Speaker Output) This connection supplies the signal for the speaker.

SYSCLK

(System Clock) The pin supplies the ISA system clock (usually 8MHz), that is, half the frequency of the ISACLK2 signal.

SMI, SMOUT0–SMOUT5, SMRAMCS, SRBTN, STPCLK, SUS_STAT

(System Power Management Interrupt, System Management Output Control, System Power Management RAM Chip Select, Suspend/Resume Button, Stop Clock, Suspend Status) These signals implement the system's power management.

FLPCS

(Floppy Chip Select) This pin provides a signal with a low level if the CPU accesses a floppy controller port.

HD7, HDCS1–HDCS0, HDEN

(Hard Disk Bus Data 7, Hard Disk Chip Select, Hard Disk Buffer Enabled) These four connections form the control bus of the IDE interface.

IMUX0

(Input Multiplex) This pin may be provided with an input signal for the gate input of timer 2 or an external audio signal for the speaker.

IRQ8, EXTRTCAS, EXTRTCDS, EXTRTCRW

(Interrupt Request 8, External RTC Address Strobe, External RTC Data Strobe, External RTC Read/Write) These connections form the interface to an external real-time clock.

EXTSMI

(External System Management Interrupt Request) A low-level potential causes an SMI request.

C8042CS, KBDA20, KBDCLK

(Keyboard Controller 8042 Chip Select, Keyboard A20 Gate, Keyboard Clock) These connections constitute the interface for driving the keyboard controller.

COMACTS, COMADCD, COMADSR, COMADTR, COMARXD, COMARI, COMARTS, COMATXD

(COM A Clear to Send, COM A Data Carrier Detect, COM A Data Set Ready, COM A Data Terminal Ready, COM A Received Data, COM A Ring Indicator, COM A Request to Send, COM A Transmit Data) These eight connections implement the first serial interface in the 82360SL.

COMBCTS, COMBDCD, COMBDSR, COMBDTR, COMBRXD, COMBRI, COMBRTS, COMBTXD

(COM B Clear to Send, COM B Data Carrier Detect, COM B Data Set Ready, COM B Data

Terminal Ready, COM B Received Data, COM B Ring Indicator, COM B Request to Send, COM B Transmit Data) These eight connections implement the second serial interface in the 82360SL.

COMX1, COMX2
(COM External Oscillator) These pins must be connected to a 1.8432 MHz oscillator, and supply the base clock for the two UARTs.

CX1, CX2
(Crystal External Oscillator) These pins must be connected to a 14.31818 MHz oscillator. After a division by 12, they provide the base clock for the timers.

$\overline{\text{ERROR}}$
(NPX Error) This signal indicates a coprocessor error.

$\overline{\text{LPTACK}}$, $\overline{\text{LPTAFD}}$, LPTBUSY, LPTD7–LPTD0, LPTDIR, $\overline{\text{LPTERROR}}$, $\overline{\text{LPTINIT}}$, LPTPE, LPTSLCT, $\overline{\text{LPTSLCTIN}}$, $\overline{\text{LPTSTROBE}}$
(LPT Acknowledge, LPT Auto Line Feed, LPT Busy, LPT Data, LPT Direction, LPT Error, LPT Initialization, LPT Paper End, LPT Selected, LPT Select In, LPT Strobe) These 18 connections implement the parallel interface.

TIM2CLK2
(Timer 2 Clock 2) This pin is provided with the clock signal for timer 2, channel 2.

TIM2OUT2
(Timer 2 Output 2) This connection supplies the output signal of timer 2, channel 2.

XD7
($\overline{\text{X}}$-Bus $\overline{\text{D}}$ata) This pin forms bit 7 of the X-bus.

$\overline{\text{XDEN}}$, XDIR
(X-Bus Data Enable, X-Bus Data Direction) These two connections provide control signals for the X-bus.

4.11 Processor Confusion by i386 Clones

The passion for copying that has hit the PC market, and which is the reason for the enormous drop in prices over the last ten years, does not exclude the heart of a PC. Only a few years ago, Intel more or less held the CPU monopoly, but today even there enormous competition is taking place (at least up to the i386 level). It is not only coprocessors that are now manufactured by competitors, but also the CPUs.

Users are happy with this, as prices seem to be in endless decline. And the CPU clones are not only equal to the Intel models, but often do better in terms of performance and power consumption. At this time there are three main microelectronics firms manufacturing i386-compatible processors: AMD (Advanced Micro Devices); Chips & Technologies; and Cyrix. The most important i386-clones are briefly discussed below.

4.11.1 AMD Processors

AMD is currently the most important manufacturer in the i386 market segment other than Intel. AMD processors are not only cheaper, but in most cases also faster and, especially, far more power efficient than Intel's models. These chip types are particularly suitable for noteboooks. Currently, AMD offers three different DX models with a complete 32-bit data bus, as well as three SX models with a 16-bit data and a 24-bit address bus.

AM386DX/AM386SX

The AM386DX is an i386DX-compatible processor available for clock frequencies from 20 MHz up to 40 MHz, that is, its clock rate and therefore the performance can be up to 20% higher than the original i386. The AM386SX is the well-known cut-down version, and has only a 16-bit data and a 24-bit address bus. Both processor types are strictly orientated to the Intel models, and have no significant differences in comparison.

AM386DXL/AM386SXL

The i386DX and i386SX-compatible processors, respectively, are implemented with a special power-saving design (the «L» in the processor name means low power). The AM386DXL/SXL consumes about 40% less power than the comparable Intel models. The DXL type may be clocked with between 20 and 40 MHz, and the SXL model with 25 MHz at most.

The main feature of the AM386DXL/AM386SXL is the static design of its circuits. The clock rate may thus be decreased to 0 MHz, that is, the clock signal can effectively be switched off. The processor does not lose its register contents in this case. With a dynamic circuit design, on the other hand, the clock frequency may not fall below a minimum value without causing a processor malfunction. If the external clock signal is switched off, then, for example, the DXL processor draws a current of only about 0.02 mA compared to 275 mA at 33 MHz. This means a reduction in power consumption by a factor of 10 000 (!). Battery-operated notebooks are very happy with this. Using the static processor design a standby mode can readily be implemented. The BIOS need not save the processor registers, but can just switch off the clock signal after the elapse of a usually programmable time period within which no key press or other action has taken place. If, for example, you then press a key to reactivate the PC, the standby logic releases the clock signal. Then the CPU again operates without the need for the BIOS for restore the registers' contents. This simplifies the implemention of a power-saving standby mode significantly.

AM386DXLV/AM386SXLV

The AM386DXLV/AM386SXLV is directed uncompromisingly towards a low power consumption. It operates with a supply voltage of only 3.3 V compared to the 5 V of an AM386DX/AM386DXL (therefore, the name LV for low voltage). The power consumption of CMOS chips is proportional to the square of the supply voltage. By decreasing the supply voltage to 3.3 V, 50% of the power is saved. But at 3.3 V the chip may only be operated up to 25 MHz; to use the maximum 33 MHz a supply voltage of 5 V is necessary. The AM386DXLV/SXLV, too, is implemented in a completely static design. Thus the external processor clock may be switched off and the AM386DXLV, for example, needs only 0.01 mA compared to 135 mA at 25 MHz.

AMD has additionally implemented a so-called *system management mode (SMM)* with the AM386DXLV to control the power consumption independently of the operating mode and the operating environment. For this purpose, the AM386DXLV/SXLV recognizes a *system management interrupt (SMI)*, which has an even higher priority than the NMI. Further, an additional address space of 1 Mbyte, which is completely separate from ordinary main memory, is available for system management mode. The SMI is issued by a signal with a low level at the $\overline{\text{SMI}}$ pin, or by setting a certain bit in the debug register 7 and executing opcode f1h. In both cases, the AM386DXLV/SXLV issues something like a major NMI, stores the current operating state of the processor at address 0006:9999 to 0006:00c8 and 0006:0100 to 0006:0124 in the SMM memory, eventually returns to real mode, and starts execution of the SMI handler at address ffff:fff0. Now all memory accesses refer only to SMM memory. The processor indicates this by the signals $\overline{\text{SMIADS}}$ and $\overline{\text{SMIRDY}}$. I/O accesses via instructions such as IN or OUT are still directed to the normal I/O address space.

To return from SMM mode to the interrupted task, and to restore the original processor state, the register pair ES:EDI must be loaded with the far address 0006:0000. Execution of the 32-bit opcode 0fh 07h then restores the processor state from the data held in SMM memory.

4.11.2 Chips & Technologies Processors

C & T became famous with its NEAT chipset for AT-compatible PCs. Meanwhile, C & T also manufacture complete (and, compared with Intel models, more powerful) CPUs. These are the 38605DX, 38605SX, 38600DX and 38600SX processors, which are together called Super386.

38605DX/38605SX
An i386 and i386SX-compatible processor, respectively, with internal instruction cache and SuperState V mode in power-saving CMOS design. The 38605SX has only a 16-bit data and a 24-bit address bus.

38600DX/38600SX
An i386 and i386SX-compatible processor, respectively, with SuperState V mode in power-saving CMOS design. The 38600SX has only a 16-bit data and a 24-bit address bus. Unlike the 38605DX/38605SX, no instruction cache is implemented.

All four processors thus have an advanced operating mode: the so-called *SuperState V mode*. This mode has an even higher privilege level than the protected mode, and implements system management functions such as driving external devices for reducing power consumption, for backing up data in advance of power-down, etc. These functions are especially valuable for notebooks.

In SuperState V mode the processor does not access ordinary main memory, but a separate memory area. Thus, normally running tasks and those tasks in protected mode are not affected; ordinary main memory and the memory area for the system management functions are completely separate from each other. This is achieved by means of two additional pins marked as free on the Intel CPUs: $\overline{\text{ANMI}}$ (alternate **NMI**, pin N15) and $\overline{\text{AADS}}$ (alternate **ad**dress **s**pace, pin P15). A low level signal at $\overline{\text{ANMI}}$ issues an NMI with an even higher priority than an ordinary NMI, and switches the 3860xDX/SX into SuperState V mode. Then the processor informs the bus controller by an active (that is, low level) $\overline{AADS}$ signal that it is attempting to access the alternate memory that is completely dedicated to the SuperState V mode. Here, for example, the handler for the ANMI may be located, which shuts down external devices or even the CPU to save power.

To activate SuperState V mode there are three options:

– Activation of the $\overline{ANMI}$ signal; the CPU issues an ANMI.
– Setting the I/O trap bit in the configuration register; every I/O access to a port switches the CPU to SuperState V mode.
– Explicitly by executing the new instruction *AENTER* (enter SuperState V mode).

The 3860xDX/SX processors may be supplied with the single (CLK1X) or double (CLK2X) clock signal by the clock signal generator. To distinguish it the processor has the USE2X connection (pin P8). In the first case, the internal processor clock PCLK coincides with the clock signal CLK1X from the generator, and USE2X is on a low level. In the second case, the CPU divides the applied clock signal internally by two, as is the case with the original Intel i386, to generate the processor clock PCLK. USE2X is on a high level for this purpose.

The 05 models of the 386xxDX/SX CPUs additionally implement an internal instruction cache with 512 bytes. That is not as much as on the i486, and the data cache is also missing, but the performance is nevertheless enhanced. Further, the 05 models have an $\overline{A20M}$ (address **20 m**ask, pin M15) connection. If an external logic applies a signal with a low level, then the processor masks the address line A20 internally, and thus emulates a wrap-around at address 1M if it addresses its internal cache. The 386xxDX CPUs may be clocked up to 40 MHz, that is, 20% higher than an original Intel i386.

4.11.3 Cyrix CPUs

Until now, Cyrix has largely been known because of its fast 80x87 coprocessors. But Cyrix has tried to get a slice of the CPU cake. The result of these efforts is the 486DLC with a 32-bit data and a 32-bit address bus, as well as the 486SLC with a 16-bit data and a 24-bit address bus. Despite the name 486, these CPUs are more an i386 than a real Intel i486. The Cyrix CPUs are optimized for low power consumption, too. The 486DLC/486SLC has an internal 1 kbyte cache but no integrated coprocessor; the i387 or compatible must be added externally. Thus, the 486DLC can be compared with a light version of the Intel i486SX. Be careful when buying a 486 notebook. You can often determine only after a close look whether a real i486 or a 486DLC/SLC is installed. The 486DLC and i387 combination is nearly as powerful as an i486, however.

4.11.4 IBM – For Members Only

IBM did not want to be behind the times, so they launched an i386-compatible processor with the name 386SLC. The 386SLC has an internal 8 kbyte cache and is implemented in a power-saving static design. At this time, the 386SLC is not freely available on the market, as IBM uses it exclusively for its own products.

5 The i486 – All in One

Currently, the most powerful member of the Intel 80x86 family is the i486. It integrates an improved i386 CPU, a more powerful i387 coprocessor, and a cache controller with an 8 kbyte-cache memory on a single chip. It is available with clock frequencies of between 25 and 50 MHz, with internal frequency doubling this up to 66 MHz. Together with its 32-bit data bus, a data transfer rate of up to 160 Mbyte/s in burst mode is possible. Unlike the i386, the i486 executes frequently used instructions (such as MOV, for example) within a single clock cycle. The i486 is thus about three times as fast as an i386 clocked with the same frequency. The number of elements used in its construction, though, is enormous: the i486 integrates more than one million transistors on a finger-nail sized semiconductor chip, nearly 50 times more than its ancestor the 8086.

Of course, the i486 is entirely downward compatible to the i386/i387 combination. It understands the same instructions and data types, runs in real, protected and virtual 8086 modes, and carries out memory segmentation and demand paging in the same way. Because the coprocessor is integrated on the same chip as the CPU, the data exchange between them also runs more quickly. The i486 can therefore be seen as the ideal candidate for intensive mathematical applications such as CAD and computer graphics.

Yet a comment has to be made about the most powerful i386 successor being used in combination with the world's most widely used operating system: DOS running on the i486 is about the same as a supertanker with an outboard motor!

5.1 i486 Terminals and Signals

The many different components of the i486 must have a continuous supply voltage. This is carried out by 24 V_{cc} and 28 V_{ss} terminals. Together with its 116 signal pins, the i486 therefore needs 168 connections; so you'll find the i486 has a monstrous pin grid array package with 168 pins. Figure 5.1 shows the i486 pin assignment.

In the following we discuss i486 connections. Pins and signals previously mentioned in connection with the i386/i387 are only listed briefly; further details can be found in the relevant chapters.

CLK
This pin is supplied with the clock signal. Unlike the i386, the i486 does not divide the external clock signal CLK by two, but uses it without alteration as the internal processor clock. The frequency of the external oscillator is thus halved when compared to an i386 with the same processor clock frequency. If this were not done, for the fastest i486 model with a 50 MHz processor clock frequency, a 100 MHz oscillator would be required. This frequency is already in the range of FM radios. The wavelength of the 100 MHz oscillation is only about 3 m, and falls into the motherboard's scale. This gives rise to disadvantageous electrodynamic effects such as signal echoes, reflections, etc., and significantly complicates the layout and operations of the boards.

Thus, halving of the external clock assists computer engineers in designing the hardware components and their connections.

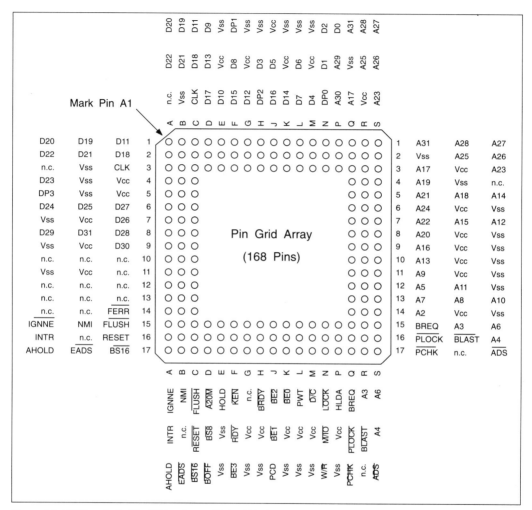

Figure 5.1: i486 terminals. The i486 package with its 168 pins is a real giant, but the chip itself is hardly larger than the 8086.

D31–D0

These 32 pins form the bidirectional 32-bit data bus of the i486 for data input/output. The data bus may be configured as a 32-, 16- or 8-bit data bus by the BS16 and BS8 signals. The signals at the BE0–BE3 pins indicate which byte of the data bus transfers valid data.

A31–A2

These 30 pins constitute the 30 high-order bits of the 32-bit address bus. The two least significant address bits, A1 and A0, must be generated by the BE0–BE3 signals.

$\overline{BE0}$–$\overline{BE3}$

(Byte Enable) The signals at these four pins (as for the i386) indicate which bytes of the 32-bit data bus are active throughout the current bus cycle, that is, which bytes transfer valid data. $\overline{BE0}$ corresponds to the least significant data byte D0–D7, and $\overline{BE3}$ to the most significant data byte D24–D31.

$\overline{BS16}$, $\overline{BS8}$

(Bus Size 16, Bus Size 8) If one of these pins is supplied with a low-level signal then the i486 operates its data bus with a width of only 16 or 8 bits respectively, instead of 32 bits, and correspondingly carries out many bus cycles to transfer, for example, a double-word with 32 bits. Thus the i486 may be directly connected to a system which has only a 16-bit or 8-bit data bus.

DP0–DP3

The i486 supports parity generation for the data bus, that is, it outputs a parity bit DP3–DP0 during all write cycles for every byte of the data bus D31–D0 so that even parity is generated. When data is read the system must apply signals to the DP3–DP0 pins, which leads to even parity. Systems that do not support this parity function fix DP3–DP0 on a V_{cc} potential. The signals supplied during the course of a data read do not affect program execution; a parity violation only activates the $\overline{PCHK}$ signal which, for example, may interrupt program execution with a hardware interrupt.

$\overline{A20M}$

(Address 20 Mask) If this pin is earthed (low-level potential), the i486 internally masks address bit A20 in advance of every memory access. Thus the i486 emulates the address wrap-around of the 8086. $\overline{A20M}$ should only be activated in real mode.

$\overline{PCHK}$

(Parity Check) After reading data, the i486 outputs a signal via this pin to indicate whether or not the transferred data bits and the parity bits are consistent. If $\overline{PCHK}$ is low, a parity error has occurred.

$M/\overline{IO}$, $D/\overline{C}$, $W/\overline{R}$

(Memory/IO, Data/Control, Write/Read) The signals at these pins define the current bus cycle. The following combinations are valid:

```
(000)          interrupt acknowledge sequence
(001)          HALT/special bus cycle
(010)          I/O is read
(011)          I/O port is written
(100)          fetching from memory (prefetching) instruction
(101)          reserved
(110)          data is read from memory
(111)          data is written into memory
```

$\overline{LOCK}$

If $\overline{LOCK}$ is active (that is, low), the i486 does not release the local bus to another bus master. The i486 does not react with an acknowledge (HLDA) to a request (HOLD) from another bus master.

$\overline{\text{PLOCK}}$

(Pseudo Lock) By means of $\overline{\text{PLOCK}}$ the i486 indicates that the current data transfer lasts for more than one bus cycle. That is the case, for example, if segment descriptors with a length of 64 bits are read from the GDT or LDT.

$\overline{\text{ADS}}$

(Address Status) The signal at this pin indicates that the i486 supplies valid bus control signals $\text{W}/\overline{\text{R}}$, $\text{D}/\overline{\text{C}}$ and $\text{M}/\overline{\text{IO}}$ as well as valid address signals.

$\overline{\text{RDY}}$

(Non-Burst Ready) If $\overline{\text{RDY}}$ is active (that is, has a low level), the addressed system has already output the data onto or taken it off the bus.

$\overline{\text{BRDY}}$

(Burst Ready) During the course of a burst cycle, $\overline{\text{BRDY}}$ has the same meaning as $\overline{\text{RDY}}$ for a normal bus cycle, that is, the addressed system has already output the data onto or taken it off the bus.

$\overline{\text{BLAST}}$

(Burst Last) $\overline{\text{BLAST}}$ indicates that the current burst cycle terminates after the next $\overline{\text{BRDY}}$.

BREQ

(Bus Request) By means of BREQ, the i486 indicates that it has requested the bus internally.

HOLD, HLDA

(Bus Hold Request, Bus Hold Acknowledge) The signals at these pins undertake bus arbitration in the well-known way, that is, passing control of the local bus among various bus masters.

$\overline{\text{BOFF}}$

(Backoff) If $\overline{\text{BOFF}}$ is supplied with a low-level signal then the i486 deactivates its bus upon the next clock cycle.

RESET

If this input is on a high level for at least 15 CLK cycles, the processor immediately aborts its operation and carries out a processor reset.

INTR

With the INTR, an interrupt controller may issue a hardware interrupt request. The checking of INTR can be prevented (masked) by clearing the interrupt flag IE.

NMI

A signal transition at this connection from low to high unavoidably issues an interrupt 2. The i486 stops program execution after completion of the current instruction.

$\overline{\text{FERR}}$

(Floating-Point Error) If an error occurs in the i486 floating-point unit, the processor activates the $\overline{\text{FERR}}$ signal. $\overline{\text{FERR}}$ is similar to the $\overline{\text{ERROR}}$ signal of the i387.

IGNNE

(Ignore Numeric Error) If this pin is supplied with a low-level signal, the i486 ignores numerical errors and executes all those instructions which do not involve the floating-point unit. But $\overline{\text{FERR}}$ is nevertheless activated. If the NE bit in control register CR0 is set, then $\overline{\text{IGNNE}}$ has no effect.

AHOLD

(Address Hold) If the AHOLD pin is supplied with a high-level signal, another bus master may access the i486 address bus to carry out a cache invalidation within the i486. Upon an active AHOLD, the i486 no longer drives its address bus, but all other bus signals continue to be active.

EADS

(External Address) If an active signal (that is, a low level signal) is applied to this pin, the i486 knows that an external bus master has supplied a valid address to its address pins. The i486 uses this address for an internal cache invalidation.

KEN

(Cache Enable) Using $\overline{\text{KEN}}$, the i486 determines whether the current cycle is cachable, and thus whether the intended address area can be transferred into the cache. If this is the case, the current read access is extended to a cache line fill cycle, that is, a whole cache line is read into the i486 on-chip cache. With $\overline{\text{KEN}}$, certain address areas can be protected against caching using hardware.

FLUSH

(Cache Flush) If $\overline{\text{FLUSH}}$ is activated by a low-level signal, the i486 writes all the contents of its cache into memory; it carries out a cache flush.

PWT, PCD

(Page Write-Through, Page Cache Disable) The signals at these two pins indicate the status of the page attribute bits PWT and PCD in the page table entry or the page directory entry. If paging is not active or if the current bus cycle is not subject to paging, PWT and PCD indicate the status of the PWT PCD bits in the control register CR3.

V$_{cc}$

These pins are supplied with the supply voltage (usually +5 V).

V$_{ss}$

These pins are grounded (usually 0 V).

5.2 i486 Internal Structure

Because three processors were integrated onto a single chip (CPU, coprocessor and cache controller), the internal structure of the i486 became more complicated than the i386. Therefore, the i486 structure is briefly explained below (and shown in Figure 5.2).

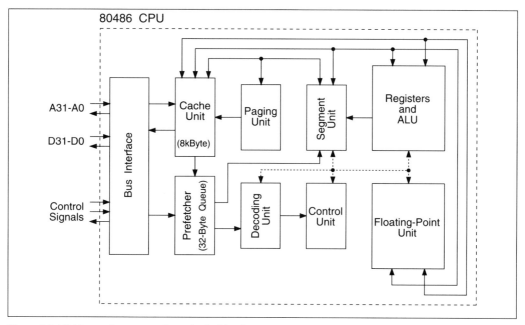

Figure 5.2: i486 internal structure. On a single chip, the i486 integrates not only an improved CPU, but also a more powerful version of the i387, a cache controller, and an 8 kbyte cache. The prefetch queue grew to 32 bytes.

Connection to the rest of the (computer) world is established by the bus unit: it accepts or supplies data via the D31–D0 data bus, addresses the two address spaces via the A31–A2, BE3–BE0 address bus, and supplies information concerning the i486's state, or accepts instructions from outside via the control bus. The bus unit is directly connected to the cache unit. The integrated 8 kbyte cache buffers data as well as instructions, and delivers them to the registers, ALU, floating point unit or the prefetcher. Unlike the memory cycles for an external cache memory (a so-called *second-level cache*), an access to the internal cache is carried out within a single bus cycle. For external cache memories, on the other hand, two bus cycles are required. Although the internal cache is rather small with its 8 kbyte capacity, this leads to a very significant increase in performance.

If data or instructions not buffered in the cache have to be read from memory, the registers or the prefetcher directly access the bus unit. This may happen if very scattered data has to be processed, or if a jump instruction to an address far away is executed.

Behind the cache the paths of the data and instruction bytes separate. The data bytes are transferred to the register or floating-point unit; the instruction bytes are handed over to the prefetch queue, which comprises 32 bytes in the i486. The decoder unit decodes the instructions held by the prefetch queue and transfers them to the control unit that controls the registers, ALU, segmentation unit and floating-point unit. Some instructions no longer need to be decoded in the i486, as was the case with the earlier 80x86 processors, but can be executed immediately. Thus, the i486 partially integrates RISC technologies to enhance performance. (The concepts and ideas behind RISC are explained later.)

If immediate operands or displacements are present in the instruction stream, the prefetcher separates them and transfers them to the ALU or segmentation unit. The data bytes fetched are supplied to the segmentation unit, registers, ALU or floating-point unit and processed there. The two 32-bit data buses form a 64-bit data bus for transferring data between the CPU core corresponding to the i386 and the floating-point unit corresponding to the i387. Unlike the i386/i387 combination, no I/O bus cycles are required for transferring data and opcodes between the CPU and the coprocessor. Further, the data exchange runs internally with a width of 64 bits compared to the 32-bit data bus on the i386/i387. This becomes noticeable, of course, in the execution speed of floating-point instructions. Thus, the i486 executes ESC instructions much faster than the i386/i387 combination.

For address evaluation the i486, like all other members of the 80x86 family, uses a segment and an offset register. In the segmentation unit the contents of the two registers are combined into a linear address. In protected mode the segmentation unit simultaneously carries out the relevant protection checks to ensure protection of the individual tasks and the system. If paging is active then the linear address evaluated in the segmentation unit is further translated into a physical address by the paging unit. Without paging, the linear address is identical to the physical address. The bus unit then supplies the physical address, and eventually the data to be written, or fetches the addressed data.

The i486 also has four write buffers. If the i486 bus is currently not available – for example, because the i486 is currently carrying out a cache line fill – the processor writes the data into a write buffer first. The buffers may be filled at a rate of one write process per clock cycle. The data is put into the four buffers in the order in which it is output by the i486. If the bus is available later, the write buffers transfer the data to the bus on their own. If, on the other hand, the i486 bus is immediately available in a write process, the write buffers are bypassed and the write data is directly transferred to the bus. If the write process leads to a cache hit, the data is stored in the on-chip cache in both cases.

Additionally, the i486 may alter the order of bus unit read and write accesses to further increase performance. This is the case if all write accesses waiting in the write buffers for execution are cache hits and the read access is a cache miss. Then the i486 carries out the read access first, followed by the write accesses. This is possible because the read access does not reference a memory location that has to be updated by one of these write accesses first.

Thus the write buffers enhance the performance of the i486 bus for several successive write accesses. If the bus is unavailable for a short time then the CPU need not wait, but simply writes the data into the buffers. The i386, on the other hand, implements no write buffers; the bus access may be delayed, and the i386 performance thus degraded.

5.3 Less is More – RISC Versus CISC

The abbreviations RISC and CISC stand for *reduced instruction set computer* and *complex instruction set computer*, respectively. The latter refers to microprocessors such as, for example, Intel's 80x86 family or Motorola's 68000 generation, which is used (besides others) in Apple Macintosh computers. Characteristic of CISC processors is their extensive instruction set of more than 300 machine instructions, the complex addressing schemes, and the *microencoding* of the processor instructions. In contrast, RISC processors such as Intel's i860, the MIPS R2000 and R3000 or the SPARC processors have a significantly reduced instruction set. But let us first turn to the concept of microprogramming.

From Figure 5.2 and the accompanying description, we already know that the instructions are read into the prefetch queue and are decoded by a decoding unit. Each instruction is not immediately executable but is available as a so-called *microprogram* in a ROM within the processor. Figure 5.3 shows the scheme of this concept that forms the basis of the technique.

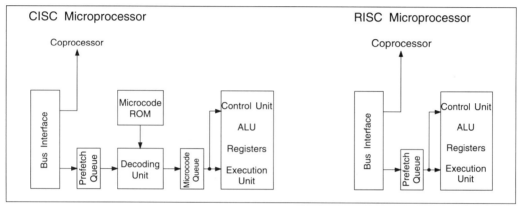

Figure 5.3: The concept of microprogramming. In the case of microprogramming (left) the processor fetches the instructions via a bus interface into the prefetch queue, which in turn delivers them to the decoding unit. The decoding unit decodes a machine instruction into a plurality of elementary microinstructions and transmits them to a microcode queue. From the microcode queue, the microinstructions are transferred to the control and the execution units so that the ALU and the registers are controlled appropriately. In a RISC microprocessor, on the other hand, the machine instructions in the prefetch queue are directly executable, and don't need to be decoded into a sequence of microinstructions.

Thus the decoding unit in the processor must decode the read instruction first, that is, separate it into instruction opcode, addressing scheme, size and type of the referred registers, etc. The control unit calls the corresponding microprogram which executes the instruction by means of the ALU, registers, etc. It is obvious that the decoding process also needs some time, which may be as long as or even longer than the actual execution time of the instruction concerned. Thus the execution time consists of the decoding and the execution time of the instruction. The prefetch queue also plays an important role in this case apart from relieving the strain on the bus unit. Because in the prefetch queue the next instructions are present prior to the execution of the current instruction, the decoding unit may work in advance and decode the next instructions, preparing them for execution in the control unit while this is still occupied by the current instruction. Thus a large prefetch queue enhances the processor's performance. Also, this is one reason why the i486 with its 32-byte prefetch queue operates faster than the i386 with a prefetch queue of only 16 bytes.

All of this works well as long as the prefetch queue is regularly refilled at the same speed at which the processor executes the instructions. In the course of a jump or procedure call that goes beyond the boundary of the prefetch queue (which frequently occurs), the processor has to cancel its prefetch queue and start fetching an instruction byte at the destination address. The same applies, of course, to RET and IRET instructions. The problem is that the next instructions not only need to be fetched but also decoded. Thus the control unit must wait quite a time before the next decoded instruction becomes available. If you are investigating a compiled program with a debugger then you will see that the program is teeming with JUMPs and CALLs. For example, compilers often encode the CASE command in C into a number of conditional JUMPs. If the target address is located outside that region which is covered by the prefetch queue, the processor also has to restart decoding from the beginning. The compilation of the source code into an unadvantageous sequence of JUMP instructions may degrade the execution time of a program significantly. (Assembler programmers should also note this.) Unfortunately, optimizing compilers manufactured by well-known firms also like to jump beyond the prefetch boundaries, sometimes for no reason.

With all of these disadvantages for microprogramming, one might get the impression that the developers didn't think very carefully. That is, of course, not true. Moreover, microprogramming developed in the historical context, and also exhibits advantages, one of which is that with a very compact instruction encoding, the instruction size (and therefore the required amount of memory in which to store them) is also low. With one byte you may encode up to 256 different instruction codes. In the early 1960s the core memory constituting the read/write memory of a computer was the most expensive – and unfortunately also the slowest – component of a computer, with an average access time of 1 μs. Today, high-quality DRAMs achieve about 0.060 μs and fast SRAMs even 0.012 μs. On the other hand, ROMs with an access time of 100 ns could already be realized at that time. Moreover, these ROMs were much cheaper than core memory, thus ten ROM accesses could be carried out in the time necessary for one access to the read/write memory. In other words, while one instruction code is read from the read/write memory, ten accesses to the microcode ROM within the CPU could be executed. Microencoding thus slowed instruction execution down only a little at that time.

Price and the low operating speed of core memory therefore supported the concept of loading only a little program code into the read/write memory. Instead, the encoding complexity was transferred to the cheaper and faster (microcode) ROM within the processor. The result was microprogramming. In the 1960s, no microprocessors existed, of course. Their functions were carried out by (in today's terms) gigantic processor boards. With the development of microprocessors, however, nothing has changed in the concept of microprogramming for a long time.

Another advantage of microprogramming is that compatibility with former processors can easily be achieved. For this only the old code must be preserved, and for more powerful new processors further instructions have to be added and stored in an eventually enlarged microcode ROM on the processor's chip. Thus it is not surprising that the «higher» members of the various processor families received more and more instructions which, moreover, became more powerful with each generation. The path to CISCs was sketched. The summit of this development is currently Intel's i486 and Motorola's 68040 processors.

The enormous advances in memory technology, and particularly the jump from core to today's semiconductor memories, has inverted the relationship of the access time for the internal microcode ROM and the external main memory slowly but steadily. Because of the huge integration density of these memory chips, and the accompanying price drop, processors are much more expensive today, and it is hardly significant whether or not an instruction code is very compact. An intensive statistical investigation carried out by IBM in the mid-1970s led to unexpected but impressive results:

- In a typical program for CISC processors only about 20% of the instructions occupy 80% of the execution time.
- There are circumstances in which the execution of a sequence of simple instructions is executed faster than a complex instruction with the same result.

For the second result, the decoding time is largely responsible, that is, the execution times indicated by the processor manufacturers are only correct under the assumption that the instruction has already been decoded and is ready for execution. The decoding time is not taken into account. For a very complex instruction the decoding time can be very long, so that several simple and speedy decodable instructions may be executed more quickly under certain circumstances.

Looking at the first result, more reasonable than reducing the number of available instructions to the 20% actually needed is optimizing these instructions as far as possible, so that they can be executed in a significantly shorter time. This led to the concept of RISC processors which are no longer microencoded. Instead, all instructions can immediately be executed by a wired logic without the intervention of a microprogram. Thus, nearly all instructions are completed within one clock cycle. The simple instruction MOV reg, reg, for example, needs two clock cycles on an i386 but only one on the i486. The i486 is in some sense a cross between the CISC and RISC processors. The often used instructions are wired as in a RISC CPU, and thus can be executed very quickly. More complex and less frequently used instructions, on the other hand, are implemented as microcode. If you are only programming for the i486, you should consider whether a sequence of simple instructions would operate more quickly than one complex instruction.

The RISC concepts of manufacturers differ, of course, but many main characteristics are equivalent:

- reducing the instruction set;
- instruction pipelining: the interleaved execution of several instructions;
- load-store-architecture: only the load and store instructions access memory; all other instructions refer to internal registers only;
- RISC processor and compiler form a single unit: the compiler is no longer developed afterwards for a certain chip, but processor and compiler form an entity from the beginning;
- a modified register concept: for a fast subroutine call in some RISC processors the registers are no longer managed statically, as AX, BX, etc., but a movable register window exists which provides a «look» into certain register files.

One main feature of RISC is the unity of processor and compiler. Until now, one team of engineers usually developed the processor and another developed the compilers and system software. The dialogue between processor and software was carried out over a well-defined interface, namely the processor's instruction set. In modern RISC concepts, on the other hand, processor and compiler form a single unit from the beginning. The RISC chip implements only those instructions which simplify the compiler's work and speed up program execution. The homogeneity of compiler and processor enables far more efficient program optimizations by the compiler than is possible with conventional CISC processors and their add-on compilers.

In summary, one could say that the concept of microprogramming is similar in some respects to a simple BASIC interpreter. There also, an instruction is separated into its components first (that is, interpreted), and then executed according to the decoded components. Microprogramming, of course, does not implement such powerful instructions as, for example, GWBASIC, nor may instructions be nested, as is possible with PRINT (STRLEN(«ww»+A$+STRING(20, «q»))+9). Program execution in RISC processors, on the other hand, can be compared to a compiled program: the instructions are immediately executed without any further intervention of a major (microcode) program. The performance differences between an interpreted and a compiled BASIC program are well known, thus it is not surprising that a RISC processor executes its instructions three to four times faster than a comparable CISC processor. Unfortunately, RISC machines are (to date) very expensive, and are therefore only used in the workstation domain. The whole host of MS-DOS programs for Intel's CISC world possibly ensures that PCs will survive for a long time to come, despite the power of modern RISC concepts.

5.4 i486 and i386/i387 – Differences and Similarities

As a member of the 80x86 family, the i486 is downward-compatible to the i386/i387 combination. In the following sections only the main differences between the two are compared, and new internals introduced.

The i486 flag register (Figure 5.4) has been expanded by the AC or alignment check flag because the i486 implements an alignment check.

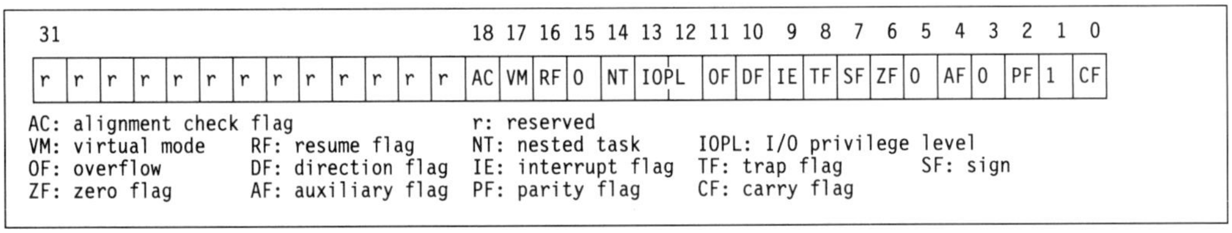

31												18 17 16 15 14 13 12 11 10 9 8 7 6 5 4 3 2 1 0

```
31                                          18 17 16 15 14 13 12 11 10  9  8  7  6  5  4  3  2  1  0
 r  r  r  r  r  r  r  r  r  r  r  r  r  AC VM RF 0  NT IOPL  OF DF IE TF SF ZF 0  AF 0  PF 1  CF

AC: alignment check flag              r: reserved
VM: virtual mode       RF: resume flag        NT: nested task      IOPL: I/O privilege level
OF: overflow           DF: direction flag     IE: interrupt flag   TF: trap flag      SF: sign
ZF: zero flag          AF: auxiliary flag     PF: parity flag      CF: carry flag
```

Figure 5.4: i486 EFLAG register.

If the *AC* flag is set (that is, equal to 1), then the i486 issues an exception corresponding to interrupt 17h if an alignment error occurs. Only programs running at privilege level 3 are affected by the alignment check; all other privilege levels ignore an alignment error. Alignment errors may occur in a word access to an odd address, a double-word access to an address which is not a multiple of four, or in an 8-byte access which is not a multiple of eight. All other flags have the same, unaltered meaning. For caching support and the protection of data on a page-level, the control registers CR0 and CR3 have been extended. CR0 incorporates five and CR3 two new bits. Figure 5.5 shows the altered control registers CR0 and CR3.

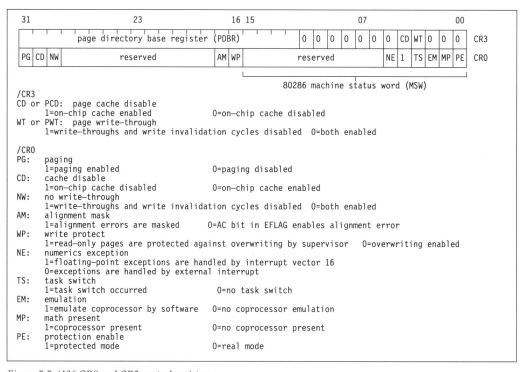

Figure 5.5: i486 CR0 and CR3 control registers.

With the *CD* and *NW* bits in the CR0 control register you can control the operation mode of the i486's on-chip cache. With a set CD-bit the cache is not refilled after a cache miss, thus it is disabled. Whether a line in the cache is replaced after a cache miss is not only dependent upon CD, but also on the signal at the $\overline{\text{KEN}}$ pin and the PCD bit in the CR3 control register. Only if all three values equal 0 does the i486 refill its cache after a cache miss. With the NW bit you can control the write behaviour of the on-chip cache if it is enabled. If the NW bit is cleared, all write data are actually output via the pins independent of a cache hit or miss, that is, written into main memory. Thus a *write-through* is carried out. Additionally, invalidation cycles are allowed which remove an entry from the cache if the invalidation address leads to a cache hit. If NW is set then all write-throughs and write invalidation cycles are disabled. In this case, the data is not written into main memory but only into the internal cache. No signal appears at the corresponding pins. Only if the address to write is not present in the cache, so that a cache miss occurs, does the i486 output the value to main memory. Invalidation cycles are ignored with a set NW bit.

With the *AM* bit it is possible to define whether the AC bit in the EFLAG register can issue an alignment exception. A set AM bit allows exceptions, and a cleared one masks the AC flag, thus the AM bit has a higher priority than the AC flag.

With the *WP* bit it is possible to protect pages marked as read-only in the page table entry against overwriting by a supervisor, that is, a program with a privilege level of 0–2. With the i386, on the other hand, read-only pages can always be overwritten by a supervisor. The more restricted protection mechanism (by segmentation in the protected mode) is not affected by this. It still has a higher priority. With the WP bit, segment areas can be protected against overwriting. The protection mechanisms of the protected mode, however, protect complete segments and not only parts of them. This is very important for operating systems with «flat» memory models (for example, UNIX), because these systems use only a single segment. On an i386/i486, this segment can comprise 4 Gbytes of memory. With the WP bit it is possible to emulate the segment-by-segment protection of the segmented memory model.

The *NE* bit controls the behaviour of the i486 when a non-masked numerics exception occurs. If NE is set then the exception is handled by means of interrupt 10h and the i486 issues an interrupt 10h. With a cleared NE bit, the exception is serviced with an external hardware interrupt, ensuring compatibility with DOS systems. For this purpose, the i486 recognizes the $\overline{\text{IGNNE}}$ and $\overline{\text{FERR}}$ signals. If an inactive (high-level) signal is applied to the $\overline{\text{IGNNE}}$ input of the i486, then the processor activates the $\overline{\text{FERR}}$ signal if a numeric error occurs. An external interrupt controller may receive the signal and issue a hardware interrupt request to the i486. During the course of its acknowledgement, the controller supplies the i486 with the handler address. In PCs, $\overline{\text{FERR}}$ is identical to IRQ13 and an interrupt 75h is issued. The LMSW instruction, supported by the i486 for compatibility reasons, does not alter the NE bit.

On the i486 the page table entries take caching into account by means of two new bits. Figure 5.6 shows the format of an i486 page table entry.

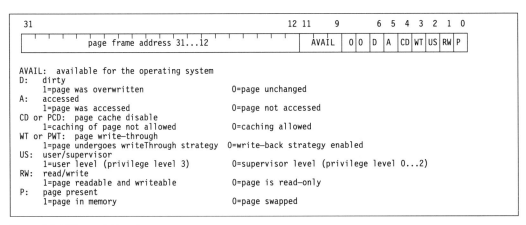

Figure 5.6: i486 page table entry.

The two new *PCD* and *PWT* bits define the cache strategy for the page concerned. With a set PCD bit, the page data is prevented from transferring to the on-chip cache. If the PCD bit is cleared then caching of the page's data is possible. If PWT is set the i486 carries out a write-through for the page concerned. If PWT is equal to 0, then in the case of a write hit the data is written only into the cache and not into main memory. In the CR3 control register (see Figure 5.5) these two bits are also implemented. They have the same meaning there, but refer to the page directory entry and not the page table entry.

If the i486 accesses a page in the external memory, it outputs signals at the PWT and PCD pins which correspond to the PWT and PCD bits in the page table or page directory entry. With paging disabled (that is, PE bit in the CR0 control register equals 0), PCD and PWT are assumed to be 0 independent of their actual value in CR3.

As well as the two test registers TR6 and TR7 for checking the translation lookaside buffer in the i386, the i486 has three more test registers, TR3–TR5, to check its own on-chip cache.

Like the i386, the i486 can conduct an internal self-test after a reset. For this the AHOLD pin must be held at a high level for two clock cycles before and after activating the RESET signal. Besides the CPU logic, the self-test also checks the on-chip cache and the floating-point unit. After completion, the high-order DX byte contains the value 04h (for i486) and the low-byte the version number. The i486 starts execution in the same way as the i386 at address ffffff0h. After the first intersegment jump or call, the address lines A31–A20 fall to a low-level and the i486 only addresses in real mode the first Mbyte of the address space available.

5.5 i486 Bus and Burst Cycles

The i486 has a very flexible bus in view of its size and cycle behaviour. The data bus can be operated with a width of 8, 16 and 32 bits by the $\overline{BS8}$ and $\overline{BS16}$ signals. The bus width can be defined separately and independently for every cycle, and need not be predefined at the time of system design. Thus the i486 can cooperate flexibly with memories and peripherals of various widths.

For the transfer of large amounts of data the i486 implements a new bus mode called *burst mode*. In normal mode one bus cycle without wait states lasts two clock cycles, as is the case for the i386. Therefore, the i486 can read or write one quantity within two processor clock cycles. In burst mode the time necessary for transferring one quantity is reduced to one clock cycle, thus the transfer rate is double. The burst mode is subject to some restrictions, though, and is therefore not always applicable.

A burst cycle is started by a first normal memory access which lasts for two clock cycles. With an inactive $\overline{BLAST}$ during the second clock cycle, the i486 indicates that it wants to execute a burst cycle. If the addressed system is able to carry out a burst cycle it reacts by activating the $\overline{BRDY}$ signal. All further accesses then last for only one clock cycle. To terminate the burst cycle the i486 activates the $\overline{BLAST}$ signal in the final access, showing that the last value of the current burst cycle is transferred with the next $\overline{BRDY}$ or $\overline{RDY}$. Figure 5.7 shows a signal diagram for a burst cycle.

The burst cycle is restricted in that the amount of data to be transferred within one burst cycle must fall into a single 16-byte area which starts at a 16-byte boundary, that is, their addresses must be in the range xxxxxxx0h to xxxxxxxfh (xxxxxxx = 0000000h to fffffffh). This corresponds to a cache line in the internal cache memory. If the intended data goes beyond this address area, then the burst cycle must be split into two cycles. Because of this address area restriction, only the A2, A3 and $\overline{BE0}$–$\overline{BE3}$ address signals change during a burst cycle; all other relevant signals like A31–A4, M/$\overline{IO}$, D/$\overline{C}$ and W/$\overline{R}$ remain the same. The addressed external system is thus able to determine the address of the succeeding transfers easily and efficiently. The decode overhead is therefore reduced, and only one clock cycle is required.

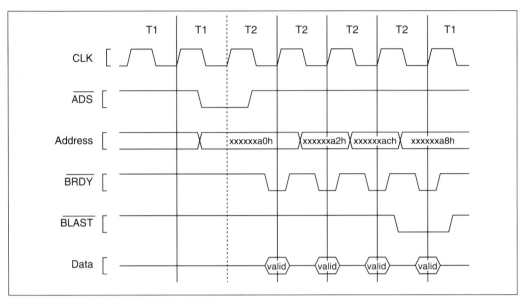

Figure 5.7: i486 burst cycle. In i486 burst mode the bus cycle for a 16-byte area is shortened from two to one processor clock cycle; only the first access needs two clock cycles. A cache line of the internal cache, for example, can thus be filled very quickly.

The burst cycle is especially suited to filling a cache line which comprises exactly 16 bytes and starts at a 16-byte boundary, or loading a TSS during the course of a task switch, as well as for descriptors. Unfortunately, write cycles can only be carried out in burst mode up to 32 bits. If the full width of the i486 data bus (32 bits) is used, then no advantages result from the burst mode for a data write. Only if the the data bus is set to a width of 8 or 16 bits by means of the $\overline{BS8}$ and $\overline{BS16}$ signals is the write operation carried out faster in burst mode. Thus, 16 bytes at most can be read in the burst mode. With a data bus width of 32 bits, four read cycles are required in total. In burst mode the i486 needs 2 + 3 = 5 clock cycles for this. The transfer rate of 16 bytes within five clock cycles on a 50 MHz i486 corresponds to a burst transfer rate of 160 Mbyte/s. However when looking at this huge number, note that this rate is only valid for 0.1 μs and, moreover, may only be achieved for read accesses. For a data write without wait states, the transfer rate reaches 100 Mbyte/s. This is, nevertheless, a remarkable value. Fast hard disk drives, on the other hand, allow only a transfer rate of about 1 to 2 Mbyte/s. Thus, the processor bus is not the bottleneck in the system; the (unfortunately very effective) breaks are located elsewhere. (These bottlenecks are discussed later.)

5.6 On-Chip and Second-Level Caches

As already mentioned, the i486 comprises an on-chip cache with a capacity of 8 kbytes. At first glance, this seems to be too small, nevertheless these 8 kbytes lead to quite a significant performance increase, especially for fetching CPU code. Besides the on-chip cache, an external cache can also be present. Common i486 motherboards typically have a cache memory with 128–256 kbytes, called second-level cache. If the i486 is unable to locate the intended data in its internal cache, it looks in the external cache memory as a second step. The external second-level cache may, in principle, be expanded to any size. The external cache controller must obviously be able to handle such a cache memory.

One main difference between on-chip and second-level cache is that the i486 can read data from the on-chip cache in a single clock cycle. An access to the second-level cache, on the other hand, has to carry out a normal bus cycle, which lasts two clock cycles. Thus an access to the on-chip cache is significantly faster. For pure CPU and memory benchmarks such as, for example, the Landmark Test, the activation of the on-chip cache increases the displayed performance by a factor of four. In practice, the on-chip cache is effective only for sequential read accesses to this extent. For data which is spread over an area of more than these 8 kbytes, the gain is not so high. Iterating mathematical calculations which are largely based on joined and frequently executed program loops are strongly accelerated by this; database accesses, on the other hand, are not.

One line of the on-chip cache is always filled by a burst cycle if the main memory can do this. On the other hand, not every cache controller is designed for such a compressed bus cycle. The 485Turbocache can execute such a cycle, others cannot. Stated briefly, the i486 operates really quickly if the current code and data are located within an 8 kbyte area loaded into the on-chip cache. A significant performance deterioration occurs if code and data are spread to such an extent that they can no longer be held in the second-level cache. Then the CPU has to carry out a longer bus cycle. Finally, another significant jump to a longer execution time occurs if the second-level cache is also no longer able to hold the data, and the i486 must carry out an ordinary main memory access. Even advanced concepts such as paging and interleaving are slow compared to the on-chip cache of a 50 MHz i486 (but they're real missiles compared to the 250 ns DRAMs from the PC's Stone Age!)

5.7 i486SX and i487SX – First Reduce, Then Upgrade

Intel has continued the SX concept with the i486 and developed an i486SX along with the accompanying i487 «coprocessor». What especially characterizes the i487SX as an upgrade instead of a coprocessor will be discussed in the following sections.

5.7.1 The i486SX – More Than an i386

Shortly after having presented the i486, Intel introduced a «light» version similar to the i386: the i486SX. Because only a few PC users are involved in highly mathematical applications like CAD or solving differential equations, the integrated coprocessor is unnecessary for most users, and only has the effect of increasing the PC's price. Thus Intel left out the coprocessor in the i486SX, but all the other features which characterize the i486 compared to the i386 (on-chip cache, RISC core, etc.) have been kept. The result is a very fast processor which can equal the i486 in normal applications (at the same clock rate, of course). Only in intensive mathematical applications is the i486SX significantly slower. This can be solved by additionally using the i487SX «coprocessor». The quote marks already indicate that the i487SX may not be classified as a pure member of the 80x87 family. Moreover, with the i487SX Intel introduced the concept of so-called *upgrades* which not only deliver a further coprocessor, but also enhance the performance of the CPU itself. Further details concerning this are given later.

Package Types

The i486SX comes in two different package types: a pin grid array with 168 pins, as well as a plastic quad flat package (PQFP) with 196 terminals. Figure 5.8 shows the layout of these two packages.

Besides the five new terminals, the PQFP version of the i486SX implements the following additional features:

– boundary scan test (JTAG),
– lower power consumption by an improved CMOS design,
– power-down mode which reduces the power consumption from about 500 mA to 50 mA.

In the following, the five additional terminals of the PQFP version are discussed. The most important is the $\overline{\text{UP}}$ pin, which is intended for upgrade support by an i487SX.

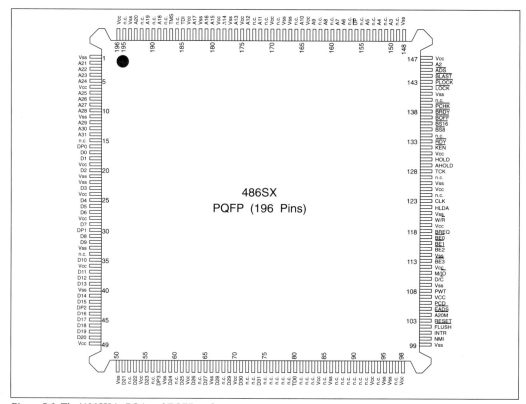

Figure 5.8: The i486SX in PGA and PQFP packages.

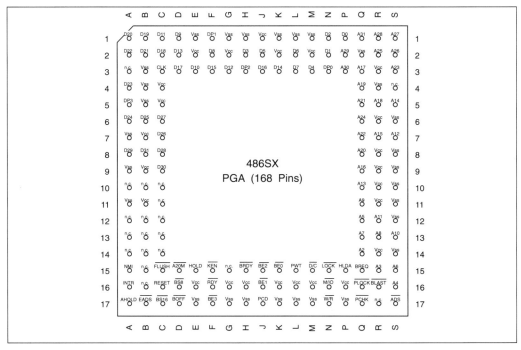

Figure 5.8: cont.

$\overline{UP}$

(Update Present) If this connection is supplied with a low-level signal, the i486SX cuts off all inputs and outputs and enters a power-down mode with significantly reduced power consumption. In other words, the i486SX is more or less disabled.

TCK

(Test Clock) The terminal is supplied with a test clock signal for the boundary-scan test.

TDI

(Test Data Input) TDI is a serial input that is provided with JTAG instructions and data.

TDO

(Test Data Output) TDO is a serial output for shifting-out JTAG instructions and data.

TMS

(Test Mode Select) If a high-level signal is applied to this connection, the TAP (tap access port) starts operation of the JTAG test logic for the boundary scan test.

JTAG Boundary Scan Test

The four terminals TCK, TDI, TDO and TMS serve to support a so-called boundary scan test according to the IEEE 1149.1 standard. This test checks the logical units in the i486SX and their wiring by means of software even after completion of manufacturing and integration into a PC. For this, the i486SX implements an internal boundary scan register and a JTAG logic which is accessed via the test access port (TAP). The test is executed by an external bus master because the i486SX is not able to drive the bus during this mode. Only the JTAG test bus with its four connections (TCK, TDI, TDO, TMS) is serviced.

The boundary scan test is executed by means of a predefined test instruction set which currently comprises five instructions. They are listed in Table 5.1 together with the 4-bit opcodes.

Instruction	Opcode	Meaning
EXTEST	0000b	tests the external connection of the i486SX
SAMPLE/	0001b	samples the current state of an i486SX unit
PRELOAD		or defines data for the output pins
IDCODE	0010b	reads the ID code of the CPU and outputs it via TDO
RUNBIST	1000b	activates the built-in self-test (BIST) of the i486SX
BYPASS	1111b	bypasses the i486SX test logic to shorten the shift path in the processor
PRIVATE	all others	

Table 5.1: JTAG opcodes

As for the test data, these instructions are also input into the i486SX serially by means of the input TDI pin. The clock signal at the TCK input serves as the test clock. After completing a test instruction, result data are available in a result register which can be output via the TDO connection. The external bus master can then check these result data and determine whether the i486SX is operating correctly.

Manufacturers also carry out a similar test with the DRAM and SRAM chips, to test whether the chips are working correctly after manufacture, or whether malfunctions have occurred. Various test patterns are written into the memory cells for this, and the data is read out again to determine whether it has changed. Some chip faults may only be detected by certain data patterns. The individual addressing of memory cells and an external data comparison would then last too long. Therefore, most modern chips have an internal test logic. The extensive test data are serially input very quickly by means of a certain pin, as is the case with the JTAG test, and only the result data (chip OK or not) are again output via another (or sometimes the same) pin.

5.7.2 Clock Frequencies

One disadvantage of the SX as compared to the i486DX is the lower clock frequency. The i486SX comes with 25 MHz at most, and the processor accordingly operates far slower. The performance reduction is only a consequence of the lower clock frequency, though, and not of a less effective SX chip construction.

Some manufacturers check CPU chips to see whether they can also stand a higher clock frequency. This is often the case, therefore i486SX boards up to clock frequencies of 33 MHz are available. Technically speaking, the DX and SX chip models do not differ much; they are manufactured at the same scale and with a comparable layout. The manufacturing tolerances are simply more generous with the SX, and thus their manufacture is easier and cheaper, leading to a higher production yield. A processor which malfunctions at 25 MHz but runs correctly at 20 MHz would be no good as a DX model, but leaves the plant as a checked 20 MHz SX chip.

As 33 MHz i486 chips exist, it might be possible, of course, that among a number of technologically equivalent i486SX chips there is one which has been manufactured just as well as the more critical i486DX by chance, and is also running at 33 MHz without any malfunction. For example, the 60 ns model DRAM chips do not differ from their 100 ns counterparts in either technology or manufacturing methods. With the 60 ns models, every manufacturing step is carried out in way the best possible way. During the course of manufacturing the 100 ns chip, there may have been the misalignment of a photo mask by 100 nm. Following completion of manufacturing it is then checked to which clock frequency the chip runs without problems, and the chip is accordingly specified then. The best ones get the *-60* stamp, the less well manufactured (but fully operable at lower clock frequencies) ones get the *-100* stamp.

5.7.3 i487SX–i486SX Upgrade

Starting with the i487SX, Intel introduced the upgrading concept. Until now the 80x87 coprocessors have only been a numerical extension of the 80x86 CPUs, and have been accessed in I/O cycles via reserved ports. With the i487SX this has changed completely. The i487SX is not only a numerical coprocessor, but also a complete i486 CPU with an addressing unit, bus unit, CPU core, cache and, of course, a numerical unit. Thus, the i487SX can be compared to a low-clocked i486DX. It is available for clock frequencies between 16 and 25 MHz, and is shipped in a pin grid array package with 169 pins. The only difference from the i486DX is the additional encoding pin and the reservation of pin B14 for the $\overline{\text{MP}}$ (**m**ath **p**resent) signal. Figure 5.9 shows the pin assignment of the i487SX.

Now the upgrade principle becomes clear. Not only is the numerical coprocessor delivered, as has been the case up to now, but the upgrades additionally integrate a powerful CPU. Thus the performance enhancement is not limited to new instructions and data formats, as is the case with the numerical 80x87 coprocessors, but the CPU itself is replaced by a more powerful CPU core integrated on the upgrade. The upgrade processor only has to inform the previous CPU that it is now present. This is carried out in the i487SX by means of the additional $\overline{\text{MP}}$ signal, indicating that an upgrade is present that now takes over all functions of the previous CPU. The old CPU is not actually necessary any more: upgrading is thus, more or less, a replacement of the old CPU by a new one without the need to remove the previous CPU. The 169th pin, D4, serves for encoding so that the i487SX may not be inserted into the upgrade socket with a wrong orientation. Intel has implemented this pin because, according to the new strategy, the general public should be able to carry out upgrading without major problems.

For combining the i486SX in the PQFP package and 196 pins with the i487SX in the PGA, connection of the CPU and upgrade is very simple (see Figure 5.10a). The $\overline{\text{MP}}$ outputs of the i487SX must be connected to the $\overline{\text{UP}}$ input of the i486SX. The i487SX outputs a low-level signal at the $\overline{\text{UP}}$ which informs the $\overline{\text{MP}}$ input of the i486SX that an upgrade is present. The i486SX then cuts off all its connections to the bus and enters a power-down mode to save power. The i486SX now draws only 50 mA instead of 500 mA, and the heat dissipation is accordingly less. The connection $\overline{\text{MP}}$ of the i487SX is pulled to a high level by means of internal resistors in the i486SX. Therefore, the i486SX operates normally without an i487SX. However, with an inserted i487SX the signal $\overline{UP}$ is stronger, and it pulls $\overline{MP}$ to low. Without an i487SX the $\overline{FERR}$ signal is always kept on a high level by means of a resistor which is connected to the supply voltage V$_{cc}$. In this case, $\overline{FERR}$ thus indicates that no floating-point error has occurred. However, an i487SX present is able to drive $\overline{FERR}$ to low.

	A	B	C	D	E	F	G	H	J	K	L	M	N	P	Q	R	S	
1	D20	D19	D11	D9	Vss	DP1	Vss	Vss	Vcc	Vss	Vss	Vss	D2	D0	A31	A28	A27	1
2	D22	D21	D18	D13	Vcc	D8	Vcc	D3	D5	Vcc	D6	Vcc	D1	A29	Vss	A25	A26	2
3	n.c.	Vss	CLK	D17	D10	D15	D12	DP2	D16	D14	D7	D4	DP0	A30	A17	Vcc	A23	3
4	D23	Vss	Vcc	Code											A19	Vss	n.c.	4
5	DP3	Vss	Vcc												A21	A18	A14	5
6	D24	D25	D27												A24	Vcc	Vss	6
7	Vss	Vcc	D26												A22	A15	A12	7
8	D29	D31	D28				487SX								A20	Vcc	Vss	8
9	Vss	Vcc	D30			PGA (169 Pins)									A16	Vcc	Vss	9
10	n.c.	n.c.	n.c.												A13	Vcc	Vss	10
11	Vss	Vcc	n.c.												A8	Vcc	Vss	11
12	n.c.	n.c.	n.c.												A5	A11	Vss	12
13	$\overline{FERR}$	n.c.	n.c.												A7	A8	A10	13
14	n.c.	$\overline{MP}$	n.c.												A2	Vcc	Vss	14
15	IGNNE	NMI	$\overline{FLUSH}$	A20M	HOLD	KEN	n.c.	$\overline{BRDY}$	$\overline{BE2}$	$\overline{BE0}$	PWT	D/C	$\overline{LOCK}$	$\overline{HLDA}$	$\overline{BREQ}$	A3	A6	15
16	INTR	n.c.	RESET	$\overline{BS8}$	Vcc	$\overline{RDY}$	Vcc	Vcc	$\overline{BE1}$	Vcc	Vcc	Vcc	M/IO	Vcc	$\overline{PLOCK}$	$\overline{BLAST}$	A4	16
17	AHOLD	$\overline{EADS}$	$\overline{BS16}$	$\overline{BOFF}$	Vss	$\overline{BE3}$	Vss	Vss	PCD	Vss	Vss	Vss	W/R	Vss	$\overline{PCHK}$	n.c.	$\overline{ADS}$	17
	A	B	C	D	E	F	G	H	J	K	L	M	N	P	Q	R	S	

Figure 5.9: i487SX pin assignment.

The circuitry gets significantly more complicated if an i486SX in the PGA package with 168 pins is used. This model has no input $\overline{UP}$, so the i487SX can't tell the i486SX of its presence. Moreover, this i486SX model implements no power-down mode. The i486SX thus draws 500 mA even with an upgrade present, although it makes no contribution to the computer's performance but waits for activation *ad infinitum*. Because of the missing $\overline{UP}$ input, we have to apply a trick to separate the i486SX from the bus. This is carried out via the $\overline{BOFF}$ connection. Additionally, an active $\overline{FLUSH}$ signal for the i486SX causes it to write back its internal cache into memory to avoid data being lost immediately after a reset or the PC's power-on. The $\overline{BOFF}$ and $\overline{FLUSH}$ pins are driven by the $\overline{MP}$ output of the i487SX. Because $\overline{BOFF}$ may also be activated by an external logic in normal i486Sx operation, the i486SX is not able to determine with $\overline{BOFF}$

whether an upgrade is present or if an external logic is the source of $\overline{BOFF}$. Thus, an eventually present power-down mode would not give rise to any advantages. With an active $\overline{BOFF}$ the i486SX lowers the power consumption by no more than 20%, because all input and output buffers for the pins are deactivated. To ensure normal operation of the i486SX without an upgrade, and that the bus arbitration and signal generation for floating-point errors with and without upgrade are carried out correctly, two additional AND gates and one OR gate are required.

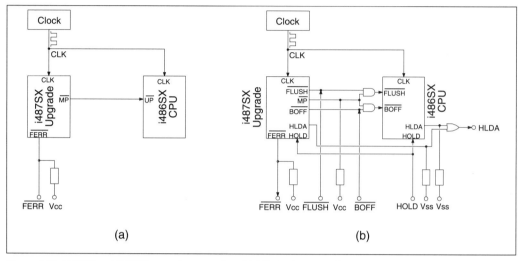

Figure 5.10: i486SX and i487SX upgrade connection. (a) i486SX in PQFP. (b) i486SX in PGA.

5.8 486DX2 Processors With Internal Frequency Doubling

Besides a variety of CPUs released in a variety of guises, recently Intel has presented the i486DX2 CPU with internal frequency doubling. The features, advantages and disadvantages of the DX2 compared to the DX are discussed in the following sections.

5.8.1 The Clock Frequencies Problem

The permanently rising CPU clock frequencies lead to two major problems. The emission of electromagnetic waves is proportional to the fourth power of the frequency. This means that for a 40 MHz i386 with an 80 MHz external clock, the emission became 80 000 times (!) larger than in the original PC with its 4.77 MHz clock. First, this requires an effective shielding of the motherboard against the environment, because otherwise you would not be able to listen to the radio any more! But much more serious are the consequences for the components in the PC or on the motherboard itself. If the resistors and capacities of the elements (and at such frequencies, also, a cable with a length of 2 cm plays an important role) are not harmonized perfectly, then signal reflexions or dampings occur which make reliable operation of the computer impossible. Therefore, with the i486 Intel decided to equalize the internal processor clock and the external clock signal. This is called a 1x-clock. The i386, on the other hand, has been externally supplied with the double processor clock frequency. The i386 then divides the external clock CLK internally by two to generate the processor clock – it is supplied with a 2x-clock. With the 50 MHz i486, even with this technique we are at a critical limit again, and if development is to go on in the same way 100 Mhz will soon be reached with a 1x-clock, too.

A further effect of these high clock rates is that the signal propagation times on the motherboard between, for example, the CPU and various buffers and drivers to the main memory are going to reach the cycle time of the clock signal even with very fast components. Even fast SRAM caches get out of step beyond 50 MHz. Only the highest quality SRAM chip (with prohibitive PC prices) allows access times down to 12 ns, corresponding to a clock frequency of 80 MHz. But these specifications are estimated very optimistically. If one adds the signal propagation delays between the CPU and SRAM via various buffers, drivers and the cache controller, then about 33 MHz to 50 MHz without wait states may be achieved. Not to talk about DRAMs....

5.8.2 The Solution – Internal Frequency Doubling

To avoid the problems indicated above, Intel had a simple but very effective idea: internal frequency doubling. This means that the i486DX2 (the «2» stands for doubling) internally doubles the supplied clock signal – a 33 MHz i486DX2 internally becomes a 66 MHz i486DX. All internal units of the CPU such as, for example, the ALU, decoding unit, floating-point unit, segmentation unit and access to the 8 kbyte cache run at twice the speed. With the 33 MHz i486DX2 this leads to 66 MHz, therefore. Only the bus unit runs from the external clock because the rest of the motherboard has to be protected from the higher clock according to this principle. Thus the i486DX2 (to keep the previous notation) is clocked by a 1/2x-clock. Doubling the clock frequency inside the processor may be achieved easily, for example, by using a switching element which is triggered by every edge of the external clock signal CLK, independently of whether the edge is rising or falling. The switching element must only be designed in a manner such that it already changes its state in advance of the next edge. For this purpose, a monostable multivibrator can be used. By choosing appropriate resistors and capacitors, the internal frequency doubling can be carried out easily. Figure 5.11 illustrates this method.

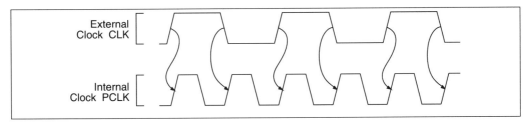

Figure 5.11: Frequency doubling by edge triggering.

Fortunately, the internally doubled clock does not give rise to the same problems as on the motherboard. For this the connections within the processor are much too short, and therefore they cannot function as antennas. With the conductor paths on the motherboard this appears to be completely different, of course.

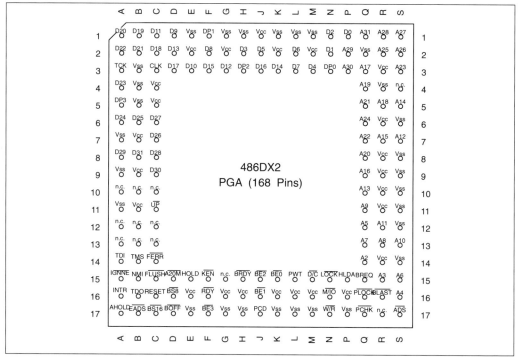

Figure 5.12: i486DX2 pin assignment.

From the outside the i486DX2 hardly differs from a normal i486DX. Figure 5.12 shows its pin assignment. The DX2 is currently available for internal clock frequencies of 50 and 66 MHz, and the external clock is 25 and 33 MHz, respectively. Thus the clock rates indicated on the chips refer to the **internal** clock frequency. All i486DX2 chips implement a boundary scan test (see Section 5.7.1). For this, the PGA comprises the four test pins TDI, TDO, TCK and TMS. Additionally, every i486DX2 is prepared so that it can accept a replacement upgrade in the future. Therefore, a connection $\overline{UP}$ (pin C11) is also present.

5.8.3 So What's the Gain?

By means of the doubled frequency of the logic units, with the exception of the bus unit all instructions are executed twice as quickly as in an i486DX which is externally clocked with the same frequency – if the data and instructions are available in time. This is fulfilled if the data required are present in a processor register or in the on-chip cache. Every access to an external memory (also to a second-level cache) slows down program execution because of the slower clocked bus unit. The access is further slowed down by the large access time if the DRAM main memory is involved. On the other hand, programs with many iteration steps such as, for example, certain mathematical applications which frequently access a small data and code area, make full use of the doubled processor clock. The 50 MHz i486DX CPU (with full external 50 MHz) carries out an access to the fast second-level cache, for example, for line fills of the internal cache significantly faster than the 50 MHz i486DX2 processor (with external 25 MHz). But for an access to main memory with the slow DRAM chips, it makes virtually no difference as to whether the processor is running with external 25 or 50 MHz. The bottleneck is located at the DRAM chips, and a «real» 50 MHz i486DX then only inserts more wait cycles.

Thus the internal frequency doubling has some major advantages. For example, it is possible to equip an existing and well-operating 33 MHz board with an i486DX2 CPU. The performance of the PC is thus enhanced significantly without any change of motherboard. This leads directly to the overdrives and the upgrade concept. Moreover, the internal frequency doubling will enable even higher frequencies in future. Instead of the 50 MHz i486DX CPU a (future) 100 MHz i486DX2 may be employed (if the internal i486DX2 circuits are still operating without any errors at this clock rate – but there are a lot of reasons to be optimistic). The required motherboard can be taken over from the 50 MHz i486DX without any alterations.

5.8.4 Clock Statements

As already mentioned, the clock statements on the processor chips always refer to the internal processor clock rate. At this time, 50 MHz i486DX and 50 MHz i486DX2 models are available in the market. Because of the double external clock rate, the DX version is somewhat faster than its DX2 counterpart. Therefore, always ask whether a DX or DX2 processor is installed. It gets even more complicated because of the huge number of i386-clones which are coming onto the market now. Remember that Cyrix' 486DLC is not a real i486. To clarify the situation, always ask for detailed and correct information from your dealer, or consult the accompanying manual.

5.8.5 Upgrading and Overdrives

The i487SX was Intel's first upgrade and referred to the i486SX. Starting with the i486DX2 CPU, Intel is continuing to upgrade as a new strategy for performance enhancement. Up to the i386, the only possibility for increasing processing power was to install an additional coprocessor. But this chip only speeds up floating-point operations; increasing the clock frequency was impossible. This has changed completely with the DX2. The so-called *overdrives* consist of an i486DX2 with the same external clock frequency as the previous processor, but by means of internal frequency doubling the processor's performance increases by 100% without the need to alter anything on the motherboard. The overdrives are inserted into an upgrade socket similar to a coprocessor but, unlike the coprocessor, they replace the previous CPU completely. Thus the CPU is disabled, and waits for its reactivation *ad infinitum*.

It's not only the older i486DX CPUs that may be replaced by an (internally) faster clocked i486DX2, but also the i486DX2 itself. Possible upgrades are, for example, the new i586. Consequently, Intel has defined an upgrade socket for the upgrade processors.

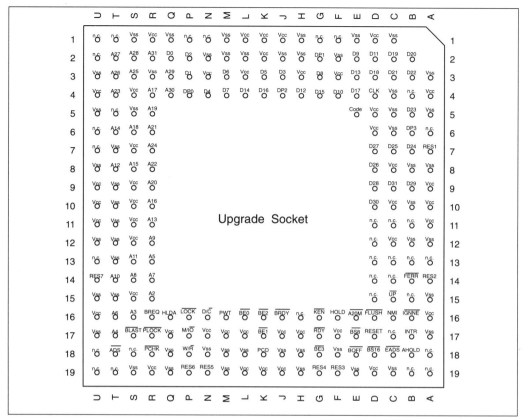

Figure 5.13: Upgrade socket layout.

Note that Figure 5.13 shows the top view of the socket in the same way as it is seen on the motherboard. The pin assignment of the processors, on the other hand, always refers to a «pin look», that is, a view from below.

As can be seen, the socket comprises four pin rows on all of the four sides, but the i486DX2 processors have only three of these rows. The outer row is therefore reserved for the additional pins of new upgrades that are not yet available in the market. Besides various connections for the supply voltages Vcc and ground Vss, these are the seven connections RES1–RES7.

Also, untrained users should be able to carry out upgrading, hence the socket has an encoding mechanism which prevents incorrect insertion of the upgrade processor (contact holes A1, A2 and B1 are missing), thus it is impossible to insert an upgrade incorrectly. Contact hole E5 (*encoding*) is present for compatibility with the i487SX, but newer upgrades no longer use it.

Because all i486DX2 processors are prepared for upgrading, they have a connection $\overline{\text{UP}}$ (**u**pgrade **p**resent, pin C11). If an upgrade is present it applies a low-level signal to the $\overline{\text{UP}}$ connection of the previous CPU to indicate that an upgrade processor is now taking over the data processing. The i486DX2 then enters power-down mode, cuts off all its outputs from the bus, and deactivates the internal function units: the power consumption thus reduces by 90%.

5.9 EISA and Microchannel – Evolution and Revolution

The introduction of the i386 and i486 32-bit microprocessors with full 32-bit data bus and 32-bit address bus also required an extension of the ISA bus. This bus was implemented for the 80286, with its 16-bit address bus and 16 Mbyte address space only. Not only is the small width of the bus system outdated today, but so are the antiquated 8-bit 8237A DMA chips, with their limitation to 64 kbyte blocks, and the rather user-unfriendly adapter configuration (using jumpers and DIP switches). Another serious contradiction between the very powerful 32-bit processors and the «tired» 8-bit AT concept is the lack of supporting bus masters on external adapter cards.

Two completely different solutions for these problems are established today: IBM's microchannel for PS/2, and EISA, which has been developed by a group of leading manufacturers of IBM-compatible PCs. IBM has gone down a completely different road with its microchannel, not only because of the new geometric layout of the bus slots, but also with the architecture implemented. Moreover, IBM has cut off the microchannel from other manufacturers by patents and other protective rights. This is a consequence of the fact that these other clone manufacturers had previously got a large part of the PC market. As IBM is rather miserly with issuing licenses, the microchannel is no longer the completely open architecture which users and manufacturers have been accustomed to with the PC/XT/AT. Together with the significantly larger functionality of the microchannel, one may speak of a radical reorganization or actually of the microchannel as a revolutionary step towards real 32-bit systems.

EISA, on the other hand, tries to take a route which might be called «evolutionary». The maxim of EISA is the possibility of integrating ISA components into the EISA system without any problems. This requires an identical geometry of the adapter cards and, therefore, unfortunately also the integration of obsolete concepts for the EISA's ISA part. With this concept, 16-bit ISA components can be integrated in an EISA system with no problems, but you don't then have any advantage. Under these conditions the EISA bus is operating more or less identically to the conventional ISA bus. Only 16- and 32-bit EISA components really take advantage of the EISA bus system, using, for example, burst cycles or 32-bit DMA. The EISA bus is capable of a data transfer rate of up to 33 Mbyte/s, compared to 8.33 Mbyte/s with an ISA bus.

In view of the technical structure, EISA is more complicated than the microchannel because it not only needs to carry out EISA bus cycles, but for compatibility reasons also ISA cycles. This applies, for example, to DMA, where the EISA system must decide whether an 8237A-compatible DMA cycle (with its known disadvantages) or a full 32-bit EISA DMA cycle has to be executed. The hardware must be able to carry out both, and thus is, of course, rather complicated. In this aspect, the microchannel has an easier life; it frees itself from the outdated PC/XT/AT concepts, and starts from a new beginning. This restriction to a new beginning makes the microchannel less complicated. However, stronger competition in the field of EISA has surely led to cheaper EISA chips, even though their technology is more complex. Additionally, as the user you have the advantage that older ISA components may also be used initially. Later you can integrate more powerful EISA peripherals. In view of the speedy development, though, who is going to use his old hard disk controller or 8-bit graphics adapter with 128 kbytes of memory when buying a computer of the previous generation?

Therefore, the more straightforward concept is surely the microchannel, which frees itself from the old traditions; but because of IBM's restrictive policy, it has been almost exclusively dedicated to IBM products up to now. On a BIOS, operating system or application level you don't notice whether you are working with an EISA or microchannel PC. Only system programmers and bit freaks have to deal with their differences.

5.9.1 EISA – The Evolution

The name EISA, as an abbreviation for *extended* **ISA,** already indicates the evolutionary concept of this 32-bit extension for the AT bus. ISA components may be used in an EISA system with no alterations. Pure EISA adapters inform the EISA system (by means of the $\overline{EX32}$ and $\overline{EX16}$ signals) that they are EISA components with the extended functions which are provided for EISA. Internally, EISA machines differ drastically from their ISA predecessors in many aspects, discussed in the following sections.

EISA Bus Structure

Figure 5.14 shows a schematic block diagram of the EISA architecture.

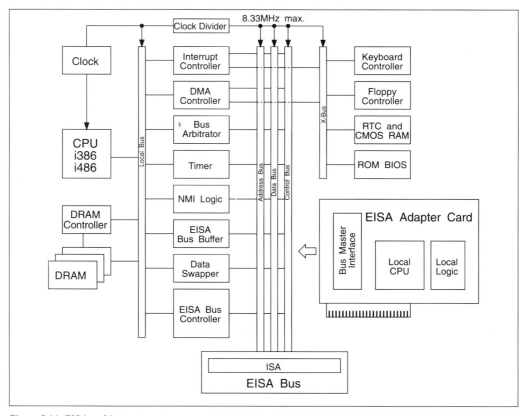

Figure 5.14: EISA architecture.

The clock generator supplies both the CPU and, after division of the frequency in the frequency divider, the EISA bus with a clock signal. Thus the EISA bus is a synchronous bus system, because the CPU and EISA bus are supplied by the same clock signal source, and are thus running synchronously. The maximum frequency of the EISA bus is 8.33 MHz. This clock rate determines the access of the CPU to all external units. On the other hand, the i386/i486 may access the main memory at the full clock frequency (with possible wait states).

The EISA bus buffer provides for a controlled data transfer between the local bus and the EISA bus. The heart of an EISA bus is the EISA bus controller. It distinguishes between EISA and ISA bus cycles, supplies all required ISA and EISA bus signals, executes normal and burst cycles, and carries out the entire bus control operation in the EISA PC. Together with the data swapper, it divides 32-bit quantities into 8- or 16-bit portions for 8- and 16-bit peripherals, or recombines such portions into a 32-bit quantity. That is necessary, for example, if you insert a 16-bit ISA adapter into an EISA slot. The EISA maxim of compatibility then requires that the EISA logic accesses the ISA adapter without any problem.

EISA adapter cards with their own bus master have a bus master interface which enables a local CPU (the bus master) to control the EISA bus. Thus, EISA is an important step towards a multiprocessor environment. Moreover, the arbitration logic and the altered assignment of DMA and interrupt channels already supports multitasking operating systems on a hardware level. It would be a pity to waste an i486 on DOS alone. Presently, there is an EISA chipset from Intel on the market that integrates the interrupt controller, DMA controller, bus arbitrator, timer and the NMI logic on a single chip: the 82357 ISP (integrated system peripheral). The bus controller is available as the 82358 EBC (EISA bus controller).

The EISA bus can carry out various bus cycles:

– standard bus cycle,
– burst cycle, and
– bus cycle with BCLK stretching.

The standard bus cycle is a normal i386 bus cycle, at least as far as the course of the participating address, data and control signals are concerned. As the EISA bus is running with a bus clock of at most 8.33 MHz, even with slow-clocked i386 CPUs a lot of CPU wait cycles are necessary. The standard bus cycle requires two BCLK cycles for transferring at most one quantity of 32 bits. The burst cycle is the same as the i486 burst cycle, but here the bus clock BCLK instead of the processor clock PCLK is decisive. A real novelty is the bus cycle with BCLK stretching. The EISA bus controller is able to stretch one half cycle of BCLK to serve slower devices at best, and to restore synchronization with the CPU clock again. Figure 5.15 illustrates this: the CPU frequency is 25 MHz, and the bus frequency BCLK is generated by dividing by three, so it is therefore 8.33 MHz. A half cycle of BCLK is stretched under two circumstances:

– synchronization of the rising BCLK edge with the falling edge of $\overline{\text{CMD}}$ if the bus master on the motherboard addresses an EISA or ISA slave;
– synchronization of the rising BCLK edge with the falling edge of $\overline{\text{CMD}}$ if an ISA master addresses an EISA slave.

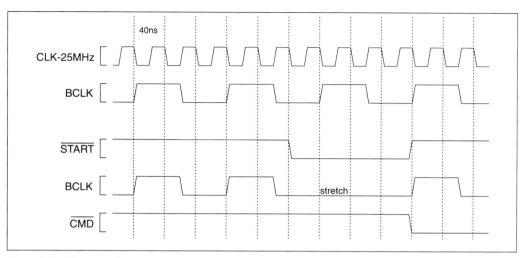

Figure 5.15: BCLK stretching. By means of stretching one half cycle of the bus clock BCLK, the bus clock can be resynchronized with slower operating devices more quickly.

By stretching BCLK, an EISA or ISA slave can be better integrated into an EISA system, as with the AT. The number of clock cycles for slower peripherals is reduced, and the system through-put is enhanced.

Arbitration

A significant advance compared to the ISA bus is *bus arbitration*. This means that an external microprocessor on an EISA adapter card can also completely control the bus, and may therefore access the system's main memory, the hard disk and all other system components on its own, without the need of support by the CPU. This is necessary for a powerful multiprocessor opera-tion if, for example, the 82596 LAN controller wants to access main memory and the hard disk. Such external *EISA bus masters* can request control of the bus by the EISA $\overline{\text{MREQ}}$ (**m**aster **req**uest) signal from the host CPU on the motherboard. The host CPU is the standard bus master in this case.

The release of the bus control to an external bus master on an adapter card was also possible with the AT, but in the AT this takes place via a DMA channel, and a powerful arbitration for several external bus masters is impossible in practice. The PC/XT and AT were only conceived of as single processor machines. Arbitration in the AT can only be a last resort, therefore. An efficient and fair arbitration model is not implemented.

On the other hand, for releasing the EISA bus to various bus masters EISA uses an arbitration model with three levels: DMA/refresh (highest level); CPU/master; other masters (lowest level). On each level several masters may be present. Within the level concerned the bus is switched in a rotating order. Refreshing the memory has the highest priority, because a lock of the refresh by another master would lead to a data loss in DRAM, and therefore to a crash of the whole system. If the refresh control requests the bus via an arbitration, it always gets control after a short reaction time period. All other bus masters have to wait until the current refresh cycle is completed.

EISA bus masters don't have to worry about refreshing the main memory on the motherboard. This is carried out by a dedicated refresh logic. On the other hand, in the AT the pseudo-ISA bus masters on an ISA adapter must also control the memory refresh if they are in control of the bus.

DMA

The DMA system has also been improved significantly compared to the AT bus. Not only is the complete 32-bit address space available for *every* DMA transfer (the AT bus allows only 64 or 128 kbyte blocks), but three new DMA operation modes with improved data throughput have also been implemented: DMA types A, B and C. The previous mode is now called the *compatible mode*. In this mode, the addresses are generated at the same clock cycles with an identical clock length, as on the ISA bus (that is, as was the case with the 8237A).

The new EISA DMA operating type A, on the other hand, shortens the memory phase of the DMA transfer, but the I/O phase remains equal. Thus, one DMA cycle is carried out within six BCLK cycles, and the maximum data throughput reaches 5.56 Mbyte/s. Most ISA devices can be operated on an EISA system with type A without causing a malfunction. With the DMA type B, the I/O cycle also needs less time so that only four BCLK cycles are necessary for one DMA transfer. The data throughput is 8.33 Mbyte/s at the most. Type B is supported by only a few ISA devices. Finally, only EISA devices which support burst cycles are able to follow burst type C. Here, one DMA transfer is executed within a single BCLK cycle. With DMA burst type C, DMA transfer rates of up to 33 Mbyte/s can be achieved if the full 32-bit width of the EISA data bus is used. This is the maximum transfer rate for the EISA bus. EISA DMA modes A to C support an 8-, 16-and 32-bit data transfer. The transfer of data read or data write from/to hard disks by means of DMA is again becoming interesting with EISA.

To address the 32-bit address space two page registers are available with EISA: the low- and high-page registers. The low-page register is completely compatible with the conventional DMA page register, known from the AT. The high-page register supplies the high-order address byte A31–A24, and often serves to distinguish ISA and EISA DMA cycles: if the high-page register is not initialized in advance of a DMA transfer, an ISA DMA cycle has to be executed which is compatible with the 8237A chip. Once the high-page register has also been initialized, the DMA control is really operating in EISA mode and the complete 32-bit address space is available. The EISA DMA chip increases or decreases the whole 32-bit address. Therefore (theoretically), a complete 4 Gbyte block can be transferred. In 8237A-compatible mode, on the other hand, only the current address register with a width of 16 bits is altered, so that only a 64 or 128 kbyte block can be moved.

With EISA the service of the DMA channels is no longer carried out according to a scheme with fixed priorities, but distributed over three levels. Within each level the channels are allocated according to a rotating scheme. This avoids the case where one peripheral with a high DMA priority locks out other devices with lower priorities by frequent DMA requests. This might be possible, for example, if a task serves a communications port where external requests are arriving continuously, but another task with a lower DMA priority accesses the hard disk. The frequent requests lock out the task which attempts to read data from the hard disk. Thus the more elaborate DMA hierarchy (as compared to the AT) supports multitasking operating systems where several tasks are competing for the DMA channels – more or less a protection of minorities in the PC. Also, the microchannel follows a similar strategy. EISA implements seven DMA channels in total, which may be programmed to serve 8-, 16- or 32-bit devices.

Interrupts

As is the case with ISA, EISA also implements 15 interrupt levels which are managed by the EISA interrupt controller. Table 5.2 lists the typical assignment of these IRQ channels.

Channel	Priority	Assigned to	Interrupt
IRQ0	1	timer 0, internal system clock	08h
IRQ1	2	keyboard	09h
IRQ2	--	cascading according to the second PIC in the AT	0ah
IRQ3	11	COM2	73h
IRQ4	12	COM1	74h
IRQ5	13	LPT2	75h
IRQ6	14	floppy controller	76h
IRQ7	15	LPT1	77h
IRQ8	3	real time clock	0bh
IRQ9	4	unused	0ch
IRQ10	5	unused	0dh
IRQ11	6	unused	0eh
IRQ12	7	unused	0fh
IRQ13	8	coprocessor	70h
IRQ14	9	hard disk controller	71h
IRQ15	10	unused	72h

Table 5.2: EISA IRQ channels

For compatibility reasons, IRQ2 is occupied by cascading. The EISA interrupt controller behaves in the same way as the two cascaded 8259A PICs in the AT. Thus you have to output a double EOI to master and slave for the IRQ8–IRQ15 channels to terminate a hardware interrupt. Unlike the AT, the interrupt channels assigned to EISA adapters may also operate with level instead of edge triggering. The level of an IRQ line above a certain threshold level issues an interrupt request in this case, and not the rise itself. It is therefore possible for several sources to share an IRQ. If one source is serviced the corresponding IRQ remains active and shows that a further device on the same IRQ line requests an interrupt. This means that in principle any number of devices may request an interrupt. Unlike the PC/XT and the AT, a line is no longer reserved for a single device. In the case of the three serial interfaces COM1, COM2, COM3, for example, previously only COM1 and COM2 could issue an interrupt via IRQ4 and IRQ3, while COM3 could only be operated with polling.

EISA Timer and Fail-Safe Timer

The EISA timer comprises six channels in total, and is equivalent and register-compatible to two 8254 chips. The first three channels 0–2 are reserved for the internal system clock, the memory refresh, and tone generation for the speaker, as was the case with the AT. One of the remaining three timers is used as a failsafe or watchdog timer. Generally, this is timer 3, that is, counter 0 of the second 8254. It issues an NMI if a certain time period has elapsed. This prevents an external bus master from keeping control of the bus too long and blocking necessary interrupts or memory refresh. If an external bus master keeps control of the EISA bus too long, in contradiction to the bus arbitration rules, this indicates a hardware malfunction or the crash of the external bus master. The failsafe timer then issues an NMI, and the arbitration logic returns control to the CPU so that it may service the NMI.

I/O Address Space

With EISA, the support and controller chips are also accessed via ports. Table 5.3 lists the new I/O address areas for EISA. Unlike ISA, the individual EISA slots, and therefore also the inserted EISA adapters, can be addressed individually. Internal registers on the EISA adapters therefore have different base addresses 1000–8000h. This is important so that EISA adapters can be automatically configured without DIP switches. The high-order byte of the I/O address is decoded by the I/O address logic of the motherboard, which uses it to drive the expansion slot concerned. The address decoder on the expansion adapters then only decodes the low-order address bytes further. Thus, an ISA adapter which knows only a 10-bit I/O address can also be inserted into an EISA slot without any problems.

I/O address	Meaning
0000h ... 00ffh	ISA motherboard
0100h ... 03ffh	ISA expansion adapter
0400h ... 04ffh	reserved for controllers on the EISA motherboard
0800h ... 08ffh	reserved for EISA motherboard
0c00h ... 0cffh	reserved for EISA motherboard
1000h ... 1fffh	expansion slot 1
2000h ... 2fffh	expansion slot 2
3000h ... 3fffh	expansion slot 3
4000h ... 4fffh	expansion slot 4
5000h ... 5fffh	expansion slot 5
6000h ... 6fffh	expansion slot 6
7000h ... 7fffh	expansion slot 7
8000h ... 8fffh	expansion slot 8
9000h ... 9fffh	reserved for additional expansion slots[*]

[*] Most EISA PCs have only eight expansion slots.

Table 5.3: EISA port addresses

CMOS-RAM

With EISA adapter cards the IRQ used, as well as the DMA channels, are programmable. The configuration information is stored in the extended CMOS RAM. EISA specifically extends the CMOS RAM by 4 kbytes for this purpose. Special installation programs provide support when configuring the EISA adapters, and automatically write data into the extended EISA CMOS RAM. Typical information is which I/O ports are used by the adapter, which IRQ and DMA channels are assigned to the adapter, etc. This EISA system information can be retrieved by means of several functions of INT 15h. Other peripherals on the motherboard are accessed via the X-bus.

EISA Adapters and Automatic Configuration

On EISA adapters you will look in vain for DIP switches, which sometimes made configuring ISA adapters appear like gambling, with an unpredictable result. EISA solves the configuration problem much more efficiently: every EISA adapter comes with a floppy disk holding a *configuration file (CFG)*. The CFG stores the system elements of the EISA PC used, such as, for example, the assigned IRQ and DMA channels. This information is used by a configuration utility which is delivered together with each EISA PC to configure both the adapter and PC correctly. Additionally, the utility is intelligent enough to detect access conflicts and to react appropriately.

Examples of this are address conflicts between two adapters whose address areas overlap, at least partially. This may occur with interfaces whose register addresses are equal, or with identical ROM base addresses of the SCSI host and VGA graphics adapters. Such address conflicts are the main reason why an AT refuses to run after installing and configuring the brand-new VGA adapter.

The CFG file was part of the EISA concept from the start. All the firms involved in EISA agreed to a standard for the file format, so incompatibilities do not arise here. The name of every CFG file must obey the following rule: !hhhpppp.CFG; where hhh is an abbreviation for the manufacturer, and pppp is a product identification. The CFG files themselves are pure ASCII files, and use a language with strictly defined commands that recall the CONFIG.SYS of MS-DOS.

Examples of CFG commands are: *NAME=???, SLOT=???, BUSMASTER=value?, COMMENTS=text*.

Manufacturers can determine all the important parameters for their EISA adapters by using the CFG commands, so that the configuration utility need only read the CFG file to configure the EISA PC correctly with details of the newly installed adapter. The user does not need detailed knowledge of occupied addresses, DMA channels, etc. and the typical cow-at-a-five-barred-gate feeling of untrained users can thus be avoided. The configuration data is stored in the extended CMOS RAM, and the EISA PC boots without additional configuration next time. If the configuration data in the CMOS RAM gets lost, for example, through a power-break of the battery, then you need simply start the configuration utility and reconfigure the system again using the CFG files for all installed adapters.

Besides the CFG files, EISA also knows another concept to support configuration, the so-called *overlay files (OVL)*. They supplement the configuration language on the level of the configuration utility, and contain instructions in a format which looks like a mixture of C and Assembler. By means of the OVL files, a very exotic EISA adapter can be integrated into an EISA system automatically. The OVL files are in about the same relationship to the configuration utility as a ROM extension is to the system ROM of the motherboard, and they extend the CFG language by new commands. An OVL file is integrated into a CFG file by means of an INCLUDE command, for example, INCLUDE=«super_ad.ovl».

5.9.2 EISA Slot

For extension of the ISA bus up to 32 bits, EISA additionally implements 90 new contacts. Presently, only 16 of them are used for data lines, 23 for address lines, and 16 for control and status lines. In addition to the 98 ISA contacts already present, these 90 new contacts would lead to a huge EISA contact strip on the motherboard (probably bigger than the motherboard itself). The microchannel solves this problem by miniaturizing the contacts and the distance between them, thus making the microchannel plug-incompatible. But EISA was launched to enable an integration of the previous ISA components without any problem.

This, of course, means that the geometry of the EISA slots is harmonized with the existing ISA adapters. The members of the EISA group negotiated these obstacles elegantly by implementing a second layer of contacts in the EISA plug which is shifted against the previous ISA contacts so that only EISA adapters can reach them. ISA adapter cards do not short-circuit the contacts because an ISA adapter cannot penetrate deep enough into the EISA slot. Thus an EISA slot is quite compact for the enormous number of contacts and, moreover, completely compatible with the ISA adapter cards having only one contact layer. Figure 5.16 schematically shows the structure of an EISA slot and the assignment of the corresponding contacts.

The signals listed on the outer sides of the figure are the new EISA signals which are supplied or accepted by the lower-lying contacts. By means of the shifted arrangement of the EISA contacts, 38 instead of 36 new contacts have been added to the previous ISA extension. Thus the EISA slot comprises 188 contacts. The encoding barriers in the slots prevent an EISA adapter card from being inserted wrongly, or an EISA card from penetrating too deep into the slot and short-circuiting the EISA contacts.

Four of these contacts are available to each manufacturer for their own purposes. Using these, a manufacturer can develop a specially adapted adapter card for applications which need signals that go beyond the EISA specification. Such adapters are, of course, no longer completely EISA compatible. On the other hand, though, the manufacturer is not restricted too much in his freedom to develop certain adapters.

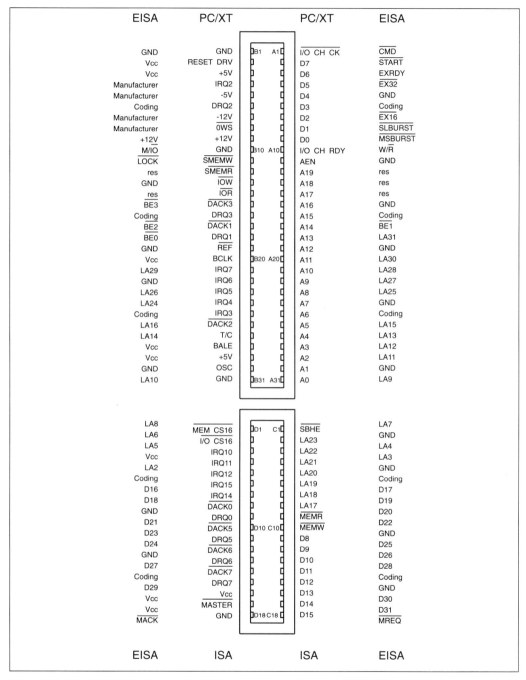

Figure 5.16: The EISA slot has lower and shifted contacts for the extension to 32 bits. Thus the slot size remains the same as for the ISA bus.

5.9.3 EISA Signals

In the following sections the new EISA contacts are discussed, as well as the meaning of the supplied or delivered signals. The ISA part's assignment of an EISA slot can be found in Section 3.6.2. The ISA contacts CLK and ALE are indicated by BCLK and BALE here, as is usual for EISA.

LA2–LA16, LA24–LA31
(Large Address) The LA2–LA16 address signals correspond to the A2–A16 signals of the ISA bus, but they are valid earlier because, unlike the A2–A16 signals, they are not latched and thus delayed. LA24–LA31 is the high-order address byte of the 32–bit EISA data bus. Together with the non-latched ISA address signals LA17–LA23, the LA2–LA16 and LA24–LA31 signals form the address bus for fast EISA bus cycles. ISA bus cycles, on the other hand, use the latched (and therefore slower) address signals A0–A16. In EISA bus cycles, the two low-order address bits corresponding to A0 and A1 are decoded from the four bits $\overline{BE0}$–$\overline{BE3}$.

$\overline{BE0}$-$\overline{BE3}$
(Byte Enable) These four signals indicate on which byte of the 32-bit data bus data is transferred. Therefore, they correspond to the A0 and A1 address bits. The signals come directly from the CPU. $\overline{BE0}$ refers to the least-significant byte D0–D7 of the data bus, $\overline{BE3}$ to the most-significant byte D24–D31.

D16-D31
The 16 bits form the high-order word of the 32-bit EISA data bus. The 16 low-order bits are transferred via the ISA bus section.

$M/\overline{IO}$
This signal serves to distinguish memory and I/O EISA bus cycles.

$W/\overline{R}$
The signal serves to distinguish write and read EISA bus cycles.

$\overline{LOCK}$
(Locked Cycle) This signal is active (low) if a bus master on the motherboard carries out a locked bus cycle with an EISA slave. Using this, the bus master has the exclusive access right to memory as long as $\overline{LOCK}$ is active. Other chips such as, for example, DMA cannot use the memory during this time period.

EXRDY
(EISA Ready) An active EXRDY signal indicates that the addressed EISA device may complete the current bus cycle. EXRDY serves to insert wait states into an EISA bus cycle.

$\overline{EX32}$
(EISA 32-Bit Device) An EISA slave activates the $\overline{EX32}$ signal if it can run with a 32-bit data bus. The EISA bus controller then accesses the device via D0–D31 with a width of 32 bits.

$\overline{EX16}$
(EISA 16-Bit Device) An EISA slave activates the $\overline{EX16}$ signal if it can run with a 16-bit data bus only. The EISA bus controller then accesses the device via D0–D15 with a width of 16 bits. The

EISA bus controller also divides all 32-bit quantities from the CPU into 16-bit portions, and combines 16-bit portions from the EISA slave into a 32-bit quantity for the CPU, respectively.

$\overline{\text{MSBURST}}$

(Master Burst) An EISA master activates $\overline{\text{MSBURST}}$ to inform the EISA bus controller that the master can carry out the next bus cycle as a burst cycle. The bus transfer rate is thus doubled. This is particularly advantageous for cache line fills and DMA transfers.

$\overline{\text{SLBURST}}$

(Slave Burst) An EISA slave activates $\overline{\text{SLBURST}}$ to inform the bus controller that it can follow a burst cycle. Typical EISA slaves which activate $\overline{\text{SLBURST}}$ are fast 32-bit main memories.

$\overline{\text{MREQ}}$

(Master Request) An external device activates the $\overline{\text{MREQ}}$ signal to take over control of the EISA bus as a bus master. The system arbitrator detects $\overline{\text{MREQ}}$ and passes control if no other master is active. Normally, the CPU on the motherboard is the active bus master.

$\overline{\text{MACK}}$

(Master Acknowledge) The system arbitrator responds with a $\overline{\text{MACK}}$ to a $\overline{\text{MREQ}}$ from an external bus master to pass over control of the EISA bus.

$\overline{\text{CMD}}$

(Command) This signal serves for clock harmonization within an EISA bus cycle by stretching a bus clock cycle BCLK appropriately. $\overline{\text{CMD}}$ is generated by the EISA bus control for all EISA bus cycles.

$\overline{\text{START}}$

This signal serves for clock signal coordination at the beginning of an EISA bus cycle. $\overline{\text{START}}$ indicates the beginning of a cycle on the local bus.

BCLK

(Bus Clock) BCLK is the clock signal for the EISA bus, and is generated by dividing the CPU frequency so that BCLK has a frequency of 8.33 MHz at most (see Figure 5.14). BCLK determines the data transfer rate. In burst mode or EISA DMA mode C, the transfer rate reaches up to 33.3 Mbyte/s (8.33 MHz∗32 bits).

5.9.4 Microchannel – The Revolution

Together with its new generation of PCs, the PS/2, IBM also implemented a new bus system and a new PC architecture, the *microchannel*. In view of its geometry as well as its logical concept, this bus is a radical departure from the AT bus, which had been very successful up to that time. Hardware compatibility to previous PC models is no longer kept, but there are some good reasons for this: the AT bus was only designed for 16-bit processors, but the new i386 and i486 CPUs run with 32 bits. Furthermore, because of its edge triggered interrupts, the AT bus is directed to singletasking operating systems such as, for example, DOS. The intended aim when designing the PS/2, on the other hand, was to go over to multitasking systems, particularly OS/2. Therefore the problems are similar to those already mentioned in connection with EISA. But it is also interesting that the microchannel was presented much earlier than EISA. EISA was supposedly designed as a reaction to the microchannel so as not to leave the 32-bit market all to IBM. Identical problems often lead to similar solutions, thus it is perhaps not surprising that the microchannel (apart from the completely incompatible bus slot) does not differ radically from EISA. After all, on the operating system and especially on the application level, a complete compatibility to the AT must be achieved. Programs which do not explicitly refer to the hardware registers also run on the PS/2 without any problems, and with no noticeable difference for the users.

MCA Bus Structure

Figure 5.17 shows a schematic block diagram of the microchannel architecture (MCA).

A significant difference from EISA is the separate system clock which supplies a frequency of 10 MHz at most for all microchannel components. Only the local bus between the CPU and the memory operates faster to carry out data accesses of the CPU to main memory at a maximum speed. Thus the microchannel is an *asynchronous bus system*; the CPU is clocked by its own CPU clock.

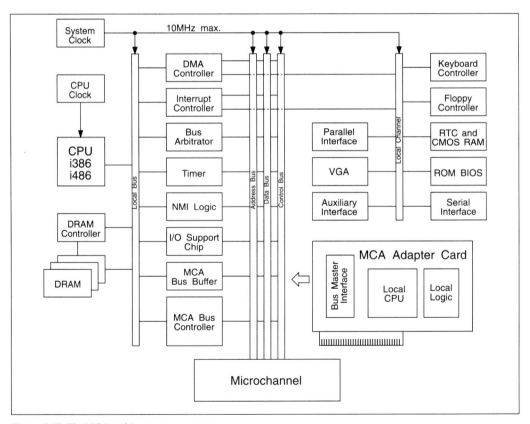

Figure 5.17: The MCA architecture.

The microchannel was initially introduced with three different bus cycles:

–   standard bus cycle,
–   synchronous extended bus cycle, and
–   asynchronous extended bus cycle.

The standard bus cycle corresponds to a conventional CPU bus cycle at 10 MHz with no wait cycles. In an extended bus cycle the device addressed inserts wait states by means of the *CHRDY* signal. If CHRDY becomes active synchronous to the data half-cycle of the MCA bus cycle, this is called a synchronous extended bus cycle, otherwise it is an asynchronous extended bus cycle. CHRDY refers to the bus clock of 10 MHz but not to the CPU clock, which may be much higher, especially with i386 or i486 processors. Because of their high clock rates, i386 and i486 always insert several CPU wait cycles which are controlled by the bus controller using the READY processor signal. One MCA bus cycle without wait cycles lasts for two bus clock cycles with 100 ns each. Thus the microchannel is presently conceived for a maximum data transfer rate of 20 Mbyte/s.

The data transfer rate can be slightly increased by the so-called *matched-memory cycles*. These are only implemented with the 16 MHz model 80, and are controlled by the $\overline{\text{MMC}}$ and $\overline{\text{MMCR}}$ signals. To carry out a matched-memory cycle the bus controller of the motherboard activates the $\overline{\text{MMC}}$ (**m**atched-**m**emory **c**ycle) signal. If the addressed device responds with an active $\overline{\text{MMCR}}$ (**m**atched-**m**emory **c**ycle **r**eturn), the bus controller shortens the cycle time of the MCA bus clock to 93.75 ns. $\overline{\text{ADL}}$ and $\overline{\text{CMD}}$ are not generated here, but $\overline{\text{MMCCMD}}$ is. Because of the shorter cycle time, a data transfer rate of at most 21.4 Mbyte/s is possible; this is an incredible increase of 7%.

No wonder, then, that IBM mothballed the matched-memory cycle, and developed the *streaming data procedure (SDP)* concept. Presently, three such SDPs have been designed:

–   32-bit SDP,
–   64-bit SDP, and
–   extended 64-bit SDP.

IBM uses the microchannel not only in its PS/2 series but also in much more powerful RISC System/6000 workstations with a basis of RISC processors with MIPS technology.

In view of the signal course, the 32-bit SDP coincides with the i486 burst mode. To request a 32-bit SDP the bus master deactivates the $\overline{\text{BLAST}}$ signal. The device addressed responds with a $\overline{\text{BRDY}}$ to indicate that it is able to carry out 32-bit burst mode. With the 32-bit SDP four bytes are transferred within a single MCA bus clock cycle. Using this the data transfer rate increases to 40 Mbyte/s for a short time. This is even more than the 33 Mbyte/s for the EISA burst mode.

A further enhancement is possible with the 64-bit SDP. Here, only during the first bus cycle is the address output. The addressed device accepts and stores it. Afterwards, the data is transferred not only via the 32-bit data bus, but also via the 32-bit address bus, that is, with a width of 64 bits or 8 bytes in total. The device addressed comprises an address counter that counts up with each 64-bit SDP automatically. It therefore only needs the start address. With the 64-bit SDP a data transfer rate of 80 Mbyte/s can be achieved. The extended 64-bit SDP is even more powerful. Here the bus cycle is reduced from 100 ns down to 50 ns, but the transfer itself is identical to that of a normal 64-bit SDP. The data transfer rate doubles to 160 Mbyte/s, that is, a medium-sized hard disk could be read within one second.

For the 64-bit SDP, further control signals are required which indicate that such a transfer is to be carried out. For this reason, IBM did not implement the SDPs in the PS/2.

Bus Arbitration

Like EISA, the MCA also supports external bus masters on adapter cards. Including the CPU, up to 16 different bus masters can be integrated. For this purpose, IBM implemented a dedicated chip, the so-called *central arbitration control point* (*CACP*), which carries out the bus arbitration and passes control to a bus master. With the MCA the motherboard's CPU, the refresh logic, the DMA controller and external bus masters on adapter cards can operate as bus masters. Table 5.4 shows the priorities assigned to these bus masters.

Priority	Device
–2d	memory refresh
–1d	NMI
00h	DMA channel 0[*]
01h	DMA channel
02h	DMA channel
03h	DMA channel
04h	DMA channel 0[*]
05h	DMA channel
06h	DMA channel
07h	DMA channel
08h	available for external bus master
09h	available for external bus master
0ah	available for external bus master
0bh	available for external bus master
0ch	available for external bus master
0dh	available for external bus master
0eh	available for external bus master
0fh	CPU on the motherboard

[*] Priority can be programmed freely.

Table 5.4: Arbitration priorities in the PS/2

The –2 priority of the memory refresh means that the arbitration logic always passes control of the bus if a refresh is requested. The memory refresh is located on the motherboard and drives the arbitration logic by an internal *refresh request* signal. The next lower priority, –1, of the NMI is also processed internally. The source of an NMI is usually an error on an adapter card, a time-out in connection with bus arbitration, or another serious malfunction. The NMI may only be serviced by the CPU on the motherboard. However, for this the CPU needs to be in control of the system bus, because the program code of the accompanying interrupt handler 2 must be read from memory. Therefore, an NMI always forces the CACP to snatch away the system bus from another active bus master, and to pass control to the CPU.

The lowest priority 0fh of the CPU means that the CPU on the motherboard is always in control of the system bus if no other bus master requests bus control. No arbitration signal line is necessary for this. Instead, the CACP automatically assigns the CPU control by means of the HOLD and HLDA processor signals, in this case.

All other bus masters can request control of the bus via the $\overline{\text{PREEMPT}}$ signal. Then, by means of ARB0–ARB3, the bus arbitration passes control to one of the requesting bus masters according to a strategy using a largely equal treatment. For this, the following steps are carried out:

–   The bus masters that want to take over control of the system bus set $\overline{\text{PREEMPT}}$ to a low level.

–   The CACP activates ARB/$\overline{\text{GNT}}$ to indicate that an arbitration cycle is in progress.

–   Each of the requesting bus masters outputs its priority code via ARB0–ARB3, and compares its code with the code on ARB0–ARB3, which consists of the priority code of all the requesting bus master.

–   If its priority code is lower then it deactivates its code on ARB0–ARB3 and rules itself out of the competition, but continues to drive $\overline{\text{PREEMPT}}$ to indicate that it wants to take over control in a later arbitration cycle.

–   After a certain time period (in the PS/2 300 ns are usually available for this purpose), only the highest priority code is still present on ARB0–ARB3.

–   The CACP pulls ARB/$\overline{\text{GNT}}$ down to a low level to indicate that the bus control has passed to a new bus master (GNT=grant) whose priority code is present on ARB0–ARB3.

–   The new bus master deactivates its $\overline{\text{PREEMPT}}$ signal. All other bus masters which were unable to take over control continue to drive $\overline{\text{PREEMPT}}$ to a low level.

–   Now the new bus master can control the bus for one bus cycle.

–   Burst bus masters that want to transfer a whole data block and are allowed to keep control of the system bus for at most 7.8 μs (the maximum allocation time for external bus masters) are an exception to this rule. Such bus masters activate the $\overline{\text{BURST}}$ signal to inform the CACP that an arbitration cycle shall not be carried out for every bus cycle. But if $\overline{\text{PREEMPT}}$ or a refresh request is active, an arbitration cycle is executed nevertheless. Thus, $\overline{\text{BURST}}$ only has an effect if the current burst bus master is the only one requesting control of the system bus.

–   Afterwards, the CACP releases control to the CPU or starts a further arbitration cycle if $\overline{\text{PREEMPT}}$ is driven low by another bus master.

Every bus master adapter has a local bus arbitrator which drives the adapter card's $\overline{\text{PREEMPT}}$ and ARB0–ARB3, and compares the priority code of the bus master adapter with the overall code ARB0–ARB3.

If the bus master does not release control after 7.8 μs, the CACP interprets this as a malfunction. It disconnects the bus master from the bus, passes control to the CPU, and issues an NMI.

The CACP can be programmed via the arbitration register at I/O address 090h (see Figure 5.18).

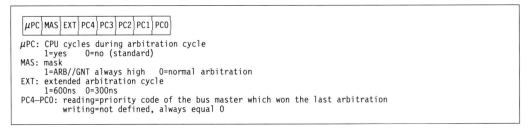

Figure 5.18: Arbitration register (Port 090h).

If you set bit μPC equal to 1, the CPU on the motherboard executes further bus cycles, for example to fetch instructions while the CACP carries out an arbitration cycle. For the bus arbitration only the lines $\overline{\text{PREEMPT}}$ and ARB0–ARB3 are required, which are not used during a CPU bus cycle. Therefore, the two cycles do not affect each other. If MAS is set the CACP always drives the ARB/$\overline{\text{GNT}}$ signal high, that is, always indicates an arbitration cycle. As long as MAS is set, only the CPU is in control of the system bus, and all other bus masters are locked out. By means of EXT, the arbitration cycle can be enhanced from the standard 300 ns up to 600 ns. This is advantageous if slow devices are present in the system. Finally, the five bits $PC4$–$PC0$ indicate the priority code of the device that last won the bus arbitration. When writing into the register, bits PC4–PC0 have no meaning and should always be set equal to 0.

Memory System

The PS/2 memory system has also been improved with the development of the microchannel. If the startup routine of the PC detects a defect in main memory, the memory is reconfigured in 64 kbyte blocks so that eventually a continuous and error-free main memory again becomes available. The block with the defect is logically moved to the upper end of the main memory and locked against access. If such a defect occurs in the lower address area in an AT, the whole of the main memory from the defective address upwards becomes unusable.

For the PS/2 models 70 and 80, two memory configuration registers at the port addresses e0h and e1h are additionally available. Using these ports, the division of the first Mbyte in RAM can be controlled so that, for example, the ROM BIOS is moved into the faster RAM (shadowing), or the memory is divided to be as RAM-saving as possible (split-memory option). These possibilities are not discussed here in detail because these setups can usually be done with the help of the extended PS/2 setup during the course of the boot process.

DMA

In terms of their functions, the microchannel's support chips differ very little from their EISA counterparts, but they are completely harmonized with this new and advanced bus system. Thus, for example, the DMA controller always carries out a 32-bit DMA transfer for the complete address space if a 32-bit microchannel is present. There is no 8237A-compatible DMA transfer. Moreover, the microchannel architecture allows all eight DMA channels to be active simultaneously. Thus, MCA is really well suited for multitasking operating systems.

Originally, in the PS/2 only a 16-bit DMA controller was intended, which could only serve the first 16 Mbyte of memory. Here again you can see the enormously fast development in the field of microelectronics. Although the microchannel and the PS/2 were intended as a new standard to replace the AT and last for years, the 16 Mbytes (which seemed astronomically large a few years ago) are no longer enough, since memory-eaters like OS/2 and Windows have appeared. Modern motherboards can usually be equipped with 32 Mbytes or even 64 Mbytes of memory.

Interrupts

As well as the bus system and the DMA controller, the interrupt controller was also harmonized with the new architecture. All interrupts are level-trigger invoked only. With EISA, on the other hand, interrupts can be level- or edge-triggered so that an ISA adapter can be operated as the serial interface adapter, which operates exclusively with edge-triggering in an EISA slot. Because of the level-triggering used in MCA, various sources can share one interrupt line IRQx. Additionally, level-triggering is less susceptible to interference, as a noise pulse only leads to a very short voltage rise but level-triggering requires a lasting high level. For the microchannel, 255 different hardware interrupts are possible, the AT allows only 15. The assignment of the IRQ lines and the correspondence of hardware interrupt and interrupt vector coincides with that in the AT and EISA.

MCA Timer and Fail-Safe Timer

The MCA timer comprises four channels in total, and is equivalent to an 8254 chip with four counters. The first three channels 0–2 are occupied by the internal system clock, memory refresh and tone generation for the speaker, as is the case in the AT. The fourth timer is used as a fail-safe or watchdog timer in the same sense as for EISA. It issues an NMI if a certain time period has elapsed, thus preventing an external bus master from keeping control too long and blocking necessary interrupts or the memory refresh. If an external bus master retains control of the MCA bus for too long, and thereby violates the bus arbitration rules, this indicates a hardware error or the crash of an external bus master. Then the fail-safe timer issues an NMI and the arbitration logic releases control to the CPU again so that it can handle the NMI.

On the PC/XT/AT, timer 1 for memory refresh is programmable, but on the PS/2 it is not. IBM thus wants to avoid nosy users who like to experiment with changing the refresh rate and crashing the PC because of too few refresh cycles. Programmers can access the timer via port 041h, but passing new values doesn't have any effect on its behaviour.

I/O Ports and I/O Address Space

As for EISA, in the PS/2 the support and controller chips are also accessed via ports. Table 5.5 lists the new I/O address areas for MCA. Unlike ISA, the MCA slots, and therefore also the inserted MCA adapters, can be addressed individually. To do this, however, you must explicitly activate a slot for a setup. This is necessary to configure MCA adapters with no DIP switches automatically.

Address	Meaning
000h-01fh	master DMA
020h-021h	master 8259A
040h-043h	timer 1
044h-047h	fail-safe timer
060h-064h	keyboard/mouse controller
070h-071h	real-time clock/CMOS RAM
074h-076h	extended CMOS RAM
080h-08fh	DMA page register
090h	CACP
091h	feedback register
092h	system control port A
096h	adapter activation/setup register
0a0h-0afh	slave 8259A
0c0h-0dfh	slave DMA
0e0h-0efh	memory configuration register
0f0h-0ffh	coprocessor
100h-107h	POS registers 0 to 7
200h-20fh	game adapter
210h-217h	reserved
220h-26fh	available
278h-27fh	2nd parallel interface
2b0h-2dfh	EGA
2f8h-2ffh	COM2
300h-31fh	prototype adapter
320h-32fh	available
378h-37fh	1st parallel interface
380h-38fh	SDLC adapter
3a0h-3afh	reserved
3b0h-3b3h	monochrome adapter
3b4h-3bah	VGA
3bch-3beh	parallel interface
3c0h-3dfh	EGA/VGA
3e0h-3e7h	reserved
3f0h-3f7h	floppy controller
3f8h-3ffh	COM1

Table 5.5: MCA port addresses

MCA Adapters and Automatic Configuration

There is also a significant advantage here compared to the old AT concept, that of the automatic identification of an adapter by the system. Microchannel adapters, like their EISA counterparts, are no longer configured by jumpers. This can instead be carried out in a dialogue with the accompanying system software. For this purpose, IBM assigns every adapter an identification number which can be read and analysed by the system. Also, third-party manufacturers get an identification number for their MCA products which is centrally managed by IBM. The configuration information is stored in an extended CMOS RAM (as is the case with EISA). Additionally, you may activate or disable individual MCA slots, thus a defective or suspicious adapter can be disabled until the maintenance technician arrives, without the need to open the PC and remove the adapter. This also allows you to operate two adapters alternately, which normally disturb each other, without pottering around the PC all the time.

To achieve these advantages, all MCA adapters and the MCA motherboard hold so-called *programmable option select (POS) registers*. They always occupy the I/O address area 0100h to 0107h. Table 5.6 lists the registers.

Number	I/O address	Meaning
0	0100h	adapter identification ID (low-byte)
1	0101h	adapter identification ID (high-byte)
2	0102h	option byte 1
3	0103h	option byte 2
4	0104h	option byte 3
5	0105h	option byte 4
6	0106h	sub-address extension (low-byte)
7	0107h	sub-address extension (high-byte)

Table 5.6: POS registers

During the boot process the POST routine of the BIOS reads the adapter identification ID and compares it with the configuration data which is held in the CMOS RAM. The adapter identification ID is awarded centrally by IBM, that is, IBM assigns every manufacturer of an MCA adapter such a number for the product concerned. The four option bytes are available for the adapter manufacturer to configure the inserted adapter and thus fulfil the functions of the former DIP switches. If the four option bytes are insufficient, the manufacturer may implement an additional configuration register on the adapter card. They are accessed by means of the two sub-address extension registers.

Three bits in the POS registers are predefined, and are listed in Table 5.7. By means of the bit *adapter activation* in the POS register 2, the adapter concerned can be disabled or activated. If it is disabled the system behaves as if the adapter were not present. Therefore it is possible, for example, to alternately operate two different graphics adapters with overlapping address areas in a PS/2. Their addresses do not then disturb each other. If a hardware error occurs on an adapter which leads to an NMI, then bit 7 in POS register 5 is set to 0 and the adapter generates an active $\overline{\text{CHCK}}$ signal. If additional status information is available in POS registers 6 and 7, the adapter also sets bit 6 to a value of 0. The remaining bits are freely available for implementing software option switches which replace the previous DIP switches.

POS register	Bit	Meaning
2	0	adapter enable
5	6	status for channel check available
5	7	channel check active

Table 5.7: Reserved POS register bits.

The POS registers are present at the same address on all adapters and the motherboard, thus access conflicts seem to be preprogrammed. To avoid this, two additional registers are implemented, the adapter activation/setup register at I/O address 096h, and the motherboard activation/setup register at I/O address 094h.

Each adapter can be operated in two different modes:

– Active mode: the POS registers are not accessible and the adapter is operating normally. You may access the ordinary control registers (the DAC colour register on a VGA, for example).

– Setup mode: here only the POS registers are accessible, not the ordinary control registers.

Using the adapter activation/setup register you may activate a slot and thus an adapter well-suited for setup of and access to its POS registers. Figure 5.19 shows the assignment of this 8-bit register.

```
┌─────────────────────────────────────────────────────────────────────┐
│  ┌───┬───┬───┬───┬───┬───┬───┬───┐                                    │
│  │CHR│res│res│res│SET│SL2│SL1│SL0│                                    │
│  └───┴───┴───┴───┴───┴───┴───┴───┘                                    │
│  CHR: channel reset                                                   │
│       0=no reset              1=reset all adapters                    │
│  res: reserved (=0)                                                   │
│  SET: adapter setup                                                   │
│       0=normal mode           1=setup mode                            │
│  SL2-SL0: adapter/slot select                                         │
│       000=slot 1   001=slot 2   010=slot 3   ...   111=slot 8         │
└─────────────────────────────────────────────────────────────────────┘
```

Figure 5.19: Adapter activation/setup register (port 096h).

The three least-significant bits define the selected slot or adapter. A set *adapter setup* bit activates this adapter for a setup. The $\overline{\text{CDSETUP}}$ signal for a slot n is thus activated, and the adapter is ready for a setup.

Example: Activate adapter in slot 3 (note: the slots are enumerated 1 to 8 but the slot selection with 0 to 7).

```
MOV al, 0000 1010b  ; slot select=2, setup active
OUT 096h, al        ; write register
```

Now you can access the POS registers of the selected adapter card and configure the adapter or read the channel check bit.

If the *channel reset* bit is set in register 096h, the CHRESET signal is activated in the microchannel and *all* adapters are reset. Thus in the setup mode, channel reset must always be equal to 0.

After completion of the configuration the *adapter activation* bit in POS register 2 must be set to enable normal functioning of the adapter. This only refers to the adapter's logic. Write the value 00h into the adapter activation/setup register afterwards to enable the adapter ($\overline{\text{CDSETUP}}$ rises to a high level). This only refers to driving the adapter.

Besides the adapters, the motherboard also comprises various setup registers which may be activated by means of the motherboard activation/setup register at I/O address 094h. Figure 5.20 shows the structure of this register.

```
/STB  res  /STV  res  res  res  res  res

/STB: setup of board units except VGA
      0=setup mode          1=normal mode
/STV: VGA setup
      0=setup mode          1=normal mode
res:   reserved (=0)
```

Figure 5.20: Motherboard activation/setup register (Port 094h).

If you clear the $\overline{\text{STV}}$ bit (set equal to 0) then you can configure the VGA option bytes. With a value of 1 in this register the VGA operates normally. To the board units belong the VGA, RAM, floppy controller, and serial and parallel interfaces. If the $\overline{\text{STB}}$ bit is set equal to 0 then you can access POS registers 2 and 3 of the motherboard units and configure them. As is the case with adapters, these POS registers are present at I/O addresses 102h and 103h. The structure of POS register 2 is shown in Figure 5.21. POS register 3 serves to configure the RAM, and is very model-dependent. Thus, only POS register 2 is described in further detail here. Information concerning POS register 3 can be found in the technical reference manual for your PS/2. For all other users, this information is of no value.

```
POS Register 2

PPX  PP1  PP0  PPE  SPS  SPE  FLE  MBE

PPX: extended mode of the parallel port
     0=no extended mode (standard)   1=extended mode
PP1, PP0: parallel port select
     00=LPT1 (standard)   01=LPT2   11=LPT3
PPE: parallel port enable
     0=disabled           1=enabled (standard)
SPS: serial port select
     0=COM1 (standard)    1=COM2
SPE: serial port enable
     0=disabled           1=enabled (standard)
FLE: floppy controller enable
     0=disabled           1=enabled (standard)
MBE: motherboard unit enable (except VGA)
     0=disabled           1=enabled (standard)
```

Figure 5.21: Motherboard POS register 2 (Port 102h).

In extended mode the parallel port can be operated bidirectionally. The remaining bits are self-evident. This adapter activation/setup register (port 096h) structure ensures that you can only activate a single slot for a setup, thus setup conflicts on the adapters are impossible. However, note that you may put an adapter and the motherboard simultaneously into the setup mode. This inevitably leads to problems, and damage to chips may even occur. Therefore, be careful when programming the setup!

As was the case for EISA, every MCA product comes with a configuration disk which holds a file containing the necessary information. This file is called the *adapter description file* (*ADF*). The filename has the format «@iiii.adf», where iiii is the four-digit adapter identification number in hexadecimal notation. Like EISA, the ADF also uses a configuration language that reminds us of CONFIG.SYS commands.

On-Board VGA and External Graphics Adapters

A main emphasis of the PS/2 concept is the integration of many units on the motherboard which previously have been located on separate adapter cards in a bus slot. To these units belong, for example, the serial and parallel interface, and especially the *video graphics array* (*VGA*). All these units are accessed by means of the *local channel* or the *peripheral standard bus*. The VGA is functionally identical to (and also available as) the *video graphics adapter* (*VGA*) for AT and EISA computers. Original VGA (that is, the video graphics *array*) is integrated on the PS/2 motherboard, but the video graphics *adapter* is implemented as an adapter for a bus slot. Thus, a PS/2 computer with an integrated VG array needs significantly fewer slots than an AT or EISA computer.

For some users even the video graphics array with a resolution of 640*480 pixels and 256 colours is not sufficient. In particular, high-resolution graphics applications like CAD need more powerful adapters. These adapters may be inserted into a bus slot, of course, but the only problem is that the VGA on the motherboard is still present and must be disabled for correct operation of the new adapter. Removing the VGA is naturally impossible. Instead, IBM had a more elegant idea. One MCA slot in every PS/2 comprises a so-called *video extension* (see Figure 5.22). An MCA graphics adapter must always be inserted into this slot to service the graphics signals. By pulling some of these signals to a low level, the inserted adapter can deactivate parts of the on-board VGA and generate the corresponding signals itself (see Section 5.8.6). For this purpose, the connected monitor need not even be plugged in differently (if it accepts the new video mode, of course); it is still driven by the same plug of the PS/2. Internally, though, the change can be immense. For example, the high-resolution 8514/A adapter with a dedicated graphics processor pulls the ESYNC, EDCLK and EVIDEO signals to a low level. Then it generates its own synchronization, pixel clock and colour signals for the monitor which it transfers by means of the contacts HSYNC, VSYNC, BLANK, DCLK and P0–P7 to the motherboard's logic to drive the monitor. Thus, the on-board VGA is more or less disabled and the monitor cut off. Only the DAC is still running, converting the digital video data P0–P7 to an analogue signal for the monitor. All control and pixel signals come from the 8514/A.

PS/2 Model 30

The PS/2 Model 30 occupies a special position. It is actually a hidden XT with the outward appearance of a PS/2 case. The model 30 thus has no microchannel, but instead the old XT bus. The only advantage is that the model 30 is already prepared for the 1.44 Mbyte floppy and hard disk drives, and thus also has a much more modern BIOS.

5.9.5 The MCA Slot

After deciding to throw the AT concept overboard, IBM was of course free to redesign the layout of the bus slots. Also, for a PS/2 there should be 8-bit adapters (for example, parallel interface adapters), 16-bit adapters for models 50 and 60 with 80286 or i386SX processors, and 32-bit adapters (for example, fast ESDI controllers for the PS/2 models with i386 or i486 CPUs). Thus, 8-, 16- and 32-bit slots are required, with the 8-bit slot already implementing all the important control lines.

The result is the MCA slot with various slot extensions, as shown in Figure 5.22.

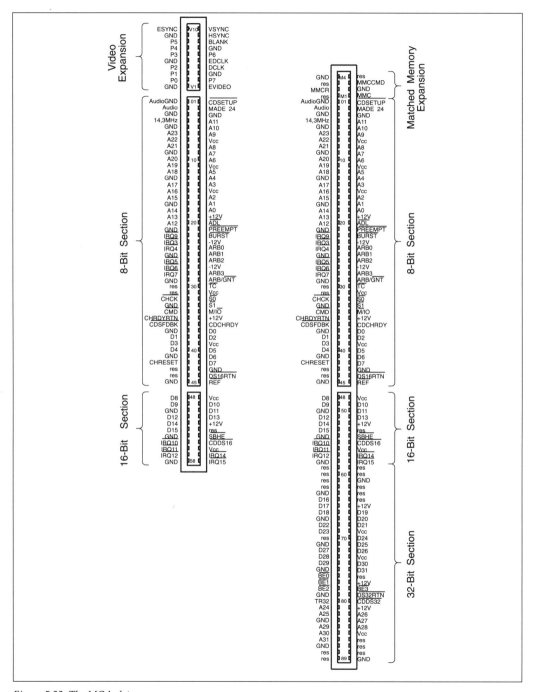

Figure 5.22: The MCA slot.

The kernel of the MCA slot is the 8-bit section with its 90 contacts. Unlike EISA, the MCA slot only has contacts on a single layer, but they are much narrower and every fourth contact of a row is grounded or at the power supply level. The ground and supply contacts on both sides are shifted by two positions so that, effectively, every second contact pair has a ground or supply terminal. By the defined potential of these contacts, the noise resistance is significantly better than on an AT. The AT had up to 31 succeeding signal contacts without any interposed ground or supply contacts. With the EISA slot, the noise sensitivity is slightly reduced because the lower EISA contact row has significantly more such contacts than the AT section of the EISA slot.

Besides the 8-bit section there are various extensions: the 16-bit section for 16-bit MCA adapters; the 32-bit section for 32-bit MCA adapters; the video extension for additional graphics adapters; and the matched-memory extension for memories with a higher access rate. The 16-bit PS/2 models do not have any 32-bit extensions, of course. Because of the narrow contacts, the MCA slot is nevertheless quite compact, although it holds up to 202 contacts.

5.9.6 MCA Signals

This section discusses the MCA contacts and the meaning of the signals which are supplied or applied.

ESYNC
(Enable Synchronization) A low level from the inserted adapter causes the VGA on the motherboard to be cut off from the three synchronization signals VSYNC, HSYNC and BLANK.

VSYNC
(Vertical Synchronization) A high-level pulse from the inserted adapter causes a vertical synchronization, that is, a vertical retrace of the electron beam.

HSYNC
(Horizontal Synchronization) A high-level pulse from the inserted adapter causes a horizontal synchronization, that is, a horizontal retrace of the electron beam.

BLANK
A high-level signal from the inserted adapter blanks the screen.

P7–P0
These eight signals form the binary video data for the video DAC (*digital to analog converter*) on the motherboard, which then generates the analogue signal for the monitor. By means of the eight bits P7–P0, the 256 simultaneously displayable colours of the VGA can be encoded.

EDCLK
(Enable DCLK) A low-level signal from the inserted adapter cuts the VGA on the motherboard off from the pixel clock line to the video DAC. Instead, the DAC uses the clock signal DCLK from the inserted adapter.

DCLK
(Data Clock) The signal from the inserted adapter supplies the pixel clock for the DAC.

EVIDEO

(Enable Video) A low-level signal from the inserted adapter cuts off the VGA on the motherboard from the palette bus. Using this, the inserted adapter can supply the video data P7–P0.

Audio, AudioGND

These two connections supply the tone signal and the accompanying tone signal ground to the motherboard. An adapter is thus able to use the speaker logic of the motherboard. The adapter applies the tone signal which the system speaker outputs to the connection Audio.

14.3 MHz

This signal is the 14 317 180 Hz clock signal for timers and other components.

A31–A0

These 32 connections form the 32-bit address bus of the microchannel.

$\overline{IRQ3}$–$\overline{IRQ7}$, $\overline{IRQ9}$–$\overline{IRQ12}$, $\overline{IRQ14}$, $\overline{IRQ15}$

(Interrupt Request) These eleven connections are available for hardware interrupt requests from peripheral adapters. The microchannel operates with level-triggered hardware interrupts. IRQ0 (system clock), IRQ1 (keyboard), IRQ2 (cascading according to the second AT PIC), IRQ8 (real-time clock) and IRQ13 (coprocessor) are reserved for components on the motherboard, and therefore do not lead into the bus slots.

$\overline{CHCK}$

(Channel Check) Via this contact the adapter cards apply error information to the motherboard to indicate, for example, a parity error on a memory expansion adapter, or a general error on an adapter card.

$\overline{CMD}$

(Command) If $\overline{CMD}$ is active (that is, low), the data on the bus are valid.

CHRDYRTN

(Channel Ready Return) A high level as the return signal from the addressed device indicates that the I/O channel is ready.

$\overline{CDSFDBK}$

(Card Select Feedback) An active (low) level indicates that the addressed adapter card is ready. $\overline{CDSFDBK}$ is the return signal for the adapter selection.

D0–D31

These 32 connections form the 32-bit data bus of the microchannel.

CHRESET

(Channel Reset) A high level at this connection resets all adapters.

$\overline{CDSETUP}$

(Card Setup) An active (low) level instructs the addressed adapter to carry out a setup.

MADE 24

(Memory Address Enable 24) A high-level signal activates the address line A24.

$\overline{\text{ADL}}$

(Address Latch) A low-level signal indicates that a valid address is present on the microchannel, and activates the address decoder latches.

$\overline{\text{PREEMPT}}$

A low-level signal issues an arbitration cycle for passing the bus to various bus masters. External bus masters activate $\overline{\text{PREEMPT}}$ to request control of the bus.

$\overline{\text{BURST}}$

A low-level signal instructs the bus system to carry out a burst cycle.

ARB0–ARB3

(Arbitration 0–3) These four signals indicate (in binary-encoded form) which of the maximum 16 possible bus masters has won the bus arbitration and gets control of the system bus.

ARB/$\overline{\text{GNT}}$

(Arbitration/Grant) If this connection is on a high level, an arbitration cycle is in progress. If ARB/$\overline{\text{GNT}}$ falls to a low level the arbitration signals ARB0–ARB3 are valid and indicate the new bus master.

$\overline{\text{TC}}$

(Terminal Count) A low-level signal at this pin indicates that the counter of the active DMA channel has reached its terminal value and the DMA transfer is complete.

$\overline{\text{S0}}$, $\overline{\text{S1}}$

These two contacts transfer the corresponding status bits of the microchannel.

M/$\overline{\text{IO}}$

(Memory/IO) A high-level signal indicates a memory cycle; a low-level signal an access to the I/O address space.

CHRDY

(Channel Ready) A high-level signal at this connection indicates that the addressed unit is ready, that is, has completed the intended access. Thus this contact transfers the ready signal from addressed devices on an adapter card. If CHRDY is low the processor or DMA chip extends the bus cycles; it inserts one or more wait states.

$\overline{\text{DS16RTN}}$

(Data Size 16 Return) A return signal with a low level from the addressed device indicates that the device is running at a data bus width of 16 bits. The bus controller thus splits 32-bit quantities into 16-bit portions, and combines two 16-bit items into a single 32-bit quantity.

$\overline{\text{DS32RTN}}$

(Data Size 32 Return) A return signal with a low level indicates that the addressed device is running at the full data bus width of 32 bits.

$\overline{\text{REF}}$

(Refresh) The signal is at a low level if the motherboard is currently executing a memory refresh. With this signal, the dynamic memory on adapter cards (for example, the video RAM) can also be refreshed synchronous to main memory. Thus the adapter does not need its own refresh logic and no additional time is wasted for refreshing DRAM on the adapters. The $\overline{\text{REF}}$ signal indicates that the address bus has a row address for the refresh.

SBHE

(System Byte High Enable) A high-level signal indicates that the high-order data bus byte D8–D15 of the 16-bit microchannel section transfers valid data.

CDDS16

(Card Data Size 16) The inserted adapter card applies a high-level signal to this connection to indicate that it is running with a data width of 16 bits. Then the bus controller operates accordingly.

$\overline{\text{BE0}}$–$\overline{\text{BE3}}$

(Byte Enable 0–3) These four signals indicate on which byte of the 32-bit data bus data are transferred. They correspond to the address bits A0 and A1, therefore. The signals come directly from the CPU. $\overline{\text{BE0}}$ refers to the least significant byte D0–D7 of the data bus, $\overline{\text{BE3}}$ the high-order byte D24–D31.

TR32

(Translate 32) A high-level signal indicates that the external bus master is a 32-bit device and drives $\overline{\text{BE0}}$–$\overline{\text{BE3}}$ instead of SBHE.

$\overline{\text{CDDS32}}$

(Card Data Size 32) If the inserted adapter card applies a low-level signal to this connection, it has a data width of 32 bits.

$\overline{\text{MMCR}}$, $\overline{\text{MMCCMD}}$, $\overline{\text{MMC}}$

These three signals control the so-called matched-memory cycles.

5.10 The Local Bus – A High-Speed Path inside the PC

For many PC users, Section 5.8 must have been a great disappointment. Even the EISA bus and the microchannel, as high-end solutions for PCs, run (in a 50 MHz i486 PC) at only a wretched 8 and 10 MHz, respectively. That is far too low for a fast screen setup with graphics-oriented operating systems, or for system extensions like Windows. Even small dialogue windows with 512∗384 pixels which occupy only one fourth of the screen in high-resolution mode contain 192 k pixels. Thus, in the 256-colour mode the first 192 k pixels must be saved and rewritten afterwards. This corresponds to 384 kbytes of image data. But the video memory can only be read if the graphics controller on the adapter doesn't carry out a read access. This is usually the case only during a horizontal and vertical retrace, thus the 384 kbytes must be transferred during the course of the relatively small retrace time windows. On a Hercules card, a complete horizontal scan inclusive of horizontal retrace lasts for about 54.0 μs and the horizontal retrace alone 8.4 μs. This means that the horizontal retrace requires about one seventh of a horizontal scan. Taking this into account, one can evaluate that the transfer of the 384 kbytes in a 16-bit ISA system lasts for about one third of a second. The user will clearly recognize this period... and refresh cycles of the video DRAM have not yet been added to this calculation.

One solution for this problem is to provide the graphics adapters with a dedicated graphics processor like the TIGA or 8514/A. Another possibility (especially if one looks at the much higher processor clock frequencies compared to the bus clock) is to operate the bus to the graphics subsystem at the same rate as the CPUs. The local bus attempts to implement exactly this. Thus the first local bus on the motherboard was nothing else but a fast interface to the video RAM so that the CPU could transfer data much faster than in a conventional system with a standard expansion bus. This concept can be readily applied to other devices which operate at a high transfer rate. One example is fast hard disk drives with integrated cache memory. But at this point another problem arises: host adapters or controllers for hard disks are usually implemented as adapter cards which must be inserted into a bus slot, but initially there was no standard, so the slots of the local bus differed from motherboard to motherboard. Compatibility among the products of various manufacturers has therefore been impossible up to now.

5.10.1 PCI and VL Bus – Two Local Bus Standards

To tackle this lack of compatibility, Intel developed the *PCI bus* (*peripheral component interconnect*) and, independently, the VESA committee designed the *VL bus* as a standard for the local bus. The following briefly discusses their concepts and features.

PCI

A significant characteristic of the PCI concept is the strict decoupling of the processor/main memory subsystem and the standard expansion bus. Figure 5.23 shows the PCI bus scheme.

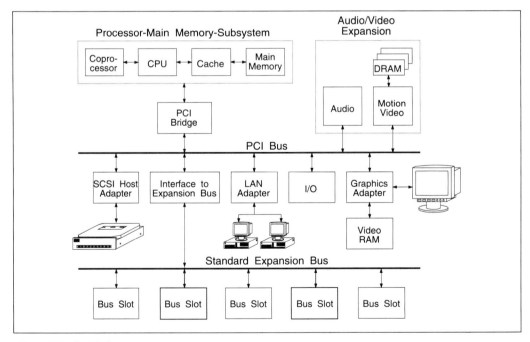

Figure 5.23: The PCI bus.

The connection between the processor/main memory subsystem and the PCI bus is established by a *PCI bridge*. Bridges in general are interfaces between two bus systems (or networks), transparent to the user. The PC bus now serves all the PCI units such as, for example, SCSI host adapter, LAN adapter, I/O device and graphics adapter (see Figure 5.23). Unlike the VL bus, here it is intended that these units are always integrated on the motherboard. Slots for these PCI devices are therefore not present. Only for an audio and motion-video device are two slots possible. Motion-video refers to moving images which require an enormous processing power. The corresponding PCI device is often very large, so that its integration is impossible. The audio/video extension also makes the PCI bus suitable for future multimedia applications.

A third class of PCI devices is the interface to the expansion bus. This means that the standard expansion bus (regardless of whether it is ISA, EISA, microchannel or another bus system) is regarded as a PCI device here. Thus, in principle, every bus system can be integrated and connected behind the PCI bus. Up to ten PCI devices may be connected to the PCI bus.

The PCI bus and its bus cycles are very similar to the i486 bus. Presently, it operates with a width of at most 32 bits and a clock rate of 33 MHz, though an extension to 64 bits is planned. The PCI bus uses a multiplexing scheme where the lines are alternately used as address and data lines. This saves lines but, on the other hand, two clock cycles are required for a single data transfer, because during the first cycle the address (and in the second cycle the data) is transferred. Thus, the data transfer rate is limited to 66 Mbyte/s. Additionally, the PCI bus implements a very powerful burst mode where the address is passed only once. Afterwards, the data's receiver and transmitter count-up the address with every clock cycle so that the address is always implicitly known. With the burst mode, 4 to 100 transfer cycles can be carried out – at a data bus width of 32 bits this means 16 to 400 bytes. The maximum data transfer rate increases in burst mode to more than 120 Mbyte/s. Whether the addressed PCI devices are capable of following this is another question, of course.

The VL Bus

The schematic concept of the VL bus is shown in Figure 5.24. Like the PCI bus, the VL bus is also located between processor and memory system on the one side and the standard expansion bus on the other. From the figure you may already recognize that the VL bus is not so strictly decoupled from the processor system and the standard expansion bus as is the case with the PCI bus. The VL bus is intended for up to three VL bus devices which can be inserted into suitable VL slots on the motherboard.

The VL slots comprise 116 contacts that look similar to the microchannel slots. They are all located 5 mm behind the slot of the standard expansion bus. That is the special feature of the VL bus: a VL adapter can not only use the signals and contacts of the VL bus, but the standard slot is also located nearby. As for the PCI bus, the standard bus width is 32 bits, but can be halved to 16 bits. For this the addressed VL device must drive the $\overline{\text{LBS16}}$ (*local bus size 16*) signal to a low level. Extension of the VL bus to a width of 64 bits is planned.

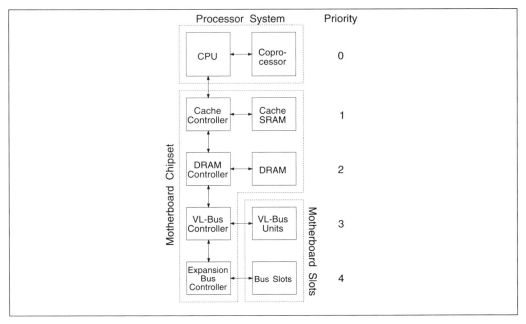

Figure 5.24: The VL bus.

The VL bus runs with the external clock frequency of the CPU, thus i486DX and i486DX2 processors supply different frequencies for it. The VL bus has been designed for a maximum clock rate of 66 MHz, but this can only be achieved if no VL bus slot is present and all VL devices are already integrated on the motherboard. Dampings, signal reflections and capacities of the VL bus slots do not allow such high frequencies. With an expansion slot the VL bus thus runs at 40 MHz at most. But this is still five times more than EISA. In the case of a CPU running at too high a clock rate, a frequency divider lowers the supply clock rate so that a 50 MHz i486 CPU can also use the VL bus with an expansion slot. The integrated bus buffers of the VL bus enable write accesses to VL devices up to 33 MHz without wait cycles, but for read accesses these buffers do not give any advantage. Thus, read cycles are always running with one wait state. Additionally, the VL bus specification provides for a burst mode and implements the necessary control signals $\overline{BRDY}$ and $\overline{BLAST}$. Thus, data transfer rates of a maximum 66 Mbyte/s (33 MHz without wait cycles or 66 MHz with one wait state at a 32-bit bus width) without burst mode and 120 Mbyte/s in burst mode for write and read accesses can be achieved. Of course, VL devices can also request additional wait cycles, for example if no access to the video RAM is currently possible because a memory refresh is in progress on the adapter. For this purpose the VL bus includes the *LRDY* (*local bus ready*) signal.

On a logical basis, the three VL devices possible are divided into so-called *local bus masters* (*LBM*) and *local bus targets* (*LBT*). An LBM can take control of the VL bus on its own and carry out data transfers similar to EISA or MCA bus masters. An LBT, on the other hand, is not capable of doing this. It is only driven in the course of a data transfer via the VL bus, but does not generate any bus signals (except LRDY). Control of the bus arbitration is carried out by the

VL bus controller, which is usually integrated on the motherboard, and carries out an arbitration similar to EISA or the microchannel.

5.10.2 Typical Local Bus Devices

As already mentioned, the local bus is aimed at devices which require or supply a large amount of data within a very short time. This is especially the case for graphics adapters and hard disks. Presently, they are also the only available local bus devices. Graphics adapters with a local bus interface are significantly faster than ISA adapters without dual-port memory or a graphics processor. In Section 12.6 a comparison of the various concepts for accelerating the picture setup can be found. Powerful hard disk drives are further candidates for local bus devices. With their cache memory they reach data transfer rates that are comparable to an EISA system.

5.10.3 Brake Blocks in the Local Bus System

Reading the last sentence in the previous section, you are surely beginning to wonder why I wrote «comparable to EISA». Wasn't the local bus introduced to increase the rather low EISA bus frequency from 8 MHz to 33 MHz, or even more with the local bus, and to enhance the data transfer rate accordingly? Obviously, we are again confronted with a «bottleneck» in the system. In the case of hard disks, this can be, for example, the transfer strategy of the data or a low number of sectors per track. In anticipation, some terms are used in the following sections that will arise in connection with hard disks later. Chapter 9 gives a detailed explanation of these terms, and in Chapter 12 the advantages and disadvantages of local bus and graphics processors are discussed.

For data transfer from and to the controller there are two possibilities: DMA and PIO (**p**rogrammed **I/O**). For an adapter with a local bus interface only PIO is applicable, as data transfer via DMA only runs at the maximum data throughput of the DMA system (about 1 Mbyte/s in an ISA system). A PIO cycle lasts for at least four bus cycles, because in the transfer controller/main memory, for example, the following cycles arise: output of the I/O address, data reading from the controller, output of the memory address, data writing into main memory. EISA controllers which transfer data by means of the DMA burst mode C require only a single EISA clock cycle for the whole process. Even if all devices in the local bus system are able to respond without wait cycles, a clock rate four times higher is necessary to achieve the same transfer rate (thus 33 MHz). Only cache SRAMs can follow this clock; all other chips, such as the DRAM chips of the main memory, the I/O registers of the adapter, etc., insert more or fewer wait states. With the 8 MHz of the EISA bus, on the other hand, no problems arise, and the data transfer rate in EISA systems is unavoidably higher.

But all these explanations are only valid so long as data is available in the on-board cache of the hard disk controller or host adapter. For larger amounts of data the drive must reload data from disk into the cache before further bytes can be transferred to main memory, or the drive has to write data onto disk before it is able to accept further bytes from main memory. This may occur, for example, if you call a program or store an extensive drawing. The transfer rate is limited in both cases (regardless of whether by the EISA or the local bus) by the rate at which the data pass below the read/write heads of the drive. With the presently typical 40 sectors per track and 3600 rpm this principal limit has a value of 1.2 Mbyte/s. With a cache controller even an ISA system achieves this long-term rate.

Every hard disk controller has a more or less powerful CPU to control the drive and to manage the on-board cache (if present). If a manufacturer now attempts to replace an existing ISA controller with a local bus interface, without any other adaptation of internal circuitry, the cache CPU which is sufficient for an ISA system can be easily overtaxed. This is reflected, of course, in the data transfer rate.

6   Memory Chips

Virtually no other computer element has been the subject of such almost suicidal competition between the world's leading microelectronic giants over the last ten years as memory chips. At the beginning of the PC-era 64 kbit chips and 16 kbit chips were considered to be high-tech. But today in our PCs, 4 Mbit chips are used, and 64 Mbit chips are already running in several laboratories.

Note that the storage capacity of memory chips is always indicated in bits and not in bytes. Today's most common 1 Mb memory chip is therefore able to hold one million bits, or 128 kbytes. For a main memory of 1 Mbyte, eight of these chips (plus one for parity) are thus required.

The technological problems of manufacturing such highly-integrated electronic elements are enormous. The typical structure size is only about 1 μm, and with the 64 Mb chip they will be even less (about 0.3 μm). Human hairs are at least 20 times thicker. Moreover, all transistors and other elements must operate correctly (and at enormous speed); after all, on a 64 Mb chip there are more than 200 million (!) transistors, capacitors and resistors. If only one of these elements is faulty, then the chip is worthless (but manufacturers have integrated redundant circuits to repair minor malfunctions that will then only affect the overall access time). Thus, it is not surprising that the development of these tiny and quite cheap chips costs several hundred million dollars.

For the construction of highly integrated memory chips the concept of dynamic RAM (DRAM) is generally accepted today. If only the access speed is in question (for example, for fast cache memories), then static RAM (SRAM) is used. But both memory types have the disadvantage that they lose their ability to remember as soon as the power supply is switched off or fails. They store information in a volatile manner. For the boot routines and the PC BIOS, therefore, only a few types of ROM are applicable. These memories also hold the stored information after a power-down. They store information in a non-volatile manner, but their contents may not be altered, or at least only with some difficulty.

6.1   Small and Cheap – DRAM

The name dynamic RAM or (DRAM) comes from the operation principle of these memory chips. They represent the stored information by charges in a capacitor. However, all capacitors have the disadvantageous characteristic of losing their charge with the lapse of time, so the chip loses the stored information. To avoid this the information must be refreshed periodically or «dynamically», that is, the capacitor is recharged according to the information held. Figure 6.1 shows the pin assignment of a 1 Mb chip as an example. Compared with the processors, we only have to discuss a few pins here.

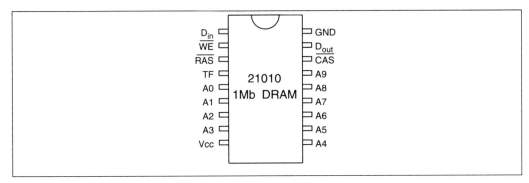

Figure 6.1: Pin assignment of a 1 Mb chip.

A9–A0 (pins 15–10, 8–5)
These ten pins are supplied with the row and column address of the memory cell.

WE (pin 2)
(Write Enable) If the signal at this pin is low the DRAM carries out a write operation; otherwise data is read from the addressed memory cell and output.

RAS (pin 3)
(Row Address Strobe) If this pin is low the DRAM accepts the supplied address and uses it as a row address.

CAS (pin 16)
(Column Address Strobe) If this pin is low the DRAM accepts the supplied address and uses it as a column address.

Din (Pin 1)
This pin is supplied with the write data during a write process.

Dout (Pin 17)
This pin provides read data during a read process.

GND (Pin 18)
The ground potential (usually 0 V) is applied to this pin.

V_{cc} (Pin 10)
The supply voltage (usually +5 V) is applied to this pin.

TF (Pin 4)
(Test Function) This pin is used by the Intel 21010 DRAM to check the DRAM during the course of manufacture. Inserted into a computer, this pin is grounded or floating.

6.1.1   Structure and Operation Principle

For data storage, reading the information, and the internal management of the DRAM, several functional groups are necessary. Figure 6.2 shows a typical block diagram of a dynamic RAM.

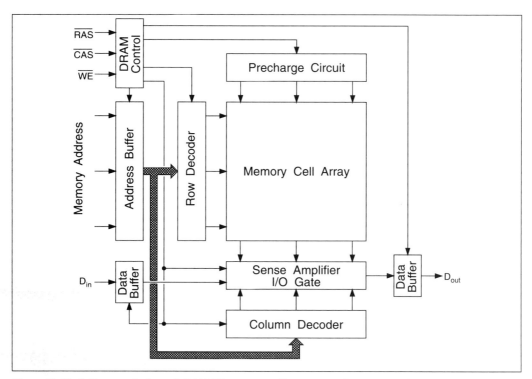

Figure 6.2: Block diagram of a dynamic RAM. The memory cells are arranged in a matrix, the so-called memory cell array. The address buffer sequentially accepts the row and column addresses and transmits them to the row and column decoder, respectively. The decoders drive internal signal lines and gates so that the data of the addressed memory cell is transmitted to the data buffer after a short time period to be output.

The central part of the DRAM is the *memory cell array*. Usually, a bit is stored in an individually addressable unit memory cell (see Figure 6.3), which is arranged together with many others in the form of a matrix with rows and columns. A 1 Mb chip has 1 048 576 memory cells arranged in a matrix of, for example, 1024 rows and 1024 columns. By specifying the row and column number, a memory cell is unambiguously determined.

The address buffer accepts the memory address output by the external memory controller according to the CPU's address. For this purpose, the address is divided into two parts, a row and a column address. These two addresses are read into the address buffer in succession: this process is called *multiplexing*. The reason for this division is obvious: to address one cell in a 1 Mb chip with 1024 rows and 1024 columns, 20 address bits are required in total (ten for the row and ten for the column). If all address bits are to be transferred at once, 20 address pins would also be required. Thus the chip package becomes very large. Moreover, a large address buffer would be necessary. For high integration, it is disadvantageous if all element groups that establish a connection to the surroundings (for example, the address or data buffer) must be powerful and therefore occupy a comparably large area, because only then can they supply enough current for driving external chips such as the memory controller or external data buffers.

Thus it is better to transfer the memory address in two portions. Generally, the address buffer first reads the row address and then the column address. This address multiplexing is controlled by the $\overline{RAS}$ and $\overline{CAS}$ control signals. If the memory controller passes a row address then it simultaneously activates the $\overline{RAS}$ signals, that is, it lowers the level of $\overline{RAS}$ to low. $\overline{RAS}$ (*row address strobe*) informs the DRAM chip that the supplied address is a row address. Now the DRAM control activates the address buffer to fetch the address and transfers it to the row decoder, which in turn decodes this address. If the memory controller later supplies the column address then it activates the $\overline{CAS}$ (*column address strobe*) signal. Thus the DRAM control recognizes that the address now represents a column address, and activates the address buffer again. The address buffer accepts the supplied address and transfers it to the column decoder. The duration of the $\overline{RAS}$ and $\overline{CAS}$ signals as well as their interval (the so-called *RAS-CAS-delay*) must fulfil the requirements of the DRAM chip.

The memory cell thus addressed outputs the stored data, which is amplified by a sense amplifier and transferred to a data output buffer by an I/O gate. The buffer finally supplies the information as read data D_{out} via the data pins of the memory chip.

If data is to be read the memory controller activates the $\overline{WE}$ signal for *write enable* and applies the write data D_{in} to the data input buffer. Via the I/O gate and a sense amplifier, the information is amplified, transferred to the addressed memory cell, and stored. The precharge circuit serves to support the sense amplifier (described later).

Thus the PC's memory controller carries out three different jobs: dividing the address from the CPU into a row and a column address that are supplied in succession, activating the signals $\overline{RAS}$, $\overline{CAS}$ and $\overline{WE}$ correctly, and transferring and accepting the write and read data, respectively. Moreover, advanced memory concepts such as interleaving and page mode request wait cycles flexibly, and the memory controller must prepare the addressed memory chips accordingly (more about this subject later). The raw address and data signal from the CPU is not suitable for the memory, thus the memory controller is an essential element of the PC's memory subsystem.

6.1.2   Reading and Writing Data

The 1-transistor-1-capacitor cell is mainly established as the common unit memory cell today. Figure 6.3 shows the structure of such a unit memory cell and the I/O peripherals required to read and write data.

The unit memory cell has a capacitor that holds the data in the form of electrical charges, and an access transistor which serves as a switch for selecting the capacitor. The transistor's gate is connected to the word line WLx. The memory cell array accommodates as many word lines WL1 to WLn as rows are formed.

Besides the word lines the memory cell array also comprises so-called bit line pairs BL, $\overline{BL}$. The number of these bit line pairs is equal to the number of columns in the memory cell array. The bit lines are alternately connected to the sources of the access transistors. Finally, the unit memory cell is the capacitor which constitutes the actual memory element of the cell. One of its electrodes is connected to the drain of the corresponding access transistor, and the other is earthed.

The regular arrangement of access transistors, capacitors, word lines and bit line pairs is repeated until the chip's capacity is reached. Thus, for a 1 Mb memory chip, 1 048 576 access transistors, 1 048 576 storage capacitors, 1024 word lines and 1024 bit line pairs are formed.

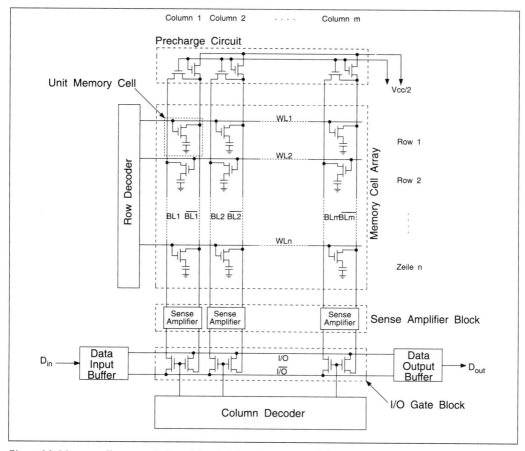

Figure 6.3: Memory cell array and I/O peripherals. The unit memory cell for holding one bit comprises a capacitor and a transistor. The word lines turn on the access transistors of a row and the column decoder selects a bit line pair. The data of a memory cell is thus transmitted onto the I/O line pair and afterwards to the data output buffer.

Of particular significance for detecting memory data during the course of a read operation is the precharge circuit. In advance of a memory controller access and the activation of a word line (which is directly connected to this access), the precharge circuit charges all bit line pairs up to half of the supply potential, that is, $V_{cc}/2$. Additionally, the bit line pairs are short-circuited by a transistor so that they are each at an equal potential. If this equalizing and precharging process is completed, then the precharge circuit is again deactivated. The time required for precharging and equalizing is called the *RAS precharge time*. Only once this process is finished, can the chip carry out an access to its memory cells. Figure 6.4 shows the course of the potential on a bit line pair during a data read.

When the memory controller addresses a memory cell within the chip the controller first supplies the row address signal, which is accepted by the address buffer and transferred to the address decoder. At this time the two bit lines of a pair have the same potential $V_{cc}/2$. The row decoder decodes the row address signal and activates the word line corresponding to the decoded row address. Now all the access transistors connected to this word line are switched on. The charges of all the storage capacitors of the addressed row flow onto the corresponding bit line (time t1 in Figure 6.4). In the 1 Mb chip concerned, 1024 access transistors are thus turned on and the charges of 1024 storage capacitors flow onto the 1024 bit line pairs.

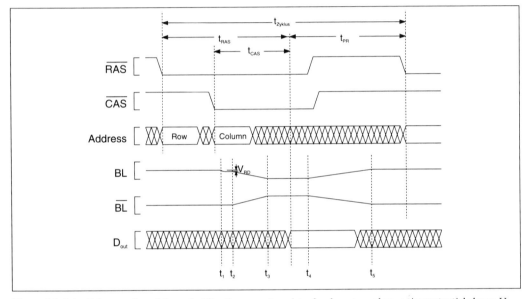

Figure 6.4: Potential course for a data read. After the access transistor has been turned on, a tiny potential charge V_{RD}, which depends on the stored value, appears on the corresponding bit line. The potential difference is amplified by the sense amplifier so that the read data becomes available after a short delay.

The problem, particularly with today's highly integrated memory chips, is that the capacity of the storage capacitors is far less than the capacity of the bit lines connected to them by the access transistors. Thus the potential of the bit line changes only slightly, typically by ±100 mV (t2). If the storage capacitor were empty, then the potential of the bit line slightly decreases; if charged then the potential increases. The sense amplifier activated by the DRAM control amplifies the potential difference on the two bit lines of the pair. In the first case, it draws the potential of the bit line connected to the storage capacitor down to ground and raises the potential of the other bit line up to V_{cc} (t3). In the second case, the opposite happens – the bit line connected to the storage capacitor is raised to V_{cc} and the other bit line decreased to ground.

Without precharging and potential equalization by the precharge circuit, the sense amplifier would need to amplify the absolute potential of the bit line. But because the potential change is only about 100 mV, this amplifying process would be much less stable and therefore more likely to fail, compared to the difference forming of the two bit lines. Here the dynamic range is ±100 mV, that is, 200 mV in total. Thus the precharge circuit enhances reliability.

Each of the 1024 sense amplifiers supplies the amplified storage signal at its output and applies the signal to the I/O gate block. This block has gate circuits with two gate transistors, each controlled by the column decoder. The column decoder decodes the applied column address signal (which is applied after the row address signal), and activates exactly one gate. This means that the data of only one sense amplifier is transmitted onto the I/O line pair I/O, $\overline{I/O}$ and transferred to the output data buffer. Only now, and thus much later than the row address, does the column address become important. Multiplexing of the row and column address therefore has no adverse effect, as one might expect at a first glance.

The output data buffer amplifies the data signal again and outputs it as output data D_{out}. At the same time, the potentials of the bit line pairs are on a low or a high level according to the data in the memory cell that is connected to the selected word line. Thus they correspond to the stored data. As the access transistors remain on by the activated word line, the read-out data is written back into the memory cells of one row. The reading of a single memory cell therefore simultaneously leads to a refreshing of the whole line. The time period between applying the row address and outputting the data D_{out} via the data output buffer is called *RAS access time* t_{RAS}, or *access time*. The much shorter *CAS access time* t_{CAS} is significant for certain high-speed modes. This access time characterizes the time period between supplying the column address and outputting the data D_{out}. Both access times are illustrated in Figure 6.4.

After completing the data output the row and column decoders as well as the sense amplifiers are disabled again, and the gates in the I/O gate block are switched off. At that time the bit lines are still on the potentials according to the read data. The refreshed memory cells are disconnected from the bit lines by the disabled word line, and the access transistors thus switched off. Now the DRAM control activates the precharge circuit (t4), which lowers and increases, respectively, the potentials of the bit lines to $V_{cc}/2$ and equalizes them again (t5). After stabilization of the whole DRAM circuitry, the chip is ready for another memory cycle. The necessary time period between stabilization of the output data and supply of a new row address and activation of $\overline{RAS}$ is called *recovery time* or *RAS precharge time* t_{RP} (see Figure 6.4).

The total of RAS precharge time and access time leads to the cycle time t_{cycle}. Generally, the RAS precharge time lasts about 80% of the access time, so that the cycle time is about 1.8 times more than the access time. Thus, a DRAM with an access time of 100 ns has a cycle time of 180 ns. Not until this 180ns has elapsed may a new access to memory be carried out. Therefore, the time period between two successive memory accesses is not determined by the short access time but by the nearly double cycle time of 180 ns. If one adds the signal propagation delays between CPU and memory on the motherboard of about 20 ns, then an 80286 CPU with an access time of two processor clock cycles may not exceed a clock rate of 10 MHz, otherwise one or more wait states must be inserted. Advanced memory concepts such as interleaving trick the RAS precharge time so that in most cases only the access time is decisive. In page mode or static column mode, even the shortest CAS access time determines the access rate. (More about these subjects in Section 6.1.)

The data write is carried out in nearly the same way as data reading. At first the memory control supplies the row address signal upon an active $\overline{RAS}$. Simultaneously, it enables the control signal $\overline{WE}$ to inform the DRAM that it should carry out a data write. The data D_{in} to write are supplied to the data input buffer, amplified and transferred onto the I/O line pair I/O, $\overline{I/O}$. The data output buffer is not activated for the data write.

The row decoder decodes the row address signal and activates the corresponding word line. As is the case for data reading, here also the access transistors are turned on and they transfer the stored charges onto the bit line pairs BLx, $\overline{BLx}$. Afterwards, the memory controller activates the $\overline{CAS}$ signal and applies the column address via the address buffer to the column decoder. It decodes the address and switches on a single transfer gate through which the data from the I/O line pair is transmitted to the corresponding sense amplifier. This sense amplifier amplifies the data signal and raises or lowers the potentials of the bit lines in the pair concerned according to the value «1» or «0» of the write data. As the signal from the data input buffer is stronger than that from the memory cell concerned, the amplification of the write data gains the upper hand. The potential on the bit line pair of the selected memory cell reflects the value of the write data. All other sense amplifiers amplify the data held in the memory cells so that after a short time potentials are present on all bit line pairs that correspond to the unchanged data and the new write data, respectively.

These potentials are fetched as corresponding charges into the storage capacitors. Afterwards, the DRAM controller deactivates the row decoder, the column decoder and the data input buffer. The capacitors of the memory cells are disconnected from the bit lines and the write process is completed. As was the case for the data read, the precharge circuit sets the bit line pairs to a potential level $V_{cc}/2$ again, and the DRAM is ready for another memory cycle.

Besides the memory cell with one access transistor and one storage capacitor, there are other cell types with several transistors or capacitors. The structure of such cells is much more complicated, of course, and the integration of its elements gets more difficult because of their higher number. Such memory types are therefore mainly used for specific applications, for example, a so-called dual-port RAM where the memory cells have a transistor for reading and another transistor for writing data so that data can be read and written simultaneously. This is advantageous, for example, for video memories because the CPU can write data into the video RAM to set up an image without the need to wait for a release of the memory. On the other hand, the graphics hardware may continuously read out the memory to drive the monitor. For this purpose, VRAM chips have a parallel random access port used by the CPU for writing data into the video memory and, further, a very fast serial output port that clocks out a plurality of bits, for example a whole memory row. The monitor driver circuit can thus be supplied very quickly and continuously with image data. The CRT controller need not address the video memory periodically to read every image byte, and the CPU need not wait for a horizontal or vertical retrace until it is allowed to read or write video data.

Instead of the precharge circuit, other methods can also be employed. For example, it is possible to install a dummy cell for every column in the memory cell array which holds only half of that charge which corresponds to a «1». Practically, this cell holds the value «1/2». The sense amplifiers then compare the potential read from the addressed memory cell with the potential of the dummy cell. The effect is similar to that of the precharge circuit. Also, here a difference and no absolute value is amplified.

It is not necessary to structure the memory cell array in a square form with an equal number of rows and columns and to use a symmetrical design with 1024 rows and 1024 columns. The designers have complete freedom in this respect. Internally, 1 Mb chips often have 512 rows and 2048 columns simply because the chip is longer than it is wide. In this case, one of the supplied row address bits is used as an additional (that is, 11th) column address bit internally. The nine row address bits select one of $2^9 = 512$ rows, but the eleven column address bits select one of 2^{11} = 2048 columns. In high-capacity memory chips the memory cell array is also often divided into two or more subarrays. In a 1 Mb chip eight subarrays with 512 rows and 256 columns may be present, for example. One or more row address bits are then used as the subarray address; the remaining row and column address bits then only select a row or column within the selected subarray.

The word and bit lines thus get shorter and the signals become stronger. But as a disadvantage, the number of sense amplifiers and I/O gates increases. Such methods are usual, particularly in the new highly-integrated DRAMs, because with the cells always getting smaller and smaller and therefore the capacitors of less capacity, the long bit lines «eat» the signal before it can reach the sense amplifier. Which concept a manufacturer implements for the various chips cannot be recognized from the outside. Moreover, these concepts are often kept secret so that competitors don't get an insight into their rivals' technologies.

6.1.3   Semiconductor Layer Structure

The following sections present the usual concepts for implementing DRAM memory cells. Integrated circuits are formed by layers of various materials on a single substrate. Figure 6.5 is a sectional view through such a layer structure of a simple DRAM memory cell with a plane capacitor. In the lower part of the figure, a circuit diagram of the memory cell is additionally illustrated.

The actual memory cell is formed between the field oxide films on the left and right sides. The field oxides separate and isolate the individual memory cells. The gate and the two n-doped regions source and drain constitute the access transistor of the memory cell. The gate is separated from the p-substrate by a so-called gate isolation or gate oxide film, and controls the conductivity of the channel between source and drain. The capacitor in its simplest configuration is formed by an electrode which is grounded. The electrode is separated by a dielectric isolation film from the p-substrate in the same way as the gate, so that the charge storage takes place below the isolation layer in the substrate. To simplify the interconnection of the memory cells as far as possible, the gate simultaneously forms a section of the word line and the drain is part of the bit line. If the word line W is selected by the row decoder, then the electric field below the gate that is part of the word line lowers the resistance value of the channel between source and drain. Capacitor charges may thus flow away through the source-channel-drain path to the bit line BL, which is connected to the n-drain. They generate a data signal on the bit line pair BL, $\overline{BL}$, which in turn is sensed and amplified by the sense amplifier.

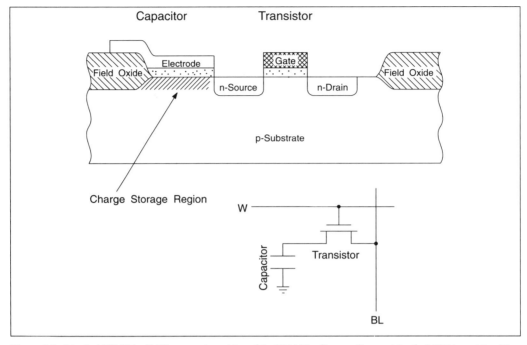

Figure 6.5: A typical DRAM cell. The access transistor of the DRAM cell generally consists of a MOS transistor. The gate of the transistor simultaneously forms the word line, and the drain is connected to the bit line. Charges that represent the stored information are held in the substrate in the region below the electrode.

A problem arising in connection with the higher integration of the memory cells is that the size of the capacitor, and thus its capacity, decreases. Therefore, fewer and fewer charges can be stored between electrode and substrate. The data signals during a data read become too weak to ensure reliable operation of the DRAM. With the latest 4 Mbit chip the engineers therefore went over to a three-dimensional memory cell structure. One of the concepts used is shown in Figure 6.6, namely the DRAM memory cell with trench capacitor.

In this memory cell type the information charges are no longer stored simply between two plane capacitor electrodes, but the capacitor has been enlarged into the depth of the substrate. The facing area of the two capacitor electrodes thus becomes much larger than is possible with an ordinary plane capacitor. The memory cell can be miniaturized and the integration density enlarged without decreasing the amount of charge held in the storage capacitor. The read-out signals are strong enough and the DRAM chip operates very reliably also at higher integration densities.

Unfortunately, the technical problems of manufacturing such tiny trenches are enormous. We must handle trench widths of about 1 μm at a depth of 3–4 μm here. For manufacturing such small trenches completely new etching techniques had to be developed which are anisotropic, and therefore etch more in depth than in width. It was two years before this technology was reliably available. Also, doping the source and drain regions as well as the dielectric layer between the two capacitor electrodes is very difficult. Thus it is not surprising that only a few big companies in the world with enormous financial resources are able to manufacture these memory chips.

To enhance the integration density of memory chips, other methods are also possible and applied, for example folded bit line structures, shared sense amplifiers, or stacked capacitors. Lack of space prohibits an explanation of all these methods, but it is obvious that the memory chips which appear to be so simple from the outside accommodate many high-tech elements and methods. Without them, projects such as the 64 Mbit chip could not be realized.

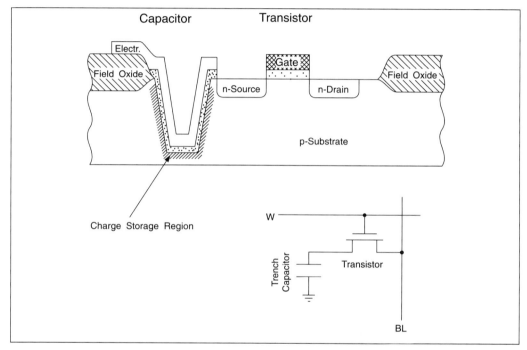

Figure 6.6: Trench capacitor for highest integration densities. To enhance the electrode area of the storage capacitor, the capacitor is built into the depth of the substrate. Thus the memory cells can move together without decreasing the stored charge per cell.

6.1.4   DRAM Refresh

From Figure 6.5 you already know that the data is stored in the form of electrical charges in a tiny capacitor. As is true for all technical equipment, this capacitor is not perfect, that is, it discharges over the course of time via the access transistor and its dieletric layer. Thus the stored charges and therefore also the data held get lost. The capacitor must be recharged periodically. Remember that during the course of a memory read or write a refresh of the memory cells within the addressed row is automatically carried out. Normal DRAMs must be refreshed every 1–16 ms, depending upon the type. Currently, three refresh methods are employed: RAS-only-refresh; CAS-before-RAS-refresh and hidden-refresh. Figure 6.7 shows the course of the signals involved during these refresh types.

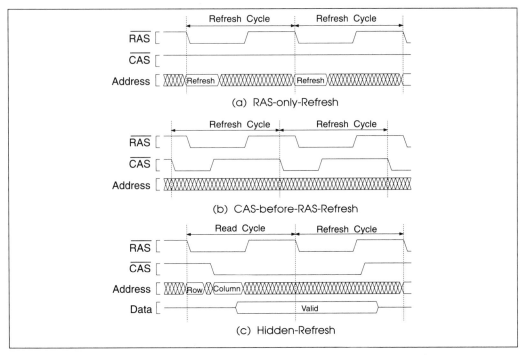

Figure 6.7: Three refresh types. (a) RAS-only-refresh; (b) CAS-before-RAS-refresh; (c) hidden-refresh.

RAS-Only-Refresh

The simplest and most used method for refreshing a memory cell is to carry out a dummy read cycle. For this cycle the $\overline{RAS}$ signal is activated and a row address (the so-called *refresh address*) is applied to the DRAM, but the $\overline{CAS}$ signal remains disabled. The DRAM thus internally reads one row onto the bit line pairs and amplifies the read data. But because of the disabled $\overline{CAS}$ signal they are not transferred to the I/O line pair and thus not to the data output buffer. To refresh the whole memory an external logic or the processor itself must supply all the row addresses in succession. This refresh type is called *RAS-only-refresh*. The disadvantage of this outdated refresh method is that an external logic, or at least a program, is necessary to carry out the DRAM refresh. In the PC this is done by channel 0 of the 8237 DMA chip, which is periodically activated by counter 1 of the 8253/8254 timer chip and issues a dummy read cycle. In a RAS-only-refresh, several refresh cycles can be executed successively if the CPU or refresh control drives the DRAM chip accordingly.

CAS-Before-RAS-Refresh

Most modern DRAM chips additionally implement one or more internal refresh modes. The most important is the so-called *CAS-before-RAS-refresh.* For this purpose, the DRAM chip has its own refresh logic with an address counter. For a CAS-before-RAS-refresh, *CAS* is held low for a certain time period before *RAS* also drops (thus CAS-before-RAS). The on-chip refresh (that is, the internal refresh logic) is thus activated, and the refresh logic carries out an automatic internal refresh. The refresh address is generated internally by the address counter and the refresh logic, and need not be supplied externally. After every CAS-before-RAS-refresh cycle, the internal address counter is incremented so that it indicates the new address to refresh. Thus it is sufficient if the memory controller «bumps» the DRAM from time to time to issue a refresh cycle. With the CAS-before-RAS-refresh, several refresh cycles can also be executed in succession.

Hidden-Refresh

Another elegant option is the *hidden-refresh*. Here the actual refresh cycle is more or less «hidden» behind a normal read access. During a hidden-refresh the $\overline{CAS}$ signal is further held on a low level, and only the $\overline{RAS}$ signal is switched. The data read during the read cycle remain valid even while the refresh cycle is in progress. Because the time required for a refresh cycle is usually shorter than the read cycle, this refresh type saves some time. For the hidden-refresh, too, the address counter in the DRAM generates the refresh address. The row and column addresses shown in Figure 6.7 refer only to the read cycle. If the $\overline{CAS}$ signal remains on a low level for a sufficiently long time, then several refresh cycles can be carried out in succession. For this it is only necessary to switch the $\overline{RAS}$ signal frequently between low and high.

New motherboards with the programmable NEAT chips often implement the option of refreshing the DRAM memory with CAS-before-RAS or hidden-refresh instead of the detour via the DMA and timer chip. This is usually faster and more effective. You should use this option, which comes directly from the field of mainframes and workstations, to free your PC from unnecessary and time-consuming DMA cycles.

6.1.5 DRAM Chip Organization

Let us look at a 16-bit graphics adapter equipped with 1 Mb chips. As every memory chip has one data pin, 16 chips are required in all to serve the data bus width of 16 bits. But these 16 1 Mb chips lead to a video memory of 2 Mbytes; that is too much for an ordinary VGA. If you want to equip your VGA with «only» 512 kbytes (not too long ago this was actually the maximum) you only need four 1 Mb chips. But the problem now is that you may only implement a 4-bit data bus to the video memory with these chips.

With the continual development of larger and larger memory chips, various forms of organization have been established. The 1 Mb chip mentioned above with its one data pin has a so-called *1Mword * 1bit organization*. This means that the memory chip comprises 1 M words with a width of one bit each, that is, has exactly one data pin. Another widely used organizational form for a 1 Mb chip is the *256kword * 4bit organization*. These chips then have 256 k words with a width of four bits each. The storage capacity is 1 Mbit here, too. Thus the first number always indicates the number of words and the second the number of bits per word. Unlike the 1M*1-chip, the 256k*4-chip has four data pins because in a memory access one word is always output or read. To realize the above indicated video RAM with 512 kbytes capacity, you therefore need four 1 Mbit chips with the 256k*4 organization. As every chip has four data pins, the data bus is 16 bits wide and the 16-bit graphics adapter is fully used. Figure 6.8 shows the pin assignment of a 256k*4-chip. Unlike the 1M*1 DRAM of Figure 6.1, four bidirectional data input/output pins D0–D3 are present. The signal at the new connection $\overline{OE}$ (output enable) instructs the DRAM's data buffer to output data at the pins D0–D3 ($\overline{OE}$ low) or to accept them from the data pins D0–D3 ($\overline{OE}$ high).

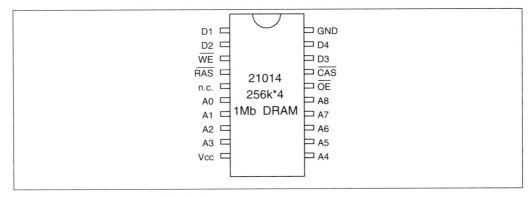

Figure 6.8: Pin assignment for a 256k*4-chip.

Besides the 256k*4-chip there is also a 64k*4-chip with a storage capacity of 256 kbits, often used in graphics adapters of less than 512 kbytes of video-RAM, as well as a 1M*4-chip with a capacity of 4 Mbits, which you meet in high-capacity SIMM or SIP modules. These chips all have four data pins that always input or output a data word of four pins with every memory access. Thus the chip has four data input and output buffers. Moreover, the memory array of these chips is divided into at least four subarrays, which are usually assigned to one data pin each. The data may only be input and output word by word, that is, in this case in groups of four bits each.

6.1.6   Fast Operating Modes of DRAM Chips

A further feature of modern memory chips is the possibility of carrying out one or more column modes to reduce the access time. The best known is the *page mode*. What is actually behind this often quoted catchword (and the less well-known static-column, nibble and serial modes) is discussed in the following sections. Figure 6.9 shows the behaviour of the most important memory signals if the chip carries out one of these high-speed modes in a read access. For comparison, in Figure 6.9a you can also see the signal's course in the conventional mode.

Page Mode

Section 6.1.2 mentioned that during the course of an access to a unit memory cell in the memory chip, the row address is input first with an active $\overline{RAS}$ signal, and then the column address with an active $\overline{CAS}$ signal. Additionally, internally all memory cells of the addressed row are read onto the corresponding bit line pair. If the successive memory access refers to a memory cell in the same row but another column (that is, the row address remains the same and only the column address has changed), then it is not necessary to input and decode the row address again. In page mode, therefore, only the column address is changed, but the row address remains the same. Thus, one page corresponds exactly to one row in the memory cell array. (You will find the signal's course in page mode shown in Figure 6.9b.)

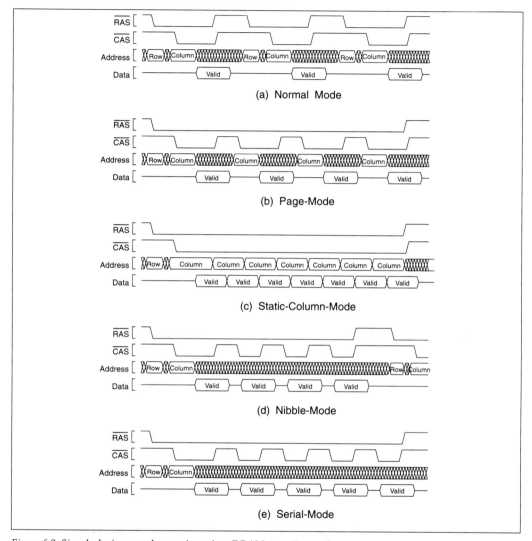

Figure 6.9: Signals during a read access in various DRAM operating modes.

To start the read access the memory controller first activates the $\overline{RAS}$ signal as usual, and passes the row address. The address is transferred to the row decoder, decoded, and the corresponding word line is selected. Now the memory controller activates the $\overline{CAS}$ signal and passes the column address of the intended memory cell. The column decoder decodes this address and transfers the corresponding value from the addressed bit line pair to the data output buffer. In normal mode, the DRAM controller would now deactivate both the $\overline{RAS}$ and $\overline{CAS}$ signals, and the access would be completed.

If the memory controller, however, accesses in page mode a memory cell in the same row of the DRAM (that is, within the same page), then it doesn't deactivate the $\overline{\text{RAS}}$ signal but continues to hold the signal at an active low level. Instead, only the $\overline{\text{CAS}}$ signal is disabled for a short time, and then reactivated to inform the DRAM control that the already decoded row address is still valid and only a column address is being newly supplied. All access transistors connected to the word line concerned thus also remain turned on, and all data read-out onto the bit line pairs is held stable by the sense amplifiers. The new column address is decoded in the column decoder, which turns on a corresponding transfer gate. Thus, the $\overline{\text{RAS}}$ precharge time as well as the transfer and decoding of the row address is inapplicable for the second and all succeeding accesses to memory cells of the same row in page mode. Only the column address is passed and decoded. In page mode access time the access time is about 50% and the cycle time up to even 70% shorter than in normal mode. This, of course, applies only for the second and all successive accesses. However, because of stability, the time period during which the $\overline{\text{RAS}}$ signal remains active may not last for an unlimited time. Typically, 200 accesses within the same page can be carried out before the memory controller has to deactivate the $\overline{\text{RAS}}$ signal for one cycle.

However, operation in page mode is not limited to data reading only: data may be written in page mode, or read and write operations within one page can be mixed. The DRAM need not leave page mode for this purpose. In a 1 Mb chip with a memory cell array of 1024 rows and 1024 columns, one page comprises at least 1024 memory cells. If the main memory is implemented with a width of 32 bits (that is, 32 1 Mb chips are present), then one main memory page holds 4 kbytes. As the instruction code and most data tend to form blocks, and the processor rarely accesses data that is more than 4 kbytes away from the just accessed value, the page mode can be used very efficiently to reduce the access and cycle times of the memory chips. But if the CPU addresses a memory cell in another row (that is, another page), then the DRAM must leave page mode and the $\overline{\text{RAS}}$ precharge time makes a significant difference. The same applies, of course, if the $\overline{\text{RAS}}$ signal is disabled by the memory controller after the maximum active period.

Static-Column Mode

Strongly related to the page mode is the static-column mode (see Figure 6.9c). Here the $\overline{\text{CAS}}$ signal is no longer switched to inform the chip that a new column address is applied. Instead, only the column address supplied changes, and $\overline{\text{CAS}}$ remains unaltered on a low level. The DRAM control is intelligent enough to detect the column address change after a short reaction time without the switching of $\overline{\text{CAS}}$. This additionally saves part of the $\overline{\text{CAS}}$ switch and reaction time. Thus the static-column mode is even faster than the page mode. But here also the $\overline{\text{RAS}}$ and $\overline{\text{CAS}}$ signals may not remain at a low level for an unlimited time. Inside the chip only the corresponding gates are switched through to the output buffer. In static-column mode, therefore, all memory cells of one row are accessible randomly. But DRAM chips with the static-column mode are quite rare on the market, and are little used in the field of PCs. Some IBM PS/2 models, though, use static-column chips instead of DRAMs with page mode.

Nibble Mode

The nibble mode is a very simple form of serial mode. By switching $\overline{CAS}$ four times, four data bits are clocked-out from an addressed row (one nibble is equal to four bits, or half a byte). The first data bit is designated by the applied column address, and the three others immediately follow this address. Internally, a DRAM chip with the nibble mode has a 4-bit data buffer in most cases, which accommodates the four bits and shifts them, clocked by the $\overline{CAS}$ signal, successively to the output buffer. This is carried out very quickly because all four addressed (one explicitly and three implicitly) data bits are transferred into the intermediate buffer all at once. The three successive bits need only be shifted, not read again. DRAM chips with the nibble mode are rarely used in the PC field.

Serial Mode

The serial mode may be regarded as an extended nibble mode. Also in this case, the data bits within one row are clocked out by switching $\overline{CAS}$. Unlike the nibble mode, the number of $\overline{CAS}$ switches (and thus the number of data bits) is not limited to four. Instead, in principle a whole row can be output serially. Thus, the internal organization of the chip plays an important role here, because one row may comprise, for example, 1024 or 2048 columns in a 1 Mbit chip. The row and column addresses supplied characterize only the beginning of the access. With every switching of $\overline{CAS}$ the DRAM chip counts up the column address internally and automatically. The serial mode is mainly an advantage for reading video memories or filling a cache line, as the read accesses by the CRT or the cache controller are of a serial nature over large address areas.

Interleaving

Another possibility to avoid delays because of the $\overline{RAS}$ precharge time is memory interleaving. For this purpose, memory is divided into several banks interleaved with a certain ratio. This is explained in connection with a 2-way interleaved memory for an i386 CPU. Because of the 32-bit i386 address bus, the memory is also organized with a width of 32 bits. With 2-way interleaving, memory is divided into two banks that are each 32 bits wide. All data with even double word addresses is located in bank 0 and all data with odd double word addresses in bank 1. For a sequential access to memory executed, for example, by the i386 prefetcher, the two banks are therefore accessed alternately. This means that the RAS precharge time of one bank overlaps the access time of the other bank. Stated differently: bank 0 is precharged while the CPU accesses bank 1, and vice versa. Figure 6.10 shows this, together with the relevant signals.

As only the access time and not the cycle time is significant for the CPU access rate, here the access rate can be doubled. Thus the effective access time for several successive memory accesses is halved. In the lower part of Figure 6.10 the same process without interleaving is shown. You can clearly see the difference.

3-way and 4-way interleaving is carried out according to the same principle, but memory is divided into three and four banks respectively, here, and the $\overline{RAS}$ and $\overline{CAS}$ shifts are only one third or one fourth of the time compared with half of the normal cycle time. Many NEAT boards allow custom setup of the interleaving factor. If your memory chips have four banks in total, you may choose either 2-way or 4-way interleaving. In the first case, two banks are always combined into one group; in the latter case, each bank is accessed individually.

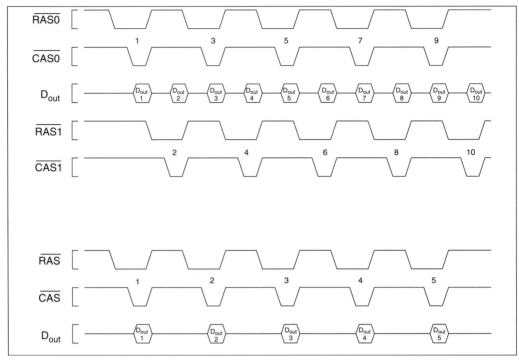

Figure 6.10: 2-way interleaving. By means of interleaving the RAS precharge time is avoided when accessing the two memory banks alternately. Therefore, only the access time of the chip is important, not the cycle time. Without interleaving, on the other hand, the nearly double cycle time is dominant so that repetitive accesses to memory are delayed.

So far I have described the concepts of page mode and interleaving in connection with a read access. But for data writing the same principles apply, of course. Moreover, read and write accesses can be mixed. The page mode does not need to be left, nor is interleaving without any value.

To use the advantages of both interleaving and page mode, many storage chips are now configured as paged/interleaved memory. Figure 6.11 shows the course of the $\overline{RAS}$ and $\overline{CAS}$ signals, as well as the output data, for a 2-way interleaved configuration with page mode.

As you can see, the $\overline{CAS1}$ signal is phase-shifted by 180° compared to $\overline{CAS0}$. Thus, bank 0 accepts column addresses, decodes them and supplies data, while for bank 1 the strobe signal $\overline{CAS1}$ is disabled to change the column address, and vice versa. The access rate is thus further increased compared to conventional interleaving or page mode. With conventional interleaving the DRAMs are interleaved according to the width of memory word-by-word or double-word by double-word. In page/interleaving this is done page-by-page. If a $\overline{RAS}$ precharge cycle is required during a page change, the access to the other bank is carried out with a probability of 50%. Thus, interleaving is effective in a way similar to conventional memory operation.

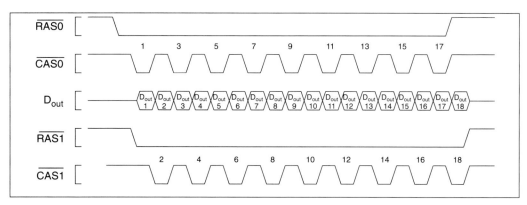

Figure 6.11: 2-way interleaving with page mode. In interleaving with page mode, successive pages are located in different banks so that a page change is executed more quickly.

However, the page mode and interleaving are not always successful, unfortunately. As mentioned, it is necessary that the memory accesses are carried out for the same page. A page change gives rise to a $\overline{\text{RAS}}$ precharge time, and thus delays the memory access. In the same way, to gain an advantage from interleaving it is required that the accesses with a 32-bit data bus are alternately carried out for odd and even double-word addresses, or alternately for odd and even word addresses in the case of a 16-bit data bus. If the CPU twice accesses an odd or even double-word or word address one after the other, in this case $\overline{\text{RAS}}$ precharge time is also required. Fortunately, program code and data tend to form blocks. Moreover, prefetching is executed sequentially so that page mode and interleaving significantly increase the memory access rate in most cases – but not always.

The hit rate is typically about 80% with page/interleaving. A very intelligent memory controller is required for this, which must be able to detect in page mode whether an access occurs within the same page, or with interleaving whether the other bank has to be accessed. If this condition is not fulfilled, the memory controller must flexibly insert wait states until the DRAMs have responded and output the required data or accepted the data supplied. Such powerful memory controllers are rather complicated, but interesting (from a technical viewpoint). Therefore, a typical member, the 82C212 for the 80286 CPU, is discussed below.

6.2   Intelligent Memory Controllers – The 82C212 Page/Interleave Memory Controller

Besides the generation of various chip signals such as $\overline{\text{RAS}}$, $\overline{\text{CAS}}$ and $\overline{\text{WE}}$, the 82C212 has the job of carrying out a page mode access with interleaving, of remapping the address space between 640 kbytes and 1 Mbyte to extended memory, of enabling shadowing of ROM BIOS code into the faster RAM, and of quickly switching the 80286 between protected and real modes.

6.2.1   Terminals and Signals

The 82C212 comes in a PLCC package with 84 terminals. Their configuration is shown in Figure 6.12. The 82C212 can serve four DRAM banks with a width of 16 data bits plus two parity bits in total. The storage capacity that the 82C212 can manage is four banks with 4 Mbytes each. This 16 Mbytes of memory is the maximum physical memory for the 80286.

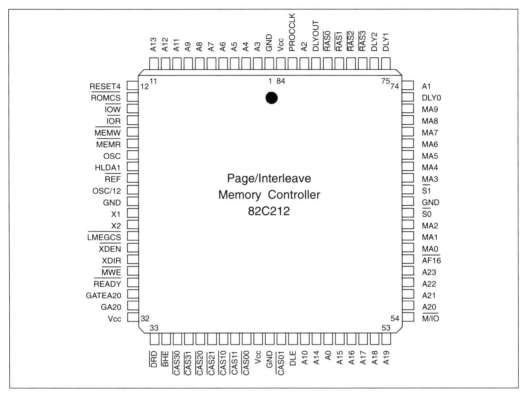

Figure 6.12: 82C212 connections. The 82C212 belongs to the modern memory controllers that support page mode and interleaving. Furthermore, the 82C212 generates the refresh addresses for the DRAM chips autonomously.

The following sections briefly describe the signals and pins of the 82C212.

PROCCLK (pin 83)
(Processor Clock) This pin is supplied with the processor clock signal from the 82C211 system controller.

X1, X2 (pins 23, 24)
These two pins are connected to a crystal oscillator, which usually generates a frequency of 14 318 180 Hz.

OSC (pin 18)
This pin outputs the oscillator clock signal with a frequency of 14.31818 MHz, which is generated by the crystal between X1 and X2.

OSC/12 (pin 21)
This pin supplies a frequency of CLK/12. The OSC/12 signal with a frequency of 1.19381 MHz is used internally to disable the $\overline{\text{RAS}}$ signal after the maximum active time in page mode of about 10 μs.

RESET4 (pin 12)
If a high-level signal is applied to this pin, the 82C212 configuration registers are reset to predefined standard values.

$\overline{\text{REF}}$ (pin 20)
(Refresh) A low-level signal at this pin issues a refresh cycle for the DRAMs.

$\overline{\text{S1}}$, $\overline{\text{S0}}$ (pins 65, 63)
The 80286 status signals are applied to these two pins. The 82C212 observes them to detect the beginning of a bus cycle.

M/$\overline{\text{IO}}$ (pin 54)
(Memory/IO) This pin is supplied with the M/$\overline{\text{IO}}$ signal from the CPU so that the 82C212 can distinguish between memory cycles and I/O cycles.

$\overline{\text{IOR}}$ (pin 15)
(I/O Read) A low-level signal at this pin informs the 82C212 that an I/O read cycle is in progress.

$\overline{\text{IOW}}$ (pin 14)
(I/O Write) A low-level signal at this pin indicates an I/O write cycle.

$\overline{\text{MEMR}}$ (pin 17)
(Memory Read) A low-level signal at this pin informs the 82C212 that a memory read cycle must be carried out.

$\overline{\text{MEMW}}$ (pin 16)
(Memory Write) A low-level signal at this pin informs the 82C212 that a memory write cycle must be executed.

HLDA1 (pin 19)
(Hold Acknowledge 1) If a high-level signal is applied to this pin the 82C212 generates $\overline{\text{RAS}}$ and $\overline{\text{CAS}}$ signals for DMA bus cycles.

$\overline{\text{ROMCS}}$ (pin 13)
(ROM Chip Select) If the 82C212 accesses an EPROM it activates the signal $\overline{\text{ROMCS}}$ to prepare the EPROM for a data output.

A23–A0 (pins 2–11, 46–53, 58–55, 74, 82)
These 24 pins are supplied with the address of the local CPU bus to address this memory. The 82C212 generates row and column addresses for the DRAM and EPROM chips from these signals.

$\overline{\text{BHE}}$ (pin 34)
(Byte High Enable) The CPU applies a low-level signal to the pin to transfer data on the high-order byte of the data bus.

$\overline{\text{READY}}$ (pin 29)

If the addressed memory has completed the data read or write then the 82C212 outputs a low-level signal at this pin. Thus the CPU can flexibly insert wait cycles if, for example, the memory has to change the page or, despite interleaving, a $\overline{\text{RAS}}$ precharge cycle is required.

$\overline{\text{AF16}}$ (pin 59)

The 82C212 outpts a low-level signal via this pin during the course of accesses to local memory. If the CPU accesses ports or memory chips located on expansion adapters, this pin is on a high level.

$\overline{\text{RAS3}}$–$\overline{\text{RAS0}}$ (pins 77–80)

(Row Address Strobe) Via these pins the 82C212 supplies the $\overline{\text{RAS}}$ signals for the DRAM chips in the four banks that the controller can serve at most. One of the banks is thus enabled for an access.

$\overline{\text{CAS00}}$–$\overline{\text{CAS31}}$ (pins 35–41, 44)

(Column Address Strobe) The 82C212 outputs a $\overline{\text{CASx0}}$ signal (x = 0,1,2,3) to select the DRAMs with the low-order data byte of bank x. Similarly $\overline{\text{CASx1}}$ accesses the DRAMs with the high-order data byte.

$\overline{\text{MWE}}$ (pin 28)

(Memory Write Enable) To carry out a write process in the addressed DRAMs, the 82C212 activates this signal. $\overline{\text{MWE}}$ is connected to the $\overline{\text{WE}}$ pin of the DRAM chips.

DLE (pin 45)

(Data Latch Enable) If the 82C212 activates this signal, the local memory buffer is enabled to accept and latch data.

$\overline{\text{DRD}}$ (pin 33)

(Data Read) With an active $\overline{\text{DRD}}$ (that is, the signal is on a low level), data is transferred from the memory bus to the local bus of the CPU. If $\overline{\text{DRD}}$ is on a high-level, data transfer occurs in the opposite direction.

DLYOUT (pin 81)

(Delay Line Out) Via this pin the 82C212 outputs a signal to a delay circuit to generate the DRAM control signals.

DLY0–DLY2 (pins 73, 75, 76)

(Delay Input) The delay circuit outputs signals to the 82C212 using these three pins to generate the DRAM control signals.

$\overline{\text{XDEN}}$ (pin 26)

(X-Data Buffer Enable) During an I/O access to ports 22h and 23h, the memory controller outputs low-level signals to enable the buffers for data transfer. Using ports 22h and 23h the CPU can access the index and data register inside the 82C212.

XDIR (pin 27)

(X-Bus Direction) The signal at this pin determines the data transfer direction between 82C212 and CPU for an access to the ports 22h and 23h.

MA0–MA9 (pins 60–62, 66–72)

(Multiplexed DRAM Address) Via these pins the 82C212 supplies the multiplexed row and column addresses that are applied to the DRAM chips. Together with the bank selection signals $\overline{RAS0}$–$\overline{RAS3}$ and $\overline{CAS00}$–$\overline{CAS31}$ and a 16-bit memory organization, 16 Mbytes of memory can thus be accessed in four banks of 4 Mbytes each. Additionally, the pins MA0–MA7 serve as a bidirectional 8-bit data bus for an access to the internal 82C212 registers.

GA20, GATEA20 (pin 31, 30)

(Gated Address Line A20, Gate Address A20) With the signal applied to the pin GATEA20, external hardware may control the masking of address line A20 to emulate a wrap-around at 1 M. Thus, strict compatibility with the 8086/88 in real mode is possible. If GATEA20 is at a low-level then address line A20 is masked, a wrap-around at 1 M occurs, and GA20 is low. If GATEA20 is at a high level, the 82C212 transfers the signal on line A20 to GA20.

$\overline{LMEGCS}$ (pin 25)

(Low Meg Memory Chip Select) If the CPU is accessing the least significant Mbyte of memory, or if a refresh cycle is carried out, then the 82C212 activates this signal.

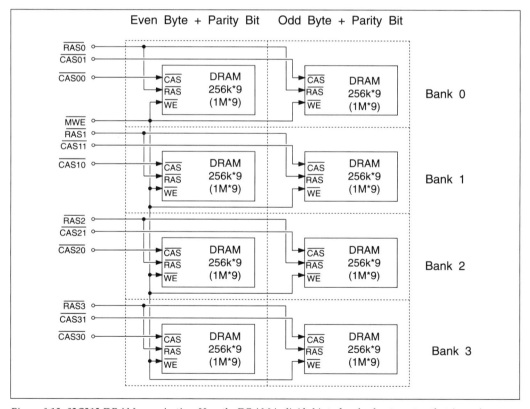

Figure 6.13: 82C212 DRAM organization. Here the DRAM is divided into four banks at most so that 4-way interleaving is possible.

V$_{cc}$ (pins 32, 42, 84)
The supply voltage is applied to these pins (usually +5 V).

GND (pins 1, 22, 43, 64)
These pins are grounded (usually 0 V).

After briefly listing the confusingly large number of signals, let us now turn to the actual application of the 82C212. Figure 6.13 shows the DRAM organization of the four banks with a width of 18 bits each. 16 bits are reserved for data and two bits for the parity of the low-order and high-order 8-bit groups. If 1 Mb chips are used for main memory then each bank may comprise up to 4 Mbyte of RAM. Thus, the maximum main memory can be 16 Mbyte in all. If you employ 256 kbit chips, each bank can only hold 1 Mbyte, so the memory can only be equipped up to 4 Mbytes.

Instead of the memory chips with 256k∗1 or 1M∗1 organization, 256k∗4 or 1M∗4 DRAMs can also be used. Now 18 chips are no longer required for every bank, only four plus two 256k∗1 or 1M∗1 chips to realize the width of 18 bits. Without interleaving you may equip the various banks with any DRAM chips. With 2-way interleaving the equipment within a bank pair must be equal, that is, banks 0 and 1 as well as banks 2 and 3 must be identically equipped. But you are free, for example, to use 256 kbit DRAMs for banks 0 and 1 and 1 Mbit chips for banks 2 and 3. For 4-way interleaving, all the four banks must be identically equipped. Higher interleaving factors are not possible with four banks, and also not useful as a performance increase is not possible any more, and the control gets only more complicated.

6.2.2   SIMM and SIP

Today, compact memory modules such as SIMM and SIP are often used instead of single chips. These modules have a standard width of nine bits, with the relevant number (∗1 or ∗4-chips) allocated to reach the indicated storage capacity (1 Mbyte, for example). Thus, a 1M∗9-module may comprise nine 1 Mb chips with the organization 1M∗1, or two 4 Mb chips with the organization 1M∗4 for data as well as one 1 Mb chip with the organization 1M∗1 for parity information. The SIMM or SIP modules must be inserted into the intended sockets of the banks. Internally the modules are often combined pair-by-pair or four-by-four to realize a main memory with a data width of 16 or 32 bits. Figure 6.14 shows a SIMM and a SIP module and the connection of the nine 1 Mbit∗1 chips to a nine bit wide module. SIMM modules have a contact strip similar to the adapter cards for the bus slots; SIP modules are equipped with pins that must be inserted into corresponding holes.

The following sections briefly discuss the terminals of the SIMM and SIP modules.

A0–A9 (connection 4, 5, 7, 8, 11, 12, 14, 15, 17, 18)
These nine connections are supplied with the row and column addresses.

DQ0–DQ7 (connection 3, 6, 10, 13, 16, 20, 23, 25)
Via these connections, the data for the eight data DRAMs are supplied or provided.

Q8 (connection 26)
The connection supplies the 9th DRAM chip signal containing the parity information.

DQ (connection 29)

Via this connection, the module accepts the parity bit for the 9th chip during the course of a data write.

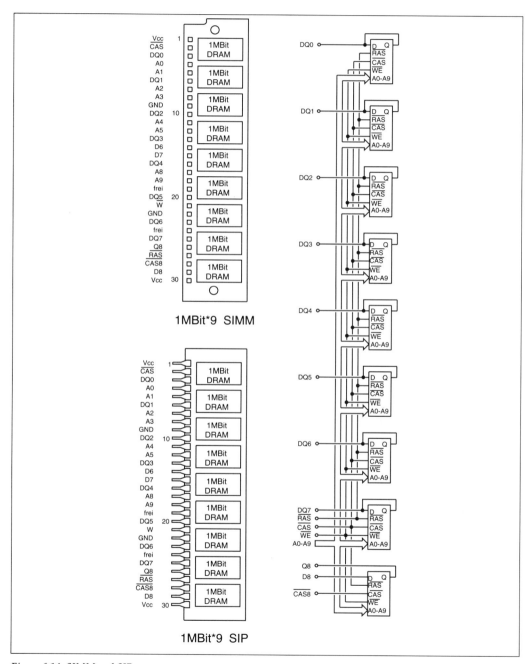

Figure 6.14: SIMM and SIP

$\overline{\text{CAS}}$ (connection 2)

(Column Address Strobe) This connection is supplied with the column address strobe signal from the memory controller for the eight data bits.

$\overline{\text{RAS}}$ (connection 27)

(Row Address Strobe) Via this connection, the row address strobe signal for all nine DRAM chips is supplied.

$\overline{\text{WE}}$ (connection 21)

If data must be written into the chips, the memory controller activates the $\overline{\text{WE}}$ signal. With a high level, data is read from the DRAM chips.

$\overline{\text{CAS8}}$ (connection 28)

The signal at this connection activates the 9th DRAM chip with the parity information.

V_{cc} (connection 1, 30)

These two connections are supplied with the supply voltage.

GND (connection 9, 22)

These two connections are grounded.

6.2.3   Internal 82C212 Structure

The signals indicated above control the 82C212 memory controller and are generated by it, respectively. Figure 6.15 shows its internal structure.

The oscillator circuit uses a 14.31818 MHz crystal to generate the OSC and OSC/12 signals. The 82C212 uses the OSC/12 clock with 1.19381 MHz to disable the $\overline{\text{RASx}}$ signal in page mode if the maximum active time period of 10 μs of each bank has elapsed.

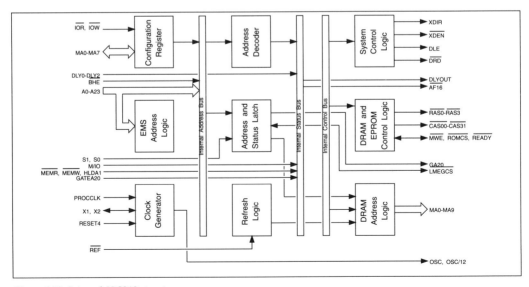

Figure 6.15: Internal 82C212 structure.

The DRAM and EPROM control logic generate the $\overline{RAS}$, $\overline{CAS}$ and $\overline{MWE}$ signals for DRAM accesses, as well as the $\overline{ROMCS}$ signal for activating the EPROM chips containing the boot and BIOS code. You may program the control logic for different numbers of wait states for DRAM or EPROM accesses by writing the intended value into the wait state register (see below). The control logic module then activates a $\overline{READY}$ signal for the CPU after completing the memory access concerned. If the access is delayed by a $\overline{RAS}$ precharge time (a page change is required, for example), then $\overline{READY}$ is not activated until more than these programmed wait cycles have elapsed. The system control module generates the signals $\overline{XDEN}$, DLE, $\overline{DRD}$ and $\overline{AF16}$ so the CPU can access the internal 82C212 registers.

To refresh the memory chips the memory controller has its an own refresh logic, which is driven by another member of the 82Cxxx chipset, the 82C211 system controller. For this purpose, the 82C211 activates the $\overline{REF}$ signal and outputs the refresh address via address lines A0–A9. The remaining 14 address signals A10–A23 are ignored. Thus with fully equipped memory the refresh is always carried in groups of $2^{14} = 16$kbytes. If less memory is installed, the block size of simultaneously refreshed cells decreases accordingly. The 82C212 outputs the refresh addresses via address lines MA0–MA9 to the DRAM chips, and issues a refresh by means of the $\overline{RASx}$ signals without activating the column addresses and the $\overline{CASx}$ signal. Internally, one memory cell row is selected within each DRAM chip, the stored data is read out onto the bit line pairs, and the sense amplifiers are activated, but the amplified data signals are not transferred through the transfer gates to the data output buffer. Thus, the refresh operation usually runs more quickly than a normal data read.

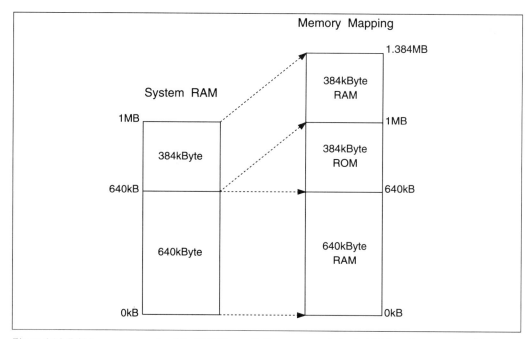

Figure 6.16: RAM memory mapping. The 82C212 can divide a memory of physical 1 Mbyte into a section of 640 kbytes between 0 k and 640 k, and a section of 384 kbytes above 1 M. The «hole» in between is filled with ROM.

Besides the modules already mentioned, the 82C212 additionally implements a memory mapping logic and accompanying registers. As you know, the address area between 640 k and 1 M is reserved for ROM chips with BIOS routines. If you have 1 Mbyte of memory installed, for example with four 256k*9 SIMMs, then the addresses from 0 bytes to 1 Mbyte are contiguous, but simultaneously the area between 640 kbytes and 1 Mbyte is reserved for ROM chips. To avoid any address conflict the addresses between 640 k and 1 M of RAM must be masked off, and 384 kbytes of RAM memory get lost. Thus, the memory controller carries out a so-called *memory mapping*. The 384 kbytes of RAM memory between 640 kbytes and 1 Mbyte are thus mapped onto the addresses between 1 M and 1.384 M. This process is shown in Figure 6.16.

Thus RAM accesses with addresses between 0 and 640 k proceed unaltered. If the address is in the range between 640 k and 1 M, the memory controller accesses the ROM chips. After addresses beyond 1 M, the memory controller accesses the 384 high-order kbytes of the 1 Mbyte RAM, thus these 384 kbytes of RAM are already in extended memory.

Another feature of modern memory controllers (and therefore also of the 82C212) is shadowing ROM data in the faster RAM, or alternatively the possibility of configuring the main memory above 1 M as extended or expanded memory, or as a mixture. More about this subject in the next two sections.

6.2.4   Shadow RAM and BIOS

One disadvantage of ROM chips compared to DRAM or SRAM is the significantly longer access time. Today, DRAM chips with access times of about 70 ns and SRAM chips with access times below 25 ns are usual. But EPROMs and other ROM types need up to 200 ns before the addressed data is available. That is an important disadvantage, because extensive BIOS routines for access to floppy and hard disk drives or the graphics adapters are located in the slower ROM. Moreover, these routines are frequently called by the operating system or application programs, and thus slow down program execution. What better solution than to move code and data from the slow ROM into the faster main memory? This process is supported by shadowing. The performance increase when BIOS routines are called can be up to 400%. Generally, the better the RAM chips and the slower the ROM the higher is the performance increase.

To move the ROM data into the RAM, two things are necessary:

- software that transfers the data from ROM to RAM;
- a memory controller that maps the ROM address space onto the RAM area to which the ROM data have been moved.

The former is carried out by the BIOS during the course of the PC's boot process. The processor simply reads the whole ROM and transfers the read data into the RAM area, which is then mapped onto the addresses of the original ROM address space by the memory controller. Then, ROM code and ROM data are still located at the same physical address. But now RAM instead of ROM chips are accessed, so no address alteration within the ROM code is required. For this purpose, the 82C212 has several registers through which the address «bending» can be carried out (more about this subject later).

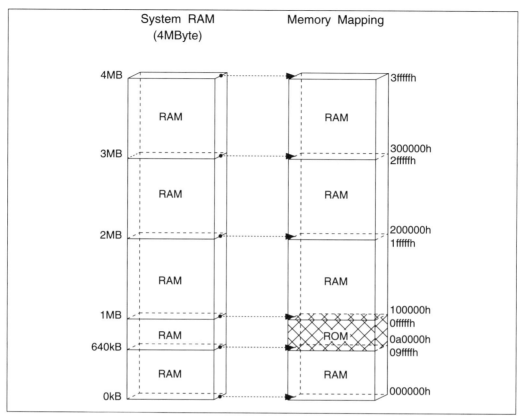

Figure 6.17: Memory mapping with more than 1 Mbyte without shadowing. Without shadowing the RAM section between 640 k and 1 M is masked-off, because the ROM chips are located at these addresses.

If more than 1 Mbyte of RAM is installed and shadowing is not active, the 82C212 maps RAM and ROM in the way illustrated in Figure 6.17.

You can see that with addresses between 640 k and 1 M, the ROM chips are still accessed. Moreover, the higher 384 kbytes of RAM memory are lost because they cannot be mapped onto the area between 1 Mbyte and 1.384 Mbyte without overlapping the installed memory between 1 M and 2 M. If shadowing is enabled, a completely different situation arises. The corresponding memory mapping is shown in Figure 6.18.

The shadow RAM is located in the address space between 640 k and 1 M; the ROM chips are completely masked off from the address space. If an application such as Word attempts to access the hard disk via BIOS interrupt 13h to read data, the CPU no longer addresses the code in ROM, but that transferred into shadow RAM. To avoid a computer crash during a BIOS call, all data needs to be transferred from the ROM to the RAM chips, of course, because application programs and the system cannot now access the ROM chips. Only a direct and therefore hardware-dependent programming of the 82C212 registers can still access the ROM.

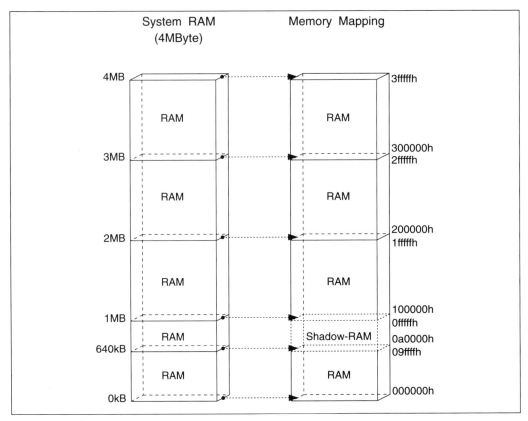

Figure 6.18: Memory mapping with shadowing enabled. With shadowing enabled the content of the ROMs between 640 k and 1 M is copied into the corresponding RAM section. Afterwards, the ROM chips between 640 k and 1 M are masked-off.

With most memory controllers you can move individual sections of ROM address space into the shadow RAM. Thus, it is not absolutely necessary to move all the 384 kbytes reserved for the ROM BIOS between 640 k and 1 M to the shadow RAM all at once. You may, for example, move the BIOS area between C0000h and C8000h, which is reserved for the EGA and VGA BIOS, to the shadow RAM to speed-up picture setup. On the other hand, it is sometimes impossible to map certain parts of the ROM address space. This especially applies to SCSI host adapters, which carry out a so-called *memory mapped I/O* for data transfer between PC and SCSI bus.

With normal XT and AT hard disk drives, sectors are read into a buffer on the controller that cannot be accessed via the normal address space. The CPU is only able to address the read data via a register port, and to transfer them into main memory. Alternatively, the data can be transferred by the DMA controller. The code in the expansion ROM on the controller adapter can be readily mapped onto the shadow RAM with no problem, because no write accesses are carried out into the ROM memory on the controller. Instead, the data is transferred directly into the main memory, whose addresses don't fall into the range between 640 k and 1 M. Thus, memory mapping for the shadow RAM plays no role in this case.

The situation is different again for SCSI adapters with memory mapped I/O. In the address range between 640 k and 1 M, which is reserved for the ROM BIOS, these adapters usually have a small RAM memory. The SCSI bus writes the data from the hard disk drive into this RAM section. The advantage is that the data is immediately transferred by the controller into the memory address space, and no additional transfer via register ports or the DMA chips is required. With shadowing this gives rise to a disaster: as the small RAM is located in the ROM address space, the RAM of the SCSI host adapter is also masked-off, and the startup routine of the BIOS transfers only the data present in the host adapter RAM into the shadow RAM before the controller enables shadowing. If a sector of the SCSI hard disk is to be read later, then the code is executed correctly, but the SCSI hard disk still transfers the read data into the RAM on the host adapter; its addresses, however, are masked-off as a part of the ROM address space. The connection between SCSI bus and the RAM on the SCSI host adapter is wired, and therefore nothing can be remapped. The SCSI bus writes into the adapter RAM, but the CPU accesses the remapped address, which still contains the data that was transferred there during the course of the shadow RAM activation process. No matter which sector is read, the CPU always finds the same data. In a favourable case the BIOS issues an error message, for example «bad track 0», because the data transferred into the shadow RAM doesn't lead to a consistent partition table. In the worst case, the BIOS interprets this «table» and carries out unpredictable processes. Therefore, you should never map the address area of an SCSI host adapter that uses memory mapped I/O into the shadow RAM.

6.2.5   Expanded Memory and Memory Mapping

Besides extended memory there is another memory type that can be used by DOS for expanding the normal base memory of 640 kbytes – the so-called *expanded memory*. Figure 6.19 shows the principle of this storage.

Expanded memory inserts a so-called EMS window with a maximum size of 64 kbytes into the first Mbyte of the real mode address space of the 80x86 CPU. EMS is the abbreviation for *expanded memory specification* or *expanded memory system*. The start address and size of this window can be chosen by means of jumpers, or via the BIOS set-up program. In most cases, the area between 640 k and 1 M that is reserved for ROM chips is not entirely occupied, so it is useful to put the EMS window into this area. But you have to be sure that the entire memory section occupied by the EMS window is really free, otherwise address conflicts occur and the PC crashes.

The EMS window is divided into four pages, with 16 kbytes at most, which are contiguous in the address space. The start address of each page can be defined by software commands that control the logic of expanded memory by means of a driver so that the four pages with 16 kbytes each can be moved within the much larger physical expanded memory. By definition, a maximum physical memory of 8 Mbytes is available for expanded memory. The principles of EMS are rather old, and were already being used more than 15 years ago on the CP/M machines with their 8-bit processors. Lotus, Intel and Microsoft decided some years ago to set up a strictly defined standard for the software control of expanded memory. The result is *LIM-EMS* (**L**otus **I**ntel **M**icrosoft **e**xpanded **m**emory specification). Today, LIM EMS 4.0 is the *de facto* standard for expanded memory systems. The hardware forming the base and the manner in which the pages in the large physical memory are inserted into the EMS window between 640 k and 1 M (that is, how the address translation is carried out) is completely hidden from the programmer who wants to use expanded memory. Together with the EMS hardware, the manufacturer delivers a driver whose software interface corresponds to LIM-EMS, and whose hardware interface is directed to the electronics used.

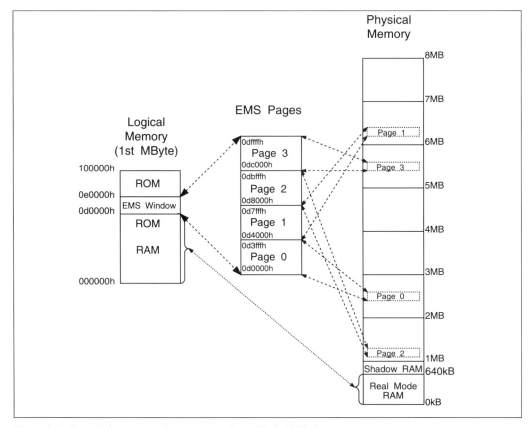

Figure 6.19: Expanded memory and memory mapping with the 82C212.

Earlier EMS systems were mainly implemented using an EMS adapter card in a bus slot. The start address of the EMS window can then be defined by means of jumpers. The EMS driver accesses the address transformation logic on the adapter card using reserved port addresses in most cases, so that, for example, the address 0d0000h (which corresponds to the first EMS page) is mapped onto the address 620000h (which is far beyond the 20-bit address space of the 8086 or the later processors in real mode, and is above 6 M). Modern memory controllers (including the 82C212) can configure the physically available main memory beyond the 1 Mbyte border as either extended or expanded memory, or as a mixture of them both. In EMS mode the 82C212 uses the EMS translation registers to remap the address bits A14–A22. You may usually choose the mode and set up the size of these two memory types using the BIOS setup program. Figure

6.19 shows a physical on-board memory of 8 Mbytes, whose first Mbyte is used as real mode RAM with 640 kbytes and as shadow RAM for ROM with 384 kbytes at most. This part of main memory is thus not available for expanded memory, but only the remaining 7 Mbytes. Analogous to an EMS memory expansion adapter with separate address translation logic, the 82C212's internal EMS logic remaps the pages of the EMS window onto these seven Mbytes. With the configuration registers, the internal EMS logic of the 82C212 can be programmed according to the EMS window's start address (0d0000h in the example), as well as the address of the EMS pages in main memory.

For addressing the physical 8 Mbyte memory of Figure 6.19, 23 address bits are required. For expanded memory the restriction to 20 address bits is bypassed by dividing the 23-bit address into two subaddresses comprising 20 bits at most. This is, on the one hand, the start address of the EMS page concerned in the physical memory. For this, nine address bits are required, as expanded memory is divided into «segments» of 16 kbytes each. On the other hand, within such a «segment» a 14-bit offset is formed. I have used the expression «segment» to indicate the analogy to the 80x86 segment and offset registers. If you load a segment register with a certain value then you need only an offset register later to access all objects within the segment concerned. After addressing an object in another segment you must reload the offset **and** the segment register with new values. A similar case arises with the EMS windows and expanded memory. To map an EMS page into expanded memory you need to write the 9-bit number (segment address) of the corresponding 16 kbyte block in expanded memory into an EMS table. If only objects within this EMS page are accessed it is sufficient to alter the 14-bit offset, but because the EMS page has to be inserted in 16 kbyte steps into the 20-bit address space of the 80x86 running in real mode, the 80x86 additionally needs to know the number of the 16 kbyte block in memory between 0 and 1024kbytes that holds the EMS page. For this purpose, six address bits are required. Thus the 80x86 needs its complete 20-bit address bus to determine the 16 kbyte block of the EMS page on the one hand, and to access objects within this page with a 14-bit offset on the other. Not until the EMS page must be moved in expanded memory (that is, another 16 kbyte block is selected), has the 80x86 to alter the 9-bit block address with the EMS driver. Afterwards, the 14-bit offset is again sufficient to address objects within the thus defined EMS page.

One characteristic of expanded memory compared with extended memory is that processors with a small address bus can also access a large memory. The 8-bit 8080 (Intel) or Z80 (Zilog) processors which played an important role in the CP/M era have only a 16-bit address bus, and can therefore only address 64 kbytes of memory. By means of the «detour» via expanded memory they can, in principle, address a memory of any size. For this, only a programmable address translation logic is required, and eventually the output of a «larger» address by repeatedly activating the 16-bit address bus.

Another advantage compared to extended memory is that the 80x86 need not be switched into protected mode to activate the complete address bus with a width of more than 20 bits. Starting with the i386, this is not important because these processors can clear the PM flag in the CR0 control register to reset the processor to real mode immediately. With an 80286 more problems occur, as a return to real mode is only possible via a time-consuming processor reset. If the expanded memory is realized using an intelligent memory controller in the fast on-board memory instead of on a slow adapter card, then on an 80286 the addressing of expanded memory can eventually be much faster than using extended memory. This especially applies if small amounts of data are to be accessed. Another advantage of expanded memory is that it can accommodate not only data code but also program code. The EMS pages are actually accessed in the processor's real mode so that the address interpretation need not be altered. The 80x86 can execute the real mode code without any change. If, on the other hand, program code needs to be stored in extended memory, the codes must be retransferred into the real mode address space and the CPU must be switched back to real mode to execute the program; otherwise the CPU has to execute the code in protected mode. That would involve generating the program for protected mode and a mixture of real mode and protected mode code. DOS is completely over-stretched with this job. Only Windows and OS/2 used this method in some way.

6.2.6   82C212 Configuration Registers

You can program the 82C212 with 12 configuration registers. To limit the number of 82C212 ports, the memory controller uses an indexing scheme. You first have to write the index of the register to be programmed into the index register port 022h. Afterwards, you write or read the value to or from the data register port 023h. Table 6.1 lists all registers and their corresponding indices.

Register	Index
version	064h
ROM configuration	065h
memory enable 1	066h
memory enable 2	067h
memory enable 3	068h
memory enable 4	069h
bank 0/1 enable	06ah
DRAM configuration	06bh
bank 2/3 enable	06ch
EMS base register	06dh
EMS address extension	06eh
miscellaneous	06fh
index register port:	022h
data register port:	023h

Table 6.1: Register ports and register indices

The version register (index 064h) contains information concerning the type and version of the memory controller used. The registers with indices 065h to 069h shadow ROM data. The bank enable registers (index 06ah, 06ch) and the DRAM configuration register give some information about the type and number of memory chips installed. The two EMS registers (index 06dh, 06eh) manage expanded memory in main memory, and the miscellaneous register holds values for various 82C212 configuration setups.

Example: `read version registers`

```
OUT 022h, 064h  ; pass index 064h of version registers to index register port
IN al, 023h     ; read contents of version register into accumulator al
```

Also, if you want to access the same configuration register twice you always have to output the index to the index register port first before you can write data into or read data from the data register port. The following discusses the various registers in more detail.

```
| ID | VR1 | VR0 | res | res | res | res | res |

ID:  NEAT identification              0=82C212
VR1, VR0: version number              00=first 82C212 version
res: reserved (res=0 standard set up)
```

Figure 6.20: Version register (index 064h).

The version register (see Figure 6.20) contains a value that identifies the 82C212 to the system or BIOS. If the *ID* bit is cleared then it is an 82C212. *VR1, VR0* hold the version of the memory controller. All other bits are reserved, and must be initialized to 0 at power-up.

Using the ROM configuration register (Figure 6.21) you can activate the ROM in address space 0c0000h to 0fffffh in 64 kbyte blocks and prepare them for shadowing. If you clear one of the bits *SH3–SH0*, the corresponding ROM area is activated. If the corresponding bit is set, the 82C212 outputs no $\overline{\text{ROMCS}}$ (**ROM** **c**hip **s**elect) signal and the memory controller accesses no ROM chips within the address area concerned, thus a shadowing in RAM can be carried out. At power-up the SH0 bit is cleared and no shadowing is enabled for the ROM BIOS between 0f0000h and 0fffffh. The remaining three SH3–SH1 bits are initialized to 1, however.

```
| WP3 | WP2 | WP1 | WP0 | SH3 | SH2 | SH1 | SH0 |
  write protection        shadow enable
   for shadow RAM           for ROM

WP3–WP0:  write protection for shadow RAM at addresses
          0c0000h–0cffffh (WP3)   0d0000h–0dffffh (WP2)   0e0000h–0effffh (WP1)   0f0000h–0fffffh (WP0)
          0=read and write (standard)    1=read only
SH3–SH0:  shadow enable for ROM addresses
          0c0000h–0cffffh (SH3)   0d0000h–0dffffh (SH2)   0e0000h–0effffh (SH1)   0f0000h–0fffffh (SH0)
          0=ROM active     1=shadowing enabled
```

Figure 6.21: ROM configuration register (index 065h).

Write accesses to ROM chips are insignificant for the crash reliability of your PC because their contents can't be altered. This situation changes if shadowing is enabled. Now all ROM data is present in a readable and writeable RAM. A program error that leads, for example, to an invalid pointer causing a write access to an address between 0c0000h and 0fffffh overwrites BIOS code and a future call of BIOS routines may therefore lead to a system crash. Thus the 82C212 enables a write protection for the 64 kbyte segments between 0c0000h and 0fffffh in shadow RAM. You can activate this write protection using the *WP3–WP0* bits. If one of these bits is set then the

corresponding shadow RAM area is protected against any overwrite. The 82C212 does not pass
write accesses to the DRAM chips.

```
┌─────────────────────────────────────────────────────────────────────────────┐
│  ┌───┬───┬───┬───┬───┬───┬───┬───┐                                            │
│  │RAM│res│res│res│res│res│res│res│                                            │
│  └───┴───┴───┴───┴───┴───┴───┴───┘                                            │
│                                                                               │
│  RAM:   RAM between 512kbyte and 640kbyte                                      │
│         0=address section in I/O channel    1=address section on system board │
│  res:   reserved (initialize res=0)                                           │
└─────────────────────────────────────────────────────────────────────────────┘
```

Figure 6.22: Memory enable register 1 (Index 066h).

The memory enable register 1 (Figure 6.22) controls the management of memory between 512
and 640 kbytes. If the *RAM* bit is cleared, the address section concerned is present in the I/O
channel (that is, in an area not managed by the 82C212). This may be an adapter card in a bus
slot. If the RAM bit is set, the accompanying memory chips are installed in a bank accessed by
the 82C212, and the memory controller also generates the DRAM control signals for this address
area. The *res* bits are reserved, and are initialized to 0 by the 82C212 at power-up.

With the memory enable registers 2, 3 and 4 (Figure 6.23) you may control the shadowing of
the address area between 0a0000h and 0fffffh in units of 16 kbyte blocks. For this purpose,
however, it is necessary that the SHx bit of the corresponding ROM address section that is
subject to shadowing is set in the ROM configuration register (index 065h); otherwise, the
82C212 does not output the ROM activation signal $\overline{ROMCS}$. If one of the *SH7–SH0* bits is set
then all accesses to the corresponding 16 kbyte block are diverted to shadow RAM. Note,
though, that the BIOS or you as the programmer are responsible for transferring all the data of
the ROM chips into the shadow RAM *before* enabling the shadowing.

```
┌─────────────────────────────────────────────────────────────────────────────────────────────┐
│  Memory Enable Register 2 (Index 067h)                                                         │
│  ┌───┬───┬───┬───┬───┬───┬───┬───┐                                                             │
│  │SH7│SH6│SH5│SH4│SH3│SH2│SH1│SH0│                                                             │
│  └───┴───┴───┴───┴───┴───┴───┴───┘                                                             │
│                                                                                                │
│  SH7-SH0:   shadow RAM enable for addresses                                                     │
│             0ac000h–0affffh (SH7)   0a8000h–0abfffh (SH6)   0a4000h–0a7fffh (SH5)   0a0000h–0a3fffh (SH4) │
│             0bc000h–0bffffh (SH3)   0b8000h–0bbfffh (SH2)   0b4000h–0b7fffh (SH1)   0b0000h–0b3fffh (SH0) │
│             0=shadow RAM disabled       1=shadow RAM enabled                                    │
│                                                                                                │
│  Memory Enable Register 3 (Index 068h)                                                          │
│  ┌───┬───┬───┬───┬───┬───┬───┬───┐                                                             │
│  │SH7│SH6│SH5│SH4│SH3│SH2│SH1│SH0│                                                             │
│  └───┴───┴───┴───┴───┴───┴───┴───┘                                                             │
│                                                                                                │
│  SH7-SH0:   shadow RAM enable for addresses                                                     │
│             0dc000h–0dffffh (SH7)   0d8000h–0dbfffh (SH6)   0d4000h–0d7fffh (SH5)   0d0000h–0d3fffh (SH4) │
│             0cc000h–0cffffh (SH3)   0c8000h–0cbfffh (SH2)   0c4000h–0c7fffh (SH1)   0c0000h–0c3fffh (SH0) │
│             0=shadow RAM disabled       1=shadow RAM enabled                                    │
│                                                                                                │
│  Memory Enable Register 4 (Index 069h)                                                          │
│  ┌───┬───┬───┬───┬───┬───┬───┬───┐                                                             │
│  │SH7│SH6│SH5│SH4│SH3│SH2│SH1│SH0│                                                             │
│  └───┴───┴───┴───┴───┴───┴───┴───┘                                                             │
│                                                                                                │
│  SH7-SH0:   shadow RAM enable for addresses                                                     │
│             0fc000h–0fffffh (SH7)   0f8000h–0fbfffh (SH6)   0f4000h–0f7fffh (SH5)   0f0000h–0f3fffh (SH4) │
│             0ec000h–0effffh (SH3)   0e8000h–0ebfffh (SH2)   0e4000h–0e7fffh (SH1)   0e0000h–0e3fffh (SH0) │
│             0=shadow RAM disabled       1=shadow RAM enabled                                    │
└─────────────────────────────────────────────────────────────────────────────────────────────┘
```

Figure 6.23: Memory enable registers for shadow RAM (index 067h, 068h, 069h).

Using memory enable register 2 you may also move address areas into the shadow RAM that correspond to the video RAM of the graphics adapters. If you do this, the CPU writes all graphics data into the shadow RAM instead of the video RAM; the graphics adapter, however, continues to access the video RAM and not the shadow RAM. The monitor seems to be dead, although the CPU actually updates its contents. All these accesses, though, are diverted to the shadow RAM, and get lost.

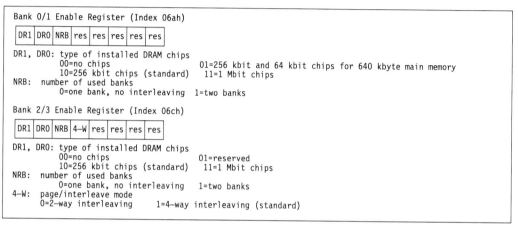

Figure 6.24: Bank enable registers (index 06ah, 06ch).

Using the two bank enable registers (Figure 6.24) you specify for the 82C212 which chips are installed, how many banks are used, as well as whether and eventually which type of interleaving is to be carried out. Register programming is usually carried out by the BIOS during the course of the boot precedure according to the configuration information that you have written with the BIOS setup program.

The *DR1, DR0* bits characterize the type of DRAM chips installed. Note that only for bank 1 are 64 kbit chips allowed to exhaust the maximum real mode main memory of 640 kbytes. The *NRB* bit indicates the number of used banks for the bank pair 0/1 or 2/3 concerned. If only one bank is so equipped, then the 82C212 can't carry out interleaving, of course. In the bank-2/3-enable register, the *4-W* bit is additionally available, with which you can choose between 2-way and 4-way interleaving; 4-way interleaving is only possible, however, if all four banks are equipped with identical DRAM chips.

The DRAM configuration register (Figure 6.25) controls the management of the installed DRAM memory. With the *P/I* bit you can disable (P/I = 0) or enable (P/I = 1) the page/interleave mode. The *REL* bit controls the relocation of the RAM between 640 kbytes and 1 Mbyte. If REL is equal to 0, the 82C212 doesn't carry out a relocation, the RAM section is masked-off and is only available as shadow RAM. If the main memory only has up to 1 Mbyte, it is better to map the RAM between 640 kbytes and 1 Mbyte onto the address area 1Mbyte to 1.384 Mbyte. Thus, 384 kbytes of extended memory is available. With the *WST* bit you can control the number of wait states that the 82C212 inserts as standard for an access to RAM.

```
┌─────────────────────────────────────┐
│P/I│REL│WST│EMS│EW1│EW0│RW1│RW0│
└─────────────────────────────────────┘
```

```
P/I:    page/interleave enable
        0=disabled (standard)      1=enabled
REL:    relocation of RAM between 640 kbyte and 1 Mbyte
        0=no relocation            1=relocation to 100000h-15ffffh
WST:    number of wait states for accesses to RAM
        0=0 wait State             1=1 wait state
EMS:    EMS activation
        0=EMS diabled (standard)   1=EMS enabled
EW1, EW0:  number of wait states for EMS memory accesses
        00=0 wait state   01=1 wait state   10=2 wait states (standard)   11=3 wait states
RW1, RW0:  number of wait states for ROM accesses
        00=0 wait state   01=1 wait state   10=2 wait states   11=3 wait states (standard)
```

Figure 6.25: DRAM configuration register (index 06bh)

Instead of extended memory you may also configure the RAM memory above 640 kbyte as either expanded memory or a mixture of extended and expanded memory. As standard the 82C212 manages the memory above 640 kbytes as extended memory if the section between 640 kbytes and 1 Mbyte is not used as shadow RAM. With the *EMS* bit you may also configure the RAM memory or a part of it as expanded memory. The *EW1*, *EW0* bits determine the number of wait states that the CPU then inserts for an access to EMS memory.

The *RW1*, *RW0* bits define the number of wait cycles for ROM accesses. As ROM chips are usually much slower than DRAMs, the 82C212 standard value at power-up is three wait states.

```
┌─────────────────────────────────────┐
│BS3│BS2│BS1│BS0│PR3│PR2│PR1│PR0│
└─────────────────────────────────────┘
```

```
BS3-BS0:   base address of EMS window
        0000=0c0000h   0001=0c4000h   0010=0c8000h   0011=0cc000h   0100=0d0000h
        0101=0d4000h   0110=0d8000h   0111=0dc000h   1000=0e0000h   1xxx=reserved
PR3-PR0:   I/O base address of EMS page registers
        0000=0208h/0209h   0001=0218h/0219h   0101=0258h/0259h   0110=0268h/0269h
        1010=02a8h/02a9h   1011=02b8h/02b9h   1110=02e8h/02e9h
```

Figure 6.26: EMS base address register (index 06dh).

Using the EMS base register (Figure 6.26) you can define the base address of the EMS windows. The *BS3–BS0* bits indicate the address of the first EMS window; all others follow at intervals of 16 kbytes. With the *PR3–PR0* bits you may determine the I/O base address of the EMS page register. (Details are described below.)

```
┌─────────────────────────────────────┐
│P01│P00│P11│P10│P21│P20│P31│P30│
└─────────────────────────────────────┘
```

```
P01, P00:   extension bits for EMS page 0
P11, P10:   extension bits for EMS page 1
P21, P20:   extension bits for EMS page 2
P31, P30:   extension bits for EMS page 3
        00=0 Mbyte to 2 Mbyte (000000h ... 1fffffh)   01=2 Mbyte to 4 Mbyte (200000h ... 3fffffh)
        10=4 Mbyte to 6 Mbyte (400000h ... 5fffffh)   11=6 Mbyte to 8 Mbyte (600000h ... 7fffffh)
```

Figure 6.27: EMS extension register (index 06eh).

The four bit pairs *Px1*, *Px0* (x = 0,1,2,3) determine in which Mbyte the corresponding EMS page x starts (Figure 6.27). Thus, the bit pairs constitute the address bits A22 and A21.

```
┌────┬────┬────┬───┬───┬───┬───┬───┐
│ES2 │ES1 │ES0 │rs1│rs0│RAS│G20│res│
└────┴────┴────┴───┴───┴───┴───┴───┘
ES2–ES0:  size of EMS memory
          000=<1 Mbyte   001=1 Mbyte   010=2 Mbyte   011=3 Mbyte   ...   111=7 Mbyte
rs1, rs0: reserved  (rs1=1, rs0=0)
RAS:      RAS time–out counter for page mode
          0=deactivated (Standard)   1=active
G20:      GA20 control
          0=A20 transmitted to GA20   1=GA20 always low (standard)
res:      reserved (res=0)
```

Figure 6.28: Miscellaneous register (index 06fh).

The three bits *ES2–ES0* specify the size of the EMS memory (Figure 6.28). The value 000 applies only to a memory provision of 1 Mbyte if the 384 kbytes above the real mode RAM of 640 kbytes is configured as expanded instead of extended memory. Bits *rs1* and *rs0* are reserved and are initialized to values 1 and 0, respectively, at power-up. With the *RAS* bit you can activate the 82C212 RAS time-out counter which disables the $\overline{RAS}$ signal after the maximum active-time in page mode to issue a $\overline{RAS}$ precharge cycle. The *GA20* bit controls the A20 address line for strict 8086 compatibility. If GA20 is cleared then the A20 address bit is transferred to the GA20 terminal of the 82C212. If, on the other hand, GA20 is set, the GA20 terminal always outputs a value of 0, thus a wrap-around at 1 Mbyte occurs.

For the address of the EMS pages in expanded memory only the two bits Px1, Px0 in the EMS extension register (see Figure 6.27) have been available up to now. Seven further address bits can be read or written via the EMS page register. Table 6.2 lists the addresses of the EMS page register for the four EMS pages.

Page	Address
0	002x8h/002x9h
1	042x8h/042x9h
2	082x8h/082x9h
3	0c2x8h/0c2x9h

x=0, 1, 5, 6, a, b, e

Table 6.2: EMS page registers

The value of x and therefore the I/O base address is defined in the EMS base register (see Figure 6.26). Table 6.3 lists the assignment of the bits in the EMS page register and the address bits A14–A20. Address bits A21 and A22 are already defined by the EMS extension register. Together, only those nine address bits required to define the address of a 16 kbyte block within 8 Mbytes of expanded memory are available.

If you set data bit 7 in one of the four EMS page registers to 0, the page is disabled and is no longer available for mapping into expanded memory.

Data bit	Meaning
0	A14
1	A15
2	A16
3	A17
4	A18
5	A19
6	A20
7	0=page disabled
	1=page enabled

Table 6.3: Entries in the EMS page register

Example: EMS page 1 shall begin at address 05a4000h in expanded memory

```
OUT 022h, 06eh   ; address EMS extension register via index register
IN  al, 023h     ; read old value via data port into accumulator al
AND al, 0c0h     ; clear P11, P10 for page 1, I/O base address at 0208h
OR  al, 020h     ; set P11=1, P10=0, because address is between 4 Mbyte and 6 Mbyte
OUT 022h, 06eh   ; address EMS extension register via index register
OUT 023h, al     ; write EMS extension register
OUT 04208h, 0a9h ; write EMS page register, page 1 enabled
```

6.3   Fast and Expensive – SRAM

In the following sections we shall examine the «racehorse» of memory chips – the SRAM. In the SRAM the information is no longer stored in the form of charges in a capacitor, but held in the state of a so-called flip-flop. Such a flip-flop has two stable states that can be switched by a strong external signal (the word flip-flop itself should tell you what's meant). Figure 6.29 shows the structure of a memory cell in an SRAM.

You can see immediately that the SRAM cell structure is far more complicated than that of a DRAM memory cell, illustrated on the right of Figure 6.29. While the DRAM cell consists only of an access transistor Tr_a and a capacitor holding the charges according to the stored data, in a typical SRAM cell two access transistors Tr_a and a flip-flop with two memory transistors Tr_s as well as two load elements are formed. Thus the integration of the SRAM memory cell is only possible with a much higher technical effort. Therefore, SRAM chips are more expensive, and usually have less storage capacity than DRAM chips. For this reason, SRAMs are mainly used for fast and small cache memories while DRAM chips form the large and slow main memory. High-quality SRAM chips for fast-clocked RISC machines or supercomputers achieve access times of no more than 12–20ns. In a PC in most cases chips with access times of 20–35 ns are used, depending on the clock rate.

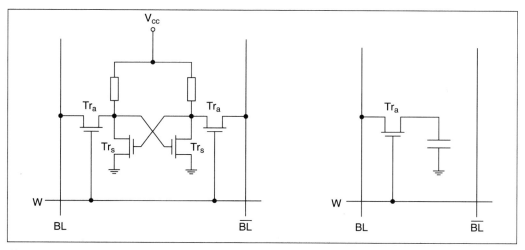

Figure 6.29: SRAM memory cell. The SRAM memory cell (left) generally consists of a flip-flop, the circuit condition of which represents the stored value. In a DRAM memory cell (right), on the other hand, the information is stored in the form of electrical charges in a capacitor.

6.3.1 The Flip-Flop

Now we turn to the flip-flop to get an understanding of the functioning of an SRAM memory cell. Figure 6.30 shows the structure of a flip-flop.

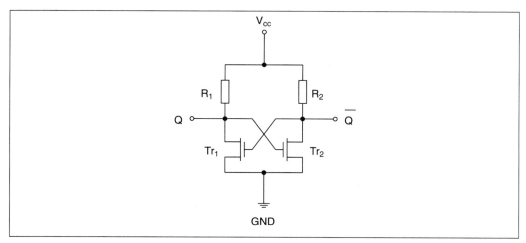

Figure 6.30: The flip-flop comprises two transistors Tr_1, Tr_2 and two load resistors R_1, R_2 .

The flip-flop is also called a *bistable multivibrator* because it can be switched between two stable internal states by external signals. The occurrence of two stable states gives rise to something like hysteresis in the flip-flop's characteristic. The higher the hysteresis the stronger is the stability of the states, and the more powerful the external signal must be to switch the flip-flop.

The simple flip-flop of Figure 6.30 consists of two feedback-coupled NMOS transistors Tr_1 and Tr_2, as well as two load elements R_1 and R_2. Feedback means that the source of Tr_1 is connected to the gate of Tr_2 and vice versa. At all outputs Q and Q two stable states may then occur. If Tr_1 is turned on then in the left branch of the flip-flop the overall voltage drops at the resistor R_1 and the output Q is grounded (low). The gate of transistor Tr_2 is therefore also supplied with a low-level voltage. Tr_2 is then turned off, and in the left branch the complete voltage drops at transistor Tr_2. Thus output Q is on a high-level of Vcc.

If, on the other hand, Tr_1 is turned off, then the complete voltage in the left flip-flop branch drops at transistor Tr_1 and the output Q is equal to Vcc (high). Therefore, a high voltage is applied to the gate of transistor Tr_2, thus Tr_2 is turned on and in the right branch the complete voltage drops at resistor R_2. The output Q is therefore grounded (low).

On the other hand, the outputs Q and Q can also be used as inputs to set up the flip-flop state, that is, switching the state of transistors Tr_1 and Tr_2 on and off. The set up of this state is equal to the storing of one bit, because the flip-flop stably supplies, for example, at output Q a high- or low-level signal.

The programming of a flip-flop state is briefly explained now with reference to an example. If transistor Tr_1 is switched on then output Q supplies a low-level signal, transistor Tr_2 is turned off, and output Q supplies a high-level signal. Every transistor has a certain resistance value even in the on state, that is, the so-called on-state resistance. The flip-flop's load elements R_1 and R_2 have a much higher resistance value than the on-state resistance of transistors Tr_1 and Tr_2. Thus, despite the on-state resistance of Tr_1 and the accompanying voltage drop, the voltage at output Q is small enough to represent a low level and, on the other hand, a voltage is applied to the gate of transistor Tr_2 which turns off Tr_2. If the value of R_1 is, for example, nine times larger than the on-state resistance of Tr_1, then 90% of the voltage Vcc drops at R_1 and only 10% at Tr_1. That's sufficient to keep the output Q at a low level and Tr_2 turned off.

To switch the state, the connection Q (which is simultaneously an output and an input) must be supplied with a signal that is so strong that the transistor turned on is unable to lead this signal to ground completely because of its on-state resistance. Thus a signal is applied to the gate of transistor Tr_2 which gives rise to a slight on-state of Tr_2. Therefore, the voltage at Q slightly decreases because of the lower voltage drop at Tr_2. This lower voltage than previously is simultaneously applied to the gate of Tr_1 so that its conductivity is somewhat degraded and the voltage drop at Tr_1 increases. By means of the feedback to the gate of Tr_2, transistor Tr_2 is further turned on and the process works itself up. During the course of this process, transistor Tr_1 turns off and transistor Tr_2 switches through more and more so that the flip-flop finally «flips» (or flops?); thus the name flip-flop. If the signal at input Q is switched off, then the output Q supplies a high-level signal and the complementary output Q a low-level signal; the flip-flop state has been altered. In other words: a new bit was written-in or programmed.

For the flip-flop's stability the ratio of the resistance values of the load elements R_1 and R_2 and the on-state resistances of the transistors Tr_1 and Tr_2 are decisive. The higher the load resistances compared to the on-state resistances, the more stable the stored states are. But it is also more difficult, then, to switch the flip-flop states. The flip-flop responds inertly to the programming signal supplied. If the resistance ratio is small then the flip-flop stability is lower.

Yet the switching can be carried out more easily and therefore more quickly. The designer of a flip-flop always treads a thin line between stability and operation speed.

If connection Q is supplied with a signal of the same level as it has just output, the new signal has no influence on the flip-flop state. If you write the same value that is already there into a memory cell, then there is, of course, no consequence for the stored value. You can also program a flip-flop by applying a signal to the complementary connection Q, which is complementary to the bit to program. Thus flip-flops are well suited as storage elements, and they are widely used, for example, in latch circuits, shift registers, etc.

In the simple flip-flop described above a new bit is always stored when the connection Q or Q is supplied with an external signal. For the clocked elements in computers this is not very favourable, because at certain times an unpredictable and invalid signal may occur on the signal lines. Therefore, clocked flip-flops are mainly used in computers. They accept the applied bit signals only if the clock signal is valid simultaneously. Such flip-flops have one or more additional access transistors controlled by the clock signal, and which transmit the applied write signal only upon an active clock signal for a store operation by the flip-flop.

Unlike the storage capacitors in DRAM memory cells, the flip-flop cells supply a much stronger data signal as transistors Tr_1 and Tr_2 are already present in the memory cell, which amplify the signal and are thus able to drive the bit lines. In a DRAM cell, however, only the tiny charge of a capacitor is transferred onto the bit line without any amplification, thus the signal is very weak. Accordingly, in a DRAM signal amplification by the sense amplifiers needs more time, and the access time is longer. For addressing memory flip-flops in an SRAM, additional access transistors for the individual flip-flop cells, address decoders, etc. are required, as is the case in a DRAM.

6.3.2   Access to SRAM Memory Cells

In an SRAM the unit memory cells are also arranged in a matrix of rows and columns, which are selected by a row and column decoder, respectively. As is the case for the DRAM, the gates of the access transistors Tr_a are connected to the word line W and the sources are connected to the bit line pair BL, $\overline{BL}$ (see Figure 6.30).

If data has to be read from such a memory cell, then the row decoder activates the corresponding word line W. The two access transistors Tr_a turn on and connect the memory flip-flop with the bit line pair BL, $\overline{BL}$. Thus the two outputs Q and Q of the flip-flop are connected to the bit lines, and the signals are transmitted to the sense amplifier at the end of the bit line pair. Unlike the DRAM, these two memory transistors Tr_s in the flip-flop provide a very strong signal as they are amplifying elements on their own. The sense amplifier amplifies the potential difference on the bit line pair BL, $\overline{BL}$. Because of the large potential difference, this amplifying process is carried out much faster than in a DRAM (typically within 10 ns or less), so the SRAM chip needs the column address much earlier if the access time is not to be degraded. SRAM chips therefore don't carry out multiplexing of row and column addresses. Instead, the row and column address signals are provided simultaneously. The SRAM divides the address into a row and column part internally only. After stabilization of the data the column decoder selects the corresponding column (that is, the corresponding bit line pair BL, $\overline{\text{BL}}$) and outputs a data signal to the data output buffer, and thus to the external circuitry.

The data write proceeds in the opposite way. Via the data input buffer and the column decoder, the write data is applied to the corresponding sense amplifier. At the same time, the row decoder activates a word line W and turns on the access transistors Tr_a. As in the course of data reading, the flip-flop tries to output the stored data onto the bit line pair BL, $\overline{\text{BL}}$. However, the sense amplifier is stronger than the storage transistors Tr_s, and supplies the bit lines BL, $\overline{\text{BL}}$ with a signal that corresponds to the write data. Therefore, the flip-flop switches according to the new write data, or keeps the already stored value depending upon whether the write data coincides with the stored data or not.

Unlike the DRAM, no lasting RAS/CAS recovery times are necessary. The indicated access time is usually equal to the SRAM's cycle time. Advanced DRAM memory concepts such as page mode, static-column mode or interleaving have no advantages for SRAMs because of the lack of address multiplexing and RAS recovery times. SRAM chips always run in «normal mode», in which both row and column address are supplied.

6.3.3   Typical SRAM – The Intel 51258

The memory controller for SRAM chips is quite simple because row and column addresses are supplied simultaneously. Because of the missing address multiplexing, more pins are required and the SRAM packages are larger than comparable DRAM chips. Further, SRAM chips don't use any high-speed operating modes (for example, page mode or static-column mode). Internal driving of the memory cells is thus easier. Because of the static design memory, a refresh is unnecessary.

The state of the memory flip-flops is kept as long as the SRAM chip is supplied with power. This simplifies the peripheral circuitry of the SRAM chips when compared to that of the DRAM chips, and compensates for the disadvantage of the much more complicated memory cell structure, to a certain degree. Nevertheless, the integration density of DRAM chips is about four times larger than that of SRAM chips using the same technology. Figure 6.31 shows the pin assignment of a typical SRAM chip – Intel's 51258.

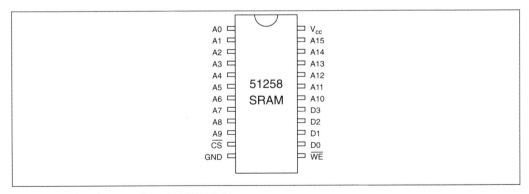

Figure 6.31: Pin assignment of a typical SRAM chip.

The 51258 has a storage capacity of 256 kbits with an organization of 64kword*4bit. Thus for addressing, the 64kword 16 address pins A15–A0 are required, because the SRAM doesn't carry out any address multiplexing. The 4-bit data is applied to or delivered by the 51258 via four data pins D3–D0. As is the case for DRAM chips, the further connections $\overline{CS}$ (chip select) and $\overline{WE}$ (write enable) are present to enable the SRAM chip ($\overline{CS}$=low) or to carry out a data write ($\overline{WE}$=low). $\overline{CS}$ instructs the SRAM to accept the supplied address, and to address its memory cell array. $\overline{RAS}$ and $\overline{CAS}$ are missing here, of course, so that $\overline{CS}$ has to carry out this triggering. If the 51258 is to be used for the cache memory of an i386 or i486, then at least eight of these chips must be installed to service the data bus with a width of 32 bits. The storage capacity of this cache memory then has 256 kbytes, sufficient for a medium-sized workstation. Because of the larger number of address pins, SRAM packages are usually much bigger than DRAM chips. Don't be surprised, therefore, if you find real SRAM memory blocks instead of tiny chips in your PC.

6.4 Long-Term Memory – ROM, EPROM and other PROMs

The disadvantage of all the memory elements discussed above is the volatility of the stored data; once switched off they lose their memory. DRAM and SRAM chips are therefore unsuitable for PC startup routines that carry out the boot process. Instead so-called *ROM* chips are employed. The storage data is written once into the ROM in a non-volatile way so that it is held all the time.

6.4.1 ROM

In ROM chips the information is not present in the form of charges, as in DRAMs, or as an alterable circuit state of electronic elements, as in SRAMs, but generally as a fixed wiring state of the elements. Often, switching elements are used that are connected between a word and a bit line, and whose switching state (on, off) is fixed.

«Pure» ROM is very rare today. In these chips the data to be stored has already been taken into account in advance of manufacturing. The data is integrated into the circuit design as either present or missing connections of nodes within the chip's circuitry. A very compact circuit design can thus be achieved, as the circuit can be optimized in view of the information to be stored. This can be carried out only at the expense of flexibility, because the change of only a single bit requires an alteration of the complete circuit.

For this reason, only programmable ROM *(PROM* for short) is used today. In these chips the information needs to be «burnt in» by the user, or at least following the last manufacturing step. In the latter case, the chip is called a *mask ROM* because programming in these ROM chips is carried out by means of a mask. Also, all other layers for gate, source and drain regions of transistors, conductive layers for word and bit lines, etc. are manufactured using such masks. The last mask then contains the connection information according to the storage data. Thus the manufacturing steps up until the last mask are equal for all ROMs, and independent from the information to be stored. Various data only needs to be handled by a single different mask. This is a significant advance compared to pure ROM.

Such mask-programmable ROMs are advantageous if a large number of identical ROM chips with the same information are to be manufactured. The main effort is in the design and manufacture of the programming mask; the production of the last layer for the ROM chips is easy. The same applies, for example, to the printing of a book: the most extensive work is in the manufacture of the printing plate. Whether 100 or 10 000 copies are to be printed is irrelevant (apart from the paper required).

The main disadvantage of mask-programmed ROMs is that the programming can be carried out only at the manufacturer's site. As you may know, the manufacturing process must be carried out in clean-rooms. The computer shop around the corner, though, which readily programs the newest BIOS version for you, cannot do this. Thus, for ROMs required only in small quantities the electrically programmable ROMs dominate.

6.4.2   EPROM

In an electrically programmable ROM (EPROM) data is written (as the name indicates) in an electrical manner, but unlike DRAMs and SRAMs, this data is stored in a non-volatile fashion. One method for achieving non-volatility is to burn a fusable link between the word and bit line. During programming a much stronger current pulse is supplied than in the future normal operating mode. As in an ordinary fuse, the pulse burns the connection between word and bit line so that they are now disconnected, and the stored value is equal to «0». All non-burned fusable links represent a «1» and data according to the open or closed connections between word and bit line is stored. The generation and supply of such strong pulses can also be carried out by the user with a so-called programmer. The chip has already been mounted in a package and therefore no further manufacturing steps are required.

Another possibility for the non-volatile storage of data is the use of a storage transistor with a so-called *floating gate*. This gate is located between the actual control gate and the substrate, and (unlike the control gate) is not connected to word, bit or other lines; it «floats» (that is, its potential has no defined value). In most cases, control and floating gate consist of the same material, for example polycristalline silicon, which is a reasonably good conductor. Figure 6.32 is a sectional view through such a storage transistor.

In memory cells with a storage transistor, the gate is usually connected to a word line, the drain to a bit line, and the source to a reference potential (V_{cc}, for example). In the above-mentioned ROM chips, the connection between word and bit line was realized by a simple conductor bridge, but now the storage transistor takes over this job. With the word line activated, a normal MOS transistor without a floating gate would always connect the bit line via drain, channel and source to V_{cc}. Storage of any values is not yet carried out by this, but here the state of the floating gate leaves permanent information on the memory cell. If the floating gate is neutral (that is, no charges are stored), then it has no influence on the electrical field that the control gate generates in the channel region between source and drain. The storage transistor operates as a normal MOS transistor, and applies the reference potential to the bit line as soon as the word line is activated.

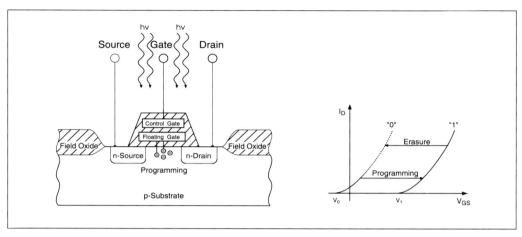

Figure 6.32: Storage transistor with floating gate. The charges in the floating gate determine the stored value.

The situation changes completely, though, if the floating gate holds electrons, that is, is charged with negative charges. The electric charges in the floating gate shield the field of the control gate and generate an electrical field in the channel region which is opposite to the field of an active control gate (the control gate is supplied with a positive voltage). Thus an activated word line cannot generate a sufficiently strong field with the control gate to turn on the transistors. The bit line is not supplied with the reference potential, and the storage transistor stores the value «0». Only with a much higher control gate potential can the storage transistor be turned on, that is, if the field of the control gate is strong enough to compensate the field of the floating gate, and to make the channel between source and drain conductive. Thus the electric charge in the floating gate shifts the storage transistor's characteristic, and therefore also the threshold voltage, to higher values (see Figure 6.32).

Loading the floating gate with electrons can be carried out by a pure electric pulse. As the floating gate is completely embedded in an isolating layer, and has no connection to other elements, the charges are held there for a long time (at least ten years). This long lifetime (and the well-isolated connections to it) is, of course, an obstacle to charging the floating gate. To program a «0» a pulse lasting 50 ms with a voltage of 20 V is applied between word and bit line, that is, between gate and drain. Thus, in the channel region fast (hot) charge carriers (electrons) are generated that have enough energy to pass the isolation region between substrate and floating gate. They accumulate in the floating gate and are held there after the programming pulse has been switched off, as the floating gate is isolated and the electrons do not have enough energy after cooling to get over the isolation layer again. Thus, the isolation layer is impermeable only to low-energy cold electrons. High-energy electrons can penetrate the isolation layer, but without destroying it. This type of storage transistor is also called *FAMOST* (*floating gate avalanche injection MOS transistor*).

The programming time of 50 ms is very long compared to the 70 ns of modern DRAMs, or even to the 20 ns of SRAM chips. But with a shorter programming time not enough electrons would be collected in the floating gate to achieve the intended effect. Remedial action might be taken by means of a higher programming voltage, but then there would be the danger of damaging the isolation layer and destroying the chip. For the timing and strength of the write pulses, therefore, a so-called *PROM programmer* is available. This is a small piece of equipment into which you may insert the PROM chips and which carries out the PROM chip programming according to your write data.

You might expect that the floating gate can be discharged and thus the data can be erased by reversing the polarity of the programming pulse. But this is not true, as in this case hot electrons are also generated in the substrate and not in the floating gate. To erase the data the ROM chip must be exposed to UV radiation. The electrons in the floating gate absorb the rays and thus take in energy. They get «hot», and can leave the floating gate in the same way as they previously got in. If the chip package is equipped with a UV-permeable quartz window then we get a so-called *EPROM* (*eraseable **PROM***). You may have already seen such chips. Through the quartz window you have a clear view of the actual chip and the bonding wires; other silicon chips are usually hidden in black or brown packages. After irradiating for about 20 minutes, all charge carriers are removed from the floating gate and the EPROM chip can be programmed again.

6.4.3 EEPROM

A quartz glass window and a UV lamp for clearing data are extensive (and also expensive) equipment for erasing EPROM chips. It would better and much easier if the chip could be cleared in the same way as it was programmed, by means of an electrical pulse. Fortunately, memory chip techniques have made considerable progress during the last few years, and now supply inexpensive *EEPROMs* (**e**lectrically **e**raseable **PROM**) as well. Figure 6.33 shows a sectional view through the storage transistor of such an EEPROM.

Loading the floating gate with electrons (that is, the programming of the memory cell) is carried out in the same way as in an EPROM: by means of a relatively long (50 ms) voltage pulse of +20 V between gate and drain high-energy charge, carriers are generated in the substrate which penetrate the gate oxide and accumulate in the floating gate. The positive potential of +20 V during programming «draws up» the negative electrons from the substrate into the floating gate. To clear the EEPROM the thin tunnel oxide film between a region of the floating gate extending downwards in direction to the substrate and the drain is important. Because of basic physical laws, isolation layers are never isolated perfectly. Instead, charge carriers can penetrate the isolation layer (with a low probability). The probability gets higher the less the thickness of the isolation layer and the higher the voltage between the two electrodes on the two sides of the layer.

For discharging the floating gate an inverse voltage is applied between gate and drain, that is, the drain is on a potential of +20 V against the gate. Thus the negative electrons in the floating gate are drawn to the drain through the thin tunnel oxide, and the stored data is thus erased. It is important to ensure that this charge drawing does not last too long, as otherwise too many electrons are drawn out of the floating gate and the gate is then charged positively. The transistor's characteristic is thus shifted to the left too much, and the threshold voltage is lowered too far, so that normal operation of the storage transistor becomes impossible.

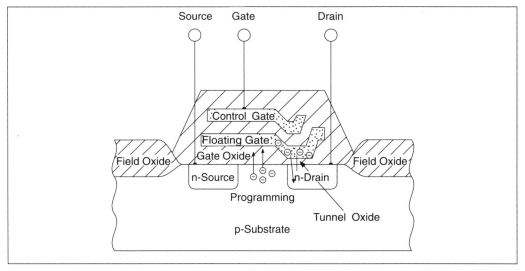

Figure 6.33: EEPROM storage transistor. In an EEPROM the charges in the floating gate can be removed by means of an electrical pulse.

A word about the storage capacities and access times of ROM chips. Because of the enormous advance in integrating electronic circuits, ROM chips with a capacity of 1 Mbit are not unusual today. On modern motherboards you will usually see only a single EPROM or EEPROM chip. The access times are between 120 ns and 250 ns in most cases, and thus are much longer than those of DRAMs or even SRAMs. You should move frequently used BIOS routines held in ROM into the faster RAM by shadowing if your PC can do this. Only the POST and boot routines must be held in ROM, as they initialize and boot the PC. The BIOS routines are needed later for supporting the operating system and application programs, therefore they may also be loaded externally, for example from a floppy disk. OS/2 currently follows this procedure. As most BIOS variants in the PC are only suited for operation in real mode, but OS/2 (except for its loading routines) runs in protected mode, all the BIOS routines in ROM are unusable. Only the advanced BIOS of some PS/2 models accommodates a protected mode BIOS. For PCs without advanced BIOS, all BIOS routines for protected mode must therefore be loaded from disk. The OS/2 that is currently freely available on the market strictly (100%) orients to IBM hardware; one reason why OS/2 has more compatibility problems than DOS.

6.5 Silicon Hard Disks – Flash Memories

In the last few years a new type of non-volatile memory has come onto the market, frequently used in small portable computers as a substitute for floppy and hard disk drives – so-called flash memories. The structure of their memory cells is fundamentally the same as that of

EEPROMs (see Figure 6.33); only the tunnel oxide is thinner than in an EEPROM memory cell. Therefore, they need an erase and programming voltage of only 12 V so that 10 000 program and erase cycles can be carried out without any problems. Despite the memory cell array, several additional control circuits and registers are formed in a flash memory, and the program and erase operations are carried out in a somewhat different way. Flash memories may thus be programmed nearly as flexibly as DRAMs or SRAMs, while they don't lose the data held. Figure 6.34 shows a block diagram of the internal flash memory structure.

The central part of the flash memory is the memory cell array, which comprises FAMOST memory cells as described in Section 6.4. The cells are addressed by an address buffer, which accepts the address signals and transfers them to a row and column decoders, respectively. Flash memories, like SRAM chips, don't carry out address multiplexing. The row and column decoders select one word line and one or more bit line pairs as in a conventional memory chip. The read data is externally output via a data input/output buffer or written into the addressed memory cell by this buffer via an I/O gate.

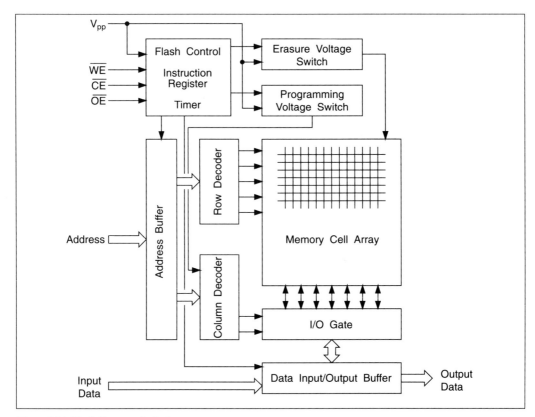

Figure 6.34: Block diagram of a flash memory.

It is important that the read process is carried out with the usual MOS voltage of 5 V, but for programming and erasing the memory cells a higher voltage V_{pp} of 12 V is required. To program a memory cell the flash control applies a short voltage pulse of typically 10 μs and

12 V. This leads to an avalanche breakthrough in the memory transistor, which loads the floating gate. A 1 Mbit flash memory can be programmed within about 2 s, but unlike the conventional EEPROM, erasure is carried out chip-by-chip. In a erasure process the flash control applies an erasure pulse to the whole memory cell array by the erasure voltage switch, so that all memory cells are erased. For an EEPROM the EEPROM programmer, on the other hand, carries out erasure cell-by-cell. The erase time for the whole flash memory is about 1 s. There are also variants of this memory available that can be erased page-by-page, that is, one complete row of memory cells is always erased.

The read, program and erase processes are controlled by means of 2-byte instructions, which the external microprocessor writes to the instruction register of the flash control. Also, for this the high voltage V_{pp} of 12 V is necessary. For a typical flash memory the following instructions are available:

- Read memory: the flash memory supplies data via the data pins.
- Read identifier code: the flash memory supplies a code at the data pins, which indicates the type and version of the chip.
- Setup erase/erase: prepares the flash memory for an erase process and carries out the erasure.
- Erase-verify: erases all memory cells and verifies this process.
- Setup program/program: prepares the programming of individual memory cells and carries out this process.
- Program-verify: executes the programming and verifies this process.
- Reset: resets the flash memory to a defined initial state.

Thus flash memories have a more extensive functionality than normal EEPROMs, and are a virtually autonomous memory subsystem. For example, unlike conventional EEPROMs they can be programmed and erased while installed in the computer. Some models even generate the high voltage V_{pp} from the supply voltage of 5 V internally. With an EEPROM you need dedicated peripheral equipment (the EEPROM programmer), and the chips must be removed from the computer in advance of programming or erasure.

Flash memories are thus mainly used as a substitute for floppy and low-capacity hard disk drives in portable computers, but also for a variety of chip cards. Because of advances in integrating electronic elements, the chips are very small and have a very low power consumption. In the non-selected state the flash chip enters a standby mode where the power consumption is again drastically reduced. Hard disks, on the other hand, require relatively large, «current-eating» electric motors to rotate the storage medium and the head actuator. *Solid state hard disks* on a base of flash memories are therefore more favourable, in terms of power consumption as well as cost, up to a size of several Mbytes. You will find them mainly as so-called *memory cards*. Compared with battery-buffered SRAM solutions, their inherent non-volatility is a big advantage. There is no battery to fail and cause a data loss. The storage time of information in a flash memory is at least ten years, and typically 100 years. Over this time period, hard disks or floppies will become demagnetized.

Flash memories are mainly used in fields where a power failure would give rise to disastrous consequences, or where the operating conditions are very rough. Hard disk drives are very sensitive to shocks and floppies to mechanical damage or humidity. Flash memories, sealed in a stable package with no mechanical movable parts, are immune against such external influences. Table 6.4 compares some values for ordinary hard disks and mass storages based on flash memories.

	Hard disk	Flash memory
Access time	24 ms	0 ms
Track-track-positioning	5 ms	0 ms
Data transfer rate	1 Mbyte/s	16 Mbytes/s
Writing a 10 kbyte block	46 ms	0.6 ms

Table 6.4: Hard disks and flash memories

You can see that inertia as well as transfer rate are far better for a flash memory. However, one disadvantage for its use as mass storage is that flash memories can usually only be erased chip-by-chip or page-by-page. This may give rise to problems if, for example, one sector of a file or a directory entry is to be updated. The driver for mass storages on a flash memory base must take this into account.

Figure 6.35 shows the pin assignment of a typical flash memory, the Intel 28F010, with a storage capacity of 128kword*8bit (1 Mbit in all). It has an access time of 120 ns, and is therefore as fast as older DRAM chips.

The chip comes in the familiar DIP or PLCC packages, but you may also find a special occupation-area-saving version in a TSOP (**t**hin **s**mall **o**utline **p**ackage), which is only 1.2 mm thick. Small and handy memory cards can thus be constructed. Most pins and signals are self-evident; the following only presents the most important ones.

A0–A16
These 17 pins are supplied with the address for accessing the 128 k words. No address multiplexing is carried out.

D0–D7
These pins supply the read data or accept the data for programming.

$\overline{\text{CE}}$
(Chip Enable) If the signal at this pin is high, the flash chip is activated and leaves the standby mode.

$\overline{\text{OE}}$
(Output Enable) If $\overline{\text{OE}}$ is low the chip outputs data.

$\overline{\text{WE}}$
(Write Enable) If the signal at $\overline{\text{WE}}$ is on a low level, commands can be written into the instruction register and the memory cells.

V_{pp}

This pin is supplied with the erase and program voltage (12 V) for writing the instruction register, for erasing the complete memory cell array, or for programming individual bytes in the memory cell array.

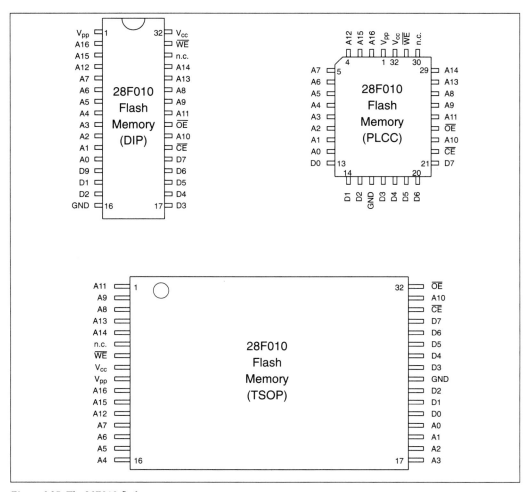

Figure 6.35: The 28F010 flash memory.

7   Peripheral and Support Chips – Nothing Runs Without Us

Peripheral and support chips belong together, and are components that support the processor for certain tasks. These chips are far less flexible than the processor, but carry out the allocated jobs at higher speed and independent of the CPU. Support chips are usually developed in close relation to a certain processor, or at least to a processor family. Together, the processor and support chips are often called a *chipset*. The following sections discuss the most important support chips used in PCs. However, because of the enormous advance in microelectronics, several of the separately described components are today usually integrated into a single chip. Therefore, don't be surprised if you can't, for example, find a chip labelled 8259A. It will be integrated as a functional unit into one of the ICs on the motherboard. These support components integrated into a single chip, though, are accessed and programmed in the same way as described below in connection with the original Intel chips.

7.1   Hardware Interrupts and the 8259A Programmable Interrupt Controller

Several components are present in PCs that only require a service by the processor from time to time. This includes the serial interface, where characters from a modem arrive asynchronously (hence the chip is also called a UART). Moreover, the time period between two successive characters or character blocks may be quite long. For this reason, the processor is often occupied by executing a program while the incoming characters are first collected in the background so as to be available for processing later.

7.1.1   Interrupt-Driven Data Exchange and Polling

If the PC expects characters to arrive at the serial interface, there are two principal possibilities for collecting them:

– the serial interface is regularly examined to see whether a complete character has arrived;
– the serial interface itself indicates that it has received a complete character.

In the first case the strategy is called *polling*. The disadvantage of this method is obvious: the processor is heavily occupied with the polling process so that execution of the foreground program proceeds slowly. Additionally, the extensive polling routine must be integrated into the program, which leads to more code and a worse performance. If the characters are arriving very quickly, the time period between two pollings may be longer than the interval between two incoming characters; data is thus lost.

The other possibility is usually realized by a hardware interrupt. The strategy is then called *interrupt-driven data exchange* or interrupt-driven communication. In this case, the serial interface activates an IRQ signal to inform the processor that a complete character has been received and is ready for transfer to the CPU. In the PC this signal is transmitted to the 8259A programmable interrupt controller (PIC), a support chip that issues an interrupt request to the processor. As the CPU in this case knows that a character is available, the interrupt handler only needs to read the character from the serial interface. The periodic examination as to whether a character is available is no longer required, thus the program overhead for servicing the serial port is less, and the performance increases. With interrupt-driven data exchange significantly higher transfer rates can therefore be achieved without lowering the execution speed of the foreground program.

Potential candidates for interrupt-driven communication, besides the serial interface, are all those components that exchange data with the main memory:

- the parallel interface;
- the floppy/hard disk controller;
- network adapter;
- the keyboard.

Also the hard disk, for example, may need quite a long time (in computer terms, of course) to position the read/write head and to read certain data. While this is carried out the computer doesn't have to wait, but can carry out other tasks. Once the drive has read the data from disk, the controller activates the interrupt signal to cause the processor to service the hard disk again. By using interrupts instead of polling, the performance and reliability of a computer system is increased.

As the processor usually only has a single interrupt input but in the PC several units for interrupt-driven data exchange are present, the 8259A PIC is implemented to manage them. The 8259A PIC is connected between the interrupt-requesting components and the processor, that is, the interrupt requests are first transferred to the PIC, which in turn drives the interrupt line to the processor. Figure 7.1 shows the pin assignment of this chip.

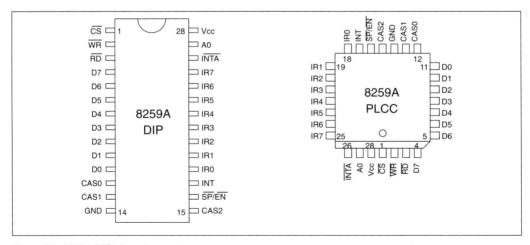

Figure 7.1: 8259A PIC pin assignment.

7.1.2   8259A Terminals and Signals

The 8259A comes in two package types, that is, as a dual in-line package and as a plastic leaded chip carrier. In the following, the pins and signals applied or provided are outlined.

$\overline{\text{CS}}$ (pin 1)
(Chip Select) If this pin is at a low level, the CPU can read data from or write data to the internal 8259A registers by means of the data bus D7–D0 and the signals $\overline{\text{RD}}$ and $\overline{\text{WR}}$. Thus the $\overline{\text{CS}}$ signal enables the PIC for read and write processes. For managing and servicing interrupts, the $\overline{\text{CS}}$ signal has no meaning.

$\overline{\text{WR}}$ (pin 2)
(Write) If this pin is supplied with a low-level signal, the 8259A accepts data from the data bus, that is, the CPU can write data into the internal PIC registers.

$\overline{\text{RD}}$ (pin 3)
(Read) If this pin is supplied with low-level signal, the 8259A outputs data onto the data bus, that is, the CPU can read data from the internal PIC registers.

D7–D0 (pins 4–11)
These eight pins form the bidirectional data bus (to/from the CPU), through which the CPU can write to or read data from internal registers. The number of the interrupt vector to be called is also transferred via D7–D0.

CAS0–CAS2 (pins 12, 13, 15)
(Cascade Lines) With these connections, and the accompanying signals, several PICs can be cascaded. Usually, a hierarchical structure of one master PIC and up to eight slave PICs is the result. The master PIC selects one of these $2^3 = 8$ slave PICs via lines CAS0–CAS2. Thus, CAS0–CAS2 form something like a local PIC address bus.

GND (pin 14)
This pin is supplied with the ground potential (usually 0 V).

$\overline{\text{SP}}/\overline{\text{EN}}$ (pin 16)
(Slave Program/Enable Buffer) Depending upon the 8259A operation mode (buffered or unbuffered), the meaning of the signal at this pin differs. In buffered mode the connection outputs a signal $\overline{\text{EN}}$ to control the external buffer. In unbuffered mode the pin recives a signal $\overline{\text{SP}}$, which indicates whether the 8259A is to be operated as a master PIC ($\overline{\text{SP}}$=1) or a slave PIC ($\overline{\text{SP}}$=0).

INT (pin 17)
(Interrupt) If a valid interrupt request is issued by a peripheral via lines IR0–IR7, the INT signal rises to a high level. INT is directly connected to the INTR input of the processor.

IR0–IR7 (pins 18–25)
(Interrupt Request) These pins are connected to those peripherals which request an interrupt. One pin may be connected to only one peripheral at most. To issue a hardware interrupt the peripheral concerned raises its IRQ output, and thus the connected IRx pin, to a high level. The input IR0 has the highest and IR7 the lowest priority. A single 8259A PIC can service a

maximum of eight different peripherals. By cascading, as is the case in the AT, however, up to 64 devices can be managed, and up to 64 interrupt levels can be realized.

$\overline{\text{INTA}}$ (pin 26)

(Interrupt Acknowledge) This pin is connected to the processor's $\overline{\text{INTA}}$ pin, through which the CPU outputs $\overline{\text{INTA}}$ pulses to carry out an interrupt acknowledge sequence for transferring the interrupt vector concerned.

A0 (pin 27)

A0 is used together with $\overline{\text{CS}}$, $\overline{\text{WR}}$ and $\overline{\text{RD}}$ to distinguish among various commands from the CPU and provide status information to the CPU.

V_{cc} (pin 28)

This pin is always supplied with the supply potential (usually +5 V).

7.1.3 Internal Structure and Interrupt Acknowledge Sequence

Figure 7.2 shows the internal structure of the 8259A programmable interrupt controller.

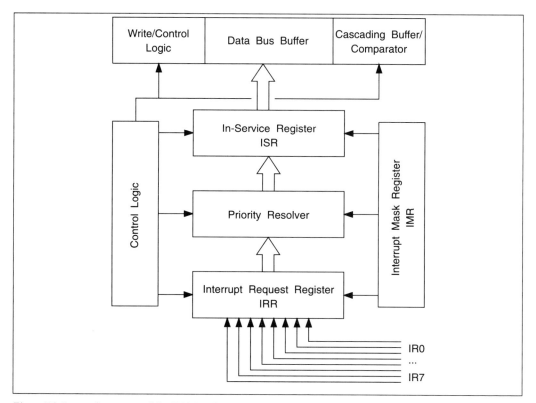

Figure 7.2: Internal structure of the 8259A PIC.

To detect and manage the interrupt requests of peripherals, three registers are available in the 8259A: interrupt request register (IRR); in-service register (ISR); and interrupt mask register (IMR). The eight interrupt lines IR0–IR7 are connected to the IRR. Each of the three registers is eight bits wide, where every bit corresponds to one of the lines IR0–IR7 (see Figure 7.3).

Figure 7.3: IRR, ISR and IMR.

To issue an interrupt request the peripheral concerned raises the signal at one of the corresponding pins IR0–IR7 to a high level. The 8259A then sets the accompanying bit in the interrupt request register. In the IRR all devices for which an interrupt request is currently pending are memorized. As it is possible for several peripherals to issue a hardware interrupt simultaneously, and therefore several bits may also be set in the IRR simultaneously, the priority encoder passes only the highest priority bit.

At the same time, the PIC activates its output INT to inform the processor about the interrupt request. This starts an *interrupt acknowledge sequence*. If the $\overline{\text{IE}}$ flag in the processor's flag register is set, then the CPU responds with the output of a first $\overline{\text{INTA}}$ pulse to the $\overline{\text{INTA}}$ input of the 8259A. The priority encoder now transfers the highest priority bit to the in-service register (ISR), and clears the corresponding bit in the IRR. The set bit in the ISR indicates which interrupt request is currently serviced (is *in-service* now). The processor outputs a second $\overline{\text{INTA}}$ pulse to instruct the 8259A to put the 8-bit number of the interrupt handler onto the data bus D7–D0. This 8-bit number consists of the three least significant bits of the number of the set bit in the ISR (see Figure 7.4).

Figure 7.4: The interrupt number. The five most significant bits are determined by the programmable offset, the three least significant bits by the number of the set bit in the ISR.

The five most significant bits can be programmed appropriately as an offset upon initializing the PIC (see below). The CPU reads the 8-bit number and calls the corresponding interrupt handler. If the 8259A is operating with automatic interrupt completion (in the so-called AEOI mode), the acknowledge sequence is completed and the ISR bit is reset. If, on the other hand, the 8259A is not operating in AEOI mode, it is the responsibility of the interrupt handler to issue an EOI command (end of interrupt) to the PIC. The set ISR bit is thus cleared manually. The various operation modes can be programmed via software.

In both cases, the 8259A is now ready to process the next hardware interrupt request (if another bit is set in the IRR). For this purpose, the priority encoder transfers the bit with the next lowest priority from the IRR into the ISR, and the described interrupt acknowledge sequence is repeated.

If a request of a higher priority occurs during the course of the $\overline{\text{INTA}}$ cycle or the servicing of an interrupt request, the 8259A completes the current $\overline{\text{INTA}}$ cycle and then services the new interrupt of higher priority.

The following actions are carried out for an interrupt request by a peripheral:

– One of the interrupt request lines IR0–IR7 is raised to a high level and thus the corresponding bit in the IRR is set.

– The 8259A detects this signal and responds with an INT signal to the processor.

– The CPU receives the INT signal and outputs a first $\overline{\text{INTA}}$ pulse if the IE flag is set.

– With the receipt of the first $\overline{\text{INTA}}$ signal from the CPU the highest priority bit in the IRR register is cleared, and the corresponding bit in the ISR register is set.

– The processor outputs a second $\overline{\text{INTA}}$ pulse and thus causes the 8259A to put an 8-bit pointer onto the data bus. The CPU reads this pointer as the number of the interrupt handler to call.

– In the AEOI mode the ISR bit is automatically reset at the end of the second $\overline{\text{INTA}}$ pulse. Otherwise, the CPU must issue an EOI command to the 8259A when executing the interrupt handler to manually clear the ISR bit.

Example: The serial interface COM1: in the XT is connected to IRQ4 corresponding to the 8259A IR4 line. The programmed offset is equal to 7. If COM1 issues an interrupt request then pin IR4 of the PIC is set to a high level and the IRR4 bit in the IRR is set. The priority encoder sets bit IS4 in the ISR and clears the bit IR4 in the IRR. During the course of the following interrupt acknowledge sequence, the 8259A outputs the value 8(offset)+4(IS4) = 12 (0ch) as the interrupt vector number. Thus the processor calls interrupt handler 0ch. During the course of servicing the interrupt the processor passes an EOI command to the 8259A, and the IS4 in the ISR is reset.

To be able to mask a certain interrupt request the interrupt mask register (IMR) is implemented. A set bit in this register masks all the interrupt requests of the corresponding peripheral, that is, all requests on the line allocated the set bit are ignored; all others are not affected by the masking.

Thus, the PIC 8259A not only activates the processor's IRQ input and manages the hardware requests according to their priority, but also, during the course of the interrupt acknowledge sequence, passes the number of the interrupt handler to be called.

7.1.4   Cascading

One characteristic of the 8259A is its *cascading* capability. For this at least two PICs are required, which form two levels: the first is formed by a master PIC, the second by 1–8 slave PICs. With this configuration interrupt requests of more than eight peripherals can be managed. Figure 7.5 shows the wiring of two 8259As as master and slave PIC, as is the case in an AT or PS/2.

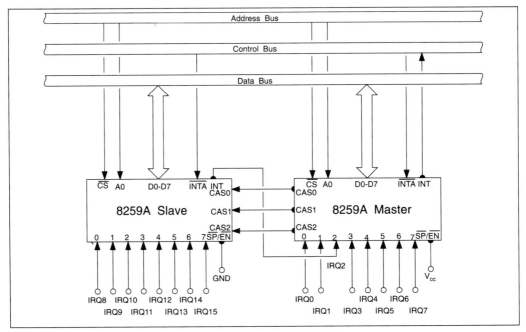

Figure 7.5: Cascading the 8259A PICs. The 8259A PICs can be cascaded so that a maximum of 64 interrupt levels is available. For this purpose, the INT output of the slave is connected to the IR input of the master, and signals CAS0–CAS2 are used for information interchange.

To realize cascading the INT output of the slave PIC is connected to one of the IR inputs of the master PIC. In the AT or PS/2, the interrupt request signal of the slave is applied to input 2 of the master PIC. The PC literature established the name IRQ0–IRQ7 (master) and IRQ8–IRQ15 (slave) for the various interrupt channels and PIC connections (see Figure 7.5). Thus the slave's INT output is redirected to IRQ2 of the master. Only the INT output of the master is connected to the INTR input of the processor via the control bus. The pins $\overline{CS}$, A0, $\overline{INTA}$ and D0–D7 are connected to the address, control and data bus, as is the case for a single-PIC configuration. Additionally, the connections CAS0–CAS2 of the master and slave are wired. The master PIC uses CAS0–CAS2 as outputs, the slave PIC, however, as inputs. This means that the master PIC supplies control signals and the slave receives them.

With a high-level signal (V_{cc}) at the $\overline{SP}/\overline{EN}$ pin, the 8259A is operated as a master and by a low-level signal as a slave. For a master, $\overline{SP}/\overline{EN}$ is therefore usually fixed to the supply voltage, and for a slave this pin is grounded. This is in general already carried out during manufacturing by soldering the pin to a corresponding supply line.

The processing of an interrupt request of a peripheral is dependent upon whether the request is running through the slave PIC or is directly managed by the master. If one of the devices connected to IRQ0, IRQ1 or IRQ3–IRQ7 requests an interrupt, the same steps as described above are carried out.

However, if the request is running over one of the lines IRQ8–IRQ15 (that is, via the slave PIC), additional steps are required:

– One of the interrupt request lines IRQ8–IRQ15 is raised to a high level, and thus the corresponding bit in the IRR of the slave PIC is set.

– The 8259A slave detects this, and responds with an INT signal to the master PIC.

– The master PIC receives the INT signal via connection 2 (IRQ2); thus bit 2 is set in the master's IRR.

– The 8259A master detects this, and responds with an INT signal to the processor.

– The CPU receives the INT signal and outputs the first $\overline{\text{INTA}}$ pulse if the IE flag is set. At the same time the master PIC activates the signals CAS0–CAS2 to address the slave PIC which manages the interrupt.

– Upon receipt of the first $\overline{\text{INTA}}$ signal from the CPU, the highest priority bit in the IRR register of the master and slave PIC is cleared, and the corresponding bits in the ISR registers are set.

– The processor outputs a second $\overline{\text{INTA}}$ pulse, and causes the slave 8259A to put an 8-bit pointer onto the data bus. The CPU reads this pointer as the number of the interrupt handler to call.

– In AEOI mode the ISR bits in the master and slave are automatically reset at the end of the second $\overline{\text{INTA}}$ pulse; otherwise, the CPU must output two EOI commands during the course of executing the handler (one to the master PIC and the other to the slave PIC) to clear the ISR bits manually.

If the 8259A is not operating in AEOI mode, then the interrupt handler needs to know whether the interrupt request is managed by the master alone or by the master-slave pair, because in the latter case two EOI commands are required. Thus, servicing a hardware interrupt depends to a great extent on the architecture forming the base of the computer. For this reason, the BIOS usually has all the necessary instructions for the appropriate handling of such requests. A programmer should therefore complete his/her own handler for hardware interrupts by chaining to the original routine instead of to their own EOI sequence.

Redirecting the INT signal from the slave's INT output to the IRQ2 input of the master leads to a shift in the priorities of the corresponding interrupt requests. As input 2 of the master has a higher priority than inputs 3–7, all interrupt requests running through the slave push their way to the front. Thus the priority in descending order is as shown in Table 7.1.

Master	Slave	Priority	PC/XT	AT/PS/2
IRQ0		highest	timer 0	timer 0
IRQ1			keyboard	keyboard
IRQ2			reserved	slave PIC
	IRQ8			real time clock
	IRQ9			reserved*)
	IRQ10			reserved
	IRQ11			reserved
	IRQ12			reserved
	IRQ13			coprocessor 80287/i387
	IRQ14			hard disk controller
	IRQ15			reserved
IRQ3			COM2	COM2
IRQ4			COM1	COM1
IRQ5			hard disk controller	LPT2
IRQ6			floppy controller	floppy controller
IRQ7		lowest	LPT1	LPT1

*) An IRQ9 leads to the call of the interrupt handler for IRQ2 (redirection of IRQ9 to IRQ2).

Table 7.1: Priorities (in descending order)

With one master and one slave 8259A PIC a maximum of 15 peripherals or interrupt channels can be handled. The IRQ2 channel is reserved for redirecting the INT signal from the slave. This 2-level cascading model can be expanded to 64 channels at most. In this case, the INT outputs of the eight slave PICs are connected to the eight inputs of the master PIC, all interrupt requests running through the slaves. For the PC, including the PS/2 and EISA models, the 15 interrupt channels that can be realized with one master and one slave are sufficient. Usually, you therefore find two chips at most. Because of the technical advances in integration, these two PICs are often integrated into a single *system controller*, together with other control chips such as DMA, timer and real-time clock. Structure and functionality, though, remain the same.

7.1.5 Initialization and Programming

For a defined operation the 8259A needs to be initialized first. This is carried out by the four *initialization command words* (*ICW*) ICW1–ICW4. Using the three *operation command words* (*OCW*) OCW1–OCW3 the 8259A PIC is instructed to operate in various modes to handle the interrupt requests. In the following description, however, the programming is only discussed for use in a PC. Other operation modes for use with the MCS–80, 85 and other systems are not described.

For accessing the 8259A registers two ports are available for the master and slave. The PIC in the PC/XT, as well as the master in the AT and PS/2, is accessed via ports 020h and 021h, and the slave PIC in the AT and PS/2 via ports 0a0h and 0a1h. Table 7.2 lists the addresses as well as the read and write data for these registers.

I/O address IRQ0 – IRQ7[1)	I/O address IRQ8 – IRQ15[2)	Read data	Write data
020h	0a0h	IRR	ICW1
		ISR	OCW2
		interrupt vector	OCW3
021h	0a1h	IMR	ICW2
			ICW3
			ICW4
			OCW1

[1) valid for PC/XT and the master PIC in the AT and PS/2.
[2) valid for slave in the AT and PS/2.

Table 7.2: 8259A PIC I/O Addresses and I/O Data

The initialization of an 8259A PIC is started by outputting the initialization command word ICW1 via port 020h (master) or 0a0h (slave). Thus the PIC recognizes that an initialization has begun, and resets the internal registers to default values. Figure 7.6 shows a flowchart for initializing the 8259A.

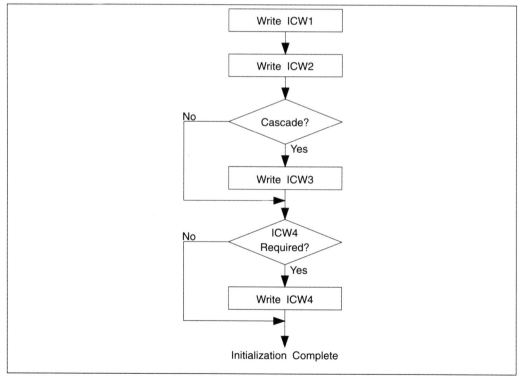

Figure 7.6: Initializing the 8259A PIC. Initializing the PIC is carried out by two to four initialization command words ICWx, depending upon the chosen operation mode.

After starting initialization by writing ICW1, the CPU supplies the initialization command word ICW2 via port 021h (master) or 0a1h (slave). If cascaded PICs are employed in the system, the processor also writes ICW3. If only one PIC is implemented, as in the PC/XT, this is not necessary. An entry in ICW1 indicates whether the PIC requires the information supplied by ICW4. If this is the case, the CPU also supplies the ICW4 word. Thus, the PIC initialization is completed with at least two and a maximum of four initialization command words.

In the following, the formats of the four ICWs is described (see Figure 7.7).

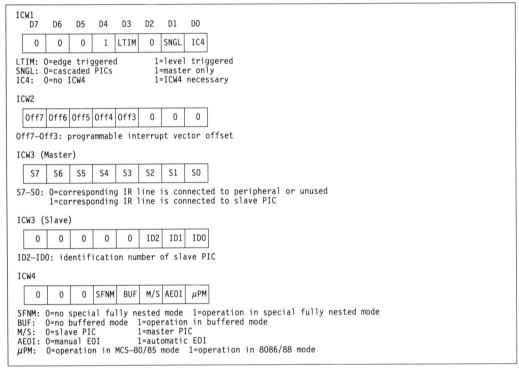

Figure 7.7: ICW formats.

Bits D7–D5 and D2 in ICW1 are equal to 0 and bit D4 is equal to 1. By means of the *LTIM* bit, the PIC is instructed to operate with either edge or level triggering. With an edge-triggered operation an interrupt request is indicated by a *transition* of the signal at the corresponding IR input from low to high. If level triggering is enabled then the interrupt request is indicated solely by a high *level*. In the PC/XT and AT, the PICs operate with edge triggering only. In PS/2 and EISA computers, level triggering can also be employed. The *SNGL* bit determines whether only a single PIC (as in the PC/XT) or at least two cascaded PICs (as in the AT and PS/2) are used. If cascaded PICs are present in addition to ICW1 and ICW2, ICW3 must be also specified. Thus with SNGL the PIC recognizes whether ICW3 is passed after transfer of ICW1 and ICW2. If *IC4* is set, then the PIC knows that later additional information is passed with word ICW4.

Bits *Off7–Off3* in ICW2 define the offset of the interrupt vector, which is passed to the CPU during the course of an interrupt acknowledge sequence. The remaining three bits of the interrupt vector number are specified implicitly by the number of the serviced request.

The meaning of the bits in the initialization word ICW3 differs from master to slave. For the master a cleared bit *S7–S0* indicates that the corresponding IR line is connected to a peripheral that is able to issue an interrupt request directly, or that line is free. A set bit, on the other hand, shows that the corresponding input is connected to the INT output of a slave PIC. For a slave PIC the three least significant bits *ID2–ID0* define the number of the master's IR input to which the slave concerned is connected. During the course of an INTA sequence the slave PICs compare their identification number (defined by means of ID2–ID0) with the number that the master PIC outputs via lines CAS2–CAS0. Only the slave PIC whose identification number matches CAS2–CAS0 responds with the output of the number of the interrupt vector to be called.

The 8259A PIC expects the transfer of ICW4 only if this is explicitly defined in ICW1. Usually, the PICs in the PC operate in the normal *nested mode*. This means that the interrupt requests managed by the PIC are structured hierarchically in the above mentioned way, that is, the request via IR line 0 has the highest priority, that via IR line 7 the lowest. Thus the interrupts are serviced according to their priority, and not according to their occurrence. For very large systems with many interrupt channels this mode can be modified by setting the *SFNM*. This prevents a slave PIC from blocking interrupt requests of a higher priority in the slave PIC while being serviced by the master. But the PC doesn't use this capability; it is only important for large computer systems. If the *BUF* bit is set then the PIC is operating in buffered mode. The $\overline{SP/EN}$ pin is not used as input to distinguish master and slave, but as an output for activating external buffers. This is necessary for large computer systems with a power-consuming system bus; the PC doesn't use this option. In buffered mode the $\overline{SP/EN}$ pin is no longer available for distinguishing master and slave. In this case, the operation mode as a master or slave is not defined by fixing the $\overline{SP/EN}$ potential on V_{cc} (master) or GND (slave), but by programming the *M/S* bit. A set M/S bit indicates that the PIC concerned is operating as a master. If the 8259A is operated in unbuffered mode then M/S has no meaning.

By means of *AEOI* you can determine whether the PIC completes the interrupt acknowledge sequence with an automatic end-of-interrupt (EOI) or expects the transfer of an EOI command by the processor. With a set AEOI bit completion is carried out automatically after the second INTA signal from the CPU. Thus the ISR bit is cleared automatically. Finally, the *μPM* (microprocessor mode) bit defines whether the PIC is installed in a system with an 8086/88 processor (*μPM* = 1) or in an MCS-80/85 system. In 8086/88 systems the PIC passes the 8-bit number of the interrupt handler to call. For this two $\overline{INTA}$ pulses from the CPU are required. In an MCS-80/85 system, however, the 8259A supplies the 16-bit address of the interrupt vector directly, and needs three $\overline{INTA}$ pulses for this.

Example: initializing master and slave PIC in the AT

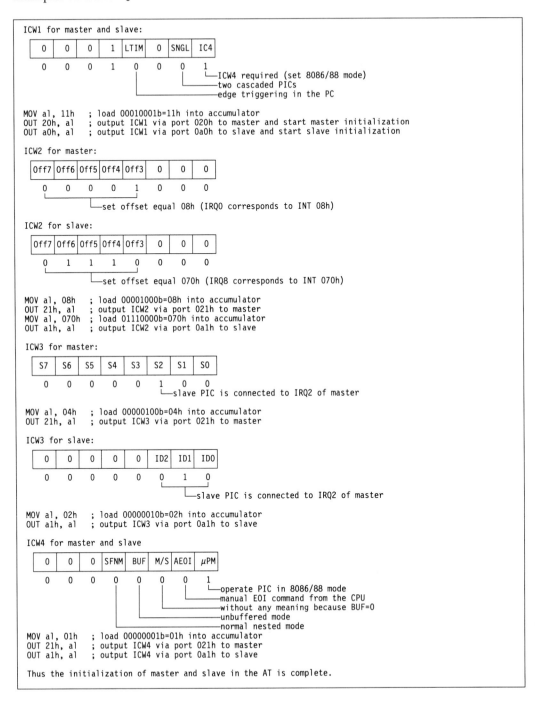

ICW1 for master and slave:

0	0	0	1	LTIM	0	SNGL	IC4

```
     0    0    0    1    0    0    0    1
                                      └──ICW4 required (set 8086/88 mode)
                                 └──two cascaded PICs
                            └──edge triggering in the PC
```

```
MOV al, 11h   ; load 00010001b=11h into accumulator
OUT 20h, al   ; output ICW1 via port 020h to master and start master initialization
OUT a0h, al   ; output ICW1 via port 0a0h to slave and start slave initialization
```

ICW2 for master:

Off7	Off6	Off5	Off4	Off3	0	0	0

```
   0     0     0     0     1    0    0    0
                          └──set offset equal 08h (IRQ0 corresponds to INT 08h)
```

ICW2 for slave:

Off7	Off6	Off5	Off4	Off3	0	0	0

```
   0     1     1     1     0    0    0    0
                          └──set offset equal 070h (IRQ8 corresponds to INT 070h)
```

```
MOV al, 08h    ; load 00001000b=08h into accumulator
OUT 21h, al    ; output ICW2 via port 021h to master
MOV al, 070h   ; load 01110000b=070h into accumulator
OUT a1h, al    ; output ICW2 via port 0a1h to slave
```

ICW3 for master:

S7	S6	S5	S4	S3	S2	S1	S0

```
   0    0    0    0    0    1    0    0
                          └──slave PIC is connected to IRQ2 of master
```

```
MOV al, 04h   ; load 00000100b=04h into accumulator
OUT 21h, al   ; output ICW3 via port 021h to master
```

ICW3 for slave:

0	0	0	0	0	ID2	ID1	ID0

```
   0    0    0    0    0    0    1    0
                               └──slave PIC is connected to IRQ2 of master
```

```
MOV al, 02h   ; load 00000010b=02h into accumulator
OUT a1h, al   ; output ICW3 via port 0a1h to slave
```

ICW4 for master and slave

0	0	0	SFNM	BUF	M/S	AEOI	μPM

```
   0    0    0    0     0    0    0    1
                                      └──operate PIC in 8086/88 mode
                                 └──manual EOI command from the CPU
                            └──without any meaning because BUF=0
                       └──unbuffered mode
                  └──normal nested mode
```

```
MOV al, 01h   ; load 00000001b=01h into accumulator
OUT 21h, al   ; output ICW4 via port 021h to master
OUT a1h, al   ; output ICW4 via port 0a1h to slave
```

Thus the initialization of master and slave in the AT is complete.

After this initialization the PIC can manage and service interrupt requests from various peripherals. Using the OCWs, additional commands can be passed to the 8259A during operation to set up various operating modes. Figure 7.8 shows the format of the three OCWs.

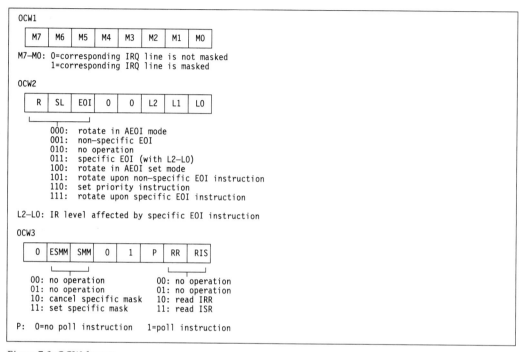

Figure 7.8: OCW formats.

OCW1 masks certain IR lines. If one of the bits $M7$–$M0$ is set, then this masks the corresponding interrupt request.

Example: `mask timer interrupt`

The timer interrupt updates the internal DOS system clock and is applied to the master PIC via IRQ0. The following C program fragment (Microsoft C 5.10) outputs the current time. After the first key hit the timer interrupt is masked and the clock stops. Upon the second keyboard operation, masking is cancelled and the clock continues to run.

```
#include <dos.h>
#include <graph.h>

void displaytime(void);

main()
{
  displaytime();       /* display time */
  outp(0x21,0x01);     /* disable timer interrupt */
  displaytime();       /* display time */
  outp(0x21,0x00);     /* enable timer interrupt */
```

```
  displaytime();      /* display time */
  exit(0);
}

void displaytime(void)
{
  struct dostime_t time;

  for (;;) {
    _dos_gettime (&time);  /* read time via DOS */
    /* display time in the middle of the screen */
    _settextposition (13,35),printf("%i:%i:%i:%i",
                                    time.hour,time.minute,time.second,time.hsecond);
    if (kbhit()) {  /* check for keyboard hit */
      getch();
      break;
    }
  }
  return;
}
```

The three high-order bits *R*, *SL* and *EOI* control the rotating and EOI modes. If, unlike the PC with its hierarchical structure, peripherals with the same priority are installed, then the PIC carries out servicing in the order of the occurring interrupt requests. This «rotating» servicing, together with the EOI mode, can be programmed via R, SL and EOI. For rotating service it may be that the PIC «forgets» which IR level has currently been serviced. To reset the set ISR bit the CPU has to issue a specific EOI command. In this case, the three least significant bits *L2–L0* indicate the ISR bit to be reset.

Example: reset ISR bit 5 in master PIC with a specific EOI command

```
MOV al, 66h  ; load 01100101b=66h into accumulator
OUT 20h, al  ; output OCW2 via port 020h to master
```

In the PC the PIC generally operates in nested mode, that is, a hierarchical servicing of the interrupt requests is carried out. Resetting the ISR bit is executed by means of an unspecific EOI command.

Example: resetting the ISR bit after servicing a coprocessor interrupt IRQ13 according to the IR line 5 in the slave PIC and IR line 2 in the master PIC (observe cascading!)

```
MOV al, 20h  ; load 00100000b=020h into accumulator
OUT a0h, al  ; output unspecific EOI command to slave PIC
OUT 20h, al  ; output unspecific EOI command to master PIC
```

If a certain interrupt request is in-service (that is, the corresponding bit in the ISR is set), all interrupts of a lower priority are disabled because the in-service request is serviced first. Only an interrupt request of a higher priority pushes its way to the front immediately after the $\overline{\text{INTA}}$ sequence of the serviced interrupt. In this case the current $\overline{\text{INTA}}$ sequence is completed and the new interrupt request is already serviced before the old request has been completed by an EOI. Thus interrupt requests of a lower priority are serviced once the processor has informed the PIC by an EOI that the request has been serviced. Under certain circumstances, it is favourable to also enable requests of a lower priority. This applies, for example, to a dynamic change of the priority structure during the course of executing an interrupt routine. For this purpose, the *ESMM* and *SMM* bits in OCW3 are implemented. They enable (ESMM = 1, SMM = 1) and disable (ESMM = 1, SMM = 0) the so-called *special mask mode*. If a bit in the OCW1 is set in this mode (thus the corresponding interrupt input is masked), all further requests of this level are disabled and all other requests of a higher *and* lower priority are enabled. In the special mask mode the interrupt requests can be masked or enabled individually.

The *RR* (read request) and *RIS* (read in-service) bits read the PIC status, and determine the requested (IRR) and currently serviced (ISR) interrupts. If you want to read the IRR status then you have to first output an OCW3 with a set RR bit via the port 020h (master) or 0a0h (slave). Afterwards, you can read the IRR byte through the same port. Determining the ISR status is carried out in the same way.

Example: determine all interrupt requests currently serviced by the master

```
MOV al, 09h   ; load 00001010b=0ah into accumulator
OUT 20h, al   ; output OCW3 to master
IN al, 20h    ; read ISR into accumulator
```

Besides the IRR and ISR, the mask register IMR can also be read. This is carried out by a simple IN instruction to the port 021h (master) or 0a1h (slave). In this case, no read command via an OCW is required.

Example: read mask status of slave PIC

```
IN al, a1h  ; read mask byte into accumulator
```

If the CPU passes the PIC an OCW3 with a set bit *P*, then the PIC operates in polling mode. The 8259A interprets the next read instruction of the processor as an acknowledge signal, and sets the corresponding bit in the ISR if a valid interrupt request of a peripheral is pending. Additionally, the PIC determines the priority level of the request, and at the same time outputs a byte with the following format onto the data bus, which is read by the CPU:

I	—	—	—	—	P2	P1	P0

If a valid interrupt request is pending, then *I* is equal to 1, otherwise equal to 0. The three least significant bits *P2–P0* indicate the level of the request of highest priority. If the PIC is investigated by polling and not by means of an automatic $\overline{INTA}$ sequence, then the INT output of the PIC must not be connected to the processor. Instead, the CPU polls the PIC(s) periodically, as already mentioned. Therefore, even more than 64 interrupt levels can be realized (but with the described disadvantages, of course). As the INT output of the PIC is no longer connected to the processor, the 8259A can also be combined with other processors such as the 8086/88 and MCS-80/85 systems.

7.1.6 Masking the NMI

The NMI also belongs to the interrupts issued by hardware. Unlike the interrupt requests IRQx, an NMI is not fed over the 8259A PIC but is directly supplied by the processor via the NMI pin. A high-level signal at this connection gives rise to an interrupt 2 immediately after the current instruction has been completed. The NMI can neither be masked by the CLI instruction nor via the IMR in the 8259A PIC. It is always enabled and has the highest priority among all hardware interrupts.

The NMI is issued in the PC by the parity checking module of the memory controller. If the module detects a parity error upon reading a byte from main memory, it raises the NMI signal to a high level. On the screen appears a message reporting the parity error. Some new ATs have a second timer chip, the so-called failsafe timer, which periodically issues an NMI to avoid a «hang» of the computer if the IRQs are masked.

But during the boot procedure a serious problem now arises. The boot routine first has to initialize all the chips and memory, and to set up the interrupt vector table. For the IRQs this gives rise to no problems; a simple CLI instruction disables all interrupt requests. If the parity check module or the failsafe timer is in an undefined state, and if one of them issues an NMI, then the processor calls the as yet uninitialized handler for interrupt 2, as the NMI is not masked by the CLI instruction. But the interrupt vector table holds only a non-initialized value (that is, a wild pointer), which points to an unknown location. You can surely imagine that the PC will already have crashed in the boot process.

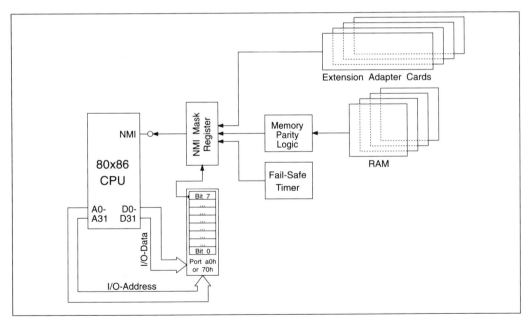

Figure 7.9: NMI and NMI mask register. The NMI issued by extension adapter cards, memory parity logic or the failsafe timer can be disabled by means of the NMI mask register. The register is controlled by bit 7 of port a0h (PC/XT) or 70h (AT).

To disable the NMI for initialization, each PC has an a NMI mask register. Figure 7.9 shows the signal path between parity module, failsafe timer and processor via the NMI mask register. In the PC/XT it is controlled by bit 7 of port a0h. Starting with the AT, bit 7 of port 70h carries out this job. If the bit is set, the NMI is masked. If the bit is cleared, the hardware can issue an NMI. Note that in the AT the address register for the CMOS RAM and the real-time clock are also located at port address 70h (see Section 7.7). If you want to alter the NMI mask bit then you need to read the port first. Now you can set or clear bit 7 and write back the byte with unchanged bits 0–6.

Example: Disable and enable the NMI in the AT; by calling nmi mask the NMI is disabled, by calling nmi unmask it is enabled.

```
/* nmi.c */
main(argc, argv)
int argc;
char *argv[];

{ int i;

  if (strcmpi(argv[1], "mask") != 0) {          /* check whether disable */
    if (strcmpi(argv[1], "unmask") != 0) {      /* check whether enable */
      printf("\n\nInvalid Argument %s", argv[1]); /* no valid argument */
      exit(1);                                  /* exit with ERRORLEVEL 1 */
    }
    else {                                      /* enable NMI */
      i = inp(0x70);                            /* read byte of port 70h */
      i = i & 0x7f;                             /* clear bit 7 */
      outp(0x70, i);                            /* write back byte to port 70h */
      printf("\n\nNMI enabled !!\n\n");         /* display message */
    }
  }
  else {                                        /* disable NMI */
    i = inp(0x70);                              /* read byte of port 70h */
    i = i | 0x80;                               /* set bit 7 */
    outp(0x70, i);                              /* write back byte to port 70h */;
    printf("\n\nNMI masked !!\n\n");            /* display message */
  }
  exit(0);                                      /* exit with ERRORLEVEL 0 */
}
```

You can easily test the consequences of masking the NMI. Disable the memory refresh by an extremely low refresh rate, or by deactivating counter 1 in the 8253/8254 PIT (see Section 7.2). After a short time the PC displays a memory parity error. If you additionally disable the NMI first by means of the command nmi mask and disable the memory refresh afterwards, then your computer crashes without displaying any message. Also here, parity errors have occurred and the hardware (the memory check module) has attempted to issue an NMI. But this NMI could not reach the CPU as the NMI mask register is locked. At some time the processor reads one or more destroyed (because they were not refreshed) bytes into the prefetch queue and hangs itself up. Don't worry; at the next hardware reset the ROM BIOS enables the NMI and the memory refresh correctly again.

7.2   8253/8254 Programmable Interval Timer

Every programmer is sometimes confronted with the problem of implementing certain delays into a program, for example to move a point slowly on-screen. Often, «dummy» loops of the following form are employed:

```
FOR I=0 TO 1000:NEXT I
```

But such delay loops have a significant disadvantage: they rely on the processor speed. The delay time can therefore be very different on a 50 Mhz i486 and on the ancestor 4.77 Mhz 8088 (namely by a factor of 100). Old computer games in particular make use of such loops, and the result is well known: while it is possible to «fly» on a PC with a 4.77 MHz 8088 with a flight simulator with no problems, the plane has crashed on a 50 MHz i486 before the pilot can operate a single key. But the problem of generating exactly defined time intervals also occurs in the system itself. DOS, for example, provides the time and date for every file, and the control of electric motors in floppy drives requires exactly defined signals. In both cases, time intervals defined by means of program loops are not suitable. Thus, the PC's designers have implemented one (PC/XT and most ATs) or sometimes two (some new ATs or EISA) *programmable interval timers (PITs)*.

7.2.1   Structure and Functioning of the 8253/8254 PIT

The PIT generates programmable time intervals from an external clock signal of a crystal oscillator that are defined independently from the CPU. The 8253/8254 is a very flexible PIT and has six operation modes in all. Figure 7.10 shows a block diagram of the 8253/8254's internal structure.

The 8253/8254 comprises three independently and separately programmable counters 0–2, each of which is 16 bits wide. Every counter is supplied with its own clock signal (CLK0–CLK2), which serves as the time base for each counter. In the original PC a 14 317 180Hz crystal provided the base clock which was divided by three to generate the 4.77 MHz clock signal for the processor. Further dividing by four leads to a signal with about 1.193180 MHz, which is applied to the three inputs CLK0–CLK2 of the 8253/8254 as the clock signal. In the PC, each of the three independent counters therefore runs with the same time base of 0.838 μs. Also today's PCs with processor clock frequencies between 4.77 MHz and 66 MHz have an oscillator that provides this 1.19318 MHz for the PIT(s).

To enable or trigger (see the section about 8253/8254 counting modes) a counter a gate signal GATE0–GATE2 is applied. Depending upon the counting mode, the counter concerned is activated by a transition low–high or a high level of the GATEx signal. Via the corresponding outputs OUT0–OUT2 the counter outputs a signal. Also, the shape of the output signals depends upon the counter's mode.

The data bus buffer together with the control/write logic reads and writes data from and to the PIT. The control register loads the counters and controls the various operation modes. Certain time intervals and signal shapes at outputs OUT0–OUT2 can thus be set. The counters may be read or written, but the control register is write-only. The 8254 also implements an additional command to read the control register (the read-back command).

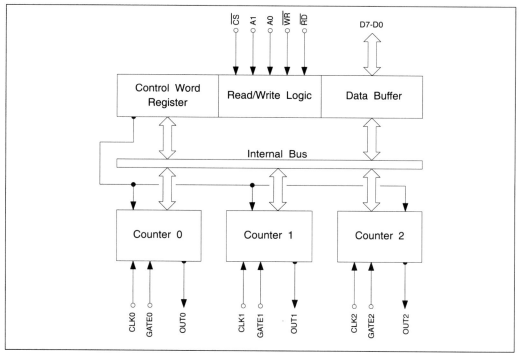

Figure 7.10: Structure of the 8253/8254 PIT. The timer chip comprises three independently operating counters 0 – 2, which are supplied separately with clock and control signals.

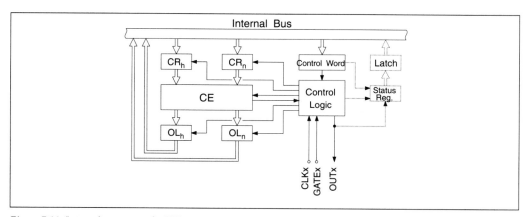

Figure 7.11: Internal structure of a PIT counter.

Figure 7.11 shows the internal structure of a counter. The central part is the counting element (CE), in which the counting process is carried out. The programmable control register defines the operation mode of the control logic, which in turn controls the counting element (CE), the high-order and low-order output latches OL_h, OL_n as well as the high-order and low-order count registers CR_h, CR_n. The 8254 additionally implements a status latch by means of which (and the read-back command) the 8254 outputs status information. When the CPU writes count values, the passed bytes are transferred into the count registers CR_h and CR_n first. Afterwards, the control logic transfers the two bytes simultaneously into the 16-bit counting element.

7.2.2 8253/8254 Terminals and Signals

8253 and 8254 coincide in view of their pin assignments and the meaning of the applied and output signals. The only difference between them is that the 8254 implements an additional command for reading the programmed status (read-back command). Figure 7.12 shows the pin assignment for the 8253/8254.

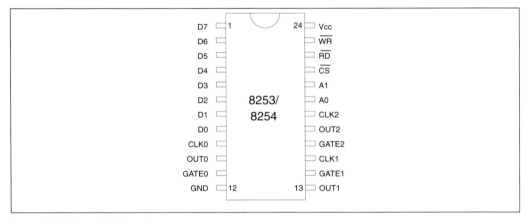

Figure 7.12: 8253/8254 pin assignment.

D7–D0 (pins 1–8)
These eight connections form the bidirectional data bus through which the 8253/8254 receives and provides data and instructions from or to the CPU.

CLK0, CLK1, CLK2 (pins 9, 15, 18)
These pins are supplied with the clock signals for the counters 0, 1 and 2, respectively.

OUT0, OUT1, OUT2 (pins 10, 13, 17)
These connections supply the output signals of the counters 0, 1 and 2, respectively.

GATE0, GATE1, GATE2 (pins 11, 14, 16)
These pins are supplied with the gate signals for the counters 0, 1 and 2, respectively, to enable the counters.

GND (pin 12)
The ground potential (usually 0 V) is applied to this pin.

V$_{cc}$ (pin 24)

The supply voltage (usually +5 V) is applied to this pin.

$\overline{WR}$ (pin 23)

(Write) If the signal at this pin is at a low level, the CPU writes data into the internal 8253/8254 registers via the data bus D7–D0.

$\overline{RD}$ (pin 22)

(Read) If the signal at this pin is at a low level, the CPU can read data from the internal 8253/8254 registers via the data bus D7–D0.

$\overline{CS}$ (pin 21)

(Chip Select) If this pin is on a low level, the CPU can read data from or write data to the internal 8253/8254 registers via the data bus D7–D0 using the $\overline{RD}$ and $\overline{WR}$ signals. Thus the $\overline{CS}$ signal enables the PIT for read and write processes. For the counting operation and the signals supplied by the PIT, $\overline{CS}$ has no meaning.

A0, A1 (pins 19, 20)

(Address) The signals at these pins indicate the number of the counter or the control register that the CPU accesses for data reading or writing. A0 and A1 are usually connected to the address bus of the system. The possible combinations of (A1, A0) have the following meanings:

```
(00)   counter 0
(01)   counter 1
(10)   counter 2
(11)   control register
```

7.2.3   Programming the 8253/8254

You may program the 8253/8254 PIT by first writing one control word via port 043h into the control register, and then one or two data bytes via the port of the intended counter. If the control register is loaded once, the counters may be overwritten with other values without accessing the control register again. Counting mode and format remain the same. Table 7.3 lists the port addresses of the various registers.

Port (1. PIT)	Port (2. PIT)	Register	Access type
040h	048h	counter 0	read/write
041h	049h	counter 1	read/write
042h	04ah	counter 2	read/write
043h	04bh	control register	write-only

Table 7.3: 8253/8254 register ports in a PC

The 8253 control register is write-only; no data can be read. For the 8254 a new command is available, the read-back command, with which certain control information can be determined.

Programming one of the three 8253/8254 counters is begun by writing a control word via port 043h (1st PIT) or 04bh (2nd PIT). Figure 7.13 shows the control word format.

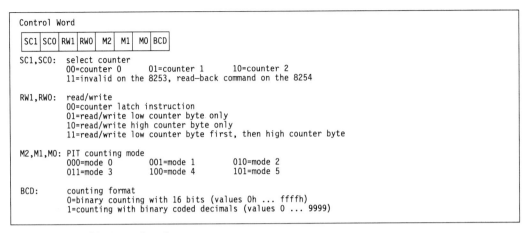

Figure 7.13: 8253/8254 control word.

7.2.4 Writing Count Values

To start a counter or load it with new values, you must first output a control word in which you define the intended counter, number and type of the byte to write, the counting mode of the counter concerned, and the counting format.

The bits *SC1* and *SC0* determine the counter to which the following entries refer. The combination SC1 = 1, SC0 = 1 is invalid on the 8253. On the 8254 this issues a read-back command for reading the control register (see below). With bits *RW1* and *RW0* you indicate which (low-order or high-order) and how many counter bytes you are going to write. If you specify that only the low-order or high-order byte is to be written, then you can also only read the low-order or high-order counter byte in a later read access. But the 8253/8254 is, nevertheless, operating as a 16-bit counter internally, that is, a high-order counter byte 10 doesn't mean a count value of 10 but $256*10 = 2560$. The counter latch command is important only for reading a counter. With the three mode bits *M2–M0* you define the counting mode of the counter selected via SC1, SC0 (details concerning the counting modes are given in the next section). Finally, the *BCD* bit determines the counting format. With a set BCD bit the counter operates with binary coded decimals, thus the range of values from 0 to 9999 is available. If BCD is equal to 0 then the counter performs a binary operation with 16 bits, and the counting range is 0 (0h) to 65 535 (ffffh).

According to bits RW1, RW0 you need to write either the low-order, the high-order, or both into the counter after passing the control word. With the combination RW1 = 0, RW0 = 1 (write low-order byte only) you provide the low-order byte via the port of the corresponding counter. According to the control word, the control logic recognizes that only the low-order byte will be passed and sets the high-order byte in CR_h automatically to 0. The same applies to the combination RW1 = 1, RW0 = 0 (write high-order byte only). In this case, the control logic sets the low-order byte in CR_n automatically to 0. If RW1 = 1, as well as RW0=1, then you first need to write the low-order byte and then the high-order byte by means of two OUT instructions. The control logic transfers the byte received first into the CR_n register and that received second into the CR_h register. For small counting values or counting values that are a multiple of 256, it is therefore sufficient to pass the low-order or high-order counter byte. You can then save one OUT instruction. This is important if you are generating ROM code, as here the available storage capacity is usually rather limited.

Example: Counter 2 shall output a square wave signal (mode 3) with a frequency of 10 kHz; the CLK frequency in the PC is 1.19318 MHz, thus the divisor has to be equal to 119. For this the low-order counter byte of counter 2 is sufficient; the high-order one is automatically set to 0.

```
MOV al, 01010110b ; load accumulator with the corresponding control word
OUT 43h, al       ; write control word via port 43h into the control register of first PIT
                  ; frequency shall be 10kHz, CLK frequency equal 1.19318MHz -> divisor 129
MOV al, 119       ; load low-order byte of counting value into accumulator
OUT 42h, al       ; write counting value into 2nd PIT
```

The maximum loadable count value is not ffffh (binary counting) or 999 (BCD counting), but 0. Upon the next CLK pulse the counter concerned jumps to ffffh or 9999, respectively, without resulting in any action. Once the value is decreased to 0 again, it outputs a signal according to the programmed mode at the OUTx pin. Thus the value 0 corresponds to 2^{16} for binary counting and 10^4 for counting with BCDs.

7.2.5 Reading Count Values

Two options for reading a counter are available on the 8253, and three on the 8254:

- direct reading by means of one or two IN instructions;
- counter latch command;
- read-back command (8254 only).

When reading a counter you should not use the first option but transfer the current state of the counting element (CE) into the output latches OL_h and OL_n, and latch there using the counter latch or read-back command. Latch OL_h then holds the high-order byte, and latch OL_n the low-order byte of the counting element. One or two successive IN instructions for the port address of the counter concerned then read these latches. If only the low-order (RW1 = 0, RW0 = 1) or high-order byte (RW1 = 1, RW0 = 0) was written when the counter was loaded with the initial counting value, then read the current counting value of the initially written byte by a single IN instruction. A succeeding IN instruction fetches the non-latched value of the low-order or high-order counter byte at the time of the IN instruction and not the corresponding second byte of the 16-bit counting element. This is only possible if you have previously written the low-order as well as the high-order counter byte. In this case you need to read the current counter value by means of two IN instructions. The PIT returns the low-order byte of the 16-bit counter with the first IN instruction, and then the high-order byte with the second IN instruction.

The processor doesn't access the counting element (CE) directly, only the output latches. If the content of CE has been transferred once by a counter latch command into the output latches, then this value is held there until the PU executes one or two IN instructions, or until the corresponding counter is reprogrammed. Successive counter latch commands are ignored if the output latches haven't been read before. The counting element, however, also continues to count after a counter latch command; the counter latch makes only a «snapshot» of the counting element CE. If you read the counter in the mode RW1 = 0, RW0 = 0 directly without the counter latch command by means of two IN instructions, then the counter value may have changed already when you issue the second IN instruction. Thus the high-order byte of the counting element CE read secondly doesn't fit the low-order byte read first. The determined values do not coincide with the actual values. As an interrupt or a memory refresh may occur between two successive IN instructions, for example, the period between the execution of two IN instructions is not predictable. Therefore, you should always issue a counter latch command or determine the counter value by means of a read-back command. Figure 7.14 shows the format of the control word for the counter latch command.

```
┌─────────────────────────────────────────────────────────────────────┐
│  ┌───┬───┬───┬───┬───┬───┬───┬───┐                                    │
│  │SC1│SC0│ 0 │ 0 │ X │ X │ X │ X │                                    │
│  └───┴───┴───┴───┴───┴───┴───┴───┘                                    │
│  SC1, SC0: counter to latch                                           │
│  X:        values without any meaning, use X=0 for compatibility      │
└─────────────────────────────────────────────────────────────────────┘
```

Figure 7.14: Counter latch command format.

To determine the current counter value you have to output a counter latch command for the counter to read via ports 043h or 04bh. According to the programmed mode, you issue one or two IN instructions for the counter concerned afterwards. But ensure that in all cases the counter has been programmed with one or two bytes before. The read 8-bit or 16-bit value then indicates the current counter value at the time of the counter latch command in the programmed counting mode (binary or BCD). If the thus determined 8-bit value is the high-order counter byte, then you need to multiply it (at least in your head) by 256 to get the «real» value that the counting element CE in the PIT uses.

Example: Determine value of counter 2; the counter has initially been loaded with low—order and high—order bytes.

```
MOV al, 10000000b ; load counter latch command for counter 2 into al
OUT 43h, al       ; output counter latch command to control register
IN al, 42h        ; read low—order counter byte into al
IN ah, 42h        ; read high—order counter byte into ah
                  ; thus ax=ah.al contains the current 16—bit counter value
```

The first IN instruction transfers the low-order byte of the counting element (CE), which is held by the latch CL_n into the least significant byte al of the accumulators ax; the second IN instruction loads the high-order byte held by the latch CL_h into the most significant accumulator byte ah. Thus, ax contains the 16-bit counter value after the two INs.

Unfortunately, there is no possibility of determining the initial value of a counter directly. This would be useful, for example, for investigating the refresh rate of counter 1. The only option is to read the counter concerned often, and to regard the maximum read value as the initial value. Another disadvantage is that on the 8253 the programmed counting mode cannot be determined. However, the interpretation of the read counter value is very different depending upon whether the counter operates with binary or BCD numbers. Further, it cannot be determined whether the counter has been loaded with a low-order and a high-order byte or only with one of them. This is necessary, though, to determine the counting rate of a PIT that is programmed in an unknown way. Without knowing the counting mode you can only speculate when interpreting the read values.

The newer PIT model, the 8254 (used first with the AT), implements the possibility of also reading the counter's mode by means of a read-back command as a significant advance. Additionally, with the read-back command you can determine the current counter value. You issue the read-back command via the control register (ports 43h or 04bh). Figure 7.15 shows the format of this new 8254 command.

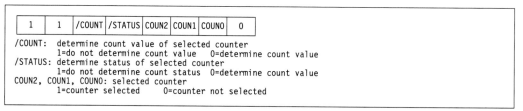

Figure 7.15: Read-back command format.

The two most significant bits define the read-back command with their value 11b (compare with Figure 7.13). $\overline{\text{COUNT}}$ indicates that the value and $\overline{\text{STATUS}}$ that the counting mode of a counter is to be determined. Note that $\overline{\text{COUNT}}$ and $\overline{\text{STATUS}}$ are complementary signals, which issue the intended action if you set the bit concerned to 0, and not 1 as usual. The bits COUN0 to COUN2 define the counter whose value or mode is to be determined.

With the read-back command you can issue several counter latch commands in parallel by indicating several counters simultaneously with the bits COUN0 to COUN2. The 8254 then behaves as if you had issued several counter latch commands (see Figure 7.14) individually, and transfers the individual CE values into the latches CL_n and CL_h of each counter. All successive counter latch commands, whether issued by its own counter latch or a further read-back command are ignored if the counter concerned hasn't been read by one or two IN instructions.

It is also possible to determine the value as well as the mode of a counter by means of the read-back command. If you only want to determine the value of a counter then set $\overline{\text{COUNT}}$=0 and $\overline{\text{STATUS}}$=1. In this case the read-back command is equivalent to one (if you set only one single COUNx = 1; x = 0, 1, 2) or more counter latch commands (if you set several COUNx = 1). For the number and interpretation of the IN instructions the same applies as for a normal counter latch command.

If, however, you want to determine the programmed mode of a certain counter, then set $\overline{\text{STATUS}}$ = 0 and $\overline{\text{COUNT}}$ = 1. Also, in this case, it is possible to select several counters simultaneously. You only need to set several COUNx to 1. The read-back command latches the current mode and supplies a status byte at the port address of the counter(s) concerned. You can fetch this status byte with an IN instruction. If you issue a new read-back command to determine the mode without having read out the counter concerned in advance, then this second command is ignored. The latches further contain the mode at the time of issuing the first command. Figure 7.16 shows the status byte format.

```
┌─────┬──────┬─────┬─────┬─────┬─────┬─────┬─────┐
│ Pin │ Null │ RW1 │ RW0 │ M2  │ M1  │ M0  │ BCD │
└─────┴──────┴─────┴─────┴─────┴─────┴─────┴─────┘
Pin:  status of OUTx pin
      1=OUTx pin high      0=OUTx pin low
Null: is count element already loaded with start value?
      1=count element not yet loaded, count value cannot be read
      0=count element loaded, count value can be read
RW1, RW0, M2, M1, M0, BCD: programmed counting mode (see Figure 7.13)
```

Figure 7.16: Status byte format.

The *Pin* bit indicates the current status of the concerned counter's OUTx pin. If Pin = 1 then the counter provides a high-level signal (+5 V), otherwise it supplies a low-level signal (0 V). The bit *Null* shows whether the last written counter value has already been transferred to the counting element CE by latches CR_n and CR_h. Depending upon the programmed counting mode, this may last some time. Not before Null = 0 is it meaningful to read back the counter value. Before this the PIT returns a value that further reflects the old state. The remaining six bits RW1, RW0, M2–M0 and BCD return the values with which they have been loaded for the counter concerned during the last write of the control register (see Figure 7.13). Thus you can determine, for example, whether you need to read the low-order or high-order byte with a single IN instruction only, or whether you must issue two IN instructions to get the current value of a counter.

Example: determine counting mode of counter 0

```
MOV al, 11100010b ; load accumulator with read-back command for mode: /COUNT=1, /STATUS=0
OUT 43h, al       ; output read-back command to control register
IN  al, 40h       ; get mode via port of counter 0
```

It is assumed that the status byte in the accumulator al has the value 00110100b. Thus the OUT pin is on a 0 V-level, the counter has been already loaded with the latest passed value, the low-order and high-order bytes are used, the counting mode is equal to 2, and the counting proceeds in a binary fashion with 16 bits. This mode is used, for example, to issue the interrupt 08h that updates the internal system clock.

In the read-back command you may also combine the determination of counter mode and value. Set $\overline{\text{COUNT}}$ as well as $\overline{\text{STATUS}}$ to 0 in this case. All counters specified by means of COUN0 to COUN2 then return information concerning the counting mode and the current count value. With the first IN instruction referring to a selected counter you get the status byte; with the second or second and third IN instructions, the PIT returns the low-order and/or high-order byte of the currently latched counter value. All further IN instructions pass non-latched counter values as they are taken from the counting element (CE) but no more status bytes. Ensure that all counters selected with bits COUN0 to COUN2 are read completely by means of two or three IN instructions; otherwise, further counter latch or read-back commands may be ignored.

If you output a counter latch command and later a read-back command to determine the counting mode without having read the counter value before, then the PIT first supplies the status byte with the first IN instructions and only afterwards the byte(s) that indicate the counter value. Thus the order of passing latched bytes is always the same. If you have read the counting value in advance of the read-back command, then the IN instruction after the read-back command of course returns the latched status byte.

7.2.6   8253/8254 Counting Modes

The 8253/8254 recognizes six different counting modes in all. Further, the PIT can count in binary or in binary coded decimals. Figure 7.17 shows the signals that are supplied by the OUTx connection in each mode, as well as the meaning of the trigger signals at the GATEx input.

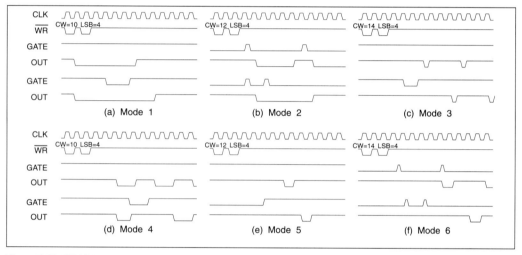

Figure 7.17: 8253/8254 operating modes.
(a) Mode 0: interrupt on terminal count; (b) Mode 1: programmable monoflop;
(c) Mode 2: rate generator; (d) Mode 3: square-wave generator;
(e) Mode 4: software triggered pulse; (f) Mode 5: hardware triggered pulse

In the following the various operation modes are briefly explained. In all modes the PIT counts from initial count values down to lower values. If you newly write the control register, then the control logic is immediately reset and the output OUT of the counter concerned is reset to a defined initial state.

You may write new counting values into one of the counters at any time, but you have to observe the last programmed mode (low-order and/or high-order counter byte, etc.). The new values, however, become effective at different times in the various modes. If a counter has reached the value 0, then it does not stop to count in the non-periodical modes 0, 1, 4 and 5, but continues with ffffh (BCD = 0) or 9999 (BCD = 1). The OUT pin, however, is not reset, and the counting operation only occurs internally without any external consequences.

In some modes the GATE signal executes the counting operation: if GATE = 1 then the 8253/8254 continues counting, otherwise it keeps the current value without any change. In other modes a low–high transition or a high level at the GATE input starts the counting operation; the GATE pulse acts as a trigger. Even if GATE then returns to a low level, the counter continues to work. The entity N in the following description names the initial counter value.

Mode 0 (Interrupt on Terminal Count)

After the control register and the initial count value have been written, the counter is loaded upon the next CLK pulse. The OUT pin is on a low level (0 V) at the start of counting. If the counter reaches the value 0, then OUT rises and remains on a high level (+5 V) until a new count value or a new control word for mode 0 is written. If GATE = 1 the counter concerned counts down; if GATE = 0 the count value is kept.

If a new count value is written into a counter it is loaded upon the next CLK pulse, and the counter continues the counting operation with the newly loaded value. Also, if GATE = 0 the counter can be loaded, but the counting operation doesn't start until GATE rises to a high level.

Mode 0 is mostly used to issue a hardware interrupt after the elapse of a certain time period. The PC uses mode 2 for the periodic timer interrupt as mode 0 is not periodic.

Mode 1 (Programmable Monoflop)

After writing the control register and the initial count value, the output OUT is on a high level (+5 V) for the moment. A trigger (transition low–high) at the GATE input loads the counter. Upon the next CLK pulse, OUT drops to a low level (0 V) and remains at that level until the counter has reached the value 0. Then OUT rises to a high level. Not until one CLK pulse after the next trigger does OUT fall again to a low level. Thus, in mode 1 the PIT generates a triggered one-shot pulse with a duration of N CLK cycles and a low level.

If another trigger pulse appears during the course of a count operation (that is, while OUT is at a low level), the PIT reloads the counter with the initial value. Thus the OUT pin is at a low level N CLK cycles after the last trigger pulse. Unlike mode 0, the PIT can be triggered in this mode.

If you write a new count value while the PIT is counting in mode 1, the new value is not effective for the current process. Not until the next trigger pulse at the GATE input is the new count value transferred to the counter. The trigger pulse can occur, of course, when the PIT has not yet completed the current counting operation. The single pulse with a low level lasts in this case until the PIT has counted the new count value down to 0.

Mode 2 (Rate Generator)

After the control word and the initial count value N have been loaded, the PIT starts counting upon the next CLK pulse. As soon as the counter reaches the value 1, OUT drops to a low level for one CLK cycle. Thus the 8253/8254 generates a short peak pulse. Afterwards, the initial count value is automatically reloaded and the PIT restarts the same counting operation again; mode 2 is therefore periodic. The distance of two OUT pulses is N CLK cycles long.

A signal GATE = 1 enables (and a signal GATE = 0 disables) the counter. If GATE drops to a low level during the counting operation and rises to a high level later, the PIT loads the initial count value at the rise and starts counting. Thus the 8253/8254 can be triggered by a hardware pulse in mode 2. On the other hand, the PIT starts immediately after writing the last data byte. With an active GATE the PIT can therefore also be triggered by software, that is, by the last write access.

Mode 2 is used for counter 2 in the PC for the periodic timer interrupt. The low–high transition during the rise of signal CLK0 issues a hardware interrupt IRQ0 corresponding to INT 08h via the 8259A PIC. The count value must not be equal to 1.

Mode 3 (Square-Wave Generator)

Mode 3 generates a periodic square-wave signal with a period of N CLK cycles. Initially, OUT is at a high level. If half of the N CLK cycles have elapsed, then OUT drops to a low level. After the counter has reached the value 0, OUT again rises to a high level, and the initial value N is reloaded into the counter. Mode 3 is therefore periodically like mode 2. But unlike mode 2, the low-phase of the OUT pin lasts N/2 CLK cycles, not only a single CLK cycle. If GATE = 1 the counter is operating; if GATE = 0 it is stopped. A drop of GATE to a low level while the OUT pin is also on a low level immediately raises OUT to a high level. A rise from a low to a high level at the GATE input (trigger pulse) loads the counter with the initial count value and starts the counting operation. Thus the PIT can be synchronized by hardware in mode 2. After the control register and the initial count value have been written, the 8253/8254 loads the counter upon the next CLK pulse. Thus, the PIT can also be synchronized by software.

A new count value supplied during the course of an active counting operation doesn't affect the current process. At the end of the current half cycle the PIT loads the new value.

The length of the low and high states differs for odd and even values of N. As a CLK cycle defines the smallest possible time resolution, no time periods with half the CLK cycle length can be generated. With an odd N the OUT pin is initially at a high level. The PIT loads the value N–1 (that is, an even number) into the counter, and begins to decrement this value (in steps) by two. Once the CLK pulse after the counter has reached a value of 0, the potential at OUT drops to a low level and the counter is reloaded with N – 1. This value is decremented (again in steps) by two. If the value of 0 is reached, then OUT rises to a high level and the whole process is repeated. Thus the signal at the OUT pin is at a high level for (N + 1)/2 CLK cycles and at a low level for (N – 1)/2 CLK cycles, that is, the signal is low somewhat longer than it is high.

With even N values, N is loaded unaltered into the counter and decremented in steps by two. If the value 0 is reached, then OUT drops to a low level and the initial value N is reloaded immediately. After the counter has counted downwards in steps of two, OUT rises again to a high level and the whole process is repeated. Thus, even with N values, the phases with high and low levels are equal in time. In both cases, the period of the square wave signal lasts N CLK cycles. The initial value must be at least equal to 2.

The generated square-wave signal can be used, for example, to transmit data via serial interfaces. The PIT then operates as a baud rate generator. In the PC, counters 1 and 2 are operated in mode 3 to drive the memory refresh and the speaker, respectively.

Mode 4 (Software-Triggered Pulse)

Initially, OUT is at a high level. If the counter has reached the value 0, then OUT drops to a low level for one CLK cycle and rises again to a high level afterwards. If GATE is at a high level the counter is operating; if GATE = 0 it is disabled. Thus the triggering is carried out by software as the PIT starts counting after the control register and initial count values are written. Because the counter is loaded upon the first CLK pulse after writing and doesn't start counting until the next CLK cycle OUT drops (if GATE = 1) to a low level N+1 CLK cycles after the write process. Unlike mode 2, the PIT doesn't operate periodically in mode 4. Only a newly written count value triggers the counter again.

If you write a new count value while a counting operation is active, the PIT loads the new value upon the next CLK cycle and continues counting, starting with the new initial value. Thus the 8253/8254 is retriggerable in mode 4 by means of software.

Mode 5 (Hardware-Triggered PULSE)

The pulse form at the OUT pin coincides with that in mode 4. But the triggering is carried out with a low–high transition of GATE. By means of this, the PIT loads the initial count value into the counter upon the next CLK cycle, and the counting process starts. If the value 0 is reached, OUT drops for a single CLK cycle to a low level, and immediately afterwards rises to a high level again. Thus, OUT drops to a low level N + 1 CLK cycles after a trigger pulse at the GATE input. If a trigger pulse occurs during a counting operation, the PIT reloads the initial value into the counter and continues counting with the initial value. Thus in mode 5 the 8253/8254 can be triggered by hardware.

If you write a new count value during the course of an active counting operation then this operation is not affected. Only after the next trigger pulse does the PIT load the new initial value.

In the following sections the application of the various counters in the PC are discussed.

7.2.7   System Clock

DOS and other operating systems use a system clock for the internal management of date and time. Using this system, the clock date and the time of the last change of directories and files are determined, alarms are issued at a certain time, etc. Besides this system clock, most PCs also have a so-called real-time clock. Unlike the PITs and the connected system clock, the real-time clock runs even if the computer is switched off. The PC queries the clock during the boot process, so you no longer need to input the date and time at power-up. Details on the real-time clock and the allocated CMOS RAM are discussed in Section 7.7.

All programming languages available for the PC implement functions to read this internal system clock. The instructions are, for example, TIMER in BASIC, _dos_gettime in C, or the direct call of INT 21h, function 2ch. This system clock is realized by counter 0 of the first (or only) 8253/8254 PIT, the 8259A PIC and the handler routines for the interrupts 08h and 1ch. Figure 7.18 shows a scheme for this.

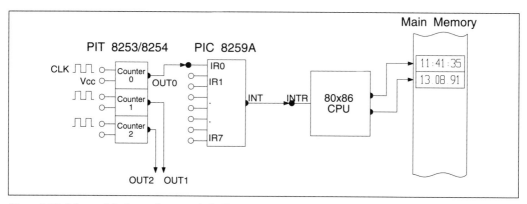

Figure 7.18: Scheme of the internal system clock. The counter 0 periodically issues a hardware interrupt via IRQ0 so that the CPU can update the DOS system clock.

The output OUT0 of counter 0 in the 8253/8254 PIT is connected to the input IR0 (corresponding to IRQ0) of the first (or only) 8259A PIC. The counter 0 operates in mode 2 (rate generator) with periodic binary counting. The CLK0 input is connected to an oscillator's output in the same way as CLK1 and CLK2, which provides a frequency of 1.19318 MHz. The GATE0 input is soldered to the supply potential V_{cc} = + 5 V so that counter 0 is always enabled. The initial count value is equal 0h or 2^{16}, that is, the PIT outputs a peak pulse exactly 1.19318 MHz/65 536=18.206 times per second. The transition from low–high at the end of the pulse issues a hardware interrupt in the 8259A PIC, which operates in the edge-triggered mode. In Section 7.1.5 the values of the PIC registers upon initialization are indicated.

An interrupt request on IR0 leads via the accompanying acknowledge sequence between PIC and 80x86 processor to an interrupt 08h. The allocated handler updates the system clock, which is a simple DOS-internal data structure, 18.206 times per second. Further, the handler calls interrupt 1ch by explicitly executing the INT 1ch instruction. This 1ch interrupt is called the user exit of the timer interrupt IRQ0. Afterwards, the handler of interrupt 08h completes the hardware interrupt by passing an EOI command to the PIC. Table 7.4 shows the structure of the BIOS data area as far as the DOS system clock is concerned.

Address	Size	Contents	Meaning
40:6c	word	low timer count	⌐number of timer pulses
40:6e	word	high timer count	⌐since 0:00 a.m.
40:70	byte	timer overflow flag	1=24h-boundary passed

Table 7.4: BIOS data area for the DOS system clock

Usually, the interrupt vector of interrupt 1ch points to a simple IRET instruction. But a programmer can redirect the entry in the interrupt vector table to his/her own routine, which is called 18.2 times per second. It is preferable to use the user exit 1ch instead of the system interrupt 08h. Popular applications are the periodic activation of TSR programs, which check the status of floppy or hard disk drives to read data. One example of such programs is the DOS command (and program) PRINT. Section 7.4 briefly describes the cooperation of timer interrupt

IRQ0 and the PIT counter 2 to output tone sequences in the background independently of the CPU.

Example: The program shall display the time according to the internal system clock; after the first keyboard hit the clock is accelerated by a factor of eight; upon the second keyboard hit the clock is updated normally.

```
main()
{
  displaytime();      /* display time in upper left corner and wait for first keyboard hit */

  /* accelerate by factor 8 */
  outp(0x43,0x34);    /* output control word 00110100b */
  outp(0x40,0x00);    /* low-order counter byte */
  outp(0x40,0x20);    /* high-order counter byte */
  displaytime();      /* display fast running time and wait for second keyboard hit */

  /* time with normal speed */
  outp(0x43,0x34);    /* output control word 00110100b */
  outp(0x40,0x00);    /* low-order counter byte */
  outp(0x40,0x00);    /* high-order counter byte */
  displaytime();      /* display normal running time */

  exit(0);
}

void displaytime(void)
{ struct dostime_t time;

  for (;;) {
    _dos_gettime (&time);        /* get time */
    /* display time in the format hour:minute:second:100th second */
    _settextposition (1, 1), printf("%i:%i:%i:%i            ",
      time.hour,time.minute,time.second,time.hsecond);
    if (kbhit()) {    /* return on keyboard hit */
      getch();
      return;
    }
  }
}
```

Note: The output of control word 00110100b via port 0x43 to the control register is not absolutely necessary as the defined mode need not be altered; it is sufficient to supply the low-order and high-order counter bytes via port 0x40.

Instead of mode 2, the PIT counter 0 may also be operated in mode 3, because in this case the transition from low–high of the square wave signal also issues a hardware interrupt via the 8259A PIC. In this case, the control word 00110100b has to be changed to 00110110b. As the other 8253/8254 modes 0, 1, 4 and 5 are not periodic, the internal clock stops if you operate the PIT in one of these modes. Try it if you like. Later, after a boot process by means of Ctrl-Alt-Del, the BIOS sets up the original mode again.

7.2.8   Memory Refresh

Besides the periodic activation of the hardware interrupt IRQ0, the PIT is also used in the PC for refreshing dynamic main memory regularly. For this purpose, PC designers have reserved counter 1, which instructs all 18 CLK cycles on a DMA chip to carry out a dummy read cycle. In the course of this dummy cycle, data is read from memory onto the data bus and the address buffers, and address decoders and sense amplifiers in the memory chips are activated to refresh one memory cell row. But the data is not taken off the data bus by a peripheral. Upon the next bus cycle it disappears. Details concerning the refreshing of dynamic memory chips (DRAMs) are discussed in Chapter 6. Here I want to explain the use of counter 1 in the 8253/8254 PIT. Figure 7.19 shows the principal connection of timer and DMA chip for memory refresh.

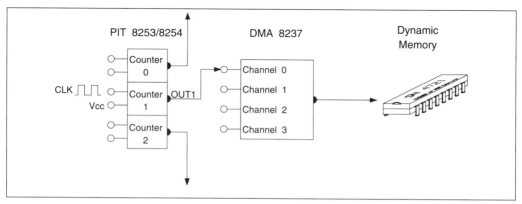

Figure 7.19: Connection of timer and DMA chip for the memory refresh. The counter periodically activates channel 0 of the 8237A DMA chip, which carries out a dummy read cycle to refresh the DRAM memory.

Counter 1 is operated in mode 3 (square-wave generator) with a count value of 18 (12h). Only the low-order counter byte is loaded (RW1 = 0, RW0 = 1), that is, the PIT generates a square-wave signal with a frequency of 1.19318 MHz/18 = 66 288 Hz. Thus, counter 1 issues a dummy read cycle every 15 μs by means of the rising edge of the generated square wave signal. The read cycle refreshes the memory. By means of the read-back and/or counter latch command, you may determine the refresh rate of your PC. Usually, you should obtain the same value as indicated above, but as the memory refresh is very hardware-dependent, other values are also possible.

System designers usually lay out the memory refresh rather carefully, that is, the memory is refreshed more often than is really necessary. The so-called *refresh overhead* (that is, the proportion of memory accesses which are caused by the refresh) can reach 10% and more. Modern and very «tight» memory chips in particular require a refresh much less frequently than older models. You may decrease the refresh rate of your PC and gain up to 5% more data throughput without degrading the reliability. Data losses because of too low a refresh rate give rise to parity errors upon reading main memory. A corresponding message then appears on the screen. Therefore, do not set the refresh rate too low.

Example: The following listing contains a program that sets up the refresh rate of your PC. The call is carried by means of "refresh <count>" where count indicates the number of CLK cycles after which the PIT shall request a memory refresh by means of the generated square wave. On the PC this value is normally equal to 18. With the program you can set values between 2 and 255 as only the low–order counter byte is loaded.

```c
main(argc, argv)  /* program called refresh.c */

int argc;
char *argv[];

{ int count;

  if (argc < 2) {                        /* no argument is passed, exit with ERRORLEVEL 2 */
    printf("\n\nArgument is missing!\nFormat:  refresh <count>\n\n");
    exit(2);
  }

  count=atoi(argv[1]);

  if (count < 0x02 || count > 0xff) {  /* invalid argument, exit with ERRORLEVEL 1 */
    printf("\n\nInvalid value %d !!\n\n", count);
    exit(1);
  }

  /* set new refresh rate */
  outp(0x43, 0x56);                    /* 01010110b, output only LSB */
  outp(0x41, count);                   /* write refresh counter value */

  printf("\n\nNew refresh value %d set.\n\n", count);
  exit(0);
}
```

The listed example program loads only the low-order byte of counter 1. The counter values are therefore limited to the range between 2 and 255. You are, of course, free to program an extension with which you can also set higher initial values. For this purpose, however, you must also use the high-order byte and load the control register with the value 01010110b instead of 01110110b, and then pass the low-order as well as the high-order byte. With high-quality chips, refresh count values of up to 1000 can be achieved without the occurrence of parity errors.

You are really free to experiment; set various refresh values and check their effects on computer performance using benchmark programs. The effect is not very significant, but you get some feeling for the «buttons» to turn to in a computer so that the performance is enhanced. After all, ten times 5% is 50%! But for permanent operation you should proceed carefully. What's the gain of 0.1% performance enhancement if your PC crashes when you are editing an important text or program? And this danger is always present while doing such experiments.

7.2.9   The Speaker

Counter 2 of the first (or only) PIT is dedicated to the tone frequency generation for the installed speaker. You may generate various frequencies with it. How this is carried out and which points you must observe is described in Section 7.4.

7.2.10 Failsafe Timer

Some newer ATs incorporate a second 8254 PIT, but only counter 0 of this PIT is used, the others usually being free. The counter's output OUT0 is connected to the NMI input of the processor via some circuitry. (See Figure 7.20 on this subject.)

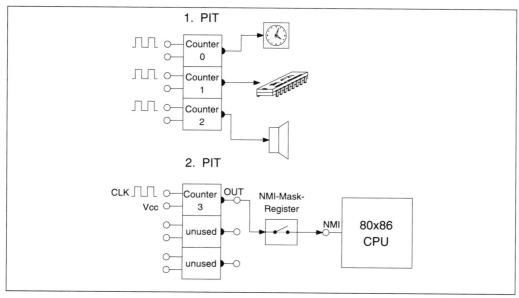

Figure 7.20: Failsafe timer wiring. Counter 3 is used as the failsafe timer which issues an NMI via the NMI mask register as soon as a certain time period has elapsed.

A signal rise from low–high at the OUT0 pin generates a non-maskable interrupt. This is useful if all hardware interrupts are intentionally blocked, or because of a program error by means of a CLI instruction or masking in the PICs, and the computer is looping. Then the PC responds neither to a keyboard hit nor to another external request, except a hardware reset – the computer hangs. Only the NMI issued by the second PIT can «free» the CPU, hence the name failsafe timer. Especially for multitasking systems such as OS/2 or UNIX, such a last resort is useful if, despite all the care taken and the use of protected mode, a program error hangs up the computer and all other tasks are affected. While developing an operating system this happens frequently, and the system programmer will certainly be very thankful for the presence of such a failsafe device.

The NMI handler (interrupt 2) can, of course, determine whether the source of the interrupt is counter 0 of the second PIT or a parity error when data is read from a memory chip. In the latter case, a serious hardware malfunction has occurred. The PC must be shut down immediately, or at least as quickly as possible to avoid extensive data loss or damage.

7.3   DMA Chip 8237A – A Detour Highway in the PC

Besides the CPU, the PC has another chip that accesses the main memory or peripherals on its own – the 8237A DMA controller chip. Compared with access via the CPU, direct memory access was placed in the background in the AT, probably because IBM was unable to make up its mind and implement a fast-clocked 16-bit DMA chip. Instead, the Stone Age era chips of the PC/XT are also used here. Only with EISA and MCA has DMA became interesting again because of the 32-bit chip employed. But first let us see what's hiding behind the often neglected and seemingly obscure term DMA.

7.3.1   Direct Memory Access with Peripherals and Memory

Powerful computers with a multitasking operating system in particular use the DMA concept to free the CPU from simple but time-consuming data transfers. The *DMA chip* or *DMA controller* establishes a second path between the peripheral and main memory in a computer system. Figure 7.21 shows the principles of the direct memory access concept.

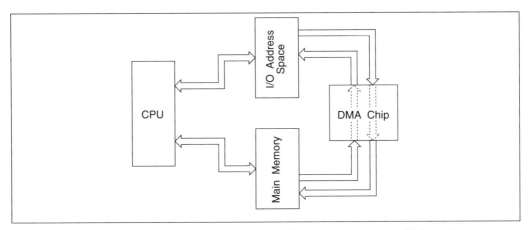

Figure 7.21: DMA. During in the course of a DMA cycle, a peripheral can exchange data with the main memory without any intervention from the CPU.

The CPU transfers data from a peripheral into an internal register, and from this register into the main memory. Of course, the transfer can also be carried out in the opposite direction. The arrows in Figure 7.21 indicate that this is a 2-step process, where an internal CPU register is always involved. If a large data block is to be transferred, the CPU can be occupied for quite a long time with this rather trivial job.

Remedial action uses the DMA chip, which establishes a second data path between the peripheral and main memory. The data transfer is not carried out via an internal register of the DMA chip, but immediately via the data bus between the peripheral and main memory. The DMA controller outputs only the address and bus control signals, thus the peripheral can access main memory directly for a read or write – hence the reason for the name DMA. The CPU is therefore freed from data transfers, and can execute other processes.

The peripherals are usually allocated a *DMA channel*, which they activate by means of a *DMA request signal (DREQ)*. The DMA chip responds to this request and carries out data transfer via this channel. This is useful, for example, when reading a sector from disk: the CPU initializes the DMA controller in a suitable manner and issues the corresponding FDC (Floppy Disk Controller) command. The FD (Floppy Disk) controller moves the read/write head to the intended sector, and activates the read head and the DMA controller. Then the DMA controller transfers the sector data into a buffer in the main memory. By means of a hardware interrupt, the FD controller informs the CPU about the completion of the command. The whole process between outputting the command to the FDC and the hardware interrupt from the FDC is carried out by the FDC and the DMA controller without any intervention from the CPU. Meanwhile, the processor has, for example, calculated the shading of a drawing or the makeup of a page to be printed.

Some DMA chips (for example, the 8237A used in PCs) additionally implement a transfer within main memory, that is, copying a data block to another memory address. Because of the very powerful i386 and i486 processors with their 32-bit data bus and the repeatable string instruction REP MOVSW, this capability is rarely used.

7.3.2 8237A Terminals and Signals

The original 8237A comes in a 40-pin DIP. Its pin assignment scheme is shown in Figure 7.22. As is the case for other chips, too, the DMA controller is often integrated together with other functional units (like the 8259A PIC or the 8253/8254 PIT) into a single LSI chip.

$\overline{\text{IOR}}$ (pin 1)
(I/O Read) In the 8237A standby state the CPU reads an internal register of the DMA chip by pulling $\overline{\text{IOR}}$ to a low level. If the 8237A is active and controls the data and address bus, then an active $\overline{\text{IOR}}$ signal indicates that the DMA chip is reading data from a peripheral via a port address. The $\overline{\text{IOR}}$ signal can be active during a write transfer (peripheral–memory).

$\overline{\text{IOW}}$ (pin 2)
(I/O Write) In the 8237A standby state the CPU writes data into an internal register of the DMA chip by activating $\overline{\text{IOW}}$. If the 8237A is active and controls the data and address bus, then an active $\overline{\text{IOW}}$ signal indicates that the DMA chip is currently writing data to a peripheral via a port address. The $\overline{\text{IOW}}$ signal can be active during a read transfer (memory–peripheral).

$\overline{\text{MEMR}}$ (pin 3)
(Memory Read) The 8237A uses the $\overline{\text{MEMR}}$ signal to inform the bus control that data is read from main memory. The $\overline{\text{MEMR}}$ signal can be active (that is, low) during a read transfer or a memory–memory transfer.

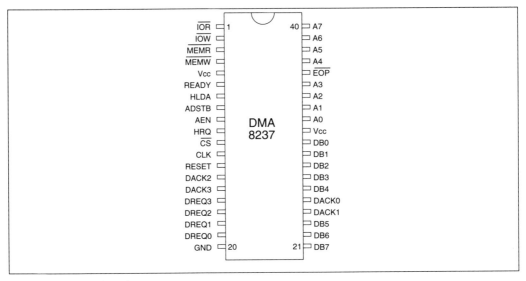

Figure 7.22: 8237A pin assignment.

$\overline{\text{MEMW}}$ (pin 4)

(Memory Write) The 8237A uses the $\overline{\text{MEMW}}$ signal to inform the bus control that data is being written into main memory. The $\overline{\text{MEMW}}$ signal can be active (that is, low) during a write transfer or a memory–memory transfer.

READY (pin 6)

Slow memories or peripherals may activate the input signal READY to extend the 8237A read and write cycles. The 80x86 processors use the same strategy during accesses to main memory and peripherals.

HLDA (pin 7)

(Hold Acknowledge) The HLDA signal from the CPU or another bus master informs the DMA chip that the CPU has released the local bus, and that the 8237A is allowed to take over control to carry out a data transfer.

ADSTB (pin 8)

(Address Strobe) The signal is used to fetch the high-order address byte A8–A15 into an external DMA address latch. The 8237A activates ADSTB if the high-order address byte A8–A15 is available on the data bus DB0–DB7.

AEN (pin 9)

(Address Enable) The 8237A provides a signal at this pin to activate the external DMA address latch. If AEN is at a high level, the DMA address latch puts the stored address as address bits A8–A15 onto the address bus. AEN can also be used to disable other bus drivers that generate address bits A8–A15 on their own, or to deactivate peripheral components.

HRQ (pin 10)
(Hold Request) With HRQ the 8237A DMA chip requests control of the local bus from the CPU or another bus master. The CPU responds with an HLDA signal. The 8237A activates HRQ if a non-masked DRQx signal or a DMA request by software occurs.

$\overline{CS}$ (pin 11)
(Chip Select) The CPU activates $\overline{CS}$ to get an access to the internal 8237A registers if command and data bytes are to be read or written. The data exchange with the CPU is then carried out via the data bus DB0–DB7. During DMA transfers, the $\overline{CS}$ input is disabled by the 8237A both internally and automatically.

CLK (pin 12)
This input is supplied with the DMA clock signal. In the PC the DMA chips usually run at 4.77 MHz, and sometimes at 7.16 MHz.

RESET (pin 13)
By means of a high-level RESET signal the 8237A is reset.

$\overline{DACK0}$–$\overline{DACK3}$ (pins 25, 24, 14, 15)
(DMA Acknowledge) An active $\overline{DACKx}$ signal indicates that the DMA channel concerned is enabled and the corresponding peripheral that issued a DMA request via DRQx is now serviced. Only a single $\overline{DACKx}$ can be active at a time. The 8237A activates a line $\overline{DACKx}$ only once it has taken over control of the local bus by means of HRQ and HLDA. The signal polarity (active–low or active–high) can be individually programmed with the mode register.

DREQ0–DREQ3 (pins 19–16)
(DMA Request) An active DREQx signal from a peripheral indicates that the device concerned requests a DMA transfer. For example, a floppy controller may activate a DREQx line to carry out the transfer of read data into main memory. Usually, DREQ0 has the highest and DREQ3 the lowest priority. A corresponding $\overline{DACKx}$ signal from the 8237A acknowledges the request. Also, the polarity of these signals (active–low or active–high) can be individually programmed by means of the mode register.

DB0–DB7 (pins 30–26, 23–21)
These eight pins form the bidirectional 8237A data bus for read and write accesses to internal registers or during DMA transfers. In DMA cycles the high-order eight bits of the DMA address are output to DB0–DB7 and latched into the external DMA address latch with ADSTB. During the course of memory–memory transfers the data byte to be transferred is first loaded into the internal temporary register (memory–DMA half cycle) and then output again by the temporary register via DB0–DB7 (DMA–memory half cycle).

A0–A3 (pins 32–35)
These four connections form a bidirectional address nibble. In the 8237A's standby state the CPU addresses internal 8237A registers. If the 8237A is active then the four low-order address bits are supplied by A0–A3.

A4–A7 (pins 37–40)
These four connections provide four address bits if the 8237A is active. In the standby state they are disabled.

EOP (pin 36)

(End of Process) The signal at this bidrectional connection indicates the completion of a DMA transfer. If the count value of the active 8237A channel reaches the value 0, then the 8237A provides an active $\overline{\text{EOP}}$ signal with a low level to inform the peripheral about the termination of the DMA transfer. On the other hand, the peripheral may also pull $\overline{\text{EOP}}$ to a low level to inform the DMA chip about the early termination of the DMA transfer. This is the case, for example, if a buffer in the peripheral that requested the DMA service has been emptied by the 8237A and all data has been transferred to main memory. By the internal as well as the external $\overline{\text{EOP}}$ condition, the TC bit in the status register is set, the corresponding request bit reset, and the DMA transfer terminated.

V_{cc} (pins 5, 31)

This pin is supplied with the supply voltage (usually +5 V).

GND (pin 20)

This pin is grounded (usually 0 V).

7.3.3   Internal Structure and Operation Modes of the 8237A

The 8237A is, despite its limited functions, a rather complex chip, which has 27 internal registers with a width between four and 16 bits. Table 7.5 lists all registers and their widths. The 8237A has four independently working DMA channels 0–3, so the base and current registers are implemented four times.

Register name	Register width	Number of registers
base address register	16 bit	4
base count register	16 bit	4
current address register	16 bit	4
current count register	16 bit	4
temporary address register	16 bit	1
temporary count register	16 bit	1
status register	8 bit	1
command register	8 bit	1
intermediate register	8 bit	1
mode register	6 bit	4
mask register	4 bit	1
request register	4 bit	1

Table 7.5: 8237A internal registers

The temporary registers hold the corresponding values for the currently active channel during the course of executing a DMA function. Only one channel may be active at any time, so one temporary register is sufficient for all four channels. By means of the status register you may read information concerning the current 8237A status; the remaining registers are for programming the DMA controller. Figure 7.23 shows the 8237A's internal structure.

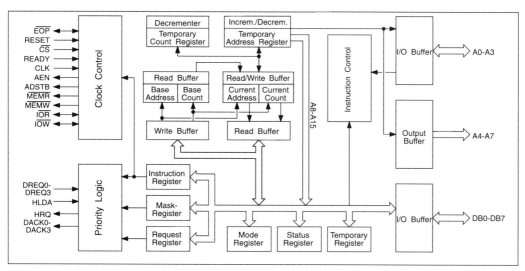

Figure 7.23: The 8237A DMA controller.

The 8237A has two different priority modes for servicing arriving DMA requests: *fixed priority* and *rotating priority*. With fixed priority channel 0 is assigned the highest and channel 3 the lowest priority. This means that requests on channel 0 are always serviced, but on channel 3 they are serviced only if no other channel is active. With rotating priority the DMA requests are serviced in the order of their occurrence. Afterwards, the currently serviced channel is assigned the lowest priority level.

From Table 7.5 you can see that the count value registers are 16 bits wide. Thus the 8237A can carry out a maximum of 64 k transfers before a wrap-around of the count register occurs. How many bytes these 64 k transfers correspond to depends upon the connection of the 8237A to the computer's data and address bus. How the DMA chip is used in the PC architecture is described in Section 7.3.4. The CPU writes a value into the count register which defines the number of DMA transfers of the channel concerned. The 8237A terminates the DMA transfer for the active channel when the count register wraps from 0000h to ffffh. Because, after every transfer, the count register is decreased by one, the actual number of DMA transfers is equal to the value written by the CPU plus one. Thus, 64 k transfers can be carried out if you initially load the count register with the value ffffh.

As soon as the count register reaches the value ffffh, this is called a *terminal count (TC)*. The end of the transfers is only reached upon a TC or an external $\overline{\text{EOP}}$ but not if the DREQ signal is disabled in a demand transfer.

If you look at the 8237A pin assignment in Figure 7.22 and compare it to Table 7.5, you can see that the 8237A address registers are 16 bits wide but the 8237A address bus comprises only eight bits A0–A7. To save terminals and to accommodate the 8237A in a standard DIP with 40 pins, the designers intended to have an external *DMA address latch* which holds the high-order address byte A8–A15 of the address registers. However, only a 16-bit address space is thus accessible – too little for a PC. For the complete address a so-called *DMA page register* is additionally required, which holds the address bits beyond A15. Figure 7.24 shows this schematically for the 24-bit AT address bus, which serves the complete 16 Mbyte address space of the 80286.

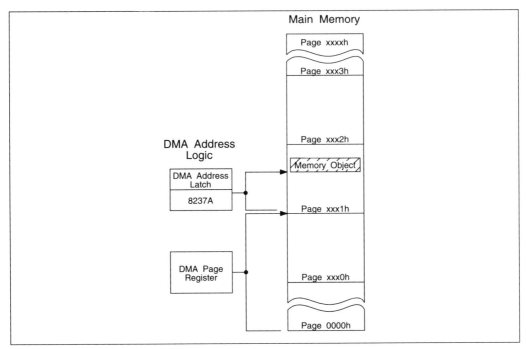

Figure 7.24: Address generation with 8237A, DMA address latch and DMA page register. The DMA page register supplies the number of the corresponding 64 kbyte page. The DMA address latch holds the high-order address byte and the 8237A address register the low-order address byte within that DMA page.

The DMA address latch is an external chip loaded by the 8237A with the high-order address byte in the address register. For this purpose, the 8237A puts address bits A8–A15 onto data bus DB0–DB7 and activates the ADSTB signal. The DMA address latch then fetches and latches the 8-bit address onto the data bus. Thus the DMA chip need only provide the low-order address byte via its address bus A0–A7.

The DMA page register, on the other hand, is loaded by the CPU and accommodates the address bits beyond A15. Each channel has its own page register, which is activated according to the active DMA channel. In a PC/XT with its 20-bit address bus, only a 4-bit page register is therefore necessary, but an AT with a fully equipped 16 Mbyte memory requires an 8-bit register. Motherboards with i386 and i486 processors that support a physical DMA address space of more than 16 Mbytes have an additional DMA page register for every channel, which holds the necessary address bits A24 and beyond. Figure 7.25 shows the scheme for DMA addressing. In a brief leap ahead to Section 7.3.4, I should mention that in the PC/XT one 8237A DMA chip for servicing 8-bit peripherals is implemented. In the AT a second 8237A was added so that three additional 16-bit channels are available there (one channel is used for cascading the two 8237As).

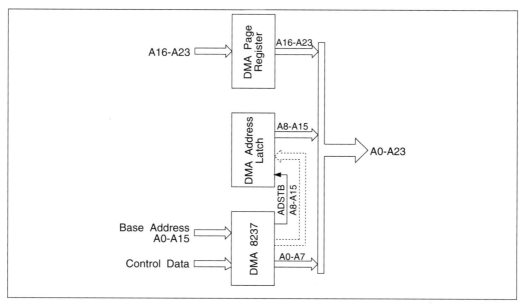

Figure 7.25: DMA addressing.

Because of the addressing structure with DMA page registers, the address space is physically divided into pages (or segments, as you like) of 64 kbytes each for 8-bit channels 0–3, or into pages of 128 kbytes each for 16-bit channels 5–7. Thus the page size is 64 kbytes for 8-bit channels 0–3 and 128 kbytes for 16-bit channels 5–7. Within these pages, the DMA address latch and the address bits A0–A7 from the 8237A indicate the offset. The DMA address cannot go beyond the current page. If for instance, you write the base address ff00h into the address register and the value 0fffh into the count register (that is, you want to transfer 4 kbytes via a DMA channel) then the address register wraps around from ffffh to 0000h during the course of this transfer. The DMA transfer is not completed by this, of course, as the count register further holds the value 0f00h. The rest of the data is therefore written to the beginning of the DMA page. This wrap-around of the address register is called a *DMA segment overflow*. Thus when programming a DMA transfer, you must always ensure that all data to be transferred can be accommodated contiguously in the remaining section of the DMA page. The DMA chip doesn't report any message if a DMA overflow occurs.

The 8237A Standby Mode

If the 8237A is in standby mode it checks with every clock cycle whether the $\overline{CS}$ signal is active and the CPU is trying to access one of its registers. If $\overline{CS}$ is active (that is, on a low level), the 8237A enters the programming state and waits for addresses and, eventually, data from the CPU to write them into the corresponding register, or to provide data from the addressed register to the CPU. Address lines A0–A3 determine the register selected. To be able to read from and write to the 16-bit 8237A registers via the 8-bit data bus DB0–DB7, the 8237A uses an internal flip-flop for switching between low-order and high-order data bytes. If you attempt to read or write a 16-bit register you must reset this flip-flop first, and then read or write the least significant and then the most significant data byte. (Details on programming the 8237A are discussed in Section 7.3.5.)

In the standby mode, the 8237A further samples its DREQ inputs upon every clock cycle to determine whether a peripheral has issued a DMA request. If the corresponding DMA channel is not masked internally then the DMA chip outputs a request for the local bus to the CPU via the HRQ pin to take over control of the local bus. After the CPU has responded with an HLDA signal and has released the bus, the requesting 8237A enters the active mode to carry out a DMA service. Depending upon the programming, it is able to operate in four different modes, explained now in brief.

Single Transfer

In this mode the 8237A carries out only a single transfer. The count register is decremented by one and the address register, depending upon the programmed state, is also decremented or incremented by one. If the count register reaches the value ffffh, starting from 0000h, then the 8237A internally issues a TC and with a corresponding programmed state also an autoinitialization of the DMA chip.

With this mode you can also move a whole block of sequentially ordered data. Unlike the block transfer mode, though, you have to start every data transfer individually by a signal DREQ or a set bit on the request register. As compensation for this restriction, however, the CPU can again get control of the local bus between two transfers.

The single transfer mode is used in the PC for transferring a data sector from the floppy disk drive into the main memory. For this purpose, the CPU has to load the count register with the value 511 (512 bytes to transfer) and the address and page register with the buffer address in the main memory. The floppy controller activates the DREQ2 line with every decoded data byte from the floppy disk to issue a single transfer cycle. After transferring 512 bytes into main memory, a wrap-around in the count register occurs, and a TC is generated. The 8237A then terminates the DMA transfer.

Block Transfer

This mode causes the 8237A to continuously transfer data after acknowledging the DREQ request and the output of $\overline{DACK}$. For this purpose, the count register is decremented by one upon each transfer, and the address register (depending upon the programmed state) decremented or incremented until a TC or an external $\overline{EOP}$ occurs. A TC is present if the count register reaches the value ffffh, starting from 0000h. With a correspondingly programmed state an autoinitialization is carried out.

Demand Transfer

In demand transfer mode the 8237A carries out data transfer continuously until a TC or an external $\overline{EOP}$ occurs, or the peripheral deactivates DREQ. Thus the demand transfer differs from the block transfer in that disabling DREQ also leads to interruption of the data transfer. In block transfer mode this has no consequences. Moreover, in demand transfer mode the data transfer continues at the location of the interruption if the peripheral activates DREQ again.

Demand transfer mode is of some importance in the PC, as the bus slots don't have a connection for $\overline{EOP}$ through which a peripheral might indicate the end of the data transfer to the DMA chip. Disabling DREQ only leads to an interruption, not to the transfer's termination. Autoinitialization is therefore not carried out. This is only possible by means of a TC or an external $\overline{EOP}$.

Cascading

One characteristic of the 8237A is its capability for cascading. The number of DMA channels can thus be extended, similar to the 8259A PIC and its interrupt channels. Unlike the PIC the extension with the 8237A works to any depth. Figure 7.26 shows a scheme for this cascading capability.

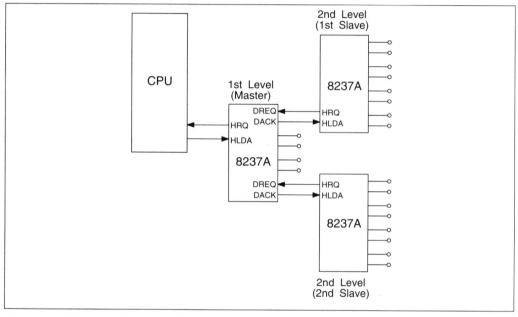

Figure 7.26: 8237A cascading. The 8237A DMA chips can be cascaded up to any level. For this purpose, the HRQ and HLDA of a slave must be connected to the master's DREQ and DACK.

Cascading is carried out by connecting one channel's DREQ and $\overline{DACK}$ of a DMA chip of a higher level with HRQ and HLDA, respectively, of a DMA chip of a lower level. Normally, an 8237A takes control of the local bus by means of HRQ and HLDA when it receives a DMA request via DREQ. With the cascading scheme, however, a DMA request to a second level DMA chip (the *master*) leads to a DMA request to the DMA chip of the first level (the *slave*), as the master's HRQ signal is passed to the DMA chip of the first level via the DREQ input. The slave takes control of the local bus by means of HRQ and HLDA, and activates its output $\overline{DACK}$, which is connected to the input HLDA of the DMA master. Thus the DMA master interprets the $\overline{DACK}$ signal from the slave as an HLDA from the CPU. Cascading therefore leads the control signals HRQ and HLDA through master and slave. The figure shows further that the cascading scheme is extendable up to any level. The AT uses one slave and one master. The slave is connected to channel 0 of the master, thus the slave channels have a higher priority than the master's channels. Channel 0 of the AT's master is usually denoted as DMA channel 4.

Besides the connections shown, the slave channel concerned needs to be programmed in cascading mode to realize cascading. It is then only used for passing the control signals from the DMA master, and doesn't provide any address or control signals for the bus.

The three transfer modes (single, block and demand) can carry out four transfer types, each of which differs in the source and target of the transfer. The following discusses these four transfer types.

Read Transfer

In read transfer, data is transferred from main memory to an I/O device, thus from memory to the I/O address space. For this purpose, the 8237A uses the $\overline{\text{MEMR}}$ and $\overline{\text{IOW}}$ signals. By activating $\overline{\text{MEMR}}$, data is read from memory onto the data bus. The data on the data bus is transferred to the I/O device by activating $\overline{\text{IOW}}$. Figure 7.27 shows a signal diagram for a read transfer.

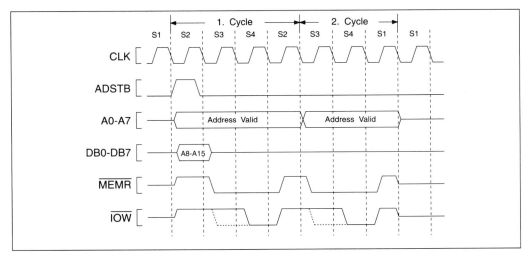

Figure 7.27: Read transfer.

During the course of the shown read transfer, the 8237A initially outputs the high-order address byte of the memory address via the data bus DB0–DB7, and activates ADSTB to latch address bits A8–A15 onto the DMA address latch. At the same time, the low-order address byte of the memory address is output via address lines A0–A7. Activating $\overline{\text{MEMR}}$ to a low level causes the memory subsystem to read data from memory, and to put it onto the system data bus. The memory buffer (see Figure 2.11) latches the read data and keeps it stable on the system data bus. By activating $\overline{\text{IOW}}$ the peripheral is advised to fetch the data on the system data bus into its I/O buffer (see Figure 2.15). The peripheral takes the data directly off the system data bus. No temporary storage in the temporary register of the 8237A is carried out.

As you can see from the figure, the 8237A doesn't generate any I/O address for the peripheral. The peripheral is only accessed via the assigned lines DREQx and $\overline{\text{DACKx}}$, while the other peripherals in the I/O address space are disabled, for example, by the active AEN signal from the DMA chip. Now only the intended device responds to the 8237A control signal. Figure 7.27 shows further that one DMA cycle lasts for four DMA clock cycles. If a slow memory or I/O device is addressed, one or more wait cycles may be inserted between S2 and S3, or between S3 and S4. The DMA cycle is then extended accordingly.

The high-order address byte A8–A15 need not be output during each DMA cycle, but only if the high-order address byte really changes. This occurs only every 256 bytes. In the second cycle of the figure, phase S2 is therefore missing, so only three clock cycles are required for a single DMA cycle. This means a time saving of 25% in the end.

Write Transfer

The write transfer is, so to speak, the opposite of the read transfer. Data is transferred from an I/O device into main memory, that is, from the I/O to memory address space. The 8237A uses the $\overline{\text{IOR}}$ and $\overline{\text{MEMW}}$ signals for this purpose. By activating $\overline{\text{IOR}}$, data is read from the I/O device onto the data bus. The data is then transferred to memory by an active $\overline{\text{MEMW}}$. The signal diagram in Figure 7.27 is also valid for a write transfer if you replace $\overline{\text{MEMR}}$ by $\overline{\text{IOR}}$ and $\overline{\text{IOW}}$ by $\overline{\text{MEMW}}$. The DMA cycle is four clock cycles long if the high-order address byte needs to be supplied to the DMA address latch, otherwise it is three clock cycles. If the DMA chip has to insert wait cycles because of slow memories or I/O devices, the DMA cycle is extended accordingly.

Verify Transfer

Verify transfer is merely a pseudo-transfer as the 8237A operates internally in the same way as in a read or write transfer, therefore it generates addresses and responds to $\overline{\text{EOP}}$ and other signals but doesn't provide any I/O and memory control signals such as $\overline{\text{IOR}}$, $\overline{\text{IOW}}$, $\overline{\text{MEMR}}$, $\overline{\text{MEMW}}$ etc. externally. Thus the verify transfer serves only for internal 8237A checking to determine whether the addressing and control logic are operating correctly. With a real verification of data this has nothing to do.

Memory–Memory Transfer

With memory–memory transfer the 8237A may move a complete data block from one address area in the main memory to another. However, this type of transfer is only available for channels 0 and 1; channels 2 and 3 only carry out the three transfer types indicated above. Channel 0 determines the source and channel 1 the destination of the data transfer. For memory–memory transfer, the temporary register is important because it accommodates the data byte read from the source area in the main memory before it is written to another location in main memory via channel 1. The memory–memory transfer is issued by a software request for channel 0, because an external DMA request with DREQ0 is not possible here. As usual, the 8237A requests control of the local bus by means of HRQ and HLDA. The memory–memory transfer is generally terminated by a TC of channel 0 or 1 if the count register reaches the value ffffh, starting with 0000h. The 8237A responds in memory–memory transfer to an external $\overline{\text{EOP}}$

signal. Through this, external diagnostic hardware, for example, may terminate the DMA transfer if the source or destination address becomes of a certain value. Figure 7.28 shows a signal diagram for a memory–memory transfer.

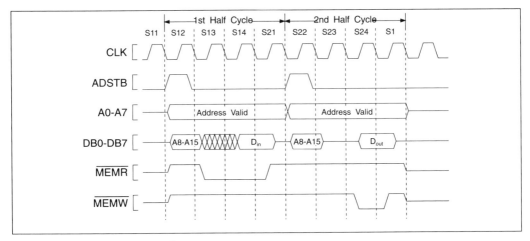

Figure 7.28: Memory–memory transfer.

During the first half cycle the DMA chip reads the data byte into the temporary register by first providing the high-order address byte A8–A15 on DB0–DB7. The address byte is then loaded into the DMA address latch by activating ADSTB. At the same time, the 8237A outputs the low-order address byte via A0–A7, and activates $\overline{\text{MEMR}}$ to read out the data byte onto the system data bus. The 8237A fetches the data, via DB0–DB7, into its temporary register. The next half cycle then writes the data byte held by the temporary register to a new address in main memory. To carry out this process, the 8237A first writes the high-order address byte into the DMA address latch and puts the data byte via DB0–DB7 onto the system bus afterwards. The following activation of $\overline{\text{MEMW}}$ instructs the memory to write the data byte to the corresponding address. Thus the memory–memory transfer is complete. As can be seen from Figure 7.28, such a transfer requires eight DMA clock cycles.

Note that CLK indicates the DMA clock and not the CPU clock. Even in i386 systems with 40 MHz, the DMA chip usually runs at 4.77 MHz. Thus a memory–memory transfer lasts for about 1680 ns. If we assume a 70 ns main memory with about 120 ns cycle time and three CPU clock cycles for the execution of one i386 MOVS instruction, then the transfer of one word via the CPU lasts only 330 ns. This is five times faster. If we further take into account that the i386 can transfer 32 bits all at once, but the 8237A only eight, then the i386 transfers data from memory to memory 20 times faster than the 8237A.

As a feature, channel 0 can be programmed to keep the same address during the course of the whole memory–memory transfer. The 8237A then carries out a memory block initialization. The size of this block is defined by the count value in the count register of channel 1.

Compressed Mode

For fast memories and I/O devices the 8237A may be programmed so that it carries out a compressed mode. The transfer time is then compressed to two DMA clock cycles. Figure 7.29 shows a signal diagram for the compressed mode.

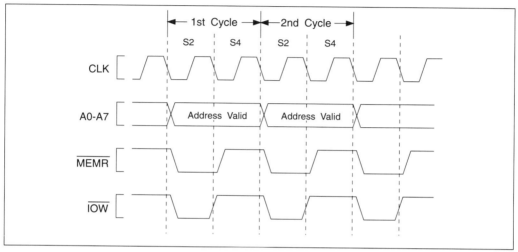

Figure 7.29: Compressed mode.

As you can see, cycle S3 is missing. It extends the read pulse with slower memories and I/O devices so that the addressed unit has enough time to provide the data. With modern devices this is no longer required, and S3 can be dropped. Note that the 8237A runs only at 4.77 MHz in the PC. Every device as slow as the 8237A can easily follow, but after 256 bytes at most an additional cycle S1 is required, because a new high-order address byte for the DMA address latch must then be supplied via DB0–DB7.

The compressed mode is only implemented for read and write transfers. For a memory–memory transfer the compressed mode is not possible, although today's RAM chips are among the fastest components in a PC.

Autoinitialization

The individual 8237A channels may be programmed so that they initialize themselves to the initial values after a TC or $\overline{\text{EOP}}$ automatically. For this purpose, the current address register and the current count register are loaded with the values from the base address register and the base count register. The base address register and base count register are not accessible, but are loaded during the course of a write to the current address register and the current count register by the CPU with the same values. The base address register and base count register are not altered by the following DMA cycles, and hold the initial values even after an $\overline{\text{EOP}}$ from which the current address register and the current count register are restored during autoinitialization. Afterwards, the 8237A channel concerned is again ready for a DMA transfer.

Autoinitialization is used if data quantities of the same size are always to be transferred to a fixed buffer in the main memory, or from the main memory. This can be the case, for example, when reading a sector from a floppy disk into the main memory. Here it would be sufficient to program the DMA chip once. For all succeeding sector transfers, the chip initializes itself again and again.

7.3.4   DMA Architecture in the PC/XT and AT

In the PC/XT a single DMA chip is present which is only able to serve 8-bit peripherals. These are devices that only have 8-bit registers, and therefore access only 8 bits of the data bus. The AT has a second DMA chip that operates as a master and which is connected to the CPU. HRQ and HLDA of the slave DMA are connected to channel 0 of the master DMA so that the slave's channels 0–3 have a higher priority than the remaining three channels of the master DMA. The master's channels 0–3 are usually denoted by DMA channels 4–7 of the AT. The four channels of the slave DMA serve 8-bit peripherals, while the three unused channels 5–7 are generally configured for 16-bit devices. The following discusses the differences between them. Table 7.6 lists the DMA channel's uses in the PC/XT and AT.

Channel	Controller	Width	Used for
0	1	8 bits	memory refresh
1	1	8 bits	available (SDLC)
2	1	8 bits	floppy disk controller
3	1	8 bits	PC/XT: hard disk controller AT: unused
4	2*)	16 bits	cascade DMA1 –> DMA2
5	2*)	16 bits	available
6	2*)	16 bits	available
7	2*)	16 bits	available

*) AT only

Table 7.6: DMA channels in PC/XT and AT

8-Bit and 16-Bit Channels

Because of the 8088 processor the PC has only an 8-bit data bus and a 20-bit address bus, thus a DMA page register with a width of only four bits is required in the PC. As an 8-bit chip, the 8237A is perfectly designed for the 8088. Because of the 8-bit data bus only 8-bit DMA channels are possible, and Figure 7.27 is applicable. During the course of a read transfer the 8237A provides the memory address and activates the $\overline{\text{MEMR}}$ signal to read a data byte from memory onto the 8-bit data bus. Afterwards, it enables the $\overline{\text{IOW}}$ signal so the peripheral can accept the data byte. A write transfer proceeds in exactly the opposite direction: the 8237A outputs the memory address and activates the $\overline{\text{IOR}}$ signal to read out a data byte from the peripheral's I/O register onto the 8-bit data bus. Afterwards, it enables the $\overline{\text{MEMW}}$ signal so that the memory can fetch the data byte.

On the XT the situation becomes more ponderous and complex. Because of the 8086 the XT has a 16-bit data bus internally. As is the case on the PC, the only DMA chip present is designed for 8-bit channels to 8-bit peripherals. Into the XT bus slot only 8-bit devices can be installed anyway, as the data bus only leads with 8 bits into them. But because of the 16-bit data bus of the 8086, memory is organized as 16-bit storage. This means that on the low-order data bus byte D0–D7 only data bytes with an even address (and on the high-order data bus byte D8–D15 only data bytes with an odd address) appear.

If the 8237A continuously counts up or down the source address during the course of a read transfer, the intended data byte appears on memory bus lines D0–D7 if an even address is supplied, and on lines D8–D15 if an odd address is output. Thus, an additional logic is required to transfer the data byte with an odd address onto data bus lines D0–D7 so that an 8-bit peripheral with an even I/O address can fetch it. At the same time, the memory only outputs the data byte with an odd address without driving the lines D0–D7. In the same way as for a peripheral with an odd I/O address, an additional logic is required to transfer the data byte with an even address onto lines D8–D15, so that the 8-bit peripheral can actually fetch it. A similar problem arises with the 8086 if it attempts to read a date byte with an odd address from or write a date byte with an odd address to the memory. The 8086 manages this by means of the control signal $\overline{\text{BHE}}$ which, together with the least significant address bit A0, disables the upper or lower half of the data bus.

On the contrary, the 8237A continuously increments or decrements the target address in memory during the course of a write transfer, and the data byte from the 8-bit peripheral always appears on the same data bus bits. With an even target address the data byte needs to appear on the low-order part D0–D7 of the memory bus; with an odd address, however, it appears on the high-order part D8–D15 of the memory bus so that the memory can write the data byte upon activation of the $\overline{\text{MEMW}}$ signal to the memory location intended.

With an 80286 and its 16-bit data bus the process works in the same way. Here also the data from the 8-bit peripheral must be put onto or taken off the low-order or high-order part of the data bus (depending upon the storage address). The situation becomes even more ponderous (hard to believe) with PCs that have an i386 or i486 chip. They usually implement main memory with a 32-bit organization. Here according to the storage address one of the now four data bus bytes is responsible for fetching or providing the 8-bit data from or to the peripheral. An additional logic that decodes the two least-significant address bits from the DMA chip can easily carry out the transfer.

The three free channels of the new second DMA chip in the AT are already designed for serving 16-bit peripherals. This can be, for example, a 16-bit controller for hard disk drives. Although the 8237A is only an 8-bit chip, it can carry out a 16-bit or even a 32-bit transfer between peripherals and main memory. How the DMA controller carries out this, at a first glance, impossible job is described below.

The descriptions up to now have shown that the internal temporary 8-bit register of the 8237A doesn't play any role in data transfer between peripherals and memory. The transfer target receives the data from the source directly via the data bus. The only problem left is that the 8237A address register provides byte addresses and no word addresses. But if the coupling of address bits A0–A15 from 8237A and the DMA address latch to the system address bus is shifted by one, which corresponds to a multiplication by a factor of two, and address bit A0 of the system bus is always set to 0, then the 8237A will generate word addresses. This also applies to the 16-bit DMA channels in the AT. A0 is always to equal 0 here. The 8237A and the DMA address latch provide address bits A1–A16, and the DMA page register supplies address bits A17–A23. Therefore, one DMA page of the 16-bit channels now has 128 kbytes instead of 64 kbytes and the data transfer is carried out in 16-bit sections. Transferring the data bytes onto the low-order or high-order part of the data bus according to an even or an odd address is not necessary.

Only on systems with a 32-bit data bus do the words need to be transferred by an additional 16/32-bit logic onto the low-order or high-order data bus word, according to whether their addresses represent double-word boundaries. This is carried out analogous to the transfer of 8-bit quantities on the XT.

For a data transfer between memory and peripherals (the main job of DMA), it is insignificant, therefore, as to whether an 8- or 32-bit chip is present. The shifting of the address bits supplied by the 8237A by one or two places leads to 16- or even 32-bit addresses. Unfortunately, the transfer can then only start and end at word or double-word boundaries, and the transferred quantities are limited to multiples of 16 or 32 bits. If a peripheral supplies, for example, 513 bytes, this may give rise to some difficulties. EISA therefore implements a 32-bit DMA controller which also runs somewhat faster than 4.77 MHz.

Memory Refresh

Channel 0 is dedicated to memory refresh. In modern ATs and other computers with intelligent DRAM controllers, the memory refresh need not be carried out by a DMA cycle; instead, the DRAM controller or even the DRAM chips themselves do this on behalf of a trigger signal from the PIT. For refresh purposes, counter 1 of the 8253/8254 PIT operates in mode 3 (square-wave generator) with a count value 18 (12h). Only the low-order counter byte is loaded (RW1 = 0, RW0 = 1), that is, the PIT generates a square-wave with a frequency of 1.19318 MHz/18 = 66 288 Hz. Counter 1 therefore issues a DREQ every 15 μs for a dummy transfer, which refreshes the DRAMs. Channel 0 of the 8237A is programmed in single transfer mode with a read transfer for this purpose. During the course of the dummy cycle, the DMA chip reads data from the memory onto the data bus, whereby the address buffers, address decoders and sense amplifiers in the memory chips are enabled. This automatically leads to the refresh of one memory cell row. But the data is not fetched by a peripheral, as no device has issued a DREQ0 and would be able to respond to $\overline{DACK0}$, $\overline{MEMR}$ and $\overline{IOW}$. The data therefore disappears upon the next bus cycle. Because all these control signals lead into the bus slots and are thus also available for the adapter cards, the dummy cycle may also refresh the memory on expansion adapters (for example, graphics adapters). Only adapters with their own refresh logic generate refresh cycles on their own.

The PIT defines the refresh time by means of the periodic square wave signal. The DMA chip is used to generate the refresh address and the control signals for reading the main memory. The startup routine of the BIOS usually loads the count register with a suitable count value, and sets channel 0 to single transfer mode and autoinitialization. Thus every request via channel 1 of the

PIT issues exactly one transfer, increments the refresh address, and decrements the count register. If the count register reaches the value ffffh, then a TC occurs and channel 0 of the DMA controller is automatically initialized. The refresh process starts from the beginning again.

Modern memory controllers handle these processes on their own. Channel 0 of the 8237A is no longer required for the memory refresh. On such motherboards you would therefore be able to use channel 0 together with channel 1 for a memory–memory transfer. However, the AT architecture thwarts your plans again.

Memory–Memory Transfers in the AT

On EACH of the channels a page register is allocated whose addresses are listed in Table 7.10. IBM, though, has implemented a common page register for channels 0 and 1 in the PC/XT. Therefore, memory–memory transfer is only possible within a single DMA page of 64 kbytes, as only channels 0 and 1 can carry out this transfer and have to share one register on the PC/XT.

But also on the AT, no memory–memory transfer is possible, for the following reasons: DMA channel 4, corresponding to the master's channel 0, is blocked by cascading from the slave DMA. Thus the master DMA chip is not available for a memory–memory transfer. Only the slave DMA remains, but also here the problems are nearly insurmountable. On the AT and compatibles the memory refresh is no longer carried out by a DMA cycle, so channel 0 would then be free for a memory–memory transfer.

But for the memory–memory transfer, the internal temporary register of the 8237A is also involved – and this is only eight bits wide. Thus, 16-bit data on the 16-bit data bus cannot be temporarily stored; for this a 16-bit DMA chip would be required. If we restrict all memory–memory transfers to 8-bit transfers, then the data byte can be temporarily stored, but depending upon an even or odd source address the byte appears on the low- or high-order part of the data bus. After temporary storage the data byte must be output by the 8237A, again depending on an even or odd target address onto the low- or high-order part of the data bus. This is possible in principle by using a corresponding external logic, but is quite complicated and expensive. Therefore, the AT or i386/i486 motherboards generally don't implement a memory–memory transfer. It could be worse, because the REP MOVS instruction moves data on an 80286 in 16-bit units and on an i386/i486 even in 32-bit units very quickly. The much higher CPU clock rate additionally enhances the effect. IBM has probably implemented the second DMA chip only because some peripherals might request a 16-bit DMA channel for data transfer. Note that the XT carries out the transfer of sector data from or to the hard disk (originally a job of the DMA) via a DMA channel but the AT employs PIO for this. Only EISA and PS/2 still use DMA for this job.

7.3.5 Programming the 8237A

For programming the 8237A five control registers are available. Additionally, you can determine the 8237A's current state by a status register. From the temporary register you may read the last transferred data byte of a memory–memory transfer. Table 7.7 lists the I/O addresses of the registers concerned. Note that the PC/XT only has the DMA 1 chip.

DMA 1[1)]	DMA 2[2)]	Read (R) Write (W)	Register name
08h	d0h	R	status register
08h	d0h	W	command register
09h	d2h	W	request register
0ah	d4h	W	channel mask register
0bh	d6h	W	mode register
0dh	dah	R	intermediate register
0fh	deh	W	mask register

1) master in PC/XT, slave in AT
2) master in AT

Table 7.7: I/O Addresses of control and status register

The read-only status register provides some information on the current state of the individual channels in the 8237A. Figure 7.30 shows the structure of this register.

7							0
REQ3	REQ2	REQ1	REQ0	TC3	TC2	TC1	TC0

```
REQ3–REQ0: DMA request for channels 3 to 0 or 7 to 4
           1=DMA request    0=no DMA request

TC3–TC0:   terminal count for channel 3 to 0 or 7 to 4
           1=TC reached, transfer complete    0=status register read or cancelled
```

Figure 7.30: Status register (08h, d0h).

The four high-order bits *REQ3–REQ0* indicate whether a request is pending via a DREQx signal for the channel concerned. Bits *TC3–TC0* show whether the 8237A has reached a terminal count of the corresponding channels according to a transition from 0000h to ffffh of each count register. If you read the status register, the four bits TC3–TC0 are automatically cleared.

Before programming an 8237A channel you should disable the whole chip, or at least the channel to be programmed. According to Murphy's law, no DMA request for this channel occurs all year – until you try to program it! If a DMA request occurs, for example after programming the low-order address register byte, then the 8237A immediately responds to the request and carries out the DMA transfer with the new low-order and the old high-order address byte. You can surely imagine what this means. Once the catastrophe is complete, the 8237A enters program mode again and the CPU can write the high-order address byte – if it is really able to do this any more. You may disable the complete DMA controller with the COND bit in the control register. An individual channel can be masked by means of the channel mask or the mask register. Figure 7.31 shows the command register.

With the *DAKP* bit you can determine the active level of the $\overline{\text{DACK}}$ signals. If DAKP is cleared, then the 8237A provides a low-level signal at the $\overline{\text{DACKx}}$ pin if it is servicing a DMA request via DRQx; otherwise, the pin outputs a high-level signal. With a set DAKP bit the 8237A supplies a high-level signal at the $\overline{\text{DACKx}}$ if it is servicing a DMA request via DRQx, otherwise a low-level signal is supplied. The standard setup after a reset is a cleared DAKP bit, which is also used by the PC. Thus, $\overline{\text{DACK}}$ signals are always active–low in the PC. The *DRQP* bit has a similar effect. With this bit you can define the active level that the 8237A assigns to the DMA request signals. A cleared DRQP bit means that the 8237A interprets a high level at its DRQx input as a DMA request for the channel x concerned. With a set DRQP bit, on the other hand, the 8237A issues a DMA transfer if a high-level signal is supplied. Thus DRQP and DAKP behave in opposite ways. The standard setup after a reset is a cleared DRQP bit, which is also used in the PC. DRQ signals are therefore always active–high in the PC.

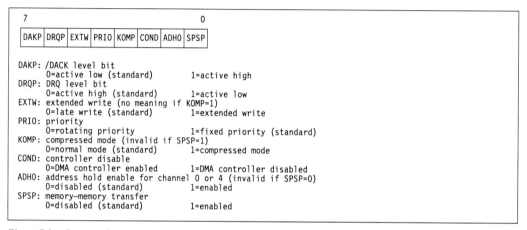

```
7                                          0
┌─────┬─────┬─────┬─────┬─────┬─────┬─────┬─────┐
│DAKP │DRQP │EXTW │PRIO │KOMP │COND │ADHO │SPSP │
└─────┴─────┴─────┴─────┴─────┴─────┴─────┴─────┘

DAKP: /DACK level bit
      0=active low (standard)          1=active high
DRQP: DRQ level bit
      0=active high (standard)         1=active low
EXTW: extended write (no meaning if KOMP=1)
      0=late write (standard)          1=extended write
PRIO: priority
      0=rotating priority              1=fixed priority (standard)
KOMP: compressed mode (invalid if SPSP=1)
      0=normal mode (standard)         1=compressed mode
COND: controller disable
      0=DMA controller enabled         1=DMA controller disabled
ADHO: address hold enable for channel 0 or 4 (invalid if SPSP=0)
      0=disabled (standard)            1=enabled
SPSP: memory–memory transfer
      0=disabled (standard)            1=enabled
```

Figure 7.31: Command register (08h, d0h).

The *EXTW* bit controls the length of the write pulse $\overline{\text{IOW}}$ or $\overline{\text{MEMW}}$ during a DMA transfer. With a set EXTW bit the write pulse will already have started one DMA clock cycle earlier during DMA phase S3; thus it is longer. You can see this in Figure 7.27: the broken line indicates an extended write, and the solid line a late write. In compressed mode (that is, with a set KOMP bit), the value of EXTW is immaterial as the S3 cycle is missing. With the *PRIO* bit you may set up the priority strategy that the 8237A uses to service incoming DMA requests. After a reset, PRIO is set so that the 8237A uses fixed priority with the order 0, 1, 2, 3. A set *KOMP* bit advises the 8237A to carry out compressed clocking where phase S3 is missing. Memory–memory transfers do not allow compressed mode – a relic of memory access times of 200 ns and more.

Using the *COND* bit you can disable the DMA controller completely. It doesn't respond to any DMA requests but must always be kept in programming mode. Thus the 8237A can only accept commands, and enables the CPU to access its internal registers.

The *AHD0* bit is important for memory–memory transfers. With a set AHD0 bit the 8237A keeps the value in the address register of channel 0 unchanged; only the address register of channel 1 is continuously increased or decreased. A whole memory block can thus be initialized with the value to which the channel 0 address register points. If AHD0 is cleared, a real memory–memory transfer of a complete data block is executed. The value of AHD0 is only effective with a set SPSP bit.

With a set *SPSP* bit the 8237A enters memory–memory transfer mode. Note that only a few motherboards support this transfer mode. For the memory–memory transfer only channels 0 and 1 are available. Channel 0 defines the source and channel 1 the target of the transfer. All other modes are defined via the mode register (see Figure 7.34).

Example: setup level, priority etc. for DMA 1 and enable DMA 1

```
OUT 08h, 18h  ; output 00011000b to command register of DMA 1:
              ; /DACK: active-low, DRQ: active-high, late write, priority: fixed
              ; clocking mode: compressed, DMA 1: enabled,
              ; address hold: disabled, memory-memory: disabled
```

```
 7                                    0
┌────┬────┬────┬────┬────┬────┬────┬────┐
│res │res │res │res │res │STCL│SEL1│SEL0│
└────┴────┴────┴────┴────┴────┴────┴────┘
res:  reserved (normally equal 0)
STCL: set/clear request bit
      1=set      0=clear
SEL1, SEL0: channel select
      00=channel 0/4   01=channel 1/5   10=channel 2/6   11=channel 3/7
```

Figure 7.32: Request register (09h, d2h).

Besides a hardware DMA request via the DRQx signals, you also have the option to start a DMA transfer by a software command. The 8237A behaves in the same way as if activated by a DRQx. DMA requests by software are imperative for memory–memory transfers, as the memory subsystem is unable to provide a DRQx signal for initiating the data transfer. The request of a DMA transfer is carried out with the request register (Figure 7.32). Bits *SEL1, SEL0* determine the channel for which the request is to be issued. The *STCL* bit defines whether the accompanying request bit is to be set or cleared. If no further DMA requests are currently active, or of a high priority, then setting the request bit immediately leads to a DMA transfer. The request is otherwise queued according the programmed priority strategy. You may remove a DMA transfer not yet initiated from the queue by clearing the corresponding request bit.

Example: issue DMA request for channel 6

```
OUT d2h, 06h  ; output 00000110b (res=0, STCL=1, SEL1/SEL0=10)
              ; to request register
```

```
 7                                    0
┌────┬────┬────┬────┬────┬────┬────┬────┐
│res │res │res │res │res │STCL│SEL1│SEL0│
└────┴────┴────┴────┴────┴────┴────┴────┘
res:  reserved (normally equal 0)
STCL: set/clear mask bit
      1=mask     0=clear
SEL1, SEL0: channel select for mask bit
      00=mask bit for channel 0/4   01=mask bit for channel 1/5
      10=mask bit for channel 2/6   11=mask bit for channel 3/7
```

Figure 7.33: Channel mask register (0ah, d4h).

The channel mask register (Figure 7.33) masks a single channel. With the related mask register, on the other hand, you can mask or release several channels all at once. Bits *SEL1, SEL0* define the channel to be masked or released. STCL determines whether this channel is to be masked or released.

Example: mask channel 1 of DMA 1

```
MOV 0ah, 05h  ; write 00000101b into channel mask register
              ; (res=0, STCL=1, SEL1/SEL0=01)
```

```
 7                                          0
┌─────┬─────┬─────┬─────┬─────┬─────┬─────┬─────┐
│MOD1 │MOD0 │IDEC │AUTO │TRA1 │TRA0 │SEL1 │SEL0 │
└─────┴─────┴─────┴─────┴─────┴─────┴─────┴─────┘
MOD1, MOD0: mode select
      00=demand   01=single   10=block   11=cascade
IDEC:  address increment/address decrement
      0=increment            1=decrement
AUTO:  autoinitialization
      0=inactive             1=active
TRA1, TRA0: transfer mode (invalid if MOD1,MOD0=11)
      00=verify   01=write   10=read   11=invalid
SEL1, SEL0: channel select
      00=channel 0/4   01=channel 1/5   10=channel 2/6   11=channel 3/7
```

Figure 7.34: Mode register (0bh, d6h).

With the mode register (Figure 7.34) you may set the operation mode and the transfer type of an 8237A channel. Bits *MOD1, MOD0* define the operation mode of the channel concerned; demand, single and block transfer as well as cascading are available, though in cascading mode the following bits are of no meaning. With *IDEC* you can define whether the address register is to be increased or decreased after each data transfer. *AUTO* activates or disables the autoinitialization of the 8237A for one channel. If you haven't selected cascading mode by means of MOD1, MOD0, then you must now define the transfer mode with *TRA1, TRA0*. *SEL1, SEL0* determine the 8237A channel for which the definitions by means of bits 7–2 hold.

Example: configure channel 2 of DMA 2

```
MOV d6h, b6h  ; load 1011 0110b into mode register of DMA 2
              ; mode: block transfer, address decrementing, autoinitialization: enabled
              ; transfer mode: write (peripheral -> memory), channel: 2
```

```
 7                                          0
┌─────┬─────┬─────┬─────┬─────┬─────┬─────┬─────┐
│ res │ res │ res │ res │STC3 │STC2 │STC1 │STC0 │
└─────┴─────┴─────┴─────┴─────┴─────┴─────┴─────┘
res:  reserved (normally equal 0)
STC3-STC0: set/clear mask bit of corresponding channel
      0=clear mask bit of channel 3,2,1,0 or 7,6,5,4
      1=set mask bit of channel 3,2,1,0 or 7,6,5,4
```

Figure 7.35: Mask register (0fh, deh).

As already mentioned, you have the option of masking or releasing several channels all at once using the mask register (see Figure 7.35). Bits *STC3–STC0* indicate whether the corresponding mask bit is set and whether the DMA request for the channels concerned is masked, or whether the mask bit is cleared and the channel released.

Example: release channels 0 and 1 of DMA 1, mask channels 2 and 3
MOV 0fh, 0ch   ; write 00001100b into mask register
               ; (res=0, STC3=1, STC2=1, STC1=0, STC0=0)

The 8237A implements three additional commands, but they are programmed as an output to a register. This means that you have to execute an OUT command with any data byte to the corresponding address to issue the command. By decoding the address bits A0–A3, the 8237A recognizes that a command and not a data write to a register has occurred. The data byte passed by the OUT instruction is ignored. Table 7.8 lists the three additional commands.

DMA 1[1]	DMA 2[2]	Command
0ch	d8h	reset flip-flop
0dh	dah	master clear
0eh	dch	clear mask register

[1] master in PC/XT, slave in AT
[2] master in AT

Table 7.8: DMA commands

You need the command *reset flip-flop* to reset the internal flip-flop in the 8237A if you want to write to a 16-bit register. Afterwards, you pass the low-order and then the high-order data byte. Without the command the flip-flop may be in an unpredictable state, and low- and high-order data bytes are possibly interchanged.

Example: reset flip–flop of DMA 1

OUT d8h, al   ; output any value to port d8h
                 ; –> command "reset flip–flop" executed

The *master clear* command has the same effect as a hardware reset of the 8237A. Command, status, request and temporary registers are cleared, and the flip-flop is reset.

Example: reset DMA 1 with master clear

OUT 0dh, al   ; output any value to port 0dh
                 ; –> command "master clear" executed
new_init   ; reinitialize DMA 1 now

The *clear mask register* command clears the mask bits of all four channels in the 8237A, and all channels are released for accepting DMA requests.

Example: release mask bits in DMA 2

OUT dch, al   ; output any value to port dch
                 ; –> command "clear mask register" executed

The above listed control registers control the operation of the 8237A. To carry out one concrete DMA transfer you must additionally initialize the address, count value and DMA page registers with appropriate values. Table 7.9 lists the I/O addresses of the address and count registers for chips DMA 1 and DMA 2.

DMA 1[1]	DMA 2[2]	Register name
00h	c0h	address register channel 0/4
01h	c1h	count register channel 0/4
02h	c2h	address register channel 1/5
03h	c3h	count register channel 1/5
04h	c4h	address register channel 2/6
05h	c5h	count register channel 2/6
06h	c6h	address register channel 3/7
07h	c7h	count register channel 3/7

[1] master in PC/XT, slave in AT
[2] master in AT

Table 7.9: Address and count register I/O addresses

Note that only the AT has two cascaded DMA chips. The PC/XT has only a DMA 1. Before you write one of these 16-bit registers you first need to reset the internal flip-flop by means of the *reset flip-flop* command.

Example: set address register of channel 6 to 1080h and write count value 0100h into the corresponding count register.

```
OUT d8h, al     ; output any value to port d8h
                ; -> command "reset flip-flop" executed
OUT c4h, 80h    ; output low-order address byte to channel 6 of DMA 2
OUT c4h, 10h    ; output high-order address byte to channel 6 of DMA 2
OUT d8h, al     ; output any value to port d8h
                ; -> command "reset flip-flop" executed again
OUT c5h, 00h    ; output low-order counter byte to channel 6 of DMA 2
OUT c4h, 01h    ; output high-order counter byte to channel 6 of DMA 2
```

For completely initializing a DMA transfer you must additionally load the page register of the channel concerned with the page address of the source and destination in the main memory. Table 7.10 lists the I/O addresses of the page registers.

Port	Page register	Port	Page register
87h	channel 0	8fh	channel 4 (refresh)
83h	channel 1[*]	8bh	channel 5
81h	channel 2	89h	channel 6
82h	channel 3	8ah	channel 7

[*] PC/XT only: simultaneously channel 0

Table 7.10: Page register I/O addresses

Note that in the PC/XT channels 0 and 1 are assigned the same physical page register. Therefore, you access the same physical register via the two different I/O addresses 87h and 83h. On the AT the page register for channel 4 – which is used for cascading – is the page address for memory refresh.

7.3.6   Example: Initialize DMA 1, Channel 2 for Floppy Data Transfer

The following program example initializes channel 2 of DMA 1 for a write transfer to transfer one floppy disk sector with 512 bytes from the controller into main memory. The segment and offset of the read buffer are passed in the registers ES:BX. A check whether a DMA segment overflow might occur is not carried out. The DMA transfer is initiated by a DREQ2 from the floppy disk controller. The program code can be part of a routine by which the CPU drives the floppy controller to transfer one sector with a read command. If several sectors are to be transferred in succession, then the value in the count registers must be increased accordingly.

```
;*************************************************************************************
;** ES: buffer segment      ssss ssss ssss ssss                              **
;** BX: buffer offset        oooo oooo oooo oooo                             **
;**                                                                           **
;** base address:     ssss ssss ssss ssss 0000                               **
;**                 +      oooo oooo oooo oooo                                **
;**                 _____                      **
;**                         pppp hhhh hhhh 1111 1111                          **
;**                                                                           **
;** pppp: entry for the DMA page register                                    **
;** hhhh hhhh: high-order byte for the DMA address register                  **
;** 1111 1111: low-order byte for the DMA address register                   **
;*************************************************************************************

dma1_disable:       ; disable DMA 1
OUT 08h, 14h        ; output 0001 0100b to command register to disable and initialize the 8237A
                    ; (/DACK: active low, DRQ: active high, late write, priority: fixed,
                    ; clocking: normal, controller: disabled, address hold: disabled,
                    ; memory–memory: disabled)

mode:               ; set up DMA mode for channel 2
OUT 0bh, 56h        ; output 0101 0110b to mode register
                    ; (mode: single transfer, address incrementation, no autoinitialization,
                    ; transfer mode: write, channel: 2)

split_address:      ; split address in ES:BX into pppp hhhh hhhh 1111 1111
MOV ax, es          ; load segment ssss ssss ssss ssss of read buffer into ax
MOV cl, 04h         ; load count value into cl
SHL ax, cl          ; shift left four times –> result ssss ssss ssss 0000
ADD ax, bx          ; add offset –> ax contains hhhh hhhh 1111 1111
JC carry            ; carry is set –> jump to carry

no_carry:
MOV bx, es          ; load segment ssss ssss ssss ssss of read puffer into bx
MOV cl, 04h         ; load count value into cl
SHR bh, cl          ; shift right bh four times –> bh contains
                    ; high-order bits ssss of buffer segment as pppp
JMP buffer_address  ; proceed with output of buffer address

carry:
MOV bx, es          ; load segment ssss ssss ssss ssss of read buffer into bx
MOV cl, 04h         ; load count value into cl
```

```
SHR bh, cl              ; shift right bh four times -> bh contains high-order bits ssss
                        ; of buffer segment
ADC bh, 00h             ; add carry

buffer_address:         ; output address to 8237A and page register
OUT 0ch, al             ; reset flip-flop
OUT 04h, al             ; output low-order address byte nnnn nnnn to address register
MOV al, ah              ; load high-order address byte hhhh hhhh into al
OUT 04h, al             ; output high-order address byte hhhh hhhh to address register
MOV al, bh              ; load page value pppp into al
OUT 81h, bh             ; load page register with pppp

count_value:            ; load count register with value 511 -> 512 bytes are transferred
OUT 0ch, al             ; reset flip-flop
OUT 05h, ffh            ; load low-order byte 255 of count value into count register
OUT 05h, 01h            ; load high-order byte 1 of count value into count register

channel_unmask:         ; release eventual channel masking
OUT 0ah, 02h            ; output 0000 0010b -> release channel 2

dma1_enable:            ; enable DMA 1
OUT 08h, 10h            ; output 0001 0000b to command register to enable 8237A again
                        ; (/DACK: active-low, DRQ: active-high, late write, priority: fixed
                        ; clocking: normal, controller: enabled, address hold: disabled,
                        ; memory-memory: disabled)
```

Alternatively, you may also mask only the channel concerned of the first DMA controller 1. All other channels remain enabled during the initialization of channel 2. Some 386 memory drivers need one or more DMA channels of the first DMA controller to access extended memory. Masking the controller, especially for a longer time period, may lead to the crash of these drivers.

7.3.7 DMA Cycles in Protected and Virtual 8086 Mode

If you want to initialize and execute a DMA transfer in protected or even virtual 8086 mode with active paging, you are confronted with many problems; in most cases, the task crashes immediately after the DMA transfer. The addresses that the 8237A, the DMA address latch, and the DMA page register provide are physical addresses. If you try to load one of these registers with a segment descriptor, the address points somewhere, but certainly not to the intended location. In virtual 8086 mode the situation doesn't get any better. Even if you succeed in eliciting the linear address from the segment descriptor, this doesn't help if paging is active. The linear address is completely replaced by the paging mechanism and the page concerned will possibly have been swapped by the operating system a long time before. The DMA controller realizes nothing, of course, as it is only running in a real mode and doesn't understand the CPU's segmentation and paging mechanisms.

In the environment of a protected mode operating system or virtual 8086 monitor, application programs have no chance of initiating a DMA transfer on their own. This is the job of the operating system only. All attempts to write the DMA registers by OUT instructions are intercepted by an exception if the IOPL flag isn't privileged enough, or the I/O port is protected by means of the I/O permission bit map. A DMA transfer is not a trivial job, especially when paging is enabled, even for the operating system or the virtual 8086 monitor, as the DMA controller overwrites the physical memory contents mercilessly without any care for the protection mechanisms of the protected mode. Therefore an incorrectly initialized DMA chip may overwrite protected memory locations even in protected mode. This inevitably gives rise to a crash of the concerned task immediately, or of the complete computer system.

7.4   About Tones and Sounds – The Speaker

During the course of each boot process, your PC outputs (hopefully) a good-tempered beep to signal that everything is OK. The installed speaker can also provide tones of various frequencies and duration, from a short glottal stop to a continuous nerve-racking squealing tone. In the following sections the two principal possibilities for driving the speaker and playing tone sequences in the background independently of the CPU are discussed. The key for operating the speaker is counter 2 of the 8253/8254 timer chip (see Section 7.2), as well as bits 0 and 1 of port B in the 8255 PPI chip (see Section 7.5). Figure 7.36 shows a diagram of the connections between PIT, port B and the speaker.

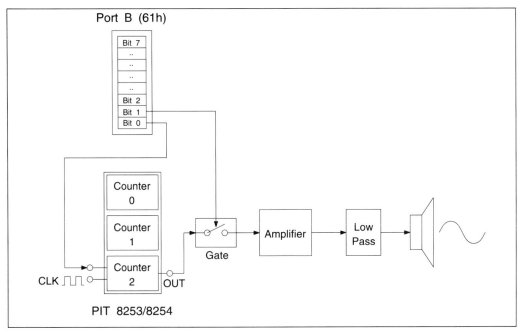

Figure 7.36: PIT, port B and speaker. Bit 0 of Port B controls the GATE input of counter 2, and bit 1 the gate that transmits the clock signal from counter 2 to the speaker.

To generate a stable tone, the output OUT of counter 2 in the 8253/8254 PIT is connected via a gate to the amplifier that drives the speaker. The low-pass filter suppresses the tones that are too high for the speaker. Like all other clock signal inputs, the PIT's CLK2 input is also connected to the 1.19318 MHz oscillator. To generate a tone, two possibilities are now available:

–   directly driving the speaker by means of counter 2 in the 8253/8254;
–   periodic activation of the amplifier with the CPU.

The first possibility is better and more direct, as the PIT carries out tone generation without any intervention from the CPU. The processor is only needed to set the tone frequency and to activate or disable the speaker. Thus the processor is free to do other jobs while the speaker is generating a tone. But don't demand high standards from the tone quality of the speaker; neither the installed amplifier nor the speaker belong to the HiFi class! For generating tones and the sounds of various instruments, synthesizer adapters (especially for multimedia applications) are now available on the market.

The audible range of tones lies between about 16 Hz and 16 kHz. Frequencies above and below this range are called infra- or supersonic: Your PC's amplifier is probably unable to generate such tones. The basis for the music scale is the so-called concert pitch A, with a frequency of 440 Hz. The scale of all octaves is deduced from this single concert pitch A. The tone A of the next lowest or next highest octave has half or twice the frequency. This applies analogously to all other tones. Table 7.11 lists the frequencies for all twelve half tones of the eight octaves. Only very modern composers use tones that are beyond the 8th octave.

Tone	Octave 1	Octave 2	Octave 3	Octave 4	Octave 5	Octave 6	Octave 7	Octave 8
C	16.4	32.7	65.4	130.8	261.6	523.3	1046.5	2093.0
C#	17.3	34.7	69.3	138.6	277.2	554.4	1108.8	2217.5
D	18.4	36.7	73.4	146.8	293.7	587.3	1174.7	2349.3
D#	19.5	38.9	77.8	155.6	311.1	622.3	1244.5	2489.0
E	20.6	41.2	82.4	164.8	329.6	659.3	1328.5	2637.0
F	21.8	43.6	87.3	174.6	349.2	698.5	1396.9	2793.8
F#	23.1	46.3	92.5	185.0	370.0	740.0	1480.0	2960.0
G	24.5	49.0	98.0	196.0	392.0	784.0	1568.0	3136.0
G#	26.0	51.9	103.8	207.7	415.3	830.6	1661.2	3322.4
A	27.5	55.0	110.0	220.0	440.0	880.0	1760.0	3520.0
A#	29.1	58.3	116.5	233.1	466.2	923.3	1864.7	3729.3
B	30.9	61.7	123.5	247.0	493.9	987.8	1975.5	3951.1

Table 7.11: The eight octaves of music

Music scale and octaves are based on the geometric mean, that is, the frequency of each tone is the geometric mean of the adjacent tones in the row as well as column directions. For example, concert pitch A: frequency 440 Hz; adjacent tones 220 Hz, 880 Hz and 415.3 Hz, 466.16 Hz; geometric mean in both cases $\sqrt{220*880} = \sqrt{415.3*466.16} = 440$Hz. Stated differently, from one octave to another the frequencies increase by a factor of two, and within the same octave by a factor of 12 2 = 1.05946. All tones are thus defined unambiguously. Of course, there are also tones of other frequencies, but an orchestra working with such tones sounds out of tune (or like Stockhausen!) After this short journey into the higher spheres of music, let's now turn back to the programming of our trivial PC speaker.

7.4.1   Direct Activation via the 8253/8254 PIT

For generating a tone only PIT mode 3 is applicable, that is, the timer chip generates a periodic square-wave signal. The other periodic mode 2 is not suitable as it only generates peak pulses with a width of 0.838 μs. The membrane of the speaker cannot follow this fast pulse, and the speaker remains quiet. To generate a square wave with the intended frequency you must put the PIT into counting mode 3 using a control word, and write one or two counter bytes afterwards. Note that the initial count value acts as a divisor, that is, the higher the value the lower the generated frequency.

Example: counter 2 shall generate a square wave of 440 Hz; thus the counter value (equal divisor) is 1,193,180 Hz/440 Hz=2712

```
MOV al, 10110110b ; counter 2, low-order and high-order counter byte, mode 3, binary counting
out 43h, al       ; write control register
mov al, 152       ; transfer low-order counter byte into al
out 42h, al       ; output low-order counter byte
mov al, 10        ; transfer high-order counter byte into al
out 42h, al       ; output high-order counter byte
                  ; now counter 2 generates a square-wave signal with 440Hz
```

Even if you generate a square-wave signal with the exact frequency of the concert pitch A (440 Hz), the result sounds somewhat different. Table 7.11 refers to pure sine oscillations; but the square wave with 440 Hz also contains, besides the 440 Hz sine signal, many other frequencies of various intensities. We as humans mainly perceive the strongest component (thus the 440 Hz), but the other additions appear as the tone «colour». Depending upon the instrument (violin, saxophone, PC speaker), the frequency and intensity of the additional tones are different, and actually characterize the sound of an instrument. Synthesizers and electronic organs use this effect to imitate various instruments by emphasizing certain additional tones.

With our PIT we are unfortunately limited to the generation of a simple tone. To cause the 8253/8254 to count in mode 3, the GATE input must be at a high level. For this purpose, bit 0 in port B of the 8255 chip is used. Port B can be accessed by port address 61h. If the value of this bit is equal to 1, then a high-level signal is applied to GATE2 and the PIT is enabled, otherwise a low-level signal is supplied and the counter is stopped. But activating the GATE input is not sufficient; a further gate is connected between PIT and the amplifier, controlled by bit 1 of port B. Only if this bit is equal to 1 is the square wave signal actually transmitted from counter 2 of the 8253/8254 to the amplifier, which in turn drives the speaker.

To generate a tone you therefore have to carry out the following steps:

–   operate counter 2 of the 8253/8254 in mode 3 with the intended frequency;
–   activate the GATE input of counter 2 by means of a set bit 0 in port B (port address 61h); and
–   turn on the gate by means of a set bit 1 in port B.

Example: To cause the speaker to actually output the 440 Hz tone in the above-indicated example, bits 0 and 1 in port B must additionally be set.

```
IN al, 61h        ; read old value of port B first
OR  al, 00000011b ; set bits 0 and 1, bits 2 to 7 remain unchanged
OUT 61h, al       ; output byte with set bits 0 and 1 to port B
```

Now the speaker constantly outputs a tone with a frequency of 440 Hz. The tone generation is carried out without any intervention of the CPU. You may call another program, but the speaker goes on sounding. A remedy is not possible until you reach the next example.

If you set only bit 0 in port B, but not bit 1, then the PIT generates the intended square-wave signal but this is not transmitted to the amplifier and the speaker remains quiet. However, if you have set bit 1 in port B but not bit 0, then the gate is turned on but there is no signal from the PIT and the speaker again remains quiet. You may load the PIT with a new count value at any time, and the speaker then outputs a tone with an accordingly altered frequency.

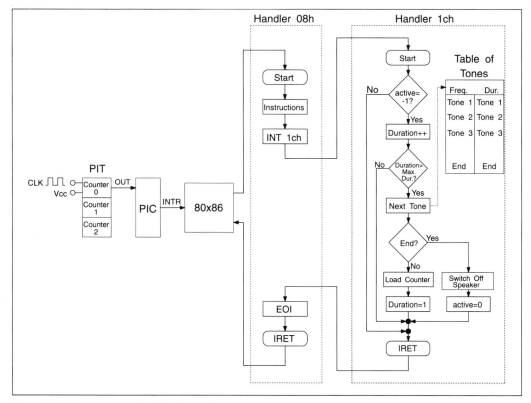

Figure 7.37: Tone sequences in the background.

Example: switch off the speaker

```
IN al, 61h        ; read old value of port B first
AND al, 11111100b ; clear bits 0 and 1, bits 2 to 7 remain unchanged
OUT 61h, al       ; output byte with cleared bits 0 and 1 to port B, speaker is switched off
```

To make the speaker quiet it is sufficient to clear one of the two bits 0 and 1.

In connection with the user exit 1ch of the periodic timer interrupt, the tone generation via the PIT is particularly powerful. Long tone sequences with tones of various durations can be played in the background while the CPU is executing another program. To achieve this a new handler for interrupt 1ch is required, which is called 18.2 times per second. Figure 7.37 shows a scheme for this.

The new handler determines with each call (that is, every 55 ms) whether the currently generated tone is to be terminated and which new tone the speaker needs to output. The handler fetches the data required from a table held in memory, where the frequencies and the duration (as the number of timer ticks) of the tones to be output are stored. Thus the CPU is taken up for a short time only every 55 ms to determine the end of the currently output tone, and to reprogram the PIT with a new frequency. The rest of the time it can process other tasks. If the stored table is extensive enough, the PC may play a complete symphony in the background while you are writing a letter, for example. Commands such as PLAY in BASIC use such a strategy to output tone sequences in the background.

7.4.2   Periodic Activation by the CPU

Another but not very powerful possibility to generate tones is the periodic activation of the speaker amplifier by the CPU. Even if counter 2 in the 8253/8254 PIT is not operating, or possibly not even in mode 3, the output OUT2 provides a voltage. This can be on a low (0 V) or high level (+5 V), depending upon the mode or signal at the GATE input. If you transmit this voltage to the amplifier via the gate that is turned on by means of bit 1 of port B, then the amplifier drives the speaker. As the signal provided by the counter is constant in time, the amplifier also generates a constant output signal. The speaker's magnet pulls or pushes away the membrane according to the polarity of the output signal. Afterwards, the membrane remains in this position until the signal from the amplifier is switched off. The membrane shoots back to the rest location.

If the amplifier turning on and off is repeated within short time intervals, the speaker outputs a tone with the frequency of this turning on and off. In other words, you may generate a tone with a certain frequency by setting and clearing bit 1 in port B in the phase of this frequency.

Example: Generate a tone by turning on and off the amplifier; program tone.c: called by "tone <count>".

```
main(argc, argv)
int argc;
char *argv[];

{ int i, count;

   count=atoi(argv[1]);      /* determine passed count value */

   while (!kbhit()) {         /* keyboard hit terminates tone generation */
                             /* enable amplifier */
      i=inp(0x61);           /* read old byte from port B */
      i=i | 0x02;            /* set bit 1 */
```

```
  outp(0x61,i);           /* write byte with set bit 1 to port B */

  for (i=0;i<count;i++); /* wait for count loops */

                          /* disable amplifier */
  i=inp(0x61);            /* read old byte from port B */
  i=i & 0xfd;             /* clear bit 1 */
  outp(0x61,i);           /* write byte with cleared bit 1 to port B */
  }

 getch();
 exit(0);
}
```

The disadvantages of this method are obvious. First, the CPU is permanently occupied by the tone generation, thus speaker operation in the background is impossible. Second, the frequency of the generated tone cannot be set up precisely as the clock frequency of the CPU is different in different PCs, and the CPU may be interrupted unpredictably by interrupts. To add a «click» to keyboards without such an in-built mechanical sound (as, for example, the Compaq keyboards), some manufacturers employ a similar method. If you are pressing a key you issue a hardware interrupt 09h whose handler fetches the character according to the depressed key into the keyboard buffer. Moreover, the handler may set bit 1 in port B for a short time. You perceive the speaker's turning on and off as a short click. The advantage compared to normal «click», keyboards is that you hear a click only if a character is actually passed. Older keyboards which have been in use for a long time may very often click without closing a corresponding contact in the scan matrix and passing a character to the PC's keyboard interface.

Example: Click on keyboard hit; keyb_echo.c generates a click sound upon every key hit.

```
main()

{ int i;

  for (;;) {
    while (!kbhit());      /* click tone upon keyboard hit */
    getch();               /* abort when Ctrl-C or Ctrl-Break */

    i=inp(0x61);           /* enable amplifier */
    i=i | 0x02;            /* by setting bit 1 */
    outp(0x61,i);          /* in port B */

    for (i=0;i<50;i++);    /* wait for 50 loops */

    i=inp(0x61);           /* disable amplifier */
    i=i & 0xfc;            /* by clearing bit 1 */
    outp(0x61,i);          /* in port B */
  }
  exit(0);
}
```

7.5   The 8255 Programmable Peripheral Interface

The 8255 PPI chip is only present in the PC/XT to establish a connection between CPU and various other components, such as the keyboard, the DIP switches for the configuration settings, and the NMI mask register.

7.5.1   PPI 8255 Terminals and Signals

The 8255 has 24 I/O pins in all, divided into three groups of eight pins each. The groups are denoted by port A, port B and port C, respectively. The PPI usually comes in a 40-pin DIP or 44-pin PLCC package. Figure 7.38 shows the pin assignment scheme of the 8255.

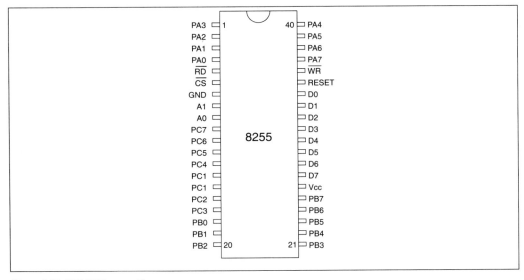

Figure 7.38: PPI 8255 connections.

PA7–PA0 (pins 37–40, 1–4)
These eight pins form port A. The lines lead to a data output latch/buffer and a data input latch, which are each eight bits wide.

$\overline{\text{RD}}$ (pin 5)
(Read) If the signal at this pin is at a low level, the CPU can read data from the 8255 PPI via the data bus D0–D7.

$\overline{\text{CS}}$ (pin 6)
(Chip Select) If this pin is at a low level, the CPU can read data from or write data to the internal 8255 registers, or access the I/O pins of the ports A, B and C by the $\overline{\text{RD}}$ and $\overline{\text{WR}}$ signals. Thus the $\overline{\text{CS}}$ signal enables the PPI for read and write processes.

A1–A0 (pins 8 and 9)

(Address) The signals at these pins, together with $\overline{RD}$ and $\overline{WR}$, select one of the three ports of the control word register. The possible combinations of (A1 A0 $\overline{RD}$ $\overline{WR}$) have the following meanings:

```
(0001)   port A -> data bus (read)
(0101)   port B -> data bus (read)
(1001)   port C -> data bus (read)
(1101)   control word -> data bus (read)
(0010)   data bus -> port A (write)
(0110)   data bus -> port B (write)
(1010)   data bus -> port C (write)
(1110)   data bus -> control word (write)
```

PC7–PC4 (pins 10–13)

These four pins form the high-order nibble of port C. The lines lead to a data output latch/buffer and a data input buffer, which are each four bits wide.

PC3–PC0 (pins 17–14)

These four pins form the low-order nibble of port C. The lines lead to a data output latch/buffer and a data input buffer, which are each four bits wide.

PB7–PB0 (pins 25–18)

These eight pins form port B. The lines lead to a data output latch/buffer and a data input buffer, which are each eight bits wide.

D7–D0 (pins 27–34)

These eight connections form the bidirectional data bus through which the 8255 receives data and commands from or outputs them to the CPU.

RESET (pin 35)

If the signal at this pin is at a high-level, the control register is cleared and the pins of all ports attain a level «1» (high).

$\overline{WR}$ (pin 36)

(Write) If the signal at this pin is at a low level, the CPU can write data into internal 8255 registers via the data bus D0–D7.

V_{cc} (pin 26)

This pin is supplied with the supply voltage (usually +5 V).

GND (pin 7)

This pin is grounded (usually 0 V).

7.5.2   8255 PPI Structure and Operating Modes

As the name PPI already indicates, the 8255 is programmable in three different modes:

- mode 0: simple unidirectional input/output without handshake;
- mode 1: unidirectional input/output with handshake via a nibble of port C;

– mode 2: bidirectional input/output via port A with handshake via the high-order nibble of
   port C.

Thus a very flexible chip for I/O purposes is available for computer designers. Figure 7.39
shows a diagram of its internal structure.

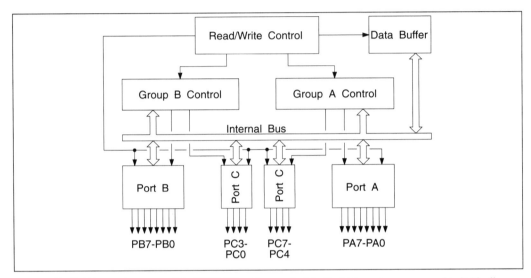

Figure 7.39: 8255 internal structure. The 8255 PPI has three ports A to C which can be programmed individually.

Ports A, B and C are combined into two groups A and B. For this purpose, port C is divided into
two sections, a high-order nibble PC7–PC4 and a low-order nibble PC3–PC0. The A-group
controls the eight I/O pins PA7–PA0 of port A, as well as the four high-order pins PC7–PC4 of
port C; the B-group controls the eight I/O pins PB7–PB0 of port B and the four low-order pins
PC3–PC0 of port C.

Port A has an 8-bit data output latch/buffer and an 8-bit input latch/buffer; port B has a data
input/output latch/buffer; and port C an 8-bit output latch/buffer, as well as an 8-bit input
buffer. Port C doesn't have a latch for the input. It can be divided into two 4-bit ports, which
may be used for outputting control signals and inputting status information for ports A and B.

Ports A, B and C may be operated separately or in the A and B combination with the high- and
low-order nibble of port C, respectively. For example, port A can be programmed for a bidirectional input and output of data to a controller with handshake and interrupt-driven data
exchange, while port B in mode 0 only observes the switching states of simple DIP switches. If
you change the mode of a port then the output register of the pins concerned is reset to «1». The
following briefly discusses the three modes.

Mode 0

Depending upon the programming for input or output, the data is simply read from or written
to the port concerned. In this mode ports A and B, as well as the high- and low-order nibbles of

port C, can be defined independently as input or output pins. Thus, the 8255 has two 8-bit and two 4-bit ports in this mode. In the PC/XT all three ports are operated in mode 0.

Mode 1

The data may be input or output in cooperation with handshake signals. In mode 1 ports A and B use the pins of port C to output the handshake signals. Ports A and B are themselves employed for the input and output of 8-bit data. Pins PC3 and PC0 provide interrupt request signals for ports A and B, respectively, if corresponding handshake signals have been received. An interrupt-driven data exchange can thus be realized with mode 1. As this 8255 capability is not used in the PC/XT and a description is only of interest for hardware developers, this mode 1 option is not described in further detail here. We shall meet interrupt-driven data exchange with handshake signals in connection with the serial and parallel interface.

Mode 2

Mode 2 is only available for Port A together with the high-order nibble of port C. In mode 2 data may be input and output; a bidirectional transfer takes place. The direction of the data flow must be inverted in certain circumstances. This is carried out by means of handshake signals, as is the case with mode 1. Further, the 8255 can also provide an interrupt request signal in mode 2 to issue a hardware interrupt. By means of mode 2, a very complex bidirectional data exchange can be realized.

One feature of the 8255 is its capability to combine modes 0, 1 and 2 for different ports. For example, you can program groups A and B in mode 1 for output and input, respectively, and connect them to the same peripheral (see Figure 7.40). Thus, you get a duplex connection between the 8255 and the peripheral. Of course, you may also realize such a bidirectional connection with port A in mode 2, but here the transfer direction must be switched according to the requirements. As a compensation, port B is available for another application.

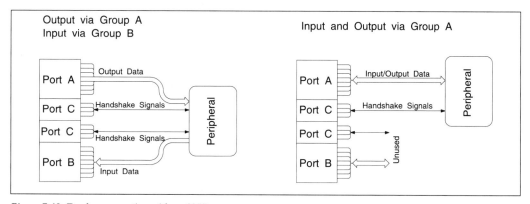

Figure 7.40: Duplex connection with an 8255.

7.5.3   Programming the 8255 PPI

Mode programming of the individual ports is carried out with a control word. You can access the control word register in the PC/XT at the port address 63h, and the three ports A, B and C with the port addresses 60h, 61h and 62h, respectively.

The ports programmed for output may be written by a simple OUT or read by an IN instruction. On the other hand, all ports programmed for input can only be read, not written. All write attempts to these ports are ignored.

Example: read port B
```
IN al, 61h  ; read port B into accumulator al
```

Example: write port A
```
MOV al, byte_value ; transfer byte_value into accumulator al
OUT 60h, al        ; write byte_value into port A; if port A is programmed
                   ; for input only then byte_value is ignored
```

For port C you have the option to set bits (and thus pins) individually to «1», or to reset to «0» by means of a control word. Also, in this case, the write commands via the control words are ignored if the port concerned is programmed for input only. Figure 7.41 shows the format of the control word.

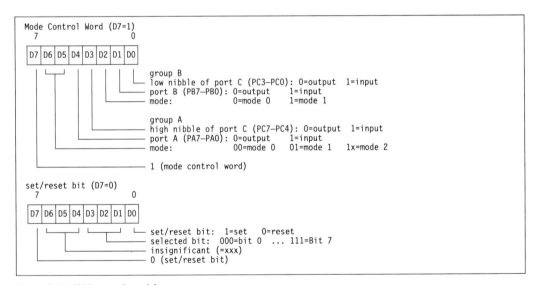

Figure 7.41: 8255 control word format.

A mode control word for setting the operation modes of ports A, B and C comprises a set bit 7 (*D7*) to distinguish this control word from a set or reset command for a single pin of port C. The three low-order bits *D2–D0* refer to the mode of group B, which consists of port B and the low-order nibble of port C. Port B and pins PC3–PC0 can be programmed separately for input or output. As for port B, only modes 0 and 1 are available – the single bit D2 is sufficient for defining the mode.

Bits *D6–D3* concern group A, which is port A and the high-order nibble of port C. Also in this case, port A and pins PC7–PC4 may be separately programmed for input and output. Besides modes 0 and 1, mode 2 with bidirectional data flow is also available for port A. For the determination of the mode, bits D5 and D6 are reserved. You may read or write the control word in the PC/XT via port address 63h. If the control word is read then *D7* is always equal to 1 as it provides mode control word information. You may thus determine the PPI's operating mode.

Example: operate all ports in mode 0; use ports A and C for data input, port B for signal output
OUT 63h, 9ch ; output control word 10011100b

Example: determine operation mode of ports A, B and C
IN al, 63h   ; read operation mode byte into accumulator al

If bit D7 in the control word is cleared (that is, equal to 0), the 8255 handles the passed byte as a set or reset command for an individual pin or individual bit of port C. Note that pins and bits can be set or reset only if the nibble to which the bit concerned belongs is operated in output mode by a mode control word; otherwise, the 8255 ignores the command. Bits D3–D1 form a 3-bit number, which defines the bit to set or reset. D0 indicates whether the selected bit is to be set to 1 or reset to 0.

Example: set bit 5 corresponding to pin 5 of port C to 1

OUT 63h, 0bh ; set bit 5 of port C by means of the control word 00001011b

Being able to set individual bits (and therefore pins) of port C is especially useful if port C is used for exchanging handshake signals in modes 1 and 2.

7.5.4   Port Assignment in the PC/XT

The 8255 PPI is used in the PC/XT to establish a connection to various components. The following figures show the port addresses of ports A, B, C and the 8255 control register, as well as the assignment of the ports in the PC/XT. Ports A, B, C may be read by a simple IN instruction and written by means of an OUT instruction if they are programmed for input and output, respectively. In the PC/XT, all three ports are operated in mode 0, that is, unidirectional input/output without handshake. Ports A and C are read-only; port B is write-only.

Port A has two main functions. If bit 7 of port B is equal to 0, then the keyboard is accessible via port A (Figure 7.42, top). Bit 7, after a keyboard interrupt 09h via IRQ1, indicates whether the key has been depressed (bit 7 equal to 1, «make-code») or released (bit 7 equal to 0, «break-code»), and the seven low-order bits contain the scan code of the key concerned. The keyboard is described in detail in Chapter 11.

If bit 7 of port B is equal to 1, the state of the DIP switches with the configuration settings can be read (Figure 7.42, bottom). Note that the assignment of port A coincides with the structure of the device byte (20, 14h) in the CMOS RAM. However, the bits *HS1* and *HS0* are reserved there; in port A they indicate the amount of main memory installed on the motherboard. Through bits *HS6–HS2* of port C you may also determine the number of 32 kbyte blocks of main memory on the motherboard installed in addition to the memory indicated by bits HS1 and HS0. Bits *FL1* and *FL0* indicate the number of floppy drives installed if the *FLP* bit is set. Through bits *GR1* and *GR0* you may determine the type of graphics adapter installed. Finally, bit *x87* indicates whether or not a coprocessor is installed.

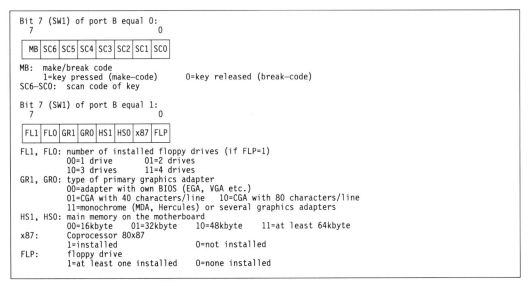

```
Bit 7 (SW1) of port B equal 0:
 7                               0

 MB SC6 SC5 SC4 SC3 SC2 SC1 SC0

MB:  make/break code
          1=key pressed (make-code)     0=key released (break-code)
SC6-SC0:  scan code of key

Bit 7 (SW1) of port B equal 1:
 7                               0

 FL1 FL0 GR1 GR0 HS1 HS0 x87 FLP

FL1, FL0: number of installed floppy drives (if FLP=1)
          00=1 drive          01=2 drives
          10=3 drives         11=4 drives
GR1, GR0: type of primary graphics adapter
          00=adapter with own BIOS (EGA, VGA etc.)
          01=CGA with 40 characters/line    10=CGA with 80 characters/line
          11=monochrome (MDA, Hercules) or several graphics adapters
HS1, HS0: main memory on the motherboard
          00=16kbyte     01=32kbyte    10=48kbyte     11=at least 64kbyte
x87:      Coprocessor 80x87
          1=installed              0=not installed
FLP:      floppy drive
          1=at least one installed    0=none installed
```

Figure 7.42: Port A (Port address 60h).

Example: Determine whether a coprocessor is installed according to the DIP switches (bit SW1 of port B assumed as 1).

```
IN  ah, 60h   ; transfer configuration byte of port A DIP switch to ah
AND ah, 02h   ; check whether bit 1 (x87) is set
```

Note that the values of the port A bits reflect the position of the DIP switches. If the switches are positioned incorrectly, then the bits also indicate an incorrect configuration, of course. The same applies to the CMOS RAM in the AT. The system is unable to determine the configuration on its own, but relies on the configuration settings according to the DIP switches or CMOS RAM during the boot process.

Port B (Figure 7.43) of the 8255 is programmed in output mode, and controls certain PC/XT registers. As already mentioned, bit *SW1* indicates whether the configuration settings or the keyboard byte can be read via port A. By means of bit *TKT*, you may deactivate or enable the clock signal for the keyboard. The keyboard is locked or released by this. Bits *NME* and *NMI* enable or disable the checking of extension adapters, for example the graphics adapter or the parity check function for main memory. The first PC came with a cassette recorder. By means of *REC* you can control its motor (an anachronism). The *SW2* bit indicates whether DIP switch 5 or DIP switches 0–3 of the second switch block can be read via port C. The *SPK* bit controls whether the output signal of the 8253 counter 2 is supplied to the cassette recorder or the speaker. Finally, the *RSG* drives the GATE input of the second counter in the 8253 PIT to enable or disable its counting function.

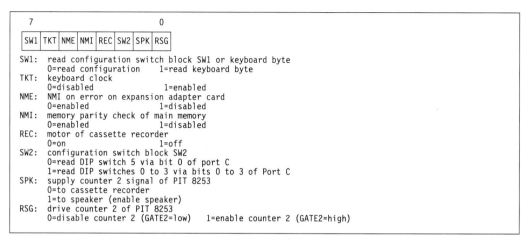

Figure 7.43: Port B (port address 61h).

Example: enable parity checking on the motherboard

```
IN  al, 61h  ; transfer byte from port B to al
OR  al, 10h  ; set bit 4 (NMI)
OUT 61h, al  ; transfer byte to port B
```

```
Bit 2 (SW2) of port B equal 0:
  7                        0
┌───┬───┬───┬───┬───┬───┬───┬───┐
│PAR│ERW│TIM│TON│HS5│HS4│HS3│HS2│
└───┴───┴───┴───┴───┴───┴───┴───┘

Bit 2 (SW2) of port B equal 1:
  7                        0
┌───┬───┬───┬───┬───┬───┬───┬───┐
│PAR│ERW│TIM│TON│res│res│res│HS6│
└───┴───┴───┴───┴───┴───┴───┴───┘

PAR:    NMI source
        0=no parity error              1=parity error in main memory
ERW:    NMI source
        0=no error on expansion card   1=error on expansion card
TIM:    counter 2 output signal of 8253 PIT
        0=low        1=high
TON:    cassette recorder signal
        0=low        1=high
HS6–HS2: size of main memory above 64 kbyte in 32 kbyte blocks
        00000=0 kbyte   00001=32 kbyte   00010=64 kbyte   00011=96 kbyte etc.
res:    reserved
```

Figure 7.44: Port C (port address 62h).

Like port A, port C (Figure 7.44) is also programmed as an input channel in the PC/XT. The *PAR* and *ERW* bits indicate whether an NMI is issued after a parity error in main memory or an error on an expansion adapter. The handler determines the source of the NMI using these bits and proceeds accordingly. With *TIM* you can read the current state of the output OUT2 of counter 2 in the 8253 timer chip. The *TON* bit indicates the level of the signal from the cassette recorder.

If bit SW2 of port B is cleared, you can read the four low-order bits of a 5-bit number via *HS5–HS2*. If you set bit SW2 of port B then you can read the most significant bit of this number via *HS6*. The 5-bit number HS6–HS2 indicates the memory installed on the motherboard beyond 64 kbytes in 32 kbyte blocks.

7.6   Modest Consumers – CMOS Elements

We have already met MOS transistors in Chapter 2. If we connect a p-channel and an n-channel MOSFET in parallel (that is, we combine them as shown in Figure 7.45), then we get a CMOS inverter. This forms the basic element of all CMOS circuits.

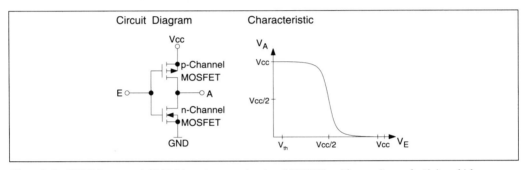

Figure 7.45: CMOS inverter. A CMOS inverter comprises two MOSFETs with opposite conductivity which are connected between ground and V_{cc}. A characteristic with sharp transition is the result.

The two MOSFETs are connected in series between the supply voltage Vcc and ground. The gate of the p- or n-channel MOSFETs is separate from the substrate, and therefore from source and drain, by a thin oxide layer so that no current may flow through the gate. For a current flow it is necessary that both transistors are conductive simultaneously to establish a current path between ground and supply voltage. But if you look at the characteristics in Figure 2.1a and 2.1b then you see that there is no overlapping in the conductivity of the p- and n-channel MOSFETs. In other words, one MOSFET is always switched off. If the voltage V_E at input E is positive enough (that is, higher than the threshold voltage V_{TO} of the n-channel MOSFET Tr_n), then the n-channel MOSFET is turned on but the p-channel MOSFET Tr_p is switched off. With a sufficiently negative voltage U_E (lower than the threshold voltage U_{TO} of the p-channel MOSFET), the p-channel MOSFET is instead conductive, and the n-channel MOSFET is turned off. In all other cases both transistors are turned off.

It is decisive for use in (digital) computer technics that the *voltage* V_A at output A is changed according to the variation of the input voltage V_E in a range between the supply voltage Vcc and ground:

– If V_E is negative enough then Tr_p is conductive and Tr_n is switched off; output A is on a Vcc-level and the CMOS inverter outputs a logical 1 (or a logical 0 if negative logic is used).

–   If V_E is sufficiently positive then Tr_n is instead conductive, and Tr_p is switched off; the output A is grounded and the CMOS inverter outputs a logical 0 (or a logical 1 if negative logic is used).

For use in computers with two clearly defined states it is good for the transition section of the characteristic between V_{cc} and ground to be very sharp (see Figure 7.45). Computers with CMOS circuits therefore operate very reliably.

A significant advantage of CMOS circuits as compared to normal MOS chips is the low power consumption. Only during the course of a switch between V_{cc} and ground does a current flow to charge or discharge the corresponding layers of the CMOS transistors, according to their capacity. The very low static power consumption is mainly the result of leak currents through the (never completely) isolating oxide layer below the gate. If the voltage V_A at output A turns over by a fast change of the input voltage V_E, then this turnover gives rise to an additional dynamic power consumption because of the regular charging and discharging of the semiconductor layers. This dynamic power consumption rises in proportion to the turnover frequency.

The content of the CMOS RAM in our real-time clock chip is rarely changed. The time update once a second is very low when compared to the rate of several MHz when the processor accesses the main memory. Thus the CMOS inverter is well suited to a static RAM with low power consumption. Of course, the chips of the usual main memory may also be implemented with the CMOS technique. As a CMOS inverter has two elements, the integration density is lower or the effort taken to integrate the same number of elements on a single chip gets higher than with normal transistors.

A serious problem in realizing ever higher integration densities (and thus, for example, higher memory chip capacities) is that the miniaturization of the elements increases the power consumption. The size and therefore the power consumption of the individual elements on the chip decreases, but as the number of these elements rises enormously, we have a higher power consumption in the end. The consumed power is nearly all converted to heat and warms up the chip. The real workaholics, and thus also current eaters, are the coprocessors. You can easily burn your fingers on an intensively used coprocessor. If the heat produced cannot be led away, the chip gets into a muddle because of calculation errors by overheated transistors. The computer crashes and is inoperable until it cools down. A further temperature increase may finally result in damaged semiconductor layers, and therefore a damaged chip. For this reason, all highly integrated processors starting with the i386 and i387 are implemented using the CMOS technique. In the conventional NMOS technique, the i387 in particular would be more of a radiator than a coprocessor!

For laptops, notebooks and other applications with a limited power source, there are also CMOS variants of the other processors. You may recognize them because of the «C» in the type name, for example 80C286 or 80C287. Compared to normal chips, these CMOS variants consume only about one third of the power.

7.7　CMOS RAM and Real-Time Clock

The old PC/XTs had several small DIP switches (sometimes mockingly called mice pianos), by means of which the user had to set the configuration of the computer. The configuration information includes the number and type of floppy drives, graphics adapter, base memory, etc. As a PC is a «personal» computer, the configurations can be very different. Because of the nearly infinite number of hard disks with different geometries (number of heads, tracks, sectors) a configuration setting by means of DIP switches is now ruled out. Another big disadvantage was the lack of a real-time clock. After every boot process the PC initialized itself to 1.1.1980, 0:00 o'clock. The user first had to input the current date and time via the DOS commands DATE and TIME. As the first PC was shipped after that date, all PCs (and therefore also DOS, by the way) don't know any earlier time than 1.1.1980, 0:00 o'clock; DOS manages all times relative to this time and date.

IBM recognized this inadequacy and installed a real-time clock as well as CMOS RAM, beginning with the successor to the PC/XT, the AT. These two elements are supplied by an accumulator or a in-built battery once the PC is switched off. Instead of CMOS RAM you will often see the name *NVR* (**n**on **v**olatile **R**AM). This indicates that the data in this memory is kept even after the power is switched off. The real-time clock is independent of the CPU and all other chips (also the 8253, 8254 PIT for the internal system clock) and keeps on updating the time and date in the background. The CMOS RAM holds the configuration data, which had to be set by means of DIP switches on the PC/XT. The ROM BIOS reads the real-time clock and the CMOS RAM during the boot process, and thus determines the current configuration as well as time and date. The TIME and DATE commands for setting time and date are now obsolete. The CMOS RAM and real-time clock are integrated in a single chip, the Motorola MC146818, or compatible. In most of today's PCs, this chip is already installed on the motherboard (or the processor card in modular machines). With a separate clock adapter card you can also equip an older PC model with this chip. If your computer has a very old BIOS that is not designed for an access to the real-time clock and CMOS RAM, this clock adapter is not very useful. You should replace the ROM or EPROM chips with the old BIOS with a newer version.

For buffering, small batteries or accumulators are largely used. Accumulators are usually soldered to the board; batteries are held in a socket. The power consumption by the CMOS RAM and the real-time clock is so low that usually it plays no role in the lifetime of the batteries or accumulators. Instead, the life is determined by the self-discharge time of the accumulator or battery, and is about three years (with lithium batteries up to ten years).

7.7.1　MC146818 Structure and Programming

The accumulator or the battery supplies the following elements with power if the PC is switched off (see Figure 7.46):

- the CMOS RAM with the configuration settings as well as time and date, which are periodically updated by the real-time clock;
- the real-time clock.

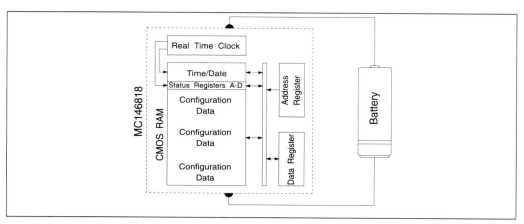

Figure 7.46: Technical structure of the MC146818. The MC146818 has a real-time clock and 64 bytes of battery-buffered RAM. The MC146818 can be programmed by an address and a data register.

The CMOS RAM in the MC146818 usually has 64 individually accessible bytes of memory. Some chips have more than these 64 bytes, especially if the data of an extended setup has to be stored. The meaning of the additional bytes, however, is no longer standardized. Of these 64 bytes, the first 14 (addresses 00h to 0dh) are reserved for the time and date, as well as the control and status registers of the real-time clock. The remaining 50 bytes hold information concerning the PC's configuration. Table 7.12 shows the memory configuration of the CMOS RAM.

Byte	Address	Contents	Byte	Address	Contents
0	00h	second*)	22	16h	base memory (high byte)
1	01h	alarm second*)	23	17h	extended memory (low byte)
2	02h	minute*)			according SETUP
3	03h	alarm minute*)	24	18h	extended memory (high byte)
4	04h	hour*)			according SETUP
5	05h	alarm hour*)	25	19h	extension byte 1st hard disk
6	06h	day of week*)	26	1ah	extension byte 2nd hard disk
7	07h	day of month*)	27–31	1bh–1fh	reserved
8	08h	month*)	32–39	20h–27h	parameter hard disk type 48
9	09h	year*)	40–45	28h–dh	reserved
10	0ah	status register A	46	2eh	check sum (low byte)
11	0bh	status register B	47	2fh	check sum (high byte)
12	0ch	status register C	48	30h	extended memory (low byte)
13	0dh	status register D			according POST
14	0eh	diagnosis status	49	31h	extended memory (high byte)
15	0fh	shutdown status			according POST
16	10h	type of floppy drives	50	32h	century*)
17	11h	reserved	51	33h	setup informations
18	12h	type of hard disk drives	52	34h	reserved
19	13h	reserved	53–60	35h–3ch	parameter hard disk type 49
20	14h	device byte	61–63	3dh–3fh	reserved
21	15h	base memory (low byte)			

*) usually binary coded decimals (1 byte)

Table 7.12: CMOS-RAM memory configuration

Note that all time and date information is usually held as binary coded decimals. You may alter this standard encoding with status register B (see Figure 7.47). If the real-time clock is running in 12-hour mode (set with status register B, see Figure 7.47), then a.m. and p.m. are distinguished by bit 7 in the entry hour or alarm hour: a cleared bit indicates a.m., a set bit p.m. DOS usually sets the time format and therefore also this bit according to the country information in CONFIG.SYS (COUNTRY=xxx). The range of values for a.m. is therefore $01–$12 and $81–$92 for p.m.

Example: 39 (= 27h) in byte 2/address 02H (minute) leads to 27 minutes

All other information is binary encoded. The quantities comprising two bytes are stored in little endian format.

Example: base memory

```
80H (= 128) in byte 21/address 15h
02H (= 2) in byte 22/address 16h
leads to 2*256 + 128 = 640 (kbyte) base memory
```

Besides the normal time and date function, the chip also has an in-built daylight saving function (activated via status register B, see Figure 7.47), as well as a function for determining the day of the week or month. The AT doesn't use these functions, however. For compatibility reasons, DOS determines the day of the week according to its own algorithm, as the PC/XT didn't incorporate such a chip.

For supervising and programming the MC146818 the four status registers A to D are of importance. Using these you can define the chip's operation mode. Figure 7.47 shows the format of these bytes.

The MC146818 updates the clock every second by updating bytes 0, 2, 4, 6, 7, 8, 9 and 50 of the CMOS RAM. While this update is in progress, bytes 0–9 cannot be accessed; an access provides possibly meaningless values. Thus the MC146818 sets the *UIP* bit in status register A to indicate this update process. Bits *B2–B0* define the time base that the real-time clock uses. In the AT the value 010b is set as standard. It provides a time base of 32 768Hz. Other values may accelerate or slow down the real-time clock. Using the four bits *T3–0* you can define the rate of the square-wave signal or the periodic interrupt (see below). The values may be in the range between 0011 and 1111. With the relation

```
frequency=65 536 Hz/2value(T3-T0)
```

rates between 8192 Hz (cycle time 122 μs) and 2 Hz (500 ms) are possible. *Value(T3–T0)* denotes the value of the rate select bits. The AT initializes the rate select to 0110b corresponding to 1024 Hz (= 65 536/2^6) or a cycle time of 976.56 μs as standard. An entry 0000b disables the rate generator. The two functions 83h and 86h of interrupt INT 15h use the 1024 Hz clock for determining wait intervals (see below).

Using the *SET* bit in the status register you can disable the update of the time and date bytes in the CMOS RAM. Thus you may initialize the MC146818 first and start the clock afterwards. The chip can not only serve as a real-time clock and an NVR, but can also generate a square-wave signal. The frequency of this signal is defined by the rate select bits T3–T0 in status register A. In the PC, the MC146818 output is not used, however, so that this capability is of only a theoretical nature as long as you don't fetch your soldering iron and use the square-wave output for your private purposes! The date and time values stored in CMOS RAM are usually held in BCD format, as already mentioned. The *DM* bit also advises the MC146818 to store all date and time values with binary encoding. But be careful: all DOS and BIOS functions assume the BCD format. Moreover, you are free to select a 12- or 24-hour clock. The *24h* bit switches the real-time clock between these two modes. Note that in the case of a 12-hour clock the most significant hour bit is set for all hours after noon (p.m.). Thus the hour counting runs from \$81 to \$92.

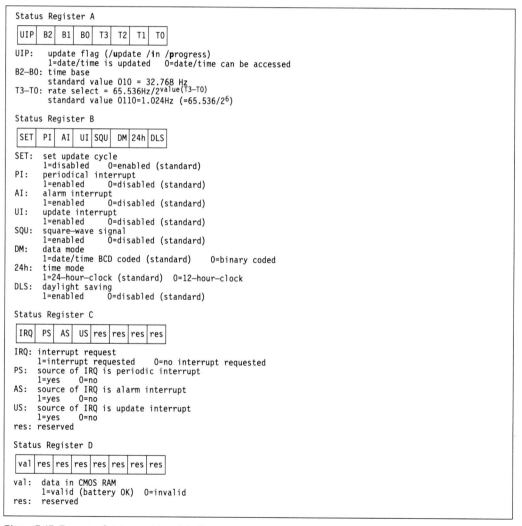

```
Status Register A

UIP  B2  B1  B0  T3  T2  T1  T0

UIP:    update flag (/update /in /progress)
        1=date/time is updated   0=date/time can be accessed
B2-B0:  time base
        standard value 010 = 32.768 Hz
T3-T0:  rate select = 65.536Hz/2^value(T3-T0)
        standard value 0110=1.024Hz (=65.536/2^6)

Status Register B

SET  PI  AI  UI  SQU  DM  24h  DLS

SET:    set update cycle
        1=disabled   0=enabled (standard)
PI:     periodical interrupt
        1=enabled   0=disabled (standard)
AI:     alarm interrupt
        1=enabled   0=disabled (standard)
UI:     update interrupt
        1=enabled   0=disabled (standard)
SQU:    square-wave signal
        1=enabled   0=disabled (standard)
DM:     data mode
        1=date/time BCD coded (standard)   0=binary coded
24h:    time mode
        1=24-hour-clock (standard)   0=12-hour-clock
DLS:    daylight saving
        1=enabled   0=disabled (standard)

Status Register C

IRQ  PS  AS  US  res  res  res  res

IRQ:  interrupt request
      1=interrupt requested   0=no interrupt requested
PS:   source of IRQ is periodic interrupt
      1=yes   0=no
AS:   source of IRQ is alarm interrupt
      1=yes   0=no
US:   source of IRQ is update interrupt
      1=yes   0=no
res:  reserved

Status Register D

val  res  res  res  res  res  res  res

val:  data in CMOS RAM
      1=valid (battery OK)   0=invalid
res:  reserved
```

Figure 7.47: Formats of status registers A to D.

Using the most significant hour bit, you may distinguish between a.m. and p.m. The *DLS* bit enables the daylight saving function of the MC146818, but the PC makes no use of it.

Bits *PI, AI* and *UI* enable various interrupt requests. A set PI bit leads to a periodic interrupt request with a rate defined by bits T3–T0 in status register A. The MC146818 then behaves like counter 0 of the PIT, which updates the internal system clock. The AI bit activates the C146817's alarm function. Upon every update of the time entries, the chip checks whether the updated time coincides with the alarm time held by bytes 1, 3 and 5. If this is true, the MC146817 issues an alarm interrupt. If you have set bit UI, then after every completed update of time and date in the CMOS RAM an interrupt request occurs. This is called the update interrupt.

The interrupt signal output of the MC146818 is connected via IRQ8 to the slave 8259A PIC in the AT. Thus all three sources lead to the same interrupt, namely interrupt 70h. Similar to the timer interrupt 08h via IRQ0, the handler of interrupt 70h calls a further interrupt as the user exit, namely interrupt 4ah. Usually, the handler consists of a simple IRET instruction, but you are free to redirect it to your own routine which, for example, tells you by the wail of a siren through the speaker and a pop-up window that it's time to have a cup of coffee.

Thus the handler of interrupt 70h or 4ah has to respond differently according to the interrupt source. If the periodic interrupt request is interpreted as an alarm interrupt, the user is unable to enjoy his computer (or life) anymore. To avoid such misunderstandings, status register C is helpful. It serves to determine the source of an interrupt request. The *IRQ* bit as an interrupt flag indicates whether the MC146818 has issued an interrupt request at all. If IRQ is set then bits *PS, AS* and *US* show whether a periodic, alarm or update interrupt has occurred. If several interrupt requests are allowed by means of several set enable bits in status register B, then they may, of course, be issued concurrently. In this case, several of the bits PS, AS and US are also set. The handler has to decide which request is serviced first.

The MC146818 has a function that permanently observes the charge state of the battery or accumulator. If the voltage drops below a critical value once, this function sets the *val* bit in status register D to indicate that the stored data is possibly invalid. The BIOS checks status register D in the course of the boot process to detect such a power break, and to display an appropriate message eventually.

Note that the time and date bytes 0–9, as well as the four status registers, are not accessible during an MC146818 update cycle (bit UIP in the status register A). However, you may always read and write the configuration bytes (described in the following) as only the setup program accesses them and not the real-time clock.

In the diagnostics status byte (see Figure 7.48) the POST routine of the BIOS stores certain check results that the PC carries out during the boot process. As already mentioned, the MC146818 sets bit val in status register D if the voltage of the battery or accumulator has once dropped below a certain minimum value. The BIOS reads this entry during the course of the boot process, and sets or clears the *STR* bit in the diagnosis status byte. In bytes 46 and 47 the BIOS stores a checksum, which is formed for bytes 16–45 (see Figure 7.57). During the course of the boot process, the PC determines whether the stored checksum coincides with the newly calculated one, and sets (checksum OK) or clears (checksum false) the *SUM* bit. Note that it is not the MC146818 but the BIOS that calculates the checksum. If you alter one of bytes 16–46 then you have to recalculate the checksum and store it in bytes 46–47. If you don't do this the BIOS displays a CMOS checksum error upon the next boot process. While booting, the BIOS further checks first whether the indicated configuration is consistent, and second, whether it coincides with the controllers, etc. actually present. The result of this check is stored in the *KFG* bit. The *MEM* bit indicates whether the POST routine has determined the same memory size as you have entered via the setup program. During the course of the boot process, the BIOS attempts to initialize all controllers. According to bit *HD* you may recognize whether or not this process was successful for hard disk drive C:. Finally, the *UHR* bit shows whether the current time is correct or invalid (indicates, for example, 12:78 o'clock).

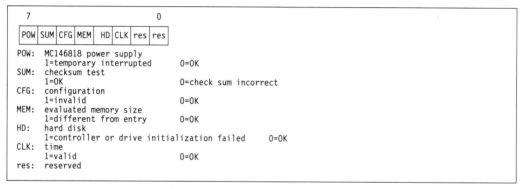

Figure 7.48: Diagnostics status byte (14, 0eh).

During a processor reset the shutdown status byte (see Figure 7.49) is loaded with a value that provides some information about the cause of the reset during the course of the following boot process. A value 00h of bits *RS7–RS0* indicates a normal reset to the BIOS which, for example, was issued by the user through the reset button. The 80286 cannot be switched back from protected to real mode, unlike the i386 and following chips; this is only possible by a processor reset. Programs such as SMARTDRV.SYS or RAMDRIVE.SYS, which access extended memory in protected mode, therefore set the shutdown status byte to a value of 09h to inform the BIOS that no «real» reset has occurred, and that only a switch back to the real mode should be carried out.

```
 7                        0
┌────┬────┬────┬────┬────┬────┬────┬────┐
│RS7 │RS6 │RS5 │RS4 │RS3 │RS2 │RS1 │RS0 │
└────┴────┴────┴────┴────┴────┴────┴────┘
RS7–RS0: reset information
    00h=normal system reset      01h=initialization for real mode
    04h=JMP to bootstrap
    05h=output EOI to PIC, clear keyboard, JMP with far pointer at 40:67h
    06h=JMP with far pointer at 40:67h without EOI
    07h=return to INT 15h, function 87h "move block in extended memory"
    08h=return to POST memory test
    09h=return to INT 15h, function 87h "move block in extended memory"
    0ah=JMP with far pointer at 40:67h without EOI
    0bh=IRET via far pointer at 40:67h
    0ch=return via far pointer at 40:67h
```

Figure 7.49: Shutdown status byte (15, 0fh).

Byte 16 in the CMOS RAM (see Figure 7.50) indicates the type of the first (high-order nibble) and second (low-order nibble) floppy drive. The values 0101 to 1111 are reserved for future types of floppy drives.

```
 7                           0
┌──┬──┬──┬──┬──┬──┬──┬──┐
│A3│A2│A1│A0│B3│B2│B1│B0│
└──┴──┴──┴──┴──┴──┴──┴──┘
A3-A0: type of first floppy drive (A:)
B3-B0: type of second floppy drive (B:)
       0000=not installed        0001=5 1/4" 360 kbyte
       0010=5 1/4" 1.2 Mbyte     0011=3 1/2" 720 kbyte
       0100=3 1/1" 1.44 Mbyte    0101-1111=reserved
```

Figure 7.50: Floppy drive types (16, 10h).

Similarly, byte 18 holds the hard disk drive types (see Figure 7.51). The high-order nibble indicates the type of the first, and the low-order nibble the type of the second hard disk. Thus, a maximum of 16 possibilities is available for every drive (including 0 for none).

```
 7          4  3           0
┌──┬──┬──┬──┬──┬──┬──┬──┐
│C3│C2│C1│C0│D3│D2│D1│D0│
└──┴──┴──┴──┴──┴──┴──┴──┘
C3-C0: type of first hard disk (C:)
D3-D0: type of second hard disk (D:)
       0000=not installed     0001-1110=type 1 ... 14
       1111=type 16 ... 255 according to hard disk extension bytes
```

Figure 7.51: Hard disk drive types (18, 12h).

In view of today's variety of hard disks, this is, of course, not sufficient. The value 15 (= 0fh) is therefore reserved as «extended». If this value is stored for one of the drives, then the actual type byte is stored at address 19h (first hard disk) or 1ah (second hard disk). The format of this hard disk extension byte is shown in Figure 7.52. The number indicated by the high-order or low-order nibble in the hard disk drive byte or in the hard disk extension byte serves as an index into a BIOS parameter table, which holds the geometry of the hard disk concerned. These BIOS tables may differ from manufacturer to manufacturer; the only solution is to look at the manual.

```
 7                           0
┌───┬───┬───┬───┬───┬───┬───┬───┐
│LW7│LW6│LW5│LW4│LW3│LW2│LW1│LW0│
└───┴───┴───┴───┴───┴───┴───┴───┘
LW7-LW0: hard disk type
```

Figure 7.52: Hard disk extension byte (25, 19h and 26, 1ah).

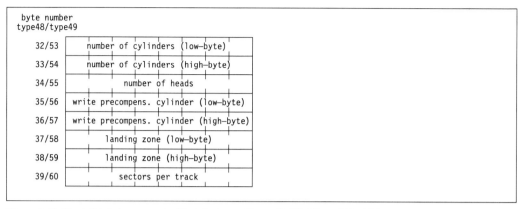

Figure 7.53: Hard disk drive parameter block for types 48 and 49 (32, 20h and 53, 35h).

Many BIOS chips allow a user-defined hard disk type. This is necessary if you have a hard disk with an exotic geometry, or a recently developed one whose parameters were unknown when the BIOS was programmed. From the viewpoint of BIOS and the operating system, PCs are designed as standard for operation with a maximum of two physical hard disks. In most cases, hard disk types 48 and 49 are reserved for freely definable types. In CMOS RAM two parameter blocks are implemented for them (see Figure 7.53). The block has eight bytes each, starting at bytes 32 and 53, respectively. The meaning of the corresponding entries is described in Section 9.1.3. Note that older BIOS versions, in particular, don't have the option to define an exotic drive geometry, and therefore neither the structure shown in Figure 7.53 nor the block addresses are strictly standardized. Fortunately, most BIOS manufacturers obey the above mentioned convention.

```
 7                          0
┌───┬───┬───┬───┬───┬───┬───┬───┐
│FL1│FL0│GR1│GR0│res│res│x87│FLP│
└───┴───┴───┴───┴───┴───┴───┴───┘
FL1, FL0: number of floppies installed (if FLP=1)
          00=1 drive        01=2 drives
GR1, GR0: type of primary graphics adapter
          00=adapter with own BIOS (EGA, VGA etc.)
          01=CGA with 40 characters/line   10=CGA with 80 characters/line
          11=monochrome (MDA, Hercules)
x87:      coprocessor 80x87
          1=installed                0=not installed
FLP:      floppy drive
          1=at least one installed   0=none installed
res:      reserved
```

Figure 7.54: Device byte (20, 14h).

In the device byte (see Figure 7.54) the setup program stores data concerning certain components of the PC. The bits *FL1, FL0* indicate the number of floppy drives installed if the *FLP* bit is set; otherwise, the entry has no meaning. Bits *GR1, GR0* define the type of the primary graphics adapter. Modern adapters with their own BIOS, such as EGA or VGA, are characterized by an entry 00b. Finally, the *x87* bit indicates whether a coprocessor is installed.

The two base memory bytes (see Figure 7.55) indicate the amount of installed base memory in kbytes as a 16-bit number in Intel format.

```
  21    base memory in kbyte (low–byte)
  22    base memory in kbyte (high–byte)
```

Figure 7.55: Base memory (21, 15h and 22, 16h).

In the setup program you normally also have to enter the size of extended memory. The program stores this value in the two extended memory bytes 23 and 24, which indicate the size of extended memory as the two base memory bytes in kbytes as a 16-bit number in Intel format (see Figure 7.56). During the course of the boot process, the POST routine of the BIOS checks how large the extended memory actually is, and stores the resulting value in extended memory bytes 48 and 49. If the two values of stored and checked extended memory don't match, then either you have entered a wrong number, the CMOS RAM has suffered a power break, or the memory chips are faulty.

```
  23/48    extended memory in kbyte (low–byte)
  24/49    extended memory in kbyte (high–byte)
```

Figure 7.56: Extended memory as stored and determined by BIOS (23, 17h and 24, 18h or 48, 30h and 49, 31h).

Bytes 46 and 47 of the CMOS RAM hold the checksum of bytes 16–45 (see Figure 7.57). This is determined by simply adding the values of bytes 16–45, and is stored by the BIOS as a 16-bit number in Intel format.

```
  46    checksum (low–byte)
  47    checksum (high–byte)
```

Figure 7.57: Checksum (46, 2eh and 47, 2fh).

Byte 50 holds the century, usually in the BCD format (see Figure 7.58). By means of the DM bit in status register B, you can also define the binary coded format. Note that in byte 9 of the CMOS RAM only the decade and the year can be accommodated, not the century.

```
   7                           0
 CE7 CE6 CE5 CE4 CE3 CE2 CE1 CE0
 CE7–CE0:   century
```

Figure 7.58: Century byte (50, 32h).

In the reserved bits and bytes some BIOS (the AMI BIOS, for example) store very hardware-dependent information, for example the clock speed of the processor, the size of the BIOS ROM, the size of the data bus, shadowing of ROM code, or caching. The use of the individual bits and bytes is not standardized in these cases so you should not attempt to use reserved bits and bytes for your own purposes, or to alter them in any way. Be aware that the entries in battery-buffered CMOS RAM are very long lived. Even a power-down and rebooting doesn't free you from faulty entries in the CMOS RAM, which let your brand new 50 MHz i486 PC with disabled caching, shadowing and paging/interleaving appear to be a slow XT.

You can access the bytes described in CMOS RAM and the four control registers A to D in two ways:

- with limited capability (only date/time and alarm) via the BIOS interrupt 1ah (see Appendix E).
- complete, by means of the address and data registers at ports 70h and 71h.

7.7.2   Access via the BIOS

Eight functions are available for the BIOS interrupt 1ah. The first two refer to the DOS-internal system clock; the other six to the real-time clock. You can thus set and clear time and date as well as set and clear an alarm time. The access via BIOS is therefore rather limited. Configuration data can neither be read nor written. Also, the other MC146818 functions, such as the periodic interrupt or generation of the square-wave signal, are not programmable. This is only possible by directly accessing the accompanying ports.

Example: set time to 12.45 o'clock without daylight saving

```
mov ah, 03h  ; function 03h
mov cl, 45h  ; 45 minutes
mov ch, 12h  ; 12 hours
mov dl, 00h  ; no daylight saving
mov dh, 00h  ; 0 seconds
int 1ah      ; set time via interrupt 1ah
```

Appendix E gives a list of all possible functions of interrupt 1ah as far as they refer to the real-time clock. Note that passing the date and time values to or from the interrupt 1ah is carried out using binary coded decimals. If the interrupt handler is unable to read the data concerned from or write it into the CMOS RAM as the MC146818 currently updates the date and time, then the carry flag is set and the values passed in the registers are meaningless.

With DOS commands DATE and TIME you can read and set the internal system clock. The real-time clock is not affected by this before DOS version 3.30. Before DOS 3.30, the system date and time are newly set, but the real-time clock is not accessed and updated. After the next boot process the system clock therefore shows the old settings again.

Besides the programming of date and time you may further use the functions 83h and 86h of interrupt 15h to set certain time intervals until an action occurs. With function 83h, the program execution is continued and a user-defined bit in the main memory is set after the wait time has elapsed. Function 86h, on the other hand, suspends program execution until the set time interval has elapsed, and therefore a real wait is carried out. Both functions are also to be found in Appendix E.

7.7.3 Access via Address and Data Register

For an access via the address and data registers ports 70h (address register) and 71h (data register) are used. Note that data bit 7 of port 70h controls the NMI mask register. Never alter its value, but read the byte from port 70h first and overwrite only the five low-order bits, which are sufficient for addressing the 64 bytes in the CMOS RAM. To read or output a data byte proceed as follows:

- fetch the old byte via port 70h and output the address of the data byte to access using the five low-order bits;

- read or write the thus accessed data byte via port 71h.

Example: read hard disk drive type

```
IN   al, 70h    ; read old byte from port 70h
AND  al, e0h    ; clear the five low-order bits
OR   al, 12h    ; load accumulator al with address of byte 18,
                ; bit 7 remains unchanged;
OUT  70h, al    ; write address of byte 18 into address register
IN   al, 71h    ; read drive type into accumulator
```

The byte read in the example then contains the type of both hard disks.

Example: determine the base memory size

```
IN   al, 70h  ; read byte from port 70h
AND  al, e0h  ; clear five low-order bits
OR   al, 16h  ; load address of high-order base memory byte into al
OUT  70h, al  ; output address to the MC146818 address register
IN   al, 71h  ; read high-order base memory byte
MOV  ah, al   ; transfer high-order base memory byte into ah
IN   al, 70h  ; read byte from port 70h
AND  al, e0h  ; clear five low-order bits
OR   al, 15h  ; load address of low-order base memory byte into al
OUT  70h, al  ; output address to the MC146818 address register
IN   al, 71h  ; read low-order base memory byte,
              ; thus ax=ah.al contains the size of base memory in kbytes
```

If you alter an entry then ensure that the CMOS RAM holds a checksum of the configuration bytes 10h to 2dh in bytes 46 and 47. Thus you also have to recalculate and write the checksum. During the course of the boot procedure the ROM BIOS checks whether configuration data and checksum conform. If this is not the case, the BIOS displays a message indicating that a CMOS RAM error has occurred and refuses to boot. This prevents the operating system from being configured incorrectly in the course of the boot process, and from damaging data or even hardware components because of a configuration error.

You may, of course, also program all functions accessible via BIOS interrupt 1ah via the ports. For setting an alarm time, for example, you have to write byte 1 (alarm second), 3 (alarm minute), and 5 (alarm hour) according to the intended alarm time and the data mode set in status register B. Further, you must enable the alarm interrupt using bit AI in status register B.

7.7.4 Extended CMOS RAM

Some ATs and i386/i486 PCs have a further battery-buffered NVR besides the conventional CMOS RAM. Its exact size will be found in your manual. Often, manufacturers use the smallest CMOS SRAM chip currently available on the market which has a capacity of 16 kbits. With the extended CMOS RAM an additional memory of 2 kbytes is available in most cases. As with a normal CMOS RAM, you may store additional information there, which should also be kept during power-down.

You may address the data in the extended CMOS RAM via ports 74h (low-order address byte) and 75h (high-order address byte), and read or write the addressed byte via port 76h. Note that no extended CMOS RAM was implemented in the IBM AT, and therefore no precisely defined standard exists. Only EISA and PS/2 have an extended CMOS RAM for storing adapter information that is clearly standardized. Unlike conventional CMOS RAM, you need two bytes for addressing, as a 1–byte address can only access 256 bytes.

Example: read byte 745 in the extended CMOS RAM

```
MOV al, 233 ; load low–order address byte into accumulator al
OUT 74h, al ; output low–order address byte via port 74h
MOV al, 2   ; load high–order address byte into accumulator al
OUT 75h, al ; output high–order address byte via port 75h
IN  al, 76h ; read byte 745 via data port 76h into accumulator al
```

Example: overwrite byte 162 of the extended CMOS RAM with the value 76

```
MOV al, 162 ; load low–order address byte into accumulator al
OUT 74h, al ; output low–order address byte via port 74h
MOV al, 0   ; load high–order address byte into accumulator al
OUT 75h, al ; output high–order address byte via port 75h
MOV al, 76  ; load data byte into accumulator al
OUT al, 76h ; write value 76 via data port 76h into byte 162 in the extended CMOS RAM
```

Part 3
Mass Storage

8   Floppies and Floppy Drives

8.1   Ferromagnetism and Induction – The Basis of Magnetic Data Recording

Pure magnetic fields in a vacuum which are generated, for example, by an electromagnet can be physically described quite easily. The situation becomes more complicated if metals or ceramics are introduced into the field, as such substances alter the magnetic field. Depending upon the strength and sign of the interaction we can distinguish three kinds of magnetism: diamagnetism, paramagnetism, and ferromagnetism. The latter is that used in most technical applications and in all magnetic data recordings (audio tape, magnetic card, floppy or hard disk).

8.1.1   Diamagnetism and Paramagnetism

All substances are diamagnetic in principle, but this effect is obscured by the frequent presence of paramagnetism. If a diamagnetic substance such as hydrogen or silver is introduced into a magnetic field, the substance weakens the magnetic field slightly (typically by 0.000001% to 0.05%). Pure diamagnetism occurs only in substances that don't have unpaired electrons, for example rare gases or metal salts. The distinctive characteristic of diamagnetism when compared to paramagnetism and ferrormagnetism is that it is completely temperature-independent.

Most atoms have at least one unpaired electron in their shell; thus paramagnetism occurs. If one introduces a paramagnetic substance, for example aluminium or liquid oxygen, into a magnetic field then this substance strengthens the magnetic field already present by 0.00001% to 0.05%. The reason for this effect is the alignment of the atoms by the external magnetic field. The lower the temperature the stronger this effect becomes, as the temperature movement of the atoms disturbs the alignment with a rising temperature.

Diamagnetism and paramagnetism have the common characteristic that the amount of magnetization is dependent upon the existence of an external magnetic field. The external field gives rise to a magnetic effect which weakens (diamagnetism) or strengthens (paramagnetism) the already existing magnetic field. If the external magnetic field is switched off, then the substances's own magnetization vanishes. Thus diamagnetic and paramagnetic substances do not generate their own permanent magnetic field, and are therefore unsuitable for the long-term recording of data.

8.1.2   Ferromagnetism

Of significant technological importance are ferromagnetic substances, the best-known of which is iron. In these materials microscopically small areas of billions of atoms, the so-called *domains*, are completely magnetized (see Figure 8.1). However, as these areas are usually aligned statistically, their effect is compensated for macroscopically and the substance seems to be unmagnetized to the exterior.

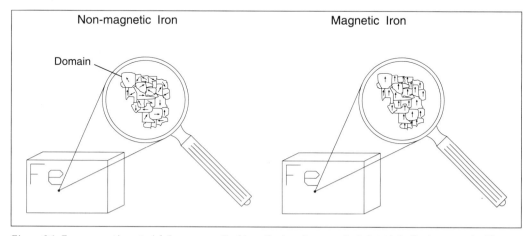

Figure 8.1: Ferromagnetic material. In unmagnetized iron the domains are oriented statistically; in magnetized iron the magnetic fields of the domains point uniformly in one direction.

If we introduce a ferromagnetic body into a magnetic field then (nearly) all domains align to the external field, and can amplify the field a million times (see Figure 8.1). Therefore, iron is used as the core for transformers, for example. The field, which is generated by the primary coil, is amplified by the iron core and induces a strong voltage in the secondary coil. The efficiency thus rises. You can see a similar effect with knives and forks made of iron, or steel scissors. If you always put them into the drawer in the same position, the earth's steadily present magnetic field magnetizes the knives and forks, and these attract other iron objects such as pins.

For data recording another characteristic of ferromagnetic substances is significant: so-called *remanence*. This is where ferromagnetic substances remain magnetic even after the external magnetic field has been «switched off». Diamagnetic and paramagnetic substances, on the other hand, lose their magnetization completely after the external magnetic field has been switched off. Figure 8.2 shows the relationship between external magnetic field H and the magnetization M of the ferromagnetic material.

With an increasing external magnetic field H, the magnetization M also rises, and sometimes reaches a saturation value J_s, which cannot be exceeded – the so-called *saturation magnetization*. Above all, domains cannot be aligned in the end. If the external magnetic field is weakened then the magnetization also decreases again, but by a smaller amount than that by which it rose during the rise of the magnetic field. If the magnetic field reaches the value 0 (that is, the external field is switched off), some magnetization remains, which is called *remanence* or *remanent magnetization.* Once a certain magnetic field of the opposite direction has been applied, the remanent magnetization also vanishes. The strength of this opposite field required for complete demagnetization is called *coercivity* or *coercitive force*. Finally, the ferromagnetic material attains a magnetization with a further rising field strength, which is opposite to the previous maximum magnetization, but has the same absolute value. If we decrease the external magnetic field again, and finally change its direction, then the magnetization follows a curve that is symmetric to the former change of magnetization. The complete curve is called a *hysteresis loop*. We say that ferromagnetic materials show a hysteresis because the magnetization is not only dependent upon the external magnetic field, but also upon the past history of the body. The generation of domains and the strong magnetization compared to paramagnetism is based on quantum-physical laws, which give rise to a strong magnetic coupling of adjacent atoms and molecules in a solid.

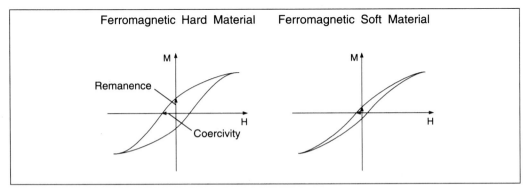

Figure 8.2: Hysteresis loop. A magnetically hard ferromagnetic material has a high remanence and coercivity, and thus the hysteresis is distinct. For a magnetically soft ferromagnetic material, on the other hand, the two curves nearly meet.

With certain additives and manufacturing methods, ferromagnetic materials can be formed which show a distinct hysteresis, that is, strong remanence and high coercivity. Such materials are called *magnetically hard*. *Magnetically soft* materials with low hysteresis, on the other hand, show a weak remanence and low coercivity.

The hysteresis properties of ferromagnetic substances are decisive for recording. Usually, one bit is represented by an area homogenously magnetized in a certain direction. This area must be at least as large as one domain. The magnetic field for magnetizing the area is mostly generated by a small electromagnet in a read/write head of the floppy or hard disk drive. Thus the domains within the area align according to the generated magnetic field and a «1» is written. By inverting the polarity of the magnetic field the domains are also aligned, but in another direction; thus a «0» is stored.

From the hysteresis loop it is apparent that for aligning the domains or overwriting old values at least a magnetic field with the strength of the coercivity is required. The data itself is stored by a magnetization with the amount of the remanence. Thus magnetically hard substances hold the data more strongly as their remanence is larger. But you need a stronger write field to generate the coercive force necessary for magnetization. Adjacent domains magnetized in opposite directions may affect each other, and demagnetize each other in the extreme. If one attempts to pack as much data as possible onto a magnetic data carrier (which, of course, become more adjacent), then one needs magnetically harder substances than with a low packing density. The 5 1/4" disks with a 1.2 Mbyte capacity are therefore coated with magnetically harder substances than the 5 1/4" disks of only 360 kbyte capacity. The accompanying 1.2 Mbyte drives generate stronger magnetic fields to format and write the 1.2 Mbyte disks. If you format a magnetically soft 360 kbyte disk in a 1.2 Mbyte drive now, the tracks may be magnetized to an amount for which a 360 kbyte drive that generates a correspondingly lower field for the soft 360 kbyte disks is unable to provide the required coercive force. You may read floppies which have been formatted and written in a 1.2 Mbyte drive, but not reformat them nor overwrite the data held on them. Only after several attempts may reformatting or overwriting happen – perhaps.

Another characteristic of ferromagnetic substances is the existence of a sharply defined temperature, the so-called *Curie temperature* T_c, or *Curie point*. Up to this temperature ferromagnetica behave in the described manner. But if, for example, iron is heated above 774°C (its Curie point), then the ferromagnetism suddenly vanishes and the iron behaves like a paramagnetic substance with a much lower magnetization. This property is used in magneto-optical drives and with magneto-optical data carriers. Chapter 9 gives more information on this.

The technically most important ferromagnetic materials are iron, cobalt, nickel, and their alloys. Table 8.1 lists the most important ferromagnetic materials, together with their Curie temperature T_c and saturation magnetization J_s.

	Tc [°C]	Js [Tesla]
Iron (Fe)	770	2.15
Cobalt (Co)	1121	1.76
Nickel (Ni)	358	0.68
Gadolinium	20	2.52
$Fe_{65}Co_{35}$	920	2.45
MnBi[*)]	360	0.78

[*)] Mangan-Wismut-Alloy

Table 8.1: Ferromagnetic materials

8.1.3   Induction

So far we have only got to know the basics of long-term data storage, but not how such magnetizations can be generated and how the data can be restored from them. It is generally known that an electric current generates a magnetic field. If a constant current is flowing through a coil then a constant magnetic field is generated, and the coil serves as an electromagnet. By means of tiny coils, domains may be aligned permanently in a ferromagnetic material and therefore – they hold data.

For detecting the aligned magnetic areas another effect of electrodynamics is used, the *induction*. This denotes the phenomenon where a changing magnetic field generates a voltage. Thus if one introduces a coil into a changing magnetic field then the induction gives rise to an electrical voltage. Remarkably, in this case only the change of the magnetic field leads to a voltage, but not the magnetic field itself. On the contrary, a constant current generates a constant magnetic field or, stated differently, an altering current leads to an altering magnetic field. Exactly these two effects are used in a transformer: the alternating current in the primary coil generates a changing magnetic field, which induces a voltage in the secondary coil by means of electromagnetic induction. This induced voltage oscillates with the same frequency as the current in the primary coil changes.

But this means that a homogenously magnetized ferromagnetic material cannot induce any voltage. If a coil is moved over such a body, no voltage is generated and no (data) signal appears. Once the ferromagnetic material has alternately magnetized areas, the magnetic field also changes in the course of the coil movement and thus generates a voltage that can be detected and amplified as a data signal. Thus for data recording, it is not a homogenous magnetization of floppies, hard disks or magnetic tapes that is required, but the formation of alternately aligned areas.

8.2   Structure and Functioning of Floppies and Floppy Drives

You probably already know the principle of an audio tape. A motor moves the tape over a recording head, which detects the information stored on the tape or writes new information onto it. Usually, music or other sound forms the information, which is output by a speaker or input by a microphone. Instead of music, every other kind of «information» can also be recorded onto the magnetic tape, for example programs or data for a computer. Magnetic tapes play an important role as an inexpensive medium for archiving data. In the field of PCs they are mainly found in the form of streamer cartridges, where the tape is installed in a case. Mainframes, on the other hand, mainly use magnetic tape reels which are handled without a case.

You have surely experienced the big disadvantage of magnetic tapes: if you want to hear a song again from the beginning or to skip it, you have to wind the tape forwards or backwards. The same applies, of course, in the field of computers. Earlier and simpler home computers only had a cassette recorder and no floppy drive. Loading a program mostly became a trial of your patience. Thus magnetic tapes are unsuitable as online mass storage, at least for more powerful computer systems, but in view of the costs unbeatable for extensive backups.

The spooling of the magnetic tape gives rise to a very long *access time*, which is defined as the time interval between an access demand and the delivery of the data. To shorten the access time, floppies and hard disks were developed. Figure 8.3 shows the structure of common 5 1/4" and 3 1/2" floppy disks.

Instead of a long and thin magnetic tape, a floppy disk consists of a flexible, circular plastic disk coated with a ferromagnetic material. To protect this data carrier from dirt and damage, the actual floppy is housed in a protective envelope or a plastic case. In the PC field today you will only find 5 1/4" floppies with a capacity of 360 kbyte and 1.2 Mbyte, and the newer 3 1/2" floppies with a capacity of 720 kbyte and 1.44 Mbyte. All of these floppies are double-sided;

thus the data are recorded on both sides. For DOS 1.x (and the original PC) single-sided floppies with a capacity of 160 or 180 kbytes were available, but they have vanished completely from the market together with their single-sided drives. Finally, the real dinosaurs were the 8" floppies, which also don't have any role in today's PCs. However, some internal DOS and BIOS structures support these floppy monsters for compatibility reasons.

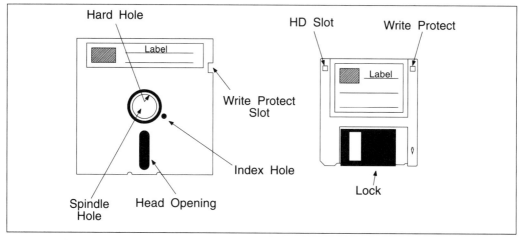

Figure 8.3: Floppy disks.

The 5 1/4" floppies are housed in a flexible envelope so that you can only see a small part of the actual data carrier through the opening for the read/write heads. Never touch the data carrier through this opening – even tiny dirt and fat particles make the floppy unusable, and the data gets lost.

To store data on or read data from the floppies you have to insert them into a floppy drive (see Figure 8.4). In the case of a 5 1/4" floppy a central mounting awl which is connected to the spindle of the drive motor takes up the floppy by means of the *spindle hole*. High-quality 5 1/4" floppies therefore have a *hard hole*. The more compact 3 1/2" floppy, on the other hand, has a gap in the metal disk. When such a floppy is inserted into a drive, the spindle meshes with this gap and locking the drive is unnecessary. Moreover, the envelopes of 5 1/4" floppies and the floppies themselves have an *index hole* that establishes an origin similar to the meridian on a globe. If you pick up a floppy the data carrier is probably rotated so you see only the data carrier's surface through the index hole in the envelope. If you carefully rotate the data carrier using the spindle and hard holes, then a small hole appears – the index hole of the data carrier.

With the *write protect hole* you can prevent data on the floppy disk from being erroneously overwritten. You only need to cover the hole with adhesive tape. All floppy drives have a photosensor assembly inside which senses this hole. If it is closed then the drive denies any write access to the inserted floppy. This denial is carried out on a hardware level and thus cannot be bypassed with a software command – a very reliable protection against computer viruses. For this reason, some manufacturers supply the original floppies of operating systems or application programs on floppies in envelopes that don't have any hole. Thus the data cannot be altered in any way – or at least as long you don't take a knife to one!

Because of the spindle hole, the index hole and the opening for the read/write heads, 5 1/4" floppies are subject to dirtying. You should therefore keep them in a clean and dust-free place, and avoid touching the actual data carrier. Even your just cleaned hand has enough fat particles to damage the surface. Furthermore, you must never write anything onto labels stuck to the floppies using a hard pen (for example, a ball-point pen or pencil) as the data carrier can be damaged through the thin protective envelope. Labels must be written before sticking them onto the floppy (even if the author himself doesn't always proceed according to these well-intended hints)!

In comparison, the newer 3 1/2" floppies are far better protected. This is necessary because of the higher data recording density. The floppies are accommodated in a stiff and stable plastic case, where the opening for the read/write heads is protected by a bolt. Once you insert the floppy into the drive, the drive's mechanism moves the bolt aside. You are free to try this by hand, but don't touch the data carrier here. Instead of the spindle hole the 3 1/2" floppy has a central metal disk with two slots: one for the motor spindle and one as the substitute for the index hole. Unlike the 5 1/4", here the floppy is not taken up by a mounting awl, but the specially formed motor spindle meshes directly with the slot. The second slot indicates the origin, in the same way as the former index hole. 3 1/2" floppies need not be locked manually in the drive, as is the case for 5 1/2" floppies. This is carried out by the drive mechanism automatically. The 3 1/2" floppies can be write-protected much more easily than their predecessors. Instead of the write protect hole they have a small *write protect slide* with which you can cover the case's hole. But note that 3 1/2" floppies, unlike the 5 1/4", are write protected if the hole is opened. Some manufacturers thus supply their software on write-protected 3 1/2" floppies, which lack the write protect slide.

The 3 1/2" floppies with a capacity of 1.44 Mbytes further have an *HD notch* to tell the floppy drive that a high-density or short HD-floppy is inserted. The problems that arise if 360 kbyte floppies are formatted or written in a 1.2 Mbyte drive can thus be avoided. As the two floppy types have an identical diameter, the data density of 1.2 Mbyte floppies must be higher, of course. Thus the magnetized areas are closer together and a higher coercivity of the magnetic coating is required to hold the data permanently. Thus, 1.2 Mbyte drives must therefore generate a stronger magnetic field to write onto the floppies, as is the case in 360 kbyte drives. As a consequence, the 360 kbyte floppies are magnetized during writing or formatting to an amount such that 360 kbyte drives have no chance of deleting the data again. The situation is similar with 720 kbyte and 1.44 Mbyte capacity 3 1/2" floppies. For the lower data density on 720 kbyte floppies a lower field strength is also required. Therefore, 3 1/2" drives have a sensor which probes the HD notch of the floppy. If you have inserted a 1.44 Mbyte floppy then the floppy drive increases the write current to generate a stronger magnetic field. If no HD notch is present (that is, you have inserted a 720 kbyte floppy), then the drive operates with a reduced write current and an accordingly weaker magnetic field. Thus, 3 1/2" drives adapt their magnetic field to the floppy type used. Problems such as those described for the older 360 kbyte and 1.2 Mbyte floppies and drives therefore don't occur here.

The drive motor rotates the inserted floppy at 300 rotations per minute for 360 kbyte floppies, or 360 rotations per minute for all other floppy types. This means that one rotation is completed every 1/5 or 1/6 second. For recording and restoring data a read/write head is additionally required, which is located at the end of an access arm. Figure 8.4 shows the scheme for a floppy drive with motor, floppy and access arm.

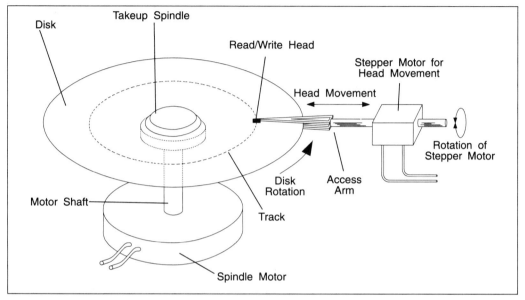

Figure 8.4: Floppy drive.

Today's common double-sided drives for double-sided floppies have two read/write heads mounted, however, on the same access arm, and they therefore cannot be moved independently, but are activated separately. The access arm is mostly moved by means of a stepper motor that drives a gear, which in turn converts the motor rotation into a linear movement of the access arm. Older models sometimes use a metal band to move the read/write heads along a rail. To move the heads to a certain position the electronic equipment of the floppy drive controls the stepper motor according to the instructions from the floppy controller, so that it carries out a certain number of angular steps. Therefore, no feedback control is carried out here. If you insert the floppy incorrectly the head may not find the addressed data, as the angular position of the stepper motor during the course of recording doesn't coincide with the stepper motor position for data reading.

Thus the one-dimensional movement of the magnetic tape past the read/write head has been converted to a two-dimensional movement; namely, the rotation of the data carrier and the linear movement of the read/write head. You may imagine a floppy disk as a rolled-up magnetic tape. On the floppy, certain data is accessible in the most disadvantageous case within one rotation of the data carrier and a complete linear movement of the access arm. One single rotation is carried out within 170–200 ms, the complete linear movement of the head typically within 200 ms. Thus 200 ms is required at most to access a data byte. With the magnetic tape you have to spool the complete tape in the most disadvantageous case, and this usually lasts longer than 200 ms. Another advantage of the floppy compared to magnetic tape is that the floppy can be removed from the drive at any position of the data carrier and the heads. Magnetic tapes, on the other hand, must be completely spooled onto a spool. Only tape cartridges are an exception.

Up to now we have only got to know the access to certain positions on the data carrier but not how the data is read or written. The basis is formed by ferromagnetism, induction, and the presence of read/write heads. Recording and restoring data is carried out only at the position of the read/write heads. Figure 8.5 shows a sectional view through a read/write head, located above the floppy.

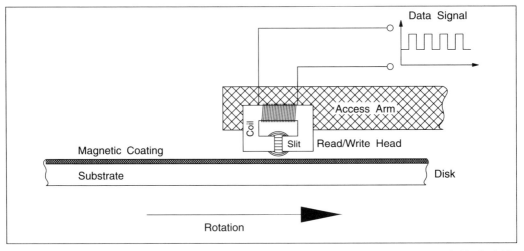

Figure 8.5: Read/write head and floppy disk. The read/write head has a coil that generates the magnetic field. The field comes out of the slit and magnetizes the coating of the disk.

Section 8.1 stated that an external magnetic field aligns the domains in a ferromagnetic material, and these domains keep their orientation even after the external magnetic field has been switched off. This effect is used for recording data. The read/write head is mainly formed of a small electromagnet with an iron core which has a tiny slit. The magnetic field lines of the electromagnet emanate from this slit during the write process, and magnetize small areas of the data carrier's coating. Depending upon the alignment of the domains, a 1 or a 0 can be represented at the location concerned.

The floppy, coated with an iron or cobalt compound, rotates below the read/write head so that the drive controller sends a short current pulse through the electromagnet of the head at a suitable moment to set up a magnetic field with the intended direction. Thus it is necessary to coordinate the rotation of the data carrier, the linear position of the access arm, and the timing of the write pulse in such a way that a defined bit can be written as the magnetization of a tiny area at any location. If several data bits are to be written in succession then the drive controller supplies a pulse stream to the read/write head in phase with the data recording, which leads to the recording of all data bits. The size of the slit and the distance between head and data carrier have a major influence on the recording density. The smaller the slit the smaller also the area of emanating field lines, and thus the area on the data carrier surface which is affected by these field lines. A small slit may thus lead to a higher data density. On the other hand, the magnetic field expands more and more with the distance from the slit. The further away the head is from the data carrier, the larger the affected area therefore becomes. Thus a small distance between head and floppy also supports a high recording density. Floppy drives and especially hard disk drives with a high capacity thus have a small read/write head with a tiny slit located as far away as possible from the data carrier.

In floppy drives the read/write head touches the floppy's surface through the force of a spring, and therefore rubs; the distance between head and data carrier is virtually zero. The floppies thus wear out in time, although the magnetic coating is further covered by a teflon layer or similar mechanically resistive material. The wearing out is limited, though, because of the low rotation speed and the fact that the data carrier is only rotated by the drive motor during the course of a data access. In the case of fast and permanently running hard disk drives, however, a head rubbing would rapidly lead to damage of the mechanical coating, and thus to a data loss. In hard disks the head, therefore, doesn't touch the data carrier's surface. You will find additional information about this subject below.

When reading recorded data the coil in the read/write head takes up the field lines of the magnetized data carrier surface which penetrate through the slit. Because of the floppy's rotation, alternating magnetizations of the data carrier's surface give rise to a variable magnetic field, which induces a voltage in the coil. The voltage reflects the data previously written. Initially, we get a stream of electric signals that are converted into a bit stream by the electronic equipment of the drive and the floppy controller. To read a certain value the controller moves the head to a certain location and drives the motor. When the intended data appear below the read/write head the controller turns on a gate to transfer the induced data signals to an amplifier. Thus data reading, a precise coordination of rotation, linear movement and the timing of gate opening is also required.

For obvious reasons, floppy drives are denoted as *drives with removable data carrier*. In this respect they differ from hard disk drives. However, the removability of the floppies is paid for with a significant data security disadvantage, as dust, fingerprints and other dirt can hardly be avoided over the course of time. Because of the floppy's rotation, this dirt acts as a scouring powder, the coating is damaged or destroyed, and data gets lost. The high-capacity 3 1/2" floppies are therefore housed in a much better protective case than was the case for the 5 1/4" floppies. Meanwhile, floppy drives and floppies with a capacity of up to 20 Mbyte have come onto the market. The recording density, increased by one magnitude, requires a further enhanced protection against dirt. Thus these floppies usually come in a hermetically sealed case. Such data carriers are more accurately called moving head disks rather than floppies, as in view of their capacity and technology they are located somewhere between floppies and hard disks.

8.3   Physical Organization of Floppies

If you cut open the protective envelope of a floppy disk then you hold the actual data carrier in your hand: a completely structureless circular disk. The sections above mentioned that the read/write head can be placed above every location of the floppy by means of the floppy rotation and movement of the access arm. But for a correct and reliable management of the written data, additionally a minimum data carrier organization is required.

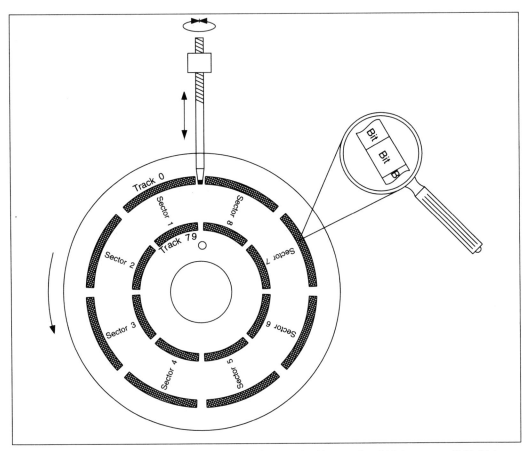

Figure 8.6: Tracks, cylinders and sectors. Every floppy disk is organized into tracks, which in turn are divided into sectors. Within one sector the bit is the smallest data unit.

Let us look at the track that a read/write head follows when viewed from the rotating data carrier. With fixed radial position of the head (that is, fixed position of the access arm) this is a circle. Its midpoint is the spindle of the drive motor. Imagine a felt-tip pen mounted on the access arm instead of the read/write head. If the radial position of the felt-tip pen is altered because of a rotation of the stepper motor, then the read/write head describes another circle with a different diameter. What's better than to take such «circles» for organizing the floppy? They are now called *tracks* which are assigned a number (see Figure 8.6). Usually, the counting starts at the outermost track (that is, the circle of largest radius) with the number 0, and proceeds to the inner ones. Between the tracks there are narrow areas that are not magnetized so the tracks can be distinguished unambiguously. Today's commonly used floppies have between 40 and 80 tracks; high-capacity hard disks have up to 2000.

With double-sided floppies and hard disks which usually comprise more than one disk, more than one read/write head is also installed. Each of these heads describes its own track called a *cylinder*. Imagine a hollow cylinder for this purpose, which intersects the floppy or all of the disks. The lines of intersection with the disk surfaces define circles or tracks of equal radius. Thus the individual tracks of a cylinder are further distinguished by the *head* to which they belong. Generally, the head counting starts with the value 0. With single-sided floppies you don't have to distinguish cylinder and track, of course.

But in connection with the track we again get similar problems as with the floppy: where is the beginning of a circle? Answer: nowhere! (This seems to be a very deep and philosophical problem, indeed.) If we look at a 1.2 Mbyte floppy with 80 tracks then we realize that every track can (roughly) accommodate 7680 bytes.

The tracks are therefore further divided, into so-called *sectors*. These sectors are enumerated in the same way as the tracks or cylinders. The beginning of every sector of a track is indicated to the drive by means of the index hole if 5 1/4" floppies are used. In the case of 3 1/2" floppies, the fixed position of the notch in the central metal plate, and in the case of hard disks a certain magnetic pattern on the disk, indicates the beginning of the first sector (or the track/cylinder). In front of every sector a so-called *address mark* is present, which indicates the number of the current track and sector. The actual data area of a sector is characterized by a *data mark*. Floppies have 8 to 18 and hard disks up to 40 sectors per track. With DOS and most other PC operating systems such as OS/2 or UNIX/XENIX, the data area of a sector usually comprises 512 bytes. DOS further groups one or more sectors logically into a so-called *cluster* or *allocation unit*. (More about this subject in the following sections.) Table 8.2 lists the parameters for the most common floppy types.

Disk	Tracks	Sectors/ track	Cluster size [sectors]	Track width [mm]	Sectors total
5 1/4" 360 kbyte	40	9	2	0.330	720
5 1/4" 1.2 Mbyte	80	15	1	0.160	2400
3 1/2" 720 kbyte	80	9	2	0.115	1440
3 1/2" 1.44 Mbyte	80	18	1	0.115	2880

Table 8.2: Floppy disk parameters

The address and data marks as well as certain synchronization patterns occupy storage area on the data carrier. Thus the formatted capacity of floppies and hard disks is lower than the unformatted capacity. Pay attention to this fact when buying one. Some manufacturers and dealers like to cheat, especially with hard disks. They sometimes specify the unformatted capacity to lead you to believe in a higher storage capacity. The 5 1/4" HD floppies, for example, have an unformatted capacity of 1.6 Mbyte, but after formatting only 1.2 Mbyte remain. The remarkable 400 kbyte difference is used for address and data marks, synchronization patterns, and other data for the controller. Data carriers are not only characterized by their capacity. More meaningful are the number of tracks per inch *(TPI)* and the number of bits per inch *(BPI)*. Table 8.3 lists these and other quantities for the most common floppy types. The 5 1/4" quad-density floppy was not used in the PC domain, but is present in the market and is mainly employed in 360 kbyte drives instead of the usual double-density floppy.

Disk type	Capacity	TPI	BPI	Coercivity [oersted]
5 1/4" double density	360 kbyte	48	5,876	300
5 1/4" quad density	720 kbyte	96	5,876	300
5 1/4" high density	1.2 Mbyte	96	8,646	600
3 1/2" double density	720 kbyte	135	8,717	300
3 1/2" high density	1.44 Mbyte	135	17,434	600

Table 8.3: Physical disk parameters

Perhaps you have wondered why new floppies have to be formatted before they can be used. The answer is very easy: during the course of formatting, magnetic patterns are written onto the floppy or hard disk which indicate the tracks, cylinders and sectors. This is denoted as *low-level formatting*. In so-called *high-level formatting* only preparations for logical data organization are carried out (details are discussed in Section 8.4). Once this formatting process is complete, it is possible to read and write data by means of the described addressing scheme. Addressing via these *physical sectors* is used by the BIOS and IO.SYS or IBMBIOS.SYS as the component of DOS closest to the hardware. DOS itself, and many other operating systems, map the physical addressing onto a logical addressing by means of *logical sectors* (details on this subject are discussed in Section 8.4.1).

With floppies the DOS command *FORMAT* carries out the job of forming tracks and sectors. It writes the value 0f6h corresponding to the character «÷» 512 times into every data sector. Therefore you don't need a special low-level formatting program here. The situation changes if a hard disk is involved. Here, FORMAT only sets up the logical structure of the data carrier but doesn't form any tracks or sectors. This is only possible by means of specialized formatting programs, for example DiskManager by Ontrack.

8.4   Logical Organization of Floppies and Hard Disks with DOS

This section discusses the logical organization of data at a system level. Knowledge of file and directory commands on a user level (for example DIR, COPY, DEL, MKDIR, CHDIR, etc.) is required. The logical organization of floppies and hard disks differs only in that hard disks additionally have a partition table. For the technical structure this is insignificant, however, so the data organization for floppies and hard disks is discussed together in the following sections.

8.4.1 Logical Sectors

As already mentioned, the BIOS uses physical sectors for organizing data. But DOS and many other operating systems employ a different scheme of so-called *logical sectors*. For this purpose the physical sectors are assigned a serial number, which starts with the value 0. Thus the scheme is: assign the first physical sector (that is, the sector with the physical «address» cylinder 0, head 0, sector 1) the logical sector number 0. Now the sectors of side 0 are counted. Afterwards, we continue with side 1 or head 1, respectively. This scheme is continued until the last side is reached. If we do the counting similarly with the next track, then every physical sector is assigned a continuous number, namely the logical sector number.

Example: Double-sided floppy with 80 tracks and 18 sectors per track according to a 3 1/2" floppy with 1.44 Mbyte capacity.

```
physical sector                    logical sector

head 0, track 0, sector 1          0
......................             .....
head 0, track 0, sector 18         18
head 1, track 0, sector 1          19
......................             .....
head 1, track 0, sector 18         36
......................             .....
head 0, track 1, sector 1          37
......................             .....
......................             .....
head 1, track 79, sector 18        2879
```

The floppy comprises 2880 sectors with 512 bytes each in total; this leads to a storage capacity of 1.44 Mbyte.

The above described mapping of physical sectors onto logical sectors with a continuous number is only valid for floppies. Hard disks have another characteristic, explained in the next section as a short leap ahead to hard disks.

Of significance for applications programmers who only use DOS functions is that the logical sectors are the smallest data entity on floppies and hard disks addressable with DOS. Only logical sectors may be accessed directly, and they are always read or written as a whole. With DOS, therefore, only logical (no physical) sectors are accessible. That is important if you have installed OS/2 or XENIX besides DOS on your hard disk.

8.4.2 The Partition

As already mentioned, other operating systems for microcomputers are on the market besides DOS. OS/2 and UNIX/XENIX are the most common. In hard disks the control electronics and the mechanics are usually much more expensive than the data carrier itself. Thus it is best to use only one high-capacity hard disk for several operating systems instead of allocating each operating system its own hard disk drive. Further, the controller hardware and the BIOS are normally only able to manage a limited number of drives. One problem that now occurs is that the data structures of DOS and XENIX are completely incompatible. Thus you must allocate every operating system its own section of the hard disk which is exclusively used and managed by each operating system. Such a section is called a *partition* (see Figure 8.7).

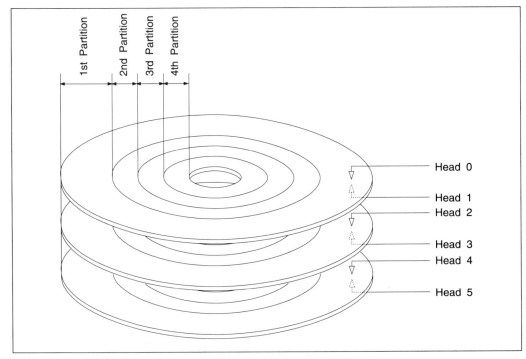

Figure 8.7: Partitions. A hard disk is divided into partitions, which generally start and end at cylinder boundaries.

Microchips are not clairvoyant, and thus the information as to whether several operating systems are present and how extensive the allocated partitions eventually are must be stored somewhere. This information is specific for a certain hard disk, and therefore it is best to write it onto the hard disk itself. You may then remove the hard disk from your PC and install it in your friend's PC without the need to reconfigure the partitions again. If you were to store the partition information in CMOS RAM, on the other hand, then you would have to reconfigure your CMOS RAM, as well as that in your friend's PC.

For storing the partition information a unique location which is definitely present on every hard disk is chosen: head 0, track 0, sector 1. This is the first physical sector of the hard disk. Hard disks may be different in size and thus may have any combination of heads, tracks and sectors. The last sector on the disk is therefore ruled out as its head, track, and sector address varies from disk to disk. Thus in the first physical sector, the so-called *partition sector*, the information about the individual partition(s) is stored by means of *partition entries* in a *partition table*.

Floppies, on the other hand, have no partition table as nothing can be saved because of their low capacity when compared to hard disks, and the data carrier can also be removed. Together with suitable drivers, you may use the same floppy drive for various operating systems. Only the form of organizing the data on the floppies differs. Floppies written with UNIX may be read with DOS, but the information is as clear as mud to DOS, which issues a corresponding error message.

Figure 8.8 shows the structure of a partition sector, partition table and partition entry. The partition table is 64 bytes long, and can accommodate four partitions at most, held in inverse order.

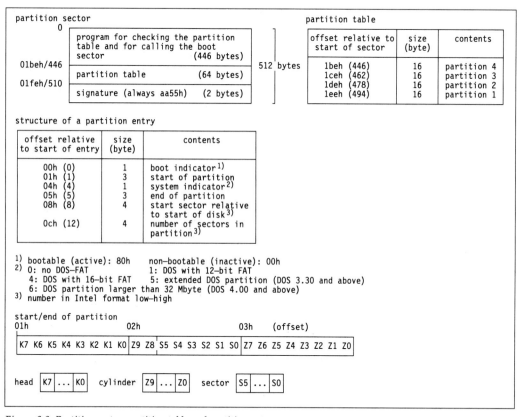

Figure 8.8: Partition sector, partition table and partition entry.

Besides the partition table the partition sector contains a small program with a maximum of 446 bytes, as well as the 2-byte signature 0aa55h. Upon power-up of the PC, the BIOS calls the partition sector program, which checks the internal consistency of the entries in the partition table, and then the bootstrap loader in the boot sector (see below). If the partition table is damaged or inconsistent, the program issues an error message and terminates the load process. Hard disks with a damaged partition sector are completely unusable as no information as to where each partition starts and ends is available to the operating system.

The partition table holds the entries for a maximum of four partitions. They specify the physical start and end sectors of each partition in a compressed 3-byte format (Figure 8.8, bottom). From the format you can see that such a partition table can only manage hard disks with up to 256 heads, 1024 cylinders and 64 sectors per track. The 256 heads haven't been reached up to now for any drive, but some high-capacity hard disks already have more than 1024 cylinders and the number of sectors per track is meanwhile getting closer to 64. Features that the controllers implement to solve these problems are discussed below.

Because of the partition table's structure, a hard disk may have up to four partitions. If several operating systems are installed in separate partitions on disk, then the PC must be able, in the course of the boot process, to determine which of the various systems is to be loaded. The boot indicator solves this problem. An entry 80h indicates a bootable active partition, an entry 00h a non-bootable inactive partition. The small program at the beginning of the partition sector determines during the boot where the bootable partition is located, and then activates its load routine. The system indicator shows which file system with or without FAT is present on disk. The use and meaning of FAT is described below.

```
Example: end of partition at 04 a2 60
    head:      04h = 4 decimal
    cylinder:  a2h = 10100010b
               60h = 01100000b
               adding the two most-significant bits 10 of a2h to 60h
               leads to 1001100000b= 260h = 608
    sector:    the six low-order bits of a2h give 100010b = 22h = 34
End of partition therefore at head 4, cylinder (track) 608, sector 34.
```

The mapping of physical onto logical sectors (described in the preceding section) is now carried out within the partition: the first sector of the partition is assigned the logical sector number 0. Afterwards, a mapping of physical sectors onto logical ones is carried out in the same way as on the floppies until the last sector (characterized by head, track, sector in the partition table) of the partition concerned is reached. Broadly speaking, one could say that the partition table divides the hard disk into smaller «floppies» so that each operating system is only able to access the floppy assigned. Some mainframe operating systems (for example VMS) divide the storage capacity of disks into such «virtual» disks, which are then available to a single user. But unlike PC partitions, the operating system itself has complete access to all data.

Modern hard disks can be very large (Seagate's model ST83050K reaches a formatted capacity of 2.84 Gbytes). Versions of DOS up to 3.30, however, use only a 16-bit number internally to indicate the logical number of the intended sector for a disk access. By means of these 16 bits, a maximum of 65 536 different numbers can be represented. The sector size of 512 bytes thus leads to partitions which hold 512 bytes*65 536 = 33 554 432 bytes = 32 Mbyte at most. This is the magic *32-MB-boundary* for DOS partitions. Starting with DOS 3.30, an advance was made which enabled DOS partitions of more than 32 Mbytes, but these partitions had to be divided into so-called *virtual drives* with a maximum size of 32 Mbytes each. Within these virtual drives DOS continued to deal with 16-bit sector numbers. To this number is added a number that indicates the offset of the virtual drive within the partition. Thus the effective size of files is further restricted to 32 Mbytes. DOS 4.00 and all higher versions actually break through this boundary, and continuous partitions of 512 Mbytes at most are possible.

It is also important that DOS can only access the logical sectors within the partition. Physical sectors located outside the DOS partition can only be accessed by means of the BIOS, or by directly programming the controller. This protects the data of other operating systems against program errors from DOS programs. Be careful if you attempt to access floppies or hard disks via the BIOS or even directly by means of the controller hardware. Erroneously overwritten sectors in other partitions can give rise to very serious trouble.

8.4.3   The Boot Sector

You may know that there are bootable system disks as well as non-bootable disks. In connection with the partition table we also learned that bootable partitions and non-bootable partitions exist as well. Moreover, you can, for example, format, write and read floppies with a capacity of 160, 320 and 360 kbytes and 1.2 Mbyte in a 5 1/4" HD drive. Thus DOS and BIOS must be able to detect the data carrier type in some way.

The key to this is the *boot sector* or *boot record*. It occupies the first sector of a floppy (head 0, track 0, sector 1) or partition, that is, the start sector of the partition. Figure 8.8 shows the structure of the boot sector.

Like the partition table of a hard disk, the boot sector is also present at an unambiguously defined location which exists on all floppies or partitions. Thus DOS and BIOS can address and read the boot sector without knowing the exact data carrier type.

As you can see in Figure 8.9, all important disk and partition parameters are located between offsets 0bh and 1eh. This area is also called the *medium descriptor table*. Most entries are self-evident, so only the most important are discussed here. Terms such as cluster and FAT are explained below.

The eight bytes of the *OEM name* contain an identity that characterizes the manufacturer and version of the operating system, for example *MSDOS4.0*. The *reserved sectors* specify the number of sectors allocated to the boot record. Usually, a value of 1 is held as the loader routine normally doesn't need more than the 488 bytes which are available after these configuration entries. Essential for determining the floppy type is the medium descriptor byte at offset 15h. The BIOS and DOS can determine the disk type with this entry (Table 8.4 shows the currently valid entries), but the medium descriptor byte is not always unambiguous so you should rely on the detailed structure as it is held by the medium descriptor table. Because of the various geometries of hard disks on the market, only the single value 0f8h is used for the medium descriptor byte to characterize a hard disk. As a hard disk cannot be removed as easily as a floppy, this is sufficient. The exact hard disk drive parameters are stored in the CMOS RAM. Alternatively, the hard disk controller may have its own BIOS which is precisely informed about the hard disk type. Details concerning the extraordinarily powerful concept of such BIOS extensions are discussed in the chapter about hard disks.

The first three bytes and the loader program at offset 1eh determine whether the floppy is bootable or not. If you boot from a floppy your PC from a floppy, the BIOS start routine branches to the first three boot sector bytes at offset 00h and calls them as a program code. These three bytes contain a near jump (DOS 2.xx) to the start address of the loader program.

Starting with DOS 3.00, the BIOS finds a short jump to the start address as well as a NOP instruction.

```
00h/0
        ┌─────────────────────────────────────────────────┬──────────────┐
        │ e9 xx xx or eb xx 90  1)                         │ (3 bytes)    │
03h/3   ├─────────────────────────────────────────────────┼──────────────┤
        │ OEM name and number                             │ (8 bytes)    │
0bh/11  ├─────────────────────────────────────────────────┼──────────────┤
        │ bytes per sector                                │ (2 bytes)    │
0dh/13  ├─────────────────────────────────────────────────┼──────────────┤
        │ sectors per allocation unit (cluster)           │ (1 bytes)    │
0eh/14  ├─────────────────────────────────────────────────┼──────────────┤
        │ reserved sectors (for boot record)              │ (2 bytes)    │
10h/16  ├─────────────────────────────────────────────────┼──────────────┤
        │ number of FATs                                  │ (1 bytes)    │
11h/17  ├─────────────────────────────────────────────────┼──────────────┤
        │ number of root directory entries                │ (2 bytes)    │
13h/19  ├─────────────────────────────────────────────────┼──────────────┤
        │ number of logical sectors                       │ (2 bytes)    │
15h/21  ├─────────────────────────────────────────────────┼──────────────┤
        │ medium descriptor byte 2)                       │ (1 bytes)    │
16h/22  ├─────────────────────────────────────────────────┼──────────────┤
        │ sectors per FAT                                 │ (2 bytes)    │
18h/24  ├─────────────────────────────────────────────────┼──────────────┤
        │ sectors per track                               │ (2 bytes)    │
1ah/26  ├─────────────────────────────────────────────────┼──────────────┤
        │ heads                                           │ (2 bytes)    │
1ch/28  ├─────────────────────────────────────────────────┼──────────────┤
        │ number of hidden sectors                        │ (2 bytes)    │
1eh/30  ├─────────────────────────────────────────────────┴──────────────┤
        │                program to load DOS                              │
        └─────────────────────────────────────────────────────────────────┘
```

1) e9h is the machine code for a near jump, xx xx characterizes the start address of the loader at 1eh/30 (DOS 2.x);
ebh is the machine code for a short jump, xx characterizes the start address; 90h is the machine code for NOP (DOS 3.x and following).
2) may be invalid with DOS 2.x and following, see Table 8.4

Figure 8.9: Boot sector.

Byte	Medium				DOS version
0f8h	hard disk				2.00
0f0h	3 1/2", double sided,	18 sectors,	80 tracks,	1.44 Mbyte	3.20
0f9h	3 1/2", double sided,	9 sectors,	80 tracks,	720 kbyte	3.20
0f9h	5 1/4", double sided,	15 sectors,	80 tracks,	1.2 Mbyte	3.00
0fah	5 1/4", single sided,	8 sectors,	80 tracks,	320 kbyte	1.00
0fah	3 1/2", single sided,	8 sectors,	80 tracks,	320 kbyte	1.00
0fbh	5 1/4", double sided,	8 sectors,	80 tracks,	640 kbyte	1.00
0fbh	3 1/2", double sided,	8 sectors,	80 tracks,	640 kbyte	1.00
0fch	5 1/4", single sided,	9 sectors,	40 tracks,	180 kbyte	2.00
0fdh	5 1/4", double sided,	9 sectors,	40 tracks,	360 kbyte	2.00
0fdh	8", double sided,	26 sectors,	77 tracks,	1.96 Mbyte	1.00
0feh	5 1/4", single sided,	8 sectors,	40 tracks,	160 kbyte	1.00
0feh	8", single sided,	2 sectors,	77 tracks,	77 kbyte	1.00
0feh	8", single sided,	6 sectors,	77 tracks,	231 kbyte	1.00
0feh	8", single sided,	8 sectors,	77 tracks,	308 kbyte	1.00
0ffh	5 1/4", double sided,	8 sectors,	40 tracks,	320 kbyte	1.10

Table 8.4: Medium descriptor byte

The loader program in the boot sector then checks whether system files IO.SYS and MSDOS.SYS (in the case of MS-DOS) or IBMBIOS.SYS and IBMDOS.SYS (in the case of PC-DOS) are present on disk. For all other operating systems the same applies. If the loader program finds the required system files, then these files and thus DOS (or another operating system) are loaded into the main memory. The computer now boots from floppy disk. If the system files are missing, the loader routine issues a message No system disk!

If you instead boot from the hard disk (more exactly, from the active partition of the hard disk) then the BIOS start routine branches to the program at offset 00h in the partition sector first (see Figure 8.8). This program now investigates the partition table and determines the bootable partition. The rest of the load process is carried out in the same way as with a floppy disk, that is, a jump to the first three boot sector bytes occurs and the boot process proceeds as described above. Your PC is thus booted from hard disk. The boot record may comprise several sectors in principle, for example, if an extensive program for loading the operating system is required. In this case only the entry at offset 0eh for the reserved sectors needs to be higher.

The boot sector of every floppy or partition contains the program for loading DOS regardless of whether the floppy or partition is bootable or not. Only the loader program in the boot sector determines whether the required system data is actually present on disk or in the partition. DOS builds up the boot sector automatically during the course of the formatting process by means of the DOS command FORMAT. The same applies to hard disks.

8.4.4 The Root Directory

By means of the entries in the boot sector, DOS knows how large the storage capacity of the floppy or partition is, and how many tracks, sectors per track and bytes per sector are present. A file management system, however, cannot be established yet. Every floppy or partition with DOS has two further fixedly defined sections besides the boot sector and the partition table: the root directory, which you meet as «\» on the user level, and the file allocation table (FAT).

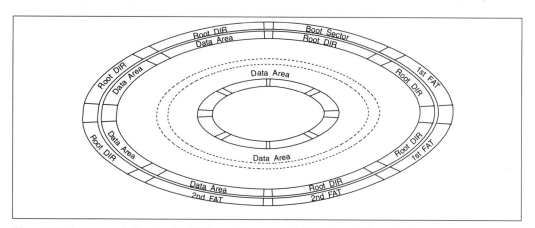

Figure 8.10: Arrangement of boot sector, FATs, root directory, subdirectories and files. On a floppy disk, from the outside to the inside are located the boot sector, the two FAT copies and the root directory. These are followed by the data area, which fills the floppy disk up to the innermost cylinder.

For file management with DOS it is necessary that the operating system knows the beginning of the data storage area. For this purpose the *root directory* is implemented, starting immediately after the boot sector and the FATs (see Figure 8.10).

If you look at the boot sector's structure in Figure 8.9, you will see that the position of the root directory is unambiguously determined by the entries in the boot sector. The root directory holds the necessary information on location, size, date and time of the last change of the files and subdirectories, as well as certain attributes in the form of a *directory entry*. Figure 8.11 shows the structure of such a 32-byte entry.

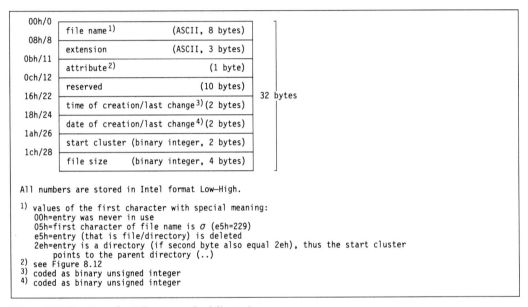

Figure 8.11: Structure of root directory and subdirectories.

The first two entries *file name* and *extension* are held in the same form as they are provided on the user level, but note that the two entries are not separated by a point from each other. Only the application program or DOS commands such as DIR insert the point for an output on-screen. Concerning the first byte of the file name, four values are reserved. If the first byte has the value 00h then the directory entry has never been used before. If the first byte is equal to e5h, which corresponds to the character σ (ASCII 229), then the directory entry concerned has been erased by a DEL or ERASE command if it pointed to a file, or by a MKDIR command if the entry pointed to a subdirectory. A value 05h for the first byte indicates that the first file name character should be σ. This character cannot be stored in this simple form as it defines an erased and therefore invalid entry. The value 2eh corresponding to the character «.» symbolizes a directory and the entry points to the directory which holds the entry itself. The DIR command displays this entry as «. <DIR>». If the second byte in the entry is also equal to 2eh (that is, the file name is «..»), then the start cluster points to the beginning of the next higher directory, the so-called *parent directory*. This is necessary to travel up the hierarchy to the next highest directory level by means of the command CD...

Time and *date* indicate the time and date, respectively, of the last alteration of the directory or file concerned. Overwriting data, extending files, and the creation of a directory (with MKDIR) or file lead to an alteration. The time is encoded as an unsigned integer in the format *time = 2048*hours+32*minutes+seconds/2*. The date, too, is stored as an unsigned integer, but in the format *date = 512*(year–1980)+32*month+day*. The date counting of DOS is always relative to 1.1.1980. This actually is no restriction, as the PC and DOS came into the market after this date, and therefore there can't be any files and directories generated on a PC before this date.

Example: 19 o'clock, 17 minutes, 32 seconds lead to
         2048 * 19 + 32 * 17 + 32/2 = 38,472d = 9a30h

Example: October 3rd, 1991 is encoded as
         512 * 11 + 32 * 10 + 3 = 5955d = 1743h

The *start cluster* entry specifies the beginning of the file or subdirectory, and the *file size* entry the length of the file. The *attribute* characterizes the type of the directory entry. The values used are listed in Figure 8.12.

```
 7                              0

 res res arc dir lab sys hid r/w

 r/w:   read-only file
        1=read only    0=readable and writeable
 hid:   hidden file
        1=hidden       0=not hidden
 sys:   system file
        1=system file  0=normal file
 lab:   volume label
        1=volume label 0=normal directory entry
 dir:   directory bit
        1=entry characterizes subdirectory   0=file
 arc:   archive bit
        1=file/directory to be archived   0=not to be archived
 res:   reserved
```

Figure 8.12: Attributes.

Read-only files or directories with a set *ver* bit cannot be overwritten by DOS; DOS denies any write access and returns an error code. The erasure of the file or subdirectory is also an overwriting process. Thus you have to reset the attribute of a read-only file to 0 before you can erase it by means of DEL or ERASE. If a file or subdirectory is hidden (that is, bit *hid* is equal to 1), then the DOS command DIR doesn't display the file or subdirectory. With DOS the two system files IO.SYS and MSDOS.SYS are always hidden and are not displayed by DIR. But utilities such as Norton Commander or PCTools can list such files and subdirectories. The attribute *sys* characterizes system files to distinguish them from normal application files. Using the DOS command LABEL you may assign a name of eleven characters at most to a floppy or hard disk. The eleven label characters are stored in the file name and extension fields of an entry in the root directory. The attribute *lab* informs DOS that this entry doesn't point to a file or subdirectory but contains the volume label. If the directory bit *dir* is set, then the directory entry concerned doesn't point to a file but a subdirectory which is one level below in the hierarchically structured DOS file system. The *arc* bit controls the backup and archiving of data. Programs such as BACKUP investigate this bit and eventually backup only those files and directories whose arc bit is set. At the same time, the arc bit is reset to 0. During the course of a write access to a file, the DOS file functions activate the arc bit automatically. This means that files with a set arc bit have been altered since the last backup. You are free to set several attributes concurrently as there are, for example, hidden and read-only system files. But ensure that the set attributes are consistent. For example, it is impossible for an entry to represent a subdirectory and a volume label simultaneously.

From Figure 8.11 you can see that the length of each entry is 32 bytes. But with DOS the logical sector derived from the physical sector of 512 bytes is the smallest readable and writeable unit, as only complete sectors can be read and written, not individual bytes. Thus the size of the root directory is always chosen so that the root directory ends on a sector boundary, otherwise storage capacity would be wasted. The boot sector entry at offset 11h, containing the number of root directory entries, is therefore always a multiple of 16. Table 8.5 lists the number of root directory entries for various floppy and hard disk fromats.

Floppy disk	Root directory entries
5 1/4" 360 kbyte	112 (7 sectors)
5 1/4" 1.2 Mbyte	224 (14 sectors)
3 1/2" 720 kbyte	112 (7 sectors)
3 1/2" 1.44 Mbyte	224 (14 sectors)
hard disk	512 (32 sectors)

Table 8.5: Number of root directory entries

If you recall a complete directory by means of the DOS command DIR, you see that most data is larger than one sector of 512 bytes. Thus it is advantageous to combine several sectors into larger groups called *cluster* or *allocation units*. Clusters are therefore of a larger granularity than sectors. The number of sectors grouped into one cluster is stored at offset 0dh in the boot sector (see Figure 8.9) of the floppy or hard disk concerned. One cluster consists of two sectors on a 360 kbyte floppy, of one sector on a 1.2 Mybte or 1.44 Mbyte floppy, and usually of four sectors on a hard disk. Thus, for example, two sectors are assigned to the first cluster on a 360 kbyte floppy, the next two sectors to the second cluster, etc. Other values are possible. If you write your own formatting program you are free to combine, for example, 16 sectors into one cluster. But remember to adapt the boot sector entry accordingly. DOS understands this cluster grouping, too, and operates accordingly.

Note that the directory entry indicates the number of the start *cluster* and not that of the start *sector* of a file or subdirectory. Every file or subdirectory is allocated a certain number of clusters by the file management routines of the operating system (hence the name allocation unit), which is sufficient to accommodate the complete contents of the file or subdirectory.

Note also that the root directory can only accommodate a limited number of entries, independent of the size of files and subdirectories, as its position and length is unambiguously and fixedly determined by the boot sector entries. If DOS reports that the floppy or hard disk is full, although according to DIR a lot of storage capacity is unused, then you have probably exhausted the root directory's capacity and DOS is unable to generate any new files or subdirectory entries in the root directory.

The root directory forms the origin of the *hierarchical file system* of DOS. This means the hierarchical grouping of subdirectories and files in each directory. As you can see from Figure 8.10, the root directory is the last static (that is, fixedly defined) area on the floppy or hard disk partition. All the remaining storage is available for dynamic allocation to subdirectories and files; it forms the so-called *data area*. In the data area, DOS carries out the grouping of sectors into clusters. The cluster counting starts with 2 – the reason for this is discussed in the following section on FAT. This means that, for example, on a hard disk with four sectors per cluster, the first four sectors of the data area form cluster 2, the next four cluster 3, etc.

Besides the boot sector and FAT, during the course of the format process FORMAT also generates the root directory as an empty directory without file or subdirectory entries. Once subdirectories are generated by MKDIR or files are opened (for example, in BASIC with the command OPEN TXT_FILE FOR OUTPUT AS #1), the root directory can be filled step-by-step.

8.4.5   The Subdirectories

With the MKDIR command you can generate subdirectories, for which DOS prepares a directory entry in the root directory. File name and extension define the name of the subdirectory, and the attribute is set to characterize the entry as a subdirectory. Like the root directory, subdirectories accommodate files and further subdirectories (that is, sub-subdirectories). For this purpose, a cluster is allocated that holds directory entries for the files or sub-subdirectories. The start cluster in the root directory points to this allocated cluster.

The first two directory entries in a subdirectory are generated by the MKDIR command. One entry points to the subdirectory itself (namely «.» if you issue DIR), and the second to the directory («..») one level above in the hierarchy, thus to the root directory in the case concerned. Therefore, the DOS command CHDIR .. moves up one level in the directory tree. For this purpose, the start cluster in this entry points to the beginning of the parent directory above. An entry 0 means that the root directory is the parent directory, that is, the current subdirectory is a first-order subdirectory.

A sub-subdirectory is generated in the same way. DOS prepares a directory entry in the subdirectory with the name of the sub-subdirectory as the file name and extension, and sets the directory attribute. Furthermore, the operating system allocates a cluster which accommodates the directory entries of the sub-subdirectory. Again, the MKDIR command generates the two first entries automatically. Figure 8.13 shows this scheme for the logical connection of the individual directories and files in a graphical manner. A further «diving» into the directory hierarchy or the directory tree is carried out analogously. Thus you are free to generate sub-sub-...-subdirectories as long as the complete access path drive:\sub\sub\...\subdirectory, including the drive's name and the backslashes, doesn't exceed 64 bytes.

The FORMAT command generates the boot sector, the FAT, and the root directory automatically. But subdirectories as dynamically allocated file structures must be prepared manually by means of the MKDIR command. Also, application programs, of course, can generate or erase subdirectories by means of certain DOS functions.

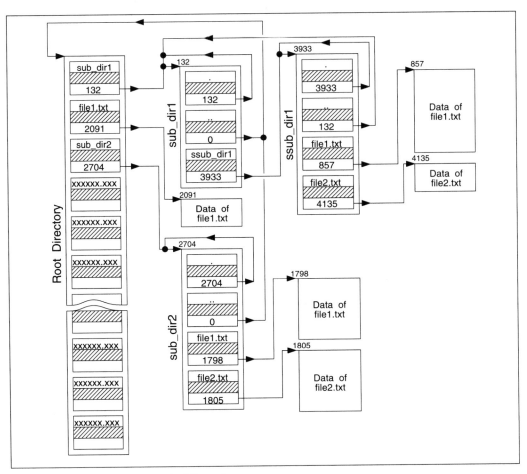

Figure 8.13: The logical connection of subdirectories.

8.4.6   The File Allocation Table (FAT)

It has already been mentioned that the files or subdirectories are allocated a cluster whose number is stored in the directory entry as the start cluster. A cluster usually has between one and four sectors, that is, a maximum of 2048 bytes. Many files are much longer, and these 2048 bytes are not enough even for short letters. But how does DOS succeed in handling large files?

The key to its strategy is the already mentioned *file allocation table (FAT)*. The FAT is located between the boot sector and the root directory (see Figure 8.10), and is automatically generated during the course of the format process (see Figure 8.14). The FAT plays a central role in data management. Any destruction of the FAT or part of it immediately leads to a complete or partial data loss. Thus every floppy or hard disk usually holds two or more FAT copies. The actual number is stored at offset 10h in the boot sector. Beginning with offset 16h, you find the FAT size in units of sectors. If you write a value higher than 2 for this word, then DOS manages all FAT copies automatically without any intervention from you or a program.

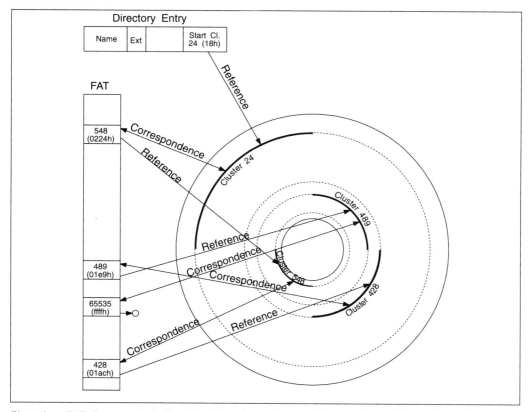

Figure 8.14: FAT. Every cluster is allocated a FAT entry, and every FAT entry points to the next cluster in the chain.

For all FATs two formats are available: 12- and 16-bit. In the first case, every cluster is assigned a 12-bit number (in the latter case a 16-bit number), enumerated starting with 0. The two first entries (that is, 0 and 1) are reserved, and are occupied by a copy of the medium descriptor byte (Table 8.5) as well as two bytes (12-bit FAT) or three bytes (16-bit FAT) with the value 0ffh. Starting with FAT entry number 2, the clusters are assigned to the cluster numbers in a definite and irreversible manner: cluster number 2 is assigned to FAT entry number 2, cluster number 3 is assigned to FAT entry number 3, etc. Thus the cluster enumeration starts with 2 and not with 0.

For example, DOS has to allocate seven clusters to a 14 kbyte file if the cluster size is four sectors, that is, 2048 bytes or 2 kbytes. In the directory entry, however, only the start, namely the first cluster of the file, is stored. Thus some information is missing as to where the file is continued, that is, a pointer to the 2nd to 7th clusters. This job is carried out by the FAT. Table 8.6 lists the meaning of the various FAT entries.

12 bit FAT	16 bit FAT	Meaning
000h	0000h	free
ff0h-ff6h	fff0h-fff6h	reserved
ff7h	fff7h	bad sector, unusable for allocation
ff8-fffh	fff8-ffffh	end of cluster chain, last cluster of file/directory
xxxh	xxxxh	next cluster of file/directory

Table 8.6: FAT entries of 12 and 16 bit FATs

Of significance for the allocation of clusters are the values xxxh and xxxxh, respectively. They specify the number of the cluster which accommodates the following section of the file or directory. If the file occupies only two clusters (that is, the file is not larger than 4096 bytes) then the FAT entry assigned to the cluster containing the second file section has a value between ff8h and fffh or fff8h and ffffh, respectively. If the file or directory is even larger, then this chaining is continued until DOS has allocated sufficient clusters to accomodate all file or directory sections. This accounts for the name file allocation table. In the example indicated, six references to clusters with their following sections as well as a value fff8h to ffffh are therefore required. The result is a so-called *cluster chain* (see Figure 8.15). Note that the cluster chain is only forward-directed. All FAT entries only point to the next cluster, never to the preceding one, that is no back-links are stored. Thus the cluster chain can only be scanned in a forward direction.

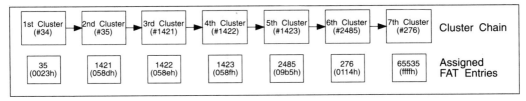

Figure 8.15: Cluster chain.

After the formatting process by means of FORMAT, all FAT entries except the first three or four bytes have the value 00h. This means that in the corresponding clusters neither files or directories are stored.

The same applies, of course, to erased files or directories. If you delete a file with DEL or ERASE or a directory with RMDIR, then the first character in the corresponding directory entry is overwritten with the value 229 (the character σ). Then, DOS resets all FAT entries of the cluster chain belonging to the file or directory to the value 000h or 0000h. Thus, the «physical» contents of a file are not erased, as only the first character in the directory entry and the FAT entries are overwritten, but the logical structure of the file or directory is invalidated. The advantage of this strategy is that the erasure process proceeds very quickly. Only the directory and FAT entries have to be overwritten with the erase character σ or deleted, respectively, but not the complete file. If you delete, for example, a 10 Mbyte file at a cluster size of four sectors, DOS has to overwrite (instead of the 10 Mbytes of the file) only about 10 kbytes in the FAT and one byte in the directory entry. This is 1/1000 of the file size. The second advantage is that erroneously deleted files and directories can sometimes be conjured up by means of certain restore programs, such as Norton Utilities or PCTools. But this is only successful if the programs can reconstruct the former logical structure. The use of 16- and 12-bit FATs is now discussed, together with two examples:

Example: 16–bit FAT

Assume that the first 16 bytes of the file allocation table of a hard disk are as follows:

f8 ff ff ff 03 00 04 00 05 00 ff ff b1 05 01 a9.

f8 is the medium descriptor byte of the hard disk (see Table 8.4); ff ff ff are the three fill bytes. The first cluster has the number two, to which the directory entry start cluster for a file or directory points. To determine the next cluster of the chain DOS must read the FAT entry for cluster 2; here it is equal 03 00. Note that the CPU also stores all FAT values in the Intel format low-high. Thus you have to interchange the two bytes to get the actual value; this leads to 0003h. The following cluster of the chain therefore has the number 3. Now DOS determines the value of the FAT entry 3; it is equal 0004h. Thus the cluster chain doesn't terminate with cluster 3 yet, but continues with cluster 4. If you proceed in the manner described you will get the cluster chain 2 -> 3 -> 4 -> 5. The 5th FAT entry now has the value ffffh; thus the cluster chain terminates with cluster 5 and the end of the file is reached. The file concerned therefore occupies four clusters in total. The FAT entries b1 05 and 01 a9 already belong to another cluster chain.

Example: 12–bit FAT

Assume that the first 16 bytes of the file allocation table of a hard disk are as follows:

f0 ff ff 03 40 00 05 60 00 07 80 00 ff 0f 00 00.

f0 is the medium descriptor byte, here of a double-sided 3 1/2" floppy with 18 sectors per track (see Table 8.4); ff ff are the two fill bytes. After them the assignment of FAT entries and clusters starts. We have to deal with a 12-bit FAT; therefore we have to combine every 12 bits corresponding to 1 1/2 bytes into one number. Unfortunately, this complicates the evaluation of the cluster chain somewhat. It is best to proceed as if the FAT bytes are to be combined as groups of three each (at least in mind). Thus we have to form pairs of FAT entries. For clusters 2 and 3 we get the three-group 03 40 00 by this process. The first 1 1/2 bytes or 12 bits in "natural" order form the FAT value for the cluster 2, the second 1 1/2 bytes the FAT entry for cluster 3. Be careful also in this case: the bytes are present in Intel format. Thus for cluster 2 we get the value 40 03 from which only the 12 *low*-order bits are significant. The FAT entry is therefore equal to 003h and points to cluster 3. For this cluster we get the value 00 40 according to the above described scheme. Here only the 12 *high*-order bits are significant as the 0 in 40 has already been "used" for cluster 2. The FAT entry for cluster 3 has the value 4. If we proceed in the manner indicated then we get the cluster chain 2 -> 3 -> 4 -> 5 -> 6 -> 7 -> 8. The 8th entry has the value fffh, thus the end of the chain is reached. The file concerned therefore occupies seven clusters in total. Further, it is interesting that the 9th entry has the value 000h, that is, the allocated cluster is free and can be allocated by DOS for a newly generated file.

In the two examples described the clusters are contiguous but this is not required. Instead, it is actually a strength of the FAT concept that the chaining also works if the clusters are spread out irregularly. The cluster chain in the first example could also be 2 -> 3 -> 3256 -> 5 -> 28 without

DOS losing the thread. Such files are called *fragmented*. The FAT entries then ensure that the successive sections of a file or directory remain chained.

But the fragmentation can give rise to some very unpleasant consequences for restoring deleted files or directories. Restore programs overwrite the erase indicator σ in the directory entry according to your inputs with the first character of the file or directory name again, and attempt to rebuild the cluster chain automatically or with your help. This only works, of course, if the cluster has been stored successively, or if you know the chaining. With extensively fragmented files all attempts to restore the original data are hopeless. An example: there are more than 3.6 million possibilities for arranging ten clusters. If we take into account that one cluster on a hard disk has four sectors then these ten clusters correspond to a maximum file size of only 20 kbytes. In the case of the above-mentioned 10 Mbyte file, the number of possibilities for arranging the required 5000 clusters largely exceeds the number of all atoms in the universe!

The characteristic that the clusters of a file need not be successive is essential if files are altered later. If, for example, you enlarge the file of the first example (which has five clusters) by a further 2 kbytes, then it is impossible to use the following 6th cluster. This cluster is already occupied by another file or directory as the corresponding FAT entry is equal to b1 05 and not 00 00. If, for example, cluster 839 is free (that is, the corresponding FAT entry has the value 00 00), then the new data can be written onto this cluster. The FAT entry 6 gets the value 839d = 0343h, or 43 03 in Intel format. Cluster 839 forms the end of the chain; thus it is assigned the value ff ff. In this way, DOS need not shift any cluster to accommodate extensions. The shortening of files is carried out analogously in the opposite direction.

The above sections make it clear that the FAT is an essential instrument for allocating files. Without FAT it would be impossible to determine the cluster of the next file or directory section if they are fragmented. Therefore, the FAT is usually present in the form of two copies (the precise number of copies is stored in the floppy or hard disk partition's boot sector). The system indicator in the partition table indicates whether you will find a 12- or 16-bit FAT. With a 12-bit FAT, 4077 clusters can be accommodated after subtracting the reserved and unused values; with a 16-bit FAT this rises to 65 517.

8.4.7   The Files

On a user level the directories only support you for organizing and managing large amounts of data. The actual information is held in the files, which may accommodate texts, business data, programs, and many other types depending upon their usage. The order of the information (that is, the data in the files) follows the route determined by the programmer. This order is not interesting, for DOS as the operating system and you as the user are not confronted with the data structure. If you output a relational data set by means of the DOS command TYPE on-screen, you may be surprised at the strange form in which the data that you normally put on-screen by means of the database program appears.

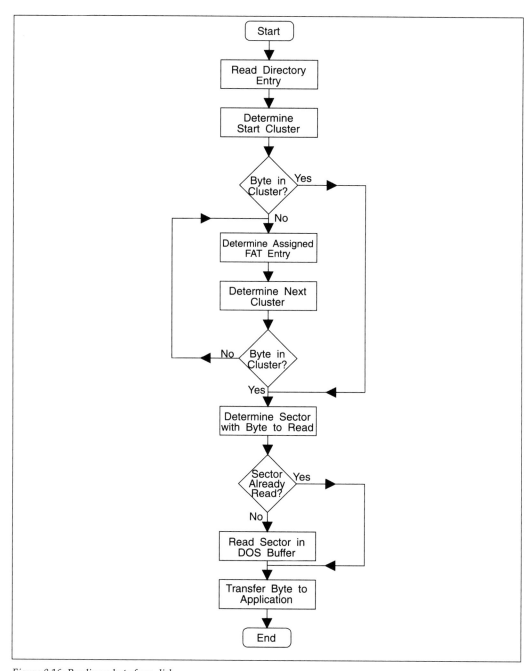

Figure 8.16: Reading a byte from disk.

Also, for every such file which uses its own data format, DOS generates a directory entry in the corresponding directory containing the start cluster of the file as well as its size. If the file is smaller than one cluster, then the start cluster accommodates the whole file and DOS sets the accompanying FAT entry to a value between ff8h and fffh (12-bit FAT) or fff8h and ffffh (16-bit FAT). If the file is larger than one cluster, then DOS distributes it in portions of one cluster to free clusters. The corresponding FAT entries are filled in such that they form a cluster chain according to the above-indicated scheme.

Under various circumstances it is possible that a file doesn't occupy the last cluster completely; it would only do so if its size is a multiple of the cluster size. Thus it is necessary to specify the file size in the directory entry. By this means, DOS is able to determine how many bytes of the last cluster are actually occupied by the file. Remember that DOS can only read and write complete sectors and allocate storage capacity in units of complete clusters because of the physical data carrier's organization into 512-byte sectors. The remaining cluster bytes are not taken into account, and can have any value. If DOS uses a cluster for a directory then it sets all cluster bytes to 0. This indicates that the directory entries are free and can be used for managing new files and subdirectories. Thus a file or directory may occupy more bytes on a floppy or hard disk than it actually comprises.

If you want to read a complete file into a word processing program, then DOS determines, according to the corresponding directory entry, the start cluster first, and reads the sectors as far as is necessary. If the file size is more than one cluster, the operating system evaluates the following clusters in the chain by means of the FAT. DOS reads the sectors until it detects an *end of the chain* entry in the FAT.

If a program attempts to read a byte or a record (for example, by the BASIC command GET #1, 1, A$), then DOS first determines in which logical sector the byte or record is located. For this the directory entry as well as the FAT is used. Afterwards, DOS reads the whole sector and determines the byte or record within the buffer that now contains the sector concerned. You may define the number of such buffers by means of the CONFIG.SYS command FILES=xx. This read procedure is shown in Figure 8.16.

DOS thus always converts any read or write access to a byte or record into an access to a certain cluster and the reading or writing of a complete sector. If you alter a byte or record by over-writing, then DOS reads the complete sector first, modifies the byte or record, and writes the complete sector back to the disk.

8.4.8   DOS version differences

You may have recognized that the directories and the underlying hierarchical structure of the file system are especially useful for organizing larger amounts of data. But the first IBM PC was only equipped with a simple cassette recorder and a single-sided 160 kbyte floppy drive at most. Therefore, the Stone Age DOS version 1.00 had no means of generating directories. Microsoft's DOS developers took over the concept of the *file control blocks* from CP/M (the successful *control program for microcomputers*) for the older 8-bit processors which didn't have any subdirectories. Because of the low storage capacity of the drives at that time, subdirectories weren't necessary; 20 files can be managed readily without any problems.

With DOS version 2.00 Microsoft introduced the concept of subdirectories. At the same time the more modern concept of so-called *handles* was implemented, which was already known from the XENIX system. Here the operating system assigns a unique number to an opened file for its internal management. The BASIC command OPEN TXT_FILE FOR RANDOM AS #1, for example, uses the handle «1» for the internal management of TXT_FILE. Application programs may access DOS system functions by calling interrupt INT 21h. The calling programs usually pass the parameters in the processor registers so that you must load certain registers with appropriate values before the call. DOS was designed for the 8086/8088 16-bit processors. Moreover, the sacred cow of compatibility should not be slaughtered, so DOS needs to be compatible not only on an 80286 but even on the advanced 32-bit i386 and i486 processors. Thus 16-bit numbers at most are available. The logical sectors, too, are managed by DOS with such a 16-bit number so that a maximum of 65,536 sectors of 512 bytes each can be accessed. Thus partitions can have a size of 32 Mbytes at most with DOS 2.00 to 3.20. With DOS 3.30 the simultaneously manageable amount of data on hard disks is also limited to 32 Mbytes. Only the complete DOS partition comprising several such logical drives can exceed the 32 Mbyte border. One might denote these logical drives by the term «subpartitions».

With DOS 4.00 Microsoft cancelled this limitation. The technical advances as well as competing and MS-DOS-compatible operating systems such as DR-DOS made this step unavoidable. Now DOS partitions can be of nearly any size; their logical sectors are managed by a 32-bit number. Today the limitation arises from the fact that a 16-bit FAT can only serve 65 517 clusters. With the usual grouping of four sectors (2 kbytes) into one cluster the data area is now limited to about 128 Mbytes. One possibility for getting larger partitions is to combine more sectors into a single cluster. This is possible up to 16 sectors per cluster. The maximum partition size is now about 512 Mbyte. Other operating systems (for example, OS/2) are free of such DOS limitations.

Besides MS-DOS and PC-DOS, several other operating systems exist (for example, Compaq DOS or DR-DOS) whose functions are compatible with MS-DOS. Some versions of these third-party operating systems have supported DOS partitions of more than 32 Mbytes for a long time, but their structures are often incompatible with MS-DOS 4.00 and higher versions. They also write a different value to the system indicator in the partition table from the original DOS. MS-DOS classifies such partitions as non-DOS partitions, and ignores them. With MS-DOS, which you may boot from a floppy, for example, you cannot access the data in such hard disk partitions.

8.4.9   Other File Systems

Besides DOS there are a lot of other operating systems. For PCs especially, OS/2 and in the future also Windows NT are of importance. Both support the FAT system used by DOS, but their increased performance requires a renovated and enhanced file system. Even the extension to partitions of up to 512 Mbytes storage capacity which has been introduced with DOS 4.00 is not enough for the future. The conceptual weak points of the FAT system concerning the fixed root directory size, the structure of the directory entries with a limited file name size of eleven characters at most, as well as the lack of any access protection, make the traditional DOS file system unsuitable for powerful, future-oriented operating systems.

Thus, with OS/2 a new file system was introduced, the so-called *high performance file system (HPFS)*. The characteristic features of HPFS are the division of a large hard disk into so-called data bands, the much more flexible arrangement of directories and files, a more efficient management strategy for free clusters, the use of sectors instead of clusters as the smallest allocation unit, a flexible length of the directory entries with 32 to 286 characters, file names up to 255 characters, and the implementation of so-called extended attributes with a size of up to 64 kbytes. In particular, the extended file names and attributes significantly help the user. Names like ANSL92_1.TXT become obsolete; now you can write ANALYSIS_SALES_1992 _VERSION_1.TXT. This file name is clear enough so that you know what's in the file even two years later. Moreover, the directory entry holds not only the date and time of the generation or last alteration, but also the date and time of the last read access. One disadvantage of the FAT system is that it is a single-chained list, that is, every entry only points to the following entry. The preceding entry can only be determined by scanning the list from the beginning again, and counting the entries. HPFS is much more powerful in this respect: all file operations proceed much faster with HPFS, a gain which is reached without any improved drive access time.

Despite all the advantages of HPFS the shortcoming remains the fact that the file system doesn't implement a protection for sensitive data. Because of the strong advance of data networks and the possibility that even unauthorized personal can get access to the file system, such protection is becoming more and more important. To reach a higher security level, Windows NT therefore implements a further improved file system with the name *NT file system (NTFS)*. The DOS FAT system and HPFS, however, are still supported.

Mass storage such as floppies and hard disks belong to the system resources of a computer, and therefore are protected in a multitasking environment against a direct access by an application. Thus with OS/2 and Windows NT you may not readily access allocation tables, directory entries, etc. any longer. The operating system cannot allow a bypassing of its protection mechanisms without losing control of the system resources. Additionally, the logical structures are more complicated than with the DOS FAT system. If you intend to program drivers or other system-near routines, you should consult a detailed manual about the various file systems.

It is important that the *physical organization* of floppies and hard disks remains unaltered even with these advanced file systems. All data carriers are organized by means of sectors, tracks and cylinders. Only the *logical organization* (that is, the strategy of storing and addressing data) has been changed.

8.5   System Configuration PC-Controller-Drive

The PC cannot read or write a single byte directly, but always has to process a complete sector, that is, the sector is the smallest addressable unit on a floppy or hard disk. To read a certain byte or bit within a byte the CPU indicates the intended cylinder first, then the required read/write head (thus the track concerned) and finally the sector with the byte to be read. The drive moves the read/write head to the corresponding cylinder and enables the indicated head. When the sector concerned appears below the enabled head, the controller turns on the transfer gate, reads the complete sector (512 bytes), and transfers the data into main memory. Then the CPU only needs to specify the location or the number of the byte within the 512-byte sector in memory to read it.

8.5.1   Controllers and Drives

Between the CPU and the floppy drive is a *floppy drive controller* which supports the CPU for accessing floppies. Figure 8.17 shows the scheme for the connection of CPU and floppy drive.

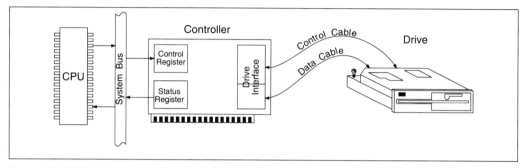

Figure 8.17: CPU-controller-drive connection. The controller is located between CPU and drive.

The floppy controller is usually located on a separate adapter card inserted into one of the bus slots. Today, often a so-called *combicontroller* is used, which can manage two hard disks as well as two floppy drives. If you have an AT-bus hard disk and the hard disk interface is already integrated on the motherboard, then it is possible that the floppy controller is also implemented on the motherboard. Then you don't need your own floppy controller any more, but may connect the floppy drive(s) immediately with the motherboard.

In principle, you are free to install more than one floppy controller in your PC, for example, to control various floppy drives such as 360 kbytes, 1.2 Mbytes and 1.44Mbytes, or a streamer. As peripherals, floppy controllers are programmed via registers, which are accessable via port addresses. If you install two standard controllers then these controllers usually disturb each other, as several registers are present at the same port address. Most controllers can therefore be configured as a primary or secondary adapter. In the first case, the base address of the control and data registers is equal to 3f0h, and to 370h in the latter case. If you want to access the floppy drives on a pure hardware level, you must select the base address 3f0h for the first controller and the base address 370h for the second.

An access via the BIOS or DOS, on the other hand, is rather disappointing in most cases. The second controller and the connected drives seem to be dead; they don't respond to any command. The reason is that most BIOS versions and DOS support a primary but not a secondary adapter. In this way you can disable, for example, the floppy controller on a combi-controller by simply configuring it as a secondary adapter. This is useful if compatibility problems occur and you have to employ a separate floppy controller.

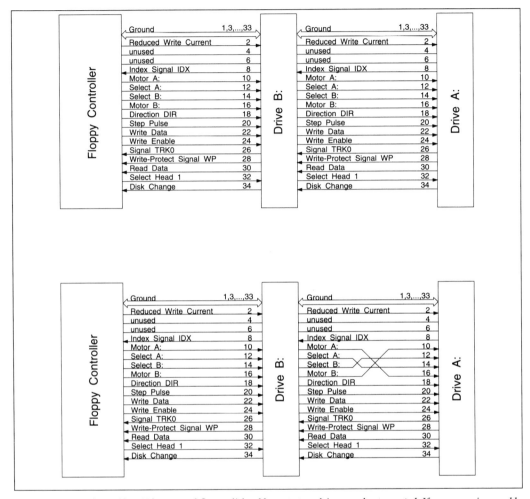

Figure 8.18: Interface cable. With a normal floppy disk cable up to two drives can be connected. If you are using a cable with twisted wires 10 to 16, drives A: and B: can both be configured as drive select 1.

The floppy drive is powered via the usual four-pole supply cable and the controller via the bus slot contacts. For 3 1/2" drives it is possible that a smaller supply plug is required. Modern power supplies therefore have cables with branching supply lines on which such small plugs are mounted. If your PC case doesn't allow you to install the small 3 1/2" drives readily and you have to insert the drive into a 5 1/4" frame first, this is not a problem as the larger frames are prepared for the large plug.

The connection between floppy drive and controller is established by a 34-pole flat cable which you must put onto the controller on one side and the drive on the other. Thus such cables have a plug for the controller and two plugs in most cases for up to two floppy drives. 3 1/2" drives often have contacts for which you need an additional adapter. Figure 8.18 shows the assignment scheme of the plugs and the signals on the individual wires of the interface cable.

There are 34-pole interface cables where wires 10 to 16 are twisted. If you use such a twisted cable it is easier to configure the floppy drives (details are given in the next section). From Figure 8.18 you can see that all control signals for activating the drives, return signals for disk change, to read and write data to and from the controller, etc. are transferred via the interface cable. One ground line with an odd number is always located between two signal lines of an even number, to avoid any influence of the signals on each other.

8.5.2   Drive Configuration

When you buy a blank drive you must configure the drive so that BIOS and DOS can access it correctly. You may install several floppy drives in your PC, so the operating system has to know how many there are and which drives are present at which address. For this purpose most drives have one or more jumpers:

- drive select jumper;
- termination resistor;
- jumper for disk change and ready;
- jumper for floppy type identification.

Via the interface cable, select signals for activating a drive are transferred. The floppy drives respond to these select signals by passing or accepting data. For this purpose it is necessary to identify every drive uniquely to achieve a unique activation. This is carried out by means of the drive select jumper. On the back side of the drive you will find a pin row with four or eight contact pairs in most cases, denoted *DS* (**d***rive* **s***elect*). The individual floppy drives in the system are assigned a number, depending upon the drive, which begins with 0 or 1, running up to 8 at most. Near the contact pairs you will therefore see the symbols DS0–DS7 or DS1–DS8. If you short-circuit a contact pair by means of the jumper, you assign the drive concerned a corresponding number. Note that you may configure the drive as A: if you short-circuit the contact pair with the lowest DS number, that is, DS0 or DS1 depending on which number the counting starts with. You configure your floppy drive as B: analogously if you short-circuit the contact pair with the next highest DS number.

Take note of whether you are using an interface cable with twisted wires 10 to 16, or not. With a non-twisted cable you must configure drives A: and B: in the manner indicated above. Whether you connect drive A: to the plug in the middle or at the end of the cable is insignificant if you use a non-twisted interface cable. You only have to note the terminating resistor (see below). The activation of the drives is carried out exclusively and correctly by the signals motor A:, select A:, select B:, motor B:.

The situation changes if you use an interface cable with twisted wires. In this case you must configure *both* drives A: and B: by means of the drive select jumper as drive B:, that is, short-circuit the contact pair with the second lowest number. Furthermore, the plug in the middle of the cable must be connected to drive B: and the plug at the end of the cable to drive A:. IBM (and other manufacturers) use cables with twisted wires so that the drives can be configured by the manufacturer as B: as standard, and the client doesn't need to carry out the configuration as drive A: or B: on his own as is required in the case of untwisted cables. Therefore, it is possibe to install a standard configured floppy drive without any drive configuration.

By twisting the wires 10 to 16, the motor and select signals for A: and the corresponding signals for B: are interchanged (see Figure 8.18, bottom). If the controller selects drive B: by means of the signals motor B: and select B:, then drive B: in the middle is accessed because it is configured as drive B: and the signals are not interchanged. As the interface cable is continuous the same select signals are also transferred to drive A:, which is also configured as B:. But because of the twisted wires the signals motor B: and select B: appear as motor A: and select A:, that is, they appear at the plug contacts for these A: signals. If the controller enables, on the other hand, drive A: using the signals motor A: and select A:, then drive B: ignores this selection because it is configured as drive B:. Because of the twisted wires, the signals motor A: and select A: appear at the plug for drive A: as signals motor B: and select B:. Drive A: has been configured as B: as is the case for drive B:, however, and accepts the two enable signals and responds to them.

The same effect is achieved if you configure the two floppy drives as A: and if you connect drive A: to the middle and drive B: to the plug at the end of the interface cable. The remaining control, return, and data signals are transferred in an unaltered manner via the untwisted wires and are always available for both drives simultaneously.

But you always have to pay attention to another configuration: the terminating resistor. In the controller such a terminating resistor is already installed, therefore you only have to configure the drives accordingly. The terminating resistor is mostly formed by a ten-pole plug inserted into a corresponding jack. To determine where this resistor is located on your drive consult the data sheet that you received with the drive (or not?). As the name indicates, the resistor must be present at the end (termination) of the interface cable, that is, on the last drive connected to the cable. As you can see from Figure 8.18, this is always drive A:. If you have additionally installed a drive B:, then remove the terminating resistor from it and store it in a safe place. You need the terminating resistor again if you remove drive B: later and want to install it as drive A: in another PC.

Some drives have an integrated terminating resistor that can be activated or disabled by means of a simple jumper. Some modern drives use another method called *distributed terminations*. Here every drive has its own terminating resistor so that the terminating resistors of all connected drives contribute to the actual terminating resistor. Thus, resistors to be installed or enabled separately are no longer required. If you don't find any terminating resistor or jumper for enabling it even after carefully investigating the drive, then you have possibly got such a drive, and you can install it without any further action.

The purpose and meaning of this terminating resistor are obscure for most users, therefore some notes on this subject are in order. Between the drives and the floppy controller a fast and busy exchange of data signals takes place, which run as very short electromagnetic pulses through the interface cable. But such pulses have the unpleasant property of being reflected at the end of the cable, and therefore generating an echo which returns to the transmitter of the pulse. You can observe the same effect in the mountains, too, if you give a cry and the echo returns from the opposite rock face after a few seconds. A strong echo on the signal lines between controller and the drive disturbs the functioning of the electronics, or even damages them because of signal interference. Thus echos should be avoided as far as possible. This is carried out with a trick. For physical reasons, the terminating resistor simulates an infinitely long interface cable. This means that for the transmitter of the pulse the cable continues infinitely beyond the receiver. Now it takes an infinite time before the echo returns from the end of the infinite cable. In other words, no echo and thus no interference occurs. If you are in London then you will also wait *ad infinitum* for an echo from the Alps!

By means of the disk change and ready jumper on some drives you may set whether the drive is to indicate a disk change via line 34 of the interface cable. This function was used starting with the AT. The PC and XT ignore the signal on line 34. Every time you open the drive's door the signal level rises to «1». The AT controller detects the level change and sets an internal bit. Now the BIOS can determine whether a disk change has occurred since the last access. If this is the case, then the internal DOS buffers that still contain information concerning the previous access must be updated using a new access to the data volume. Without a disk change the internal DOS buffers may be used, and the access is carried out much more quickly. In the PC and XT this function is not implemented: DOS always accesses the disk even if it hasn't been removed. Some controllers further handle a ready signal from the drive. This is usually not used in the PC. As the floppy drives of the same type and model are also used in other computers, some drives implement this function; by means of the jumper(s), in most cases you can choose between a no disk change and a ready function.

Note that a drive with a standard ready signal (SR signal) may give rise to some problems in an AT. The SR signal is also passed via line 34, but always provides the opposite level of the disk change signal. «1» indicates that the drive is ready, that is, the flap is closed. Interpreted as a disk change signal this means that the floppy has been changed. That's not a tragedy yet. The AT access then always accesses the floppy instead of using the internal buffers, and the access proceeds more slowly. The situation becomes more critical if you open the flap and remove the floppy. Now the SR signal drops to «0» to indicate that the drive is not ready. But the AT interprets this signal as if no disk change had occurred, and reads the internal DOS buffer. This may give rise to strange behaviour: you have listed the directory by means of DIR, opened the drive flap, removed the floppy and called DIR again. Although you hold the floppy in your hand, the AT goes on displaying the same «ghost» directory without grumbling. You can only use such a drive in an AT if you disconnect line 34 from the drive and fix it at a potential of +5 V indicating «1». The AT then always assumes that a disk change has occurred and always reads the data from disk.

Some ATs with an older BIOS version that doesn't interpret the disk change signal correctly demonstrate other awkward behaviour. Many manufacturers of large program packets thankfully began to supply a reasonable installation program with their software. Today's program packets often need a storage capacity far beyond 1 Mbyte, that is, the programs come on a whole packet of floppies. Some installation procedures now use the disk change signal by means of function 16h of the BIOS interrupt INT 13h to determine whether the user actually has inserted the next floppy before they proceed with the installation. But if the drive doesn't provide a correct signal then the installation procedure denies continuation of the installation process, and keeps asking you for the next floppy after you have inserted the first one. This next floppy has been in the drive for half an hour now, but the installation program doesn't copy or install any further files. Even opening and closing the flap isn't successful, only a new drive or the soldering iron (admittedly a rather radical solution...).

Some 3 1/2" drives further have a jumper for enabling the identify floppy type function. The jumper enables a mechanism on 1.44 Mbyte drives which detects the HD signature on the right side of a 1.44 Mbyte floppy (see Figure 8.3) to enhance the field strength of the write field.

8.6   Recording Formats and CRC

Up to now we have only learned that data is written in tracks and sectors onto the disk. How these tracks and sectors appears in detail (that is, «looking through a microscope») is discussed in the following sections.

8.6.1   Sector Layout

Figure 8.19 shows the format of a floppy track in IBM format for MFM and FM encoding. Details concerning these two recording formats are discussed in the following sections.

```
MFM sector format                       FM sector format
start of track                          start of track
GAP 4A: 80 byte 4eh                     GAP 4A: 40 byte ffh
SYNC:   12 byte 00h                     SYNC:    6 byte 00h
IAM:     4 byte c2h c2h c2h fch         IAM:     1 byte fch
GAP 1:  50 byte 4eh                     GAP 1:  26 byte ffh


sector                                  sector
SYNC:   12 byte 00h                     SYNC:    6 byte 00h
IDAM:    4 byte a1h a1h a1h feh         IDAM:    1 byte feh
ID:      4 byte tr hd sc sz*)           ID:      4 byte tr hd sc sz*)
CRC:     2 byte CRC value               CRC:     2 byte CRC value
GAP 2:  22 byte 4eh                     GAP 2:  11 byte ffh
SYNC:   12 byte 00h                     SYNC:    6 byte 00h
DAM:     4 byte a1h a1h a1h fbh         DAM:     1 byte fbh
      or 4 byte a1h a1h a1h f8h              or 4 byte f8h
Data: 512 data byte                     Data: 512 data byte
CRC:     2 byte CRC value               CRC:     2 byte CRC value
GAP 3:  80 byte 4eh                     GAP 3:  40 byte ffh

/EOT                                    /EOT
GAP 4B:  xx byte 4eh                    GAP 4B:  xx byte ffh

*) the four byte identify the corresponding sector in the format
track–head–sector–sector size
```

Figure 8.19: Track layout.

Here I want to explain only the MFM format as it superseded the FM format completely. As you see, a sector accommodates not only the 512 data bytes but the tracks and sectors have many additional bytes for addressing and synchronization. A track always starts with *GAP 4A*. This gap contains 80 bytes of value 4eh, which can also be found in all other gaps. A floppy indicates the beginning of a track by means of the index hole, but its position is far less precise for exactly determining the beginning. Two data bits are separated on a 5 1/4" floppy with 15 sectors per track by about 2 μm only, and such precision can't be achieved with a hole of 1 mm in diameter. The pattern of the 80 4eh bytes informs the controller about the beginning of the track and gives it enough time for its electronics to be able to respond to the beginning of the track. The next 12 bytes *SYNC* with the value 00h synchronize the decoder elements in the controller with the floppy's rotation. The individual bits are passing below the read/write head, and they generate a pulse pattern for the controller through electromagnetic induction. Thus the controller must adapt itself to the clocking of this pattern, as minor rotation variations cannot be avoided. All synchronization patterns on the disk comprise a 12-byte chain with the value 00h. The four bytes of the *index address mark (IAM)* inform the controller that now the sectors of the track are following. Immediately afterwards, another gap appears, *GAP 1*. The IAM consists of three bytes of value a1h and a fourth byte of value fch which identifies the address mark as an index address mark. The IAM characterizes the beginning of the track far more precisely than the index hole in the floppy. As you will see below, the track contains further address marks.

After this track start, which already occupies 146 bytes, the sector area begins. Every sector contains ten sections; the first is a synchronization pattern SYNC consisting of 12 bytes of value 00h in the same way as for the start of the track. SYNC is followed by the *ID address mark (IDAM)*, which indicates the start of the identification field for the sector concerned. The IDAM has three bytes a1h and one byte feh. After the ID address mark the controller finds the *sector identification (ID)*. It identifies the sector concerned in the format track-head-sector-sector size. When you are formatting a floppy (see Section 8.7.3) you have to supply a format buffer for every track to be formatted which contains exactly this information. The controller calculates from the four IDAM bytes and the sector identification ID a CRC check value in the course of formatting, and stores it in the two bytes of the *CRC* section. Cyclic redundancy check (CRC) undertakes consistency checking of data (similar to parity checking) but CRC is much more powerful.

The CRC section is followed by another gap, *GAP 2*, with 22 bytes. GAP 2 is necessary as the controller must first calculate a CRC check value from the read bytes IDAM, ID and CRC, and compare to this calculated value with the stored one. This lasts a certain time, and without the gap the values that come after it would have already passed below the head. After GAP 2 another synchronization field SYNC appears to enable resynchronization of the controller with the disk rotation after the CRC calculation. The *data address mark (DAM)* finally indicates the beginning of the sector data area *data*. It comprises 512 bytes which you write as the physical sector onto the data carrier. But besides the standard 512 bytes, other sizes for the sector data area are also possible, which you may define during the formatting process of the track. Valid sizes are 128, 256, 512 bytes up to 16 kbytes. Large values may give rise to difficulties in synchronization, as the controller must operate during reading or writing a sector for a long time without any synchronization pattern SYNC. With small sector sizes you waste storage capacity, because the controller generates the above-mentioned and the following data sections for every large or small sector on disk. As was the case for IDAM and ID, the controller also calculates a CRC check value for the sector data area and stores it in *CRC* behind the field data. During the course of reading a sector, the check value is calculated again and the controller compares the calculated and stored values. At the termination of a sector you find another gap, *GAP 3*. Thus a sector not only comprises 512 bytes, but may grow up to 654 bytes because of all the marks that are automatically generated by the controller. If you look at Figure 8.19 you will readily see why the formatted capacity is lower than the unformatted.

GAP 3 has a special job. As the recording of data is a rather delicate procedure and needs to be carried out very precisely, GAP3 as an elastic bufferserves as an elastic buffer between two sectors. If a drive has elongated a sector because of thermal deformation, rotation variations, or incorrect timing of the write signals (like a rubber band), then GAP 3 prevents the data of the sector concerned from overlapping with the data of the next sector and damaging them. Such an elongation can be caused, for example, if the rotation rate of the floppy disk increases suddenly due to reduced friction. But the controller assumed a certain rotation rate in advance by means of SYNC before DAM. The controller keeps this rotation rate throughout the complete sector. Thus the increased rotation rate leads to a slight elongation of the sector data area, which may be up to 5%. This is, technically speaking, not a serious value. Instead, it shows the power and flexibility of modern microchips.

The other sectors of the track now follow the sector described. After 8 to 18 sectors in total, one rotation is complete and the controller detects a number of bytes of value 4eh located as *GAP 4B* between the end of the track (EOT) and the start of the track. Their number is not exactly defined. Instead, GAP 4B serves as an elastic buffer between the end and the beginning of the track, as was the case for GAP 3 between the individual sectors.

8.6.2   FM and MFM

The described track and sector layout only defines the number and value of the individual data bytes, but not how they are brought onto the floppy surface as magnetizations of the ferromagnetic coating. The information is written as a continuous bit stream onto the surface. For floppies, two recording methods exist: FM and MFM. In the following sections these two methods are briefly explained. As the MFM method enables twice the information density with the same recording density, only the MFM method is used today. For compatibility reasons, all floppy controllers still support the older FM recording (or encoding) format. Figure 8.20 shows the encoding of the byte 01101001 in FM and MFM format.

The data bits are stored in a so-called *bit cell*. A bit cell is a certain section on the floppy's surface which accommodates a single bit. For the FM recording format, every bit cell is divided into two half cells which hold a *clock bit* and a *data bit*, respectively. Remember that only a flux change in the magnetic data carrier medium is able to generate a signal. Thus every pulse is generated by a flux change (usually a reversal of the magnetization), and therefore a set clock or data bit must comprise a reversal. The granularity of the magnetic recording medium and the size of the read/write head limit the size of such a bit cell (towards smaller sizes). Typical values for the size of a bit cell are about 1 μm to 3 μm for floppies.

Characteristic of the FM format is that every bit cell contains a set clock bit. The actual information stored in the clock bits appears between two successive clock bits as an active or inactive signal, corresponding to a value of 1 or 0, respectively. Thus, writing data in the FM encoding format is very easy. You only need a clocked counter that outputs a clock pulse for all odd count pulses, and for all even clock pulses supplies a pulse to the read/write head if the value of the bit to write is equal to 1, or no pulse if the value concerned is equal to 0.

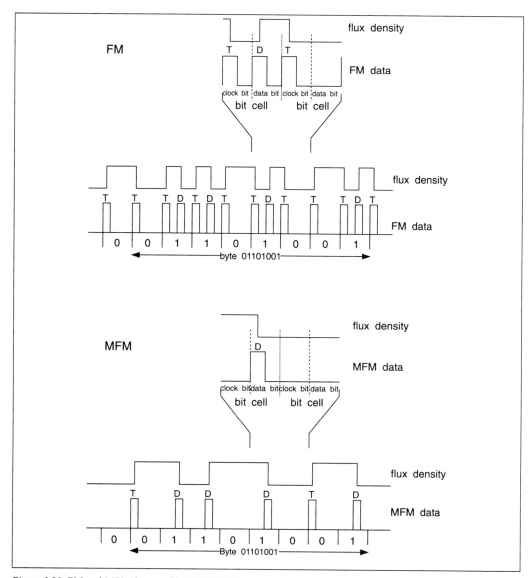

Figure 8.20: FM and MFM format of byte 01101001.

Also, restoring the data bits is very easy. A read signal logic equipment detects the clock bits and determines whether an active signal according to a set bit or an inactive signal corresponding to a bit value of 0 appears between two successive clock bits. Thus the FM method operates quite simply and reliably, but the information density on the data carrier is not very exciting. The MFM method increases the density by a factor of two without the need to raise the density of the clock and data bits.

Figure 8.20 shows the same data byte as it is written with MFM encoding format onto the data carrier. It is obvious at once that the number of clock bits is much smaller, and the distance between two active bits is much larger than is the case for the FM method. The reason for this is the encoding rule for MFM data recording:

- A clock bit is only written if the preceding as well as the current bit cell doesn't have a set data bit.
- A data bit is always written if it is equal to 1.

For encoding data in the MFM format, not only the current data bit is taken into account, as is the case with the FM method, but also the preceding data bit. Thus the value stored in a bit cell is the result of two successive data bits. Accordingly, the electronic equipment for executing this encoding, and especially for restoring the data, is much more complicated (and expensive). As a compensation, fewer active bits must be written into the bit cells. With the FM method every bit cell has a set clock bit; with the MFM method active clock bits only occur if at least two data bits of value 0 are successive. As you may see from Figure 8.20, the result is that the distance between two successive active bits, regardless of whether clock or data bits and thus the distance between two successive flux changes, is at least as large as one bit cell and at most as large as two bit cells. On the contrary, the distance between two active bits with the FM method is as large as half a bit cell at least and a whole bit cell at most. In other words, the bit cells can be made half as large without increasing the bit and flux change rate compared to the FM encoding method. Thus the information density now becomes twice as large as with the FM method, and this is achieved without increasing the flux change density on the data carrier surface. The additional expenditure affects only the encoding and decoding electronics of the controller, a problem which modern microelectronics can solve without problems and very reliably.

The method for restoring the original data from the MFM data is quite interesting, and is important for understanding the error recovery strategies of hard disk controllers. Therefore, how the controller decodes the MFM data from the flux changes on the data carrier by means of various clock signals is explained. Figure 8.21 shows the scheme for restoring data byte 01101001 from the MFM data of Figure 8.20 (bottom).

Figure 8.21 (top) shows the flux density with the flux changes for inducing a voltage pulse in the read/write head. Note that every flux change gives rise to a pulse, but a regular magnetization doesn't generate any voltage. The read/write head continuously detects the signals and transfers them to two gates: a data and a clock gate. The data gate is supplied with a data clock signal so that the high signal levels form a periodically opened *data window*. The data gate then simply turns on and lets the signals pass. In the same way, a clock signal is supplied to the clock gate, but this clock signal is shifted in phase against the data clock signal by 180°. The high levels of the clock signal define a periodically opened *clock window*. The clock gate then simply turns on and lets the signals pass. The phase shift is chosen so that the signal, because of a flux change, can pass the data gate if it is a data bit. The signal, on the other hand, passes through the clock gate if it is a clock bit. As you can see from Figure 8.21, the data gate provides the originally encoded data bits and the decoding process has been carried out. The clock bits running through the clock window keep the synchronization if the data bits are equal to 0, and therefore no data signals appear at the data gate. With set data bits the MFM decoder uses the data bits to keep the synchronization. This is important if many set bits are arriving in succession, for example 512 bytes of value ffh.

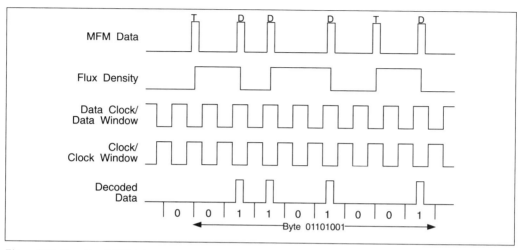

Figure 8.21: Decoding MFM data.

The most delicate point with MFM recording is that synchronization becomes more difficult because of the partially missing clock bits. As already mentioned, a clock bit only appears if at least two bits of value 0 are successive. For this reason, the synchronization fields of the tracks and sectors all have the value 00h (see Figure 8.19). Floppies used for the MFM method are formatted with longer synchronization fields than is the case with FM floppies. If the MFM method is used, then the SYNC fields typically comprise 12 bytes; with the FM method, on the other hand, they are only 6 bytes long (see Figure 8.19). Also, the values for IAM, IDAM and DAM in the sector format generate bit patterns with the MFM method that can easily and reliably be decoded by the controller to identify the corresponding bit sequences as address marks.

8.6.3   CRC – Nothing Can Hide From Me

The CRC fields have a mysterious feel as one usually doesn't get any information other than that they can detect data errors very efficiently. In the following sections the veil will be lifted.

You may know the method of checking, by means of a so-called *parity bit*, whether or not a transmitted character has arrived correctly. For this purpose, transmitter and receiver have to agree upon whether the parity is to be odd or even. If you want to transfer the basic principle to other check methods then you can see that a check value (the parity bit in the case of the parity check) and a checking rule (in the case of the parity check the agreement as to whether an odd or even parity should be generated and how it is determined) are required. The analogous rules of the CRC check indicate that a 16- or 32-bit check value must be formed by dividing the value by a divisor, and that this has to be carried out by means of modulo-2-division. First, a few words on modulo-2-division.

Usually, a larger value DIVIDEND is divided by a smaller value DIVISOR by taking into account as many places of the dividend as the divisor has, and determining how often the divisor is included in the dividend. Afterwards, this multiple is subtracted from the places used. Now the next lower place of the dividend is added on the right side of the subtraction result. The division is continued accordingly. Finally, we get the quotient and a remainder:

`DIVIDEND ÷ DIVISOR = QUOTIENT + REMAINDER`

For dividing binary numbers only the subtraction is required, as one immediately recognizes whether the divisor is larger or smaller than the partial dividend.

Example: a209h ÷ 9bh (1010 0010 0000 1001b ÷ 1001 1011b or 41.481d ÷ 155d); numbers pulled down step by step are represented in bold face

```
1010001000001001 ÷ 10011011 = 100001011 + 1100000
10011011
 00001110
 00000000
  00011100
  00000000
   00111000
   00000000
    01110000
    00000000
     11100001
     10011011
      10001100
      00000000
       100011000
        10011011
         11111011
         10011011
          1100000
```

Thus the quotient is 100001011b=10bh=267d, the remainder 1100000b=60h=96d.

In the example indicated the division has been carried out step-by-step by means of «normal» subtraction. Here, normal means that the subtraction follows the rules you learnt at school. A carry occurs if a digit of the subtrahend is larger than the corresponding place of the minuend. For CRC calculations this normal arithmetic is not used, but the so-called *modulo-2-arithmetic*. Here the subtractions are no longer carried out in the normal way, but XOR values (see below) of minuend and subtrahend are evaluated. In the same way, the addition is also carried out by XORing the individual places of the two summands. Addition and subtraction are therefore identical, and provide identical results. At a first glance this seems to be contradictary, as addition and subtraction usually behave in an opposite way. But it is exactly this that is very interesting from a mathematical view. Additionally, the technical realization of the modulo-2-arithmetic is much easier than that of normal arithemtic, as no carries need to be taken into account. With ordinary addition and subtraction, every place of the sum or difference is the result of the corresponding places of the two summands or minuend and subtrahend **as well as** of a possible carry. The modulo-2-arithmetic can therefore be realized by means of simple XOR gates and registers. Thus the electronic circuitry operates much faster than with conventional arithmetic. This is very advantageous for time-critical applications, to which the on-line evaluation of CRC checksums during the course of reading from or writing to floppies and hard disks also belongs.

The name XOR means that the result of two values is evaluated by means of an exclusive-or operation. The logical XOR operation thus corresponds more to our «common OR» than the ordinary logical OR. The result of an XOR operation is true (equals 1) if either the first or the second value is true. Table 8.7 shows the truth table for this operation.

---

0 XOR 0 = 0
0 XOR 1 = 1
1 XOR 0 = 1
1 XOR 1 = 0

Table 8.7: XOR truth table

Division with modulo-2-arithmetic is carried out in the same way as ordinary division, but instead of the successive normal differences modulo-2-differences are formed, that is, the bit by bit XOR values.

Example: as in the example above a209h ÷ 9bh (1010 0010 0000 1001b ÷ 1001 1011b or 41.481d ÷ 155d); numbers pulled down step by step are represented in bold face

```
1010001000001001 ÷ 10011011 = 101111011 + 1101100
10011011
 01110010
 00000000
  11100100
  10011011
   11111110
   10011011
    11001010
    10011011
     10100011
     10011011
      01110000
      00000000
       111000000
       10011011
        11110111
        10011011
         1101100
```

Thus the quotient is 101111011b or 17bh or 379d, the remainder is equal to 1101100b or 6ch or 108d.

The quotient and the remainder differ from the result above. But before you say that this result is now wrong, remember that the values have been generated by a completely different calculation rule than we are accustomed to in our everyday life. The calculation process and the results are denoted by the same terms only for reasons of analogy. If you try on your own to calculate the quotient and remainder of two binary numbers, then you will readily realize that the division with modulo-2-arithmetic is much easier and therefore also much faster, as no error-prone carries must be handled. The same applies, of course, to the electronic circuitry for executing the divisions. Thus it is not surprising that mathematicians looked for meaningful ways in which to apply this simpler kind of arithemtic to checksum calculations. One result of this search is CRC.

Of course, for modulo-2-arithmetic the above-mentioned expression DIVIDEND ÷ DIVISOR = QUOTIENT + REMAINDER also holds, but the values for QUOTIENT and REMAINDER differ for modulo-2-arithmetic from the above evaluated results. In both cases, however, it is true that QUOTIENT and REMAINDER say more about DIVIDEND than a simple parity bit is able to do.

For CRC checksums, therefore, the remainder of a modulo-2-division of the value to be checked by a fixed divisor is calculated. The quotient is not suited for that, as its length is dependent upon the value of the dividend, and thus varies significantly according to the number and value of the data bytes for which the CRC check value is to be calculated. The remainder, on the other hand, is always equal to DIVISOR -1 at most. If it were to be larger then the remainder could again be divided by the divisor for at least one time. Thus the length of the divisor in bits determines the length of the CRC checksum. In computers, a 17-bit divisor is usually used for ordinary and a 33-bit divisor for more critical applications. The divisors are called the *generators* of the CRC, as they generate the CRC checksums. The 17- and 33-bit generators lead to 16- and 32-bit CRC values, respectively. The evaluation of CRC checksums can be carried out by means of hardware, but you are free to execute the CRC calculations by software, too (for example, if you want to carry out a data communication via the serial interface and to check the transferred data in more detail, as this is possible with a simple parity bit.)

The power of CRC checksums for detecting data errors is enormous. For a 16-bit CRC-CCITT (described below) the following holds:

- single bit errors: 100%
- double bit errors: 100%
- errors with an even number of bits: 100%
- burst errors less or equal 16 bits: 100%
- burst errors with 17 bits   99.9969%
- all other burst errors: 99.9984%

The parity check, on the other hand, may fail with two erroneous bits, for example if the two erroneous bits have been complemented compared to the original ones. The relatively simple calculation on the one hand and the enormous power on the other have positioned CRC checksums as an instrument for error checking. They are not only used for floppies and hard disks but also for data communication, for example. Here, mainly 17-bit generators are used which lead to 16-bit checksums. Generally, the following are employed:

- 10001000000100001: the value (11021h or 68,665d) has been defined by the CCITT; thus the CRC result is often called CRC-CCITT;

- 11000000000000101: the value (11005h or 68,637d) is used by IBM for its BYSYNC data communications protocol.

The first generator is somewhat more powerful for detecting errors than the second used by IBM. The CCITT generator is employed by floppy controllers for calculating the CRC checksum in the sectors.

To carry out data checking using CRC values, the data transmitter must evaluate the CRC values from the data bytes and additionally transfer them to the data bytes. The receiver detects the data bytes, determines a CRC checksum from them by applying the same rule, and then? One would expect, of course, that the receiver compares the calculated CRC value with the received value. If they coincide then the data bytes are correct with a probability of at least 99.9969%. This strategy is also possible, of course, and successful.

A better option uses the special properties of the modulo-2-arithmetic and the CRC codes. If you look at the sector layout of Figure 8.19 then you can see that, for example, the 512 data bytes and the two CRC bytes are in succession. Thus, 514 bytes are transferred to the controller in succession, which then have to be split by the CRC logic into 512 data bytes for calculating the CRC checksum as well as two received CRC bytes. But it is easier to combine the two CRC bytes and the 512 data bytes into a single 514-byte value, and to carry out the CRC calculation with these 514 bytes. For this purpose the 512 data bytes need to be filled with two 0-bytes at the right side *before* the CRC calculation. Thus the data bytes are extended by two bytes of value 0 at that position in the 514-byte block where the CRC bytes are to be placed. This corresponds to a multiplication by 65 536 and the quotient also increases by this factor. The CRC check value is now calculated by means of these 514 bytes, which have the two 0-bytes at the right side.

One feature of the CRC calculation with modulo-2-arithmetic is that the CRC value of these 514 bytes is exactly equal to 0 if the CRC value calculated before from the 512 data bytes plus the two 0-bytes coincides with the two received CRC bytes. Fantastic, isn't it? The same applies, of course, to 32-bit CRC values. You only have to fill the data bytes on the right side with 32 0-bits in advance of calculating the CRC value that is to be written onto disk.

For data exchange with a CRC check, transmitter and receiver therefore proceed as follows:

– The transmitter extends the data bytes on the low-order side by that number of 0-bytes which corresponds to the intended number of CRC bytes. The transmitter then determines a CRC value from the data bytes plus the 0-bytes, and transmits the data bytes as well as the CRC value as a continuous data stream.

– The receiver regards the received data (which comprise the data bytes as well as the CRC value) as a continuous data block, and determines a CRC value for the whole block. If this CRC value is equal to 0 then the calculated and the received CRC checksum coincide; otherwise, a data error has occurred.

The scheme is valid for data communication, for example, and also for the CRC checksums on disk, of course. The controller calculates the accompanying CRC values while writing the data onto disk, and puts them after the sector data. During the course of reading a sector, the controller handles the sector data plus the CRC bytes as a continuous data block, and calculates its CRC checksum. If this sum is equal to 0, then the 512 data bytes are correct.

Example: The four data bytes a2 50 b9 09h corresponding to 10100010010100001011100100001001
shall be transmitted; the CRC checksum is calculated with the CCITT generator
10001000000100001.

CRC checksum of the four data bytes only:
10100010010100001011100100001001 ÷ 10001000000100001 = 1010100011001001 remainder
1001100011100000
quotient a8c9h, remainder=CRC checksum 98e0h
CRC checksum of the four data bytes plus two 0–bytes:
1010001001010000101110010000100100000000000000000 ÷ 10001000000100001
= 101010001100100110010001111101100 remainder 0110110001101100
quotient a8c991ech, remainder=CRC checksum 6c6ch
The quotient has increased by two bytes because of the extension from four to six bytes. The
four data bytes a250b909h, as well as the two CRC bytes 6c6ch, are transmitted; thus the data
block is a250b9096c6ch or 1010001001010000101110010000100101101100011011100b.
CRC checksum of the four data bytes plus two CRC bytes, that is, of data block a250b9096c6ch:
1010001001010000101110010000100101101100011011100 ÷ 10001000000100001
= 101010001100100110010001111101100 remainder 0000000000000000
quotient a8c991ech, remainder=CRC checksum 0000h
The CRC checksum 0000h indicates that the four data and two CRC bytes are consistent; the
quotient is equal to the above indicated value.

But the CRC and the even more powerful *ECC codes* (**e**rror **c**orrecting **c**odes or **e**rror *checking and correcting*) are not only used for magnetic data recording with floppy or hard disk drives. ECC codes are, in principle, CRC codes whose redundancy is so extensive that they can restore the original data if an error occurs that is not too disastrous (for example, a burst error with eleven destroyed data bits). Very fail-safe RAM memory systems also use them.

Usually, the control logic of the main memory in a PC only checks whether the parity of every stored data byte is consistent with the stored parity bit. There are memory controllers available that store a CRC or ECC value instead of the parity bit, and which are therefore able to detect (CRC) or even correct (ECC) a memory data error. One example of such a memory controller with embedded ECC logic (sometimes also called EDC logic for **e**rror **d**etecting and **c**orrecting) is AMD's AM29C660. The controller is able, for example, to repair soft-errors in DRAM chips caused by natural radioactivity in the air or tiny amounts of radioactive substances in the chip substrate (for example, thorium). The ionizing effect of the emitted α-rays causes additional charges in the charge storage area of a DRAM memory cell, and thus distorts the held value.

8.6.4   For Freaks Only – Some Amazing Features of CRC Codes

The following sections briefly present the mathematical background of CRC codes.

At the beginning we started with the expression

data = quotient * divisor + remainder

With modulo-2-arithmetic the ordinary + must be replaced by the modulo-2-plus ++:

data = quotient * divisor ++ remainder

This expression doesn't exhibit any exciting feature yet; but after a modulo-2-addition of the remainder, on both sides we get

```
data ++ remainder = quotient * divisor ++ remainder ++ remainder
```

If two identical values (here remainder) are added by means of modulo-2-arithmethic, then a 0-bit always meets a 0-bit and a 1-bit a 1-bit. According to the truth table for the XOR operation, all matching sum bits are set to 0. Thus the result is equal to 0. We then get the following expression:

```
data ++ remainder = quotient * divisor
```

or in a rearranged form

$$\text{quotient} = \frac{\text{data ++ remainder}}{\text{divisor}}$$

This doesn't mean anything, but with a modulo-2-addition of the remainder (that is the CRC checksum) the result of the addition can be divided by the divisor without any remainder. Thus the remainder is equal to 0 with this division.

If you meet CRC checksums, in most cases the generator is indicated by means of which the CRC checksums are calculated. Without knowing the generator you are not able to check the data block for consistency, of course. But the generator appears on the data sheets for controllers or communication protocols in most cases as a polynomial. The *generator polynomial* of CRC-CCITT, for example, is $x^{16}+x^{12}+x^5+1$, and that of CRC-16 $x^{16}+x^{15}+x^2+1$.

The assignment of generator polynomials and binary divisors for modulo-2-division is very simple:

- The exponent of the each polynomial term indicates the position of the corresponding bit in the divisor.

- All terms which correspond to a divisor bit of 0 are neglected.

Example: `CRC–CCITT` $x^{16}+x^{12}+x^5+1$ means
$1*x^{16}+0*x^{15}+0*x^{14}+0*x^{13}+1*x^{12}+0*x^{11}+0*x^{10}+0*x^9+0*x^8+0*x^7+0*x^6+1*x^5+0*x^4+0*x^3+0*x^2+0*x^1+1*x^0$
thus the binary divisor is equal to 10001000000100001

`CRC–16` $x^{16}+x^{15}+x^2+1$ means
$1*x^{16}+1*x^{15}+0*x^{14}+0*x^{13}+0*x^{12}+0*x^{11}+0*x^{10}+0*x^9+0*x^8+0*x^7+0*x^6+0*x^5+0*x^4+0*x^3+1*x^2+0*x^1+1*x^0$
thus the binary divisor is equal to 11000000000000101

The deeper reason for this assignment is that the modulo-2-division can be put down to the division of polynomials with binary coefficients, that is, coefficients that may only have the values 0 and 1. In a strict mathematical treatment of CRC codes (with which I don't want to torture you), such polynomials are used.

Which generator polynomials and thus which divisors are especially suited to maximize the error detection properties is not a trivial mathematical question. But characteristic of all generator polynomials is that the power x^0 (that is, the summand 1) must always be present.

Strictly speaking, CRCs are not only checksums but codes that serve to encode information. The fact that the codes incorporate redundant information makes them so valuable for error checking. Redundant information means that some part of the information can be determined along with the rest of the information. This also applies to parity: the parity bit can be determined from the other bits, that is, the data bits. Also, the ASCII code serves (as the name already implies) for encoding information, but it is not redundant as each of the 256 different codes is assigned exactly one character, that is, a single piece of information. All of the eight ASCII bits are needed, and no bit is left for any redundant information. Thus with a redundant code there are always fewer codewords than would be possible because of the number of available bits. Eight data bits plus one parity bit enable 512 different code words, on the one hand; but only 256 are actually used and valid – those whose parity bit is consistent with the corresponding data bits (that is, all code words with odd **or** even parity, but not both).

The same applies to the CRC codes. Here the generator polynomials generate the various CRC codes. Let's look at the following example for a generator polynomial: x^3+x^2+1. This means a generator of 1101. Thus the generator polynomial has four digits. The degree of the polynomial (that is, the highest power) is denoted by m; thus the length of the accompanying polynomial is m+1. Using the generator polynomial, the code words are generated in two steps.

In the first step, code words longer than m+1, containing only zeroes except the generator, and which are formed by cyclic shifts of the generator are formed. No 1s may go beyond the beginning or end of the word. The code words must be longer than the generator, as they don't carry any information otherwise. Let's assume codewords with a length of six. With the generator 1101 only the basic words 001101, 011010 and 110100 are possible. With 101001 the leading 1 would go beyond the beginning and be added at the end again; but this is not allowed according to the rule indicated above.

In the second step, all further code words are formed by means of modulo-2-addition. We get eight code words in total: 001101, 011010, 110100, 010111, 111001, 101110, 100011, 000000. Thus the code of length 6 according to the generator 1101 comprises eight valid code words. By means of six bits, $2^6=64$ code words can otherwise be represented. The remaining 56 code words are invalid. The generated code is therefore highly redundant. The probability that a statistically constructed 6-bit word represents a code word of this special CRC code is only 1:8.

If the degree of the generator polynomial is increased from three to a higher value, the redundancy also rises further. The probability that a statistically constructed code word is a valid code word of a CRC code generated by a polynomial of degree m is equal to $1/2^m$, in general. Stated differently: the probability that a statistically generated code word is detected to be erroneous is equal to $1-1/2^m$. All damaged data bytes on a floppy represent such statistical code words, as the alteration of the data bytes is unpredictable and thus completely statistical. Any error is detected by the CRC logic of a floppy controller employing the CRC-CCITT generator $x^{15}+x^{12}+x^5+1$ with a probability of $1-1/2^{16}=0.999984$ or 99.9984%. The value coincides with the above indication. Some statistical code words generated by an unpredictable change of part of a valid code word (for example, by a simple bit error) can be detected with an even higher probability.

For storing data onto disk or communication with CRC checksums one therefore generates valid code words (according to the CRC rules indicated above) which are written onto disk or transmitted to the receiver. During the course of checking the inner consistency of data and the CRC value, an important property of valid code words with ECC codes comes in useful: a code word is valid if it can be divided by the generator of the CRC code without remainder. For example, the above-indicated 6-bit code words generated by generator 1101 can be divided by generator 1101 without a remainder. For all other 6-bit values, such as 111111, this is not true. Remember that the CRC check was successful if, for a modulo-2-division of the data block made of the data bytes and the CRC value, the remainder is equal to 0. Thus the addition of the CRC sum to the actual data always generates a valid code word. In other words: in a CRC check (for example, in floppy drives) the CRC logic investigates whether the 514-byte data blocks made of 512 data bytes and two CRC bytes represent valid code words or not. Mathematics and computer science are therefore no mystery at all.

The cyclic shifts during the course of generating the code words from the generator, as well as the fact that the code words contain redundant information, lead to the name CRC or cyclic redundancy codes. Also, the seemingly very trivial parity compared to the CRC codes represents a cyclic code. If you use the generator polynomial x+1 you may generate all code words with an even parity. As the degree of the generator polynomial is equal to 1 the probability of detecting a statistical error by means of the parity bit according to the formula indicated above is $1–1/2^1 = 1/2$. Statistically generated code words are therefore detected only half of all cases.

8.7 Programming Floppy Drives-Access Levels and Compatibility

The following sections discuss the various interfaces to floppy drives and controllers. Unfortunately, minor repetitions of subjects already covered by Chapter 1 are unavoidable. Appendices F and G summarize the most important functions.

8.7.1 Application Programs

If you access a file as a user of, for example, dBASE or Word then you usually select a program function and mark the intended file or input its name manually. You don't get to know the characteristics that distinguish your PC from a home or supercomputer: as the user you are only confronted by the user shell of each program. If this shell is ported to other machines and systems, then you don't see any difference between a slow XT and a terrifically fast Cray Y-MP3, the current top dog computer for computer freaks and serious scientific applications. The hardware-near characteristics remain hidden. Thus application programs define the highest access level to floppies and hard disks (see Figure 1.27 in Chapter 1).

8.7.2   High-Level Languages and Operating Systems

However, application programs have to be programmed in some way; they don't arrive on their own, unfortunately. Application programmers use so-called *high-level languages* in most cases (for example, C, Pascal, BASIC or COBOL). Some program packages such as Lotus 1-2-3 are also written in hardware-near assembler, but the maintenance of the program code gets rather difficult then. High-level languages or the function libraries of C and assembler usually have more or less extensive file and directory functions which enable a high-level access to floppies and hard disks without the need to handle the underlying technical characteristics. System programmers who supply these functions can tell you a thing or two about that! By means of the functions mentioned you may access files and the directory concerned via its usual name, read and write records or lines of data, etc. By combining several of these functions you may construct a more complex function, for example loading a long piece of text or storing an altered entry in a database. As the classification of DOS as an *operating system* already indicates, it is responsible for the operation of the PC and therefore for managing the data and directories, the input and output of characters via the keyboard and monitor, the provision of date and time, etc. Application programs should not rely on direct hardware accesses as they try to bypass the operating system. This works well with DOS (provided your programs are free of bugs), but with a more powerful operating system such as OS/2 or UNIX/XENIX the protected mode system aborts the application in most cases, as such a strategy is an obvious violation of the protection mechanisms.

The compilation of high-level languages on certain computers (in our case the PC) must therefore rely on the capabilities and the functions of the operating system. ANSI-C as a reasonably standardized language appears very similar to a PC programmer and a programmer using the above cited CRAY Y-MP3, but the generated codes have nothing to do with each other. In view of the multi-processor architecture and the several hundred times higher processing speed of the CRAY, this seems to be evident. But let's turn back to DOS now.

DOS supplies three interrupts for disk-oriented functions, that is, interrupts 25h and 26h as well as the *function distributor* interrupt 21h. By means of interrupts 25h and 26h you may read and write logical sectors within the DOS partition. Thus you have a low-level access to the DOS data organization, namely the boot sector, the FATs, the root directory, and the subdirectories. The partition table is outside the DOS partition and remains unreachable even with the help of interrupts 25h and 26h. For application programmers who don't deal with the file organization on a operating system level, the file and directory functions of the INT 21h are much more comfortable. They provide the basis for processing and managing data by means of the commands and subroutine libraries of high-level languages or assembler. You can, of course, achieve the same results by means of an access to the logical sectors via interrupts 25h and 26h. As DOS always converts any data access into an access to logical sectors via INT 25h and INT 26h, and then into an access to a physical sector via the BIOS, you would be building your own operating system functions, functions which Microsoft has already incorporated into DOS! The data-oriented functions of INT 21h have the further advantage that you don't have to pay attention to DOS-internal changes of the file and directory structure among various DOS versions. For example, you access data with DOS 5.00 by means of INT 21h in the same way as you do with DOS 3.00. However, the situation changes as far as interrupts 25h and 26h are concerned. The extension of the DOS area to more than 64k sectors also required a change in accessing the logical sectors by means of INT 25h and INT 26h. Before DOS 4.00 came onto the market the application passed the number of the intended sector in a 16-bit register. Starting with DOS 4.00, this is carried out by a pointer to a 32-bit data structure in main memory, which holds the number of the intended sector. This is characteristically for the «small operating system» DOS, as mainframes don't allow any access to the internal data structure of the mass storage by an application – this is the exclusive right of the system programs and the operator who controls the machine. Section 8.8 describes the data access by means of interrupts INT 21h, INT 25h and INT 26h in more detail.

The DOS functions more or less form a translator between the application programs and the PC hardware. DOS programs have to run correctly on such different machines as a Stone Age PC with an 8088 processor, a 4.77 MHz clock rate and an 8 bit data bus and, on the other hand, on an i486 machine with a 32-bit EISA bus and a 50 MHz clock rate. This really is a hard job. To adapt DOS to such very different computers it is divided into three parts (see Figure 1.28 in Chapter 1).

From Chapter 1 you know that the part of DOS with which you are confronted as a user is called the *command interpreter COMMAND.COM*. COMMAND.COM outputs the well-known and infamous prompt C:\>, processes the internal DOS commands as DIR, and calls application programs. Even COMMAND.COM relies on DOS functions in the same way as application programs for inputting and outputting characters as well as for loading and executing programs. These functions are embedded in the second part, called *MSDOS.SYS* (or *IBMDOS.SYS* if you are working with IBM's PC-DOS). In this part you also find the routines for handling interrupts 21h, 25h, and 26h. For adapting to various hardware environments, DOS further has a third part called *IO.SYS* or *IBMBIOS.SYS*. Computer manufacturers such as Compaq, Tandon and others adapt this part to the characteristic behaviour of their computers to ensure correct operation. IO.SYS contains specific code for accessing the drives and graphics adapters of these manufacturers. But you may also operate 100% IBM-compatible PCs from Taiwan with the «normal» DOS, without the need of special adaptations to the machine. Unfortunately, there is at least one crash per day between 99.99% and 100% compatibility.

The adaptation of IO.SYS to various hardware environments is made as compatible as possible. Of course, it is always possible to program a certain computer in the intended manner; but if your program has to run without any change on several computers then the PCs have to be compatible. This actually is, besides the open architecture, the reason for the PC's success. As an off-the-peg suit is cheaper then a made-to-measure suit, of course, individually programmed word processing systems would be impossibly expensive. The comparison with the made-to-measure suit is also correct in another sense. No program fulfils exactly your requirements, only the average ones. Application programmers must rely on the operating system functions. In this sense, all DOS versions are compatible. A later version is always able to carry out what a former was able to do. But be careful: the inverse doesn't hold! Remember that with DOS 2.00 directories, with DOS 3.00 network functions, and with DOS 4.00 partitions of more than 32 Mbyte capacity were introduced.

MSDOS.SYS and IO.SYS are located on floppies and hard disks as hidden system files immediately after the root directory. Using the «hidden» attribute prevents MSDOS.SYS and IO.SYS from being deleted erroneously. DIR doesn't display the files IO.SYS and MSDOS.SYS; this is only possible with tools such as Norton Commander or PCTools.

8.7.3   BIOS and Registers

With IO.SYS or IBMBIOS.SYS we are already much nearer the hardware level than with an application program. The software at the lowest level that can be accessed by a program is formed by the *BIOS* (**b**asic **i**nput/**o**utput **s**ystem). As the name indicates, the routines of the BIOS implement an interface for inputting and outputting data or accessing and investigating peripheral hardware devices; graphics adapter, parallel and serial interface, EMS expansion adapters as well as (what else?) floppy and hard disk controllers, which in turn control the drives belonging to them.

Each of these peripherals has its own dedicated BIOS interrupt. In the case of floppy and hard disk drives, this is interrupt INT 13h. Section 8.9 and Appendix F discuss its functions. INT 13h exclusively works with physical sectors; thus we are already on the level of the physical data carrier organization and the partition table becomes accessible. For calling and executing the BIOS functions, a *de facto* standard has been established which orients to the assumptions of IBM BIOS. Among all DOS parts only IO.SYS accesses the BIOS, thus such a standard would not necessarily be required as IO.SYS, as the very hardware-dependent part of DOS, can always be adapted to every BIOS. Because of the standardization of the BIOS functions, even an application programmer can call BIOS functions and be sure in most cases that the called function will be carried out correctly on another PC.

As you already know, the ports form the interface to peripherals such as the controller and graphics adapters, and access their control and data registers. Note that most peripherals have a (more or less) complex microprocessor that often has its own BIOS. Thus powerful peripherals more or less form their own «computer» in the PC, to which you pass commands via the ports. As different controllers from different manufacturers for different floppy or hard disk drives with different encoding formats can also have very different ports and a different «command set», direct programming by means of the registers or ports is out of the question. Direct programming gives rise to maximum performance at maximum control of the hardware, but porting the program to another PC (which may even have the same name) often fails because of minor but nevertheless decisive differences in hardware. The BIOS offers a good compromise between performance and control on the one hand, and compatibility on the other. Unlike DOS, it is always tailored especially for the actual computer type. The functions of INT 13h (for example, move head) are passed to the floppy controller via the corresponding port as a suitable «command sequence».

Unfortunately, DOS gives hardly any possibilities for programming the serial and parallel ports, or even the graphics adapter, so that they are suitable for powerful applications. If you want to employ, for example, the features of EGA and VGA adapters, or even those of the new graphics adapters with fast graphics processors, then you are forced to use BIOS functions. The same applies for accesses to data beyond the DOS partition (for example, the partition table). Here only a direct call of BIOS functions solves the problem. As already mentioned, nearly all BIOS interrupts have become *de facto* standards today. This means that in modern PCs the BIOS functions of all manufacturers carry out the same functions, thus compatibility generally holds right down to the BIOS level.

8.8 Programming Floppy Drives – Access via DOS

DOS provides three interrupts (25h, 26h and 21h) for access to floppy and hard disks. Interrupts 25h and 26h form the lower level as you may address logical sectors directly by means of them. But note that a direct access to logical sectors may lead to disastrous results in the case of an access error. For example, incorrect FAT entries destroy the logical structure of the file system, and make the data completely inaccessible. Figure 8.22 shows the call and return formats for the interrupts INT 25h for reading and INT 26h for writing a logical sector. By means of these interrupts you may read or write several successive sectors all at once. For hard disks a new call format via parameter blocks was introduced with DOS version 4.00 to access sectors with a number beyond 65 535, but this applies only to hard disks, as 65 536 sectors with 512 bytes each correspond to 32 Mbytes of data. Further details about this format are discussed in Chapter 10.

```
partitions up to 32Mbyte or 65536 sectors
INT 25h – read one or more logical sectors      INT 26h – write one or more logical sectors
```

register	call value	return value		register	call value	return value
AL AX CX DX BX DS Carry	drive number[1] number of sectors first sector offset of read buffer segment of read buffer	error code[2] error if <> 0		AL AX CX DX BX DS Carry	drive number[1] number of sectors first sector offset of write buffer segment of write buffer	error code[2] error if <> 0

[1] value 0 = drive A, value 1 = drive B, etc.
[2] see Table 8.8

Figure 8.22: INT 25h and INT 26h formats.

Note that interrupts 25h and 26h leave a status byte on the stack after a call that you must remove (and use) with a POP instruction. If the intended sector cannot be read or written for some reason, then DOS sets the carry flag and returns an error code in register AX. The code specifies the cause for the failed read or write attempt. Table 8.8 lists the valid error codes.

Code	Error
01h	invalid command
02h	incorrect address mark
04h	sector not found
08h	DMA overflow
10h	CRC or ECC error
20h	controller error
40h	seek error
80h	drive not ready

Table 8.8: INT 25h and INT 26h error codes

Example: read logical sector 519 with INT 25h from floppy in drive B: (programming language: C)

```
unsigned char far buffer[512];
void read_log_sector_519(void)
{ union REGS inregs, outregs;
  struct SREGS segregs;

  inregs.h.al=0x01                              /* drive B: */
  inregs.x.cx=0x0001                            /* read only one sector */
  inregs.x.dx=0x0207                            /* first sector is 519 */
  inregs.x.bx=FP_OFF(buffer)                    /* transfer offset of buffer to bx */
  segregs.ds=FP_SEG(buffer)                     /* transfer segment of buffer to ds */
  int86x(0x25, &inregs, &outregs, &segregs)     /* call interrupt, sector is transferred
                                                   to buffer */
  if ((outregs.x.cflag & 0x01) == 0x01) {       /* check whether carry is set */
    printf("\nerror code: %x", outregs.x.ax);   /* display error code */
  }
}
```

Example: write logical sector 1482 with INT 26h onto floppy in drive A: (programming language: C)

```
unsigned char far buffer[512];
void write_log_sektor_1482(void)
{ union REGS inregs, outregs;
  struct SREGS segregs;

  inregs.h.al=0x00                              /* drive A: */
  inregs.x.cx=0x0001                            /* write only one sector */
  inregs.x.dx=0x05ca                            /* first sector is 1482 */
  inregs.x.bx=FP_OFF(buffer)                    /* transfer offset of buffer to bx */
  segregs.ds=FP_SEG(buffer)                     /* transfer segment of buffer to ds */
  int86x(0x26, &inregs, &outregs, &segregs)     /* call interrupt, sector is written
                                                   from buffer */
  if ((outregs.x.cflag & 0x01) == 0x01) {       /* check whether carry is set */
    printf("\nerror code: %x", outregs.x.ax);   /* display error code */
  }
}
```

If you want to write, for example, byte 6294 of the file TEXT.TXT in directory \S_DIR\SS_DIR\SSS_DIR by means of interrupt INT 26h, then this would be very cumbersome (but not impossible, of course). First you have to look for S_DIR in the directory entries of the root directory by reading the corresponding sector with INT 25h. Then the start cluster of S_DIR must be read; eventually, an access to the FAT via INT 25h is required to determine the accompanying cluster chain. In S_DIR you have to look for the directory entry for SS_DIR analogously, etc. until you have found the entry for TEXT.TXT in SSS_DIR. With the start cluster in the directory entry and the corresponding cluster chain, which you determine by means of the FAT, you have to determine the logical number of the 13th sector of TEXT.TXT. The 6294th byte is located in the 13th sector of the cluster chain, as one sector is able to hold 512 bytes. Now you must read this sector by means of INT 26h into a 512-byte buffer, alter the byte with the number 150 as intended, and write the whole sector by means of INT 26h back to disk again. To update the date and time marks in the directory entry of TEXT.TXT, the sector with the directory entry must be read, altered, and stored. If you want to enlarge the file by the write process then you first need to look for one or more free clusters and mark them appropriately in the FAT. You can see that interrupts INT 25h and INT 26h are only interesting for programming tools or for computer freaks who really want to know every detail. But they are completely unsuitable for file-oriented programming of applications.

With the file-oriented functions of INT 21h, DOS offers an essential simplification in the tasks of searching, reading and writing sectors, updating date, time and file size, and allocating free clusters. As a user or application programmer you therefore do not need to keep struggling with multiple sector accesses and the organization structure of the data with DOS. Instead, DOS internally converts every file or directory access into sector accesses as described above.

A significant alleviation of INT 21h is that you may access files with the common name drive:path\filename.ext. Moreover, an access to certain bytes or records is possible by indicating the position relative to the beginning of the file or relative to the location of the last write or read process. Thus, DOS defines something like a «cursor» within an opened file, indicating the location of the read and write accesses. Table 8.9 lists the most important file and directory functions of INT 21h, but a detailed description would go far beyond the scope of this book.

Number	Function	DOS version
39h	create subdirectory	2.00 ff.
3Ah	delete subdirectory	2.00 ff.
3Bh	change directory	2.00 ff.
3Ch	create file	2.00 ff.
3Dh.	open file	2.00 ff.
3Eh	close file	2.00 ff.
3Fh	read file (device)	2.00 ff.
40h	write file (device)	2.00 ff.
41h	delete file	2.00 ff.
42h	move file cursor	2.00 ff.
43h	set/read file attribute	2.00 ff.
45h	duplicate handle	2.00 ff.
46h	adapt handle	2.00 ff.
47h	determine current directory	2.00 ff.
4Eh	find first directory entry	2.00 ff.
4Fh	find next directory entry	2.00 ff.
56h	rename file	2.00 ff.
57h	set/read date/time of file	2.00 ff.
5Ah	create temporary file	3.00 ff.
5Bh	create new file	3.00 ff.
67h	determine max. handle number	3.30 ff.
68h	forced write of DOS buffers	3.30 ff.

Only the handle-oriented functions are listed since FCB-oriented functions are internally converted by DOS into handle-oriented functions.

Table 8.9: INT 21h file and directory functions

Originally, DOS was designed as a successor of CP/M for the 16-bit 80x86 microprocessor family. In the first DOS version 1.00, the designers therefore used the concept of *file control blocks*

(FCB) for file management. But CP/M's FCBs have a serious disadvantage: they don't allow any directory structure, and all files are, so to speak, located in the root directory. DOS 2.00 (according to Bill Gates, the first «real» DOS) replaced this outdated concept by so-called *handles*. While opening a file in any directory using the function 3Dh of INT 21h, DOS (or more precisely, the INT 21h) provides a number, namely the handle, which unambiguously characterizes the opened file.

Instead of the nearly infinite litany drive:path\filename.ext you only have to pass this number to DOS to access data in an opened file or to extend the file. The rest of the work is done by the operating system for you. DOS searches the relevant sectors, reads them into the transfer buffer, transfers the intended byte or the intended record to the user program, writes the byte or record after the alteration back to the transfer buffer, writes the buffer as a sector onto the disk, eventually allocates a new cluster in the FAT, and finally updates date, time, archive attribute and file size in the directory entry when closing the file. Note that it does not update the directory entries until the file is closed. If you switch off the PC with opened files or issue a boot process (by means of Ctrl-Alt-Del), then DOS may possibly leave an erroneous directory entry and CHKDSK reports lost clusters or allocation errors.

8.9   Programming Floppy Drives – Access via BIOS Interrupt INT 13h

It has already been mentioned above that the BIOS is usually the level nearest the hardware where compatibility among various computers can still be expected for an access to floppy and hard disk drives. The access is carried out via the functions of interrupt INT 13h, listed in Appendix F. Note that for floppy drives only the six first functions 00h–05h are available. Most functions with a higher number are exclusively dedicated to hard disks. Starting with the AT, the BIOS additionally recognizes functions 15h–18h. Some modern BIOS versions also support function 08h for determining the parameters of the floppy drive concerned. In the PC/XT BIOS this function was not implemented for floppies.

The following sections briefly discuss the functions for floppy drives. The precise call and return parameters are listed in Appendix F. The called interrupt handler checks the validity of most of the parameters passed in the registers, and carries out the function requested. Note that the BIOS counting for the floppy drives starts with 00h corresponding to A: with DOS. For hard disks, bit 7 of the drive's number is additionally set so that the first hard disk has the BIOS number 80h.

If the BIOS has completed the requested function, it passes an indicator in the carry flag as to whether or not the operation was successful. If the carry flag is set (=1) then an error has occurred and the register ah contains an error code. Appendix F.2 lists the possible error codes and their meaning. However, note that not all codes are valid for both floppies and hard disks. For example, a hard disk may not be write-protected by hardware; the corresponding error message is senseless for a hard disk.

The most important INT 13h functions are:

- function 00h – initialize drive
- function 01h – read status of last operation
- function 02h – read sector(s)
- function 03h – write sector(s)
- function 04h – verify sector(s)
- function 05h – format track
- function 08h – determine drive parameters
- function 15h – determine DASD type
- function 16h – determine disk change (AT only)
- function 17h – determine floppy format (AT only)

The 04h (verify sector) function shows somewhat mysterious behaviour. According to all the available information, this function compares one or more sectors on disk with the contents of a verification buffer in the main memory. But no controller actually does this, so I'm of the opinion that the function code is only implemented for reasons of compatibility with the original PC BIOS, and the BIOS doesn't carry out a real comparison. Instead, the controller seems to check only whether the CRC or ECC bytes are correct.

Using two examples, I want to briefly explain the use of INT 13h functions. The function calls and their formats are described in Appendix F.

– **Function 02h – Read Sector(s)**

Example: Read sector 1 of track 0, head 0 of the floppy in drive B:; this sector contains the boot record of the floppy (assembler MASM 5.1).

```
buffer DB 512 DUP (?)        ; provide read buffer with 512 bytes (=1 sector)
mov ah, 02h                  ; function 02h (read sector)
mov dl, 01h                  ; second floppy drive B:
mov dh, 00h                  ; head 0
mov ch, 00h                  ; track 0
mov cl, 01h                  ; sector 1
mov al, 01h                  ; read only one sector
mov es, SEG buffer           ; segment address of read buffer
mov bx, OFFSET buffer        ; offset address of read buffer
int 13h                      ; read sector by means of interrupt 13h into buffer
```

– **Function 05h – Format Track**

Example: format one track of a floppy with 15 sectors/track in drive A:

```
struct format_buffer {                        /* define format buffer structure */
  unsigned char track;
  unsigned char side;
  unsigned char sector;
  unsigned char bytes;
};

/*======================================*/
/* format floppy with 15 sectors/track */
/*======================================*/
```

```
format_track(track, side)
int track, side;

{ union REGS inregs,outregs;
  struct SREGS segregs;
  struct format_buffer far *form_buffer;
  int i;

  form_buffer = (struct format_buffer far *)_fmalloc(60);  /* generate format buffer */

  for (i=0; i<15; i++) {                      /* configure format buffer */
    form_buffer[i].track = track;
    form_buffer[i].side = side;
    form_buffer[i].sector = i;
    form_buffer[i].bytes = 2;                 /* 512 bytes/sector */
  }

  inregs.h.ah=0x05;                           /* function 0x05 */
  inregs.h.dl=0x00;                           /* floppy drive A: */
  inregs.h.dh=side;
  inregs.h.ch=track;
  inregs.h.al=0x0f;                           /* 15 sectors/track */
  segregs.es=FP_SEG(form_buffer);
  inregs.x.bx=FP_OFF(form_buffer);
  int86x(0x13,&inregs,&outregs,&segregs);     /* issue interrupt */

  if ((outregs.x.cflag & 0x01) == 0x01) {     /* check whether error occurred */
    printf("\nerror: %x", outregs.h.ah);
  }

  _ffree(form_buffer);
}
```

During the course of an access to disk on a BIOS level, you alone are responsible for inter-cepting errors. The succinct error message «(a)bort, (r)etry, (i)gnore», well-known from DOS, is not output by the BIOS. If, for example, a non-recoverable read error occurs in a read access, then the BIOS function returns to the calling program with a set carry flag, and the register ah contains the value 10h as an error indicator for *read error*. If you don't carry out an error check immediately after returning from the BIOS interrupt, your program may use incorrect data, namely that which was already in the read buffer before the call was issued. In the best case, your PC now processes gibberish. Under the worst circumstances, data may now be destroyed; for example, if your program erroneously determines a «free» location on disk because of an incorrectly read FAT sector and writes another data sector to this place. Also, always make sure that the read or write buffer is of a sufficient size to accommodate all read sectors or data to be written.

Besides the above indicated examples, you can also read, write or verify several sectors at once. You only have to pass to the INT 13h the number in register al. But be careful: some BIOS variants don't support function calls that span more than one cylinder.

In a more technical view, this means that most BIOS variants are able to switch among several heads, but don't move the read/write head to another track. If you try, for example, to read more than 30 sectors all at once from a double-sided floppy with 16 sectors per track, then you surely pass a cylinder boundary. If your read attempt doesn't start at sector 1, head 0 of a cylinder, then you pass the cylinder boundary even earlier, of course. Depending upon the BIOS type, the BIOS can behave unpredictably. For example, users of PC-DOS have had such experiences: this DOS version doesn't worry about passing cylinder boundaries, and on some PCs this leads to a system crash whose cause isn't immediately apparent; or the word processor seems to have a bug as the text previously written onto disk later has utterly confused contents which suddenly appears normal on-screen after a further attempt to load the text.

The behaviour described is called a *multi-track problem*. If you intend to use the BIOS interrupt INT 13h for programming your floppy drives, you should always check for maximum compatibility and operation reliability before you call a BIOS function that passes a cylinder boundary. Another possibility is to always process only a single sector. Of course, you never pass a cylinder boundary then. But reading many individual sectors is much slower than handling complete cylinders. It's up to you which strategy you use as the programmer: real problems sometimes favour this strategy and sometimes the other.

Table 8.10 lists all the sections of the BIOS data area that concern floppies and floppy operations.

Address	Size	Structure 76543210	Content	Meaning
40:10	byte	xx	installed hardware	number of installed floppies if bit 0 is equal to 1 (00=1, 01=2, 10=3, 11=4)*)
		1		floppy installed
40:3e	byte	1	calibration status floppy drives	interrupt requested
		xxx		reserved (=0)
		1		calibrate DR3*)
		1		calibrate DR2*)
		1		calibrate DR1
		1		calibrate DR0
40:3f	byte	x	motor status floppy drives	1=write/format
				0=read/verify
		1		reserved
		xx		selected drive (00=A, 01=B, 10=C, 11=D)1)
		1		motor DR3 on*)
		1		motor DR2 on*)
		1		motor DR1 on
		1		motor DR0 on
40:40	byte		time-out value of drive motors	value in timer-ticks
40:41	byte	1	status of last floppy operation	drive not ready
		1		seek error
		1		general controller error
		xxxxx		error code:

Table 8.10: BIOS data area for floppy drives

Address	Size	Structure 76543210	Content	Meaning
				01h=invalid function number
				02h=address mark not found
				03h=write protection
				04h=sector not found
				06h=disk change
				08h=DMA overflow
				09h=DMA segment error
				0ch=invalid media type
				10h=CRC error
40:42	7byte		result status	max. 7 result status bytes of floppy controller
40:8b	byte	xx	transfer rate controller	rate last set (00=500kbit/s, 01=300kbit/s, 10=250kbit/s, 11=reserved)
		xx		step rate
		xx		transfer rate (00=500kbit/s, 01=300kbit/s, 10=250kbit/s, 11=reserved
		xx		reserved,
40:94	byte		current track drive 0	
40:95	byte		current track drive 1	

[*) The Personal Computer only supports two floppy drives

Table 8.10: cont.

8.10 Programming Floppy Drives – Direct Access via Registers

The most immediate control of the floppy controller and connected drives you have is through the controller's control and data registers. The following discusses how a floppy controller is constructed, and how it carries out certain actions.

8.10.1 Structure and Functioning of a Floppy Controller

Figure 8.23 shows a simple block diagram of a controller with an SA-450 interface, which is used in most PCs. The SA-450 interface was developed by Shugart Associates in the 1970s, and taken over later by IBM for the PC. Since that time, all PC floppy drives have worked with this interface. Note that the interface specification only defines the layout and the signals of the connections, but not its shape. 3 1/2" drives can eventually have a completely different plug so that you may need an adapter to connect a 3 1/2" drive to your floppy controller.

To communicate with the rest of the PC the controller needs access to the bus. This is established via the PC interface, which is also present in a similar form on all other adapter cards. The C interface accepts data as commands or write data from the bus, and transfers data as status or read data to the bus. The controller has a buffer that holds one or more bytes to be transferred from the drive to main memory, or vice versa. Unlike hard disk controllers, the floppy controller has no sector buffer, in most cases, which accommodates a complete sector of data plus the accompanying CRC or ECC bytes.

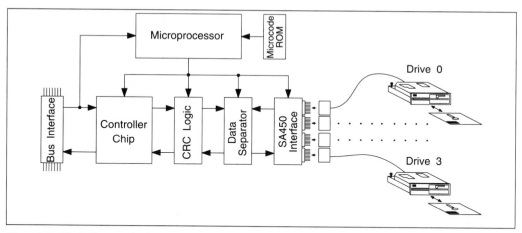

Figure 8.23: Block diagram of a floppy controller.

A floppy controller is quite a powerful peripheral device which has to carry out far more extensive control tasks than, for example, the parallel interface. The controller therefore usually has its own microprocessor with a program ROM. In the case of your PC's floppy controller, this is usually the NEC µPD765 or compatible. The AT can also incorporate an Intel 82072A and the PS/2 an 82077A. µPD765 and the program ROM together form a so-called *microcontroller*, which handles a main part of the control job. The microprocessor controls the individual components on the controller adapter and partially the electronics on the drives according to the program in the ROM. The µPD765 can encode data in the FM and MFM recording formats. Nearly all of today's floppy drives use the MFM method, however. As the µPD765 is an older but nevertheless powerful chip, the FM method is still integrated. The differences between FM and MFM are not serious enough to warrant two fundamentally different chips. Because all floppy drives in the PC only work with the MFM method, all further values for recording density, data transfer rate, etc. refer to MFM encoding. You get the corresponding values for FM by dividing the MFM values by two, as the recording density for MFM is twice as large as for FM.

The main part of the drive control is carried out by the *storage controller*. It does the heavy labour and controls, for example, the read and write functions, converts parallel data from the CPU into serial data for recording on disk (and vice versa), and executes the CRC check of the read data. The bus actually transmits the data in byte or word format with eight or 16 bits. But on the floppy disk the data is present as a continuous bit stream. Individual bits according to the magnetized areas passing below the read/write head, but not complete bytes, follow each other. All data for or from the floppy run through this storage controller. The *data separator* or *data synchronizer* carries out the encoding into FM or MFM data, which is then transferred to the drive for recording on disk. Furthermore, the data is synchronized according to the FM or MFM encoding format, and address marks for the sectors are generated or read. The feedback signals from the drives enable the microcontroller to respond to the dynamic behaviour of the electronic elements and the drives.

In a data write the data therefore goes through the following data path:

- the data is transferred from the bus into the bus interface;

- the storage controller determines the CRC bytes, converts the parallel submitted data into serial data, and formats it in a suitable manner;

- the data separator converts this regular serial data stream into a data stream according the FM or MFM recording format, and generates an address mark;

- the SA-450 interface transfers the encoded data stream to the floppy drive;

- the drive's read/write head writes the encoded data stream as tiny magnetized areas onto the disk's surface.

All components are continuously controlled by the microcontroller on the floppy adapter. To read data from a floppy disk the microcontroller inverts the above indicated course of events. It detects the address marks and reads the sector concerned. The data separator separates the data and clock signals (hence the name separator). Note that FM and MFM refer only to the encoding method, and not the interface between controller and drive. There are MFM drives that you cannot connect to your MFM floppy controller, as the interface between them doesn't follow the SA-450 standard.

I would like to mention that because of the advances in miniaturizing electronic components over the last ten years, today several components are often integrated on a single chip. Thus you will rarely find more than two chips on your floppy controller or combicontroller. All functions of μPD765, program ROM, storage controller etc. are now integrated into one or two chips, but the functions remain the same. The same applies (fortunately) to the command set of the microcontroller. In the AT and PS/2 the registers and some of the commands have been extended.

8.10.2 Configuration of a PC Floppy Controller

So far we have got to know the principal structure and data flow in a controller. The following sections discuss the configuration and programming of the floppy controller in connection with an example, namely the reading of one sector. You can access the control and data registers on a PC/XT by means of three, on the AT by four and on the PS/2 by five ports. Table 8.11 lists all the important information concerning configuration and port addresses. The base addresses differ depending upon whether you have configured the controller as a primary or secondary adapter. The PS/2 model 30 differs slightly in its port assignment from all other PS/2 machines, because it follows the XT's architecture.

All floppy controllers use DMA channel 2 to transfer data between the controller and main memory during the course of a read or write. After completing a command the controller issues a hardware interrupt via IRQ6 during the so-called result phase (see below). The interrupt is serviced by the interrupt handler 0eh, but you are free to configure the controller in another way.

	Primary	Secondary	Write (W) Read(R)
base address	3f0h	370h	
status register A (PS/2)	3f1h	371h	R
status register B (PS/2)	3f1h	371h	R
digital output register DOR	3f2h	372h	R/W
main status register	3f4h	374h	R
data rate select register (PS/2)	3f4h	374h	W
data register	3f5h	375h	R/W
digital input register DIR (AT)	3f7h	377h	R
configuration control register (AT)	3f7h	377h	W
DMA channel	2	2	
IRQ	6	6	
INTR	0eh	0eh	

Table 8.11: Floppy controller port addresses and configuration data

8.10.3 Floppy Controller Registers

The digital output register can only be written. It controls the drive motors, selects a drive, and resets the controller. Figure 8.24 shows the structure of this register.

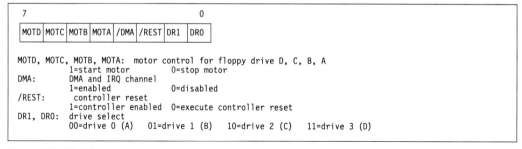

Figure 8.24: Digital output register.

Using the *MOTD–MOTA* bits you can turn the motors of drives D to A on and off. A set bit activates the corresponding spindle motor. The *DMA* bit enables the DMA and IRQ channels on the controller, through which it issues a data exchange between controller and main memory as well as a hardware interrupt request to the CPU. But this only applies to the PC/XT and AT; on a PS/2 this bit has no effect – the data transfer is always carried out by means of DMA. With a set $\overline{REST}$ bit the floppy controller is enabled to accept and execute commands. If $\overline{REST}$ is equal to 0, then the controller ignores all commands, including the motor activations via the digital output register; it carries out an internal reset of all registers except the POR. With the *LW1*, *LW0* bits you select the drive you want to access. A µPD765 can manage up to four floppy drives A: to D:.

The main status register is read-only and contains the status information of the floppy controller. Don't confuse this register and status registers ST0–ST3 that contain the status information concerning the last executed command, and which you may read via the data register. Figure 8.25 shows the structure of the main status register. Unlike the data register, the main status register can always be read, even if the controller is currently executing a command and, for example, is placing the head above a certain track.

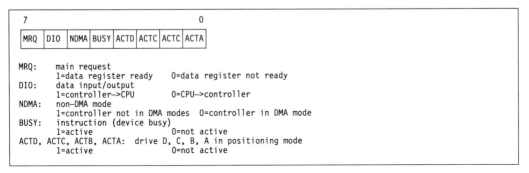

Figure 8.25: Main status register.

If the *MRQ* bit is set, the data register can receive or provide commands and data from and to the processor. Using *DIO*, the controller indicates whether it expects data from the CPU or whether it wants to hand over status information to it. If the *NDMA* bit is set, the floppy controller doesn't operate in DMA mode, that is, it doesn't transfer data via DMA channel 2 to or from main memory. The data transfer is carried out by means of a read or write command to the data register. The controller then always issues a hardware interrupt with every expected data byte or every data byte that is being supplied. If you find a set *BUSY* bit then the controller is currently executing a command. According to bits *AKTD–AKTA*, you can determine which drive is currently positioning the read/write heads.

The data register is eight bits wide, and is actually a whole stack of registers. Newer, powerful floppy controllers such as Intel's 82077A have a 16-byte FIFO memory instead of a simple data register, which accelerates the data throughput and doesn't subject the response time of the main system (that is, CPU and DMA) to the rather strict range of the μPD765. Controller commands are one to nine bytes long. According to the first command byte, the controller recognizes how many bytes the command concerned comprises. Therefore, you do not need to index the registers of the stack by means of an index register, as is the case, for example, with the video controller MC6845. The controller automatically transfers the command bytes for the data register internally to the corresponding command registers to carry out the command concerned. The controller's command formats are listed in Appendix G.

In the AT and PS/2, the digital input register (DIR) and the configuration control register are additionally available at port addresses 3f7h and 377h, respectively. But note that the register assignment differs among AT, model 30 and all other PS/2 models (see Figure 8.26). With these registers you can detect a disk change, determine the data transfer rate between controller and drive, and investigate the DMA mode of the controller.

The detection of a disk change was implemented in the AT to accelerate the access to floppies. If you don't change the floppy between two successive DIR commands, then DOS fetches the sector with the directory entries from an internal DOS buffer in main memory for the second call, but doesn't reread the sector concerned from disk. This is carried out much faster, but only if you did not change the floppy in the meantime. The PC/XT doesn't support the disk change function, but DOS always reads the sector concerned from disk. Thus the AT carries out floppy access much faster on average than the PC/XT.

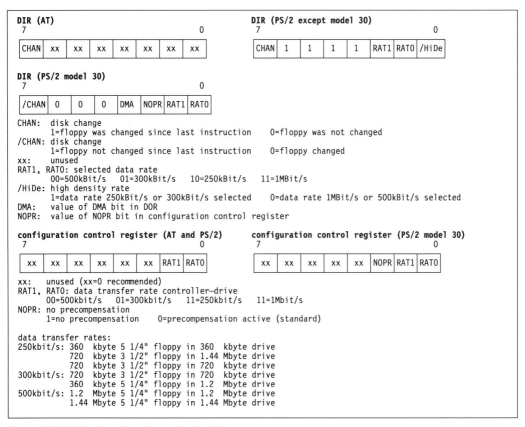

Figure 8.26: DIR and configuration control register.

Additionally, the HD drives and the accompanying floppies introduced with the AT require a much higher data transfer rate between controller and drive, as the number of revolutions has increased from 300 to 360 revs/min and, on the other hand, the number of sectors per track has risen to 15 with a 1.2 Mbyte floppy (and even 18 with a 1.44 Mbyte floppy). With an effective sector length of 654 bytes plus 146 bytes for the start of the track, as well as nine sectors per track for a 5 1/4" floppy with a capacity of 360 kbytes, the amount of data passing below the read/write head reaches about 250 kbits/s. If you insert the same floppy into a 1.2 Mbyte drive with 360 revs/min, then the data transfer rate increases to 300 kbits/s. The increase of the sector number up to 18, together with the higher rotation speed of 360 revs/min, leads to a data transfer rate of 500 kbits/s for a 1.44 Mbyte floppy. Depending upon the drive you connect to an AT floppy controller and which floppy you are using in such a drive (360 kbyte floppy in an HD drive, for example), you need to program the floppy controller for the respective data transfer rate. This is carried out by the configuration control register at port address 3f7h or 377h. The structure of DIR and the configuration control register is shown in Figure 8.26.

With the *CHAN* or $\overline{CHAN}$ (PS/2 model 30) bit you can determine a disk change. If CHAN is set then the data medium has possibly been changed since the last access. Note that the meaning of $\overline{CHAN}$ on a PS/2 model 30 is inverted compared to all other computers. With the two *RAT1*, *RAT0* bits and the help of the configuration control register, you can program the data transfer rate between controller and drive. The selected rate can be determined by the DIR. Note that not all AT controllers and drives support a data transfer rate of 1 Mbit/s. On all PS/2s except model 30, you can determine via $\overline{HiDe}$ whether the controller has set up the high-density rate of 500 kbit/s or 1 Mbit/s. On a PS/2 model 30, the *DMA* and *NOPR* bits additionally indicate the values of the corresponding bits in the DOR and configuration control register, respectively.

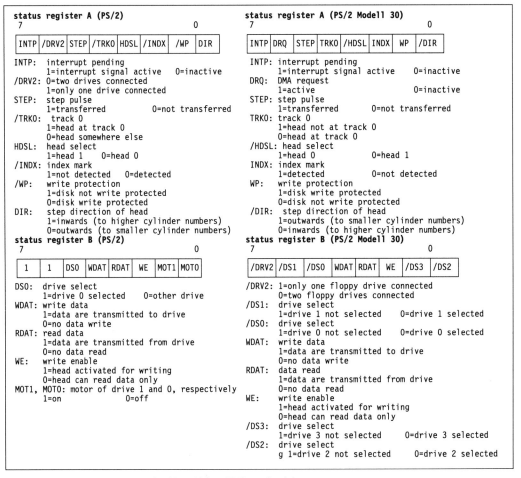

Figure 8.27: Status registers A and B (Port 3f1h or 371h, read-only).

The bit NOPR on a PS/2 model 30 controls the activation of the so-called precompensation; the standard value is 0.

On a PS/2 there are two more status registers A and B. But note also that here the structure of the two registers differs between model 30 and all other PS/2 models. Figure 8.27 shows the structure of the status registers A and B.

From the two status registers A and B you can read the status of the control lines between floppy controller and floppy drive on a PS/2. The register bits DRV2, TRK0, INDX, WP and RDAT directly indicate the status of the corresponding data lines. But in the case of status registers A and B, note the different bit values between model 30 and all other PS/2 models.

8.10.4 Floppy Controller Commands and Command Phases

On the μPD765 15 different commands are available. The PS/2 implements some further commands oriented to the hard disk controllers. All commands proceed according to three phases:

- command phase: the controller is activated and the CPU passes the command;

- data phase: the controller searches one or more sectors and transfers the data to or from the PC if required;

- result phase: the controller issues an interrupt and provides status information concerning the last executed command.

In the following sections I want to discuss the three command phases using an example concerning the reading of one sector into main memory.

If you are programming a command that gives rise to a data transfer between main memory and controller, you must set up the DMA controller before activating the command so that the DMA controller transfers the data correctly after DRQ2 is activated. Depending upon the number of sectors to be transferred, you therefore have to provide a buffer in main memory which is able to accommodate the data. The DMA base address must point to the beginning of the buffer, and the count direction must be set for counting up. After DRQ2 has been activated by the controller, the DMA controller responds with a $\overline{\text{DACK2}}$ and transfers the data from the buffer to the controller, or vice versa. A program example for this is provided in Section 7.3 which discusses the 8237A DMA controller.

Command Phase

The command phase is issued by activating the floppy controller via the digital output register (DOR), and selecting the intended drive. As in the PC many floppy drive operations issue an interrupt after command completion, and the data transfer is carried out via the DMA chip, you should also set the DMA bit in the DOR. If you want to access not only the controller but also the floppy, then you have to start the corresponding drive motor by means of a set MOTx bit (x = A, B, C, D).

Example: issue command phase (assembler MASM 5.1)
```
mov dx, 3f2h        ; load port address into dx
out dx, 1ch         ; output 0001 1100 (MOTA=1, DMA=1, AKTV=1, LW1/LW0=00) to DOR
```

```
(C, Microsoft C5.1)
outp (0x3f2, 0x1c); /* output 0001 1100 (MOTA=1, DMA=1, AKTV=1, LW1/LW0=00) to DOR */
```

The controller now expects the supply of a command via the data register. Appendix G summarizes all commands. In the following section I therefore want to discuss only the command for reading one sector; its format is shown in Figure 8.28. Nine command bytes are required in total. Note that the controller accepts a command byte only if the MRQ bit in the main status register is set; otherwise the controller ignores the passed command byte and gets into a muddle. Thus you have to read the main status register before passing a command byte, and check whether the MRQ bit is set. A fast CPU can pass the command bytes much faster than the rather slow floppy controller is able to accept and transfer them to the corresponding internal register according to the command selected.

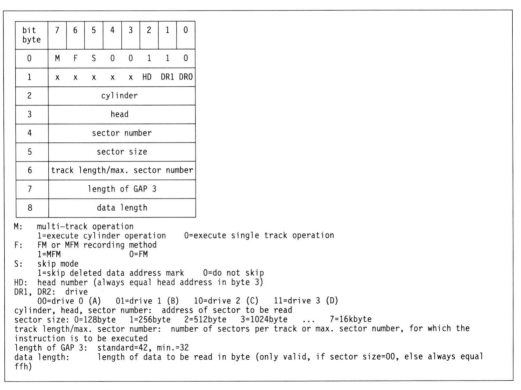

Figure 8.28: Sector read.

With the *M* bit you may also instruct the μPD765 to carry out the same command for the other track. The controller then not only reads the sector(s) concerned on one side of the floppy, but also that on the other. As, during the course of the data transfer for the first sector, the DMA controller continuously counts up the target address, the sector read later doesn't overwrite the previously read data but is appended to the data of the first sector. Thus you can read several sectors all at once with this command. Such multi-track operations are also available for other commands, for example writing sectors, reading tracks, etc. With the *F* bit you determine the encoding format. The PC exclusively uses the MFM method for floppies; thus the F bit must be set, otherwise the controller cannot read the data correctly, or it writes them onto disk in a format which is not understandable for other functions. If you set the skip bit *S*, the controller ignores deleted data address marks and skips the accompanying sectors. If, on the other hand, the controller detects a deleted data address mark with the S bit cleared, it aborts the current command and returns an error message. You may access data with a deleted address mark only by means of the two commands *read deleted data* (opcode MFS01100) and *write deleted data* (opcode MF001001). These functions are also listed in Appendix G. The remaining five bits 00110 in the first command byte represent the opcode for *read sector*. From 00110 the controller recognizes that eight additional command bytes will follow.

The *HD* bit informs the controller about the intended head. As floppy drives only have two heads with the numbers 0 and 1, one bit is sufficient. Note that HD always coincides with the head address in byte 3. With *LW1, LW0* you select one of the four possible drives connected to the controller. *Cylinder, head* and *sector number* are self-evident, I think.

The *sector size* entry informs the controller about how many bytes it can expect in the addressed sector, and therefore how many it has to transfer into main memory. The value 2, indicating 512 bytes per sector, is used as standard. *Track length/max. sector number* indicates the number of the last sector in the track or cylinder (that is, the length of a track in sectors), or the maximum sector number for which the command is to be carried out. The controller executes all commands by starting with that sector which is determined by the cylinder, head and sector numbers. If it has carried out the command for this start sector, it reads the next sector and transfers it into main memory. The controller continues with this operation until it has read and transferred the sector indicated by the entry track length/max. sector number. If you specify a sector here which is no longer present in the track, the controller attempts to read a sector which would be located beyond the end of the track. This, of course, doesn't work, and the controller aborts the command with an error code. If you specify the same value as in the entry sector number, then the controller reads only one sector.

A further possibility to abort the reading of sectors before the end of the track is reached is to supply the controller with a TC (terminal count) signal from the DMA controller. The programmed DMA chip always activates this signal if its count value has been decremented to 0. If you only want to read a single sector and select DMA for the data transfer, then you have to specify a count value that corresponds to the sector size of, generally, 512 bytes. Because of the TC signal generated after the transfer of 512 bytes, the sector read command is aborted. The opposite applies, of course, if you want to transfer two or more sectors into main memory.

With the *length of GAP 3* byte you inform the controller about the length of GAP 3 as it is to be used for data reading. The value for reading and writing data is different from that for formatting the drive. For formatting the PC uses a GAP-3-length of 80 bytes for a 5 1/4" drive, and 84 bytes for a 3 1/2" drive, as standard. For a read or write access, only 42 bytes and 27 bytes, respectively, are used. Some 5 1/4" drives may only use a value of 32 for reading or writing, thus these values are not defined very strictly. Remember the meaning of GAP 3 as described in

Section 8.6: because of rotation variations and timing deviations of the write pulses, the actual length of a sector may vary. GAP 3 then serves as a buffer. If you overwrite an already formatted sector which has been elongated because of a slightly increased rotation speed during the course of the fomatting process with new data, and the rotation speed is somewhat lower than in the formatting process because of an increased friction, then the controller has already written the sector up to the last CRC field onto disk before GAP 3 begins. In the next read process, the controller becomes confused, as it expects only the values 4eh of GAP 3 and not the actually overwritten old data. Thus the sector cannot be read without an error. The controller therefore also writes a GAP 3 onto disk with every write process even after the floppy has been formatted. This ensures that on a slower rotating floppy the formerly held data is also overwritten, and cannot cause any distortion. Let us assume the inverse case. During formatting the rotation speed was somewhat too low and the sector has therefore been compressed. If the floppy is now rotating faster in the course of writing a sector, then the last CRC data of the sector already overlaps GAP 3. If the controller additionally writes all the 80 bytes of GAP 3 onto disk, then it damages the beginning of the next sector as the end of GAP 3 overlaps SYNC or even IDAM of the next sector. You can see that it is necessary, on the one hand, to write GAP 3 additionally to the write data onto disk with every write process but, on the other hand, this GAP 3 may not be as long as for formatting the floppy. A reasonable value for its length is therefore about half the formatting length of 80 or 84 bytes. Thus the floppy drives in the PC use the value 42 for a 5 1/4" drive and 27 for a 3 1/2" drive as standard. Newer and more reliably controlled 5 1/4" drives don't need more than 32 bytes, though. It is more important to specify the length of GAP 3 for a formatting or write process, and less so for reading data.

If the number of bytes per sector is defined as 00, corresponding to 128 bytes per sector, then you inform the controller by means of *data length* about the actual number of bytes you want to read. If the actual data length for writing data is less than the sector size of 128 bytes, then the remaining bytes are all filled with zeroes. For calculating the CRC checksum, these fill bytes are also used. The PC employs a sector size of 512 bytes as standard, so the command byte *data length* is without meaning. But you must nevertheless pass a value as the controller expects nine command bytes for the command *read sector*. It will not start the programmed command until you have passed the 9th byte. Use the value ffh in this case.

Example: read sector 12, head 1, track 40 of the 1.2 Mbyte floppy in drive B:; the DMA controller programming required in advance is described in Chapter 7.3.6 (programming language: Microsoft C 5.1).

```
main()
{ unsigned char opcode[9];
  int index;

  outp(0x3f2, 0x2d); /* enable motor B:, controller, DMA and IRQ */

  opcode[0]=0x46;    /* 0100 0110, no multi-track operation (M=0), MFM (F=1), no skip mode
                        (S=0) */
  opcode[1]=0x05;    /* 0000 0101, head 1, drive B (01) */
  opcode[2]=0x28;    /* cylinder (track) 40 */
  opcode[3]=0x01;    /* head 1 */
  opcode[4]=0x0c;    /* sector 12 (0ch) */
```

```
opcode[5]=0x02;    /* 512 bytes per sector */
opcode[6]=0x0f;    /* 1.2Mbyte floppy, thus maximum 15 (0fh) sectors per track */
opcode[7]=0x2a;    /* 42 (2ah) bytes for Gap 3 */
opcode[8]=0x00;    /* data length insignificant as 512 bytes per sector */

for (index=0; index<9; index++) {
  write_controller(opcode[index]);  /* pass command byte to controller */
}

outp(0x3f2, 0x00); /* disable motor B:, controller, DMA and IRQ */
exit(0)
}

void write_controller(command_byte)
unsigned char command_byte;
{ int mrq;

for ( ; ; ) {                    /* wait until controller is ready */
  mrq=inp(0x3f4) && 0x80;        /* determine status of MRQ */
  if (mrq==0x80) {               /* check whether controller is ready */
    outp(0x3f5, command_byte); /* output command byte to data register */
    return;                      /* return to main program */
  }
}
}
```

The controller decodes the received command bytes and proceeds to the data phase if the input command bytes are consistent and data is to be transferred. If the input command bytes are inconsistent, however, then the controller jumps directly to the result phase. Thus the command phase is completed and the PC waits for a hardware interrupt from the controller, which indicates that the command has been completed. In a multitasking environment, the CPU can meanwhile carry out other tasks.

Data Phase

After the last command byte has been passed, the controller waits (in the discussed example) until the head-load time has elapsed and then lowers the read/write head onto the disk. Afterwards, head and controller start to read the ID address marks from the rotating floppy. If the controller detects an ID address mark that coincides with the programmed sector address, then the controller reads the data area of the sector and the CRC checksum and transfers the data into main memory. If this process has finished, the controller increments the sector address and reads the next sector. This process continues until the controller receives a TC signal from the DMA chip, or the controller issues an implicit TC signal as the end of the track is reached, or the data cannot be transferred into main memory quickly enough, or the sector with the programmed maximum sector number has been read and transferred. After completing the read process, the read/write head remains on the data carrier until the head-unload time has elapsed. If the CPU issues another command within this time period, the heads are already on the floppy and the head-load time is saved. Thus the data access is carried out more quickly.

If the controller receives two IDX pulses via the IDX line from the drive without having detected the programmed ID address mark in the meantime, it sets the interrupt code IC1, IC0 to a value of 01, indicating an abnormal command termination. Additionally, the controller sets the ND bit in status register 1 to indicate that it hasn't found the programmed sector. A twice repeated IDX pulse thus means only that the index hole of the floppy disk has passed the drive's photosensor assembly twice, or that the controller has detected the index address mark (IAM) at the start of the track twice, and therefore the floppy has carried out at least one complete rotation.

During the course of the command phase, direct action by the CPU is required as it must activate the controller and pass the command bytes. But in the data phase, controller and floppy drive work undependently as the head positioning, searching for the selected cylinder, the physical reading or writing and all other controller and drive processes are carried out without any intervention from the CPU. Even transferring the data of a read sector or sector to be written proceeds without any CPU activity. The DMA controller, programmed in advance, carries out this job alone, but you must set the DMA bit in the digital output register for this purpose so that the controller actually generates the DRQ2 and IRQ6 signals. Additionally, the NDM bit in the second byte of the *specify drive parameters* command must be cleared to enable the DMA transfer capability in the controller. In a data read process the controller first reads the data from the floppy, and then enables the DRQ2 signal to issue a data transfer via channel 2 of the DMA controller. During the course of a data write, the controller activates the DMA control to transfer data from main memory to the controller via DMA channel 2, and writes the sector data together with the self-generated control data, for example the GAPs, IDAM, CRC, etc. onto disk.

If you have programmed a command that moves data, then the DMA chip cuts off the CPU from main memory and takes over control of the data and address bus. During the course of data transfer via the DMA controller, the CPU can continue to execute instructions which don't require a memory access, for example the multiplication of two register values. This means that the moving of large amounts of data is not carried out via the CPU.

OS/2 or UNIX/XENIX, as multitasking operating systems, enable the concurrent execution of several programs or, in the case of UNIX/XENIX, even the servicing of several users. As a processor can carry out a lot of work within the 100 ms that a floppy drive needs on average to address the intended sector, it is a waste of time to wait for the completion of the sector search and the transfer of data. Instead, the processor passes the controller the corresponding command (for example, read sector), and prepares a channel of the DMA controller for data transfer between controller and main memory. The floppy controller and the floppy drive then work autonomously and read a sector. The DMA controller transfers the sector data to the location in main memory determined in advance. The CPU is not burdened with this process at all, but can execute other tasks. Once the command has been completed the controller issues a hardware interrupt to get the attention of the CPU and operating system again. This is not the case with DOS, because as a single-tasking operating system no other programs execute concurrently.

However, there are other possibilities for the transfer of data between main memory and controller: interrupt-driven data exchange and polling. For interrupt-driven data exchange you must set the NDM bit in byte 2 of the *specify drive parameters* command and the DMA control bit in the POR to a value of 1. As standard, NDM is cleared so that the controller transfers the data to or reads it from main memory by means of DMA. If a data byte in the data register is ready for output, or if the controller needs another data byte from main memory, it issues an interrupt request via IRQ6, but no DRQ signal for a DMA request. The interrupt handler of interrupt 0eh must then be able to determine the cause of the interrupt and to transfer the data byte from the controller to main memory or vice versa. According to bits IC1, IC0 and SE in status register ST0, the handler can determine the cause of an interrupt (see Table 8.12).

SE	IC1/0	Interrupt source
0	11	polling
1	00	normal termination of seek or calibration command
1	01	abnormal termination of seek or calibration command

Table 8.12: Interrupt sources

For data transfer the CPU reads the data byte with an IN instruction from the data register of the controller, and writes it into main memory using a MOV instruction. If data is to be transferred from main memory to the controller, then the CPU reads a data byte with a MOV instruction from main memory and writes it with an OUT instruction into the controller's data register. Note that the controller also issues an interrupt upon entering the result phase (after completing the data phase), if you are programming such a handler for interrupt 0eh. The second interrupt is used to inform the main system about the command's completion, and to indicate that status data is available in the status registers.

If you want to carry out the data transfer using polling you must additionally clear the DMA bit in the POR to disable the IRQ drivers in the controller. Then the floppy controller doesn't generate an IRQ or a DRQ signal. The only possibility of determining whether data is available in the data register, or is to be transferred into it, is a periodic investigation of the MRQ bit in the main status register. If MRQ is set then the controller expects the transfer of a byte or the reading of its data register. If the DIO bit in the main status register is set, the controller wants to provide data to the CPU. With a cleared DIO bit, it expects data from the CPU. The polling program has to determine whether the data consists of command bytes, read data, write data, or status bytes. Although the timing problems are serious enough with interrupt driven data exchange, they become virtually unsolvable in polled operation of several powerful drives connected to the one controller. The data register will not wait until the end of time, of course, for a service by the CPU, which additionally is carrying out other tasks such as supervising the hard disk drives, the timer chips, and the execution of the foreground program. Thus, data exchange using DMA is surely the best solution. In all Personal Computers it is carried out via DMA channel 2.

After the completion of the transfer the data phase is finished, and the controller now proceeds to the result phase to inform the host of success or failure using appropriate status information.

Result Phase

At end of the data phase, or if you have programmed a command that doesn't have a data phase such as *check drive status*, the controller issues a hardware interrupt. The CPU then recognizes that the command has been completed, and that result status bytes are available in the data register.

The floppy controller has four status registers ST0–ST3 in all, which you may extract in this order from the data register. The exact number of status registers with a status byte depends upon the command concerned. Appendix G lists the number and type of the status bytes for every command. Additionally, the data register provides some information about the head, drive, etc. of the last processed sector (you will also find this information in Appendix G). The structure of the four status registers is shown in Figure 8.28.

The following discusses the status and result bytes of the example command *read sector*. This command provides seven status and result bytes during the course of the result phase, and these are shown in Figure 8.29.

```
7                              1
┌─────┬─────────────────────┐
│  0  │         ST0         │
├─────┼─────────────────────┤
│  1  │         ST1         │
├─────┼─────────────────────┤
│  2  │         ST2         │
├─────┼─────────────────────┤
│  3  │       cylinder      │
├─────┼─────────────────────┤
│  4  │        head         │
├─────┼─────────────────────┤
│  5  │    sector number    │
├─────┼─────────────────────┤
│  6  │     sector size     │
└─────┴─────────────────────┘

ST0, ST1, ST2:  status register 0...2
cylinder, head, sector number:  address of sector last read
sector size:    0=128byte   1=256byte   2=512byte   ... 7=16kbyte
```

Figure 8.29: Status and result bytes of «read sector» command.

The seven result bytes can be read via the data register by an IN instruction. As is the case for writing the command bytes, here also you have first to check whether the data register is ready. The following example shows this procedure.

Example: Read sector 12, head 1, track 40 of the 1.2Mbyte floppy in drive B:; DMA controller programming required in advance is described in Section 7.3.6 (programming language: Microsoft C 5.1).

```
main()
{ unsigned char st0, st1, st2, cylinder, head, sector, byte_per_sector;

  st0=read_controller();              /* read result byte st0 from controller */
  st1=read_controller();              /* read result byte st1 from controller */
  st2=read_controller();              /* read result byte st2 from controller */
  cylinder=read_controller();         /* read cylinder concerned from controller */
  head=read_controller();             /* read head concerned from controller */
  sector=read_controller();           /* read sector concerned from controller */
  byte_per_sector=read_controller();  /* read sector size from controller */

  exit(0)
}
```

```
unsigned char read_controller(void)
{

int mrq;
  unsigned char result-byte;

  for ( ; ; ) {                    /* wait until controller is ready */
    mrq=inp(0x3f4) && 0x80;        /* determine status of MRQ */
    if (mrq==0x80) {               /* check whether controller is ready */
      intp(0x3f5, result_byte);    /* output command byte to data register */
      return(result_byte);         /* return result byte */
    }
  }
}
```

Now the corresponding bytes contain the status ST0–ST2 of the read command. According to ST0–ST2, you may determine whether the command was executed correctly, and if not, analyse the reasons for a failure. The interrupt handler for IRQ6 corresponding to interrupt 0eh of the BIOS stores the maximum of seven status bytes for a floppy operation in the seven bytes at address 0040:0042 and above. Note that you must read out all completion status bytes from the status register before the controller is ready to accept and execute a new command. This also applies if the status registers ST0–ST3 indicate a failure.

8.10.5 Specify Drive Parameters

Before you can read or write data you have to set up some drive parameters that directly affect the electromechanical behaviour of the read/write heads using the controller command *specify drive parameters*. As an addition to the above discussed example, I therefore want to describe the technical background of this command. Figure 8.30 shows its format.

The *step rate time* entry determines the time interval between two pulses to the stepper motor of the floppy drive. Each pulse leads to a certain rotation of the motor and thus to a certain movement of the read/write head (usually to the adjacent track). Thus, by means of the step rate time entry, you can influence the drive's access time. If you specify a value that is too small then the stepper motor will have already received the next step pulse before it can respond to the last one. As in floppy drives, access to the tracks is solely controlled by the number of step pulses to the stepper motor of the read/write head (starting from track 17, 20 pulses, for example, lead to track 37); seek errors are the consequence, and the controller responds with a read/write error.

The two entries *head-load time* and *head-unload time* control the loading and unloading of the read/write head onto and from the disk. The value for head-load time defines the time interval that the μPD765 waits before it instructs the floppy drive to load the read/write head onto the data carrier. Waiting is necessary to give the head and access arm enough time to settle down (that is, to damp all oscillations) after an access movement. Any radial movement of the head, and therefore damage to the data carrier, can thus be prevented. With the head-unload time entry you control the time interval that the controller waits before it instructs the drive to unload the head from the data carrier after a read or write access. If the controller were to unload the heads immediately after an access, then no continuous reading or writing of successive sectors would be possible. The time required for unloading and then reloading the heads is longer than the time interval until the next sector appears below the head. With a head-unload time different from zero, the drive is therefore able to read or write a complete track or a complete cylinder. Once this process is complete, the heads are unloaded and possibly moved to another cylinder. The *NDM* bit defines whether a DMA channel (NDM = 0) or interrupt-driven data exchange is employed. The PC always uses DMA channel 2 for data transfer, thus NDM is always equal to 0 here. Note that in the AT and PS/2 the effective values for step rate time, head-unload time, and head-load time are also dependent upon the programmed data transfer rate as well as on the entries in the command bytes. With a PC/XT floppy controller this rate is always set to 250 kbits/s, thus the effective values are only determined by the command bytes here. The BIOS stores these values (as well as others) in the floppy parameter table (see Appendix F.5). The entry of the pseudo-interrupt vector 1eh points to the beginning of this table.

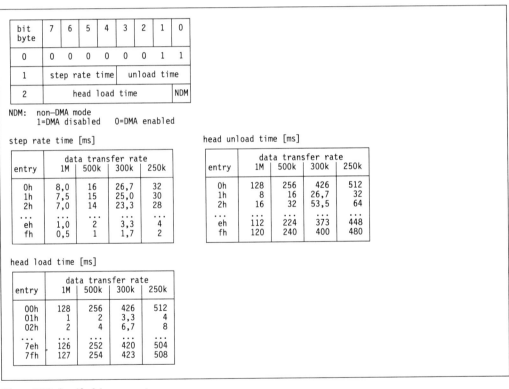

bit byte	7	6	5	4	3	2	1	0
0	0	0	0	0	0	0	1	1
1	step rate time				unload time			
2	head load time							NDM

NDM: non-DMA mode
           1=DMA disabled   0=DMA enabled

step rate time [ms]

entry	data transfer rate			
	1M	500k	300k	250k
0h	8,0	16	26,7	32
1h	7,5	15	25,0	30
2h	7,0	14	23,3	28
...	...	...	...	...
eh	1,0	2	3,3	4
fh	0,5	1	1,7	2

head unload time [ms]

entry	data transfer rate			
	1M	500k	300k	250k
0h	128	256	426	512
1h	8	16	26,7	32
2h	16	32	53,5	64
...	...	...	...	...
eh	112	224	373	448
fh	120	240	400	480

head load time [ms]

entry	data transfer rate			
	1M	500k	300k	250k
00h	128	256	426	512
01h	1	2	3,3	4
02h	2	4	6,7	8
...	...	...	...	...
7eh	126	252	420	504
7fh	127	254	423	508

Figure 8.30: Specify drive parameters.

Finally, a few words on reading, writing, and formatting 360 kbyte floppies in 1.2 Mbyte drives. As you know, it is not only possible to read and write a 360 kbyte floppy with 40 tracks and 9 sectors per track in an HD drive with a capacity of 1.2 Mbyte, but also to format it. While it is quite easy for you to set up the controller to a track length of nine sectors, by means of the *track length* entry, for example, in the *read sector* command of the above mentioned example, there is no possibility of reducing the number of tracks from 80 to 40. The problem must thus be bypassed. During the course of a read, write, or formatting process, only every second track is accessed. To format a 360 kbyte floppy in a 1.2 Mbyte drive you therefore have to generate tracks 0, 2, ..., 78. In the same way, the drive must access tracks 0, 2, ..., 78 for data reading and writing. DOS and the BIOS do this for you if you remain at their level. For programming a direct access to the floppy controller by means of its registers, you thus have to pay attention to many critical technical details. Determining whether the machine is a PC/XT, AT, PS/2 model 30 or another PS/2 machine is a really difficult job. The fixed installed BIOS need not worry about determining the computer type, as it knows it in advance. Therefore, this BIOS can be tailored for the PC as the programmer knows in which computer the ROM chips are to be installed.

8.10.6 Error Recovery Strategy

Unlike the hard disk controllers, floppy controllers don't have an in-built error recovery strategy. If a read or write error has occurred you should repeat the read or write attempt at least twice to exclude an unintended start delay of the spindle motor as a possible reason. If this doesn't help, or if a seek error has occurred, then it is best to recalibrate the drive. For this purpose, move the head back to track 0 and repeat the access. Sometimes, the tolerance may be so high that the read/write head reaches the edge or even the middle of two adjacent tracks. This is especially the case if the drive has carried out multiple relative seeks, or seeks over a large distance (from track 0 to track 70, for example). The signals from the address marks are no longer strong enough for the controller to determine the position correctly. Unlike hard disk drives, floppy drives operate with an open-loop positioning scheme, that is, the positioning electronics don't receive any feedback signals to indicate the current location of the head.

9   Hard Disk Drives

Many PC users see the hard disk as the most important and valuable part of their computer. This is justifiable if no data backup is made and all the last three years' work is on the hard disk. Besides the memory chips and processors, hard disks have been the subject of much development towards higher and higher capacities (with steadily falling prices) in the last ten years. Remember that the first hard disk for the XT (with its exciting capacity of 10 Mbytes!) cost more than $3,000 when introduced; an access time of more than 100 ms was included in this price. If you wanted to spend $3,000 on a hard disk today you'd have trouble in getting hold of one!

In spite of the low price, some dealers continue to sell their i386s with a 40 Mbyte hard disk and Windows. As everyone knows graphics, and therefore also graphics-oriented shells, occupy a large amount of storage, so 40 Mbytes are only enough for an older 80286 without Windows. When you buy a new PC, multiply the estimated storage requirements by at least three. In less than a year, your disk will be full (this is a tip based on my own long-suffering experiences!). If installing Windows and a graphics application such as CorelDRAW!, then 100 Mbytes at least are required.

Another common name for the hard disk drive is the *winchester drive*, for historical reasons: in the 1960s IBM introduced a cupboard-sized disk drive with an overall capacity of 60 Mbytes onto the market. 30 Mbyte were installed, and the other disk (also with 30 Mbytes) could be removed and changed. You may have seen pictures where this cooking-pot-sized 30 Mbyte disk pack is screwed onto the drive spindle. As an abbreviation, the drive was also called a 30–30 (30 Mbyte installed and 30–30 Mbyte removable storage capacity). John Wayne fans may remember that he always had his Winchester 30 ready! Thus the mental leap to calling the 30–30 drive a Winchester was not too far. This has nothing to do with guns, of course, but the term has remained until today, and is particularly used in the field of mainframes as «insider» slang.

The advances made in the last decade can be seen by the fact that Seagate's ST506 drive, introduced onto the market in 1980 with its 5 1/4" disks, only had a capacity of 5 Mbytes, but nevertheless required full height. The ST412 successor already had a capacity of 10 Mbytes. (By the way, the name ST506/412 interface comes from these drives.) With its four heads and 17 sectors per track the ST412 had only 150–300 cylinders. Today's powerful IDE, ESDI and SCSI models have up to 70 sectors per track, and 2000 cylinders with a disk size between 2" and 3 1/2". Advanced interface concepts that take into account the advancing development of microelectronics and encoding methods therefore became absolutely necessary. In the following sections, information concerning the ST506/412 standard and also the more advanced concepts such as IDE, ESDI and SCSI are discussed.

9.1   Structure and Functioning of Hard Disk Drives

9.1.1   The Head-Disk Assembly (HDA)

The differences between floppy drives and hard disks are, in terms of principle, not very significant, but the latter are far more powerful. Also, in a hard disk drive the actual data carrier is a stiff rotating disk, unlike flexible floppies. The data is organized in tracks and sectors, as is the case for floppies, while access to data is also carried out by read/write heads moved by an actuator. But the mechanical equipment and the control of hard disk drives is far more elaborate so as to achieve the larger capacity and higher performance. Figure 9.1 shows the interior of a hard disk. For the figure, the cover of the *head-disk assembly (HDA)* has been removed, but *never* do that on your own; you have to scrap your hard disk afterwards and all the stored data is lost. I recommend that nosy users go to a computer exhibition and admire the drives under glass at the stands of hard disk manufacturers, or otherwise open an old and no longer used drive.

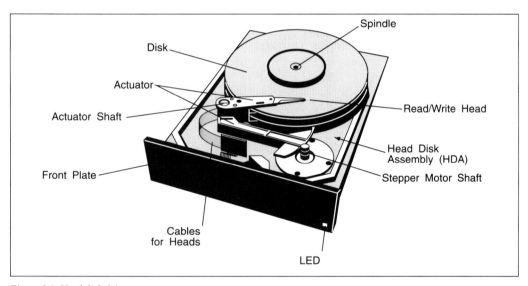

Figure 9.1: Hard disk drive.

The HDA consists of all mechanical and electronic components, which have to be specially protected against external dirt. Disks, heads, actuator and drive spindle belong to the HDA. The electronic controller, however, is located on a board at the drive peripheral. The rotation speed of the hard disk's spindle motor is stabilized by a feedback control circuit so the disks rotate with a constant speed of about 3600 revolutions per second. The control circuit reduces the revolution variations to about ±0.3%, and on high-quality drives to even ±0.1%. This means that the data carrier of a hard disk moves ten times faster than a floppy. Even the simplest drives accommodate 17 sectors per track, and powerful high-end drives have up to 70. Together with the increased rotation speed, this gives rise to 80 times the data amount which passes per second below the head compared to an old 360 kbyte floppy. Thus, drive and controller electronics need to be much more powerful than for floppy drives.

While you can insert a floppy disk with two sides at most into a floppy drive, most hard disk drives accommodate two to eight disks. Only very small 2" hard disk drives for notebooks have one (high-capacity) disk. As every disk has two sides, between four and 16 heads are required, located at the end of an access arm as is the case for the floppy drive. All heads are fixed to the same *actuator*, and are in moved in common by it. Thus the heads interpose the disks in the form of a comb or pincers. Figure 9.2 shows this in a graphical manner.

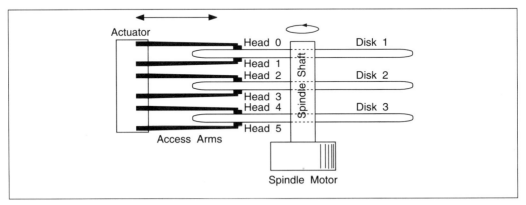

Figure 9.2: Heads and disks. Each disk surface is allocated a head, which is fixed to the end of an access arm. All arms and heads are moved in common and simultaneously by a single actuator.

As is the case for floppy drives, usually one head is active at most to read or write data. Only extremely powerful models for mainframes activate several heads simultaneously to increase the data rate. In the PC such drives are not used because they are very expensive and, in any case, with the new ESDI and SCSI drives the bottleneck is no longer located in the drive but at the 8 MHz PC system bus.

The actuator is operated by a stepper or linear motor. The latter is also often called a *voice coil actuator*. Both carry out positioning of the heads above the track or cylinder concerned. Details on disks, heads, and actuators are given below.

Most hard disks come with a front plate that usually accommodates an LED. Every time the controller accesses the drive to read or write data or to move the heads, only this diode lights up. You can remove this front plate without any problems if the drive doesn't fit into your PC's case with it.

The Disk

Today's hard disk drives usually come with a disk size of 5 1/4" or 3 1/2". The smaller disks have the advantage that the heads don't need to be moved so far, thus smaller actuators and spindle drivers are sufficient, and the head positioning time is shorter. Additionally, smaller drives are usually quieter. With some larger and, especially, older hard disks you have the impression that a coffee grinder is working in your PC and not a high-tech product! For small notebooks, 2" drives are also available, and even midgets of only one inch in diameter exist (with a comparably incredible storage capacity). On the other hand, you can also buy hard disk drives with 8" or even 14" disk diameters, but they are largely used for mainframes.

To accommodate data in the form of tiny magnetizations, at least the surface of the disks must be magnetizable. Today, aluminium alloys are mainly used as the disk material, as they are light but nevertheless mechanically stable. The low mass of the aluminium disks compared to disks made of iron, for example, and therefore the low inertia, gives rise to the fact that the operational revolution speed is reached more quickly after power-up. This is especially important for hard disks that are switched off regularly to save power in laptops and note-books, and which must be accelerated again if an access is required.

A magnetizable coating (the data medium) is deposited on the aluminium carrier. The high bit density when compared to floppies requires magnetically hard substances; usually, cobalt or certain ferro-ceramics are therefore employed. For coating the aluminium disks there are two main methods. With the *ferrite coating* a solvent with the ferrite is squirted near to the disk's centre and the disk itself is rotated at a high speed. By means of centrifugal force, the solvent and therefore also the ferrite material moves towards the circumference. After the solvent has vaporized, an only 1–2μm thick and regular ferrite layer remains on the alumium carrier. Afterwards, the ferrite layer is hardened or a very thin but hard protective layer is deposited on it. Finally, the disk is polished so that even the smallest unevenness which might disturb the head passing above it vanishes. Because of the ferrite material, the disk becomes a russet or brown colour. This colour is an unambiguous hint that the disk has been coated with a ferrite material. The method is used for disks of a low to medium data density.

For disks with more than 20 Mbytes capacity per disk side, the magnetic layer is deposited by galvanization or by sputtering. You may also find the *galvanization method* with chromium-plated car bumpers or for pieces of jewellery. The object to be galvanized is immersed in a salt solution containing ions of the material with which the object is to be coated. If a negative voltage is applied to the object to be galvanized, the metal ions move to it, are discharged there, neutralized to atoms, and deposited regularly on the object. Thus, for example, car bumpers can be coated with chromium, copper jewellery with gold, and the aluminium disk for a hard disk drive with cobalt. The result is a hard, regular cobalt layer with a thickness of only 0.1–0.2 μm. This corresponds to only a few hundred atom layers. The thickness can be controlled easily by the galvanization current and the time of the galvanization process.

In *sputtering* the metal with which the carrier is to be coated is atomized by ion irradiation in a vacuum. The atoms move to the object to be coated (here the aluminium disk), and deposit there as a very regular and hard layer with a thickness of 0.05–0.2 μm. Also, in this case, the thickness can be easily controlled by means of the ion irradiation strength and the sputtering time.

Afterwards, a thin graphite layer is deposited to protect the magnetic medium against mechanical damage. A hard disk coated by means of galvanization or sputtering shines like a mirror, and is more resistant to a head-crash (that is, an unintentional hard bouncing of the heads onto the disk while the disk is rotating) than ferrite-coated disks.

Usually, the data bits are recorded in a linear way, thus the magnetizations lie within the disk plane. If you imagine the magnetization for a data bit as a bar magnet, then this means that the bar magnet is either aligned to the track direction or in an opposite direction to it, depending upon the bit value. Besides this method there also exist hard disks with *vertical recording*. Here the «bar magnets» are no longer collinear to the track, but instead are perpendicular or vertical to the aluminium disk. Thus the recording takes place into the depth of the data carrier medium and much higher bit densities can be achieved. But today, hard disks with horizontal recording are largely used.

The number of flux changes that can be accommodated is decisive for the capacity of a disk. Remember that only the change of the magnetization (a flux change) may generate a signal in the read/write heads. The number of flux changes is indicated as *FCI* (**F**lux **C**hanges per **I**nch). Note that the bit density *(BPI)* not only depends upon the maximum number of flux changes FCI, but also on the encoding method used. On RLL hard disks the number of flux changes is about 50% *lower* than the number of BPI. The RLL encoding method is so powerful that a bit can be encoded with less than a single flux change. In contrast, the very old FM method requires two flux changes for every bit, namely one for the clock and one for the data signal. Without increasing the mechanical quality of a disk (which is expressed by FCI), just the use of another recording method raises the storable data amount by a factor of three. The disk remains the same; only the electronics used become more complex because of the more extensive encoding method. Details concerning RLL are discussed below.

The Heads

As is the case for floppy drives, the read/write heads write data onto disk as tiny magnetizations, or detect these magnetizations as data bits. But the significantly higher bit density on hard disks requires new technologies when compared to floppy drives. As already seen in Figure 9.2, for every disk side a dedicated head is available, but all heads are moved in common by a single actuator. The smaller the heads, the tinier the magnetizations can get. A small head also means a low mass, and therefore low inertia. Thus the heads may be positioned more quickly.

For generating and detecting small magnetization areas on the data carrier, it is necessary that the heads are at a distance which is as small as possible above the disks. Figure 9.3 shows the reason.

The magnetic field generated by the read/write head may not be focused as is shown in Figure 9.3 (left side). Instead, it spreads out nearly hemispherically with a slight vertical concentration towards the disk (Figure 9.3, right side). You can see that the horizontal size of the magnetic field on the disk surface is about the same as the distance between head and disk, but the size of the magnetic field directly determines the smallest region of the medium that can be magnetized in one direction, that is, one bit. This means that the recording density can be increased solely by a reduced head/disk distance. Therefore, one tries to make the heads as small as possible, and also to position them as near to the disk as possible. Of course, the magnetic medium must also be sufficiently fine-grained so that the domains don't get larger than one of these elementary bits.

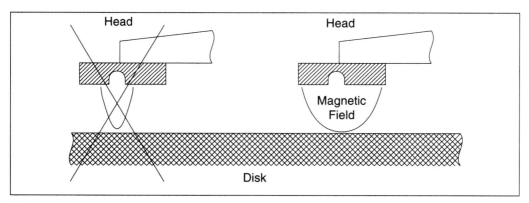

Figure 9.3. Head–disk distance and size of the magnetized region. The magnetic field is not emanating from the slit in a certain direction, but more likely in a half circle form. Thus the distance between head and disk determines the elementary magnetizing region.

Presently, there are two main head technologies: ferrite heads and thin-film heads. The *ferrite heads* are low-cost and reliable members of the older head generation. They generate the magnetic field by means of a coil with a ferrite core, as already described in connection with floppy drives. The heads act as a simple conventional electromagnet. The winding, however, may not be miniaturized to any extent, so the size of the ferrite heads is limited towards smaller sizes. Because of the rather heavy ferrite core, ferrite heads are of a higher mass than the thin-film heads. The power expenditure of the actuator becomes larger. Therefore, today ferrite heads are still employed, but only for hard disks in the lower and middle capacity ranges (up to about 10 Mbytes per disk side).

The modern concept of *thin-film heads* is virtually a waste product of microelectronics and its manufacturing methods. Semiconductor chips are formed by depositing and etching various layers. What better, therefore, than also to apply this reliable technique to the read/write heads of a hard disk drive. Here the heads are no longer formed by winding a wire around a ferrite core, but by means of various thin layers. The result is a microscopically small and very light head which is, nevertheless, able to generate a rather strong magnetic field. Because of the low distance between head and disk the field generated by the head need not be as strong as is the case for the ferrite heads. Thus, in the data medium the thin-film heads generate a sufficiently strong field to magnetize the cobalt domains.

When the drive is switched off the heads rest on the disk. Most of today's drives «park» their heads on a track reserved for this purpose which is not in use for data recording. This prevents the heads from scratching off the coating in areas occupied by stored data during acceleration at power-up. When the spindle motor starts the disk rotation, they take up the surrounding air similar to a ventilator, and an air stream occurs. This air stream is strong enough to generate an air cushion above the disk, thus the heads take off from the disk surface and ride a microscopic distance from the disk's surface on this air cushion without actually touching the disk. Typical distances are 1 μm for ferrite heads and 0.2–0.5 μm in the case of thin-film heads. Figure 9.4 shows a comparison between the size of a thin film head, its distance from the disk, a human hair, and various dirt particles.

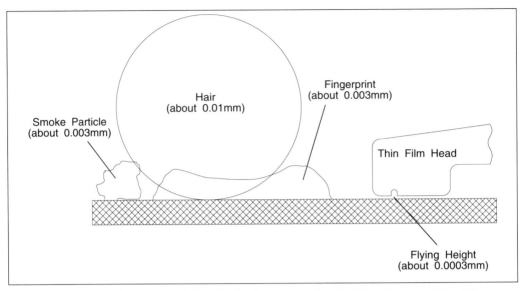

Figure 9.4: Comparison of various typical sizes of the head, its distance from the disk, and various dirt particles.

The disk-head distance is mainly dependent upon the head shape. According to their aerodynamic properties, they fly quite high. Thus a hard disk can be operated in a vacuum only with some difficulties, as the springy air cushion between head and disk is missing. The thickness of the cushion is, by the way, dependent upon the air pressure: the lower the pressure the thinner the cushion gets. Thus on a high mountain the heads fly lower than at the coast. This is one reason why data sheets for hard disks contain an entry for the hard disk's operation range concerning altitude. If Reinhold Messner intends to take a notebook up Mt Everest (which seems improbable), he would be very surprised. Because of the low air pressure of less than 400 mbar, the air cushion is so thin that the heads permanently touch the disk's surface, and the stored data is destroyed within a short time.

Actuators with a Stepper or Linear Motor

As already mentioned, the read/write heads are moved in common by an actuator. An actuator means all mechanical components necessary for the head's movement. Presently, actuators with a stepper or linear motor are used.

Figure 9.1 shows an *actuator with a stepper motor*. In the figure you can only see the spindle of the stepper motor, however. As is the case with the floppy drive, the stepper motor in hard disk drives is also rotated step-by-step in one or other direction by means of stepper pulses. These steps are fixed, and mean a fixed alteration of the motor spindle's angular position. Intermediate rotation angles are impossible: if, for example, the stepper motor can make a complete rotation with 180 steps, then this means that every stepper pulse turns the motor spindle by 2°. Thus only angular positions of 0°, 2°, 4°, ... 358° can be realized; an intermediate position of, for example, 3° is not possible. The rotation of the motor spindle is transferred onto the actuator by friction. In Figure 9.1, the actuator can rotate around the actual axis. The stepper motor rotation is transferred to the arc-like actuator element, and the actuator rotates around the actuator axis.

Thus the heads fixed to the actuator end are moved radially, and a head positioning occurs. By rotating the motor step-by-step, the actuator and thus the heads are also moved step-by-step. Usually, one motor step corresponds to a movement of the heads one track inwards or outwards.

It is characteristic of actuators with a linear motor that no feedback between the actuator's position and the stepper motor is implemented. If the motor has to move the heads from track 0 to track 219, for example, then the motor control simply provides 219 stepper pulses. Upon each pulse the motor is rotated one step, and thus the head moves one track. After 219 stepper pulses the head reaches track 219. That this doesn't work very exactly and reliably seems to be obvious. On floppy drives with a track width of at least 0.1 mm, problems seldom occur: such precision can be governed very easily. But even on simple hard disk drives with a stepper motor (for example, the formerly widely used Seagate ST225 with its 615 tracks), the track width reaches only 1/10 of that for floppies. Such a positioning precision can just be reached with a stepper motor. For the smaller 3 1/2" disks with more than 1000 tracks, the stepper motor is not suitable because of its poor positioning precision.

For an exact positioning of the heads, not only the precision but also the reproducibility is decisive, that is, a reliable repeatability of the head positioning to the same track – and this is the main problem for actuators with a stepper motor. The coupling between stepper motor spindle and actuator is done via the friction between the spindle and the arc-shaped element. Although the spindle is usually coated with a gum or plastic layer to keep the slippage as low as possible, it may be that the actuator temporararily slides on the stepper motor spindle, especially during large actuator accelerations. But now the strict correspondence of rotation angle and actuator position is lost, and positioning errors occur because the heads are moved to the wrong tracks, or at least to the edges of the tracks. This problem may be solved quite easily by returning the actuator to the abut position corresponding to track 0. For this purpose, the *recalibrate drive* command is used. The abutting actuator position is assigned to track 0, and the actuator control then restarts track and pulse counting.

A much more unpleasant problem concerning stepper motor actuators is heat deformation. Assume the following situation. Immediately after power-up you format your hard disk. All drive components are cold at that time. Thus upon every step pulse you generate the next track. After your PC has been operating for several hours, suddenly positioning and read errors occur. The reason is simply the heat deformation of the mechanical components. For example, the actuator enlarges with rising temperature, and therefore the arm between the actuator spindle and head gets longer. This means that the amount of the head's track-to-track movement becomes slightly larger than the actual track distance generated in advance by formatting with a cold actuator. Although the heat deformations are very low, and the manufacturers try to compensate for these deformations by certain material combinations, they are sufficient to make at least cylinders with a higher number inacessible. If, on the other hand, you format your hard disk in a warm state, the PC may report positioning errors during power-up when all mechanical components are still cold. You can't even boot your PC then! You don't recognize many access failures directly as the controller carries out an in-built error recovery routine in the background which comprises seek retries and other procedures. Even then you may recognize access failure only indirectly by a nearly infinite access time for storing a short letter or the loud workings of the actuator motor and the drive mechanics.

The deeper cause for such failures is that no feedback between the head position and the motor control is implemented. The motor control passes the motor the seemingly required number of step pulses, and the stepper motor positions the head on the off-chance. If the head is located between two tracks, then an access is impossible, although only a further movement of half a track would be required.

Another disadvantage of hard disks with a stepper motor is that the manufacturers didn't implement an automatic head parking device, as these are low-cost models. The automatic head parking device moves the actuator into a transport position by means of a spring. In operation, the stepper motor exceeds the spring force to move the head accordingly. Some drives use the spindle motor as a generator that generates a sufficiently strong current pulse by means of the remaining rotation to move the actuator into the parking position when the drive is switched off.

Without a parking device the heads touch down onto tracks that usually contain data. At power-up the heads which are at rest scratch the disk's surface until the air cushion is strong enough to lift the heads. This is not very serious if you leave your PC in the same place all the time without moving it, but the missing automatic parking may give rise to a medium-sized disaster if you take your PC home in your car and you drive into a pothole. The shock of the hard heads onto the smoother disk may possibly destroy a data sector in that case. Manufacturers generally indicate the maximum allowed accelerations on the data sheets for their drives in g (which means the earth's gravitational acceleration of 9.805 m/s^2). Any shock that exceeds the limit in operation or switched-off state may give rise to serious damage. But the accelerations and shock forces actually occurring can hardly be estimated.

Fortunately, many PC manufacturers deliver a floppy disk with the setup program and a park routine for moving the hard disk heads to a safe location. If you are not sure whether your hard disk has an autopark device, then call the program in advance of each transportation. The programs are usually called *park*, *diskpark*, or something like this. It is also recommended that you call the program every time before you switch off the PC. You can recognize hard disks that park their heads automatically at power-down by a short scratch or knock, which indicates the positioning of the heads in their parking position.

High-quality hard disk drives use a linear motor instead of the stepper motor. Additionally, a control circuitry is implemented which compares the current head position to the intended one. Thus the read/write heads are always positioned above the correct track. According to the operation principle, two types of actuators with a linear motor (also called voice-coil actuators) can be distinguished (see Figure 9.5): linear and rotating.

The operation principle of such a voice-coil actuator is similar to that of the membrane drive in a speaker. A coil surrounds a permanent magnet or moves between two permanent magnets. If a current flows through the coil then a magnetic field occurs which is, depending upon the current direction, parallel to the field of the permanent magnet, or antiparallel to it. In the first case, the coil is pushed away; in the latter it is attracted. This leads to a linear movement of the coil, and thus of the actuator, which is connected to the coil. By means of a speedy electronic control of the coil current, coil and actuator can thus be moved and positioned along the permanent magnet.

With the linear voice-coil actuator the coil moves on two rails in a linear direction. The head at the actuator's end is directly moved in the same way as the actuator coil and radially shifted relative to the disk. Even rather low current pulses in the coil generate remarkable magnetic forces and actuator accelerations. Therefore, more and more the *rotating voice-coil actuator* is used as standard. Here the actuator is held in rotation around the actuator axis similar to the stepper motor actuator. On one end the read/write heads are mounted; at the other is the coil that carries out an arc-shaped movement in or around an arc-shaped permanent magnet. Because of a larger arm length between actuator axis and head compared to the distance of actuator axis and coil, a short coil movement is converted to an extensive head movement. This is favourable as the coil and the thus connected actuator part are rather heavy, and therefore inert, especially compared to the tiny thin-film heads. In this way, a modest movement of the massive parts with a low power expenditure can be converted to a fast positioning movement of the heads. Thus the rotating actuator type allows shorter positioning times at a lower power consumption by the coil.

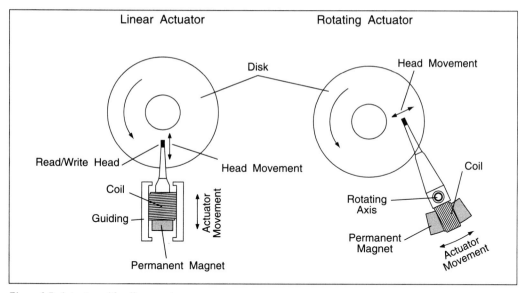

Figure 9.5: Actuator with a linear motor.

Unfortunately, the linear motor described has a significant disadvantage compared to the stepper motor: the positionings are not absolute. A short current pulse in the coil moves the actuator, but by how much can't be precisely predicted. Moreover, the magnetic fields generated by the coil slightly alter the magnetic properties of the permanent magnet. One has to choose another strategy and implement an active feedback loop that always leads to an absolute position of the read/write head and the actuator.

This is carried out by so-called *servo tracks* and a *servo head* (also called *index tracks* and *index head*, respectively). Perhaps you have been surprised by the fact that some hard disks have an odd number of heads. Why didn't the engineers simply add another head to use the last remaining disk side, as all other parts are already present? The answer is simple: the head is actually present but is dedicated to detecting the servo tracks, and is therefore part of the feed-back loop for the head positioning. At the manufacturer's site the seemingly unused disk side is provided very precisely with the servo tracks. Their only job is to implement a reference for head positioning.

When the drive attempts to access a certain track, the servo head is positioned above the servo track concerned. Thus, all other read/write heads that are intended for data recording are also located at this track. As the user you cannot alter the servo tracks. Also, all low-level formatting programs orient according to these servo tracks, and generate the data tracks on all disks at the same radial position as the servo tracks. If the drive attempts to position the head above a certain track, then the drive control energizes the coil of the linear motor and the servo head permanently detects the number of that track which is currently present below the servo head. When the servo head has reached the intended track, the drive aborts this rough positioning, turns off the current, and carries out a fine positioning. For this purpose, the servo head is moved forwards and backwards in tiny steps by means of small current pulses until the signal from the servo track is maximal. Therefore, the head is exactly in the middle of the track concerned.

It is obvious that positioning with a servo head and servo tracks is much more precise and especially temperature-independent. However, the feedback of the servo signal to the drive control requires more electronic equipment. Furthermore, the precise generation of the servo tracks is complicated. High-capacity hard disk drives with a linear motor and servo tracks are therefore much more expensive than their stepper motor counterparts. With a capacity of more than 20 Mbytes per disk side, such a technology cannot be avoided any longer. Here I also want to mention that higher-capacity drives for mainframes and supercomputers exist, which carry out the servo track detection optically. The principle is similar to that of a CD player or CD ROM drive, where a laser beam with a diameter of only about 1 μm scans the disk surface and provides information on the servo tracks to the drive control. The magnetic read/write heads can thus be positioned with an even higher precision than is possible with magnetic servo tracks and magnetic servo heads. However, don't confuse this method with optical drives; the data recording and restoring is carried out in a purely magnetic and not an optical manner.

Air Filtering and Ventilation

All hard disk drives have an air filter. This filter serves not for filtering the air from outside which penetrates into the HDA, but for internally filtering the air already in the case. An air exchange with the environment takes place only to a small degree if the air pressure is changing. Figure 9.6 shows a scheme for the air circulation in a hard disk drive.

To avoid the HDA being blown up by a low environmental pressure or being pressed by a high air pressure, every case has a ventilation slit which leads to an air filter. Depending upon the environmental pressure, air can penetrate from or escape to the outside via the air filter. This is essential: if you take a 5 1/4" hard disk onto an aeroplane with a pressurized cabin you would expose the cover to a force which is higher than 100 pounds! I don't think you would ever wish to put such a heavy load on your hard disk. But it could become worse: in an aeroplane without a pressurized cabin your hard disk would really explode!

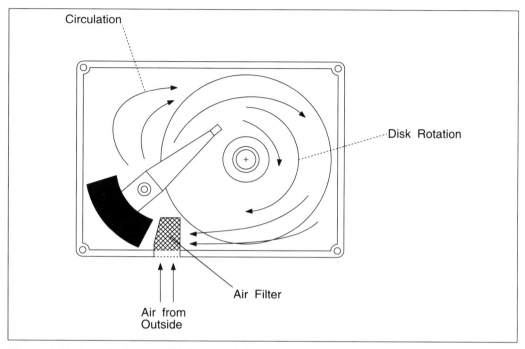

Figure 9.6: Air circulation in a hard disk drive. The disk rotation takes up the air in the drive; because of this a circulation stream is generated.

The air filter of a hard disk drive largely serves to filter the air already in the HDA. Because of slight head touches onto the disk or general wear-out of the rotating elements, microscopic dirt particles are formed, but they still are large enough to act as a scouring powder if they come between the head and the disk. The rotating disks therefore take up the air and generate an air circulation. The air filter is located within the streaming area of this circulation and filters off these small particles.

The air exchange with the environment is usually insignificant, and the internal wear-out is small. Thus the air filters of hard disks are designed as permanent filters that don't need to be replaced by you. This is completely different with large disk drives for mainframes, the so-called disk-packs. Here air is intentionally pressed through the whole drive to blow out all the dirt which has entered the drive during a disk change. This air must be filtered, of course, and because of the extensive air stream the filters have to be regularly replaced.

9.1.2 Interleaving

During reading or writing, the intended sector passes below the head because of the floppy or disk rotation and the controller enables the read/write head. Then the sector data is written into or read from the controller's sector buffer. If, for example, more data is to be read, then the data of the just read sector must be transferred into the main memory of the PC before the sector buffer can be filled with the data of the next sector. The controller-internal sector buffer usually has only a capacity sufficient for one sector plus the additional redundancy bytes. To be able to read the next sector, this sector data must be transferred within that short time interval which corresponds to the passage of the gap between the two sectors below the head. Only very fast ATs with a powerful controller succeed in doing this. On old XTs or on slow hard disk controllers, the new sector has already passed partially below the head by the time the sector buffer is ready to accommodate the new one. Thus the CPU must wait for a complete disk revolution before the new sector again appears below the read/write head. On a hard disk running at about 3600 rpm, this lasts about 16 ms. If you want to read a small file with 100 kbytes of data corresponding to 200 sectors, the read process would last for 200*16ms = 3.2 seconds. This is too long, of course, and makes a nonsense of the high transfer rate of the hard disks.

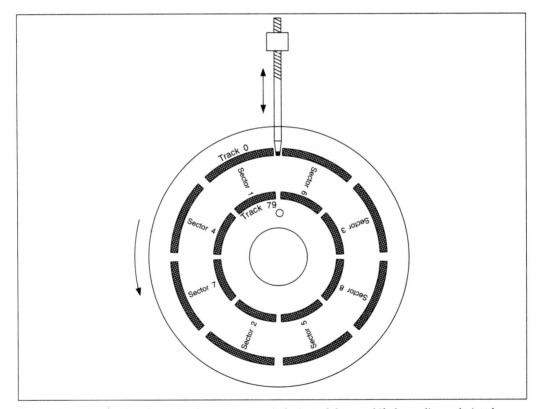

Figure 9.7: Interleaving doesn't position the sectors successively; instead they are shifted according to the interleave factor.

The solution to these problems is called *interleaving*. Here the sectors are not positioned successively, as is the case for floppies, but they are shifted by one or more sectors. Figure 9.7 shows the scheme. The amount of sector shifting is indicated by the *interleave factor*. A factor of three, for example, means that the sector with the next successive number N+1 is the third sector after the sector numbered N. One could also say that two sectors come between two successively enumerated sectors. For a hard disk with N sectors per track, interleave values between one (which means no shifting) and N – 1 are allowed. Between two successively enumerated sectors, zero to N–2 sectors are located.

The effect of interleaving is readily explained. When two succcssively enumerated setors are to be read, then controller and system bus have enough time to transfer the data in the sector buffer into main memory before the next sector appears below the read/write head. On the XT the interleave factor was equal to 6; on the AT equal to 3; and on the PS/2 machines only one (that is, no interleaving). Turbo ATs or i386/i486-machines can also have an interleave factor of one. Floppies are always handled with an interleave factor of one, as their data transfer rate doesn't inconvenience even a 4.77 MHz PC. Additionally, floppy drives transfer the sector data more or less online into main memory without temporary storage in a sector buffer. On hard disks this is not possible, as they not only carry out a CRC-check by means of their redundancy bytes, but they can even correct the data by additional ECC-bytes. However, this correction can only be carried out when all bytes have been read into the sector buffer; otherwise, an erroneous byte may already have been transferred to main memory when the ECC logic is just detecting the error by means of the previously read ECC bytes. Details on this subject are discussed below.

It is important that the interleave factor of a hard disk is defined during the course of the low-level formatting procedure. You may determine the optimum interleave value only by testing. For this purpose, you start to format your disk with a large value and check the data transfer rate. But note that too small a value has more fatal consequences than too large a value. With too large a value the controller waits longer for the next sector than is required. The time may be in the range for the passage of two sectors but in the case of too low a value the sector has just disappeared and the controller must wait nearly one complete revolution (that is, N – 1 sectors) until the intended sectors appear again. You may ascertain this on your own: while the transfer rate rises slowly up to a maximum value with a decreasing interleave value at first, the rate sharply drops to the worst value you can get after the interleave value falls below the optimum value. Some programs (for example, Spinrite) carry out such a check automatically, and determine the optimum value for your system.

While you get hardly any problems on conventional ST506/412 hard disks if you carry out low-level formatting and determine the interleave value by means of a special formatting program such as DiskManager or Spinrite, this is usually not possible with the modern IDE or SCSI drives. As a compensation, these disks are usually preformatted with an interleave value of one. High-performance hard disks may have up to 70 sectors per track today and, nevertheless, operate with an interleave factor of one. This is possible because a cache memory is implemented on them, which can accommodate a complete track, or even more. Thus the data is first written from disk into the sector buffer, and during the course of a disk revolution, the sectors of one track are written into the cache memory. The host system can now read the cache memory at its leisure. Here, too low an interleave value no longer plays a role.

9.1.3   Controller and Interfaces

For the driving head and actuator you need a controller to carry out the commands from the CPU, as well as the encoding and decoding of data. Figure 9.8 shows a schematic block diagram for the controller-drive combination.

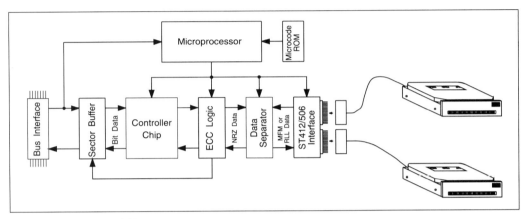

Figure 9.8: Controller and drive.

The bus interface establishes the connection of the controller to the PC. Read and write data for the drive as well as command data for the controller are exchanged via the interface. The controller itself consists of a microprocessor for controlling the drive interface and the controller-internal logic elements. For this purpose, a machine program is stored in the microcode ROM that the microprocessor uses. The data which is to be written into or read from a sector is held by the sector buffer, which always accommodates one complete sector. The interface to the drive can be formed very differently depending upon whether it is an ST412/506, ESDI, or embedded controller. Embedded controllers are integrated (embedded) on the drive, and exclusively control this single drive. On the other hand, ST412/506 and ESDI controllers can be connected to virtually any ST412/506 and ESDI drive, respectively. The drive interface supplies the connected drive with all the required control and data signals, and also accepts the corresponding return and data signals from the drive.

Let's discuss the principal functioning of a hard disk controller in relation to a read process. To read one sector the CPU passes a command block that has several command and parameter bytes to a register in the PC interface. The controller's microprocessor detects the command block and interprets the codes. The controller carries out the relevant command (here reading one sector) under the control of the program in microcode ROM. For this purpose, it drives the drive interface to position the drive's head above the intended track by means of precise stepper pulses. The drive head now continuously reads the signals passing below the head, and transfers the corresponding signals via the drive interface to the data separator. Depending upon the recording method, the data separator converts the MFM or RLL encoded data into an intermediate format called *NRZ* (**n**on-**r**eturn to **z**ero). The microprocessor determines, by means of the programmable storage controller, whether an address mark, a gap, or another field is currently passing below the head. If the microprocessor has detected an address mark, then it determines whether track and sector numbers coincide with the intended values. If the track number is not as intended, then it directs the drive to carry out another positioning; if only the sector number doesn't coincide, the microprocessor simply waits for the next address mark. If the sector number becomes equal to that intended, the controller opens the read gate and accepts the read data from disk (and converted to NRZ data by the data separator). The completely decoded data is then transferred into the sector buffer.

At the same time, the ECC circuitry checks whether the sector data conforms to the ECC bytes. If this is not the case, then the data is corrected by means of the ECC bytes. Unlike floppy controllers, which because of their CRC bytes are only able to check whether the data is correct, hard disk controllers can not only check for errors but even correct them with their ECC (**error correcting code**) bytes as long as the error is not too serious. The principle behind the ECC codes is similar to that of the CRC checksums, but more complex generator polynomials are used. Correspondingly adapted circuits recover the original data bytes from the erroneous data and ECC bytes. A hard disk controller with an ST412 interface usually uses a 4-byte ECC with the generator polynomial

$$ECC = x^{32}+x^{28}+x^{26}+x^{19}+x^{17}+x^{10}+x^6+x^2+1$$

Powerful hard disks with RLL encoding also employ longer ECC codes, with up to six or even eight bytes. But even with a 4-byte ECC, burst errors up to eleven bits can be corrected.

If the read data in the sector buffer is held in a correct or corrected form, then it may be transferred into the main memory. XT controllers use DMA channel 3 for this purpose. Thus, similar to floppy drives, a data transfer by means of the DMA chip takes place. On the other hand, the AT controller uses interrupt-driven data exchange with IN and OUT commands. For this purpose, the controller issues a hardware interrupt via IRQ14 after the sector has been read into the sector buffer. Now the handler transfers all 512 read data bytes from the sector buffer into main memory via programmed I/O.

When writing a sector the process is inverted. First, the 512 data bytes to be written are transferred from main memory to the sector buffer. The controller then carries out the positioning of the head and the search for the correct track and the intended sector in the same way as was the case for data reading. If the microprocessor has detected the address mark of the correct sector by the signals from the read/write head, it opens the write gate and continuously transfers the data via the storage controller. The storage controller now generates data address marks and other gap information, calculates the ECC bytes, converts the sector data into the NRZ format, and transfers the NRZ data stream to the data separator. In the data separator the encoding to MFM or RLL data is carried out, and this the data separator then transfers to the drive and thus to the activated read/write head via the drive interface. The head writes the data signals arriving from the data separator, without any further alterations, onto disk. If all address marks, sector data, and gaps have been written then the write process is complete, and the microprocessor may detect and process the next command.

A legitimate question is why IBM has implemented a second DMA chip in the AT, but unlike the XT doesn't use the DMA controller for data transfer between controller and main memory. The reason may possibly be that the AT with its 80286, and in particular the i386 and i486 PCs with an ISA bus, can carry out much faster data transfer using the IN, OUT and MOV commands than relatively low-clocked (4.77 MHz or 5 MHz) 8-bit DMA chips. Only in the environment of a multitasking operating system might the DMA transfer be more advantageous to free the CPU from such boring jobs. The PS/2 has thus been designed for multitasking operation.

Some magnetic media show the unpleasant property that a slight movement of the magnetized areas, and thus of the stored data bits, occurs if the magnetized areas are very close together. These *bit-shiftings* therefore occur only on the inner cylinders with high cylinder numbers, and further also depend upon the magnetization patterns on the disk. This means that the shifting only occurs for certain bit sequences. These critical bit sequences are well-known and can thus be handled by so-called *write-precompensation*. For this purpose, certain bits are written onto the disk slightly earlier or later, depending on the preceding and following bit, as this would actually be correct according to the encoding method used. The precompensation logic thus investigates online the data stream running to the drive for critical bit patterns, and delays or accelerates the corresponding signals. The time values for delay or acceleration for a hard disk with 17 sectors per track are in the range of 12–15 ns, that is, about 6% of an MFM bit cell. But note that many hard disks don't require a precompensation. Embedded controllers handle this problem without your intervention, as they are designed for each drive and therefore know its behaviour best. For some other hard disks you have to enter the start cylinder of the precompensation in the setup.

Another possibility for handling these bit shiftings is to reduce the write current for the inner cylinders with the closely adjacent data bits. You will therefore find, in the setup for your hard disk controller if it is not directly fixed on the drive, a *reduced write current* entry. By this reduction the data bits on the disk are not magnetized so strongly, and therefore affect each other less; the bit shifting is suppressed. Also, for this quantity you will find an entry in the setup where you have to enter the start cylinder at which the write current is to be reduced. A value that is larger than the maximum hard disk cylinder means in both cases that no precompensation and no reduced write current, respectively, is present, because the start cylinder cannot be reached.

Which of the components shown in Figure 9.8 is actually present on the controller adapter or the drive depends upon the interface standard and the actual implementation used. The widely used controllers with an ST412/506 interface accommodate all components from the bus to the drive interface on a separate controller board. The drives themselves are connected to the controller via the ST412/506 interface. Characteristic of this interface is that the read and write data runs via the physical connection controller-drive already in MFM or RLL-encoded form, and therefore as an asynchronous signal pattern. Further details are discussed in Section 9.4.

In ESDI systems the data separator is already integrated on the drive. Between drive and controller only the synchronous NRZ data is exchanged, thus raising the maximum achievable data transfer rate. Finally, controller and drive form a unit in IDE and SCSI systems. The connection to the PC bus is carried out by a host adapter which, in principle, is only an extended PC bus interface in the form of a small adapter board. Every manufacturer is free to implement the connection between controller and drive in any form.

9.1.4 Capacity, Data Transfer Rate, and Reliability

Manufacturers and dealers like to shower their clients with a lot of catchwords and accompanying data to show their products in the most favourable light. Lies are seldom told, but leaving out some background information may give rise to a wrong impression. The following sections therefore investigate some of the frequently recited and «decisive» properties of hard disks.

Storage Capacity

The first characteristic of a hard disk is, of course, the *storage capacity*. Here, four different combinations are possible, which differ in their amount by nearly one quarter (!), but nevertheless refer to the same hard disk on which you can store the same number of bytes in all four cases. A popular cheat is to indicate the unformatted capacity. As you already know from the floppies, the controller generates several address fields and gaps apart from the data area, thus the formatted capacity is about 20% less, on average. Therefore, note whether the manufacturer or dealer indicates the (unformatted) gross or the (formatted) net capacity. As a user only the formatted data capacity is decisive for you, of course. Depending on the formatting parameters and the sector size, the formatted capacity may vary only slightly. In the PC today, only hard disks with a sector size of 512 bytes are used, so that the formatted capacity enables a better comparison of various hard disks.

A further possibility to make the capacity of a hard disk appear to be larger without being dishonest is to indicate the capacity not in Mbytes but miobytes (million bytes). Remember that 1 kbyte is 1024 bytes, not 1000 bytes. In the same way, 1 Mbyte is equal to $1024*1024 = 1\ 048\ 576$ bytes and not 1 000 000 bytes – a remarkable difference of 5%. If you buy a hard disk with an unformatted capacity of 100 miobytes, which is already a reasonable size, you will not be able to accommodate more data than your friend who got one with a net capacity of 80 Mbytes.

Access Time

Another popular quantity, especially at the time of hard disk dinosaurs, is the *access time*. But which one is meant? There are four different access times: track-track, positioning, random, or full-stroke. The first time indicates the time interval that the actuator requires to move the head from the current to an adjacent track. The value includes the so-called *settle time*. When actuator and head are accelerated by the actuator motor and decelerated shortly before the destination track, they tend to oscillate. Once this oscillation has been dampened (that is, the head has settled), the head can access the track correctly. Typical values for track-track access times are about 2.5–5 ms today. A small value for this access time is important, as most data is held by successively enumerated sectors. If the capacity of one cylinder is exhausted, then the file continues on the next cylinder. Thus the head must be moved by one track. Finally, after optimization with a disk optimizer (for example, Compress or SpeedDisk), the directories are also grouped so that often only a few track movements are necessary to access all the data in a directory. Thus a low track-track access time is favourable.

The *average positioning time* indicates the time interval required on average to move the head from the current track to a randomly selected destination track. This time indication includes the head settle time, but not the so-called *latency*. When you attempt to access a certain sector of the disk by a controller command, then the drive must position the head above the intended track first. But now the sector is usually not accessible yet. Only in a few rare cases will the sector appear below the read/write head immediately after the head settlement. However, it may also be that the intended sector has just passed and the controller must wait for one complete revolution. On average this wait time or latency is just the time interval required for half a disk revolution. As all hard disks rotate at 3600 rpm, the latency is usually equal to 8.3 ms. Stone Age hard disks and modern ESDI disks don't differ here. The latency becomes especially dominant on drives with low positioning times.

Positioning time and latency together lead to the *random* or *average access time*. This is the time required for a random access to a certain sector, thus the average time for a completely random head movement from the current track to the destination, and the wait until the sector concerned appears below the head after the elapse of the latency time. The old and formerly widely used ST225 drive required 65 ms; typical values today are between 12 ms and 28 ms. A low average access time is important if you work with many applications that use randomly distributed data or contain index data for searching the data actually required. Spreadsheets and database programs belong to this group. To locate one byte in a database, several disk accesses and therefore accompanying head movements may be required. A low access time is then very important.

Also, the interpretation of the average access time requires some care. There is an elegant possibility to reduce this time remarkably: disk caches. These are cache memories integrated on the drive or controller which can accommodate a complete track or individual sectors before the track or sector data is transferred into main memory, or the data delivered by the main memory is written onto disk. The access to disk caches is, of course, very fast; the access times are significantly below 1 ms. However, the average mechanical access time remains the same, and is further composed of the average (mechanical) positioning time as well as the latency. Sequential disk accesses in particular are significantly accelerated by the disk cache. Some manufacturers assume, rather arbitrarily, that 40% of all accesses are sequential with the cache access time, 40% are random accesses with the average mechanical access time, and 20% are write accesses, also with the average mechanical access time, for example. The weighted average is thus equal to 40% * cache access time + 60% * average mechanical access time. Together with an average mechanical access time of 20 ms, an average access time of 12 ms is the result – a value which looks rather good. I want to leave judgement as to the 40%–40%–20% distribution up to you. Always ask when you buy a hard disk drive whether the access time with cache or only with the mechanical access time is indicated. A disk with a 30% longer mechanical access time usually leads to better system performance than its counterpart which achieves the shorter access time only with the help of a cache.

The disk caches become really effective starting at a size beyond 1 Mbyte. The corresponding cache controller for hard disks speeds up, for example, link processes remarkably, as during the course of these processes many library files must be opened and closed. A real alternative for i386/i486 computers with a large main memory are software caches that emulate a disk cache in main memory. Programs like SmartDrive, DiskCache, etc. belong to this class. On fast-clocked i386/i486 PCs these software caches are even faster, as a lot of data is already present in the fast accessible main memory, and need not be fetched from the controller cache via the slowly clocked PC system bus. But the significant disadvantage is that a hang-up of the PC because of a system failure also leads to a loss of the data just written onto the «disk» if it was temporarily stored in the cache and the hang-up occurred before it was written onto disk. Only a write-through strategy can avoid this problem, but this is very unfavourable if programs swap data blocks as the cache now has virtually no effect. Hardware caches on the controller are not affected by such system crashes. Their logic is separated from the main system, and even works when the PC has already hung-up. You should only wait for a few seconds after the last write access before you switch off your PC and turn off the current supply for the cache before all cache data has been written.

Besides these access times, manufacturers often also indicate the *full-stroke time*. This is the time required to move the head from track 0 to the track with the maximum cylinder number, or vice versa. The value is significant for an access to data which is very far away from each other. Such very strongly fragmented data can appear with DOS, for example, if you extend an old file and nearly all clusters up to the end of the disk are already occupied by other files and directories. DOS then allocates a sector on a track in the very innermost part of the disk for the additional data. Thus the heads must be moved quite far.

Data Transfer Rate

Another way of showing certain hard disks in a more favourable light by insufficient explanation is the *data transfer rates*. They generally refer to the quotient from the transferred amount of data and the time required for this. If you are leaving the City of London on Friday afternoon at 4pm to go in your Lotus to Bournemouth for the weekend, you surely don't tell your friends that you drove to Bournemouth at a speed of 150 mph only because it was possible to go at this speed for a few miles because the traffic jam cleared for a short time! For a distance of about 150 miles you need at least three hours on a Friday afternoon! But this doesn't hinder some hard disk manufacturers (like some printer manufacturers) from indicating data transfer rates which are as realistic as the above car·journey! By the term data transfer rate I would understand a value with which a realistic (that is, medium-sized) file is transferred from the drive into main memory. All other definitions may also be correct in the strict context for which they are defined, but for practical use they often don't tell you anything.

Three components mainly contribute to the transfer rate: disk-controller transfer, processing in the controller, and controller–main memory transfer. The first part is limited by the number of bytes passing below the read/write head every second. With 17 sectors per track at 3600 rpm, this value (together with the address fields, gaps, etc.) reaches about 600 kbytes/s. This actually corresponds to the 5 Mbits/s specification for the ST412 interface of MFM-encoded data. The controller separates all bytes which don't belong to the sector data field, thus only about 510 kbytes remain. First, these 510 kbytes/s are only valid for a single sector; we ought to write 512 bytes/980 μs as one sector comprises 512 data bytes and the sector together with all address fields and gaps passes within about 980 μs below the head. Now the data is in the sector buffer and has to be further transferred into main memory. If the controller and main system are fast enough to carry out this job before the next sector appears (that is, with an interleave of 1:1), then this transfer rate remains the same for the complete track. The transfer rate is effectively equal to 510 kbytes/s. But with an interleave factor of two, already two complete revolutions are required to transfer all the data of a track into main memory. Thus the transfer rate reduces to 255 kbytes/s. On an XT the interleave of 6:1 used leads to a ridiculous transfer rate of only 85 kbytes/s; a value which is nearly reached by a 1.2 Mbyte drive.

The processing time in the controller is usually very short, as the CRC and ECC checking and the ECC correction is carried out within a very short time. The processing time thus only slightly affects the transfer rate.

But the transfer rate between the controller and main memory via the PC system bus is, during the short time interval until the next sector appears and within which all the sector data must be transferred from the controller into main memory, significantly larger, of course. The distance between two sector data fields is only 100 μs. Thus, the transfer rate into main memory must be equal to 512 bytes/100 μs, or about 5 Mbytes/s! The PC system bus must therefore be able to handle at least such a rate so that an interleave value is possible. ISA and EISA buses only run at a frequency of 8.33 MHz at most, according to their specification. Together with a width of 16 bits for the ISA and 32 bits for the EISA bus, the data transfer rate of the bus system is thus limited to a maximum of 8.33 Mbytes/s and 16.67 Mbytes/s, respectively, as the processor requires two bus clock cycles for one bus cycle. Only the burst mode of the EISA bus with an i486 processor or the DMA mode C enables a doubled transfer rate of 33.3 Mbytes/s for a short time. Therefore, already the RLL-encoded data with an ST412 interface and 26 sectors per track exhausts the ISA bus capacity. Don't think that your PC doesn't operate well if your hard disk test program reports a transfer rate not very much above 800 kbytes/s, even with the brand new high-performance controller. The transfer rate between two sectors is much higher and needs the complete ISA bus capacity. An average value over long time intervals always smears out peak values completely.

Now it becomes clear why high-capacity drives with up to 70 sectors per track and an interleave of 1:1 have a disk cache (or at least a track instead of a sector buffer). The cache operates much faster than the transfer via the ISA or EISA bus and can therefore accommodate a complete track. The transfer into main memory via the PC bus can be carried out continuously, and the transfer capacity of 8.33 Mbytes/s or 16.67 Mbytes/s can be used for a longer time than the 100 μs between two sectors in the case of MFM-encoded disks with an ST412 interface. With a low number of sectors per track, the number of passing sector data bytes (and with a high number of sectors per track, the transfer capabilities of the ISA or EISA bus) limits the transfer rate. The buffering between the two asynchronously operating system elements, hard disk and PC system bus, raises the transfer rate remarkably. Also, here it becomes obvious that the performance of a complete system is governed by the performance of the weakest member. The disk cache on the drive thus serves mainly for enhancing the data transfer rate, and not for reducing the access time. But up to now, the access time has been valid as the exclusive performance characteristic and sacred cow, for hard disk manufacturers tend to gloss over the access time of their hard disks by means of the cache instead of emphasizing the much more important function for the transfer rate.

You may determine the various access times and data transfer rate by means of a hard disk test program such as the CORETEST. Disable any software cache for this purpose to avoid any distortion of the transfer rate. With an active software cache you get values only concerning the data transfer capacity of your system bus and the performance of the cache driver.

Benchmark programs for determining the data transfer rate usually only read the same data block repeatedly. If this block is no larger than the on-board cache then the drive must read the data from the disk only once. All further accesses refer solely to the FATS cache. You thus only investigate the transfer rate from cache-main memory, that is, the performance of the connection. If the size of the data block exceeds the storage capacity of the controller cache, then the data transfer rate is brought to its knees; in some cases it can be decreased by a factor of ten! You can recognize this clearly when you are looking at the frequently shown data transfer diagrams in computer magazines. Large files, and also small files or file fragments that can be readily accommodated by the cache but have to be fetched first, are transferred only at this significantly lower transfer rate.

Reliability and MTBF

As a user of hard disks, the drive's reliability is of particular importance. Where is the gain if you access data within 15 ms and this data can theoretically be transferred with a rate of 1 Mbytes/s, but your drive is out of order because of a hardware failure? Manufacturers therefore generally indicate some reliability information. The time interval between two complete failures of the drive which requires some repair is described by *MTBF* (**M**ean **T**ime **B**etween **F**ailures). The MTBF must be interpreted as follows: if we assume a plurality of identical drives, then on average one failure occurs within the MTBF. Thus MTBF is a statistical quantity, and statistical quantities have to be handled with care. For this reason some astronomical values for MTBF are discussed in brief here. I have already seen MTBF values of 150,000 hours, which is more than 17 (!) years of uninterrupted 24-hour operation. To get a trustworthy average value for the MTBF one would have to operate a plurality of identical drives for a much longer time than the MTBF indicates. How is it possible otherwise to indicate a time average value if the test time is much below this? With an MTBF of 17 years this is, of course, impossible, as the drive would be outdated long before reaching the MTBF test time. Instead, manufacturers make certain assumptions and elaborate statistical failure models that rely on experience with other and older drives. Afterwards, a test is carried out that may stretch over six months. From the failure rate in this time interval and the comparison with the failure rate of older drives for which some experience values exist, one extrapolates the MTBF for the investigated drive. The manufacturers prefer, of course, a linear dependency, but this doesn't correctly reflect the technical behaviour in all cases. For example, the failure rate of a car rises remarkably with its age. With a linear extrapolation of the failure rate, within the first two years each car would become at least (statistically) 30 years old. Thus be careful when interpretating the MTBF values. It's better that you rely on well-informed (!) consultants, who may provide you with global experience and no statistical average values.

Besides a complete failure which is characterized by the MTBF, there are other ordinary and more or less troublesome read and positioning errors. Write errors are not detected by the drive in most cases. They manifest themselves only by later read errors. On average, the number of recoverable read errors for good hard disks is about 1 per 10^{10} read bits. Note that the error rate is indicated as *error per read bits* but a read access is always carried out sector by sector with 512 bytes and eight bits per byte. Converted to the number of read accesses, a value 4000-times larger arises. The number of recoverable read errors then reaches 1 per $2*10^6$ read accesses; a value which no longer looks as trustworthy as the one indicated above. Performance and reliability infomation should therefore always be investigated precisely. But nevertheless, the above indicated value is quite good. You may read 1 Gbyte of data before a recoverable read error occurs, but as a user you don't recognize such an error because the ECC bytes correct it. Only the BIOS detects the ECC correction and sets a corresponding indicator. Much more troublesome are the non-recoverable read errors. A typical rate for a high-quality drive is 1 error per 10^{14} read bits or 1 failure per $2*10^{10}$ read commands. But such errors characterize only the so-called *soft errors*. They assume error-free working mechanics and a damage-free disk surface. Mechanical damage because of natural wear-out or a head crash, as *hard errors*, increase the error rate by several powers of ten. The most likely failure reason is an incorrect head positioning. The rate of such *seek errors* is about 1 per 10^6 positionings with linear motors. Stepper motors show an error rate that is about ten times higher. All these values seem to be rather good, but take into account the fact that the heads of hard disks must be moved frequently and quickly – one million head movements are reached within a short time. But as a compensation, the error recovery strategies built into the controller handle such positioning errors automatically. For example, in most cases it's sufficient to move the head back to track 0 to recalibrate the drive and then repeat the positioning. Generally speaking, today's hard disks are very reliable devices if you handle them with care.

9.1.5 BIOS Configuration

This section discusses the BIOS setup configuration for all presently used interface standards.

First, a few words about hard disk entries in the BIOS entries. If you're using an ST412/506 controller that can be accessed by the on-board BIOS of the AT and which does not have its own BIOS, you usually have to define the drive geometry with the setup program. Normally, one of the entries available in the BIOS fits your drive. If this is not the case, then most PCs allow you to enter the geometry parameters using a user-definable entry. Consult the data sheet of your hard disk drive for this purpose. There you will find the number of tracks, heads and sectors per track. Furthermore, the sheets also indicate where the write precompensation and the reduced write current starts. If the data sheet doesn't contain any information about them, then always enter a value that is higher than the maximum cylinder number to disable the precompensation and the reduced write current. If read errors occur, especially with high cylinder numbers, it's best then to enter about 2/3 of the maximum cylinder number.

On new IDE hard disks, which can be directly accessed by the AT BIOS as the ST412/506 controller, the precompensation and reduced write current entries are without meaning. The embedded controllers of these drives are best adapted to the hard disks concerned. Whether and in which way, for example, the precompensation is carried out is hidden from you. The controller does this internally. On the other hand, you usually have to enter the drive geometry into the setup table as the IDE hard disk appears to the system. Always consult the data sheet of your hard disk and obey the manufacturer's indications of the physical geometry with various zones. Some IDE drives are intelligent enough to use any geometry indicated by you, as long as the resulting number of sectors doesn't exceed the number of sectors physically present on the drive.

ESDI and SCSI hard disks cannot be accessed by the AT BIOS directly, as their register assignment isn't compatible with the AT bus standard. Such hard disks have a BIOS extension on the controller or host adapter which replaces the former INT 13h interrupt and carries out all hard disk functions. As more or less intelligent drives, these hard disks identify their geometry to the controller and BIOS by an identify command. You should therefore not enter any value in the BIOS setup for them, but indicate that no hard disk is present. If you use, for example, a SCSI hard disk as drive C: then you must enter for the first hard disk in the setup that no drive is present; otherwise, you may provoke a conflict between the controller and the system BIOS. With the BIOS extension engagement, during the course of booting, the ESDI and SCSI drives are integrated into the system, and you may access the hard disks with no problem.

9.2 Recording Formats, Low-Level Formatting, and Bad-Sector Mapping

This section discusses the «low-level properties» of hard disk drives and controllers. Here, I want to present a new and very powerful recording or encoding method, RLL. Moreover, you will gain an insight into the various tasks and strategies of the controller for managing hard disks.

9.2.1 MFM and RLL

The use of MFM instead of FM already leads to a significant increase of the data density BPI without the need to enhance the flux change density FCI. Thus it's not surprising that the developers of hard disks searched for other ways in which to realize higher and higher storage capacities. One way to achieve this is the *RLL method* which seems to be surrounded by even more mystery than the MFM method. RLL is the abbreviation for *run length limited*. This means that the number of zero bits between two set bits is limited. With the MFM method this is not the case. You may fill a 512-byte sector with 4096 zero bits with no problem. With the MFM method only clock but no data bits are then recorded. This is already the main difference to RLL: the MFM method records a clock bit if two zero bits occur in succession. The RLL method, on the other hand, gets along without any clock bit. The RLL logic determines, solely from the time interval between two set bits, how many zero bits were interposed. Because of synchronization problems, rotation variations, etc., which give rise to a variation of the period between the zero bits, this doesn't work for all numbers of zero bits. Therefore, their number is limited (hence the name RLL) to avoid the RLL logic losing the beat.

With the most widely used RLL method there are, by definition, at least two and at most seven zero bits between two set bits. The method is therefore called *RLL 2,7*. But now a problem arises: a 16-bit integer with the value 0 consists of 16 zero bits. That's too much for RLL. The data bits must therefore be re-encoded so that at least two and at most seven zero bits are in succession. Table 9.1 shows the encoding table for RLL 2,7.

data bit	RLL 2,7 code
000	000100
10	0100
010	100100
0010	00100100
11	1000
011	001000
0011	00001000

Table 9.1: RLL 2,7 encoding

You can see that data bit groups of different lengths are encoded into RLL codes also of different lengths. In the RLL codes a maximum of four zero bits is in front and a maximum of three zero bits behind a 1. Thus seven zero bits at most can meet. Furthermore, behind every 1 at least two zero bits occur. Therefore, between two 1s there are always at least two zero bits and the requirements for RLL 2,7 are fulfilled.

From Table 9.1 you can also see the disadvantage of the RLL method: the RLL codes are much longer than the data bit groups by a factor of two. We now discuss, in connection with Figure 9.9, why RLL enables a higher data density BPI with the same flux change density FCI.

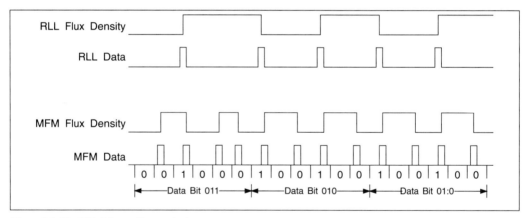

Figure 9.9: The RLL 2,7 encoding method.

In Figure 9.9, the same data byte 01101001 as in Figure 8.20 is encoded in RLL format. I have assumed the first bit of the following data byte to be equal to 0. From Table 9.1 you can deduce that the RLL code for the nine data bits 01101001 I 0 is as follows: 001000100100100100. Figure 9.1 (bottom) shows the data and (above) the flux density, as well as flux changes, for the case where the RLL code is recorded by the MFM method. The MFM flux density also comprises, besides the set RLL bits, clock bits if two zero bits are in succession.

The RLL method, on the other hand, records only the set RLL bits. According to the RLL code 001000100100100100, these are only of four set bits. In data reading the zero bits in-between are generated by the RLL logic purely from the time delay between two set RLL bits and added to the 1-bits. For recording the nine data bits by means of the MFM method, twelve flux changes are required; with the RLL method, on the other hand, only five flux changes are necessary. A precise mathematical analysis of the RLL method shows that in the statistical average the MFM method requires three times the flux changes for data recording compared to the RLL method. With the same packaging density of flux changes, three times more data can thus be accommodated by means of the RLL method compared to MFM.

But as already mentioned, the RLL codes are unfortunately twice as long as the data bit groups so that the three times higher packaging density is halved again by the twice as long RLL codes. As the net gain a factor of 1.5 remains, or stated differently: with the RLL method, 50% more data can be accommodated on the disk than is possible with MFM. On average, thus only two flux changes are required for recording three data bits. As was the case for the replacement of the FM by the MFM method, this data density increase is achieved largely by nothing as the flux change density, and thus the quality of the disk and read/write head, need not be improved. The enhancement is exclusively packed into the encoding method, and therefore into the RLL logic of the controller.

But the RLL logic becomes significantly more complicated than the electronics for encoding and decoding by means of the MFM method. The difficulties arise in that the code words are comprised of between four and eight RLL bits. With the MFM method the code word length was uniformly equal to one bit. If the RLL logic gets into a muddle even only for a single RLL bit, then burst errors of up to five data bits are the result. Thus, RLL controllers must have a much more powerful ECC logic to be able to correct such errors reliably. High-quality RLL controllers therefore use a 6-byte instead of a 4-byte ECC code.

An RLL controller has not yet finished its work with the decoding of the flux changes to RLL data, but additionally it has to convert the RLL data into the actual data bits. This contrasts with an MFM controller where the bit stream behind the data gate can be directly used as a serial data stream. The same applies, of course, to data writing when the data stream to be written has to be converted into RLL data first, and then the RLL data must be encoded into flux changes according to the set RLL bits.

Besides the described and proved RLL 2,7 method there exist further RLL methods, called *advanced RLL (ARLL)*. Examples are the RLL 1,7 and the RLL 3,9 method. In both cases, the encoding overhead for the data bit groups into RLL code is much higher and, in addition, the larger number of zero bits between two set RLL bits makes great demands on the stability of the RLL electronics. With ARLL a data density increase of up to 90% compared to MFM can be realized, so that a single flux change encodes nearly two data bits.

9.2.2   High-Level Formatting of Hard Disks with FORMAT

Unlike floppies, for hard disks the FORMAT command doesn't generate any tracks or sectors. During the course of *high-level formatting* with FORMAT, only the logical structure of the partition concerned is established. The generation of the boot sector, the two FAT copies, and the root directory belong to this process. All entries in the FAT are set to 00h to indicate that the partition is free of data. In particular, the sectors of the subdirectories and files are not over-written with a certain data pattern. On hard disks you can only format individual partitions, but not the complete hard disk with FORMAT. Thus you must first partition the hard disk and generate the partition table by means of *FDISK*, or another suitable program. The FORMAT command itself doesn't affect the partition table, but only reads the information stored there to determine the beginning and size of the partition to be formatted, and to carry out the formatting accordingly.

Reformatting hard disks with FORMAT only erases their logical structure, similar to the DEL and RMDIR commands. Physically, the data is still present. Some utilities (for example, PCTools or Norton Utilities) can then even recover an erroneously formatted hard disk partition. Because of the destruction of more than a single file (as is the case with DEL) or a single sub-directory (with RMDIR), the reconstruction of the original directory and file structure is much more complicated here. If the original directories and files were fragmented, then even these tools have no chance. Therefore, resident programs exist that intercept all hard disk operations and store the logical structure of the hard disk in certain sectors reserved for this purpose. One example is the MIRROR program of PCTools. The accompanying recovery program recognizes the reserved sectors, and because with high-level formatting only the logical structure of the hard disk, but not the data itself, has been destroyed the program can recover the logical structure of the hard disk from the information held in the reserved sectors.

Unlike low-level formatting, you don't have the opportunity to replace damaged sectors and tracks with FORMAT. When FORMAT detects a damaged sector, the corresponding cluster is simply marked as *bad*. But a single hard disk cluster usually has eight sectors with DOS 2.xx and four sectors with DOS 3.00 and above. Thus, FORMAT wastes between three and seven intact sectors when marking a cluster as bad. The low-level formatting, together with the bad-sector mapping, solves the problem of defect sectors much more intelligently. Details are given in the following section.

9.2.3   Low-Level Formatting and Bad-Sector Mapping

To emboss tracks and sectors on a hard disk you have to carry out a low-level format. But note that most hard disks come in a preformatted form already.

Advice: Generally, you must not reformat intelligent drives with an embedded controller that carries out translating, such as IDE drives.

The usual formatting programs such as DiskManager or Spinrite are overtaxed with the various recording zones of the drives and the translating which the controller carries out. The only effect they have is that they probably destroy the drive structure. This especially applies to AT bus hard disks, as they can be accessed by the utilities in the same way as the ST412/506 hard disks. With the ST412/506 this works excellently as the programs are particularly tailored for this kind of drive and controller. But the AT bus interface is only register-compatible; the internal conversion in the drives differs significantly from the ST412/506 drives, as every AT bus hard disk has it own controller. AT bus drives and others (for example, SCSI) may only be formatted with specially adapted programs. As the user you should not try to do this on your own.

The first job of the low-level fomatting procedure is to generate tracks and sectors. This is carried out by positioning through rotation steps of a stepper motor, which moves the head from track to track, or by orienting the data tracks according to the servo tracks on the servo disk on drives with a linear motor. After every positioning the head writes the passed track format data onto the data carrier according to the commands from the controller. Figure 9.10 shows the typical layout of a hard disk track of ST412/506 drives for MFM and RLL encoding.

```
MFM sector format                           RLL sector format
beginning of track                          beginning of track
SYNC:    10 byte 00h                        SYNC:    11 byte 00h
IAM:      2 byte a1h fch                     IAM:      2 byte a1h fch
GAP 1:   11 byte 4eh                        GAP 1:   12 byte ffh

sector                                      sector
SPD:      7 byte 4eh
SYNC:    10 byte 00h                        SYNC:    10 byte, 00h
IDAM:     2 byte a1h feh                     IDAM:     2 byte 5eh a1h
ID:       4 byte cy hd sc f1*)              ID:       4 byte cy hd sc f1*)
ECC:      4 byte ECC value                  ECC:      4 byte ECC value
GAP 2:    5 byte 00h                        GAP 2:    5 byte 00h
SYNC:    10 byte 00h                        SYNC:    11 byte 00h
DAM:      2 byte a1h f8h                     DAM:      2 byte 5eh a1h
data: 512 data byte                         data: 512 data byte
ECC:      4 byte CRC value                  ECC:      4 byte ECC value
GAP 3:   15 byte 00h                        GAP 3:    3 byte 00h and 17 byte ffh

EOT                                         EOT
GAP 4:    ca. 56 byte 00h                   GAP 4:    ca. 93 byte 00h

*) the four bytes identify the corresponding sector in the format
cylinder-head-sector-sector flag
```

Figure 9.10: Layout of a hard disk track.

The fields of the sectors and the track are essentially the same as those on floppies (see Figure 8.19). Therefore, only the significant differences are discussed. First, the gaps between the sectors as well as between the end and start of the track are smaller. This is possible as the rotation of the hard disk is stabilized by means of an electronic feedback loop, and the rotation variations are lower because of the missing friction between head and disk. Gaps acting as «speed buffers» between the individual sectors are therefore virtually unnecessary. Additionally, hard disks don't have an index hole like the floppies to mark the beginning of the track. On hard disks this is carried out exclusively by an *index address mark (IDAM)*, which indicates the beginning of the track and activates the index signal line *IDX* to the controller. The value for the fields differs only a little between MFM and RLL. Only the address marks have different identifiers.

Of significance for establishing the bad-sector mapping are the *ID fields*. They have four bytes, and at first specify the number of the cylinder, head and sector. The two most significant bits of the 10-byte cylinder number are always stored as high-order bits of the sector number. Unlike the format of a floppy track, the 4th byte doesn't contain any information concerning the sector size, but the sector flag. Table 9.2 shows the structure of the sector flag.

Thus a set bit 0 indicates that the sector concerned is damaged. Bit 1 characterizes the track to which the sector belongs as defective and no alternative track is assigned. A set bit 2 indicates that the track is defective but the controller has assigned an alternative track. The identification of the alternative track is stored in the ID field of the sectors, that is, the three bytes sc hd sc in the ID field don't characterize the current track, but define the alternative track. If bit 3 in the sector flag is set, this means that the track concerned represents an alternative track and has been assigned to a defective track as a substitute. Finally, bits 4–7 are reserved.

Bit	Meaning
0	bad sector
1	bad track without reassignment
2	track ID points to alternative track
3	alternative track
4–7	reserved

Table 9.2: Sector flag structure

The reason for the bad-sector mapping is that absolutely error-free disk surfaces can only be manufactured with difficulty. Even a microscopic defect of the medium destroys a data bit and makes the accompanying sector unusable. The manufacturers therefore check their disks intensively for several hours, thus detecting defective spots that would not give rise to any problems in normal operation. You get such a *manufacturer defect list* for every drive. The list specifies the error location in the format cylinder, head, sector. The defect list usually comes as a data sheet, or the defects are listed on a label attached to the drive's case. Even if such a defect list contains several dozens of error locations, this is not very serious as the bad-sector mapping removes them. This works as follows.

If the controller detects a defect on the disk according to the two defect lists (see below) that only affects a single sector of the track, the controller simply shifts the sectors slightly so that the error is now outside the sector (or between two sectors, or at the beginning and end of the track). Thus the error no longer disturbs the data in the track. This process is called *sector slipping*. Not a single byte of the storage capacity gets lost through this.

Alternatively, the controller can mark the sector concerned as bad by setting bit 1 in the sector flag. But here the storage capacity is reduced by one sector. Some controllers format a normally unused spare sector in addition to the usual 17 or 26 sectors per track for ST412/506 hard disks. This sector can be employed instead of the marked sector. In this case, no storage capacity gets lost even if one sector is marked as bad. Thus, errors that only affect one single sector can easily be recovered.

The situation becomes more complicated if a medium's errors affect more than one sector. Such damage can no longer be handled within the track. The controller marks the complete track as bad by setting bit 2 in the sector flag of all sectors in the track. By doing this, the track is marked as bad. Furthermore, the controller assigns an alternative track, beginning with the highest cylinder.

The identification cy hd sc fl of this alternative track is stored in the ID fields of all sectors of the damaged track. When a controller command addresses the bad track, the controller recognizes, according to the sector flag, that the complete track is marked as bad and is assigned an alternative track. It reads the identification of the alternative track from the ID field and moves the head to the alternative track. Thus the controller carries out another positioning; all accesses to the defective track are diverted to the alternative track. The alternative track itself is defined as an alternative track by a set bit 3 in the sector flag of all sectors in the track. Such alternative tracks are no longer available for a normal access, that is, direct addressing by the «actual» track number.

It is less favourable to mark a defective track as bad solely by setting bit 1. The controller thus detects that the track is damaged and cannot be used anymore, but no alternative track has been assigned. A «hole» therefore appears in the address space of sectors and tracks.

The capacity of the hard disk is reduced if a defective track is assigned an alternative track, but you get the advantage that the whole continuously formatted area is now error-free. In this way we get something like a «sector address space» which is continuous and free of holes, that is, damaged sectors or tracks. It is thus much easier to manage such a seemingly error-free area, even if some accesses are diverted to other tracks, than to handle a plurality of defect sectors. Then the hard disk always comprises 17 or 26 sectors per track, and not, for example, 17 sectors in this track, only 14 in another, 16 in the next, etc. As most medium errors are only very small today, and mainly affect only a single sector, the controller has to replace a complete track only in a very few cases. Normally, sector slipping is sufficient to repair the defect.

Controllers that carry out such a bad-sector mapping usually reserve the first physical cylinder of the connected hard disk for their own purposes. This cylinder is assigned the number –1 (that is, a negative number) so that only the controller can access the information stored there. Using the normal controller commands, such as read sector, this cylinder cannot be accessed. The lowest possible cylinder number 0 already addresses the second physical cylinder. Thus the partition table and other important areas are not shifted logically. Some manufacturers write the manufacturer defect list and the geometry information concerning the drive onto cylinder –1 before the hard disk is shipped. The geometry information is very important for autoconfiguring controllers (see Section 9.2.5 for details). Table 9.3 shows the layout of the controller cylinder –1.

Sector Number	Track 0	Track 1
1	geometric information (1st copy)	geometric information (3rd copy)
2	geometric information (2nd copy)	geometric information (4th copy)
3 – 8	reserved	reserved
9 – 10	manufacturer defect list (1st copy)	reserved
11 – 12	manufacturer defect list (2nd copy)	reserved
13 – 14	known defects (1st copy)	reserved
15 – 16	known defects (2nd copy)	reserved
17	reserved	reserved

Table 9.3: Controller cylinder layout

From the first physical cylinder only the first two tracks corresponding to heads 0 and 1 are used, as every hard disk at least has these two tracks. The geometry information is stored in four identical copies for redundancy purposes. If one copy is destroyed then the controller can access the other three. The manufacturer defect list is also present as two identical copies in sectors 8 and 9 as well as 10 and 11. The structure of this list is shown in Table 9.4. In the same way, the list of known defects is also stored twice; its structure is shown in Table 9.5.

Byte	Contents	
0–1	signature 0beedh of manufacturer defect list	
2–4	reserved	
5–6	bad cylinder or ffh for end of list	
7	bad head	1 defect entry
8–9	number of bytes from IDAM up to defect	
10–509	max. 100 more defect entries	
510–511	reserved	

Table 9.4: Manufacturer defect list structure

The manufacturer defect list is (as the name implies) written by the manufacturer onto track 0 after checking the hard disk. The list can accommodate up to 101 entries, and is closed by an entry ffffh for the section defective cylinder. The entries characterize the defects by indicating the cylinder, head and number of bytes located between the index address mark IDAM at the beginning of the track, and the defect itself. The controller uses this defect list during the course of formatting to carry out sector slipping or to assign an alternative track.

Byte	Contents	
0–1	signature 0fabeh of list of known defects	
2–4	reserved	
5–6	bad cylinder or ffh or end of list	
7	bad head	
8	first bad physical sector	1 defect entry
9	second bad physical sector (or ffh if not present)	
10–509	max. 100 more defect entries	
510–511	reserved	

Table 9.5: Structure of the grown defect list

The *grown defect list* is generated and extended during the course of the formatting procedure by the controller or by explicit controller commands for assigning alternative sectors or tracks. Unlike the manufacturer defect list, the defects are characterized by the values for cylinder, head and sector number. Both lists together indicate all known defects on the hard disk, and the controller uses them during the course of a formatting process to carry out the bad-sector mapping and the assignment of alternative tracks automatically and independently. Note that this remapping is carried out by the hard disk controller's microcode, and not by the CPU.

For characterizing defective tracks and sectors, and for assigning alternative tracks, three commands are usually available for an ST412/506 controller:

– *Format defective track* (opcode 07h): this command formats a track and sets bit 1 in all sector flags of the track to mark the track as defective. An alternative track is not assigned by this command.

– *Reassign sector* (opcode 09h): the sector is added to the grown defect list so that each sub-sequent formatting procedure attempts to repair the sector defect by means of sector slipping or by assigning an alternative sector within the track. If the track already has a defective sector, then any subsequent formatting process marks the whole track as bad and assigns an alternative track.

– *Reassign alternative track* (opcode 11h): this command marks a track as defective and explicitly assigns a certain other track as the alternative track. Unlike the above indicated command, the reassignment is therefore carried out at once, and not during the course of the next formatting process.

Special formatting programs are unnecessary for IDE or SCSI drives, as a later reformatting only improves the interleaving or carries out a bad-sector mapping of bad sectors with the grown defect list. The first aim is irrelevant, as all IDE and SCSI drives are always preformatted with an interleave of 1:1. Furthermore, the controllers of these drives are intelligent enough to carry out a dynamic bad-sector remapping. This means that the controller marks a sector or track as bad, and reassigns an alternative sector or track automatically and on its own if it has detected a persistent read error. Such errors usually indicate damage to the data carriers at the corresponding location.

9.2.4   Error Recovery Strategies

Because of the extremely high data density of the hard disks, even on high-quality drives, read and seek errors frequently occur. But drive manufacturers have taken into account such errors by implementing certain error recovery procedures in the controller. Head crashes that don't destroy a sector completely, but only give rise to some problems for a data read, can be diminished somewhat by this. Finally, the hard disk medium demagnetizes itself slowly but continuously. If a sector is only read for a long time but never written, as is the case, for example, for the boot sector, then after several years demagnetization may be rather serious. At first, only recoverable read errors occur, which can be overcome by the implemented error recovery procedure. Later, though, the whole sector becomes inaccessible. An early reading and rewriting of the sector's contents may counteract such data losses. Elaborate hard disk test programs such as HDTEST or DiskTechnician may determine such sneaking demagnetization, and repair it simply by rewriting the sector's contents.

The following sections discuss which extensive procedures the controller carries out for error recovery in order to be able read the data anyway. The procedures are enabled on the XT controller, for example, using the 5th command byte in a 6-byte command block, and on the AT bus controller by a set R bit in the command code (see Section 9.6.4). The procedures that a controller actually carries out depend upon the microcode which controls the controller's microprocessor, and thus on the manufacturer and the controller model. Therefore, a typical error recovery procedure which is used, for example, by the ST412/506 hard disk controllers ST11x and ST21x is discussed.

The procedures differ depending upon whether an error has occurred while reading a data or address field of a sector. The controller cannot detect a positioning error absolutely, but only by comparing the entries in the ID field of the sector with the intended ones. If the two cylinder numbers don't coincide then a positioning error has occurred. The same applies to errors in the data area. If the sector area has been damaged, for example, by a head crash, then the controller is unable to detect this reason directly. Instead, it accepts further signals from the head and decodes them according to the recording method. From the damaged sections it gets only confusing information which is decoded in the same way at first. Using the ECC bytes, the controller can then, however, recognize that part of the sector which contains invalid data. Whether the reason for this is a head crash, a former write error or a sneaking demagnetization, the controller is not able to determine. For the outcome (erroneous data), this is, of course, insignificant.

If the controller has detected an error in the data area because of some inconsistencies between the sector data and the ECC bytes, it proceeds as follows. If an attempt is successful (that is, the sector concerned can be read without any error), then the controller terminates the procedure and transfers the data into main memory.

– Read sector eight times: the controller repeats the read attempt up to eight times without applying an ECC correction. If the failure reason is only a synchronization problem or too extensive a rotation variation, then the first retry is successful in most cases.

– Shoe shining: the controller first moves the head back to track 0, then to the track with the maximum cylinder number, and finally positions the head above the track with the addressed data sector again. Errors can thus be recovered which result from a tiny mis-positioning of the head, that is, the head is at the side and not in the middle of the track, so that certain data signals are too weak.

– Reread sector and carry out ECC correction: if the error can be recovered only by means of the ECC bytes, then the controller corrects the data, and sets an indicator in the status byte that shows a recoverable ECC error has occurred. Minor write errors or damage because of weak head crashes can thus be recovered.

– Read the sector six times shifting the data and clock window: the controller attempts to read the sector but shifts the data as well as the clock window (see Section 9.6.2) by +1.5%, +6%, +7.5%, 1.5%, –6% and (at the last attempt) –7.5%. Errors caused by bit shifting with missing precompensation can thus be recovered.

– Microstepping and reading the sector eight times without ECC correction: the controller moves the head in tiny steps and tries to read the sector without applying any ECC correction eight times. Therefore, errors because of small deviations of the track from the originally defined position can be recovered. The reasons are mostly heat deformations and temperature differences between formatting and the read process. Drives with a stepper motor are particularly affected by this.

– Microstepping and reading the sector eight times with ECC correction: the controller moves the head in tiny steps and attempts to read the sector while carrying out an ECC correction eight times.

Thus, the six procedure steps carry out up to 31 (!) read accesses before the controller finally gives up and indicates a non-recoverable read error to the host. This has many advantages, but also a few disadvantages. One advantage is that because of the extensive recovery attempts the controller can nearly always restore the data if the errors and damage are only minor. The disadvantage is that neither you, DOS nor the BIOS recognize nearly complete failures, as such. Only a lasting and in most cases also loud head activity points to such dangers. Errors because of minor damage, a sneaking demagnetization, or the mechanical wear of the drive are hidden until the catastrophe occurs. Some elaborate hard disk test programs such as HDTEST and DiskTechnician can detect such errors, which are normally corrected by the controller early enough, and take precautions or display some warning.

I particularly want to point out that CHKDSK is not able to detect such failures in any way. CHKDSK checks only the logical structure of the disk, that is, the consistency of directories and FAT. Also, many other hard disk test programs (for example, DiskTest of Norton Utilities) read the sectors only on a DOS or maybe BIOS level. In both cases, the error recovery procedures of the controller are enabled and the programs detect (following the 31 failed attempts) that something is wrong with the drive. This cannot be called a precaution by any stretch of the imagination.

Another source of errors is positioning failures (also called seek errors), which particularly occur on drives with a stepper motor or old and mechanically worn drives. The controller recognizes them according to a missing or incorrect ID address mark:

– No ID address mark found: recalibrate drive and reseek. In most cases the cause is a head positioning between two tracks or a non-formatted drive.

– Wrong ID address mark found: recalibrate drive four times and reseek.

Thus persistent seek errors are reported faster than data errors, but they can usually be recovered more quickly by means of a drive recalibration as they are independent of the data carrier.

Note that intelligent drives with an embedded controller often carry out a dynamic bad-sector remapping: after a persistent read error these controllers mark the sector concerned, or the whole track, as bad and reassign an alternative sector or track automatically and on their own. The whole process is executed without your intervention or any command from DOS or the BIOS.

9.2.5 Autoconfiguration

One problem when installing a new hard disk is adjusting the correct drive parameters in the BIOS setup. Besides the drive geometry (that is, the number of cylinders, heads and sectors per track) you additionally need to know the start cylinder for the write precompensation, for example, and to select the corresponding entry in the setup. But that's not sufficient. A drive that has come onto the market after the BIOS has been programmed can have a geometry that hasn't been implemented. A maximum of 271 different disks can be held in CMOS RAM if we take into account the 15 regular and 256 extended entries, but integrating 271 different parameter tables into a ROM is a pure waste of storage capacity. Some manufacturers of compatible PCs have therefore reserved a free definable entry, because at some time the number of possible parameter values becomes too large for the BIOS ROM or the CMOS RAM. But as the user, you have to know the geometry of your drive exactly to be able to employ this user-specific entry.

IBM and other manufacturers had a better idea; autoconfiguring controllers and drives. On these hard disks the geometry information is stored in the first physical cylinder. All information required is held by sectors 1 and 2 of tracks 0 and 1 in the form of four identical copies (Table 9.3). Table 9.6 shows the structure of these four geometry sectors.

Byte	Contents
0–1	signature 0dabeh of geometric information
2–3	number of cylinders
4	number of heads
5	number of sectors per track
6–7	reserved
8	interleave factor
9	BIOS flag byte
10	number of cylinders for alternative tracks
11	reserved
12–13	start cylinder of write precompensation
14–20	manufacturer's name (ASCII)
21–39	product name
40–511	reserved

Table 9.6. Structure of geometric information

The information starts with the signature 0dabeh so the controller can be sure that the sector concerned actually holds geometric information, and doesn't erroneously interpret some data bytes. As you can see from Table 9.6 all the required parameters are stored. Thus the controller only needs to read the first physical drive sector at power-up to determine the correct drive parameters.

9.3   Integrating Exotic Drives and Translating

If you look at the market for hard disk drives you'll see that a virtually infinite variety of different drive geometries exists. But BIOS and DOS need to know precisely how many sectors per track, cylinders and heads the installed hard disk has to access it correctly. The PC implements two possibilities for integrating non-standardized drives: function 09h of INT 13h, and BIOS extensions.

9.3.1   BIOS Interrupt 13h, Function 09h Set Drive Parameters

In the CMOS RAM you store information concerning the hard disk type by selecting the corresponding hard disk type with the setup program. Then the BIOS looks for the accompanying drive parameters which are stored in an internal BIOS table. Perhaps you have already noticed that most setup programs also have, besides many «in-built» hard disks one free entry that you can fill with the number of heads, cylinders, etc. of your drive, that is, all those parameters which unambiguously characterize your hard disk. But how does the BIOS process such an entry? The key is the function 09h *set drive parameters* of interrupt 13h as well as interrupts 41h and 46h that point to parameter tables. In this way you can also integrate quite exotic hard disks into your system.

The entries for interrupts 41h and 46h in the interrupt table, however, don't point to a handler (that is, executable program code) which can be called by means of an INT instruction; the instruction INT 41h would lead to a system crash immediately. Instead, the addresses segment:offset point to two tables with the user-defined geometry parameters of the hard disks concerned. Interrupt 41h is reserved for the first hard disk, interrupt 46h for the second. The tables have 16 bytes, and are called *hard disk parameter tables*. Figure 9.11 shows the structure of these tables.

Figure 9.11: Hard disk parameter table.

The entries *number of cylinders* and *number of heads* define the geometry. After formatting, the number of sectors per track is unambiguously defined by the generated address marks so that this information is not required. The values for *start cylinder of reduced write current* and *start cylinder of precompensation* control the write current and the precompensation (see Section 9.1.3). The *maximum ECC data burst length* defines the length of burst errors which can be corrected using the ECC code used. Usually, this value is equal to 11. The *control byte* determines the controller's behaviour in the case of an error. With the three *time-out* values you inform the BIOS when, depending upon the process concerned, it should report a time-out error. The last four bytes of the table are reserved, and should always be set to 0.

During the course of a call to function 09h of interrupt INT 13h, the handler reads the address corresponding to interrupt 41h or 46h and determines the entries in the tables. For all accesses to the first or second hard disk, the BIOS then uses the geometries as they are indicated in the tables. If you replace the addresses stored in the interrupt table for interrupts 41h and 46h by the addresses in your own tables, you can integrate hard disks with nearly any geometry into the system. But this, of course, is only possible if controller and hard disk use the same recording method (for example MFM or RLL 2,7) and the same interface format as the ST412/506, AT-Bus, etc. Otherwise, the combination is impossible for physical reasons.

To integrate an exotic hard disk into your system so that the BIOS and DOS are able to access it, you must therefore first generate the corresponding hard disk parameter table, store the address of that table in the entry for interrupt 41h or 46h in the interrupt table, and then call function 09h of interrupt INT 13h. Also, the BIOS start routine does the same when initializing the hard disks. It reads the hard disk parameters from the CMOS RAM and generates one or two tables for INT 41h or INT 46h using this information, depending upon how many drives are installed. Afterwards, the start routine calls function 09h of INT 13h and the drive parameters are now available to the system.

Inversely, you can also determine the parameters of a connected hard disk by function 08h of INT 13h, for example, when you attempt to check whether the BIOS has carried out the integration correctly. Format and return values of this function are indicated in Appendix F.

9.3.2   BIOS Extensions and Booting

The execution of an INT 13h function for an MFM-encoded disk with an IDE interface can be very different from that for an SCSI hard disk with the SCSI command set defined by ANSI. If you replace your old MFM disk by a modern SCSI disk, then you would also need to replace the BIOS. But the PC's designers had a better idea to avoid such problems, one which is more suited for the open concept of the PC: so-called *BIOS* or *ROM extensions*. As you know, the PC and XT didn't have a hard disk as a standard; only the AT was already prepared for such a drive. Thus the PC/XT BIOS doesn't implement any INT 13h functions for hard disks, only floppy drive functions. At the time when the AT came onto the market, the ST412/502 interface was the measure to live up to. Thus in the AT BIOS the access to such a hard disk with an AT bus interface is already implemented. If you attempt to expand a PC/XT with a hard disk you must use a controller with its own hard disk BIOS; for the AT, a controller without BIOS is sufficient. Without a BIOS extension the PC/XT ignores all hard disk accesses; controller and drive thus seem to be dead.

Now you can see why BIOS functions are called by interrupts: to replace the former routines stored in the old BIOS by the new ones of the BIOS extension, only the interrupt address has to be altered so it points to the BIOS extension. This *interception* is carried out during the course of the boot process. As you know, all ROM chips with the BIOS are located between the segment addresses c000h and ffffh. The area above f600h is reserved for the standard BIOS with startup routines. To additionally detect installed BIOS extensions, the startup routine scans the segment area between c000h and f5ffh in steps of 2 kbytes during system initialization. This searching for BIOS extensions and their initialization is shown in Figure 9.12.

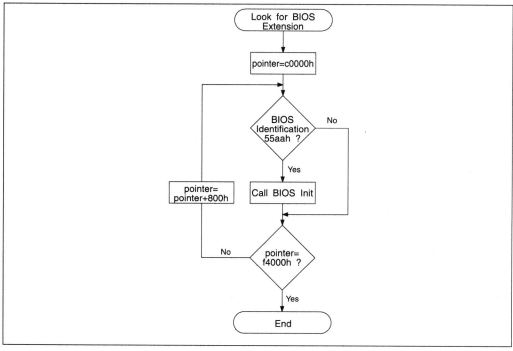

Figure 9.12: Integrating a BIOS extension.

Note that BIOS extensions always begin with the identifier 55aah. If the initialization routine detects such an identifier then the BIOS extension is initialized. Figure 9.13 shows the structure of this 5-byte header of BIOS extensions.

```
00h ┌─────────────────────────────────────┐
    │ ROM identifier 55aah                │
    │                          (2 bytes)  │
02h ├─────────────────────────────────────┤
    │ ROM size in units of 512-byte       │
    │ blocks                   (2 bytes)  │
04h ├─────────────────────────────────────┤
    │ start of initialization (1 byte)    │
    └─────────────────────────────────────┘
```

Figure 9.13: BIOS identifier.

The first two bytes accommodate the ROM BIOS identifier 55aah. The two following bytes specify the size of the ROM extension in units of 512-byte blocks. Finally, the 5th byte holds the start address of the initialization routine for the BIOS extension as an offset relative to the ROM beginning. Note that according to the IBM standard the sum of all bytes in the ROM extension, determined by the number of the 512-byte blocks in the BIOS identifier, must be equal to 0. Thus every ROM extension has at least one check byte so that the sum actually has a value of 0.

Example: Scan ROM area from segment c000h to f400h and call initialization routine if present (language: Microsoft C 5.10).

```
main()
{ unsigned char far *rom_pointer;
  void far *init_pointer();
  unsigned char sum;

  rom_pointer = 0xc0000;                   /* initialize rom_pointer to beginning of ROM area */
  while(rom_pointer < 0xf6000) {           /* scan while rom_pointer is in the range between */
                                           /* c000:0000 and f400:1fff */
    if ((int) *rom_pointer == 0x55aa) {    /* check for BIOS identifier */
      blocks = (unsigned int) *rom_pointer /* determine number of 512-byte blocks */
      sum = checksum(rom_pointer, blocks); /* check whether checksum is equal to 0 */
      if (sum == 0) {                      /* yes, checksum is equal to 0 */
        init_pointer = rom_pointer+4;      /* load start address of initialization routine */
        init_pointer();                    /* call initialization routine */
      }
    }
    rom_pointer = rom_pointer+0x800;       /* next block 2kbyte later */
  }

  exit(0);                                 /* end */
}

unsigned char check_sum(rom_pointer, blocks)
  unsigned far *rom_pointer;
  unsigned int blocks;

{ unsigned char sum;
  unsigned int index, blocknr;

  sum=0                                                   /* initialize sum */
  for (blocknr = 0; blocknr < blocks; blocknr++) {        /* scan all blocks */
    for (index = 0; index < 512; index++, rom_pointer++) { /* block size equal to 512 bytes */
      sum = sum + *rom_pointer;                            /* form checksum, ignore carry */
    }
  }
  return(sum);                                            /* return checksum */
}
```

The initialization routine of the BIOS extension now executes an initialization, which refers to the BIOS extension itself and the peripherals which the extension is to serve. The initialization routine completes the integration of the BIOS extension by detouring one or more interrupts to routines that are part of the BIOS extension. All BIOS extensions on hard disk controllers detour, for example, the existing INT 13h for floppy drives integrated into the BIOS on the motherboard to interrupt 40h. If a program issues an interrupt 13h then the BIOS first checks whether a request to a hard disk or a floppy drive has occurred. If the program wants to access a hard disk then the BIOS extension proceeds with the execution of the intended routine; otherwise it branches to interrupt 40h, which now carries out the function for the floppy drive concerned.

By means of the engagement of BIOS extensions the standard routines of the BIOS on the system board have been replaced by the new routines of the BIOS extension on the new controller. According to this scheme, the BIOS extension of, for example, an SCSI host adapter replaces INT 13h of the system BIOS in an AT. Therefore, you may access an SCSI hard disk drive using INT 13h in the conventional manner. With the help of a suitable BIOS extension, a tape drive can also be programmed as a floppy drive, for example. The engaged BIOS routines convert the commands for hard disk or floppy drives into commands for tape drives.

By means of function 08h of interrupt 13h you can determine the format of the hard disk in which it appears to the system. This is particularly important for high-capacity hard disks with more than 1024 tracks, or a variable number of sectors per track. Such hard disks appear to the system with a completely different geometry to that which the drive actually has. The 08h function converts the «hard disk» drive into a transparent peripheral.

Example: My SCSI hard disk with 105 Mbytes storage capacity comprises physically six heads, an outer group with 831 cylinders, and 35 sectors per track, as well as an inner group with 188 cylinders and 28 sectors per track. But to the BIOS and the user the drive appears as a hard disk with 12 heads, 1005 cylinders and 17 sectors per track.

But the BIOS extension is not only effective when installing a new hard disk drive. It is a very general and therefore also a very powerful concept. For example, the BIOS extension on EGA and VGA adapters replaces the INT 10h of the standard BIOS to make the specialized and powerful functions of these graphics adapters available to the system. The BIOS on the mother-board recognizes only the simple, and for programmers, not very exciting functions of the monochrome and CGA adapters. On the other hand, EGA and VGA boards support many functions on a hardware base (for example, scrolling of the screen contents or zooming of several sections). With older adapters these functions had to be programmed by software, and were thus quite slow. Very new graphics adapters with a graphics processor or a video RAM of more than 128 kbytes cannot be accessed conventionally. They need their own BIOS, as the interface to the PC system bus is incompatible with conventional adapters. The open and powerful concept of BIOS extensions enables the integration of such graphics adapters into a PC without any problems. As long as you remain on a BIOS level, no difficulties arise; the BIOS extension handles all the problems. That is, of course, no longer the case if you program the adapter directly using the registers. For graphics adapters, *de facto* standards are not yet established to the same extent as is the case for floppy and hard disk controllers concerning addresses and the meanings of the registers. BIOS extensions for hard disks usually start at address c800:0000, those for graphics adapters at c000:0000. In most cases, you can alter the start address of ROMs extensions by means of a jumper on the adapter board. This is useful if two ROMs disturb each other.

It is not impossible that certain BIOS variants are more powerful than others. Particularly with new technical developments, it takes some time for a standard to become established. For example, all 8086/88 machines don't recognize an interrupt 15h/function 89h for switching the processor into protected mode, as the 8086/88 CPU is not capable of this. If you attempt to detect by software whether a BIOS supports certain functions, this can get quite laborious and error-prone. Depending upon the quality of the BIOS, it returns an error message, the registers are not changed, or the registers are filled with unpredictable values.

As already mentioned, compatibility on a register level among various interface and drive specifications is very rare. But within a certain type the controllers and floppy/hard disk drives fortunately get along with one another, in most cases. You may, for example, connect a no-name controller with an ST412 interface for RLL drives to an NEC RLL hard disk with an ST412 interface without problems, and access it by means of the AT system BIOS.

9.3.3 Translating and Zone Recording

You may know that the circumference of a circle rises with increasing radius. Applied to hard disks, this means that the length of a track gets larger the lower the cylinder number is, because the outermost cylinder with the largest diameter is assigned the number 0 and the innermost cylinder with the smallest diameter has the highest possible number.

But now the number of bytes per track is dependent upon the length of the track, that is, the circumference of the cylinder, and thus the cylinder number. It seems absurd to fill the large outer cylinders only with the same number of sectors as the smaller inner ones: the outer sectors would be elongated by this. To use the storage capacity of a disk best it would be more favourable, therefore, to raise the number of sectors per cylinder with increasing cylinder diameter. However, this gives rise to the fact that the fixed number of sectors per track must be given up. Accordingly, the BIOS functions become more complicated as you must additionally know for every hard disk how many sectors each cylinder accommodates.

Thus, simpler unintelligent drives without their own controller are content with a fixed number of sectors per track throughout the whole disk. High-quality and intelligent drives such as SCSI and AT bus hard disks, on the other hand, carry out such a conversion. These drives have their own controller which is fixed to the drive and is no longer inserted as an additional board into a bus slot. The connection to the host is established by a so-called *host adapter*, which is often but erroneously called a controller. The controller now knows which track accommodates how many sectors; but to the user the disk appears on a BIOS level homogenously with a fixed number of sectors per track. This means that the controller converts the indicated values for head, cylinder, sector of a BIOS call into the actual values for head, cylinder, sector on the hard disk without any external intervention. This process is completely hidden from the user. Usually you can't affect this *translation* even on a register level, but some IDE hard disk drives allow a variable translation.

In practice, a hard disk is usually divided into an inner and an outer zone which each have a fixed number of sectors per track. Thus the number of sectors per track changes only from zone to zone, and not from track to track. This is called *zone recording*.

Because of the extensive translation, the logical format used by the BIOS has virtually nothing to do with the actual physical format. But this seems to be more complicated than it really is. A controller separated from the drive, as was usual a few years ago, must of course be able to control many different drives. But a controller that is integrated into the drive's case can best be adapted to this single hard disk on which it is mounted. The rapidly falling prices in the field of microelectronics now means that every hard disk has its own controller without raising the costs too much.

But the BIOS (and also you as the programmer) want to know, of course, with which geometrical format you can now access the hard disk. For this purpose, function 08h *determine drive parameters* of interrupt INT 13h is also implemented. The function returns the geometric parameters that you can use for accessing the hard disk. The function call is carried out by the BIOS on the host adapter of the intelligent hard disk which has intercepted the already existing interrupt 13h at power-up.

When you look at the hard disk functions of INT 13h in Appendix F, you can see that the cylinder number has only 10 bits. Only 1024 cylinders can thus be represented, while powerful ESDI or SCSI drives accommodate far more cylinders. The ESDI interface is designed for up to 4096 cylinders as standard. With translation, the BIOS can be altered in such a way that 4096 cylinders can actually be accessed. For this purpose, translating increases the virtual head number until the cylinder number has been decreased to 1024 or less. The increase of the head number together with the decrease of the cylinder number keeps the drive capacity constant, and makes it possible for the physical cylinders beyond 1024 to be accessed via the BIOS in the same format as before.

Another note on translation and the formatting of hard disks. During the course of a low-level formatting the controller generates sectors and tracks on the data carrier. Depending upon the translation and the boundary between the areas of different sector numbers per track, different formatting parameters must be passed to the controller. The conversion of BIOS sectors and the physical sectors on disk within the controller does not depend on any rule from the hard disk used: there is no standard which determines how many sectors per track must be generated up to which track, etc. If you now try to format such a hard disk by means of direct register commands, then you will usually cause chaos, but nothing more. SCSI and IDE hard disks therefore always come preformatted, and can be successfully reformatted on a low level by the user only in some rare cases. Even professional utilities such as DiskManager, Spinrite or Norton Utilities usually assume a fixed format. These very popular and useful utilities for conventional hard disks cannot be employed here. It's best to refrain from such formatting attempts if you are not absolutely (really 100%) sure that you know everything about the translating of your hard disk, and you are also absolutely sure that your formatting routine is free of any bugs.

Also, be somewhat sceptical when interpreting benchmark results concerning, for example, the access time of a hard disk whose controller carries out translation. In many head positionings the logical head only «moves» one track but the physical one remains on the same track. On the other hand, it is also possible that the physical head is moved although the program accesses only a single logical track, for example to read a complete track. The access times and transfer rate determined may therefore differ from the actual properties of the investigated drive.

9.4 Access via DOS and the BIOS

The variety of hard disk interfaces unavoidably gives rise to incompatibilities. Here the hierarchical access scheme DOS-BIOS-register comes to the rescue again, because you can access logical sectors by the two DOS interrupts 25h and 26h, and physical sectors via the BIOS interrupt 13h, without the need to take the interface actually used into account in detail. Of course, you achieve a higher execution speed with direct register programming, and you can further use the features of the interface concerned which are not accessible with the BIOS. The BIOS standard functions orient to the first XT and AT models, and cannot, in the nature of things, cope with the much more advanced ESDI, IDE or SCSI interfaces. For programs that are to be executed on as many PCs as possible and have to be compatible (unfortunately reduced to a common denominator), the DOS interrupts 25h and 26h as well as the BIOS interrupt 13h are indispensable.

9.4.1   DOS Interrupts 25h and 26h

With the DOS interrupts 25h and 26h (already presented in Chapter 8 in connection with floppy drives), you can read and write the logical sectors within the DOS partition. Thus you may access all data areas, including the boot sector and the FAT. The partition table as well as other partitions, however, remain unreachable. The calling procedure for the two interrupts in the case of sectors with numbers lower than 65 536 is the same as already discussed in this chapter.

partitions up to 32 Mbyte or 65536 sectors
INT 25h – read logical sector(s)   INT 26h – write logical sector(s)

register	call value	return value	register	call value	return value
AL	drive number[1]		AL	drive number[1]	
AX		error code[2]	AX		error code[2]
CX	number of sectors		CX	number of sectors	
DX	first sector		DX	first sector	
BX	offset read buffer		BX	offset write buffer	
DS	segment read buffer		DS	segment write buffer	
Carry		error when <> 0	Carry		error when <> 0

[1] value 0 = drive A, value 1 = drive B, etc.
[2] see Table 9.7

partitions larger than 32 Mbyte or more than 65536 sectors
INT 25h – read logical sector(s)   INT 26h – write logical sector(s)

register	call value	return value	register	call value	return value
AL	drive number[1]		AL	drive number[1]	
AX		error code[2]	AX		error code[2]
CX	0ffffh		CX	0ffffh	
DX			DX		
BX	offset parameter[3]		BX	offset parameter[3]	
DS	segment parameter[3]		DS	segment parameter[3]	
Carry		error when <> 0	Carry		error when <> 0

[1] value 0 = drive A, value 1 = drive B, etc.
[2] see Table 9.7
[3] parameter block

first sector (4 bytes)
number of sectors   (2 bytes)
address of read/write buffer (4 bytes)

Figure 9.14: INT 25h and INT 26h calling formats.

But with DOS 4.00 a new calling format was introduced to serve partitions comprising more than 65 536 sectors or 32 Mbytes. Figure 9.14 shows the two calling formats with and without the new parameter block.

When using interrupts 25h and 26h, note that they leave a status byte on the stack that you must remove with a POP instruction. If the intended sector cannot be read or written for some reason, then DOS sets the carry flag and returns an error code in register ax, indicating the cause of the failed read or write attempt. Table 9.7 lists the valid error codes.

Code	Error
01h	invalid command
02h	incorrect address mark
04h	sector not found
08h	DMA overflow
10h	CRC or ECC error
20h	controller error
40h	seek error
80h	drive not ready

Table 9.7: INT 25h and INT 26h error codes

The following sections discuss only the extended function call via the new parameter block for accessing sectors with a number beyond 65 535. The conventional calling format is discussed in Chapter 8.

According to an entry ffffh in the register cx, DOS 4.00 and above recognizes that the extended calling format is to be used. The calling program must pass the offset and segment of the parameter block in the registers bx and ds for this purpose. The parameter block defines the first sector, the number of sectors, and the address of the read or write buffer for these sectors. With the conventional format these quantities are passed by registers cx, dx, bx and ds. Now the use of the extended form is explained using an example.

Example: Read three sectors beginning with sector 189,063 from hard disk C: (language: Microsoft C 5.10).

```
type parm_block {
  unsigned long start_sector;
  unsigned num_of_sectors;
  char far *buffer;
}

main()
{
  union REGS inregs, outregs;
  struct SREGS segregs;
  struct far parm_block p_block;

  /* construct parameter block */
  p_block.start_sector = 189063;
  p_block.num_of_sectors = 3;
```

```
p_block.buffer = (char far *) _fmalloc(1536);  /* buffer for three sectors */

/* call function */
inregs.h.al = 0x02;                            /* drive C: */
inregs.x.cx = 0xffff;                          /* extended calling format */
inregs.x.bx = FP_OFF(p_block);                 /* transfer parameter block offset into bx */
segregs.ds = FP_SEG(p_block);                  /* transfer parameter block segment into ds */
int86x(0x25, &inregs, &outregs, &segregs);     /* call interrupt, sectors are read into */
                                               /* p_block.buffer */

if ((outregs.x.cflag & 0x01) == 0x01) {        /* check whether carry is set */
  printf("\nError code: %x", outregs.x.ax);    /* display error code */
  exit(1);                                     /* abort with ERRORLEVEL 1 */
}

.......................................        /* process read sectors */

  exit(0);
}
```

9.4.2   Hard Disk Functions of BIOS Interrupt 13h

This section briefly discusses the most important functions of INT 13h that you haven't already met in connection with the floppy drives, or which differ significantly from that case. All functions are summarized in Appendix F.

When the BIOS has completed the requested function it indicates (by means of the carry flag) whether the operation could be carried out successfully. If the carry flag is set (CF = 1) then an error has occurred and register ah contains the error code. You will find all possible error codes and their meaning in Appendix F.2. Note that not all codes are valid for both floppy and hard disk; because of their more elaborate intelligence, hard disk controllers can classify the errors in more detail.

Note also that for the hard disk functions the two most significant bits of the sector register cl represent the two most significant bits of a 10-bit cylinder number which is composed of the two cl bits mentioned and the eight bits of the cylinder register ch. Thus you may access a maximum of 1024 cylinders by means of the BIOS.

You must *never* call any of functions listed below which refer to the formatting of a track or whole drive if you use an embedded controller or a drive which carries out translation. By doing this you would only disturb the internal management of the tracks and the translation, or even the bad-sector mapping of these intelligent drives. I cannot to predict the consequences for every drive, but take into consideration that a logical track as you can access it via the BIOS may possibly be only part of a physical track, or may be distributed over two tracks or even two cylinders. If you attempt to format such a partial track or a divided track, then this can only fail, of course.

– Function 05h – Format Track or Cylinder

Unlike floppy drives, in the case of hard disks the interleave is also of importance. You may adjust the interleave factor using the format buffer. It successively contains the track, head, sector number and sector size entries in the same way as they are written into the address field of the sector concerned of an ST412/506 hard disk. Note that you can only format a complete track, not individual sectors. The BIOS passes the controller the entries in the format buffer for every sector to format. If you don't count up the sector number by one from entry to entry, but arrange it in such a way that it corresponds to the intended interleave value, then you also achieve a corresponding sector shift (that is, interleaving) on the hard disk. Thus you may alter the interleave value for a track without any major problems, for example to determine the optimum interleave factor.

Advice: if you own an already preformatted hard disk that carries out translation then you must never call this function.

The drive may behave completely unpredictably, especially if you alter the interleave value. The number of sectors per track with which the drive appears to the system, and therefore to your program, has nothing to do with the drive's actual geometry. If you attempt to format a certain (logical) track with function 05h you may refer to some unintended location on the disk or even cross a cylinder boundary. You can imagine that you would cause confusion.

Example: Format track 0 of the first hard disk with interleave 3 (language: Microsoft C 5.10).

```
type format_buffer {
  unsigned char cyl;
  unsigned char head;
  unsigned char sector;
  unsigned char byte_p_sector;
}

struct far format_buffer f_buffer[17];   /* format buffer for 17 sectors */
int sector;

/* construct format buffer */
for (sector = 0; sector < 17; sector++) {
  f_buffer[sector].cyl = 0;               /* cylinder 0 */
  f_buffer[sector].head = 0;              /* track 0 */
  f_buffer[sector].byte_p_sector = 0x02;  /* 512 bytes per sector */
}
/* set interleave 3:1 */
f_buffer[0].sector = 0, f_buffer[1].sector = 6, f_buffer[2].sector = 12;
f_buffer[3].sector = 1, f_buffer[4].sector = 7, f_buffer[5].sector = 13;
f_buffer[6].sector = 2, f_buffer[7].sector = 8, f_buffer[8].sector = 14;
f_buffer[9].sector = 3, f_buffer[10].sector = 9, f_buffer[11].sector = 15;
f_buffer[12].sector = 4, f_buffer[13].sector = 10, f_buffer[14].sector = 16;
f_buffer[15].sector = 5, f_buffer[16].sector = 11;

inregs.h.al = 17;                    /* 17 sectors per track */
inregs.h.ch = 0x00;                  /* cylinder 0 */
inregs.h.dh = 0x00;                  /* Head 0 according to track 0 */
inregs.h.dl = 0x80;                  /* first hard disk */
```

```
segregs.es = FP_SEG(f_buffer);          /* segment address of format buffer */

for (sector = 0; sector < 17; sector++) {
  inregs.h.ah = 0x05;                   /* function 05h */
  inregs.h.cl = sector;
  inregs.x.bx = FP_OFF(f_buffer);       /* offset address of format buffer */
  int86x(0x13, &inregs, &outregs);      /* format sector by means of interrupt 13h */
  f_buffer++;                           /* next entry in format buffer */
}
```

– Function 06h – Format and Mark Bad Track

This function manages bad tracks within the frame of the bad-sector mapping if the track has more than one defect sector, and thus the whole track is unusable. The 06h function writes address marks onto the track whose flags indicate a defective track. The controller then skips this track for data recording and assigns an alternative track automatically. The function can be employed only for ST412/506 controllers and drives. Intelligent hard disks with an embedded controller and translation carry out the bad-sector mapping automatically. Unlike function 05h, you may pass the interleave value directly via register ah. You don't need a format buffer; no rearrangement of the sector numbers in that buffer according to the interleave value is therefore required.

Advice: never use this function if your drive has its own controller or carries out translation.

The BIOS track length doesn't coincide with the physical track length if translation is in force. Therefore, you would only mark part of the track as bad, or two partial tracks if a cylinder boundary is crossed. What your controller does with your drive in this case is unknown.

Example: Mark bad drive 80h, cylinder 951, head 2 with interleave 2.

```
inregs.h.al = 2;                        /* interleave 2 */
inregs.h.ch = 183;                      /* 8 low-order cylinder bits */
inregs.h.dh = 2;                        /* head 2 */
inregs.h.dl = 0x80;                     /* first hard disk */
for (sector = 0; sector < 17; sector++) {
  inregs.h.ah = 0x06;                   /* function 06h */
  inregs.h.cl = 0xc0 + sector;          /* 2 high-order cylinder bits plus 6 sector bits */
  int86x(0x13, &inregs, &outregs);      /* mark track by means of interrupt 13h */
}
```

– Function 07h – Format and Mark Drive

This command formats the complete drive, from the start cylinder indicated up to the physical end of the drive. For the formatting process, the interleave value passed in register al is used. Set the head and sector number in registers cl and dh to a value of 0 so that the formatting procedure starts at the beginning, and not in the middle of the start cylinder.

Example: Format drive 81h beginning with cylinder 100 (interleave=3).

```
inregs.h.ah = 0x07;                     /* function 07h */
inregs.h.al = 3;                        /* interleave 3 */
inregs.h.ch = 100;                      /* 8 low-order cylinder bits */
inregs.h.cl = 0;                        /* 2 high-order cylinder bits plus sector 0 */
```

```
inregs.h.dh = 0;                    /* head 0 */
inregs.h.dl = 0x81;                 /* second hard disk */

int86x(0x13, &inregs, &outregs);    /* format drive */
```

Advice: never use this function if your drive has its own controller or carries out translation.

Functions 08h (determine drive parameters) and 09h (set drive parameters) are discussed in Section 9.3.

The following INT 13h functions are described in Appendix F:

- function 08h – determine drive parameters
- function 09h – set drive parameters
- function 0ah – read extended sectors
- function 0bh – write extended sectors
- function 0ch – seek
- function 0dh – hard disk reset
- function 0eh – read sector buffer
- function 0fh – write sector buffer
- function 10h – check drive ready
- function 11h – recalibrate drive
- function 19h – park read/write heads

The functions *12h (check controller RAM)* and *13h (controller diagnostics)* listed in Appendix F are not implemented for all BIOS variants. Table 9.8 shows the BIOS data area as far as hard disks and hard disk operations are concerned.

Address	Size	Structure 76543210	Contents	Meaning
40:74	byte		status of last hard disk operation	see app. F.2
40:75	byte		number of installed hard disks	
40:76	byte		control byte of hard disk	
40:77	byte		offset address of hard disk port	
40:8c	byte	0	status of hard disk controller	command phase
		0		controller transmits data
		1		IRQ of controller
		1		DRQ of controller
		1		controller selected (active)
		1		data phase
		1		controller receives data
		1		controller ready
40:8d	byte		error code of hard disk controller	see Table 9.9
40:8e	byte	1	IRQ/DMA control of hard disk controller	IRQ enabled
		1		DMA enabled

Table 9.8: BIOS data area for hard disks

The controller error codes differ from the error codes which are returned by the BIOS. Table 9.9 shows the valid controller error codes.

Code	Description	Code	Description
00h	no error	19h	bad track without alternative track
02h	no seek signal	1ah	error reading data
03h	write error	1bh	error writing data
04h	drive not ready	1ch	alternative track not marked
06h	track 0 not found	1dh	squencer error
10h	ECC error in ID field	1eh	invalid access to alternative track
11h	ECC error in data field	20h	invalid opcode
12h	no ID address mark found	21h	invalid logical block address
13h	no data address mark found	22h	invalid parameter
14h	no ID field	23h	overflow of defect list
15h	seek error	30h	error in sector buffer
16h	internal controller error	31h	ROM check error
17h	DMA error	33h	internal microprocessor error
18h	correctable data error		

Table 9.9: Controller error codes

Finally, I want to mention that the BIOS detours all floppy calls internally to interrupt INT 40h if a hard disk is installed, or if a hard disk BIOS replaces INT 13h during the course of the boot process. For this purpose, the interrupt vector of INT 13h is moved to INT 40h. This causes the handler of INT 13h always to check first whether the request refers to a hard disk or a floppy drive. In the first case, the function call is processed within that handler. In the latter case, the handler issues (via instruction INT 40h) another software interrupt. The INT 40h handler comprises all necessary routines to serve the function call for a floppy drive.

9.5   ST412/506 and ESDI

The interface most widely in use is still the ST412/506, but it is more and more being superseded by the IDE or AT bus. Because of the close relationship between ESDI and ST412/506, both are discussed. An extensive description of every detail would go beyond the scope of this book.

9.5.1   ST412/506 Interfaces and the Connection Between Drive and Controller

The name ST412/506 interface has a historical background. Seagate introduced the ST506 system in 1980 with a storage capacity of 5 Mbytes and a strictly defined interface to the controller. One year later, in 1981, the successor model ST412 system with a storage capacity of 10 Mbytes and a slightly altered interface came onto the market. The interface concept was adapted by IBM for the PC and is known today as the ST412/506 interface.

For the transfer rate between drive and controller the ST412/506 standard *requires* a value of 5 Mbits/s for MFM encoding and 7.5 Mbits/s for RLL encoding. These values must not be under stood as a minimum specification but as an «exact» specification. The 5 Mbits/s and 7.5 Mbits/s, respectively, also contain, besides the actual data bit, address marks, CRC and ECC bytes, as well as gap bits.

With a sector length of about 575 bytes, MFM-encoded hard disks with an ST412/506 interface can thus accommodate 17 sectors and RLL-encoded hard disks 26 sectors per track. An increase of the sector density, which is technically quite easy today, would be a Pyrrhic victory as the required transfer rate of 5 Mbits/s or 7.5 Mbits/s doesn't allow any more sectors. The only solution is the use of another interface such as ESDI, IDE or SCSI.

Although ST412/506, strictly speaking, only defines the interface between drive and controller, but doesn't make any assumption for the integration of controller and drive into the PC system, the following configuration has been established. The controller is located on a separate adapter card which is inserted into a bus slot; a maximum of two hard disk drives are connected to the controller by a control and data cable. The controller adapter card establishes a connection to the PC bus simultaneously; a host adapter is not required here. Many ST412/506 controllers also accommodate a floppy controller besides the hard disk interface; they are then called a *combicontroller*. Unlike floppies, where the connection between drive and controller was effected by a single flat conductor cable, in the hard disk system the control and data signals run through separate cables. The wider cable with 34 wires is the control cable, and the narrow one with only 20 wires the data cable. Figure 9.15 shows the assignment of the corresponding wires.

You can connect a maximum of two hard disks with the control cable. On the other hand, for every hard disk its own data cable is necessary. Note also that for hard disks control cables which have twisted wires between the plug in the middle and the end of the cable (similar to the cable for floppy drives) do exist. But unlike floppies, wires 25–29 are twisted here. Therefore, don't mix the control cables for hard disks and for floppy drives; the cables for floppy drives have twisted wires 10–16. From Figure 9.15 you can see that the control cable for the ST412/506 interface is designed for up to four drives. But on the PC, the signals *drive select 3* and *drive select 4* are not used, so you may connect a maximum of two hard disks. Among all hard disk interfaces used on the PC, the ST412/506 is the least «intelligent». It is a pure signal interface, thus the controller is unable to pass any command to the drive. The drive itself accommodates only the control circuitry for stabilizing the disk rotation and the head positioning. All other control functions are carried out by the controller itself, for example interpretation of the commands from the PC system, the encoding and decoding of the read and write data, the generation of address marks, etc. This means that the controller passes the drive the write data immediately in the form the head writes them onto disk. In the drive itself, neither a synchronization of the signals nor any improvement in the pulse forms of the write pulses is carried out.

ST412/506 controllers and drives were used first in the XT, and later also in the AT. Because the XT BIOS was not designed as standard for the support of hard disks, all XT controllers must have their own BIOS with the hard disk functions of INT 13h. The start address of this BIOS extension is usually c8000h. The AT, on the other hand, supported hard disks from the first day, and the required routines are already implemented in the system BIOS at address f0000h. But there are other differences between XT and AT controllers with an ST412/506 interface:

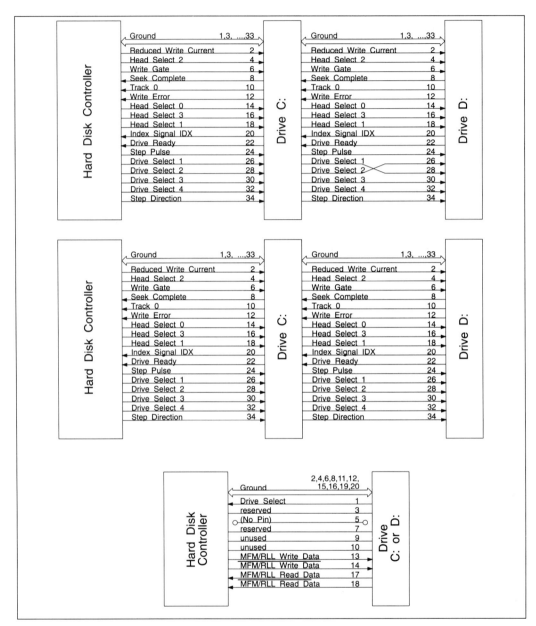

Figure 9.15: ST412/506 interface control and signal cable. The drives are connected to the controller with a control cable with 34 wires, and a data cable with 20 wires.

– The XT controller uses DMA channel 3 for transferring data between sector buffer and main memory; in the AT, on the other hand, the BIOS carries out a programmed I/O by means of the port instructions IN and OUT without using any DMA channel.

– The XT controller employs IRQ5 for issuing a hardware interrupt, the AT controller IRQ14.

– The XT controller is accessed via the XT task file, the AT controller via the AT task file; the register assignment and addresses of these two task files are incompatible; drivers for XT hard disk controllers with an ST412/506 interface cannot be used for an AT controller.

– The commands for an XT controller always consist of a 6-byte command block to a single register; the AT controller, on the other hand, is programmed by means of single command bytes to several individual registers.

You will find a detailed description of the AT bus interface in Section 9.6. Today, XT hard disk controllers have nearly vanished from the market (as is the case for the XT itself). Therefore, the XT task file is not discussed in detail.

9.5.2 Connecting and Configuring ST412/506 Hard Disk Drives

One remark in advance: all plugs and cable connectors are identical for MFM and RLL hard disks with an ST412/506 interface; thus you can connect, for example, an RLL disk to an MFM controller. But the different transfer rates of 5 Mbits/s and 7.5 Mbits/s, as well as the different design of the electronics for MFM and RLL, lead to frequent read, write and seek errors. If you connect an MFM disk to an RLL controller, then this works even worse as the drive responds far too slowly to the RLL data pulses from the controller. In some unfavourable cases, electric equipment may be damaged because of the extensive design differences. Thus you may operate MFM hard disks only with an MFM controller, and RLL hard disks only with an RLL controller; mixtures between RLL and MFM are *never* allowed.

The connection of ST412/506 hard disks by means of the control cable to the controller is carried out in the same way as with floppy drives. You must connect the first hard disk to the end of the control cable, an eventual second hard disk to the connector in the middle. If you are using a control cable without twisted wires, then configure drive C: as *drive select 0* and drive D: as *drive select 1* by means of the corresponding jumpers on the drives. If you are using a control cable with twisted wires then you may configure both hard disks as *drive select 1*, as was the case for floppy drives. Because of the exchange of the select signals, the intended disk is always enabled. Don't forget, too, to remove the terminating resistor (if present) from drive D: in the middle. Finally, connect the data cable with the data connection of the drive and the data connector on the controller. The ST412/506 hard disk system is now configured correctly.

You will see that the data cables are normally much shorter than the control cables. The reason is that long cables are very sensitive to external noise as no shielded wires are used for the connection of drive and controller. The data runs at 5 Mhz between drive and controller, a range in which some other internal components of the computer are active (for example, the 4.77 MHz signal for the processor or the 8 Mhz bus clock). But external noise sources such as short-wave transmitters emit electromagnetic waves in this frequency range. The data cable as an antenna may receive these signals. By shortening the cable the antenna effect, and thus the influence of noise on the sensitive MFM and RLL signals, will be reduced. But this is hardly possible at higher frequencies or data transfer rates. Thus ESDI as the immediate successor of ST506/412 follows another concept.

9.5.3   The ESDI Interface

ESDI was conceived by Maxtor in 1983 as a powerful and intelligent successor to the ST412/506 interface. The main problem of the long transfer distances between hard disk and data separator was solved, in that ESDI already integrates the data separator on the drive. Thus, the asynchronous MFM or RLL data which gives rise to read and write errors if minor signal distortion occurs must not be transferred between drive and controller. Instead, synchronous NRZ data run through the cables, which are much more resistent against such signal alterations. The ESDI cables may be up to 3 m long.

ESDI is designed for a transfer rate of up to 24 Mbits/s between drive and controller; typically 10–15Mbits/s are achieved. A sector density of 34 sectors per track and interleave 1:1 leads to a maximum data transfer rate between drive and main memory of 1020 kbytes/s. ESDI hard disks are therefore high-end drives; for data encoding the RLL method is mainly used. Furthermore, an ESDI controller is intended for connecting up to seven ESDI drives, and may access hard disks with a maximum of 64 heads in four groups of 16 heads each, as well as a maximum of 4096 cylinders. The controller of its predecessor interface (ST412/506), on the other hand, only allowed a maximum of 16 heads and 1024 cylinders.

An ESDI controller may also pass complete commands which are decoded and executed by the drive. Therefore, it's obvious that an ESDI controller cannot be supported by the AT-BIOS; every ESDI adapter has its own BIOS extension with the hard disk functions of INT 13h and internal diagnostics and configuration routines for serving the connected ESDI drives. Although the ESDI controller may also pass complete commands, the generation of address marks, synchronization pattern, and the decoding of the NRZ into parallel bit data for the PC system bus is carried out by the controller. Thus an ESDI controller is neither a pure controller which takes over *all* control functions, nor a host adapter which solely establishes a connection to the system bus; instead, it is something like an intermediate product between controller and host adapter.

The following sections briefly discuss the ESDI signals and commands. The connection between ESDI controller and the drives is established, similar to the ST412/506 interface, by means of a common 34-wire control cable and an individual 20-wire data cable for every drive. To the ESDI control cable up to seven drives can be connected. Figure 9.16 shows the assignment of the control and data cable.

The controller selects one of the 16 heads with numbers 0–15 from a group of 16 heads by means of the lines $\overline{\text{head select } 2^3}$ to $\overline{\text{head select } 2^0}$. Note that the signals are complementary; for example, head 15 is selected by the signal combination 0000. ESDI drives may have up to four such groups, that is 64 heads. A certain group is selected by the command *select head group* (see below). The lines for the head select determine the head within the selected group. In a similar way, the controller can select one of the seven possible drives by means of the signals $\overline{\text{drive select } 2^2}$ to $\overline{\text{drive select } 2^0}$. These signals are also active low (complemented); thus drive 1 is selected by the signal combination 110. The signal combination 111 corresponding to drive address 0 means that the controller has currently not selected any drive. The two control signals $\overline{\text{write gate}}$ and $\overline{\text{read gate}}$ control the activation of the write and read gate in the selected drive so that data can be written by the controller onto or read from the data carrier. $\overline{\text{Index signal IDX}}$

indicates that the beginning-of-track mark has just passed below the head. The $\overline{\text{drive ready}}$ signal shows that the addressed hard disk is rotating at the indended rpm and is read to execute commands.

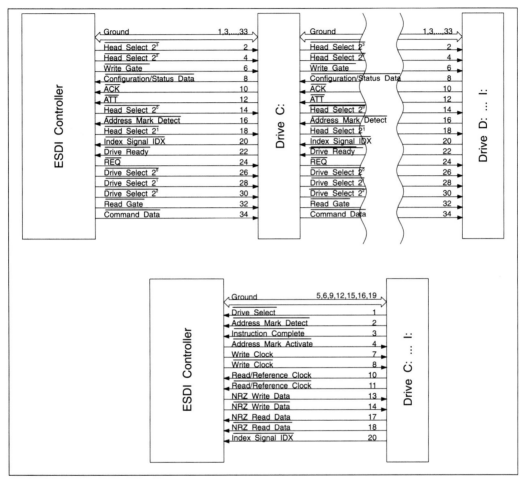

Figure 9.16. The ESDI cable. The drives are connected to the controller by means of a control cable with 34 wires and a data cable with 20 wires. Up to seven ESDI drives can be connected to a single ESDI controller.

The other signals implement the protocol for the command transfer to the selected drive and the return of status data from the addressed hard disk. The two signals $\overline{\text{ACK}}$ (acknowledge) and $\overline{\text{REQ}}$ (request) form the handshake signals for an ordered transfer of command and status data between controller and drive. The transfer is carried out in two cases:

– The controller passes a command to the selected drive; commands are always transferred via the line $\overline{\text{command data}}$ as a serial stream of 16 command bits plus one parity bit so that odd parity occurs; the handshake signals serve to agree on a correct course for this serial data transfer.

- The drive transfers status or configuration data to the controller; after a corresponding command the drive returns 16 status bits plus one parity bit (odd parity) via the line configuration/status data, which indicates the configuration of the addressed drive or the status of the last command.

Don't confuse this data transfer with the transfer of NRZ data between drive and controller via the data cable. The NRZ data is decoded in the controller, and is data that has been read from the hard disk or which is to be written onto it. On the contrary, the exchange of command, configuration and status data is carried out via the control cable, and the transferred data is neither written onto nor read from the disk. It is used exclusively by the hard disk control, or generated by this control for the controller.

The $\overline{\text{ATT}}$ (attention) signal is activated by the drive if an error occurs and the controller is to read the command status via the line configuration/status data. Finally, the signal address mark found indicates that the hard disk control has detected an address mark. The NRZ data now following on the data cable thus indicates the corresponding address.

The transfer of the read and write data from or to the addressed drive is carried out similar to ST412/506 via a separate data cable. But ESDI occupies far more wires with a signal. As is the case for ST412/506, the drive select signal indicates that the drive to which the data cable concerned is connected has been selected by the controller by means of the control lines $\overline{\text{drive select 2}^x}$. Accordingly, the address mark found signal shows that the drive has detected an address mark and the following NRZ data represents address data. By means of the signal activate address mark the drive is instructed to write the NRZ data passed afterwards as an address mark onto the data carrier. $\overline{\text{Index signal IDX}}$ indicates that the beginning-of-track mark has just passed below the head. When the drive has completed a command, it activates the line command complete to inform the controller that it can now read status data from the drive.

The other signals and lines of the data cable synchronize and transfer the NRZ data from or to the drive, and are always passed as complementary signals. The *NRZ write data* is transferred from the controller to the drive to write them onto the data carrier. On the contrary, during the course of a read process the drive transfers *NRZ read data* to the controller. The drive generates the *read/reference clock* to define the data transfer rate. ESDI, unlike ST506/412, doesn't fix the transfer rate to a certain value, but implements three different classes instead: transfer rate lower than 5 Mbits/s, between 5 Mbits/s and 10 Mbits/s and above 10 Mbits/s. Depending upon the requested class the connected controller must be more or less powerful. The drives can identify their transfer rates, corresponding to one of the classes, to the controller by means of a command. Usually, the BIOS extension on the ESDI adapter carries out this job to check whether the controller can service the connected drive or whether their transfer rate is too high. The read/reference clock then determines the transfer rate exactly. For this reason, the number of sectors per track is not so strictly defined with ESDI hard disks as is the case with the 17 or 26 sectors for the ST412/506 interface. ESDI disks usually have 34 sectors per track which corresponds to a transfer rate of about 10 Mbits/s. But high-end ESDI drives can accommodate up to 70 sectors per track if the connected controller can stand a transfer rate of 20 Mbits/s. Originally, ESDI was intended for a transfer rate of 15 Mbits/s at most, but this maximum value has recently been increased up to 24 Mbits/s. Only SCSI, with a maximum of 6 Mbytes/s equal to 48 Mbits/s in synchronous mode, provides an even higher data transfer rate. But note that all these values only refer to the transfer between controller and hard disk: they don't say anything about the speed at which the data can be shovelled into or out of main memory, however. All the remarks of Section 9.1.4 are also valid for ESDI.

The controller further generates the write clock from the read/reference clock, which determines at which speed the controller transfers the write data to the drive. Thus the term *reference clock* is quite correct. Unlike the read/reference clock, the write clock need not be active all the time; it is sufficient if the controller drives this line during write processes.

You can see that the ESDI interface between controller and drive is a mixture of a low-level interface because of the physical signals $\overline{\text{head select}}$ 2^3–2^0, $\overline{\text{drive select}}$ 2^2–2^0, $\overline{\text{ACK}}$, $\overline{\text{REQ}}$, etc., and a high-level interface because of the command and status codes. The ST412/506, on the other hand, is a purely physical interface, which is only realized by means of electrical signals; and SCSI is a high-level interface, as the complete drive control including drive selection is carried out with logical commands.

9.5.4 ESDI Commands and Configuration Data

The 16-bit ESDI commands appear in two formats, depending upon whether the controller passes command parameters. Figure 9.17 shows the ESDI command format.

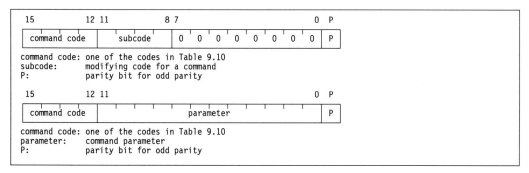

Figure 9.17: ESDI command data word.

Note that in addition to the 16 command bits a parity bit P is passed to generate odd parity. The following sections list the ESDI commands in brief to give an impression of the intelligence of this advanced interface. I have neglected an extensive description of every individual command in favour of the IDE and SCSI interface. Table 9.10 shows all the commands, as well as the accompanying command codes. According to the listed ESDI commands, you can clearly see that the ESDI controller is neither a pure controller, because it passes high-level commands (for example, *seek head* to the drive) and doesn't control the positioning itself by means of stepper pulses, nor a host adapter because, for example, no command *read sector* is implemented. To read a sector the ESDI controller must first transfer a seek-head command, and afterwards a parameter which indicates the intended track to the ESDI drive. When the drive has activated the line $\overline{\text{command complete}}$ on the data cable to indicate completion of the seek command then it is the job of the controller to observe the lines $\overline{\text{address mark found}}$ and $\overline{\text{NRZ read data}}$ to detect the address mark of the intended sector first, to filter the sector data out of the NRZ data stream, and to transfer it into the sector buffer afterwards. Thus the head positioning is carried out by means of a command, as is the case with a host adapter. The following sector data read, though, is executed in the same way as with a conventional controller. ESDI thus achieves much higher performance data than an ST412/506 drive, but is nowhere near as flexibile as the SCSI.

Command code	Subcode	Parameter	Command name
0 0 0 0	no	yes	seek head
0 0 0 1	no	no	calibrate drive
0 0 1 0	yes	no	request sense
0 1 0 0	yes	no	request configuration
0 1 0 1	no	yes	select head group
0 1 1 0	yes	no	control drive
0 1 1 1	yes	no	set data sense offset
1 0 0 0	yes	no	set track offset
1 0 0 1	no	yes	start diagnostics
1 0 1 0	no	yes	set byte/sector
1 1 1 0	no	yes	set configuration
others	—	—	reserved

Table 9.10: ESDI commands and command codes

To give you an impression of what configuration data ESDI drives provide for a struggling system programmer, I have listed in Table 9.11 the configuration word that is transferred to the controller as a 16-bit word plus parity by the drive via the line $\overline{\text{configuration/status data}}$. For this purpose, the controller must pass a *request sense* command with the subcode 0000b to the drive. This configuration word is called a *general configuration word*.

Bit	Meaning
0	1=sectors hard-sectored by byte pulses from controller
1	1=sectors hard-sectored by drive, sector pulses from drive
2	1=sectors soft-sectored by controller with address marks, address mark pulses from drive
3	0=drive uses MFM encoding 1=drive uses other encoding method (usual RLL)
4	1=head switch time > 15 μs
5	1=drive supports control of spindle motor for motor switch off/on
6	1=hard disk drive (non-removable volume)
7	1=drive with removable volume
8	1=data transfer rate < 5 Mbits/s
9	1=data transfer rate between 5 Mbits/s and 10 Mbits/s
10	1=data transfer rate > 10 Mbits/s
11	1=rotation deviation > ±0.5%
12	1=drive supports data sense offset
13	1=drive supports track offset
14	1=GAP 3 necessary to compensate rotation deviation
15	0=magnetic disk drive 1=no magnetic disk drive

Table 9.11: General configuration word

Table 9.12 further lists the *special configuration words* that the drive transfers to the controller if the subcode in the command word differs from 0000b. The drive returns the configuration data in the same way as above, as a 16-bit word plus parity bit via the line configuration/status data to the controller.

Subcode	Meaning
0001	number of fixed drive cylinders
0010	number of removable drive cylinder
0011	number of heads bit 15..8: removable heads; bit 7...0: fixed heads
0100	min. number of unformatted bytes per track (hard-sectored drives only)
0101	actual number of unformatted bytes per track (hard-sectored drives only)
0110	sectors per track (hard-sectored drives only) bit 15...8: reserved; bit 7...0: sectors per track
0111	min. number of bytes in intersector gap ISG
	bit 15...8: ISG bytes after index or sector pulse
	bit 7...0: byte per ISG
1000	min. number of bytes per PLO synchronization field bit 15...8: reserved; bit 7...0: byte per PLO field
1001	number of words of manufacturer-own status bit 15...4: reserved; bit 3...0: number of words
1111	manufacturer identification
others	reserved

Table 9.12: Special configuration word

From Tables 9.11 and 9.12 you can easily recognize that an ESDI drive can identify its geometry and formatting parameters to the system in a very detailed way. The nearly infinite variety of drive entries in the AT setup is now obsolete. If you install an ESDI controller with its own BIOS and ESDI drives, then the BIOS routines determine the geometry and all other important drive parameters on their own, and initialize the system accordingly. Thus ESDI systems are self-configuring, as is the case for SCSI drives.

9.5.5   Connecting and Configuring ESDI Hard Disk Drives

For the connection of ESDI hard disks in principle the same rules as for an ST506/412 drive apply. First you must configure the drives, that is, adjust their ESDI address. This is carried out by a *drive select jumper* with which you assign the drive a number. The drive concerned then responds to a corresponding address drive select 2^x on the control cable and becomes active. Also, make sure that you don't assign an address twice, and thus give rise to an address conflict. Because of the different uses of the cable wires and the binary encoding of the drive address on the control cable, no cables with twisted wires are available for ESDI to free you from this drive configuration. With ESDI you always need to assign every drive an ESDI address. On the contrary, it is insignificant here which plug of the control cable you connect with which ESDI drive. You only have to remove the terminating resistor (if present) from all except the last drive to terminate the control cable.

Also ensure that you actually connect the data cable of a drive to the corresponding plug on the controller when installing the data cable. Unlike the ST412/506, ESDI can manage up to seven drives, so you have much more opportunity to mix the cables. There is nothing else to do for configuring the system. By means of the BIOS extension on the ESDI controller and the in-built intelligence of the ESDI drives, you don't even need to adjust the BIOS setup. Simply enter *no drive* in the setup to avoid any conflicts between the system BIOS and the BIOS extension. During the course of the boot procedure, the ESDI BIOS intercepts interrupt 13h automatically, and all programs may access the ESDI hard disk(s) without any problem.

9.6　　Drives with IDE, AT Bus or ATA Interface

Recently, a new hard disk interface standard was established for PCs which is overtaking the ST412/506 standard more and more: the so-called *IDE* or *AT bus* interface. IDE is the abbreviation for *intelligent drive electronics* – an indication that the connected drives are intelligent on their own. With the conventional controller-hard disk combination, the drive itself has only those electronic elements required to drive the motors and gates of the drive. The more extensive control for executing commands (for reading a sector, for example, a head seek, the reading of the encoded signals, the separation of data and clock signal, the transfer into main memory, etc. must be carried out) is taken over by the electronic equipment on a separate adapter, that is, the hard disk controller. Thus the drive itself is rather «stupid». A further disadvantage of this solution is that the still encoded signals must run from the drive via the data cable to the controller to be decoded there. The transfer path worsens the signals; a high data transfer rate between drive and controller fails because of the relatively long signal paths. Further, the exploding market for hard disk drives gave rise to a nearly infinite variety of drive geometries and storage capacities, so that a separate controller (which possibly comes from a third-party manufacturer) is simply overtaxed to serve all hard disk formats.

The falling prices for electronic equipment during the last few years, in parallel with a remarkable performance enhancement, gave a simple solution: modern and powerful hard disk drives already integrate the controller, and it is no longer formed by a separate adapter card. The signal paths from disk to controller are thus very short, and the controller can be adapted in an optimized way to the hard disk it actually controls. The IDE and SCSI interfaces follow this method of integrating drive and controller into a single unit. But SCSI has another philosophy in other aspects; details concerning SCSI are discussed in the next chapter. ESDI, as a middle course, integrates the data separator on the drive but the rest of the controller (for example, the sector buffer and drive control) is still formed on a separate adapter.

The IDE interface (discussed in the following sections) lies, in view of its performance, between the conventional solution with a separate controller and an ST412/506 interface to the drive on the one side, and the SCSI and ESDI hard disks as high-end solutions on the other.

At the end of 1984, Compaq initiated the development of the IDE interface. Compaq was looking for an ST506 controller which could be directly mounted onto the drive and connected to the main system by means of simple circuitry. In common with hard disk manufacturers such as Western Digital, Imprimis and Seagate, the AT bus interface arose in a very short time. Too many cooks spoil the broth, and so in the beginning incompatibilities were present everywhere. To take remedial action several system, drive and software manufacturers founded an interest group called CAM (common access method), which elaborated a standard with the name ATA (AT attachment) in March 1989. Besides other properties, the command set for IDE drives was also defined. As well as the eight commands with several subcommands already present on the AT controller, 19 new commands were added, which mainly refer to the drive control in view of low power consumption. For example, the sleep command for disabling the controller and switching off the drive if no access has been carried out for a while is one of these. Appendix H lists all the necessary and optional commands. Today, all manufacturers orient to this specification, so that incompatibilities are (nearly) a thing of the past. You may use the terms AT bus, IDE and ATA synonymously. Presently, ANSI is working on an obligatory standard for this interface.

9.6.1 The Physical CPU-Drive Interface

IDE is a further development of the AT controller with an ST506 interface so that the AT bus hard disks orient to the register set and the performance of such hard disks. Thus, IDE is a logical interface between system and hard disk, and accepts high-level commands (for example, read sector or format track). ESDI and ST412/506, on the other hand, are physical interfaces between controller and drive and refer, for example, to the control signals for the drive motors to move the head to a certain track. As with IDE the controller and hard disk form an inseparable unit, it is the job of every manufacturer to design the control of the drive and the transfer of the data. The definition of a physical interface is therefore obsolete.

The physical connection between the AT bus in the PC and the IDE interface of the drives (or better, the controllers on the drives) is established by a so-called *host adapter*. The motherboard plays the role of host here. The host adapter accommodates only a few buffers and decoder circuits, which are required to connect the IDE drives and the AT system bus. Newer motherboards already integrate these host adapters, otherwise they need a separate adapter card which is inserted into a bus slot. Many host adapters further have a floppy controller so that they are often called an AT bus controller. That's not correct as the controller is located immediately on the board of the drive; the adapter only establishes the connection betweend the drive and system bus. To the system and you as a programmer, the AT bus drives appear to be the usual controllers and drives with an ST412/506 interface which had been operating in your PC up to now. Thus AT bus drives can be accessed by the routines of INT 13h implemented in the conventional AT BIOS. Unlike ESDI or SCSI hard disk drives, no BIOS extension is required.

For connecting the drives, only a single 40-wire flat conductor cable is used, with which you connect the host adapter and the drives. The IDE interface can serve a maximum of two drives, one of which must be the master, and other the slave (adjust the jumper or DIP switch accordingly). The master drive is assigned address 0, the slave address 1. Table 9.13 lists the assignment of the 40 wires and the signals running on them.

Pin 20 of the cable is locked to avoid a misinsertion of the plug. Most of the 40 IDE lines are grounded or can be directly connected to the AT system bus. This explains the name AT bus interface. Between host adapter and IDE drive there are only five signals, $\overline{\text{CS1Fx}}$, $\overline{\text{CS3Fx}}$, SPSYNC, $\overline{\text{DASP}}$ and $\overline{\text{PDIAG}}$, which control the IDE drives and are not connected to the AT bus. The two first signals $\overline{\text{CS1Fx}}$ and $\overline{\text{CS3Fx}}$ are chip select signals generated by the host adapter to select the register group with the base address 1f0h or the register group with the base address 3f0h. Which meaning the accompanying registers have is described below.

IDE signal	Pin	Signal meaning	AT signal direction	Signal
RESET	1	reset drives	RESET DRV[1]	host–>drive
GND	2	ground	—	—
DD7	3	data bus bit 7	SD7	bidirectional
DD8	4	data bus bit 8	SD8	bidirectional
DD6	5	data bus bit 6	SD6	bidirectional
DD9	6	data bus bit 9	SD9	bidirectional
DD5	7	data bus bit 5	SD5	bidirectional
DD10	8	data bus bit 10	SD10	bidirectional
DD4	9	data bus bit 4	SD4	bidirectional
DD11	10	data bus bit 11	SD11	bidirectional
DD3	11	data bus bit 3	SD3	bidirectional
DD12	12	data bus bit 12	SD12	bidirectional
DD2	13	data bus bit 2	SD2	bidirectional
DD13	14	data bus bit 13	SD13	bidirectional
DD1	15	data bus bit 1	SD1	bidirectional
DD14	16	data bus bit 14	SD14	bidirectional
DD0	17	data bus bit 0	SD0	bidirectional
DD15	18	data bus bit 15	SD15	bidirectional
GND	19	ground	—	—
[2]	20	pin 20 mark	—	—
DMARQ[3]	21	DMA request	DRQx	drive–>host
GND	22	ground	—	—
DIOW	23	write data via I/O channel	IOW	host–>drive
GND	24	ground	—	—
DIOR	25	read data via I/O channel	IOR	host–>drive
GND	26	ground	—	—
IORDY[3]	27	I/O access complete (ready)	IOCHRDY	drive–>host
SPSYNC	28	spindle synchronization	—	drive–>drive
DMACK[3]	29	DMA acknowledge	DACKx	host–>drive
GND	30	ground	—	—
INTRQ	31	interrupt request	IRQx	drive–>host
IOCS16	32	16 bit transfer via I/O channel	I/OCS16	drive–>host
DA1	33	address bus 1	SA1	host–>drive
PDIAG	34	passed diagnostic from slave	—	drive–>drive
DA0	35	address bus 0	SA0	host–>drive
DA2	36	address bus 2	SA2	host–>drive
CS1Fx	37	chip select for base addr. 1f0h	—	host–>drive
CS3Fx	38	chip select for base addr. 3f0h	—	host–>drive
DASP	39	drive active/slave present	—	drive–>host
GND	40	ground	—	—

[1] inverted signal of AT bus signal
[2] pin locked to prevent incorrect insertion of plug
[3] optional

Table 9.13: IDE interface cable layout

With the spindle synchronization signal SPSYNC the spindle motor rotation of master and slave can be synchronized. This is advantageous if, for example, drive arrays are formed or a mirroring is carried out. But many IDE drives don't implement this, and the SPSYNC pin is not used. The two signals $\overline{\text{DASP}}$ (**d**rive **a**ctive/**s**lave **p**resent) and $\overline{\text{PDIAG}}$ (**p**assed **diag**nostic) return acknowledge signals by the slave to the master during the course of initialization. Also, these signals are not implemented in many older IDE models manufactured before the ATA standard became effective. That's not very serious; only some diagnostics routines are not always executed correctly. If your diagnostics software reports some obscure errors, although your drives have been running error-free for several months, then the reason may be the lack of one or both signals.

An optional but, nevertheless, important signal is $\overline{\text{IORDY}}$. With a low level a drive can inform the CPU that it requires additional clock cycles for the current I/O cycle, for example, for reading the sector buffer or transferring the command code. The CPU then inserts wait states. But many IDE drives don't use this signal, and always fix the corresponding line at a high level.

For performance enhancement the IDE standard defines two more signals, which were not to be found on an ST506 controller in the original AT: DMARQ (**DMA req**uest) and $\overline{\text{DMACK}}$ (**DMA ack**nowledge). In the AT, the data exchange between main memory and the controller's sector buffer was not carried out via a DMA channel, as was the case on the PC/XT, but by means of the CPU; a so-called *programmed I/O (PIO)* is executed. If, for example, a sector is to be read, then the sector data read into the sector buffer is repeatedly transferred via the data register into a CPU register by an IN instruction, and from there into main memory by a MOV instruction, until the sector buffer is empty. Thus the AT controller didn't carry out a DMA transfer, and therefore didn't provide any DMA control signals. As with modern and powerful DMA chips, the transfer rate between sector buffer and main memory is much higher (a factor of two can readily be achieved) and the development of multitasking systems like OS/2 request a relief from such «silly» data transfer operations, the two optional DMA control signals are implemented in the new IDE standard. Some AT bus hard disks can be instructed by a software command or a jumper to use a DMA channel instead of PIO for exchanging data between sector buffer and main memory. But as the programmer, you must then take into account the preparations for carrying out such a DMA transfer.

The integration of the controllers on the drives makes it possible to integrate more intelligence into the hard disk control. To this belongs, for example, intelligent retries if an access has failed. It is especially important that many IDE drives carry out an automatic *bad-sector remapping*. Usually, you can mask defective sectors and cylinders during the course of a low-level formatting process via the defect list, and use error-free alternative sectors and tracks instead. But if, after such a low-level formatting, a sector or track is damaged, the mapping is no longer possible and the sector is lost for data recording. This becomes fiendish, especially in the case of sneaking damage. The controller then always needs more retries to access the sector concerned correctly. Using the in-built retry routine, the operating system seldom recognizes anything about this as the data is read or written correctly after several retries. But at some time the point is reached where even the retry routine is overtaxed, the sector is completely inaccessible, and all data is lost. Many IDE drives are much more clever: the controller reserves several sectors and tracks of the hard disk for later use during the course of bad-sector remapping. If the controller detects several failed accesses to a sector, but finally leads to a correct data access, then the data of the sector concerned is written into one of the reserved spare sectors and the bad sector is marked. Afterwards, the controller updates an internal table so that all future accesses to the damaged sector are diverted to the reserved one. The system, or you as its user, doesn't recognize this procedure. The intelligent IDE drive carries out this remapping without any intervention, in the background.

The emergence of battery-powered laptops and notebooks gave rise to the need for power-saving drives. In a computer, powerful hard disks are one of the most power-consuming components, as they require strong current pulses for fast head seeks, and unlike floppy drives the hard disks are continuously running. Most specialist drives for portable computers can be switched off or disabled by software commands to minimize power consumption. Also, for the IDE hard disks according to the ATA standard such commands are optionally implemented. In the order of decreasing power consumption such hard disks can be operated in the active, idle, standby and sleep modes. Of course, it takes the longest time to «awaken» a drive from sleep into the active state. For this purpose the disk has to be accelerated from rest to the operation rpm, the head must be positioned, and the controller needs to be enabled.

9.6.2   Features of IDE Hard Disk Drives

Intelligent drives with an embedded controller, the most powerful among all IDE hard disks, carry out a translation from logical to physical geometry. The high recording density allows drives with up to 50 sectors per track in the outer zone with a large radius. IDE hard disks run virtually exclusively with an interleave of 1:1. To reduce the average access time of the drives, some hard disks are equipped with a cache memory which accommodates at least two tracks, in most cases. Even if your PC is unable to stand an interleave value of 1:1 as the transfer via the slowly clocked AT bus is not fast enough, this is not a disaster. Because of the 1:1 interleave, the data is read very quickly into the controller cache which is acting as a buffer. The CPU fetches the data from the cache with the maximum transfer speed of the AT bus. An interleave value which is adjusted too low, therefore, has no unfavourable consequences as it would do without the cache.

For high-capacity IDE hard disks, the RLL encoding method is mainly used; simpler ones may also use the MFM method. High performance IDE drives enable data transfer rates between drive and main memory of up to 1 Mbyte/s; a value which comes near the top of the practical values of SCSI and ESDI. On average, transfer rates of about 700 kbytes/s are realistic for usual IDE drives. Thus they are located between the older ST412/506 controllers and the high-end SCSI and ESDI solutions. The simpler interface electronics of the IDE host adapter and the support of the AT bus drives by the AT's on-board BIOS make it appear that the IDE hard disks are a rather good solution for Personal Computers in the region of medium performance.

An IDE interface manages a maximum of two drives. As long as the connected drive meets the IDE interface specification, the internal structure of the drive is insignificant. For example, it is possible to connect a powerful optical drive by means of an IDE interface. Usually, one would select an SCSI solution as this is more flexible in a number of ways than the AT bus.

One restriction of IDE is the maximum cable length of 18" (46 cm); some manufacturers also allow up to 24" (61 cm). For larger systems which occupy several cabinets, this is too little, but for a Personal Computer even in a large tower case it is sufficient. These values are part of the IDE standard. Thus, it is not impossible that the cables may be longer; but the IDE standard does not guarantee this.

Another disadvantage is that (especially older) but even also some present implementations of the IDE standard don't operate absolutely error-free in view of the signal timing. With an unfavourable combination of drive, host adapter and driver it may be (for example, with network software running in protected mode) that the IDE drive doesn't respond to instructions from the processor quickly enough. The consequences are rather unnerving, with unpredictable crashes during the course of an access to the IDE drives, even though no problems had occurred before with an ST412/506 controller. Thus IDE is not identical to an ST506 AT controller, but is a new product. Because of the market development during the last three years, and the attempts to form a clearly defined and obligatory standard, such problems are now vanishing more and more.

9.6.3   The AT Task File

The CPU accesses the controller of the IDE hard disk by means of several data and control registers, commonly called the *AT task file*. The address and assignment of these registers is identical to that of the hard disk controller with an ST506 interface in the IBM AT, but note that the registers are not compatible with the XT task file, or other interfaces such as ESDI or SCSI. The AT task file is divided into two register groups with port base addresses 1f0h and 3f0h. The following sections describe the registers of the AT task file and their meaning in more detail. Table 9.14 lists all the registers concerned.

Register	Address [bit]	Width Write(W)	Read (R)
data register	1f0h	16	R/W
error register	1f1h	8	R
precompensation	1f1h	8	W
number of sectors	1f2h	8	R/W
sector number	1f3h	8	R/W
cylinder LSB	1f4h	8	R/W
cylinder MSB	1f5h	8	R/W
drive/head	1f6h	8	R/W
status register	1f7h	8	R
command register	1f7h	8	W
alternate status register	3f6h	8	R
digital output register	3f6h	8	W
drive address	3f7h	8	R

Table 9.14: The AT task file

The data register, which is the only 16-bit register of the AT task file, can be read or written by the CPU to transfer data between main memory and the controller. The AT interface supports only programmed input/output via registers and ports, but no data transfer by means of DMA. The reading and writing is carried out in units of 16 bits; only the ECC bytes during the course of a read-long command are passed byte-by-byte. In this case, you must use the low-order byte of the register. Note that the data in the data register is only valid if the DRQ bit in the status register is set.

The CPU can only read the error register; it contains error information concerning the last active command if the ERR bit in the status register is set and the BSY bit in the status register is cleared; otherwise, the entries in the error register are not defined. Note that the meaning of this register differs for the diagnostics command. Figure 9.18 shows the structure of the error register.

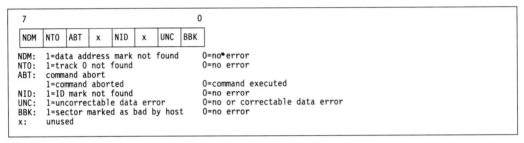

Figure 9.18: Error register (1f1h)

A set *NDM* bit indicates that the controller hasn't found a data address mark on the data carrier. If *NT0* is set this means that after a corresponding command the drive was unable to position the read/write head above track 0. If the controller had to abort execution of the active command because of an error, the *ABT* bit is set. If the *NID* bit is equal to 1, the controller was unable to detect the ID address mark concerned on the data carrier. A set *UNC* bit shows that an uncorrectable data error has occurred; the data is invalid even after applying the ECC code. If *BBK* is equal to 1 then the CPU has earlier marked the sector concerned as bad; it can no longer be accessed.

The precompensation register (1f1h) is only implemented for compatibility reasons with the AT task file of the original AT. All data passed by the CPU is ignored. The intelligent IDE hard disk drives with an embedded controller process the precompensation internally without any intervention by the CPU.

The sector count register (1f2h) can be read and written by the CPU to define the number of sectors to be read, written or verified. If you pass the register a value of 0, then the hard disk carries out the command concerned for 256 sectors, and not for 0 sectors. After every transfer of a sector from or into main memory, the register value is decreased by one. Thus the register's contents, which can be read by an IN instruction, indicates the number of sectors still to be read, written or verified. Also, during the course of a formatting process, the controller decrements the register value. Note that the meaning of the register differs somewhat for the command *set drive parameters*.

The sector number registers (1f3h) specifies the start sector for carrying out a command with disk access. After processing every sector the register contents is updated according to the executed command. Thus the register always indicates the last processed sector independently of whether the controller was able to complete the concerned command successfully or not.

The two registers cylinder MSB (1f5h) and cylinder LSB (1f4h) contain the most-significant (MSB) and least-significant byte (LSB) of the 10-bit cylinder number. The two most-significant bits are held by the register cylinder MSB, the eight least-significant ones by the register cylinder LSB. The six high-order bits of register cylinder MSB are ignored, thus the registers are able to represent cylinder numbers between 0 and 1023, as is also the case for the original AT. Because many IDE hard disks carry out a translation, the physical cylinders of the hard disk are not limited to this range. The physical drive geometry is then converted into a logical one, which has a maximum cylinder number of 1023. After processing of each sector, the contents of both registers are updated, thus the registers always indicate the current cylinder number.

By means of the registers drive/head (1f6h) you can determine the drive for which the command concerned is to be carried out. Furthermore, head defines the start head with which the disk access begins. Figure 9.19 shows the format of this register.

Figure 9.19: Drive/head register (1f6h).

The three most-significant bits always have value of 101b. The *DRV* bit defines the addressed drive, and the bits *HD3–HD0* specify the number of that head with which the command concerned starts to execute. A maximum of 16 heads can therefore be accessed.

The status register (1f7h) can only be read by the CPU, and contains status information concerning the last active command. The controller updates the status register after every command, or if an error occurs. Also, during the course of a data transfer between main memory and controller, the register is updated to carry out handshaking. If the CPU reads the status register an eventually pending interrupt request (via IRQ14 in the PC) is cancelled automatically. Note that all bits of this register except BSY and all registers of the AT task file are invalid if the BSY bit is set in the status register. Figure 9.20 shows the structure of the register.

The *BSY* bit is set by the drive to indicate that it is currently executing a command. If BSY is set then no registers may be accessed except the digital output register. In most cases you get any invalid information; under some circumstances you disturb the execution of the active command. A set *RDY* bit shows that the drive has reached the operation rpm value and is ready to accept commands. If the revolution variations of the spindle motor are beyond the tolerable range, for example because of an insufficient supply voltage, then the controller sets the RDY bit to 0. A set *WFT* bit indicates that the controller has detected a write fault. If the *SKC* bit is equal to 1, then the drive has completed the explicit or implicit head positioning. The drive clears the SXC bit immediately before a head seek. A set *DRQ* bit shows that the data register is ready for outputting or accepting data. If DRQ is equal to 0 then you may neither read data from the data register nor write data into it. The controller sets the *CORR* bit to inform the CPU that it has corrected data by means of the ECC bytes. Note that this error condition doesn't abort the reading of several sectors. Upon the passage of the track beginning below the read/write head of the drive, the controller sets the *IDX* bit for a short time. If the *ERR* bit is set, the error register contains additional error information.

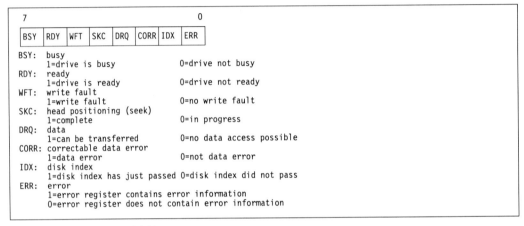

Figure 9.20: Status register (1f7h).

The command register (1f7h) passes command codes; the CPU is only able to write to it. The command register is located at the same port address as the read-only status register. The original AT has eight commands in total with several variations. The new IDE standard additionally defines some optional commands, but I want to restrict the discussion to the requested command set which is already implemented on the IBM AT. The execution of a command starts immediately after you have written the command byte into the command register. Thus you have to pass all other required data to the corresponding registers before you start the command execution by writing the command byte.

Command	NS	SN	CY	DR	HD
calibrate drive				xx	
read sector	xx	xx	xx	xx	xx
write sector	xx	xx	xx	xx	xx
verify sector	xx	xx	xx	xx	xx
format track			xx	xx	xx
seek head			xx	xx	xx
diagnostics					
set drive parameters	xx			xx	

NS: number of sectors   SN: sector number   CY: cylinder MSB and LSB
DR: drive (in register drive/head)
HD: head (in register drive/head)
xx: parameter necessary for corresponding command

Table 9.15: Command parameter registers

Table 9.15 lists the requested IDE commands as well as the parameter registers that you must prepare for the corresponding commands.

Besides the status register under the port address, additionally an alternate status register is implemented at I/O address 3f6h. It has the same structure as the normal status register, and contains the same information. The only difference between them is that a read-out of the alternate status registers doesn't cancel a pending interrupt request via IRQ14.

Under the same port address 3f6h you also find the digital output register DOR; the CPU is only able to write to it. The DOR defines the controller's behaviour; its structure is shown in Figure 9.21.

Figure 9.21: Digital output register (3f6h).

If you set the *SRST* bit you issue a reset for all connected drives. The reset state remains active until the bit is equal to 1. Once you clear the SRST bit again, the reset drives can accept a command. With the $\overline{\text{IEN}}$ bit you control the interrupt requests of the drives to the CPU. If $\overline{\text{IEN}}$ is cleared (that is, equal to 0) then an interrupt is issued via IRQ14 after every command carried out for one sector, or in advance of entering the result phase. If you set $\overline{\text{IEN}}$ to 1 then IRQ14 is always masked and the drives are unable to issue an interrupt. In this case, the CPU may only supervise the controller by polling.

With the read-only drive address register (3f7h) you may determine which drive and which head are currently active and selected. Figure 9.22 shows the structure of this register.

```
 7                                            0
┌───┬──────┬─────┬─────┬─────┬─────┬─────┬─────┐
│ x │ /WTGT│ /HS3│ /HS2│ /HS1│ /HS0│ /DS1│ /DS0│
└───┴──────┴─────┴─────┴─────┴─────┴─────┴─────┘
x:          unused
/WTGT:      write gate
            1=no write operation    0=writing to disk active
/HS3-HS0:   1'complement of currently active head
            0000=head 15   0001=head 14   ...   1111=head 0
/DS1:       drive select 1
            0=drive 1 active    1=drive 1 inactive
/DS0:       drive select 0
            0=drice 0 active    1=drive 0 inactive
```

Figure 9.22: Drive address register (3f7h).

If the $\overline{\text{WTGT}}$ bit is cleared (that is, equal to 0), the write gate of the controller is open and the read/write head is currently writing data onto disk. The bits $\overline{\text{HS3}}$–$\overline{\text{HS0}}$ indicate the currently active head as 1'complement. Similarly, the bits $\overline{\text{DS1}}$ and $\overline{\text{DS0}}$ determine the currently selected drive.

9.6.4   IDE Interface Programming and Command Phases

The programming and execution of the commands for an IDE interface proceed similar to a floppy controller or other hard disk interfaces in three phases:

−   Command phase: the CPU prepares the parameter registers and passes the command code to start the execution.

−   Data phase: for commands involving disk access, the drive positions the read/write heads and eventually transfers the data between main memory and hard disk.

−   Result phase: the controller provides status information for the executed command in the corresponding registers, and issues a hardware interrupt via IRQ14 (corresponding INT 76h).

The controller's command and register are written and read by the CPU via ports, but unlike the PC/XT, the IBM AT and all compatibles don't use the DMA controller for transferring the sector and format data between main memory and controller. Instead, this data transfer is also carried out by *programmed I/O* via CPU and data register. This means that the CPU writes sector and format data into or reads them from the data register in units of 16 bits. Only the ECC bytes are read and written in 8-bit portions via the low-order byte of the data register. To synchronize CPU and controller for a data exchange, the controller issues a hardware interrupt at various times via IRQ14:

−   Read sector: the controller always enables IRQ14 when the CPU is able to read a sector, eventually together with the ECC bytes, from the sector buffer. Unlike all other commands, this command doesn't issue an interrupt at the beginning of the result phase, thus the number of hardware interrupts is the same as the number of read sectors.

−   Write sector: the controller always activates IRQ14 when it expects sector data from the CPU. Note that the first sector is transferred immediately after issuing the command, and the controller doesn't issue an interrupt for this purpose. Furthermore, the controller activates, via IRQ14, a hardware interrupt at the beginning of the result phase. Thus the number of hardware interrupts coincides with the number of written sectors.

−   All other commands: the controller issues a hardware interrupt via IRQ14 at the beginning of the result phase.

The interrupt handler for INT 76h corresponding to IRQ14 in the PC must therefore be able to determine whether the controller wants to output data, is expecting it or whether an interrupt has occurred which indicates the beginning of a result phase. If you intend to program such a handler, use the status and error register to determine the interrupt source. The IRQ14 controller is disabled as soon as the CPU reads the status register (1f7h). If IRQ14 remains active, you must read the status information via the alternate status register (3f6h).

Note for your programming that the controller of the addressed drive starts command execution immediately after the CPU has written the command code into the command register. Thus you have to load all necessary parameter registers with the required values before you start command execution by passing the command code.

Appendix H lists all requested controller commands for the IDE interface, and the three optional commands for identifying the controller as well as reading and writing the sector buffer. As an example one command is dicussed here in more detail: write four sectors beginning with cylinder 167, head 3, sector 7 with ECC bytes. The format for this command is shown in Figure 9.23.

AT task file register		bit							
		7	6	5	4	3	2	1	0
command	(1f7h)	0	0	1	1	0	0	L	R
sector count	(1f2h)	number of sectors to write							
sector number	(1f3h)	S7	S6	S5	S4	S3	S2	S1	S0
cylinder LSB	(1f4h)	Z7	Z6	Z5	Z4	Z3	Z2	Z1	Z0
cylinder MSB	(1f5h)	0	0	0	0	0	0	Z9	Z8
drive/head	(1f6h)	1	0	1	DRV	HD3	HD2	HD1	HD0

Figure 9.23: Write sector command.

If the L bit is set then the four ECC bytes are also supplied by the CPU and not generated internally by the controller. The ECC logic then doesn't carry out an ECC check. For a single sector you therefore have to pass 516 bytes. If L is equal to 0 then this means a normal write command. The CPU only passes the 512 data bytes, and the controller generates the four ECC bytes internally and writes them, together with the data bytes, onto disk. The R bit controls the internal retry logic of the controller. If R is set, then the controller carries out an in-built retry procedure if it detects a data or address error during the course of the command execution. Only if these retries are also unsuccessful does the controller abort the command and return an error code. If R is cleared, the controller aborts the command immediately without any retry if an error has occurred.

With *sector count* you may determine the number of sectors to be written onto disk. Possible values are between 0 and 255; a value of 0 writes 256 sectors onto disk. The sector numbers $S7$–$S0$ indicate the number of the start sector to be written first. If the number of sectors to write is larger than 1, the controller automatically counts up the sector number until it detects the end of the track. Afterwards, it proceeds with the next head, and eventually with the next cylinder, until all sectors have been written or an error occurs. The values $Z9$–$Z0$ of the cylinder number define the start cylinder for the write process. The two bits Z_9 and Z_8 represent the two most significant bits of the 10-bit cylinder number. Using *DRV* you can select one of the two drives, and with *HD3*–*HD0* the head of the drive for which the command is to be carried out.

Immediately after the command byte has been written, the controller starts the command execution, that is, the data phase. It sets the BSY bit in the status register to indicate that it has decoded the command and prepared the sector buffer for accomodating the 512 data bytes, as well as the four ECC bytes. If this is finished, the controller clears the BSY bit and sets the DRQ bit in the status register to inform the CPU that it now expects the sector data. The CPU first transfers the 512 data bytes word-by-word, and afterwards the four ECC bytes byte-by-byte. If all 516 sector bytes have been passed the controller sets the BSY bit again and clears the DRQ bit. Now it begins to write the data onto disk.

If the first sector has been written then the controller issues an interrupt 76h via IRQ14. The handler concerned now transfers the 516 bytes of the following sector data via the data registers to the controller in the same manner as described above. This process is repeated four times until all four sectors, together with their ECC bytes, have been written.

Example: Write four sectors starting with cylinder 167, head 3, sector 7 together with ECC bytes onto master drive (language: Microsoft C 5.10).

```
unsigned int word_buffer[1024];
unsigned char byte_buffer[16];
unsigned int *word_pointer;
unsigned char *byte_pointer;
int int_count;

main()

{ int word_count, byte_count;
  void far *old_irq14;

  word_pointer = &word_buffer;     /* initialize */
  byte_pointer = &byte_buffer;     /* pointer    */

  init_buffers();                  /* initialize buffer */

  old_irq14=_dos_getvect(0x76);    /* set new interrupt  */
  _dos_setvect(0x76, new_irq14()); /* for IRQ14          */

  while((inp(0x1f7) & 0x80) == 0x80); /* wait until BSY in status register is cleared */
  outp(0x1f2, 0x04);                  /* register sector count: 4 sectors */
  outp(0x1f3, 0x07);                  /* register sector number: 7 */
  outp(0x1f4, 0xa7);                  /* register cylinder LSB: 167 */
  outp(0x1f5, 0x00);                  /* register cylinder MSB: 0 */
  outp(0x1f6, 0xa3);                  /* register drive/head: DRV=0, head=3 */
  outp(0x1f7, 0x33);                  /* register command: opcode=001100, L=1, R=1 */

  /* write first sector (512 data bytes + 4 ECC bytes */
  while((inp(0x1f7) & 0x80) == 0x80 || (inp(0x1f7) & 0x08) != 0x08);  /* wait until BSY in
                                              status register is cleared and DRQ is set */
  word_pointer = word_buffer;      /* initialize pointer */
  for (word_count = 0; word_count < 256; word_count++, word_pointer++) {
    outpw(0x1f0, *word_pointer);   /* transfer 256 words = 512 data bytes */
  }

  byte_pointer = byte_buffer;      /* initialize pointer */
  for (byte_count = 0; byte_count < 4; byte_count++, byte_pointer++) {
    outp(0x1f0, *byte_pointer);    /* transfer 4 ECC bytes */
  }

  int_count=0;                     /* initialize interrupt count */

  while (int_count < 4);           /* wait until all four sectors are transferred */
```

```
  _dos_setvect(0x76, old_irq14());        /* set old IRQ14 */

  status_check();                         /* check status information and determine error code*/

  exit(0);
}

void interrupt far new_irq14()
{ int word_count, byte_count;

  int_count++;

  if (int_count < 4) {                    /* ignore interrupt at the beginning of result phase */
    for (word_count = 0; word_count < 256; word_count++, word_pointer++) {
      outpw(0x1f0, *word_pointer);        /* transfer 256 words = 512 data bytes */
    }
    for (byte_count = 0; byte_count < 4; byte_count++, byte_pointer++) {
      outp(0x1f0, *byte_pointer);         /* transfer 4 ECC bytes */
    }
  }
  return;
}
```

In the example, the handler for IRQ14 serves only for transferring the data; a more extensive function, for example for determining the interrupt source, is not implemented. The 2048 data bytes in 1024 data words as well as the 16 ECC bytes must be suitably initialized. This is not carried out here because of the lack of space. Furthermore, the procedure status_check() for checking the status information is not listed in detail.

AT task file register		bit 7	6	5	4	3	2	1	0
error	(1f1h)	NDM	NTO	ABT	x	NID	x	UNC	BBK
sector count	(1f2h)	number of written sectors							
sector number	(1f3h)	S_7	S_6	S_5	S_4	S_3	S_2	S_1	S_0
cylinder LSB	(1f4h)	Z_7	Z_6	Z_5	Z_4	Z_3	Z_2	Z_1	Z_0
cylinder MSB	(1f5h)	0	0	0	0	0	0	Z_9	Z_8
drive/head	(1f6h)	1	0	1	DRV	HD_3	HD_2	HD_1	HD_0
status	(1f7h)	BSY	RDY	WFT	SKC	DRQ	COR	IDX	ERR

```
NDM:  1=data address mark not found       0=no error
NTO:  1=track 0 not found                 0=no error
ABT:  instruction abort
      1=instruction aborted               0=instruction executed
NID:  1=ID mark not found                 0=no error
UNC:  1=not-correctable data error        0=no or correctable data error
BBK:  1=sector marked bad by host         0=no error
DRV:  drive
      1=slave     0=master
Z9-Z0, S7-S0, HD3-HD0: sector identification of last written sector
```

Figure 9.24: Result phase of «Write Sector» instruction.

Upon the last interrupt the result phase is entered. Figure 9.24 shows the task file registers that contain valid status information after the command has been completed. The entries in the error register are only valid if the ERR bit in the status register is set and the BSY bit is cleared.

According to the sector identification, you can determine the last written sector or the sector which gave rise to the command abortion. The *sector count* register specifies the number of sectors still to be written, that is, a value of 0 if the command has been terminated without any error.

9.7 SCSI

A very flexible and powerful option for connecting hard disks to a PC is SCSI (*small computer systems interface*). The term already indicates that SCSI is intended for the PC and other small systems (for example, workstations or the Mac). SCSI was derived from the SASI interface of Shugart Associates (**S**hugart **A**ssociates **s**ystems **i**nterface). SCSI comes with a somewhat older standard SCSI-I, which is not strict enough in some aspects, resulting in compability problems when implementing SCSI-I. The new standard SCSI-II determines the properties more precisely, and additionally defines some more commands and operation modes. SCSI follows a different philosophy to those hard disk interfaces already discussed; this section gives more information on this subject.

9.7.1 SCSI Bus and Connection to the PC

SCSI defines a bus between a maximum of eight units, as well as the protocol for data exchange among them. Such SCSI units may be hard disks, tape drives, optical drives, or any other device that fulfills the SCSI specification. Thus, SCSI drives are intelligent, as are the IDE hard disks; the unit's controller is always integrated on the drive. For connection to the PC a *SCSI host adapter* is required, which establishes the connection to the PC's system bus similar to the IDE interface. The host adapter itself is also a SCSI unit, so that only seven «free» units remain. Unlike an IDE host adapter, the SCSI host adapter is thus rather complex, as it must recognize all the functions of the SCSI bus and be able to carry them out. But the advantage is that SCSI is not limited to the AT bus. There are also host adapters for EISA or the Mac. The enormous data transfer rate as well as the high-end performance of the SCSI hard disks doesn't suggest its use in a PC/XT, however. With an accordingly adapted host adapter the same SCSI devices can also be integrated into workstations or an Apple. The Mac has a SCSI interface as standard to connect up to seven external SCSI devices. Apple thus elegantly bypasses its lack of flexibility compared with the IBM-compatible PCs.

Thus the SCSI bus serves only for a data exchange among the SCSI units connected to the bus. A maximum of two units may be active and exchange data at any one time. The data exchange can be carried out between host adapter and a drive, or (as a special feature of SCSI) also between two other SCSI devices (for example, a tape drive and a hard disk). It is remarkable that this data exchange is carried out without the slightest intervention from the CPU; the SCSI drives are intelligent enough to do this on their own. Figure 9.25 shows a scheme of the SCSI bus in the case of integrating SCSI into a PC.

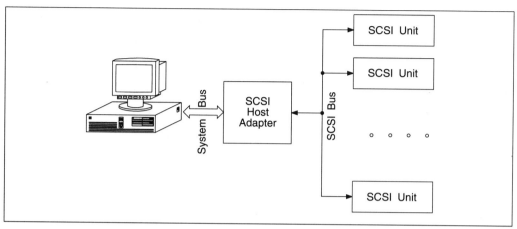

Figure 9.25: SCSI bus and PC integration. The SCSI bus is connected to the PC system bus by a SCSI host adapter. Up to seven SCSI units can be served.

Every SCSI unit is assigned a SCSI address, which you can set by a jumper on the drive. Addresses in the range 0–7 are valid; according to the SCSI standard, address 7 is reserved for a tape drive. The address is formed by bytes where the least significant bit 0 corresponds to the address or SCSI-ID 0, and the most significant bit 7 to the address or SCSI-ID 7. SCSI addresses are transferred via the data section of the SCSI bus (see Table 9.16).

But don't confuse the SCSI address or SCSI-ID with the logical unit number (LUN). Every target can accommodate up to eight logical units, which you identify in a SCSI command with the LUN. An example of this would be a SCSI controller which serves several drives. The controller establishes the connection to the SCSI bus, and further carries out all control functions. Thus the controller is the target. Additionally, the target is assigned several drives (the logical units), which are distinguished by the LUN. Today, external SCSI controllers are rare; most hard disks and also other drives integrate the SCSI controller directly. If you attempt to access such a hard disk you always have to set LUN to a value of 0, as the drive is the first and only logical unit of the target.

Be careful not to cause an address conflict between two drives. The controller of a drive determines its SCSI address at power-up, and then responds to commands that concern this SCSI address. As the host adapter is a SCSI unit, too, with a corresponding SCSI address, several host adapters may access the same SCSI bus. In this way, it is possible for several PCs to share a common SCSI bus, and thus the same drives. They can exchange data via the host adapters without the need for the usual network. Unfortunately, the SCSI bus is restricted to a length of 6 m; a value which is still quite high when compared to the IDE cables with their maximum of about 0.5 m.

The connection between SCSI units is established by means of a 50-wire flat conductor cable with 50-pole plugs. You may also see cables with 25 twisted cable pairs; here one ground line is always twisted around one signal line, similar to Centronics cables. Table 9.16 shows the assignment of the lines and plug pins.

Signal	Pin	Meaning	Signal	Pin	Meaning
GND	1	ground	TERMPWR	26	termination
$\overline{DB(0)}$	2	data bit 0	GND	27	ground
GND	3	ground	GND	28	ground
$\overline{DB(1)}$	4	data bit 1	GND	29	ground
GND	5	ground	GND	30	ground
$\overline{DB(2)}$	6	data bit 2	GND	31	ground
GND	7	ground	$\overline{ATN}$	32	attention
$\overline{DB(3)}$	8	data bit 3	GND	33	ground
GND	9	ground	GND	34	ground
$\overline{DB(4)}$	10	data bit 4	GND	35	ground
GND	11	ground	$\overline{BSY}$	36	busy
$\overline{DB(5)}$	12	data bit 5	GND	37	ground
GND	13	ground	$\overline{ACK}$	38	acknowledge
$\overline{DB(6)}$	14	data bit 6	GND	39	ground
GND	15	ground	$\overline{RST}$	40	reset
$\overline{DB(7)}$	16	data bit 7	GND	41	ground
GND	17	ground	$\overline{MSG}$	42	message
$\overline{DB(P)}$	18	parity bit	GND	43	ground
GND	19	ground	$\overline{SEL}$	44	select
GND	20	ground	GND	45	ground
GND	21	ground	$\overline{C/D}$	46	command/data
GND	22	ground	GND	47	ground
GND	23	ground	$\overline{REQ}$	48	request
GND	24	ground	GND	49	ground
1)	25	—	$\overline{I/O}$	50	I/O

1) no connection

Table 9.16: SCSI interface cable layout

As you can see from Table 9.16, eight data bits $\overline{DB(0)}$–$\overline{DB(7)}$ together with one parity bit $\overline{DB(P)}$ as well as nine control signals are transferred. The SCSI logic generates the parity bit automatically if the unit supports parity; this is not always the case. Using a jumper, you can often determine whether the parity bit should be generated and checked. All signals are active low. TERMPWR drains surplus charges and damps the SCSI bus. Although the data bus has only eight bits, SCSI is designed for a data transfer rate of up to 6 Mbytes/s in asynchronous and 7 Mbytes/s in synchronous mode. In asynchronous mode, handshake signals are used for data exchange; in synchronous mode the data transfer is carried out with the handshake signals as clock signals, which leads to a higher transfer rate. But note that not all SCSI units support the synchronous mode. Only in the newer drives orienting to the SCSI-II standard is the synchronous mode implemented. Moreover, the indicated data transfer rates refer only to the SCSI bus. At which speed the data is passed from or into the PC's main memory via the PC system bus is another question, and it is not determined by the SCSI transfer rates. The overall transfer rate essentially depends upon the quality of the host adapter and the firmware in the adapter's ROM BIOS; a realistic value is 1 Mbyte/s. Also, it is decisive, of course, at which speed the data can be read from disk or tape. The principle of the data transfer on a SCSI bus is shown in Figure 9.26.

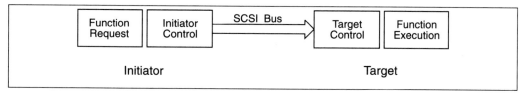

Figure 9.26: Data transfer on the SCSI bus.

Any SCSI unit can carry out the function of an *initiator* and take control of the SCSI bus by means of control signals. With a SCSI address the initiator activates a certain unit called the *target* which carries out certain funtions. It is of further importance that the initiator occupies the SCSI bus only for command and data transfer, otherwise the bus is free and can be used by other SCSI units. This also applies if the target unit carries out a command (for example, reading a block), and during this time doesn't require a connection to the initiator. Following the command execution, the target unit establishes the connection to the initiator again and transfers the data. The control of the bus is executed by the following control signals:

– $\overline{\text{BSY}}$ (busy): the signal indicates whether the bus is currently busy.

– $\overline{\text{SEL}}$ (select): the signal is used by the initiator to select the target device; on the contrary, the target may also use SEL to re-establish the connection to the initiator after a temporary release of the bus control.

– $\overline{\text{C/D}}$ (control/data): the signal is exclusively controlled by the target, and indicates whether control information or data is present on the SCSI bus. An active signal (with a low level) denotes control information.

– $\overline{\text{I/O}}$ (input/output): the signal is exclusively controlled by the target device, and indicates the direction of the data flow on the data bus relative to the initiator. An active signal (with a low level) means a data transfer to the initiator.

– $\overline{\text{MSG}}$ (message): the signal is activated by the target during the message phase of the SCSI bus.

– $\overline{\text{REQ}}$ (request): the signal is activated by the target unit to indicate the handshake request during the course of a $\overline{\text{REQ/ACK}}$ data transfer.

– $\overline{\text{ACK}}$ (acknowledge): the signal is activated by the initiator to indicate the handshake acknowledge during the course of a $\overline{\text{REQ/ACK}}$ data transfer.

– $\overline{\text{ATN}}$ (attention): an initiator activates the signal to indicate the attention condition.

– $\overline{\text{RST}}$ (reset): an active signal resets all connected SCSI devices.

You may already recognize that an extensive activation and deactivation procedure with a data transfer by means of handshake signals is carried out. The following sections discuss the various phases of the SCSI bus, but note that they are only of importance during the course of a data transfer via the SCSI bus. The CPU access to a SCSI device is only affected by this indirectly, as the SCSI logic implemented in the host adapter detects the various bus phases and generates the corresponding control signal automatically. The SCSI bus recognizes eight bus phases in total:

– bus-free
– arbitration
– selection
– reselection
– command
– data
– message
– status.

The last four bus phases (command, data, message and status) together are also called the information transfer phase.

Bus-Free Phase

This bus phase indicates that no SCSI unit is currently using and controlling the bus, thus the SCSI bus may be taken over by any connected SCSI unit. This phase is effective when both $\overline{\text{SEL}}$ and $\overline{\text{BSY}}$ are disabled (high).

Arbitration Phase

In this bus phase a SCSI unit may take control of the bus so that the unit acts as an initiator or target for a bus operation. For this purpose the following procedure is carried out:

– The SCSI bus must be in the bus-free phase as otherwise no unit except the active one is able to take control of the bus; thus $\overline{\text{BSY}}$ and $\overline{\text{SEL}}$ are both active.

– The unit activates $\overline{\text{BSY}}$ and puts its SCSI-ID onto the data bus.

– After a short arbitration delay, the unit investigates the data bus. If another SCSI-ID with a higher priority is active (that is, with a higher SCSI_ID number than its own), then the unit is not allowed to take cotrol of the bus. If this is not the case, then the unit may control the bus; it has won the arbitration and activates $\overline{\text{SEL}}$.

– After a short bus-clear delay, the SCSI unit is now able to control the SCSI bus and change the bus signals.

Selection Phase

In this phase an initiator selects a target unit and advises the target to carry out certain functions (for example, reading and writing data blocks). During the selection phase, the $\overline{\text{I/O}}$ signal is inactive to distinguish this phase from the reselection phase of a target. The initiator now outputs the OR-value of its SCSI-ID and the SCSI-ID of the target onto the data bus. Therefore, the two data bits which characterize initiator and target are active.

The thus addressed target must now detect that it has been selected by an initiator and an activate $\overline{\text{BSY}}$ within a certain time period. If this doesn't happen, then the selection phase has failed and the initiator deactivates $\overline{SEL}$; the SCSI bus enters the bus-free phase. As the initiator has also output its own SCSI-ID besides the target-ID onto the data bus, the target unit is able to identify the initiator. This is important so that the target unit, after a bus-free phase, can activate the correct initiator in the following reselection phase.

Reselection Phase

With the reselection phase a target may re-establish the connection with the original initiator to continue the interrupted operation. This is the case, for example, if a host adapter issues a read command to a target drive. Head positioning and reading the sector concerned takes up to 40 ms, even on fast hard disks; this is a very long time for a computer. Therefore, the target unit releases the SCSI bus and carries out head positioning and reading on its own, but remembers the initiator's SCSI-ID. Thus a bus-free phase occurs, which other devices may use to exchange data. If the target drive has completed the read operation, then it re-establishes the contact to the original initiator by means of a reselection phase and transfers the read data.

The reselection phase proceeds similar to an arbitration and selection phase. The target unit takes over the SCSI bus in an arbitration phase of the SCSI bus, activates $\overline{BSY}$ $\overline{SEL}$ and then the $\overline{I/O}$ signal to identify the phase as a reselection phase and itself as the target. Afterwards, the target outputs its own and the SCSI-ID of the original initiator. The initiator detects that it is selected, and sets up the connection to the target again; now the data exchange can start.

During the course of the four information transfer phases command, data, message and status, phase data and control information are transferred via the data bus. The signals $\overline{C/D}$, $\overline{I/O}$ and $\overline{MSG}$ are used to distinguish the individual transfer phases. If $\overline{I/O}$ is active, then information is transferred from the target to the initiator, otherwise the data transfer proceeds in the opposite direction. Each data transfer in one of these four phases is carried out by handshake. The transmitter puts the data onto the data bus $\overline{DB(0)}$–$\overline{DB(7)}$, and eventually the parity information onto $\overline{DB(P)}$, and activates $\overline{REQ}$ to indicate the validity of the data to the receiver. The receiver fetches the data and activates $\overline{ACK}$ afterwards to inform the transmitter that the data has been accepted. As a result, the transmitter deactivates $\overline{REQ}$. Now the receiver also negates the signal $\overline{ACK}$ (that is, both handshake signals are deactivated), and the next transfer of a data byte by means of a handshake can be carried out.

MSG	C/D	I/O	Phase	Transfer direction
0	0	0	data-out	initiator–> target
0	0	1	data-in	target–> initiator
0	1	0	command	initiator–> target
0	1	1	status	target–> initiator
1	0	0	invalid	–
1	0	1	invalid	–
1	1	0	message-out	initiator–> target
1	1	1	message-in	target–> initiator

Table 9.17: SCSI bus phases

It is important here that the target unit controls the three signals $\overline{C/D}$, $\overline{I/O}$ and $\overline{MSG}$. The initiator, though, may request a message-out phase by activating $\overline{ATN}$. Table 9.17 shows the connections between the $\overline{MSG}$, $\overline{C/D}$ and $\overline{I/O}$ signals on the one hand, as well as the phase and transfer directions on the other.

Command Phase

In the command phase the addressed target may request command data from the initiator. For this purpose, the target unit activates the $\overline{C/D}$ signal and deactivates the $\overline{MSG}$ and $\overline{I/O}$ signals. The initiator now transfers the command data.

Data Phase

During the course of the data phase, the target may instruct the initiator to transfer data to the target (the data-out phase), or it can provide data for the initiator (the data-in phase).

Message Phase

In the message phase, the target may advise the initiator to transfer messages to the target (the message-out phase), or it can provide messages for the initiator (the message-in phase).

Status Phase

During the course of the status phase, the target supplies status information to the initiator.

Besides the control signals for issuing the various phases, there are the two further signals, $\overline{ATN}$ (attention) and $\overline{RST}$ (reset). With $\overline{ATN}$ the initiator informs the target that it intends to pass a message. The target fetches the message with a message-out phase. However, the target can transfer a message simply by issuing a message-in phase; only the initiator uses the attention signal. When a SCSI unit activates the $\overline{RST}$ signal, all units are separated from the SCSI bus, all operations are aborted, and the units are set to a defined state.

According to the SCSI specification every initiator implements two sets of three pointers each, called the *current pointers* and the *saved pointers*, respectively. The current pointers point to the next command, data and status byte which are to be transferred between the initiator and the target. They are used by the target currently connected to the initiator. As the connection between initiator and target can be interrupted during an active command and re-established later (reselection phase), the saved pointers are also of further importance. For every active command there is in fact a set of saved pointers, independently of whether the corresponding connection between initiator and target is currently established. The saved command pointer points to the beginning of the command block for the active command, and the saved status pointer to the beginning of the status area of the active command. The pointers are usually realized by means of registers, which accommodate the corresponding pointer values.

At the beginning of every command the saved data pointer refers to the beginning of the data area until the target unit passes the initiator a message *save data pointer*. Upon this instruction, the initiator shifts the current data pointer into the saved data pointer. Inversely, the target may load the active pointer with the saved pointer by passing the initiator the message *restore pointer*. If a SCSI unit is separated from the bus, only the saved pointers are kept; the active ones are reloaded with new values upon connection with another unit. If the separated SCSI unit is reconnected to the initiator by a reselection phase, then the current pointers are restored from the saved ones.

Messages coordinate the connection of the various SCSI units, and pass status information indicating the state of the currently active commands. Thus the protocol of the SCSI bus comprises the physical control signals as well as the logical messages. On the other hand, the commands of the command phase issue certain operations of the SCSI target unit and do not determine the connection of initiator and target. It is only essential for the SCSI units to support the message *command complete* (00h); all other messages are optional.

An initiator informs the target that it also supports the other messages by activating the $\overline{\text{ATN}}$ signal in the course of the selection phase before $\overline{\text{SEL}}$ is activated and $\overline{\text{BSY}}$ is disabled. Then the first message of the initiator to the target after the selection phase is the identification, in the same way as the target must pass the initiator this message after a reselection phase.

The SCSI standard defines the following messages:

–   Command complete (00h): the target passes the initiator this message in a message-in phase to indicate whether or not a command or a linked command has been completed success-fully, and status information has been transferred to the initiator during the course of a status phase. After transferring this message, the target enters the bus-free phase.

–   Save data pointer (02h): the target passes the initiator this message to instruct it to save the current data pointers for the currently connected SCSI unit in the saved data pointers.

–   Restore data pointers (03h): the target passes the initiator this message to instruct it to restore the current data pointers from the saved ones.

–   Separate (04h): the target passes the initiator this message to indicate that the target is going to interrupt the current connection, that is, to deactivate $\overline{\text{BSY}}$. Later, a new connection is required by means of the reselection phase to complete the command successfully.

–   Abortion (06h): the initiator transfers this message to the target to advise it to abort the current operation, to delete the current data and status information, and to enter the bus-free phase.

–   Message rejected (07h): this message can be supplied by the initiator or the target to indicate that the last received message was invalid, or is not implemented in the SCSI unit.

–   No operation (08h): the message has no result.

–   Linked command complete (0ah): the target outputs the message to the initiator to indicate that a linked command has been completed, and that status information has been trans-ferred to the initiator during the course of a status phase.

–   Linked command with flag complete (0bh): the target outputs the message to the initiator to indicate that a linked command with a set flag has been completed, and that status infor-mation has been transferred to the initiator during the course of a status phase.

−   Reset bus unit (0ch): the message is passed to the target by the initiator to reset the target.

−   Identify (80h to ffh): the message is output by the initiator or target for its own identification. Bit 7 of the message is always set to characterize it as an identification. The remaining seven bits contain the identification code (see Figure 9.27).

```
7                          0
┌───┬───┬───┬───┬───┬───┬───┬───┐
│ 1 │D/R│res│res│res│LU2│LU1│LU0│
└───┴───┴───┴───┴───┴───┴───┴───┘
D/R: disconnect/reconnect
     1=initiator can carry out disconnection/reconnection
     0=initiator cannot carry out disconnection/reconnection
res: reserved (normally equal 0)
LU2–LU0: logical unit number
     000=0   001=1   ...   111=7
```

Figure 9.27: Identification code.

Besides the messages the target also transfers a status code to the initiator once a command has been completed. Figure 9.28 shows the structure of this status byte.

```
7                          0
┌───┬───┬───┬───┬───┬───┬───┬───┐
│res│res│res│ST3│ST2│ST1│ST0│ 0 │
└───┴───┴───┴───┴───┴───┴───┴───┘
res: reserved (normally equal 0)
ST3–ST0: status code
     0000=o.k.    0001=check status    0100=busy
     1000=intermediate status/o.k.     1100=reservation conflict
```

Figure 9.28: Status code.

The code 0000 indicates that the SCSI unit has executed the command successfully. If a *check status* code is output then an error, an exception, or an abnormal command termination has occurred. You should use the command request sense to determine the cause of this condition. If the target is busy, the status code 0100 is passed. If a linked command is active, the target passes the status code 1000 for every completed individual command except the last one. Thus the status code 1000 confirms the link and takes care that the command sequence is not interrupted. If an error occurs, the status code 0001 is supplied and the linked command is aborted. Finally, a code 1100 means a reservation conflict, that is, a SCSI device has attempted to access a logical unit that is already reserved for another SCSI unit.

Messages are usually not accessible for you as the programmer; they only coordinate the SCSI units among themselves. You can see that SCSI defines a high-level protocol that is not only based on physical signals but also on logical messages. SCSI is therefore very flexible; but presently there is a lack of a strictly defined standard for connecting the SCSI bus to the system bus of a PC. All users of an operating system or an operating system extension (for example, UNIX, OS/2 or Windows) running at least partially in protected mode could tell you a thing or two about that! The problem here is not the SCSI standard, but the appropriate programming of the host adapter to get an access.

The following two sections therefore discuss the programming of the SCSI host adapters ST01 and ST02. With these you may transfer data via the SCSI bus to or from your PC's main memory to access, for example, SCSI hard disks or tape drives.

9.7.2   Memory-Mapped I/O and SCSI Task File of Host Adapters ST01 and ST02

The two host adapters only differ in that the ST02 additionally has a floppy controller for a maximum of two drives; the ST01 does not. All SCSI functions of these host adapters are identical. If, in the following, the host adapter is discussed then the information concerned is also valid for the ST02. The adapters come in two versions, each with an 8 kbyte or a 16 kbyte BIOS. The following description is restricted to an ST01 with an 8 kbyte BIOS. For the other adapter and BIOS sizes the analogous information applies. You can configure the adapters by means of a jumper so that they issue a hardware interrupt via IRQ3 or IRQ5 if another SCSI unit activates the SEL line of the SCSI bus, for example the target for reselecting the initiator.

Both host adapters operate with so-called *memory-mapped I/O* to allow an access to their internal control and status registers. With memory-mapped I/O the registers concerned are located in the normal memory address space of the CPU; thus they are accessed with common memory commands (for example, MOV). With *I/O-mapped I/O*, on the other hand, the registers are addressed via port addresses (that is, IN and OUT instructions); the registers are located in the CPU's I/O address space. It seems to be impossible at first glance to access a control register by means of a memory command. But remember that the access to a memory chip is carried out in the same way as that to the I/O address space by means of electrical signals. And these signals don't care whether the transistor of a memory cell or the transistor of a register is on the end of the line. Apple Macs, for example, use only memory-mapped I/O, while on the PC most register accesses are carried out by means of I/O-mapped I/O because of Intel's processor architecture and the powerful I/O protection mechanisms in protected mode.

Besides a ROM BIOS with the INT 13h routines and internal diagnostics and initialization programs, the host adapter has a control and status register as well as a SCSI data port and static RAM, which are all in a continuous address area. As is the case for most adapters with their own BIOS, you may also select the start address by means of a jumper on the ST01. The following description therefore uses that value as the base address, where usually the ROM BIOS of a hard disk controller begins (namely c8000h or segment c800h). Figure 9.29 shows the corresponding address organization for an ST01 with 8 kbytes of ROM BIOS. Thus all addresses of BIOS, registers, and RAM are located within a range of 8 k.

Between the addresses c8000h and c9800h there is the ROM BIOS comprising a maximum of 6 kbytes of code and data. The 128 bytes above are occupied by the RAM, which is used by the BIOS routines for temporarily storing data. Thus the ST01 adapter doesn't use any system memory for executing its in-built routines. You can, of course, read and write this adapter RAM on your own, but the results cannot be predicted. The control and status register area starts at c9a00h and comprises 512 bytes. Finally, the 1024 bytes at c9c00h accommodate the SCSI data port for transmitting and receiving data from the SCSI bus. Note that you must not move the area of the control and status register and the SCSI data port by shadowing into RAM, although they are located in the ROM address area. The registers are physically present at this address. If the addresses are detoured during the course of shadowing, then memory chips are present at these addresses and not the required adapter registers (remember that memory-mapped I/O is used here).

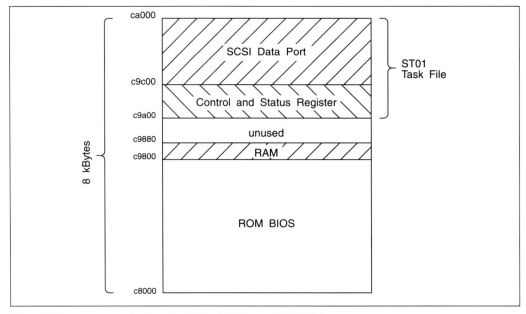

Figure 9.29: Memory organization of an ST01 with 8 kbytes ROM BIOS.

If you carry out a write process with an address between c9a00h and c9bffh, you automatically write the control register. If you read data from the same address range (for example, by an instruction *MOV memory, register*), you automatically read the status register. Thus for an access to these two adapter registers the nine least significant address bits are not decoded. The same applies for the SCSI data port through which you may read or write data bytes from or onto the SCSI bus. A read or write access to the address range between c9c00h and cbfffh leads directly to an access to the data bits of the SCSI bus; here the ten least significant address bits are not decoded. The advantage is that you can rapidly read or write a complete data block using the string instructions and the prefix *REP* without the need to initialize the address for every byte. The structure of the control register is shown in Figure 9.30, that of the status register in Figure 9.31.

Using the control register you may control certain control lines of the SCSI bus directly, besides adapter activation. The *SCSI ENAB* bit advises the host adapter to drive the data bits of the SCSI bus to output data. The same is carried out implicitly when you start an arbitration phase with ARB STRT; the host adapter as the initiator then puts its SCSI-ID onto the SCSI bus. If the *INTR ENAB* bit is set, the host adapter issues an interrupt via IRQ3 or IRQ5 if another SCSI unit activates the SEL line of the SCSI bus. The handler serves a reselection phase of a previously addressed target or completes an arbitration phase. *PAR ENAB* enables the parity generator on the host adapter so that it generates a parity bit upon every data transfer to a target. The *ARB STRT* bit starts an arbitration phase of the host adapter to establish a connection to a target. The remaining four bits *SCSI ATTN, SCSI BUSY, SCSI SEL* and *SCSI RST* directly control the signals on the corresponding lines of the SCSI bus. A set bit leads to an activated SCSI line, that is, to a low level.

```
 7                                              0

 SCSI INTR PAR  ARB   SCSI SCSI SCSI SCSI
 ENAB ENAB ENAB STRT  ATTN BUSY SEL  RST

SCSI ENAB: SCSI bus enable
           1=SCSI bus drivers of host adapter enabled    0=disabled
INTR ENAB: interrupt enable
           1=interrupt is issued when SEL line active
           0=interrupt disabled
PAR ENAB:  SCSI parity
           1=generate and check parity bit          0=not parity check
ARB STRT:  SCSI arbitration
           1=start arbitration, ARB line of SCSI bus active (low)
           0=inactive (high)
SCSI ATTN: SCSI attention
           1=ATN line of SCSI bus active (low)      0=inactive (high)
SCSI BUSY: 1=BSY line of SCSI bus active (low)      0=inactive (high)
SCSI SEL:  SCSI selection
           1=SEL line of SCSI bus active (low)      0=inactive (high)
SCSI RST:  SCSI reset
           1=reset all SCSI units
```

Figure 9.30: ST01 control register (c9a00h to c9bffh).

```
Example: Reset all SCSI units by means of an active RST line.
MOV ax, c800h;       ; load control register segment via
MOV es, ax           ; ax into extra segment register es
MOV ES:[1b00], 01h   ; output set SCSI RST bit via an
                     ; address between c9a00h and c9bffh
```

The status register, which is located in the same address area as the control register, reads status information concerning host adapter operations and the signals on SCSI control lines (see Figure 9.31).

If the *ARB CMPL* bit is set then the SCSI host adapter has completed the arbitration phase and taken over control of the SCSI bus as the initiator. Now you can transfer a command block via the SCSI data port to the SCSI bus and thus to the target. If a parity error occurs during the course of a read process then the adapter sets the *SCSI PARF* bit. All other bits *SCSI SEL, SCSI REQ, SCSI C/D, SCSI I/O, SCSI MSG* and *SCSI RST* directly indicate the status of the corresponding control lines of the SCSI bus. According to this information, you may determine whether the target, for example, expects data or attempts to output a message to the initiator, that is, the host adapter. It is up to you to handle the corresponding situations by suitably programming the SCSI data port and the control register according to the SCSI protocol.

```
Example: read status register
MOV ax, c800h;       ; load control register segment via
MOV es, ax           ; ax into extra segment register es
MOV ah, ES:[1a90]    ; read status byte from status register via
                     ; an address between c9a00h and c9bffh into ah
```

```
7                                          0
┌─────┬─────┬─────┬─────┬─────┬─────┬─────┬─────┐
│ ARB │SCSI │SCSI │SCSI │SCSI │SCSI │SCSI │SCSI │
│ CMPL│PARF │SEL  │REQ  │C/D  │I/O  │MSG  │RST  │
└─────┴─────┴─────┴─────┴─────┴─────┴─────┴─────┘

ARB CMPL:  arbitration complete
           1=host adapter took over control of SCSI bus
SCSI PARF: SCSI parity error
           1=parity error when reading data     0=no parity error
SCSI SEL:  SEL line status of SCSI bus
           1=selection phase
SCSI REQ:  REQ line status of SCSI bus
           1=request in REQ/ACK handshake
SCSI C/D:  C/D line status of SCSI bus
           1=command phase       0=data-out or data-in phase
SCSI I/O:  I/O line status of SCSI bus
           1=in phase            0=out phase
SCSI MSG:  MSG line status of SCSI bus
           1=message phase
SCSI RST:  RST line status of SCSI bus
           1=reset all SCSI units
```

Figure 9.31: ST01 status register (c9a00h to c9bffh).

The SCSI host adapter frees you from carrying out a REQ/ACK handshake; the ST01 generates the corresponding control signals automatically. For example, to transfer a 512-byte block during the course of a *write block* command to the target, you only need to write a corresponding data byte 512 times into the data port. The host adapter's logic generates all the control signals required such as *I/O CH RDY* and *0WS* for the PC system bus to confirm receipt of the data byte to the CPU, and to instruct the CPU to insert wait states if necessary. Thus the control signals REQ of the SCSI bus and MEMW and MEMR of the PC system bus are synchronized. Moreover, the adapter also generates the REQ signals for the SCSI bus and waits for the ACK signal from the target to carry out a handshake for the data byte transfer to the target. You access the data bits of the SCSI bus via the SCSI data port between addresses c9c00h and cbfffh. When you attempt to output a data byte, for example of a command, parameter block, message or data block to the target, you always need to write the byte into the data port. If you want to read a byte, for example of a status message or data block, from the SCSI bus, you must read the byte from the data port. Because of the extensive size of the data port with its 1024 bytes, you may, for example, write a 512-byte data block using the string instruction MOVSB together with the prefix REP, and loading the value 512 into the count register CX. Now the CPU can transfer a complete block from a buffer in the main memory to the SCSI bus, and thus to the target, all at once. The same procedure can be carried out, of course, in the opposite direction. By the same instruction, you may read 512 data bytes from the SCSI bus and transfer them into a buffer in the main memory. Because of the REP prefix, source and destination addresses are counted up or down in the same way, according to the value of the direction flag. If you suitably initialize the start address for the SCSI data port, then the address doesn't pass beyond the value c9fffh and you are always accessing the data port.

Example: transfer 512 data bytes from a buffer in main memory via the SCSI data port to the SCSI bus

```
buffer DB 512 DUP (?)  ; provide a buffer with 512 bytes (1 data block)
.................      ; initialize buffer with suitable data
MOV ax, c800h;        ; load SCSI data port segment via
MOV es, ax            ; ax into extra segment register es
```

```
MOV di, 1c00h           ; initialize destination index to the beginning of SCSI data port
MOV si, OFFSET buffer   ; load buffer offset into source index
MOV CX, 200h            ; transfer 512 bytes
CLD                     ; clear direction flag, address counting to higher addresses
MOVSB                   ; transfer 512 bytes from buffer to SCSI data port
```

The host adapter handles all requests for CPU wait cycles, as well as the generation and detection of the handshake signals.

9.7.3   Programming and Command Phases

Unlike previous hard disk interfaces (for example, ST412/506 and IDE), SCSI doesn't deal with tracks and sectors, but regards the complete storage capacity of a hard disk as a continuous list of data blocks with a fixed size. In view of the logical structure, these data blocks are similar to the logical sectors of DOS, which are assigned a logical sector number between 0 and ∞. How a SCSI unit manages this list appearing on the SCSI level internally is the exclusive job of the intelligent controller. On hard disks the logical block number is converted into tracks and sectors, often using zone recording. A SCSI tape drive, on the other hand, can use the logical block numbers in a virtually unaltered form, as on the magnetic tape the data blocks are in succession.

On a PC running under DOS an enormous conversion process is carried out between logical and physical structures:

– the logical DOS sectors must be converted into cylinder, head and sector for INT 13h;

– INT 13h must convert the values for cylinder, head, and sector into a logical block number for the SCSI host adapter;

– the addressed hard disk drive converts the logical block number into a value comprising the physical cylinder, head, and sector, of the SCSI drive.

Thus it is not surprising that every SCSI host adapter has its own BIOS extension to establish the connection between system and SCSI bus, and to carry out the conversion of the physical sectors of INT 13h into logical block numbers for SCSI. The BIOS extension identifies the drive geometry via function 09h of INT 13h to the system. Register addresses and meanings, as well as the programming schemes for the various host adapters, don't coincide in most cases with any known programming interface, for example the AT task file. Another deficit of SCSI is the lack of a standard for programming the host adapter. On IDE this was no problem, as the AT task file known from the IBM AT was simply taken.

For a PC with DOS this is not yet a serious problem, as the host adapters are equipped with an extension ROM for the BIOS routines for INT 13h. The BIOS extension intercepts the INT 13h during the course of the boot process, and replaces the standard routines that are incompatible with the host adapter. But with operating systems running in protected mode (for example, OS/2 or UNIX/XENIX), enormous problems arise. The shipped ROM code is largely only executable in real mode, but cannot support the protected mode operating system. For this reason you always get problems with adapters that have their own BIOS extensions when installing them in a computer running under OS/2 or UNIX/XENIX. Only PS/2 machines with advanced BIOS implement a BIOS running in protected mode. Therefore, the BIOS is also loaded from disk, and not just the operating system, if you are using OS/2 on an IBM-compatible PC. If this BIOS doesn't support the installed adapter (and this applies not only to hard disk controllers but to all other adapters, too), then the adapter is not operating correctly, or the BIOS extension prevents you from working in protected mode.

Also, the lack of a defined programming interface to the host adapter means that instead of the ROM code the operating system can be equipped with a universal driver, which can access all SCSI drives according to the SCSI specification. As long as the boot routine is running in real mode, the system data can be read from the SCSI drive to boot the computer. But in that moment when the initialization routine switches the processor into protected mode, the hard disk becomes «dead» as the real-mode-BIOS denies the access when the hard disk is addressed, or hangs-up the PC. Such problems cannot occur with IDE or ESDI hard disks, as they are programmed via registers. These registers, though, are located in the I/O address space for which even in protected mode no address transformation is carried out: only the access rights are checked by the operating system. Therefore, the system can manage its own accesses, and problems hardly ever arise.

Similar problems result from the use of network software, such as Novell NetWare, which runs in protected mode. However, you get suitable driver software for most host adapters. Unfortunately, the enormous flexibility of SCSI when installing various drives and units is at least partially compensated for by the lack of a programming standard. This is one reason why SCSI could not become dominant in the market. Instead, for IBM-compatible PCs, the IDE interface is usually used, although it is much less powerful and flexible. Meanwhile, most SCSI manufacturers have recognized this, and are working on a strictly defined standard for programming SCSI host adapters.

At the end of every command the target (that is, the drive) returns a status byte to the initiator (the host adapter). If this byte indicates an error condition, then you should investigate the cause using the *request sense* command. With a single byte the cause cannot be described exactly enough, and the SCSI host adapter doesn't implement a status register with error information, as was the case, for example, for IDE.

The SCSI commands follow a strict scheme. The first command byte always contains the command code, the second the number of the addressed target, and the third a control byte. SCSI commands always have six, ten or twelve bytes. The 10- and 12-byte commands are denoted as extended. The command code is divided into a 3-bit group code and a 5-bit code with the command within that group (see Figure 9.32).

Figure 9.32: Command byte structure.

The structure of the command byte gives rise to eight different command groups; only three of them (0, 1 and 5) are currently in use. The five command bits allow 32 commands per group; thus a maximum of 256 different commands is possible. You must set all reserved bits of the command codes to a value of 0. Most SCSI host adapters support only 6-and 10-byte commands. Figure 9.33 shows their structure.

6–byte command										10–byte command									
bit byte	7	6	5	4	3	2	1	0		bit byte	7	6	5	4	3	2	1	0
0	command code									0	command code								
1	LUN			LBA (MSB)						1	LUN			reserved				REL
2	logical block address									2	logical block address (MSB)								
3	logical block address (LSB)									3	logical block address								
4	transfer length/parameter list/ allocation length									4	logical block address								
5	control byte									5	logical block address (LSB)								
										6	reserved								
										7	transfer length/parameter list/ allocation length (MSB)								
										8	transfer length/parameter list/ allocation length (LSB)								
										9	control byte								

Figure 9.33: Structure of the 6- and 10-byte commands.

The first byte of the command block represents the command code, consisting of the 3-bit group and the 5-bit command. The logical unit number *(LUN)* specifies the address of the logical unit to access within the target. For drives with an embedded controller this is always equal to 0. The logical block address *(LBA)* has 21 bits for a 6-byte command and 32 bits for a 10-byte command. It indicates the number of the intended data block. Thus, with a 6-byte command you can access a maximum of 2 M blocks and with a 10-byte command a maximum of 4 G blocks. For hard disks where one block usually corresponds to a 512-byte sector, a 6-byte command is sufficient in most cases. You can then access 1 Gbyte of data. If you set the *REL* bit for relative addressing then the block address is relative to the block referred to in the previous process. The block address is interpreted in this case as the 2'complement of a signed number. Most SCSI units and hard disks, though, don't support relative addressing. Note that this option is missing on 6-byte commands.

The *transfer length* specifies the amount of data to be transferred. Usually, this is the number of intended blocks, but some commands also use the number of bytes. Details on this subject are discussed in Appendix H, together with a list of all SCSI commands. Six-byte commands with a byte for the transfer length allow the transfer of a maximum 256 blocks, where a value of 0 means that 256 blocks are transferred. Thus you can read or write up to 256 blocks all at once, for example. On an IDE interface this means a multi-sector transfer. With the use of a 10-byte command, which reserves two bytes for the transfer length, up to 65 535 blocks may be transferred with a single command. A value of 0 here really means that no block is transferred. Thus, SCSI commands are very powerful; 65 535 sector blocks with 512 bytes each corresponds to nearly 32 Mbytes of data, after all! Thus you may transfer, for example, a complete DOS partition (before version 3.30) by means of a single SCSI command.

The *parameter list* entry usually indicates the number of bytes transferred during the data-out phase of a command as a parameter list to the target. This applies, for example, to the *mode select* command.

If you issue a command used for returning sense data such as request sense or inquiry, then you need to enter in the *allocation length* field the number of bytes that the initiator is to receive from the target. The target terminates the transfer of the sense data when the value indicated in the field allocation length is reached. If the value is higher than the number of transferred sense bytes, then the target terminates the data-in phase earlier. The remaining bytes are not defined.

Every command block is terminated by a control byte, which mainly controls the linking of several commands. Figure 9.34 shows its format.

```
 7      6 5           2 1     0
┌─────────────────────────────────┐
│┌──────┬───────────┬───┬───┐     │
││manufac│ reserved  │ F │ L │     │
│└──────┴───────────┴───┴───┘     │
│ manufac:   manufacturer (insignificant)          │
│ reserved:  0                                     │
│ F:     flag                                      │
│        1=message "linked command with flag complete" output │
│        1=message "linked command complete" output│
│ L:     link                                      │
│        1=command link      0=no command link     │
└─────────────────────────────────┘
```

Figure 9.34: Control byte structure.

The two most significant bits *manufac* are available for the manufacturers of SCSI units; their value is ignored by the target. The four reserved bits must be set to 0. If the link bit *L* is set, then the initiator requests a command link. The target then returns only an intermediate status after completing a command, and requests the next command. The connection is not interrupted (as is the case for individual commands) and re-established by means of a bus-free and a selection phase, but remains effective so that the initiator can pass the next command block at once. Closely related to the link bit is the flag bit *F*. If L is cleared then F should also be equal to 0. With an enabled link a cleared flag bit F indicates that the target passes the initiator a message *linked command complete* after successfully completing a partial command. If the flag bit is set then a message *linked command with flag complete* is transferred instead.

You start a command execution by transferring a 6- or 10-byte command block to the target. Some commands additionally require a parameter list, which is transferred during the course of a data-out phase. If you employ the ST01 then you must therefore proceed as follows:

−   Clear the SCSI ENAB bit in the control register and set SCSI ENAB to activate the SCSI bus; write the SCSI-ID of the host adapter into the SCSI data port, and start an arbitration phase of the host adapter by means of the ARB STRT bit in the control register.

- Observe the ARB CMPL bit in the status register to determine the end of the arbitration phase, and to confirm that the host adapter has gained control of the SCSI bus.

- Issue a selection phase to select the intended target by activating the SEL line with the SCSI SEL bit of the control register, and by outputting the target's SCSI-ID via the SCSI data port.

- Observe the SCSI BSY bit in the status register afterwards to determine whether the addressed target has responded to the selection phase and has taken control of the bus.

- Observe the SCSI C/D, SCSI MSG and SCSI I/O bits in the status register to determine the beginning of a command phase; for this purpose, SCSI MSG and SCSI I/O must be cleared, but SCSI C/D must be set.

- Transfer the six or ten command bytes of the command block via the SCSI data port to the target to start command execution.

- If, additionally, a parameter list has to be transferred for the command concerned (mode select, for example), then observe the bits SCSI MSG, SCSI C/D and SCSI I/O to determine the beginning of a data-out phase (SCSI MSG, SCSI C/D and SCSI I/O cleared), and provide the parameter list via the SCSI data port.

- If a command (write block, for example) requires the transfer of a data block, then observe the SCSI MSG, SCSI C/D and SCSI I/O bits to determine the beginning of a data-out phase (SCSI MSG, SCSI C/D and SCSI I/O cleared), and provide the data block via the SCSI data port.

- If a command (read block, for example) returns a data block to the initiator (that is, the host adapter), then observe the bits SCSI MSG, SCSI C/D and SCSI I/O to determine the beginning of a data-in phase with cleared bits SCSI MSG, SCSI C/D and set bit SCSI I/O, and to fetch the data block via the SCSI data port.

- Observe SCSI MSG, SCSI C/D and SCSI I/O bits in the status register to determine the beginning of a status phase when SCSI MSG is cleared and SCSI C/D and SCSI I/O are set; the status byte is read via the SCSI data port.

- Observe the SCSI MSG, SCSI C/D and SCSI I/O bits in the status register to determine the beginning of a message-in phase (SCSI MSG, SCSI C/D and SCSI I/O are set), and to fetch the message via the SCSI data port.

You can see that the data exchange via host adapter and the SCSI bus is a rather extensive operation. All the details concerning correct programming of the host adapters would go far beyond the scope of this book. I have no other choice than to refer the SCSI freaks among you to the original literature on this subject. I hope, nevertheless, that the basic concepts and idea behind the very powerful and flexible SCSI interface have become somewhat clearer now. Consider that you can, by means of SCSI, integrate hard disks, tape drives, optical drives, and all the other revolutions that will surely arise in the future into your PC without the need of a hardware adapter or memory-eating driver for every single device. A general interface standard gives rise to an enormous flexibility but the concrete programming, unfortunately, becomes somewhat ponderous.

More powerful SCSI host adapters than the ST01 and ST02 implement a major portion of the SCSI bus control, which has to be programmed explicitly on an ST01 or ST02, by means of a processor, which is in turn controlled by firmware or exclusively by means of hardware, that is, an ASIC. The data exchange between host adapter and drive is then carried out very quickly. EISA SCSI host adapters often transfer the data from the host adapter by means of an EISA DMA channel operating in burst DMA mode C at the full width of 32 bits. Such SCSI systems achieve the highest transfer rates of up to 10 Mbytes/s if the host adapter has an on-board cache. But the 10 Mbytes/s refers only to the pure DMA transfer, that is, the path host-adapter-cache to main memory, or vice versa. The transfer rates on the SCSI bus are significantly lower but, nevertheless, impressive (up to 4 Mbytes/s).

9.8   Optical Mass Storage

For several years (and especially since the appearance of the CD in the audio and video fields) a triumphant progress has been predicted for optical mass storage. But as with all great prophesies – the reality is usually far more leisurely (fortunately, if we consider the daily end-of-the-world' prophesies!). The fact that optical mass storage hasn't already superseded magnetic media, and especially hard disks, is largely due to two reasons: the storage capacity of the hard disks has increased remarkably in the past five years, and further, re-writeable and high-capacity optical data carriers have been under development for years, or very expensive. The following section discusses the presently most widely used optical mass storage in brief.

9.8.1   CD-ROM

The common CD is well-suited as a read-only memory for extensive amounts of data. Even the music held in digital form on CDs is nothing more than a certain kind of information, after all. The high storage capacity of the CD and the well-tested techniques of the optical and mechanical components make the CD-ROM a reasonable alternative for data which is very extensive and will not be altered. To this group of data belong, for example, large program and data packs; Windows applications in particular come with a box full of floppies, which significantly contributes to the price. The difference between a CD player and a CD-ROM drive is not very extensive. Only a data interface for transferring data to the PC system bus and a very poor control interface so that the CPU has the opportunity to access certain data with software commands have been added. The interface is accessed by means of a suitable driver. With the driver a CD-ROM drive can be integrated into a PC system without any major problems. Further, CD-ROM drives are quite cheap; you can get high-quality drives for less than $500. Most drives have a SCSI interface, or can be directly connected to the floppy controller, but SCSI offers higher flexibility and more power. The disks typically have a capacity of 300 Mbytes or more. As is the case for all optical drives (this applies to WORMs as well as magneto-optical drives, too), the data transfer rate of a maximum of 150 kbytes/s and the access time of about 50 ms are not very exciting.

Especially for multimedia PCs, which enable the concurrent input, processing and output of data, the generation and output of visual information (for example, pictures that are part of an encyclopedia), as well as the input, processing and output of audio information (for example, speech and music), a certain variant of the CD-ROM has been developed, *CD-I (CD-interactive)*. CD-I supplies a significantly improved and more powerful programming interface to the actual computer so that the enormous amounts of data on a CD can be managed in a better way. Which multimedia capabilities are rapidly arising you may recognize, for example, by the fact that recently PC adapter cards with an integrated TV receiver have come onto the market. With a suitable driver and Windows you can watch the news in one window while you are working in another.

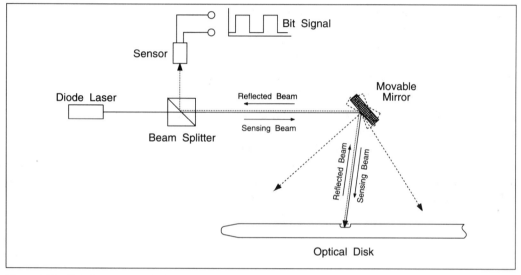

Figure 9.35: CD-ROM. A precisely focused laser beam emitted by a laser diode is radiated onto the surface of an optical disk by an optical assembly with a movable mirror. The intensity of the back-scattered beam is detected by a sensor, which converts the optical signal into a bit signal.

The operating principle of CD-ROM is quite easy, and corresponds largely to that of a conventional CD player (see Figure 9.35). Inside the drive a small semiconductor laser emits a very thin laser beam with a wavelength of about 850 nm. The beam is invisible, therefore, as the wavelength is in the near-infrared. Via an optical mirror assembly, which is precisely moved with some control elements, the laser beam is focused onto the surface of the CD-ROM disk. The disk usually accommodates the information in the form of small depressions. If the laser beam hits such a dip then the beam is not back-reflected in a well-directed way, as is the case between the dips, but is instead scattered. Thus the back-reflection intensity is much lower if the beam hits such a depression. (You see the same effect in connection with a mirror and a rough wall: although the amount of reflection of the mirror is not significantly higher than that of a white wall, you are dazzled by the sun reflected by the mirror but not by the white wall.) In the drive a sensor detects the intensity of the back-reflected beam, which varies according to the passing dips (that is, according to the information bits), and thus converts this variation into a data bit pattern.

Unlike floppies and hard disks, the information is not arranged in concentric circles (the tracks) but as a single spiral from the beginning of the disk up to its end. Thus, CD-ROM cannot deny that it has been developed from the CD player. After all, music is usually output as a continuous stream of tones from the beginning to the end; an organization according to tracks and sectors is therefore unneccessary.

CDs are well suited for the mass distribution of large amounts of data. At first a master-CD made of copper or another stable material is formed by depositing a photoresist on it, writing the information by means of a laser beam, and thus exposing certain locations. These exposed locations of the photoresist are removed and the disk is then etched so that part of the carrier material is removed at the exposed locations. Thus we get a disk that already contains dips at the right positions. Afterwards, a reverse disk is formed which contains the information as tiny bumps instead of dips. By pressing, a positive disk can be formed easily. For this purpose, a blank CD is put on the reverse disk and they are pressed together under high pressure. The bumps of the reverse disk form dips in the blank CD and a CD for CD-ROM is complete. For protection purposes, the disk is afterwards coated with an infrared-transparent layer.

In principle, dips are not essentially required for recording. Two different reflection types are sufficient, no matter how they are achieved. These may, for example, be two different phases (cristalline or amorphous) or two different magnetizations of the carrier's surface. The first method is used for WORMs, the latter for magneto-optical drives. (More about these in the following sections.) The main disadvantage of CD-ROM cannot be overlooked: the information held must be burnt-in during the manufacturing process. As the user you can't extend the stored data. Therefore, a first advance are the WORMs.

9.8.2   WORM

WORM has nothing to do with worms either in the biological or in the computer sense, but is simply the abbreviation for **write once, read many** (times). You may write on the WORM data carrier once and read it in principle until the end of time. Thus WORMs are well suited for archiving large amounts of data (for example, the correspondence of legal chambers or the credit transfers of banks). The stability of the written information is good, and remains readable for a longer time than on magnetic data carriers.

In addition to a sense laser beam, a WORM drive has a second, the so-called write laser beam, which is much more intensive than the sense laser beam. If information is written then the write laser generates a short but, nevertheless, very powerful laser pulse. Depending upon the structure and surface, the coating at the hit location vaporizes and exposes the surface of the data carrier itself, located below. This surface has a different reflection coefficient from the vaporized data carrier coating. Alternatively, the coating of the data carrier or the data carrier itself may only be melted at the location concerned, but not vaporized. At the end of the write laser pulse, the melted coating cools down very rapidly and solidifies in an amorphous form, that is, without any regular arrangement of the atoms. This amorphous form usually has a different reflection coefficient from the previously present crystalline or polycristalline coating. In both cases, another intensity of the sense laser beam is reflected which the sensor converts into a corresponding bit signal. Thus reading is carried out similar to the CD-ROM.

The disadvantage of WORMs is that the information, once written, cannot be erased. If you alter a single bit in an allocation unit, the complete allocation unit must be rewritten at another location. Thus WORMs are only suitable for archiving data that is hardly altered later. WORM data carriers achieve storage capacities of up to 500 Mbytes per disk side (that is, ten times more than a current high-end hard disk). But as is the case for CD-ROMs, you pay for the high capacity with a poor transfer rate of typically 150 kbytes/s and an average access time of 50 ms.

9.8.3 Magneto-Optical Drives

The only optical drives with erasable and rewriteable data carriers that have made the leap from development onto the market are magneto-optical drives. They use the influence of a magnetic field onto the polarization of an electromagnetic wave. Light and infrared beams are a form of electromagnetic radiation, as radio or radar waves are. Normal light is depolarized and the electrical as well as the magnetic field of the wave can have any direction perpendicular to the beam direction.

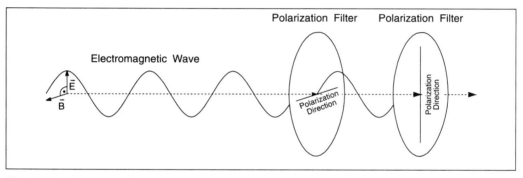

Figure 9.36: Polarization and polarization filter. An electromagnetic wave (for example, light) consists of a periodically changing field E and a periodically changing magnetic field B. The direction of B is called the polarization. Polarization filters only let pass waves whose polarization meets the polarization direction of the filter.

In polarized (or better, linearly polarized) light, the electric field of the wave only points in one direction, perpendicular to the propagation direction (see Figure 9.36). In the same way the magnetic field of the wave also points solely in a certain direction, the so-called *polarization direction*, which is perpendicular to the electric field as well as the propagation direction. The light of a laser, for example, is always polarized in a certain direction. A *polarization filter* only lets a polarized wave with certain polarization direction pass, but no light polarized perpendicularly thereto. Thus polarization filters can be used for determining the polarization direction: if the detector behind the polarization filter detects some light, it is polarized according to the filter direction; if the polarization filter doesn't let any light pass, it is polarized perpendicular to the filter direction.

When an electromagnetic wave passes through a body located in a magnetic field, the external magnetic field affects the electromagnetic field of the wave and turns the electrical and magnetic field of the wave, that is, its polarization direction. This phenomenon is called the *Faraday effect*. The same applies to the reflection at the surface of a magnetized substance. The magnetic field generated by the magnetization of the substance turns the polarization direction of the reflected wave relative to the incoming one. The direction of the polarization turn depends upon the magnetization direction of the substance.

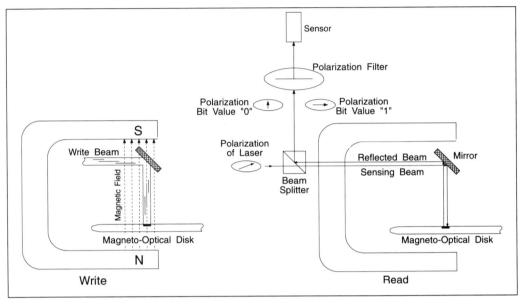

Figure 9.37: Magneto-optical disk. When writing data an intensive write beam warms up the surface of the disk. Under the influence of an external magnetic field, this spot cools down and magnetizes according to the external magnetic field. When reading data the external magnetic field is switched off and a weak sensing beam scans the disk. A sensor determines the magnetization direction of the disk with a polarization filter.

Magneto-optical drives now use the Faraday effect to record data. This works as follows: a magneto-optical disk at first has a uniformly magnetized coating made of a ferromagnetic lanthan-alloy. When the polarized laser beam hits the surface, the polarization direction of the reflected beam is turned according to the magnetization of the surface. A polarization filter serves as an analyser for the polarization direction of the back-reflected beam, and the sensor behind the filter detects the intensity passed through the polarization filter (see Figure 9.37).

If a bit is to be written onto disk, then a short but intensive write pulse from the laser heats up the surface at the corresponding location above the *Curie-point* T_C. As you know from Chapter 8, the magnetization of the ferromagnetic disk coating vanishes completely. At the same time, an electromagnet generates a magnetic field whose direction depends on the value of the bit to write; for a «1» the magnetic field is opposite to that for a «0». The direction of this magnetic field now determines the direction in which the elementary magnets (domains) of the heated spot orient when they are again cooled down below the Curie-point. Thus the value of the written bit is also decided. The coating freezes the direction of the magnetic field more or less at the time of writing; thus the writing of a bit is complete.

When reading a bit the laser beam scans the surface of the disk and the polarization system detects the direction of the polarization turn for the reflected beam. If the laser beam hits the above written bit, then the direction of the polarization turn for the reflected beam is dependent upon the magnetization direction of the surface coating. For example, the polarization direction for a «0» is turned to the left, and for a «1» turned to the right. In the first case, for example, no light can pass through the polarization filter, and the sensor detects a bit of value «0». In the latter case, the full intensity of the reflected beam reaches the sensor, and it detects a bit of value «1». Thus the information is also held here in the form of a tiny magnetization; but unlike a hard disk, the localization of a certain bit on the disk is carried out by means of a laser beam, that is, in an optical way.

By warming up the relevant spot later, and with a corresponding direction of the magnetic field generated by the electromagnet, the written bit can be erased again without any problem. Multiple write processes are thus possible, but presently their total number doesn't reach the possible number of erasures for pure magnetic disks. The stability of the written information is somewhere between 10 and 25 years.

Also, magneto-optical drives pay for their high storage capacity with a comparably poor transfer rate for high-performance drives of significantly less than 1 Mbyte/s and an average access time of typically 50 ms. But you should consider that a magneto-optical disk accommodates up to 30,000 (!) tracks. The enormous capacity of the optical data carriers is thus not achieved by increasing the bit density bpi, but mainly by raising the track density tpi – a hint that optical systems with mirrors which only need to position a completely massless and inertless laser beam operate much more exactly than magnetic ones. Compared to a laser beam, they have to move a very heavy read/write head.

Part 4
Externals and Peripherals

10 Interfaces – Connection to the Outside World

The chapter title already outlines the purpose of interfaces; to establish a connection with the rest of the world. The original concept of the PC was to supply users with their own complete computer system. But even in this case interfaces are required – for example, to connect a printer or plotter. You can break the isolation of an autonomous PC from its environment by installing a serial interface and a modem or network adapter; your PC becomes an intelligent telecommunications device with local computing power.

Generally, the term «interface» characterizes a hardware or software unit that establishes a connection between two (in most cases) different units. The following chapters discuss components that are usually called the interfaces of a PC. In particular, the parallel and serial interfaces, as well as network adapters, belong to this group.

10.1 Parallel Interface

Every PC is equipped with at least one parallel and one serial interface. Unlike the serial interface, for which a lot of applications exist, the parallel interface ekes out its existence as a wallflower, as it's only used to serve a parallel printer. Which undreamt-of possibilities the parallel interface can further offer are discussed in Section 10.1.4. But let's first turn to the «standard job» of parallel interfaces.

10.1.1 Printing

BIOS and DOS can usually serve up to four parallel interfaces in a PC, denoted LPT1, LPT2, LPT3 and LPT4 (for *line printer*). The abbreviation PRN (for **prin**ter) is synonymous (an alias) for LPT1; all commands with the target PRN are equivalent to commands with the target LPT1. The interface name already indicates the job of the parallel interface: to access a printer. (Whether you actually connect a printer to the interface is another question, of course.) Also, a robot which you program using the first parallel interface, for example, has the «address» LPT1.

The connection between interface and parallel printer is carried out by a Centronics cable. Centronics succeeded in the 1970s as the first printer manufacturer to establish a clearly defined interface standard for printers. Until then printing was its own science! Usually, a Centronics cable has 36 wires, and thus also 36 pins or contacts. 18 wires serve as ground lines and are twisted around the corresponding signal wire to provide at least a minimum of shielding and a simple protection against signal crosstalk. This still holds for the printer's cable connector; it has a two-sided contact strip with 36 contacts in total. Figure 10.1 shows the plugs on the side of the printer and PC, respectively.

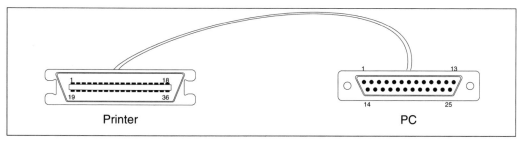

Figure 10.1: Centronics plug.

For the transfer of data and control signals to the printer only half (18) of the contacts are required. IBM therefore used only 25 contacts on the side of the PC instead of 36 to reduce the plug size (and to decrease the cost). The other ground lines required can easily be formed by internally splitting a ground line; the number of contacts is reduced and the plugs get smaller (and cheaper, of course). Because of the smaller jack and plugs, more interfaces can be implemented within the same installation space. An interface board usually has a jack each for the parallel and serial interfaces additionally implemented on the board on its reverse. When using an original Centronics plug, only a single jack would be possible.

The connection of a printer is very easy: you only have to connect the corresponding plugs on the cable ends to the jacks of the printer and PC. Confusion is impossible because of the different shape. But make sure that you don't try a similarly formed but otherwise incompatible jack, such as the connection for an external floppy drive or the SCSI bus.

Note also that the length of cable may not exceed 5 m, as otherwise data transfer errors occur and the cable sometimes seems to slur the data. The specification of the parallel interface and the structure of the Centronics cable doesn't allow large distances, unlike the serial interface and the serial data transfer. If you insist on operating a printer in your cellar (because of the noise, perhaps) which is 20 m away from your computer desk then you have no choice but to use the serial interface. This allows distances of up to 200 m but the serial data transfer is about ten times slower.

10.1.2 Printing Via DOS

In most cases you can print text and other data with no problem using the application program concerned. Usually, you only need to select the corresponding menu item. However, ensure that the printer is actually installed at the relevant interface!

Another possibility for printing data via DOS is the DOS commands COPY, PRINT and TYPE. With COPY file PRN, for example, you print the file on the first parallel printer. The same effect is achieved with PRINT file /d:PRN. Finally, you have the opportunity to input TYPE > PRN using the TYPE command and redirection to PRN. A detailed description of these commands is included in your DOS manual. The principle behind the use of PRN as something like a «file» is that DOS manages all units, whether they be a hard disk, a floppy, the screen, or here the parallel interface, by a device driver. The power of this concept is that the driver's interface to DOS is the same for all units, thus DOS can access a file on an optical disk in the same way as a parallel interface and pass data. DOS doesn't care whether you input on a COMMAND.COM-level C:\> the command COPY file a:new_file or COPY file PRN. DOS recognizes, according to the (reserved) name PRN, that no file on the standard drive but the first parallel interface is the target. Further reserved device names are LPT1–LPT4, COM1–COM4, CON and AUX. (See your DOS manual for further details.)

Programmers further have the opportunity to print data using the DOS function interrupt INT 21h. For this purpose, the two following functions are implemented whose call format is indicated in Appendix I.

– *Function 05h printer output*: this old 05h function dates from the CP/M era, and outputs one character to PRN; LPTx can't be accessed. If a printer error occurs then DOS calls INT 24h as the hardware error handler.

Example: print character 'a' on PRN

```
MOV ah, 05h   ; load function number into ah
MOV dl, 'a'   ; load ASCII code of 'a' into dl
INT 21h       ; call DOS interrupt
```

– *Function 40h write file/device*: this function uses the more modern concept of handles, and outputs a whole string. Note that the DOS device PRN is assigned handle 4 as standard. All other devices LPTx must be opened in advance with the 3dh function *open file/device* for a write access (that you are not able to read anything from the printer by means of function 3fh seems to be obvious). For PRN this is not necessary; but jokers readily have the opportunity to let PRN disappear from the scene by means of a function call 3eh, *close file/device*. A future call of function 40h with the target handle 4 corresponding to PRN fails.

Example: print character 'a' on PRN

```
buffer DB 1 DUP('a')  ; load buffer with byte 'a'
MOV ah, 40h           ; load function number into ah
MOV bx, 04h           ; load handle 4 for PRN into bx
MOV cx, 01h           ; write one character
MOV dx, OFFSET buffer ; load offset of buffer into dx
                      ; segment of buffer already in ds
INT 21h               ; function call
```

The main advantage of function 40h is that you can output a whole string quite easily, and get an error code in register ax. As is usual for such high-level functions, you cannot, for example, determine the status of the parallel interface and the connected printer. This is only possible using the BIOS.

10.1.3 Printing Via BIOS Interrupt INT 17h

Another possibility for accessing the parallel interface is the three functions of BIOS interrupt 17h. With function 00h you can output a character similar to the 05h function of INT 21h; the 01h function initializes the interface and printer, and function 02h determines the current status. Every function provides a status byte in the ah register. Its structure is shown in Figure 10.2.

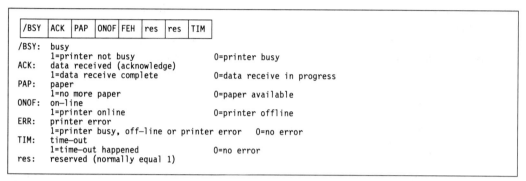

```
 /BSY  ACK  PAP  ONOF FEH  res  res  TIM

 /BSY:  busy
        1=printer not busy              0=printer busy
 ACK:   data received (acknowledge)
        1=data receive complete         0=data receive in progress
 PAP:   paper
        1=no more paper                 0=paper available
 ONOF:  on-line
        1=printer online                0=printer offline
 ERR:   printer error
        1=printer busy, off-line or printer error   0=no error
 TIM:   time-out
        1=time-out happened             0=no error
 res:   reserved (normally equal 1)
```

Figure 10.2: Printer status byte.

If $\overline{BSY}$ is set (= 1) then the printer accepts further data; it is not busy. The printer itself signals, via a set *ACK* bit, that it has received a character correctly, and can receive further data bytes. If no more paper is available in the printer then the *PAP* bit is set. The *ONOF* checks whether the printer concerned is on or off-line, perhaps because of an erroneously operated printer key, a paper or another error, or it is even switched off. The *ERR* bit is always set if an error has occurred in the printer, for example because of exhausted paper, a stuck printing head, or an error during the course of data transfer. You may define a time-out value for the printer or parallel interface (as a standard, 20 s are set). If the printer is not ready (bit $\overline{BSY}$) or if the BIOS doesn't receive an ACK signal after the lapse of this time interval, then the BIOS sets the *TIM* bit. On a DOS level you have the opportunity to set an infinite time-out value by the command MODE LPTx ,,P. The system always retries the data transfer after a time-out value.

The values of the individual bits in the printer status byte, except ACK and ERR, reflect the status of the corresponding lines or pins. A bit value of 1 corresponds to a high signal level of about +5 V, a bit value of 0, on the other hand, to a signal level of about 0 V. With ACK and FEH the situation is inverted; a value of 1 corresponds to a high, a bit value of 0 to a low signal level. With the exception of the TIM bit, the printer status byte indicates the contents of the parallel interface concerned; but ACK and FEH are inverted by the BIOS. Further information on the status register and the signals is presented in Section 10.1.5.

Use function 00h of the BIOS interrupt 17h for outputting a character to a printer. But also note that other devices may be connected to a parallel interface. Meanwhile, programs exist through which you may exchange data between two computers via the parallel interface, but these programs directly access the interface registers; a data output by means of BIOS interrupt 17h doesn't succeed in most cases.

Example: output character 'a' via the BIOS to the first parallel printer.

```
MOV ah, 00h    ; load function number 00h into ah
MOV al, 'a'    ; print character 'a'
MOV dx, 00h    ; transmit character to LPT1
INT 17h        ; call interrupt
```

Before you can use a parallel interface to output a character, for example after booting, you first need to initialize the interface. Depending upon the printer type, the printer may also carry out an initialization. You may also reset the printer by passing an explicit initialization command. The 01h function, on the other hand, issues an initialization by activating a signal on the interface cable while the reset command is passed over the eight data lines as a normal print character, and interpreted by the printer as a command code and not as a character to be printed.

Example: initialize second parallel printer.

```
MOV ah, 01h    ; load function number 01h into ah
MOV dx, 01h    ; initialize LPT2
INT 17h        ; call interrupt
```

You get the status byte with every command in register ah. Through the 02h function of interrupt 17h you also have the opportunity to determine the status without any further action. This is advantageous, for example, if you want to detect in advance whether the printer is ready.

Example: determine status of the third parallel printer.

```
MOV ah, 02h    ; load function number 02h into ah
MOV dx, 02h    ; determine status of LPT3
INT 17h        ; call interrupt
```

The BIOS interrupt 17h thus returns more status information concerning the corresponding parallel interface than DOS functions 05h and 40h. Of significance for precisely detecting the cause of a printer error is function 02h. But you don't get ultimate control over the function capabilities of the parallel interface until you have programmed the registers directly. The strategy and the exciting capabilities of the parallel interface beyond plain printing on a parallel printer are discussed in the following sections.

Address	Size	Structure 76543210	Contents	Meaning
40:08	word		base address LPT1	
40:0a	word		base address LPT2	
40:0c	word		base address LPT3	
40:0e	word		base address LPT4	
40:11	byte	xx......	installed hardware	number of parallel interfaces (00=0, 01=1, 10=2, 11=3)
40:78	word		time-out LPT1	time-out value in seconds
40:79	word		time-out LPT2	time-out value in seconds
40:7a	word		time-out LPT3	time-out value in seconds
40:7b	word		time-out LPT4	time-out value in seconds

Table 10.1: BIOS data area and parallel interface

Table 10.1 lists all the relevant sections of the BIOS data area as far as the parallel interface is concerned. The base addresses indicate the beginning of the three interface registers (see Section 10.1.5). By altering the time-out values you can determine how long the BIOS should try to access the printer concerned before a time-out error is reported. Finally, the *installed hardware* byte indicates how many parallel interfaces are present in your system. The startup routine of the BIOS determines the base addresses and the number of interfaces present during the course of booting and writes the corresponding values to the BIOS data area.

10.1.4 Structure, Function and Connection to Printers

The parallel interface demonstrates a quite simple structure, as it is normally used in a PC only for data output to a printer. Figure 10.3 shows a block diagram of this interface.

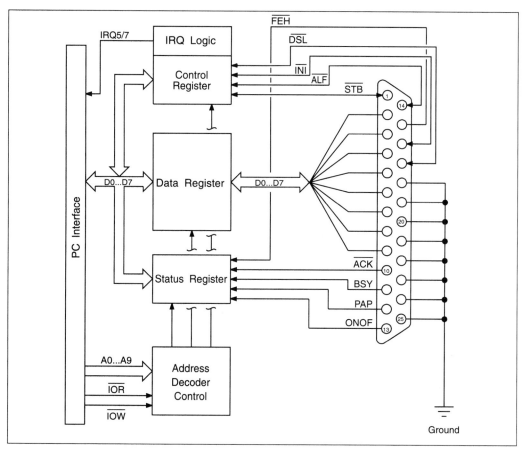

Figure 10.3: Block diagram of the parallel interface.

Connection to the PC system bus is established as usual by a PC interface. Note that the interface adapter cards have only an 8-bit data bus and thus will run even in an ISA or EISA computer with a width of eight bits. This is sufficient, as data is always passed to printers in units of eight bits, and the internal registers of the interface are only eight bits wide. The address decoder decodes address bits A0–A9 if one of the $\overline{IOR}$ and $\overline{IOW}$ signals is enabled to determine whether the interface, and eventually which register, is selected. The control supervises all input and output operations of the registers, and thus of the whole interface.

The central part of the parallel interface is the 8-bit data register, which can be read and written by the CPU (that is, it is bidirectional). The CPU passes the data register the data bytes for the printer. If the processor reads out the data register then it gets the OR-value of the last written byte and the signals which are externally applied to interface pins 2–9. Usually, a printer doesn't drive lines 2–9 onto a high level, so that an IN instruction referring the data register simply returns the last written value. The situation changes if an external device drives the lines concerned onto a high level. The high level then overwrites a possible 0 bit in the data register, and you get the corresponding OR-value. If you write a 0-byte into the data register in advance of an IN instruction, then this instruction always supplies the signal levels at pins 2–9. You may thus realize, for example, a data exchange with another parallel interface, that is, another PC (see below). If you only want to access a printer (the standard job of the parallel interface), then you simply need to load the data register with the value to be passed.

The status register reflects the current status of the connected printer, which returns status values to the interface via various lines (see Table 10.2). The CPU can only read the status register (it is unidirectional). Using the control register, you may determine the behaviour of the interface, as well as control the printer, via several control signals. The control register can be read and written, and serves particularly to control data transfer to the printer. You can configure the interface so that the IRQ logic issues a hardware interrupt request as soon as the printer is ready to accept another character. The next section discusses further details concerning programming the interface in more detail.

The connection to the printer is established with a Centronics cable. Table 10.2 lists the assignment and the signals on the pins and plug contacts.

Most printers fix the $\overline{DSL}$ signal internally to ground, that is, the printer is always selected. In older systems, the CPU was able to select or deselect the printer explicitly by this signal. The eight data pins D0–D7 transfer a data byte to the printer; but you may also receive data if the circuitry of the interface is implemented bidirectionally. By means of lines $\overline{STR}$, $\overline{ALF}$ and $\overline{INI}$, the printer is controlled by the CPU and the interface. A transition of the $\overline{STR}$ (strobe) signal from a high to a low level instructs the printer to accept the data byte on lines D0–D7 as the data byte to be transferred. With a low level of connection $\overline{ALF}$ the printer carries out an automatic line feed after every printed line. Finally, a transition of the signal $\overline{INI}$ from a high to a low level gives rise to an initialization of the connected printer if it supports the $\overline{INI}$ signal.

The other control signals are usually passed by the printer to the interface, and indicate the printer's current state. If the CPU attempts to transfer a byte to the printer by activating $\overline{STR}$, then the printer responds with the activation of the $\overline{ACK}$ signal to acknowledge reception. It pulls $\overline{ACK}$ to a low level to indicate that the interface is allowed to pass further data. An activated BSY signal indicates that the printer is currently busy and cannot receive any character. If the printer is out of paper then it raises the PAP signal to a high level. When you are switching the printer online it enables the ONOF signal. You can try this if you like, and read the printer's status by means of function 02h of the BIOS interrupt 17h. Finally, the $\overline{\text{FEH}}$ signal indicates, with a low level, that an error has occurred; for example, the printing head is stuck.

25 pin	36 pin	Signal	Description
1	1	$\overline{\text{STR}}$	low signal level transmits data to printer
2	2	D0	data bit 0
3	3	D1	data bit 1
4	4	D2	data bit 2
5	5	D3	data bit 3
6	6	D4	data bit 4
7	7	D5	data bit 5
8	8	D6	data bit 6
9	9	D7	data bit 7
10	10	$\overline{\text{ACK}}$	low level indicates that printer received one character and is able to receive more
11	11	BSY	high level of signal indicates – character received – printer buffer full · – printer initialization – printer offline – printer error
12	12	PAP	high level indicates out of paper
13	13	OFON	high level indicates that printer is on-line
14	14	$\overline{\text{ALF}}$	auto line feed; low level indicates that printer issues line feed automatically
15	32	$\overline{\text{FEH}}$	low level indicates – out of paper – printer offline – printer error
16	31	$\overline{\text{INI}}$	low level initializes printer
17	36	$\overline{\text{DSL}}$	low level selects printer
18–25	19–30,33	ground	ground 0 V
—	16	0V	—
—	17	case	protective ground of case
—	18	+5V	—
—	34,35	—	unused

Table 10.2: Layout and signals of 25 and 36 pin plugs

Note that not all listed signals are actually supported by all printers. In particular, the $\overline{\text{INI}}$ and $\overline{\text{DSL}}$ signals are not used often. Furthermore, the parallel interface inverts some signals internally. The meaning of a signal and the accompanying register bit is then inverted; therefore, pay attention!

10.1.5 Programming the Registers Directly

The parallel interface has three registers with which you can transfer data and control the printer as well as the interface. The base address of the registers for all interfaces LPT1–LPT4 is stored in the BIOS data area (see Table 10.1). The data register (Figure 10.4) is located at offset 00h, the status register (Figure 10.5) at offset 01h and the control register (Figure 10.6) at offset 02h. Generally, the base address of LPT1 is 378h and that of LPT2 278h. The parallel interface on a Hercules or monochrome adapter card starts at 3bch, but may still represent LPT1. Further,

2bch can be used as a fourth possibility, so the registers can serve a maximum of four parallel interfaces. During the course of booting, the BIOS checks in the I/O address order 3bch, 378h, 278h and 2bch whether a parallel interface is physically present at the corresponding I/O addresses, and assigns those actually found the names LPT1, LPT2, etc. in succession. But some BIOS variants support only two parallel interfaces, and don't recognize any others. A configuration check by means of the BIOS interrupt INT 11h then returns only two installed parallel interfaces, even though you have installed four, for example. The following sections discuss the meaning of the registers in more detail.

7							0	
D7	D6	D5	D4	D3	D2	D1	D0	printer signal
9	8	7	6	5	4	3	2	pin number

D7–D0: data bit 7...0

Figure 10.4: Data register (bidirectional, offset 00h).

The data register is eight bits wide, and accommodates the data bits to be transferred. You may read and write this register simply by using an IN or OUT instruction.

The status register is read-only, and returns control information from the printer. Upon a cleared $\overline{BSY}$ bit the printer is currently busy (that is, the printer buffer is full), a character transfer is in progress, or the printer carries out an initialization. The interface may not transfer another character, but has to wait until the $\overline{BSY}$ bit is set. The $\overline{ACK}$ bit, together with the STR bit of the control register (see Figure 10.6), is of significance for a correct data transfer. If the interface has transferred a data byte to the printer, then the printer activates the $\overline{ACK}$ line to acknowledge receipt of the character. Accordingly, the $\overline{ACK}$ bit in the status register is cleared. If $\overline{ACK}$ is set, this shows the printer is still occupied with the reception (if $\overline{BSY}$ is cleared simultaneously), or that the previous character transfer was a long time ago (with a set $\overline{BSY}$ bit). To determine whether the printer is ready to receive data, you must therefore use $\overline{BSY}$, and for the character transfer itself the $\overline{ACK}$ bit.

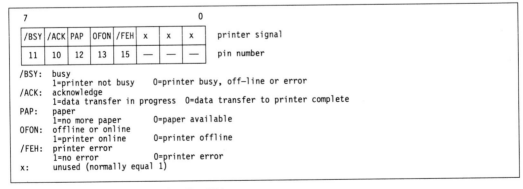

7							0	
/BSY	/ACK	PAP	OFON	/FEH	x	x	x	printer signal
11	10	12	13	15	—	—	—	pin number

/BSY: busy
       1=printer not busy   0=printer busy, off-line or error
/ACK: acknowledge
       1=data transfer in progress 0=data transfer to printer complete
PAP: paper
       1=no more paper   0=paper available
OFON: offline or online
       1=printer online   0=printer offline
/FEH: printer error
       1=no error   0=printer error
x: unused (normally equal 1)

Figure 10.5: Status register (read-only, offset 01h).

If the printer is out of paper the *PAP* bit is set to 1. At the same time, the *OFON* bit is cleared and the $\overline{\text{FEH}}$ bit is set to indicate this error, and to tell you the printer is now offline. By investigating the OFON bit you can therefore determine whether the printer is online at all, for example, in the case of a time-out error.

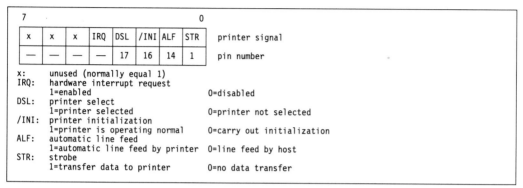

Figure 10.6: Control register (bidirectional, offset 02h).

The control register controls the printer behaviour and the generation of hardware interrupts by the parallel interface. If the *IRQ* bit is set, then the interface issues a hardware interrupt via IRQ5 (LPT2) or IRQ7 (LPT1) corresponding to INT 0dh and INT 0fh, respectively, if a transition of the $\overline{\text{ACK}}$ signal from a high to a low level occurs. Thus an interrupt occurs exactly when the printer acknowledges receipt of the character. The accompanying handler can then transfer the next character to the ready printer. But the PC BIOS doesn't usually use this interrupt-driven data transfer, but simply investigates the $\overline{\text{ACK}}$ bit to detect the acknowledgement by the printer. With the IRQ bit you can, for example, implement an interrupt driven and bidirectional data exchange via the parallel interface. Details on this subject are discussed in the following section.

Note that the IRQ channel of the interface is usually set by a jumper or DIP switch. In the case of polling by the BIOS, this is insignificant as an interrupt never occurs. But if you program a handler, for example for the IRQ channel of LPT1 to realize a hardware-driven data transfer in the background, you must ensure that IRQ7 is actually used for the LPT1 board. The situation gets even more complicated if all four possible parallel interfaces can issue an interrupt. As only two IRQ channels, and therefore also only two handlers, are available, the interrupt handler must be able, for example by reading the status bits, to determine which interface has actually issued the interrupt request.

Printers that strictly orient to the Centronics standard must be explicitly activated by setting the *DSL* bit. On IBM-compatible parallel printers the corresponding line is not used, and the printer is always enabled when you switch it on or press the online button. A cleared $\overline{\text{INI}}$ bit gives rise to a printer initialization. You also achieve the same effect on most printers by passing an explicit reset command; the only difference here is that an electrical signal of the interface, and not a command code, is used. If you set the *ALF*, the printer carries out an automatic line feed after printing each line.

For the data transfer to printers besides $\overline{ACK}$ the *STR* bit is also of significance. A set STR bit generates a short *strobe pulse* that instructs the printer to accept the signals on the data lines, according to the data register, as the transfer data. Thus, STR clocks the data transfer from the interface to the printer. Note that setting the STR bit only gives rise to a single strobe pulse. If you want to pass another data byte it is not, therefore, sufficient only to load the data register. Additionally, you must clear and set the STR bit again to generate a strobe pulse. The following example illustrates the strategy for printing a character out to a printer by directly programming the interface registers:

Example: routine for outputting a character to printer LPT1 (language: Microsoft C 5.10); the routine returns with an error code.

```
int parall_output(char character)
{
  int i, code;

  for (i = 0; i < TIMEOUT_COUNT; i++) {  /* wait until printer no more busy */
    code = inp(0x379);                   /* read status register */
    if ((code & 0x80) == 0x80) break;    /* check whether BSY bit is set */
  }
  if (i == TIMEOUT_COUNT) return (1);    /* BSY timeout error, error code 1 */

  outp(0x378, (int) character);          /* load data register */

  code = inp(0x37a);                     /* read control register */
  code = code | 0x01;                    /* set STB bit */
  outp(0x37a, code);                     /* strobe high */

  for (i = 0; i < STROBE_WAIT) ;         /* wait a short time */

  code = inp(0x37a);                     /* read control register */
  code = code & 0xfe;                    /* clear STB bit */
  outp(0x37a, code);                     /* strobe low, data are transferred */

  for (i = 0; i < TIMEOUT_COUNT; i++) {  /* wait for ACK from printer */
    code = inp(0x379);                   /* read status register */
    if ((code & 0x40) == 0x00) break;    /* check whether ACK bit is cleared */
  }
  if (i == TIMEOUT_COUNT) return (2);    /* ACK timeout error, error code 2 */

  return(0);                             /* character passed correctly, error code 0 */
}
```

If you compare the meaning of the bits in the control and status registers with the assignment of the corresponding lines, then you see that the bits $\overline{BSY}$, DSL, ALF and STR are inverted compared to their corresponding signals. Thus the parallel interface inverts the signals at pins 11, 17, 14 and 1, respectively. Why especially these signals are inverted I don't know, but maybe you have a good idea?

10.1.6 More About LPTx – General Interface Assignment

All the descriptions above only refer to the use of the parallel interface for accessing a parallel printer. For example, the receiving interface inside the printer is responsible for pulling the $\overline{\text{ACK}}$ signal to a low level if the printer has received the character correctly. But, of course, you are free to connect any other device to the parallel interface, too; for example, a small robot. This robot doesn't need to generate an active-low signal $\overline{\text{ACK}}$ in any way when data has been transferred. Instead, the 12 pins 1–9, 14, 16 and 17 are available to you without restriction for output and the 17 pins 1–17 for fetching signals. Thus the parallel interface is very flexible, and you have the opportunity to use it in some way which differs significantly from its very limited use as a printer interface.

To access an external device connected to the parallel interface, you need to know what conseqences a set or cleared bit in the data or control register for the signals at the corresponding pins has, and which signal level a set or cleared bit in one of these three registers means. Exactly these points are discussed in the following sections. Some precautions are demanded as the parallel interface inverts several signals before they are output at or read from the corresponding pin. This applies (as already mentioned) for pins 1, 11, 14 and 17.

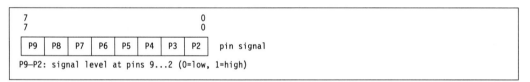

Figure 10.7: Data register (bidirectional, offset 00h).

The eight bits of the bidirectional data register (Figure 10.7) correspond to the pins with numbers 9–2. The assignment of bit value and signal level is not inverted, that is, a set bit corresponds to a high-level signal of about +5 V. Ensure, when reading the register value, that the value of a bit is determined by OR-ing the last written bit and the level of the applied signal. If you want to determine the «pure» pin signal, then you must first set the register bit to 0; afterwards, you may determine the signal level at the accompanying pin correctly. The same also applies for all bidirectional registers.

```
 7                              0
 ┌──────┬────┬────┬────┬────┬────┬────┬───┐
 │/P11* │P10 │P12 │P13 │P15 │ x  │ x  │ x │  pin signal
 └──────┴────┴────┴────┴────┴────┴────┴───┘
 P10...P15: signal level at pins 10...15 (0=low, 1=high)
```

Figure 10.8: Status register (read-only, offset 01h).

The status register (Figure 10.8) is read-only, even for a general use of the parallel interface. The three low-order register bits are not used and usually provide a value of 1. The four most significant bits 3–6 indicate the signal levels at pins 15, 13, 12 and 10 in non-inverted form. On the other hand, the interface inverts the signal level at pin 11, that is, a set bit $\overline{\text{P11}}$ corresponds to a low, a cleared bit to a high signal level.

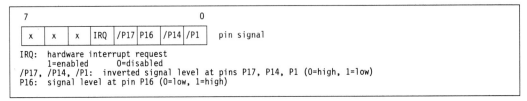

Figure 10.9: Control register (partially bidirectional, offset 02h).

The control register (Figure 10.9) is partially bidirectional. The IRQ bit has a meaning only for write accesses; you can use it for defining whether the interface is to issue a hardware interrupt via IRQ5 or IRQ7 if the signal at pin 10 (see status register) drops from a high to a low level. Reading the IRQ bit always returns the last written value. The three most significant bits are not used, and return a value of 1 during the course of a read access. The four low-order bits of the register, on the other hand, are bidirectional. But note that only the bit P16 corresponding to pin 16 is not inverted. The other three bits indicate the inverted ones of the signals at pins 17, 14 and 1 when read. If you are writing some values then the interface sets the signal levels at these pins so that they appear inverted compared to the bit values in the control register.

Another possible application of the parallel interface is the control of an external device. Suitable signal levels at the programmable output pins then drive the device accordingly. Via the input pins, the device can also return information to the PC. With a soldering iron and some skill you can, for example, construct a computer-controlled irrigation plant for your garden where the parallel interface controls magnetic valves and pumps to irrigate the garden, depending upon signals that humidity and sunshine sensors apply to the input pins.

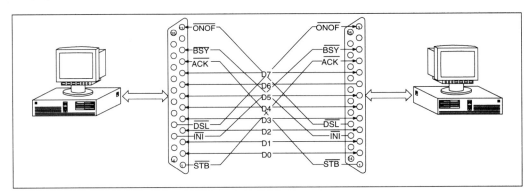

Figure 10.10: Data exchange via the parallel interface. For a data exchange, several control and status lines must be interchanged to enable a handshake.

A somewhat more serious application is the exchange of data between two computers via the parallel interface. This works much faster than by means of a serial interface, as the data is transferred in portions of one byte and not only of a single bit (if you use only one of the output lines for transferring control information then you may even transfer eleven bits at a time). Besides the continuous access to another computer, this data exchange is advantageous particularly if no data exchange by means of floppies is possible, for example because the floppy sizes are incompatible. Figure 10.10 shows a scheme for a possible data transfer via the parallel interface.

As you can see from Figure 10.10, data pins 2–9 of the two interfaces are connected to each other, and pins 1 ($\overline{STB}$), 17 ($\overline{DSL}$) and 16 ($\overline{INI}$) are connected crossways to pins 10 ($\overline{ACK}$), 13 (ONOFF) and 11 (BSY). The data exchange proceeds as follows:

1. The transmitter raises line 17 ($\overline{DSL}$) to a high level by clearing bit $\overline{P17}$ in the control register to indicate that it wants to transfer data to the receiver.

2. The receiver detects this selection by means of the set bit P13 in the status register, and activates the line $\overline{INI}$ by setting bit P16 in the control register.

3. The transmitter detects this acknowledgement by the receiver through the cleared bit P11 in the status register; the connection is therefore established, the roles as transmitter and receiver are unambiguously defined, and the transmitter is now able to transfer data to the receiver.

4. The transmitter loads the character to be transmitted into the data register and lowers the potential of the $\overline{STB}$ line by means of a set bit $\overline{P1}$ in the control register to a low level, and clears the bit $\overline{P1}$ afterwards to raise the potential of the line $\overline{STB}$ to a high level again. Because of the short pulse, the data transfer is started and an IRQ is issued in the receiver.

5. The called IRQ handler of the receiver reads the data register and thus the transmitted data, and transfers it into a buffer in main memory.

6. Afterwards, the receiver lowers the potential of the $\overline{STB}$ line by means of a set $\overline{P1}$ bit on the control register to a low level, and clears the $\overline{P1}$ bit to raise the potential of the $\overline{STB}$ line again to a high level. This short pulse acknowledges the reception of the data and issues an IRQ in the transmitter.

7. The called IRQ handler of the transmitter returns control to the transfer program, which repeats steps 4–6 until all data has been transferred.

8. The transmitter disconnects itself by setting bit $\overline{P17}$ in the control register.

9. The receiver responds to the disconnection by clearing bit P16 in the control register; now the roles as transmitter and receiver can be distributed again.

Steps 1–9 outline the data transfer only, of course. For the receiver's response to the selection by the transmitter or the acknowledgement by the receiver, several check steps for determining time-out errors should additionally be implemented. With the remaining pins 12, 14 and 15, for example, an additional error signal, an attention signal (if the receiver has important data ready for the transmitter), or other status information may be transmitted. Clever programming of the steps required enables a data transfer rate of more than 100 kbytes/s. Not very exciting when compared to «real» networks, but nevertheless significantly more than via a serial interface. The main disadvantage, though, is that the connection length must not exceed 5 m. Additionally, you are forced to fetch your soldering iron to form the necessary wirings.

10.2   Serial Interface

Besides the parallel interface for accessing parallel printers, the serial interface is of great importance on a PC because of its flexibility. Various devices such as a plotter, modem, mouse and, of course, a printer can be connected to a serial interface. The structure, functioning and programming of the serial interface are the subject of the following sections.

10.2.1 Serial and Asynchronous Data Transfer

We have already met parallel data transfer in the previous section. Characteristic of parallel data transfer is that the bits of a data byte, and eventually a parity bit, are transmitted in parallel, that is, simultaneously via a plurality of data lines. Thus for a data byte and a parity bit, nine data lines are required. In a serial data transfer the individual data bits and the eventual parity bit are, however, transferred successively, that is, in a serial manner via a single data line. One objection to this might be that the parallel interface also passes the data bytes successively (that is, serially) when printing a large document. But the difference is that in a parallel data transfer the individual data units (that is, the data bytes) are transmitted as a whole, while the serial data transfer splits even the data units into single bits and transfers them bit-by-bit.

Synchronous and Asynchronous Transfer

The serial data transfer is further distinguished according to whether the data exchange is carried out synchronously or asynchronously. The difference is quite simple: in a synchronous transfer one or more additional signals are transmitted, which indicate when the next bit is valid on the data line. These signals may be formed by clock signals of a clock signal source or by handshake signals of the form *request* and *acknowledge*. The main advantage of synchronous transfer is that the receiver responds to various clock rates, as long as its maximum frequency is not exceeded. For this purpose it simply detects, for example, the low-high transition of the clock signal.

In contrast, in an asynchronous data transfer the data bits themselves accommodate a minimum of synchronization information; receiver and transmitter must operate at the same clock frequency here. The embedded synchronization information comprises a so-called *start bit*, which indicates the beginning of a data unit, and at least one *stop bit*, which indicates the end of the data unit concerned. If the parity information (which is also frequently used for a parallel data transfer) is taken into account, too, then a *serial data unit (SDU)* consists of a start bit, the data bits, eventually one parity bit, and at least one stop bit. Thus, compared to the synchronous serial data transfer we have an overhead because of the start and stop bits here.

Parity and Baud Rate

The parity is a simple and, unfortunately, also a poor protection against transmission errors. Parity can only detect single-bit errors reliably; burst errors with several disturbed bits are not detected with a probability of 50%. Thus the parity is only suitable for short and less error-prone transfer paths; for other applications, CRC codes are much more reliable, but are more complicated to calculate. The advantage of parity is that nearly all serial interface chips support the generation and checking of parity bits on a hardware level. Five different parities in total are distinguished:

– no parity: no parity bit is embedded at all;

– even parity: the parity bit is set so that in the data bits and the parity bit together an even number of 1s appears.

– odd parity: the parity bit is set so that in the data bits and the parity bit together an odd number of 1s appears.

– mark: the parity bit is always set to a value of 1.

– space: the parity bit is always set to a 0.

At this point, a few remarks are needed on the apparently pointless parities mark and space. Mark and space are actually suitable only for detecting errors in the parity bit itself. When an SDU with a cleared or set parity bit arrives, and a mark or space parity should actually be valid, an error of the parity bit has occurred. This doesn't say anything about whether the data bits are correct or not, of course. Inversely, the data bits can be destroyed, but the receiver doesn't notice that at all if the parity bit is OK. But nevertheless mark and space are frequently used, and I don't know why: perhaps you have a good idea (if so, please tell me)! Mark and space are thus only of minor value. Leave out the parity in this case, although no parity seems to be less reliable than the parities mark and space (but this only *seems* to be).

Another measure in connection with serial data transfer which frequently gives rise to misunderstandings is the *baud rate*. Named after the French mathematician J.M.E. Baudot, it means the number of signal changes of a transfer channel per second. As for the usual serial interfaces, the signal changes are equidistant in time and a very simple binary data encoding is carried out (a logical high level equal to mark corresponds to a «1», a logical low level equal to space to a «0»), the baud rate here is equal to the number of transferred *bits per second (bps)* if one also includes the start, parity and stop bits. For more powerful encodings, and by using data compression methods, the data rates (in bps) may exceed the baud rate significantly.

SDU and Serialization

Before an asynchronous serial data transfer between two devices can take place, transmitter and receiver must be set up to the same formats. To the format belong the number of data bits, whether and eventually which parity is to be established, as well as the number of stop bits. Valid specifications for the number of data bits are five, six, seven, and eight. If you choose five data bits the serial interface chip in your PC automatically adds 1 1/2 stop bits. This means that the active-time of the stop bit is as long as 1 1/2 bits; otherwise you may choose one or two stop bits. Moreover, you must set the baud rate for transmitter and receiver to the same value. As an example, Figure 10.11 shows an SDU with one start bit, seven data bits, odd parity and one stop bit. Note that the start bit always has a value of 0 corresponding to space and the stop bit(s) is (are) always equal to 1 corresponding to mark.

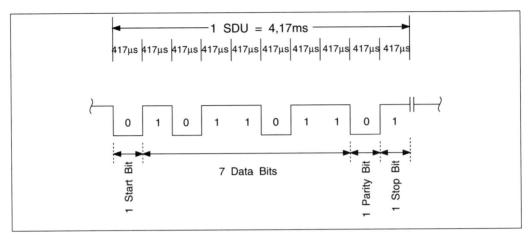

Figure 10.11: SDU. The serial data unit shown has one start bit, seven data bits, one parity bit, and one stop bit. At the selected baud rate of 2400, each bit is transferred within 417 µs.

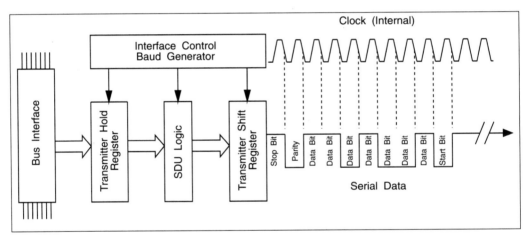

Figure 10.12: Transmitting an SDU.

But how is the SDU generated inside the interface, and output or received, and the received SDU separated into its components? Figure 10.12 shows a scheme for generating the SDU. The interface chip has a transmitter hold register for transmitting data, which first fetches the data bytes from the CPU. According to the selected data format, the SDU logic puts the start bit in front of the set number of data bits, eventually calculates the parity bit, and appends it together with the set number of stop bits to the data bits. The thus formed SDU is transferred into the transmitter shift register. The transmitter shift register is now operated by a clock source according to the phase of the baud rate, and thus provides (beginning with the start bit and the least significant data bit) the individual bits of the SDU at its serial output. For this purpose, the AND-value of the clock signal and the current least significant SDU bit at the output of the transmitter shift register are formed. The operation mode of the transmitters causes first the low-order and then the high-order data bits to be supplied. If no further data is to be output, the chip provides a mark signal (that is, a level corresponding to a logical «1»), and drives the transmission line to a logical high level.

The reception of an SDU proceeds inversely. The start bit with a logical value of 1 corresponding to space is an unambiguous signal for an incoming SDU, as the reception line is usually held on mark by the transmitter. Thus the start bit acts as a trigger pulse, and starts the receiver in the serial interface chip. The SDU bits are loaded into the receiver shift register according to the phase of the setup baud rate. This means that in the receiver shift register first the low-order and then the high-order data bits arrive. The receiver logic separates start bit, parity bit (if present) and the stop bit(s) from the received SDU bits, eventually calculates the parity of the received bits, and compares it to the setup parity. Afterwards, the extracted data bits are transferred into the receiver buffer register from which they may be read out as the received data byte by the CPU. This reception scheme is illustrated in Figure 10.13.

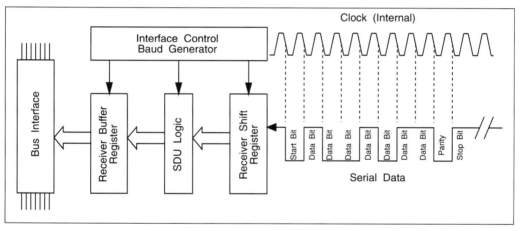

Figure 10.13: Receiving an SDU.

From the description of the transmission and reception process, it can be readily seen that transmitter and receiver must be set to the same baud rate. Additionally, the set data formats (that is, number of data bits, parity and number of stop bits) must also coincide, otherwise the receiver may reassemble possibly a different byte from that which the transmitter was passed for transmitting. Upon reception of an SDU, various errors may occur, discussed briefly in the following:

– Framing error: if the receiver has detected an invalid stop bit then the received SDU doesn't fit into the «frame» that the setup data format and the setup baud rate define. Thus the receiver has detected a framing error.

– Break error: if the reception line is at a logical low level (corresponding to space) for a longer time than an SDU usually lasts then the receiver assumes that the connection to the transmitter is broken, as the transmitter usually drives the line to a logical high level as long as no data is transferred.

– Overrun error: if data is arriving in the receiver faster than it is read from the receiver buffer register by the CPU, then a later received byte may overwrite the older data not yet read from the buffer. This is called an overrun error.

– Parity error: if none of the above indicated errors has occurred and the SDU has been received seemingly in a correct form, a parity error may still be present, that is, the calculated parity doesn't coincide with the set one. The reason is either damage to the SDU in the course of the transmission (for example by noise), or a different setup for the parity at the transmitter's and the receiver's sites.

10.2.2 RS-232C Interface

Most PC interfaces for serial data exchanges follow the RS-232C standard of the EIA (Electronic Industries Association, the publisher of the RS-232C specification). In Europe you will often find the term V.24, which is identical to RS-232C, but published by the CCITT. (The following uses RS-232C.) The standard defines the mechanical, electrical, and logical interface between a data terminal equipment (DTE) and a data carrier equipment (DCE). The DTE is usually formed by a computer (in our case, the PC), and the DCE by a modem. The RS-232C standard defines 25 lines between DTE and DCE, and thus a 25-pin plug. Most are reserved for a synchronous data transfer. To remain on the chosen path of the PC, the discussion is restricted to its typical use in a Personal Computer: this is serial, asynchronous data exchange. For this purpose, only eleven of the RS-232C signals are required. Furthermore, IBM defines a 9-pin connection for its serial interface, where two of the usually present RS-232C lines are missing. Table 10.3 shows the corresponding assignments and signals for 25- and 9-pin plugs.

On the 9-pin connector the protective ground and the signal for the data signal rate are missing, but the remaining nine signals are sufficient for a serial asynchronous data exchange between a DTE and a DCE in accordance with the RS-232C standard. The pins 3/2 and 2/3 transfer the data signals; the rest of the connections are intended for the control signals.

25 pin	9 pin	Signal	Direction	Description
1	—	—	—	protective ground
2	3	TD	DTE–>DCE	transmitted data
3	2	RD	DCE–>DTE	received data
4	7	RTS	DTE–>DCE	request to send
5	8	CTS	DCE–>DTE	clear to send
6	6	DSR	DCE–>DTE	data set ready
7	5	—	—	signal ground (common)
8	1	DCD	DCE–>DTE	data carrier detect
20	4	DTR	DTE–>DCE	data terminal ready
22	9	RI	DCE–>DTE	ring indicator
23	—	DSRD	DCE<–>DTE	data signal rate detector

Table 10.3: Layout and signals of 25 and 9 pin plugs

For controlling the data transfer between DTE and DCE the five control signals RTS (request to send, pin 4/7), CTS (clear to send, pin 5/8), DCD (data carrier detect, pin 8/1), DSR (data set ready, pin 6/6) and DTR (data terminal ready, pin 20/4) are decisive. The meaning of the signals and their use is as follows:

RTS (Request to Send):
This signal from the DTE instructs the DCE to prepare for a data transfer from the DTE to the DCE. Thus the DTE signals to the DCE that it intends to output data that is be accepted by the DCE. The DCE activates its carrier frequency to transmit data to the target.

CTS (Clear to Send): this signal from the DCE indicates to the DTE that the DCE is ready to accept data from the DTE. The DCE usually activates the CTS signal as a response to an activation of the RTS signal from the DTE. If the DCE has activated the signal, the DTE can begin to output data.

RTS and CTS distribute the roles of the two communication partners as transmitter and receiver for a half-duplex connection, and switch the two partners between transmitting and receiving. Thus RTS and CTS form something like handshake signals.

DCD (Data Carrier Detect): the DCE activates the DCD signal if it has detected the carrier signal from the transmission target and the connection is going to be set up. DCD remains active while the connection remains established. In the half-duplex mode, only the receiving DCE outputs an active DCD signal.

DSR (Data Set Ready): the DCE (usually a modem) informs the DTE by an active DSR signal that it is switched on, has completed all preparations for a connection to the target, and can communicate with the DTE. Data set generally denotes an external data terminal equipment.

DTR (Data Terminal Ready): the signal from the DTE indicates the general readiness of the DTE, and is usually activated at power-up of the DTE. The DCE may be connected to the line afterwards, but DTR doesn't explicitly instruct this connection; this is carried out by RTS. If the connection between DTE and DCE is established once, then DTR must remain active throughout the whole connection time. Thus DTR and DSR are responsible for *establishing the connection*; RTS and CTS, on the other hand, are responsible for the *data transfer* (and the transfer direction in the case of a half-duplex connection). Without an active DTR signal the RTS and CTS signals have no effect; the DCE doesn't respond in any way to the control signals, and doesn't output or accept data. Thus DTR represents something like a «main switch». Deactivating DTR or DSR breaks the connection, but note that RI works independently of DTR; a modem may activate the RI signal even if DTR is not active.

The RI (**ring indicator**) signal informs the DTE that a ring has occurred at the DCE. This is the case, for example, if an external computer system calls the modem via the telephone line as it wants to set up a connection to your PC. If you operate a public database then your clients may dial your database via the telephone network and fetch data.

The 25-pin connector may additionally transmit a DSRD (**d**ata **s**ignal **r**ate **d**etector; pin 23) signal which allows switching between two different baud rates. The signal can be passed between the DTE and DCE in both directions, thus it is possible, for example, that the DTE instructs the DCE to select a high baud rate or that the DCE informs the DTE about the baud rate of the transmission channel. The use of the five indicated control signals differs depending upon the connection type. The following sections discuss the meaning and use of the control signals for a simplex, half-duplex, and full-duplex connection.

Simplex Connection

In principle, there are two possibilities here: data transfer from the DTE to the DCE, or vice versa. In the first case, only the DTE transfers data to the DCE via the TD line. The RD line is not connected. The DCE doesn't use RTS or the DTE holds the RTS signal active all the time. In the same way, the DTE doesn't use the return signal CTS from the DCE, or the DCE holds CTS constantly on an active level. The DCE always outputs an inactive DCD signal as it can only receive data from the DTE and transfer it to the destination, but cannot receive a data carrier signal from the destination. DSR is either always active or is activated when the destination is called. By means of DTR, the DTE can indicate to the DCE that it is ready for operation as usual and may activate or disable the DCE. The RI signal has virtually no meaning with this simplex connection, because normally the transmitter calls the receiver. Nevertheless, it is possible that the target via the DCE requests the DTE by means of RI to transfer data. One example for such a simplex connection is the access of a serial printer via the serial interface. Then the printer responds with a return signal (via DSR, for example) only to control the data transfer so that its internal buffer doesn't overflow.

In the latter case, however, only the DCE transfers data to the DTE via the RD line. The TD line is not connected. The DCE doesn't use RTS either, or the DTE holds the RTS signal active all the time. In the same way, the DTE doesn't use the return signal CTS from the DCE, or the DCE holds CTS constantly at an active level. The DCE may output an active DCD signal as it can detect a carrier signal from an external device and transfer data to the DTE. DSR is either always active or is activated when the external device gets ready. By means of DTR, the DTE can indicate that it is ready for operation, and it can activate or disable the DCE as usual. The RI signal has a meaning again, as the external device may call the DTE via the DCE.

Half-Duplex Connection

On a half-duplex connection both the DTE and the DCE can operate as receiver and transmitter, but only one data line is available, which is alternately used by the DTE and DCE. The TD and RD lines thus output and receive data, respectively, in a strictly ordered manner. For assigning the roles as receiver and transmitter between the DTE and DCE, the handshake control signals RTS and CTS are used. If the DTE device wants to act as a transmitter, then it activates the RTS signal and waits for an acknowledgement of the other DCE device by means of the CTS signal. Now data can be exchanged while the DTE is acting as the transmitter and the DCE as the receiver, otherwise the DCE may operate as a transmitter and the DTE as a receiver. The DCE can output an active DCD signal because the data transfer may be carried out to the DTE. DSR is either active or activates when the target is called. The DTR signal indicates (as usual) the operation readiness of the DTE, and enables or disables the DCE. In a half-duplex connection, the transfer direction can be switched by means of the RTS and CTS signals; also, the RI signal is of importance again, to inform the DTE that an external device wants to establish a connection to the DTE via the DCE. The output and reception of data is then controlled by means of RTS and CTS (in a somewhat ponderous way, however). Figure 10.14 shows the course of the signal levels for a connection of DTE and DCE in time.

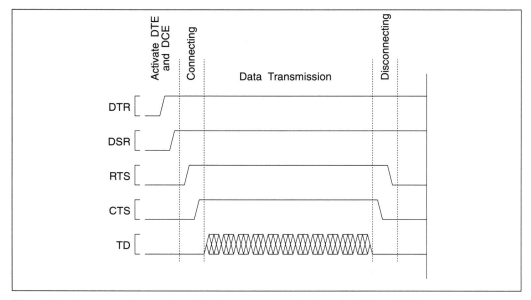

Figure 10.14: The course of the signal levels in the case of a connection between DTE and DCE.

Full-Duplex Connection

Most microcomputer modems are full-duplex, and transfer data in both directions simultaneously; thus DTE and DCE act simultaneously as receiver and transmitter. Whether physically two data lines are actally present or only two separate logical channels exist is insignificant. It is important that neither of the two transmitters (and simultaneously receivers) needs to wait for transmission enabling by its partner. The RTS and CTS signals thus are without meaning: RTS is usually not used, or is always active as CTS. Further, the DSR signal is also enabled all the time on most modems, but on other DCEs, DSR may be active only if the preparations for calling the destination device are completed. The signal is normally activated by the DCE only if it has detected a carrier signal from the destination device. Also in this case, the DTR signal acts as a main switch, and RI indicates that an external device wants to establish a connection with the DTE via the DCE. A full-duplex connection is very comfortable, as you as the programmer do not need to pay attention to the roles of receiver and transmitter, that is, you may keep the RTS signal active all the time while ignoring the CTS and DSR signals.

Figures 10.15a–f show an example for the various activations of the control signals if an incoming call reaches your PC via a full-duplex modem.

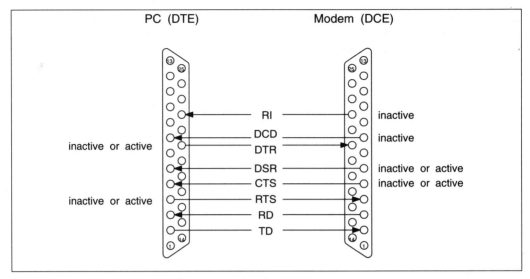

Figure 10.15 (a): Stand-by condition of PC (DTE) and modem (DCE).

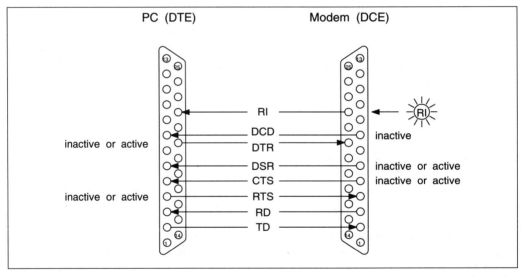

Figure 10.15 (b): An external unit attempts to call the PC via the modem; the modem activates signal RI each time the external unit is ringing.

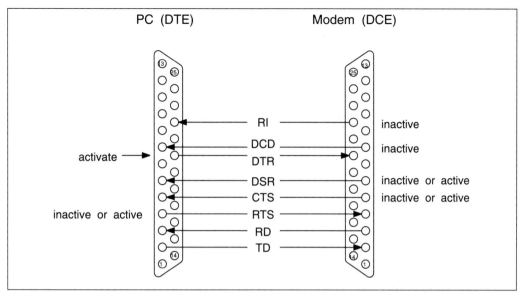

Figure 10.15 (c): The PC detects RI and activates DTR to show its ready state and to activate and instruct the modem to accept the incoming call; also, the modem has to establish a connection to the calling unit.

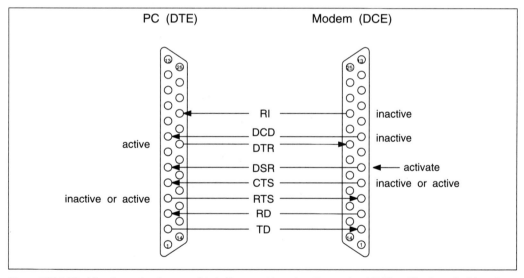

Figure 10.15 (d): After the modem has completed all preparations, it activates signal DSR and begins to build up the connection to the calling unit.

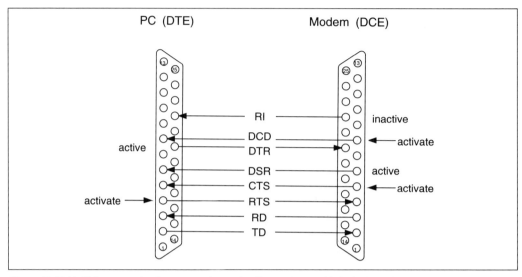

Figure 10.15 (e): If the connection between modem and calling unit is established, the modem activates signal DCD to inform the PC that the connection is usable, and the PC is allowed to transmit or receive data. The PC activates RTS to output data, that is, to carry out a bidirectional data exchange. The modem responds with CTS to indicate that it is ready to accept the transmission data from the PC.

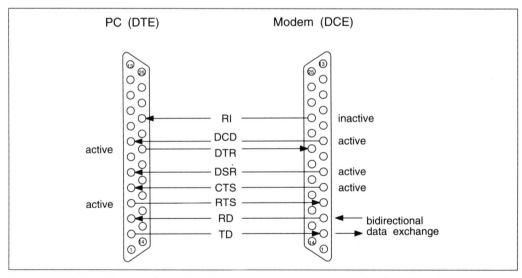

Figure 10.15 (f): The PC outputs data to the calling unit via the modem or accepts data from this unit until the connection is broken by deactivating DCD, DSR or DTR.

RS-232C Logic Levels and Transfer Rates

Unlike the logic signals normally used on a PC, the RS-232C signals are bipolar. This means that a level of 0 V (which corresponds to GND) doesn't indicate a logical low level but a negative voltage value. Thus a «1» is represented by positive voltage relative to ground, and a «0» as a negative voltage. For output signals, the voltage value for a «1» is between +5 V and +15 V, and for a «0» between –5 V and –15 V. Concerning input signals, a «1» is represented by a voltage between +3 V and +15 V, and a «0» by a voltage between –3 V and –15 V. These values are called *EIA signal levels*. The rather extensive voltage range and the relatively high maximum voltage ±15 V enables a noise-free signal transmission even over large distances. The parallel interface represents a «1» by a voltage of about +5 V and a «0» by a voltage of 0 V. Thus the difference between «0» and «1» may be up to six times larger on an RS-232C interface than on a parallel interface. As the power supplies in Personal Computers provide a voltage level of ±5 V and ±12 V only, the installed serial interface here supplies only voltages up to ±12 V.

The RS-232C standard allows a transfer rate up to 20,000 baud according to its specification. But the interface chips in the PC enable up to 115 200 baud if the cables between DTE and DCE don't get too long. An even higher value is impossible, because the UART 8250/16450 used cannot generate higher baud rates.

10.2.3 Connection to Printers and the Zeromodem

From the above description of the serial interface you can see that RS-232C is unambiguously directed to a modem as the DCE. This modem is then usually connected to a destination modem, which in turn connects to another computer (not necessarily to a PC, but perhaps to a Cray, for example). The interface is therefore also called a *communications port*.

If you connect a serial printer or another PC peripheral with a serial interface (for example, a plotter) to your RS-232C, then the peripheral represents a DTE but not a DCE. This DTE is therefore formed by a printer controller. The DCD and RI signals on the PC's side are meaningless, and also for most other signals other interpretations hold. Figure 10.16 shows a typical connection between the serial interface of a PC and your printer.

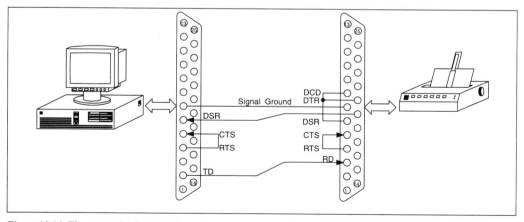

Figure 10.16: The connection between the serial interface and a printer. As a printer is not a DCE, various control and status lines have to be connected or interchanged to emulate the behaviour of a DCE.

The transmission data of the PC become the received data of the printer. Thus, serial printer cables connect the TD line from the PC to the RD pin of the printer plug. On the PC's side, RTS and CTS are connected to each other so that a transmission request from the PC immediately enables the transmission. Printers cannot output data; therefore we are confronted with the prime example for a simplex connection from the PC to the printer. Because of its RS-232C compatibility, the printer as the DTE refuses to print anything as long as no active signal is present at the inputs CTS, DSR and DCD. This problem is readily solved by connecting RTS with CTS and DTR with DCD and DSR. Thus, activating RTS immediately gives rise to an activation of CTS, and that of DTR to an activation of DCD and DSR.

But the main problem here is that the PC can transmit data much faster than the printer can print it, that is, the internal printer buffer gets full. On the parallel interface this problem is easily solved as the printer activates the BUSY signal, thus informing the PC that it can't accept data temporarily. Unlike this, the serial interface is not directed to serving a printer. Only a trick can help to solve the problem: the printer uses, for example, pin 19 (not used for asynchronous data exchange) to output a «buffer-full signal». On the PC's side, the connection DSR would provide an input for this signal, as according to the RS-232C standard the DSR signal from the DCE tells the DTE whether the target is ready to accept data. If the printer buffer is full, the printer simply disables the handshake signal at pin 19, and the DTE knows that temporarily no additional data can be transferred. If enough room is available in the buffer again, the printer enables the signal once more; the «data set» is ready, and the PC may transfer further data to the printer.

Warning: most but unfortunately not all printers with a serial interface provide such a buffer-full signal at pin 19. If your printer stubbornly refuses to print something even though you have connected it to the correct interface and the connection is OK, then the cause may be a different use of the RS-232C pins and signals. Consult the printer handbook or use a printer cable that the printer manufacturer supplies together with the printer concerned. Thus, cables for connecting a printer with the serial interface are *never* RS-232C interface cables. If you want to connect a «real» RS-232C DCE to your PC you must not use a printer cable but a standard RS-232C cable.

Another non-standard but, nevertheless, interesting application of the serial interface is the connection between two computers to exchange data. Directly connecting them by means of the conventional serial interface cables is impossible, of course, because both interfaces are configured as a DTE; not even the plug fits into the jack of the second PC. Another problem is that, for example, TD meets TD, RD meets RD, DTR meets DTR, etc. This means that outputs are connected to outputs and inputs to inputs. With this no data transfer is possible, of course. As both computers are of the same types, only another trick solves the problem. Figure 10.17 shows the scheme for such a zeromodem.

The transmission data of the PC represents the received data of the other computer, of course. Thus it is required to twist the TD and RD lines. In this way, the transmission data of one PC become the received data of the other, and vice versa. Also, on a normal RS-232C connection between a DTE and a DCE, the transmission data of the DTE is the received data of the DCE, and vice versa. But there no crossing of the lines is required, as the DCE interface internally processes the data arriving on TD as received data and outputs the transmission data onto the RD line. But here we have to handle two DTEs, and not the combination DTE/DCE.

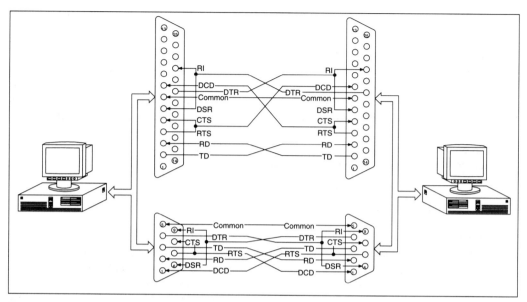

Figure 10.17: A zeromodem serves for data exchange between two DTEs, and therefore the interconnection is rather complicated.

The other signals comply with the RS-232C standard for the control signals of a data transfer. When you look at Figure 10.17 you see that the activation of RTS to begin a data transfer gives rise to an activation of CTS on the same DTE, and to an activation of DCD on the other DTE. Via this a data transfer connection is simulated as it usually happens, for example, between a DCE and an external device. Furthermore, an activation of DTR leads to the rise of DSR and RI on the other DTE so that a «call» is registered there. By means of the interconnection shown in Figure 10.17, for every DTE it is simulated that a DCE is on the end of the line, although a connection between two DTEs is actually present.

In principle, it would be sufficient to connect one control output of the DTE (for example, RTS) with one control input of the other DTE (for example, CTS), and to cross the data lines. The two programs which serve the DTEs on both sides must only be structured accordingly to detect when the destination DTE is ready to receive data. But the advantage of the connection shown in Figure 10.17 is that the control signals strictly comply with the RS-232C requirements. Thus the zeromodem can be operated with standard DOS or standard BIOS functions, while otherwise a specialized program would be necessary. One prime example for this are mice connected to a serial interface. For integrating them into the PC system, you need a certain mouse driver as the mouse electronics doesn't meet the RS-232C specification in any form. For signal transfer the mouse only uses the RD line. All other lines are usually disabled (that is, they are on a low level). But this level corresponds to a voltage of –12 V for the DTR and RTS line, which the mouse uses as its power supply. Thus here the RS-232C control lines are used for supplying a peripheral with energy. That this doesn't comply with the RS-232C specification at all seems to be obvious; the mouse cannot be accessed either by DOS or by the BIOS, but only by direct register programming.

By means of a zeromodem you can always use the neglected DOS command CTTY, for example, to control a second PC from your desk. If you input the CTTY COM1 command on the second PC then this computer reads all commands from the first serial interface and outputs all data to COM1 instead of the first serial interface. In other words, COM1 becomes the standard input/output device. But programs which bypass DOS and access, for example, the keyboard buffer or the video memory directly don't work correctly any more. However, you may work with the usual DOS commands such as DIR or COPY on a second PC by means of a zeromodem and CTTY. You will only get a return message if your first computer accepts data from the serial interface and can display them (for example, in a dedicated window), otherwise your serial interface slurs the message arriving from the second PC.

10.2.4 Access Via DOS

Unfortunately, the access possibilities to the serial interface are rather limited with DOS. By means of the DOS interrupt 21h, you may not even initialize the interface, for example, and set up the baud rate. On a DOS level, this is only possible with the external command MODE (consult your DOS manual), which uses a call to the BIOS interrupt 14h. With DOS you can only output a single character via the serial interface or read one, for example, to output a character on the printer, to draw on a plotter, or to receive data from a modem.

DOS manages the serial interface in the same way as the parallel interface, by means of a device driver. Thus you can also access COM1–COM4 like every other DOS device and, for example, print a file with the internal DOS command COPY file.txt COM1 on a printer connected to the first serial interface. If you have connected a modem via COM1 then you may «copy» the file file.txt to a PC in New Zealand, for example. COM1 belongs to the reserved device names, as is the case for LPT1 to LPT4, COM2 to COM4, CON and AUX. (Consult your DOS manual for details.)

As a programmer you may further use the DOS function interrupt INT 21h to output data via the serial interface, or to receive data from it. For serial interfaces four functions are available (listed in Appendix I.2). These are:

-   Function 03h – read character from the serial interface.
-   Function 04h – output character via the serial interface.
-   Function 3fh – read file/device.
-   Function 40h – write file/device.

Example: read one character from AUX by means of function 03h.

```
MOV ah, 03h    ; load function number into ah
INT 21h        ; call DOS interrupt, character is read into al
```

Don't be too demanding as to the performance of the serial interface with DOS. Because of the enormous program overhead, you may achieve only up to 2400 or maybe 4800 baud even on fast ATs if the data transfer is to be carried out error-free. A direct programming via registers, on the other hand, enables up to 115 200 baud.

The main advantage of the functions 3fh and 40h is that you can easily read or output a whole string, and that you get an error code in the ax register. As usual for such high-level functions, you don't have the opportunity, for example, to determine the status of the serial interface, or that of the connected modem or printer. This is only possible via the BIOS.

10.2.5 Access Via the BIOS

Another possibility for accessing the serial interface is the functions of BIOS interrupt 14h. Via function 00h, you may initialize the serial interface and set up the data format as well as the transfer rate, for example. The new functions 04h and 05h, beginning with the PS/2 BIOS and BIOS variants of most compatible PCs, further allow you to extend initialization as well as directly access the modem control register (see Section 10.2.6). By means of the functions 01h and 02h, you can output and receive a character, respectively. With the function 03h the status of the serial interface concerned can be determined.

Every function returns a transfer status byte in the ah register. Some functions also supply a modem status byte in the al register. Figure 10.18 shows their structures.

For the DCE or serial interfaces you may define a time-out value (20 s are set up as a standard), which the BIOS uses to determine how long at most to wait for a response. If no connection can be established, or if no character can be output or received within this interval time, then the *TIM* bit is set. On a DOS level you have the opportunity to set an infinite time-out interval by means of the command MODE COMx ,,P. The remaining seven bits, TSR to EMP, define the current status of the interface and the signals concerned, respectively. If the *TSR* bit is set then the transmitter shift register is empty, but with a set *THR* bit only the hold register, which accommodates the next character to be output, is empty. If the interface detects a break of the connection between DCE and DTE, then the *BRK* bit is set. A general framing error gives rise to a set *FRM* bit. The cause may be a different baud rate of the transmitter and receiver, so that the receiver receives, for example, more signal bits than should be present according to the SDU format definition. A parity error is indicated by a set *PAR* bit, and an overrun error by means of a set *OVR* bit. An overrun error only occurs if the data is arriving more quickly at the interface than the CPU is able to read it from the receiver buffer. If received data is available that has been assembled by the interface into a complete data byte, then the *EMP* bit is set to inform the CPU that it may fetch the next data byte.

Tha values of the individual bits in the transfer status byte, except TIM, reflect the value of the corresponding bit in the serialization status register. Further information concerning the serialization status register and the meanings of the individual bits are discussed in Section 10.2.6. The modem status byte finally represents, in an unaltered form, the contents of the modem status register. This register is discussed in detail in Section 10.2.6.

Among all seven functions of the BIOS interrupt 14h, only the initialization of the serial interface, the determination of the interface status and reading one character from a serial interface are discussed here. The meaning and programming of the other functions is obvious.

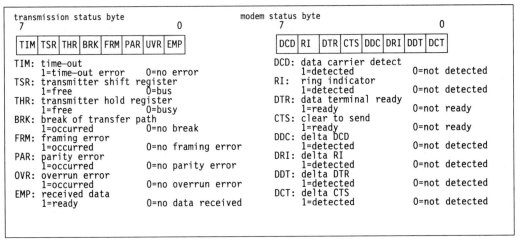

Figure 10.18: Transmission status and modem status byte.

Before you can use a serial interface (for example, after booting the PC for outputting a character or reading a data byte), you have to initialize it. This is carried out by function 00h and the transfer of a status byte which unambiguously defines the configuration of the interface. Figure 10.19 shows the format of this parameter byte.

BDR	BDR	BDR	PAR	PAR	STP	DBT	DBT

BDR: baud rate
    000=110 baud   001=150 baud   010=300 baud   011=600 baud
    100=1200 baud   101=2400 baud 110=4800 baud 111=9600 baud
PAR: parity
    00=none   01=odd   10=none   11=even
STP: number of stop bits
    0=1 stop bit   1=2 stop bits
DBT: number of data bits
    10=7 bits   11=8 bits

Figure 10.19: Parameter byte.

The three most significant *BDR* bits define the baud rate. With function 00h you may set up a maximum baud rate of 9600 baud; by the extended function 04h (see Appendix I.2), up to 19 200 baud are possible. Direct programming via registers, on the other hand, enables up to 115 200 baud. The two *PAR* bits determine the parity for the data transfer; the function 04h additionally allows the parities mark and space. The *STP* bit defines the number of stop bits. Finally, the two *DBT* bits define the number of data bits; valid entries are seven or eight data bits. But by means of the 04h function you are also free to set five or six data bits. Generally, the 04h function reflects the register values of the interface chip UART 8250/16450 far more directly than the 00h function. Details on this are discussed in Section 10.2.6.

Example: Initialize COM2 with 4800 baud, even parity, 2 stop bits, 7 data bits.

```
MOV ah, 00h    ; load function number 00h into ah
MOV al, deh    ; parameter byte 11011110b
MOV dx, 01h    ; COM2
INT 14h        ; call interrupt
```

The transfer status byte is returned in register ah with every command, the modem status byte, on the other hand, only with function 00h. With function 03h of interrupt 14h you have the opportunity to determine both status bytes without any further action. This is advantageous, for example, if you want to determine in advance whether a modem or plotter is ready for operation.

Example: determine status of first serial interface.

```
MOV ah, 03h    ; load function number 03h into ah
MOV dx, 00h    ; determine status of COM1
INT 14h        ; call interrupt
               ; transfer status is returned in ah, modem status in al
```

Thus the BIOS interrupt 14h already returns much more status information concerning the corresponding serial interface and the connected devices than the DOS functions 03h, 04h, 03fh and 40h. Of interest is function 03h, for example, to determine the cause of an interface failure. But only directly programming the registers allows ultimate control over the interface, and the use and optimization in view of its non-standard applications.

Via BIOS interrupt 14h you may also read one character from the serial interface. For this purpose, the function 02h waits until either a character has arrived or the time-out value has elapsed. Of importance concerning the performance of function 02h is that for *every* character the BIOS establishes the connection to the connected device strictly according to the RS-232C standard, via RS-232C control signals CTS, RTS, DSR and DTR, and disconnects afterwards. This, of course, affects the transfer rate enormously, so you may hardly achieve more than 19 200 baud using the BIOS functions. Also in this case, a direct register access provides much higher rates for well-trained programmers, which may reach the hardware limit of 115 200 baud without the CPU being occupied only by the serial interface.

Example: read one character by means of the BIOS from COM3.

```
MOV ah, 02h    ; load function number 02h into ah
MOV dx, 02h    ; fetch character from COM3
INT 14h        ; call interrupt
               ; function waits and returns character in register al
```

Table 10.4 lists all the important sections of the BIOS data area for the serial interface. The base addresses indicate the beginning of the interface registers (see Section 10.2.6). By altering the time-out values you can determine how long the BIOS will try to access the DCE via the interface concerned before a time-out error is reported. Finally, the *installed hardware* byte specifies how many serial interfaces are installed in your system. The BIOS startup routine determines the base addresses and the number of interfaces during the course of booting and writes the corresponding values into the BIOS data area.

Address	Size	Structure 76543210	Contents	Meaning
40:00	word		base address COM1	
40:02	word		base address COM2	
40:04	word		base address COM3	
40:06	word		base address COM4	
40:11	byte	....xxx.	installed hardware	number of serial interfaces (000= 0,001= 1,010=2, 011=3, 100=4)
40:7c	word		time-out COM1	time-out value in seconds
40:7d	word		time-out COM2	time-out value in seconds
40:7e	word		time-out COM3	time-out value in seconds
40:7f	word		time-out COM4	time-out value in seconds

Table 10.4: BIOS data area and serial interface

10.2.6 The UART 8250/16450

For the complex functions of the serial interface, such as the conversion of parallel data from the system bus into serial data at a certain baud rate, restoring the parallel data from the serial data, etc., you will find a single chip in your PC: the *UART 8250* or *UART 16450* (UART is the abbreviation for **u**niversal **a**synchronous **r**eceiver and **t**ransmitter). The name already outlines the job and function of the chip. It acts as a programmable and thus «universal» receiver and transmitter for an asynchronous data transfer. The 8250 version was used in the PC/XT; starting with the AT and on all of today's interface adapter boards, the improved 16450 or 82450 are employed. The early 8250 version has a bug which leads to an interrupt after an interface access, although there is no reason for that (interrupt sources are discussed below). Known bugs are harmless, and these unfounded interrupts are ignored by the PC/XT BIOS. In the first successor, version 8250A, this bug was fixed; but now the PC/XT BIOS, which expected an unfounded interrupt, did not cooperate correctly with the 8250A. On the second successor, 8250B, the bug was fixed, but the 8250B issues an unfounded interrupt in the same way as the 8250 to retain compatibility. Here you can clearly see the strange effects the surge towards compatibility may produce: for compatibility reasons, a bug-free chip is deliberately equipped with the bug again. That's not very good if we consider that rail companies could equip all modern high-speed trains with steam engines for compatibility with R.L. Stevenson's first engine!

The 8250 enables a maximum transfer rate of 9600 baud. That makes it clear why the BIOS interrupt 14h allows only an initialization of maximum 9600 baud. The improved 16450 successor for the AT can stand up to 115 200 baud, but the PS/2 BIOS allows, even by means of the extended initialization, only 19 200 baud, as the INT 14h for servicing serial interfaces can hardly operate faster because of all the ponderous setups for every transferred or received character. You can achieve the 115 200 baud only by means of direct register accesses. This subject is discussed as a main point in the following sections, but first a short glance at the chip's structure and its integration into the PC system.

Connection Scheme and EIA Line Drivers

The UART 8250/16450 comes in a standard DIP case with 40 pins. Figure 10.20 shows the corresponding pin assignment.

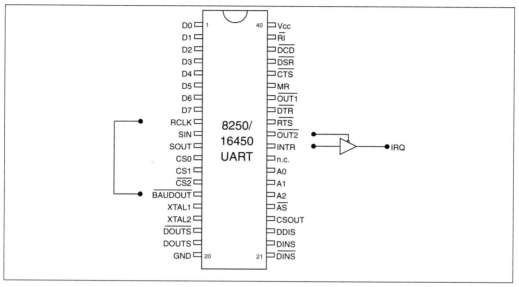

Figure 10.20: UART 8250/16450 connections. The UART is the heart of a serial PC interface. Normally $\overline{BAUDOUT}$ and RCLK are connected to each other so that receiver and transmitter operate at the same baud rate. The INTR output is combined with $\overline{OUT2}$ by a logic gate.

The following sections discuss the terminals, and briefly describe the meaning of the provided or output signals.

D0–D7 (pins 1–8)
These eight pins form the bidirectional data bus between CPU and 8250/16450 through which data, control words and status information is transferred.

RCLK (pin 9)
(Receiver Clock) This connection is supplied with 16 times the receiver baud rate.

SIN (pin 10)
(Serial In) This pin is supplied with the serial input data.

SOUT (pin 11)
(Serial Out) This connection provides the serial transmission data.

CS0, CS1, $\overline{CS2}$ (pins 12–14)
(Chip Select x) If CS0 and CS1 are at a high level and $\overline{CS2}$ is at a low level, then the UART is selected by the CPU to transfer data to or from the CPU.

$\overline{\text{BAUDOUT}}$ (pin 15)

This pin outputs a signal with 16 times the frequency of the transmitter baud rate. If $\overline{\text{BAUDOUT}}$ is connected to RCLK, the receiver and transmitter operate at the same baud rate.

XTAL1, XTAL2 (pins 16, 17)

To these pins either an external crystal or an external oscillator is connected, which determines the UART's main reference frequency.

$\overline{\text{DOUTS}}$, DOUTS (pins 18, 19)

If $\overline{\text{DOUTS}}$ is supplied with a low or DOUTS with a high level, the CPU writes data or control words into internal registers of the UART.

GND (pin 20)

This pin is supplied with the ground potential (usually 0 V).

$\overline{\text{DINS}}$, DINS (pins 21, 22)

If $\overline{\text{DINS}}$ is on a low or DINS is on a high level, the CPU reads data or status words from internal registers of the UART.

DDIS (pin 23)

If the CPU is reading data from the UART then the level at this pin becomes low. Thus, for example, an amplifier between UART and the data bus can be switched off if the CPU doesn't read data.

CSOUT (pin 24)

(Chip Select Out) If the signal at this connection is at a high level, the CPU has selected the UART using CS0, CS1 and $\overline{\text{CS2}}$.

$\overline{\text{AS}}$ (pin 25)

(Address Strobe) An active $\overline{\text{AS}}$ signal with a low level indicates the validity of address signals A0–A2 and the chip select signals CS0–$\overline{\text{CS2}}$.

A2–A0 (pins 26–28)

These three address or register select signals determine the register that the CPU accesses for reading or writing. Note that for an access to the divisor latch register the DLAB bit must additionally be set (see also Table 10.6).

INTR (pin 30)

The UART raises this signal to a high level if it has detected an interrupt condition, and the bit concerned in the interrupt enable register is set.

$\overline{\text{OUT2}}$ (pin 31)

This pin can be freely programmed by the user. In the PC $\overline{\text{OUT2}}$ is used as the master interrupt enable via a logic gate.

$\overline{\text{RTS}}$ (pin 32)

(Request to Send) The terminal outputs an active-low signal according to the RTS bit in the modem control register.

$\overline{\text{DTR}}$ (pin 33)

(Data Terminal Ready) This terminal outputs an active-low signal according to the DTR bit in the modem control register.

$\overline{\text{OUT1}}$ (pin 34)

This pin can be freely programmed by the user.

MR (pin 35)

(Master Reset) If a high-level signal is applied to this pin then the UART carries out a reset of all registers except the receiver buffer, the transmitter hold register, and the divisor latch register.

$\overline{\text{CTS}}$ (pin 36)

(Clear to Send) This terminal is supplied with an active-low signal according to the state of the CTS line.

$\overline{\text{DSR}}$ (pin 37)

(Data Set Ready) This terminal is supplied with an active-low signal according to the state of the DSR line.

$\overline{\text{DCD}}$ (pin 38)

(Data Carrier Detect) This terminal is supplied with an active-low signal according to the state of the DCD line.

$\overline{\text{RI}}$ (pin 39)

(Ring Indicator) This terminal is supplied with an active-low signal according to the state of the RI line.

V_{cc} (pin 40)

This pin is supplied with the supply voltage (usually +5 V).

The RS-232C control signals are output or processed by the UART 8250/16450 in inverted form, and the serial data signals SIN and SOUT in normal form. Furthermore, the chip is supplied with a voltage V_{cc} of only +5 V so that an EIA level of ±12 V cannot be generated with the UART alone. For these reasons, so-called EIA line drivers are connected between UART and the transmission lines. They amplify the signals from or to the UART so that the EIA levels of ±12 V are available at the output. Additionally, the incoming signals are converted to 0 V or +5 V. The drivers are implemented as inverters so that on the 9-pin or 25-pin plug of the adapter signals are actually present which correspond to the bit values in the control and status registers. If you check the potentials at the RS-232C pins of your serial interface using a voltage meter, you will see that a logically low level of the control and status signals is represented by a voltage of about –12 V and a logically high level by a voltage of about +12 V. On the contrary, a voltage of –12 V on the TD and RD lines indicates a mark state of the serial data, and a voltage of +12 V a space state. Thus, SIN and SOUT are also guided through inverter cicuits, but these signals are not output in a complementary form by the UART so that the difference described between control and status signals on the one hand and the serial data on the other arises.

When using the UART 8250/16450 in the PC, the output signal **OUT2** is combined with the INTR output signal by a logic gate (see Figure 10.20, right side). In this way, the IBM engineers have implemented something like a master interrupt enable bit OUT2 in the modem control register (see Figure 10.27). If OUT2 is cleared then all interrupts of the UART are globally masked; if OUT2 is set, the individual interrupt sources are enabled. Thus the interrupt requests from the UART may be blocked during critical program sequences without destroying the interrupt mask.

Structure and Functioning

The UART 8250/16450 has to carry out a lot of functions and is therefore a rather complex chip. Figure 10.21 shows a block diagram of its internal structure.

As a receiver and transmitter the UART has a receiver section (Figure 10.21, upper part) as well as a transmitter section (Figure 10.21, lower part). A feature of the 8250/16450 is that the transmitter and receiver on the chip can be operated with different baud rates. The UART first generates from the main reference frequency (which is either supplied externally or formed internally by the crystal at inputs XTAL1 and XTAL2) the reference frequency for the baud rate by dividing the main reference frequency by the divisor, which is stored as a 16-bit value in the divisor latch register. The generated baud rate reference frequency is output as a complementary signal at the $\overline{\text{BAUDOUT}}$ pin. By further dividing the reference frequency by 16, the UART finally determines the transmission baud rate. In the PC, the main reference frequency is generated by an external oscillator, and is equal to 1.8432 MHz. The aim and object of this factor of 16 is discussed below.

Unlike this procedure, the receiver baud rate is generated externally and applied to the terminal RCLK as 16 times its intended value. If one connects the output $\overline{\text{BAUDOUT}}$ with the inout RCLK, as is actually the case for the PC, then receiver and transmitter operate at the same baud rate. The separation of receiver and transmitter baud rate is advantageous, for example, if the data transfer is to be carried out at a high speed, but the return channel for control signals from the destination is operated at a significantly lower rate. Then it is possible to further process the $\overline{\text{BAUDOUT}}$ signals and, for example, to divide them by a factor of 100 before it is applied to the RCLK input. Alternatively, RCLK can also be supplied by an external oscillator, but as already mentioned, $\overline{\text{BAUDOUT}}$ is directly connected to RCLK in the PC (Figure 10.20, left side).

The receiver control detects and separates the start bit, parity bit (if present), and the stop bit(s) from the data bits arriving in the receiver shift register via the SIN input. The receiver control further controls the assembly of a data byte from the extracted serial data bits. If the receiver shift register has received all data bits, then the whole data byte is transferred to the receiver buffer register. With a data length of eight bits no problems occur, but the situation becomes more difficult if the data has seven, six or even only five bits. The corresponding one, two or three high-order data bits are not defined in this case, and can take any random value. If you read data with a transfer length of less than eight bits from the receiver buffer register then you should mask the corresponding high-order data bit(s).

On the transmitter side, the transmitter shift register outputs the individual data bits at the programmed transmission baud rate at the SOUT output under the supervision of the transmitter control. The transmitter control automatically inserts the start bit, and eventually the parity bit and the stop bit(s) into the serial data stream. If the transmitter shift register is empty, then the control loads the data byte to be transferred next from the transmitter hold register (if available) into the transmitter shift register and outputs it via SOUT. If no transmission data is available in the transmitter shift register, then the transmitter control holds the SOUT output in the mark state.

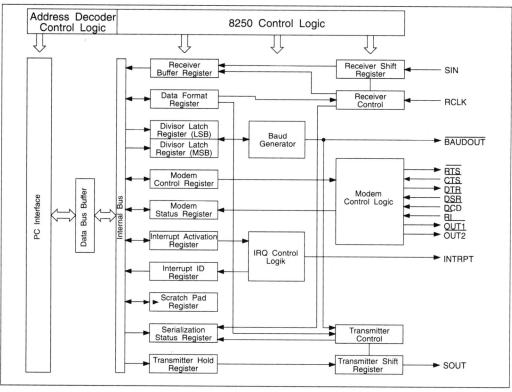

Figure 10.21: UART 8250/16450 block diagram.

The modem control logic provides and accepts the RS-232C control signals. The IRQ control logic detects the changes of the RS-232C control lines, the status of the receiver buffer and the transmitter hold register, the state of the line to the transmission partner, as well as possible transfer errors. Depending upon the programmed interrupt enable mask, the IRQ then raises the INTRPT output to generate a hardware interrupt, and writes the interrupt cause into the interrupt ID register. COM1 is usually assigned to IRQ4 and COM2 to IRQ3.

Baud rate generator, modem control logic, IRQ control logic and the receiver control can be configured and controlled by the two divisor latch registers accommodating the most significant (MSB) and the least significant (LSB) divisor byte, the modem control register, the interrupt enable register and the data format register. You may read the state of these chip groups via the modem status register, the interrupt ID register, and the data format register.

The data received can be fetched by a simple IN instruction from the receiver buffer register so that there is enough room for the next data byte. Similarly, you can write a data byte to transfer into the transmitter hold register via an OUT instruction. The data byte is automatically transferred to the transmitter shift register afterwards, and output via SOUT as a serial data stream. The 16450 additionally implements a scratch-pad register which has no function in the UART but can be used as a temporary storage for a data byte. The value in the scratch-pad register has no effect on the 16450's behaviour.

All registers are connected to each other via an internal data bus and to the PC system bus by means of the data bus buffer. They can be read or written, respectively, with the port instructions IN and OUT.

If you add all of the registers you will get a total of eleven. To address them address bits A2–A0 are available, but they can encode only eight different registers. This problem is solved as follows: the most significant bit DLAB in the data format register (see Figure 10.26) indicates whether addresses 000b and 001b access the two divisor latch registers or the receiver buffer register. Moreover, an IN instruction referring to the 000b address automatically accesses the receiver buffer register, and an OUT instruction to this address writes the transmitter hold register. Thus, all eleven registers can be addressed.

Detecting the Start Bit and the Factor 16

The reliable detection of the start bit with which every SDU begins is a significant problem in connection with asynchronous data transfer. As you know, the value of the start bit is always equal to 0, that is, an SDU always starts with a decrease of the logic level from «1» to «0». With Figure 10.22, which shows an SDU with one start bit, seven data bits, one parity bit for odd parity, and one stop bit, I want to discuss in detail the detection of the start bit and the associated factor of 16.

As already mentioned, the start bit begins with a drop of the logic level to «0», that is, a transition from mark to space. This drop serves as a trigger pulse for an internal circuit that starts the UART receiver. One would now expect the thus started circuitry to sample the arriving signal stream at regular time intervals corresponding to the programmed baud rate, so as to restore the bit values. From the figure it is apparent that this sampling of the individual bits should be carried out in the middle of every bit pulse to supply the best results. Put differently, the receiver should wait for 1 1/2 bits after detecting the falling edge of the start bit before it samples the first data bit. Those of you who have seen the real signals of an incoming SDU on an oscilloscope would agree that the signal course shown in Figure 10.22 is somehat idealized. In particular, the signal edges are often rather smeared out, and actually the first signal edge is decisive for detecting the start bit. Thus a strongly smeared edge, which may possibly reach to the middle of the start bit (and this can particularly happen for high baud rates), leads to significant problems for the subsequent detection of the data bits. Another problem is short spikes on the transmission line, which give rise to short pulses, and may lead the UART to believe in a start bit where none is actually present.

The problem can be solved in a simple but ingenious way: the serial data stream at the SIN terminal is not sampled at a frequency corresponding to the baud rate, but with a frequency 16 times higher. In other words, every individual SDU bit is sampled not once but 16 times, and the average value of all 16 samples leads to the value of the bit concerned. The individual bits can thus be restored even from heavily disturbed signals.

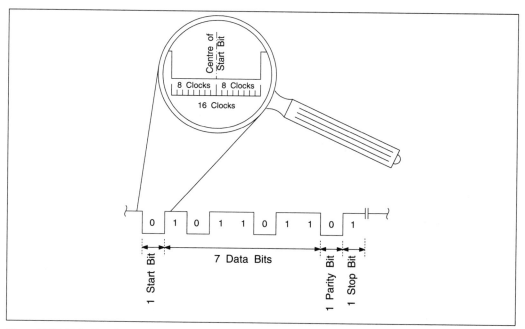

Figure 10.22: Detecting the start bit. The bits are sampled at a frequency 16 times the baud rate to enhance the reliability of data detection.

But this strategy not only holds for the start bit, of course. Figure 10.22 shows the start bit in an enlarged view. When the signal drops to a level «0» a synchronization circuitry inside the UART is started by this trigger pulse. But the circuitry first waits for eight sample cycles; thus we are exactly in the middle of the start bit (at least theoretically). Even if the edge of the start bit is not very good, the middle of the start bit can be determined much more precisely than if we were simply to wait for a time interval corresponding to half an SDU bit. After eight sampling cycles (that is, in the middle of the start bit), where the signal should be expressed best, the synchronization circuitry detects the signal level again. If it is still on «0» then a real start bit has appeared and the synchronization circuitry starts the receiver, which samples the serial data stream with 16 times the baud rate now and determines the individual SDU bits. If, on the other hand, the signal level has already increased to «1» or nearly «1» again at the time of the second sampling in the middle of the start bit, then only a short noise pulse has occurred; the synchronization circuitry is reset and the receiver is not enabled. Thus the reference frequency 16 times higher than the baud rate increases the transfer reliability. Of course, other values such as eight or 32 are also possible in principle, but the UART 8250/16450 always uses the factor of 16.

8250/16450 Registers and Programming

The UART 8250 has ten control and status registers, and the 16450 additionally has the scratchpad register. All registers have successive addresses, and can be accessed by three address bits, that is, the offsets are in the range between 0–7. The base addresses of the UARTs and thus also of the registers are stored in the BIOS data area (see Table 10.4). Usually, you find the base addresses and IRQ assignments as indicated in Table 10.5.

Interface	Base address	IRQ
COM1	3f8h	IRQ4
COM2	2f8h	IRQ3
COM3	3e8h	IRQ4[*]
COM4	2e8h	IRQ3[*]

[*] or polling

Table 10.5: COMx base addresses and IRQ channels

On most interface adapter cards you may set up the base address and IRQ line with a jumper or DIP switch. Thus you might configure COM1 with IRQ4. As long as the handler for COM1 doesn't use an interrupt, this doesn't give rise to any problem. But some difficulties occur if you have installed a mouse on COM1 and you set up IRQ3 for COM1. The mouse driver knows to which COM interface the mouse is connected, and attempts to serve IRQ4 corresponding to INT 0ch. But there will never be any signal from COM1 because you have configured your interface with an incorrect IRQ, and the mouse seems to be dead. Some older BIOS versions further have problems managing more than two serial interfaces. It may be that COM3 and COM4 are not accessible, or can only be operated with polling. But polling is unsuitable, for example, for using the corresponding interface as a mouse port.

Starting with the base address of the interface concerned, you additionally need the register offsets to actually address the various registers. Table 10.6 lists the information required.

Register	Offset	DLAB	A2 A1 A0
receiver buffer register	00h	0	0 0 0
transmitter hold register			
interrupt enable register	01h	0	0 0 1
interrupt identification register	02h	-	0 1 0
data format register (line control register)	03h	-	0 1 1
modem control register (RS-232 output)	04h	-	1 0 0
serialization status register (line status reg.)	05h	-	1 0 1
modem status register(RS-232 input)	06h	-	1 1 0
scratch-pad register	07h	-	1 1 1
divisor latch register (LSB)	00h	1	0 0 0
divisor latch register (MSB)	01h	1	0 0 1

DLAB=divisor latch access bit

Table 10.6: UART 8250 register addresses

With offset 00h you can access both the receiver buffer and the transmitter hold register (Figure 10.23) assuming that the most significant DLAB bit in the data format register (see Figure 10.26) is cleared.

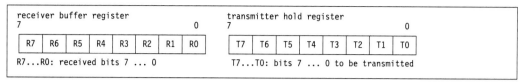

Figure 10.23: Receiver buffer and transmitter hold register (offset 00h).

After a serial data stream at the SIN input of the UART has been converted into a byte internally, the thus received byte is transferred into the receiver buffer register. The E0 bit corresponds to the last received data bit. With an IN instruction you may now fetch the data byte. Note that possibly one or more high-order bits are not defined if you use a data length of less than eight bits, but an IN instruction, on the other hand, always reads one byte of eight bits. With a smaller data length you should always mask the high-order bits, that is, set to 0. By reading the receiver buffer register with IN you automatically empty the register so that it may accommodate the next data.

Example: read receiver buffer register of COM1.

```
MOV dx, 3f8h   ; load address of receiver buffer register into dx
IN al, dx      ; read contents of receiver buffer register into al
```

If you write a byte into the transmitter hold register using an OUT instruction, it is automatically transferred to the transmitter shift register and output as a serial data stream at SOUT. Note that the S0 bit is output first. The UART's transmitter control inserts start, parity, and stop bits automatically.

Example: write transmitter hold register of COM1 to output character 'a'.

```
MOV dx, 3f8h   ; load address of transmitter hold register into dx
MOV al, 'a'    ; load byte 'a' for output into al
OUT dx, al     ; write 'a' into transmitter hold register and output via SOUT
```

```
 7                           0
 ┌───┬───┬───┬───┬────┬────┬───┬────┐
 │ 0 │ 0 │ 0 │ 0 │SINP│ERBK│TBE│RxRd│
 └───┴───┴───┴───┴────┴────┴───┴────┘
 SINP:  RS-232 input
        1=interrupt on state-change of a RS-232 input line
        0=no interrupt
 ERBK:  error & break
        1=interrupt on parity, overrun, framing error or BREAK
        0=no interrupt
 TBE:   transmitter buffer empty
        1=interrupt on transmitter buffer empty    0=no interrupt
 RxRD:  received data ready
        1=interrupt when one byte is ready in receiver buffer register
        0=no interrupt
```

Figure 10.24: Interrupt enable register (offset 01h).

As already mentioned, the UART 8250/16450 issues a hardware interrupt request under certain circumstances. With the interrupt enable register (Figure 10.24) you may control the interrupt requests. The high-order nibble register is always equal to 0 and cannot be altered. If you set the *SINP* bit, then the UART activates its INTRPT line if the state of one of the RS-232C input signals $\overline{\text{CTS}}$, $\overline{\text{DSR}}$, $\overline{\text{DCD}}$ or $\overline{\text{RI}}$ changes. Thus, for example, a ringing $\overline{\text{RI}}$ signal can get attention via a hardware interrupt. If you set the *ERBK* bit then the UART issues an interrupt if the receiver control detects a parity, overrun, or framing error, or a break of the connection during the course of an incoming byte.

The two other bits *TBE* and *RxRD* communicate between CPU and UART in the case of a normal data transfer. If you set TBE then the UART issues an interrupt as soon as the data byte to be transmitted has been transferred from the transmitter hold register to the transmitter shift register, and the transmitter hold register can accommodate the character to be transmitted next. The RxRD bit has a similar function: if RxRD is set then the 8250/16450 issues a hardware interrupt as soon as a complete data byte is available in the receiver buffer register, that is, the receiver control has assembled a data byte from the signals at SIN in the receiver shift register, and has transferred it into the receiver buffer register. You must fetch the data byte from the receiver buffer register, as otherwise an overrun error occurs with the next received data byte.

Example: issue interrupt upon an empty transmitter hold register, or if a data byte is available in the receiver buffer register for COM1, that is, set bits TBE and RxRD.

```
MOV dx, 3f9h    ; load address of interrupt enable register into dx
IN al, dx       ; read register into al
OR al, 03h      ; set TBE and RxRD
OUT dx, al      ; write register
```

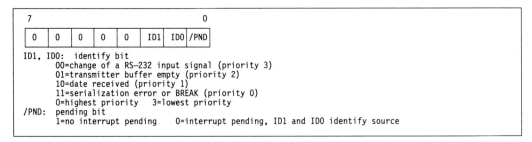

Figure 10.25: Interrupt identification register (offset 02h).

With the interrupt identification register (Figure 10.25) you can determine, using an IN instruction, whether an interrupt is currently pending or not. An active interrupt is indicated by a cleared $\overline{\text{PND}}$ bit. This is especially useful if polling is used for the interface concerned, because you may readily determine, according to the $\overline{\text{PND}}$ bit, whether an interrupt is required; the two bits *ID1* and *ID0* then indicate the source of the interrupt request. Of course, you can only identify interrupts in the interrupt status register that you have enabled in advance by means of the interrupt activation register. Polling is also effective if the IRQ line is connected to the 8259A PIC, but the interrupt handler simply consists of an IRET instruction. You can use identification bits ID1 and ID0, for example, as index bits into a jump table to handle the interrupt cause.

The interrupt sources are assigned various priorities; level 0 corresponds to the highest priority, and level 3 to the lowest. Note that all interrupts of a lower priority are locked as long as an interrupt of a higher priority is pending. As long as, for example, a parity error (priority 0) has not been serviced, the RS-232C control signals may change to any extent, but no further interrupt is issued because of this change.

Interrupt source	ID1 ID0	Clear pending interrupt by
change of a RS-232C input signal	0 0	reading of RS-232C status register
transmitter hold register empty	0 1	writing data byte into transmitter hold register or reading interrupt identification register
data byte in receiver buffer register	1 0	reading data byte from receiver buffer register
receiver error or break	1 1	reading of serialization status register

Table 10.7: Clear pending interrupts

The handler must be able to actually clear a pending interrupt. The actions needed for this are shown in Table 10.7. As you can see, the interrupt can be cleared by reading the accompanying status register or receiver buffer register, or by writing the transmitter hold register. In the case of an interrupt because of an empty transmitter hold register, you have a choice between writing a new data byte into the transmitter hold register or reading the interrupt identification register. The reason is obvious: if you could clear the interrupt by writing the transmitter hold register only, then an endless data transmission would be the consequence. As you will usually read the interrupt identification register first after an interrupt has occurred to determine the interrupt source, an interrupt request because of an empty transmitter hold register has already been acknowledged by this.

Example: determine whether an interrupt is pending for COM1 and jump to the handler according to the addresses in the jump table jp_tab.

```
MOV dx, 3fah      ; load address of interrupt identification register into dx
IN al, dx         ; read register into al
TEST al, 01h      ; test PND bit
JNZ further       ; jump to further if PND is set

MOV bx, jp_tab[al] ; load D1, D0 as index for jump table jp_tab into bx
JMP bx             ; jump to the corresponding handler address

further:
.....................................
```

Using the data format register (Figure 10.26) you may define the SDU format, and further determine whether an access with the offset addresses 00h and 01h accesses the receiver buffer/transmitter hold register and the interrupt enable register or the two bytes of the divisor latch register. If the divisor latch access bit *DLAB* is cleared, then an access with offset 00h leads to reading the receiver buffer register or writing the transmitter hold register. Moreover, the offset 01h addresses the interrupt enable register.

If you set bit *BRK* then the signal at the UART output SOUT is always held on the break state, that is, logical 0 corresponding to space. This also applies if you write a data byte into the transmitter hold register to output it via SOUT. Once you clear BRK again, data can be supplied via

SOUT. Note that SOUT usually outputs a signal according to a logical 1 or mark if the transmitter shift register is empty, and the UART will not provide a serial data stream. Thus, a set BRK bit simulates a break of the connection for the receiver.

```
  7                                          0
 ┌─────┬─────┬─────┬─────┬─────┬─────┬─────┬─────┐
 │DLAB │ BRK │PAR2 │PAR1 │PAR0 │STOP │DAB1 │DAB0 │
 └─────┴─────┴─────┴─────┴─────┴─────┴─────┴─────┘
 DLAB:   divisor latch access bit
         1=access to divisor latch
         0=access to receiver/transmitter registers and interrupt activation register
 BRK:    BREAK
         1=on    0=off
 PAR2, PAR1, PAR0: parity
         000=none  001=odd   011=even   101=mark   111=space
 STOP:   number of stop bits
         1=2 stop bits     0=1 stop bits
 DAB1, DAB0:  number of data bits
         00=5 data bits  01=6 data bits  10=7 data bits  11=8 data bits
```

Figure 10.26: Data format register (offset 03h).

Using the three parity bits *PAR2–PAR0* you can determine which parity (if any) the transmitter control generates for the data bytes. PAR0 is sometimes called the parity enable bit, PAR1 the parity select bit, and PAR2 the forced-parity bit. With *STOP* you define the number of stop bits, and with *DAB1, DAB0* the number of data bits. Valid data lengths are five, six, seven, and eight data bits. Note that the UART 8250/16450 automatically selects 1 1/2 stop bits upon a data length of five bits. This means that the active phase of the stop bit lasts for 1 1/2 times that of «normal» bits. Half a bit seems to be senseless.

With a set *DLAB* bit you can access the least significant (offset 00h) as well as most significant (offset 01h) byte of the divisor latch register. The divisor latch register is a 16-bit counter register, containing the divisor that the baud generator in the UART uses to generate the reference frequency. The baud rate rises by further dividing the reference frequency by the above described divisor 16. In general, the baud rate is therefore as follows:

$$\text{baud rate} = \frac{\text{main reference frequency}}{16*\text{divisor}} = \frac{\text{reference frequency}}{\text{divisor}}$$

In the PC a main reference frequency of 1.8432 MHz is usually used, generated by an external oscillator and applied to the two 8250/16450 terminals XTAL1 and XTAL2 so that the following holds (main reference frequency = 1.8432 MHz, reference frequency = 115 200 Hz):

$$\text{baud rate} = \frac{115\ 200}{\text{divisor}}$$

Thus you can operate your UART in the PC with a maximum rate of 115 200 baud if you write the value 1 into the divisor latch register. With one start bit, eight data bits, and one stop bit, this corresponds to a transfer rate of 10 520 bytes per second. Thus the CPU has 86 μs at most to read the receiver buffer register if no overrun error occurs.

Example: set COM1 to 300 baud; divisor = 384.

```
MOV dx, 3fbh    ; load address of data format register into dx
IN al, dx       ; read data format register into al
OR al, 80h      ; set DLAB
OUT dx, al      ; write data format register

MOV dx, 3f8h    ; load address of divisor latch register (LSB) into dx
MOV al, 80h     ; load low-order divisor byte (128) into al
OUT dx, al      ; write divisor latch register (LSB)

INC dx          ; set up address of divisor latch register (MSB)
MOV al, 01h     ; load low-order divisor byte (256) into al
OUT dx, al      ; write divisor latch register (MSB)

MOV dx, 3fbh    ; load address of address of data format register into dx
IN al, dx       ; read data format register into al
AND al, 7fh     ; clear DLAB
OUT dx, al      ; write data format register
```

Note that the level of the output signals of the UART 8250/16450 modem control logic and the values of the corresponding bits in the modem control register and the modem status register are complementary to each other. But the RS-232C output signals are further amplified by the EIA line drivers before they appear at the RS-232C terminal of your PC; moreover, the RS-232C input signals from the RS-232C connector of your PC have been amplified by these line drivers before they are applied to the UART terminals. As already mentioned, the EIA line drivers in your PC generally operate as inverters, so that the signal levels at the RS-232C connector of your PC corresponds to the bit values in the modem control or modem status register; a set bit means a high signal level, a cleared bit a low signal level. Thus, in the following description, note whether the bit values, the signal levels at the UART terminal, or the signal levels at the RS-232C connector of your PC are meant.

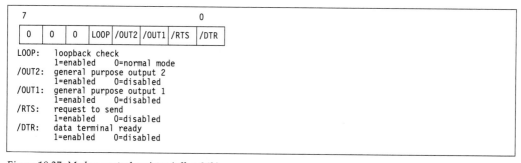

Figure 10.27: Modem control register (offset 04h).

The modem control register (Figure 10.27) supervises the UART modem control logic. The three most significant bits are not used; a reading access always returns a value of 0. By setting the *LOOP* bit you enable the feedback-loop check of the UART 8250/16450. This is a special test and diagnostics mode implemented in the 8250/16450, in which the four modem control logic outputs are internally connected to the RS-232C inputs of the modem control logic as follows:

$\overline{\text{RTS}}$ to $\overline{\text{CTS}}$, $\overline{\text{DTR}}$ to $\overline{\text{DSR}}$, $\overline{\text{OUT1}}$ to $\overline{\text{RI}}$ and $\overline{\text{OUT2}}$ to $\overline{\text{DCD}}$. Moreover, the transmitter output SOUT is set to a logical 1 corresponding to mark, the receiver input SIN is cut off from the rest of the UART, and the transmitter shift register is directly connected to the receiver shift register. Thus, with a set LOOP bit you can test the modem control functions and the generation of interrupts in the UART, as well as the serializations in the transmitter shift register and the data assembly in the receiver shift register. If you write, for example, a data byte into the transmitter hold register, it is transferred to the transmitter shift register; eventually an interrupt «TBE» is issued upon an enabled interrupt; the serial data stream is directly transferred according to the format defined in the data format register into the receiver shift register and converted into a data byte there; the data byte is transferred into the receiver buffer register; and finally, an interrupt «RxRD» is issued if the interrupt enable register has been programmed accordingly. A comparison of the data byte that you have written into the transmitter hold register in advance with the byte that is now available in the receiver buffer register indicates whether the transmitter and receiver logic is operating correctly.

With a cleared LOOP bit the UART 8250/16450 operates normally as a serial, asynchronous receiver and transmitter. The two bits OUT2 and OUT1 then control the logic level that the corresponding UART outputs provide: a set bit leads to a low, a cleared to a high level. Thus the bit values and signal levels at the UART output are complementary. Note that in the PC the output signal OUT2 is combined with the INTRPT signals by a logic gate; the OUT2 bit therefore acts as a master interrupt enable bit. You cannot mask the interrupt internally using OUT2 (that is, the corresponding bits in the interrupt identification register are set as usual), but using the logic gate you block transmission of the INTRPT signal to the 8259A PCI, and thus the generation of a hardware interrupt with a cleared OUT2 bit. OUT1, on the other hand, is not used in the PC.

The two bits RTS and DTR control the levels of the UART's RS-232C output signals $\overline{\text{RTS}}$ and $\overline{\text{DTR}}$ directly. A set bit leads to a low level at the UART outputs $\overline{\text{RTS}}$ and $\overline{\text{DTR}}$, respectively, and with the inverting line drivers to a high level of +12 V at the RTS or DTR output of the PC's RS-232C connector.

Example: set master interrupt bit to enable individual interrupts.

```
MOV dx, 3fch   ; load modem control register address into dx
IN al, dx      ; read modem control register into al
OR al, 08h     ; set OUT2
OUT dx, al     ; write modem control register
```

The serialization status register (Figure 10.28) contains information on the status of the receiver and transmitter section in the UART 8250/16450. The most significant bit is not defined, and always returns a value of 0. A set TXE bit indicates that the transmitter hold register and the transmitter shift register are empty. If TXE is equal to 0, then data is still present either in the transmitter hold register or in the transmitter shift register. If the TBE bit is set then the transmitter hold register is empty, otherwise a data byte is being held there.

The next four bits refer to the state of the connection and eventual reception errors. If the BREK bit is set, then the receiver logic has detected a break in the connection. This happens if SIN is on the space logic level for more than one SDU. A set FRME bit indicates a framing error, a set PARE bit a parity error, and a set OVRR bit an overrun error of the receiver buffer register. If the *RxRD* bit is set, then a data byte is available in the receiver buffer register. Thus you can use the serialization status register, for example, together with the interrupt identification register, to determine the cause of an error interrupt in detail, or to determine the UART status in polling mode even if the interrupts are masked.

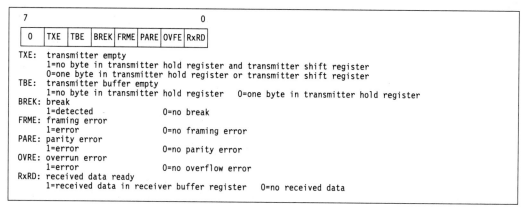

Figure 10.28: Serialization status register (offset 05h).

Example: determine whether a data byte is available in the receiver buffer register and read the data byte if so.

```
MOV dx, 3fdh    ; load address of serialization status register into dx
IN al, dx       ; read serialization status registers into al
TEST al, 01h    ; test RxRD
JZ further      ; jump to further if RxRD is cleared
MOV dx, 3fdh    ; load address of receiver buffer register into dx
IN al, dx       ; read data byte in receiver buffer register into al
further:
```

. . . .

```
 7                            0
┌──────┬─────┬──────┬──────┬──────┬─────┬──────┬──────┐
│ /DCD │ /RI │ /DSR │ /CTS │ DDCD │ DRI │ DDSR │ DCTS │
└──────┴─────┴──────┴──────┴──────┴─────┴──────┴──────┘

/DCD:  data carrier detect
       1=DCD active       0=DCD inactive
/RI:   ring indicator
       1=RI active        0=RI inactive
/DSR:  data set ready
       1=DSR active       0=DSR inactive
/CTS:  clear to send
       1=CTS active       0=CTS inactive
DDCD:  delta data carrier detect
       1=DCD change since last read   0=DCD not changed
DRI:   delta ring indicator
       1=RI change since last read    0=DCD not changed
DDSR:  delta data set ready
       1=DSR change since last read   0=DSR not changed
DCTS:  delta clear to send
       1=CTS change since last read   0=CTS not changed
```

Figure 10.29: Modem status register (offset 06h).

Using the modem status register (Figure 10.29) you can determine the status of the RS-232C input signals. The high-order nibble provides the current signal levels, and the low-order nibble gives information on the level change since the last register read. An IN instruction referring to the modem status register thus clears the low-order nibble register.

The four bits DCD, RI, DSR, and CTS indicate the signal levels at the UART input terminals $\overline{DCD}$, $\overline{RI}$, $\overline{DSR}$ and $\overline{CTS}$ directly; a set bit corresponds to a low signal level, a cleared bit to a high signal level. Note that the levels are inverted by the EIA line drivers. At the RS-232C connector of your PC, a set bit therefore corresponds to a high signal level of +12 V again, and a set bit to a low signal level of –12 V.

If the *DCD* bit is set, then the modem has detected a carrier signal (or has simply set the DCD signal to a high level). If a call is arriving at the modem it raises the RI line to a high level and the UART sets the RI bit. Similarly, a set *DSR* bit signals that the modem is ready, and a set *CTS* bit that the UART is ready to output data to the modem.

The bits *DDCD, DRI, DDSR,* and *DCTS* finally indicate whether the signals DCD, RI, DSR, and CTS at the RS-232C connector (or accordingly the DCD, RI, DSR, and CTS bits in the modem status register) have been altered since the last register read; a set DXXX bit means a bit change.

Example: determine whether the DCD bit has changed, and eventually transfer a new DCD into the least significant bit of the al register.

```
MOV dx, 3feh    ; load address of modem status registers into dx
IN al, dx       ; read modem status register into al
TEST al, 08h    ; test DeltaDCD
JZ further      ; jump to further if DeltaDCD is cleared
AND al, 80h     ; clear all bits except DCD
CLC             ; clear carry
RCL al          ; transfer DCD from most-significant al bit into carry
RCL al          ; transfer DCD from carry into least-significant al bit
further:
.........................................................
```

7							0
SPR7	SPR6	SPR5	SPR4	SPR3	SPR2	SPR1	SPR0

SPR7...SPR0: bit 7 ... 0 in register

Figure 10.30: Scratch-pad register (offset 07h).

The scratch-pad register (Figure 10.30) is implemented only on the 16450, and can be used as a 1-byte memory for temporary data, for example if you don't want to use the main memory in an IRQ handler. The values of the bits *SPR7–SPR0* don't affect the functioning and the behaviour of the UART 16450 in any way.

10.3 Other Interfaces

10.3.1 IBM Adapter for Computer Games

A further and very simply structured interface is the adapter for computer games. Two joysticks with release buttons for machine guns, missiles and other pedagogically valuable toys can be connected. The structure and functioning of the adapter is quite simple (see Figure 10.31). You may access the adapter with IN and OUT instructions referring to port address 201h.

The adapter is connected to the PC system bus via only the eight low-order bits of the data bus, the ten low-order bits of the address bus, and the control lines $\overline{IOR}$ and $\overline{IOW}$. On the reverse the adapter has a jack with 15 contacts, to which a maximum of two game consoles can be connected. Some adapter cards also have two jacks so that joysticks can be connected individually. The assignment of the standard adapter connector is shown in Table 10.8.

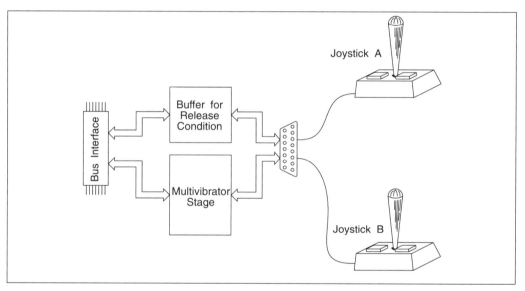

Figure 10.31: Structure of the game adapter. The game adapter has a buffer, in which the current release status of the joystick buttons is stored, and a multivibrator for determining the joystick position.

Each of the two joysticks has two potentiometers with a resistance value between 0 Ω and 100 kΩ arranged perpendicular to each other, indicating the X and Y positions, respectively, of the joystick. Additionally, every joystick has up to two buttons. They are usually open, and the corresponding lines are pulled to a high level by the joystick's internal circuitry (see Figure 10.32).

You can determine the *pressed* or *released* state of the buttons easily with an IN instruction referring to address 201h. The game adapter returns a data byte with the structure shown in Figure 10.32. The high-order nibble indicates the button's status. As the adapter doesn't use an IRQ line, and thus isn't able to issue an interrupt, you have to investigate the status byte regularly to determine the current status, that is, the game adapter operates only in polling mode.

Pin	Used for
2	1st button of joystick A (BA1)
3	X-potentiometer of joystick A (AX)
6	Y-potentiometer of joystick A (AY)
7	2nd button of joystick A (BA2)
10	1st button of joystick B (BB1)
11	X-potentiometer of joystick B (BX)
13	Y-potentiometer of joystick B (BY)
14	2nd button of joystick B (BB2)
1,8,9,15	supply voltage Vcc (+5 V)
4,5,12	ground GND (0 V)

Table 10.8: Layout of game adapter connector

```
7                                                    0

 BB2  BB1  BA2  BA1   BY    BX    AY    AX

 BB2, BB1, BA2, BA1: status of buttons B2, B1, A2 und A1
                     1=button released   0=button pressed
 BY, BX, AY, AX:     multivibrator status according to the corresponding potentiometer
```

Figure 10.32: Game adapter status byte.

Example: determine whether the 2nd button of joystick A has been operated.

```
MOV dx, 201h    ; load game adapter address into dx
IN al, dx       ; read status byte into al
TEST al, 20h    ; check whether BA2 is set
```

It is more ponderous to detect the current position of the joysticks; you must determine the current resistance value of the potentiometer concerned. The multivibrator element is implemented for this purpose. If you issue an OUT instruction referring to port address 201h with any output value, then a one-shot multivibrator in the multivibrator element is started. The values of the four low-order bits BY, BX, AY, and AX in the status byte rises to 1. The one-shot multivibrator mainly has a capacitor, which is discharged via a 2.2 kΩ resistor on the adapter board and the corresponding joystick potentiometer. If the capacitor voltage is decreased below a certain threshold value by the discharge process, then the multivibrator outputs a 0 instead of a 1. Depending upon the potentiometer resistance value, this requires more or less time; the exact relation is as follows.

time interval = 24.2 μs + 0.011 μs * resistance[Ω]

or

$$resistance[\Omega] = \frac{time\ interval - 24.2\ \mu s}{0.011\ \mu s}$$

Thus the time interval may be in the range between 24.2 μs for the potentiometer position 0 Ω, and 1124 μs corresponding to 100 kΩ. To determine the resistance value of the individual potentiometers you output any data byte to the 201h port first to start the one-shot multivibrator. The corresponding bit in the status byte rises to 1. Afterwards, you continuously determine (according to the status byte) whether the value of the bit corresponding to the potentiometer investigated has fallen to 0 by regularly reading port 201h. You may determine the time interval, for example, by reading counter 0 of the 8253/8254 PIT timer chips in advance of the first and after the last IN instruction. On counter 0 a wrap-around occurs only every 55 ms; thus the time interval corresponding to a potentiometer position is always significantly smaller than the cycle time of counter 0. Of course, you can load, for example, counter 2 of the PIT with appropriate count values and use counter 2 for determining the time interval. From this time interval and the above indicated relation, you can determine the resistance value and thus the joystick position.

Example: determine resistance value of the potentiometer AX corresponding to the X position of joystick A.

```
MOV dx, 201h      ; load game adapter address into dx
OUT dx, al        ; write any value to port 201h to start one-shot multivibrator

MOV al, 00h       ; load counter-latch command referring counter 0 into al
OUT 43h, al       ; output counter-latch command to PIT control register
IN al, 40h        ; read low-order counter byte into al
IN ah, 40h        ; read high-order counter byte into ah
                  ; thus ax=ah.al holds the current 16-bit counter value
MOV bx, ax        ; transfer counter value into bx

check_status:
IN al, dx         ; read status byte from port 201h
TEST al, 01h      ; check whether bit AX is still set
JZ check_status   ; if bit AX is set then check again

MOV al, 00h       ; load counter-latch command referring counter 0 into al
OUT 43h, al       ; output counter-latch command to PIT control register
IN al, 40h        ; read low-order counter byte into al
IN ah, 40h        ; read high-order counter byte into ah
                  ; thus ax=ah.al holds the current 16-bit counter value
MOV cx, ax        ; transfer counter value into cx

..............    ; determine counter difference from bx and cx and
                  ; thus time difference and resistance value
```

In principle, the game adapter can also be used for other purposes than the connection of a joystick. For example, you can measure resistance values in general, and you are not limited to the range 0–100 kΩ. Also, for example, the high-order nibble of the status byte could indicate the bell button state in your apartment if you take a soldering iron and connect the bell via the game adapter to your PC. Together with a speech synthesizer this may give rise to some funny experiences... but Figure 10.33 shows only the usual wiring for joysticks!

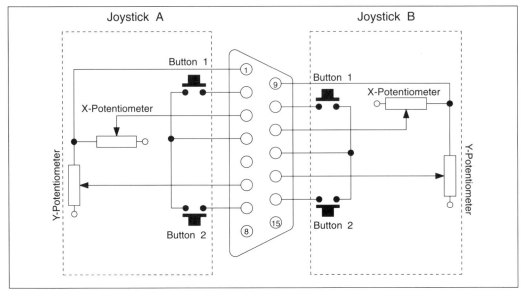

Figure 10.33: Joystick wiring.

Starting with the AT and PS/2, you also have the opportunity to determine the status of the buttons as well as the multivibrator state using the BIOS instead of a direct register access. For this purpose, function 84h of INT 15h is implemented. Figure 10.34 shows the call format of this function.

register	call value	return value
AH	84h	
AL		button status (bit 7..4)
AX		AX value
BX		AY value
CX		BX value
DX	00h: button status	BY value
	01h: multivibrator status	
carry		set if error occurred

Figure 10.34: Calling format of INT 15h, function 84h.

The function carries out two different checks. If the DX register holds the value 00h upon the function call, the function determines only the button status and returns this in the high-order nibble of register al corresponding to Figure 10.32. If DX is set to a value of 01h, the function reads the state of the multivibrators and returns it in registers AX to DX.

10.3.2 Network Adapters

Network adapters are also interfaces in the narrower sense, because they establish a connection to other computers or peripherals (for example, a laser printer in the network). For connecting

Personal Computers to each other, Ethernet has largely become established, on which, for example, Novell NetWare is built. If you want to connect your PC via a network to a larger computer system, for example a UNIX system or an AS/400, you will often meet IBM's Token Ring. Both networks are comparable in view of their performance. The various network standards are not discussed here; interested readers will find a large amount of specialized literature on this subject.

10.3.3 Datanets, Packet Switching, and PAD Adapters

Parallel to the public telephone network, for several years there has been a pure data network, too, which has various names in different countries; for example, DATEX in Germany, or Datapac in Canada. Unlike the telephone network which works in an analog manner, large parts of the data networks were implemented for pure data transfer from the beginning. They are therefore much more reliable and also more powerful than the combination of a telephone and a network-modem (DATEX P10 reaches 48 000 baud, while the telephone network doesn't reach much more than 1200 to 2400 baud without errors). Of course, in principle you are also free to transmit a conversation in binary-encoded form with CD quality, but the datanets are usually exclusively employed for worldwide data transfer. In many countries there are similar datanets, so you can exchange data with computer systems throughout the world in the same way as you talk with your friend in Australia via a telephone line.

Some datanets still operate with line switching, that is, your PC is connected to the destination computer by means of a line which is exclusively dedicated to it throughout the whole connection time. Thus you are occupying a line (for example, to a database) even if you are thinking which command you should input next. This is, of course, a pure waste, and very expensive especially if you have a connection to another continent via satellite. While you are thinking about the next command another communication member could be using the line without disturbing you.

For this reason, telecommunication companies have established so-called *packet-switching networks*. This means that all data and commands are transferred in the form of data packets after the destination has been called and the connection established. International datanets comply with the CCITT X.25 standard, which defines the calling procedure, transmission, and other network parameters. A data packet consists of the destination address and the data, and usually comprises 128 bytes. If you issue, for example, a read command referring to a database, then the command is first converted into one or more packets which are transferred to the destination via the network. Which route the packet takes (which line is used) is insignificant here; the transmission path can be very different from packet to packet. For example, it may be that your command packet is running via the path London – New York – Los Angeles – Stanford, but the second packet via the path London – Chicago – San Francisco – Stanford. The switching system must be able, of course, to handle problems; for example, depending upon the transmission time, the second packet may arrive in advance of the first one! But you nevertheless have the illusion that a data line is always reserved for you. The big advantage of packet switching is the much more efficient use of transmission paths, as the switching system is free to select the connection lines for every packet, and always uses a currently available physical line. These datanets thus operate with so-called *virtual connections*. The switching systems usually comprise a large computer with enormous storage capacity for transferring and temporarily storing the data packets. As the user you pay only for the number of transferred data packets if packet switching is effective, that is, the bill is calculated according to the amount of data (and, of course, the distance to the destination device). If you don't output or receive packets then you don't have to pay (or only a very low amount), even if the connection to the destination device is still established. With line switching, on the other hand, you have to pay according to the connection time because you occupy the line even if you don't accept or provide data.

Data networks often operate with normal modems that you can connect directly to the serial interface of your PC. With a suitable terminal program (and an account, of course) you are ready to exchange data via the public datanet now and access databases or mail boxes, etc.

Access to packet switching networks is not so easy, however, as the data that is to be output by your PC must first be converted into a suitable number of packets with corresponding addresses. The incoming data packets must also be separated into an address and actual data. This job is carried out by a so-called *PAD adapter* (**p**acket **a**ssembler/**d**isassembler, that is, a hardware device that assembles a transmission packet from the data and the address, or disassembles a data packet into address and data). The PAD adapter is connected to the modem, which transfers the data packet to the datanet or receives packets from the network; thus, the PAD forms a DCE. In most cases, you may access the PAD by means of suitably adapted terminal software and a serial interface on the PAD adapter. But some PAD adapters (for example, IBM's X.25 adapter) employ an interface chip other than the UART 8250, namely Zilog's Z80 SIO. It carries out many of the same functions as the 8250, but its register layout and addresses are incompatible with the 8250. When buying a PAD adapter, make sure that the terminal software is actually programmed for the adapter concerned; otherwise you remain separated from the (datanet) world. PADs are quite intelligent components, and implement commands that you may pass by means of the terminal program. You use these PAD commands to control the PAD's access to the data network or the disconnection of the destination device.

The calling of a destination device is as simple as using the telephone. If you have logged into the datanet (which is already carried out on some datanets with switching on the PC and the modem) you need only input the datanet number of the destination. Now the switching system establishes a connection to the destination (for example, a database). As soon as the (possibly virtual) connection is established, your PC behaves in the usual form as a terminal of the connected database (but which can be several thousand kilometres from the database).

The public datanet, with its higher reliability against noise, provides significant advantages compared to data exchange via the public telephone network, especially for users who regularly transfer large amounts of data over long distances, or who intend to use databases frequently. The higher base cost for a datanet account will pay for itself for all those who frequently use the datanet, because of the lower transfer costs.

10.3.4 Fax Adapter Cards

Another interesting interface for your PC are facsmile adapters, which are controlled by an appropriate fax program. You don't need to print text or a drawing, go to the fax and insert the sheet into the fax machines; instead you instruct your fax mouem directly on-screen to transmit the document to another fax device. For example, you may form a drawing including text with CorelDRAW! and export the result into a file; the fax program only needs to read the file, and provide corresponding fax data to the installed fax modem. This saves time and paper. If you already own a scanner you can also fax in the usual way by scanning in drawings and other documents and sending them via the fax program and the fax adapter.

For incoming faxes, your fax adapter doesn't print the documents on the very expensive thermopaper, but writes them into a file. Thus you may edit the fax, rotate or process it, or, for example, read it into your business graphics program. Also in this case you save paper, time and money.

11   Keyboards and Mice

This chapter discusses the most common and most important input devices for PCs – the keyboard and the mouse.

11.1 The Keyboard

Despite all the «new-fangled» input devices such as the mouse, scanners, and voice input systems, the keyboard still plays the major role if commands are to be issued or data input to a computer. Well-trained typists can enter a lot of bytes/s, but we lesser mortals get minor muscle spasms after a few hours of intensive programming, or after writing a book manuscript using four fingers exclusively! How important the keyboard is can be seen, for example, because the computer refuses to load the system during booting if it doesn't recognize a keyboard. This is reasonable, of course: why run a computer that accepts neither commands nor data and continues to display C:\> until the end of time?

Depending upon whether you use a keyboard with American, British or some other language assignment, some control, shift or other keys may be named differently. Furthermore, in the literature you will sometimes find different names for the same key, for example the enter or CR keys. Therefore, Table 11.1 lists some different names for these keys. In the following I will only use the names given in the first column of Table 1.11.

Key	Name	Alternative names
⏎	enter key	CR key
Ctrl	control key	
Alt	alternative key	
	shift key	
	shift-lock key	caps-lock
↑	cursor up	
↓	cursor down	
←	cursor left	
→	cursor right	
Ins	insert	
Del	delete	
Home	cursor home	clear-home
End	end	
Page↑	page up	
Page↓	page down	
SysReq	system request	

Table 11.1: Alternative key names

11.1.1 Structure and Functioning of Intelligent and Less Intelligent Keyboards

The keyboard and the accompanying keyboard interface, especially those for the AT and today's widely used MF II keyboard (**m**ultifunction keyboard), are more complex devices than they seem from the outside. Contrary to the widely held opinion, *every* keyboard has a keyboard chip, even the previous model of the less intelligent PC/XT keyboard with the 8048. The chip in the keyboard case supervises a so-called *scan matrix*, formed of crossing lines. At each crossing small switch is located. If you press the key then the switch is closed. The micro-program of the keyboard chip is intelligent enough to detect a *prelling* of the keys. Prelling is the phenomenon whereby the accompanying switch is first closed when a key is pressed, then the switch reopens and closes again. The reason for this behaviour is the sprung reaction force of the key switches. The chip must be able to distinguish such a fast prelling from an intentional and slower double key press by the user.

Figure 11.1 shows a scheme for the principle structure of a keyboard and the accompanying keyboard interface in the PC.

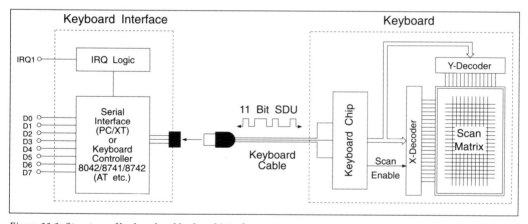

Figure 11.1: Structure of keyboard and keyboard interface.

The keyboard chip regularly checks the status of the scan matrix to determine the *open* or *closed* state of the switches. For this purpose, it activates successively and individually the X lines and detects from which Y terminal it receives a signal. By means of these X and Y coordinates, the newly pressed or released switch (that is, the newly pressed or released key) is unambiguously identified. The keyboard chip determines whether a key – and eventually which one – has been pressed or released, and it writes a corresponding code into a keyboard-internal buffer (details concerning these make and break codes are discussed in Section 11.1.2). Afterwards, the key-board transmits the code as a serial data stream via the connection cable to the keyboard inter-face in the PC. Figure 11.2 shows the structure of the accompanying SDU for the data transfer, as well as the assignment of the keyboard jack on your PC.

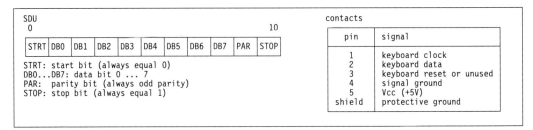

Figure 11.2: Keyboard SDU.

The line keyboard clock transfers the data clock signal for the data exchange with the keyboard interface on the motherboard. Thus the transfer is carried out synchronously, unlike the UART 8250. Activating the signal keyboard reset on some interfaces gives rise to a keyboard initialization. Via the line keyboard data, the data is exchanged between the keyboard and the keyboard interface in the PC.

In a PC/XT the keyboard interface is essentially formed of a simple serial interface that only accepts the serial data stream from the keyboard. Here no data transfer to the keyboard is possible. The 8048 in the PC/XT keyboard is therefore not prepared to accept data from the keyboard interface in the PC. Thus the PC/XT keyboard cannot be programmed. Upon receipt of a code from the keyboard, the interface issues a hardware interrupt via IRQ1 corresponding to INT 09h, and provides the data at port B of the 8255 PPI.

In the AT, instead of the primitive serial interface a keyboard controller has been installed. In older ATs you will find the 8042 chip, in newer ones the 8741 or 8742 (or compatible) chip. Thus the keyboard interface became intelligent, and is able to do more than simply accept a serial data stream and issue an interrupt. The keyboard controller can be programmed, for example, to disable the keyboard. Moreover, a bidirectional data transfer between keyboard and keyboard controller is possible here; thus the keyboard controller can transfer data to the keyboard interface. The keyboard chip's microcode is therefore prepared for receiving control commands through which you may, for example, set the repetition rate of the keyboard. Details concerning the programming of the AT or MF II keyboards are discussed in Section 11.1.5.

In IBM's PS/2 models an additional mouse port for a PS/2 mouse is integrated into the keyboard interface. A brief description of the PS/2 mouse interface is given in Section 11.2.4.

11.1.2 Scan codes – A Keyboard Map

You may have wondered how a keyboard with a British keyboard layout can be connected to a Taiwanese PC without the PC always mixing Chinese and English. The reason is quite simple: every key is assigned a so-called *scan code* that identifies it. For the scan code one byte is sufficient, as even the extensive MF II keyboards have a maximum of 102 keys. Only once the keyboard driver is effective is this position value converted into a character. Of course, this need not always be an ASCII code as, for example, for 'F1' no ASCII code exists.

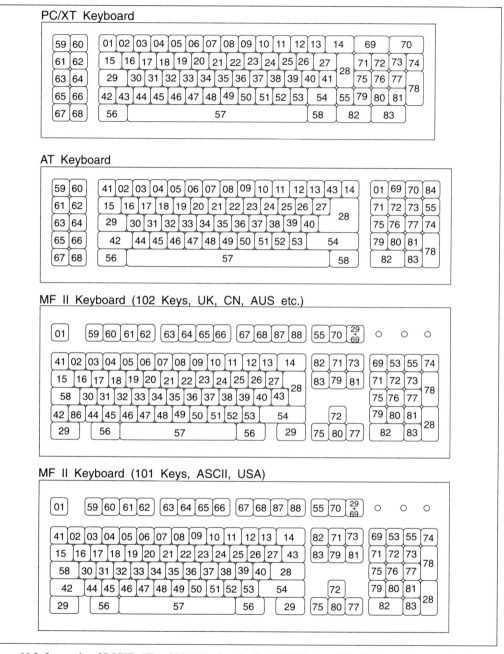

Figure 11.3: Scan codes of PC/XT, AT and MF II keyboards. The PC/XT keyboard has 83 keys with scan codes from 01 to 83. The AT keyboard additionally has a SysReq key. The MF II keyboard has several new control keys in separate blocks, and three LEDs to indicate the status of the shift keys.

Additionally, it is required that, depending upon the pressed SHIFT keys, various characters are output if you press, for example, the key «7»: without SHIFT you get the digit '7', with SHIFT the character '/', and with the ALT GR-key pressed the bracket '{' is output. On the PC/XT keyboard the individual keys are simply enumerated continuously. The principle of key enumeration and scan codes has been kept for the AT and MF II keyboards; only some new keys were added and the layout changed so that some keys are shifted. Figure 11.3 shows the layouts of these keyboards, together with the scan codes assigned to the individual keys.

If you press a key (also a «silent» key such as Ctrl) then the keyboard first generates a so-called *make-code*, which is equal to the scan code of the pressed key, and transfers this make-code to the PC's keyboard interface. There a hardware interrupt INT 09h is usually issued via IRQ1 and the handler fetches the make-code from the keyboard interface. The handler routine processes the code differently, depending upon whether SHIFT (which can affect a following key press), a function or a control key such as HOME, or a normal key such as 'A', has been pressed.

Example: press SHIFT first and afterwards 'C' without releasing SHIFT.

transferred make–codes: 42 (SHIFT) and 46 ('C')

Note that here uppercase and lowercase is not distinguished. Only the keyboard driver combines the two make-codes into one ASCII code for the character 'C'. Further, a repetition function is implemented in every keyboard that continuously repeats and transfers the make-code of the pressed key to the keyboard interface so that you don't need, for example, to press and release the 'A' key 80 times if you want to fill a whole line with 'a'. On a PC/XT keyboard the repetition rate is fixed and equal to 10 characters/s; on AT and MF II keyboards you can program the rate with values between 2 and 30 characters/s.

If, on the other hand, you release a pressed key then the keyboard generates a so-called *break-code*, which is transferred to the keyboard interface in the same way as the make-code. Also in this case, the interface issues an interrupt INT 09h via IRQ1, and calls the handler of the keyboard driver. The break-code is simply the scan code with a set bit 7, that is, the most significant bit is equal to 1. Thus the break-code is equal to the make-code plus 128. According to the break-codes, the handler can determine that a key hasn't been pressed but released, and also which key has been released. In connection with a SHIFT key, the effect of the SHIFT key is cancelled for the following character. Now lowercases instead of uppercases are output again.

Example: the keys SHIFT and 'C' of the above example are released in the opposite order.

transferred break–codes: 174 (=46+128 corresponding to 'C') and 170 (=42+128 corresponding to SHIFT)

Compared to the PC/XT keyboard, on the AT keyboard only the SysReq keyboard with scan code 84 was added. All other keys were assigned the same make/break-codes as before, but some control keys are located at another place, and the numerical keypad was implemented as a separate block. Compatibility thus remains, even on the hardware level, as the only difference from the outside is the new SysReq key, and new components do not give rise to any incompatibility with older programs.

The situation becomes somewhat more complicated with the new MF II keyboard. This keyboard not only has a completely different layout (for example, the function keys are no longer arranged on the left hand side but on the top), but it has been extended by the two function keys F11/F12 as well as separated control keys. On a PC/XT and AT keyboard the use of the numerical keypad with enabled NumLock is rather ponderous if the cursor has to be moved simultaneously. For this reason, IBM implemented the control keys on its extended or MF II keyboard in a separate control block between the alphanumerical and numerical keypads. Moreover, the keyboard has been extended by a second Ctrl and Alt key, as well as PRINT and PAUSE keys.

If these new keys (as is actually the case) are assigned the same scan code as the former keys with the same function, then a program cannot distinguish whether you have pressed, for example, the left or right Alt key. But with DOS this is of significance as, by means of the right Alt key (Alt Gr), you have access to the third keyboard level with characters {, [, etc. But for this purpose the new keys must differ from the former ones. A new scan code now gives rise to the problem that older programs that access the keyboard directly (for example, former versions of the BASIC interpreter) cannot detect and process the new keys. The engineers had (again) a good idea: if you press or release one of the new MF II keys then the precode byte e0h or e1h is output first, followed by the make or break-code. Make and break-codes thus remain the same compared to the former AT keyboards. The precode byte e1h is output if the PAUSE key is operated, the precode byte e0h for all other new keys of the MF II keyboard. Thus the keyboard driver can distinguish, for example, between the left and right Alt keys.

The MF II keyboard additionally attempts to imitate and behave like the AT keyboard. This means that the new control keys, whose equivalents are also present in the numerical keypad, output other make and break-code sequences if the NumLock function is enabled. With a disabled NumLock function you have to press only the intended control key.

Example: `cursor left with disabled NumLock function.`

`make–break sequence: 4bh (cursor make) cbh (cursor break)`

If, on the other hand, the NumLock function is enabled, then you have to press the SHIFT key first, and afterwards the intended control key, to avoid outputting a number because of the enabled NumLock function.

Example: `cursor left with enabled NumLock function.`

`make–break sequence: 2ah (SHIFT make) 4bh (cursor make) cbh (cursor break) aah (SHIFT break)`

To simulate the AT keyboard the MF II keyboard therefore outputs another make-break sequence if the NumLock function is enabled. If you press and release the key cursor left in the separate control block with the NumLock function disabled, then the MF II keyboard outputs the make-break sequence e0h 2ah e0h aah. The two precode bytes e0h in front of the actual scan code indicate that you have pressed a new key of the MF II keyboard. If you press the same cursor key with the NumLock function enabled, the chip in the MF II keyboard automatically generates the sequence e0h 2ah e0h 4bh e0h cbh e0h aah. The same applies, of course, for the other control keys.

Another special role is played by the PAUSE key. On the PC/XT and AT keyboard a program is paused by pressing Ctrl+NumLock. The MF II keyboard therefore supplies the following make-break sequence: e1h 1dh 45h e1h 9dh c5h. e1h characterizes the new MF II key, 1dh and 9dh are the make and break-code, respectively, for Ctrl, as well as 45h and c5h the make and break-code, respectively, for NumLock. Even if you keep the PAUSE key pressed the complete make-break sequence is output.

If you program a keyboard driver you have, in principle, every freedom to assign a scan code, depending upon the pressed shift keys, etc., a certain character. However, there is no effect if you remove the individual keys from the switches and rearrange them; even if you have arranged the keys in alphabetical order beginning in the upper left corner of your keyboard, the first key on the MF II keyboard will not return an 'a' but a '^', as before.

A keyboard driver uses an internal conversion table to assign the keyboard's scan codes an ASCII code, and thus a character, or to carry out certain functions. Using another conversion table, for example, a Spanish keyboard can easily be connected to a PC. The technical structure and the passed scan codes remain the same, but the keyboard driver converts them to another ASCII code. Also operating a shift-lock key such as NumLock is processed only by software: the driver sets an internal indicator that indicates the status and enables the LEDs with a certain command. Only on the MF II keyboard is an internal circuit really switched if the NumLock key is operated so that the keyboard actually outputs corresponding make-break sequences if you operate a control key in the separate control block. After a keyboard reset the NumLock function is always enabled. Every operation and the following switching of the internal circuit is registered by the keyboard driver via the issued interrupt, so that the BIOS-internal NumLock indicator always corresponds to the NumLock state of the keyboard – until you disable IRQ1 once, press the NumLock key, and reactivate IRQ1 again. The internal keyboard status and the NumLock indicator of the keyboard driver are then complementary.

11.1.3 Keyboard Access Via DOS

For accessing the keyboard seven functions of the DOS interrupt INT 21h are available: 01h, 06h, 07h, 08h, 0ah, 0bh, and 3fh. You will find a list containing the calling formats as well as the returned characters in Appendix J. Note that these functions don't access the keyboard itself, but only read and write a 32-byte buffer in the BIOS data area. Accordingly, they are inflexible and less powerful if you want to use the complete function palette of modern MF II keyboards. The first six keyboard functions are relics from the CP/M era, and always serve the standard input device only. If you make, for example, the printer at the serial interface COM1 erroneously the standard input device by using the redirection program.exe < COM1, then you will wait until the end of time. Your printer is unable to output any character, and because of the redirection you have «disabled» the keyboard. The keyboard hits are registered and the characters are written into the keyboard buffer; DOS doesn't pass them to the program, but waits for a character from the printer. The only way out is the 3-finger input Ctrl-Alt-Del.

Significantly better is the 3fh function *(read file/device)*, which uses the concept of the handles. The standard input/output device is denoted by the reserved name *CON* (for console) with DOS, and is assigned the handle 0 as standard. We have already met the 3fh function, for example when reading a character from the serial interface. Thus you can see the power of handles in connection with device drivers: for an access to files, interfaces, and the keyboard, a single function is sufficient.

The functions of INT 21h differ in how they process an input character. In the so-called raw mode, which the functions 06h, 07h, 0ah as well as function 3fh (if configured accordingly) use, the control characters ^C, ^P, etc. are not processed accordingly, but simply passed to the calling program. But the functions 08h and 3fh correspondingly set up, on the other hand, interpret these control characters and, for example, call INT 23h for a program abortion if ^C was input.

Example: buffered character input with a maximum of 80 characters (function 0ah; language: Microsoft C 5.10).

```
char *ch_input(void)
{ char *buffer, *string;
  union REGS inregs, outregs;

  buffer = (char *) malloc(82);    /* provide buffer */
  *buffer=80;                      /* first byte indicates maximum number of characters */

  inregs.h.ah = 0x0ah;             /* function 0ah */
  inregs.x.dx = FP_OFF(buffer);    /* buffer offset; segment already in DS */
  int86(0x21, &inregs, &outregs);  /* call function */

  string = buffer + 2              /* pointer string to beginning of string */
                                   /* further: *buffer=80  *(buffer+1)=length of input string */
  return(string);                  /* return pointer to input string */
}
```

Consult Appendix J or a good DOS reference for details concerning the various DOS functions.

11.1.4 Keyboard Access Via the BIOS

The BIOS writes the characters passed by the keyboard into a temporary buffer called the *keyboard buffer*, which as standard starts at address 40:1e, has 32 bytes, and thus ends at address 40:3d. Every character is stored in the buffer as a 2-byte value whose high-order byte represents the scan code and whose low-order byte indicates the ASCII code. Thus the buffer can temporarily store 16 characters. All input characters are first accepted by the INT 09 (the handler of IRQ1), which determines the ASCII code from the scan code by means of a conversion table and writes both codes into the keyboard buffer afterwards.

Structure and Organization of the Keyboard Buffer

The keyboard buffer is organized as a ring buffer managed by two pointers. The pointer values are stored in the BIOS data area at addresses 40:1a and 40:1c (see Table 11.2). The write pointer indicates the next free write position in the keyboard buffer, where the character input next will be stored. The read pointer refers to the character in the keyboard buffer to be read first, that is, to the character that will be passed to a program next. Because of the ring organization it may be that the value of the read pointer is higher than that of the write pointer. In this case, all words between the read pointer and the physical end of the buffer at 40:3d, as well as the characters between the physical beginning of the buffer at 40:1e and the write pointer, are valid characters from the keyboard. However, all words between the write and the read pointer are empty, and may accept further characters from the keyboard.

From the buffer organization it is apparent that the keyboard buffer is empty if the beginning and the end of the buffer coincide. On the other hand, the buffer is full if the write pointer refers to the character that precedes the character to which the read pointer points. If you press a further key a short beep sounds. This means that the keyboard buffer has 32 bytes but because of its organization is only able to accommodate 15 characters with 2 bytes each. If one were to exhaust the full capacity of 16 characters with 2 bytes each, then the write pointer might refer to the same character as the read pointer, that is, read and write pointers coincide. But this is, as I have already mentioned, characteristic if the keyboard buffer is empty. Figure 11.4 shows this behaviour. Thus you can recognize an empty keyboard buffer simply by the fact that the values for the read and write pointers coincide while a full buffer is present if the write pointer refers to the character immediately preceding the character referred to by the read pointer.

Upon every keyboard hit the keyboard controller issues an interrupt 09h via IRQ1, which accepts the scan code of the character and converts it into an ASCII code if this is possible. Afterwards, scan code and ASCII code are written to that location in the keyboard buffer to which the write pointer refers, and the write pointer is updated to the next character position in the buffer. If you read a character using the BIOS functions discussed below the function passes the character referred to by the read pointer to the calling program and updates the read pointer. The character is thus logically removed from the buffer, although ASCII and scan code are still physically held by the buffer. A program can, of course, write back one character into the keyboard buffer by writing the character in front of the word which is referred to by the read pointer, and updating the read pointer accordingly. The written character is passed to a program in advance of the already stored characters. Alternatively, a character may also be written behind the already present characters, and the pointer is updated afterwards to point to the next location in the buffer. The thus written character is passed to a program once all characters present have been transferred.

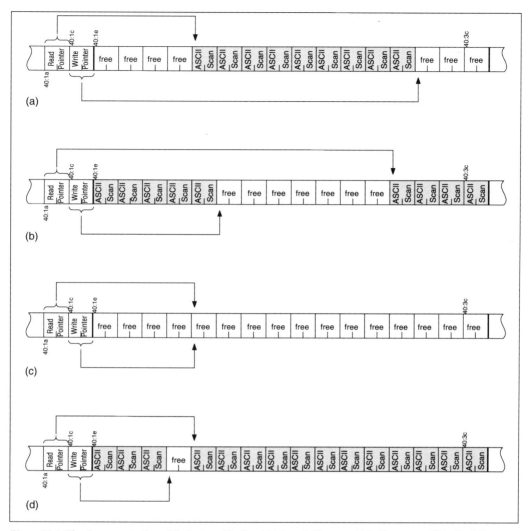

Figure 11.4: The ring organization of the keyboard buffer. (a) Normal, (b) wrap, (c) buffer empty, (d) buffer full.

Keyboard Status and BIOS Data Area

In the BIOS data area, besides the keyboard buffer and the pointers for the beginning and the end of the buffer, several bytes are also stored which indicate the keyboard's status. Table 11.2 indicates the use of the BIOS data area as far as the keyboard is concerned.

Address	Size	Structure 76543210	Content	Meaning
40:17	byte	1	first shift status byte	insert mode active
		1		shift lock mode active
		1		NumLock mode active
		1		scroll active
		1		Alt key pressed
		1		Ctrl key pressed
		1		left shift key pressed
		1		right shift key pressed
40:18	byte	1	second shift status byte	insert key pressed
		1		shift lock key pressed
		1		NumLock key pressed
		1		scroll key pressed
		1		pause mode active
		1		SysReq key pressed
		1		left Alt key pressed
		1		left Ctrl key pressed
40:19	byte		alternative keyb. input	
40:1a	word		read pointer	points to character in buffer next to be read
40:1c	word		write pointer	points to next free location in buffer
40:1e	32 bytes		keyboard buffer	16 characters, but only 15 are used
40:80	word		begin of keyboard buffer	offset in segment 0040h
40:82	word		end of keyboard buffer	offset in segment 0040h
40:96	byte	1	keyboard status byte	ID code is read
		1		last character was ID code
		1		activate NumLock when reading ID and extended code
		1		MF II keyboard installed
		1		right Alt key pressed
		1		right Ctrl key pressed
		1		last code equal E0h
		1		last code equal E1h
40:97	byte	1	general keyboard status	error keyboard data
		1		LEDs are updated
		1		ACK sent back
		1		ACK received
		0		reserved
		x		shift LED: 1=on, 0=off
		x		NumLock LED: 1=on, 0=off
		x		scroll LED: 1=on, 0=off

Table 11.2: BIOS storage area and keyboard

The bytes 40:17 and 40:18 refer to the keyboard status for the PC/XT and the AT keyboard. Because of several shift keys being present on the extended MF II keyboard, additional status bytes are required, for example to distinguish the left and right Alt key. This and other status information is held in bytes 40:96 and 40:97. With the words 40:80 and 40:82, DOS or another program can define an alternative keyboard buffer, which the BIOS then uses instead of the buffer starting at 40:1e. Note that the buffer address is limited to segment 0040h. The alternative buffer may exceed a size of 32 bytes, corresponding to 16 characters.

Functions 4fh and 85h of BIOS Interrupt 15h

Starting with the AT, and on the PS/2, two functions have been implemented in the INT 15h system interrupt which are effective before the input character is written into the keyboard buffer. The handler of the hardware interrupt 09h corresponding to IRQ1, which accepts a character from the output buffer of the keyboard controller, internally calls the function 4fh of INT 15h for every character using the following instruction sequence. The function therefore forms a hook for the keyboard input. This is carried out as follows:

```
MOV ah, 4fh     ; load function number into ah
MOV al, scan    ; load scan code of key into al
STC             ; set carry flag
INT 15h         ; call interrupt 15h, function 4fh
```

Normally the handler for INT 15h, function 4fh consists of a simple IRET instruction. Thus the scan code in al remains unchanged, and INT 09h writes it together with the corresponding ASCII code into the keyboard buffer in the BIOS data area. But the situation becomes more interesting if you intercept INT 15h, function 4fh; now you can alter the passed scan code and fool the PC into recognizing an X for a U. For this purpose, you only have to load the al register with the new scan code 45 (corresponding to X) if a scan code 22 indicating U is passed during the call. The handler fragment of the following example carries out this process explicitly:

Example: replace U (scan code 22) by an X (scan code 45).

```
CMP ah, 4fh    ; check whether function 4fh is called
JNE further    ; other function, therefore jump
CMP al, 16h    ; check whether scan code is equal 22=16h
JNE return     ; return if scan code is not equal 22
MOV al, 2dh    ; load new scan code 45=2dh into al
return:
IRET
further:
   ...........  ; something else
```

A more serious application would be to replace the period in the numeric keypad of the MF II keyboard by a comma, which is the decimal sign in some languages (for example, German). But you have to carry out more checks to confirm that the user really has operated the period key in the numeric block, and not the Del key in the separate control block, with the same scan code but the precode byte 0eh.

Function 4fh of INT 15h can «slur» a character. For this purpose, you must simply clear the carry flag and return with a RET 2 command, or manipulate the carry flag on the stack before you issue an IRET instruction. (Remember that an INT instruction pushes the flags onto the stack, and that an IRET instruction reloads the flags from the stack into the flag register; see Chapter 2.) INT 09h then ignores the key hit and doesn't write any code into the keyboard buffer.

Another keyboard hook is the function 85h of INT 15h, which the handler of INT 09h calls if you press or release the SysReq key on an AT keyboard or Alt+SysReq on an MF II keyboard. The standard routine comprises a simple IRET instruction, and the keyboard driver normally ignores the key hit. But you may intercept the call, for example to open a window as a consequence of the SysReq hit, which allows an access to a resident program with system commands. Most pop-up programs (for example, Sidekick) don't use function 85h of INT 15h, but intercept INT 09h to supervise the keyboard before the handler of INT 09h processes the input character. A certain key combination (for example, Ctrl+Alt+F1) then gives rise to the activation of the TSR program. The reason for this strategy is that the PC/XT doesn't have a SysReq key, and thus the BIOS doesn't implement a call to INT 15h, function 85h. Actually, SysReq is aimed at use in a multitasking operating system to switch between various applications.

If the handler of INT 09h detects that you have operated the key combination *Ctrl-Break*, then it calls interrupt 1Bh. The BIOS initializes the accompanying handler to a simple IRET instruction so that Ctrl-Break is ignored. But DOS and application programs have the opportunity to install their own routine, and may intercept and process a Ctrl-Break accordingly. Note that Ctrl-C is intercepted only on a DOS level, and doesn't give rise to a call of INT 23h, but Ctrl-Break is intercepted on a BIOS level. With the entry BREAK = ON in CONFIG.SYS, you instruct DOS to replace the simple IRET instruction by its own handler.

Two further reserved key combinations recognized by the INT 09h are *Ctrl-Alt-Del* for a warm boot and *Print* or *Shift-Print* for printing the screen contents. With a Ctrl-Alt-Del the handler of INT 09h calls interrupt INT 19h *load bootstrap*; with Print INT 05h is issued.

Functions of BIOS Interrupt 16h

A much better keyboard control than the DOS functions is offered by the BIOS interrupt INT 16h, which provides eight keyboard functions. All functions of interrupt 16h are listed in Appendix J. In principle, you may determine the same values that the BIOS functions return (that is, scan code, ASCII code, and shift status) by directly accessing the keyboard buffer or the keyboard status byte in the BIOS data area. This way is much faster than via INT 16h, but you have to take care. Furthermore, you lose compatibility to a significant extent. Nearly all BIOS manufacturers comply with the formats indicated in Appendix J.

The functions 10h, 11h, and 12h have been implemented in the newer BIOS versions (since the end of 1985) to support the new function and control keys of the extended MF II keyboard. Usually, the BIOS functions return an ASCII value of 0 if a function or control key has been pressed, for example a cursor key, F1 or HOME.

Example: read character by means of INT 16h, function 00h; assume that key "A" has been pressed.

```
MOV ah, 00h    ; execute function 00h, that is read character
INT 16h        ; issue interrupt

Result:  ah=30 (scan code for key "A"); al=97 (ASCII code for 'a')
```

Example: read character by means of INT 16h, function 00h; assume that key "HOME" in the separate control block of a MF II keyboard has been pressed.

```
MOV ah, 00h    ; execute function 00h, that is, read character
INT 16h        ; issue interrupt
```

Result: ah=71 (scan code of key "HOME"); al=00 (characterizes function and control keys which is not assigned an ASCII code)

Thus, function 00h doesn't distinguish between the operation of a «normal» and the operation of a new function or control key of the MF II keyboard. But if you use function 10h for the extended keyboard instead of function 00h, then the interrupt returns an indicator e0h in the al register, which indicates the operation of an extended key.

Example: read character by means of INT 16h, function 10h; assume that the key "HOME" in the separate control block of a MF II keyboard has been pressed.

```
MOV ah, 10h    ; execute function 10h, that is, read character
INT 16h        ; issue interrupt
```

Result: ah=71 (scan code of key "HOME"); al=e0 (indicator for a separate function or control key of the MF II keyboard which is not assigned an ASCII code)

The only key that you cannot access even with the extended functions is the PAUSE key. This key is already intercepted by the handler of INT 09h (corresponding to IRQ1) and converted to an endless program loop. When you press another key the CPU leaves this loop and continues program execution.

On a PS/2 and some ATs you can set both the repetition rate at which the keyboard transfers characters if a key is kept pressed, as well as the delay until the first character repetition occurs, using function 03h of the BIOS interrupt 16h.

Example: set a repetition rate of 20 characters/s and a delay of 500 ms.

```
MOV ah, 03h    ; load function number 03h into ah
MOV bl, 04h    ; 20 characters/s
MOV bh, 01h    ; 500 ms delay
INT 16h        ; call function
```

11.1.5 Programming the Keyboard Directly via Ports

As already mentioned, you can program the AT and MF II keyboard similar to other peripheral devices. On the PC/XT keyboards this is not possible because this model doesn't implement a keyboard controller able to transfer commands and data to the keyboard. Here, all transfers proceed in one direction; only the keyboard transfers scan codes to the keyboard interface on the motherboard. Thus the following description focuses mainly on the AT and MF II keyboards. With PS/2 models you can also access the PS/2 mouse via the keyboard controller. Figure 11.5 shows the scheme for an AT, MF II or PS/2 keyboard controller with a mouse.

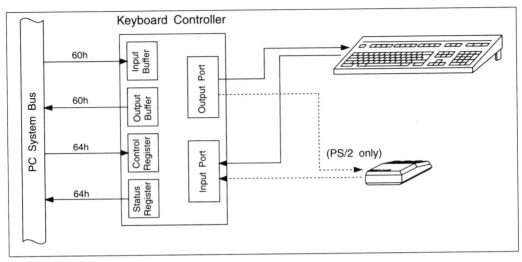

Figure 11.5: AT, MF II or PS/2 keyboard controller.

Registers and Ports

For directly programming the AT and MF II keyboards the two port addresses 60h and 64h are available. Using these you may access the input buffer, the output buffer and the control register of the keyboard controller. Table 11.3 lists the addresses of the corresponding registers. The PC/XT keyboard is only able to transfer the scan codes via port address 60h and to issue a hardware interrupt. Note that the SW1 bit in port A of the 8255 must be set for this purpose. The following descriptions refer exclusively to AT and MF II keyboards.

Port	Register	Read (R) Write (W)
60h	output buffer	R
60h	input buffer	W
64h	control register	W
64h	status register	R

Table 11.3: Keyboard controller registers

Using the status register you may determine the current state of the keyboard controller. The structure of the read-only status register is shown in Figure 11.6. You can read the status register by a simple IN instruction referring to the port address 64h.

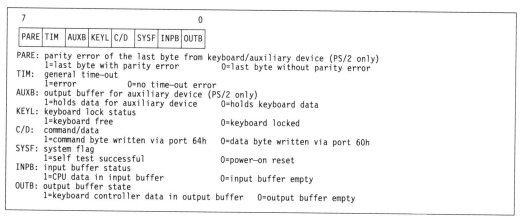

Figure 11.6: Status register (64h).

The *PARE* bit indicates whether a parity error has occurred during the course of transferring the last SDU from the keyboard or the auxiliary device (beginning with PS/2). If *TIM* is set then the keyboard or mouse didn't respond to a request within the defined time period, that is, a time-out error occurred. In both cases, you should request the data byte once more using the controller command *Resend* (see below). The *AUXB* bit shows whether a data byte from the mouse is available in the output buffer. If *OUTB* is set, a data byte from the keyboard is available in the output buffer. When the CPU reads the byte from the output buffer, AUXB or OUTB, respectively, is cleared automatically. Before you read the output buffer using an IN instruction you should always check (according to OUTB or AUXB) whether or not the controller has already transferred a byte into the output buffer. This may take some time, for example if you carry out a keyboard self-test and wait for the result byte. The keyboard is unable to transfer another character via the input port to the keyboard controller before the CPU has read the last passed character from the output buffer. Inversely, the *INPB* bit indicates whether a character is still in the input buffer of the keyboard controller, or whether the CPU can pass another. The *C/D* bit shows whether the last written byte was a command byte that has been transferred by the CPU via the port address 64h, or a data byte that the CPU has written via the port address 60h. *KEYL* and *SYSF*, finally, indicate whether the keyboard is locked or not, and whether the self-test could be completed successfully.

Example: read status register.

```
IN al, 64h  ; the IN instruction referring port address 64 transfers
            ; the contents of the status register into al
```

```
7                                           0
┌────┬────┬────┬────┬────┬────┬────┬────┐
│ C7 │ C6 │ C5 │ C4 │ C3 │ C2 │ C1 │ C0 │
└────┴────┴────┴────┴────┴────┴────┴────┘
C7...C0: command bit 7 bis 0
```

Figure 11.7: Control register (64h).

You access the write-only control register (Figure 11.7) by an OUT instruction referring to the port address 64h. The keyboard controller interprets every byte you pass in this way as a command. Note that commands for the keyboard are written via the input buffer, that is, by an OUT instruction with the keyboard command code referring to the port address 60h. Table 11.4 lists the commands valid for the keyboard controiller.

Code	Command	Description
a7h	disable auxiliary device	disables the auxiliary device
a8h	enable auxiliary device	enables the auxiliary device
a9h	check interface to auxiliary device	checks the interface to auxiliary device and stores the check code in the output buffer (00h=no error, 01h=clock line low, 02h=clock line high, 03h=data line low, 04h=data line high, ffh=no auxiliary device)
aah	self-test	the keyboard controller executes a self-test and writes 55h into the output buffer if no error is detected
abh	check keyboard interface	the keyboard controller checks the keyboard interface and writes the result into the output buffer (00h=not error, 01h=clock line low, 02h=clock line high, 03h=data line low, 04h=data line high, ffh=general error
adh	disable keyboard	disables the keyboard
aeh	enable keyboard	enables the keyboard
c0h	read input port	reads input port and transfers the data into the output buffer
c1h	read out input port (low)	reads bit 3-0 of input port repeatedly and transfers the data into bit 7-4 of status register until INPB in the status register is set
c2h	read out input port (high)	reads bit 7-4 of input port repeatedly and transfers the data into bit 7-4 of status register until INPB in the status register is set
d0h	read output port	reads output port and transfers the data into the output buffer
d1h	write output port	writes the following data byte into the output port
d2h	write keyboard output buffer	writes the following data byte into the output buffer and clears AUXB in the status register
d3h	write output buffer of auxiliary device	writes the following data byte into the output buffer and sets AUXB in the status register
d4h	write auxiliary device	writes the following data byte into the auxiliary device
e0h	read test input port	the keyboard controller reads its test input and writes T0 into bit 0 and T1 into bit 1 of output buffer
f0h– ffh	send pulses to output port	pulls low bits 3–0 of output port corresponding to low nibble 00h to 0fh of command for 6ms

Table 11.4: Controller commands (AT, PS/2)

Example: disable keyboard.

```
start:
IN al, 64h    ; read status byte
TEST al, 02h  ; check whether input buffer is full
JNZ start     ; some byte still in the input buffer
OUT 64h, adh  ; disable keyboard
```

Note that afterwards you have no opportunity to input something via the keyboard; even Ctrl–Alt–Del doesn't work any more.

Using the input and output buffer you can transfer data to the keyboard controller, as well as pass commands and data to the keyboard, and you can receive data from the keyboard controller or the keyboard itself. The structure of these two buffers is illustrated in Figure 11.8.

Figure 11.8: Input and output buffer (60h).

You may access the input buffer with an OUT instruction, referring to the port address 60h, if the INPB bit of the status register is cleared. Via the input buffer, data bytes are eventually transferred to the keyboard controller, which belong to a controller command issued in advance via port address 64h.

Example: write byte 01h into the output port.

```
OUT 64h, d1h    ; pass code for the controller command "write output port"
                ; via the control register to the keyboard controller
wait:
IN al, 64h      ; read status register
TEST al, 02h    ; check whether input buffer is full
JNZ wait        ; input buffer full thus wait
OUT 60h, 01h    ; pass data byte 01h for the controller command
```

In the same way, you pass control commands to the keyboard by writing the code of the intended keyboard command into the input buffer of the keyboard controller. The keyboard controller then transfers the command byte to the keyboard, which in turn interprets and executes it. You will find a list of all keyboard commands and their interpretation in the next section.

The keyboard controller writes all data that the CPU has requested by means of a controller command into the output buffer. If you have pressed a key then the keyboard passes the scan code in the form of an SDU to the keyboard controller, which extracts the scan code byte and writes it into the output buffer. In both cases the keyboard controller issues (via IRQ1) a hardware interrupt corresponding to INT 09h if it has received a byte from the keyboard and written it into the output buffer. The handler of this hardware interrupt can then fetch the character by means of an IN instruction referring to the address 60h, determine the corresponding ASCII code, and put both into the keyboard buffer of the BIOS data area or process the return codes for ACK, etc. accordingly. Details concerning the transfer of scan codes are discussed below.

The input and output ports of the keyboard controller not only establish a connection to the keyboard or (in the case of PS/2) a mouse, but also control other gate chips in the PC or output status information from other devices. Don't confuse the input and output ports with the input and output buffers. Figure 11.9 shows the structure of the input port, Figure 11.10 that of the output port.

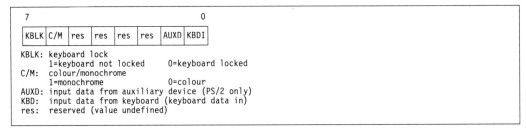

Figure 11.9: Input port.

You can read the input port by passing the keyboard controller the command *read input port* via port 64h. The keyboard controller then transfers the contents of the input port to the output buffer, from which you may read the byte with an IN instruction referring to port 60h. The most significant *KBLK* bit indicates whether the keyboard is locked or not. On the first ATs, the user had to set a switch to inform the system about the installed graphics adapter type (colour or monochrome) for booting. The *C/M* bit indicates the corresponding switch position if your PC is still equipped with such a switch; otherwise this value is not defined, or provides the same information as is stored in the CMOS RAM. Using the two *AUXD* and *KBD* bits you can read the serial data stream of the mouse (PS/2 only) and the keyboard.

Example: read the input port.

```
OUT 64h, c0h   ; output command "read input port" to keyboard controller
wait:
IN al, 64h     ; read status register of keyboard controller
TEST al, 01h   ; check whether byte is available in the output buffer
JZ wai         ; wait until byte is available
IN al, 60h     ; read input port byte from the keyboard
               ; controller's output buffer into al
```

```
 7                                 0
┌─────┬─────┬─────┬─────┬─────┬─────┬─────┬─────┐
│KBDO │KCLK │AUXB │OUTB │ACLK │AXDO │GA20 │SYSR │
└─────┴─────┴─────┴─────┴─────┴─────┴─────┴─────┘
KBDO: output data to keyboard
KCLK: keyboard clock
AUXB: output buffer of auxiliary device full (PS/2 only)
OUTB: output buffer full
ACLK: auxiliary device clock (PS/2 only)
AXDO: output data to auxiliary device (PS/2 only)
GA20: gate for A20
      1=on (A20 enabled)      0=off
SYSR: processor reset
      1=execute reset         0=no reset
```

Figure 11.10: Output port.

The output port of the keyboad controller not only supervises the keyboard via *KBDO* and *KCLK* bits (and on a PS/2 also the mouse via the *AXDO* and *ACLK* bits), but can additionally lock address line A20 of the 80286 and above via the *GA20* bit to emulate the 8086/88 address wrap-around. If you want to access the 64 kbytes of the high-memory area above the 1 Mbyte border, you must set bit GA20. HIMEM.SYS does this automatically when you access this storage area. As you know, you don't have the option on the 80286 to switch the processor back to real mode by simply clearing the PM flag. This is possible on the 80286 only by a processor reset, which must be carried out by hardware. For this purpose, the *SYSR* bit is implemented in the keyboard controller's output port. If you set SYSR to 1 then the 80286 carries out a processor reset. But the start routine of the AT BIOS recognizes (according to the shutdown status byte in the CMOS RAM) whether a boot process is in progress, or whether a program has issued a processor reset via SYSR to switch the 80286 back to real mode. In the latter case, the BIOS start routine returns control immediately back to the calling program, for example to the HIMEM.SYS or RAMDRIVE.SYS drivers which access extended memory to store and read data there. The *OUTB* and *AUXB* bits indicate whether the output buffers for the keyboard or the mouse (PS/2 only) are available.

Example: issue processor reset.

```
OUT 64h, d0h    ; output command "read output port" to keyboard controller
wait:

IN al, 64h      ; read status register of keyboard controller
TEST al, 01h    ; check whether byte is available in the output buffer
JZ wait         ; wait until byte is available
IN al, 60h      ; read output port byte from the keyboard
                ; controller's output buffer into al
OR al, 01h      ; set bit SYSR
OUT 64h, d1h    ; output command "write output port" to keyboard controller
OUT 60h, al     ; issue processor reset
```

Receiving Keyboard Characters

If you didn't issue a certain keyboard command for which the keyboard returns some data bytes, you will only receive the make and break codes according to the keys pressed or released. The keyboards have a small buffer memory, which usually holds about 20 bytes. Depending upon which keys you are operating, the buffer can therefore accommodate more or fewer key operations, as the scan code for a new MF II key occupies far more bytes than for the ordinary 'A' key, for example. If the internal keyboard buffer is overflowing because the CPU doesn't read data from the keyboard controller's output buffer (for example, if IRQ1 in the 8259A PIC is disabled), then the keyboard places the value 00h or ffh into the internal buffer to indicate the overflow condition. Table 11.5 shows the return codes of the keyboard.

Code	Meaning
00h	⎡ overflow error or
ffh	⎣ key error
41abh	keyboard ID of MF II keyboard
aah	BAT complete code
eeh	echo after echo command
fah	ACK
fch	BAT error
feh	resend request
1h–58h	make and break codes of keys

Table 11.5: Keyboard return codes

If the output buffer of the keyboard controller is empty (that is, bit OUTB in the status register is cleared), then the keyboard transfers a scan code (or return code) from the internal buffer as a serial bit stream to the keyboard controller. The controller in turn places the character into its output buffer, sets bit OUTB in the status register, and issues a hardware interrupt via IRQ1 (corresponding to INT 09h).

On a PC/XT keyboard the handler should first set the SW1 bit of port B so that port A really contains the scan code from the keyboard and not the data from the configuration DIP switches. As is the case for the other keyboards, the scan code can then be fetched by a simple IN instruction referring to the port address 60h. Thus the character has been removed from the output buffer so that the keyboard may pass the next scan code from its internal buffer.

The following example illustrates the principle of character passing between keyboard controller and the CPU. To disable IRQ1, bit 1 in the IMR of the 8259A PIC is masked. If you try this small program you may clearly see the amount of make and break-codes the MF II keyboard generates for SHIFT and other keys if you operate one of the new MF II keys.

Example: detect passed scan codes and display them on the screen until ESC is pressed.

```
main()
{ int status, scan code;

  outp(0x21, 0x02);                    /* lock IRQ1 */
  for (;;) {                           /* endless loop for reading characters */
    for (;;) {                         /* wait until character is available in output buffer */
      status = inp(0x64);              /* read status register */
      if ((status & 0x01) == 0x01) break;  /* leave wait loop if character in output buffer */
    }
    scan code = inp(0x60);             /* read scan code from output buffer */
    printf("\t%d", scan code);         /* output scan code in tab-steps */
    if (code == 0x01) break;           /* leave endless loop if ESC is pressed */
  }
  outp(0x21, 0x00);                    /* release IRQ1 */
  exit(0);
}
```

Commands for the Keyboard

The AT and MF II keyboards implement several commands that you pass via the input buffer of the keyboard controller. But note that, for example, the command *turn on/off LEDs* is meaningless for an AT keyboard, as this keyboard doesn't have any LED. Table 11.6 summarizes all keyboard commands for the AT and MF II keyboard.

Code	Command	Description
edh	turn on/off LEDs	turns on/off the MF II keyboard LEDs
eeh	echo	returns a byte eeh
f0h	set/identify scan codes	sets one of three scan code sets and identifies the present scan code set

Table 11.6: Keyboard Commands (AT, PS/2)

Code	Command	Description
f2h	identify keyboard	identifies the keyboard (ACK=AT, ACK+abh+41h=MF II)
f3h	set repetition rate/ delay	sets repetition rate and delay of keyboard
f4h	enable	enables the keyboard
f5h	standard/disable	sets the standard values and disables the keyboard
f6h	standard/enable	sets the standard values and enables the keyboard
feh	resend	the keyboards transfers the last transmitted character once more to the keyboard controller
ffh	reset	executes an internal keyboard reset and afterwards the BAT

Table 11.6: cont.

The following briefly discusses the most important commands. Generally, the keyboard returns an ACK corresponding to fah after every command except echo and resend. Every character from the keyboard to the controller issues an interrupt via IRQ1. Normally, the keyboard drivers process only codes between 0 and 127. Thus, ACK and all other return messages are slurred by the keyboard driver. Only if you suppress the generation of INT 09h, for example by masking IRQ1 in the IMR of the 8259A PIC, can you actually detect the return messages; otherwise the interrupt snatches away the return byte from you, as the keyboard controller issues the interrupt immediately after receiving the byte.

– **Turn On/Off the LEDs (edh):** After passing the command the keyboard responds with an ACK to the controller, aborts scanning the scan matrix, and waits for the indicator byte from the controller, which you must also pass to the controller via the input buffer. Figure 11.11 shows the structure of the indicator byte.

```
 7                            0
┌───┬───┬───┬───┬───┬────┬────┬────┐
│ 0 │ 0 │ 0 │ 0 │ 0 │CPSL│NUML│SCRL│
└───┴───┴───┴───┴───┴────┴────┴────┘
CPSL: LED for CapsLock or ShiftLock
        1=on        0=off
NUML: LED for NumLock
        1=on        0=off
SCRL: LED for ScrollLock
        1=on        0=off
```

Figure 11.11: Indicator byte.

Example: switch on LED for NumLock, switch off all others.
```
OUT 60h, edh    ; output command for turning on/off the LEDs
wait:
IN al, 64h      ; read status register
TEST al, 02h    ; check whether input buffer is empty
JNZ wait        ; input buffer full thus wait
OUT 60h, 02h    ; switch on LED for NumLock
```

– **Echo (eeh):** this command checks the transfer path and the command logic of the keyboard. As soon as the keyboard has received the command it returns the same response byte eeh corresponding to an echo back to the keyboard controller.

– **Set/Identify Scan Codes (f0h):** this command selects one of three alternate scan code sets of the MF II keyboard; 01h, 02h, and 03h are valid. The standard setup is the scan code set 02h. After outputting the command the keyboard responds with an ACK, and waits for the transfer of the option byte. The values 01h, 02h, and 03h select sets 1, 2, or 3; a value of 00h instructs the keyboard to return, besides the ACK, another byte to the keyboard controller upon receiving the option byte which specifies the active scan code set.

– **Identify Keyboard (f2h):** this command identifies the connected keyboard. A PC/XT keyboard without a controller doesn't respond in any way, that is, a time-out error occurs. An AT keyboard returns only an ACK, but an MF II keyboard returns an ACK followed by the two bytes abh and 41h, which are the low as well as high bytes of the MF II ID word 41abh.

Example: `identify keyboard`.

```
int keyb_ident(void)           /* function returns indicator:0=PC/XT, 1=AT, 2=MF II, 3=error
*/

{ int status, code, ret_code;

  outp(0x21,0x02);             /* lock IRQ1 */

  outp(0x60, 0xf2);            /* output command */

  timeout_wait();              /* wait loop for ACK */
  status=inp(0x64);            /* read status register */
  if ((status & 0x01) != 0x01) {
    ret_code=0;                /* no ACK from keyboard -> PC/XT keyboard */
  }
  else {
    code=inp(0x60);            /* fetch character */
    if (code != 0xfa) {        /* error */
      ret_code=4;
    }
    else {
      timeout_wait();          /* wait loop for 1st ID byte */
      status=inp(0x64);        /* read status register */
      if ((status & 0x01) != 0x01) {   /* no ID byte from keyboard -> AT keyboard */
        ret_code=1;
      }
      else {
        code=inp(0x60);        /* fetch 1st ID byte */
        if (code != 0xab) {    /* error */
          ret_code=5;
        }
        else {
          timeout_wait();      /* wait loop for 2nd ID byte */
          status=inp(0x64);    /* read status register */
          if ((status & 0x01) != 0x01) {   /* no 2nd ID byte from keyboard -> error */
            ret_code=6;
          }
          else {
            code=inp(0x60);        /* fetch 2nd ID byte */
```

```
            if (code != 0x41) {  /* error */
              ret_code=7;
            }
            else {
              ret_code=2;
            }
          }
        }
      }
    }
  }
}
outp(0x21,0x00);          /* release IRQ1 */
return(ret_code);         /* return keyboard identifier */
}
```

– **Set repetition rate/delay (f3h):** with this command you may set the repetition rate as well as the delay of an AT or MF II keyboard. After outputting the command the keyboard returns an ACK and waits for the data byte, which you may pass via the input buffer to the keyboard. Figure 11.12 shows the structure of the data byte.

```
 7                                    0
┌───┬────┬────┬────┬────┬────┬────┬────┐
│ 0 │DEL1│DEL0│RAT4│RAT3│RAT2│RAT1│RAT0│
└───┴────┴────┴────┴────┴────┴────┴────┘

DEL1, DEL0:  delay [ms]
00=250ms    01=500ms   10=750ms    11=1000ms
RAT4...RAT0: repetition rate [characters/s]
00000=30.0   00001=26.7   00010=24.0   00011=21.8   00100=20.0   00101=18.5   00110=17.1   00111=16.0
01000=15.0   01001=13.3   01010=12.0   01011=10.9   01100=10.0   01101=9.2    01110=8.5    01111=8.0
10000=7.5    10001=6.7    10010=6.0    10011=5.5    10100=5.0    10101=4.6    10110=4.3    10111=4.0
11000=3.7    11001=3.3    11010=3.0    11011=2.7    11100=2.5    11101=2.3    11110=2.1    10111=2.0
```

Figure 11.12: Repetition rate and delay.

Example: set 30 characters/s and 150 ms delay

```
int max_rate(void)   /* routine for maximum keyboard rate; return code: 0=o.k., -1=error */
{ int status, ret_code;

  outp(0x21,0x02);              /* lock IRQ1 */
  outp(0x60, 0xf3);             /* output command */
  timeout_wait();               /* wait loop for ACK */
  status=inp(0x64);             /* read status register */
  if ((status & 0x01) != 0x01) {
    ret_code=-1;                /* no ACK from keyboard -> error */
  }
  else {
    outp(0x60, 00h);            /* output data byte */
    ret_code=0;                 /* everything o.k. */
  }
  outp(0x21,0x00);              /* release IRQ1 */
  return(ret_code);             /* return code */
}
```

– **Resend (feh)**: if an error has occurred during the course of transferring data between the keyboard and keyboard controller, you can instruct the keyboard with this command to pass the last character once again.

– **Reset (ffh)**: this command carries out an internal self-test of the keyboard. After receiving the command byte the keyboard first outputs an ACK for this purpose. The keyboard controller must respond by raising the data and clock line to the keyboard to a high level for at least 500 μs. Afterwards, the keyboard carries out the in-built BAT (**b**asic **a**ssurance **t**est). Upon the BAT's completion, it transfers a code aah (test passed) or fch (keyboard error) to the controller. You can set the data and clock line to a high level using bit 6 and 7 in the output port.

11.2   Mice and Other Rodents

For a long time, mice have been indispensable on Apple computers for using programs there. But on IBM PCs the mouse made its debut only once Windows came onto the market, as handling Windows with the usual keyboard and without a mouse is quite ponderous. On programs that allow an operation both by hot-keys and by a mouse, well-trained users work faster if they use only the hot-keys (that is, the keyboard) when selecting menu items. Thus, mice are surely not the ultimate solution, but they are at least very useful for graphics-oriented applications or drawing programs. Some mice can confidently be called rats if they exceed a weight of one pound or the required space for their movement is at least as large as your desk! In the following, however, we only discuss mice.

11.2.1 Structure and Function

A mouse is structured quite simply. The central part is a steel ball, coated with gum or plastic, which rotates as the mouse is moved. This movement is transmitted to two small rollers perpendicular to each other, which convert the mouse movement in the X and Y directions into a rotation of two disks, with holes. These disks alternately close or open a photosensor assembly when rotated, that is, the mouse is moved. Thus the number of interruptions and releases of the photosensor assembly is an unambiguous quantity for the amount of the mouse's movement in the X and Y directions, and the number of these interruptions and releases per second specifies the speed of this movement. Such mechanical mice are used most today.

A newer concept is the so-called optical mouse, where sensors on the bottom detect the mouse's movement on a specially patterned mouse pad. A special patterning is required so that the mouse's logic can determine the direction and speed; a normal mouse pad would only confuse the mouse. All mice further have two or three buttons. Originally, Microsoft intended three buttons as the standard, but actually implemented only two on its own (Microsoft) mice. Many compatible mice therefore also only have two buttons. The information as to how far the mouse has moved and which buttons have been pressed or released is passed to the PC via a cable or an infra-red beam.

11.2.2 Mouse Driver and Mouse Interface

Most mice are connected to the serial interface. Via the various control lines, the mouse is then supplied with energy; wireless infra-red mice need a battery, of course. When you move your mouse or press or release a button, the mouse generally passes a mouse data packet to the interface, which in turn issues an interrupt. For handling this interrupt a *mouse driver* is needed, which intercepts the interrupt for the corresponding serial interface, reads the mouse data packet, and updates internal values that concern the current keyboard status as well as the mouse's position. Moreover, the mouse driver provides a software interface via mouse interrupt 33h for interpreting these internal values. You will find a list of all INT 33h functions in Appendix J.

The mouse driver is not only responsible for servicing the interface interrupt and providing the mentioned values, but also for moving the *mouse pointer* over the screen. This pointer seems to follow the mouse's movement. To clear up a common misconception: don't move the mouse pointer over the screen using the mouse itself; you only continuously issue interrupts when moving the mouse, during the course of which the amount of mouse movement is passed to the interface. The mouse driver detects these positional signals from the mouse and converts them into a movement of the mouse pointer on-screen. For this purpose, it deletes the mouse pointer at the current location, writes the old screen contents at this location again, reads the screen contents at the new location, and overwrites the location with the mouse pointer.

For the mouse driver you can choose from three options: hardware and software mouse pointer in text mode, as well as a graphics mouse pointer in graphics mode. You may define the type and shape of the mouse pointer by means of functions 09h and 0ah of INT 33h. The hardware mouse pointer is nothing more than the conventional cursor that the mouse driver moves on-screen according to the mouse's movements. For the software mouse pointer you can select any character; as a standard an inverted space character is defined. Thus in text mode the mouse pointer always has one character corresponding to a video memory word of two bytes (attribute and character code). The functions of INT 33h for reading the mouse pointer positions returns the position in units of pixels, that is, in the case of a character box with 8*16 pixels for a VGA adapter, the X coordinate by the values 0, 8, 16, ... 472. You must first divide these quantities by the X dimension of the character box to determine the row and column of the mouse pointer in text mode.

The mouse pointer is not simply output on-screen, but combined bit-by-bit via the so-called screen and cursor masks of the mouse pointer with the video memory word at the mouse pointer's location:

```
new video memory word = (old word AND screen mask) XOR cursor mask
```

The combination is carried out in two steps. First, the mouse driver forms the AND value of the old video memory word and the screen mask. Thus, using the screen mask you can clear individual bits in the video memory word. Second, the XOR value of the AND result and the cursor mask is formed.

Example: `old word 'A' corresponding to ASCII code 41h with attribute 01h, thus old word is equal to 4101h; screen mask 4040h, cursor mask 0f1fh.`

```
new word = (4101h AND 4040h) XOR 0f1fh
        = (4000) XOR 0f1fh
        = 4f1fh
```

Resulting mouse pointer: character 4fh corresponding to '0', attribute equal to 1fh.

Thus, with the cursor mask you define the character and colour of the mouse pointer. Table 11.7 shows the combination table for this.

Screen bit	Screen mask bit	Cursor mask bit	Resulting bit
bit	0	0	0
bit	0	1	1
bit	1	0	bit (unchanged)
bit	1	1	$\overline{bit}$ (inverted)

Table 11.7: Combining screen bit, screen and cursor mask

You may clear, set, leave unchanged, or invert individual bits in the video memory word. Figure 11.13 shows the structure of the video memory word for a character in text mode. In Section 11.2.3 an example for using the screen and cursor mask is discussed.

```
┌─────────────────────────────────────────────────────────────────────────────┐
│  15                                  7                                  0     │
│  ┌────┬────┬────┬────┬───┬────┬────┬────┬────┬────┬────┬────┬────┬────┬────┐  │
│  │BLNK│BAK2│BAK1│BAK0│INT│FOR2│FOR1│FOR0│CHR7│CHR6│CHR5│CHR4│CHR3│CHR2│CHR1│CHR0│ │
│  └────┴────┴────┴────┴───┴────┴────┴────┴────┴────┴────┴────┴────┴────┴────┘  │
│  BLNK:  blink                                                                 │
│         1=on              0=off                                               │
│  BAK2...BAK0: background colour (from present palette)                        │
│  INT:   intensity                                                             │
│         1=high intensity    0=normal intensity                               │
│  FOR2...FOR0: foreground colour (from present palette)                        │
│  CHR7...CHR0: character code                                                  │
└─────────────────────────────────────────────────────────────────────────────┘
```

Figure 11.13: Video memory word structure for a character in text mode.

In graphics mode the the mouse pointer is represented similarly. Also in this case, the mouse driver first forms the AND value of the present screen bit and the screen mask, and afterwards the XOR value of this result and the cursor mask when displaying the mouse pointer. In graphics mode, one pixel is assigned one or more bits; if you are defining the mouse pointer you thus have to note the number of bits per pixel. Furthermore, the mouse pointer size here is always 16*16 pixels, and as standard an arrow is defined, which you may alter by means of function 09h. An example of this is discussed in the next section.

Many mouse drivers have problems with a Hercules card in graphics mode. The 720*348 resolution, differing from the geometry of standard IBM adapters, as well as the character box of 9*14 pixels, often gives rise to a phenomenon whereby the individual points of the graphics mouse pointer are widely spread over the whole screen, and therefore don't form a coherent mouse pointer.

Besides mice connected to a serial interface, there are further so-called bus mice which come with an adapter for a bus slot. They access the PC system bus directly, and therefore don't occupy a serial interface. The structure and functioning are largely the same as for conventional mice connected to a serial interface; INT 33h provides the same results. On the PS/2 the mouse was integrated into the system from the beginning, so that here, besides a keyboard connector, a connection for a PS/2 mouse is also implemented as standard.

11.2.3 Programming the Mouse

For programming and interrogating the mouse the functions of mouse interrupt 33h are available. INT 33h is a software interface to the mouse driver to determine the position of the mouse pointer and the number of «mouse clicks», as well as to define the shape and behaviour of the mouse pointer. Appendix J.2 lists all the functions of INT 33h. Only a few less obvious ones are discussed here because of the lack of space. To display the mouse pointer on-screen you always have to enable it with function 01h.

– **Function 09h – Define Mouse Pointer in Graphics Mode**: with this function you define the shape and behaviour of the mouse pointer in graphics mode. The screen and cursor mask are held in a buffer. The action point defines, relative to the upper left corner of the mouse pointer, which value is to be returned during the course of an inquiry referring to the mouse pointer's position. The mouse pointer always has 16*16 pixels that must be covered by the screen and cursor mask. Thus, depending upon the screen mode and the number of colours used, a quite large buffer is necessary to accommodate the mask bits.

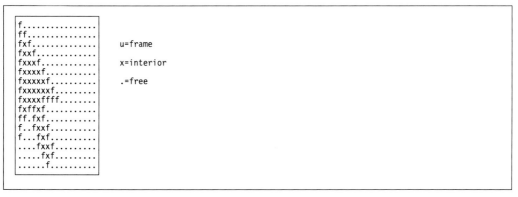

Figure 11.14: Arrow mask.

Example: arrow pointer in the high–resolution VGA mode with 256 colours, that is, 1 byte per pixel.

Figure 11.14 shows the mask for the arrow pointer which comprises frame, interior and free fields. The arrow pointer shall completely cover all underlying pixels, and in the free fields the background shall appear unaltered. For both the screen mask and the cursor mask, 256 bytes (16 characters * 16 points/row) are required. Assume the colour of the frame to be ffh and that of the interior 88h. The action point shall be the upper left tip of the arrow. With the combination (screen bit AND screen mask) XOR cursor mask, the following values are required in the screen and cursor mask for the pixels u, x and . of the arrow pointer:

```
pixel           screen mask      cursor mask

u               00h              ffh
x               00h              88h
.               ffh              00h
```

Thus the buffer has the following contents:

```
00h ffh ffh ffh ffh ffh ffh ffh ffh ffh ffh ffh ffh ffh ffh ffh ffh┐
00h 00h ffh ffh ffh ffh ffh ffh ffh ffh ffh ffh ffh ffh ffh ffh ffh
00h 00h 00h ffh ffh ffh ffh ffh ffh ffh ffh ffh ffh ffh ffh ffh ffh
00h 00h 00h 00h ffh ffh ffh ffh ffh ffh ffh ffh ffh ffh ffh ffh ffh
00h 00h 00h 00h 00h ffh ffh ffh ffh ffh ffh ffh ffh ffh ffh ffh ffh
00h 00h 00h 00h 00h 00h ffh ffh ffh ffh ffh ffh ffh ffh ffh ffh ffh
00h 00h 00h 00h 00h 00h 00h ffh ffh ffh ffh ffh ffh ffh ffh ffh ffh
00h 00h 00h 00h 00h 00h 00h 00h ffh ffh ffh ffh ffh ffh ffh ffh ffh ├─ screen mask
00h 00h 00h 00h 00h 00h 00h 00h 00h ffh ffh ffh ffh ffh ffh ffh ffh
00h 00h 00h 00h 00h 00h ffh ffh ffh ffh ffh ffh ffh ffh ffh ffh ffh
00h 00h ffh 00h 00h 00h ffh ffh ffh ffh ffh ffh ffh ffh ffh ffh ffh
00h ffh ffh 00h 00h 00h 00h ffh ffh ffh ffh ffh ffh ffh ffh ffh ffh
00h ffh ffh ffh 00h 00h 00h ffh ffh ffh ffh ffh ffh ffh ffh ffh ffh
ffh ffh ffh ffh 00h 00h 00h 00h ffh ffh ffh ffh ffh ffh ffh ffh ffh
ffh ffh ffh ffh ffh 00h 00h 00h ffh ffh ffh ffh ffh ffh ffh ffh ffh
ffh ffh ffh ffh ffh ffh 00h ffh ffh ffh ffh ffh ffh ffh ffh ffh ffh┘
ffh 00h 00h 00h 00h 00h 00h 00h 00h 00h 00h 00h 00h 00h 00h 00h 00h┐
ffh ffh 00h 00h 00h 00h 00h 00h 00h 00h 00h 00h 00h 00h 00h 00h 00h
ffh 88h ffh 00h 00h 00h 00h 00h 00h 00h 00h 00h 00h 00h 00h 00h 00h
ffh 88h 88h ffh 00h 00h 00h 00h 00h 00h 00h 00h 00h 00h 00h 00h 00h
ffh 88h 88h 88h ffh 00h 00h 00h 00h 00h 00h 00h 00h 00h 00h 00h 00h
ffh 88h 88h 88h 88h ffh 00h 00h 00h 00h 00h 00h 00h 00h 00h 00h 00h
ffh 88h 88h 88h 88h 88h ffh 00h 00h 00h 00h 00h 00h 00h 00h 00h 00h
ffh 88h 88h 88h 88h 88h 88h ffh 00h 00h 00h 00h 00h 00h 00h 00h 00h ├─ cursor mask
ffh 88h 88h 88h 88h ffh ffh ffh ffh 00h 00h 00h 00h 00h 00h 00h 00h
ffh 88h ffh ffh 88h ffh 00h 00h 00h 00h 00h 00h 00h 00h 00h 00h 00h
ffh ffh 00h ffh 88h ffh 00h 00h 00h 00h 00h 00h 00h 00h 00h 00h 00h
ffh 00h 00h ffh 88h 88h ffh 00h 00h 00h 00h 00h 00h 00h 00h 00h 00h
ffh 00h 00h 00h ffh 88h ffh 00h 00h 00h 00h 00h 00h 00h 00h 00h 00h
00h 00h 00h 00h ffh 88h 88h ffh 00h 00h 00h 00h 00h 00h 00h 00h 00h
00h 00h 00h 00h 00h ffh 88h ffh 00h 00h 00h 00h 00h 00h 00h 00h 00h
00h 00h 00h 00h 00h 00h ffh 00h 00h 00h 00h 00h 00h 00h 00h 00h 00h┘
```

Function call to INT 33h, function 09h.

```
MOV ax, 09h         ; define function
MOV bx, 00h         ; upper left tip
MOV cx, 00h         ; upper left tip
MOV dx, SEG puffer  ; load buffer segment into dx
MOV es, dx          ; load segment into es
MOV dx, OFF puffer  ; load buffer offset into dx
INT 33h             ; call function
```

–   **Function 0ah – Define Mouse Pointer in Text Mode**: this function defines the shape and behaviour of the mouse pointer in text mode. Thus the definition of the mouse pointer is much easier here than in graphics mode. You may choose from between a hardware mouse pointer (that is, the conventional cursor) and a software mouse pointer, for which you are free to select any character. If you choose a software mouse pointer then the video memory word of the character onto which the mouse pointer is mapped is combined with the screen and cursor mask as follows: *(video memory word AND screen mask) XOR cursor mask.* Therefore, the mouse pointer's colour as well as its character can change.

Example: bright, blinking software mouse pointer with colour 3 of the active palette of constant character -.

```
MOV ax, 0ah    ; select function
MOV bx, 00h    ; software mouse pointer
MOV cx, 00h    ; screen mask (clear screen character completely -> constant character -)
MOV dx, 8b02h  ; cursor mask (BLNK=1b, BAKx=000b, INT=1b, FORx=011b, CHRx=00000010b)
INT 33h        ; function call
```

Example: software mouse pointer with scan lines between 3 and 8

```
MOV ax, 0ah    ; select function
MOV bx, 01h    ; hardware mouse pointer
MOV cx, 03h    ; first scan line
MOV dx, 08h    ; last scan line
INT 33h        ; function call
```

- **Function 0ch – Define Call Mask for User-Defined Procedure:** with this function you can define a condition for which the mouse driver calls a user-defined procedure. An application program is thus always activated if, for example, you move the mouse or operate a mouse button. Thus a continuous inquiry is not necessary; the mouse gets attention on its own. The procedure is passed a mask in register ax according to the call mask in which the bit is set that gave rise to the procedure call. The bc, cx, and dx registers define the current button state and the mouse pointer position.

Example: the mouse driver shall call the procedure mouse_handler if the mouse is moved or the left button is pressed.

```
MOV ax, 0ch                    ; select function
MOV cx, 03h                    ; call mask (left button pressed, mouse moved)
MOV dx, OFF mouse_handler      ; load procedure offset into dx
MOV bx, SEGMENT mouse_handler; ; load procedure segment into bx
MOV es, bx                     ; load segment into es
INT 33h                        ; call function

mouse_handler    PROC    FAR
   ..............              ;
TEST ax, 01h                   ; check whether mouse has been moved
JNZ movement                   ; jump
TEST ax, 02h                   ; check whether left button pressed
JNZ button                     ; jump
   ..............
movement:
   ..............              ; process mouse movement
```

```
button:
    ..............           ; process button press
RETF                         ; far return to the mouse driver
END PROC
```

11.2.4 The PS/2 Mouse

In view of the success of graphics-oriented user shells (to which the OS/2 presentation manager also belongs), IBM has already implemented a mouse port into the keyboard controller of its PS/2 models. The mouse is generally denoted as the *pointing device* here. In principle, other pointing devices (for example, a trackball) can also be connected to the mouse port, as long as they comply with the PS/2 mouse interface. Because of the PS/2 mouse's interface integration, you can also access the PS/2 mouse via the keyboard controller ports 60h and 64h. The mouse passes the controller the data in the form of an 8-byte mouse data packet. Its structure is shown in Figure 11.15.

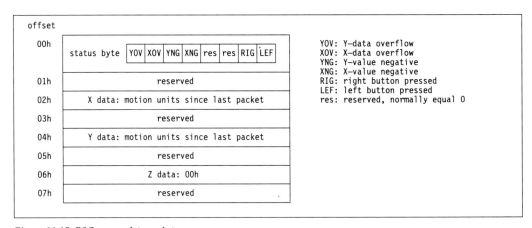

Figure 11.15: PS/2 mouse data packet.

The following discusses the mouse programming via the controller ports, as well as the new mouse functions of the PS/2 BIOS.

Programming the PS/2 Mouse Via Ports

To transfer data or commands to the mouse (or the auxiliary device in general) you must first pass the keyboard controller the command *write auxiliary device*, corresponding to the command code d4h. The following byte to the port address 60h is then transferred to the auxiliary device. If you write the command byte to port 60h, as you do for the keyboard, then the command is not transmitted to the mouse but the keyboard. Note that you don't instruct the keyboard controller permanently to transfer all data to the auxiliary device. The command code is only effective for the immediately following data byte to port 60h. Table 11.8 lists all valid command codes for the PS/2 mouse.

Code	Command	Description
e6h	reset scaling	resets X-Y-scaling factor to 1:1
e7h	set scaling	sets X-Y-scaling to 2:1
e8h	set resolution	sets mouse resolution corresponding to following data byte (00h=1 count/mm, 01h=2 counts/mm, 02h=4 counts/mm, 03h=8 counts/mm)
e9h	determine status	supplies a 3-byte status:

```
byte 3: sample rate          byte 2: resolution
byte 1:
        res MOD ENA SCL res LFT res RIG

                                      └── right mouse button (1=pressed)
                                      ─── left mouse button (1=pressed)
                                      ─── scaling (0=1:1, 1=2:1)
                                      ─── mouse (0=disabled, 1=enabled)
                                      ─── mode (0=stream, 1=remote)
```

Code	Command	Description
eah	set stream mode	sets stream mode
ebh	read data	transfers a data packet from mouse to controller
ech	reset wrap mode	resets mouse from wrap mode to normal mode
eeh	set wrap mode	sets mouse to wrap mode
f0h	set remote mode	sets remote mode
f2h	indentify unit	supplies an identification code (00h=mouse)
f3h	set sample rate	sets sampling rate of mouse according to following data byte (0ah=10 samples/s, 14h=20 samples/s, 28h=40 samples/s, 3ch=60 samples/s, 50h=80 samples/s, 64h=100 samples/s, c8h=200 samples/s
f4h	enable	enables data transfer in stream mode
f5h	disable	disables data transfer in stream mode
f6h	set standard	initializes mouse with standard values (100 samples/s, scaling 1:1, stream mode, resolution 4 counts/mm, data transfer disabled)
feh	resend	mouse transmits the last transferred data packet to the controller once more
ffh	reset	executes an internal mouse test

Table 11.8: Commands for the auxiliary device mouse (PS/2)

The PS/2 mouse can be operated in two different modes: *stream mode* and *remote mode*. In stream mode the mouse always passes data when you operate a mouse button or move the mouse a predefined distance. The programmable sample rate determines how often the mouse may transfer data to the controller per second at most. In remote mode, on the other hand, the mouse data is transferred only after an explicit request by the *read data* command, corresponding to code ebh. In both cases, the mouse writes data into the output buffer of the keyboard controller, which then issues a hardware interrupt corresponding to IRQ1. The interrupt handler determines (according to the AUXB bit in the status register of the keyboard controller) whether the output buffer contains keyboard or mouse data. The following briefly discusses the PS/2 mouse commands.

– **Reset Scaling (e6h)**: this command restes the scaling factor to 1:1.

– **Set Scaling (e7h)**: this command sets the scaling factor in stream mode to a value of 2:1, so that the X and Y values from the mouse are doubled. In remote mode the command has no effect.

Example: set scaling.

```
OUT 64h, d4h  ; command "write auxiliary device" for controller
wait:
IN al, 64h    ; read status register
TEST al, 02h  ; check whether input buffer is empty
JNZ wait      ; input buffer full, thus wait
OUT 60h, e7h  ; command "set scaling" for mouse
```

– **Set Resolution (e8h)**: with this command you can set the resolution of the mouse. The following values are possible: 00h = 1 count/mm, 01h = 2 counts/mm, 02h = 4 counts/mm, 03h = 8 counts/mm. After the command byte you must also write the data byte to port 60h.

Example: resolution 4 counts/mm.

```
OUT 64h, d4h  ; command "write auxiliary device" for controller
wait1:
IN al, 64h    ; read status register
TEST al, 02h  ; check whether input buffer is empty
JNZ wait1     ; input buffer full, thus wait
OUT 60h, e8h  ; command "set resolution" for mouse
wait2:
IN al, 64h    ; read status register
TEST al, 02h  ; check whether input buffer is empty
JNZ wait2     ; input buffer full, thus wait
OUT 60h, 02h  ; set resolution to 4 counts/mm
```

– **Determine Status (e9h)**: with this command you may determine the current mouse status. The status byte is passed in the controller's output buffer.

– **Set Stream Mode (eah)**: this command sets the mouse to stream mode.

– **Read Data (ebh)**: this command forces the transfer of a mouse data packet. The command is valid in stream as well as in remote mode. Moreover, in remote mode this is the only option for the CPU to receive data from the mouse.

– **Reset Wrap Mode (ech)**: this command resets the mouse to the normal operation mode.

– **Set Wrap Mode (eeh)**: this command sets the mouse to wrap or echo mode. In wrap mode the mouse returns every command or data byte which it receives from the controller back to the controller, except the commands *reset wrap mode* (code ech) and *reset* (code ffh).

– **Set Remote Mode (f0h)**: this command sets the mouse to remote mode. The mouse then transfers a data packet to the controller only after an explicit request via the *read data* (code ebh) command.

– **Identify Device (f2h)**: This command instructs the mouse to return an identification code to the controller's output buffer.

– **Set Sampling Rate (f3h)**: using this command you may set the sampling rate via a data byte, which is transferred to the mouse after the command code f3h via port 60h. The following values are possible: 0ah = 10 samples/s, 14h = 20 samples/s, 28h = 40 samples/s, 3ch = 60 samples/s, 50h = 80 samples/s, 64h = 100 samples/s and c8h = 200 samples/s.

– **Enable(f4h)**: this command enables data transfer if the mouse is in stream mode. In remote mode the command has no effect.

– **Disable (f5h)**: this command disables the data transfer if the mouse is in stream mode. In remote mode the command has no effect.

– **Set Standard (f6h)**: this command initializes the PS/2 mouse. The standard state is as follows:

```
sampling rate: 100 samples/s
scaling:       1:1
mode:          stream mode
resolution:    4 counts/mm
transfer:      disabled
```

– **Resend (feh)**: this command instructs the mouse to pass the controller the last data packet once again.

– **Reset (ffh)**: this command resets the mouse and carries out an internal self-test.

After the receipt of every valid command from the controller the mouse provides an ACK to acknowledge reception. This is not the case for the *reset wrap mode* (code ech) and *reset* (code ffh) commands. In both cases, the mouse doesn't output an ACK. Table 11.9 lists the valid mouse return codes.

Code	Meaning
00h	mouse identification
fah	ACK
feh	resend request

Table 11.9: Mouse return codes

The CPU must respond to a return code feh with the repeated transfer of the last command or data byte because a transmission error has occurred.

Programming via BIOS Interrupt 15h

In the PS/2 BIOS, eight subfunctions are implemented for interrupt INT 15h, function c2h which support the PS/2 mouse. Using these functions you may access the mouse the same way as is possible via the controller ports. Appendix J.3 summarizes all the PS/2 mouse functions of the BIOS, so they are not all discussed in detail here.

Before you can use a PS/2 mouse and the accompanying BIOS routines, you have to specify the entry address of the driver which is to process the mouse data packet from the PS/2 mouse. You can do this using the subfunction *pass driver address* (subcode 07h) of INT 15h, function c2h. Afterwards, you must adjust the size of the mouse data packet by means of the subfunction *initialize mouse* (subcode 05h). Now mouse and BIOS are prepared so that you may activate the mouse with the subfunction *enable mouse* (subcode 00h).

When using the PS/2 BIOS routines, the mouse data transfer to a driver or an application proceeds as follows:

–   The BIOS interrupt handler, corresponding to IRQ1, determines whether mouse or keyboard data is available, and pushes the one to eight bytes of the mouse data packet onto the stack.

–   Afterwards, the BIOS executes a far-call to the program.

–   The called program processes the mouse data and returns to the BIOS routine with a far-return using the BIOS return address held on the stack.

11.3   Trackball

The trackball is a space-saving alternative to the mouse, and is sometimes already integrated into the keyboard. With cheap and therefore low-resolution mice, the mouse pointer movement is similar to a mouse marathon on the desk! The structure of the trackball is like that of a mouse lying on its back, so that the ball is now on the top. To allow users with clumsy fingers to use the trackball, the ball is usually much larger than that of a mouse. On the trackball you are directly moving the ball, not indirectly via mouse movements. But the internal structure essentially remains the same; also here, the ball's movement is transmitted onto rollers, which in turn drive disks with holes for closing and opening photosensor assemblies. Connection of the trackball to the PC system is usually carried out via a serial interface and the trackball driver, which provides the same software interface as the mouse via INT 33h. Further discussion is not, therefore, necessary.

11.4   Digitizer or Graph Tablet

For CAD applications that need the very precise positioning of pointers on a high-resolution screen, so-called *digitizer tablets* are available on which you move a *cross hair glass*. The digitizer tablets and glass form a unit, as is the case for an optical mouse and its mouse pad; they may not be operated separately. Below the surface of the tablet a very dense X-Y matrix made of thin wires is usually formed. The tablet processor successively sends short sense pulses through the X and Y wires by activating the first X wire and scanning all Y wires in succession with pulses, then activating the next X wire and successively sending a sense pulse through all Y wires, etc. The sense pulses give rise to a short pulse in the glass if it is exactly above the crossing of an X and Y wire through which a sense pulse is running simultaneously at that time. Through this pulse, and the time at which it occurred, the processor can then determine the position of the glass very precisely. The accompanying driver then locates the CAD cross-hair on the screen, or another pointer, accordingly.

The glass of the digitizer tablet usually has four buttons, with which certain reactions and actions of the CAD program are issued. Which actions occur is, of course, up to the programmer. For most CAD programs, the tablet comes with various templates that divide the tablet logically into a central part for positioning the cross-hair, and a peripheral section with certain function symbols. A button operation in the central area sets a point in most cases, while a button operation in the peripheral section calls the function above whose symbol the glass is currently located.

12   Graphics Adapters

This chapter mainly discusses graphics adapters. As you know, there is a virtually infinite variety of such adapters on the market, from the simple monochrome board that can only display text, up to high-resolution and rapid professional adapters for CAD applications, that incorporate dedicated graphics processors. A detailed discussion of all adapters is therefore far beyond the scope of this book, and probably impossible. For this reason, discussion is restricted mainly to the most-widely used adapters, that is, the Hercules card as the low-cost beginner's model, and the VGA adapter as the colour model for Windows and other graphics-oriented applications.

12.1   Displaying Images on a Monitor and the General Structure of Graphics Adapters

The display of images (including text as well as graphics) on a computer monitor is similar to the method used in a conventional TV. Figure 12.1 schematically illustrates the generation of images on a *cathode ray tube (CRT)*.

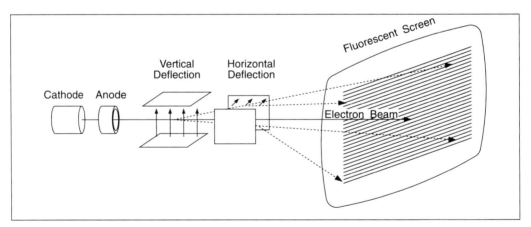

Figure 12.1: Displaying images on a monitor with a cathode ray tube. The electrons emitted by the cathode are accelerated by the anode and deflected in the deflection units. Afterwards, they hit and thus illuminate the fluorescent screen.

The screen's content is divided into many horizontal rows, where every row has a plurality of points, so-called *pixels* or *picture elements*. The tube is emptied so that the electrons emitted by the cathode (hence cathode ray tube) are rapidly accelerated by the electric field of the anode and hit the screen. This screen is coated with a fluorescent material that illuminates when the fast electrons hit it. The negatively charged electrons are deflected by electrical fields generated by electrical voltages at the deflection plates, thus forming so-called *scanlines*.

If the electron beam has reached the right-hand end of row then it must return to the beginning of the next scanline; this is called a *horizontal retrace*. In the same way, the electron beam must return to the upper left corner when it has reached the lower right one; it carries out a *vertical retrace*.

To actually display an image consisting of many pixels the intensity of the electron beam is modulated accordingly. At the locations where a strong beam hits a bright pixel appears, and at positions hit by a less intensive beam, darker points are generated. Because of the persistence of the fluorescent layer, the points still emit light when the electron beam is already at another location, and because of the inertia of our eyes we get the impression that there is a steady image on the screen. With the electron beam just described, only monochrome or grey shaded images can be generated. These monitors usually have a fluorescent coating which emits green, amber, or white light.

If you attempt to display coloured images, three electron beams are required, each of which hits points on the screen surface lighting up in three different colours. Usually, coatings are used today that provide the three primary colours red, green, and blue. With these three primary colours all known colours can be generated by means of *additive colour mixing*. A white point, for example, results if all three colour elements of a pixel are illuminated at the same intensity. Thus, on colour monitors all three electron beams are modulated according to the image information, where the absolute beam intensity determines the brightness and the relative beam intensity the colour of the corresponding pixel.

You can imagine that the modulation of the electron beam as well as the horizontal and vertical retraces have to be synchronized so that, for example, the vertical retrace occurs exactly when the electron beam has reached the end of the last scanline with the pixel to be displayed last, and a horizontal retrace would be required anyway. Scanning of the screen is carried out line-by-line, therefore, and the image is displayed on the monitor in the same way. The graphics adapter has to provide the video signals required for the individual pixels (that is, the intensity and colour signal), as well as the synchronization signals for the horizontal and vertical retrace.

Example: on a VGA monitor with a resolution of 640*480 pixels, every line has 640 pixels and the image is generated by 480 scanlines. Thus, after 480 horizontal retraces a vertical retrace occurs. The image is built up 60 times per second, that is, a vertical retrace occurs every 16.7 ms.

For the VGA adapter at the resolution indicated, IBM specifies a video bandwidth of 25.175 MHz, which corresponds to the rate at which the pixels are written onto the screen. This means that every second more than 25 million points have to be be written, thus the video amplifiers of the monitor must operate very quickly. At even higher resolutions (today we already have a *de facto* standard of 1024*768 pixels) the video bandwidth rapidly rises up to 100 MHz; also, high-quality circuits and the tube itself become overtaxed with such frequencies, and only very expensive CAD monitors can stand such rates. But there is a simple and quite cheap way out: *interlacing*. The interlacing method writes in two passes; first only those scanlines with an odd number are written, and in the second pass all those lines with an even number. The line frequency and thus the video bandwidth is halved, but the picture frequency (the number of vertical retraces) remains the same. This is necessary as the eye would recognize a halving of the image frequency as a flicker, but it can be tricked by alternately writing odd and even scanlines. Figure 12.2 shows the electron beam path in interlaced and non-interlaced modes. For a perfect image in the interlace mode, it is essential that the electron beam hits the screen's surface exactly between two scanlines of the previous pass. The precise adjustment is not very simple, so the image in interlaced mode is usually significantly worse than in non-interlaced mode.

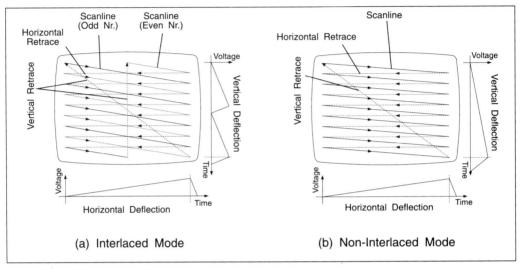

Figure 12.2: Interlaced and non-interlaced mode. (a) In interlaced mode, the scanlines with an odd number are first written, and afterwards all scanlines with an even number. The voltage of the vertical deflection unit carries out two cycles for one complete image; (b) in non-interlaced mode the lines are written in succession.

If you think that the interlace display method is new then I must disappoint you. This method has been used since the start of the TV era to prevent the bandwidths of TV channels from going beyond all possible bounds. In Europe one TV image consists of 625 lines, separated into two partial images of 312.5 lines each. The partial images are transmitted 50 times per second, so that the TV effectively displays 25 complete images per second.

LCD and gas-plasma monitors generate the picture similar to a cathode ray tube, but here no electron beam forms the picture; instead the individual pixels are assigned elements that may be addressed in succession. Therefore, on these monitors the image is also generated line-by-line. Retraces don't play any role here, as the retrace can be carried out simply by an address change during the course of addressing the elements.

In their principal structure the graphics adapters don't differ significantly, despite all the differences concerning the capabilities of displaying colours and the various resolutions. Figure 12.3 shows a block diagram for the general structure of a modern graphics adapter.

The central part is the video controller or graphics control chip CRTC (**cathode ray tube** controller), which supervises the functions of the adapter and generates the necessary control signal. The CPU accesses the video RAM via the bus interface to write information that defines the text or graphics the monitor is to display. The CRTC continuously generates addresses for the video RAM to read the corresponding characters, and to transfer them to the character generator.

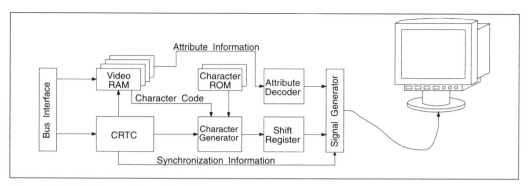

Figure 12.3: Block diagram of a graphics adapter.

In text mode the characters are usually defined by their ASCII codes, which are further assigned a so-called attribute. The attribute defines the display mode for the character concerned more precisely – for example, whether it is to be displayed in a blinking or inverted manner. The character ROM, for every ASCII code, holds a pixel pattern for the corresponding character. The character generator converts the character codes using the pixel pattern in the character ROM into a sequence of pixel bits, and transfers them to a shift register. The signal generator generates the necessary signals for the monitor, using the bit stream from the shift register, the attribute information from the video RAM and the synchronization signals from the CRTC. The monitor processes the passed video signals and displays the symbolic information in the video RAM in the usual form as a picture. The character information in the video RAM thus modulates the electron beam of the monitor through the intermediate stages of character ROM, character generator, shift register, and signal.

In graphics mode the information in video RAM is directly used for generating characters, that is, the entries don't define an index into the character ROM, but already represent the pixel pattern itself with the corresponding colour or grey scale information. Because of this, attribute information is no longer required; the signal generator generates from the bit values in the shift register the brightness and colour signals for the monitor.

12.2   Screen Modes and the 6845 Graphics Controller

Modern graphics adapters may be operated in two completely different (and incompatible) modes: text and graphics modes. Older display adapters such as IBM's monochrome display adapter (MDA) only allow pictures in text mode. Graphics adapters, on the other hand, can display free graphics with possibly very different resolutions. All of these functions are carried out under the control of the graphics controller. The following discusses the basic principles of text and graphics mode and presents a typical member of the graphics controller chips, Motorola's CRTC 6845.

12.2.1 6845 Video Controller

This video controller can be found as the original or compatible chip on nearly all graphics adapters (for example, the Hercules card). Exceptions are VGA and graphics adapters with a dedicated graphics processor. The CRTC 6845 comes in a standard 40-pin DIP case; its connection scheme is shown in Figure 12.4.

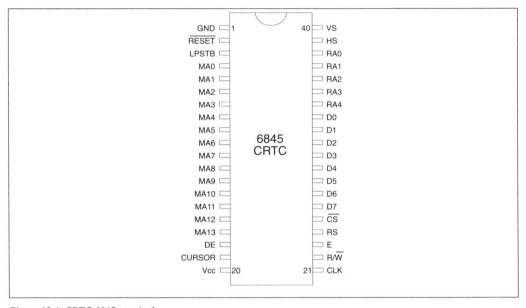

Figure 12.4: CRTC 6845 terminals.

The following briefly presents and discusses the terminals and signals of the 6845. Using the 6845 in text and graphics mode is described in Sections 12.2.2 and 12.2.3.

$\overline{\text{RESET}}$
A low-level signal at this pin resets the 6845.

LPSTB
(Light Pen Strobe) A pulse from the light pen instructs the 6845 to store the current address for the video RAM in the light pen register. The CPU reads this register and thus determines the position of the light pen on-screen.

MA0–MA13
(Memory Address) These 14 terminals provide the memory addresses for the video RAM. MA0–MA13 continuously increase with the line scanning to address the corresponding characters in video RAM successively.

DE
(Display Enable) A high-level signal at this pin indicates that the 6845 CRTC is currently providing address and control signals for the displayed region of the screen.

CURSOR

A high-level signal shows that the cursor position is currently scanned.

VS

(Vertical Synchronization) At this terminal the 6845 outputs the signal for vertical synchronization, and thus causes a vertical retrace.

HS

(Horizontal Synchronization) At this terminal the 6845 outputs the signal for horizontal synchronization, and thus causes a horizontal retrace.

RA0–RA4

(Row Address) These five connections specify the current scanline of a character in text mode. Thus, RA0–RA4 characters with a maximum of 32 scanlines can be displayed. In graphics mode RA0–RA4 is often combined with MA0–MA13 into a «large» address, and addresses, for example, the banks of the video RAM.

D0–D7

The eight terminals form the bidirectional data bus for an access by the CPU to the internal 6845 registers.

$\overline{\text{CS}}$

(Chip Select) A low-level signal at this connection enables the 6845 for an access by the CPU.

RS

(Register Select) A low-level signal (RS = 0) selects the address register, and a high-level signal (RS = 1) selects the 6845 data register for the next read or write access by the CPU.

E

(Enable) A high–low transition of this signal activates the data bus, and serves as a clock pulse for the 6845 to read data from or write it into the internal registers.

R/$\overline{\text{W}}$

(Read/Write) A high-level signal means that the CPU reads internal 6845 registers; a low-level signal, on the other hand, means that the CPU writes an internal 6845 register.

CLK

(Clock) The clock signal is used for synchronizing the 6845 monitor signals, and is usually equal to the rate at which the characters are displayed on screen.

V_{cc}

This pin receives the supply voltage (usually +5 V).

GND

This pin is earthed (usually 0 V).

Of particular importance for displaying texts and graphics on the monitor are the memory address MA0–MA13 and the scanline address RA0–RA4. The following sections discuss how the remaining hardware of a graphics adapter uses these address signals in text and graphics mode.

12.2.2 Character Generation in Text Mode

In text mode every character on-screen is assigned a word of two bytes in video RAM. The low-order byte contains the character code, the high-order byte the attribute. The signal generator on the graphics adapter then displays the character, depending upon the attribute byte value – for example, blinking, with high intensity, inversely, or with a certain colour. Figure 12.5 shows the structure of the video memory word.

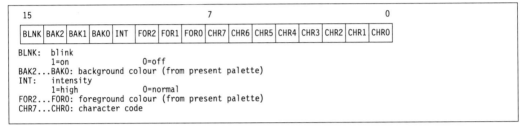

Figure 12.5: Video RAM word structure for a character in text mode.

If the *BLNK* bit is set, the character concerned is displayed blinking. Depending upon the graphics adapter and its manufacturer, the character blinks at a rate of between 1 Hz and 3 Hz. The bits *BAK2–BAK0* define the background colour of the character; eight different colours are possible. The actual colour not only depends on the value of the bits BAK2–BAK0, but also on the graphics adapter, the selected colour palette, whether a monochrome or colour monitor is used, and on the current resolution of the adapter. A set *INT* bit displays the character with a high intensity, that is, bright. The bits *FOR2–FOR0* determine the character's foreground colour, as BAK2–BAK0 do for the background colour. Also here, the colour actually displayed depends upon the graphics adapter, the colour palette selected, whether a monochrome or colour monitor is used, and on the current resolution of the adapter. The eight low-order bits *CHR7–CHR0* define the code of the displayed character, and serve as an index into the character table in character ROM, or into a character RAM containing the pixel pattern for the characters concerned.

```
    1        9              1        8
 1  000000000           1  00000000
    001110000              00111000
    011011000              01101100
    110001100              11000110
 5  110001100           5  11000110
    110001100              11000110
    110001100              11000110
    110001100              11000110
    011011000              01101100
10  001110000          10  00111000
    000000000              00000000
    000000000              00000000
    000000000              00000000
14  000000000          14  00000000
      (a)                    (b)
```

Figure 12.6: Pixel pattern "O" in text mode. (a) on-screen; (b) in character ROM.

In text mode, every text row is generated by a certain number of scanlines. The Hercules card, for example, uses 14 scanlines for one text row; every character is represented in text mode by a pixel block comprising a height of 14 scanlines and a width of nine pixels. As every character is separated by a narrow space from the next character, and every row by a few scanlines from the next row, the complete block is not occupied by character pixels. For the actual character a 7*11 matrix is available, the rest of the 9*14 matrix remains empty. Also in text mode, every alpha-numerical character is displayed as a pixel pattern held in the character ROM or RAM. Figure 12.6 shows, for example, the pixel pattern for an «O» on a Hercules card as it appears on screen (Figure 12.6a).

A «1» means that at the location concerned a pixel with the foreground colour is written, and a «0» that a pixel with the background colour appears. For technical reasons, only eight of the nine pixel columns are actually held in the ROM (Figure 12.6b). The 9th pixel column on the screen is formed for ASCII characters 0–191 and 224–255 by internally generating an empty column in the character generator, and for the block graphics characters with ASCII codes 192–223 by repeating the 8th column to generate the 9th one. The doubling of the 8th column to form the 9th is necessary so that for the horizontal graphics characters, no breaks appear between the individual characters. Thus, in the character ROM every pixel line of a character is eight bits, or exactly one byte, long. How many pixel lines a character comprises is defined by an entry in the 6845 control register *max. scanline.*

In the character ROM the pixel matrices for the 256 different characters are arranged so that the character code as the first index specifies the beginning of the character in ROM. The number of the current scanline for the character is then the second index or the offset, which determines the pixel line (that is, the byte) within the character.

The graphics adapter displays a character in text mode as follows. The 6845 outputs continuous addresses for the video RAM via MA0–MA13. The character in the upper left corner corres-ponds to the lowest address that the 6845 provides immediately after a vertical retrace. The adapter logic addresses the video RAM by means of this address, and fetches the character code and the attribute. The character code serves for the character generator as the first index into the character ROM. The line address is equal to 0 at this moment, that is, the 6845 addresses the first scanline of the character matrix. According to the timing of the video frequency, the bits of the pixel matrix are now transferred from the shift register to the signal generator. If the signal generator receives a «1» from the shift register, then it generates a video signal corresponding to the foreground colour of the character. If, on the other hand, a «0» arrives then it supplies a video signal corresponding to the background colour. The first scanline is thus displayed on the monitor according to the pixel matrices of the characters in the first text line.

When the electron beam reaches the end of the scanline, the 6845 activates the output HS to issue a horizontal retrace and a horizontal synchronization. The electron beam returns to the beginning of the next scanline. After every scanline (after every horizontal retrace) the 6845 increases the RA0–RA4. This line address forms the offset within the pixel matrix for the char-acter to be displayed. Upon every scanline of the monitor a pixel line of the characters in the text row concerned is thus displayed on the monitor. This means that with the above indicated 9*14 pixel matrix for one character the first text row has been displayed after 14 scanlines. The line address RA0–RA4 returns to the value 0, the 6845 provides new addresses MA0–MA13, and the next text row is output in the same way. If the end of the last scanline is reached, the 6845 resets the address MA0–MA13 and the line address RA0–RA4 to the initial values and enables the output VS to issue a vertical retrace and a vertical synchronization. Exactly one picture has thus been formed on-screen. Because the screen image cannot persist, and as the CPU may overwrite the video RAM with new values, the screen must be refreshed within a short time interval (typically 50 Hz). The above-described procedure starts again.

EGA and VGA hold the pixel patterns in a character RAM into which you can also load user-defined characters, and thus define your own characters. For this purpose, you have to fill the character RAM with appropriate pixel matrices. How this works in principle is discussed in Section 12.5.2.

Because of the 5-bit line address RA0–RA4, characters with a maximum height of 32 scanline are possible. The 14-bit memory address MA0–A13 further enables the addressing of video memories up to 16 k word. In graphics mode, MA0–A13 and RA0–RA4 can be combined into one 19-bit address. The 6845 can then address a video memory of up to 512 k objects.

12.2.3 Character Generation and Free Graphics in Graphics Mode

In graphics mode the bytes in video RAM are no longer interpreted as a character code and attribute. Instead, they directly determine the intensity and colour of the corresponding pixel. The 6845 also outputs the memory addresses MA0–MA13, as well as the line addresses RA0–RA4 in this case. How the hardware of the graphics adapter interprets these values for addressing the video memory depends upon the adapter card used, and may differ significantly. In most cases the video RAM is divided into several banks addressed by the line address RA0–RA4. The memory address MA0–MA13 then specifies the offset within each bank.

In graphics mode the data in the video RAM is directly transferred to the shift register and the signal generator; character ROM and hardware character generator don't play any role here, and are disabled. If you write, for example via the BASIC command PRINT "A", the character «A» (ASCII 65) in graphics mode onto the screen, then BASIC doesn't write ASCII code 65 to the corresponding location in the video RAM but copies the pixel matrix for the character «A» to the corresponding location in the video RAM.

The power of the graphics mode is not displaying text, but the capability of drawing free graphics and lines. For this purpose, the program must write appropriate values to the corresponding locations in the display memory. A line, for example, is represented by a plurality of identical bit groups or bytes in the video RAM.

Depending upon the number of displayable colours, one pixel on the monitor is assigned more or fewer bits. Monochrome graphics requires only a single bit corresponding to bright (bit = 1) or dark (bit = 0) per pixel. Multi-colour graphics usually assign several bits per pixel; on a VGA with 256 different colours, eight bits or one byte per pixel is required. Thus the storage capacity of the video RAM must increase rapidly with increasing resolution and the rising number of colours in the pictures. VGA boards with a 1 Mbyte video RAM are therefore not unusual today; high-resolution graphics adapters for CAD applications may accommodate up to eight Mbtyes of video RAM.

12.2.4 General Video RAM Organization and Structure

The video RAM is organized differently, depending upon the operation mode and graphics adapter used. The following discusses in brief the usual organization. On graphics adapters with a video RAM up to 128 kbytes you may address the whole display memory via the CPU as the normal main memory. But if the video RAM gets larger, then it would overlap the ROM extensions at address c0000h and disturb them. Thus, EGA and VGA boards with more than 128kbytes of display RAM implement a switch that can be set by software to access various 128 kbyte windows into the much larger video RAM. How these switches are used is not standardized, and is thus manufacturer-dependent. If you don't know the switch address and method, then there is nothing left but to use the BIOS.

RAM Organization in Text Mode

In text mode the video RAM is regarded as a linear array; the first word is assigned the character in the upper left corner, that is, the character in row 1, column 1. The second word then describes the character in row 1, column 2, etc. Depending upon the text resolution, a varying number of words is necessary to accommodate the whole screen's contents.

Example: the standard resolution of 25 rows with 80 characters each requires 2000 display memory words with two bytes each, thus a total of 4 kbytes of video RAM; high-resolution SuperVGA adapters with 60 rows of 132 characters each need 15,840 bytes.

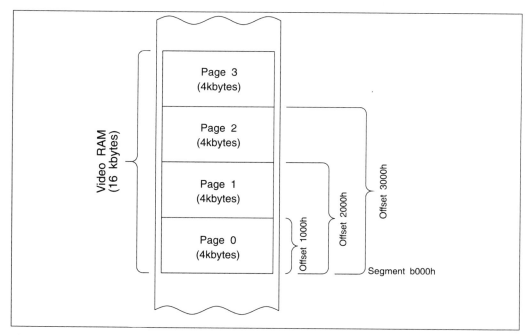

Figure 12.7: Video RAM in text mode divided into several pages.

You can see that the video RAM of most adapters is much larger than a single screen page requires. On an EGA or VGA in text mode the video RAM is therefore divided into *pages*, which can accommodate a whole screen page. The size of the pages depends upon the screen mode and the maximum number of pages, plus, of course, the size of the video RAM. Figure 12.7 shows the division of the video RAM into pages in text mode.

The 6845 can be programmed so that it starts after a vertical retrace with a memory address MA0–MA13 different from 0. If the start address meets the beginning of a page, then several pages that are separated from each other can be managed in video RAM. Moreover, by altering the start address in the 6845 the pages can be switched rapidly. If the CPU changes the contents of a page that is currently not displayed, then the screen doesn't change. Thus you must distinguish between the active displayed page and the processed one. The PC's BIOS is prepared for managing up to eight pages; for each of them its own cursor is defined.

Example: the first and only page of the Hercules card begins at address b0000h. A blinking character "A" shall be written into the upper left corner with the foreground colour 7 and the background 0 at a high intensity.

```
MOV ax, b000h      ; load ax with the segment address of the video RAM
MOV es, ax         ; transfer segment address into ES
MOV ah, f8h        ; load attribute 1111 1000 into ah
MOV al, 41h        ; load character code for "A" into al
MOV es:[00h], ax   ; write attribute and character code into video RAM
```

In general, the address of the display memory word for the character in row i, column j of page k is given by the following equation:

```
address = video segment + page_size * k + 2 * characters_per_row * i + 2 * j
```

Video segment denotes the start address of the video RAM in the PC's address space, and *page_size* denotes the size of a page in the video segment (i, j and k start with 0).

RAM Organization in Graphics Mode

In graphics mode, the situation is more complicated. For example, on the Hercules card the video RAM is divided in graphics mode into four banks per page. The first bank accommodates the pixels for scanlines 0, 4, 8, ... 344, the second bank pixels for scanlines 1, 5, 9, ... 345, the third bank pixels for scanlines 2, 6, 10, ... 346, and the fourth bank pixels for scanlines 3, 7, 11, ... 347. The video RAM of the Hercules card in graphics mode has 64 kbytes, and is divided into two pages of 32 kbytes each. The resolution in graphics mode is 720*348 pixels; every pixel is assigned one bit. Thus 90 bytes are required per line (7120 pixels/8 pixels per byte). For the Hercules card, the address of the byte containing the bit corresponding to the pixel in line i and column j of page k is expressed by the following equation:

```
address(i,j,k) = b0000h + 8000h * k + 2000h * (i MOD 4) + 90 * INT(i/4) + INT(j/8)
```

b0000h characterizes the video segment, 8000h the size of a page, MOD 4 the modulo-4-division by 4, 2000h * (i MOD 4) the offset of the bank which contains the byte, INT the integer part of the corresponding division, 90 * INT(i/4) the offset of line i in the bank, and INT(j/8) the offset of column j in the bank. Figure 12.8 illustrates the decision of the video RAM in various pages in graphics mode of the Hercules card.

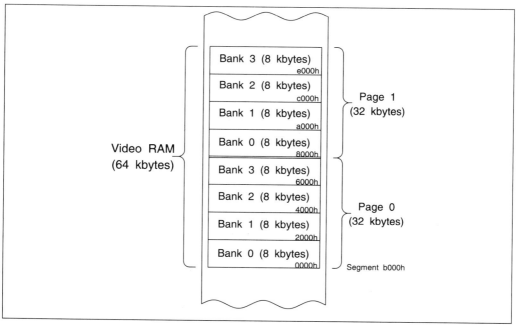

Figure 12.8: Hercules card video RAM splitting into several pages in graphics mode.

You can see that addressing one pixel in the video RAM requires a quite extensive procedure. The above-indicated expression is, by the way, only valid on a Hercules card. On a CGA the video memory is divided in graphics mode into only two banks; on an EGA or VGA the situation becomes even more complicated. Details are discussed in Section 12.5.3.

Access Conflicts

As just mentioned, the CPU can access the video RAM using a simple memory cycle. But besides the CPU, the logic on the graphics adapter also carries out an access to the video RAM according to memory addresses MA0–MA13 provided by the 6845. This may give rise, of course, to conflict if the CPU and the adapter logic address the same chip. The situation becomes particularly critical if the CPU attempts to overwrite an entry while the adapter is just reading it to display it on screen. Whether, finally, the old or the new value gets the upper hand is unpredictable. On the first PC graphics adapter, the CGA, no protection against a simultaneous access to video RAM by the CPU and the adapter logic was implemented; the result was the infamous CGA snow. The CPU access disturbs the read process by the adapter logic (especially in graphics mode) so seriously that the logic determines completely incorrect values, and on the screen bright points appear for a short time; the observer has the impression that snowflakes are blowing over his monitor!

On more modern graphics adapters, the engineers have implemented a gate that blocks an access of the CPU to a video RAM bank if the adapter logic is currently reading the same bank. The CPU then inserts more or fewer wait cycles until access to the video RAM is possible. Depending upon the organization of the video RAM and the adjustment of the adapter to the PC system bus, many wait cycles may therefore occur. Benchmark programs that test the access to the display memory report up to 40 wait cycles on a fast 33 MHz Personal Computer. The only two time periods when the CPU has unlimited access to the video RAM (if the adapter doesn't carry out a refresh of its on-board DRAMs, however) are the horizontal and vertical retraces. During these retrace periods the adapter doesn't access the video RAM. The EGA/VGA board and some other graphics adapters can be configured so that they activate IRQ2 at the beginning of a retrace period. The CPU is thus informed, via a hardware interrupt, that an access to the display memory is possible now without disturbing the screen picture.

The best solution of all these problems is to use *dual-port RAM*, which is often also called *VRAM* (**video RAM**). Normal RAM chips have a single data port through which they accept write data and provide read data. Depending upon the organization of the RAM chips, one or more data pins are implemented for this port. Whether a read or write access to the RAM occurs, and thus whether the data port is acting as a read or write port, is determined by the DRAM controller via the RAM control signal $\overline{WE}$.

Dual-port RAM chips now have two data ports instead of a single switching data port, so that accesses of two different devices can be serviced concurrently without disturbing each other. On some dual-port memories the function of these two ports as a read and write port, respectively, is fixed. Via the first port, data is only output (read port), and via the second data is only accepted (write port). Some other dual-port memories implement the first port as a parallel and the other as a serial port. Via the first port, the data is input and output in parallel (parallel port), via the other exclusively in a serial manner (serial port). The serial port then provides (beginning with a start address) a certain number of internal memory cells synchronously to an external clock signal. By means of the parallel port, however, any memory cell can be accessed by means of an address. Such dual-port memories are especially suited for graphics adapters, as here the CPU carries out random accesses to the video RAM to read or write data, while the adapter logic is reading the memory in a more or less serial manner to display a row on the monitor.

12.2.5 The Hercules Card and Programming the 6845

With the Hercules card as an example, the programming of the 6845 CRTC for text and graphics modes is discussed in detail.

Advice: if you do not program the control register of the graphics adapter and the 6845 correctly and quickly enough, then your monitor or graphics adapter may be damaged. Carry out such programming only if you are sure that you haven't made any mistake.

During the course of a mode change, monitor and graphics adapter are more or less «up in the air», as far as the synchronization and video signals are concerned. Strong synchronization signals at the wrong time can damage the circuits or the monitor burns completely; therefore be careful!

Table 12.1 lists the I/O ports of the video system on the Hercules card. The I/O ports for the additionally implemented parallel interface are not specified, however.

Port	Register	Write (W) Read(R)
3b4h	6845 index register	W
3b5h	6845 data register	R/W
3b8h	mode control register	W
3b9h	set light pen flip-flop	W
3bah	status register	R
3bbh	reset light pen flip-flop	W
3bfh	configuration register	W

Table 12.1: Hercules card I/O port

For programming the display mode of the Hercules card, besides the 6845 registers, the mode control register, the status register and the configuration register are also important. The two «ports» 3b9h and 3bbh are not real I/O ports, but the addresses 3b9h and 3bbh represent command codes that give rise to the action indicated. To instruct the Hercules card according to these two commands, you simply need to issue an OUT instruction referring to the specified I/O addresses with any value. Figure 12.9 shows the structure of the write-only mode control register.

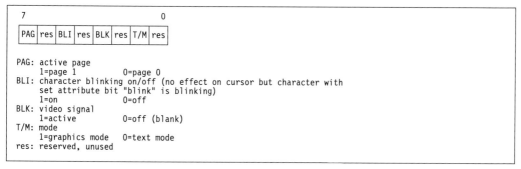

Figure 12.9: The mode control register.

With the *PAG* bit you can define the active page to be displayed on-screen. Page 0 is located between addresses b0000h and b7fffh, and page 1 between b8000h and bffffh. Note that page 1 overlaps with the address area of the video RAM on a CGA. If you only use page 0 then you can install two graphics adapters in the same PC, that is, a Hercules card and a CGA. By setting the *BLI* bit you enable the blinking of characters that have a set blink attribute BLNK in the accompanying display memory word. The *BLK* bit determines whether the video signal from the Hercules card is actually transferred to the monitor. A set bit enables the screen display, a cleared one blanks the screen. Thus you can make a monitor safer with BLK by, for example, clearing bit BLK if no keyboard hit has occurred for more than three minutes. After operating any key BLK is set again and the previous picture appears again. This avoids character burn-in on the fluorescent layer of the tube.

The *T/M* bit determines the operation mode of the Hercules card. If T/M is set the adapter operates in graphics mode; if T/M is cleared the Hercules card runs in text mode. But be careful: for changing the operation mode it is not sufficient only to clear or set T/M. Instead, you must additionally load the 6845 with parameters that are adjusted according to the intended operation mode. Table 12.3 lists the standard values for the 6845 register in text and graphics mode. The T/M bit in the mode control register mainly controls the character generator, the decoder logic, and the oscillator on the Hercules card, as the memory addresses MA0–MA13 and the line addresses RA0–RA4 output by the 6845 must be interpreted differently in graphics mode and text mode.

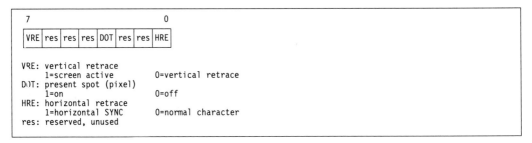

```
7                              0
VRE res res res DOT res res HRE

VRE: vertical retrace
     1=screen active          0=vertical retrace
DOT: present spot (pixel)
     1=on                     0=off
HRE: horizontal retrace
     1=horizontal SYNC        0=normal character
res: reserved, unused
```

Figure 12.10: The status register.

The status register of the Hercules card is read-only, and provides some information concerning the current adapter status. If the *VRE* bit is cleared, the monitor is currently executing a vertical retrace, that is, the 6845 has activated the vertical synchronization signal VS. Otherwise the electron beam is writing information onto the screen. The *DOT* bit indicates whether the electron beam is currently writing a bright (DOT = 1) or a black point (DOT = 0). Finally, you can determine, according to *HRE*, whether the monitor is currently carrying out a horizontal retrace, and the 6845 has activated the horizontal synchronization signal HS for this purpose. If HRE is cleared then a normal character is written onto the screen.

```
7                              0
res res res res res res MSK GEN

MSK: masking of page 1
     1=page 1 corresponding to addresses b8000h–bffffh is masked off the address space;
        setting of bit PAG in mode control register is prevented
     0=page 1 is not masked off; setting of bit PAG in mode control register is enabled
GEN: graphics activation (graphic enable)
     1=graphics mode can be enabled by setting bit T/M in mode control register
     0=graphics mode cannot be enabled by setting bit T/M in mode control register;
        Hercules card is operating in text mode only
```

Figure 12.11: The configuration register.

The write-only configuration register serves to avoid an erroneous switching into graphics mode, and to enable page 1 starting at address b8000h. If the *MSK* bit is set, then page 1 is physically masked off from the PC's address space. This is necessary, for example, if you have additionally installed a CGA on your system and want to use it concurrently with the Hercules card to display coloured graphics at a low resolution. Activating page 1 would give rise to certain disturbances of the CGA and Hercules card. With a cleared MSK bit, page 1 of the Hercules card can also be accessed. If you set bit *GEN*, you can switch between text and graphics mode by means of the T/M bit in the mode control register. If GEN is cleared, T/M has no effect on the operation mode of the adapter; it is always running in text mode, and thus emulates IBM's MDA (**m**onochrome **d**isplay **a**dapter).

The main job when switching between text and graphics mode is the programming of the 6845. For adjusting all necessary parameters it comprises 19 registers; one index register and 18 control registers. To avoid a wide range being occupied in the I/O address space, the 6845 uses an indexed scheme for addressing its control registers. You first need to input the index of the intended register using the index register at port 3b4h before you access the 6845 control register concerned via the data register at port 3b5h. Table 12.2 lists all 6845 registers together with their indices.

Index	Register	R/W^{*)}	Meaning
0	horizontal total	W	number of characters per line including SYNC minus 1
1	horizontal displayed	W	displayed characters per line
2	HSYNC position	W	position of character where HSYNC is issued
3	SYNC width	W	number of characters for HSYNC per line
4	vertical total	W	number of scanlines including line during vertical retrace minus 1
5	vertical adjust	W	number of scanlines additional to number of character lines
6	vertical displayed	W	number of displayed lines
7	VSYNC position	W	line where vertical retrace starts
8	interlace mode	W	non-interlaced, interlaced or interlaced/video mode
9	max scanline	W	number of scanlines per character line minus 1
10	cursor start	W	first scanline of cursor
11	cursor end	W	last scanline of cursor
12	start address (high)	W	⌐ start address of MA0-MA13
13	start address (low)	W	⌐ after vertical retrace
14	cursor (high)	R/W	⌐ offset of cursor position
15	cursor (low)	R/W	⌐ in video RAM
16	light pen (high)	R	⌐ offset of light pen position
17	light pen (low)	R	⌐ in video RAM

^{*)} R=read, W=write

Table 12.2: 6845 data register indices on the Hercules card

Notes to Table 12.2:
- For monochrome monitors the horizontal scan period is 54 μs corresponding to 18.43 kHz.
- The monitor has to be refreshed 50 times per second; the total number of character lines and scanlines has to be adapted to this value.

– The oscillator of the Hercules card generates in text mode a time base per character of 0.5625 μs corresponding to 1.778 MHz and in graphics mode a time base of 1.00 μs per character corresponding to 1.00 MHz.
– In text mode the character size is 9x14 pixels and in graphics mode 16x4 pixels.

The following presents the registers and the meaning of their entries in brief. All entry values specified in the example refer to the text mode of the Hercules card, with 25 rows of 80 characters each and a screen refresh rate of 50 Hz. The time base CLK in text mode is equal to 0.5625 μs per character, corresponding to 1.778 MHz.

Horizontal Total (Index 0)
This register defines the line frequency, that is, the frequency of HS. The line frequency is specified in units of character periods. If the 6845-internal character counter has counted up to the value that the register contains, then a new line begins. For one line all characters including HSYNC contribute.

Example: 97
```
Upon the 97th character the new line begins; thus one line is scanned within
96*0.5625 µs=54.0 µs, the line frequency is about 18.45 kHz.
```

Horizontal Displayed (Index 1)
This register contains the number of visible characters per row. With every character row the 6845 increments the memory address MA0–MA13 by this value, but keeps the address constant during a horizontal retrace. If the next scanline belongs to the same character row again, then MA0–MA13 is reset to the old value at the beginning of the row, that is, the value of this register is subtracted from the current memory address MA0–MA13. If, on the other hand, the next scanline already belongs to the next character row, then the memory address MA0–MA13 is not altered and is further incremented with every character after the horizontal retrace, that is, after HSYNC. The value in this register must be less than that in the register horizontal total. The less these two values differ, the more rapid is the horizontal retrace. Note that not all monitors can follow such a fast horizontal retrace; interference or even monitor damage may be the consequence.

Example: 80
```
Thus every row displays 80 characters.
```

HSYNC Position (Index 2)
This register controls the position in the line where the 6845 activates the HS signal, and thus issues a horizontal retrace; it contains the position of the character concerned. The horizontal retrace may occur after the last displayed character of the line at the earliest, thus the value in this register is always at least equal to the value in the horizontal displayed register; additionally the sum of the register values HSYNC position and SYNC width is lower than the value in the horizontal total register. Increasing the register value gives rise to a left-shift of the screen picture, and vice versa.

Example: 82
```
The activation of HS and the horizontal retrace occurs with the 83rd character of the line.
Thus one line comprises 80 displayed characters, one dummy character and 15 characters for the
```

horizontal retrace, so that the horizontal retrace HSYNC requires a time period that corresponds to 15 characters, equal to 8.4375 μs.

SYNC Width (Index 3)

This register determines the width, that is, the time period of the HS pulse for the horizontal
retrace in units of character periods. The synchronization signal VS for the vertical retrace, on
the other hand, is fixed to a time period which corresponds to 16 complete scanlines. The register may be loaded with values between 1 and 15 character periods to comply with the requirements of various monitors. A value of 0 means that no HS is provided.

Example: 15
The Hercules card provides an HS signal with a width of 15*0.5625 μs=8.4375 μs. Thus HS is
active for nearly the whole horizontal retrace, which lasts for 15 character periods.

According to the values of the four registers indicated above, a line is displayed in the following
manner. After a horizontal retrace the 6845 internally counts up the characters starting with 1,
and continuously increases the memory address MA0–MA13 to actually output the number of
displayed characters on the monitor. When as many characters have been output as are specified by the horizontal display register, then the 6845 stops counting up the memory address, but
the beam continues to move. If the internal counting reaches the value in the HSYNC register
position, then the 6845 activates the HS signal for the time period specified by the SYNC register width, and thus issues a horizontal retrace. As soon as the time corresponding to the characters indicated by the horizontal total register has passed, the 6845 begins to output the
memory address for the next scanline.

Vertical Total (Index 4)

This register, together with the vertical total adjust register, defines the screen refresh frequency, that is, the frequency of VS. If we calculate the number of character rows necessary to
keep a refresh frequency of exactly 50 Hz, for example, then we will get a value in most cases
which comprises an integer and a fractional part. On many monitors the refresh rate is generated by means of the mains voltage frequency; in Europe we have 50 Hz, in North America 60
Hz. Thus the 6845 must adapt to this, and may enable the signal VS only at times which comply
with the request for a refresh frequency of 50 Hz. For this purpose, this register determines the
integer part of the above-mentioned value minus one. The fine-tuning corresponding to the
fractional part is carried out by the next register, vertical total adjust.

Example: 25
The integer part corresponds to 26 character rows of 760 μs each.

Vertical Total Adjust (Index 5)

This register carries out the fine-tuning corresponding to the above-mentioned fractional part
and specifies that number of scanlines in addition to the total number of rows so that the
request for a fixed refresh frequency for the vertical synchronization signal VS is fulfilled.

Example: 6
The Hercules card supplies 6 dummy scanlines in addition to the 26 character rows to fulfil the
requested frequency of 50 Hz for the signal VS.

Vertical Displayed (Index 6)

This register specifies the number of visible rows. Note that the register may only contain values that are less than or equal to the value in the vertical total register.

Example: 25
```
The Hercules card displays 25 visible rows.
```

VSYNC Position (Index 7)

This register controls the position where the 6845 activates the VS signal, and thus issues a vertical retrace. It contains the position of the row concerned minus 1. The vertical retrace can be carried out after the last displayed row at the earliest. Thus the value in this register is always at least equal to the value in the vertical displayed register. Increasing the register value gives rise to a shift of the screen picture upwards, and vice versa.

Example: 25
```
The Hercules card issues a vertical retrace after 25 rows, that is, immediately after the
beginning of the 26th row.
```

Interlace Mode (Index 8)

The 6845 can drive the monitor in interlaced and non-interlaced modes. For adjusting the modes the two low-order bits with the following meaning are used:

bit 1	bit 0	mode
0	0	non-interlaced
1	0	non-interlaced
0	1	interlaced
1	1	interlaced/video

Thus the 6845 carries out one non-interlaced mode as well as two different interlaced modes. Figure 12.12 shows the display of character «O» in both cases.

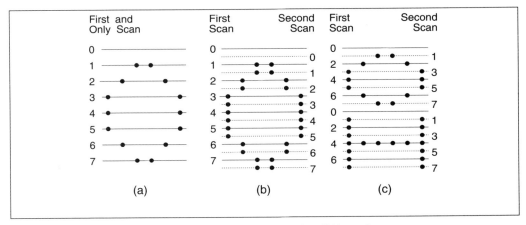

Figure 12.12: (a) Non-interlaced mode; (b) interlaced mode; (c) interlaced/video mode.

In interlaced mode (Figure 12.12b) the VS signal is delayed by half a scanline period, and the two passages of the electron beam write the same information. This enhances the readability of the characters but the character is not displayed at a higher resolution in principle.

Also in interlaced/video mode (Figure 12.12c) the VS signal is delayed by half a scanline period, but the two electron beam passages write different information. As is apparent from the figure, the two passages display the odd and then the even-numered scanlines of the character. The readability of the characters is thus not improved, but the monitor achieves a better resolution at the same bandwidth. The figure shows this by the «H» shown below the «O».

For programming an interlaced mode you must pay attention to the following:

– The horizontal total register must contain an odd value.

– For the interlaced/video mode the max. scanline register must contain an odd value, that is, an even number of scanlines must be defined.

– For the interlaced/video mode the vertical displayed register must indicate a value equal to half of the actually required number of visible rows.

– For the interlaced/video mode the two registers cursor start and cursor end must both hold odd or even values.

Example: 2
The Hercules card uses non–interlaced mode.

Max. Scanline (Index 9)
This register defines the number of scanlines per character row; the value is equal to the number of scanlines per character row, minus 1. Upon every scanline of a character row the line address RA0–RA4 is increased by one. Thus 32 scanlines for one character row can be realized at most by means of this 5-bit register. If the electron beam jumps to the next scanline which already belongs to the following character row, then the line address RA0–RA4 is reset to 0. In text mode, the line address serves to address the character's scanline in character ROM, and in graphics mode for addressing that bank in video RAM which contains the entry for the current scanline.

Example: 13
The character matrix in text mode comprises 14 scanlines.

Cursor Start (Index 10)
This register determines the first scanline of the cursor and its behaviour. Bits 0–5 specify the start line, and bits 6 and 7 the behaviour as follows:

bit 6	bit 5	cursor behaviour
0	0	no blinking
0	1	cursor not displayed
1	0	blinking with 16∗refresh rate
1	1	blinking with 32∗refresh rate

The refresh rate is the time interval between two VS signals. Not all graphics adapters use bits 5 and 6 to define the cursor blinking. This may also be carried out by an external adapter logic and the CURSOR signal. This strategy synchronizes the cursor blink rate with the character blinking.

Example: 11
```
The cursor starts with scanline 11.
```

Cursor End (Index 11)
This register defines the last scanline of the cursor.

Example: 12
```
The cursor ends with scanline 12, that is, comprises two scanlines (see example above).
```

Start Address High/Low (Index 12/13)
This register pair, with its total of 14 bits (8 bits of the LSB register and 6 bits of the MSB register) defines the start address that the 6845 provides after a vertical retrace as the memory address MA0–MA13. It is thus possible to define several pages in video RAM. If a certain page is to be displayed on-screen, then you have to load the register pair start address with the offset of the intended page relative to the video segment. By altering the start address you can carry out very fast hardware scrolling.

Example: 0
```
The active page starts at offset 0.
```

Cursor High/Low (Index 14/15)
The contents of the register pair, with a total of 14 bits (8 bits of the LSB register and 6 bits of the MSB register) defines the position of the cursor in video RAM. For a page change you must also alter the position of the cursor within this new page, relative to the beginning of the video segment. If the 6845 detects that the current memory address MA0–MA13 coincides with the entry in this register pair, then it displays the cursor on-screen and enables the CURSOR signal. But the cursor lines actually appear on screen only if the current scanline corresponding to the line address RA0–RA4 is within the range defined by the registers cursor start and cursor end: otherwise, the pixel pattern of the character underlying the cursor is output.

Example: 0
```
The cursor is located at the beginning of the video RAM, that is, in the upper left corner of
the screen.
```

Light Pen High/Low (Index 16/17)
The register pair with a total of 14 bits (8 bits of the LSB register and 6 bits of the MSB register) holds the internal 6845 memory address MA0–MA13 upon the rising edge of a signal applied to the input terminal LPSTB. Usually, this is a signal from a light pen that has detected the electron beam. Because of the signal propagation times and the consequent delays compared to the «real» light pen position, the values must be further corrected by software for one or two locations to the left.

Example: 40
```
Without correction the light pen is located in column 40 of row 1; after correcting the value,
this corresponds to column 38 or 39 of row 1.
```

Table 12.3 summarizes the standard values of the 6845 control register for text and graphics mode of the Hercules card. You can see that the values differ significantly. The reason is the completely different character generation and organization of the video RAM in text and graphics mode.

Register index	Text	Graphics	Register index	Text	Graphics
0	97	53	7	25	87
1	80	45	8	2	2
2	82	46	9	13	3
3	15	7	10	11	0
4	25	91	11	12	0
5	6	2	12	0	0
6	25	87	13	0	0

Table 12.3: Standard values for text and graphics mode

In text mode the adapter logic reads for every character (for every memory address MA0–MA13) two bytes from the video RAM: the character code as well as the attribute. The character code is used by the character generator as an index into character ROM containing the pixel matrices for the various characters. The 6845 specifies the scanline of each pixel matrix using the line address RA0–RA4. The attribute byte is transferred to the attribute decoder and the signal generator without any further intermediate stage. This gives rise to a displayed character box of 9*14 pixels per character (the register max. scanline contains an entry 13 for this purpose).

Also in graphics mode, the adapter logic fetches two bytes for every memory address MA0–MA13; but here every bit corresponds to exactly one pixel on-screen. Moreover, the video RAM is divided into four banks of 8 kbytes each for every page, which are addressed by the line address RA0–RA4. Thus a character that forms the definition base for the synchronization signals in graphics mode comprises 16*4 pixels. The time base for one character is therefore equal to 1 µs instead of the 0.5625 µs in text mode. Because of the significantly different form of the character matrix, altered entries in the 6845 control registers are also required. The number of displayed characters is therefore only equal to 45; with the character box width of 16 pixels, this corresponds exactly to 720 points on-screen, namely the horizontal resolution of the Hercules card. The number of displayed rows is a result of the smaller row's «thickness» of only four scanlines per character row – larger than in text mode – namely equal to 87. This corresponds to 87*4 = 348 scanlines, that is, the vertical resolution of the adapter in graphics mode. The max. scanline register contains the value 3, corresponding to four scanlines. Thus every line's address corresponds to one bank of the video RAM; the division into banks is now clear. The other register values, too, are adapted to the altered character format.

By changing the various register values you can therefore generate different screen formats. But remember that fixed-frequency monitors cannot always stand the programmed mode, and may be damaged by incorrect register values. Only the so-called multisync monitors, which can adjust to a very broad range of horizontal and vertical frequencies, carry out such experiments without being damaged.

12.3　Most Important Adapter Types and Their Characteristics

The following discusses the currently most important graphics adapters. Compatible adapters, particularly, usually have a nearly infinite number of display modes. The following list therefore mainly refers to the original adapters, and doesn't make any claim for completeness. Table 12.4 summarizes the possible standard video modes, together with the accompanying resolutions and the adapters required. As is the case for the other PC components, here also downward compatibility holds. For example, the EGA can carry out all CGA video modes, but not the new modes of the VGA.

Mode number	Mode type	Text lines	Text columns	Resolution	Colours	Pages	MDA	CGA	HGC	EGA	VGA
0	text	25	40	320*200	16	8		x			
0	text	25	40	320*350	16	8				x	
0	text	25	40	360*400	16	8					x
1	text	25	40	320*200	16	8		x			
1	text	25	40	320*350	16	8				x	
1	text	25	40	360*400	16	8					x
2	text	25	80	640*200	16	4		x			
2	text	25	80	640*350	16	4				x	
2	text	25	80	720*400	16	4					x
3	text	25	80	640*200	16	4		x			
3	text	25	80	640*350	16	4				x	
3	text	25	80	720*400	16	4					x
4	graphics	25	40	320*200	4	1		x		x	x
5	graphics	25	40	320*200	4	1		x		x	x
6	graphics	25	80	640*200	2	1		x		x	x
7	text	25	80	720*350	mono	1	x		x	x	
7	text	25	80	720*400	mono	8					x
–	graphics	25	80	720*348	mono	1			x		
13	graphics	25	40	320*200	16	8				x	x
14	graphics	25	80	640*200	16	4				x	x
15	graphics	25	80	640*350	mono	2				x	x
16	graphics	25	80	640*350	16	2				x	x
17	graphics	30	80	640*480	2	1					x
18	graphics	30	80	640*480	16	1					x
19	graphics	25	40	320*200	256	1					x

Table 12.4: Standard video modes

12.3.1　MDA – Everthing is Very Grey

The first PCs and XTs were equipped with IBM's MDA (*monochrome display adapter*). The MDA can only be operated in text mode. It is very interesting that IBM intended the MDA for professional use, but the graphics-capable CGA for home use. I think the reason was that the MDA has a character matrix of 9*14 pixels, but the CGA only one of 8*8 pixels. Table 12.5 lists the main adapter parameters.

	Text mode
video segment	b000h
size of video RAM	4 kbyte
screen pages	1
video controller	CRTC 6845
port addresses of 6845	3b0h–3bfh
character matrix	9*14
effective character size	7*9
resolution (pixels)	720*350
colours	mono
monitor control signals	digital
horizontal frequency[*)]	18.432 kHz
vertical frequency[*)]	50 Hz
video bandwidth[*)]	16.257 MHz
own BIOS	no

[*)] if connected to a standard monochrome monitor with fixed frequency

Table 12.5: MDA parameters

The specified frequencies refer to the usual MDA use with a monochrome monitor of a fixed horizontal and vertical frequency. By altering the 6845 register values, other values may also be adjusted. At the respective port addresses the same 6845 registers are present as on the Hercules card. The MDA doesn't have its own BIOS, but is accessed via the system BIOS on the motherboard. The video RAM is organized linearly; every text character on the screen is assigned a word in video RAM which specifies character code and attribute.

12.3.2 CGA – It's Getting to Be Coloured

	Text mode	Graphics mode
video segment	b800h	b800h
size of video RAM	16 kbytes	16 kbytes
screen pages	4 ... 8	1
video controller	CRTC 6845	CRTC 6845
port addresses of 6845	3d0h–3dfh	3d0h–3dfh
character matrix	8*8	8*8
effective character size	7*7, 5*7	7*7, 5*7
max. resolution (pixels)	640*200	640*200
colours	16	4
monitor control signals	digital	digital
horizontal frequency[*)]	15.75 kHz	15.75 kHz
vertical frequency[*)]	60 Hz	60 Hz
video bandwidth[*)]	14.30 MHz	14.30 MHz
own BIOS	no	no

[*)] if connected to a standard colour monitor with fixed frequency

Table 12.6: CGA parameters

The CGA (*colour graphics adapter*) was the first graphics-capable adapter from IBM (but with a very poor resolution of a maximum at 640*200 pixels). Just as bad is the representation of characters in text mode, as the character matrix consists of 8*8 pixels only. Table 12.6 summarizes the most important CGA parameters.

In text mode the video RAM is divided (depending upon the resolution) into eight (25 rows with 40 columns each) or four (25 rows with 80 columns each) pages of 2 kbytes or 4 kbytes each. Within the page concerned, the characters are addressed linearly. The CGA can display 16 different colours in text mode. Figure 12.13 shows the assignment of attribute bits and the displayed colour.

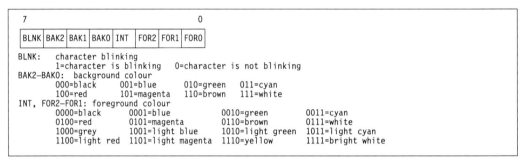

Figure 12.13: Attribute bits and corresponding colours in CGA text mode.

The CGA attribute decoder decodes the attribute byte and provides a corresponding RGBI signal (**r**ed-**g**reen-**b**lue-**i**ntensity) to actually display the colour on the monitor. The colour and intensity of the pixels is therefore passed in a digital form to the monitor; you may only connect a digital RGB monitor to a CGA. The pixel colours in the three CGA graphics modes are generated differently. The mode control register at port 3d8h, as well as the colour select register at port 3d9h, are decisive. Table 12.7 lists the CGA I/O ports.

Port	Register	Write (W) Read (R)
3d4h	6845 index register	W
3d5h	6845 data register	R/W
3d8h	mode control register	W
3d9h	colour select register	W
3dah	status register	R
3dbh	clear light pen flip-flop	W
3dch	set light pen flip-flop	W

Table 12.7: CGA I/O ports

12.3.3 Hercules – The Non-Fitting Standard

The Hercules graphics card (HGC) in text mode emulates the MDA precisely; all parameters coincide. This also means, for example, that in text mode a video RAM of only 4 kbytes is available, although the Hercules card is equipped as standard with 64 kbytes. Unlike the MDA, it may also be operated in monochrome graphics mode, whose resolution corresponds to about the pixel resolution in text mode. Only the two last lines 348 and 349 are no longer displayed, but used already for the vertical retrace. The resolution incompatible with the CGA and the different register addresses are the reason why the Hercules card cannot be serviced by the motherboard's system BIOS. As this adapter, moreover, doesn't have its own BIOS either, a driver is required or the graphics programs must program the Hercules card directly. Earlier this gave rise to many problems. But meanwhile, the Hercules resolution became a *de facto* standard, supported by nearly all programs. Only some mouse drivers have difficulties in displaying the mouse pointer on a Hercules. Details on the adapter programming and the division of the video RAM in graphics mode are discussed in Sections 12.2 and 12.5.3. Table 12.8 summarizes all the main adapter parameters.

	Text mode	Graphics mode
video segment	b000h	b000h
size of video RAM	4 kbytes	64 kbytes
screen pages	1	2
video controller	CRTC 6845	CRTC 6845
port addresses of 6845	3b0h–3bfh	3b0h–3bfh
character matrix	9∗14	9∗14
effective character size	7∗9	7∗9
resolution (pixels)	720∗350	720∗348
colours	mono	mono
monitor control signals	digital	digital
horizontal frequency[*]	18.432 kHz	18.432 kHz
vertical frequency[*]	50 Hz	50 Hz
video bandwidth[*]	16.257 MHz	16.257 MHz
own BIOS	no	no

[*] if connected to a standard monochrome monitor with a fixed frequency

Table 12.8: Hercules adapter parameters

The second screen page starts at address b8000h, and thus overlaps with the CGA video RAM. On a Hercules card you have the option to block and mask the second page out of the CPU's address space. You can thus use two graphics adapters in a PC, a CGA and a Hercules with a blocked second page. Some debuggers use this to display the investigated code on one monitor and the current screen contents of the program on the other.

12.3.4 EGA – More Colours and a Higher Resolution

The really very poor graphics capabilities of the CGA (only suitable really in the children's room but not for the office), and the advance of business graphics, required an enhanced graphics adapter very soon. For this purpose, the CGA was extended to get an EGA. This adapter allows a maximum resolution of 640∗350 pixels, and 16 colours out of a palette of 64 colours can be displayed simultaneously. I will discuss soon what the meaning of the somewhat dubious palette is, but let's first look at few useful but largely neglected features of the EGA:

- User-defined character sets: unlike MDA, HGC and CGA which operate with the fixed defined character sets in the ROM of the character generators, on an EGA you can define and load your own character matrices. Thus you are not limited to the characters defined by the BIOS.

- Two concurrently usable character sets: by redefining the blink bit 3 in the attribute byte (with function 10h, subfunction 03h of INT 10h) into a bit for distinguishing two character sets, you can display 512 different characters instead of 256 with an EGA. For this purpose, a 9-bit code composed of the 8-bit character code and the 1-bit «blink» code is used.

- Screen splitting: the screen can be split by hardware into two partial screens; the EGA displays information in them from two completely different video RAM locations.

- Video RAM division into several image layers: in the three new 16-colour EGA modes 13, 14, and 16, the image is divided into four layers which can be enabled or disabled by a simple register access. Some CAD programs use this multilayer technique to overlap several drawings by hardware.

Compatibility as the main and, often also cursed, maxim of PCs is also valid for EGA, of course: all CGA modes can also be carried out by the EGA. With the MDA's text mode, however, the EGA has some problems, as the requested resolution of 720*350 points corresponding to a character matrix of 9*14 pixels doesn't fit the internal EGA timing at all. But text modes 2 and 3 of the CGA are revamped to a resolution of 640*350 points corresponding to a character matrix of 8*14 pixels. This is nearly as good as the MDA text, and is additionally coloured (with 16 possible colours). The register addresses in CGA-compatible modes are equal to 3dxh; in pure EGA modes, on the other hand, they are equal to 3cxh. You will find these and other parameters given in Table 12.9.

	Text mode	Graphics mode
video segment	b800h	a000h
size of video RAM	64–256 kbyte	64–256 kbyte
screen pages	1 ... 8	1 ... 8
video controller	EGA–CRTC	EGA–CRTC
port addresses	3d0h–3dfh	3c0h–3dfh
character matrix	8*14, 8*8	8*14, 8*8
effective character size	7*9, 7*7	7*9, 7*7
resolution (pixels)	640*350	640*350
colours	16 of 64	16 of 64
monitor control signals	digital	digital
horizontal frequency	15.7–21.8 kHz	15.7–21.8 kHz
vertical frequency	60 Hz	60 Hz
video bandwidth	14.3–16.3 MHz	14.3–16.3 MHz
own BIOS	yes	yes

Table 12.9: EGA parameters

As a further feature, the EGA has its own BIOS which controls the adapter in the new modes, and is usually present in the CPU's address space starting at the segment address c000h. The system BIOS on the motherboard only supports MDA and CGA, as you know; thus the new operation modes cannot be set up by this BIOS as the EGA has a vast number of new registers which deal, for example, with the setup of the colour palette not implemented on the CGA. Table 12.10 summarizes the EGA I/O ports.

Port	Register	Write (W) Read (R)
3c0h	index/data register of attribute controller	W
3c2h	input status register 0	R
3c4h	sequencer index register	W
3c5h	sequencer data register	W
3cah	graphics position register 2	W
3cch	graphics position register 1	W
3ceh	graphics controller index register	W
3cfh	graphics controller data register	W
3b4h	CRTC index register	W
3b5h	CRTC data register	W
3bah	input status register 1	R
3d4h	CRTC index register	W
3d5h	CRTC data register	W
3dah	input status register 1	R

Table 12.10: EGA I/O ports

You can see that there is a large number of I/O ports and because of the three index/data register pairs, even more registers at these ports. Note that most of the registers are write-only. Thus the CPU is unable to determine the current video mode with its register values. With a detailed description of all EGA registers, a whole book could be filled; and this has actually already been done by others. Therefore, I restrict myself to the most important facts here.

With the CRTC index and data register you can access the registers of the CRTC chip. On an EGA you will find a controller that is improved compared to the 6845 and adapted to the special EGA's requirements.

The EGA, besides the usual monitor, also has an additional so-called feature connector. Using the feature connector an external device has the opportunity to affect the picture setup of the EGA and, for example, to provide its own clock signal: but I don't know of any important device that makes use of this.

The registers of the attribute controller are responsible for the displayed palette colours. On an EGA the attribute decoder can therefore be programmed to display various colours. The programmable sequencer controls the read-out of the video RAM and the conversion of the byte data into serial data for the generation of pixels on-screen. The CRTC provides the control signals for the monitor, as usual.

Despite its compatibility, the physical organization of the video RAM is very different between the EGA and the previous adapters. On an EGA the complete video RAM is divided into four parallel memory layers. This means that every one of these four layers starts at address a0000h; thus the four layers overlap. A write access to the byte address a0000h transfers the byte value into all four layers simultaneously. Under the control of the map mask and the read map select register, you may enable the various layers for a read or write process. How you may use these two registers is discussed in Section 12.5.3. Figure 12.14 shows a diagram for the four parallel memory layers described.

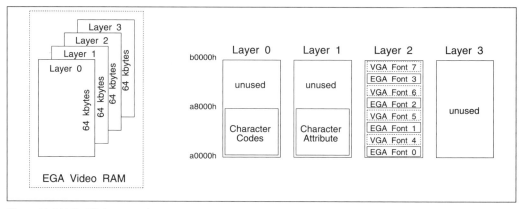

Figure 12.14: The EGA memory layers.

Although at a first glance this physical arrangement of the four layers appears strange, nevertheless, it does make sense: in the real mode address space of the PC the range between a0000h and bffffh is reserved for the graphics adapter. These 128 kbytes are far too little for a fully equipped EGA with 256 kbytes of display memory. Therefore, one has two possibilities:

–   Divide the 256 kbytes into two or more banks, and switch between them with a programmable register; expanded memory follows a similar concept.

–   Divide the 256 kbytes into two or more parallel layers, and enable or disable certain layers for an access.

The second possibility has a major advantage for a graphics adapter: if, for example, all layers are enabled in parallel for a write access, then writing one byte on an EGA, with its four parallel layers, gives rise to a simultaneous transfer of four bytes into all memory layers. If fewer layers are enabled, then the byte is transferred to correspondingly fewer memory layers. In the 16-colour EGA modes that assign one pixel four bits, the video RAM is organized in this way, in which every one of the four pixel bits is located in its own layer. By enabling or disabling the various layers, for example, three of the four pixel bits can be set or cleared at once. If one employs the first of the two methods indicated above, one would have to switch the banks more often. Furthermore, with parallel memory layers the adapter logic has to supply only a single byte address to fetch four bytes in a single cycle. Thus the graphics adapter requires fewer address lines and operates more quickly.

Figure 12.14 shows what information the four memory layers holds in text mode. Character codes and attributes are stored in the parallel layers 0 and 1. But how can compatibility with the RAM organization of the CGA be kept when it requires a linear array of code-attribute pairs? Very simply: the EGA has an address transfomation logic that connects layers 0 and 1 in such a way that they appear to the CPU in the usual manner, that is, in the order code_0(layer 0), attribute_0(layer 1), code_1(layer 0), attribute_1(layer 1), etc. But the adapter logic itself accesses the video RAM according to its physical organization, as parallel memory layers, when reading data for displaying it on the monitor.

A further significant difference compared to MDA, HGC and CGA is that on the EGA in text mode, part of the video RAM is reserved for the character generator; that is, the complete layer 2. There the character generator stores the character definition table for converting the character code into pixel patterns on-screen. RAM may be overwritten, of course, so that new character tables can be loaded, or the loaded ones can be altered. It's best to use the 10h function of INT 10h for this purpose. Details on this subject are given in Section 12.5.2. From Figure 12.14 it is apparent that on an EGA a maximum of four character definition tables can be installed; on a VGA eight are possible.

On a CGA you may only choose from 16 colours. In text mode they are unrestrictedly available for the foreground, but in graphics mode you may choose from only four colours, each dependent upon the selected CGA palette; that is, only four of the 16 possible colours can be displayed simultaneously. The EGA also extends the number of simultaneously displayable colours to 16 in text mode. They can be selected from a palette of 64 different colours. This corresponds to the four foreground bits in the attribute of the text mode, or the four bits in the four memory levels in graphics mode.

For the colours actually displayed the palette register is decisive. It is connected between the «colour value» and the monitor driver (see Figure 12.15).

```
5                                    0
┌────┬────┬────┬────┬────┬────┐
│SRED│SGRE│SBLU│PRED│PGRE│PBLU│
└────┴────┴────┴────┴────┴────┘

SRED: secondary red            PRED: primary red
      1=on     0=off                 1=on     0=off
SGRE: secondary green          PGRE: primary green
      1=on     0=off                 1=on     0=off
SBLU: secondary blue           PBLU: primary blue
      1=on     0=off                 1=on     0=off
```

Figure 12.15: Colour generation with palette registers.

On the CGA the four colour bit values (for example, in the attribute byte in text mode) specify the colour to be displayed directly. On the EGA, however, the colour value points to one of 16 entries in the palette register. This entry finally determines the colour actually displayed. Every entry has six bits, and can therefore specify one of $2^6 = 64$ different colours. This happens as follows:

– The 64 colours are formed from all possible combinations of three primary and three secondary colours; the primary colours are much brighter than the secondary ones.

– A set bit in the palette register gives rise to an activation of the corresponding signal line to the monitor if the colour value of the current pixel or character points to the corresponding register.

It thus becomes apparent that on the EGA 64 different colours are possible using the six bits in the palette register, but with the four colour value bits only 16 different registers can be addressed. In the CGA-compatible video modes 4–6 with fewer than four bits per pixel, and thus fewer than 16 colour values, only the corresponding palette registers with the colour values 0–3 (modes 4 and 5) or 0 and 1 (mode 6) are addressed. The remaining palette registers are unused here. For changing the palette register entries the function 10h of INT 10h is available (see Section 12.5.2).

By altering the palette registers you can change the colour of the screen display instantaneously. The change affects all characters or pixels whose colour value points to the altered register; no change of the colour value itself is required for this. For example, you can program a seemingly rotating torus by outputting a circle or ellipse on-screen, which consists of line parts with alternating colour values. Now you only need to continuously switch the corresponding palette register entries and the observer gets the impression that the torus is rotating. The other possible strategy, to alter the colour values themselves, continuously requires much more programming overhead and execution time. The observer therefore gets the impression of a flickering torus.

12.3.5 VGA – Colours and More Colours

Starting with the PS/2, IBM introduced a new and, compared to the earlier models, significantly improved adapter: the *video graphics adapter* or the *video graphics array* (VGA). The main characteristic is not the resolution extended to 640*480 pixels, but the extension of the colour palette to $2^{18} = 262\,144$ different colours, from which a maximum of 256 can be displayed simultaneously. This, of course, is no longer possible with a digital colour signal to the monitor, as 18 colour signal lines would be required. VGA, therefore, outputs an analog signal that drives an analog monitor. With the 262 144 different colours very realistic images can be generated. VGA is equipped as standard with a display memory of 256 kbytes; newer VGA adapters even have a video memory with 1 Mbyte of RAM. They can display 1024*768 pixels with 256 different colours. Table 12.11 summarizes the main parameters of the standard VGA.

	Text mode	Graphics mode
video segment	b000h	a000h
size of video RAM	256 kbytes	256 kbytes
screen pages	1 ... 8	1 ... 8
video controller	VGA–CRTC	VGA–RTC
port addresses of 6845	3b0h–3dfh	3b0h – 3dfh
character matrix	9*16	9*16
effective character size	7*9	7*9
resolution (pixels)	640*480	640*480
colours	256	256
monitor control signals	analog	analog
horizontal frequency	31.5 kHz	31.5 kHz
vertical frequency	50-70 Hz	50-70 Hz
video bandwidth	28M Hz	28 MHz
own BIOS	yes	yes

Table 12.11: VGA parameters

For compatibility reasons, the VGA can carry out all CGA and EGA modes, and in contrast to EGA the VGA also recognizes the MDA text mode 7. The resolution in this mode is 720*400 pixels, corresponding to a character box of 9*16 points. This is 50 scanlines more in the vertical direction than the original MDA text mode. Of course, you are free to install your own character sets, too, as was the case on the EGA. But the VGA allows up to eight different character definition tables.

On the VGA all control registers can also be read, so that the CPU has the opportunity to determine the current video mode and the accompanying parameters and to store them for future use. The VGA BIOS implements the function 1ch which exclusively backs up and restores the video status. This is, for example, of importance for a multitasking operating system if the various programs frequently alter the video mode.

On the EGA the set bits in the palette registers give rise to an activation of the corresponding colour signal lines to the monitor. On a VGA this is no longer possible, but the colour generation is controlled by means of 256 registers in a video DAC (*digital-analog converter*). Every register is divided into three groups of six bits each. The first bit group specifies the red, the second the green, and the third the blue contribution to the colour. Every primary colour can be added to the actual colour with $2^6 = 64$ shades; this leads to the 262 144 different VGA colours. As only 256 video DAC registers exist, only 256 of these 256 k colours can be displayed simultaneously. You may access the DAC colour registers using function 10h of INT 10h, beginning with subfunction 10h.

The conversion of the colour values in the text attribute or the pixel values in graphics mode differs in the various modes. Figure 12.16a shows how the conversion of a colour value into a colour signal to the monitor is carried out if the VGA operates in text mode or a graphics mode (except VGA mode 19).

As is the case on the EGA, the colour value first selects one of 16 palette registers. Unlike the EGA, the palette registers don't determine the colours directly with their bits, but the value held by the selected palette register represents an index that selects one of the 256 video DAC colour registers. Then the selected DAC colour register determines the actual colour and the DAC provides an analog signal to the monitor according to the 18-bit colour value stored there.

Also on a VGA, the palette registers are six bits wide so that $2^6 = 64$ video DAC registers may be addressed. The other 192 registers remain unreachable at first, but you can change this situation with the VGA's colour select register; it is available with index 14h via the index register 3c0h at data port 3c0h. The 256 video DAC registers are divided into four pages of 64 colours each, and the colour select register provides the address 0–3 of the currently enabled colour page. The value of the palette register then serves as an offset within such a colour page. The bits 2 and 3 of the colour select register specify the current colour page; all other bits are equal to 0. Four different colour pages can thus be managed.

Example: enable colour page 2 corresponding to the DAC colour registers 128 to 191.

```
OUT 3c0h, 14h  ; address colour select register
OUT 3c0h, 08h  ; select page 2 corresponding 00001000b (bit 3=1, bit 2=0)
```

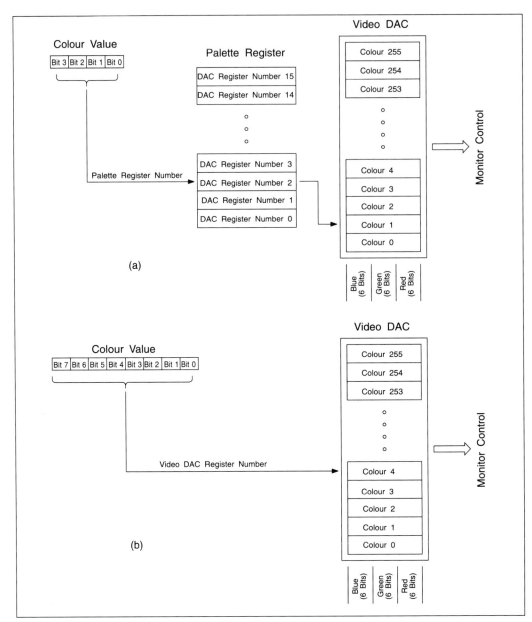

Figure 12.16: The colour generation with the video DAC registers. (a) Colour generation in text mode and graphics modes (except Mode 19); (b) colour generation in VGA Mode 19 with 256 colours.

But note that the VGA BIOS (except VGA mode 19) preloads only the first 64 DAC colour register with EGA-compatible colour values. If you want to use the other 192 colour registers, then you must load them with the intended values using function 10h of INT 10h.

In VGA mode 19 with its 256 different colours, the pixel values 0–255 select one of the 256 different DAC colour registers directly (see Figure 12.16b). The palette registers don't play any role here, but transfer the address values 0–15 to the video DAC unaltered. Address values 16 – 255 bypass the palette register in this mode in any case.

12.3.6 TIGA and 8514/A – Faster, Higher, Further

With 256 colours and a resolution of 1024∗768 pixels, VGA systems reach their limit. All the graphics adapters discussed up to now are rather stupid and cannot form their own graphics objects; this is the exclusive job of the CPU. As you know, the PC's bus system operates at 8.33 MHz at most, so the CPU, even on a 50 MHz i486 AT, can only transfer data into the video RAM of the adapter at this rate. Additionally, the CPU must calculate all points itself when drawing lines, circles, etc., switch the memory layers of EGA and VGA adapters, and set the corresponding bits in the video RAM. This requires a very long time, of course, compared to the operation speed of modern processors. What better, then, than to equip the graphics adapter with some intelligence so that it can form, for example, lines, circles and other geometric functions on its own?

The result of this line of thought is graphics adapters using TIGA (*Texas Instruments graphics architecture*) or IBM's 8514/A standard. Both adapter types have a dedicated and specialized graphics processor, which also masters, besides simple arithmetical instructions, extensive graphics commands. TIGA and 8514/A are compatible with each other neither on the hardware level nor in the way in which they are accessed by software. Both, however, effectively free the CPU from extensive graphics calculations; to draw a line, for example, the CPU only has to pass the graphics processor the coordinates of the end points and the graphics processor carries out all other work. A further advantage is that the CPU no longer has problems with the video RAM organization; the video RAM's management and organization is taken over by the graphics processor.

If you are now of the opinion that the use of a graphics processor for supporting the CPU is a very new concept I must disappoint you. Your PC is teeming with such support processors. One rather old but nevertheless still used processor is the FDC μPD765 which controls the floppy drives. In principle, the CPU would also be able to carry out these functions using several registers, for example, to control the positioning of the read/write heads above a certain track. The FDC does nothing else but execute a specialized microprogram to free the CPU from this job. Analogous to the passing of the end point coordinates of a line to the graphics processor, the CPU only has to provide the number of the intended track (and the command code, of course). To retrieve the graphics processor's honour, I must mention that you as the programmer have many more options to instruct the graphics processor than is possible for a μPD765. For example, you can swap complete programs onto the graphics adapter which are then to be executed by the graphics processor. It is thus possible to support certain programs (for example, CAD or business chart programs) by appropriate programs for the graphics processor.

One characteristic feature of graphics processors is the very high clock rate; the TMS 34020 on TIGA adapters runs at a remarkable 60 MHz. Simple operations such as filling rectangles with a certain colour value thus proceed very quickly. But presently you should not expect miracles, especially in connection with Windows and other graphics-oriented programs. The reason is often an insufficiently optimized adaptation (or should one speak of misadaptation?) of the programs to the capabilities of the graphics processor used. It is realistic to expect accelerations by a factor of three for outputting high-resolution graphics. Some processes, for example the drawing of circles or the filling of rectangles, however, proceed up to ten times faster than on a good but conventional VGA adapter.

Note that the graphics processor adds some intelligence to the adapter, but the adapter requires, besides other components, a CRTC, a colour controller and a memory controller, as usual. For TIGA and 8514/A adapters, as mainly high-end products, dual-port memories are used for the video RAM. The graphics processor is not then slowed down by the accesses to the video RAM necessary for refreshing the display. Besides this memory, the TIGA and 8514/A adapters also have a conventional DRAM for storing the graphics processor's programs and data. You can see that these adapters are very complex and thus rather expensive. Presently, high-quality adapters with a graphics processor cost about $1,000, but for this money you usually get at least 1 Mbyte of display RAM as well as 500 kbytes of program and data DRAM (and the processor, of course).

12.4   Accessing the Screen via DOS

The response to this section's heading is very short and disappointing: pitiful. DOS doesn't implement a single function for accessing the adapter in graphics mode. Only in text mode are the usual CP/M-compatible and the handle functions of INT 21h available, which display text on the monitor. But you have no opportunity, for example, to specify the colour of the displayed characters with INT 21h.

Starting with DOS 4.00 you can slightly affect the screen's output using a somewhat enhanced MODE command. For example, you can adjust the number of text columns to 40 or 80, and on an EGA or VGA the number of lines to values between 25 and 50. Consult your DOS manual for further details on the MODE command.

To display text on the monitor you can use the DOS commands COPY, TYPE and PRINT on the COMMAND.COM level. DOS summarizes the keyboard and the monitor under the reserved device name CON (for console); a write access to CON is always transferred to the monitor, a read access from CON expects characters from the keyboard. You can therefore output text on-screen by selecting CON as the target for one of the above-mentioned commands. If you want to display the contents of the file output.txt on the monitor, you have the three following opportunities:

```
COPY output.txt CON
TYPE output.txt > CON
PRINT output.txt /D:CON
```

Instead of the second line you can also specify, of course, the usual command TYPE output.txt, as DOS directs the source of the TYPE command automatically to the standard output device corresponding to handle 1. This is usually the monitor. With TYPE output.txt > CON you redirect the output from the standard output device to CON, that is, normally from CON to CON.

As a programming freak you have some further options for outputting data using the function interrupt INT 21h. For this purpose, four functions are available (their calling formats are listed in Appendix K):

– function 02h – output on-screen;
– function 06h – direct character output;
– function 09h – string output;
– function 40h – write file/device.

The main advantage of function 40h is that you may output a whole string quite easily, and the function returns an error code in the ax register.

As DOS passes all the above-indicated function calls to the corresponding BIOS routines, you may use the functions in text as well as in graphics mode to display text. But now all capabilities for accessing the screen are exhausted. Setting and clearing individual pixels in graphics mode via DOS is impossible; only direct access to the BIOS graphics functions or even an immediate access to the video RAM and the graphics controller registers remain.

12.5   Accessing the Screen Via the BIOS

A much more powerful access to the graphics adapter compared to the DOS function interrupt INT 21h is offered by the BIOS interrupt INT 10h. Its functions serve, for example, to set the current video mode, which requires an extensive programming of the graphics controller. Furthermore, the INT 10h manages various screen pages automatically; you don't, therefore, need to know details of the video RAM's organization. Another significant advantage of BIOS functions over direct access to the video RAM is that you may specify points on-screen by their line and column coordinates. Thus the organization of the video RAM differing from adapter to adapter and mode to mode will only concern you if you attempt to access the video RAM directly.

Appendix K summarizes all the BIOS functions of INT 10h. The system BIOS on the motherboard has all the routines for the MDA and CGA adapters. The HGC in text mode emulates the MDA, and can therefore be accessed via the BIOS routines of the standard BIOS. But in graphics mode you have to read and write the video RAM directly to set and clear individual points. The HGC is incompatible with all IBM adapters in this mode. Meanwhile, nearly all compilers come with function libraries for programming the Hercules card.

The much more powerful EGA and VGA graphics adapters have their own BIOS so that you can use their improved and extensive capabilities. During the course of the boot process, the EGA/VGA BIOS intercepts INT 10h and replaces the handler by its own routine. The old INT 10h address is transferred into the interrupt vector table as INT 42h (the BIOS extension of hard disk controllers follows a similar strategy, as you know, which moves the old INT 13h of the system BIOS to INT 40h).

12.5.1 Graphics Routines of Standard BIOS

The system BIOS on the motherboard comprises all those functions required for accessing the MDA and CGA; Appendix K.2 lists them all. The corresponding functions are extended by the EGA/VGA BIOS to the advanced EGA/VGA operation modes, while the calling formats don't change. The EGA/VGA BIOS only allows a more extensive range of values, for example for positioning the cursor, which are adapted to the enhanced resolution.

One of the most important BIOS functions of INT 10h is function 00h for setting the video mode. As you have seen in Section 12.2 in connection with the quite simple 6845 graphics control chip, for a mode change many and sometimes very critical programming steps are required to load the 6845 registers with appropriate values. Function 00h carries out all of this dangerous work for you. However, you can emulate the other functions of INT 10h quite simply if you know the video RAM structure in detail.

Example: setup graphics mode 6 with 640*200 pixels on the CGA.

```
MOV ah, 00h     ; setup function 00h
MOV al, 06h     ; setup mode 6
INT 10h         ; call function
```

Address	Size	Structure 76543210	Contents	Meaning
40:10	byte	..xx....	installed hardware	video adapter (00=EGA/VGA, 01=40x25colour, 10=80x25colour 11=80x25monochrome)
40:49	byte		video mode	
40:4a	word		number of columns	
40:4c	word		size of active page	size in bytes
40:4e	word		offset of active page	
40:50	word		cursor position page 0	low=column, high=row
40:52	word		cursor position page 1	low=column, high=row
40:54	word		cursor position page 2	low=column, high=row
40:56	word		cursor position page 3	low=column, high=row
40:58	word		cursor position page 4	low=column, high=row
40:5a	word		cursor position page 5	low=column, high=row
40:5c	word		cursor position page 6	low=column, high=row
40:5e	word		cursor position page 7	low=column, high=row
40:60	word		cursor type	low=end scanline high=start scanline
40:62	byte		active page	low=column, high=row
40:63	word		6845 I/O port	03b4h=monochrome, 03d4h=colour
40:65	byte		mode control register	register value
40:66	byte		actual palette	actual palette value
40:100	byte		status print screen	00h=INT 05h not active 01h=INT 05h active, print screen in progress ffh=error

Table 12.12: BIOS data area of system BIOS (MDA, CGA)

This simple 1-line code fragment gives rise to a rather extensive 6845 initialization by the BIOS and updates various parameters in the BIOS data area which characterize the current video mode. Table 12.12 lists the structure of the BIOS data area as far as the routines of INT 10h in the standard BIOS are concerned.

Note that the entries in the BIOS data area are correct only if you don't bypass the BIOS and program some 6845 registers directly, for example. Depending upon the adapter type and the resolution, the BIOS can manage up to eight different screen pages, each with its own cursor. Using function 05h, for example, you can display one of the eight pages and edit another page in the background with functions 02h, 03h, 08h, 09h, 0ah, 0ch, 0dh and 0eh. By switching the pages, animation effects can be achieved seemingly without any delay. All INT 10h functions are explained in detail in Appendix K.2, so they are not discussed here.

The last byte in the table actually already belongs to the DOS data area, and indicates the current status of INT 05h. The handler of INT 05h (the so-called *print-screen routine*) is called if you press the PRINT key, or SHIFT+PRINT. The routine then writes the current screen contents onto the printer. But this only works if the graphics adapter is running in text mode. In graphics mode, the routine simply reads the first 4,000 bytes from the video RAM, interprets them as character code-attribute pairs, and outputs the seeming character codes on the printer. That you get nonsense if the CGA is operating in graphics mode (for example, if a circle is displayed on screen) seems to be obvious. Only after a call to the external DOS command GRAPHICS has installed a handler for INT 05h can the graphics contents be output on an IBM-compatible graphics printer.

12.5.2 Trouble Support – The EGA and VGA BIOS

A detailed description of all EGA/VGA BIOS functions would go far beyond the scope of this book. Therefore, only a few essential functions that can also be applied with some basic knowledge of the EGA/VGA features are discussed. Readers more interested in these subjects will find many books available which describe EGA/VGA programming precisely, particularly concerning the variety of EGA/VGA control registers and their meaning.

The EGA/VGA BIOS intercepts INT 10h during the course of the boot process and replaces the handler, which points to the motherboard's system BIOS using its own routine. The old handler is redirected to INT 42h, and all calls to INT 10h are redirected by the EGA/VGA BIOS to INT 42h if the EGA/VGA adapter is running in a strictly MDA or CGA-compatible mode. These are operation modes 0–7. Note that EGA and VGA may display text modes 0–3 and 7 with a different vertical resolution from MDA and CGA. You can adjust these vertical resolutions, and thus the height of the character matrix, using function 30h.

Moreover, the EGA and VGA BIOS additionally uses the storage location 40:84h to 40:88h in the BIOS data area and stores EGA/VGA-specific parameters there. Table 12.13 shows the structure of this EGA/VGA parameter area.

ddress	Size	Structure 76543210	Contents	Meaning
40:84	byte		text rows-1	displayed text rows minus 1
40:85	word		character height	height of one character in scanlines
40:87	byte	x		video RAM not cleared at last mode setting
		xx		size of video RAM (00=64 kbyte, 01=128 kbyte, 10=192 kbyte, 11=256 kbyte)
		x		reserved
		x		EGA disabled
		x		BIOS has to wait for HSYNC
		x		EGA and monochrome monitor
		x		no cursor emulation
40:88	byte	xxxx		feature control bits (EGA only)
		xxxx		status of DIP switches

Table 12.13: BIOS data area of EGA/VGA BIOS extension

The EGA/VGA BIOS extension expands the already existing functions of INT 10h to the enhanced resolutions and the more extensive colour variety of the new adapters. It is thus possible, for example, to locate the cursor in text mode in line 30 if you are using the alphanumerical resolution 80*43. Most standard BIOS versions simply ignore such a function call. Additionally, the EGA/VGA BIOS has the following new functions with several subfunctions each:

– function 10h: accessing the palette and colour registers;
– function 11h: installing new character definition tables;
– function 12h: configuring the video subsystem;
– function 1ah: video combination;
– function 1bh: video BIOS function capabilities and status information (VGA only);
– function 1ch: save/restore video status (VGA only).

The following briefly discusses some functions and subfunctions that are not immediately self-evident.

Function 10h, Subfunction 03h – Enable/Disable Blink Attribute

Usually, bit 3 in the attribute byte of a character determines in text mode whether the character is to be displayed in a blinking (bit 3 set) or non-blinking (bit 3 cleared) manner. If you disable the meaning of this blink bit in the attribute byte (BL equal 0) using this function, then bit 3 selects one of two character sets that you have selected in advance using function 11h, subfunction 03h from four (EGA) or eight (VGA) possible character sets. If bit 3 in the attribute byte is cleared then the character code refers to the corresponding character in the primary character set. If, on the other hand, bit 3 in the attribute byte is set, then the character code points to the corresponding character in the secondary character set. Thus you can display 512 instead of 256 different characters; but the «blink capability» of the characters gets lost. The meaning of the bits 7–4 and 2–0 is not affected by this.

Example: disable blink attribute.

```
MOV ah, 10h    ; use function 10h
MOV al, 03h    ; use subfunction 3
MOV bl, 00h    ; disable blinking
INT 10h        ; call function
```

Function 11h – Interface to the Character Generator

This function implements 12 (EGA) or 15 (VGA) subfunctions for loading and activating character definition tables. Every table entry always has 32 bytes, where each byte corresponds to a scanline of the respective character even if the character matrix doesn't require 32 bytes per character (less than 32 scanlines, for example). In the EGA BIOS, two character definition tables for the two character matrices 9*14 and 8*8 are stored; the VGA BIOS additionally holds a character definition table for the character matrix 9*16. You can also load user-defined tables and thus display virtually any character in text mode.

If you load a table, using subfunctions 00h to 04h, which has a character height that differs from the current mode, then the graphics controller is not reprogrammed for the new character size. In the case of a larger character height than the current mode uses, the lower scanlines are simply cut off. But if the new character size is less than the former one, empty scanlines appear at the lower part, that is, the visible character distance gets larger. The EGA can hold four, the VGA eight different character tables in the character generator RAM. Thus you always need to specify the number under which the character definition table is to be stored when calling an installation subfunction.

Example: load 8*14 character definition table without reprogramming the CRTC.

```
MOV ah, 11h    ; use function 11h
MOV al, 01h    ; load 8*14 character table from ROM BIOS into character generator RAM
MOV bl, 03h    ; assign table the number 3
INT 10h        ; call function
```

Note that the loaded table doesn't become active until you explicitly enable it, by means of subfunction 03h, as the active character table. The same applies to functions 10h to 14h and 20h to 24h. You may specify a primary and a secondary character definition table. The secondary table only becomes active if you have disabled the blink attribute with function 10h, subfunction 03h. As standard, the table 0 forms the primary as well as the secondary character definition table.

Example: enable table 1 as the primary, table 7 as the secondary definition table.

```
MOV ah, 11h    ; use function 11h
MOV al, 03h    ; select subfunction character definition table
MOV bl, 2dh    ; enable tables 1 and 7 with 0010 1101b
INT 10h        ; call function
```

The example is valid only for a VGA, as the EGA can only hold four tables, and thus no table with number 7 exists. Subfunctions 10h to 14h, on the other hand, reprogram the video controller and thus adjust it to the new character height. The calling procedure for these functions doesn't differ from that for the functions 00h to 04h in any way.

Also in graphics mode you can install character definition tables using the subfunctions 20h to 24h. When outputting a character, the BIOS copies the corresponding table entry for the character into the video RAM and thus displays the corresponding pixel pattern. The subfunction 20h installs a 8*8 character definition table for codes 128–255, to which the pseudo-interrupt vector 1fh points. This is required in CGA-compatible mode, as in the system BIOS ROM no pixel patterns are stored for codes 128–255. You can install these patterns on a DOS level with the GRAFTABL command.

For every function group 0xh, 1xh, and 2xh you have the opportunity to install its own character definition table. Happily, this is quite easy. You have only to note the fact that every character *always* occupies 32 bytes, as the maximum character height is 32 scanlines even if the actual character height has only eight or even fewer scanlines. Thus, each scanline of the character is represented by exactly one byte; a set bit means a pixel appearing with the foreground colour and a cleared one that the pixel has the background colour. A complete character set consists of 256 characters with 32 bytes each, that is, occupies 8 kbytes of memory. But you don't need to specify a whole set; instead, one or more characters are sufficient. If you define the number of an already loaded table upon the call to subfunctions 00h, 10h, or 21h, one or more table entries are overwritten, but the others remain unaltered. Thus you can specifically modify individual characters.

Example: for the ASCII code 128 (normally the character "Ç") of the character set table 0 a rectangle shall appear in the 9*16 character matrix. The installation is carried out without reprogramming the CRTC.

```
The character matrix for the rectangle is as follows:
  scanline    pixel        byte value
         1  xxxxxxxx           ffh
            x000000x           81h
            x000000x           81h
            x000000x           81h
         5  x000000x           81h
            x000000x           81h
            x000000x           81h
            x000000x           81h
            x000000x           81h
        10  x000000x           81h
            x000000x           81h
            x000000x           81h
            x000000x           81h
            x000000x           81h
            x000000x           81h
        16  xxxxxxxx           ffh
```

All further scanlines don't have any set pixels, that is, the value of bytes 17–32 is equal to 00h. The 9th column is generated internally by the character generator; because the ASCII code is equal to 128 a blank column appears. Thus the buffer matrix has the following contents:

```
ffh 81h 81h 81h 81h 81h 81h 81h 81h 81h 81h 81h 81h 81h 81h ffh
00h 00h 00h 00h 00h 00h 00h 00h 00h 00h 00h 00h 00h 00h 00h 00h
```

The character matrix is installed as follows:

```
MOV bh, 20h          ; 32 bytes per table entry
MOV bl, 00h          ; complete table 0
MOV cx, 01h          ; install 1 character
MOV dx, 80h          ; install character starting with ASCII code 128
MOV bp, OFFSET matrix ; store character matrix offset in bp
MOV ax, SEG matrix   ; store character matrix segment in ax
MOV es, ax           ; load character matrix segment into es
MOV ah, 11h          ; use function 11h
MOV al, 00h          ; use subfunction 00h – install user-defined
                     ; character definition table
INT 10h              ; call function
```

If you load the bh register in the above example with the value 16 instead of 32, the last 16 bytes of the buffer matrix can be omitted. In this case, the corresponding bytes in the character generator RAM are not overwritten, but remain unaltered. In an analogous manner you may install a complete character set; only the necessary work to set up the buffer becomes more extensive. The installation of one or more characters, or even a complete character set, by means of subfunctions 10h and 21h is carried out in the same way as described above.

You may use the installation of the user-defined character set, for example, to also display in text mode a small graphic in a window on-screen. If you reserve ASCII codes 128–255 for this purpose, then a graphics window of, for example, 16*8 text characters or 144*128 pixels is possible. This corresponds to a quarter of the screen in the CGA graphics mode with 320*200 points. To be able to actually output the graphics in text mode onto the screen, you must define a buffer in the main memory that you use like a virtual screen in which to store the pixel values for the character matrices. By installing this virtual screen as the character definition table in the character generator RAM, you can output simple graphics in text mode. If you work with a primary and a secondary character set and use more than 128 characters from the 512 possible, you can integrate quite complicated graphics without the need to use the more complicated and time-consuming graphics mode. The only disadvantage is that the 9th pixel column is generated by the character generator without any possibility of intervention.

Further, subfunction 30h is useful to determine the parameters and the storage location of the predefined ROM character tables in the EGA/VGA BIOS. You can thus, for example, read the predefined character matrices and alter them when defining new character definition tables.

Example: determine parameter and storage location of 8*8 ROM table.

```
MOV ah, 11h    ; use function 11h
MOV al, 30h    ; use subfunction 30h
MOV bh, 03h    ; select 8*8 ROM table
INT 10h        ; call function
```

After the call, cx contains the number of bytes per defined character, dl the number of scanlines displayed on-screen for the corresponding character matrix, and es:bp points to the table in ROM.

Function 12h, Subfunction 20h – Select Alternate Print Screen Routine
Using this subfunction you can replace the standard handler for INT 05h by a routine that can serve the new EGA/VGA resolutions.

Example: enable new routine for printing the screen.

```
MOV ah, 12h    ; use function 12h
MOV bl, 20h    ; use subfunction 20h
```

Pressing PRINT or SHIFT+PRINT now calls the newly installed print routine.

Function 12h, Subfunction 31h – Load Standard Palette (VGA Only)
Using this subfunction you may determine whether the VGA is to load the standard palette or keep the current palette values when a graphic mode change by means of INT 10h, function 00h occurs. Normally, the palette registers are loaded with the standard values upon every mode change.

Function 1ch – Save/Restore Video Status (VGA Only)
One problem during the course of programming resident pop-up programs or graphics programs in a multitasking environment is that the activated program has virtually no opportunity to determine the current graphics status and restore it later. The reason is the many write-only registers of graphics adapters from CGA to EGA. Only on a VGA can all essential registers be read, and the VGA BIOS implements the 1ch function, with which you can save all important graphics parameters en bloc into a buffer and restore them later, also en-bloc. As the number of parameters to be saved is not always the same you have to determine the size of the buffer required first by calling subfunction 00h.

12.5.3 Help for Self-Help – Accessing the Video Memory Directly

Using BIOS INT 10h you can output characters in text mode and pixels in graphics mode in any colour at any location on the screen, but you won't break any records! To set a single point on-screen, the BIOS works very hard, but if you attempt to write a whole window onto the screen, or try to save one before it is overwritten by another, you have no choice but to access the video RAM directly. But now we have to pay for the fact that neither IBM nor Microsoft defined a reasonable standard for access to the PC's video system early enough. Fortunately, direct access to the display memory is not very complicated.

MDA

In MDA text mode with BIOS mode number 7, the 4 kbytes video RAM is organized as a linear array containing 2000 contiguous screen memory words attribute:character code for the 25 rows with 80 columns each. The character code forms the low-order, the attribute the high-order byte of the screen memory word. The video RAM starts at segment b000h; the character in the upper left corner is represented by the first word in the video RAM (as is the case for all video modes of all graphics adapters). Thus every character is encoded by two bytes, every row by 160 bytes (a0h bytes). The address of the screen memory word corresponding to the character in row i, column j (i = 0 to 24, j = 0 to 79) is given by the following expression:

```
address(i,j) = b0000h + a0h * i + 02h * j
```

CGA

The structure and organization of the video RAM on a CGA differ significantly between text and graphics mode.

Text Mode (Modes 0, 1, 2, 3)

In CGA text mode with mode numbers 0 and 1, the 16 kbytes of video RAM is divided into eight pages of 2 kbytes (800h bytes), each of which is organized as a linear array and contiguously accommodates the 1000 screen memory words attribute:character code for the 25 rows of 40 columns each. As is the case for all text modes, the character code forms the low-order and the attribute the high-order byte of every screen memory word. The video RAM on a CGA starts at segment b800h; the character in the upper left corner is represented by the first word of a page in the video RAM. Each character is encoded by two bytes, that is, every row by 80 bytes (50h bytes). The address of the screen memory word corresponding to the character in row i, column j of the page k (i = 0 to 24, j = 0 to 39, k = 0 to 7) is given by the following expression:

```
address(i,j,k) = b8000h + 800h * k + 50h * i + 02h * j
```

In text modes 2 and 3, on the other hand, the 16 kbytes of video RAM is divided into four pages of 4 kbytes (1000h bytes), each of which is organized as a linear array and contiguously accommodates the 2000 screen memory words attribute:character code for the 25 rows of 80 columns each. Also here, the video RAM starts at segment b800h. Every character is encoded by two bytes, and every row by 160 bytes (a0h bytes).

The address of the screen memory word corresponding to the character in row i, column j of the page k (i = 0 to 24, j = 0 to 79, k = 0 to 7) is given by the following expression:

```
address(i,j,k) = b8000h + 100h * k + a0h * i + 02h * j
```

Graphics Mode (Modes 4, 5, 6)

In graphics mode the video RAM is divided into two banks of 8 kbytes (2000h bytes) each. Bank 0 accommodates all scanlines with an even number, bank 1 all scanlines with an odd number. In graphics mode, only one page is available, which occupies the whole video RAM. The first bank has memory addresses b800:0000 to b800:1fffh, the second bank memory addresses b800:2000 to b800:3fffh. Figure 12.17 shows the division of the video RAM into banks for all three CGA graphics modes.

In the 4-colour modes 4 and 5, one pixel is assigned two bits to encode the four colours. Thus, one byte in video RAM is able to accommodate four pixels. The pixel with the higher number (that is, the pixel appearing more on the right of the monitor) is encoded by the low-order bits. The k-th byte accommodates pixels 4k, 4k+1, 4k+2 and 4k+3. Figure 12.18a shows this arrangement.

Thus, in modes 4 and 5, 80 bytes (50h bytes) are required to encode one line (320 pixels/4 pixels per byte). The address of that byte which accommodates the pixel in line i and column j (i = 0 to 199, j = 0 to 319) is given by the following expression:

```
address(i,j) = b0000h + 2000h * (i MOD 2) + 50h * INT(i/2) + INT(j/4)
```

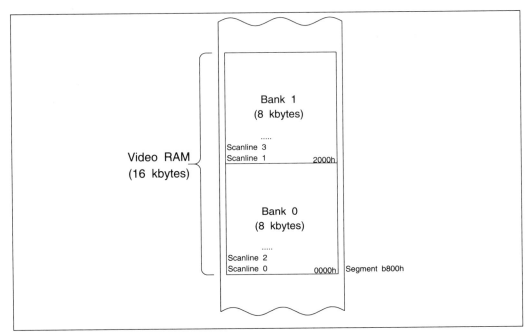

Figure 12.17: Video RAM bank structure for the three CGA graphics modes.

In high-resolution mode 6 («high» refers to the time when the first PC came onto the market) with only two colours, one pixel is assigned only one bit, that is, one video RAM byte can accommodate eight pixels. As is the case for the low-resolution mode, the pixels with a higher number are encoded by the low-order bits. Thus the k-th byte holds the pixels 4k, 4k+1, 4k+2, 4k+3, 4k+4, 4k+5, 4k+6, and 4k+7. Figure 12.18b shows this arrangement.

```
  7              byte #k              0        7                 byte #k                   0
 ┌────┬────┬─────┬─────┬─────┬─────┬─────┬─────┐  ┌────┬─────┬─────┬─────┬─────┬─────┬─────┬─────┐
 │P4k │P4k │P4k+1│P4k+1│P4k+2│P4k+2│P4k+3│P4k+3│  │P4k │P4k+1│P4k+2│P4k+3│P4k+4│P4k+5│P4k+6│P4k+7│
 └────┴────┴─────┴─────┴─────┴─────┴─────┴─────┘  └────┴─────┴─────┴─────┴─────┴─────┴─────┴─────┘

P4k:    pixel number 4k                         P4k:    pixel number 4k     P4k+4: pixel number 4k+4
P4k+1: pixel number 4k+1                        P4k+1: pixel number 4k+1    P4k+5: pixel number 4k+5
P4k+2: pixel number 4k+2                        P4k+2: pixel number 4k+2    P4k+6: pixel number 4k+6
P4k+3: pixel number 4k+3                        P4k+3: pixel number 4k+3    P4k+7: pixel number 4k+7
      (a) low resolution modes 4 and 5                    (b) high resolution mode 6
```

Figure 12.18: Pixel arrangement in the video byte of the CGA graphics modes.

In mode 6 also, 80 bytes (50h bytes) are necessary for one line (640 pixels/8 pixels per byte). The address of that byte which accommodates the pixel in line i and column j (i = 0 to 199, j = 0 to 639) is given by the following expression:

```
address(i,j) = b0000h + 2000h * (i MOD 2) + 50h * INT(i/2) + INT(j/8)
```

Hercules Graphics Card

On the Hercules card also, the structure and organization of the video RAM in text and graphics mode differs significantly.

Text Mode (Mode 7)

In text mode the Hercules card emulates the MDA precisely, so that all statements concerning the MDA apply to the Hercules card as well. Thus the address of the screen memory word corresponding to the character in row i, column j (i = 0 to 24, j = 0 to 79) is given by the following expression:

```
address(i,j) = b0000h + a0h * i + 02h * j
```

Graphics Mode

As already mentioned, the video RAM on the Hercules card is divided in graphics mode into four banks per page. The first bank accommodates the pixels for scanlines 0, 4, 8, ... 344, the second bank that for scanlines 1, 5, 9, ... 345, the third bank that for the scanlines, 6, 10, ... 346, and the fourth bank that for scanlines 3, 7, 11, ... 347. The Hercules card video RAM in graphics mode has 64 kbytes, and is divided into two pages. The resolution is 720*348 pixels. Because of the monochrome display, every pixel is assigned one bit, thus 90 bytes are required per line (720 pixels/8 pixels per byte). The address of the byte which accommodates the pixel in line i and column j of page k (i = 0 to 347, j = 0 to 719, k = 0 to 1) is given by the following expression:

```
address(i,j,k) = b0000h + 8000h * k + 2000h * (i MOD 4) + 90 * INT(i/4) + INT(j/8)
```

b0000h specifies the video segment, 8000h the size of one page (32 kbytes) and 2000h the size of one bank (8 kbytes). Figure 12.8 in Section 12.2.4 illustrates this division of the Hercules card's video RAM into pages if the graphics mode is active.

EGA

The EGA is downward-compatible to the CGA, so that all expositions concerning text modes 0–3 and graphics modes 4–6 apply here, too. In particular, the segment addresses and the division into screen pages, as well as RAM banks, remain the same in these modes.

Text Mode (Modes 0 to 3)

The character codes are stored in memory layer 0 and the accompanying attributes in memory layer 1 of the EGA video RAM. But the address transformation logic on the EGA board carries out a certain combination of the actually parallel storage layers, so that the organization and structure of the video RAM, as well as the address calculation, are identical for the CPU, as on a CGA. The EGA is unable to carry out MDA's text mode 7, however.

Graphics Mode (Modes 4–6 and 13–16)

The EGA can operate in CGA graphics modes 4–6 because of its downward-compatibility. Also in this case, the address transformation logic on the EGA card carries out a combination of the actually parallel memory layers so that the organization and structure of the video RAM, as well as the address calculation, are identical to the CGA.

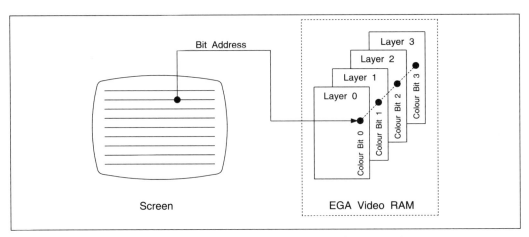

Figure 12.19: Distribution of the 4 bit/pixel to the memory layers in EGA modes 13, 14 and 16.

On the other hand, nearly all parameters of the video RAM and its organization differ from the CGA if one of the EGA graphics modes 13–16 is effective. In all of these EGA modes, the video RAM begins at segment address a000h. Except for monochrome mode 15 every pixel can be displayed in 16 different colours from a palette of 64 colours. Thus four bits per pixel are required in modes 13, 14, or 16. Unlike CGA graphics modes, the video RAM is not divided into two banks here, but the pixels are contiguous in video RAM. The four bits per pixel are distributed to the four parallel memory layers of the EGA. Thus the address of one of these four bits per pixel not only comprises video segment and offset but additionally the memory layer. This is shown in Figure 12.19.

For the CPU the pixels follow one another bit-by-bit while every bit address is assigned four memory layers. Layer 0 accommodates bit 0 of the pixel concerned, layer 1 bit 1 of the pixel concerned, etc. To display pixels with all 16 possible colours on screen, you not only need to calculate the bit addresses, but additionally an access to the four memory layers is required. For this purpose, the EGA map mask register is implemented. It is addressed via the index port 3c4h with index 02h, and can be written via data port 3c5h. Figure 12.20 shows the structure of this map mask register.

Figure 12.20: The map mask register (index 02h, index port 3c4h, data port 3c5h).

Using the map mask register you can enable several layers simultaneously for a write. A set one of the bits *EB3–EB0* enables the corresponding layer. If you now carry out a write access to the corresponding bit address, then the value is transferred into one or more layers.

Example: set bit 0 of the byte at address a000:0000h for the layers 0, 1 and 3.

```
MOV ax, a000h    ; load video segment into ax
MOV es, ax       ; transfer video segment into es
MOV bx, 0000h    ; load offset 0000h into bx
OUT 3c4h, 02h    ; index 2 -> address map mask register
OUT 3c5h, 0bh    ; write 00001011b into map mask register
                 ; -> enable layers 0, 1 and 3
MOV [es:bx], 01h ; set bit 0 in layers 0, 1 and 3
```

For saving screen contents so that you can, for example, restore the original state after a window has appeared and then disappeared again, it is necessary to read the bit values of the four layers. For this purpose, the read map select register is implemented. It is addressed with index 04h via index port 3ceh, and can be written via data port 3cfh. Figure 12.21 shows the structure of the read map select register.

```
 7                           0
┌───┬───┬───┬───┬───┬───┬───┬───┐
│res│res│res│res│res│res│LY1│LY0│
└───┴───┴───┴───┴───┴───┴───┴───┘
LY1, LY0: read access enabled for
          00=layer 0   01=layer 1   10=layer 2   11=layer 3
```

Figure 12.21: The read map select register (index 04h, index port 3ceh, data port 3cfh).

Unlike the map mask register, the read map select register enables access to only a single layer, as the four layers may actually hold different bit values. Therefore, reading all four layers simultaneously is impossible.

Example: read byte at address a000:0000h for layer 2.

```
MOV ax, a000h    ; load video segment into ax
MOV es, ax       ; transfer video segment into es
MOV bx, 0000h    ; load offset 0000h into bx
OUT 3ceh, 04h    ; index 4 -> address read map select register
OUT 3cfh, 02h    ; write 0000 0010b into read map select register
                 ; -> enable layer 2
MOV al, [es:bx]  ; load byte in layer 2 into al
```

Because of the distribution of the four bits per pixel to the four layers, the CPU has the impression that every pixel is assigned one bit in the address space. These four bits of one pixel are addressed by additionally specifying the layer via the map mask or the read map select register. Figure 12.22 shows the pixel bit arrangement in the screen byte for modes 13, 14, and 16.

```
 7                    k-th byte                 0
┌─────┬──────┬──────┬──────┬──────┬──────┬──────┬──────┐
│ P4k │P4k+1 │P4k+2 │P4k+3 │P4k+4 │P4k+5 │P4k+6 │P4k+7 │
└─────┴──────┴──────┴──────┴──────┴──────┴──────┴──────┘
P4k:    pixel number 4k      P4k+4: pixel number 4k+4
P4k+1: pixel number 4k+1     P4k+5: pixel number 4k+5
P4k+2: pixel number 4k+2     P4k+6: pixel number 4k+6
P4k+3: pixel number 4k+3     P4k+7: pixel number 4k+7
```

Figure 12.22: Distribution of the 4 bits/pixels to the memory layers in EGA graphics modes 13, 14 and 16.

In mode 13, 40 bytes (25h bytes) are required per line (320 pixels/8 pixels per byte). Every screen page comprises 8 kbytes (2000h bytes). The address of the byte with the pixel in line i, column j of the screen page k (i = 0 to 199, j = 0 to 319, k = 0 to 7) is therefore:

```
address(i,j,k) = a0000h + 2000h * k + 25h * j + INT (i/8)
```

Mode 14, with a higher resolution, requires 80 bytes (50h bytes) per line, corresponding to 640 pixels/8 pixels per byte. One screen page here comprises 16 kbytes (4000h bytes). The address of the byte with the pixel in line i, column j of the screen page k (i = 0 to 199, j = 0 to 639, k = 0 to 3) is:

```
address(i,j,k) = a0000h + 4000h * k + 50h * j + INT (i/8)
```

In the best high-resolution EGA mode 16, every line also needs 80 bytes (50h bytes) per line (640 pixels/8 pixels per byte); each screen page comprises 32 kbytes (8000h bytes). The address of the byte with the pixel in line i, column j of the screen page k (i = 0 to 349, j = 0 to 639, k = 0 to 1) is as follows:

```
address(i,j,k) = a0000h + 8000h * k + 50h * j + INT (i/8)
```

The EGA mode 15 drives a TTL monochrome monitor instead of the RGB monitors or extended EGA colour monitors usually employed with an EGA. This mode is something like an extended monochrome mode with the four monochrome intensities black, normal, bright and blinking. But note that although bright and blinking can be active, this mode is a graphics and not a text mode. Thus every pixel is assigned two bits, which are distributed to layers 0 and 2. Layers 1 and 3 are not used in this mode. This quite high resolution EGA monochrome mode 15 requires 80 bytes (50h bytes) per line corresponding to 640 pixels/8 pixels per byte. Every screen page comprises 32 kbytes (8000h bytes). The address of the byte with the pixel in line i, column j of the screen page k (i = 0 to 349, j = 0 to 639, k = 0 to 1) is therefore:

```
address(i,j,k) = a0000h + 8000h * k + 50h * j + INT (i/8)
```

VGA

The VGA is downward-compatible with the CGA, EGA, and MDA so that all expositions concerning text modes 0–3 and 7 as well as the graphics modes 4–6 and 13–16 are also valid. In particular, the segment addresses and the division into screen pages, as well as RAM banks, remain the same in these modes.

Text Mode (0–3, 7)

The character codes are stored in memory layer 0 and the accompanying attributes in memory layer 1 of the VGA video RAM, as is the case on the EGA. The VGA address transformation logic carries out a certain combination of the actually parallel storage layers so that the organization and structure of the video RAM, as well as the address calculation, are identical for the CPU, as on a CGA or MDA. Unlike the EGA, the VGA can also carry out MDA's monochrome text mode 7 with an enhanced resolution of 720*400 pixels corresponding to a character matrix of 9*16 pixels.

Graphics Mode (Modes 4–6, 13–19)

The VGA carries out CGA graphics modes 4–6 and EGA graphics modes 13–16 in the same way as on the original adapters. The organization and structure of the video RAM, as well as the address calculation, are identical to the CGA and EGA in these compatible modes.

Additionally, the VGA implements three new VGA modes: graphics modes 17, 18, and 19. VGA mode 17 serves mainly for compatibility to the graphics adapter of the PS/2 model 30, the MCGA (multi colour graphics array). The bits for the individual pixels are located only in layer 0 – the three layers 1, 2, and 3 are not used. Every pixel is assigned one bit, that is, two colours may be displayed.

In VGA mode 17, 80 bytes per line (50h bytes) are required (640 pixels/8 pixels per byte). Every screen page comprises 40 kbytes (a000h bytes). The address of the byte with the pixel in line i, column j (i = 0 to 479, j = 0 to 639) is therefore:

`address(i,j) = a0000h + 50h * j + INT (i/8)`

In VGA mode 18 the four bits of a pixel are distributed to the four memory layers, as is the case for the EGA. For setting one pixel with the intended colour you must therefore additionally address the four layers besides the byte.

In the high-resolution VGA mode 18 with 16 different colours per line, 80 bytes (50h bytes) are also required (640 pixels/8 pixels per byte). Every screen page comprises 40 kbytes (a000h bytes). Thus the address of the byte with the pixel in line i, column j (i = 0 to 479, j = 0 to 639) is therefore:

`address(i,j) = a0000h + 50h * j + INT (i/8)`

In VGA mode 19 with 256 colours per pixel, the video RAM is again organized very simply as a linear array, in which one byte corresponds to one pixel. The byte value specifies the colour of the pixel. The bits are not distributed to various memory layers here. This mode requires 320 bytes (140h bytes) per line corresponding to 320 pixels/1 pixel per byte. The single screen page thus comprises 64 kbytes (10000h bytes), but only 64 000 bytes are actually used. The remaining 1536 bytes remain free. The addres of the pixel in line i, column j (i = 0 to 199, j = 0 to 319) then is:

`address(i,j) = a0000h + 140h * j + i`

Summary

Table 12.14 summarizes the addresses of the characters or pixels in line i, column j of the screen page k in the video RAM.

Mode	Addresses	i[1]	j[2]	k[3]	Layer
0, 1	addr(i,j,k) = b8000h + 800h*k + 50h*i + 02h*j	0..24	0..39	0..7	–
2, 3	addr(i,j,k) = b8000h + 1000h*k + a0h*i + 02h*j	0..24	0..79	0..4	–
4, 5	addr(i,j) =b0000h + 2000h*(i MOD 2) + 50h*INT(i/2) + INT(j/4)	0..199	0..319	0	–
6	addr(i,j) =b0000h + 2000h*(i MOD 2) + 50h*INT(i/2) + INT(j/8)	0..199	0..639	0	–

Mode	Addresses	i[1]	j[2]	k[3]	Layer
7	addr(i,j) =b0000h + a0h∗i + 02h∗j	0..24	0..79	-	–
13	addr(i,j,k) = a0000h + 2000h∗k + 25h∗j + INT (i/8)	0..199	0..319	0..7	0..3
14	addr(i,j,k) = a0000h + 4000h∗k + 50h∗j + INT (i/8)	0..199	0..639	0..3	0..3
15	addr(i,j,k) = a0000h + 8000h∗k + 50h∗j + INT (i/8)	0..349	0..639	0..1	0, 2
16	addr(i,j,k) = a0000h + 8000h∗k + 50h∗j + INT (i/8)	0..349	0..639	0..1	0..3
17	addr(i,j) =a0000h + 50h∗j + INT (i/8)	0..479	0..639	-	–
18	addr(i,j) =a0000h + 50h∗j + INT (i/8)	0..479	0..639	-	0..3
19	addr(i,j) =a0000h + 140h∗j + i	0..199	0..319	-	–
HGCG[4]	addr(i,j,k) = b0000h + 8000h∗k + 2000h∗(i MOD 4) + 90h∗INT(i/4) + INT(j/8)	0..347	0..719	0..1	–

[1] line number
[2] column number
[3] screen page number
[4] graphics mode of the Hercules card

Table 12.14: Video RAM addresses

12.6   Graphics Processor Versus Local Bus

The two concepts of a graphics adapter with a dedicated graphics processor and local bus have the same intention: to accelerate the screen setup. But now all common grounds are already exhausted. While the local bus enables the fast transfer of a vast amount of data generated by the CPU into the video RAM (or vice versa), the graphics processor actually attempts to use the opposite method, to pass only a few commands and parameters to describe the contents of that screen part which is to be displayed. The generation of extensive amounts of data for display on screen is transferred to the adapter by this strategy; the amount of data passed is typically about a factor of 100 less and the transfer time is accordingly lower.

With the local bus the CPU further has to calculate the values for all pixels, and is regularly interrupted by processes such as the periodic timer interrupt, main memory refreshes, mouse movement, etc. A relatively long task switch in a multitasking operating system such as OS/2 or NT Windows may slow down the screen setup significantly. Moreover, for generating the pixel data no intelligent CPU is required; a simple but highly specialized (and therefore very fast) chip can do that better. Thus the local bus concept loads the CPU with rather stupid jobs and blocks it for complicated calculations which require some higher intelligence. Many of the present graphics adapters for the local bus have an external 32-bit interface, but access the video RAM internally only at a width of 16 or even 8 bits. The reason for this is that the manufacturers employ the known and presently available graphics chips that mainly come from the 16-bit ISA world. One example is the very successful and widely used ET4000 (Tseng) with its 16-bit technique. For an ISA adapter the chip is sufficient, but it causes a bottleneck in a local bus graphics adapter. It is replaced by the 32-bit successor ET4000-W32, which really uses all the advantages of the local bus with its width of 32 bits. Finally, the CPU speed limits the screen setup. For example, for displaying a rectangle not only repeated MOV commands are necessary, but also comparison and conditional jumps to define the borders of the rectangle. The switching between the various memory layers in many EGA and VGA modes slows down the picture setup once again.

Graphics processors can free the CPU from a significant part of this unnecessary work. To generate a rectangle with a unique colour, for example, it is sufficient to fill a rather large part of the video RAM with a unique data pattern. For this purpose, the CPU passes only the coordinates of two corners and the intended colour value. Because of the very high clock rate of such a specialized processor with up to 60 MHz and more, simple graphics patterns such as lines, rectangles and circles are generated very quickly. A possible lower data transfer rate between CPU and graphics adapter doesn't play a significant role, as the graphics processor needs much more time to generate the pixel data than the data transfer to the graphics processor lasts. The graphics processors come in useful particularly in connection with multitasking operating systems if task switches, main memory refresh cycles or hardware interrupts occur. While the CPU is handling these requests, the graphics processor keeps setting up the picture in the background and in parallel to the CPU operation.

Additionally, the graphics processor can also be programmed to carry out certain «screen programs». It is thus also capable of generating complicated patterns. Moreover, these adapters can save screen windows in an on-board memory, that is, the screen data need not be transferred into main memory and saved there if, for example, a new window appears with Windows or the OS/2 presentation manager. The on-board program execution and on-board program and data memory already gives some aura of multiprocessing.

A further problem is that normal video RAM is usually only accessible for a short time window. The RAM chips on the adapter can thus be either read or written. If the adapter's CRTC chip continuously reads the video RAM when displaying a line then the CPU cannot also access the display memory with the local bus; the processor has to wait for the next horizontal or vertical retrace. For this purpose, the adapter disables the bus signal RDY and causes the CPU to insert a lot of wait cycles. This also applies in principle to the adapters with a graphics processor. But here the accesses of the CRTC and the graphics processor can be adjusted so that the graphics processor, for example, writes a RAM bank of the display memory which is currently not read by the CRTC controller for displaying the present scanline. With an external CPU this is not possible, as the CPU doesn't know which address is currently read and therefore not accessible at the moment. Also in this case, we see a clear advantage for those adapters with a dedicated graphics processor. The problem can be reduced by using dual-port memories for the video RAM. Now the video memory is only locked during the refresh cycles; the reading by the CRTC controller no longer blocks the access. ISA graphics adapters with a dual-port memory thus achieve about the same results in various practice-oriented benchmarks as local bus graphics adapters with conventional DRAM chips. Presently, 32-bit EISA adapters are even better in most cases, because their technique is directed to the 32 bits of the EISA bus without any compromise. But in future this may change when new graphics adapters designed for the 32-bit local bus come onto the market.

Appendices

A   ASCII and Scan Codes

A.1   ASCII Code

Ctrl	dec	hex	char	code
^@	0	00		NUL	Null Character
^A	1	01	▼	SOH	Start of Header
^B	2	02	–	STX	Start of Text
^C	3	03	♥	ETX	End of Text
^D	4	04	♦	EOT	End of Transmission
^E	5	05	♣	ENQ	Enquiry
^F	6	06	♠	ACK	Acknowledge
^G	7	07	.	BEL	Bell
^H	8	08	.	BS	Backspace
^I	9	09		HT	Horizontal Tabulation
^J	10	0A		LF	Line Feed
^K	11	0B		VT	Vertical Tabulation
^L	12	0C		FF	Form Feed
^M	13	0D		CR	Carriage Return
^N	14	0E		SO	Shift Out
^O	15	0F		SI	Shift In
^P	16	10	►	DLE	Data Link Escape
^Q	17	11	◄	DC1	Device Control 1
^R	18	12	↕	DC2	Device Control 2
^S	19	13	‼	DC3	Device Control 3
^T	20	14	¶	DC4	Device Control 4
^U	21	15	§	NAK	Negative Acknowledgement
^V	22	16	▬	SYN	Synchronous Idle
^W	23	17	↨	ETB	End of Transmission Block
^X	24	18	↑	CAN	Cancel
^Y	25	19	↓	EM	End of Medium
^Z	26	1A	→	SUB	Substitute
^[	27	1B	.	ESC	Escape
^\	28	1C	∟	FS	File Separator
^]	29	1D	↔	GS	Group Separator
^^	30	1E	▲	RS	Record Separator
^_	31	1F		US	Unit Separator

dec	hex	char	dec	hex	char	dec	hex	char	dec	hex	char
32	20		64	40	@	96	60	'	128	80	Ç
33	21	!	65	41	A	97	61	a	129	81	ü
34	22	"	66	42	B	98	62	b	130	82	é
35	23	#	67	43	C	99	63	c	131	83	â
36	24	$	68	44	D	100	64	d	132	84	ä
37	25	%	69	45	E	101	65	e	133	85	à
38	26	&	70	46	F	102	66	f	134	86	å
39	27	'	71	47	G	103	67	g	135	87	ç
40	28	(	72	48	H	104	68	h	136	88	ê
41	29	)	73	49	I	105	69	i	137	89	ë
42	2A	*	74	4A	J	106	6A	j	138	8A	è
43	2B	+	75	4B	K	107	6B	k	139	8B	ï
44	2C	,	76	4C	L	108	6C	l	140	8C	î
45	2D	–	77	4D	M	109	6D	m	141	8D	ì
46	2E	.	78	4E	N	110	6E	n	142	8E	Ä
47	2F	/	79	4F	O	111	6F	o	143	8F	Å
48	30	0	80	50	P	112	70	p	144	90	É
49	31	1	81	51	Q	113	71	q	145	91	æ
50	32	2	82	52	R	114	72	r	146	92	Æ
51	33	3	83	53	S	115	73	s	147	93	ô
52	34	4	84	54	T	116	74	t	148	94	ö
53	35	5	85	55	U	117	75	u	149	95	ò
54	36	6	86	56	V	118	76	v	150	96	û
55	37	7	87	57	W	119	77	w	151	97	ù
56	38	8	88	58	X	120	78	x	152	98	ÿ
57	39	9	89	59	Y	121	79	y	153	99	Ö
58	3A	:	90	5A	Z	122	7A	z	154	9A	Ü
59	3B	;	91	5B	[	123	7B	{	155	9B	¢
60	3C	<	92	5C	\	124	7C	|	156	9C	£
61	3D	=	93	5D	]	125	7D	}	157	9D	¥
62	3E	>	94	5E	^	126	7E	~	158	9E	₧
63	3F	?	95	5F	_	127	7F	⌂	159	9F	ƒ

dec	hex	char	dec	hex	char	dec	hex	char
160	A0	á	192	C0	└	224	E0	α
161	A1	í	193	C1	┴	225	E1	ß
162	A2	ó	194	C2	┬	226	E2	Γ
163	A3	ú	195	C3	├	227	E3	π
164	A4	ñ	196	C4	─	228	E4	Σ
165	A5	Ñ	197	C5	┼	229	E5	σ
166	A6	ª	198	C6	╞	230	E6	μ
167	A7	º	199	C7	╟	231	E7	τ
168	A8	¿	200	C8	╚	232	E8	Φ
169	A9	⌐	201	C9	╔	233	E9	θ
170	AA	¬	202	CA	╩	234	EA	Ω
171	AB	½	203	CB	╦	235	EB	δ
172	AC	¼	204	CC	╠	236	EC	∞
173	AD	¡	205	CD	═	237	ED	ϕ
174	AE	«	206	CE	╬	238	EE	$\in$
175	AF	»	207	CF	╧	239	EF	$\cap$
176	B0	░	208	D0	╨	240	F0	$\equiv$
177	B1	▒	209	D1	╤	241	F1	$\pm$
178	B2	▓	210	D2	╥	242	F2	$\geq$
179	B3	│	211	D3	╙	243	F3	$\leq$
180	B4	┤	212	D4	╘	244	F4	$\int$
181	B5	╡	213	D5	╒	245	F5	$\int$
182	B6	╢	214	D6	╓	246	F6	$\div$
183	B7	╖	215	D7	╫	247	F7	$\approx$
184	B8	╕	216	D8	╪	248	F8	°
185	B9	╣	217	D9	┘	249	F9	•
186	BA	║	218	DA	┌	250	FA	·
187	BB	╗	219	DB	█	251	FB	$\surd$
188	BC	╝	220	DC	▄	252	FC	ⁿ
189	BD	╜	221	DD	▌	253	FD	²
190	BE	╛	222	DE	▐	254	FE	■
191	BF	┐	223	DF	▀	255	FF	

A.2 Scan Codes UK

key	scan code		ASCII/extended			ASCII/extended with shift			ASCII/extended with ctrl			ASCII/extended with alt		
	dec	hex	dec	hex	char	dec	hex	char	dec	hex	char	dec	hex	char
ESC	1	01	27	1b		27	1b		27	1b		1	1	NUL
1 !	2	02	49	31	1	33	21	!				120	78	NUL
2 "	3	03	50	32	2	34	22	"	3	03	NUL	121	79	NUL
3 £	4	04	51	33	3	156	9c	£				122	7a	NUL
4 $	5	05	52	34	4	36	24	$				123	7b	NUL
5 %	6	06	53	35	5	37	25	%				124	7c	NUL
6 ^	7	07	54	36	6	94	5e	^	30	1e		125	7d	NUL
7 &	8	08	55	37	7	38	26	&				126	7e	NUL
8 *	9	09	56	38	8	42	2a	*				127	7f	NUL
9 (	10	0a	57	39	9	40	28	(				128	80	NUL
0)	11	0b	48	30	0	41	29	)				129	81	NUL
− _	12	0c	45	2d	−	95	5f	_	31	1f		130	82	NUL
= ∓	13	0d	61	3d	=	43	2b	∓				131	83	NUL
BKSP	14	0e	8	08		8	08		127	7f				
TAB	15	0f	9	09		15	0f							
Q	16	10	113	71	q	81	51	Q	17	11	^Q	16	10	NUL
W	17	11	119	77	w	87	57	W	23	17	^W	17	11	NUL
E	18	12	101	65	e	69	45	E	5	05	^E	18	12	NUL
R	19	13	114	72	r	82	52	R	18	12	^R	19	13	NUL
T	20	14	116	74	t	84	54	T	20	14	^T	20	14	NUL
Y	21	15	121	79	y	89	59	Y	25	19	^Y	21	15	NUL
U	22	16	117	75	u	85	55	U	21	15	^U	22	16	NUL
I	23	17	105	69	i	73	49	I	9	09	^I	23	17	NUL
O	24	18	111	6f	o	79	4f	O	15	0f	^O	24	18	NUL
P	25	19	112	70	p	80	50	P	16	10	^P	25	19	NUL
[{	26	1a	91	5b	[	123	7b	{	27	1b				
] }	27	1b	93	5d	]	125	7d	}	29	1d				
ENTER 2)	28	1c	13	0d		13	0d		10	0a		28	1c	NUL
ENTER 2)	28	1c	13	0d		13	0d		10	0a		28	1c	EXT
ctrl le	29	1d												
ctrl ri 1)	29	1d												
A	30	1e	97	61	a	65	41	A	1	01	^A	30	1e	NUL
S	31	1f	115	73	s	83	53	S	19	13	^S	31	1f	NUL
D	32	20	100	64	d	68	44	D	4	04	^D	32	20	NUL
F	33	21	102	66	f	70	46	F	6	06	^F	33	21	NUL
G	34	22	103	67	g	71	47	G	7	07	^G	34	22	NUL
H	35	23	104	68	h	72	48	H	8	08	^H	35	23	NUL
J	36	24	106	6a	j	74	4a	J	10	0a	^J	36	24	NUL
K	37	25	107	6b	k	75	4b	K	11	0b	^K	37	25	NUL
L	38	26	108	6c	l	76	4c	L	12	0c	^L	38	26	NUL
; :	39	27	59	3b	;	58	3a	:						
, @	40	28	44	2c	,	64	40	@						
¬ '	41	29	170	aa	¬	96	60	'						
shift le	42	2a												
# ~	43	2b	35	23	#	126	7e	~						
Z	44	2c	122	7a	z	90	5a	Z	26	1a	^Z	44	2c	NUL
X	45	2d	120	78	x	88	58	X	24	18	^X	45	2d	NUL
C	46	2e	99	63	c	67	43	C	3	03	^C	46	2e	NUL
V	47	2f	118	76	v	86	56	V	22	16	^V	47	2f	NUL
B	48	30	98	62	b	66	42	B	2	02	^B	48	30	NUL
N	49	31	110	6e	n	78	4e	N	14	0e	^N	49	31	NUL
M	50	32	109	6d	m	77	4d	M	13	0d	^M	50	32	NUL
, <	51	33	44	2c	,	60	3c	<						
. >	52	34	46	2e	.	62	3e	>						
/ ?	53	35	47	2f	/	63	3f	?						
/2)	53	35	47	2f	/	47	2f	/						
shift ri	54	36												
print scr * 2)	55	37	42	2a	*	INT 5h 4)								
* 2)	55	37	42	2a	*	42	2a	*	150	96	EXT	55	37	NUL SysReq 5)
alt le	56	38												
alt ri 1)	56	38												
blank	57	39	32	20	SPC	32	20	SPC	32	20	SPC	32	20	SPC
CAPS−Lock	58	3a												

key	scan code		ASCII/extended			ASCII/extended with shift			ASCII/extended with ctrl			ASCII/extended with alt		
	dec	hex	dec	hex	char	dec	hex	char	dec	hex	char	dec	hex	char
F1	59	3b	59	3b	NUL	84	54	NUL	94	5e	NUL	104	5e	NUL
F2	60	3c	60	3c	NUL	85	55	NUL	95	5f	NUL	105	5f	NUL
F3	61	3d	61	3d	NUL	86	56	NUL	96	60	NUL	106	60	NUL
F4	62	3e	62	3e	NUL	87	57	NUL	97	61	NUL	107	61	NUL
F5	63	3f	63	3f	NUL	88	58	NUL	98	62	NUL	108	62	NUL
F6	64	40	64	40	NUL	89	59	NUL	99	63	NUL	109	63	NUL
F7	65	41	65	41	NUL	90	5a	NUL	100	64	NUL	110	64	NUL
F8	66	42	66	42	NUL	91	5b	NUL	101	65	NUL	111	65	NUL
F9	67	43	67	43	NUL	92	5c	NUL	102	66	NUL	112	66	NUL
F10	68	44	68	44	NUL	93	5d	NUL	103	67	NUL	113	67	NUL
NUM–Lock	69	45												
NUM–Lock [6]	69	45												
Pause [7]	69	45												
Scroll [6]	70	46												
home [3]	71	47	71	47	NUL	55	37	7	119	77	NUL			
home [3]	71	47	71	47	EXT	71	47	EXT	119	77	EXT	151	97	EXT
cursor up [3]	72	48	72	48	NUL	56	38	8						
cursor up [3]	72	48	72	48	EXT	72	48	EXT	141	8d	EXT	152	98	EXT
page up [3]	73	49	73	49	NUL	57	39	9	132	84	NUL			
page up [3]	73	49	73	49	EXT	73	49	EXT	132	84	EXT	153	99	EXT
– [8]	74	4a	45	2d	–	45	2d	–						
cursor le [3]	75	4b	75	4b	NUL	52	34	4	115	73	NUL			
cursor le [3]	75	4b	75	4b	EXT	75	4b	EXT	115	73	EXT	155	9b	EXT
5 [8]	76	4c				53	35	5	143	8f	NUL			
cursor ri [3]	77	4d	77	4d	NUL	54	36	6	116	74	NUL			
cursor ri [3]	77	4d	77	4d	EXT	77	4d	EXT	116	74	EXT	157	9d	EXT
+ [8]	78	4e	43	2b	+	43	2b	+	144	90	NUL	78	4e	NUL
End	79	4f	79	4f	NUL	49	31	1	117	75	NUL			
End [3]	79	4f	79	4f	EXT	79	4f	EXT	117	75	EXT	159	9f	EXT
cursor dg [3]	80	50	80	50	NUL	50	32	2	145	91	NUL			
cursor do [3]	80	50	80	50	EXT	80	50	EXT	145	91	EXT	160	a0	EXT
page do [3]	81	51	81	51	NUL	51	33	3	118	76	NUL			
page dg [3]	81	51	81	51	EXT	81	51	EXT	118	76	EXT	161	a1	EXT
ins [3]	82	52	82	52	NUL	48	30	0	146	92	NUL			
ins	82	52	82	52	EXT	82	52	EXT	146	92	EXT	162	a2	EXT
del [3]	83	53	83	53	NUL	44	2c	,	147	93	NUL			
del	83	53	83	53	EXT	83	53	EXT	147	93	EXT	163	a3	EXT
\ | [1]	86	56	92	5c	\	124	7c	|						
F11	87	57	133	85	EXT	135	87	EXT	137	89	EXT	139	8b	EXT
F12	88	58	134	86	EXT	136	88	EXT	138	8a	EXT	140	8c	EXT

[1] alphanumeric block; MF II with precode byte 0eh only

[2] numeric block; MF II with precode byte 0eh only

[3] in separate control block of MF II

[4] print screen via INT 05h with DOS

[5] SysReq according to INT 15h, function 85h

[6] MF II with precode byte e0h

[7] MF II with precode byte e1h only

[8] numeric block

A.3   Scan Codes USA

key	scan code		ASCII/extended			ASCII/extended with shift			ASCII/extended with ctrl			ASCII/extended with alt		
	dec	hex	dec	hex	char	dec	hex	char	dec	hex	char	dec	hex	char
ESC	1	01	27	1b		27	1b		27	1b		1	1	NUL
1 !	2	02	49	31	1	33	21	!				120	78	NUL
2 @	3	03	50	32	2	64	40	@	3	03	NUL	121	79	NUL
3 #	4	04	51	33	3	35	23	#				122	7a	NUL
4 $	5	05	52	34	4	36	24	$				123	7b	NUL
5 %	6	06	53	35	5	37	25	%				124	7c	NUL
6 ^	7	07	54	36	6	94	5e	^	30	1e		125	7d	NUL
7 &	8	08	55	37	7	38	26	&				126	7e	NUL
8 *	9	09	56	38	8	42	2a	*				127	7f	NUL
9 (	10	0a	57	39	9	40	28	(				128	80	NUL
0)	11	0b	48	30	0	41	29	)				129	81	NUL
− _	12	0c	45	2d	−	95	5f	_	31	1f		130	82	NUL
= +	13	0d	61	3d	=	43	2b	+	127	7f		131	83	NUL
BKSP	14	0e	8	08		8	08		127	7f				
TAB	15	0f	9	09		15	0f							
Q	16	10	113	71	q	81	51	Q	17	11	^Q	16	10	NUL
W	17	11	119	77	w	87	57	W	23	17	^W	17	11	NUL
E	18	12	101	65	e	69	45	E	5	05	^E	18	12	NUL
R	19	13	114	72	r	82	52	R	18	12	^R	19	13	NUL
T	20	14	116	74	t	84	54	T	20	14	^T	20	14	NUL
Y	21	15	121	79	y	89	59	Y	25	19	^Y	21	15	NUL
U	22	16	117	75	u	85	55	U	21	15	^U	22	16	NUL
I	23	17	105	69	i	73	49	I	9	09	^I	23	17	NUL
O	24	18	111	6f	o	79	4f	O	15	0f	^O	24	18	NUL
P	25	19	112	70	p	80	50	P	16	10	^P	25	19	NUL
[{	26	1a	91	5b	[	123	7b	{	27	1b				
] }	27	1b	93	5d	]	125	7d	}	29	1d				
ENTER	28	1c	13	0d		13	0d		10	0a		28	1c	NUL
ENTER 2)	28	1c	13	0d		13	0d		10	0a		28	1c	EXT
ctrl le 1)	29	1d												
ctrl ri 1)	29	1d												
A	30	1e	97	61	a	65	41	A	1	01	^A	30	1e	NUL
S	31	1f	115	73	s	83	53	S	19	13	^S	31	1f	NUL
D	32	20	100	64	d	68	44	D	4	04	^D	32	20	NUL
F	33	21	102	66	f	70	46	F	6	06	^F	33	21	NUL
G	34	22	103	67	g	71	47	G	7	07	^G	34	22	NUL
H	35	23	104	68	h	72	48	H	8	08	^H	35	23	NUL
J	36	24	106	6a	j	74	4a	J	10	0a	^J	36	24	NUL
K	37	25	107	6b	k	75	4b	K	11	0b	^K	37	25	NUL
L	38	26	108	6c	l	76	4c	L	12	0c	^L	38	26	NUL
; :	39	27	59	3b	;	58	3a	:				39	27	NUL
, @	40	28	44	2c	,	64	40	@				40	28	NUL
¬ '	41	29	35	23	#	126	7e	~				41	29	NUL
shift le 1)	42	2a												
\ | 1)	43	2b	95	5c	\	124	7c	|						
Z	44	2c	122	7a	z	90	5a	Z	26	1a	^Z	44	2c	NUL
X	45	2d	120	78	x	88	58	X	24	18	^X	45	2d	NUL
C	46	2e	99	63	c	67	43	C	3	03	^C	46	2e	NUL
V	47	2f	118	76	v	86	56	V	22	16	^V	47	2f	NUL
B	48	30	98	62	b	66	42	B	2	02	^B	48	30	NUL
N	49	31	110	6e	n	78	4e	N	14	0e	^N	49	31	NUL
M	50	32	109	6d	m	77	4d	M	13	0d	^M	50	32	NUL
, <	51	33	44	2c	,	60	3c	<						
. >	52	34	46	2e	.	62	3e	>						
/ ? 2)	53	35	47	2f	/	63	3f	?						
/ 2)	53	35	47	2f	/	47	2f	/						
shift ri	54	36												
print scr	55	37	42	2a	*	INT 5h 4)						SysReq 5)		
★ 2)	55	37	42	2a	*	42	2a	*	150	96	EXT	55	37	NUL
alt le 1)	56	38												
alt ri 1)	56	38												
blank	57	39	32	20	SPC	32	20	SPC	32	20	SPC	32	20	SPC
CAPS−Lock	58	3a												

key	scan code		ASCII/extended			ASCII/extended with shift			ASCII/extended with ctrl			ASCII/extended with alt		
	dec	hex	dec	hex	char	dec	hex	char	dec	hex	char	dec	hex	char
F1	59	3b	59	3b	NUL	84	54	NUL	94	5e	NUL	104	5e	NUL
F2	60	3c	60	3c	NUL	85	55	NUL	95	5f	NUL	105	5f	NUL
F3	61	3d	61	3d	NUL	86	56	NUL	96	60	NUL	106	60	NUL
F4	62	3e	62	3e	NUL	87	57	NUL	97	61	NUL	107	61	NUL
F5	63	3f	63	3f	NUL	88	58	NUL	98	62	NUL	108	62	NUL
F6	64	40	64	40	NUL	89	59	NUL	99	63	NUL	109	63	NUL
F7	65	41	65	41	NUL	90	5a	NUL	100	64	NUL	110	64	NUL
F8	66	42	66	42	NUL	91	5b	NUL	101	65	NUL	111	65	NUL
F9	67	43	67	43	NUL	92	5c	NUL	102	66	NUL	112	66	NUL
F10	68	44	68	44	NUL	93	5d	NUL	103	67	NUL	113	67	NUL
NUM–Lock	69	45												
NUM–Lock [6]	69	45												
Pause [7]	69	45												
Scroll [6]	70	46												
home [3]	71	47	71	47	NUL	55	37	7	119	77	NUL			
home [3]	71	47	71	47	EXT	71	47	EXT	119	77	EXT	151	97	EXT
cursor up [8]	72	48	72	48	NUL	56	38	8						
cursor up [3]	72	48	72	48	EXT	72	48	EXT	141	8d	EXT	152	98	EXT
page up [8]	73	49	73	49	NUL	57	39	9	132	84	NUL			
page up [3]	73	49	73	49	EXT	73	49	EXT	132	84	EXT	153	99	EXT
– [8]	74	4a	45	2d	–	45	2d	–						
cursor le [8]	75	4b	75	4b	NUL	52	34	4	115	73	NUL			
cursor le [3]	75	4b	75	4b	EXT	75	4b	EXT	115	73	EXT	155	9b	EXT
5 [8]	76	4c				53	35	5	143	8f	NUL			
cursor ri [8]	77	4d	77	4d	NUL	54	36	6	116	74	NUL			
cursor ri [3]	77	4d	77	4d	EXT	77	4d	EXT	116	74	EXT	157	9d	EXT
+ [8]	78	4e	43	2b	+	43	2b	+	144	90	NUL	78	4e	NUL
End [8]	79	4f	79	4f	NUL	49	31	1	117	75	NUL			
End [3]	79	4f	79	4f	EXT	79	4f	EXT	117	75	EXT	159	9f	EXT
cursor do [8]	80	50	80	50	NUL	50	32	2	145	91	NUL			
cursor do [3]	80	50	80	50	EXT	80	50	EXT	145	91	EXT	160	a0	EXT
page do [8]	81	51	81	51	NUL	51	33	3	118	76	NUL			
page do [3]	81	51	81	51	EXT	81	51	EXT	118	76	EXT	161	a1	EXT
ins [8]	82	52	82	52	NUL	48	30	0	146	92	NUL			
ins [3]	82	52	82	52	EXT	82	52	EXT	146	92	EXT	162	a2	EXT
del [3]	83	53	83	53	NUL	44	2c	,	147	93	NUL			
del	83	53	83	53	EXT	83	53	EXT	147	93	EXT	163	a3	EXT
F11	87	57	133	85	EXT	135	87	EXT	137	89	EXT	139	8b	EXT
F12	88	58	134	86	EXT	136	88	EXT	138	8a	EXT	140	8c	EXT

[1] alphanumeric block; MF II with precode byte 0eh only

[2] numeric block; MF II with precode byte 0eh only

[3] in separate control block of MF II

[4] print screen via INT 05h with DOS

[5] SysReq according to INT 15h, function 85h

[6] MF II with precode byte e0h

[7] MF II with precode byte e1h only

[8] numeric block

B   80x86 Processor Machine Instructions

B.1   8086/88

AAA	*ASCII Adjust After Addition* Adjusts the result of a BCD addition.
AAD	*ASCII Adjust Before Division* Converts non-packed BCD to binary number.
AAM	*ASCII Adjust After Multiplication* Converts 8 bit binary number to non-packed BCD.
AAS	*ASCII Adjust After Subtraction* Converts the result of a subtraction to BCD.
ADC	*Add with Carry* Adds source operand, destination operand and carry flag.
ADD	*Add* Adds source and destination operand.
AND	*Logical AND* Bit by bit logical AND of two operands.
CALL	*Call Procedure* Calls a procedure.
CBW	*Convert Byte to Word* Converts signed byte to signed word.
CLC	*Clear Carry Flag* Sets carry flag to zero.
CLD	*Clear Direction Flag* Clears direction flag for string instructions.
CLI	*Clear Interrupt Flag* Blocks out maskable interrupts.
CMC	*Complement Carry Flag* Complements the carry flag.
CMP	*Compare* Compares two operands.
CMPS *CMPSB* *CMPSW*	*Compare String* Compares two strings.

CWD	*Convert Word to Double* Converts signed word to signed double word.
DAA	*Decimal Adjust After Addition* Converts result of addition to packed BCD.
DAS	*Decimal Adjust after Subtraction* Converts result of subtraction to packed BCD.
DEC	*Decrement* Subtracts 1 from destination operand.
DIV	*Unsigned Divide* Divides destination operand by source operand.
ESC	*Escape* Supplies instruction and optional operand for coprocessor.
HLT	*Halt* Halts the processor.
IDIV	*Signed Divide* Divides signed destination operand by signed source operand.
IMUL	*Signed Multiply* Multiplies signed destination operand with signed source operand.
IN	*Input from Port* Transfers byte, word or double word (i386 and above) from port to accumulator.
INC	*Increment* Adds 1 to destination operand.
INT	*Interrupt* Issues a software interrupt.
INTO	*Interrupt on Overflow* Issues interrupt 4 if overflow flag is set.
IRET	*Interrupt Return* Returns control from interrupt handler to interrupted program.

JB/JNAE	*Jump Conditionally*	
JAE/JNB	Executes a jump depending upon a certain condition.	
JBE/JNA		
JA/JNBE		
JE/JZ		
JNE/JNZ		
JL/JNGE		
JGE/JNL		
JLE/JNG		
JG/JNLE		
JS		
JNS		
JC		
JNC		
JO		
JNO		
JP/JPE		
JNP/JPO		
JCXZ	*Jump if CX is Zero*	
JECXZ	Jumps if value of CX is equal zero.	
JMP	*Jump Unconditionally*	
	Jumps always.	
LAHF	*Load Flags into AH Register*	
	Transfers bits 0 to 7 into register AH.	
LDS	*Load Far Pointer*	
LES	Reads and stores the far pointer of source memory operand in a segment/register pair.	
LEA	*Load Effective Address*	
	Calculates the effective address (offset) of the source memory operand.	
LOCK	*Lock the Bus*	
	Locks out other processors from the bus.	
LODS	*Load String Operand*	
LODSB	Loads a string from memory into accumulator.	
LODSW		
LOOP	*Loop*	
	Returns repeatedly to a certain label and executes one or more loops.	
LOOPE/	*Loop if xxx*	
LOOPZ	Executes a loop conditionally.	
LOOPNE/		
LOOPNZ		

MOV	*Move Data*
	Copies the value of the source into the destination operand.
MOVS	*Move String Data*
MOVSB	Copies a string from one memory area into another memory area.
MOVSW	
MUL	*Unsigned Multiply*
	Multiplies two unsigned operands.
NEG	*Two's Complement Negation*
	Replaces the operand by its 2's complement.
NOP	*No Operation*
	Doesn't execute any process.
NOT	*One's Complement Negation*
	Replaces each operand bit by its complementary value.
OR	*Inclusive OR*
	Bit by bit logical OR of two operands.
OUT	*Output to Port*
	Transfers a byte, word or double word from the accumulator to a port.
POP	*Pop*
	Pops the last value off the stack and transfers it to the operand.
POPF	*Pop Flags*
	Transfers the last value on the stack into the flag register.
PUSH	*Push*
	Transfers the operand onto the stack.
PUSHF	*Push Flags*
	Transfers the flag register onto the stack.
RCL	*Rotate*
RCR	Rotates the bits of the operand.
ROL	
ROR	
REP	*Repeat String*
	Repeats the string instruction CX-times.
REPE	*Repeat String Conditionally*
REPNE	Repeats the string instruction until the condition is true.
RET	*Return from procedure*
RETN	Returns from a procedure to the calling program.
RETF	

SAHF	*Store AH into Flags*	
	Transfers AH into bits 0 to 7 of the flag register.	

SAL	*Shift*	
SAR	Shifts the operand bits.	
SHL		
SHR		

SBB *Subtract with Borrow*
Subtracts the source from the destination operand and additionally subtracts the carry flag.

SCAS *Scan String Flags*
SCASB Scans a string for a certain value.
SCASW

STC *Set Carry Flag*
Sets carry flag to 1.

STD *Set Direction Flag*
Sets direction flag to 1.

STI *Set Interrupt Flag*
Sets interrupt flag to 1.

STOS *Store String Data*
STOSB Writes the accumulator value into a string.
STOSW

SUB *Subtract*
Subtracts two operands.

TEST *Logical Compare*
Tests certain bits of an operand.

WAIT *Wait*
Halts the CPU until a corresponding signal from the coprocessor is received.

XCHG *Exchange*
Exchanges the value of two operands.

XLAT *Translate*
XLATB Translates a value from one encoding system into another encoding system.

XOR *Exclusive OR*
Bit by bit exclusive OR of two operands.

B.2   80186

Only the new 80186 instructions are listed.

BOUND	*Check Array Bounds* Checks whether a value is within the preset boundaries of an array.
ENTER	*Make Stack Frame* Generates a stack frame for a local variable of a procedure.
INS *INSB* *INSW*	*Input from Port to String* Transfers a string from a port into a string.
LEAVE	*High Level Procedure Exit* Opposite to ENTER.
OUTS *OUTSB* *OUTSW*	*Output String to Port* Transfers a string to a port.
POPA *POPAD*	*Pop All* Transfers the last eight values from the stack into the general purpose registers.
PUSHA *PUSHAD*	*Push All* Transfers the general purpose registers onto the stack.

B.3   80286

Only the new 80286 instructions are listed.

ARPL	*Adjust Requested Privilege Level (Privileged)* Adjusts the requested privilege level.
CLTS	*Clear Task-Switched Flag (Privileged)* Clears the task-switched flag in the machine status word MSW.
LAR	*Load Access Rights (Protected Mode)* Loads the access rights of a selector into a certain register.
LGDT *LIDT* *LLDT*	*Load Descriptor Table (Privileged)* Loads the value of an operand into a descriptor table register.
LMSW	*Load Machine Status Word (Privileged)* Loads the value of a memory operand into the machine status word.
LSL	*Load Segment Limit (Protected Mode)* Loads the segment limit of a selector into a register.

LTR	*Load Task Register (Privileged)*
	Loads the value of an operand into the current task register.
SGDT	*Store Descriptor Table (Privileged)*
SIDT	Stores a descriptor table register in a certain operand.
SLDT	
SMSW	*Store Machine Status Word (Privileged)*
	Stores the machine status word in a memory operand.
STR	*Store Task Register (Privileged)*
	Stores the current task register in an operand.
VERR	*Verify Read or Write (Protected Mode)*
VERW	Verifies that a certain segment selector is valid and can be read or written.

B.4 i386

Only the new i386/i386SX instructions are listed.

BSF	*Bit Scan Forward or Bit Scan Reverse*
BSR	Scans the operand in forward or reverse direction to look for the first bit set (=1).
BT	*Bit Test*
BTC	Copies the value of a certain bit into the carry flag.
BTR	
BTS	
CDQ	*Convert Double to Quad*
	Converts signed double word into signed quad word.
CMPSD	*Compare String*
	Compares two strings.
CWDE	*Convert Word to Extended Double*
	Converts a signed word to a signed double word.
INSD	*Input from Port to String*
	Transfers a string from a port to a string.
IRETD	*Interrupt Return*
	Returns the control from an interrupt handler to the interrupted program.
LFS	*Load Far Pointer*
LGS	Reads and stores the far pointer of the source memory operand in a
LSS	segment/register pair.
LODSD	*Load String Operand*
	Loads a string from the memory into the accumulator.

MOVSD	*Move String Data* Copies a string from one memory area to another.
MOVSX	*Move with Sign-Extend* Copies an operand and extends its sign to 16/32 bits.
MOVZX	*Move with Zero-Extend* Copies an operand and extends its value with zeros.
OUTSD	*Output String to Port* Transfers a string to a port.
POPFD	*Pop Flags* Transfers the last value on the stack into the flag register.
PUSHFD	*Push Flags* Transfers the flag register onto the stack.
SCASD	*Scan String Flags* Scans a string for a certain value.
SETB/ SETNAE SETAE/SETNB SETBE/SETNA SETA/SETNBE SETE/SETZ SETNE/SETNZ SETL/SETNGE SETGE/SETNL SETLE/SETNG SETG/SETNLE SETS SETNS SETC SETNC SETO SETNO SETP/SETPE SETNP/SETPO	*Set Conditionally* Sets the byte of the operand conditionally.
SHLD SHRD	*Double Precision Shift* Shifts the bits of an operand into another operand.
STOSD	*Store String Data* Stores the value of the accumulator in a string.

B.5 i486

Only the new i486 CPU core instructions are listed.

BSWAP
Byte Swap
Swaps two bytes.

CMPXCHG
Compare and Exchange
Compares and exchanges source and destination operand, depending upon the comparison result.

INVD
Invalidate Cache
Invalidates the entries in the on-chip cache.

INVPG
Invalidate TLB Entry
Invalidates the entries in the translation lookaside buffer of the paging unit.

WBINV
Write-Back and Invalidate Data Cache
Writes the contents of the on-chip data cache back into main memory and invalidates the cache entries.

XADD
Exchange and Add
Exchanges and adds source register and destination register or memory operand and destination register and writes the result into the destination register.

C   80x87 Processor Machine Instructions

Many 80x87 instructions have a format with or without WAIT. Instructions without WAIT are characterized by an N after the beginning F (for floating, i.e. ESC instruction).

C.1   8087

F2XM1	*2 to X minus 1* Calculates y=2^x–1 with $0 \le x \le 0,5$. x is taken from TOP and the result y is stored in TOP again afterwards.
FLD FILD FBLD	*Load* Loads a value from memory or a register into a register.
FABS	*Absolute* Converts the value in TOP to its absolute value.
FADD FADDP FIADD	*Add/Add and Pop* Adds source and destination operand.
FCHS	*Change Sign* Changes the sign of TOP.
FCLEX FNCLEX	*Clear Exceptions* Clears the exception flags, busy flag and bit 7 in the status word.
FCOM FCOMP FCOMPP FICOM FICOMP	*Compare* Compares source with TOP.
FDECSTP	*Decrement Stack Pointer* Decrements the pointer to the register (TOP) on top of the register stack.
FDISI FNDISI	*Disable Interrupts* Masks off all interrupts; only valid on the 8087, all other coprocessors ignore FDISI/FNDISI.
FDIV FDIVP FIDIV	*Divide* Divides the destination by the source operand and stores the result in the destination operand.
FDIVR FDIVRP FIDIVR	*Divide Reversed* Divides the source by the destination operand and stores the result in the destination operand.

FENI *FNENI*	*Enable Interrupts* Clears the IE flag in the control word and thus enables the interrupts; only valid on the 8087, all other 80x87 processors ignore FENI/FNENI.	
FFREE *FREE*	*Free* Changes the tag entry of a register to empty without changing the register value.	
FIADD *FISUB* *FISUBR* *FIMUL* *FIDIV* *FIDIVR*	*Integer Add/Subtract/Multiply/Divide* Carries out addition, subtraction, multiplication and division using integers.	
FICOM *FICOMP*	*Compare Integer* Compares two integers.	
FINCSTP	*Increment Stack Pointer* Increments the pointer referring to the register (TOP) on top of the register stack.	
FINIT *FNINIT*	*Initialize Coprocessor* Initializes the coprocessor and resets all registers and flags.	
FLD *FILD* *FBLD*	*Load* Converts the operand to the temporary real format and pushes it onto the register stack.	
FFLD1 *FLDZ* *FLDPI* *FLDL2E* *FLDL2T* *FLDLG2* *FLDLN2*	*Load Constant* Loads +1, +0, π, $\log_2(e)$, $\log_2(10)$, $\log_{10}(2)$ and $\log_e(2)$, respectively, onto the register stack.	
FLDCW	*Load Control Word* Loads the control word from memory into the control register of the coprocessor.	
FLDENV	*Load Environment State* Loads the environment state from memory into the coprocessor. The environment state comprises control word, status word, tag word, instruction pointer and operand (data) pointer.	
FMUL *FMULP* *FIMUL*	*Multiply* Multiplies the source with the destination operand and stores the result in the destination operand.	

FNOP	*No Operation* Doesn't carry out any process.
FPATAN	*Partial Arctangent* Calculates z = arctan (y/x). y is taken from register TOP, x from register TOP+1, x is popped off the stack, and the result is stored in the new TOP (y).
FPREM	*Partial Remainder* Calculates the partial remainder of TOP when divided by TOP+1. The result is stored in TOP.
FPTAN	*Partial Tangent* Calculates y/x = tan(z); z is taken from register TOP; y is pushed into register TOP and x into register TOP–1.
FRNDINT	*Round to Integer* Rounds broken TOP to an integer.
FRSTOR	*Restore Saved State* Restores the coprocessor state from the data stored memory.
FSAVE FNSAVE	*Save Coprocessor State* Saves the current coprocessor state as a data array in memory.
FSCALE	*Scale* Scales with powers of 2 by calculating y=y*2^x. y is taken from TOP+1, y from register TOP. The result is stored in TOP.
FSQRT	*Square Root* Calculates the square root of TOP.
FST FSTP FIST FISTP FBSTP	*Store Real/Store Real and Pop/Store Integer/Store Integer and Pop/Store BCD and Pop* Writes the value in TOP in memory or a register.
FSTCW FNSTCW	*Store Control Word* Writes the control word into a memory operand.
FSTENV FNSTENV	*Store Environment State* Stores the coprocessor environment state in memory. The environment state comprises control word, status word, tag word, instruction and operand (data) pointer.
FSTSW FNSTSW	*Store Status Word* Writes the status word into a memory operand.

FSUB *FSUBP* *FISUB*	*Subtract* Subtracts the source from the destination operand and stores the difference in the destination operand.
FSUBR *FSUBPR* *FISURB*	*Subtract Reversed* Subtracts the destination from the source operand and stores the difference in the destination operand.
FTST	*Test for Zero* Compares TOP with +0.
FUCOM *FUCOMP* *FUCOMPP*	*Unordered Compare* Compares the source operand with TOP.
FWAIT	*Wait* Halts the CPU operation until the coprocessor has completed the current process.
FXAM	*Examine* Examines the contents of TOP and stores the result in condition code C3–C0 of the status word.
FXCH	*Exchange Registers* Exchanges the contents of the destination register and TOP.
FXTRACT	*Extract Exponent and Mantissa* Stores the exponential part of TOP in TOP and pushes the mantissa into TOP–1.
FYL2X	$Y \log_2(X)$ Calculates $z = y \log_2(x)$. x is taken from the register TOP and y from the register TOP+1. After a pop the result is stored in the new TOP.
FYL2XP1	$Y \log_2(X+1)$ Calculates $z = y \log_2(x+1)$. x is taken from the register TOP and y from the register TOP+1. After a pop the result is stored in the new TOP.

C.2   80287

Only the new 80287 instructions are listed.

FSETPM	*Set Protected Mode* Switches the 80287 into protected mode. The 80387 ignores this instruction as it handles addresses equally in real and protected mode.

C.3   80287XL and i387/i387SX

Only the new 80287XL/i387/i387SX instructions are listed.

FCOS   *Cosine*
                          Calculates the cosine of TOP.

FPREM1   *Partial Remainder (IEEE)*
                          Calculates the remainder of TOP when divided by TOP+1 according to the
                          IEEE standard. The result is stored in TOP.

FSIN   *Sine*
                          Calculates the sine of TOP.

FSINCOS   *Sine and Cosine*
                          Calculates the sine and cosine of TOP. The sine is stored in TOP and the
                          cosine is pushed onto the register stack, i.e. into TOP–1.

C.4   i486

Only the new instructions of the i486 floating-point unit are listed.

FSTSW AX   *Store Status Word into AX*
                          Stores the floating point unit's status word in the accumulator of the CPU
                          core.

D Interrupts

D.1 PC Hardware Interrupts

Interrupt	PC/XT	AT and PS/2
08h	IRQ0 timer chip	IRQ0 timer chip
09h	IRQ1 keyboard	IRQ1 keyboard
0Ah	unused	IRQ2 slave 8259
0Bh	IRQ3 COM2	IRQ3 COM2
0Ch	IRQ4 COM1	IRQ4 COM1
0Dh	IRQ5 hard disk	IRQ5 LPT2
0Eh	IRQ6 floppy disk drive	IRQ6 floppy disk drive
0Fh	IRQ7 LPT1	IRQ7 LPT1
70h		IRQ8 real-time clock
71h		IRQ9 redirected to IRQ2
72h		IRQ10 reserved
73h		IRQ11 reserved
74h		IRQ12 reserved
75h		IRQ13 coprocessor
76h		IRQ14 hard disk drive
77h		IRQ15 reserved

D.2 PC Software Interrupts

Interrupt	Description
5h	print screen[1]
10h	BIOS video functions
11h	determine system configuration
12h	determine memory size
13h	floppy/hard disk drive functions
14h	serial interface
15h	cassette recorder (PC) or extended memory functions (AT)
16h	BIOS keyboard functions
17h	BIOS printer functions (LPTx)
18h	ROM BASIC
19h	load and execute bootstrap
1Ah	timer/real-time clock functions
1Bh	program abortion[2]
1Ch	timer interrupt (user exit)
1Dh	address of BIOS video parameter table
1Eh	address of BIOS floppy disk parameter table
1Fh	address of BIOS graphics character table
20h	DOS program termination

Interrupt	Description
21h	DOS system functions
22h	DOS program termination address
23h	DOS program abortion[3]
24h	DOS handler for hardware errors
25h	read logical sectors (DOS)
26h	write logical sectors (DOS)
27h	terminate program resident (DOS)
28h	DOS idle (no file functions currently in progress)
29h	TTY output (DOS)
2Ah	critical section (DOS)
2Fh	DOS multiplexer
40h	redirected INT 13h for floppy drive functions
41h	address of parameter table for hard disk 0
42h	redirected INT 10h for video functions (EGA)
43h	address of EGA video parameter table
44h	address of the first 128 CGA graphics characters
46h	address of parameter table for hard disk 1
4Ah	alarm interrupt of real-time clock (user)
50h	periodic/alarm interrupt (AT)
5Ah	cluster functions
5Bh	redirected INT 19h for PC cluster
5Ch	network functions
60h–67h	reserved for application programs

[1] activated by PrScr or Shift PrScr
[2] activated by Ctrl-Break
[3] activated by Ctrl-C

D.3   80x86 Exceptions

Interrupt	Description
0h	division by zero
1h	single step
3h	breakpoint
4h	overflow detection with INTO
5h	BOUND
6h	invalid opcode
7h	coprocessor not present
8h	double fault
9h	segment overflow coprocessor
Ah	invalid task state segment
Bh	segment not present
Ch	stack exception
Dh	general protection error
Fh	reserved by Intel
10h	coprocessor error
11h–19h	reserved by Intel

E   BIOS Clock Interrupt 1ah and Functions 83h/86h of INT 15h

- The functions 00h and 01h of INT 1ah are related to the DOS-internal system clock only, but not to the MC146818 real-time clock.

- The access to the real-time clock is carried out by functions 02h to 07h of INT 1ah.

- The functions 83h and 86h of INT 15h set time intervals.

E.1   BIOS Interrupt INT 1ah

Function 00h – Read Time Counter (DOS-Internal System Clock)

This function returns the number of timer ticks since 0:00 a.m. If more than 24 hours have elapsed since power-up, the value of AL is different from 0. In DX:CX the function returns the high and low timer values, respectively, at 40:6eh and 40:6ch in the BIOS data area and the timer overflow flag 40:70h in register AL. After a call to this function, the timer overflow flag will be cleared.

Register	Call value	Return value
AH	00h	
AL		24 hour indicator
CX		high count value
DX		low count value

Function 01h – Set Time Counter (DOS-Internal System Clock)

This function 00h sets the number of timer ticks since 0:00 a.m. The function stores the high and low timer values, respectively, which are passed in DX:CX into 40:6eh and 40:6ch in the BIOS data area and resets the timer overflow flag 40:70h.

Register	Call value	Return value
AH	01h	
CX	high timer count	
DX	low timer count	

Function 02h – Read Time (Real-time Clock)

This function reads the time from the real-time clock chip MC146818.

Register	Call value	Return value
AH	02h	00h
CL		minute $^{*)}$
CH		hour $^{*)}$
DH		second $^{*)}$
Carry		error if $< > 0$

$^{*)}$ binary coded decimal

Function 03h – Set Time (Real-time Clock)

This function sets the time of the real-time clock chip MC146818.

Register	Call value	Return value
AH	03h	00h
CL	minute $^{*)}$	
CH	hour $^{*)}$	
DL	daylight saving (1=yes, 0=no)	
DH	second $^{*)}$	
Carry		error if $< > 0$

$^{*)}$ binary coded decimal

Function 04h – Read Date (Real-time Clock)

This function reads the date from the CMOS RAM in the real-time clock chip MC146818.

Register	Call value	Return value
AH	04h	
CL		year $^{*)}$
CH		century $^{*)}$
DL		day $^{*)}$
DH		month $^{*)}$
Carry		error if $< > 0$

$^{*)}$ binary coded decimal

Function 05h – Set Date (Real-time Clock)
This function sets the date in the CMOS RAM of the real-time clock chip MC146818.

Register	Call value	Return value
AH	05h	
CL	year[*]	
CH	century[*]	
DL	day[*]	
DH	month[*]	
Carry		error if < > 0

[*] binary coded decimal

Function 06h – Set Alarm Time (Real-time Clock)
This function sets the alarm time of the real-time clock chip MC146818. If the alarm time is reached, the MC146818 issues an interrupt 4ah. Before setting a new alarm time you have to clear an active alarm time via function 07h.

Register	Call value	Return value
AH	06h	
CL	minute[*]	
CH	hour[*]	
DH	second[*]	
Carry		error if < > 0

[*] binary coded decimal

Function 07h – Clear Alarm Time (Real-time Clock)
This function clears an active alarm time and has to be called before setting a new alarm time.

Register	Call value	Return value
AH	07h	
Carry		error if < > 0

E.2   Wait Functions 83h and 86h of BIOS Interrupt INT 15h

Function 83h – Set or Clear Wait Time Interval
If AL = 00h this function sets the high bit of a byte in main memory at a user-defined address when the programmed time interval has expired. After a call to this function, the calling program continues at once. After expiry of the wait time interval, the real-time clock issues an interrupt. The wait time interval has to be specified in units of one microsecond, but because of the usually programmed real-time clock frequency of 1024 Hz the actual time resolution is about 976 µs, i.e. 1/1024 Hz. If AL = 01h the active wait time is disabled.

Subfunction 00h – Set Wait Time Interval

Register	Call value	Return value
AH	83h	00h
AL	00h	register B of MC146818
CX	time interval (high)[1]	
DX	time interval (low)[1]	
BX	offset of target byte[2]	
ES	segment of target byte[2]	
Carry		error if < > 0

1) in μs
2) bit 7 of target byte will be set after expiration of time interval

Subfunction 01h – Clear Wait Time Interval

Register	Call value	Return value
AH	83h	
AL	01h	

Function 86h – Wait Until Time Interval Has Elapsed

This function suspends execution of the calling program until the programmed time interval has elapsed. Afterwards, the program execution continues. The wait time interval must be specified in units of one microsecond, but because of the usually programmed real-time clock frequency of 1024 Hz, the actual time resolution is about 976 μs, i.e. 1/1024 Hz.

Register	Call value	Return value
AH	86h	
CX	time interval (high)[1]	
DX	time interval (low)[1]	
Carry		error if < > 0

1) in μs

F   BIOS Interrupt INT 13h

If you are using the BIOS Interrupt 13h, which is available for floppy drives as well as for hard disk drives, you should observe the following rules:

- With functions that refer to hard disk drives, bits 6 and 7 of the sector register CH represent bits 8 and 9 of a 10-bit cylinder number; the remaining eight bits of the cylinder number are passed in CH; therefore, cylinder numbers 0–1023 are possible.

- For read, verify, or write operations you have to provide a buffer large enough to accommodate all the sectors to be read, compared, or written.

- The drive count starts with 00h; for hard disk drives, additionally bit 7 is set so that here the drive number count starts with 80h.

- The error codes are returned in the AH register and simultaneously stored in the BIOS data area at 40:41h (floppy disk) and 40:74h (hard disk), respectively.

The first floppy drive A: has the drive number 00h, the second drive the number 01h. The first hard disk is assigned number 80h, the second 81h. For every sector to be read, verified, or written you have to provide 512 bytes. To read three sectors, for example, a buffer comprising 1536 bytes is required. If you have to format four sectors, for example, you have to pass four format buffers.

F.1   The Functions

Function 00h – Initialize (Floppy/Hard Disk)
This function initializes the addressed drive.

Register	Call value	Return value
AH	00h	error code[1]
DL	drive[2]	
Carry		error if < > 0

[1] see F.2
[2] floppy disk drives: 00h

Function 01h – Read Status (Error Code) of Last Floppy or Hard Disk Operation (Floppy/Hard Disk)
This function determines the termination status of the last hard disk or floppy drive operation.

Register	Call value	Return value
AH	01h	error code[1]
DL	drive[2]	
Carry		error if < > 0

[1] see F.2
[2] floppy disk drives: 00h

Function 02h – Read Sectors (Floppy/Hard Disk)

One or more sectors are read from floppy/hard disk into the read buffer.

Register	Call value	Return value
AH	02h	error code[*]
AL	number of sectors to read	
CH	track/cylinder	
CL	sector	
DH	head	
DL	drive	
ES	segment of read buffer	
BX	offset of read buffer	
Carry		error if < > 0

[*] see F.2

Function 03h – Write Sectors (Floppy/Hard Disk)

This function writes one or more sectors from the write buffer in main memory onto the floppy or hard disk.

Register	Call value	Return value
AH	03h	error code[*]
AL	number of sectors to write	
CH	track/cylinder	
CL	sector	
DH	head	
DL	drive	
ES	segment of write buffer	
BX	offset of write buffer	
Carry		error if < > 0

[*] see F.2

Funcion 04h – Verify Sectors (Floppy/Hard Disk)

This function compares the contents of the verify buffer in main memory with the contents of one or more sectors on the floppy or hard disk, or determines whether one or more sectors can be found and read, and whether they return a valid CRC code. In the last case, no data is compared.

Register	Call value	Return value
AH	04h	error code[*]
AL	number of sectors to verify	
CH	track/cylinder	
CL	sector	
DH	head	
DL	drive	
ES	segment of verify buffer	
BX	offset of verify buffer	
Carry		error if < > 0

[*] see F.2

Function 05h – Format Track or Cylinder (Floppy/Hard Disk)

This function formats the sectors of one track or one cylinder. On an AT you have to fix the medium type with function 17h or 18h first.

Register	Call value	Return value
AH	05h	error code[1]
AL	number of sectors per track	
CH	track/cylinder	
CL	sector number	
DH	head	
DL	drive	
ES	segment of format buffer [2]	
BX	offset of format buffer [2]	
Carry		error if < > 0

[1] see F.2
[2] see F.4

Function 06h – Format and Mark Track Bad (Hard Disk)

This function marks a track with more than one bad sector entirely as bad so that this track is not used for further data recording. The function is only valid for an XT hard disk controller.

Register	Call value	Return value
AH	06h	error code[*]
AL	interleave	
CH	cylinder	
CL	sector	
DH	head	
DL	drive	
Carry		error if < > 0

[*] see F.2

Function 07h – Format Drive (Hard Disk)

This function formats the drive beginning with the specified start cylinder. The function is only valid for an XT hard disk controller.

Register	Call value	Return value
AH	07h	error code[*]
AL	interleave	
CH	cylinder	
CL	sector	
DH	head	
DL	drive	
Carry		error if < > 0

[*] see F.2

Function 08h – Determine Drive Parameters (Floppy Drive)

This function determines the geometric parameters of a floppy.

Register	Call value	Return value
AH	08h	error code[1]
BH		0
BL		drive type [2]
CH		number of cylinders − 1
CL		sectors per track − 1
DH		number of heads − 1
DL	drive	number of drives
ES		parameter table segment
DI		parameter table offset
Carry		error if < > 0

[1] see F.2
[2] 0=hard disk, 1=360 kbytes, 2=1.2 Mbytes, 3=720 kbytes, 4=1.44 Mbytes

Function 08h – Determine Drive Parameters (Hard Disk)

This function determines the geometric parameters of a hard disk drive.

Register	Call value	Return value
AH	08h	error code[1]
AL		0
CH		number of cylinders − 1
CL		sectors per track − 1
DH		number of heads − 1

Register	Call value	Return value
DL	drive	number of drives
ES		parameter table segment
DI		parameter table offset
Carry		error if < > 0

[1]) see F.2

Function 09h – Specify Drive Parameters (Hard Disk)

This function specifies and adapts the geometric parameters of a hard disk drive.

Register	Call value	Return value
AH	09h	error code[*])
DL	drive	number of drives
Carry		error if < > 0

[*]) see F.2

Function 0Ah – Extended Read (Hard Disk)

This function reads one or up to 127 sectors together with their ECC check bytes from the hard disk into the read buffer in main memory. The controller's ECC logic does not carry out any ECC correction.

Register	Call value	Return value
AH	0Ah	error code[1])
AL	number of sectors to read	
CH	cylinder	
CL	sector	
DH	head	
DL	drive	
ES	read buffer segment [2])	
BX	read buffer offset [2])	
Carry		error if < > 0

[1]) see F.2
[2]) the read buffer must have 516 bytes for each sector to be read (512 sector bytes plus 4 check bytes)

Function 0Bh – Extended Write (Hard Disk)

This function writes one or up to 127 sectors together with their ECC check bytes from the write buffer in main memory onto the hard disk. The controller's ECC logic does not generate ECC bytes on its own, but writes the passed ECC bytes without any changes into the ECC field of the sector.

Register	Call value	Return value
AH	0Bh	error code[1]
AL	number of sectors to write	
CH	cylinder	
CL	sector	
DH	head	
DL	drive	
ES	write buffer segment[2]	
BX	write buffer offset[2]	
Carry		error if < > 0

[1] see F.2
[2] the write buffer must have 516 bytes (512 sector bytes plus 4 check bytes) for each sector to be written; the check bytes are not calculated by the controller, but are written directly from the buffer

Function 0Ch – Seek (Hard Disk)

This function moves the read/write head to a certain track or cylinder.

Register	Call value	Return value
AH	0Ch	error code[*]
CX	cylinder	
DH	head	
DL	drive	
Carry		error if < > 0

[*] see F.2

Function 0Dh – Hard Disk Reset (Hard Disk)

This function resets the addressed drive.

Register	Call value	Return value
AH	0Dh	error code[*]
DL	drive	
Carry		error if < > 0

[*] see F.2

Function 0Eh – Read Buffer (Hard Disk)

This function transfers 512 bytes from the controller's sector buffer into the read buffer in main memory. No data is read from the volume. The function mainly checks the data path between controller and main memory.

Register	Call value	Return value
AH	0Eh	error code*)
DL	drive	
ES	read buffer segment	
BX	read buffer offset	
Carry		error if < > 0

*) see F.2

Function 0Fh – Write Buffer (Hard Disk)

This function transfers 512 bytes from the write buffer in main memory into the controller's sector buffer. No data is written onto the volume. The function mainly checks the data path between controller and main memory.

Register	Call value	Return value
AH	0Fh	error code*)
DL	drive	
ES	write buffer segment	
BX	write buffer offset	
Carry		error if < > 0

*) see F.2

Function 10h – Test Drive Ready (Hard Disk)

This function determines whether the hard disk is ready, and if not, determines the error status.

Register	Call value	Return value
AH	10h	error code*)
DL	drive	
Carry		error if < > 0

*) see F.2

Function 11h – Calibrate Drive (Hard Disk)

This function moves the read/write head to track 0.

Register	Call value	Return value
AH	11h	error code*)
DL	drive	
Carry		error if < > 0

*) see F.2

Function 12h – Check Controller RAM (Hard Disk)

This function checks the controller RAM, and investigates controller errors.

Register	Call value	Return value
AH	12h	error code*)
DL	drive	
Carry		error if < > 0

*) see F.2

Function 13h – Drive Diagnostics (Hard Disk)

The controller checks the drive and determines the error status, if necessary.

Register	Call value	Return value
AH	13h	error code*)
DL	drive	
Carry		error if < > 0

*) see F.2

Function 15h – Determine Drive Type (Floppy Drive)

This function determines the type of the addressed drive (AT and PS/2).

Register	Call value	Return value
AH	15h	type*)
DL	drive	
Carry		error if < > 0

*) 00h=no drive installed, 01h=drive without connection for disk change
02h=drive with connection for disk change, 03h=hard disk

Function 16h – Determine Disk Change (Floppy Drive)

This function determines whether the disk has been changed (AT and PS/2).

Register	Call value	Return value
AH	16h	change flag*)
DL	drive	
Carry		error if < > 0

*) 00h=no change, 01h=invalid drive number, 06h=disk changed

Function 17h – Fix Floppy Disk Format (Floppy Drive)

This function fixes the controller-drive data transfer rate by means of the disk format. This is necessary, for example, to use a 360 kbyte floppy disk in a 1.2 Mbyte high density drive.

Register	Call value	Return value
AH	17h	type or error code[1]
AL	disk format[2]	
Carry		error if < > 0

[1] drive type or see F.2
[2] 1=320/360 kbyte disk in 320/360 kbyte drive
   2=320/360 kbyte disk in 1.2 Mbyte drive
   3=1.2 Mbyte disk in 1.2 Mbyte drive
   4=720 kbyte disk in 720 kbyte drive

Function 18h – Fix Floppy Disk Format (Floppy Drive)

This function fixes the disk type for formatting. This is necessary, for example, to format a 360 kbyte floppy disk in a 1.2 Mbyte high density drive.

Register	Call value	Return value
AH	18h	type or error code[1]
CH	number of tracks	
CL	sectors per track	
DL	drive number	
DI		parameter table offset[2]
ES		parameter table segment[2]
Carry		error if < > 0

[1] 00h=no error, 0ch=medium unknown, 80h=no disk in drive
[2] see F.5

Function 19h – Park Read/Write Heads (Hard Disk)

This function moves the read/write heads to a certain cylinder and parks them.

Register	Call value	Return value
AH	19h	error code[*]
DL	drive	
Carry		error if < > 0

[*] see F.2

F.2   Error Codes

Error code (AH value)	Meaning	Valid for floppy	Valid for hard disk
00h	no error	yes	yes
01h	invalid function number	yes	yes
02h	address mark not found	yes	yes
03h	disk write-protected	yes	no
04h	sector not found	yes	yes
05h	unsuccessful reset	no	yes
07h	erroneous initialization	no	yes
08h	DMA overflow	yes	no
09h	DMA segment overflow	yes	yes
10h	read error	yes	yes
11h	data read error, ECC correction successful	no	yes
20h	controller error	yes	yes
40h	track not found	yes	yes
80h	no drive response	yes	yes
BBh	BIOS error	no	yes
FFh	unknown error	no	yes

F.3   Hard Disk Drive Parameter Table

AT Controller

Offset	Size	Contents
00h	word	number of cylinders
02h	byte	number of heads
03h	word	reserved
05h	word	precompensation start cylinder
07h	byte	reserved
08h	byte	control byte*)
09h	3 bytes	reserved
0Ch	word	landing zone for head parking
0Eh	byte	number of sectors per track
0Fh	byte	reserved

*) Bits 0–2: reserved, Bit 3: 1=more than 8 heads
   Bit 4: reserved
   Bit 5: defect list at max.cylinder+1
   Bit 6: disable ECC retries
   Bit 7: disable seek retries

XT Controller

Offset	Size	Contents
00h	word	number of cylinders
02h	byte	number of heads
03h	word	reduced write current start cylinder
05h	word	precompensation start cylinder
07h	byte	max. ECC data burst length
08h	byte	control byte [1]
09h	byte	standard time-out value [2]
0Ah	byte	formatting time-out [2]
0Bh	byte	drive check time-out [2]
0Ch	4 bytes	reserved

[1] bits 0–2: drive option, bits 3–5: reserved
   bit 6: disable ECC retries
   bit 7: disable seek retries
[2] in units of timer ticks

F.4 Format Buffer

Offset	Size	Contents
00h	byte	track of sector to format
01h	byte	head of sector to format
02h	byte	sector number
03h	byte	number of bytes per sector [1]

[1] 0=128, 1=256, 2=512, 3=1024

F.5 Floppy Disk Parameter Table

The parameter table is located in the DOS data area at address 50:22h.

Offset	Size	Contents
00h	byte	first specification byte [1]
01h	byte	second specification byte [2]
02h	byte	number of timer pulses until drive motor is off
03h	byte	number of bytes per sector [3]
04h	byte	sectors per track [4]
05h	byte	gap length in bytes [5]
06h	byte	data length in bytes [6]
07h	byte	gap length for formatting [7]
08h	byte	fill byte for formatting [8]
09h	byte	head settle time after seek [ms] [9]
0Ah	byte	motor start time in 1/8 seconds

1) bit 7...4=step rate [ms]

Entry	Data transfer rate			
	1M	500k	300k	250k
0h	8.0	16	26.7	32
1h	7.5	15	25.0	30
2h	7.0	14	23.3	28
...	...	...	...	...
eh	1.0	2	3.3	4
fh	0.5	1	1.7	2

bit 3...0=head unload time [ms]

Entry	Data transfer rate			
	1M	500k	300k	250k
0h	128	256	426	512
1h	8	16	26.7	32
2h	16	32	53.5	64
...	...	...	...	...
eh	112	224	373	448
fh	120	240	400	480

2) bit 7...1: head load time [ms]

Entry	Data transfer rate			
	1M	500k	300k	250k
00h	128	256	426	512
01h	1	2	3.3	4
02h	2	4	6.7	8
...	...	...	...	...
7eh	126	252	420	504
7fh	127	254	423	508

bit 0=non-DMA mode: 1=no DMA, 0=DMA used
3) 0=128, 1=256, 2=512, 3=1024
4) 08h=8 sectors/track, 09h=9 sectors/track, 15h=15 sectors/track, 18h=18 sectors/track
5) 1bh for 1.2 Mbyte and 1.44 Mbyte, else 2ah
6) insignificant, mostly equal ffh
7) 50h for 360 kbytes/720 kbytes, 54h for 1.2 Mbyte, 6ch for 1.44 Mbyte
8) standard: f6h corresponding to '÷'
9) standard: 0fh

G Floppy Disk Controllers

G.1 The Commands

- The specifications cylinder, head, sector number, and sector size are called the *sector identification*.

- Before you can transfer a command byte or read a status byte in the result phase, you must read bit MRQ in the main status register to determine whether the data register is ready to receive or supply a byte.

- All command and status bytes are transferred via the data register (port 3f7h or 377h).

- The transfer of the read data or data to be written between main memory and controller is normally done via DMA; for this you have to program the DMA control before the transfer of a command.

- If you want to use interrupt-driven data exchange or polling instead of DMA transfer, read the notes in Section 9.7.5.

- Read and write commands concern all sectors from the start sector up to the end of the track; you can abort the read or write operation earlier by setting the count value of the DMA controller such that the DMA chip issues a TC signal after the desired number of sectors, or by setting the command byte *track length/max. sector number* to a value that indicates the last sector to be handled.

- If you set the multiple track bit M the controller executes the specified command not only for the programmed head but for the other head (i.e. for the opposite disk side) too; after the end of the track corresponding to the programmed head, the controller continues with the beginning of the track on the other disk side.

- After the command completion the status registers ST0 to ST3 contain status information which helps you confirm the correct execution of the command, or determine the cause of an error.

- In advance of a read, write, or format operation, you first have to fix the drive format.

- The commands are divided into data transfer commands, control commands, and extended commands, which are available on an AT or PS/2.

G.1.1   List of Valid Commands

- Data transfer commands
  read sector
  read deleted sector
  write sector
  write deleted sector
  read complete track
  format track

- Control commands
  read identification
  calibrate drive
  check interrupt status
  fix drive data
  check drive status
  seek
  invalid command

- Extended commands
  verify
  determine controller version
  seek relative
  register summary

G.1.2   Data Transfer Commands

Read Sector

This command reads one or more sectors with a valid data address mark from disk and transfers the data into main memory.

Command Phase

bit byte	7	6	5	4	3	2	1	0
0	M	F	S	0	0	1	1	0
1	x	x	x	x	x	HD	LW1	LW0
2	cylinder							
3	head							
4	sector number							
5	sector size							
6	track length/max. sector number							
7	length of GAP 3							
8	data length							

M: multi-track operation
    1=carry out cylinder operation   0=carry out single track operation
F: FM or MFM recording method
    1=MFM (standard)   0=FM
S: skip mode
    1=skip deleted data address marks   0=do not skip
HD: head number (always equal head address in byte 3)
LW1, LW2: drive
    00=drive 0 (A)   01=drive 1 (B)   10=drive 2 (C)   11=drive 3 (D)
Cylinder, head, sector number: address of first sector to read
Sector size: 0=128 bytes   1=256 bytes   2=512 bytes   ...   7=16kbytes
Track length/max. sector number: number of sectors per track or max. sector number, for which the
                                   command shall be carried out
Length of GAP 3: standard value=42, minimal value=32 (5 1/4") or standard value=27 (3 1/2")
data length: length of data to read in bytes (only valid if sector size=00), else equal ffh

Result Phase

	7 0
0	ST0
1	ST1q
2	ST2
3	cylinder
4	head
5	sector number
6	sector size

ST0, ST1, ST2: status register 0 to 2 (see G.2)
Cylinder, head, sector number, sector size: sector identification according to Table G.1

Read Deleted Sector

This command reads one sector with a deleted data address mark from disk and transfers the data into main memory. Sectors with a correct data address mark cannot be accessed by means of this command.

Command Phase

bit byte	7	6	5	4	3	2	1	0
0	M	F	S	0	1	1	0	0
1	x	x	x	x	x	HD	LW1	LW0
2	cylinder							
3	head							
4	sector number							
5	sector size							
6	track length/max. sector number							
7	length of GAP 3							
8	data length							

M: multi—track operation
     1=carry out cylinder operation   0=carry out single track operation
F: FM or MFM recording method
     1=MFM (standard)   0=FM
S: skip mode
     1=skip deleted data address marks   0=do not skip
HD: head number (always equal head address in byte 3)
LW1, LW2: drive
     00=drive 0 (A)   01=drive 1 (B)   10=drive 2 (C)   11=drive 3 (D)
Cylinder, head, sector number: address of first sector to read
Sector size: 0=128 bytes   1=256 bytes   2=512 bytes   ...   7=16 kbytes
Track length/max. sector number: number of sectors per track or max. sector number, for which the
                                   command shall be carried out
Length of GAP 3: standard value=42, minimal value=32 (5 1/4") or standard value=27 (3 1/2")
Data length: length of data to read in bytes (only valid if sector size=00), else equal ffh

Result Phase

	7 0
0	ST0
1	ST1
2	ST2
3	cylinder
4	head
5	sector number
6	sector size

ST0, ST1, ST2: status register 0 to 2 (see G.2)
Cylinder, head, sector number, sector size: sector identification according to Table G.1

Write Sector

This command transfers the data to be written from main memory to the controller, and writes one or more sectors with valid data address marks onto the disk.

Command Phase

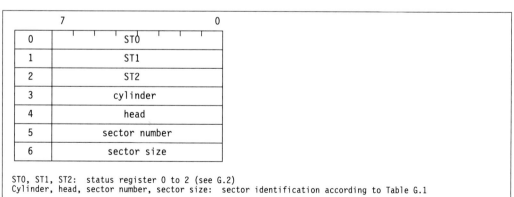

bit byte	7	6	5	4	3	2	1	0
0	M	F	0	0	0	1	0	1
1	x	x	x	x	x	HD	LW1	LW0
2	cylinder							
3	head							
4	sector number							
5	sector size							
6	track length/max. sector number							
7	length of GAP 3							
8	data length							

```
M:   multi-track operation
     1=carry out cylinder operation      0=carry out single track operation
F:   FM or MFM recording method
     1=MFM (standard)                    0=FM
HD:  head number (always equal head address in byte 3)
LW1, LW2:  drive
     00=drive 0 (A)   01=drive 1 (B)   10=drive 2 (C)   11=drive 3 (D)
Cylinder, head, sector number:  address of first sector to write
Sector size:      0=128 bytes   1=256 bytes   2=512 bytes   ...   7=16 kbytes
Track length/max. sector number:   number of sectors per track or max. sector number, for which the
                                   command shall be carried out
Length of GAP 3:  standard value=42, minimal value=32 (5 1/4") or standard value=27 (3 1/2")
Data length:      length of data to write in bytes (only valid if sector size=00), else equal ffh
```

Result Phase

	7	0
0	ST0	
1	ST1	
2	ST2	
3	cylinder	
4	head	
5	sector number	
6	sector size	

```
ST0, ST1, ST2:  status register 0 to 2 (see G.2)
Cylinder, head, sector number, sector size:  sector identification according to Table G.1
```

Write Deleted Sector

This command transfers the data to be written from main memory to the controller and writes one or more sectors onto disk. Simultaneously, the data address mark of the sector concerned is deleted so that this sector can be accessed only by the *read deleted sector* command.

Command Phase

bit byte	7	6	5	4	3	2	1	0
0	M	F	0	0	1	0	0	1
1	x	x	x	x	x	HD	LW1	LW0
2	cylinder							
3	head							
4	sector number							
5	sector size							
6	track length/max. sector number							
7	length of GAP 3							
8	data length							

```
M:   multi-track operation
     1=carry out cylinder operation      0=carry out single track operation
F:   FM or MFM recording method
     1=MFM (standard)                     0=FM
HD:  head number (always equal head address in byte 3)
LW1, LW2:  drive
     00=drive 0 (A)   01=drive 1 (B)   10=drive 2 (C)   11=drive 3 (D)
Cylinder, head, sector number:  address of first sector to write
Sector size:     0=128 bytes   1=256 bytes   2=512 bytes   ...   7=16 kbytes
Track length/max. sector number:   number of sectors per track or max. sector number, for which the
                                   command shall be carried out
Length of GAP 3:  standard value=42, minimal value=32 (5 1/4") or standard value=27 (3 1/2")
Data length:      length of data to write in bytes (only valid if sector size=00), else equal ffh
```

Result Phase

	7 0
0	ST0
1	ST1
2	ST2
3	cylinder
4	head
5	sector number
6	sector size

```
ST0, ST1, ST2:  status register 0 to 2 (see G.2)
Cylinder, head, sector number, sector size:  sector identification according to Table G.1
```

Read Track

This command reads the data of one complete track, starting with the first sector after the index address mark (IDAM), sector-by-sector without attention to the logical sector number given in the ID address mark. The track is regarded as a contiguous data block, and multi-track operations are not allowed; the command is limited to one single disk side. The read operation starts as soon as a signal on the IDX line indicates the passing of the index hole, i.e. the beginning of the track. Note that the available read buffer in main memory is large enough to accommodate all sectors of the track continuously. The sector specification in the command phase is ignored.

Command Phase

bit byte	7	6	5	4	3	2	1	0
0	M	F	S	0	0	0	1	0
1	x	x	x	x	x	HD	LW1	LW0
2	cylinder							
3	head							
4	sector number							
5	sector size							
6	track length/max. sector number							
7	length of GAP 3							
8	data length							

```
M:   multi-track operation
       1=carry out cylinder operation     0=carry out single track operation
F:   FM or MFM recording method
       1=MFM (standard)                   0=FM
S:   skip mode
       1=skip deleted data address marks  0=do not skip
HD:  head number (always equal head address in byte 3)
LW1, LW2:  drive
       00=drive 0 (A)   01=drive 1 (B)    10=drive 2 (C)   11=drive 3 (D)
Cylinder, head, sector number:  address of first sector to read, but ignored here
Sector size:      0=128 bytes   1=256 bytes   2=512 bytes   ...   7=16 kbytes
Track length/max. sector number:   number of sectors per track or max. sector number, for which the
                                   command shall be carried out
Length of GAP 3:  standard value=42, minimal value=32 (5 1/4") or standard value=27 (3 1/2")
Data length:      length of data to read in bytes (only valid if sector size=00), else equal ffh
```

Result Phase

	7 0
0	STO
1	ST1
2	ST2
3	cylinder
4	head
5	sector number
6	sector size

ST0, ST1, ST2: status register 0 to 2 (see G.2)
Cylinder, head, sector number, sector size: sector identification according to Table G.1

Format Track

This command formats one track. For each sector of the track to be formatted you have to provide a 4-byte format buffer which holds the sector identification of the corresponding sector (see Figure G.1). Note that you specify a sufficiently large and continuous format buffer for all sectors of the track. Before issuing the command you have to program the DMA control so that the controller can read the format buffer data successively via DMA channel 2. Alternatively, you can transfer the format data by means of interrupt-driven data exchange; the controller issues a hardware interrupt before formatting each sector. The handler then may transfer the 4-byte format information for the sector to be formatted next. The formatting starts after the drive has indicated the beginning of the track by providing a signal on the line IDX at the time the index holes passes through the photosensor. The sectors are formatted continuously until the drive again indicates the passage of the index hole by a signal on the IDX line. For the formatting process, the length of GAP is larger than is the case for reading or writing data. The bytes cylinder, head, sector number, and sector size don't have any meaning in the result phase here, but you have to read them out before you can program a new command.

Command Phase

bit byte	7	6	5	4	3	2	1	0
0	0	F	0	0	1	1	0	0
1	x	x	x	x	x	HD	LW1	LW0
2	sector size							
3	track length							
4	length of GAP 3							
5	fill byte							

```
F:   FM or MFM recording method
     1=MFM (standard)                 0=FM
HD:  head number (always equal head address in byte 3)
LW1, LW2:  drive
     00=drive 0 (A)   01=drive 1 (B)   10=drive 2 (C)   11=drive 3 (D)
Sector size:    0=128 bytes   1=256 bytes   2=512 bytes   ...   7=16 kbytes
Track length:   number of sectors per track
Length of GAP 3: standard value=80 (5 1/4") or 84 (3 1/2")
Fill byte:      byte to fill the sector's data area of the sectors (standard=0f6h corresponding to "÷")
```

Result Phase

	7 0
0	ST0
1	ST1
2	ST2
3	cylinder
4	head
5	sector number
6	sector size

```
ST0, ST1, ST2:  status register 0 to 2 (see G.2)
Cylinder, head, sector number, sector size:  invalid values, but have to be read in advance of a new
                                             command
```

00h	track
01h	head
02h	sector number
03h	sector size[1]

```
1) 0=128 bytes, 1=256 bytes, 2=512 bytes, 3=1024 bytes, ..., 7=16 kbytes
```

Figure G.1: Format buffer for one sector.

G.1.3 Control Commands

Read Sector Identification

This command reads the sector identification of the first ID address mark that the controller is able to detect. Thus you can determine the current position of the read/write head. If the controller cannot read any ID address mark between two pulses on the IDX line (i.e. after a complete disk revolution), it issues an error message. The bytes cylinder, head, sector number, and sector size in the result phase characterize the read sector identification.

Command Phase

bit byte	7	6	5	4	3	2	1	0
0	0	F	0	0	1	0	1	0
1	x	x	x	x	x	HD	LW1	LW0

```
F:    FM or MFM recording method
      1=MFM (standard)              0=FM
HD:   head number (always equal head address in byte 3)
LW1, LW2:  drive
      00=drive 0 (A)   01=drive 1 (B)   10=drive 2 (C)   11=drive 3 (D)
```

Result Phase

	7 0
0	ST0
1	ST1
2	ST2
3	cylinder
4	head
5	sector number
6	sector size

```
ST0, ST1, ST2:  status register 0 to 2 (see G.2)
Cylinder, head, sector number, sector size:  sector identification read
```

Calibrate Drive

This command moves the read/write head to cylinder 0. If a seek error has occurred in the course of a sector access you can move the head to an absolute cylinder to calibrate the drive again. The command doesn't implement a result phase, but issues an interrupt after completion. Immediately afterwards you should employ a command *check interrupt status* to determine the status information of the calibration operation.

The controller executes the command by setting the DIR signal to 0, passing the drive 79 step pulses at most, and checking the TRK0 signal of the drive after each step pulse. If the signal is active (i.e. the head is on track 0), the controller sets bit SE in status register 0 and aborts the command. If the TRK0 signal is not active even after 79 step pulses, the controller sets bits SE and EC in status register 0 and terminates the command. To calibrate the drive you may have to issue several calibration commands. That's especially true for floppy drives that handle more than 80 tracks. After completion of the command you should always determine, by means of a command *check interrupt status*, whether the head is correctly positioned over track 0. After power-up a calibration command is necessary to initialize the head position correctly.

Command Phase

bit byte	7	6	5	4	3	2	1	0
0	0	0	0	0	0	1	1	1
1	x	x	x	x	x	0	LW1	LW0

```
LW1, LW2:  drive
      00=drive 0 (A)    01=drive 1 (B)    10=drive 2 (C)    11=drive 3 (D)
```

Check Interrupt Status

This command returns status information about the controller state in the result phase if the controller has issued an interrupt. Interrupts are issued:

– at the beginning of the result phase of the commands
   read sector
   read deleted sector
   write sector
   write deleted sector
   read track
   format track
   read sector identification
   verify

– after completion of the following commands without the result phase
   calibrate drive
   seek
   seek relative

– for data exchange between main memory and controller, when interrupt-driven data exchange is effective and the controller doesn't use DMA.

The command resets the interrupt signal and determines the source of the interrupt via status register ST0. If you issue the command and no interrupt is pending, the status register ST0 returns a value 80h corresponding to the message *invalid command*.

Command Phase

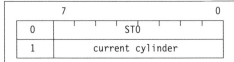

bit byte	7	6	5	4	3	2	1	0
0	0	0	0	0	1	0	0	0

Result Phase

7						0
0			STO			
1		current cylinder				

STO: status register 0 (see G.2)
current cylinder: current position of read/write head

Fix Drive Data

With this command you pass the controller mechanical control data for the connected drives. Note that the effective values are also dependent upon the selected data transfer rate. With a PC/XT controller the values are fixed, because the data transfer rate cannot be programmed and doesn't vary in this case. The command doesn't have a result phase.

Command Phase

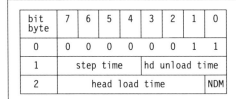

bit byte	7	6	5	4	3	2	1	0
0	0	0	0	0	0	0	1	1
1	step time				hd unload time			
2	head load time							NDM

NDM: non–DMA mode
       1=data transfer not via DMA   0=data transfer via DMA

step pulse time [ms]

entry	Data transfer rate			
	1M	500k	300k	250k
0h	8.0	16	26.7	32
1h	7.5	15	25.0	30
2h	7.0	14	23.3	28
...	...	...	...	...
eh	1.0	2	3.3	4
fh	0.5	1	1.7	2

head unload time [ms]

entry	Data transfer rate			
	1M	500k	300k	250k
0h	128	256	426	512
1h	8	16	26.7	32
2h	16	32	53.5	64
...	...	...	...	...
eh	112	224	373	448
fh	120	240	400	480

head load time [ms]				
	Data transfer rate			
entry	1M	500k	300k	250k
00h	128	256	426	512
01h	1	2	3.3	4
02h	2	4	6.7	8
...	...	...	...	...
7eh	126	252	420	504
7fh	127	254	423	508

Check Drive Status

In the result phase the command provides status information concerning the state of the connected drives.

Command Phase

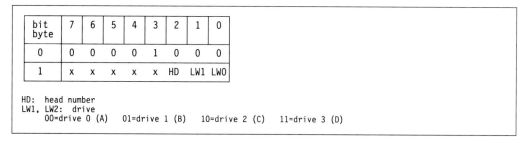

bit byte	7	6	5	4	3	2	1	0
0	0	0	0	0	1	0	0	0
1	x	x	x	x	x	HD	LW1	LW0

```
HD:  head number
LW1, LW2:  drive
         00=drive 0 (A)   01=drive 1 (B)   10=drive 2 (C)   11=drive 3 (D)
```

Result Phase

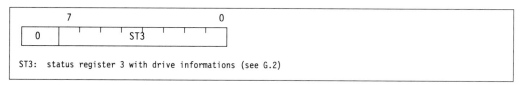

```
ST3:  status register 3 with drive informations (see G.2)
```

Park Read/Write Head

This command moves the read/write head to the park cylinder. For command execution the controller compares the current cylinder number with the programmed number, sets the direction signal (DIR) for the drive accordingly, and issues step pulses until both cylinder numbers coincide. The command has no result phase; you should therefore verify the head position immediately after command completion with the *check interrupt status* command.

Command Phase

```
HD:   head number
LW1, LW2:  drive
      00=drive 0 (A)    01=drive 1 (B)    10=drive 2 (C)    11=drive 3 (D)
Cylinder:  cylinder where the head should be moved to
```

Invalid Command

If you specify an invalid opcode, the controller switches to a standby state and sets bit 7 of status register ST3. The same applies if you issue a *check interrupt status* command and no interrupt is pending.

Command Phase

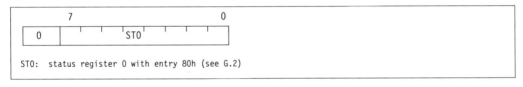

Result Phase

```
        7                        0
  ┌───┬──────────────────────────┐
  │ 0 │          ST0             │
  └───┴──────────────────────────┘

ST0:  status register 0 with entry 80h (see G.2)
```

G.1.4   Extended Commands

Verify

This command reads one or more sectors with valid data address marks from disk, calculates the CRC check sum, and compares the calculated and the read CRC values to check the internal consistency of the data. The command therefore behaves like a read command without data transfer to main memory. Thus the command cannot be aborted by a TC signal from the DMA controller. On the other hand, you must set bit EC to »1« to issue an implicit TC signal when the count value *data length/verify sectors* is decremented to 0. *Data length/verify sectors* therefore indicates the number of sectors to be verified; a value 00h checks 256 sectors. If you set EC equal to 0, you should give *data length/verify sectors* a value of ffh.

Command Phase

bit byte	7	6	5	4	3	2	1	0
0	M	F	S	1	0	1	1	0
1	EC	x	x	x	x	HD	LW1	LW0
2	cylinder							
3	head							
4	sector number							
5	sector size							
6	track length/max. sector number							
7	length of GAP 3							
8	data length/verify sectors							

```
M:   multi-track operation
     1=carry out cylinder operation    0=carry out single track operation
F:   FM or MFM recording method
     1=MFM (standard)                  0=FM
S:   skip mode
     1=skip deleted data address marks  0=do not skip
EC:  enable count value
     1=command byte 8 specifies the number of sectors to verify
     0=command byte 8 specifies the data length if sector size=00
HD:  head number (always equal head address in byte 3)
LW1, LW2:  drive
     00=drive 0 (A)    01=drive 1 (B)    10=drive 2 (C)    11=drive 3 (D)
Cylinder, head, sector number:  address of first sector to verify
Sector size:    0=128 bytes    1=256 bytes    2=512 bytes   ...   7=16 kbytes
Track length/max. sector number:   number of sectors per track or max. sector number, for which the
                                   command shall be carried out
Length of GAP 3:  standard value=42, minimal value=32 (5 1/4") or standard value=27 (3 1/2")
Data length/verify sectors:  length of data to read in bytes (valid only if sector size=00)
                             if EC=0 or number of sectors to verify if EC=1
```

Result Phase

	7 0
0	ST0
1	ST1
2	ST2
3	cylinder
4	head
5	sector number
6	sector size

```
ST0, ST1, ST2:  status register 0 to 2 (see G.2)
Cylinder, head, sector number, sector size:  sector identification according to Table G.1
```

Determine Controller Version

This command determines whether an extended controller which supports the extended commands is installed. A normal µPD765 regards the command code 00010000 as invalid opcode, and issues an error message.

Command Phase

bit byte	7	6	5	4	3	2	1	0
0	0	0	0	1	0	0	0	0

Result Phase (only if an extended controller is installed)

	7							0
0	1	0	0	1	0	0	0	0

Seek Relative

This command moves the read/write head relative to the current cylinder. The command doesn't have a result phase.

Command Phase

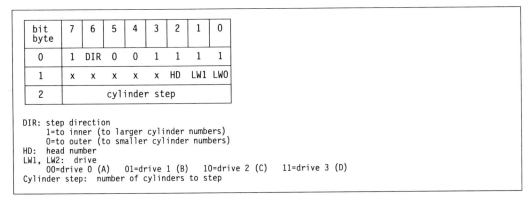

bit byte	7	6	5	4	3	2	1	0
0	1	DIR	0	0	1	1	1	1
1	x	x	x	x	x	HD	LW1	LW0
2	cylinder step							

```
DIR: step direction
     1=to inner (to larger cylinder numbers)
     0=to outer (to smaller cylinder numbers)
HD:  head number
LW1, LW2:  drive
     00=drive 0 (A)   01=drive 1 (B)   10=drive 2 (C)   11=drive 3 (D)
Cylinder step:  number of cylinders to step
```

Register Summary

This command reads internal controller registers, and provides their values in the result phase.

Command Phase

bit byte	7	6	5	4	3	2	1	0
0	0	0	0	0	1	1	1	1

Result Phase

	7　　　　　　　　　　　　　　　　0
0	current cylinder DR0
1	current cylinder DR1
2	current cylinder DR2
3	current cylinder DR3
4	step time ∣ hd unload time
5	head load time ∣ NDM
6	number of sectors/track length

Current cylinder DR0, DR1, DR2, DR3:　cylinder where the read/write head is currently positioned
Step time, head unload time, head load time: mechanical characteristics set by the command *fix drive data*
NDM: non—DMA mode
　　1=DMA disabled　0=DMA enabled
Number of sectors/track length:　number of sectors per track

MT	size	HD_{prog}	Last sector affected by command	Sector identification in the result phase			
				Cylinder	Head	Sector	Sector
0		0	before end of track	cyl_{prog}	HD_{prog}	sec_{prog}	siz_{prog}
0		0	end of track	$cyl_{prog}+1$	HD_{prog}	1	siz_{prog}
0		1	before end of track	cyl_{prog}	HD_{prog}	sec_{prog}	siz_{prog}
0		1	end of track	$cyl_{prog}+1$	HD_{prog}	1	siz_{prog}
1		0	before end of track	cyl_{prog}	HD_{prog}	sec_{prog}	siz_{prog}
1		0	end of track	cyl_{prog}	$\overline{HD}_{prog}$	1	siz_{prog}
1		1	before end of track	cyl_{prog}	$\overline{HD}_{prog}$	sec_{prog}	siz_{prog}
1		1	end of track	$cyl_{prog}+1$	$\overline{HD}_{prog}$	1	siz_{prog}

HD_{prog}:　programmed head　　　　cyl_{prog}: programmed cylinder
sec_{prog}:　programmed sector　　　siz_{prog}: programmed sector size
$\overline{HD}_{prog}$:　inverted value of HD_{prog} corresponding to opposite head

Table G.1: Sector identification in the result phase

G.2   Status Registers ST0 to ST3

The indicated status values are valid only if the corresponding status bit is set.

Status Register ST0

IC1, IC0: interrupt code
00=normal termination of controller command; the command was executed correctly and without any error
01=abnormal termination of the command; the controller has started the command execution but was not able to terminate it correctly
10=invalid command; the controller did not start command execution
11=abnormal termination by polling

SE: seek end
The controller has terminated a seek or calibration command or has correctly executed a read or write command with implicit seek.

EC: unit check
In a calibration command the TRK0 signal from drive was not set after 79 step pulses, thus the head did not reach track 0 after 79 pulses.

NR: drive not ready

HD: currently active head
1=head 1   0=head 0

US1, US0: currently selected drive (unit select)
00=drive 0 (A:)   01=drive 1 (B:)
10=drive 2 (C:)   11=drive 3 (D:)

Status Register ST1

EN: end of cylinder
The controller attempted to access a sector behind the end of the track, i.e. the last sector of the track. EN is set if, after a read or write command, no external or implicit TC signal is issued before the sector count exceeds the end of the track.

xx: bit unused; value always equal 0

DF: data error
The controller detected an error in the ID address field or the data field of a sector.

TO: time-out
The controller did not receive a signal from the DMA controller or the CPU within the required time period.

NDAT: no data
–   The controller cannot find the addressed sector in a *read sector* or *read deleted sector* command.
–   The controller cannot read the ID address mark in a *read identification* command without error.
–   The controller cannot determine the sector sequence in a *read track* command correctly.

NW: not writeable
The write-protection signal of the drive is active, i.e. the disk is write-protected while the controller is executing a write command.

NID: no address mark
–   The controller did not find an ID address mark after two IDX pulses, i.e. one complete disk revolution.
–   The controller cannot find a data address mark DAM or a deleted data address mark DAM on the specified track.

Status Register ST2

xx: bit unused; value always equal to 0

DADM: deleted address mark
–   The controller detected a deleted data address mark DAM when executing a *read sector* command.
–   The controller detected a valid data address mark DAM when executing a *read deleted sector* command.

CRCE: CRC error in data field
The controller detected a CRC error in the data field of the sector.

WCYL: wrong cylinder
The contents of the track address in the ID address mark differs from the track address in the controller.

SEQ: seek equal
- With a µPD765 the condition *seek equal* is fullfilled.
- Otherwise SGL is not used and is always equal to 0.

SERR: seek error
- With the µPD765 the controller did not find the corresponding sector when seeking on the cylinder.
- Otherwise SFEH is not used and is always equal to 0.

BCYL: bad cylinder
The track address in the ID address mark differs from the track address in the controller. The value is equal ffh and indicates a bad track with a physical error according to the IBM soft sector format.

NDAM: not data address mark DAM
The controller cannot find a valid or deleted data address mark DAM.

Status Register ST3

The bits in the status register ST3 directly indicate the state of the control lines of the selected drive.

7							0
ESIG	WPDR	RDY	TRK0	DSDR	HDDR	DS1	DS0

ESIG: error
- With a µPD765 the error signal of the drive is active, i.e. an error has occurred.
- Otherwise ESIG is not used and is always equal 0.

WPDR: write-protection
The write-protection line is active, thus the inserted disk is write-protected.

RDY: ready
- With a µPD765 the ready signal of the drive is active, i.e. the drive is ready.
- Otherwise RDY is not used and is always equal 1, thus the drive is always ready.

TRK0: track 0
The TRK0 signal of the drive is active, thus the head is above track 0.

DSDR: double sided disk
The DSDR signal of the drive is active, thus the drive is double-sided.

HDDR: head
The bit indicates the status of the HDSEL signals of the drive: 1=head 1 active 0=head 0 active

DS1, DS0: drive select
Both bits indicate the status of the select signals DS1 and DS0 of the drive: 00=drive 0 (A:) 01=drive 1 (B:) 10=drive 2 (C:) 11=drive 3 (D:)

H   Hard Disk Drive Controllers

H.1   The IDE Interface Commands

– The specifications cylinder, head, sector number and sector size are called the *sector identification*.

– The data and status registers are together called the AT task file.

– Before you can access a register you have to determine whether the BSY bit in the status register (1f7h) is cleared.

– The transfer of a command byte to the command register (1f7h) starts the corresponding command; therefore you have to load the parameter registers with the necessary values in advance.

– All sector and format data is read and written via the data register (1f0h) by means of programmed I/O (PIO); a data exchange is only possible if the BSY bit in the status register is cleared and the DRQ bit is set.

– The DRQ bit remains set until the sector, format and, eventually, ECC data are completely read or written.

– Read and write commands can last across several sectors, starting with the start sector if the value in the sector number register (1f1h) is larger than 1; a value of 0 in this register means that the corresponding command is executed for 256 sectors.

– After command completion, the status register (1f7h) and, eventually, the error register (1f1h) contain status information, which enables you to confirm the correct execution of the command or to determine the reason for a malfunction or command abortion.

– If erroneous read data is correctable by the ECC bytes, the controller sets the CORR error bit in the status register (1f7h), but the command execution is not aborted.

– The sector identification after command completion or abortion indicates the last handled sector or the sector where the error occurred, respectively.

– Most IDE hard disks can be operated in native and translation mode: in native mode the logical drive geometry coincides with the physical geometry; in translation mode the translation logic of the controller translates the physical geometry to a completely different logical geometry.

– Be careful when using the format command because drives in translation mode can behave unpredictably if you program this command; the IDE hard disk comes preformatted with the best interleave factor; the dynamic bad sector remapping remaps defect sectors to good ones, and later reformatting of the drive is therefore unnecessary.

– The multiple sector commands read sector and write sector issue an interrupt 76h via IRQ14 before or after processing each sector.

– The result phase of each command starts with a hardware interrupt via IRQ14.

– The IDE interface supports two physical drives at most; the master (drive select 0) and the slave (drive select 1).

– For the IDE interface, the eight commands of the original AT are required; in Appendix H.1.4 you will find the optional commands, introduced with the new IDE specification.

H.1.1   Summary of Listed Commands

– Required commands
calibrate drive
read sector
write sector
verify sector
format track
seek
diagnostics
set drive parameters

– Optional commands
read sector buffer
write sector buffer
identify drive

H.1.2   Required Commands

Calibrate Drive

This command moves the read/write heads to cylinder 0. After issuing the command by transferring the command byte to the command register, the controller sets the BSY bit in the status register and moves the head to track 0. When the seek is complete the controller clears the BSY bit and issues a hardware interrupt via IRQ14. After a seek error, the command can be used to recalibrate the drive.

Command Phase

```
┌─────────────────────────────────────────────────────────────────────┐
│  AT task file                          bit                            │
│  register                  7 │ 6 │ 5 │ 4 │ 3 │ 2 │ 1 │ 0             │
│ ─────────────────────────────────────────────────────────           │
│  command      (1f7h)       0   0   0   1   x   x   x   x             │
│ ─────────────────────────────────────────────────────────           │
│  drive/head   (1f6h)       1   0   1  DRV  x   x   x   x             │
│                                                                       │
│  x:    values insignificant (recommendation: 0)                       │
│  DRV: drive                                                           │
│       1=slave    0=master                                             │
└─────────────────────────────────────────────────────────────────────┘
```

Result Phase

AT task file register		bit 7	6	5	4	3	2	1	0
error	(1f1h)	x	NTO	ABT	x	NID	x	x	x
cylinder LSB	(1f4h)	0							
cylinder MSB	(1f5h)	0							
drive/head	(1f6h)	1	0	1	DRV	HD_3	HD_2	HD_1	HD_0
status	(1f7h)	BSY	RDY	x	SKC	DRQ	x	x	ERR

```
NTO:   1=track 0 not found              0=no error
ABT:   command abortion
       1=command aborted                0=command completed
NID:   1=ID mark not found              0=no error
DRV:   calibrated drive
       1=slave     0=master
HD₃-HD₀: active head (unchanged)
BSY:   busy
       1=drive busy        0=drive not busy
RDY:   ready
       1=drive ready       0=not ready
SKC:   seek
       1=complete          0=in progress
DRQ:   data request
       1=data can be transferred    0=no data access possible
ERR:   error
       1=error register contains additional error information
x:     unused, invalid
```

Read Sector

This command reads 1–256 sectors according to the value in the *sector count* register; a value of 0 means 256 sectors. The first sector is specified by the sector number, cylinder MSB, cylinder LSB, and head registers. After transfer of the command code, the controller sets the BSY bit in the status register, the addressed drive carries out an implicit seek, activates the corresponding read/write head, and reads the sector, eventually together with the ECC bytes, into the sector buffer. After the read of each sector the DRQ bit is set, and the controller issues a hardware interrupt 76h via IRQ14. The interrupt handler transfers the sector data into main memory. If all data words are transferred and at least one more sector is to be read, the controller sets the BSY bit again, clears DRQ and reads the next sector, etc. The sector identification is automatically updated, and always indicates the currently processed sector.

If a non-correctable data error occurs, the controller aborts the command and the sector identification defines the sector with the error. If the data error can be corrected by the ECC bytes, only the CORR bit in the status register is set, but the command is not aborted. If the long-bit L is set the controller executes a read-long command and the sector data, together with their ECC bytes, are read. In this case, the controller does not carry out an ECC check. DRQ is active until the last ECC byte is read by the host. The ECC data is transferred byte-by-byte, all other data is transferred word-by-word (16 bits).

Command Phase

AT task file register		bit 7	6	5	4	3	2	1	0
command	(1f7h)	0	0	1	0	0	0	L	R
sector count	(1f2h)	number of sectors to read							
sector number	(1f3h)	S_7	S_6	S_5	S_4	S_3	S_2	S_1	S_0
cylinder LSB	(1f4h)	Z_7	Z_6	Z_5	Z_4	Z_3	Z_2	Z_1	Z_0
cylinder MSB	(1f5h)	0	0	0	0	0	0	Z_9	Z_8
drive/head	(1f6h)	1	0	1	DRV	HD_3	HD_2	HD_1	HD_0

```
L:    long-bit
      1=sector data and ECC bytes are read      0=only sector data are read
R:    retry disable
      1=automatic command retry is not executed
      0=automatic command retry is executed
S7-S0: sector number
Z9-Z0: cylinder number (10-bit binary number)
DRV:   drive
      1=slave      0=master
HD3-HD0:  head number (binary number)
      0000=head 0    0001=head 1    0010=head 2    ...    1111=head 15
```

Result Phase

AT task file register		bit 7	6	5	4	3	2	1	0
error	(1f1h)	NDM	x	ABT	x	NID	x	UNC	BBK
sector count	(1f2h)	$0^{*)}$							
sector number	(1f3h	S_7	S_6	S_5	S_4	S_3	S_2	S_1	S_0
cylinder LSB	(1f4h)	Z_7	Z_6	Z_5	Z_4	Z_3	Z_2	Z_1	Z_0
cylinder MSB	(1f5h)	0	0	0	0	0	0	Z_9	Z_8
drive/head	(1f6h)	1	0	1	DRV	HD_3	HD_2	HD_1	HD_0
status	(1f7h)	BSY	RDY	x	x	DRQ	COR	x	ERR

```
*) in the case of command abortion, the register indicates the number of sectors still to be read
NDM:  1=data address mark not found     0=no error
NTO:  1=track 0 not found               0=no error
ABT:  command abortion
      1=command aborted                 0=command completed
NID:  1=ID mark not found               0=no error
UNC:  1=uncorrectable data error        0=no or correctable data error
BBK:  1=sector marked bad by host       0=no error
DRV:  drive
      1=slave      0=master
Z9-Z0, S7-S0, HD3-HD0: sector identification of sector last read
BSY:  busy
      1=drive is busy      0=drive not busy
RDY:  ready
      1=drive ready        0=not ready
DRQ:  data
      1=can be transferred      0=no data access possible
COR:  correctable data error
      1=occurred                0=no data error
ERR:  error
      1=error register contains additional error information
x:    unused, invalid
```

Write Sector

This command writes 1–256 sectors according to the value in the *sector count* register onto disk. The first sector is specified by the sector number, cylinder LSB, cylinder MSB, and head registers. After transfer of the command code, the controller sets the BSY bit in the status register, the addressed drive carries out an implicit seek and prepares the sector buffer for receiving the write data from main memory. Afterwards, the controller sets the DRQ bit and clears the BSY bit. The CPU must now transfer the sector data, eventually together with the ECC bytes, via the data register (1f0h) into the sector buffer. When the write data is transferred the controller clears the DRQ bit and sets the BSY bit again. Then the drive writes the data onto disk. If at least one more sector is to be written, the controller sets the DRQ bit, clears the BSY bit, and issues a hardware interrupt 76h via IRQ14. The interrupt handler now transfers the write data for the next sector from main memory to the data register, etc. The sector identification is automatically updated, and always indicates the current processed sector. After all sectors are written, the controller once again issues an interrupt via IRQ upon entering the result phase.

If a write error occurs, the controller aborts the command and the sector identification defines the sector with the error. If the long-bit L is set the controller carries out a write-long command, and the sector data together with the ECC bytes are written. In this case, the controller does not generate the ECC byte itself, but writes the tranferred byte onto disk without any change. DRQ is active until the last ECC byte is transferred by the host. The ECC data is transferred byte-by-byte, all other data is transferred word-by-word (16 bit).

Command Phase

AT task file register		bit 7	6	5	4	3	2	1	0
command	(1f7h)	0	0	1	1	0	0	L	R
sector count	(1f2h)	number of sectors to write							
sector number	(1f3h)	S_7	S_6	S_5	S_4	S_3	S_2	S_1	S_0
cylinder LSB	(1f4h)	Z_7	Z_6	Z_5	Z_4	Z_3	Z_2	Z_1	Z_0
cylinder MSB	(1f5h)	0	0	0	0	0	0	Z_9	Z_8
drive/head	(1f6h)	1	0	1	DRV	HD_3	HD_2	HD_1	HD_0

```
L:   long bit
     1=sector data and ECC bytes are written    0=only sector data are written
R:   retry disable
     1=automatic command retry is not executed
     0=automatic command retry is executed
S7–S0: sector number
Z9–Z0: cylinder number (10-bit binary number)
DRV:   drive
     1=slave    0=master
HD3–HD0:  head number (binary number)
     0000=head 0   0001=head 1   0010=head 2   ...   1111=head 15
```

Result Phase

AT task file register		bit 7	6	5	4	3	2	1	0
error	(1f1h)	NDM	x	ABT	x	NID	x	x	BBK
sector count	(1f2h)				$0^{*)}$				
sector number	(1f3h)	S_7	S_6	S_5	S_4	S_3	S_2	S_1	S_0
cylinder LSB	(1f4h)	Z_7	Z_6	Z_5	Z_4	Z_3	Z_2	Z_1	Z_0
cylinder MSB	(1f5h)	0	0	0	0	0	0	Z_9	Z_8
drive/head	(1f6h)	1	0	1	DRV	HD_3	HD_2	HD_1	HD_0
status	(1f7h)	BSY	RDY	WFT	x	DRQ	x	x	ERR

```
*) in the case of command abortion, the register indicates the number of sectors still to be written
NDM:  1=data address mark not found      0=no error
ABT:  command abortion
      1=command aborted                  0=command completed
NID:  1=ID mark not found                0=no error
BBK:  1=sector marked bad by host        0=no error
DRV:  drive
      1=slave     0=master
Z9-Z0, S7-S0, HD3-HD0: sector identification of sector last written
BSY:  busy
      1=drive is busy     0=drive not busy
RDY:  ready
      1=drive ready       0=not ready
WFT:  write fault
      1=occurred                    0=no write fault
DRQ:  data
      1=can be transferred          0=no data access possible
CORR: correctable data error
      1=occurred                    0=no data error
ERR:  error
      1=error register contains additional error information
x:    unused, invalid
```

Verify Sector

This command checks one or more sectors. The controller reads one or more sectors into the sector buffer and performs the ECC check, but doesn't transfer the read sector data to main memory. Therefore, the check is carried out based on the ECC bytes only; the written sector data is not compared with the data in an external buffer. At the beginning of the result phase, the command generates a hardware interrupt 76h via IRQ14. Between the individual sector checks no interrupts are issued.

Command Phase

AT task file register		bit 7	6	5	4	3	2	1	0
command	(1f7h)	0	1	0	0	0	0	0	R
sector count	(1f2h)	number of sectors to verify							
sector number	(1f3h)	S_7	S_6	S_5	S_4	S_3	S_2	S_1	S_0
cylinder LSB	(1f4h)	Z_7	Z_6	Z_5	Z_4	Z_3	Z_2	Z_1	Z_0
cylinder MSB	(1f5h)	0	0	0	0	0	0	Z_9	Z_8
drive/head	(1f6h)	1	0	1	DRV	HD_3	HD_2	HD_1	HD_0

R: retry disable
   1=automatic command retry is not executed
   0=automatic command retry is executed
S_7–S_0: sector number
Z_9–Z_0: cylinder number (10–bit binary number)
DRV: drive
   1=slave   0=master
HD_3–HD_0: head number (binary number)
   0000=head 0   0001=head 1   0010=head 2   ...   1111=head 15

Result Phase

AT task file register		bit 7	6	5	4	3	2	1	0
error	(1f1h)	NDM	x	ABT	x	NID	x	UNC	BBK
sector count	(1f2h)	$0^{*)}$							
sector number	(1f3h)	S_7	S_6	S_5	S_4	S_3	S_2	S_1	S_0
cylinder LSB	(1f4h)	Z_7	Z_6	Z_5	Z_4	Z_3	Z_2	Z_1	Z_0
cylinder MSB	(1f5h)	0	0	0	0	0	0	Z9	Z8
drive/head	(1f6h)	1	0	1	DRV	HD_3	HD_2	HD_1	HD_0
status	(1f7h)	BSY	RDY	x	x	DRQ	COR	x	ERR

*) in the case of command abortion, the register indicates the number of sectors still to be verified
NDM: 1=data address mark not found   0=no error
ABT: command abortion
     1=command aborted   0=command completed
NID: 1=ID mark not found   0=no error
UNC: 1=uncorrectable data error   0=no or correctable data error
BBK: 1=sector marked bad by host   0=no error
DRV: drive
     1=slave   0=master
Z_9–Z_0, S_7–S_0, HD_3–HD_0: sector identification of sector verified last
BSY: busy
     1=drive is busy   0=drive not busy
RDY: ready
     1=drive ready   0=not ready
DRQ: data
     1=can be transferred   0=no data access possible
COR: correctable data error
     1=occurred   0=no data error
ERR: error
     1=error register contains additional error information
x: unused, invalid

Format Track

This command formats one track of the hard disk. On most IDE drives the command can be used in native and translation modes, but the behaviour is rather different in these modes.

In native mode a low-level formatting of the addressed track is carried out. Immediately after you have passed the command byte, the controller sets the BSY bit and prepares the sector buffer for receiving the format data from the CPU. Then the controller clears the BSY bit, sets the DRQ bit, and waits for the transfer of 256 words with format data from the CPU. The CPU may now transfer the data via the data register (1f0h) to the sector buffer. The format data consists of two bytes for every sector of the track, where the low byte indicates the sector flag and the high byte the sector number. A sector flag 00h means a sector to format normally; a value 80h indicates a sector that has to be marked as bad. The format data is written into the format buffer with the low byte, i.e. the sector flag, first. Note that the format buffer always has to contain 512 bytes, even if the number of sectors per track is less than 256. The remaining format bytes are ignored by the controller, but have to be transferred so that the controller sets the BSY bit and starts the format operation.

If the transfer of the format data is complete, the DRQ bit is cleared and the BSY bit is set. The controller now starts the format operation of the addressed track. After detecting the index pulse that indicates the physical beginning of the track, the ID fields of the sectors are rewritten and the sector data fields are filled with the byte values 6ch corresponding to the character »l«. By means of the ID fields sectors or complete tracks can be marked as bad. After the formatting, the controller clears the BSY bit and issues a hardware interrupt 76h via IRQ14.

For a format operation in native mode you must therefore know the physical drive geometry very well. On a drive with zone recording, for example, it is absolutely necessary that you know all the borders of the individual zones and the number of sectors of each zone. You must transfer this number to the sector count register.

When formatting in translation mode the controller writes only the sector data filled with the byte values 6ch; the ID marks are not changed. That is actually not a real formatting operation, because the structure of the volume is not changed. For example, it is not possible to adjust the interleave value by this. For the number of sectors per track in this case you have to specify the logical sector number per track; the borders of the zone recording are insignificant. With other values most controllers respond with an error message *ID mark not found* and abort the formatting operation. In some cases, the controller can do something unpredictable. Low level formatting of IDE hard disks in translation mode is therefore very critical, and the normally very useful tools such as DiskManager or PCTools are of no value. To overwrite all sectors with 512 bytes, 6ch has the same effect as a format operation in translation mode.

Command Phase

AT task file register		bit 7	6	5	4	3	2	1	0
command	(1f7h)	0	1	0	1	0	0	0	0
sector count	(1f2h)	number of sectors per track							
cylinder LSB	(1f4h)	Z_7	Z_6	Z_5	Z_4	Z_3	Z_2	Z_1	Z_0
cylinder MSB	(1f5h)	0	0	0	0	0	0	Z_9	Z_8
drive/head	(1f6h)	1	0	1	DRV	HD_3	HD_2	HD_1	HD_0

Z_9–Z_0: cylinder number (10–bit binary number)
DRV: drive
    1=slave   0=master
HD_3–HD_0: head number (binary number)
    0000=head 0   0001=head 1   0010=head 2   ...   1111=head 15

Result Phase

AT task file register		bit 7	6	5	4	3	2	1	0
error	(1f1h)	NDM	x	ABT	x	NID	x	x	x
sector number	(1f3h)	S_7	S_6	S_5	S_4	S_3	S_2	S_1	S_0
cylinder LSB	(1f4h)	Z_7	Z_6	Z_5	Z_4	Z_3	Z_2	Z_1	Z_0
cylinder MSB	(1f5h)	0	0	0	0	0	0	Z_9	Z_8
drive/head	(1f6h)	1	0	1	DRV	HD_3	HD_2	HD_1	HD_0
status	(1f7h)	BSY	RDY	x	x	DRQ	x	x	ERR

NDM: 1=data address mark not found   0=no error
ABT: command abortion
       1=command aborted   0=command completed
NID: 1=ID mark not found   0=no error
Z_9–Z_0, S_7–S_0, HD_3–HD_0: sector identification of sector formatted last
DRV: drive
       1=slave   0=master
BSY: busy
       1=drive is busy   0=drive not busy
RDY: ready
       1=drive ready   0=not ready
WFT: write fault
       1=occurred   0=no write fault
DRQ: data
       1=can be transferred   0=no data access possible
ERR: error
       1=error register contains additional error information
x: unused, invalid

Seek

This command moves the read/write heads to the programmed track and selects the addressed head. Immediately after transfer of the command code, the controller sets the BSY bit and executes the seek. If the seek is completed correctly, the controller clears the BSY bit, sets the SKC bit, and issues a hardware interrupt 76h via IRQ14. Note that the disk need not be formatted for carrying out the command correctly. In translation mode the passed logical cylinder number is converted to a physical cylinder number, and the head is moved to the physical cylinder.

Command Phase

AT task file register		bit 7	6	5	4	3	2	1	0
command	(1f7h)	0	1	1	1	x	x	x	x
cylinder LSB	(1f4h)	Z_7	Z_6	Z_5	Z_4	Z_3	Z_2	Z_1	Z_0
cylinder MSB	(1f5h)	0	0	0	0	0	0	Z_9	Z_8
drive/head	(1f6h)	1	0	1	DRV	HD_3	HD_2	HD_1	HD_0

```
Z9-Z0: cylinder number (10-bit binary number)
DRV:   drive
       1=slave    0=master
HD3-HD0:  head number (binary number)
       0000=head 0   0001=head 1   0010=head 2   ...   1111=head 15
x:     unused, invalid
```

Result Phase

AT task file register		bit 7	6	5	4	3	2	1	0
error	(1f1h)	NDM	NTO	ABT	x	NID	x	x	x
cylinder LSB	(1f4h)	Z_7	Z_6	Z_5	Z_4	Z_3	Z_2	Z_1	Z_0
cylinder MSB	(1f5h)	0	0	0	0	0	0	Z_9	Z_8
drive/head	(1f6h)	1	0	1	DRV	HD_3	HD_2	HD_1	HD_0
status	(1f7h)	BSY	RDY	x	SKC	DRQ	x	x	ERR

```
NDM:   1=data address mark not found        0=no error
NTO:   1=track 0 not found                  0=no error
ABT:   command abortion
       1=command aborted                    0=command completed
NID:   1=ID mark not found                  0=no error
DRV:   drive
       1=slave    0=master
Z9-Z0, HD3-HD0: track identification of sector where head is moved to
BSY:   busy
       1=drive is busy    0=drive not busy
RDY:   ready
       1=drive ready    0=not ready
SKC:   seek
       1=complete    0=in progress
DRQ:   data
       1=can be transferred        0=no data access possible
ERR:   error
       1=error register contains additional error information
x:     unused, invalid
```

Diagnostics

This command starts the controller-internal diagnostics routine to check the controller electronics. The CPU can issue this command if the BSY bit is cleared. The RDY bit concerns only the drives, and is insignificant for the diagnostics command because only the controller and not the mechanical drives are checked. Note that the diagnostic information is returned in the error register (1f1h). The meaning of the individual error bits differs from the normal case; furthermore, after completion of the diagnostics command the ERR bit in the status register (1f7h) is always equal to 0. The seven low order bits in the error register contain a binary diagnostics code for the master drive; the high order bit indicates a summary error code for the slave drive.

Command Phase

AT task file register		bit 7	6	5	4	3	2	1	0
command	(1f7h)	1	0	0	1	0	0	0	0

Result Phase

AT task file register		bit 7	6	5	4	3	2	1	0
error	(1f1h)	SLF	MD_6	MD_5	MD_4	MD_3	MD_2	MD_1	MD_0
status	(1f7h)	BSY	x	x	x	DRQ	x	x	0

SLF: slave diagnostics code
            0=slave o.k. or slave not present
            1=error of slave in at least one diagnostics function
MD_6–MD_0: binary master diagnostics code
            1=master drive o.k.
            2=formatting circuit error in master drive
            3=buffer error in master drive
            4=ECC logic error in master drive
            5=microprocessor error in master drive
            6=interface circuit error in master drive
BSY: busy
            1=drive is busy   0=drive not busy
DRQ: data
            1=can be transferred   0=no data access possible
x: unused, invalid

Set Drive Parameters

This command sets the logical geometry of the addressed drive. In the sector count register you specify the number of logical sectors per logical track, and in the drive/head register you specify the number of logical heads of the drive. In translation mode the translation logic of the controller then translates the logical geometry to the real physical geometry of the drive. In translation mode, the drive uses this logical geometry to carry out those commands involving a disk access. The number of logical cylinders of the drive is an automatic result of the request that the number of all logical sectors cannot be larger than the physical sectors actually present. A change of the logical geometry of a hard disk, where data is already stored, inevitably results in complete data loss as the changed geometry destroys the logical structure of the file system.

Command Phase

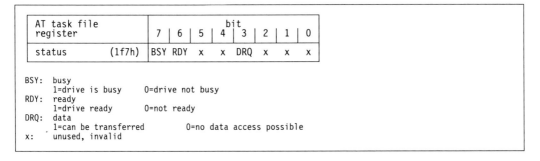

DRV: drive
     1=slave   0=master
HD$_3$–HD$_0$: number of logical heads of the drive

Result Phase

AT task file register		bit							
		7	6	5	4	3	2	1	0
status	(1f7h)	BSY	RDY	x	x	DRQ	x	x	x

BSY: busy
      1=drive is busy   0=drive not busy
RDY: ready
      1=drive ready   0=not ready
DRQ: data
      1=can be transferred   0=no data access possible
x: unused, invalid

H.1.3   Optional Commands

The following three commands are supported by most of the IDE hard drives, although they are optional commands and were not implemented in the original AT controller.

Read Sector Buffer

This command reads out the contents of the controller's sector buffer. Immediately after you have passed the command code, the controller sets the BSY bit and prepares the buffer for a read operation by the CPU. Afterwards, the BSY bit is cleared, the DRQ bit is set, and the controller issues a hardware interrupt 76h via IRQ14. The CPU now can read the sector buffer and transfer the data to main memory. The command serves mainly for checking the data path between controller and main memory. You can use the command in self-programmed diagnostic routines to determine the source of drive faults.

Command Phase

```
 AT task file              bit
 register          7 | 6 | 5 | 4 | 3 | 2 | 1 | 0
 command   (1f7h)  1   1   1   0   0   1   0   0
 drive/head (1f6h) 1   0   1  DRV  x   x   x   x

DRV: drive
     1=slave     0=master
```

Result Phase

```
 AT task file              bit
 register          7 | 6 | 5 | 4 | 3 | 2 | 1 | 0
 status    (1f7h) BSY RDY  x   x  DRQ  x   x   x

BSY:  busy
      1=drive is busy     0=drive not busy
RDY:  ready
      1=drive ready       0=not ready
DRQ:  data
      1=can be transferred     0=no data access possible
x:    unused, invalid
```

Write Sector Buffer

This command writes data into the controller's sector buffer. Immediately after passing the command code the controller sets the BSY bit and prepares the buffer for a write operation by the CPU. Afterwards, the BSY bit is cleared, the DRQ bit is set, and the controller issues a hardware interrupt 76h via IRQ14. The CPU can now transfer data from main memory to the sector buffer. The command serves mainly for checking the data path between controller and main memory. You can use the command in self-programmed diagnostic routines to determine the source of drive faults.

Command Phase

```
 AT task file              bit
 register          7 | 6 | 5 | 4 | 3 | 2 | 1 | 0
 command   (1f7h)  1   1   1   0   1   0   0   0
 drive/head (1f6h) 1   0   1  DRV  x   x   x   x

DRV: drive
     1=slave     0=master
```

Result Phase

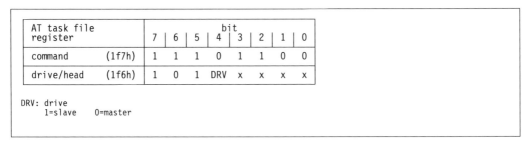

Identify Drive

This command reads parameters and other information from the addressed drive. Immediately after you have passed the command code, the controller sets the BSY bit, loads the information into the sector buffer, and prepares the buffer for a read operation by the CPU. Afterwards, the BSY bit is cleared, the DRQ bit is set, and the controller issues a hardware interrupt 76h via IRQ14. The interrupt handler has to read all 256 data words of 16 bits each out of the sector buffer. The structure of the 512 byte information is shown in Table H.1.

Command Phase

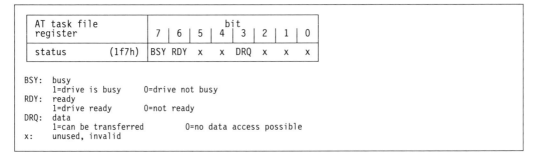

Result Phase

Word*)	Meaning
00	constant value 025ch
01	number of cylinders
02	reserved
03	number of heads
04	number of unformatted bytes per physical track
05	number of unformatted bytes per sector
06	number of physical sectors per track
07–08	reserved
09	constant value 0000h
10–19	ASCII serial number
20–21	reserved
22	number of ECC bytes which are transferred in read / write-long operation
23–26	ASCII identification of controller firmware
27–46	ASCII model number
47–255	reserved

*) 16-bit words

Table H.1: Sector buffer identification information

H.1.4   Optional IDE Commands

In the following table you will find all the IDE commands, together with the hex command codes, which are optional according to the newest IDE interface specification.

Command	Command code
check for active, idle, standby, sleep	98 e5
identify drive	ec
idle	97 e3
idle immediate	95 e1
read sector buffer	e4
read sector with DMA (with retry)	c8
read sector with DMA (without retry)	c9
read multiple sectors	c4
set features	ef
set multiple mode	c6
set sleep mode	99 e6
set standby mode	96 e2
standby immediate	94 e0
write sector buffer	e8
write sector with DMA (with retry)	ca
write sector with DMA (without retry)	cb
write multiple sectors	c5
write same sector	e9
write verification	3c
available for manufacturer	9a, c0–c3, 80–8f, f5–f
reserved	all other codes

H.2   SCSI Commands

–   All *reserved* fields have to be set to 0.

–   LSB characterizes the least significant byte, MSB the most significant byte of a multiple byte quantity.

–   The command codes are uniformly 6, 10, or 12 bytes long.

–   A command is executed in the following phases: transfer of the command code from the initiator to the target in the command phase –> transfer of the parameters and/or data from the initiator to the target in the data-out phase –> transfer of the result data from the target to the initiator in the data-in phase –> transfer of the status from the target to the initiator in the status phase –> transfer of messages from the target to the initiator in the message phase.

–   LUN indicates the logical unit within one target or one logical unit which is connected to the target. Examples are two hard disks (LUNs) connected to one SCSI controller (target).

–   SCSI manages all drives by means of so-called *logical blocks* which are continuous and equal in size. It is the job of the target to convert the logical block address, for example, in the case of a hard disk into physical cylinder, head, and sector numbers.

–   The error codes are provided at two levels: as a status key which indicates the error group; and the status code with a detailed error description.

H.2.1   Summary of Listed Commands

–   Only the SCSI-I commands are listed. The new and extended SCSI-II commands are omitted because a detailed description of these SCSI commands would really be far too much for this book.

–   6-byte commands
    test unit ready
    rezero unit
    request sense
    format unit
    reassign blocks
    read
    write
    seek
    read usage counters
    inquiry
    mode select
    reserve
    release
    mode sense

start/stop
read long
write long

– 10-byte commands
write and verify
read capacity
extended read
read defect data
extended write
extended seek
verify
write buffer
read buffer

H.2.2   6-Byte Commands

Test Unit Ready

With this command you can determine whether the addressed target drive is ready. If so, the target completes the command with the status *everything o.k.* A *request sense* command returns only a *no status*. Note that the status key is valid only after an extended request sense command to determine the cause of a not-ready state of the addressed drive.

bit byte	7	6	5	4	3	2	1	0
0	0	0	0	0	0	0	0	0
1	LUN			reserved				
2	reserved							
3	reserved							
4	reserved							
5	reserved						F	L

```
LUN:   logical unit number 0 to 7
F:     flag
       1=return messages with flag, if L=1    0=messages without flag
L:     link
       1=linked commands          0=single commands
```

Rezero Unit

This command moves the target back to the zero position, i.e. mostly to the beginning of the drive. On a hard disk this means that the read/write heads are moved to track 0.

bit byte	7	6	5	4	3	2	1	0
0	0	0	0	0	0	0	0	1
1		LUN			reserved			
2	reserved							
3	reserved							
4	reserved							
5	reserved						F	L

```
LUN:  logical unit number 0 to 7
F:    flag
      1=return messages with flag, if L=1    0=messages without flag
L:    link
      1=linked commands              0=single commands
```

Request Sense

This command instructs the target to return status data about the last executed command to the initiator. The target aborts the transfer of the status data if all available bytes have been transmitted to the initiator, or if the allocation length is exhausted. Note that the status data is only valid with a message *check status* for the preceding command as long as the target has not received any further command. The target transfers status data to the initiator during the course of a data-in phase. The status data consists of an 8-byte header and eventually of 14 or 19 more status bytes in accordance with the preceding command and the error. Only with an allocation length of 27 bytes (or more) can you be sure that all status bytes are transferred by the target. Whether and, if so, how many additional status bytes the target transfers in an extended form depends upon the entry *additional status length* in byte 7 of the status data. With an entry 14, additional status bytes are transferred, which indicates the physical location of the error; with an entry 19, on the other hand, the additional status bytes with the usage counter values are returned. The cause of the fault is the overflow of one or more of these counters.

bit byte	7	6	5	4	3	2	1	0
0	0	0	0	0	0	0	1	1
1		LUN			reserved			
2	reserved							
3	reserved							
4	allocation length							
5	reserved						F	L

```
LUN:  logical unit number 0 to 7
allocation length: number of bytes which the initiator reserves for the target's status data
      0=4 status bytes (SCSI-I)    0=0 status bytes (SCSI-II)
      1 ... 255: number of status bytes to transfer
F:    flag
      1=return messages with flag, if L=1    0=messages without flag
L:    link
      1=linked commands              0=single commands
```

head

byte bit	content
	7 | 6 | 5 | 4 | 3 | 2 | 1 | 0
0	VAL | class | error code
1	reserved
2	reserved | status key
3	logical block address (MSB)
4	logical block address
5	logical block address
6	logical block address (LSB)
7	additional status length

```
VAL:    valid
        1=logical block address (byte 3-6) valid    0=LBA not valid
class:  error class, for extended status class equal 7
error code: for extended status equal 0
status key: error group, see H.2.4
logical block address: identification of the block where the error occurred
additional status length: number of additional status bytes
        14=additional status bytes
        22=additional status bytes with usage counters

Additional status bytes
Byte    Contents
8       reserved
9       reserved
10      reserved
11      reserved
12      additional status code
13      reserved
14      reserved
15      reserved
16      reserved
17      retries
18      physical cylinder (MSB)
19      physical cylinder (LSB)
20      physical head
21      physical sector

Additional status code: see H.2.5
retries:    number of retries for read or write errors until the operation was successful;
            valid only for corrected errors, i.e. status key 01h
Physical cylinder, head, sector: physical identification of the sector where the error
                        occurred

Additional status bytes with usage counters
Byte    Contents
18      number of read blocks (MSB)
19      number of read blocks
20      number of read blocks (LSB)
21      number of seeks (MSB)
22      number of seeks
23      number of seeks (LSB)
24      number of uncorrectable read errors
25      number of correctable read errors
26      number of seek errors

Number of read blocks
Number of seeks                             see Table H.6:
Number of uncorrectable read errors         usage counter format
Number of correctable read errors
Number of seek errors

byte 8-17 are equal to above
```

Table H.2: Status

Format Unit

This command formats the whole drive by writing all ID and sector data fields. You must specify the block size and the geometric drive parameters, such as sectors per track, etc., in advance by a *mode select* command. If you do not, the target uses the same parameters as for a preformatted drive and the predetermined standard parameters for a non-formatted drive. Most SCSI hard disks contain a so-called manufacturer defect list, stored in one or more reserved tracks, which is managed by the controller. The target uses this list to correct the known defects by reassigning blocks. If you reformat a hard disk which has been in use for a long time, it may be possible that the function of the intelligent bad sector remapping has detected further defects and has repaired them by reassigning blocks in the background. Such defect entries are called a *grown defect list*, and are also stored in reserved tracks by the controller. In a format operation the initiator may further transfer additional defect parameters in a data-out phase. The data transferred by the initiator consists of a 4-byte header and zero or more 4-byte defect descriptors, whose structure is shown in Table H.4. The format command can be executed in one of three modes, which is determined by the bits *FMT* and *CMP* (Table H.3).

bit byte	7	6	5	4	3	2	1	0
0	0	0	0	0	0	1	0	0
1	LUN			FMT	CMP	defect form		
2	reserved							
3	interleave (MSB)							
4	interleave (LSB)							
5	reserved						F	L

```
LUN:  logical unit number 0 to 7
FMT:  format data             ┐
CMP:  complete                ├─ format mode, see Table H.3
defect form: defect list format ┘
interleave:  interleave value
     0=standard value (normally equal 1)
     valid values: 1 to (sectors per track − 1)
F:    flag
     1=return messages with flag, if L=1    0=messages without flag
L:    link
     1=linked commands             0=single commands
```

FMT	CMP	Defect form bit			Command	Description
		2	**1**	**0**		
0	x	x	x	x	P&G	format with **p**rimary and **g**rown defect list; no data-out phase with defect list from initiator
1	0	0	x	x	P&G&I	format with **p**rimary, **g**rown and defect list from **i**nitiator; data-out phase with defect list from initiator
1	1	0	x	x	P	format only with **p**rimary defect list; grown defect list is ignored; no data-out phase with defect list from initiator

x: value insignificant (recommendation: 0)

Table H.3: FMT, CMP and defect list

Header

Byte	Contents
0	reserved
1	reserved
2	length of defect list (MSB)
3	length of defect list (LSB)

The entry length of defect list indicates the total number of bytes in the following defect descriptors.

Descriptor

Byte	Contents
0	defect block address (MSB)
1	defect block address
2	defect block address
3	defect block address (LSB)

Table H.4: Initiator defect list

Reassign Blocks

This command instructs the target to replace defect logical blocks by intact blocks in a certain area of the drive which is reserved for this purpose. The initiator passes to the target a defect list which contains the blocks to reassign. The defect blocks are thus mapped to intact blocks so that all further accesses are diverted to the intact blocks. The data in the defective blocks is lost. If the capacity of the drive is not sufficient to reassign all specified defective blocks, the command aborts with a *check status* and the error key is set to *medium error*. The target automatically adds all blocks reassigned by this command to the known defect list. The defect list, which is transferred in a data-out phase by the initiator, consists of a 4-byte header followed by one or more defect descriptors with a length of 4 bytes each. The structure of head and descriptor is shown in Table H.5.

bit byte	7	6	5	4	3	2	1	0
0	0	0	0	0	0	1	1	1
1	LUN			reserved				
2	reserved							
3	reserved							
4	reserved							
5	reserved						F	L

```
LUN:  logical unit number 0 to 7
F:    flag
      1=return messages with flag, if L=1    0=messages without flag
L:    link
      1=linked commands              0=single commands
```

Header

Byte	Contents
0	reserved
1	reserved
2	defect list length (MSB)
3	defect list length (LSB)

The entry length of defect list indicates the total number of the bytes in the following defect descriptors.

Descriptor

Byte	Contents
0	defect logical block address (MSB)
1	defect logical block address
2	defect logical block address
3	defect logical block address (LSB)

Table H.5: Head and descriptor of the defect list

Read

This command instructs the target to read one or more blocks from the drive, and to transfer the data in a data-in phase to the initiator.

bit byte	7	6	5	4	3	2	1	0
0	0	0	0	0	1	0	0	0
1	LUN			LBA (MSB)				
2	logical block address							
3	logical block address (LSB)							
4	transfer length							
5	reserved						F	L

```
LUN:  logical unit number 0 to 7
logical block address:  number of block to read first
transfer length:        number of logical blocks to read
F:    flag
      1=return messages with flag, if L=1    0=messages without flag
L:    link
      1=linked commands              0=single commands
```

Write

This command instructs the target to receive one or more blocks from the initiator in a data-out phase, and to write it onto the medium.

Bit Byte	7	6	5	4	3	2	1	0
0	0	0	0	0	1	0	1	0
1	LUN			LBA (MSB)				
2	logical block address							
3	logical block address (LSB)							
4	transfer length							
5	reserved						F	L

```
LUN:  logical unit number 0 to 7
logical block address:  number of block to write first
transfer length:        number of logical blocks to write
F:    flag
      1=return messages with flag, if L=1    0=messages without flag
L:    link
      1=linked commands              0=single commands
```

Seek

This command positions the target at the specified logical block. In the case of a hard disk, the read/write head is moved to the track which contains the corresponding block (sector).

bit byte	7	6	5	4	3	2	1	0
0	0	0	0	0	1	0	1	1
1	LUN			LBA (MSB)				
2	logical block address							
3	logical block address (LSB)							
4	reserved							
5	reserved						F	L

```
LUN:  logical unit number 0 to 7
logical block address:  number of the block where the target is to be positioned
F:    flag
      1=return messages with flag, if L=1    0=messages without flag
L:    link
      1=linked commands              0=single commands
```

Read Usage Counters

Using this command you can read the usage counters of a target to determine the number of the read blocks, seeks, correctable as well as uncorrectable read and seek errors. The command also determines the load of a target in a SCSI system. After command completion, all counters are reset to 0. If an overflow has occurred, the target generates an error message in the next command. You can enable and disable the generation of an overflow error message with a mode select command. The counter values are transferred to the initiator in a data-in phase; the formats are shown in Table H.6. Alternatively, you can read the usage counters via an extended command *check status*.

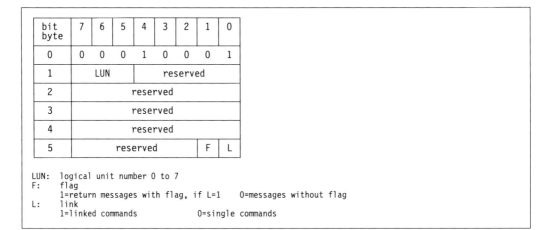

bit byte	7	6	5	4	3	2	1	0
0	0	0	0	1	0	0	0	1
1	LUN			reserved				
2	reserved							
3	reserved							
4	reserved							
5	reserved						F	L

```
LUN:  logical unit number 0 to 7
F:    flag
      1=return messages with flag, if L=1    0=messages without flag
L:    link
      1=linked commands              0=single commands
```

Byte	Contents
0	number of read blocks (MSB)
1	number of read blocks
2	number of read blocks (LSB)
3	number of seeks (MSB)
4	number of seeks
5	number of seeks (LSB)
6	number of uncorrectable read errors
7	number of correctable read errors
8	number of seek errors
Read blocks:	number of blocks which are read since power-on, the last read usage counters command or the last transfer of the values as status bytes
Seeks:	number of head seeks
Uncorrectable read errors:	number of uncorrectable read errors
Correctable read errors:	number of correctable read errors
Seek errors:	number of retry procedures to restore data

Table H.6: Usage counter format

Inquiry

This command transfers target parameters to the initiator in a data-in phase. The inquiry parameters comprise a 5-byte header and additional information. The format is shown in Table H.7. The target aborts the data-in phase as soon as all target parameters have been transferred or the reserved bytes are exhausted. The additional information depends upon the type and manufacturer of the target, and typically indicates the manufacturer's name, the product name, the version number, and the serial number. Therefore, the length of the additional information is manufacturer-dependent; SCSI host adapters use the *inquiry* command for initialization, and in many cases display the additional information on–screen during the course of the boot procedure.

bit / byte	7	6	5	4	3	2	1	0
0	0	0	0	1	0	0	1	0
1	LUN			reserved				
2	reserved							
3	reserved							
4	allocation length							
5	reserved						F	L

```
LUN:   logical unit number 0 to 7
allocation length:   number of bytes which are reserved by the initiator to receive the target parameters;
                     a value of 0 means that no target parameters are transferred
F:     flag
       1=return messages with flag, if L=1    0=messages without flag
L:     link
       1=linked commands              0=single commands
```

byte bit	7	6	5	4	3	2	1	0
				contents				
0	unit type code							
1	RMB	unit type indicator						
2	ISO		ECMA			ANSI		
3	reserved				0	0	0	1
4	additional length							

Unit type code: 00h=LUN 0   7fh=else
RMB: bit for removable medium
       1=removable medium (tape drive, optical drive etc.)
       0=non-removable medium (hard disk drive etc.)
Unit type indicator: user-specific code which can be set via a command mode select
ISO, ECMA, ANSI: modification number of the corresponding implemented standard according to
                 ISO, ECMA or ANSI; most SCSI drives use ANSI standard
Additional length: number of following additional information bytes

Table H.7: Target parameter header

Mode Select

This command enables the initiator to set or alter the target parameters. The initiator transfers a list of mode parameters to the target in a data-out phase. The list comprises a 4-byte header which may be followed by a block descriptor and zero or more page descriptors. In Table H.8 you can see their formats. Each page descriptor holds information for the target concerning a certain function class, the descriptions of which are shown in Table H.9. The descriptors can be transferred in any order, and the target uses class-specific standard settings if no descriptor is passed for a class. Many parameters depend upon the drive type and the manufacturer, so that no generally valid statements are possible.

Bit Byte	7	6	5	4	3	2	1	0
0	0	0	0	1	0	1	0	1
1	LUN			PF	reserved			SP
2	reserved							
3	reserved							
4	length of parameter list							
5	reserved						F	L

LUN: logical unit number 0 to 7
PF: page format (ignored in most cases as the mode select parameters are always processed in page
      format)
      1=page format
SP: save mode parameters (ignored in most cases as the mode select parameters are always stored by the
      target)
      1=save parameters   0=do not save
length of parameter list: number of mode select data bytes
F: flag
      1=return messages with flag, if L=1   0=messages without flag
L: link
      1=linked commands   0=single commands

```
Head

Byte    Contents

0       reserved
1       medium type
2       reserved
3       block descriptor length

Medium type:            00h=hard disk
Block descriptor length: length of the following block descriptors in byte

Block descriptor

Byte    Contents

0       density code
1       number of blocks (MSB)
2       number of blocks
3       number of blocks (LSB)
4       reserved
5       block length (MSB)
6       block length
7       block length (LSB)

Density code:  standard medium density
               00h=hard disk
Number of blocks:  number of formatted blocks or blocks to be formatted; 0=max. number of possible blocks
                   for the chosen block length
Block length:  size of each block in byte

Page descriptor
```

Byte	Contents
0	0 0 page code
1	page length
2	dependent on page code*)
....	....
n	dependent on page code

```
*) see below
page code:  00h=operation parameters (dependent on drive type and manufacturer)
            01h=error recovery parameters   02h=separation parameters   03h=format parameters
            04h=geometry parameters    05h...1fh=reserved
            20h=serial number of drive   21h ... 3fh=reserved
            30h=customer identification   3ch=software identification
page length: length of page (entries 2 to n) in byte
```

Table H.8: Mode select parameters

Operation parameters (page code=00h, page length=2)

byte bit	7	6	5	contents 4	3	2	1	0
2	USG	0	0	ATN	reserved			
3	unit type indicator							

USG: usage
    1=overflow of usage counters leads to error message in the following command
    0=error message disabled
ATN: attention
    1=condition check state is not transferred when attention condition is active
unit type indicator: user-specific information which is additionally transferred with an
                     inquiry command

Error recovery parameters (page code=01h, page length=6)

byte bit	7	6	5	contents 4	3	2	1	0
2	0	0	TB	0	0	PER	DTE	DCR
3	reserved							
4	reserved							
5	reserved							
6	reserved							
7	reserved							

TB: transfer block
    1=bad data block is transferred to initiator
    0=bad data block is not transferred to initiator
PER: post error bit
    1=message check state is provided for corrected error
    0=message is not provided
DTE: disable transfer on error
    1=retry disabled (if PER=1)
    0=retry possible
DCR: disable correction
    1=error correction disabled
    0=normal error correction procedure with retry and ECC

Separation parameters (page code=02h, page length=10)

Byte	Contents
2	reserved
3	reserved
4	reserved
5	reserved
6	reserved
7	reserved
8	reserved
9	reserved
10	reserved
11	reserved

No special data; reserved for future use

Table H.9: Page descriptors

Format parameters (page code=03h, page length=22)

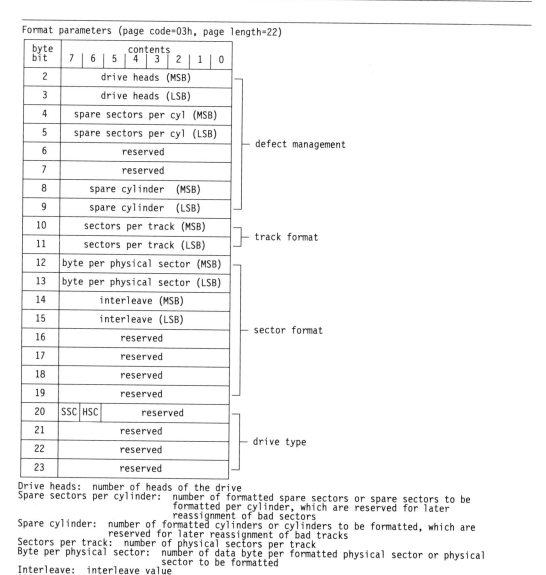

byte bit	contents
	7 | 6 | 5 | 4 | 3 | 2 | 1 | 0
2	drive heads (MSB)
3	drive heads (LSB)
4	spare sectors per cyl (MSB)
5	spare sectors per cyl (LSB)
6	reserved
7	reserved
8	spare cylinder (MSB)
9	spare cylinder (LSB)
10	sectors per track (MSB)
11	sectors per track (LSB)
12	byte per physical sector (MSB)
13	byte per physical sector (LSB)
14	interleave (MSB)
15	interleave (LSB)
16	reserved
17	reserved
18	reserved
19	reserved
20	SSC | HSC | reserved
21	reserved
22	reserved
23	reserved

- defect management (bytes 2–9)
- track format (bytes 10–11)
- sector format (bytes 12–19)
- drive type (bytes 20–23)

Drive heads: number of heads of the drive
Spare sectors per cylinder: number of formatted spare sectors or spare sectors to be formatted per cylinder, which are reserved for later reassignment of bad sectors
Spare cylinder: number of formatted cylinders or cylinders to be formatted, which are reserved for later reassignment of bad tracks
Sectors per track: number of physical sectors per track
Byte per physical sector: number of data byte per formatted physical sector or physical sector to be formatted
Interleave: interleave value
SSC: soft sector
       1=drive supports soft sector format
HSC: hard sector
       1=drive supports hard sector format

Table H.9: cont.

Geometry parameters (page code=04h, page length=18)

Byte   Contents

  2   number of cylinders (MSB)
  3   number of cylinders
  4   number of cylinders (LSB)
  5   drive heads
  6   reserved
  7   reserved
  8   reserved
  9   reserved
 10   reserved
 11   reserved
 12   reserved
 13   reserved
 14   reserved
 15   reserved
 16   reserved
 17   reserved
 18   reserved
 19   reserved

Number of cylinders: number of cylinders of the drive for data and defect management
Drive heads: number of read/write heads of the drive

Serial number (page code=20h, page length=9)

Byte   Contents

  2   serial number (MSB)
  3   serial number
  4   serial number
  5   serial number
  6   serial number
  7   serial number
  8   serial number
  9   serial number
 10   serial number (LSB)

Serial number: number in ASCII format

Soft ID (page code=3ch, page length=1)

byte bit	contents							
	7	6	5	4	3	2	1	0
7	ENA	reserved			SCSI ID		

ENA: software enable
          1=target uses SCSI ID of bits 0–2 as SCSI address and SCSI ID, respectively
SCSI–ID: target ID

Table H.9: cont.

Reserve

This command reserves the corresponding logical unit for a SCSI device. This command, together with *release*, is the base for preventing access conflicts in systems with several initiators (host adapters). The command has two modifications: with a cleared PTY bit the logical unit is reserved for the initiator of the command; on the other hand, if PTY is set the unit is reserved for a third initiator, which is characterized by the SCSI ID. The complete logical unit and not just one block is affected by the reservation, which can only be cancelled by a release command of the corresponding initiator, by a reset message, or by a hardware reset.

bit byte	7	6	5	4	3	2	1	0
0	0	0	0	1	0	1	1	0
1	LUN			PTY	unit ID			0
2	reserved							
3	reserved							
4	reserved							
5	reserved						F	L

```
LUN:  logical unit number 0 to 7
PTY:  1=reservation for a third initiator
      0=reservation for the current initiator
unit ID:  SCSI ID of the third unit for which the LUN is reserved if PTY is set
F:    flag
      1=return messages with flag, if L=1    0=messages without flag
L:    link
      1=linked commands            0=single commands
```

Release

This command cancels the reservation of a logical unit for the initiator. If the unit has been reserved by a command from a third device the reservation can be cancelled only by a release command from the same initiator. For this the unit ID has to meet the ID of the initiator that issued the reserve command before.

bit byte	7	6	5	4	3	2	1	0
0	0	0	0	1	0	1	1	1
1	LUN			PTY	unit ID			0
2	reserved							
3	reserved							
4	reserved							
5	reserved						F	L

```
LUN:  logical unit number 0 to 7
PTY:  1=reservation for a third initiator
      0=reservation for the current initiator
unit ID:  SCSI ID of the third unit for which the LUN was reserved if PTY is set
F:    flag
      1=return messages with flag, if L=1    0=messages without flag
L:    link
      1=linked commands            0=single commands
```

Mode Sense

This command returns the medium and drive parameters of the target. By means of certain page parameter values, you can determine all changable parameters and standard values for the parameters. The status data is transferred from the target to the initiator in a data-in phase. The status data comprises a 4-byte header followed by zero or more block descriptors, and eventually additional drive parameters. Their formats are shown in Table H.10. The structure of the pages is indicated in Table H.9.

bit byte	7	6	5	4	3	2	1	0
0	0	0	0	1	1	0	1	0
1		LUN		PF		reserved		
2	PGP			page code				
3				reserved				
4			allocation length					
5			reserved				F	L

```
LUN:  logical unit number 0 to 7
PF:   page format (bit is ignored; mode data are always returned in page format)
      1=mode data are returned in page format
PGP:  returned page parameter values
      00b=current values      01=changeable values
      10b=standard values     11b=saved values
allocation length: number of bytes which are reserved by the initiator for the mode data
F:    flag
      1=return messages with flag, if L=1    0=messages without flag
L:    link
      1=linked commands              0=single commands
```

Mode data header

Byte	Contents
0	length of mode data
1	medium type
2	reserved
3	block descriptor length

Length of mode data: mode data in bytes excluding this byte 0
Medium type: 00h=hard disk
Block descriptor length: length of block descriptors in bytes

Block descriptor

Byte	Contents
0	density code
1	number of blocks (MSB)
2	number of blocks
3	number of blocks (LSB)
4	reserved
5	block length (MSB)
6	block length
7	block length (LSB)

Density code: standard medium density
                   00=hard disk
Number of blocks: number of formatted blocks or blocks to be formatted; a value equal 0 means the max.
                   number of blocks possible with the chosen block size
Block length: size of a block in bytes

Table H.10: Mode data

Page descriptor

byte	contents		
0	1	0	page code
1	page length		
2	dependent on page code*)		
....	....		
n	dependent on page code		

*) see below

Page code: 00h=operation parameters (dependent on drive type and manufacturer)
               01h=error recovery parameter   02h=separation parameter   03h=format parameter
               04h=geometry parameter   05h ... 1fh=reserved   20h=serial number of drive
               21h...3eh=reserved   3fh=all pages transferred
Page length: length of a page (entries 2 ... n) in bytes

Table H.10: cont.

Start/Stop

This command instructs the target to move the heads into transport position, or to move the heads out of this position. On many drives, additionally the spindle motor is switched off or on.

bit byte	7	6	5	4	3	2	1	0
0	0	0	0	1	1	0	1	1
1	LUN			reserved				IMM
2	reserved							
3	reserved							
4	reserved							STR
5	reserved						F	L

LUN: logical unit number 0 to 7
IMM: immediate
       1=status is transferred immediately after the beginning of the command execution
       0=status is transferred after command completion
STR: start
       1=position head on track 0 or equivalent track
       0=move head into transport position
F: flag
       1=return messages with flag, if L=1   0=messages without flag
L: link
       1=linked commands   0=single commands

Read Long

This command reads one block together with the ECC bytes from the target and transfers them in a data-in phase to the initiator. No error check and error correction is carried out by the target by means of the ECC bytes.

Bit Byte	7	6	5	4	3	2	1	0
0	1	1	1	0	0	1	0	1
1	LUN			LBA (MSB)				
2	logical block address							
3	logical block address (LSB)							
4	reserved							
5	reserved						F	L

```
LUN:  logical unit number 0 to 7
logical block address:  number of the block to read first
transfer length:        number of logical blocks to read
F:    flag
      1=return messages with flag, if L=1    0=messages without flag
L:    link
      1=linked commands             0=single commands
```

Write Long

This command instructs the target to receive one or more blocks together with the ECC bytes from the initiator in a data-out phase, and to write them onto the medium. The target doesn't generate the ECC bytes itself, but writes the data transferred by the initiator without any change onto the medium.

bit byte	7	6	5	4	3	2	1	0
0	1	1	1	0	0	1	1	0
1	LUN			LBA (MSB)				
2	logical block address							
3	logical block address (LSB)							
4	reserved							
5	reserved						F	L

```
LUN:  logical unit number 0 to 7
logical block address:  number of the block to write first
transfer length:        number of logical blocks to write
F:    flag
      1=return messages with flag, if L=1    0=messages without flag
L:    link
      1=linked commands             0=single commands
```

H.2.3   10-Byte Commands

Write and Verify

This command instructs the target to write the data received from the initiator in a data-out phase onto the medium. Afterwards, the target has to verify whether the data has been written correctly. With the CHK bit you can choose between two different verify modes. With the CHK bit cleared the target verifies the write operation by comparing the written data with the data which has been transferred by the initiator before. If CHK is set, the target only performs a medium verification, i.e. the target only checks whether the ECC bytes conform to the written data. If the verification leads to an error, the status key is set to compare error.

bit byte	7	6	5	4	3	2	1	0
0	0	0	2	0	1	1	1	0
1	LUN			reserved			CHK	0
2	logical block address (MSB)							
3	logical block address							
4	logical block address							
5	logical block address (LSB)							
6	reserved							
7	transfer length (MSB)							
8	transfer length (LSB)							
9	reserved						F	L

```
LUN:  logical unit number 0 to 7
CHK:  byte check
      1=verify by comparison     0=medium verification only via ECC
      logical block address: block to start write and verification with
      transfer length: number of logical blocks to write and verify
F:    flag
      1=return messages with flag, if L=1    0=messages without flag
L:    link
      1=linked commands          0=single commands
```

Read Capacity

The target returns information concerning the drive's capacity to the initiator. There are two execution forms of the command: if the PMI bit is cleared, the command transfers the logical block address (LBA) and the block length of the last logical block on the drive. LBA in the command code has to be equal to 0 in this case. If the PMI bit is set, the target transfers the LBA and the block length of the last logical block after the LBA in the command, after which a significant delay in data transfer occurs. This can be a cylinder boundary which requires a repositioning of the head. The capacity information is transferred during the course of a data-in phase. Table H.11 gives the structure of the capacity information.

bit byte	7	6	5	4	3	2	1	0
0	0	0	1	0	0	1	0	1
1	LUN			reserved				
2	logical block address (MSB)							
3	logical block address							
4	logical block address							
5	logical block address (LSB)							
6	reserved							
7	reserved							
8	reserved							PMI
9	reserved						F	L

LUN: logical unit number 0 to 7
PMI: partial medium indicator
  1=logical block address and block length of last block before a significant data transfer delay occurs
  0=logical block address and block length of last block
F: flag
  1=return messages with flag, if L=1   0=messages without flag
L: link
  1=linked commands   0=single commands

Byte	Contents
0	logical block address (MSB)
1	logical block address
2	logical block address
3	logical block address (LSB)
4	block length (MSB)
5	block length
6	block length
7	block length (LSB)

Table H.11: Capacity information

Extended Read

This command instructs the target to read one or more blocks from the drive, and to transfer the data in a data-in phase to the initiator. Unlike the normal reading of a block, here the logical block address comprises 32 bits and the transfer length 16 bits. Thus you can access volumes with a capacity of 4 G blocks and read 64 k blocks all at once.

bit byte	7	6	5	4	3	2	1	0
0	0	0	1	0	1	0	0	0
1	LUN			reserved				
2	logical block address (MSB)							
3	logical block address							
4	logical block address							
5	logical block address (LSB)							
6	reserved							
7	transfer length (MSB)							
8	transfer length (LSB)							
9	reserved						F	L

```
LUN:   logical unit number 0 to 7
logical block address:  number of the first block to read
transfer length:        number of logical blocks to read
F:     flag
       1=return messages with flag, if L=1    0=messages without flag
L:     link
       1=linked commands               0=single commands
```

Read Defect Data

This command instructs the target to transfer the medium defect data stored on the medium to the initiator in a data-in phase. The defect data comprises a 4-byte header and (depending upon the P and G bit of the command) a defect list, or additionally a reassign list, which indicates the reassignment of the defect blocks. The reassign list is passed after the defect list. In this case, defect and reassign lists are separated by four bytes of value ffh. Table H.12 gives the corresponding formats.

bit byte	7	6	5	4	3	2	1	0
0	0	0	1	1	0	1	1	1
1	LUN			reserved				
2	reserved			P	G	reserved		
3	reserved							
4	reserved							
5	reserved							
6	reserved							
7	allocation length (MSB)							
8	allocation length (LSB)							
9	reserved						F	L

```
LUN: logical unit number 0 to 7
P:   1=transfer manufacturer defect list only
G:   grown defect list (bit is valid only if P is also set)
     1=transfer defect list added by host and entries about the reassigned blocks
Allocation length: number of bytes which the initiator has reserved for the defect data to be transmitted
F:   flag
     1=return messages with flag, if L=1    0=messages without flag
L:   link
     1=linked commands               0=single commands
```

List head

byte bit	contents								
	7	6	5	4	3	2	1	0
0	reserved								
1	reserved			P	G	reserved			
2	length of defect list (MSB)								
3	length of defect list (LSB)								

P, G: type of transferred defect list
                               10=defect list only
                               11=defect list and reassignment list
                               00, 01=invalid
length of defect list: defect list length in bytes

Defect entry

Byte	Contents
0	cylinder (MSB)
1	cylinder (LSB)
2	head
3	sector

Cylinder, head, sector: defect sector identification

Reassignment entry

Byte	Contents
0	logical block address (MSB)
1	logical block address
2	logical block address
3	logical block address (LBA)
4	cylinder (MSB)
5	cylinder (LSB)
6	head
7	sector

Logical block address: block address of sector
Cylinder, head, sector: identification of sector which has been reassigned the block **address**

Table H.12: Defect list

Extended Write

This command instructs the target to receive one or more blocks in a data-out phase from the initiator, and to write them onto the medium. Unlike the normal writing of a block, here the logical block address comprises 32 bits and the transfer length 16 bits. Thus you can access volumes with a capacity of 4 G blocks and write 64 k blocks all at once.

bit byte	7	6	5	4	3	2	1	0
0	0	0	1	0	1	0	1	0
1	LUN			reserved				
2	logical block address (MSB)							
3	logical block address							
4	logical block address							
5	logical block address (LSB)							
6	reserved							
7	transfer length (MSB)							
8	transfer length (LSB)							
9	reserved						F	L

```
LUN:  logical unit number 0 to 7
logical block address:  number of the block to write first
transfer length:        number of logical blocks to write
F:    flag
      1=return messages with flag, if L=1   0=messages without flag
L:    link
      1=linked commands           0=single commands
```

Extended Seek

This command moves the target to the specified logical block. In the case of a hard disk drive, the read/write head is positioned on that track which contains the corresponding block (sector). Unlike the normal seek, here the logical block address is 32 bits wide, thus you can access volumes with a capacity of 4 G blocks.

bit byte	7	6	5	4	3	2	1	0
0	0	0	1	0	1	0	1	1
1	LUN			reserved				
2	logical block address (MSB)							
3	logical block address							
4	logical block address							
5	logical block address (LSB)							
6	reserved							
7	reserved							
8	reserved							
9	reserved						F	L

```
LUN:    logical unit number 0 to 7
logical block address:  number of the block where the drive is to be positioned
F:      flag
        1=return messages with flag, if L=1    0=messages without flag
L:      link
        1=linked commands                   0=single commands
```

Verify

This command instructs the target to verify the data written onto the medium. Using the CHK bit, you can choose between two different verify modes. With the CHK bit cleared the target verifies the write operation by comparing the written data with data transferred by the initiator in a data-out phase. If CHK is set the target only performs a medium verification; the target only checks whether the ECC bytes conform to the written data. If the verification leads to an error, the status key is set to compare error. The command is similar to *write and verify*, but the data transferred with a deleted CHK bit are not written onto the medium.

bit byte	7	6	5	4	3	2	1	0
0	0	0	1	0	1	1	1	1
1	LUN			reserved			CHK	0
2	logical block address (MSB)							
3	logical block address							
4	logical block address							
5	logical block address (LSB)							
6	reserved							
7	verify length (MSB)							
8	verify length (LSB)							
9	reserved						F	L

```
LUN:    logical unit number 0 to 7
CHK:    byte check
        1=verify by comparison     0=medium verification only via ECC
logical block address: block where to start verification
transfer length: number of logical blocks to verify
F:      flag
        1=return messages with flag, if L=1    0=messages without flag
L:      link
        1=linked commands               0=single commands
```

Write Buffer

This command instructs the target to write the data transferred by the initiator in a data-out phase into its buffer memory. The transferred write data comprises a 4-byte header and the write data itself. The header format is shown in Table H.13.

bit byte	7	6	5	4	3	2	1	0
0	0	0	1	1	1	0	1	1
1	LUN			reserved				
2	reserved							
3	reserved							
4	reserved							
5	reserved							
6	reserved							
7	allocation length (MSB)							
8	allocation length (LSB)							
9	reserved						F	L

```
LUN:  logical unit number 0 to 7
allocation length: number of max. transferred data including header which are stored by the target
F:    flag
      1=return messages with flag, if L=1    0=messages without flag
L:    link
      1=linked commands              0=single commands
```

Byte	Contents
0	reserved
1	reserved
2	reserved
3	reserved

Table H.13: Buffer data header

Read Buffer

This command instructs the target to transfer the indicated number of bytes in a data-in phase from its buffer memory to the initiator. The transferred read data comprises a 4-byte header and the read data itself. The header format is shown in Table H.14.

bit byte	7	6	5	4	3	2	1	0
0	0	0	1	1	1	1	0	0
1	LUN			reserved				
2	reserved							
3	reserved							
4	reserved							
5	reserved							
6	reserved							
7	allocation length (MSB)							
8	allocation length (LSB)							
9	reserved						F	L

```
LUN:  logical unit number 0 to 7
allocation length:  max. number of data transferred by the target including header
      1=return messages with flag, if L=1    0=messages without flag
L:    link
      1=linked commands              0=single commands
```

Byte	Contents
0	reserved
1	reserved
2	available size (MSB)
3	available size (LSB)

available size: number of bytes that can be stored in the data buffer

Table H.14: Buffer data header

H.2.4   Status Key

Key	Meaning	Cause
0h	no status	no special status information necessary
1h	corrected error	last command completed successfully after recovery procedure of target
2h	not ready	drive cannot be accessed
3h	medium error	command aborted because of an uncorrectable error; cause probably bad medium
4h	hardware error	target detected an uncorrectable hardware error of controller, drive, etc.
5h	invalid request	invalid parameter in command descriptor block or in the additional parameters
6h	attention/reset	reset occurred since the last selection by the initiator

Key	Meaning	Cause
7h	data protected	the data on the volume is protected against the current access
9h	reserved for manufacturer	(the manufacturers may use this code for their own puposes)
ah	copy operation aborted	the copy operation between initiator and target has been aborted
bh	command aborted	the current command has been aborted
dh	volume overflow	the volume is full
eh	compare error	an error occurred during a verify operation
fh	reserved	

H.2.5 Additional Status Codes

Code	Meaning
00h	no status information
01h	no index or sector signal
02h	no seek signal
03h	write error
04h	drive not ready
06h	track 0 not found
10h	CRC or ECC error in ID
11h	uncorrectable read error of data blocks
12h	no address mark found in ID field
13h	no address mark found in data field
14h	no data record found
15h	seek error
17h	recovered data after retries of target without ECC correction
18h	recovered data after ECC correction by target (without retries)
19h	error in the defect list
1ah	parameter overflow
1ch	primary defect list not found
1eh	recovered ID after ECC correction by target
20h	invalid command code
21h	invalid logical block address LBA; address bigger than read drive capacity
24h	invalid entry in command descriptor block
25h	invalid logical unit number LUN
26h	invalid entry in parameter list
29h	power-on, reset or bus-reset occurred
2ah	mode select parameters changed
32h	no spare sector available for defect sector
40h	RAM error
42h	power-on diagnostics error
44h	internal controller error

Code	Meaning
45h	error in selection or reselection phase
46h	unsuccessful software reset
47h	parity error of the SCSI interface
48h	initiator has detected an error
49h	invalid defect list
80h	usage counter overflow
0h-ffh	reserved for manufacturer-own codes (for example error codes of the controller diagnostics routines)

I Access to Interfaces

I.1 Parallel Interface

To access the parallel interface four functions of DOS interrupt 21h and three functions of BIOS interrupt 17h are available.

I.1.1 DOS Functions

The functions are accessed by a call to DOS interrupt 21h.

Function 05h – Printing
This function transfers one character to the parallel interface PRN.

Register	Call value	Return value
AH	05h	
DL	ASCII code of character to print	
Carry		

Function 40h – Write File/Unit
This function transfers one or more characters from a buffer to the parallel interface. Usually, PRN is assigned handle 4, otherwise you must use the handle returned by function 3dh *open file/device*.

Register	Call value	Return value
AH	40h	
AX		error code / byte number[*]
BX	handle	
CX	number of bytes to write	
DX	write buffer offset	
DS	write buffer segment	
Carry		error if < > 0

[*] system error code if carry is set, or the number of actually written bytes

I.1.2 BIOS Functions

The functions are accessed by calling BIOS interrupt 17h.

Function 00h – Output Character to Parallel Interface and Printer
This function outputs a character to the parallel interface.

Register	Call value	Return value
AH	00h	status[1]
AL	character's ASCII code	
DX	interface/printer number [2]	

[1] see I.1.3
[2] 0=LPT1=PRN, 1=LPT2, 2=LPT3, 3=LPT4

Function 01h – Initialize Parallel Interface and Printer
This function initializes the parallel interface and the connected printer.

Register	Call value	Return value
AH	01h	status[1]
DX	interface/printer number [2]	

[1] see I.1.3
[2] 0=LPT1=PRN, 1=LPT2, 2=LPT3, 3=LPT4

Function 02h – Determine Printer Status
This function determines the current status of the parallel interface and the connected printer.

Register	Call value	Return value
AH	02h	status[1]
DX	interface/printer number [2]	

[1] see I.1.3
[2] 0=LPT1=PRN, 1=LPT2, 2=LPT3, 3=LPT4

I.1.3   Printer Status Byte

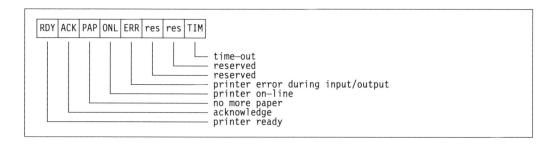

I.2   The Serial Interface

For the serial interface four functions of DOS interrupt 21h and seven functions of BIOS interrupt 14h are available.

I.2.1   DOS Functions

The functions are accessed by a call to DOS interrupt 21h.

Function 03h – Read Character From the Serial Interface
This function reads one character from the serial interface COM1 corresponding to AUX.

Register	Call value	Return value
AH	03h	
AL		received character

Function 04h – Output Character Via the Serial Interface
This function outputs one character via the serial interface COM1 corresponding to AUX.

Register	Call value	Return value
AH	05h	
DL	ASCII code of character to output	
Carry		

Function 3fh – Read File/Device
This function reads one or more characters from a serial interface into a buffer. Usually, AUX corresponding to COM1 is assigned handle 3, otherwise you must use the handle returned by function 3dh, *open file/device*, for the interface concerned.

Register	Call value	Return value
AH	3fh	
AX		error code/byte number[*]
BX	handle	
CX	number of bytes to read	
DX	read buffer offset	
DS	read buffer segment	
Carry		error if < > 0

[*] system error code if carry is set, or number of the bytes actually read

Function 40h – Write File/Device

This function outputs one or more characters from a buffer via a serial interface. Usually, AUX corresponding to COM1 is assigned handle 3, otherwise you must use the handle returned by function 3dh, *open file/device,* for the interface concerned.

Register	Call value	Return value
AH	40h	
AX		error code/byte number[*]
BX	handle	
CX	number of bytes to write	
DX	write buffer offset	
DS	write buffer segment	
Carry		error if < > 0

[*] system error code if carry is set, or number of the bytes actually written

I.2.2   BIOS Functions

These functions are accessed via a call to BIOS interrupt 14h.

Function 00h – Initialize Serial Interface

This function initializes the serial interface.

Register	Call value	Return value
AH	00h	transmit status[1]
AL	parameter byte [2]	modem status [3]
DX	interface number [4]	

[1] see I.2.3
[2] see I.2.5
[3] see I.2.4
[4] 0=COM1=AUX, 1=COM2, 2=COM3, 3=COM4

Function 01h – Output Character Via Serial Interface

This function outputs a character via the serial interface.

Register	Call value	Return value
AH	01h	transmit status[1]
AL		character
DX	interface number [2]	

[1] see I.2.3
[2] 0=COM1=AUX, 1=COM2, 2=COM3, 3=COM4

Function 02h – Read Character Via Serial Interface

This function reads one character via the serial interface.

Register	Call value	Return value
AH	02h	transmit status[1]
AL		character
DX	interface number[2]	

[1] see I.2.3
[2] 0=COM1=AUX, 1=COM2, 2=COM3, 3=COM4

Function 03h – Determine Status of Serial Interface

This function determines the current status of the serial interface.

Register	Call value	Return value
AH	03h	transmit status[1]
AL		modem status[2]
DX	interface number[3]	

[1] see I.2.3
[2] see I.2.4
[3] 0=COM1=AUX, 1=COM2, 2=COM3, 3=COM4

Function 04h – Initialize Serial Interface Extended (PS/2 Only)

This function carries out an extended initialization of the serial interface. The function is available on the PS/2 only.

Register	Call value	Return value
AH	04h	transmit status[1]
AL	break setting	modem status[2]
BH	parity	
BL	stop bits	
CH	data bits	
CL	baud rate	
DX	interface number[3]	

[1] see I.2.3
[2] see I.2.4
[3] 0=COM1=AUX, 1=COM2, 2=COM3, 3=COM4

```
Break setting: 00h=no break   01h=break
Parity:    00h=none   01h=odd   02h=even   03h=mark   04h=space
Stop bits: 00h=one stop bit    01h=two stop bits or 1 1/2 with 5 data bit
Data bits: 00h=5   01h=6   02h=7   03h=8
Baud rate: 00h=110 baud    01h=150 baud    02h=300 baud    03h=600 baud
           04h=1200 baud   05h=2400 baud   06h=4800 baud   07h=9600 baud
           08h=19200 baud
```

Function 05h, Subfunction 00h – Read Modem Control Register

This function reads the modem control register of the serial interface. The function is available on the PS/2 only.

Register	Call value	Return value
AH	05h	
AL	00h	
BL		modem control register[1]
DX	interface number [2]	

[1] 0=COM1=AUX, 1=COM2, 2=COM3, 3=COM4
[2] see I.2.6

Function 05h, Subfunction 01h – Write Modem Control Register

This function writes the modem control register of the serial interface. The function is available on the PS/2 only.

Register	Call value	Return value
AH	05h	transmit status[1]
AL	01h	modem status [2]
BL	modem control register [4]	
DX	interface number [3]	

[1] see I.2.3
[2] see I.2.4
[3] 0=COM1=AUX, 1=COM2, 2=COM3, 3=COM4
[4] see I.2.6

I.2.3   Transmit Status

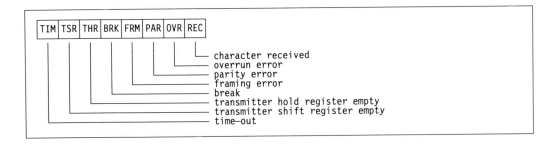

I.2.4   Modem Status

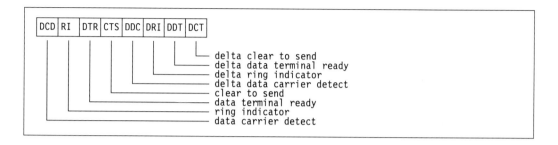

I.2.5   Parameter Byte

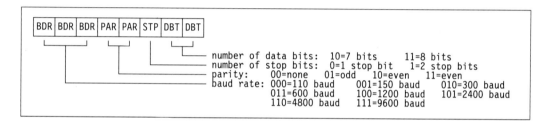

I.2.6   Modem Control Register

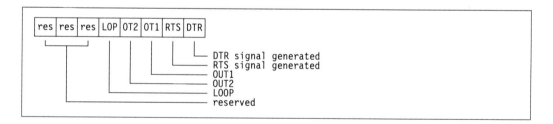

J   Keyboard and Mouse Access

J.1   The Keyboard

– The seven DOS functions are accessed via a call to DOS interrupt 21h.

– The keyboard can be accessed directly by means of BIOS interrupt 15h.

– With many BIOS versions, the hardware interrupt handler 09h calls function 4fh of INT 15h and passes a scan code to the handler.

– If you press or release the SysReq key, the handler of interrupt 09h calls function 85h of INT 15h.

J.1.1   DOS Functions

Function 01h – Character Input With Echo
This function reads one character byte from the keyboard buffer and outputs the character via the standard output device at the same time. For non-ASCII characters like the function key, you have to call the function twice; the first call returns code 00h, the second call the scan code of the key.

Register	Call value	Return value
AH	01h	
AL		ASCII code

Function 06h – Character Input From Standard Input Device Without Check
This function attempts to read one character from the keyboard buffer, and doesn't wait for an available character. With non-ASCII keys like F1 the first call returns a code equal to 0, and the second call the scan code of the pressed key. The function reads the keyboard as long as it is the standard input device. If redirection like < file or < device is active, all characters are read from the file or device. Control characters like Ctrl-C are not interpreted, but only passed.

Register	Call value	Return value
AH	06h	
AL		ASCII code
DL	ffh	
zero		1=character read
		0=no character available

Function 07h – Direct Character Input From Keyboard

This function attempts to read one character from the keyboard buffer and waits for an available character. With non-ASCII keys like F1, the first call returns a code equal to 0 and the second call the scan code of the key concerned. Unlike the 06h function, this function waits until a key is pressed if the keyboard buffer is empty. Control characters like Ctrl-C are not interpreted but only passed.

Register	Call value	Return value
AH	07h	
AL		ASCII code

Function 08h – Character Input From Standard Input Device With Check

This function attempts to read one character out of the keyboard buffer. The function waits until a character is available. With non-ASCII keys like F1, the first call returns a code equal to 0, and the second call the scan code of the pressed key. The function reads from the keyboard as long as it is the standard input device. If redirection such as < file or < device is active, all characters are read from the file or device. Control characters like Ctrl-C are interpreted accordingly.

Register	Call value	Return value
AH	08h	
AL		ASCII code

Function 0ah – Buffered Character Input From Standard Input Device With Echo

This function reads a character string into a buffer. The input is terminated by pressing RETURN. Character codes except Ctrl-C (program abortion) and Ctrl-P (echo on printer) are passed with a preceding »^« (for example, Ctrl-R as ^R). The first byte of the buffer indicates the max. length of the input, and the second byte the actual length. Therefore, the buffer has to comprise max.length+2 bytes. The function reads from the keyboard as long as it is the standard input device. If redirection such as < file or < device is active all characters are read from the file or device.

Register	Call value	Return value
AH	0ah	
DX	buffer offset	
DS	buffer segment	

Function 0bh – Check Status of Standard Input Device

This function determines whether a character has been input via the standard input device. The function accesses the keyboard as long as it is the standard input device. If redirection such as < file or < device is active, all characters are read from the file or device.

Register	Call value	Return value
AH	0bh	
AL		00h=no character available
		ffh=one character available

Function 3fh – Read File/Device

This function reads one or more characters from the keyboard into a buffer. Usually, the keyboard (CON) is assigned handle 0.

Register	Call value	Return value
AH	3fh	
AX		error code / byte number[*)
BX	handle	
CX	number of bytes to read	
DX	read buffer offset	
DS	read buffer segment	
Carry		error if < > 0

[*) system error code if carry is set, or number of bytes actually read

J.1.2   BIOS Interrupt INT 16h

Function 00h – Read Next Character

This function reads the next character out of the keyboard buffer and updates the corresponding pointer. If the keyboard buffer is empty, the function waits for the next key.

Register	Call value	Return value
AH	00h	scan code
AL		ASCII code

Function 01h – Determine Buffer Status

This function determines the status of the keyboard buffer, and indicates whether a character is available. Unlike function 01h, the keyboard pointer is not updated.

Register	Call value	Return value
AH	01h	scan code
AL		ASCII code
zero		0=character available
		1=no character available

Function 02h – Determine Shift Status

This function determines the status of the shift keys by checking the keyboard flag at 0040:0017.

Register	Call value	Return value
AH	02h	
AL		shift status[*]

[*] see J.1.4

Function 03h – Set Typing Rate And Delay (PS/2 And Some ATs)

This function sets the typing rate and the delay of the AT or MF II keyboard.

Register	Call value	Return value
AH	03h	
BL	typematic rate[1]	
BH	delay [2]	

[1] 00h=30.0 01h=26.7 02h=24.0 03h=21.8 04h=20.0 05h=18.5 06h=17.1 07h=16.0
 08h=15.0 09h=13.3 0ah=12.0 0bh=10.9 0ch=10.0 0dh=9.2 0eh=8.5 0fh=8.0
 10h=7.5 11h=6.7 12h=6.0 13h=5.5 14h=5.0 15h=4.6 16h=4.3 17h=4.0
 18h=3.7 19h=3.3 1ah=3.0 1bh=2.7 1ch=2.5 1dh=2.3 1eh=2.1 1fh=2.0
[2] 00=250 ms 01=500 ms 10=750 ms 11=1000 ms

Function 05h – Write Character and Scan Code Back to Keyboard Buffer

This function writes an ASCII character and a scan code back to the keyboard buffer to emulate a key press.

Register	Call value	Return value
AH	05h	
AL		status[*]
CH	scan code	
CL	ASCII code	

[*] 00h=o.k. 01h=keyboard buffer full

Function 10h – Read One Character from Extended Keyboard

This function reads one character from the extended (MF II) keyboard. The function is similar to function 00h, but supports the codes of the extended keyboard, i.e. for the codes of the new function and control keys a precode byte 0eh is passed instead of the value 00h. Thus the new keys can be distinguished from conventional ones.

Register	Call value	Return value
AH	10h	
AL		scan code
		ASCII code

Function 11h – Determine Buffer Status for the Extended Keyboard

This function determines the buffer status for the extended keyboard. This function is similar to function 01h but supports the codes of the extended keyboard, i.e. for the codes of the new function and control keys a precode byte 0eh is passed instead of the value 00h. Thus the new keys can be distinguished from conventional ones.

Register	Call value	Return value
AH	11h	scan code
AL		ASCII code
zero		0=character available
		1=no character available

Function 12h – Determine SHIFT Status of the Extended Keyboard

This function determines the status of the SHIFT keys by checking the keyboard flags at 0040:0017 and 0040:0018. The function corresponds to function 021h, but supports the additional SHIFT keys of the extended keyboard.

Register	Call value	Return value
AH	12h	2nd shift status byte[1]
AL		1st shift status byte [2]

[1] see J.1.4
[2] see J.1.5

J.1.3   BIOS Interrupt INT 15h

Function 4fh (AT and PS/2) – Keyboard Hook

The interrupt 09h calls this function if it receives a scan code from the keyboard. Normally, the function only clears the carry flag and executes a RET, but you can intercept the function and replace the scan code returned in AL with another code.

Register	Call value	Return value
AH	4fh	
AL	keyboard scan code	new scan code
carry		0b (ignore key press) or
carry	1b	1b (process key)

Function 85h (AT and PS/2) – SysReq Hook

The interrupt 09h calls this function if you press or release SysReq on a PC/XT or AT keyboard, or if you press or release Alt+SysReq on an MF II keyboard. Normally, the function only sets AX to 00h and clears the carry flag, but you can intercept the function.

Register	Call value	Return value
AH	85h	00h
AL	00h (SysReq pressed) or 01h (SysReq released)	
carry		0b

J.1.4   First Shift Status Byte

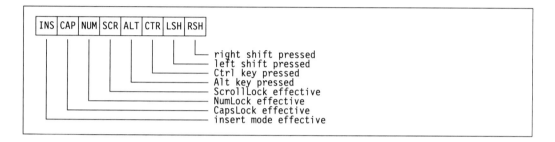

J.1.5   Second Shift Status Byte

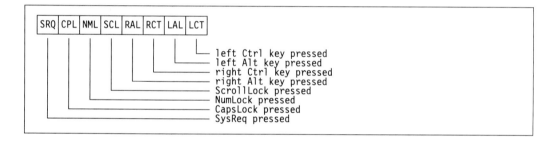

J.2   The Mouse Interrupt 33h

Mouse and mouse driver can be accessed via mouse interrupt 33h.

J.2.1   Functions of INT 33h

Function 00h – Check Mouse Present
This function determines whether a mouse is present, and resets the mouse driver to its standard settings. In the BX register the number of available mouse buttons is returned.

Register	Call value	Return value
AX	00h	status[1]
BX		mouse buttons [2]

[1] 0=mouse present; 1=no mouse present
[2] 2=two buttons (Microsoft); 3=three buttons

Function 01h – Display Mouse Cursor/Increment Cursor Flag

This function increments the cursor flag by one. The mouse cursor is displayed on-screen if the flag is equal to 0. Normally, the cursor flag has a value of –1.

Register	Call value	Return value
AX	01h	

Function 02h – Clear Mouse Cursor/Decrement Cursor Flag

This function decrements the cursor flag by one, and therefore clears the mouse cursor on the screen. The mouse cursor is displayed on-screen if the flag is equal to 0. Normally, the cursor flag has a value of –1.

Register	Call value	Return value
AX	02h	

Function 03h – Determine Status of Mouse Buttons and Position of Mouse Cursor

This function determines the current status of the mouse buttons and the current position of the mouse cursor on-screen.

Register	Call value	Return value
AX	03h	
BX		button byte[*]
CX		X-value of cursor position
DX		Y-value of cursor position

[*] see J.2.2 (1=corresponding button pressed, 0=corresponding button released)

Function 04h – Set Mouse Cursor Position

This function sets the position of the mouse cursor on-screen.

Register	Call value	Return value
AX	04h	
CX	X-value of cursor position	
DX	Y-value of cursor position	

Function 05h – Determine Number of Mouse Button Clicks and Mouse Cursor Position

This function determines how often a certain mouse button has been pressed, and where the mouse cursor was on-screen at the time the last click occurred.

Register	Call value	Return value
AX	05h	button byte[1]
BX	mouse button [2]	count value [3]
CX		X-value of cursor position
DX		Y-value of cursor position

[1] see J.2.2 (1=corresponding button pressed, 0=corresponding button released)
[2] 1=check left button, 2=check right button, 4=check middle button
[3] number of clicks (0 to 32,767)

Function 06h – Determine Number of Mouse Button Releases and Mouse Cursor Position

This function determines how often a certain mouse button has been released since the last inquiry and where the mouse cursor was on-screen at the time the last release occurred.

Register	Call value	Return value
AX	06h	button byte[1]
BX	mouse button [2]	count value [3]
CX		X-value of cursor position
DX		Y-value of cursor position

[1] see J.2.2 (1=corresponding button pressed, 0=corresponding button released)
[2] 1=check left button, 2=check right button, 4=check middle button
[3] number of releases (0 to 32,767)

Function 07h – Define Horizontal Borders for Mouse Cursor

This function defines the horizontal borders for the mouse cursor movement. The mouse cursor cannot move outside them, even if the mouse is moved further. Thus, together with function 08h, you can define a window for the mouse cursor.

Register	Call value	Return value
AX	07h	
BX		
CX	left border	
DX	right border	

Function 08h – Define Vertical Borders for Mouse Cursor

This function defines the vertical borders for the mouse cursor's movement. The mouse cursor cannot move outside them, even if the mouse is moved further. Together with function 07h, you can define a window for the mouse cursor.

Register	Call value	Return value
AX	08h	
BX		
CX	upper border	
DX	lower border	

Function 09h – Define Mouse Cursor in Graphics Mode

This function defines the shape and behaviour of the mouse cursor in graphics mode. Screen and cursor mask are provided in this order in a buffer. The action point defines, relative to the upper left corner of the mouse cursor, which value is to be returned in an inquiry of the mouse cursor position.

Register	Call value	Return value
AX	09h	
BX	action point horizontal[*]	
CX	action point vertical[*]	
DX	mask buffer offset	
ES	mask buffer segment	

[*] range of values: –16...+16

Function 0ah – Define Mouse Cursor in Text Mode

This function defines the shape and behaviour of the mouse cursor in text mode.

Register	Call value	Return value
AX	0ah	
BX	mouse cursor type[1]	
CX	screen mask [2]	
DX	cursor mask [3]	

[1] 0=software mouse cursor, 1=hardware mouse cursor
[2] software mouse cursor: screen mask code, hardware mouse cursor: first scan line of mouse cursor
[3] software mouse cursor: cursor mask code, hardware mouse cursor: last scan line of mouse cursor

Function 0bh – Read Movement Counter of Mouse

This function reads the movement counter of the mouse and determines how far the mouse has been moved since the last function call. One count value is equal to one mickey, i.e. 1/200" or 0.13 mm.

Register	Call value	Return value
AX	0bh	
CX		count value horizontal[*]
DX		count value vertical[*]

[*] range of values: –32768 ... +32767

Function 0ch – Define Call Mask for User Procedure

This function defines the conditions for which the mouse driver calls a user-defined procedure via a far call.

Register	Call value	Return value
AX	0ch	
CX	call mask[1]	
DX	procedure offset	
ES	procedure segment	

1)

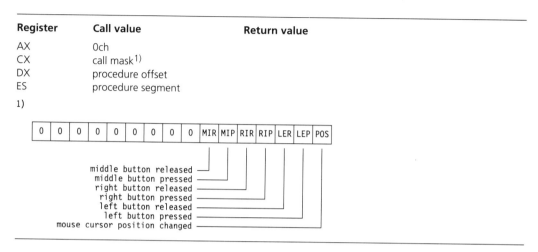

The procedure is passed the following parameters:

Register	Contents
AX	mask with set bit which led to the call
BX	current status of mouse buttons (see J.2.2)
CX	X-value of mouse cursor position
DX	Y-value of mouse cursor position

Function 0dh – Enable Light Pen Emulation

This function enables the light pen emulation of the mouse driver. The light pen appears on-screen if the left and right mouse buttons are pressed.

Register	Call value	Return value
AX	0dh	

Function 0eh – Disable Light Pen Emulation

This function disables the light pen emulation of the mouse driver.

Register	Call value	Return value
AX	0eh	

Function 0fh – Define Mickey/Pixel Ratio

This function defines the number of mickeys per pixel. The horizontal standard value is equal to 8, the vertical equal to 16.

Register	Call value	Return value
AX	0fh	
CX	horizontal ratio*)	
DX	vertical ratio*)	

*) range of values: 1 ... 32,767

Function 10h – Disable Mouse Cursor Conditionally

This function defines the borders within which the mouse cursor is cleared from the screen. If the mouse cursor enters the defined window it will be cleared. For re-displaying the mouse cursor you must use function 01h.

Register	Call value	Return value
AX	10h	
CX	X-value of right border	
DX	Y-value of lower border	
SI	X-value of left border	
DI	Y-value of upper border	

Function 13h – Define Threshold Value for Double Speed

This function defines the threshold in mickeys/s for which the mouse cursor is moved on-screen with double speed. The standard threshold value is equal to 64.

Register	Call value	Return value
AX	13h	
DX	threshold value	

J.2.2   Button Byte

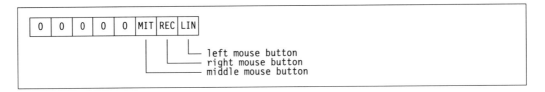

J.3   PS/2 Mouse Support via BIOS Interrupt INT 15h, Function c2h

– The PS/2 mouse support on a hardware level is carried out by subfunctions 00h to 07h of INT 15h, function c2h.

– Before using the routines you must pass the jump address of the mouse driver or the corresponding application program which handles the mouse packets to the BIOS via subfunction 07h – *pass driver address*. Afterwards, the mouse must be initialized via subfunction 05h – *initialize mouse*. Then the mouse can be enabled or disabled by subfunction 00h – *enable/disable mouse*.

J.3.1   Subfunctions of INT 15h, Function c2h

Subfunction 00h – Enable/Disable Mouse
This function enables or disables the mouse. Before activation the program must pass the address of the mouse driver or the program to the BIOS via subfunction 07h, and initialize the mouse with subfunction 05h.

Register	Call value	Return value
AH	c2h	status*)
AL	00h	
BH	00h enable mouse	
	01h disable mouse	
carry		error if < > 0

*) see J.3.2

Subfunction 01h – Reset Mouse
This function resets the mouse.

Register	Call value	Return value
AH	c2h	status*)
AL	01h	
BH		mouse identification 00h
carry		error if <> 0

*) see J.3.2

Subfunction 02h – Set Sample Rate
This function sets the sample rate for the mouse.

Register	Call value	Return value
AH	c2h	status[1]
AL	02h	
BH	sample rate [2]	
carry		error if <> 0

[1] see J.3.2
[2] 00h =10 samples/s   01h =20 samples/s   02h =40 samples/s   03h=60 samples/s
      04h =80 samples/s   05h =100 samples/s   06h =200 samples/s

Subfunction 03h – Set Resolution
This function sets the resolution of the mouse.

Register	Call value	Return value
AH	c2h	status[1]
AL	03h	
BH	resolution [2]	
carry		error if <> 0

[1] see J.3.2
[2] 00h=1 unit/mm   01h=2 units/mm   02h=4 units/mm   03h=8 units/mm

Subfunction 04h – Determine Mouse Identification
This function determines the identification code of the connected mouse (or another connected device).

Register	Call value	Return value
AH	c2h	status[*]
AL	04h	
BH		identification code
carry		error if <> 0

[*] see J.3.2

Subfunction 05h – Initialize Mouse
This function initializes the mouse and adjusts the size of the mouse data packet.

Register	Call value	Return value
AH	c2h	status[1]
AL	05h	
BH	data packet size [2]	
carry		error if <> 0

[1] see J.3.2
[2] see J.3.3

Subfunction 06h – Extended Mouse Status

This function determines the extended mouse status and sets the X-Y-scaling factor of the mouse.

Register	Call value	Return value
AH	c2h	status[1]
AL	06h	
BH	function to execute [2]	
BL		first status byte [3]
CL		second status byte [3]
DL		third status byte [3]
carry		error if <> 0

[1] see J.3.2
[2] 00h=determine status   01=scaling factor 1:1   02=scaling factor 2:1
[3] if equal 00h on call

Subfunction 07h – Pass Driver Address

This function passes the BIOS the address of the PS/2 mouse driver.

Register	Call value	Return value
AH	c2h	status[*]
AL	07h	
BX	offset address of driver or application program	
ES	segment address of driver or application program	
carry		error if <> 0

[*] see J.3.2

J.3.2   Status Byte

Status	Meaning
00h	no error
01h	invalid function call
02h	invalid input
03h	interface error
04h	resend necessary
05h	no device driver present

J.3.3   Mouse Packet on the Stack

The table below indicates the data on the stack where the BIOS pushes the mouse packet. The offsets are calculated relative to SP. The actual mouse packet therefore consists of a maximum of eight bytes of Z-data, Y-data, X-data, and status.

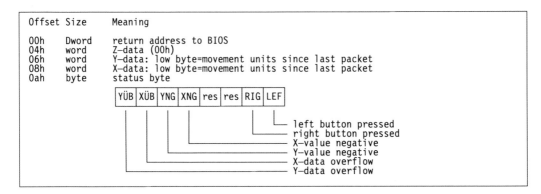

```
Offset Size      Meaning

00h    Dword     return address to BIOS
04h    word      Z-data (00h)
06h    word      Y-data: low byte=movement units since last packet
08h    word      X-data: low byte=movement units since last packet
0ah    byte      status byte

          YÜB XÜB YNG XNG res res RIG LEF

                                        └─ left button pressed
                                      ──── right button pressed
                                  ──────── X-value negative
                              ──────────── Y-value negative
                          ──────────────── X-data overflow
                      ──────────────────── Y-data overflow
```

K   Access to Graphics Adapters

- DOS functions are called via DOS interrupt 21h.

- The system BIOS comprises the standard functions for text and graphics mode of the graphics adapter.

- EGA and VGA have a BIOS extension with further powerful routines for adapter logic control, as well as character and graphics output in the new text and graphics formats.

K.1   DOS Functions

Function 02h – Character Output
This function outputs a character to the standard output device (usually CON). The character codes 07h (bell), 08h (backspace), 09h (tab), 0ah (line feed), and 0dh (carriage return) are interpreted as control characters, and the BIOS carries out a corresponding process.

Register	Call value	Return value
AH	02h	
DL	ASCII character code	

Function 06h – Character Output to Standard Output Device Without Check
This function outputs a character to the standard output device (usually CON). If redirection of the form < file or < device is in effect, all characters are output to the file or device. DOS control characters of the form Ctrl-C are not interpreted, but only transferred. But the character codes 07h (bell), 08h (backspace), 09h (tab), 0ah (line feed) and 0dh (carriage return), which are recognized by the BIOS, are actually interpreted by the BIOS.

Register	Call value	Return value
AH	06h	
DL	ASCII character code	

Function 09h – String Output
This function outputs a complete string to the standard output device (usually CON). The string must be terminated by the character »$« (ASCII code 36). DOS control characters of the form Ctrl-C are not interpreted, only transferred. But the character codes 07h (bell), 08h (backspace), 09h (tab), 0ah (line feed), and 0dh (carriage return), which are recognized by the BIOS, are actually interpreted by the BIOS.

Register	Call value	Return value
AH	09h	
DX	string offset	
DS	string segment	
AL		'$'

Function 40h – Write File/Device

This function outputs a string by means of a handle. The handle for the standard output device is equal to 1. If the standard output device is not CON anymore, and you still want to output one or more characters on-screen, you must open CON first with a call to function *open file/device* for a write access.

Register	Call value	Return value
AH	40h	
AX		error code/byte number[*]
BX	handle (01h)	
CX	number of bytes to output	
DX	write buffer offset	
DS	write buffer segment	
carry		error if < > 0

[*] system error code if carry is set, or number of actual written bytes

K.2   BIOS Interrupt INT 10h – Standard Functions of the System BIOS

The listed functions are implemented in the system BIOS on the motherboard.

Function 00h – Set Video Mode

This function sets a certain video mode of the grahics adapter by loading the mode and control registers of the grahics chip with appropriate values. High resolution EGA and VGA adapter cards have plenty of resolution for text and graphics mode, which you can find in the manual of your adapter card. After a call to the 00h function, the cursor is in line 0, column 0, the palette is reset to standard colours, and the screen is cleared.

Register	Call value	Return value
AH	00h	
AL	video mode[*]	

Mode no.	Mode type	Text lines	Text columns	Char. matrix	Resolution	Colours	Pages	Page size	Video segment	MDA	CGA	HGC	EGA	VGA
0	text	25	40	8*8	320*200	16	8	800h	b800h		x			
0	text	25	40	8*14	320*350	16	8	800h	b800h				x	
0	text	25	40	8*16	360*400	16	8	800h	b800h					x
1	text	25	40	8*8	320*200	16	8	800h	b800h		x			
1	text	25	40	8*14	320*350	16	8	800h	b800h				x	
1	text	25	40	8*16	360*400	16	8	800h	b800h					x
2	text	25	80	8*8	640*200	16	4	1000h	b800h		x			
2	text	25	80	8*14	640*350	16	4	1000h	b800h				x	
2	text	25	80	9*16	720*400	16	4	1000h	b800h					x
3	text	25	80	8*8	640*200	16	4	1000h	b800h		x			
3	text	25	80	8*14	640*350	16	4	1000h	b800h				x	
3	text	25	80	9*16	720*400	16	4	1000h	b800h					x
4	graphics	25	40	8*8	320*200	4	1	4000h	b800h		x		x	x
5	graphics	25	40	8*8	320*200	4	1	4000h	b800h		x		x	x
6	graphics	25	80	8*8	640*200	2	1	4000h	b800h		x		x	x
7	text	25	80	9*14	720*350	mono	1	1000h	b000h	x		x	x	
7	text	25	80	9*16	720*400	mono	8	1000h	b000h					x
13	graphics	25	40	8*8	320*200	16	8	2000h[1]	a000h				x	x
14	graphics	25	80	8*8	640*200	16	4	4000h[1]	a000h				x	x
15	graphics	25	80	8*14	640*350	mono	2	8000h[1]	a000h				x	x
16	graphics	25	80	8*14	640*350	16	2	8000h[1]	a000h				x	x
17	graphics	30	80	8*16	640*480	2	1	a000h	a000h					x
18	graphics	30	80	8*16	640*480	16	1	a000h[1]	a000h					x
19	graphics	25	40	8*8	320*200	256	1	10000h	a000h					x

[1] per video RAM layer

Function 01h – Set Cursor Size (Text)

This function sets the cursor size in text mode. If the value of the start scan line is more than the value of the end scan line, a divided cursor is displayed. If the values of the scan lines are out of the range given by the character box in the active video mode, no cursor is displayed. The cursor parameters are stored in the BIOS data area at 40:60h. The standard settings for a CGA are start scan line = 6, end scan line = 7 and for an MDA start scan line = 11, end scan line = 12.

Register	Call value	Return value
AH	01h	
CH	start scan line of cursor[1]	
CL	end scan line of cursor [2]	

[1] bit 7: reserved (=0); bits 6,5: 00=normal, 01=cursor not displayed
   bits 4–0: start scan line of cursor
[2] bits 7–5: reserved (=0); bits 4–0: end scan line

Function 02h – Set Cursor Position (Text/Graphics)

This function sets the cursor position of the active screen page. The screen page need not be displayed; also, a hidden page can be addressed. In text mode, the text cursor appears at that location; in graphics mode, the cursor remains invisible, but defines the coordinates where, for example, a point is to be set. The function stores the cursor coordinates at 40:50h.

Register	Call value	Return value
AH	02h	
BH	screen page	
DH	row	
DL	column	

Function 03h – Read Cursor Position (Text)

This function determines the cursor position of the active screen page. The screen page need not be displayed; also, a hidden page can be addressed. The function reads the cursor type from the BIOS storage area at 40:60h and the cursor coordinates at 40:50h.

Register	Call value	Return value
AH	03h	
BH	screen page	
CH		start scan line of cursor
CL		end scan line of cursor
DH		row
DL		column

Function 04h – Read Light Pen Position (Text/Graphics)

This function determines the position and status of the light pen. Nowadays, the light pen has been replaced by mouse and trackball.

Register	Call value	Return value
AH	04h	status[1]
BX		pixel column (graphics mode)
CH		pixel line 0 to 199 (graphics mode)
CL		pixel line 0 to xxx[2] (graphics mode)
DH		row (text mode)
DL		column (text mode)

[1] 00h=switch of light pen open,
   01h=switch closed, coordinates valid
[2] for modes with more than 200 lines (xxx ≥ 200)

Function 05h – Select Screen Page (Text/Graphics)

This function specifies the active screen page, i.e. the displayed screen page. The number of available screen pages depends upon the video mode and the graphics adapter used.

Register	Call value	Return value
AH	05h	
AL	screen page	

Function 06h – Scroll Window Up (Text/Graphics)

This function defines a window on-screen and scrolls the window contents up the number of specified rows. With AL = 00h the window can be cleared. The blank rows appearing at the bottom of the window are filled with ' ' (blank) characters. These blank characters are assigned the attribute passed in register BH.

Register	Call value	Return value
AH	06h	
AL	number of rows to scroll	
BH	attribute of blank rows	
CH	upper row of window	
CL	left column of window	
DH	lower row of window	
DL	right column of window	

Function 07h – Scroll Window Down (Text/Graphics)

This function defines a window on-screen and scrolls the window contents down the number of specified rows. With AL = 00h the window can be cleared. The blank rows appearing at the top of the window are filled with ' ' (blank) characters. These blank characters are assigned the attribute passed in register BH.

Register	Call value	Return value
AH	07h	
AL	number of rows to scroll	
BH	attribute of blank rows	
CH	upper row of window	
CL	left column of window	
DH	lower row of window	
DL	right column of window	

Function 08h – Read Character/Attribute From Screen (Text/Graphics)

This function reads the character at the current cursor position. Eventually, you must locate the cursor at the desired position in advance with function 02h. In text mode the function returns not only the character code, but also the character attribute. In graphics mode, the character matrix at the specified cursor position is compared with the active character table to determine a character code. If the matrix pattern does not meet a character in the table, the function returns a code 00h.

Register	Call value	Return value
AH	08h	character attribute (text mode only)
AL		character code
BH	screen page	

Function 09h – Write Character/Attribute Onto Screen (Text/Graphics)

This function writes a character starting at the current cursor position and repeats the process CX-times. The cursor position is not altered by this. In text mode BL specifies the attribute, and in graphics mode the foreground colour of the character to be written. If characters are written in graphics mode and bit 7 of BL is set, the character matrix of the character to be written is XOR-ed with the contents of the video RAM at that location.

Register	Call value	Return value
AH	09h	
AL	character code	
BH	screen page	
BL	character attribute	
	or foreground colour	
CX	number of repetitions	

Function 0ah – Write Character Onto Screen (Text/Graphics)

This function writes one character, starting with the current cursor position, and repeats the process CX-times. The cursor position is not altered by this. The character attribute at the concerned location is not modified. If characters are written in graphics mode and bit 7 of BL is set, the character matrix of the character to be written is XOR-ed with the contents of the video RAM at that location.

Register	Call value	Return value
AH	0ah	
AL	character code	
BH	screen page	
CX	number of repetitions	

Function 0bh – Set Colour Palette (Graphics)

This function sets the colours for medium resolution of the CGA. Depending upon the value of the BH register, the BL register has a different meaning. By modifying the palette the colour of the displayed screen can be changed instantaneously, and the user has the impression of a blinking screen.

BH=00h

Register	Call value	Return value
AH	0bh	
BH	00h	
BL	colour 0–31[*)]	

[*)] mode 4,5: background colour equal to BL
mode 0,1,2,3: margin colour equal to BL
Mode 6,11: foreground colour equal to BL

BH=01h

Register	Call value	Return value
AH	0bh	
BH	01h	
BL	palette[*)]	

[*)] 00h: palette = green (1), red (2), yellow (3)
01h: palette = cyan (1), magenta (2), white (3)

Function 0ch – Write Pixel Onto Screen (Graphics)

This function writes one pixel onto the screen at a desired location. Bit 7 of register AL serves as the inverting bit, i.e. the colour in AL is XOR-ed with the pixel currently located at the addressed location. If you write the pixel in the same manner again, it has disappeared from the screen. Thus objects can seemingly be moved on-screen.

Register	Call value	Return value
AH	0ch	
AL	colour	
BH	screen page[*)]	
CX	pixel column	
DX	pixel line	

[*)] only necessary if the video mode supports more than one page

Function 0dh – Read Pixel From Screen (Graphics)

This function reads one pixel at a certain location on the screen.

Register	Call value	Return value
AH	0dh	
AL		colour of read pixel
BH	screen page*)	
CX	pixel column	
DX	pixel line	

*) only necessary if the video mode supports more than one page

Function 0eh – Write in TTY Mode (Text/Graphics)

This function writes one character onto the screen while the screen behaves like a serial terminal from the system's point of view (therefore, TTY mode). This function does not display the four characters with codes 07h (bell), 08h (backspace), 0ah (line feed) and 0dh (carriage return) but executes a corresponding action. For example, a code 08h deletes the character left of the cursor and moves the cursor one position to the left. After each character the cursor is moved implicitly.

Register	Call value	Return value
AH	0eh	
AL	character code	
BH	screen page	
BL	foreground colour*)	

*) graphics mode only

Function 0fh – Determine Video Status (Text/Graphics)

This function determines the current video mode and video status.

Register	Call value	Return value
AH	0fh	number of column from 40:4ah
AL		video mode from 40:49h
BH		active screen page from 40:62h

Function 13h – Write String (Text/Graphics)

This function writes a whole string onto the screen. The bits 0 and 1 of register AL determine the behaviour of the function. The string may contain character codes and character attributes alternately, or character codes only. In the second case, the attribute passed in register BL is used.

Register	Call value	Return value
AH	13h	
AL	function behaviour[1]	
BH	screen page	
BL	character attribute[2]	
CX	length of string without attributes	
DH	start cursor row	
DL	start cursor column	
BP	string offset	
ES	string segment	

[1] bit 0: 1=cursor points to last written character after function call
          0=cursor points to start after function call
  bit 1: 1=string contains character codes and character attributes alternately
          0=string contains character code only, the attribute is taken from BL; codes 07h (bell), 08h (backspace), 0ah (line feed)
          and 0dh (carriage return) are interpreted as control commands
[2] graphics mode only

K.3   BIOS Interrupt INT 10h – Additional Functions of the EGA/VGA BIOS

–   The functions listed are implemented in the BIOS extension of EGA and VGA adapters.

–   The EGA and VGA BIOS redirects the start address of the handler for INT 10h of the system BIOS on the motherboard to INT 42h upon booting.

Function 10h – Set Palette Registers
This function sets the palette registers of EGA and VGA. With an EGA, 64 different colours are possible; with a VGA, $2^{18} = 262.144$.

Subfunction 00h – Set Individual Palette Registers (EGA/VGA)
This function updates the specified palette register in the attribute controller.

Register	Call value	Return value
AH	10h	
AL	00h	
BH	new register value	
BL	palette register	

Subfunction 01h – Set Overscan Register (EGA/VGA)
This function determines the overscan colour, i.e. the border colour. The value in BH is transferred into the overscan register.

Register	Call value	Return value
AH	10h	
AL	01h	
BH	new register value	

Subfunction 02h – Set All Registers (EGA/VGA)

This function loads all 16 palette registers and the overscan register with values which are passed in a table. The bytes 0–15 of the table contain the new values for the registers 0–15, and byte 16 of the table holds the new value for the overscan register.

Register	Call value	Return value
AH	10h	
AL	02h	
DX	register table offset	
ES	register table segment	

Subfunction 03h – Enable/Disable Blink Attribute (EGA/VGA)

This function determines the value of bit 3 in the mode control register. If bit 3 is set, a character with a set blink attribute is displayed on the monitor in a blinking manner. If bit 3 is cleared the blink bit in the attribute has no effect; the character is always displayed non-blinking. In this case, bit 3 of the attribute byte selects one of two active character definition tables. Therefore, 512 instead of 256 characters are available.

Register	Call value	Return value
AH	10h	
AL	03h	
BL	blinking (1=on, 0=off)	

Subfunction 07h – Read Palette Register (VGA)

This function reads the value of the indicated palette register.

Register	Call value	Return value
AH	10h	
AL	07h	
BH		palette register value
BL	palette register	

Subfunction 08h – Read Overscan Register (VGA)

This function reads the value of the overscan register.

Register	Call value	Return value
AH	10h	
AL	08h	
BH		value of the overscan register

Subfunction 09h – Read All Registers (VGA)

This function reads all 16 palette registers and the overscan register into a table. Bytes 0–15 of the table contain the values of the registers 0–15, and byte 16 of the table holds the value of the overscan register.

Register	Call value	Return value
AH	10h	
AL	09h	
DX		register table offset
ES		register table segment

Subfunction 10h – Write Video DAC Colour Register (VGA)

This function writes new colour values into the specified video DAC colour register. Only the six lower bits are significant. There are 256 video DAC colour registers.

Register	Call value	Return value
AH	10h	
AL	10h	
BX	colour register number	
CH	green value	
CL	blue value	
DH	red value	

Subfunction 12h – Write Block of Video DAC Colour Registers (VGA)

This function loads one block of video DAC colour registers with the values indicated in a table. All 256 colour registers can thus be written at one time. Only the six lower bits of each table entry are significant.

Register	Call value	Return value
AH	10h	
AL	12h	
BX	first register to write	
CX	number of registers	
DX	table offset*⁾	
ES	table segment*⁾	

*⁾ table entry structure:

```
    offset
          ┌──────────────────────┐
     02h  │ blue value  (1 byte) │
          ├──────────────────────┤
     01h  │ green value (1 byte) │
          ├──────────────────────┤
          │ red value   (1 byte) │
     00h  └──────────────────────┘
```

Subfunction 13h – Set Colour Select State of Attribute Controller (VGA)

This function sets the colour selection of the attribute controller. This is carried out by the colour select and mode control registers.

Register	Call value	Return value
AH	10h	
AL	13h	
BL	register selection*⁾	
BH	value of colour select register or bit 7	

*⁾ 1=set colour select register, 0=set bit 7 of mode control register

Subfunction 15h – Read Video DAC Colour Register (VGA)

This function reads the value of the indicated video DAC colour register.

Register	Call value	Return value
AH	10h	
AL	15h	
BX	colour register number	
CH		green value
CL		blue value
DH		red value

Subfunction 17h – Read Block of Video DAC Colour Registers (VGA)

This function reads the values of a block of video DAC colour registers into a table. All 256 registers can thus be read at one time.

Register	Call value	Return value
AH	10h	
AL	17h	
BX	first register to read	
CX	number of registers	
DX	table offset*)	
ES	table segment*)	

*) table entry structure:

```
    offset
         ┌─────────────────────────┐
         │ blue value   (1 byte)   │
    02h  ├─────────────────────────┤
         │ green value (1 byte)    │
    01h  ├─────────────────────────┤
         │ red value   (1 byte)    │
    00h  └─────────────────────────┘
```

Subfunction 18h – Write Video DAC Mask Register (VGA)

This function loads the video DAC mask register with a new value.

Register	Call value	Return value
AH	10h	
AL	18h	
BL	new mask value	

Subfunction 19h – Read Video DAC Mask Register (VGA)

This function reads the video DAC mask register.

Register	Call value	Return value
AH	10h	
AL	19h	
BL		mask value

Subfunction 1ah – Read Colour Select Register of Attribute Controller (VGA)

This function reads the colour select register of the attribute controller.

Register	Call value	Return value
AH	10h	
AL	1ah	
BL		bit 7 of mode control register
BH		colour select register*)

*) bits 2 to 3, if BL=0; bits 0 to 3, if BL=1

Subfunction 1bh – Carry Out Grey Scale Mapping For a Block of Video DAC Colour Registers (VGA)

This function carries out a grey scale mapping for the colour values of a colour register block.

Register	Call value	Return value
AH	10h	
AL	1bh	
BX	first colour register	
CX	number of colour registers	

Function 11h – Interface to the Character Generator

This function serves as an interface to the character generator of the EGA and VGA. You may thus define your own character sets.

Subfunction 00h – Load User-Defined Character Definition Table for Text Mode (EGA/VGA)

This function loads a user-defined character definition table from the main memory into the character generator RAM. The character definition table holds the pixel pattern for each of the character codes. The video controller is not reprogrammed for an eventually new character height.

Register	Call value	Return value
AH	11h	
AL	00h	
BH	bytes per defined character	
BL	table number in character generator RAM	
CX	number of defined characters	
DX	ASCII code of first defined character	
BP	offset of table in main memory	
ES	segment of table in main memory	

Subfunction 01h – Load 8∗14 Character Definition Table From EGA/VGA ROM For Text Mode (EGA/VGA)

This function loads the 8∗14 character definition table from EGA/VGA ROM into the character generator RAM. The character definition table holds the pixel pattern for each of the character codes. The video controller is not reprogrammed for an eventually new character height.

Register	Call value	Return value
AH	11h	
AL	01h	
BL	table number in character generator RAM	

Subfunction 02h – Load 8∗8 Character Definition Table From EGA/VGA ROM For Text Mode (EGA/VGA)

This function loads the 8∗8 character definition table from EGA/VGA ROM into the character generator RAM. The character definition table holds the pixel pattern for each of the character codes. The video controller is not reprogrammed for an eventually new character height.

Register	Call value	Return value
AH	11h	
AL	02h	
BL	table number in character generator RAM	

Subfunction 03h – Select Active Character Definition Table (EGA/VGA)

This function selects one of the loaded character definition tables in the character generator RAM for displaying characters on the monitor. With EGA, bits 0 and 1 of the BL register determine the primary of four character tables, which is used if bit 3 of the character attribute is equal to 0. Bits 2 and 3 of register BL indicate the secondary character table, which the character generator uses if bit 3 of the character attribute is equal to 1. With VGA, bits 0, 1, and 4 of the BL register determine the primary of eight character tables, which is used if bit 3 of the character attribute is equal to 0. Bits 2, 3, and 5 of register BL indicate the secondary character table, which the character generator uses if bit 3 of the character attribute is equal to 1. Bit 3 of the attribute byte determines the primary or secondary character tables only if you have disabled the blink attribute with INT 10h, function 10h, subfunction 03h.

Register	Call value	Return value
AH	11h	
AL	03h	
BL	value of character map select register*)	

*)

```
┌───┬───┬───┬───┬───┬───┬───┬───┐
│res│res│SE2│PR2│SE1│SE0│PR1│PR0│
└───┴───┴─┬─┴─┬─┴─┬─┴─┬─┴─┬─┴─┬─┘
          │   │   │   └───┴───┴── primary character table (PR2 only on VGA)
          └───┴───┴────────────── secondary character table (SE2 only on VGA)
```

Subfunction 04h – Load 8∗16 Character Definition Table From VGA ROM For Text Mode (VGA)

This function loads the 8∗16 character definition table from VGA ROM into the character generator RAM. The character definition table holds the pixel pattern for each of the character codes. The video controller is not reprogrammed for an eventually new character height.

Register	Call value	Return value
AH	11h	
AL	04h	
BL	table number in character generator RAM	

Subfunction 10h – Load User-Defined Character Definition Table For Text Mode and Reprogram CRT Controller (EGA/VGA)

This function loads the user-defined character definition table from main memory into the character generator RAM, and programs the CRT controller. The character definition table holds the pixel pattern for each of the character codes.

Register	Call value	Return value
AH	11h	
AL	00h	
BH	bytes per defined character	
BL	table number in character generator RAM	
CX	number of defined characters	
DX	ASCII code of first defined character	
BP	offset of table in main memory	
ES	segment of table in main memory	

Subfunction 11h – Load 8∗14 Character Definition Table From EGA/VGA ROM For Text Mode and Program CRT Controller (EGA/VGA)

This function loads the 8∗14 character definition table from EGA/VGA ROM into the character generator RAM, and programs the CRT controller. The character definition table holds the pixel pattern for each of the character codes.

Register	Call value	Return value
AH	11h	
AL	11h	
BL	table number in character generator RAM	

Subfunction 12h – Load 8∗8 Character Definition Table From EGA/VGA ROM For Text Mode and Program CRT Controller (EGA/VGA)

This function loads the 8∗8 character definition table from EGA/VGA ROM into the character generator RAM, and programs the CRT controller. The character definition table holds the pixel pattern for each of the character codes.

Register	Call value	Return value
AH	11h	
AL	12h	
BL	table number in character generator RAM	

Subfunction 14h – Load 8*16 Character Definition Table From EGA/VGA ROM For Text Mode and Program CRT Controller (VGA)

This function loads the 8*16 character definition table from VGA ROM into the character generator RAM, and programs the CRT controller. The character definition table holds the pixel pattern for each of the character codes.

Register	Call value	Return value
AH	11h	
AL	14h	
BL	table number in character generator RAM	

Subfunction 20h – Load 8*8 Character Definition Table From EGA/VGA ROM For INT 1fh in Graphics Mode (EGA/VGA)

This function loads the 8*8 character definition table from EGA/VGA ROM. The character definition table holds the pixel pattern for the character codes 80h to ffh (128 to 256) if the EGA/VGA carries out a CGA-compatible graphics mode.

Register	Call value	Return value
AH	11h	
AL	20h	
BP	offset of table in main memory	
ES	segment of table in main memory	

Subfunction 21h – Load User-Defined Character Definition Table For Graphics Mode (EGA/VGA)

This function loads the user-defined character definition table from main memory into the character generator RAM. The character definition table holds the pixel pattern for each of the character codes.

Register	Call value	Return value
AH	11h	
AL	21h	
BL	screen rows*)	
CX	bytes per defined character	
DL	screen rows (if BL=0)	
BP	offset of table in main memory	
ES	segment of table in main memory	

*) 0=DL valid, 1=14 screen rows, 2=25 screen rows, 3=43 screen rows

Subfunction 22h – Load 8∗14 Character Definition Table From EGA/VGA ROM For Graphics Mode (EGA/VGA)

This function loads the 8∗14 character definition table from EGA/VGA ROM into the character generator RAM. The character definition table holds the pixel pattern for each of the character codes.

Register	Call value	Return value
AH	11h	
AL	22h	
BL	screen rows*)	
DL	screen rows (if BL=0)	

*) 0=DL valid, 1=14 screen rows, 2=25 screen rows, 3=43 screen rows

Subfunction 23h – Load 8∗8 Character Definition Table From EGA/VGA ROM For Graphics Mode (EGA/VGA)

This function loads the 8∗8 character definition table from EGA/VGA ROM into the character generator RAM. The character definition table holds the pixel pattern for each of the character codes.

Register	Call value	Return value
AH	11h	
AL	23h	
BL	screen rows*)	
DL	screen rows (if BL=0)	

*) 0=DL valid, 1=14 screen rows, 2=25 screen rows, 3=43 screen rows

Subfunction 24h – Load 8∗16 Character Definition Table From VGA ROM For Graphics Mode (VGA)

This function loads the 8∗16 character definition table from VGA ROM into the character generator RAM. The character definition table holds the pixel pattern for each of the character codes.

Register	Call value	Return value
AH	11h	
AL	24h	
BL	screen rows*)	
DL	screen rows (if BL=0)	

*) 0=DL valid, 1=14 screen rows, 2=25 screen rows, 3=43 screen rows

Subfunction 30h – Determine Current Parameters of the Character Definition Table (EGA/VGA)

This function determines the current parameters of the indicated character definition table in EGA/VGA ROM.

Register	Call value	Return value
AH	11h	
AL	30h	
BH	character table*)	
CX		bytes per defined character
DL		screen rows
BP		offset of character definition table
ES		segment of character definition table

*) 0=contents of INT 1fh, 1=contents of 43h, 2=address of 8*14 ROM table
   3=address of 8*8 ROM table, 4=address of second half of 8*8 ROM table
   5=address of alternate 9*14 ROM table, 6=address of 8*16 ROM table,
   7=address of alternate 9*16 ROM table

Function 12h – Configuration of Video Subsystem (EGA/VGA)

This function selects various configuration parameters for the EGA/VGA. Function 12h is often called alternate select.

Subfunction 10h – Determine Video Configuration (EGA/VGA)

This function determines the EGA or VGA configuration.

Register	Call value	Return value
AH	12h	
BL	10h	
BH		size of video RAM[1]
		standard mode[2]
CH		feature bits
CL		position of configuration switches

[1] 0=64 kbytes, 1=128 kbytes, 2=192 kbytes, 3=256 kbytes
[2] 0=colour, 1=monochrome

Subfunction 20h – Select Alternate Routine For Print Screen (EGA/VGA)

This function enables the alternate routine for print screen to support the new screen modes with more than 25 rows.

Register	Call value	Return value
AH	12h	
BL	20h	

Subfunction 30h – Set Scan Line Number For Text Mode (VGA)

This function defines the number of scan lines in text mode.

Register	Call value	Return value
AH	12h	
AL	scan lines*)	12h
BL	30h	

*) 0=200 scan lines, 1=350 scan lines, 2=400 scan lines

Subfunction 31h – Load Standard Palette (VGA)

This function defines whether the standard palette is to be loaded, or whether the current palette values should be kept if the video mode is changed by a call to INT 10h, function 00h.

Register	Call value	Return value
AH	12h	
AL	command code*)	12h
BL	31h	

*) 0=load standard palette, 1=do not load standard palette

Subfunction 32h – Control CPU Access to Video RAM and I/O Ports (VGA)

This function determines whether or not the CPU can access the video RAM and the corresponding I/O ports.

Register	Call value	Return value
AH	12h	
AL	command code*)	12h
BL	32h	

*) 0=access enabled, 1=access disabled

Subfunction 33h – Control Grey Scale Mapping (VGA)

This function determines whether or not the VGA carries out a grey scale mapping.

Register	Call value	Return value
AH	12h	
AL	command code*)	12h
BL	33h	

*) 0=enable grey scale mapping, 1=disable grey scale mapping

Subfunction 34h – Control Cursor Emulation (VGA)

This function determines whether or not the VGA is to carry out a cursor emulation. The BIOS then adjusts the start and end scan lines if the character size is changed (for example, by a change from 9∗16 to 8∗8 character matrix) so that the cursor keeps the same form. That is advantageous if, for example, you have defined lines 14 and 15 as cursor scan lines for a 9∗16 character matrix because these lines are no longer valid for an 8∗8 character matrix. Without cursor emulation the cursor would disappear from the screen.

Register	Call value	Return value
AH	12h	
AL	command code*)	12h
BL	34h	

*) 0=enable cursor emulation, 1=disable cursor emulation

Subfunction 36h – Enable or Disable the Monitor Control Signals (VGA)

This function enables or disables the monitor control signals by enabling or disabling the reading of the video RAM and transfer of the control signals to the monitor. A disable shortens the access time for several successive accesses to the video RAM.

Register	Call value	Return value
AH	12h	
AL	command code*)	12h
BL	35h	

*) 0=enable monitor control signals, 1=disable monitor control signals

Function 1ah – Video Combination (EGA/VGA)

Subfunction 00h – Determine Video Combination (EGA/VGA)

This function determines the current video combination of graphics adapter and monitor as it is set by means of the DIP switches of the adapter.

Register	Call value	Return value
AH	1ah	
AL	00h	1ah
BH		inactive combination*)
BL		active combination*)

*) see below

Subfunction 01h – Set Video Combination (EGA/VGA)

This function sets the current video combination of graphics adapter and monitor and stores the information in the BIOS data area.

Register	Call value	Return value
AH	1ah	
AL	01h	1ah
BH	inactive combination*)	
BL	active combination*)	

*) Value	Meaning
00h	no monitor connected
01h	MDA with monochrome monitor
02h	CGA with colour monitor
03h	reserved
04h	EGA with colour monitor
05h	EGA with monochrome monitor
06h	PGA (professional graphics adapter)
07h	VGA with analog monochrome monitor
08h	VGA with analog colour monitor
09h	reserved
0ah	MCGA with digital colour monitor
0bh	MCGA with analog monochrome monitor
0ch	MCGA with analog colour monitor
ffh	video system not recognized

Function 1bh – Determine Video BIOS Function Capabilities and Status Informations (VGA)

This function provides exhaustive information about the capabilities of your video BIOS by determining the VGA BIOS function capabilities and the corresponding status information, and storing them in a 64-byte buffer. After the function call, the buffer contains a pointer segment:offset to a 16-byte table with a description of the BIOS function capabilities, and to 60 bytes which describe the current video status.

Register	Call value	Return value
AH	1bh	
AL		1bh
BX	0	
DI	buffer offset	*)
ES	buffer segment	*)

*) **buffer contents:**

Offset	Size	Contents
00h	dword	address of table with BIOS function capabilities (segment:offset)
04h	byte	video mode
05h	word	number of displayed character columns
07h	word	length of displayed range of video RAM (in bytes)
09h	word	start address of upper left corner on monitor in video RAM
0bh	16 bytes	8 cursor positions (column:line) for 8 screen pages
1bh	byte	cursor end (scan line)
1ch	byte	cursor start (scan line)
1dh	byte	number of active screen page
1eh	word	I/O address of CRTC address register

*) **buffer contents:**

Offset	Size	Contents
20h	byte	value of mode select register (I/O address 3b8h/3d8h)
21h	byte	value of palette register (I/O address 3b9h/3d9h)
22h	byte	number of displayed character lines
23h	word	height of displayed character matrix in scan lines
25h	byte	code for active video combination
26h	byte	code for inactive video combination
27h	word	number of simultaneously displayed colours (monochrome: 0)
29h	byte	maximum number of screen pages
2ah	byte	number of scan lines: 0=200, 1=350, 2=400, 3=480
2bh	byte	character table if attribute bit 3 equal 0 (VGA only)
2ch	byte	character table if attribute bit 3 equal 1 (VGA only)
2dh	byte	general status information:

```
                 res res BLK CEM STP MON GRY MOD

blink attribute enabled ┘      │       │  └ all modes on all
                               │       │    subsystems possible
     cursor emulation ─────────┘       └─── grey scale mapping
            enabled                         enabled
  loading of standard ──────────────────── monochrome monitor
     palette enabled                        connected
```

2eh–30h	3 bytes	reserved
31h	byte	size of video RAM: 0=64 kbytes, 1=128 kbytes, 2=192 kbytes, 3=256 kbytes
32h	byte	save status:

```
                 res res EXT POV GOV TOV DYN CH2

        extended video ┘      │       │  └ two character sets
combination code active       │       │    enabled (VGA only)
    palette overwrite ────────┘       └─── dynamic save area
              active                        enabled
    graphics character ──────────────────── text character set
      overwrite active                      overwrite enabled
```

| 33h–3fh | 12 bytes | reserved |

Table with BIOS function capabilities

Offset	Size	Contents
00h	byte	supported video modes:

```
          M07 M06 M05 M04 M03 M02 M01 M00

mode 07h ┘     │       │  └ mode 00h
mode 06h ──────┘       └─── mode 01h
mode 05h ───────────────── mode 02h
mode 04h ───────────────── mode 03h
```

| 01h | byte | supported video modes: |

```
          M0f M0e M0d M0c M0b M0a M09 M08

mode 0fh ┘     │       │  └ mode 08h
mode 0eh ──────┘       └─── mode 09h
mode 0dh ───────────────── mode 0ah
mode 0ch ───────────────── mode 0bh
```

Offset	Size	Contents

02h byte supported video mode:

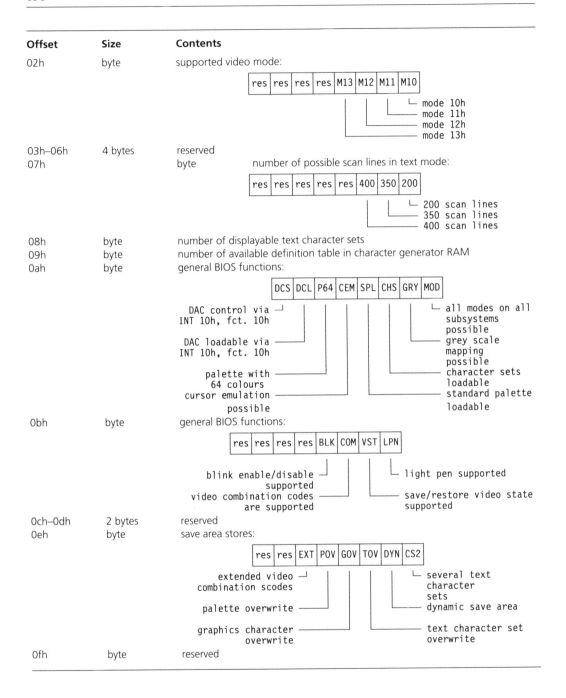

03h–06h 4 bytes reserved
07h byte number of possible scan lines in text mode:

08h byte number of displayable text character sets
09h byte number of available definition table in character generator RAM
0ah byte general BIOS functions:

0bh byte general BIOS functions:

0ch–0dh 2 bytes reserved
0eh byte save area stores:

0fh byte reserved

Function 1ch – Save/Restore Video Status (VGA)

Subfunction 00h – Determine Size of Save/Restore Buffer (VGA)

This function returns the required size necessary for the save/restore buffer to hold the specified status information.

Register	Call value	Return value
AH	1ch	
AL	00h	1ch
BX		buffer size in 64-byte blocks
CX	status information*)	

*)

```
| res | res | res | res | res | DAC | BDT | HDW |
                                  |     |     └─ video hardware status
                                  |     └─────── video BIOS data area
                                  └───────────── video DAC status
```

Subfunction 01h – Save Status (VGA)

This function saves the specified status in the save/restore buffer.

Register	Call value	Return value
AH	1ch	
AL	01h	
CX	status to save*)	
BX	offset of buffer	
ES	segment of buffer	

*)

```
| res | res | res | res | res | DAC | BDT | HDW |
                                  |     |     └─ video hardware status
                                  |     └─────── video BIOS data area
                                  └───────────── video DAC status
```

Subfunction 02h – Restore Status (VGA)

This function restores the specified status from the information in the save/restore buffer.

Register	Call value	Return value
AH	1ch	
AL	02h	
CX	status to restore*)	
BX	buffer offset	
ES	buffer segment	

*)

```
┌────┬────┬────┬────┬────┬────┬────┬────┐
│res │res │res │res │res │DAC │BDT │HDW │
└────┴────┴────┴────┴────┴────┴────┴────┘
                              │    │   └─ video hardware status
                              │    └───── video BIOS data area
                              └────────── video DAC status
```

L   Functions 89h and 87h of Interrupt 15h

– Function 89h switches the processor to protected mode.

– Function 87h switches the processor to protected mode, moves a block of data so that extended memory is accessible, and resets the processor to real mode.

Function 89h – Switch to Protected Mode

This function switches the processor to protected mode and transfers control to the code segment to which the GDT points. For this purpose, the GDT has to be built up in real mode by the calling program. The passed interrupt numbers for IRQ0 and IRQ8 are used to adjust the interrupt offsets of the 8259A PICs. Note that the 80286 and i386/i486 processors have different GDT formats. The function uses the entries in the GDT for initializing the IDTR and the SS register.

Register	Call value	Return value
AH	89h	*)
BH	interrupt number for IRQ0	
BL	interrupt number for IRQ8	
SI	GDT offset	
ES	GDT segment	
carry	error if <> 0	

*)00h=switch was successful, processor now in protected mode
  ffh=switch was not successful, processor in real mode

Function 87h – Move Block

This function moves a block of data in memory by switching the processor to protected mode, moving the block, and resetting the processor back to real mode. By means of this function, extended memory becomes accessible and data can be copied from standard memory to extended memory, and vice versa. The function moves the data in units of two bytes, or one word. In addition to the descriptor for source and target segments, the BIOS builds up the required four descriptors in the GDT. For this purpose, the calling program has to reserve 48 bytes for a GDT with the entries needed. The source and target descriptors which comprise the entries segment limit (in bytes), base address and access rights (always equal to 93h) must be generated by the calling program. These have to be written into the 48-byte table at offset 10h and 18h, respectively. Note the differences between 80286 and i386/i486 descriptors.

Register	Call value	Return value
AH	87h	1)
CX	number of words to copy	
SI	GDT offset 2)	
ES	GDT segment 2)	
carry		error if <> 0

1) 00h=move was successful, 01h= RAM parity error
   02h=unexpected exception, 03h=error concerning address line A20

2)

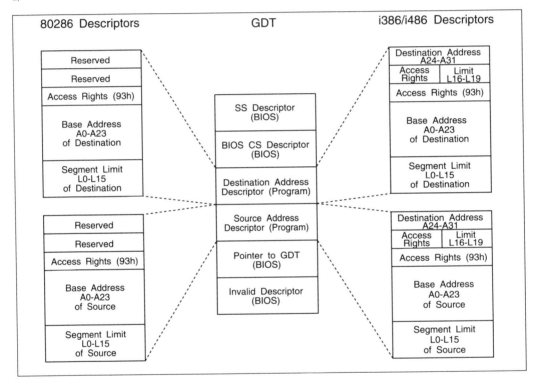

Glossary

1"
Abbr. for 1 inch; equals 2.54 cm.

14.318.180 Hz
This frequency forms the base clock in the PC/XT. Dividing by three generates the processor frequency of the 8086/88. For compatibility reasons, this frequency is still used today for the timer chips and the real-time clock after dividing by twelve.

16450/16550
The improved successor of the UART 8250. It is used in the AT and newer PC models, and enables a transmission rate of up to 115.200 baud.

38605DX/38605SX
An i386-compatible processor from Chips & Technologies with an internal instruction cache and a new operating mode for reducing power consumption, the SuperState V Mode. The 38605SX has only a 16-bit data bus and a 24-bit address bus.

38600DX/38600SX

An i386-compatible processor from Chips & Technologies with a new operating mode for reducing power consumption, the SuperState V Mode. The 38600SX has only a 16-bit data bus and a 24-bit address bus. Unlike the 38605DX/38605SX, no cache is implemented.

386SL
An Intel chipset which comprises the 386SL and the 82360SL I/O-subsystem. The 386SL integrates an i386 CPU, a cache controller and tag RAM, an ISA bus controller and a memory controller on a single chip. On the 82386SL a real-time clock, two timers with three channels each, a memory decoder, two DMA controllers, a parallel interface, two interrupt controllers, and two serial interfaces are integrated. With the 386SL chip set, very compact notebook ATs can be constructed.

386SLC
An i386-compatible processor from IBM with significantly increased performance compared to Intel's original. The 386SLC includes an internal 8 kbyte cache and is implemented in a power-saving static design. Currently, the 386SLC is not freely supplied, but reserved by IBM for its own products.

4.77 MHz
This frequency was the processor clock for the 8088/86 in the original PC/XT.

486DLC/486SLC
An i386-compatible and power-saving CMOS processor from Cyrix. Unlike its Intel counterparts, it incorporates an internal 1 kbyte cache, an enhanced processor kernel similar to the i486,

and an internal power management unit for reducing power consumption. The SLC is the SX-model of the DLC with a 16-bit data bus and a 24-bit address bus.

640 kbyte-boundary

In the PC the video RAM and various ROMs are located at the upper end of the real mode address space. They normally start at address a0000h. With DOS only the lower 640 kbytes of memory are available for operating system, drivers, and application programs.

6502

A common 8-bit microprocessor for CP/M, which was mainly used as the CPU in the legendary C64.

68000 family

A CISC processor family from Motorola, which is mainly used in Apple computers. They are the counterparts to the Intel 80x86 family.

6845

A graphics controller chip or CRTC, which is used in various forms in nearly all graphics adapters. Besides other jobs, it generates the control and synchronization signals for the monitor.

8042

A microchip used as a keyboard controller in the AT.

8048

A microchip used as a keyboard chip in PC/XT keyboards.

8080/85

A well-known 8-bit processor for CP/M, and the predecessor of the 8086/88.

8086

A 16-bit processor with 16-bit registers, a 16-bit data bus, and a 20-bit address bus. It is employed in the XT, and is the ancestor of the 80x86 family. The 8086 operates in real mode only. The address space comprises 1 Mbyte.

8088

A 16-bit processor with 16-bit registers, a 16-bit data bus, and a 20-bit address bus. It is used in the PC, and apart from the smaller data bus width is identical to the 8086.

80186/88

These processors are the successors to the 8086/88. Besides improved and extended instructions, an interrupt controller, a DMA chip and a timer chip are integrated on the 80186/88.

80286

The second generation of the 80x86 family. The 80286 represents a 16-bit processor with 16-bit registers, a 16-bit data bus, and a 24-bit address bus. With the 80286 protected mode was introduced, in which an address space of up to 16 Mbytes is enabled.

80287/80287XL

The mathematical coprocessor for the 80286. The 80287XL is improved compared to the normal 80287, and has all i387 functions.

80386/80386SX

Another name for i386/i386SX (see i386/i386SX).

80387/80387SX

Another name for i387/i387SX (see i387/i387SX).

80486/80486SX

Another name for i486/i486SX (see i486/i486SX).

80486DX2

Another name for i486DX2 (see i486DX2).

80487SX

Another name for i487 (see i487).

8087

The mathematical coprocessor for the 8086/88.

80x86 family

The family of the downward-compatible 80x86 chips. Presently, the family comprises the 8086/88, 80186/88, 80286, i386/i386SX, and i486/i486SX. They all are CISC processors with an extensive and micro-encoded instruction set.

82072A

A floppy disk controller for the AT.

82077A

A floppy disk controller for the PS/2 with a microchannel, and the successor to the 82072A.

82284

The clock generator for the 80286.

82288

The bus controller for the 80286.

8237A

An 8-bit DMA controller with four independently programmable DMA channels. In the PC/XT one such chip is present; in the AT two chips are cascaded so that seven DMA channels are available.

82450

A UART chip and improved successor to the 8250 for the AT.

8250

A UART chip used in the PC/XT. There are several versions with the names 8250, 8250A, 8250B, and 8250C.

8253

A programmable interval timer (PIT) with three independent counters. The 8253 is used in the PC/XT and in many ATs.

8254

A programmable interval timer (PIT) with three independent counters, and the improved successor to the 8253. The 8254 is used in most ATs, and in EISA and microchannel PCs.

8255A

A programmable peripheral interface (PPI) with three 8-bit ports A, B, and C. Port C can be divided into two nibbles that extend ports A and B by four bits. The 8255A was used in the PC/XT for reading DIP switches and for transferring the scan codes from the PC/XT keyboard. The 8255A is not used in the AT any more.

8259A

A programmable interrupt controller (PIC) with eight different interrupt lines. In the PC/XT one such chip is used; in the AT two 8259As are cascaded so that here 15 different interrupt levels are available.

8284

The clock generator for the 8086/88 and 80186/88.

8288

The bus controller for the 8086/88 and 80186/88.

8514/A

An IBM graphics adapter with an in-built graphics processor.

8741

A microchip often used as a keyboard controller in the AT.

8742

A microchip often used as a keyboard controller in the PS/2.

ABIOS

Abbr. for **a**dvanced **BIOS**. The ABIOS of the PS/2 comprises the BIOS routines for the PC operation in protected mode.

Access Time

The time period between the supply of an access signal and the output or acceptance of the data by the addressed subsystem. Examples are the access times for DRAMs, SRAMs, or hard disks.

Accumulator

A CPU register which is optimized in view of the execution of some instructions. In former processors the accumulator was the only register that could be used as the instruction destination, i.e. for providing the operation result.

ACK

Abbr. for **ack**nowledge.

active-high

A signal is called active-high if a high potential level has the effect or shows the status which is indicated by the signal's name. For example, the 8086's READY signal is active-high because a high potential level indicates that the addressed unit is ready. On the other hand, a low level states that the unit is not ready yet.

active-low

A signal is called active-low if a low potential level has the effect or shows the status which is indicated by the signal's name. For example, the 8086's $\overline{RD}$ signal is active-low because a low potential level indicates that data is being read. On the other hand, a high level states that data is being written. Active-low signals are usually characterized by a cross bar ($\overline{RD}$), a preceding slanted line (/RD), a succeeding star (RD*), or in a few cases, by a succeeding tilde (RD~).

Actuator

Comprises all components of a drive necessary for positioning the read/write head. Normally, these are at least the access arm and the access motor.

Adapter Card

Also called an extension card or plug-in card. A board with electronic circuitry which is inserted into a bus slot to enhance the capabilities of the PC. Typical representatives are interface adapter cards, graphics adapter cards, and controller cards.

ADC

Abbr. for **a**nalog to **d**igital **c**onverter. An ADC converts an analog signal into a predetermined number of bits, which represent the value of the analog signal.

Address

A quantity which describes the location of an object. Specifically, an address is a word or a number that characterizes a storage location or a port.

Address Bus

A number of generally parallel lines that transmit an address.

Address Space

The number of objects that a CPU or another chip can address.

ALU

Abbr. for **a**rithmetical and **l**ogical **u**nit. The ALU is part of a CPU, and executes the arithmetical and logical operations.

AM386DX/AM386SX

An i386-compatible processor from AMD with increased performance compared to Intel's original. The AM386SX only has a 16-bit data bus and a 24-bit address bus.

AM386DXL/AM386SXL

An i386-compatible processor from AMD with increased performance compared to Intel's original and a power-saving static design. The AM386SXL has only a 16-bit data bus and a 24-bit address bus.

AM386DXLV/AM386SXLV

The low-voltage model of AMD's AM386DX. The AM386DXLV operates at only 3.3 V, and therefore consumes 50% less power. The AM386SXLV has only a 16-bit data bus and a 24-bit address bus.

AMD

Abbr. for **A**dvanced **M**icro **D**evices. A US firm that produces microelectronic components such as processors, ASICs, RAM chips, etc. AMD became known through its Intel-compatible 80x86 and 80x87 processors, and it could win a considerable market share with its 386 clones.

Analog

Without intermediate steps, continuously. An analog signal, for example, can have continuous values without intermediate steps.

Analog Monitor

A monitor for displaying text or graphics which is driven by an analog signal. A VGA adapter would be an example of a graphics adapter that drives an analog monitor.

ANSI

Abbr. for **A**merican **N**ational **S**tandards **I**nstitute. An authority in the US that sets up technical standards. ANSI is comparable with the German DIN.

Arbitration

The transfer of control over a unit from the present holder of the control rights to another unit that wants to take over control. This is done by arbitration signals and an arbitration strategy.

Architecture

The overall concept for the design and structure of a computer or a computer system.

ARRL

Abbr. for **a**dvanced **RLL**. An RLL recording method which operates with a more complex encoding than RLL 2,7, and thus enables higher data densities. Compared to MFM, ARRL achieves an increase of up to 90%.

ASCII code

Abbr. for **A**merican **s**tandard **c**ode for **i**nformation **i**nterchange. A 7-bit code that encodes 32 control characters for data transfer, and additionally 96 alphanumeric characters.

ASCIIZ string

A string that is terminated by the ASCII character \0, i.e. a null.

ASIC

Abbr. for **a**pplication **s**pecific **IC**. An integrated circuit focused to a specific application. ASICs are often manufactured by gate arrays.

Assembler

A program that translates mnemonic code and symbolic addresses into machine code. Assemblers are the programming option which is closest to the machine and still accepts symbolic addresses and quantities.

Associative Memory

See CAM.

Asynchronous

Not corresponding to a phase or clock signal, or without a clock signal.

AT

1. Abbr. for **a**dvanced **t**echnology.
2. The successor of the PC/XT with an 80286 CPU and 16-bit bus slots.

AT bus

The AT bus system with various support chips (DMA, PIC, PIT, etc.) and a 16-bit bus slot. The AT bus is strictly defined by ISA.

ATA

Abbr. for **AT a**ttachment. A standard for mainly connecting hard disk drives to an AT bus; synonymous with IDE.

Attribute

1. A quantity which is added to another quantity, and which further defines the properties of this quantity.

2. The high byte of the video word which has information on the brightness, colour and background of the character to be displayed. The character code is stored in the low byte of the video word.

Autopark

A function of better quality hard disk drives which moves the actuator and the read/write heads into the park position upon switching off the drive. Any damage of the data medium can thus be prevented.

AUX

Abbr. for **aux**iliary. With DOS synonymous with COM1, else generally an additional signal or an additional line.

Average Access Time

The average value for the time period between the output of an access instruction and the delivery of the data. The average access time is mainly used to characterize the speed of the positioning mechanism in hard disk drives and similar mass storages devices.

Bad Sector Mapping

The logical replacement of defective sectors or tracks by intact spare sectors or spare tracks when formatting the drive. This is done either by shifting the sectors within one track (sector slipping), or by diverting the accesses to the corresponding spare track if the defects are too serious. The capacity of the hard disk drive can thus be maintained in spite of defective spots. The bad sector mapping is carried out by the controller, and therefore transparent for BIOS, DOS and all other software.

BASIC

Abbr. for **b**eginners **a**ll-purpose **s**ymbolic **i**nstruction **c**ode. A very simple structured programming language with easy to remember instruction names like »PRINT«. Very often, BASIC is implemented in the form of an interpreter, but nowadays there exist several powerful BASIC compilers which have some structural elements of C or Pascal.

Baud Rate

The number of state changes of a transmission channel per second. On binary data channels the baud rate is usually equal to the number of transmitted bits per second (bps).

BCD

Abbr. for **b**inary **c**oded **d**ecimal. BCD encodes a decimal digit as a binary value of one byte. Example: BCD = 04h corresponds to decimal 4. BCD wastes a lot of storage because one byte is able to encode 256 different values, but BCD uses only ten (0–9) of them.

Bidirectional

In the case of a bidirectional transmission, data can be exchanged in either direction between the communication participants. Thus the two participants can serve both as a transmitter and a receiver.

Big Blue

Nickname for IBM, because IBM is a big business group and the company's emblem is blue.

Big Endian Format

In the big endian format the high bytes of a multiple-byte quantity are stored at lower addresses, and the low bytes are stored at higher addresses. Motorola's 68000 family uses the big endian format.

BIOS

Abbr. for basic input/output system. The BIOS comprises the system programs for the basic input and output operations, and represents the software interface to the PC hardware. Typical BIOS functions are accesses to the floppy disk, hard disk drive, interfaces, and graphics adapters.

Bit

Abbr. for binary digit. A digit, number, or a value that can show only two different conditions. These are normally named 0 and 1 or 0 and L. Very often, the bit is also called the smallest information unit.

Bit Line

The line in the column direction of a memory cell array in a RAM or ROM to which the stored value of a selected memory cell is transferred. The bit line is usually connected to the source terminal of the selection transistor.

BNC

A special plug form for transmitting high frequency signals. By means of an extensive shielding of the BNC plugs, a BNC connection is very noise-safe. Very high resolution graphics adapters and monitors are often connected via BNC plugs and jacks.

Board

A stiff card which comprises electronic elements and wiring for connecting them.

Booting

Loading the BIOS and the operating system into a computer. The booting is normally the result of the operations of BIOS, bootstrap, and operating system loader.

Bootstrap

A small program on a bootable disk or partition which controls and executes the loading of the operating system. The name bootstrap has a somewhat fairy-tale background: just as the braggart Baron Münchhausen pulled himself by his own bootstraps out of the swamp, the computer also boots itself via the bootstrap.

Bouncing
The phenomenon whereby when pressing a key the corresponding switch first closes, then opens, and afterwards closes again. The reason for this is the elastic reacting force of the key switch, and therefore this is not an intentional double key pressing.

bpi
Abbr. for **b**its **p**er **i**nch.

bps
Abbr. for **b**its **p**er **s**econd.

Break-Code
See scan code.

Burst Mode
A special high-speed mode for the transmission of larger data blocks in the form of an uninterrupted burst of smaller data units. For example, a cache line of 16 bytes can be transferred as a burst of four data units with 4 bytes each.

Bus
A number of generally parallel signal lines which transmit control, data, and address signals.

Bus Master
A device or chip that can control a bus autonomously. Examples are the CPU and DMA chips.

Bus Slot
A dual contact strip in a PC into which adapter cards can be inserted. The bus slot comprises the contacts for all necessary control, data, and address signals.

Byte
A group of eight bits.

C
A very flexible programming language which is very close to the machine, but comprises all elements of a high-level language. Characteristic of C is that there are almost no reserved names and commands. Instead, all extensive commands which are known from other languages are implemented in the form of function libraries.

Cache
A very fast intermediate memory between a fast CPU and a slower memory subsystem.

Cache Flush

Writing the cache contents into main memory or to another data medium. Cache flushes are necessary only for cache systems which do not support a write-through strategy.

Cache Miss

See cache hit.

Cache Hit

If a CPU in a computer system with a cache outputs an address to read data, and if the thus addressed data is already in the cache SRAM and doesn't have to be read out of the slow main memory but may be read out of the fast cache SRAM, this is called a cache hit. If this is not true and the addressed data is in the main memory only but not in the SRAM, this is called a cache miss.

CAD

Abbr. for **c**omputer-**a**ided **d**esign. CAD concerns the drawing of plans and all secondary jobs with the aid of a computer. CAD is applicable in mechanical and electrical engineering, and for architects or building engineers.

CAM

Abbr. for **c**ontents **a**dressable **m**emory; often called associative memory. CAM concerns a memory or memory chip in which the information is not addressed by means of an address, but via a part of the information itself, thus by part of the memory contents. The CAM thus associates further data with this partial information so that eventually a range of information is addressed. Then the information can be ambiguous. CAMs are mainly used for cache systems.

CAS

Abbr. for **c**olumn **a**ddress **s**trobe. A control signal for a DRAM memory chip, which instructs the chip to accept the address provided as the column address and to interpret the address accordingly.

CCITT

Abbr. for **C**omité **C**onsultatif Internationale de **T**élégraphique et **T**éléphonique, an international committee for telegraph and telephone. A suborganization of the UN which sets up international mandatory standards for telecommunication services. You can thus telephone Australia or Europe without any problems caused by incompatibilities between different telephone networks.

CD-ROM

Abbr. for **c**ompact **d**isk **ROM**. An optical mass storage where the information is unchangeably written onto a compact disk. Typical capacities are 500 Mbytes per disk side.

CD-I

Abbr. for **CD** interactive. A modification of CD-ROM with an improved (interactive) interface.

Centronics

A US printer manufacturer who was the first to set up a standard for connecting a printer to a parallel interface. Today all parallel printers are connected via a Centronics cable to the PC's parallel interface.

Character Generator

An electronic circuitry on a graphics adapter which in text mode supplies an alphanumeric character according to the corresponding bit mask stored in ROM or RAM. Thus the character generator generates the pixels for displaying the character from the character code in the video RAM. In graphics mode, however, each pixel is individually stored in the video RAM.

Chip

A fingernail-sized silicon plate with up to several million circuits and electronic elements.

Chipset

A group of integrated circuits which serve for a certain job, for example to build an AT. A chipset integrates the function of many discrete elements, for example CPU, PIC, PIT, DMA, etc., on a small number of chips.

CISC

Abbr. for complex instruction set computer. Microprocessors that comprise a very extensive instruction set of 100 to 400 machine instructions. Characteristic of CISC is the micro-encoding of the machine instructions.

CMOS

Abbr. for complementary metal oxide semiconductor. CMOS is a technology for semiconductor elements with very low power consumption. Generally, this is achieved by connecting one NMOS and one PMOS element.

COBOL

Abbr. for common business oriented language. COBOL is a programming language which is specifically designed for banking and business applications.

Coercivity

That magnetic field which is necessary to de-magnetize a completely magnetized ferromagnetic body.

COM1, COM2, COM3, COM4

The DOS name for the various serial interfaces in a PC. COM is derived from communications port.

Combicontroller

A combination of floppy and hard disk controller on a single adapter card. Normally, one combicontroller manages two hard disk and two floppy disk drives.

Compiler

A program which translates the commands written in a high-level language such as C or Pascal into a series of machine instructions for the computer.

CON

The DOS name for keyboard and monitor. CON is derived from **con**sole. Formerly, the console was the »workstation« for the operator who controlled and supervised the computer.

Console

See CON.

Control Bus

A number of lines that transmit control information or control signals, generally in parallel.

Controller

1. An electronic device which controls and supervises the function of a peripheral; examples are the floppy disk controller, hard disk controller, LAN controller, etc.

2. An electronic device which executes a certain function; for example, a DMA controller.

Coprocessor

Also called processor extension. A microchip specially designed for a certain CPU to enhance or support the functions of that CPU. Examples are numerical coprocessors which enhance the capabilities of the CPU by calculating numerical expressions with floating-point numbers.

CP/M

Abbr. for **c**ontrol **p**rogram for **m**icrocomputers. A simple operating system for 8-bit processors such as the 8080/85 or Z80. CP/M was the predecessor of DOS, therefore DOS still uses some concepts of CP/M (the FCBs, for example).

CPU

Abbr. for **c**entral **p**rocessing **u**nit. The CPU is the heart of a computer, and is also often called the (central) processor. Examples are the Intel 80x86 family and the Motorola 68000.

CR

Abbr. for **c**arriage **r**eturn. CR is an ASCII control character with the code 0dh, which leads to the carriage return of a serial printer or to a cursor movement to the beginning of the line.

CRC

Abbr. for **c**yclic **r**edundancy **c**heck or **c**yclic **r**edundancy **c**ode. A family of redundant codes that can detect data errors very efficiently. Burst errors, for example, are detected with a probability of more than 99.99%. CRC is especially applied to data recording and data transfer.

CTS

Abbr. for clear to send. With CTS a DCE indicates its transmission readiness, and that the DTA may transmit data to the DCE now.

CU

Abbr. for control unit. The CU is part of a processor or CPU and controls the ALU, registers, and other components.

Curie Point/Curie Temperature

The sharp defined temperature T_c where the ferromagnetic properties of a material disappear.

Cyrix

A US-manufacturer of microelectronic components. Cyrix became famous with its 80x87-compatible coprocessors for the 80x86 family. Now Cyrix is also manufacturing 80x86-compatible microprocessors, especially power-saving models for portable PCs.

DAC

Abbr. for digital analog converter. A DAC converts a digital signal made of a certain number of bits into an analog signal, which represents the value of these bits.

Data Bus

A number of lines that transfer data generally in parallel.

Data Communication Equipment

See DCE.

Data Medium

A device on which data can be durably stored. Examples are floppy disks, hard disks, magnetic tapes, and optical disks.

Data Terminal Equipment

See DTE.

Datex P

A public data network of the Deutsche Bundespost for transmitting data (Data Exchange), which operates with packet switching (P).

DCD

Abbr. for data carrier detect. With DCD a DCE informs a DTE that it has detected a data carrier signal from another DCE.

DCE

Abbr. for data communication equipment. A device for transmitting data, generally a modem.

DD
Abbr. for **d**ouble **d**ensity.

Descriptor
An 8-byte data block which describes a segment or gate in protected mode.

Diamagnetism
A form of magnetism which somewhat weakens the external magnetic field (typically by 0.000001% to 0.05%). Pure diamagnetism appears only in materials with paired electrons.

Digital
With intermediate steps, discontinuously, divided in discrete steps. A digital signal, for example, can only reach certain values on a scale, but no intermediate values.

Digital Monitor
A monitor for displaying text or graphics which is driven by a digital signal. The HGC adapter is an example of a graphics card which drives a digital monitor.

DIN
Abbr. for **D**eutsche **I**ndustrie **N**ormenausschuß or **D**eutsche **I**ndustrie**n**orm. An organization which sets up obligatory technical standards in Germany.

DIP
Abbr. for **d**ual **i**nline **p**ackage. A package with contacts on the two opposite lateral sides.

DIP Switch
A small switch block in a DIP package which has several small switches. Jokingly often called a mice piano.

Display Memory
See video RAM.

DMA
Abbr. for **d**irect **m**emory **a**ccess. Besides the CPU, DMA forms a second data channel between peripherals and main memory through which a peripheral can directly access the main memory without the help of the CPU and read or write data. In the PC, DMA is implemented by the 8237A DMA controller.

Domain
The elementary region of uniform magnetization in a ferromagnetic material. Often also called the white domain.

DOS
Abbr. for **d**isk **o**perating **s**ystem. The most-installed operating system for IBM-compatible PCs. DOS operates only in the 80x86 real mode.

Doping

The introduction of other atoms into a semiconductor to affect the electrical properties of it.

Double Word

A 4-byte quantity, therefore 32 bits.

dpi

Abbr. for **d**ots **p**er **i**nch.

Drain

One conduction terminal of a field effect transistor.

DRAM

Abbr. for **d**ynamic **RAM**. DRAM is a direct accessible memory (RAM) where the information is usually stored in the form of charges in a capacitor. Because all capacitors are gradually discharged by leak currents, the storage capacitor and therefore the whole DRAM must be periodically refreshed, hence the name dynamic.

DRDOS

Abbr. for **D**igital **R**esearch **DOS**. An MS-DOS compatible operating system from Digital Research.

Drive Array

A group of physically different drives combined into one logical drive. The storage capacity of the drive is thus increased, the average seek time is reduced, and the data transfer rate grows because the drives of the drive array operate in parallel.

Driver

A software or hardware unit for driving a software or hardware component. The driver usually has a clearly defined interface so that, for example, a program can access the device without the need to know the device's structure and functioning in detail.

DSR

Abbr. for **d**ata **s**et **r**eady. Using DSR a DCE informs a DTE that it is in general ready.

DTE

Abbr. for **d**ata **t**erminal **e**quipment. A device located at the end of a transmission line which provides or receives data. Examples are a PC, a telephone and a fax.

DTR

Abbr. for **d**ata **t**erminal **r**eady. With DTR a DTE informs a DCE that it is in general ready.

Dual-Port RAM

A RAM chip which has two independent access ports to the memory cells in the RAM chip. Two devices can thus access the information in RAM without disturbing each other. Dual-port memories are mainly used for the video RAM of graphic adapters, where CPU and adapter logic access the display memory concurrently. Another application is their use as communication memory in a multiprocessor system, so that two or more processors can exchange data through this memory.

Duplex
The concurrent data transmission capability of a channel in both directions.

DWord
Abbr. for **D**ouble **W**ord. See double word.

EBCDIC Code
Abbr. for **e**xtended **b**inary **c**oded **d**ecimal **i**nterchange **c**ode. An 8-bit character code corresponding to the ASCII code which is mainly used in IBM mainframes.

ECC
Abbr. for **e**rror **c**orrecting **c**ode. Sometimes also called self-correcting code. A form of cyclic redundancy code where the redundancy is so extensive that errors can not only be detected but also corrected. The ECC codes are mainly applied to data recording on hard disk drives.

ECL
Abbr. for **e**mitter **c**oupled **l**ogic. A certain family of logic circuits.

EEPROM
Abbr. for **e**lectrically **e**rasable **PROM**. A programmable read-only memory which can be erased by a high level voltage pulse. EEPROMs are mainly implemented with FAMOST technology.

EGA
Abbr. for **e**nhanced **g**raphics **a**dapter. An IBM graphics adapter with, compared to CGA, enhanced resolution and more colours. Standard EGA comprises 640*400 pixels.

EIA
Abbr. for **E**lectronic **I**ndustries **A**ssociation. A US organization which sets standards for the electronics industry.

EISA
Abbr. for **e**xtended **ISA**. EISA defines a 32-bit extension for the ISA or AT bus to integrate the i386/i486 32-bit processors. EISA is downward-compatible with the XT and AT bus, therefore XT and ISA adapters can be used without any problems (theoretically).

EISA Master
A bus master which can carry out EISA bus cycles.

EISA Slave
A device which serves EISA bus cycles.

EMS Window
A 64 kbyte block in the address space of the PC between 640 k and 1 M which can be overlaid by four EMS pages with 16 kbytes each. The EMS window is therefore something like a window into the much larger address space of expanded memory.

ENIAC
Abbr. for electronic numerical integrator and calculator. One of the first fully electronic digital computers which ran with vacuum tubes. It was developed in the US between 1943–1946.

EPROM
Abbr. for erasable **PROM**. A programmable read-only memory that can be erased by irradiation of UV-light. EPROMs are mainly implemented with FAMOST technology.

ESC Instruction (Coprocessor)
All opcodes for the 80x87 numerical coprocessor start with the bit sequence 11011, corresponding to 27. This is the ASCII code for the character ESC, therefore they are called ESC instructions.

ESDI
Abbr. for enhanced small device interface. ESDI is an interface between a hard disk controller and a hard disk drive. ESDI was introduced by Maxtor in 1983 as the more powerful successor to the ST506/412 interface. The main characteristic of ESDI is that the data separator no longer resides on the controller, but is integrated into the drive itself. ESDI is designed for data transfer rates up to 24 Mbits/s, equal to 3 Mbytes/s.

Ethernet
A local area network (LAN) with a data transfer rate of up to 10 Mbits/s via coaxial cables.

EU
Abbr. for execution unit. That part of a CPU which actually executes the instructions under the control of the control unit (CU).

Exception
If an internal processor error occurs, the CPU issues an interrupt called an exception. The source of an exception can, for example, be a segment which is not present in memory, an unloaded page, a division by zero, a set breakpoint, or a protection error.

Expanded Memory
A memory system accessed by bank switching. More than 1 Mbyte of memory is thus available for the 80x86 in real mode. From expanded memory only that part which is within the EMS window can be accessed at a given time.

Extended ASCII Code

An 8-bit code whose codes from 0–127 meet the standard ASCII code. The codes 128–255 are allocated block graphics and other characters.

Extended Memory

The memory above 1 M. Extended memory, except the first 64 kbytes immediately above the 1 Mbyte boundary, can be accessed in protected mode only.

FAMOST

Abbr. for floating gate avalanche injection MOS transistor. A FAMOST has a floating gate that can be loaded with electrons by a high-level voltage pulse which leads to an avalanche breakthrough. The characteristic of the FAMOST is thus changed. FAMOSTs are mainly used for EPROMs, EEPROMs and flash memories.

Faraday Effect

The effect whereby the polarization of an electromagnetic wave (for example, light) is rotated if the wave passes a magnetized medium.

FCB

Abbr. for file control block. A data structure under CP/M which describes an opened file. With DOS the FCB is replaced by the more modern handle concept.

fci

Abbr. for flux changes per inch.

FDC

Abbr. for floppy disk controller.

Fault Current Protection Switch

An electronic device which compares the current running through the phase wire with the back current in a house or office. If the difference becomes larger than a predetermined amount, the switch assumes that a human is in contact with the phase and current is flowing through his body directly to mass, i.e. the human suffers an electric shock. Then the fault current protection switch cuts off the current flow.

Ferromagnetic Material

A material which shows ferromagnetic properties. Examples are iron, cobalt, nickel, or permanent magnets.

Ferromagnetism

The phenomenon whereby microscopic regions of a material, the so-called domains, are completely magnetized. If such a body is moved into a magnetic field, all domains straighten according to the external field and the body is magnetized. A feature of ferromagnetism is that this magnetization remains even if the external field is switched off.

FET

Abbr. for field effect transistor. In a FET the control of the conductivity is carried out by an electrical field between the gate and source.

FIFO

Abbr. for first-in, first-out. FIFO memories are often used as buffers.

Flip-Flop

Also called a bistable multivibrator. An electronic circuit with two stably defined states that can be switched by a strong write pulse. Flip-flops are used as latches or SRAM memory cells.

Floppy Disk

A data carrier which consists of a circular disk made of a flexible material. The floppy disk is usually located in a protective envelope or a case. For the PC, 5 1/4" floppy disks with 360 kbytes and 1.2 Mbytes storage capacity and 3 1/2" floppy disks with 720 kbytes and 1.44 Mbytes of storage capacity are currently in use.

Floppy Disk Drive

A drive to read and write floppy disks with a drive motor, one or two read/write heads, and an access arm for positioning the heads.

FM

Abbr. for frequency modulation. A data encoding method for magnetic data carriers.

Full Stroke Time

The time a disk drive needs to move the read/write head from cylinder 0 to the cylinder with the maximum cylinder number.

G

Symbol for Giga (i.e. one billion of a quantity), for example in 1 GW = 1 000 000 000 W. Note that 1 Gbyte usually means 2^{30} bytes = 1 073 741 800 bytes.

Gallium Arsenide

Abbr. GaAs. A semiconductor material for extremely fast operating circuits.

Galvanization

The deposition of metals on a substrate by introducing the substrate into a solution with ions of the desired coating metal and applying a certain voltage.

Gate

The control terminal of a field effect transistor. By changing the gate voltage the conductivity of the transistor can be varied.

Gate Array

A microchip with a number of logic gates. To carry out a certain function the connection of the gates is determined by a mask after the last manufacturing step. The gate array can thus be adapted very easily to various jobs, because the function concerned affects only a single step of the manufacturing process. Today, gate arrays are mainly used for ASICs or highly integrated controller chips in the PC.

Gbyte

2^{30} bytes = 1 073 741 800 bytes; **not** 1 000 000 000 bytes.

GDT

Abbr. for **g**lobal **d**escriptor **t**able. A table of 8-byte entries (the descriptors), which describe segments and gates in protected mode.

GDTR

Abbr. for **g**lobal **d**escriptor **t**able **r**egister. A memory management register from the 80286 which holds the base address and the limit of the GDT in memory.

Gradual Underflow

A floating point number that is different from zero, but which cannot be represented in normalized form any more.

Graphics Adapter

An adapter for a PC bus slot to display graphics and text on a monitor. Examples are CGA, HGC, EGA, VGA, 8514/A, and TIGA.

Graphics Mode

A certain operating mode of a graphics adapter where each point on the screen is allocated one or more bits. Each picture element (pixel) can be addressed individually. The image is not restricted to a certain font, but any characters and graphics may be displayed. Text characters are written into the video memory in bit-mapped form, and are not generated by the hardware character generator.

Graphics Processor

A specialized microprocessor which processes graphics commands. The processor can thus draw, for example, lines and geometric objects with only the coordinates of a few characterizing points, without any intervention from the CPU. With a graphics processor the CPU is relieved from ordinary graphics tasks.

Graphics Control Chip

A microchip which generates all the necessary control and data signals to display text and graphics on a monitor.

Half Duplex
The transmission of data in one direction where, however, the transmission direction can be switched. The two communication participants may therefore operate as receiver and transmitter alternately.

Handle
A number which DOS internally allocates to an opened file or device, for example the keyboard (handle 0).

Handshake
The beginning of a data or control signal transmission by a request signal and the acknowledgement of the data or control signal's delivery by an acknowledge signal.

Hard Disk/Hard Disk Drive
A drive for data recording which uses a stiff data carrier in the form of a fast rotating disk. The read/write heads of the drive are moved by a common actuator. Generally, hard disks are located in a case.

HD
1. Abbr. for **h**ard **d**isk.
2. Abbr. for **h**igh **d**ensity.

HDA
Abbr. for **h**ead **disk a**ssembly. That part of a hard disk drive which comprises the disks, the heads, and the actuator. Normally, the HDA is surrounded by a case, and the incoming air is filtered so that no pollution may penetrate into the HDA.

HDC
Abbr. for **h**ard **d**isk controller.

Hercules Card or Hercules Graphics Card
Abbr. HGC. A monochrome adapter card with graphics capabilities for the PC. In text mode it is compatible with the MDA; in graphics mode it supports a resolution of 720*348 pixels.

HEX
Abbr. for **hex**adecimal number.

HGC
Abbr. for **H**ercules **g**raphics **c**ard.

High-Level Formatting
The formatting of a data carrier or medium if only the logical structure of the file system is established, but no tracks and sectors are physically generated. For a hard disk, the command FORMAT carries out a high-level formatting only.

Host

Also called a central computer. A computer or computer element which represents the kernel of a computer system.

Host Adapter

An adapter card which establishes the interface between a host and an external bus. Examples are SCSI host adapters for the connection of a SCSI bus with SCSI drives or IDE host adapters for the connection of the AT bus with IDE drives to the PC system bus.

Hz

Symbol for Hertz. 1 Hz = 1 period/s.

i386/i386SX

The third generation of the 80x86 family. The i386 has a 32-bit processor with 32-bit registers, a 32-bit data bus, and a 32-bit address bus. With the i386 the virtual 8086 mode was introduced. The physical address space comprises 4 Gbytes. The SX modification, i386SX, is internally identical to the i386, but has only a 16-bit data bus and a 24-bit address bus.

i387/i387SX

The mathematical coprocessor for the i386 and i386SX, respectively.

i486/i486SX

The fourth and, up to now, last generation of the 80x86 family. The i486 has a 32-bit processor with 32-bit registers, a 32-bit data bus, and a 32-bit address bus. Further, it has an improved i387 coprocessor, a cache controller, and an 8 kbyte cache SRAM. The i486SX only lacks the coprocessor.

i486DX2

An i486 with internally doubled processor frequency, i.e. the internal processor clock is twice the external clock supplied by the clock generator. The bus interface and therefore the bus cycles, on the other hand, run with the external clock only.

i487SX

The upgrade for an i486SX. The i487SX not only supplies the coprocessor, but is a complete i486 CPU with on-chip cache, etc. If the i476SX is installed it disables the i486SX CPU and takes over its jobs, too.

IC

Abbr. for integrated circuit. A circuit consisting of several electronic elements which is provided on a single carrier (substrate). DRAMs and microprocessors belong to the highest integrated ICs.

IDE

Abbr. for intelligent drive electronics. A standard for connecting intelligent hard disks or other drives with an embedded controller to the AT bus. The IDE interface is also called an AT bus or ATA interface.

IDT

Abbr. for interrupt descriptor table. A table of 8-byte entries (the descriptors) which describe gates for handling interrupts in protected mode.

IDTR

Abbr. for interrupt descriptor table register. A memory management register from the 80286 which holds the base address and limit of the IDT in memory.

IEEE

Abbr. for Institute of Electrical and Electronics Engineers; sometimes called IE^3 (I-triple-E). An engineering organization in the US which defines standards.

IIL

Abbr. for integrated injection logic; also called I^{2}L. A family of logic elements.

Induction

The phenomenon whereby a varying magnetic field generates an electrical field and thus a voltage. The magnitude of the voltage is proportional to the flux change of the magnetic field.

Inert Gas

A chemical gas which does not, or only weakly, react (i.e. inert). Inert gases are helium, neon, argon, krypton, xenon, and the radioactive radon.

Intel

An important US firm which manufactures microelectronic components, for example memory chips and processors. The most important processor family is the 80x86. Intel is regarded as the inventor of the microprocessor.

Interlock

If a stage in a pipeline needs the result or the system element of another stage which is not yet available, this called an interlock. Interlocks arise, for example, if in the course of calculating a composite expression the evaluation of the partial expressions is still in progress. The requesting pipeline-stage then has to wait until the other pipeline-stage has completed its calculations.

Interrupt (Software, Hardware)

A software interrupt is issued by an explicit interrupt instruction INT; a hardware interrupt, however, is transmitted via an IRQ line to the processor. In both cases, the processor saves flags, instruction pointer and code segment on the stack, and calls a certain procedure, the interrupt handler.

Interrupt Handler
See interrupt.

I/O
Abbr. for input/output.

I/O-Mapped I/O
With I/O-mapped I/O the registers of peripherals are accessed via the I/O address space, i.e. ports.

IRQ
Abbr. for interrupt request. A line or signal which is activated by a peripheral to issue a hardware interrupt to the CPU.

ISA
Abbr. for industrial standard architecture. A defined standard which has replaced the vague AT bus specification. ISA defines the bus structure, the architecture of CPU and support chips, and the clock frequency of the ISA bus.

ISA Master
A bus master which can carry out ISA bus cycles.

ISA Slave
A device which serves ISA bus cycles.

IU
Abbr. for instruction unit. A portion of the CPU which drives the execution unit.

Joystick
A stick with buttons frequently used for computer games.

k
Symbol for kilo (i.e. one thousand of a quantity), for example, in kW = 1000 W. Note that kbyte generally means 2^{10} bytes = 1024 bytes.

kbit
2^{10} bits = 1024 bits.

kbyte
2^{10} bytes = 1024 bytes.

Keyboard
An input device for computers. A keyboard is usually connected to a keyboard controller or a keyboard interface on the motherboard via a serial interface. The keyboard consists of a scan

matrix, a keyboard chip and several keys. If a key is pressed the keyboard chip transmits a scan code to the computer, which unambiguously characterizes the pressed key.

kHz
1000 Hz = 1000 periods/s.

LAN
Abbr. for local area network. LANs are data networks which are restricted in space. Typical distances are less than 500 m. Mainly Ethernet and Token-Ring LANs are used.

Lanthanoide
Also called rare earth. Certain metallic chemical elements which show very similar chemical properties. There are 14 different lanthanoides; the element lanthanum gave the name for this element group.

Laser
1. Abbr. for light amplification by stimulated emission of radiation, a phenomenon of quantum physics.
2. Light sources which emit a sharply focused beam of high optical quality.

Latch
A circuit which largely consists of two antiparallel connected inverters. The latch holds (latches) data which has been written once, even after deactivating the external signal (data). The data writing is usually controlled by a clock signal.

Latency
The average time between the positioning of the read/write head and the appearance of the desired sector below the head. On average, this takes half a disk rotation. Hard disks with 3600 rpm therefore show a latency of 8.3 ms, and floppy disk drives with 360 rpm a latency of 83 ms.

LDT
Abbr. for local descriptor table. A table of 8-byte entries (the descriptors) which describe segments in protected mode. These segments are local for the task concerned.

LDTR
Abbr. for local descriptor table register. A memory management register from the 80286 that holds a selector, which in turn indicates the descriptor for the local descriptor table in the global descriptor table.

LF
Abbr. for line feed. LF is an ASCII control character with the code 0ah. LF leads to a line feed in a serial printer, or to a positioning of the cursor in the next line but the same column.

Little Endian Format

In the little endian format the high-bytes of a multiple byte quantity are stored at higher addresses, and the low-bytes are stored at lower addresses. Intel's 80x86 family uses the little endian format. When writing multiple byte entities in the usual way, with the highest order bit left and the lowest order bit right, the arrangement in memory seems to be exchanged.

Local-Bus

A new bus system for the Personal Computer which operates with 32 bits and, unlike EISA, up to 50 MHz. Unfortunately, the local-bus is not applicable as universally as the ISA, EISA, or MCA buses, but is currently only used for the integration of fast graphics adapters and hard disk controllers. There exist two new standards for the local-bus: Intel's PCI, and the VESA VL-bus.

Local Network

See LAN.

Login

To announce oneself to a mainframe as a user. The login is usually carried out by a LOGON command, as well as inputting a user identification and password.

Low-Level Formatting

The formatting of a data carrier involving the generation of physical tracks and sectors, but not the logical structure of the file system. With FORMAT and a floppy disk you may carry out a low and high-level formatting simultaneously. With a hard disk drive, however, only high-level formatting is possible with FORMAT.

LPT1, LPT2, LPT3, LPT4

The DOS names for the various parallel interfaces in a PC. LPT is derived from line printer.

LSB

Abbr. for least-significant bit or least-significant byte.

LSI

Abbr. for large scale integration. This means the integration of 10 000 to 100 000 elements on a single chip.

μ

Symbol for micro, i.e. one millionth of a quantity. Example: 1 μm = 0.000 001 μm

M

Symbol for Mega, i.e. one million of an unit as, for example, in MW=1 000 000W. Note that Mbyte usually means 2^{20} bytes=1 048 576 bytes.

m

Symbol for milli, i.e. one thousandth of a quantity. Example: 1mm=0.001m

Magneto-Optical Drive
A writeable and erasable mass storage where the recording and reading of data is carried out by a laser beam, i.e. in an optical manner. The information itself is written in the form of tiny magnetizations: the data medium has a ferromagnetic coating. Magneto-optical drives use the Curie point for writing and the Faraday effect for reading the information.

Mainframe
A very powerful computer which serves many users (up to 1000 or more), and which may execute several tasks in parallel.

Main Memory
That memory of a computer which stores the program and the data necessary for program execution, or which are processed by the program. Generally, the main memory is implemented with DRAM.

Make-Code
See scan code.

Mantissa
The number by which the power in scientific notation is multiplied to give the value of the expression. Example: $1.83*10^4$; 1.83 is the mantissa, 10 the base, and 4 the exponent of the number 18300 in scientific notation.

Mark
A form of parity where the parity bit is always equal to 1 independently of the data value.

Machine Instruction
An instruction for a microprocessor which is decoded and interpreted by the processor without further modification or translation by software or hardware. Machine instructions consist of a variable-length sequence of bits that specify the operation type, the addressing scheme, the affected registers, etc. The machine instruction is the lowest level of processor instruction accessible by a programmer. Assembler and high-level language instructions are translated into machine instructions by the assembler and compiler, respectively.

Matrix
A generally two-dimensional arrangement of objects, for example numbers or memory cells. An individual object within the matrix is determined by specifying its line and column.

Mbit
2^{20} bits = 1048576 bits.

Mbyte
2^{20} bytes = 1048576 bytes.

MC146818

A CMOS RAM and real-time clock chip from Motorola which is contained in the AT and its successors as the original or a compatible chip.

Memory Bank

A group of memory chips which are accessed in common.

Mega

See M.

Memory-Mapped I/O

With memory-mapped I/O all registers of the peripherals are located in the normal address space, and thus are accessed via the normal memory instructions such as MOV.

MF II Keyboard

Abbr. for **m**ultifunction II keyboard. An extended and programmable keyboard which has separate blocks with control keys and LEDs to indicate the shift status of various keys.

MFM

Abbr. for **m**odified **f**requency **m**odulation. An encoding method to record data on a magnetic data carrier with twice the data density of FM.

MHz

$1\,000\,000$Hz$=1\,000\,000$ periods$/$s.

Mickey

$1/200$", i.e. $1/200$ inch (equal to 0.127 mm.)

Micro

See μ.

Microchip

A highly integrated circuit on a single substrate plate – the chip. More particularly, microchip means ICs with extensive logic, for example, microprocessors or DRAMs.

Microcoding or Micro-encoding

The encoding of machine instructions of a processor into a sequence of more elementary instructions to the instruction and execution unit in a CPU. The microcode is stored in the processor's microcode ROM and is not accessible to the programmer but is burnt-in during the course of manufacture.

Microchannel

A modern bus system from IBM for PS/2 Personal Computers. The microchannel is designed for an 8- to 32-bit data and address bus, and the support of multitasking operating systems on a hardware level. Unlike EISA, the microchannel is incompatible with the PC/XT and ISA bus.

Microprocessor

A microchip with high intelligence for the execution of instructions. Therefore, a microprocessor is programmable and the program is usually stored in a ROM or main memory.

MIPS

1. Abbr. for **m**illion **i**nstructions **p**er **s**econd. MIPS indicates the number of instructions executed by a processor within one second, and sometimes serves as a (not very powerful) degree for the performance of the CPU.

2. Abbr. for **m**icroprocessor without **i**nterlocked **p**ipeline-**s**tages. A RISC architecture where no interlocks occur between the pipeline stages. Well-known MIPS implementations are Siemens R3000/4000 and IBM's R6000 processors.

Mirroring

The simultaneous and identical recording of data on two different mass storage mediums, for example, hard disks. This prevents data being lost if one drive is damaged.

µm

Symbol for micrometer, i.e. one millionth of a metre or 0.000 001 m.

MMU

Abbr. for **m**emory **m**anagement **u**nit. The MMU is either part of a processor or integrated on a separate chip, and carries out the address transformations for segmentation and paging.

Mnemonics

Easy-to-remember abbreviations which characterize the machine instructions of a processor, and which are translated by an assembler according to the addressing scheme, the operands, etc. into machine instructions, e.g. MOV.

Modem

Abbr. for **mo**dulator/**dem**odulator. Modem means a device which modulates a carrier signal with a data signal and extracts the data signal from the modulated carrier signal, respectively. Data can thus be transmitted over a data network or radio network.

Monitor

1. A device for computers to display text and graphics.
2. A supervision program for a hardware or software unit. Example: virtual 8086 monitor; a system program to supervise the i386 and successive processors and one or more tasks in virtual 8086 mode.

MOS

Abbr. for **m**etal **o**xide **s**emiconductor. A technology for manufacturing electronic components or integrated circuits which have a layer structure of the form indicated.

MOSFET

Abbr. for **m**etal **o**xide **s**emiconductor **FET** (field effect transistor).

A field effect transistor which has a control gate (metal), a substrate (semiconductor), and an isolating film (oxide) which separates gate and substrate.

Motherboard

Also called a mainboard. That board in a PC housing the central components such as CPU, main memory, DMA controller, PIC, PIT, etc., as well as the bus slots.

Motorola

An important US manufacturer of microelectronic components, for example, memory chips and processors. The most important Motorola processor family is the 68000. Presently, Motorola is very involved in the telecommunications field.

Mouse

A pointing device in the form of a small housing with two or three buttons. In the housing is embedded a ball, rotated by a movement of the mouse by the user. The rotation of the ball is detected by sensors, and a logic can determine the direction and amount of the movement. Optical mice don't have a ball, but only optical sensors that detect the mouse's movement over a special mouse pad.

Mouse Cursor

An object in the form of a cursor or an arrow which is moved on the screen seemingly in accordance with the mouse's displacement. The location of the mouse cursor on-screen can be evaluated by software.

µP

Abbr. for microprocessor.

µPD765

The floppy disk controller chip in the PC/XT.

MS-DOS

Abbr. for **M**icro**s**oft-DOS, the DOS implementation from Microsoft.

MSB

Abbr. for **m**ost-**s**ignificant **b**it or **m**ost-**s**ignificant **b**yte.

MSI

Abbr. for **m**edium **s**cale **i**ntegration. It characterizes the integration of 100 to 10 000 elements on a single chip.

MSW

Abbr. for **m**achine **s**tatus **w**ord. A 80286 control and status register for protected mode.

MTBF

Abbr. for mean time between failures. MTBF indicates the average value for the time period between two complete failures of the corresponding device. MTBF is mainly used to characterize the reliability of hard disk drives.

Multimedia PC

A PC which has various extensions to provide, receive and process information in the form of data, image, and audio concurrently.

Multiplexer

A device which transfers the data of several input channels to a smaller number of output channels in a strictly defined way. Example: the 20-bit memory address of the 80286 is divided into two successive 10-bit packets (the row and the column address) by the DRAM controller; here the number of input channels is equal to 20, but the number of output channels is only equal to 10. The DRAM controller therefore represents a multiplexer, and the described multiplexing manner is called time-divisional multiplexing.

Multitasking

The concurrent execution of several tasks in a computer. Users have the impression that the tasks are executed in parallel; actually, the computer only switches between the tasks very quickly.

Multitasking Operating System

An operating system which can manage several tasks in a computer system simultaneously, activating them for a short time period and interrupting them again later. Examples are OS/2, UNIX, or mainframe operating systems such as VMS or BS2000.

n

Symbol for nano (i.e. one billionth of a quantity). Example: 1 nm=0.000 000 001 m.

NAN

Abbr. for not a number. A floating-point number which is different from zero but doesn't meet the IEEE definitions for the representation of floating-point numbers in a computer.

Nano

See n.

Nanometre

One billionth of a metre, i.e. 0.000 000 001 m.

Nanosecond

One billionth of a second. i.e. 0.000 000 001 s.

NEC

A major Japanese manufacturer of electrotechnical and electronic devices (**N**ippon **E**lectric **C**ompany).

Netnode

A station in a network. Netnodes are, for example, workstations, switching computers, or printers.

Network

Transmission equipment with a server, netnodes and transmission devices which enable communication between individual network users.

Network Adapter

An adapter card enables the access to a network. Generally, you also need drivers and network software.

Nibble

A group of four bits, i.e. half a byte.

nm

Abbr. for nanometre, i.e. one billionth of a metre, or 0.000 000 001 m.

NMI

Abbr. for **n**on-**m**askable **i**nterrupt. A hardware interrupt request to a CPU which cannot be masked internally in the processor by a bit, but must be serviced immediately.

NMOS

Abbr. for **n**-channel **MOS**. A technology for manufacturing MOS transistors where the channel conductivity is based on negative charged electrons.

Normalized Representation

In normalized floating-point number representation, it is assumed that the leading digit is always equal to 1. Because the leading digit is always known implicitly, it is omitted and the exponent is adjusted accordingly, so that the value of the number remains equal. The precision is thus increased by one digit without enlarging the number format.

NRZ

Abbr. for **n**onreturn to **z**ero. An encoding method for binary data where the signal for two successive 1's doesn't return to zero.

ns

Abbr. for nanosecond, i.e. one billionth of a second or 0.000 000 001 seconds.

NVR

Abbr. for **n**onvolatile **RAM**. A memory which doesn't lose its contents even after the power has been switched off.

Offset

The address within a segment, i.e. the number of bytes from the beginning of the segment.

Operating System

Hardware-near software which controls and supervises the operation of a computer, establishes an interface between application programs and the hardware and file system, and which manages the various tasks.

OS/2

Abbr. for Operating System/2. The multitasking successor to DOS for IBM-compatible personal computers.

Overdrive

An upgrade for i486DX/SX processors. See upgrade.

Overflow

The condition where the result of an arithmetical operation is too large for the reserved memory location. For example, the multiplication of two integers may cause an overflow if the destination register can only accept an integer, but the result is longer than 16 bits.

P5

The short form or development name for the i586/Pentium.

Packed BCD

Binary coded decimal numbers where each nibble of a byte encodes a decimal digit. Example: 72h = decimal 72. Packed BCD saves much storage area when compared to ordinary BCD.

PAD

Abbr. for **p**acket **a**ssembler/**d**isassembler. A hardware or software device in a network with packet switching which generates one or more data packets with corresponding addresses from data to be transmitted, or reconstructs the entire information from such received packets.

Page

A section of an address space which is handled as a unit.

Page Directory

The first-order page table in a system with paging which holds the addresses of the second-order page table. The page directory is always in memory and is, unlike the second-order page tables, not swapped onto disk.

Page Mode

A certain operating mode of modern DRAM chips which leads to a very fast access to the memory cells, and therefore to the data of one page. In page mode, the DRAM must only be supplied with the column address to address data within one page. Thus the RAS precharge time is saved. If the intended data is outside the active page, a lengthy page change is necessary.

Page Table

A table which holds the addresses of the corresponding pages in a system where paging is effective. The first-order page table is called a page directory. Unlike the first-order page table, the second-order page tables can be swapped like ordinary pages.

Paging

1. Generally, the division of an address space into smaller units – the pages.
2. Demand paging: the swapping of pages in main memory onto an external mass storage if the data stored there are currently not needed by the program. If the CPU wants to access the swapped data, the whole page is transferred into memory again and another currently unused page is swapped. A much larger virtual address space than that actually present physically can thus be generated.

Palette

The total of all possible colours which a graphics adapter (for example, EGA or VGA) is able to display.

Parallel Interface

A PC interface which provides or receives data in the parallel form of one byte.

Paramagnetism

A form of magnetism where the external magnetic field is slightly enhanced (typically by 0.00001% to 0.05%). Paramagnetism appears in all materials with unpaired electrons.

Parity

A simple means of detecting errors in data recording or transmission. For that purpose, a data quantity is allocated a parity bit whose value is computed from the data bits. With even parity the number of 1's of all data and parity bits is even, thus the modulo-2 sum of all bits is equal to 0. With odd parity, however, the number of 1's is odd, thus the modulo-2 sum of all bits is equal to 1. In addition, mark and space parities exist.

Pascal

A common structured programming language.

PC

1. Abbr. for **P**ersonal **C**omputer.
2. IBM's first personal computer with an 8088 processor and an 8-bit data bus.

PC-DOS
Abbr. for Personal Computer-DOS; IBM's DOS implementation.

Peripheral
A device or unit located outside the system's CPU/main memory.

PGA
Abbr. for pin grid array. A package where the terminals are provided in the form of pins at the bottom of the package.

Physical Address Space
The number of physically addressable bytes, determined by the number of address lines of a processor or the amount of installed memory.

PIC
Abbr. for programmable interrupt controller. A chip for the management of several hardware interrupts and the ordered transfer of the requests to a CPU which usually has only one input for such an interrupt request. Thus the PIC serves as a multiplexer for hardware interrupts. In the PC you will find the 8259A.

PIO
Abbr. for programmed I/O. With PIO data are exchanged between the main memory and a peripheral not by means of DMA, but with IN and OUT instructions via the CPU.

Pipeline-Stage
A unit or stage within a pipeline which executes a certain partial task. A pipeline for a memory access may include the four pipeline-stages address calculation, address supply, reading the value, and storing the value in a register.

Pipelining
Starting the execution of a function of the next cycle before the function of the current cycle has been completed. For example, the 80286 provides the address for the next read cycle in advance of receiving the data of the current cycle. This is called address pipelining or pipelined addressing. Similarly, a processor can start the execution of parts of a complex instruction in an early pipeline stage before the preceding instruction has been completed in the last pipeline stage.

PIT
Abbr. for programmable interval timer. A chip which outputs a pulse as soon as a programmed time period has elapsed. In the PC you will find the 8253 or its successor, the 8254.

Pixel
Short form of picture element; a point on a monitor. Usually the name pixel is only used in graphics mode. The pixel may be allocated one or more bits which define the colour and brightness of the picture element.

PLA

Abbr. for **p**rogrammable **l**ogic **a**rray. A highly integrated chip with logic gates which is employed as an ASIC, and whose logic can be freely programmed during manufacturing or by the user. A PLA usually has a field of AND gates and a field of OR gates. By combining AND and OR, any logical combination can be realized. This is similar to the fact that all natural numbers can be generated with 0 and 1.

PLCC

Abbr. for **p**lastics **l**eaded **c**hip **c**arrier. A package where the contacts are formed on all of the four sides.

PMOS

Abbr. for **p**-channel **MOS**. A technology for manufacturing MOS transistors where the channel conductivity is based on positively charged holes.

Polarization

If the electric or magnetic field of an electromagnetic wave is oscillating in one direction only, the wave is linearly polarized. The direction of the magnetic field is called the polarization direction.

Polarization Filter

A device for separating the part of a certain polarization direction from an electromagnetic wave. Only that part whose polarization direction coincides with the polarization direction of the filter passes through the filter.

Port

An address in the 80x86 I/O address space. Usually, registers in peripherals are accessed via ports.

Positioning Time

The time period between an instruction to position the read/write head and the head being moved to the indicated track.

POST

Abbr. for **p**ower-**o**n **s**elf **t**est. A program in ROM which detects and checks all installed components during power-on.

PPI

Abbr. for **p**rogrammable **p**eripheral **i**nterface. A chip which establishes a connection to peripherals such as the keyboard or the DIP switches of the PC/XT. In the PC/XT you will find the 8255.

PQFP

Abbr. for **p**lastics **q**uad **f**latpack **p**ackage. A package where the contacts are formed on all four sides.

Prefetch Queue
A small intermediate memory in a CPU where the prefetcher stores the following instructions before the processor has executed the current instruction. The prefetch queue relieves the bus system, and predecodes the instructions in CISC processors.

PRN
The DOS name for the first parallel printer. PRN is synonymous with LPT1.

Process Computer
A small computer usually without a monitor and a keyboard for controlling machines such as automobile engines, robots, or chemical reactors.

Processor
An intelligent microchip which is highly programmable. Often used synonymously for CPU.

Program
A group of instructions to a CPU to process data or to control machines.

PROM
Abbr. for **p**rogrammable **ROM**. A read-only memory where the stored data can be programmed during the last manufacturing step, or in the field by the user.

Protected Mode
An advanced operating mode from the 80286 on, where the access of a task to code and data segments and the I/O address space is automatically checked by processor hardware. The address generation in protected mode is incompatible with that in real mode. Thus real mode applications like DOS cannot be executed in protected mode.

PS/2
An IBM Personal Computer series with microchannel; conceived as the AT's successor.

RAM
Abbr. for **r**andom **a**ccess **m**emory. In a RAM data can be directly and randomly read or written (i.e. with any choice of the address).

RapidCAD
An i386/i387 upgrade with an i486 processor kernel (CPU and coprocessor), but without an on-chip cache.

RAS
Abbr. for **r**ow **a**ddress **s**trobe. A control signal for a DRAM chip which instructs the chip to accept the address supplied as a row address, and to interpret it accordingly.

Read/Write Head

A magnetically activated component at the tip of an access arm in a floppy disk or hard disk drive. The read/write head writes data as tiny magnetic regions onto the data medium or reads the data from the medium.

Real Mode

An 80x86 operating mode where the segment value is just multiplied by 16 and the offset is added to generate the physical memory address. In real mode no access checks are carried out for the code and data segments and the I/O address space. All 80x86 CPUs up to the i486 support the real mode for compatibility reasons.

Real-Time Clock

A chip that regularly updates time and date without any intervention from the CPU.

Reduced Write Current

In hard disk drives there may be so-called bit shifts on the inner cylinders which disturb the writing and reading of data. By reducing the write current on these cylinders, this effect can be prevented.

Register

1. Internal memories of a CPU whose contents can be loaded or modified by instructions or the CPU itself.

2. Components or intermediate memories of peripherals whose value issues a certain action in the device (control register), or whose value indicate the status of the device (status register). The registers are accessed either via ports (i.e. the I/O address space (I/O-mapped I/O)), or via the ordinary address space (memory-mapped I/O).

Remanence

The remaining magnetization of a ferromagnetic body if the external magnetic field is switched off. Materials with a high remanence are called magnetically hard; materials with low remanence magnetically soft. The remanence is the basis of all magnetic data recording methods.

REQ

Abbr. for **req**uest.

RGB

Abbr. for **r**ed **g**reen **b**lue.

RI

Abbr. for **r**ing **i**ndicator. With RI a DCE informs a DTE that an external unit wants to establish a connection for data transmission.

RISC

Abbr. for reduced instruction set computer. Microprocessors which have a significantly reduced instruction set compared to a CISC (typically less than 100 machine instructions). Characteristic of RISC is that the machine instructions no longer microcoded, but may be executed immediately without decoding. Well-known representatives of RISC processors are MIPS (microprocessor without interlocked pipeline stages) and SPARC.

RLL

Abbr. for run length limited. A very efficient encoding method for hard disks or magneto-optical drives where the number of successive zeroes is restricted to a certain range. With RLL 2,7 at least two (but at most seven) zero bits may be in succession. No clock bits are therefore necessary, and the number of required flux changes is reduced to one third. A disadvantage is that the data to record must be re-encoded to fulfil the RLL condition. Therefore, RLL 2,7 allows a data density increase of only 50% compared to MFM. But note that this is achieved without any improvement of the magnetic quality of the disk; the gain is exclusively a consequence of the better encoding method. However, the data retrieval is much more complicated, and because of the burst susceptibility of RLL also more error-prone.

ROM

Abbr. for read-only memory. ROM characterizes a memory chip from which data that has been written in advance can be read but cannot be written in the field. The stored data is determined once, and cannot be modified afterwards (or only with some special equipment). The data stored in a ROM remains, even if the power is switched off.

ROM BIOS

The PC BIOS routines in the ROM on the motherboard.

RS 232C

A generally accepted standard for serial interfaces which defines the signal levels, the signal meanings, the plug layout, and the procedure to establish a connection between a DCE and a DTE.

RTC

Abbr. for real-time clock.

RTS

Abbr. for request to send. With RTS a DTE tells a DCE that it wants to transmit data. The DCE then responds with a CTS.

Scan code

A code which characterizes the keys on a keyboard unambiguously. The scan code is transmitted as make-code to the keyboard interface or the keyboard controller on the motherboard when the key is pressed. If the key is released, the key transmits the same scan code with bit 7 set as a so-called break-code.

Scan matrix
A matrix made of intersecting lines. In a keyboard small switches are located at these intersections which connect the matrix at these locations if the corresponding key is pressed. The pressed key can thus be determined. In a tablet the controller activates the individual lines in succession so that the position of the moving cross-hair glass may be detected.

Scanner
A reading device with a sensor row which scans an original document (for example, an image, a drawing or text) in a graphical manner and transmits the bit pattern to a computer.

Stepper Motor
A motor that rotates a fixed angle upon every step pulse. Intermediate positions are not possible.

SCSI
Abbr. for small computer systems interface. SCSI is an instruction-oriented, high-level interface for external mass storages (for example, hard disk drives, tape drives or CD-ROM). The data transfer is carried out at a width of eight bits. SCSI interfaces are designed for data transfer rates up to 7 Mbytes/s in synchronous mode.

SDLC
Abbr. for synchronous data link control. A protocol developed by IBM for synchronous data exchange. It is implemented by the SDLC adapter.

SDU
Abbr. for serial data unit. The smallest data quantity which is provided by a serial interface or a UART. It comprises one start bit, the data bits, eventually one parity bit, and one, one and a half or two stop bits.

Segment
A section in memory which is described by a segment register or a segment descriptor. Within the segment the objects are addressed by an offset.

Sector Slipping
The shifting of the start of the sector within a hard disk track during the course of bad sector mapping to repair a small defect.

Selector
An index into a descriptor table to select the segment or gate which is described by the descriptor.

Serial Interface
A PC interface that provides or accepts data in serial form as the bits of an SDU.

Server

A central computer in a network which manages the common data and supplies it to the workstations in the network. Usually, it controls access of the individual network nodes to peripherals such as printers or modems.

Shadowing

The transfer of ROM code into RAM, where the ROM is masked out of the address space and the RAM is overlaid by the initial ROM address region thereafter. All ROM accesses are now redirected to the faster operating RAM.

Silicon

Chemical symbol Si. A semiconductor which has attained an outstanding importance in microelectronics. By introducing impurity atoms (doping) such as arsenic or phosphorus, the electrical properties of silicon can be varied across a very wide range. Silicon is the main part of quartz (i.e. ordinary sand), and is therefore available in unrestricted amounts.

SIMM

Abbr. for single in-line memory module. A form of memory module with a contact strip to insert the module into a slot like adapter cards.

Simplex

The transmission of data in one direction where the transmission direction, unlike half duplex, cannot be switched. The role of the communication participants as transmitter or receiver is therefore fixed.

SIP

Abbr. for single in-line package. A form of memory module with a pin row.

Slot

See bus slot.

Source

One conduction terminal of a field effect transistor.

Space

A form of parity where the parity bit is always equal to 0 independent of the data.

SPARC

A RISC architecture which includes, as a specific feature, a number of registers (up to 2048 or more), the ring-like organized register set. But a task or a routine is only allocated a register window of 32 registers. SPARC processors can carry out a task switch very quickly because only the register window has to be moved, and no storage of the task environment in memory is necessary (at least as long as the register set is not exhausted).

Sputtering

In sputtering a metal which is intended to coat a substrate is atomized in vacuum by ion irradiation. The atoms move to the substrate and are deposited as a very regular and hard coating.

SRAM

Abbr. for static **RAM**. SRAM is a random access memory (RAM) where the information is usually stored as the state of a flip-flop. Because the circuit state of the flip-flop is not changed without a write pulse, an SRAM need not be refreshed as is the case with a DRAM. This is the reason for the name static.

SSI

Abbr. for small scale integration. This means the integration of fewer than 100 elements on a single chip.

ST506/412

A physical interface between a hard disk controller and a hard disk drive. The standard requires a transfer rate of 5 Mbits/s for MFM encoding, and 7.5 Mbits/s for RLL encoding.

Start Bit

The first bit of an SDU which serves as a trigger for the receiver of the SDU.

Static Electricity

When rubbing two different materials (for example, a cat's fur on a glass stick) the separation of charges occurs. One body is charged with positive and the other with negative charges.

Stop Bit

The last bit of an SDU.

Streamer

A tape drive which mainly serves for archiving and the backup of hard disks. The hard disk data is »streamed« as an uninterrupted bit stream to the streamer.

String

A group of successive characters terminated by \0 (ASCIIZ), or whose length is stored in a string descriptor.

Strobe

A signal that instructs a device such as a DRAM or a latch to read another signal as an address.

Structure Size

The size of the elementary components of a microchip in its smallest extension, therefore usually the width of these components. Source, drain, and gate of MOSFETs, bit lines, etc., belong to the elementary components. The most highly integrated chips have structure sizes of less than 1 μm.

Substrate

The carrier of the microchip circuitry. On the substrate the transistors and connections are formed. In most cases, silicon is used as the substrate material which is doped to adjust the electrical properties as intended.

Super386

A family of i386-compatible Chips & Technologies (C&T) processors. It comprises the processors 38600DX, 38605DX, 38600SX, and 38605SX.

Superscalar

A RISC processor architecture which may start more than one instruction in separate pipelines; for example, a comparison instruction in the ALU pipeline and a floating-point calculation in the floating-point pipeline. Using this, and some skilful programming techniques, some instructions need less than one clock cycle for execution. Intel's P5 and i860 and Motorola's MC88110 apply this superscalar principle.

Synchronous

Corresponding to a phase or clock signal, or with the use of a clock signal.

System Clock

A functional group in a PC (or another computer) which generally comprises a PIT, a PIC channel, and a data structure. The group is periodically activated by the PIT to automatically update the data structure so that it always indicates the current time and date. The system clock is part of the operating system. The operating system uses the system clock to provide all files and directories with a time and date mark.

T

Symbol for Tera; (i.e. one trillion of a quantity), for example in THz = $1\,000\,000\,000\,000$ Hz. Note that Tbyte generally means 2^{40} bytes and not 10^{12} bytes.

Task

Also called a process or job. A task is a called program loaded into memory which is managed by the operating system. The operating system activates the individual tasks periodically, and interrupts them. Each task has its own environment. The distinction between task and program is only significant with multitasking operating systems.

Task State Segment

A data structure in protected mode which describes one task.

Task Switch

Switching from one active task to another task which is currently interrupted. For this purpose the active task is interrupted, all important parameters are saved in the TSS, and the new and up to now inactive task is activated by the operating systm.

Tbyte
2^{40} bytes, **not** 1 000 000 000 000 bytes.

Terminal
1. A device for data input and output which has only a rather simple local logic and is usually connected via a serial interface to the computer. Terminals are employed in multi-user systems.

2. A connection of a chip, interface or other device for inputting or outputting signals or supply voltages.

Text Mode
An operating mode of a graphics adapter where only the characters of a certain character set can be displayed on the monitor. The pixels cannot be addressed individually. The pixels are generated by a hardware character generator.

TIGA
Abbr. for **T**exas **I**nstruments **g**raphics **a**rchitecture (or **a**dapter). A graphics adapter with an in-built graphics processor.

Timer Chip
See PIT.

Token-Ring
A local area network (LAN) developed by IBM for connecting Personal Computers to main-frames or multi-user systems.

tpi
Abbr. for **t**rack **p**er **i**nch.

TR
Abbr. for **t**ask **r**egister. A memory management register from the 80286 onwards that contains a selector which in turn indicates the descriptor for the active TSS in the global descriptor table.

Trackball
A pointing device which is similar to a mouse lying on its back, and which has two or three buttons. The user rotates an embedded ball. By detecting the ball's rotation using sensors, the track ball logic can determine the direction and amount of the movement.

Track-Track Access Time
The time period necessary to move the read/write head from the current to the adjacent track.

Triggering
The start or stop of a process by an external signal.

TSOP
Abbr. for thin small outline package. A very flat package with contacts on two sides. TSOP packages are mainly used for flash memories.

TSS
See task state segment.

TTL
Abbr. for transistor-transistor logic. A family of logic elements.

Two's Complement
Also 2'complement. A representation of negative numbers where the negative number is generated by complementing all bits of the corresponding positive number and adding the value 1 afterwards.

UART
Abbr. for universal asynchronous receiver and transmitter. A UART is an intelligent microchip for a serial interface which carries out the serialization of parallel data and the insertion of start, parity, and stop bits, or the parallelization of serial data and the separation of start, parity, and stop bits. Typical representatives are the 8250 and the Z80SIO.

ULSI
Abbr. for ultra large scale integration. This means the integration of more than 1 000 000 elements on a single chip.

Underflow
The condition where the result of an arithmetical operation is too small for the reserved memory location. That is possible, for example, if the divisor in the division of two single-precision real numbers is so big that the result can no longer be represented as a single-precision real number, but the result, however, is different from null. If the result is representable by a single-precision real number but not in normalized form, this is called a gradual underflow.

UNIX
A multitasking operating system for simultaneously serving several workstations. UNIX is manufacturer-independent, and therefore its importance for more powerful computers (workstations) has been growing in the last few years.

Upgrade
Unlike the coprocessor, the upgrade not only supplies an enhancement for floating-point operations, but also takes over the previous CPU's jobs. Therefore, an upgrade is a complete and usually much more powerful CPU. In the case of the i486SX, which lacks the coprocessor, the corresponding upgrade (the i487SX) supplies a coprocessor as well as a faster CPU.

USART

Abbr. for **u**niversal **s**ynchronous and **a**synchronous **r**eceiver and **t**ransmitter. Unlike the UART, a USART additionally has a logic for serial data transmission.

VGA

Abbr. for **v**ideo **g**raphics **a**rray or **v**ideo **g**raphics **a**dapter. VGA was introduced by IBM with the PS/2 series as a successor for EGA. Unlike the other graphics adapters, VGA supplies an analog signal. Therefore, 256 different colours from a palette of $262\,144$ (= 2^{18}) colours may be displayed simultaneously.

Video Memory

See video RAM.

Video RAM

Also called video memory or display memory. In text mode the screen words, and in graphics mode the pixel values, are stored in video RAM. With most of the graphics adapters, the video RAM is divided into several pages. The graphics control chip then reads the video RAM continuously to display the written information as text or graphics on the monitor.

Virtual 8086 Mode

An advanced operating mode from the i386 where the access of a task to code and data segments and the I/O address space is automatically checked by the processor hardware. But the address generation with segment and offset is done in the same manner as in real mode. Real mode applications can thus be executed in a protected environment. With paging, several virtual 8086 tasks are possible in parallel.

VLSI

Abbr. for **v**ery **l**arge **s**cale **i**ntegration. This means the integration of $100\,000$ to $1\,000\,000$ elements on a single chip.

VMS

Abbr. for **v**irtual **m**achine **s**ystem. An operating system for DEC mainframes which operates using the concept of a virtual machine for each user.

Voice Coil Actuator

Also called linear motor. A driving device for the access arm of a hard disk drive where a permanent magnet on the access arm moves in a coil which is energized from a driver circuit. The access arm is thus moved by the magnetic action of a coil and permanent magnet in the same way as the membrane of a speaker.

VRAM

Abbr. for **v**ideo **RAM**. Specifically, dual-port RAM chips used for the video RAM of graphics adapters.

WE
Abbr. for write enable. A control signal for a RAM chip which indicates that the access is a write cycle and the RAM chip should store the data supplied at the specified address.

Weitek
A US firm which became known by its 80x87-compatible coprocessors for the 80x86 family. Many Personal Computers have a Weitek socket as well as the 80x87 socket for inserting a Weitek 80x87.

Wide Area Network
A data network which is not restricted in terms of distance. Typical distances are larger than 100 km. The scientific networks or the NASA data network for the supervision of missile starts and flight trajectories are wide area networks.

Word
Two bytes, i.e. 16 bits.

Word Line
The line in the row direction within a memory cell array of a RAM or ROM which turns on the access transistors of one memory row or page. The word line is usually connected to the gate of the access transistors.

WORM
Abbr. for write once, read many (times). A WORM is usually an optical drive where the data carrier may be written by the user without any restriction. Unlike magneto-optical drives, here the data medium cannot be erased.

Wrap-around
If the address exceeds the maximum possible value, a wrap-around occurs because the highest order address bit cannot be put into the address register or onto the address bus. This applies to the 8086 if the segment register also holds the value ffffh and the offset register holds the same value ffffh. The result is the 20-bit address 0ffefh. The leading 1 is, as the 21st address bit, neglected, and the address jumps from a value at the top of memory to a value very near to the bottom of memory.

Write Precompensation
On hard disks there may be bit shiftings in the inner cylinders with high cylinder number which disturb the reading and writing of data. By an intended shifting of the individual bits when writing data, this effect is prevented. This is called write precompensation.

Write-Through
Also write-thru. Write-through characterizes a cache strategy where the data is always written into main memory when data is written by the CPU. Therefore, the write-through is carried out through the cache system. Additionally, the data may be written into the cache SRAM but this is not necessary.

X-Bus

That part of the PC/XT/AT system bus which accesses the I/O ports on the motherboard, for example the registers of the PIC, PIT or the keyboard controller.

XENIX

Microsoft's UNIX implementation for Personal Computers.

XT

1. Abbr. for extended technology.
2. The successor of the PC with an 8086 processor and an internal 16-bit data bus.

Z4

The first freely programmable digital computer from Konrad Zuse. It operated with an electro-mechanical relay.

Z80

A common 8-bit microprocessor for CP/M which was, for example, used in the well-known Sinclair.

Index